# The Baltic Sea and Approaches

1. Approaches to the Baltic
2. Sweden
3. Finland
4. Russia
5. Poland
6. Kaliningrad
7. Lithuania
8. Latvia
9. Estonia
65°N
60°N
55°N
10°E
20°E
30°E
Haparanda
Luleå
Skellefteå
Vaasa
Sundsvall
Gulf of Bothnia
Söderhamn
Gävle
NORWAY
FINLAND
Åland Is
Turku
Vyborg
Helsinki
Gulf of Finland
St Petersburg
Oslo
Mariehamn
Hanko
Norrtälje
Lake Vänern
RUSSIA
Tallinn
Stockholm
Hiumaa
ESTONIA
Sea
Göta K
Pärnu
Skagerrak
Vättern
Trollhätte
Saaremaa
Gulf of Rīga
Göteborg
Västervik
Visby
North Sea
Kattegat
SWEDEN
Ventspils
Gotland
LATVIA
Rīga
Kalmar
Liepāja
DENMARK
Öland
Århus
Karlskrona
Baltic
LITHUANIA
Copenhagen
Malmö
Klaipėda
Simrishamn
Bornholm
Kaliningrad
Gdynia
RUSSIA
Rügen
Kiel
Gdańsk
Lübeck
Rostock
POLAND
GERMANY
Hamburg
Szczecín

# THE BALTIC SEA AND APPROACHES

ROYAL CRUISING CLUB PILOTAGE FOUNDATION

Andy Beharrell

Imray Laurie Norie & Wilson

Published by
Imray Laurie Norie & Wilson Ltd
Wych House The Broadway St Ives Cambridgeshire
PE27 5BT England
✆ +44 (0)1480 462114
ilnw@imray.com
www.imray.com
2025

1st edition 1992
2nd edition 2003
3rd edition 2010
4th edition 2017
5th edition 2025



ISBN 978 178679 522 9

British Library Cataloguing in Publication Data. A catalogue record for this title is available from the British Library.



Printed in Croatia by Denona

## CAUTION

Whilst the Royal Cruising Club Pilotage Foundation, the author and the publishers have used reasonable endeavours to ensure the accuracy of the content of this book, it contains selected information and thus is not definitive. It does not contain all known information on the subject in hand and should not be relied on alone for navigational use: it should only be used in conjunction with official hydrographical data. This is particularly relevant to the plans, which should not be used for navigation. The Royal Cruising Club Pilotage Foundation, the authors and the publishers believe that the information which they have included is a useful aid to prudent navigation, but the safety of a vessel depends ultimately on the judgment of the skipper, who should assess all information, published or unpublished. The information provided in this pilot book may be out of date and may be changed or updated without notice. The Pilotage Foundation cannot accept any liability for any error, omission or failure to update such information. To the extent permitted by law, the Pilotage Foundation, the author and the publishers do not accept liability for any loss and/or damage howsoever caused that may arise from reliance on information contained in these pages.

### Positions and Waypoints

All positions and waypoints are to datum WGS 84. They are included to help in locating places, features and transits. Do not rely on them alone for safe navigation.

### Bearings and Lights

Any bearings are given as °T and from seaward. The characteristics of lights may be changed during the lifetime of this book. They should be checked against the latest edition of the UK Admiralty *List of Lights*.

# CONTENTS

## BOOK SUPPLEMENTS WITH UPDATES AND CORRECTIONS

The quality of Imray and Royal Cruising Club Pilotage Foundation publications is enhanced by contributions from sailors visiting the area. We welcome all feedback for updates and new editions. If you notice any updates, errors or omissions, please let us know via **rccpf.org.uk/Provide-Feedback**

Reports are posted on the Cruising Notes page of the Pilotage Foundation website and incorporated into an annual supplement available free of charge from **imray.com** or **rccpf.org.uk**.

## FIND OUT MORE

For a wealth of further information, including passage planning guides and cruising logs for this area visit the Royal Cruising Club Pilotage Foundation website at **rccpf.org.uk**

Imray is the leading publisher of nautical information for leisure sailors. Combining the latest official hydrographic data with verified first-hand research, Imray charts, books and digital products present quality information to the highest standard.

Imray was formed in 1904 when three nautical publishing firms, each with a history from the mid 18th century, joined. Today, it works with well-known authors and organisations, covering popular sailing areas worldwide. It has been publishing Royal Cruising Club Pilotage Foundation books since the 1970s: **imray.com**.

**ROYAL CRUISING CLUB PILOTAGE FOUNDATION**

Following the priority established by the Royal Cruising Club (RCC) to publish pilotage information, the Royal Cruising Club Pilotage Foundation was established as an independent charity in 1976 with the objective 'to advance the education of the public in the science and practice of navigation'. The Foundation's principal activity is to collate and publish pilotage information for the benefit of cruising sailors worldwide.

Benefitting from the copyrights donated by RCC members and others and working with its team of dedicated authors and editors, the Pilotage Foundation has developed a portfolio of cruising guides available both in printed format and through its website, covering a wide range of cruising areas including some of the more remote areas of the world.

The Foundation's website gives full details of its activities and provides a portal for the sale or download of its publications, including some free eBooks, as well as Cruising Notes comprising up-to-date navigational and other reports.

TRINITY HOUSE

The Royal Cruising Club Pilotage Foundation is privileged to have Trinity House as its Patron. The ongoing safety of navigation and education of mariners are common goals of both organisations: **trinityhouse.co.uk**.

## FOREWORD

The area covered by *The Baltic Sea and Approaches* encompasses unlimited places to tie up or anchor in a number of diverse cruising grounds, including the densest archipelago in the world. It would be impossible for one book to provide in depth coverage of every region and this book does not pretend to supplant the detailed pilot books available for each country or coastline. Instead the hope is that *The Baltic Sea and Approaches* gives a valuable overview to the area, with sufficient pilotage detail to enable the reader to passage plan effectively, either for a single cruise or for multiple seasons. Further pointers are given towards the sources of more detailed cruising information for each region, available either in book form or electronically.

It would be a herculean task to produce a book of this coverage without a dedicated team of authors, each of whom have spent time cruising the Baltic, some of them for many, many years. The Pilotage Foundation is immensely grateful to the following people who have worked so hard to bring this edition up to date:

**Germany & Denmark** Nicholas Hill & John Sadd

**Sweden**

**West Coast** Nicholas & Ragnhild Torsteinsrud-Smith and John Sadd

**Gota Kanal** Dick Beddoe

**South and East Coasts** Andy Beharrell and John Sadd

**Gulf of Bothnia** Robin Matthews and Bob & Fiona Slay

**Finland (incl. Åland Islands)** Anne & Andy Fleck and John Sadd

**Poland** Andy Beharrell

The Royal Cruising Club Pilotage Foundation is particularly grateful to Andy Beharrell who has worked closely with the team to pull this edition together so effectively.

The team at Imray, led by Lucy Wilson, have spun their usual magic in turning an enormous and complex bundle of text and images into such an attractive and well-presented treasure trove of information. We are all extremely grateful to them for their hard work and expertise.

The Pilotage Foundation continues to depend on all of the yachtsmen and women who cruise the Baltic to help to keep this book up to date by contributing information based on their own experience of the region. If you have some information or photographs for us we would love to hear from you at info@rccpf.org.uk. Any feedback will be published on our website at rccpf.org.uk and annual correctional supplements to the book will be available via the Imray website at imray.com.

Emily Winter
Editor in chief
2025

## ACKNOWLEDGEMENTS

This fifth edition has built on the work of previous authors and contributors and we remain very grateful to them all for this firm foundation, in particular Nigel Wollen who guided the teams in the past. Andy Beharrell and the current team of authors would also like to thank the following contributors who have been so generous in sharing Baltic information for this edition, whether in the form of photographs, updates to chart information, or sections of text: Robin Matthews, Bob & Fiona Slay, Viv Fox, John Sadd, Nicholas & Ragnhild Torsteinsrud-Smith, Anne & Andy Fleck and Dick Beddoe. Individual photographs are credited with each image. The book would not have been possible without this valued input from so many fellow cruisers. The authors are also very grateful to Lucy Wilson, Emilie Crabb, Anna Wilson, Victor Fajardo Calvache, Debbie Wilson, Dawn Oliphant and the rest of the team at Imray for deciphering all of their submitted information and converting it all, so beautifully, into a coherent whole.

Andy Beharrell
2025

## Key to symbols used on plans

- depths in metres
- shallow water with a depth of 1m or less
- rocks with less than 2m depth over them
- rock just below or on the surface
- a shoal or reef with the least depth shown
- wreck partially above water
- wreck
- dangerous wreck with depth over it
- eddies
- rock ballasting on a mole or breakwater
- above-water rocks
- cliffs
- church
- mosque
- windmill
- wind turbine
- chimney
- pine
- trees other than pine
- waypoint
- fish farm
- anchorage
- prohibited anchorage
- harbour with yacht berths
- yacht harbour / marina
- visitors' berths
- port of entry
- customs
- harbourmaster's office

water
electricity
shower
waste pump-out
fuel
travel-hoist
slipway
post office
tourist information

airport
castle
ruins
houses / buildings
yacht berth
local boats (usually shallow or reserved)
ferry
beacon
port hand buoy

starboard hand buoy
mooring buoy

**Light characteristics**

light
white light
red light
green light
sectored light
lighthouse
F fixed

Fl. flash
Fl(2) group flash
Oc. occulting
R red
G green
W white
M miles
*s* sand
*m* mud
*w* weed
*r* rock

Bönhamn on the Swedish High Coast
(Höga Kusten) *Andy Beharrell*

# INTRODUCTION

The Baltic has much to offer the cruising yachtsman. Incorporating nine countries, each with their own distinctive features, it provides a fascinating variety of scenery, pilotage, traditions and history.

This fifth edition of *The Baltic Sea and Approaches* owes much to the groundwork, research and effort that has formed the basis of previous editions, but has been completely revised to cover the many changes that have taken place, including many new harbours and anchorages.

The overall objective of the book is to provide a general introduction to the Baltic Sea and its adjoining countries, to capture the flavour of the places and the people, and to act as a reference to the more detailed pilot books, charts and other sources of information. It is therefore intended to be a useful planning guide to what is, at first sight, quite a confusing cruising ground. It is not possible to cover such a large and varied area in one volume, and it does not pretend to be a comprehensive pilot book. However, it is hoped that it includes sufficient detail of the main harbours and approaches for it to have a place in the cockpit or at the chart table as well as an aid to passage planning.

There is always some debate as to where the Baltic Sea begins and ends and many argue that the island of Bornholm marks its western extremity. However, for the purposes of this book, we have also included the whole south and west coast of Sweden and the eastern area of Denmark. We have also included routes through Germany and Denmark to get to this region, to ensure that it represents a full guide to passage planning. For those intending to do lengthier cruises around Germany and Denmark, the Pilotage Foundation and Imray publish a specific guide to these countries which it would be very worthwhile to add to your cruising library. The sequence of chapters runs in a northerly arc between Germany and Russia, then from Poland to Estonia along the southern shore.

## Why go to the Baltic?

The attractions of the Baltic to the cruising yachtsman are very varied, and really include something for everyone.

- Although subject to the normal vagaries, the summer weather is governed by continental weather patterns and is generally far warmer than one might expect in those latitudes.
- The days are long during the main season, and there is little need for night sailing. For the Scandinavians, the season starts late (on or around Midsummer on 21 June), and the harbours are less crowded in the earlier and later parts of the season. The holiday season ends by mid-August when school holidays end, but it is perfectly possible to continue cruising well into September or even later.
- There is no tide, so no need to crawl out of one's bunk in the early hours. There are, however, some currents, which may be used to good effect. These are generally wind driven and are dealt with in more detail on page 7.
- There are hundreds of anchorages, and a huge variety of harbours with well developed facilities. The latter tend to become busy during the holiday season but it is nearly always possible to find a quiet anchorage.
- In the sheltered waters of the archipelagos there is relatively flat water and very little swell, with short distances between anchorages. This makes it ideal for sailing with young children or less experienced crew.
- All the Baltic countries have a rich and eventful history, which is evidenced by the number of great castles and churches as well as beautiful historic towns and cities which provide plenty to do if the weather turns nasty. (For more details of Baltic history see below, and the introductory section for each country.)
- Each country has its own distinctive food culture, such as the famous Scandinavian smörgåsbord. Fish dishes feature prominently, with excellent fish smokeries operating in many harbours.
- There are plenty of places to leave a yacht, or to lay up for the winter, but early booking is strongly advised. See further information below.

The beautiful Blå Kusten (Blue Coast) in eastern Sweden
*Andy Beharrell*

## EARLY HISTORY OF THE BALTIC

*Contributed by John Langdon*

Geologically, the Baltic first became recognisable as a region when it broke away from the super-continent Concordia in the southern hemisphere 1,800 million years ago. It then drifted around on its own tectonic plate as other super-continents came and went, before reaching its current position between the Eurasian and North American plates. The land remains low lying except for the mountains of Norway that were created by pressure from the North American plate.

Evidence of the earliest known Baltic inhabitants has been found in Wolf Cave in west Finland and dated to 125,000BCE. By then humans had evolved in Africa, but Europe and the near east were Neanderthal territory. Then came the last ice age glaciation in 110,000BCE, which continued until 10,000BCE. Scandinavia was covered by 2km of snow and ice, with even more over Canada. Sea levels correspondingly fell by 120m, leaving considerably more dry land around the world than today, and the ice-covered lands were crushed lower into the earth's magma. Even now the north Baltic countries are still "rebounding" at a rate of a metre per century, leaving harbours from as recently as Viking times well inland.

It was halfway through the ice age that at most 5,000 humans left Africa steadily to populate the world. After 15,000 years some had reached Australia, a journey that at that time would have only crossed 40M of water. Only then did humans head for Neanderthal Europe, and for whatever reason, 5,000 years later the Neanderthals were extinct.

From 10,000BCE humans could follow the now rapidly receding ice from north Germany and northwest Russia into the Nordic countries. The forests, lakes and marshlands, however, kept them in small, isolated communities of hunter-gatherers until quite late on. There is little sign of planted crops or domesticated farm animals much before 2,000BCE.

Coastal communities made votive ship models to hang in churches to protect those who went to sea *Andy Beharrell*

The early human civilisations developed in warmer climes. Even the Romans, who had successfully colonised France and Britain, could make little progress through the cold, wet forests of Germany, let alone any further north. Indeed, even the medieval Teutonic Knights sometimes had to squeeze their armies in single file through the forests of Latvia. Alexander Nevsky's great set-piece battle against them had to be fought on the winter ice.

There was, however, still plenty of contact between the Baltic peoples and the more sophisticated south. The Baltic Sea and its rivers, just like the Mediterranean, soon became the most convenient highway. Baltic amber was found in Tutankhamun's Tomb, for example, and the Roman historian Tacitus speaks very highly of the tall, fine-looking Baltic people, their noble way of life and their longboats.

Kalmar Castle, Sweden *C.N. Hill*

It was the Vikings who put the Baltic firmly on the world map. Their heyday was between 800 and 1,100CE when as raiders, traders or settlers, they sailed further and further from home. Norwegian Vikings followed the North Atlantic to Scotland and Ireland and then on to Iceland, Greenland and Canada. The Danes went to England, France, Spain and the Western Mediterranean. The Swedes headed east along the Gulf of Finland and south through the rivers to the Caspian, the Black Sea and the Eastern Mediterranean and were connected to the Middle East and Asia via the old trade routes.

'Going a-Viking' was usually a small, local, freelance affair. The Vikings never made any attempt to co-ordinate and merge their conquests into a single great empire. Indeed the Danish Norsemen, or Normans, who conquered Northern France and then England, soon adopted the language of their subject peoples and lost all ties with their original homeland. Similarly the Swedish Vikings, or Rus, who created Russia, were soon defending their territory against their fellow Swedes.

By the later Middle Ages, having seen for themselves what the more advanced Roman, Byzantine and Islamic civilisations had achieved, local Baltic leaders were slowly conquering or merging with their neighbouring tribes to create nations with similar prosperity and stability.

They also sought to exploit their Baltic trade as Europe's main supplier of grain and ship-building materials, with first Denmark, then the German Hanseatic League, then Sweden and then Russia dominating the region. At the end of the Second World War, the Soviet Union occupied all of the southern and eastern Baltic, leaving only Denmark, Sweden and Finland independent. Following the fall of the Berlin Wall in 1989 came the break up of the Soviet Union in 1991. Now all of the Baltic countries are free market democracies and all but Russia (including Kaliningrad) are members of the EU. With their new-found status the Baltic states are developing quickly and facilities for yachtsmen are changing fast.

*More detailed histories from the Middle Ages onwards are to be found in the sections on the individual countries which follow.*

## Useful sources of information

Contact details and websites for sources of information in specific countries are listed in the text for each country. The internet is a valuable resource when planning a Baltic cruise, and is also an excellent source of weather information.

The Cruising Association (CA) deserves a special mention as its Baltic Section provides its members with an outstanding source of information, including pilot books for each of the Baltic countries, newsletters and access to 37 local representatives (known as HLRs) as well as seminars and social events. Its Cruising Almanac, published annually by Imray, also contains a section on the Baltic (theca.org.uk).

The Royal Yachting Association will advise on a wide range of issues, including the International Certificate of Competence, VHF Operator Certificate, and VAT (for further details see rya.org.uk).

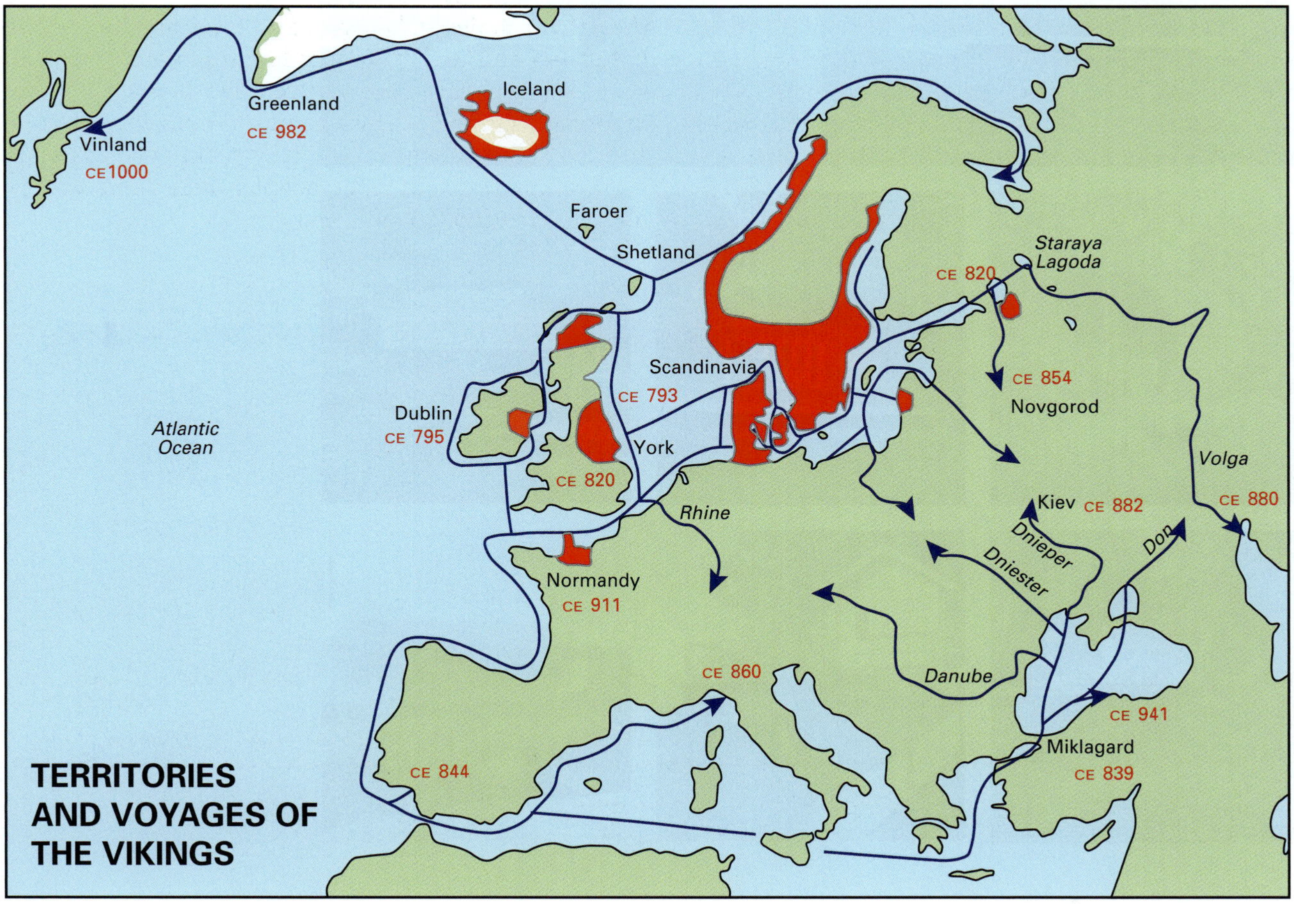

## THE SAUNA EXPERIENCE

*Contributed by John Dare, sauna enthusiast*

For many people a wonderful extra to cruising in the Baltic is the sauna experience. Almost everywhere one goes – hotels, marinas, yacht clubs and even fairly remote islands – one will find a sauna to enjoy. After a few days at sea, particularly if the weather has been a little unfriendly, there are few things more pleasant than a relaxing sauna bath. It is a great delight to get warm, clean and relaxed all at the same time.

So what happens? The sauna experience varies from the well-organised facility with showers, jacuzzis and swimming pools adjacent, to the little sauna hut in the woods with a simple, wood-burning stove. The latter are perhaps the most enjoyable, particularly if they are on the edge of the water with a lovely view as they often are. In any case the experience is basically the same. First, wash yourself in the shower, sea, pool or other available water. Then sit and relax in the sauna and the heat (most likely between 60°C and 90°C) should have you perspiring freely in 5mins or so. A first stay of around 10mins serves most people, but step out for a break if you feel at all uncomfortable. During the break the most traditional thing to do is to enter the sea, which you will find remarkably refreshing. Then return to the sauna for some more heat and repeat as you wish. Also, during the break, especially where you have the sauna to yourself, it is very relaxing to simply sit outdoors enjoying a snack or perhaps a cold beer. Remember, the essence of the experience is to relax and take your time – a hurried sauna is a waste of time.

There are no hard and fast rules about sauna etiquette, but a few general guidelines should be observed. Drinking and eating in the sauna is not done. Traditionally saunas are mixed, but in busy or more public places you will come across designated hours for men and women, or even different saunas for each. Normally saunas are taken naked, but if modesty dictates you can certainly wrap a towel around yourself or even wear a swimsuit - and you should, of course, respect the privacy of others using the sauna before you. If you are using a wood-burning sauna you will doubtless find wood and wood-cutting tools close to hand, and you are expected to replace the wood you have used. Saunas by definition are clean places, and you should certainly leave the area as clean as you found it. In some marinas use of the sauna is included in your harbour dues while in other places a charge is made, and it may sometimes be necessary to book, usually for 1hr. The situation varies and one simply has to enquire.

Above all, saunas are social places to be enjoyed with friends and/or family. The sauna experience is an essential part of the Baltic cruise, so relax and enjoy it!

Saunas take many and varied forms in the Baltic countries
*Andy Beharrell and Fiona Slay*

## REACHING THE BALTIC

The three main routes into the Baltic are:

**A** via Kiel Canal
**B** via Limfjord/Kattegat
**C** via Skagerrak/Kattegat

The entrance to the Kiel Canal can be reached in a few days from the English Channel, whilst the Limfjord or Skaggerak routes are alternatives if crossing from Northern England or Scotland.

The Göta Kanal can be a useful and interesting route across Sweden if starting or returning from a Baltic cruise.

Full details of the Kiel Kanal, Limfjord and Göta Kanal are included in the text.

The detail of passages to and from the Baltic is outside the remit of this book but extensive details can be found on the Pilotage Foundation website (available to all) at www.rccpf.org.uk and to members of the Cruising Association on their website www.theca.org.uk.

### Travel

*By sea*

For those who leave their yachts in the Baltic, it can make sound economic sense to drive out with a laden car at the beginning of each season. One possible route is to take a car through the Eurotunnel or via one of the many ferries to France or the Netherlands. Ferries are available from Newcastle to Amsterdam or Harwich to the Hook of Holland. Alternatively, the choice of Dover - Calais ferries is extensive. Once in Europe, there are then a host of ferry options into the Baltic from one of the German, Danish or Polish ports, with numerous different ferry operators.

The range of inter-island and international ferries in the Baltic is extensive *Andy Beharrell*

Stena Line has a significant choice of routes (www.stenaline.co.uk/routes). For Sweden, one possibility is an overnight ferry from Kiel to Gothenburg, or shorter routes include Rostock to Trelleborg and Grenaa to Halmstad. TT Line is another operator (www.ttline.com/en) with routes from Rostock or Travemünde to Trelleborg.

Brightly coloured boat houses at Seglinge in the Åland Islands *Hugh Rayment-Pickard*

There is a very comprehensive ferry service between the Baltic countries, and within each country. Some of them are huge vessels, and their sudden appearance is enough to keep the unwary yachtsman on his toes.

*By air*

All the Baltic countries are well served by both national and budget airlines, as well as internal flights. Individual country details are given in the text, but the following resumé of airports may be helpful when planning crew changes or visits home .

| | |
|---|---|
| **Germany** | Hamburg, Lübeck and Berlin |
| **Denmark** | Esbjerg, Billund, Århus, Ålborg, and Copenhagen |
| **Sweden** | Göteborg (Landvetter) and Malmö in the West. On the East coast, Stockholm (Arlanda, Skavsta or Västeräs), Karlskrona (Ronneby), Kalmar, Gotland (Visby), and, further north, Örnsköldsvik, Umeå and Luleå |
| **Finland** | Helsinki, Vaasa, Mariehamn, and Turku. On the Saimaa lakes, Lappeenranta and Savonlinna |
| **Poland** | Warsaw, Gdańsk, Kraków and Szczecin |
| **Lithuania** | Vilnius, Palanga, and Kaunas |
| **Latvia** | RIga, Liepaja |
| **Estonia** | Tallinn, Kärdla, Roomassaare, Parnu |

*By land*

Details for individual countries will be found in the text. Both rail and bus services are generally very good throughout the Baltic countries and most of the major ports mentioned in this book are on national rail networks or can be reached by bus or ferry. The European Rail Timetable is an invaluable guide for planning rail travel in Europe or Scandinavia.

www.europeanrailtimetable.eu

'The Man in Seat Sixty One' is also a very useful website for helping to plan rail journeys around Europe and around the Baltic region.

www.seat61.com

## Navigation

*Search and rescue*

The Global Maritime Distress Safety System (GMDSS) is fully established in the Baltic and the Baltic countries communicate and coordinate in maritime rescue. Area A1 (20–30M off the coast) is covered by VHF Ch 70. Area A2 (up to 150M off the coast) MF-DSC 2187.5 kHz. Otherwise, communication is on Ch 16 or MF 2182 kHz. In practice, the maritime services monitor VHF Ch 16/70.

### EMERGENCY PHONE NUMBERS

**All countries** ✆112
(this number applies to all EU countries, together with Russia and Kaliningrad, and can be dialled from mobiles. It is free)
**Germany** ✆+49 124124
**Finland** ✆+358 204 1000
**Latvia** ✆+371 673 23103
**Russia** ✆+7 8123274146

*Buoyage*

The IALA System A has been adopted by all countries. In Finland and Sweden the cardinal and lateral marks may not have topmarks, so it is important to be able to identify by colour alone (which, in turn, may be faded and can be difficult to see if sailing towards the sun). Many of the buoys are small by UK standards, and a good pair of binoculars is essential. Transits are also common, usually taking the form of a vertical yellow stripe against a red background, or occasionally a less visible black and white. Daymarks are often used to mark rock channels or outlying dangers and these marks take a range of forms. Some are lit and some not, but all are marked on charts and can make useful confirmation of a position.

*Waypoints/positions*

Positions of lights and other marks given in this book have been taken from a variety of sources and will not necessarily agree exactly with GPS positions. The positions given beneath each harbour name (or on the chartlets or plans) are intended purely to facilitate planning, and are NOT intended as a waypoint unless specifically stated.

*GPS accuracy*

The conflict between Russia and Ukraine at the time of writing has occasionally caused some issues with the GPS system. While most modern sets will use Galileo (or differential GPS), there is not complete clarity on the extent to which these systems are affected. It may be worth checking websites like gpsjam.org occasionally to review the situation. Where the map is green, there

Leading marks often take the form of a vertical yellow stripe against a red background *Andy Beharrell*

A beautiful sunset in the Åland Islands *Hugh Rayment-Pickard*

is interference of between 0–2%, yellow indicates 2–10%, but there have been very occasional days where sites in the eastern Baltic have gone red indicating an interference level of more than 10%. Whilst this is not expected to be frequent, it is something to check occasionally when relying on GPS systems for tight navigation.

### *Chart datum*

In 2005 a new national height system was introduced by all the countries around the Baltic. Height references are now made from land-based marks and so, as the land rises the reference system also rises. All the EU countries around the Baltic will also use a common vertical chart datum known as Baltic Sea Chart Datum 2000 (BSCD 2000). The various hydrographic offices have therefore begun the process of adapting their databases and products to the new datum. This transition will be gradual and care should therefore be taken to check the datum on any charts which you are using.

### *Tides & currents*

There is no appreciable tide within the Baltic, but prolonged winds in one direction and changes in atmospheric pressure can produce significant variations in depth.

Because the Baltic collects more fresh water than evaporates from its surface, there is a weak but steady surface outflow of less dense, less saline water through the Kattegat and Skagerrak into the North Sea, partially balanced by a return flow of more saline water at a lower level. Within the Baltic, surface currents are weak and tend to run towards Denmark, parallel to the associated coastline. Wind patterns can produce their own surface currents. Currents can flow in almost any direction, even upwind, since their direction is influenced not only by the wind but also by the shapes of the basins. Following a blow which may change sea levels, surface and sub-surface currents may be markedly different.

Long term prediction is not possible, and the best course is to consider the effect of the weather pattern of the previous days. Ask locally when in doubt.

### *Charts & pilot books*

British Admiralty charts are useful for passage planning, notably charts 259 (the Baltic Sea), 2816 (the Baltic Sea – Southern Sheet) and 2817 (the Baltic Sea – Northern Sheet) and possibly 2252 (Gulf of Bothnia).

However, it is essential to carry the detailed large scale charts published in each country, and details of these (and of local pilot books) are given in the chapters covering the individual countries. In complex areas where each island looks much like its neighbour, as do the buoys on the chart, it is vitally important to be able to find your place at a glance and a supply of small removable adhesive markers or arrows may help.

### Electronic chartplotters

There has been very rapid development and improvement of electronic charts and their associated equipment, with tablets or even smartphones performing a useful role. These are useful for passage-making provided that the user is aware of the need to scroll in to a large enough scale to see the detail. They are also useful for planning purposes but this is limited by the loss of detail when you scroll out to a smaller scale. They should not be regarded as a substitute for detailed paper charts.

### Traffic separation schemes (TSS)

There are a number of TSS in the Baltic, all of which are shown on the charts. They are monitored closely and the regulations should be strictly observed.

### VHF stations around the Baltic

Stockholm Radio publishes a chart of all the VHF stations around the Baltic and their approximate transmission range. This can be accessed on www.stockholmradio.se/kartor-och-kanalplan-vhf and should be regularly checked as there are occasional changes.

## Weather

### Weather forecasts

There is extensive weather information for most of the Baltic countries. See main text for each country for details. The Swedish Meteorological Office (SMHI) issues a forecast for all the Baltic sea areas on their website www.smhi.se/en/weather/forecasts/sea-weather-forecast. This is a very helpful site as it also shows the names and coverage of each of the sea areas.

Many forecasts give wind speeds in metres per second (m/s); multiply by two for the approximate equivalent in knots (kn), and divide by two for Beaufort.

### Weather information

Since most harbours now have WiFi, and with mobile data readily available, the internet is now undoubtedly the best source of weather information. Apps and websites like Windfinder.com, Predictwind.com, Windy.com and Windy.app are increasingly the best way to access weather data and some will give comparative forecasts from all the different forecasting models.

### Expected temperatures

The temperatures around the Baltic are heavily influenced by the sea temperature. In late spring this will be affected by the melting of the ice but by May temperatures will be starting to rise. The average daily maximum temperature in Stockholm in May is around 16°C rising to 19° in June, 22° in July and 21° in August. From then on it will fall significantly as the days draw in.

The pattern will be similar in the eastern Baltic and in Tallinn the average daily maximum temperature in May is around 15°C rising to 19° in June, 21° in July and 20° in August.

Once the ice has melted the sea temperatures can also be expected to rise fairly quickly. In the southern part of the Baltic where temperatures are less affected by the ice 10 or 11°C in May can be expected to be 17 to 18° by August. On the east coast of Sweden around Öland and Gotland temperatures of 5 or 6° in May become about 16° in August while in the Gulf of Finland temperatures may start at just 1°C in May rising to 16° or higher around Helsinki in August. Localised temperatures in archipelagos can be higher than these in good weather as the warming of the rocks creates warmer patches in some anchorages.

### Algal bloom (Cyanobacteria)

In the Baltic there are two types of cyanobacteria and when there are higher summer temperatures and sunny, calm weather, these can result in huge algal blooms across various parts of the Baltic. While eastern and northern parts of the Baltic are often the most vulnerable, these blooms can also appear elsewhere. They are most likely during July and August. The toxicity of the blooms depends on the species of the cyanobacteria, but it is best to avoid swimming where blooms are present. The presence of algal blooms is measured by SMHI and can be checked on their website www.smhi.se/en/weather/observations/the-algae-situation/algae.

## Formalities

### General

As a result of no longer being part of the EU, UK boats must now check out of the UK using form C1331 and then check into the EU/Schengen area at an Official Port of Entry. British Citizens arriving through airports or on ferries will need to get stamped into the EU/Schengen area. Schengen rules mean that you are allowed to stay in the Schengen area for a maximum of 90 days in each of the previous 180 days. The 180-day period is a rolling window, so you must count back 180 days from each day of your stay. To help with this, there is a Schengen visit calculator on home-affairs.ec.europa.eu/policies/schengen-borders-and-visa/border-crossing/short-stay-calculator_en

In late-2025 the European Travel Information and Authorization System (ETIAS) system will be implemented. ETIAS will require citizens of approximately 60 countries who currently enjoy visa-free access to Europe's Schengen Area to obtain advanced authorization before travelling. This system is similar to the ESTA required for travelling to the USA. It is not a visa but advance security clearance for short-term visitors. There will be a transitional period for at least 6 months from late-2025 when people will be advised to get an ETIAS authorization, but it will not be a requirement. There will then be a 6-month grace period when ETIAS will be compulsory for most travellers, but first-time visitors since the end of the transitional period will still be granted entry. Application will be online and should be fairly quick and straightforward. The cost is expected to be €7 with a validity of three years.

### Customs & immigration

The individual requirements of each country are set out in the relevant chapters.

All countries require a valid passport for each person aboard. Visitors are advised to check visa or other requirements before departure.

All the countries except Russia are members of the EU and passage between those countries should be free from customs formalities for EU citizens in boats on which VAT has been paid or exempted. Holders of non-EU passports should check the position. Customs and Immigration requirements are quite distinct from Schengen clearance, which is dealt with in the next paragraph.

### Schengen area

All the Baltic countries except Russia are parties to the Schengen agreement, which allows citizens of those countries freedom to travel between member countries without formality. It is important to understand that the UK and the Republic of Ireland are not members of the Schengen area (and never have been). Skippers arriving from the UK or another non-Schengen area country are required to check in or out. Skippers should enquire of the harbourmaster, Police or Customs at the first Schengen port of entry, and be prepared to present a crew list containing name, nationality, date of birth and passport number for each. In practice this requirement seems to have been applied with a light touch in the past, but it should be noted that, at the time of publication, the whole future of Schengen was being called into question, with some member countries (Scandinavian and others) starting to assert more control over their borders. Readers are advised to check the up to date position well before departure (see www.schengenvisainfo.com).

### Ship's papers

All yachts should carry a registration document (either under Part I of the Merchant Shipping Act 1995 or the Small Ships Register (SSR), or the national equivalent, together with a VAT receipt or exemption (the EU Single Administrative Document), evidence of marine insurance (specifying the areas covered and period of cover), and a VHF Ships Radio Licence.

### Restrictions on duration of visits

A VAT-paid yacht registered in an EU country can be kept in any other EU country indefinitely. Non-EU registered yachts (which now includes UK yachts which were not in the EU when Brexit happened on 31 January 2020) can be kept in the EU (and moved between EU countries) for a period of up to 18 months and this period can be extended to allow for lay-up periods or similar, after which they must clear out of the EU and clear back in. The regulations are subject to frequent change, and owners should check before arrival. In the UK details are available from HM Revenue and Customs (www.hmrc.gov.uk).

### Courtesy flags

A courtesy flag for the country being visited should be flown from the starboard spreader. (Note that the Åland Islands have their own flag).

### Ensigns

The national ensign of the visiting yacht should be flown. The red ensign is widely recognised, whilst the blue or the white can lead to some entertaining but sometimes exhausting attempts to explain the niceties of British ensign etiquette.

## Skipper & crew

### VHF Operator's Certificate

At least one person aboard should hold a VHF Operator's Certificate of Competence, with GMDSS endorsement if appropriate.

### International Certificate of Competence (ICC)

There is no general requirement for skippers of visiting yachts to hold a certificate of competence, but in practice it is desirable for skippers to hold an ICC (or equivalent), especially if visiting Poland, Lithuania, Latvia or Estonia. Although skippers of boats registered in the Baltic States require a certificate, this does not apply to skippers of boats whose flag state does not require them to have such qualifications (such as the UK). In practice, the crew should carry whatever certificates they do hold.

### Documentation

Cruising the Baltic, you would be well advised to carry a copy of the following documentation for the boat and for the skipper and crew as appropriate:

- The ship's VHF radio licence
- Insurance certificate – boat insurance and travel insurance for individuals
- Original boat VAT receipt (or letter/document proving the EU tax status of the boat)
- The boat registration documents (Part 1 registration or SSR)
- Passports
- Any qualifications – ICC, Yachtmaster, VHF user certificate

It may also be worth taking driving licences for crew members in case of hiring a car.

### GHIC cards / health insurance

UK nationals should carry a Global Health Insurance Card (GHIC), which entitles them to medical treatment under reciprocal agreements with the health services of the home country. It should be noted that GHIC cards must be renewed every five years (see www.nhs.uk/using-the-nhs/healthcare-abroad/apply-for-a-free-uk-global-health-insurance-card-ghic/ for details as to how to apply or renew). Appropriate health insurance is also advisable, but be alert for restrictions on the duration of visits or policies that restrict or exclude pursuits such as sailing.

## Health risks

### Tick bites

Visitors should be aware of the health risk from tick bites. Ticks are most prevalent in, but not confined to, areas of woodland and long grass. Ticks may be infected with TBE (Tick Borne Encephalitis) and/or Lyme Disease. TBE is the most serious and can lead to death in rare cases. A course of injections with annual top-ups will give immunisation. Injections can only be obtained privately in the UK and can possibly be arranged via a GP surgery. The risks are taken very seriously by the locals and there is a travelling vaccination facility on a yacht in the Stockholm archipelago (www.vaccinkliniken.se). Lyme disease is less serious but there is no immunisation available against it. Both diseases can show similar symptoms at the beginning, including fatigue, aching limbs, fever and (in the case of Lyme Disease) a red ring around the bite. If there is any sign of such symptoms medical advice should be sought without delay.

### Mosquitoes

Can be a nuisance in certain areas, especially in late evening. Netting is available from most camping shops and can be draped over open hatches like a wedding veil, or fitted nets can be made. Mosquito repellent should be carried.

## Preparing and equipping the boat

### Motor/sailing cone

To be displayed in the foretriangle when motor sailing: this is mandatory and strictly enforced in Germany (and in the Netherlands if visiting that country en route to the Baltic).

### Holding tanks

The regulations differ between the various countries, but are becoming stricter each year. Sweden, for instance, now imposes an absolute prohibition on the discharge of sewage from pleasure craft within 12M of the shore, regardless of nationality or flag status, and all countries impose regulations concerning the discharge of sewage in harbours or in close proximity to the land. It is therefore becoming increasingly difficult to cruise in the Baltic without fitting a holding tank capable of discharge at a pump-out facility. Given the fact that the sea is almost tideless, and given the Scandinavian love of swimming, the regulations are entirely understandable. It may be possible to comply by using a portable chemical toilet ('porta potty') or composting toilet (C-Head), if an owner wishes to avoid fitting a holding tank. Pump out facilities are becoming more generally available and in many archipelago areas you will find pump-out barges moored in popular spots.

A pump-out barge in Sweden. These will often be found around the archipelago areas in the Baltic *Andy Beharrell*

### Mobile phones

In general, mobile coverage in the Baltic is excellent. All the Baltic countries except Russia are in the EU, which since June 2017 has abolished 'roaming' charges. The new rules mean that EU citizens travelling within the EU are able to call, text and browse the internet on mobile devices at the same price they pay at home. With the UK's departure from the EU some mobile operators have been re-instating roaming charges. Mobile users should check the detail of their tariffs with their phone providers to avoid being caught out by surprise charges. In some countries it is possible to buy a local SIM card and use that, but it is worth being aware that this can be increasingly difficult. Many of the Baltic countries are clamping down on the ability of visitors to purchase pay-as-you-go SIM cards. At best this may mean having your passport with you to register the SIM card, while at worst, it may mean that this is no longer a viable option. E-sim cards may be an alternative – see www.moneysavingexpert.com/mobiles/what-is-an-esim/ for further information.

### Internet access

WiFi is widely available in Scandinavia, in cafés, tourist offices and marinas. The signal in marinas is sometimes weak, especially when moored some distance from the aerial, and there is often a charge to use it.

### Bottled gas

This is a complex muddle. Butane gas is not widely available in the north or east Baltic because it remains liquid at low temperatures but both butane and the popular Campinggaz are widely available in Germany and Denmark, and in certain harbours in Sweden and Finland. Supplies are often limited and expensive.

Calor gas is not available as either butane or propane outside the UK and EU safety regulations preclude refilling of bottles (although there may still be facilities to refill propane cylinders at Stenungsund and Kalmar in Sweden). On no account should butane bottles be refilled with propane because propane stores at a higher pressure and could cause the bottle to explode. Note that the British 'colour code' of blue bottles for butane and orange bottles for propane does not hold good around the Baltic.

The alternative is to purchase a local bottle and connecting regulator (but refills may only be available

Midsummer around the Baltic – practices vary, but it is enthusiastically celebrated all around the Baltic region *Andy Beharrell*

in the country of origin), or the solution may be to buy a set of worldwide connectors.

Gas consumption can be reduced by the use of a pressure cooker or thermal cooker. Portable barbecues are very popular in Scandinavia, and are in use quite regardless of the weather. Alternatively a small electrical induction cooker could be carried for use when plugged into a 220/240V network.

### *Electricity*

A 220Volt electricity supply is available in most yacht harbours throughout the Baltic, usually with the familiar circular blue European standard connectors. However, older facilities still have continental 2-pin plugs and other variations will occasionally be encountered. It is advisable to carry a very long connecting cable, as berths are often some distance from the nearest socket. A residual current device (RCD) to trip the supply if any leakage occurs to earth may provide an additional safety measure if the yacht is connected to an aged harbour circuit.

### *Fuel*

Diesel fuel is readily available throughout the Baltic. However, a few yacht harbours do not have diesel pumps on site and so some 20 litre containers may be useful. In Sweden, many fuel points are unmanned and instructions are generally given in English as well as Swedish. Tax-free fuel is not available. If there is red diesel in the tanks, skippers should carry receipts showing that tax has been paid. Red diesel should only be in the boat's tanks and not in cans.

Skippers need to be aware of the risk of 'diesel bug' caused by fuel containing a Bio component, which can cause blockages of filters and fuel lines. This can be countered by the use of a biocide to discourage bug growth. Storage time of the fuel is a compounding factor.

### *Water*

Water is available on the pontoons in most of the Baltic guest harbours, and where this is not the case it is noted in the text. Quality is generally good. It will often be necessary to provide your own hose, with a variety of different connectors.

Bergskils or rock anchors are a useful addition to your Baltic mooring armoury *Andy Beharrell*

Rock mooring involves tying your bow to any convenient mooring point *Andy Beharrell*

Mooring to rocks is popular throughout the archipelagos of Sweden and Finland *Fiona Ferguson*

There are many good yards for leaving boats around the whole Baltic region
*Andy Beharrell*

### *Chandlery*

Where possible, details of chandlers are given for individual countries. There has been a trend towards chandlery becoming more of a mail order/internet business but, although chandlery shops are quite scarce, they are generally available in the main yacht harbours. The best are to be found in Sweden, Finland, Germany and Denmark, but they are also becoming more common in Poland and the Baltic States. They can have variable ranges of stock, but if they do not stock a particular item, they can often order it.

### *Laundry*

Many yacht harbours have on-site launderettes, which may need to be booked in advance. The machines are often operated on eco-cycles at low temperatures and can take two hours or more for a standard wash.

### *Provisioning & alcohol*

All the main towns and cities are well served with supermarkets and stores, and open markets can be found in many places. However, few, if any, shops will be found near the more remote anchorages. It is therefore necessary to plan ahead, and stock up when the opportunity arises.

If, having transited the Kiel Canal, you are headed towards Denmark, Sweden and Finland, considerable savings are to be made by provisioning the boat before leaving Germany.

It should be noted that Midsummer (21 June) marks the start of the holidays, and many of the shops and restaurants in the smaller communities remain closed until then. Midsummer's Day is cause for great celebrations, usually around the maypole.

Alcohol prices are often the subject of concern for visiting yachts and the situation varies from one country to another. In Sweden and Finland, alcoholic drinks can only be purchased from government owned shops, known as Systembolaget in Sweden (where minimum age for purchase is 20 years old) and Alko in Finland, although beer not exceeding 3.5% alcohol is available in Swedish and Finnish supermarkets. These shops are only to be found in the larger towns or shopping centres. These restrictions do not apply in the other Baltic countries. As a general comment, alcohol is expensive in Sweden and Finland, less so in Denmark, and even less in Germany, Poland and the Baltic States, though costs will always depend on the prevailing exchange rates.

### *Laying up*

There are a great many excellent yards where yachts may be laid up for the winter. They are too numerous to list in detail, and it is important to obtain up to date information as standards can change very quickly upon a change of ownership. If possible, seek personal recommendation, or obtain details via yacht clubs or marinas. The Cruising Association provides a very useful directory for members which is reviewed at regular intervals.

Prices in Sweden, Finland and Denmark tend to be higher than in Germany (and remember that VAT rates are higher than in the UK for all of the countries concerned except Germany). The price also depends on whether the yacht is stored in a shed (heated or unheated), or outside. The cold winter temperatures mean that it is important to drain all systems unless in a heated shed, and electrical equipment should be disconnected.

Above all, it is very important to book early, as space in the good yards is reserved several months ahead.

## BERTHING SYSTEMS

### *Baltic mooring*

There is little or no tide in the Baltic, and this means that there is a variety of mooring techniques. These are described below and some may take a bit of getting used to. With practice though, you will often come to find them easier than tidal equivalents.

One essential for many of these Baltic moorings is to be able to climb off the yacht from the stern or the bow. Most yachts based in the Baltic have a split pushpit but those with easy stern access will often berth stern first. The jetty (or shore) is often well below the level of the bow, and a bow ladder will avoid the need for a potentially dangerous gazelle-like leap ashore.

### *Alongside*

Mooring alongside is possible in many harbours, and no allowance needs to be made for tides. Some quaysides may be protected by large motor tyres, or be rather rough or damaged, in which case a fender board is useful. Be prepared for yachts to raft up. Do always check though as in some areas mooring alongside will be charged at a higher rate than mooring bow or stern-to. In the low season this is not often enforced, but in high season it will be.

### *Box moorings*

These are particularly prevalent in Denmark and Germany, but are also found in the other Baltic countries, and provide an interesting challenge, especially in a cross wind. They are formed with a series of vertical posts, usually of timber but increasingly of steel, piled into the harbour bed and separated from the quay by a distance of 8–15m (sometimes more).

Moored in box berths *Andy Beharrell*

To moor in these, the yacht is steered in between two posts, with long lines (20m minimum is recommended) attached to the stern cleat. These lines should have large bowline loops at the end. The loops are dropped over the posts as the boat passes between them. It usually pays to target the windward post as a priority to ensure not being blown too far to leeward. When the boat reaches the staging or jetty, a crew member leaps off the bow with lines and ties them off – once again, ensure the windward bow line is attached first. The crew member on the bow should also be calling the distance from the jetty back to the helmsman. The lines from the stern can then be tightened to hold the boat in place. Sometimes there will be a line between the jetty and the pile and securing a warp to this as you enter can help hold the boat in position until you have had a chance to tension your mooring lines.

Fenders should be hung either side so as to protect your boat from those in adjacent boxes. If the adjoining

Rock mooring in the Stockholm Archipelago *Andy Beharrell*

berth is occupied by another yacht it is perfectly acceptable to lie alongside it during the berthing process, and there is much to be said for selecting a box that lies to windward of an occupied berth, so as not to be blown downwind.

It is important to select a box which is not too narrow, and to have the fenders tied on but left on deck until the widest part of the yacht has passed the posts. In many places the width of the box berth will be marked. Sometimes on the jetty and occasionally on the posts themselves.

This is not an easy manoeuvre to carry out in a strong crosswind. To avoid being blown sideways, concentrate on securing the windward lines first, and sort the others out afterwards. If you get the opportunity, it is a good idea to practise your technique in an empty harbour on a quiet day.

### *Stern buoy*

A row of mooring buoys is laid 2 to 3 boat lengths off a jetty or pontoon. Most buoys have a ring on a stalk, to which a long stern line is secured on approach and then lines from the bow are made up ashore. It is best to approach to windward of the chosen buoy. There are various devices which can help, including having a stern line on a reel, and using a Scandinavian buoy hook. Once the bow is made fast, the line back to the buoy can then be tightened to hold the boat away from the jetty.

It is common practice for stern buoys to be shared if all are in use.

### *Stern anchor*

This system involves deploying a stern anchor 3–4 boat lengths out and taking a bow line to the jetty or shore. As with the stern buoy system, it can help to have the stern line or tape on a reel attached to the pushpit.

Yachts frequently use this technique to moor direct to the rocky shores in the sheltered waters of the archipelagos, in which case the anchor is dropped on the approach and a crew member has to jump ashore and make fast to convenient trees or rings or hammer in rock pegs (bergskils). This should only be attempted where the shore is sufficiently steep-to, and it is always advisable to reconnoitre the chosen place first to ensure that there are no shallow areas or hidden rocks.

### *Booms*

These are narrow (perhaps only 10cm wide) finger pontoons laid at right angles to the main pontoon, and often only 5–6m long. Lines have to be attached from the yacht to the outer (and sometimes the inner) end of the boom and to the main pontoon. Use of sheet winches can help. Access the shore via the bow as the boom will not take your weight. Do not try it!

Sometimes there is space for two yachts between each set of booms, but often they are individual slots.

### *Lazy lines*

In this case, a line is tied to the jetty and runs to a heavy weight some distance from it. Approach the jetty, pick up the line, preferably with a boat hook, and take it back to the stern and secure it to a stern cleat. At the same time, a member of crew should have jumped ashore and secured the bow lines.

The line will have spent all season in the water and may well be muddy and weedy. A pair of heavy waterproof gloves will be useful.

Care should be taken to determine whether this system is in use, since dropping a stern anchor could lead to it becoming seriously fouled on the ground chains. Harbours which employ this particular system may well have a sign (an anchor with a red line across it). This is not intended to forbid mooring but means 'Do not use a stern anchor'.

Y-boom berths on the Göta Kanal *Andy Beharrell*

**Note:** In this chapter we are only covering the main routes into the Baltic via the Skaggerak and Kattegat, through the Limfjord and the Kiel Canal. For a more extensive guide to Germany and Denmark see the separate Pilotage Foundation guide *Germany and Denmark* (Imray).

# 1. APPROACHES TO THE BALTIC

## ROUTES TO THE BALTIC

Access to the Baltic can be from the north (around the tip of Jutland) or through the Limfjord. If coming from the UK, it is possible to cross directly from the east coast of the UK or from Scotland to Thyboron to access the Limfjord, but this route is only viable in onshore winds of less than a Force 6. An alternative is to cross from Lerwick in the Shetlands to Bergen (a crossing of around 180M) and then work south towards the Baltic from there.

From the south, the main route is via the River Elbe and into the Kiel Canal, though an interesting alternative is to head through the River Eider and join the Kiel Canal further east.

In this chapter we cover all these options and give a range of stopping points in both Denmark and Germany, though if you are planning to make more stops in Germany and/or Denmark we would recommend the separate Pilotage Foundation guide *Germany and Denmark* as this gives much more extensive coverage and also includes the Great and Little Belt areas of Denmark along with the remainder of the east coast of Jutland not covered in this book.

## GERMANY

Germany's Baltic coastline (known as the *Ostsee* in German) falls naturally into two parts – the former West German province of Schleswig-Holstein and the former East German province of Mecklenburg-Vorpommern. Neither has any dramatic physical features, but they are both very interesting in many other respects and have much to offer the cruising yachtsman.

In this chapter we look mainly at the eastern part as this is a key route through to the Baltic. This area has seen much redevelopment since reunification in 1990, but one can still enjoy large areas of countryside which remains untouched and where wildlife has been protected and left undisturbed. The coast has spits, bars and islands enclosing irregular inland seas known as Bodden, often backed by sand dunes planted with Norwegian spruce. There are a number of historically significant towns, each with its own character.

In the 13th century Lübeck became the centre of the Hanseatic League and Wismar, Rostock, Stralsund and Danzig (Gdansk) all received their city charters in the same era. This results in an area brimming with history and towns which still display their legacy from the Hanseatic era. Indeed, the old town of Stralsund, together with Wismar, is a UNESCO World Heritage Site.

The Hanseatic Cogs (trading ships) carried a wide range of cargoes including beeswax, furs, timber, tar, flax, honey, wheat, and rye from the east to England and other western countries. Cloth and manufactured goods moved in the opposite direction. Metal ore (mainly copper and iron) and herring were traded from Sweden and Lübeck also had a vital role in the salt trade. The Hanseatic League also traded in beer and the beer from the Hanseatic towns themselves was often the most valuable. This could still be considered a recommendation for a visit to the area!

If heading through Bremerhaven then the Maritime Museum is worth a visit as they have the best preserved example of a Hanseatic Cog. The Cog has been dated to 1380 and it was found in 1962 in the river at Bremen.

Economically now, the mainstays of Mecklenburg-Vorpommern are agriculture, fishing and tourism, together with shipbuilding at Rostock and Wismar. There is very little manufacturing industry apart from that associated with shipping. The tourist industry has been established since the end of the 19th century when the extensive beaches of the province became popular.

Throughout the whole area, major restoration work continues to be undertaken to preserve the many historic buildings and towns, and there has also been massive investment in the infrastructure such as roads and railways. English is widely spoken throughout this part of Germany, especially among the business community, but there are still some areas, especially in Mecklenburg-Vorpommern, where it may not as widespread. It is likely that younger Germans have a better grasp of English than their older counterparts who would have had to learn Russian in school as their main language.

# GERMANY KEY INFORMATION

## Rescue/Safety services

**Emergency** ✆ 112

**Police** ✆ 110

**MRCC Bremen Rescue Radio** monitors VHF Ch 16/70, DSC MMSI 00 211 1240, ✆ 124 124 (without prefix). Call Sign '**Bremen Rescue**'.

This is operated by the German national lifeboat organisation DGzRS and coordinates rescues in both the German North Sea and the Baltic.

## Charts and chart packs

UKHO Admiralty charts, or their German equivalents, are excellent for yachts on passage. However, for more leisurely cruising, and particularly to explore the area between Darsser Ort and the Polish border, three series of chart packs are available – the BSH Sportschiffahrtskarten 3000 series published by the German Hydrographic Office, the NV Sportschiffahrtskarten series and the Delius Klasing Sportbootkarten series. These are also sold digitally.

The German Hydrographic Office (BSH) Sportschiffahrtskarten 3000 Series covers all of the German Baltic Coast but the sets for Rugen (3006), the Peenestrom and Stettiner Haff (3007) and the Zalew Szczecinski and Szczecin (3020) are particularly useful.

There are two excellent series of chart packs (size A2). They are published annually and come with electronic versions on CD and complementary pilot books:

**Nautische Veröffentlichung (NV)**
Serie 1 Fünen – Kiel
Serie 2 Lübeck – Bornholm – Kopenhagen
Serie 4 Rügen – Bodengewässer – Stettin
Serie 6 Poland – Litauen – Lettland
NOK Nord-Ostsee Kanal. A chart (A2) of the Kiel Canal.

**Delius Klasing Sportbootkarten**
Satz 1: Kieler Bucht, Mecklenburger Bucht, Schlei – 12 charts and 78 harbour plans covering the coast as far east as Warnemünde.
Satz 2: Mecklenburg, Vorpommern, Bornholm – 10 charts and 85 harbour plans covering the coast from Darsser Ort to the Polish border.

The advantages of the series type of chart are that one pack covers a large area and many harbour plans are included. The charts include a combination of large and small scales which can take a little getting used to.

## Pilots and cruising guides

**In English**

*The Baltic Pilot Volumes I and II* (NP 18 and 19) are useful for reference, but they are not ideally suited to the needs of the yachtsman.

*The Cruising Almanac* Imray/Cruising Association www.imray.com

*Admiralty List of Lights and Fog Signals*, Vols. B and C NP75 and 76

*Admiralty List of Radio Signals*, Vols 1,2,3,5, and 6

*Admiralty Maritime Communications United Kingdom and the Baltic*, NP291

*Germany and Denmark*, Nicholas Hill (Imray, 2023) is very useful

*Yachtsman's Ten Language Dictionary*, Barbara Webb & Michael Manton (Adlard Coles Nautical)

*Wie erreich ich wen in Allen deutsche Häfen* (How Do I Reach Whom in all German Harbours) (Storck Verlag 2014, 56th edition)

The Cruising Association publishes an excellent guide *Cruising in Baltic Germany* (available to non-members), which includes the Kiel Canal and many harbours as well as general information

**In German**

There are several pilot books available in German covering the Baltic coast, including:

*Ostseeküste Travemünde bis Flensburg* by Jan Werner published by Delius Klasing as companion to their Satz 1 chart series, and *Ostseeküste Travemünde bis Stettin* by Jan Werner published by Delius Klasing as companion to their Satz 2 chart series

The NV Nautische Veröffentlichung chart series (NV Ostsee) include their *Hafenlotse* guides which complement the charts and contain harbour plans

The Delius Klasing-Sportbootkarten series also has excellent supplements with harbour plans and aerial shots

*Sejlerens Marina Guide Volume 4, Ostsee, Nordsee, Elbe and Weser* covers both North Sea and Baltic marinas. Revised annually and available free at marina offices

*Hafenhandbuch* Vols Ostsee 1 and Mecklenburg-Vorpommern und Polen (Delius Klasing)

Guidance for Pleasure Craft in the Kiel Canal - *Merkblatt für Spoortbootfahrer* obtainable at the canal or download from **www.wsa-kiel.wsv.de**

## Time

Germany uses UT+1 in winter and UT+2 in summer.

## € Money

Germany uses the Euro. Cash dispensers are widespread. Credit cards are often not accepted, but the Mastercard Maestro debit card is quite widely used.

### Other regulations

- Children under 15 are not permitted to steer a vessel in German waters. In certain rivers the age limit is 21 or 23.
- Animals microchipped, blood tested, with a passport, current health certificate and Rabies vaccination, issued by a recognised vet prior to entry, are allowed in under the Pet Travel Scheme (PETS).
- Vessels over 25T are treated as merchant ships and must carry a pilot through most state waterways unless the skipper has a Master's Certificate. However, in practice, this does not seem to be applied to yachts. Some inland waterways require special permission before entry for power vessels and sometimes sailing yachts.
- Motor/sailing cones are taken seriously and failure to display one when required can lead to an immediate fine.

Non EU-registered yachts can stay in the EU for a maximum of 18 months.

Customs enquiries ✆+49 351 44834 530, enquiries.english@zoll.de

**Germany Embassy** 23 Belgrave Square, London SW1X 8PZ ✆+44 20 7824 1300 consularl@german-embassy.org.uk

**The Consulate General** (to which visa enquiries should be addressed) is round the corner at 1–6 Chesham Place, Belgrave Mews West, London SW1X 8PZ ✆+44 20 7824 1463 pass@lond.diplo.de
The website for both is **www.london.diplo.de**

**British Embassy** Wilhelmstrasse 70, 10117 Berlin ✆+49 30 204570
**www.gov.uk/government/world/organisations/british-embassy-berlin.de**

## Public holidays

Official public holidays in Germany include:
1 Jan, Good Friday, Easter Sunday and Monday, 1 May (Labour Day), Ascension Day (May), Whit Sunday and Monday (May or June), 3 Oct (German Unification Day), 24–26 Dec, 31 Dec. A number of regional holidays are also held.

## Communications

The country code for Germany is 49. Mobile coverage is generally very good. To make an international call, dial 00 followed by the country code, area code (omitting any initial 0) and number. WiFi is now installed at most larger marinas.

## Travel

There are major **airports** serving the Baltic coast area at Hamburg, Lübeck, Berlin and Rostock.

There are good **train** services throughout Germany and on to Poland, and excellent express coach services from London to Hamburg and Travemünde.

**Ferry** services operate on the following routes: Kiel – Klaipeda, Kiel – Oslo, Kiel – Göteborg, Puttgarden – Rødby; Travemünde – Trelleborg; Travemünde – Helsinki; Travemünde – Riga; Rostock – Gedser; Rostock – Trelleborg, Rostock – Helsinki, Rostock – Ventspils, Sassnitz/Mukran – Trelleborg; Sassnitz/Mukran – Baltysk, Sassnitz/Mukran – Klaipeda.

## WC Holding tanks

Toilets must not be discharged within 12M of the shore. Holding tanks are not compulsory for foreign yachts which are staying in Germany for one season. Yachts built before 1980 or less than 10.5m LOA/2.8m beam built before 2003 are also exempt.

## Websites

**www.germany.travel/en/** – The German National Tourist Office. All the usual links, weather information etc. Includes pages on both Schleswig-Holstein and Mecklenburg-Vorpommern. English version

**www.visits-to-germany.com** – A general tourist site, but with attractive graphics and much of interest. English version

**www.dwd.de** – The German Meteorological Office. Useful forecasts in English

**www.bsh.de** – The German Hydrographic Office. Includes an (apparently complete) listing of German charts and official publications. Impeccable English version

**www.kiel-canal.de** – The (commercial) United Canal Agency. Some history, webcams etc. English version

**www.wsa-kiel.wsv.de** – Kiel canal site with guidance for pleasure craft

**www.visit-luebeck.com** – Tourist guide to Travemünde and Lübeck, with full English translation

**www.mvp.de** – An excellent site covering the Mecklenburg-Vorpommern region, with English translation and many useful links

**www.rostock.de/en** – Warnemünde/Rostock city

**www.ycstr.de** – The Yacht Club of Strelasund. In German only

**www.ruegen.de** – A very useful website covering Rügen island, with links to many of its towns and villages. Full English translation

## Firing range information

**www.bsh.de/EN/TOPICS/Shipping/Navigational_information/Warnings_and_notices/shooting-areas/shooting-areas_node.html**

## Radio communications & weather information

The coast has continuous **VHF** coast radio station coverage which is run by a private company, DP07 (Delta Papa Null Sieben). Areas: Kiel Bay north VHF Ch 67, Kiel Bay south VHF Ch 23, Lübeck Bay VHF Ch 24. Rostock transmits on VHF Ch 60 and Arkona on VHF Ch 66. Weather forecasts in slow German are issued on these channels at 0745, 0945, 1245, 1645 and 1945 local time, add an hour for Mar to Oct. Vital navigational warnings are broadcast on VHF Ch 16 every hour and H+30 until cancelled. Coastal areas covered are Flensburger Forde to Fehmarn, East of Fehmarn to Rugen, and East of Rugen. Sea areas are: Belte und Sund (Belts and Sound), Westliche Ostsee (Western Baltic), Sudliche Ostsee (Southern Baltic) and Boddengewasser Ost (Boddengewasser East).

**Navtex**, 518kHz is perhaps the best and most reliable method of receiving weather information in English.

**The German Met Service**, DWD (Deutscher Wetter Dienst) provides forecasts in English for the North Sea and Baltic Sea, www.dwd.de. It also has a useful 3-day forecast for winds and wave heights. There is an English translation button.

*Note* Wind speeds are sometimes given in metres per second. As a very approximate guide, double them to convert to knots and halve them to convert to Beaufort.

## PRACTICALITIES

### Yacht services & chandleries

Mooring fees are generally considerably lower than in the UK, and in ports with few facilities there may well be no charges at all for overnight mooring.

Berthing will usually be in box berths, or sometimes bows-to with the stern secured to a buoy, or alongside a jetty or, in recently built marinas, against a finger pontoon (see main introduction for details of berthing systems, page 14). The concept of visitors' berths is uncommon, and a vacant berth will usually be indicated by a green plaque at its head. A red one indicates that it is reserved and that its owner will soon be returning. Communication with marinas is generally conducted over the telephone rather than by VHF.

In Schleswig-Holstein yachts are well provided for. Chandlery, fuel and bottled gas (including Campinggaz) are readily available.

In Mecklenburg-Vorpommern facilities have improved significantly with the development of many new marinas. Obtaining fuel and bottled gas is no longer a problem and chandlery is available in the major harbours.

### Shopping

The availability and choice of consumer goods in the entire region is as extensive as anywhere in Europe though it is worth bearing in mind that most shops are closed on Saturday afternoons and on Sundays.

As prices throughout Germany are lower than in Scandinavia, yachts bound in that direction might well consider stocking up with non-perishable stores before leaving Germany. This applies particularly to beer, wines and spirits as these are expensive in Denmark and even more so in Sweden and Finland.

### Diesel

Non-bio red diesel is not available, and any that is bought in the UK should be kept in the main tank (not cans) and the receipt retained. At the time of publication German diesel contains a 7% bio component, though rules and regulations are in a constant state of flux and this may change in future.

### Gas

Gas cylinders, including Calor gas, can be refilled in northern Germany (www.faerbergas.de).

### Health

See main Introduction page 9 concerning GHIC cards. Some prescription drugs may be banned so it is best to keep a doctor's note on board confirming your need for particular medicines. See German Customs website for up to date information in English (zoll.de/EN/Private-individuals/Travel/travel_node.html).

The Bremen Cog has been dated to 1380 and was discovered in 1962 in the river at Bremen *Olga Ernst/Wikimedia Commons (https://commons.wikimedia.org/wiki/File:Bremer_Kogge,_Schifffahrtmuseum_Bremerhaven.jpg)*

# CRUISING

## The cruising areas

The coast east of Kiel is low-lying and well populated. Yachts aiming for the Mecklenburg area will sail past the mammoth Heiligenhafen yacht harbour before passing under the impressive Fehmarnsund bridge (clearance 23m, but winds from north or east can raise sea level by up to 1.5m) connecting Fehmarn island to the mainland. Those heading for southern Sweden can either skirt the northern coast of Fehmarn or stop on the south of Fehmarn before heading across to Gedser in Denmark. Neither route holds much of shore interest, but if choosing the German coast Travemünde and particularly Lübeck are well worth a visit.

East of Wismar the coast features hills and woods for some 6M but then flattens out. Further east it is again wooded between Warnemünde and the promontory of Darsser Ort. Darsser Ort is designated as an 'emergency only' haven for use under duress of weather and yachts are not welcome. The local SAR vessel is sometimes based here. Inland lies the Mecklenburg lake district. It is densely wooded and has over a thousand lakes. This unspoilt region is ideal for walking, cycling or indeed exploring by boat, via a system of shallow canals linking major lakes but the maximum draft is around 1.2m, so this will be too restrictive for most cruising yachts.

The coastline is low lying and seemingly featureless from seaward, but behind the tree-lined spits and sandbars which form much of this coast lie the Boddens. These large unspoilt lagoons, often bordered by immense expanses of reeds, are remarkable for their birds, isolation, shoal waters and small fishing ports. Local ferries run day-trippers out to them and they have become popular tourist destinations, but they still have a special ambience derived from their isolation and tranquillity.

For navigation in the Boddens, German charts (and perhaps one of the German pilot books) are necessary, and the small craft folios, which are available in electronic form as well as on paper, are clear and accurate.

Behind the coasts of Darss and Zingst the three Boddens of Barther, Bodstedter and Saaler may be entered from the eastern end. Dredged, buoyed channels up to 25m wide are maintained with depths of 3.2m up to Barth and 2.4m beyond (the offshoot to Prerow carries 2.1m, that to Wustrow 1.5m and that to Ribnitz 1.6m). But it must be remembered that, depending on the winds and atmospheric conditions, sea levels may change by as much as +2m to -1m.

The coastal islands of Hiddensee, Rügen and Usedom, have long, wide, sandy beaches alternating with steep cliffs. Away from the resorts there are secluded fishing villages and large nature reserves full of birdlife. Hiddeensee has no cars and lovely bike riding. Vitte has good facilities, and the view from the Dornbusch lighthouse is worth the walk up the hill from Kloster.

Behind the western and northern coasts of Rügen is another area of Bodden which can be entered from the north or the south, with depths of 3m in the dredged channels, but very shoal and sometimes stony outside them.

At the southern tip of Hiddensee, approached via the Gellenstrom, lies the entrance to the Strelasund, a buoyed channel separating Rügen from the mainland. Just inside the entrance is a major breeding ground for wild geese and swans, which may be seen in their thousands. The clearly-marked channel winds past the small yacht and fishing harbour of Barhöft (where the local SAR vessel is stationed).

The Libben Channel to the northeast of Hiddensee is a useful alternative approach in strong onshore winds, giving access to sheltered waters. It saves continuing on to the more distant Sassnitz if the Gellenstrom passage is felt to be untenable.

The Strelasund leads to the charming town of Stralsund, which has undergone considerable restoration and is also an excellent shopping centre. It has impressive churches with far reaching views, an award-winning aquarium (the Ozeanum) and direct trains to Berlin. The double lifting road and rail bridge, the Ziegelgrabenbrücke, leads through to the Strelasund south, which meanders through marshes and meadows to Stahlbrode and Palmer Ort where the comparatively deep (8m) Greifswalder Bodden begins.

The seaward side of Usedom, from Peenemünde to the approaches to Świnoujście, is generally low – less than 60m – and featureless, with no harbours. The best marks are the churches of Zinnowitz, Heringsdorf and Ahlbeck (the border lies about 1.5M southeast of Ahlbeck church).

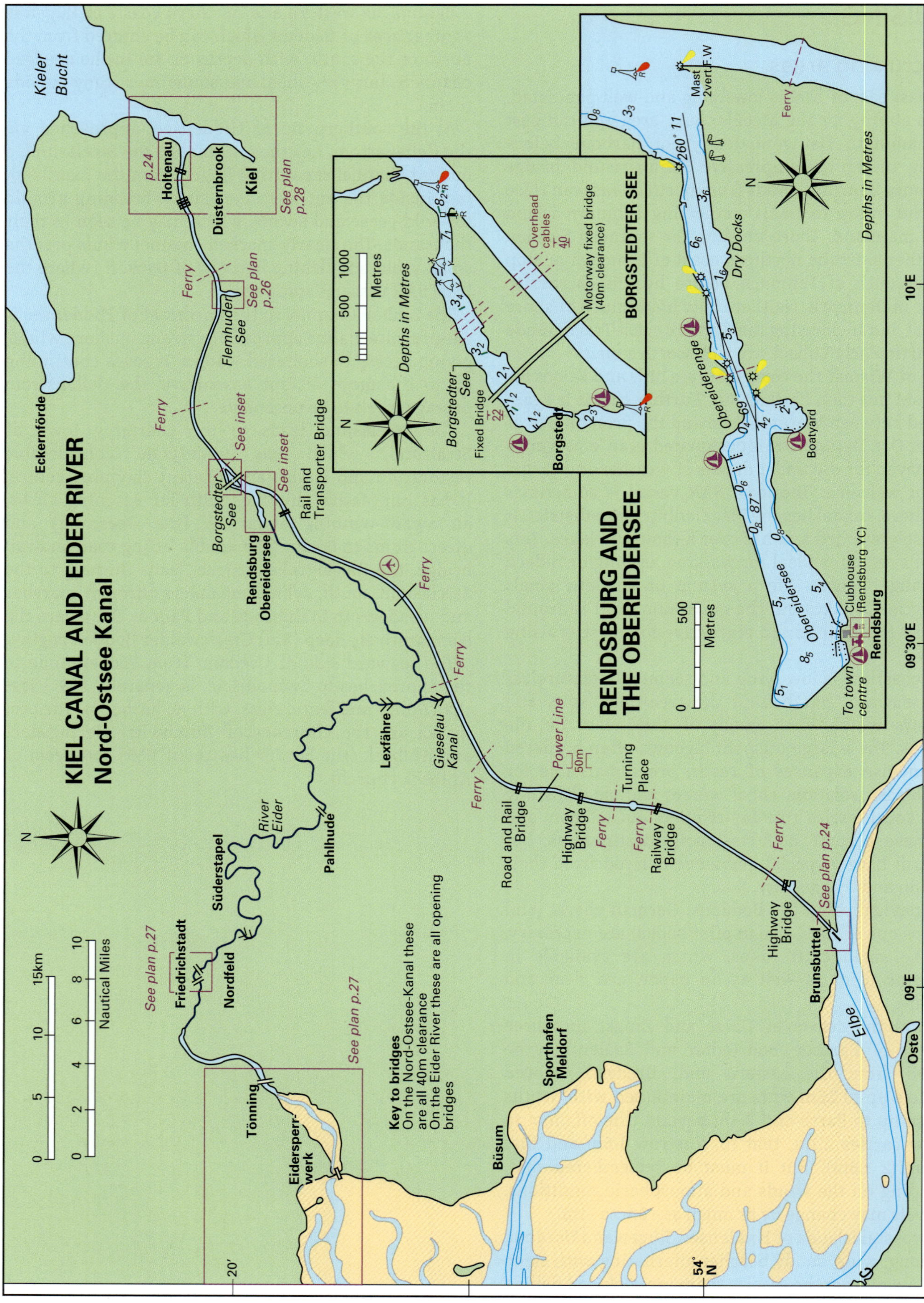
KIEL CANAL AND EIDER RIVER
Nord-Ostsee Kanal
Kieler Bucht
Holtenau
p.24
Düsternbrook
Kiel
See plan p.28
Eckernförde
Ferry
Flemhuder See
See plan p.26
See inset
Borgstedter See
Rendsburg Obereidersee
Rail and Transporter Bridge
Lexfähre
Gieselau Kanal
Power Line 50m
Road and Rail Bridge
Highway Bridge
Turning Place
Railway Bridge
Highway Bridge
See plan p.24
Brunsbüttel
Elbe
Oste
River Eider
Pahlhude
Süderstapel
Friedrichstadt
See plan p.27
Nordfeld
Tönning
Eidersperr-werk
Büsum
Sporthafen Meldorf
Key to bridges
On the Nord-Ostsee-Kanal these are all 40m clearance
On the Eider River these are all opening bridges
0 5 10 15km
0 2 4 6 8 10
Nautical Miles
20'
54°N
09°E
09°30'E
10°E
Borgstedter See
Fixed Bridge
Borgstedt
Motorway fixed bridge (40m clearance)
Overhead cables 40
Depths in Metres
0 500 1000 Metres
BORGSTEDTER SEE
RENDSBURG AND THE OBEREIDERSEE
0 500 Metres
To town centre
Rendsburg
Clubhouse (Rendsburg YC)
Obereidersee
Obereiderenge
Boatyard
Dry Docks
Mast 2vert.F.W
260°
69°
87°
Depths in Metres

# 1A. APPROACH TO THE BALTIC VIA THE KIEL CANAL AND THE RIVER EIDER

## The Kiel Canal

The Nord-Ostsee Kanal (NOK), also known as the Kiel Canal, is one of the major routes from the North Sea into the Baltic and is a formidable feat of engineering. Built so that the German fleet could move between the Baltic and the North Sea without having to pass through the Kattegat, it was opened in 1895. It is just over 53M long with a minimum bridge clearance of 39.6m. It is very wide, and dredged to 11m. Near Rendsburg, roughly halfway along the canal, is one of the last remaining transporter bridges in the world. Its moving section crosses the canal just a few metres above the canal.

Ships up to 235m can use the canal, so expect to have some substantial company both in the locks and on the canal itself. The canal carries an annual average of 32,000 ships (approximately 90 each day), transporting approximately 100 million tonnes of goods.

There are two pairs of locks at each end - the western at Brunsbüttel, at the entrance from the Elbe, and the eastern at Holtenau (a suburb of Kiel) where the canal enters Kiel Hafen. At Brunsbüttel yachts are usually directed to the southern lock, and at Holtenau to the northern lock, except in winter.

If approaching from the west, the waiting area is to the southeast of the moles (see plan page 24), where you stem the tide, which can run very hard here, until you are allowed to enter.

A confusing array of lights may be displayed from the locks (see table below).

The locks at both ends of the canal have been subject to considerable change in recent years with a fifth lock being built at the Brunsbüttel end and additional developments at Holtenau. For up-to-date information on the status of the locks, see www.nok-wsa.de/?lang=en.

Whilst in the canal, there are notices along the side which indicate which VHF channel to use to contact the canal authorities.

| Yacht relevant signals at locks | |
|---|---|
| Fixed single white light | No entry |
| White over red | Prepare to enter |
| One white occulting light on the signal mast at the lock island | Entry for pleasure craft permitted into the approach area |
| One white occulting light on the signal mast at the lock | Entry for pleasure craft permitted into the outer harbour and the locks |
| White over green | Entry permitted for vessels exempt from pilotage |

| Lock and canal communications | |
|---|---|
| Canal stretch between Brunsbüttel and Breiholz | VHF Ch 2, call "Kiel Canal 2" |
| Canal stretch between Breiholz and Kiel-Holtenau | VHF Ch 3, call "Kiel Canal 3" |

The canal is marked in kilometres.

*Kiel Canal websites*

www.yumpu.com/en/document/view/40435259
www.wsa-kiel.wsv.de
www.wsv.de

## Contacts

Holtenau lock keeper ☏+49 431 3603 152
Brunsbüttel lock keeper ☏+49 4852 885-252
Kiel Canal wsa-nord-ostsee-kanal@wsv.bund.de

A loudspeaker also instructs yachts regarding entry. The lock keepers are very busy, so avoid calling them if possible. Yachts caught in sudden fog or poor visibility may moor inside the dolphins on the mooring rings. Pleasure craft drawing over 3.1m are subject to mandatory pilotage. Pleasure craft of 20m or more must operate a class A or B AIS transponder during

The new locks at Holtenau. Note the very low floating wooden pontoons and horizontal fenders *John Sadd*

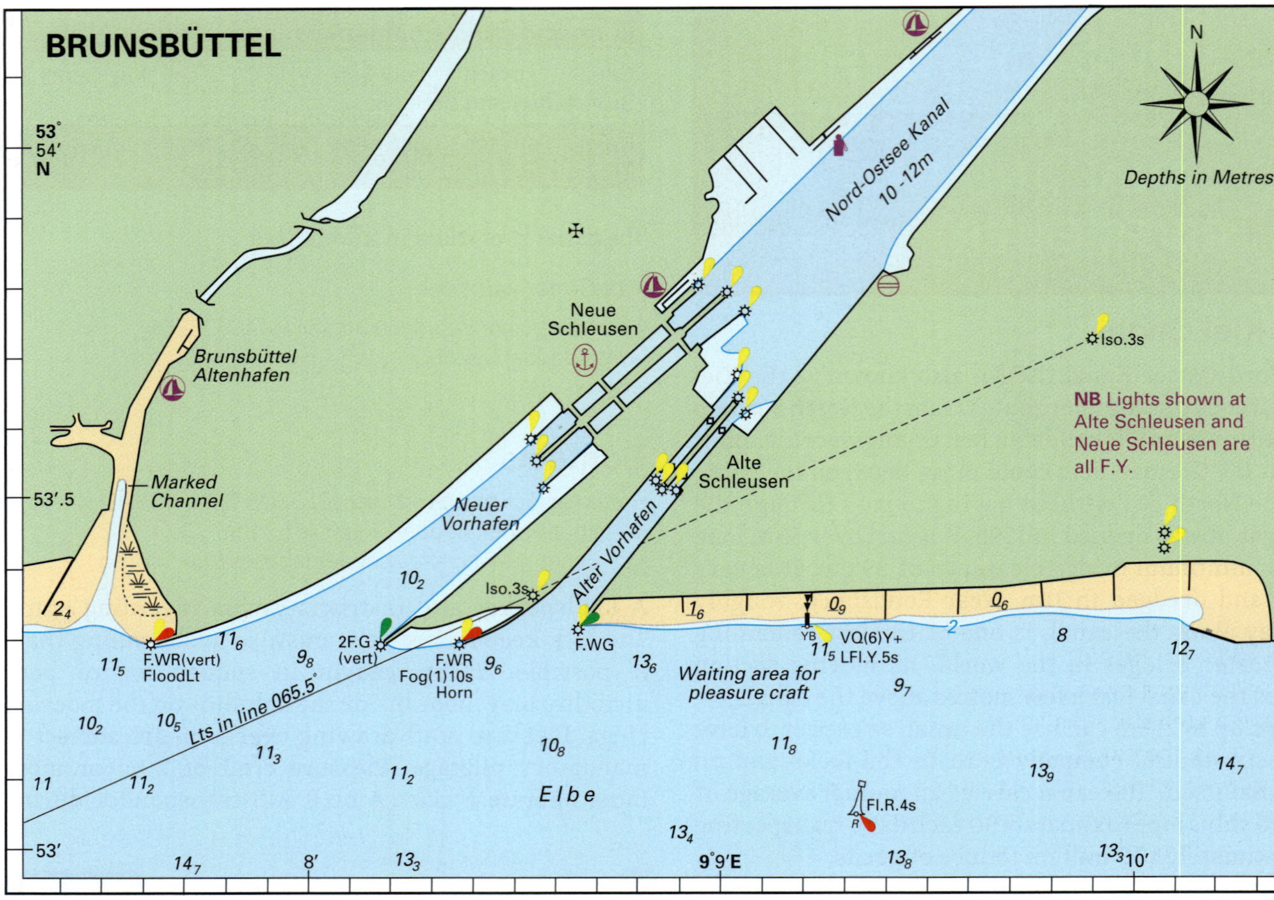


their transit, rentable at the canal entrance locks if necessary. Recreational multihulls up to 12m wide and under 20m long are exempt from the mandatory pilotage requirement.

There is a defined waiting area for yachts at Brunsbüttel, and you may well get into trouble with the *Wasserschutzpolizei* if you linger elsewhere. The waiting area is on the upstream side of the locks (the Hamburg side).

In the locks, mooring is to very low floating wooden rafts, so fenders need to be at water level, preferably weighted. The rise and fall is very small at both ends and there is no turbulence – indeed, it is generally not even possible to distinguish whether the lock is being filled or emptied. Be prepared to share the lock with ships and expect associated propeller wash.

It is essential to keep well clear of commercial shipping whilst in the canal, generally by keeping to

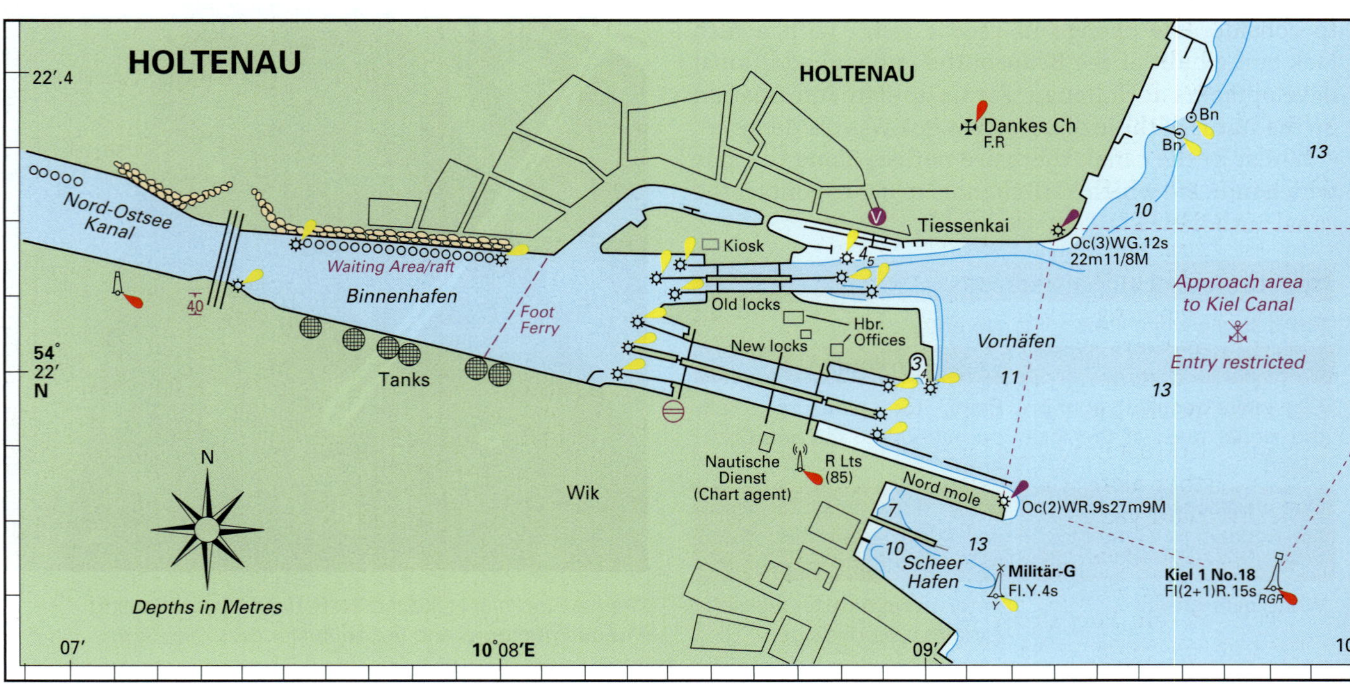

You will have company as you go along the Kiel Canal - keep close to the starboard bank to stay out of the way of ships *Viv Fox*

the starboard side. Even so it is wise to keep well clear of the bank, as passing ships can create a great deal of wash which may even ground a yacht.

A good watch should also be kept for the many ferries which cross the canal along its length and have right of way over yachts. Should three vertical red lights be seen all yachts should keep to starboard and stop, usually to allow a large vessel to pass. A good watch on AIS will give plenty of warning of ships approaching.

The modest canal dues are payable at Holtenau. New cash/card machines are located at the new waiting area to the north, and also on the Tiessenkai. Charts can be bought at Holtenau at Kapitän Stegmann's office which is on the south side of the locks. Unfortunately, it is forbidden to cross the canal on foot across the locks so if westbound it is necessary to moor alongside the quay at Tiessenkai just east of the locks and walk to the foot ferry.

Although the canal can be traversed in one day at a speed of 5kn (the maximum speed is 8.1kn or 15km/h), it is quite an effort to do so as hand-steering is required throughout. Shorthanded yachts will find it easier to stop overnight (see below). Motorsailing is permitted, providing a speed of at least 3.25kn (6km/h) is maintained. Pure sailing and tacking are not permitted. When motor-sailing the regulation downward-pointing cone must be displayed.

Yachts are not permitted to proceed through the canal between sunset and sunrise or in bad visibility, and will not be locked in unless there is time to reach one of the authorized mooring places, marked by yellow buoys. Kilometre markers standing on the banks of the canal indicate the distance from Brunsbüttel. There are the following options for an overnight stay:

A. Brunsbüttel just inside the locks on the north side (A little further along the canal on the north side is a fuel berth for yachts).

B. The best facilities are to be found in Rendsburg, at Km66 (see plan page 22). The yacht harbour, Regatta-Verein Rendsburg ☎+43 31 23961 is at the head of the bight, near the Rendsburg Yacht Club www.regatta-verein-rendsburg.de and convenient for the town centre and mainline station. It has good marina facilities, fuel, a restaurant, food shops and a chandlery and is convenient for crew changes.

C. Dückerswisch Siding at 20.5km, or Oldenbüttel Siding at 40.5km.

D. A peaceful spot is the entrance to the Gieselau Kanal on the waiting pontoon just before the lock at 40.5Kms.

E. The Marina Schreiber Borgstedt at 67.5km (the latter has a pontoon berth and diesel is available).

F. There is an attractive anchorage in the entrance to the Flemhuder at Km85.5 (48M from Brunsbüttel and 7M from Holtenau) where the anchorage carrying about 2.5m depth is marked out by four yellow buoys (see plan page 26).

When exiting the sidings and rejoining the canal the lights on signal masts must be obeyed in case a ship is approaching.

The Rendsburg transporter bridge – built between 1911 and 1913 *Andy Beharrell*

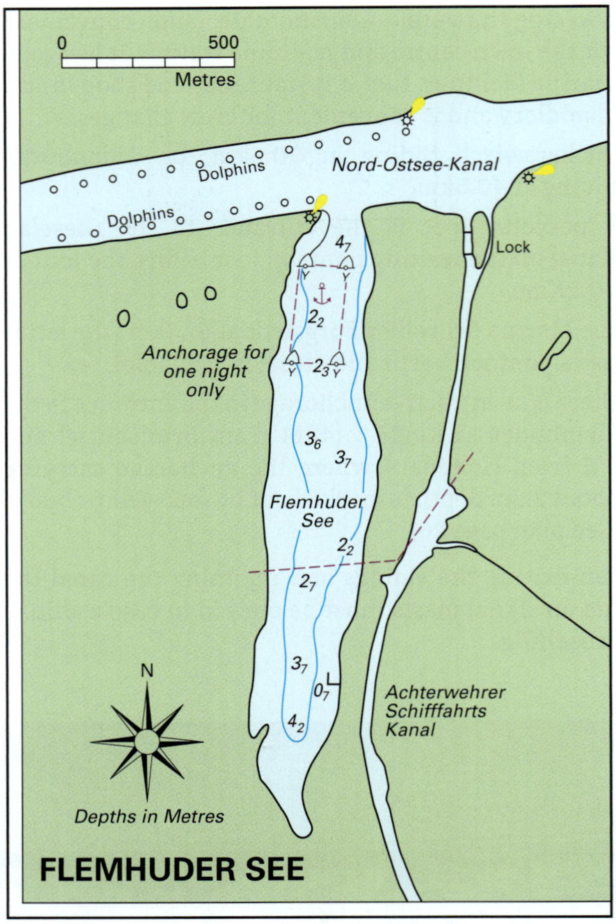

The quays at Tönning *Miranda Delmar-Morgan*

Friedrichstadt façade *Miranda Delmar-Morgan*

## Approach to the Baltic via the River Eider

The slow-flowing and meandering River Eider is an alternative mast-up route to the Baltic for those with time to spare. It does not bypass the Kiel Canal entirely as one has to join the Kiel Canal just past the 40km mark via the 1M-long Gieselau Kanal. However, it is a very attractive route which includes the charming towns of Tönning and Friedrichstadt.

It is 85M from the entrance to the river to Holtenau as opposed to 54M from Brunsbüttel to Holtenau. There are four locks and four opening bridges and apart from the Eidersperrwerk lock (Eiderdamm), which is manned continuously, they are not manned at night and only at set times on Sundays and public holidays (see www.wsa-elbe-nordsee.wsv.de/Webs/WSA/Elbe-Nordsee/DE/5_Service/2_Haefen_Schleusen/bszsEider.pdf for details of opening times). The river is tidal as far as the lock at Nordfeld.

It is 21M from Helgoland to the River Eider landfall buoy at 55°14'.5N 08°27'.6E and from there another 16M along the shallow buoyed channel to the lock at Eiderdamm. There is a waiting basin on the seaward side and a quay on the landward side of the lock. The lock is open 24hrs but currents of 2–5kn run seaward when the sluices are opened (HW+0230) It is essential to arrange to tackle the buoyed approach channel during the second half of the flood and to avoid the route altogether in strong onshore winds because of the bar (1.5–3m). HW at Eiderdamm is HW Helgoland +0120.

Once through the Eiderdamm lock it is another 5M to Tönning by unlit buoyed channel but if it is getting late there is a good anchorage in the river between red buoys No. 62 and 64. No anchoring is permitted within 2km of the dam. Westbound from Tönning you should leave before HW in order to allow for arrival at the Eiderdamm locks near HW for best of use of the ebb and tidal height into the North Sea.

### Tönning

This is an attractive old fishing town and berthing is possible alongside in the river. The quays in the inner harbour channel dry to soft mud at LW. Basic facilities but no fuel berth.

### Friedrichstadt

This charming town was built by the Dutch when they were brought in to sort out the drainage problems of the area in the 17th century. Consequently, the town has a very Dutch appearance with a network of canals, bridges and gabled houses. Berth in the Neuerhafen in 3m or the Alterhafen in 1.7m by going through the lock, but the approach to the lock can carry as little as 1m at LW. Basic facilities.

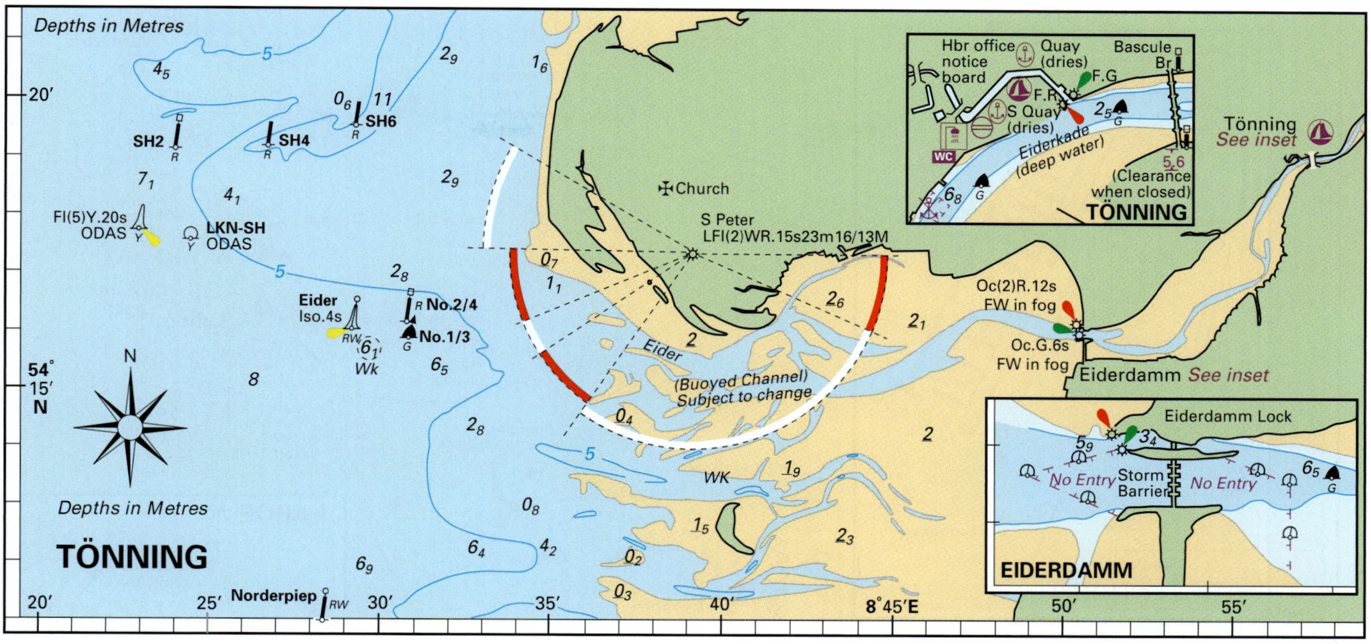
Depths in Metres
TÖNNING
Depths in Metres
20′
54° 15′ N
20′
25′
30′
35′
40′
8°45′E
50′
55′
SH2
SH4
SH6
Fl(5)Y.20s
ODAS
LKN-SH
ODAS
Eider
Iso.4s
No.2/4
No.1/3
Wk
WK
Norderpiep
Church
S Peter
LFl(2)WR.15s23m16/13M
Eider
(Buoyed Channel)
Subject to change
Oc(2)R.12s
FW in fog
Oc.G.6s
FW in fog
Eiderdamm See inset
Tönning
See inset
Hbr office
notice
board
Quay
(dries)
Bascule
Br
F.G
F.R
S Quay
(dries)
Eiderkade
(deep water)
(Clearance
when closed)
WC
TÖNNING
Eiderdamm Lock
No Entry
Storm
Barrier
No Entry
EIDERDAMM

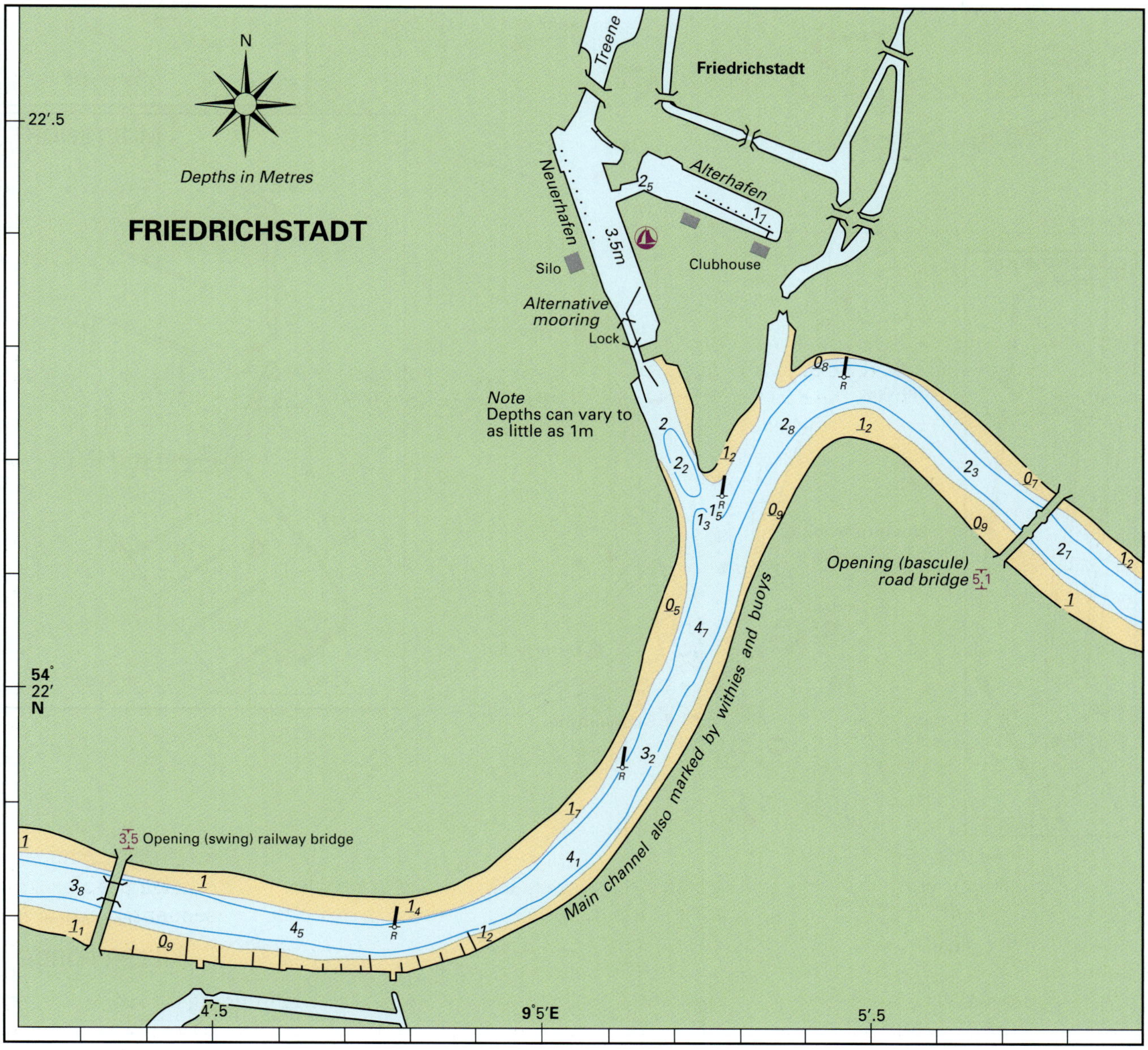
Depths in Metres
FRIEDRICHSTADT
22′.5
54° 22′ N
4′.5
9°5′E
5′.5
Treene
Friedrichstadt
Alterhafen
Neuerhafen
3.5m
Silo
Clubhouse
Alternative
mooring
Lock
Note
Depths can vary to
as little as 1m
Opening (bascule)
road bridge
Opening (swing) railway bridge
Main channel also marked by withies and buoys

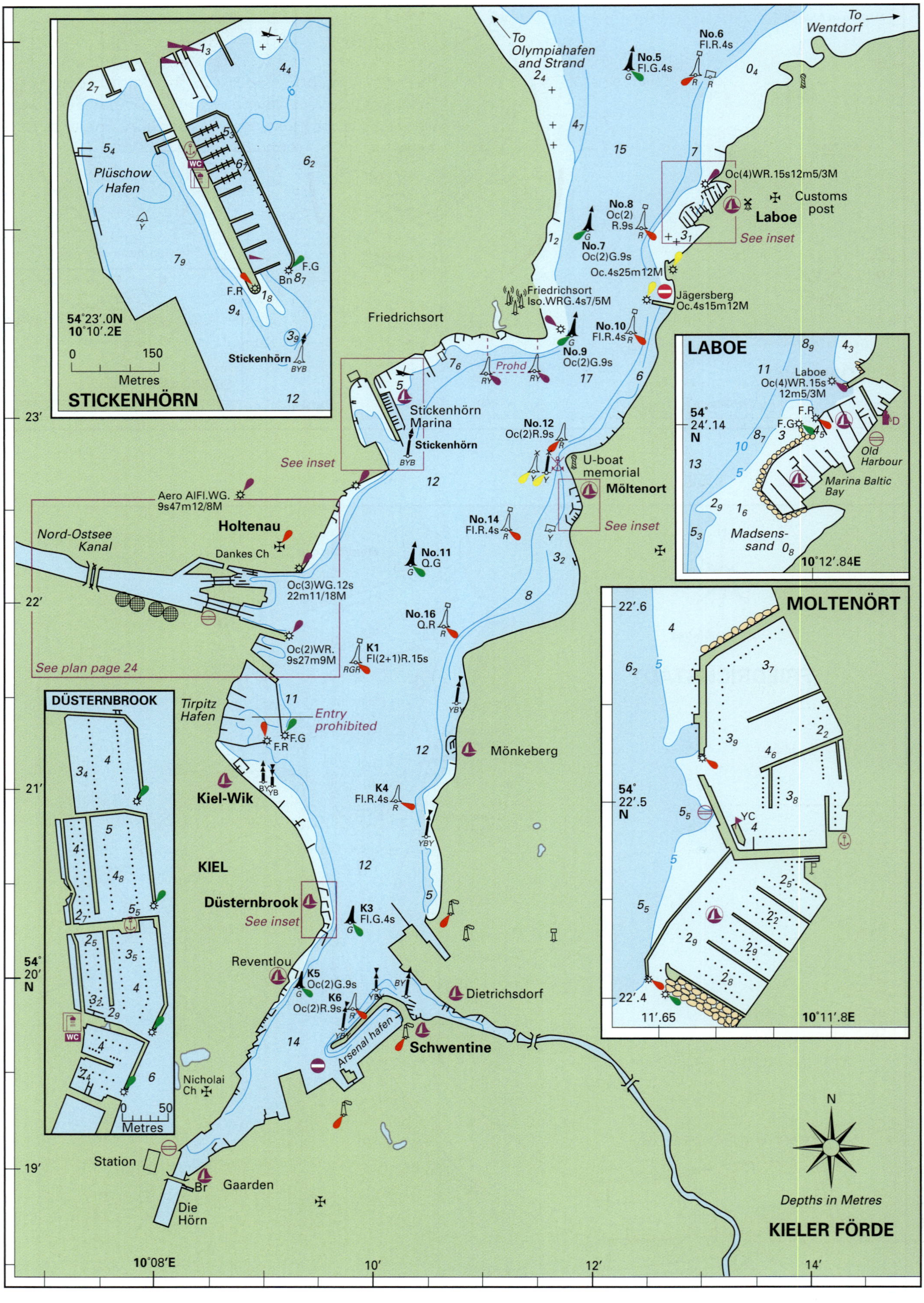
STICKENHÖRN
Plüschow Hafen
54°23′.0N
10°10′.2E
0 150 Metres
Stickenhörn
F.R
F.G
Bn
LABOE
Laboe
Oc(4)WR.15s 12m5/3M
F.R
F.G
Old Harbour
Marina Baltic Bay
Madsens-sand
54° 24′.14 N
10°12′.84E
MOLTENÖRT
22′.6
54° 22′.5 N
22′.4
11′.65
10°11′.8E
YC
DÜSTERNBROOK
0 50 Metres
To Olympiahafen and Strand
To Wentdorf
No.5 Fl.G.4s
No.6 Fl.R.4s
Oc(4)WR.15s12m5/3M
Customs post
Laboe
See inset
No.8 Oc(2) R.9s
No.7 Oc(2)G.9s
Oc.4s25m12M
Jägersberg Oc.4s15m12M
Friedrichsort Iso.WRG.4s7/5M
Friedrichsort
No.10 Fl.R.4s
No.9 Oc(2)G.9s
Prohd
Stickenhörn Marina
Stickenhörn
See inset
No.12 Oc(2)R.9s
U-boat memorial
Möltenort
See inset
Aero AlFl.WG. 9s47m12/8M
Holtenau
Nord-Ostsee Kanal
Dankes Ch
Oc(3)WG.12s 22m11/18M
No.14 Fl.R.4s
No.11 Q.G
No.16 Q.R
Oc(2)WR. 9s27m9M
K1 Fl(2+1)R.15s
See plan page 24
Tirpitz Hafen
Entry prohibited
F.G
F.R
Mönkeberg
Kiel-Wik
K4 Fl.R.4s
KIEL
Düsternbrook
See inset
K3 Fl.G.4s
Reventlou
K5 Oc(2)G.9s
K6 Oc(2)R.9s
Dietrichsdorf
Arsenal hafen
Schwentine
Nicholai Ch
Station
Br
Gaarden
Die Hörn
N
Depths in Metres
KIELER FÖRDE
23′
22′
21′
54° 20′ N
19′
10°08′E
10′
12′
14′

# 1B. KIELER FÖRDE TO MECKLENBURGER BUCHT

## KIELER FÖRDE INCLUDING KIEL

54°21'N 10°10'E

### Distances (from Kiel)

Heiligenhafen 35M, The Schlei 25M, Flensburg Förde 50M, Travemünde 65M, Gislövs Läge 130M, Copenhagen 145M, Stubbekøbing 85M

### Lights

**Kiel light tower** 54°30'N 10°16'.5E Iso.WRG.6s29m17–13M
Horn Mo(KI)30s Racon Red round tower, white band on grey base 33m. Floodlit

**Friedrichsort** 54°23'.4N 10°11'.6E Iso.WRG.32m7–5M
White round tower, green bands on gallery and base 32m. Floodlit

The marina breakwater south head, 1M southwest, is lit

**Scheerhafen (Holtenauer Schleusen, S side)** 54°21'.8N 10°09'.1E Oc(2)WR.9s23m9M
Red beacon, white band, grey lantern, masonry base 20m

**Nord-Ostsee Kanal (Holtenauer Schleusen, N side)** 54°22'.2N 10°09'.2E Oc(3)WG.12s22m11/8M
Red round tower 20m

### Contacts

**Port Office** ☎+49 4319 011173, VHF Ch 11 (0730–1600 LT), ☎+49 1716 497373 (outside office hours)
www.port-of-kiel.de

**Kieler Förde Vessel Traffic Service** ☎ +49 4313 603456, VHF Ch 67 Call Sign "Kiel Marine Traffic"

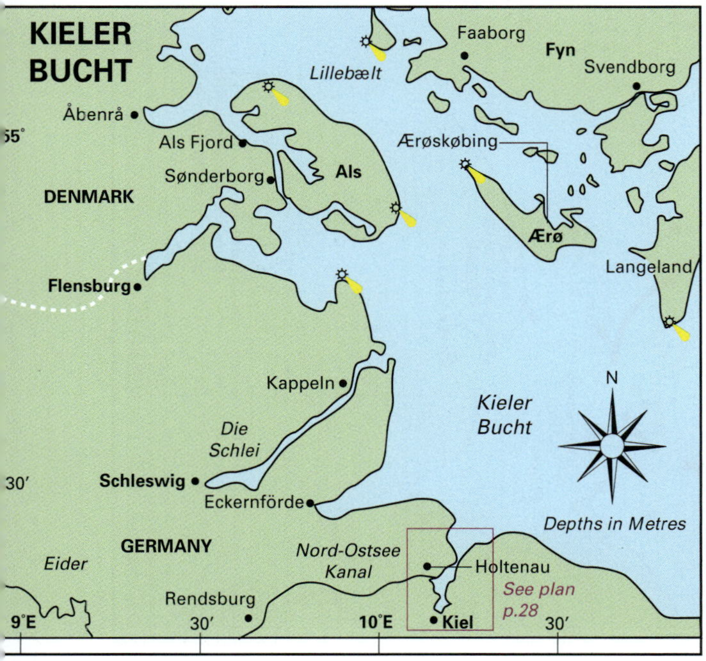


### General

Kieler Förde is the approach to Kieler Hafen, with Kiel, a major naval base, a commercial port and easily the largest yachting centre in the Baltic, at its head. Holtenau, the eastern end of the Kiel Canal, lies on the western side of Kieler Hafen, and there are numerous yacht harbours around its shores.

Kiel has a superb shopping centre – modern, busy and with great variety. For yachts entering the Baltic it is an excellent place to store ship for the whole Baltic cruise or to have repairs carried out and, having first-class travel facilities, it is an ideal place for crew changes.

The spectacular Kiel Week (Kielerwoche) takes place during the last full week in June, when the entire waterfront will be packed with tall ships and other vessels, so book a berth well in advance.

### Approach

From north and northwest 54°30'N 10°15'E
From east or northeast 54°28'N 10°20'E

It should be noted that there are military firing ranges (Todendorf and Putlos) between Kieler Förde and Heiligenhafen. The ranges are likely to be in use on

The port-hand of the two Kieler Bucht light structures, marking the Baltic approach to Kiel *A. and A. Fleck*

Holtenau Lighthouse *Miranda Delmar-Morgan*

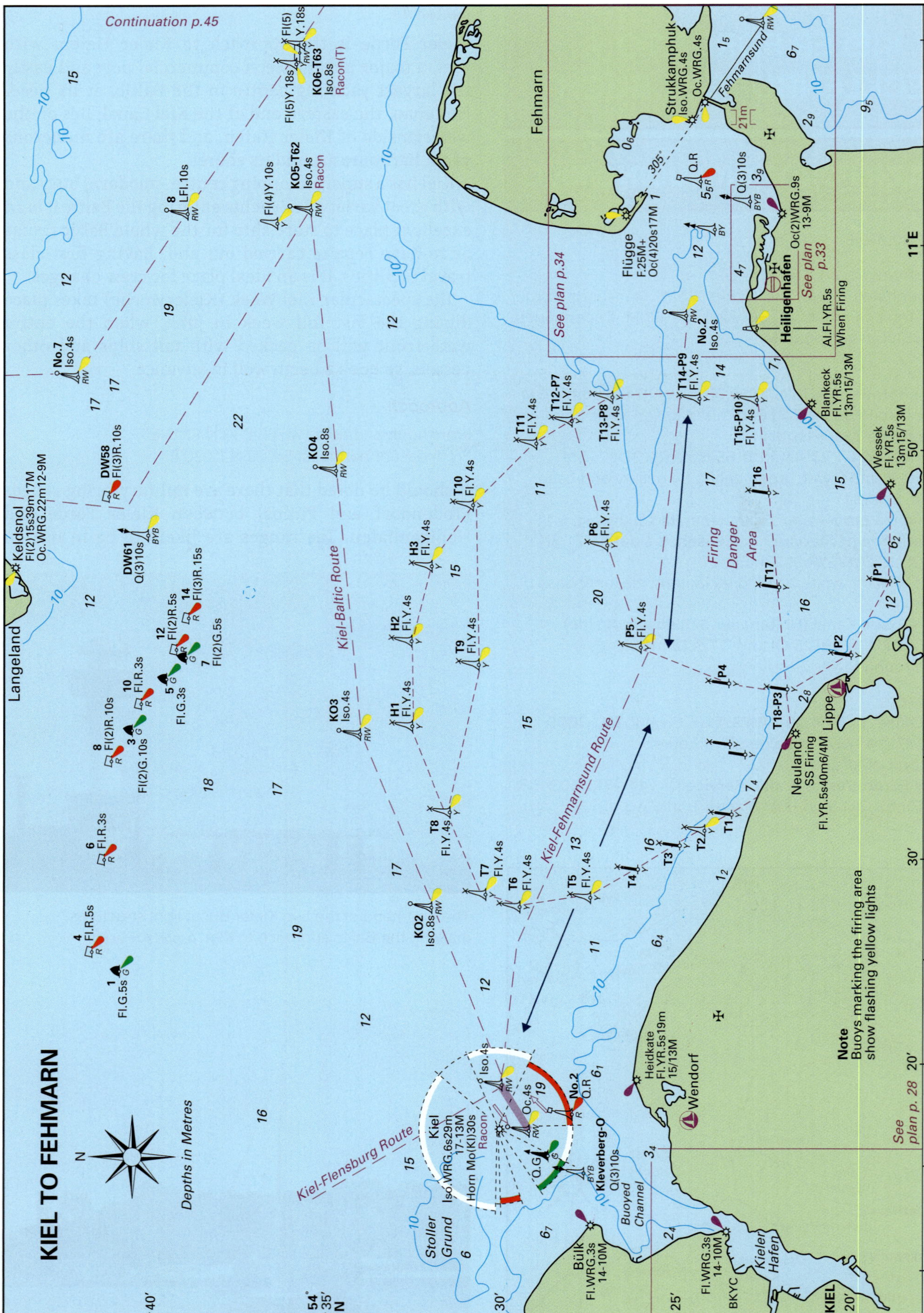
KIEL TO FEHMARN
Depths in Metres
N
Continuation p.45
Langeland
Keldsnol
Fl(2)15s39m17M
Oc.WRG.22m12-9M
Fehmarn
See plan p.34
Flügge
F.25M+
Oc(4)20s17M
Strukkamphuk
Iso.WRG.4s
Oc.WRG.4s
Fehmarnsund
Heiligenhafen
See plan p.33
Oc(2)WRG.9s
13-9M
Al.Fl.YR.5s
When Firing
Blankeck
Fl.YR.5s
13m15/13M
Wessek
Fl.YR.5s
13m15/13M
Firing Danger Area
Lippe
Neuland
SS Firing
Fl.YR.5s40m6/4M
Kiel-Baltic Route
Kiel-Fehmarnsund Route
Kiel-Flensburg Route
Kiel
Iso.WRG.6s29m
17-13M
Horn Mo(Kl)30s
Racon
Stoller Grund
Bülk
Fl.WRG.3s
14-10M
Kleverberg-O
Q(3)10s
Buoyed Channel
Kieler Hafen
Fl.WRG.3s
14-10M
BKYC
KIEL
Heidkate
Fl.YR.5s19m
15/13M
Wendorf
Note
Buoys marking the firing area show flashing yellow lights
See plan p. 28
54°35'N
11°E

Looking south from Laboe over the Kieler Förde. Baltic Bay marina at Laboe is visible *Andy Beharrell*

weekdays, but not at weekends. When in use Alt.Y.R.5s lights are shown on towers on the shore at 54°26'N 10°19'E and 54°23'N 10°56'E and at five other locations in between.

Range control boats are stationed at the east and west ends of the range when in use to intercept yachts and pass instructions to them on VHF Ch 16. A situation broadcast by Todendorf Naval Coastal Radio Station is transmitted at 0730, 1100, and 1530 LT Mon–Fri (and exceptionally at 0730 and 1100 on Saturdays) on VHF Ch 11 announced 5mins beforehand on VHF Ch 16. The range is crossed by the Kiel-Fehmarnsund route and it is a long way around the outermost buoys. NATO exercises use the extended area.

There is a major TSS just outside the Kieler Förde and major landmarks include the Kiel light tower and (in daylight) the impressive German Navy war memorial just north of Laboe. The Förde is very well buoyed throughout, but there is a large area of shoal water extending from the shore near the naval war memorial. Friedrichsort light is a prominent landmark when approaching Stickenhörn Marina. The entrance to the canal is about 1M further south

### *Anchorage, berthing & facilities*

There are no restrictions on anchoring in Kieler Hafen, but because of the heavy volume of commercial traffic it is strongly recommended that yachts should seek a berth at one of the many yacht harbours.

In view of the extensive choice of yacht harbours and associated facilities to be found in the Kieler Förde area, this section merely highlights a selection.

### *Communications & travel*

The nearest international airports are Hamburg and Lübeck. There are good train and coach services to all parts of Europe.

## Düsternbrook

54°20'.4N 10°09'.5E (outer mole)
Situated about 1.5M south of the canal entrance.

**Contacts**

Düsternbrook Sporthafen ✆+49 4312 604 84 26
www.sporthafen-kiel.de/sporthaefen
duesternbrook@sporthafen-kiel.de

This is the nearest harbour to the excellent shopping centre of Kiel, which can be reached on foot via the promenade and the Oslokai. Constructed for the 1938 Olympics, it has 288 berths in 2-4m and all normal marina facilities. It is a good base from which to stock up or change crews. Large yachts berth in the northernmost basin. The Kieler Yacht Club (✆+49 431 85021 www.kyc.de) has its headquarters on the other side of the main road and welcomes (well dressed!) visiting yachtsmen.

## Laboe

54°24'.1N 10°12'.8E (east mole)

**Contacts**
www.schiffswerftlaboe.de/en/marina

Laboe is a pleasant small town with an old fishing and yacht harbour ☎+49 4343 427556 and the Marina Baltic Bay ☎+49 4343 421151 (hafenmeister@schiffswerftlaboe.de) immediately south of it on the eastern side of Kieler Förde. Beware the frequent ferry traffic from the inner side of the outer mole of the old harbour. It is best not to round the molehead too close.

The fuel berth is in the old harbour to port as you enter but it is worth checking opening times with the harbourmaster. There are engineers, a marine electrician and sailmaker on site and Campinggaz is available. Laboe is the closest place from which to visit the conspicuous U-Boat Memorial. Bikes are available for hire.

## Strande

54°26'.1N 10°10'.3E

**Contacts**
☎+49 4349 8988, (0800–1200 and 1600–1800 LT)
VHF Ch 11
www.hafen-strande.de
Olympiahafen Schilksee marina ☎+49 431 371 021 or
+49 431 2604 84 *Mobile* +49 172 8024352

Strande is situated on the western side of Kieler Förde, about 4M north of Holtenau. Like Laboe, it is a good place to obtain fuel as well as being worth considering in its own right as a pleasant first or last night stop in the Baltic. Good bathing beach. Close by is the Olympiahafen Schilksee marina built for the 1972 Sailing Olympics. It has all facilities.

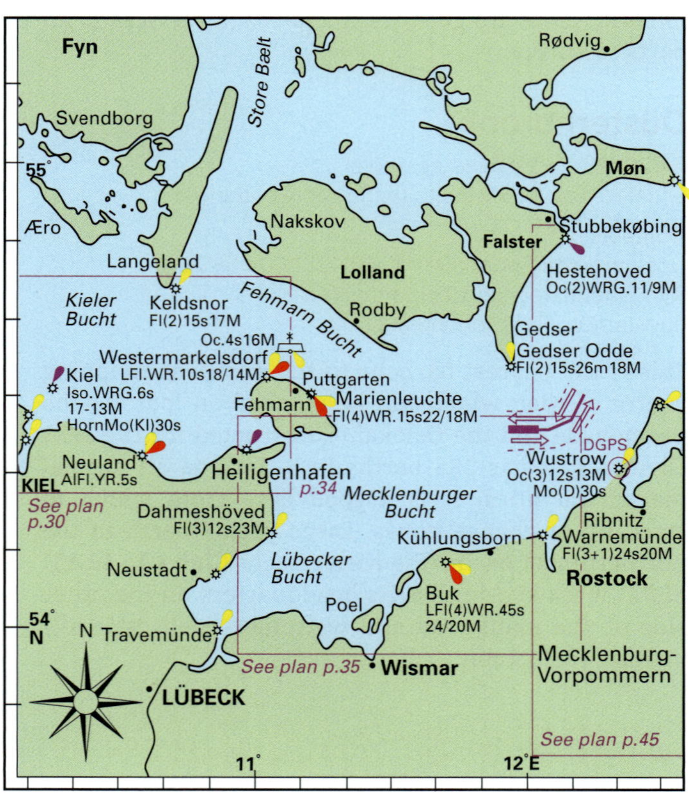


## HEILIGENHAFEN

54°23'N 11°00'E

**Distances**
Kiel 35M, Travemünde 33M, Wismar 38M, Warnemünde 43M

**Lights**
**Heiligenhafen (S side of Heiligreede)** 54°22'.2N 11°01'.2E
Oc(2)WRG.9s16m13–9M
Red tower, platform, white lantern, red and white dwelling 13m
**Outer Leading Lights 268.5°** Front 54°22'.4N 10°59'.6E
Oc.4s13m17M White g with red border on white mast 11m
*Rear* 312m from *front* Oc.4s19m17M White v with red border on grey warehouse
Inner Leading Lights 279.2° *Front* 54°22'.6N 10°59'.1E
Iso.3s13m17M Red g on white mast 14m
*Rear* 195m from front, Iso.3s13m17M Red v on white mast 16m

**Contacts**
**Heiligenhafen Harbourmaster** ☎+49 4362 5034 24
www.marina-heiligenhafen.de
**Marina Heiligenhafen** ☎+49 174 586 68 71
www.marina-heiligenhafen.de

### *General*

*See notes regarding Firing Ranges under Kieler Förde on page 19.*

Heiligenhafen is a major yacht and fishing harbour strategically placed for yachtsmen making eastwards from Kieler Förde. In strong northeasterly conditions the approach may become unpleasant, and in these circumstances it may be preferable to seek a harbour on Fehmarn Island such as Orth (54°27'N 11°03'E), or Burgtiefe (54°25'N 11°12'E) and Burgstaaken (54°25'N 11°11'E) in the Burger See to the east of Fehmarnsund bridge (see plan page 34). Burgtiefe has a useful set of 'boxes' in a circular pattern to accommodate berthing in any wind direction.

### *Approach & entrance*

Approach is made in the white sector of Heiligenhafen light on a bearing of approximately 210° to pick up the outer leading lights in the vicinity of Heiligenhafen No. 1 buoy. By day a useful guide to the entrance is the 134m radar tower about 1M south-southwest of Heiligenhafen light. By night this tower has red lights. After following the outer leading lights for about 0.7M the inner leading lights will be picked up.

### *Anchorage & berthing*

It is possible to anchor off Heiligenhafen light in 5m or 6m in suitable conditions but most yachts will wish to continue to the main yacht harbour. It may be possible to find an alongside berth in the old harbour to the south of the yacht harbour and if the charter fleet is out their berths may be unofficially available.

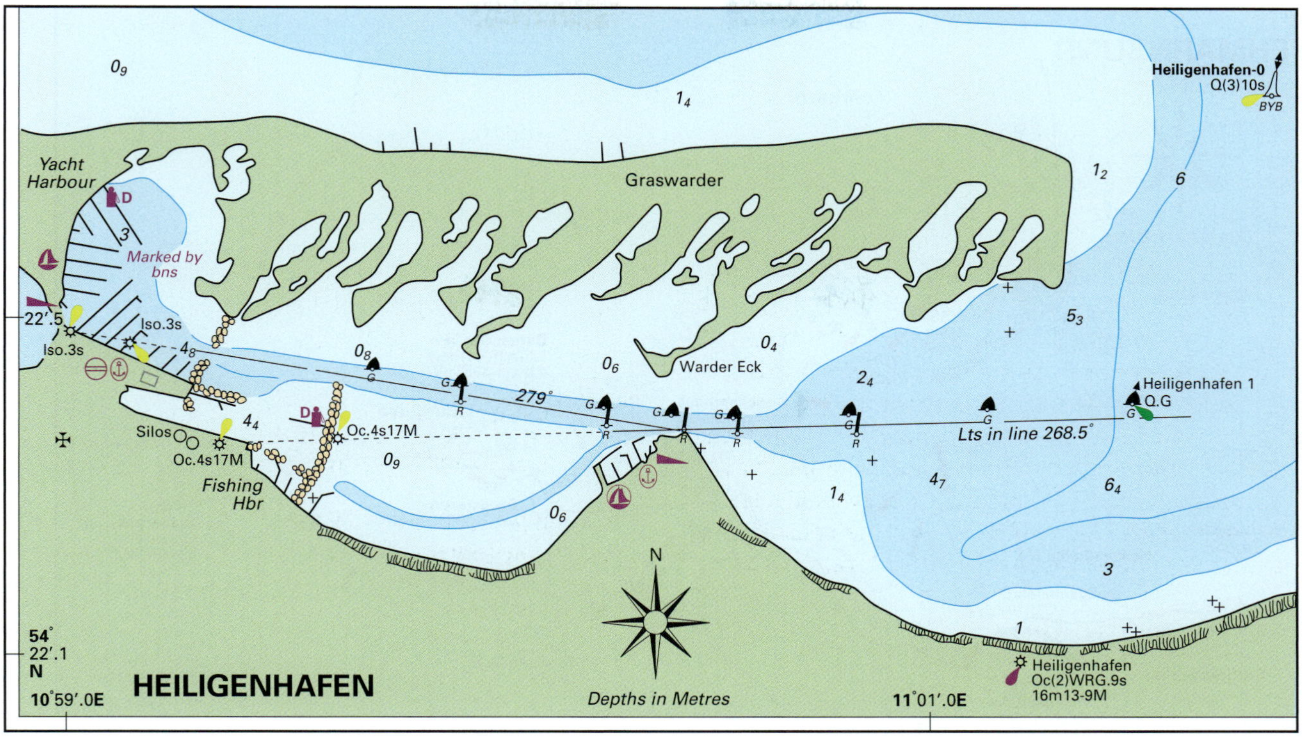


*Formalities*

The harbourmaster's office is between the yacht harbour and old harbour.

*Facilities*

Heiligenhafen is an attractive small holiday town with all shopping facilities convenient to the harbour. It has a sizeable charter fleet and a full range of yacht services, including chandlery, diesel and WiFi.

The yacht club sometimes has bikes for hire, and there are good restaurants and fresh fish. Excellent bird watching on the Graswarder nature reserve.

*Communications & travel*

There are regular buses to Grossenbrode where you can catch trains to Berlin and Fehmarn.

The Blue House, Graswarder *Miranda Delmar-Morgan*

Heligenhafen Graswarder looking seaward *Miranda Delmar-Morgan*

Heligenhafen entrance from east *Miranda Delmar-Morgan*

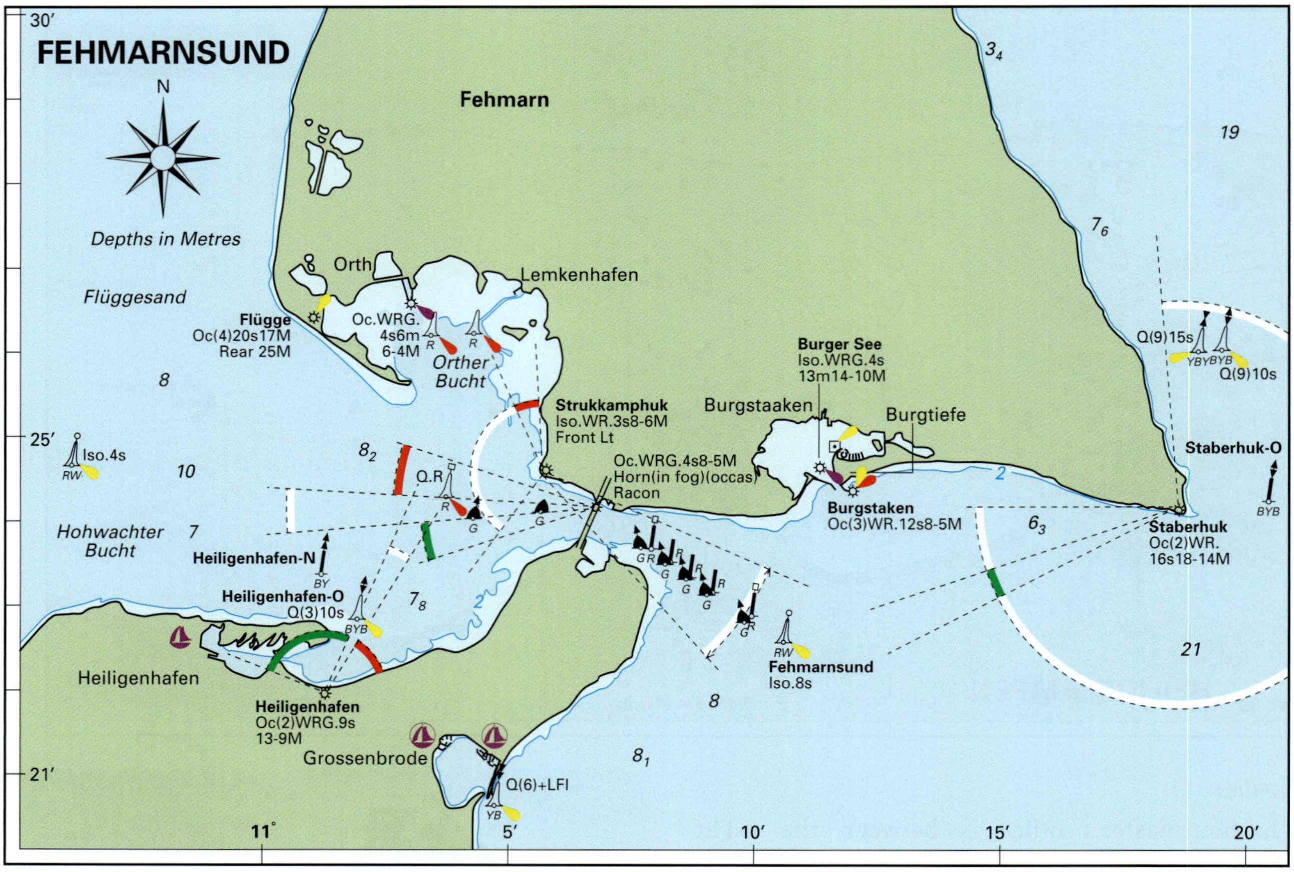


## Fehmarnsund

This is the channel between the island of Fehmarn and the mainland. It is crossed by a combined rail and road bridge with a clearance of 22m. but this can vary by up to 2m depending on wind conditions. Clearance is indicated at water level on each side of the bridge. There are sometimes currents up to 4kn if there have been persistent strong winds from the east or west.

The approach from the west is wide and straightforward but from the east the channel is very narrow and closely buoyed. It carries a depth of 5m. Neustadt, in the Lübecker Bucht, has a Schengen clearance facility. Ancora Marina at Neustadt has diesel.

## TRAVEMÜNDE (INCLUDING LÜBECK)

North mole 53°57'.7N 10°53'.3E

### Distances

Kiel 65M, Heiligenhafen 35M, Wismar 25M

### Lights

**Travemünde (Hochhaus)** 53°57'.8N 10°53'E
Fl.WR.4s114m19/15M Building 118m

**Priwall Leading Lights** 215.9° *Front* 53°57'.5N 10°53'.2E
Oc(2)9s14m17M White g with red border on white mast 13m
*Rear* 380m from front Oc(2)9s24m17M
White v with red border on white framework tower 21m

**North molehead** 53°57'.8N 10°53'.4E
Oc.RG.4s10m6/5M+F.Y in fog
White tower, black bands with glass bricks 9m Floodlit

### Contacts

**Travemünde Port Authority** ✆+49 4502 74362
VHF Ch 16/19
**Travemünde/Lübeck Vessel Traffic Service** Call Sign "Trave Traffic" ✆+49 4502 84750, VHF Ch 13 (broadcasts every 3hrs from 0600–2100 LT)
**Trave Bridge (Herrenbrüke)** VHF Ch 13
**Lübeck Hubbrucken** VHF Ch 18
**Passathafen Marina** ✆+49 45 11 22 87 610
Mobile ✆+49 15 12 04 02 479 / 16 09 31 34 967
passathafen@luebeck.de
**Böbs Werft Marina** ✆+49 4502 5051
www.boebs-werft.de
**Marina Baltica** ✆+49 4502 86010
www.marina-baltica.de
info@marina-baltica.de
**Eric Warburg Bridge** summer opening times: 0930, 1200, 1730, 1930.

### *General*

Travemünde is the outer port for Lübeck. It is a holiday resort and a busy ferry and commercial port with three major yacht harbours and was once on the border between the former East and West Germany. Its shopping centre is adequate though not extensive. Travemünde is an ideal base from which to visit Lübeck by public transport.

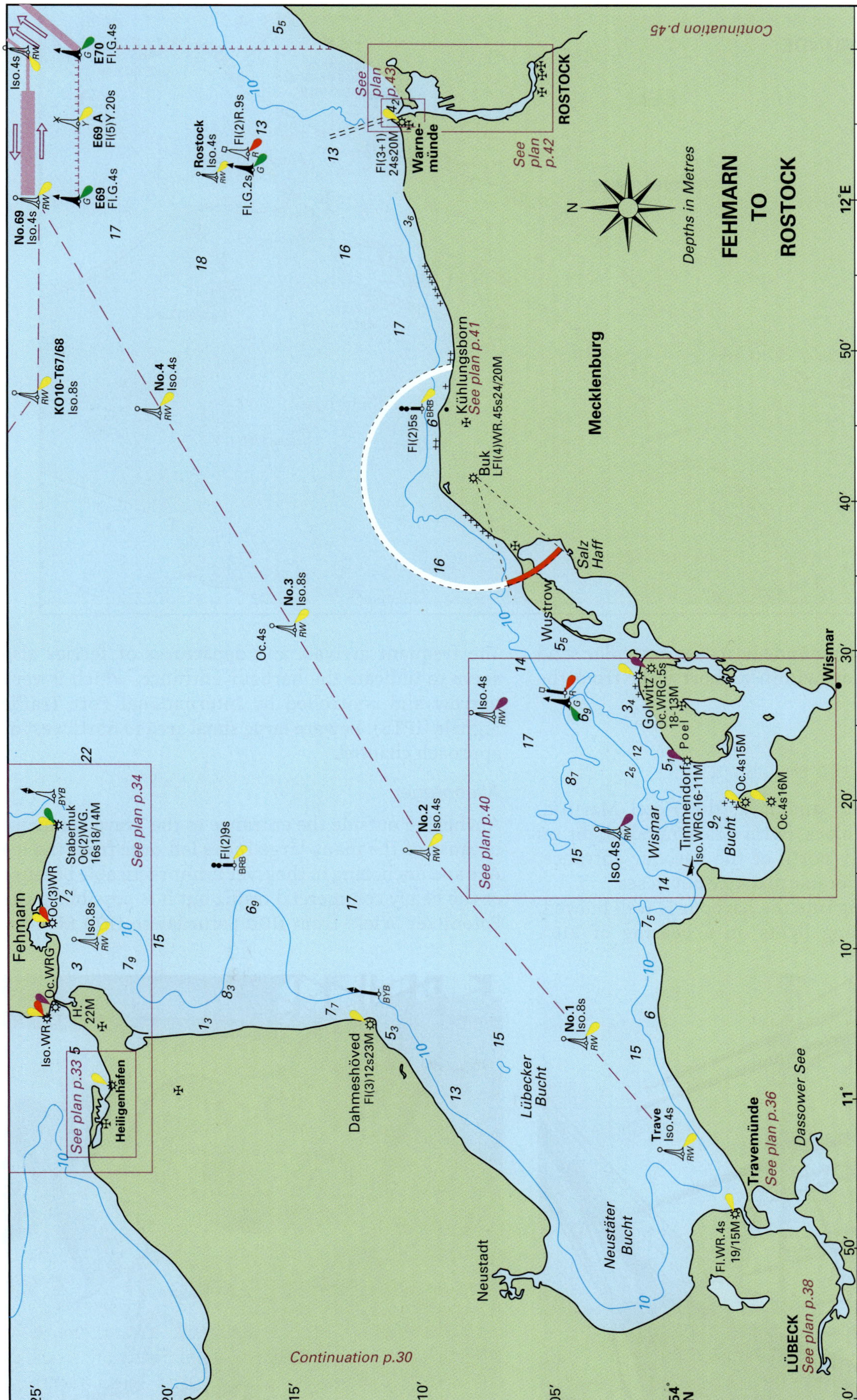
FEHMARN
TO
ROSTOCK
Depths in Metres
N
Continuation p.45
Continuation p.30
Mecklenburg
ROSTOCK
See plan p.42
See plan p.43
Warne-
münde
Fl(3+1)
24s20M
Kühlungsborn
See plan p.41
Buk
LFl(4)WR.45s24/20M
Fl(2)5s
Salz
Haff
Wustrow
Wismar
See plan p.40
Golwitz
Oc.WRG.5s
18-13M
Poel
Timmendorf
Iso.WRG.16-11M
Wismar
Bucht
Oc.4s15M
Oc.4s16M
Travemünde
See plan p.36
Dassower See
LÜBECK
See plan p.38
Fl.WR.4s
19/15M
Neustadt
Neustäter
Bucht
Lübecker
Bucht
Trave
Iso.4s
No.1
Iso.8s
No.2
Iso.4s
No.3
Iso.8s
Oc.4s
No.4
Iso.4s
KO10-T67/68
Iso.8s
No.69
Iso.4s
E69
Fl.G.4s
E69 A
Fl(5)Y.20s
E70
Fl.G.4s
Rostock
Iso.4s
Fl(2)R.9s
Fl.G.2s
Dahmeshöved
Fl(3)12s23M
Fehmarn
Oc.WRG
Iso.WR
22M
Oc(3)WR
Iso.8s
Staberhuk
Oc(2)WG.
16s18/14M
See plan p.34
Heiligenhafen
See plan p.33
Fl(2)9s
Iso.4s
12°E
11°
54°N
50′
40′
30′
20′
10′
25′
15′
05′

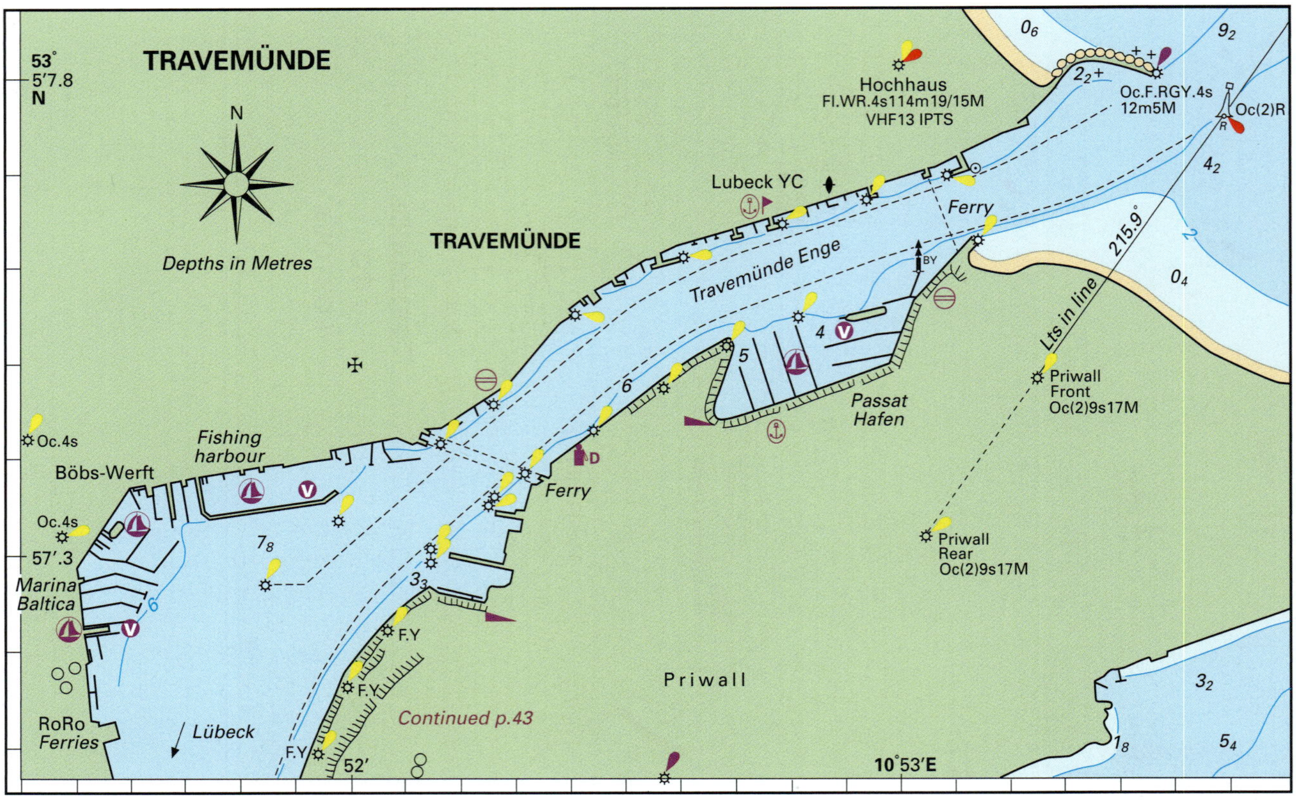


Every summer Travemünde hosts a spectacular sand sculpture competition within a short walk from the waterfront.

### *Approach*

The Trave RW SWM: 53°59'.8N 10°56'°7E

The most prominent landmark, the Hotel Maritim, is a 37-floor tower block (with Travemünde light on the top) immediately north of the harbour entrance, visible from a considerable distance out to sea.

The fairway leading into the harbour is well buoyed, with powerful leading lights on a bearing of 216°. The frequent arrivals and departures of ferries also serve to indicate the harbour entrance, which is very narrow and controlled by International Port Traffic Signals (IPTS). Beware large shoal area to northwest of approach channel.

### *Anchorage*

Anchoring outside the entrance to the Trave is unwise because of the many large rocks left over from the Ice Age and anchoring in the river is impracticable because of the heavy commercial traffic but it is possible in the Potenitzer Wiek, from 1100 Saturday to 1100 Monday

*The Passat* – a German four-masted steel barque and one of the Flying P-Liners *Andy Beharrell*

One of the sand sculptures at the annual Travemünde sand sculpture festival *Andy Beharrell*

An unusual marker at the entrance to Travemünde
*Andy Beharrell*

between the four yellow anchorage buoys (beware submarine cables). The Dassower See is a nature reserve and permission for entry is needed.

### Berthing

There are three major yacht harbours – the Passathafen, immediately to port on entry behind the permanently-moored square-rigger Passat, or the Marina Baltica and adjacent Böbs Werft marina, both about 0.5M further in on the starboard hand. All carry depths of up to 7m.

It is also possible to berth in the fishing harbour, to starboard just before reaching the Marina Baltica, where there is a more traditional ambience but fewer facilities.

### Services

All three yacht harbours have excellent facilities. The Passathafen is perhaps slightly more attractive visually, but all are efficient. There is a crane at the Passathafen if it is necessary to step the mast after emerging from the Elbe-Lübeck Canal. On the north side, Lübeck YC halfway along the strand manages the box berths, and the Harbourmaster office is below the yacht club. Berths operate on the red/green card system.

Marina Baltica can accommodate yachts up to 30m length and 5m draught. It has boat-building facilities with engineers and onshore storage.

Fuel can be obtained at the bunker station, on the Priwall side of the river close to the car ferry, and Campinggaz can bought from the hardware store in the town centre. There is no full-scale chandlery shop, but there are several boatyards equipped for most repairs.

### Facilities

There is a shopping centre on the north bank, about 10mins walk from Marina Baltica and a short ferry ride across the river from the Passathafen. Banks, restaurants, hotels and a tourist information office will be found in the centre of the town. Customs post.

### Communications & travel

There are good bus and rail services to Hamburg, where there is an international airport. Ferries to Trelleborg, Helsinki and Riga.

Passathafen at Travemünde *Andy Beharrell*

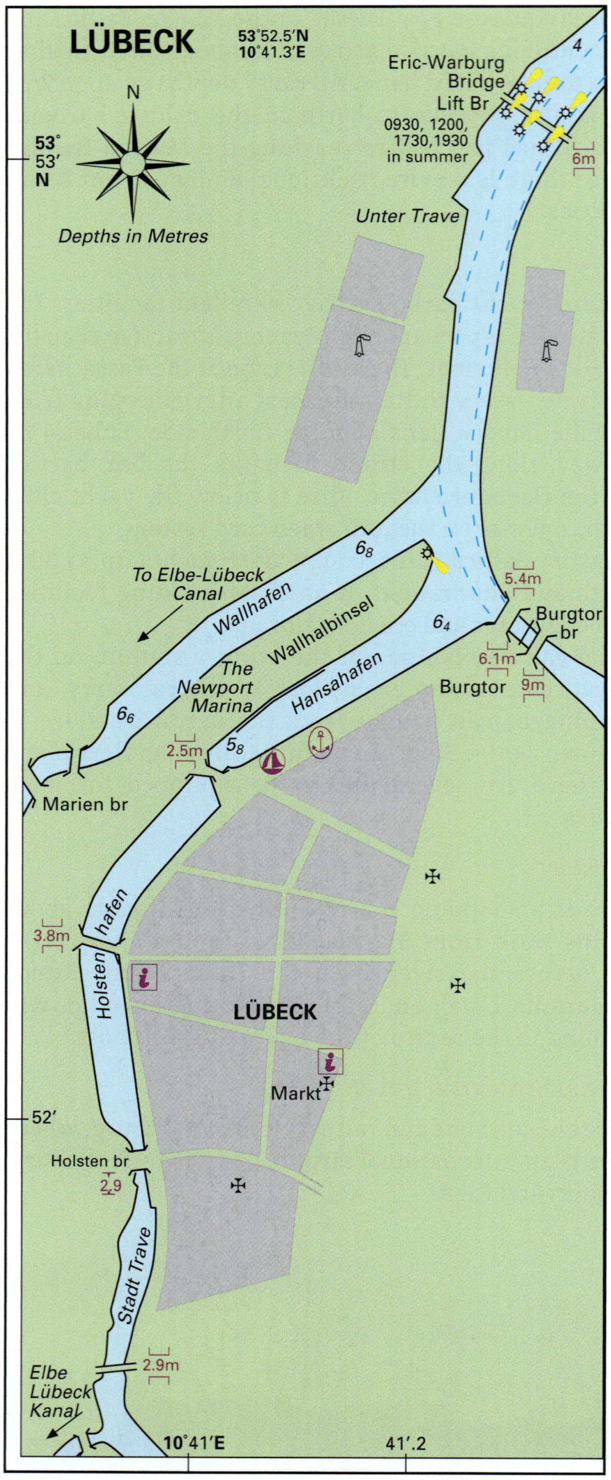


## Upriver to Lübeck

The Hanseatic city of Lübeck, 11M up the River Trave from Travemünde, is easily reached by bus or train from Travemünde, and should not be missed. The city has a population of 200,000 and it is full of historic buildings which have been painstakingly restored and maintained following the bomb damage of the Second World War. There is also an interesting historic-ship harbour, the Hansahafen, where a number of carefully preserved old ships lie.

The trip up the River Trave is interesting. It once formed the east/west German border. The undeveloped surroundings alter from rural to industrial as you progress and beyond the marinas at Herreninsel and Schlutup, the river becomes increasingly industrialized. There are ship turning circles to observe, before you pass through the Eric Warburg lifting bridge after which you may spot the *Lisa von Lübec*, a replica of a Hanseatic trading ship, which berths on the north side of the Hansahafen.

### The Newport Marina

53°52'.4N 10°41'.0E

**Contacts**

www.the-newport.de
✆+49 451 16 08 53 52
marina@the-newport.de

The Hansa marina, which was run by the city, is no longer there. Instead, on the opposite bank, is a new private development, the Newport Marina and restaurant. This has large finger pontoons with at least 50 berths. There is a floating shower block with the usual amenities, although not a washing machine. However, there is a launderette about 500m away.

Lübeck, approach to Hansahafen *Miranda Delmar-Morgan*

The Holsten Gate is a city gate in the old Hanseatic city of Lübeck. It was built in 1464 *Andy Beharrell*

The "Strandkorb" beach-chair was invented in 1882 by German basket maker Wilhelm Bartelmann in Rostock. They are very popular on north German beaches *Andy Beharrell*

## WISMAR

53°54'N 11°26'E

### Distances

Travemünde 25M, Warnemünde 35M

### Lights

**Timmendorf** 53°59'.5N 11°22'.6E Iso.WRG.6s21m16–11M White round tower, red and brown top, white lantern, red cupola, with white dwelling 21m

**Gollwitz** N 54°01'.4N 11°28'E Iso.WRG.4s13m19–14M White tower with red and green lantern on white building

**Hohen Wieschendorf** Leading Lights 180.3° *Front* 53°57'.6N 11°20'E Oc.4s20m15M White lattice mast 16m
*Rear* 1500m from front Oc.4s39m16M White v with red surround on white lattice mast 21m

**Walfisch** Leading Lights 123.9° *Front* 53°56'.7N 11°25'.1E Oc(2)9s10m7M Red and white g on white tubular metal mast 10m
*Rear* 1.35M from front, Oc(2)9s30m7M Red and white tubular metal mast 30m

**Wismar** Leading Lights 149.9° *Front* 53°54'N 11°27'.1E Oc.R.4s28m12M Framework tower on promontory on west side of harbour 26m
*Rear* 700m from front Oc.R.4s46m12M Framework tower 43m

### Contacts

**Harbour Office** ✆+49 3841 224491 (0700–1530 Monday–Friday, 0800–1200 LT Saturday) *Mobile* +49 162/4720355
**Wismar Vessel Traffic Service** VHF Ch 12 (broadcasts on VHF Ch 12 every 3hrs from 0630–2130 LT in German or English on request)
**Wismar Tourist office** www.wismar.de/tourismus
**Wismar Alter Hafen** ✆+49 3841/2513260
**Wismar Westhafen** ✆+49 3841 224491
www.marina-westhafen-wismar.de
**Wismar Brunkowkai** ✆+49 3841 251 3261
hafen.wismar.de/Liegeplätze/Wasserwanderrastplatz
hafenamt@wismar.de

### General

Wismar, a historic town of some 60,000 inhabitants, is principally engaged in shipbuilding and repairs. The old town has remarkable baroque and Gothic architecture and the Alte Markt is a reminder of the greatness of the Hanseatic League. It has one of the largest squares in Germany, with many gabled houses including the 'Alte Schwede', built in 1380 though taking its name from the pub opened there in the late 19th century, a reminder that Wismar belonged to Sweden in the 17th and 18th centuries.

The old town has a preservation order and much restoration has been carried out, though of the medieval fortifications only the Wassertor and bits of the town wall remain. The church of St Nicholas and the museum in the Schabbelhaus are worth visiting. The town is listed as a UNESCO World Heritage site.

An attraction of Wismar from the yachtsman's viewpoint is that it is possible to moor within easy walking distance of the centre of this comparatively small and memorable town. The new Marina Westhafen has most modern facilities, a Netto supermarket a short walk to the southwest, bike hire nearby, a petrol station and an ATM to the west up Lübsche Strasse about 300m away. There is also an Edeka supermarket in town.

The Alterhafen is home to the fishing boat stalls with their fantastic array of smoked and fresh fish for sale. From Wismar, ships of the White Fleet (Weisse Flotte) take an hour to run to the island of Poel, which is popular for its beaches. Poel also has a museum showcasing the island. Schwerin, on the edge of the Mecklenburg Lake District, is some 30km by rail from Wismar. Its castle, inspired by Chateau Chambord, was the seat of the Dukes of Mecklenburg until they were thrown out in 1918 - it is both amazingly grand and unsatisfactorily dull, though its gardens and orangery are pleasant enough. Outside the town, Schweriner See is, at 65km$^2$, the largest of many lakes which contribute to a pretty countryside.

### Approach

The Grossestief channel is entered about 3M north of the island of Poel on about 165° (in the white sector of Gollwitz north light) before swinging west at the second pair of channel buoys on to 230° south of

The view from St George's church in Wismar over Westhafen *Andy Beharrell*

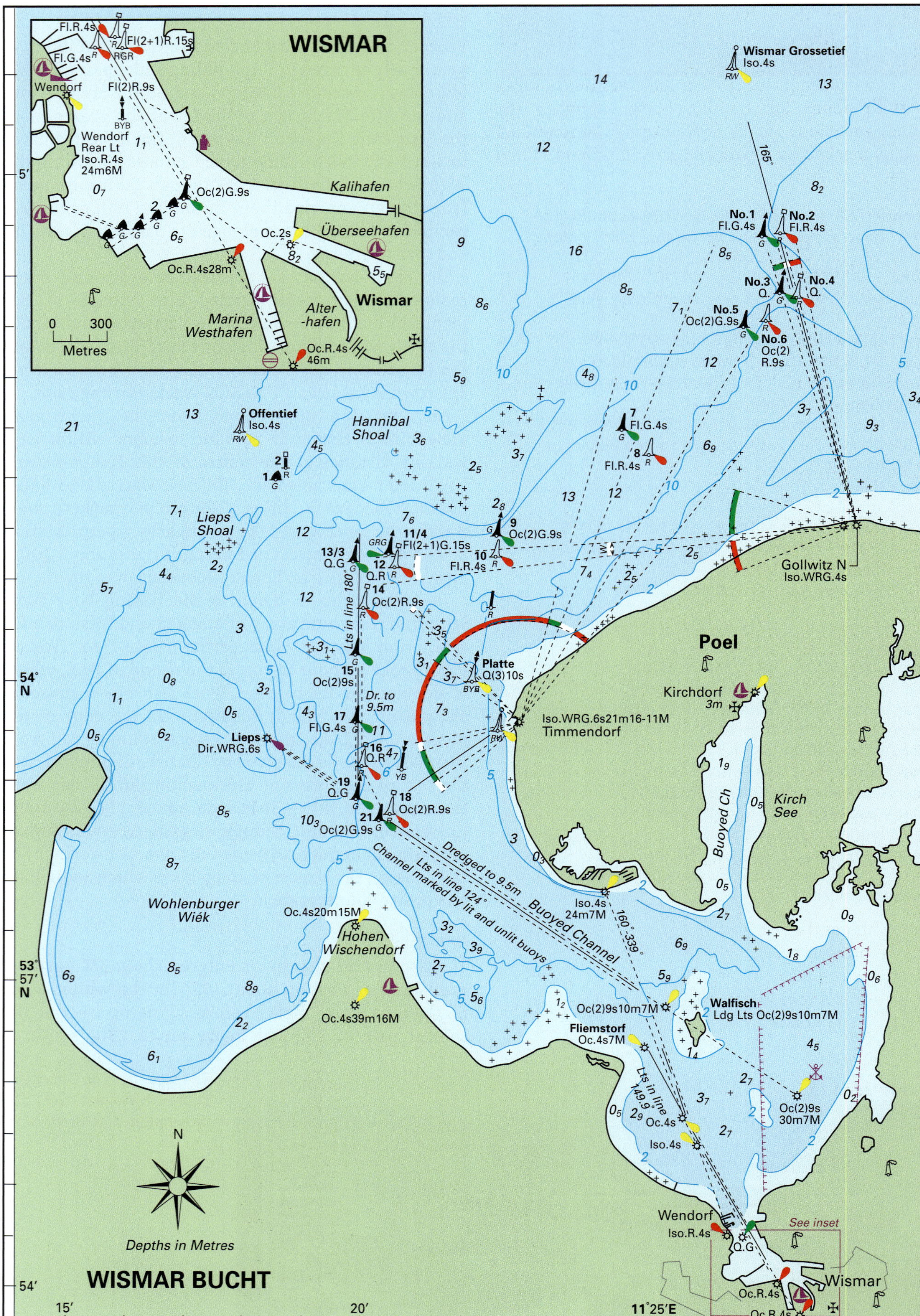
WISMAR
Fl.R.4s
Fl(2+1)R.15s
Fl.G.4s
Wendorf
Fl(2)R.9s
Wendorf Rear Lt Iso.R.4s 24m6M
Oc(2)G.9s
Kalihafen
Oc.2s
Überseehafen
Oc.R.4s28m
Marina Westhafen
Alter -hafen
Wismar
Oc.R.4s 46m
0 300 Metres
Wismar Grossetief Iso.4s
No.1 Fl.G.4s
No.2 Fl.R.4s
No.3 Q.
No.4 Q.
No.5 Oc(2)G.9s
No.6 Oc(2) R.9s
Offentief Iso.4s
Hannibal Shoal
7 Fl.G.4s
8 Fl.R.4s
Lieps Shoal
13/3 Q.G
11/4 Fl(2+1)G.15s
12 Q.R
9 Oc(2)G.9s
10 Fl.R.4s
14 Oc(2)R.9s
Gollwitz N Iso.WRG.4s
Poel
Lts in line 180°
15 Oc(2)9s
Platte Q(3)10s
Kirchdorf 3m
Dr. to 9.5m
17 Fl.G.4s
Iso.WRG.6s21m16-11M Timmendorf
Lieps Dir.WRG.6s
16 Q.R
19 Q.G
18 Oc(2)R.9s
21 Oc(2)G.9s
Buoyed Ch
Kirch See
Dredged to 9.5m
Lts in line 124°
Channel marked by lit and unlit buoys
Buoyed Channel
Iso.4s 24m7M
160° 339°
Wohlenburger Wiék
Oc.4s20m15M
Hohen Wischendorf
Oc.4s39m16M
Oc(2)9s10m7M
Walfisch Ldg Lts Oc(2)9s10m7M
Fliemstorf Oc.4s7M
Lts in line 149.9°
Oc.4s
Iso.4s
Oc(2)9s 30m7M
Wendorf Iso.R.4s
Q.G
See inset
Wismar
Oc.R.4s
Depths in Metres
WISMAR BUCHT
N
54°N
53°57′N
54′
15′
20′
11°25′E

Hannibal Shoal. Thereafter the channel is marked by buoys and leading lights. The vast ship-building shed of Nordic Yachts is clearly visible.

An alternative approach, from the Offentief landfall buoy with about 5m depth, crosses between the Hannibal and Lieps shoals northwest of Timmendorf light. It is marked by a pair of unlit buoys and is in a white sector of Timmendorf light.

### Anchorage

Anchor outside the shipping channel (but display anchor ball and light as there is considerable commercial shipping in Wismarbucht). If visiting the attractive little village of Kirchdorf on the island of Poel do not consider anchoring in the dredged approach channel as the holding is bad in very soft mud and ferries take up most of the fairway. Visiting yachts can moor on the western pontoon in 2m at the outer end.

### Berthing

In Wismar visiting yachts can berth alongside on the east side of the Alten Hafen but this is more suitable for larger vessels. Berthing for yachts is available at the Westhafen or Brunkowkei marinas which are not much further from the city centre.

### Services

Water, electricity and shower/toilet facilities are available at both marinas although facilities at Brunkowkei are minimal. There are laundry facilities at Westhafen and there is a fuel station on the north side of the harbour basin between the oil jetty and the chemical works. Weather forecasts are available on request from the harbourmaster's office. There is a black water pump out station to starboard as you enter the Alter Hafen.

In the event of any problems NC Marine (www.ncmarine.de) or Yachtwerft Ostsee (www.yachtwerft-ostsee.de) could be approached.

### Facilities

There is water and electricity on the pontoons, showers, toilets, laundry and a diesel berth. Groceries, gas and most other supplies are available in the town centre, where there is a tourist information office and banks, restaurants and hotels abound.

### Communications & travel

There are good train services to Hamburg, Berlin and Rostock.

Wismar channel marker
*Miranda Delmar-Morgan*

## KÜHLUNGSBORN

53°09'.2N 11°46'.4E outer mole

**Distances**
Wismar 27M, Heiligenhafen 30M,
Warnemünde 12M, Gedser 25M, Stralsund 64M

**Lights**
**Buk** 54°07'.9N 11°41'.6E LFl(4)WR.45s95m24–20M Red and brown round tower, red cupola
**Kuhlungsborn** E Mole Head FR.6m4M Red Mast
N Mole Head FG.6m4M Green Mast
**Warnemünde** 54°10'.9N 12°05'.1E Fl(3+1)W.24s 34M 20M White round tower with black bands, two galleries, copper cupola

**Contacts**
**Harbourmaster** ✆+49 38 2934 1055
*Mobile* +49 151 12110565
www.bootshafen-kuehlungsborn.de
info@bootshafen-kuehlungsborn.de

### General

A large marina with several hundred berths just to the east of Kühlungsborn, the largest seaside resort in Mecklenburg, amongst much new housing development.

### Approach

Straightforward by day or night from a northeasterly direction and around the eastern end of the north breakwater.

### Berthing

Berth at new pontoons in 3.0 to 3.5m.

### Facilities

Water/electricity on the pontoons. Showers/toilets. Laundry, diesel berth. Shops, restaurants and banks are all available in the town.

From Kühlungsborn the Molli, a steam railway, which has a gauge of only 90cm and is a great tourist attraction, runs through Heiligendamm and beautiful countryside into the centre of Bad Doberan, which has the Doberaner Munster, a great brick church built by the Cistercians between 1294 and 1368. It has never been bombed and remains beautifully intact and preserved.

Heiligendamm was established in 1793 as a spa, it is known as 'The White Town by the Sea' because of its white-painted, period buildings.

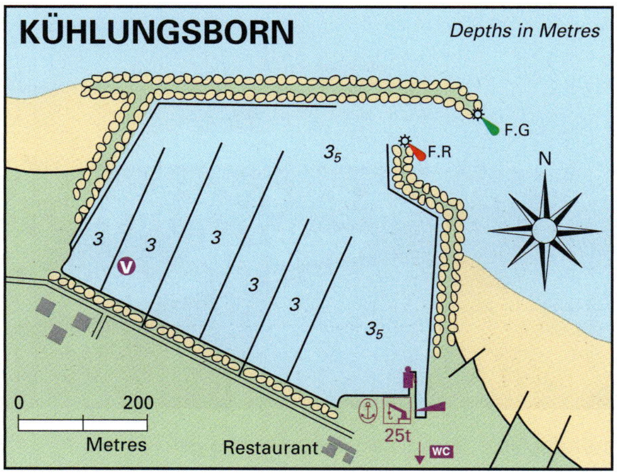

## WARNEMÜNDE (WITH ROSTOCK)

54°11'.2N 12°05'.2E west mole

**Distances**
Wismar 35M, Kühlungsborn 12M, Rostock 6M, Darsser Ort 30M, Stralsund 54M

**Lights**
**Warnemünde**, W side of entrance 54°10'.9N 12°05'.1E Fl(3+1)24s34m20M White round tower, black bands, two galleries, copper cupola 31m
**Petersdorf Leading Lights** 161.6° *Front* 54°08'.7N 12°06'.8E Oc.R.4s24m12M Striped metal mast, red top 21m
*Rear* 0.84M from front Oc.R.4s45m15M Striped metal mast, red top 33m
**West mole head**, E arm 54°11'.2N 12°05'.2E Iso.G.4s14m6M Green tower, white band, two galleries 12m Floodlit
**East mole** 54°11'.2N 12°05'.5E Iso.R.4s14m6M Red tower, white band, two balconies 12m Floodlit

**Contacts**
**Warnemünde/Rostock Vessel Traffic Service** ✆+49 381 2067 1141/2 VHF Ch 73/16 (vessels must maintain a listening watch on VHF Ch 73 – broadcasts on VHF Ch 73 every 2hrs from 0515–2115 LT in German, English on request)
**Rostock Port Authority** ✆+49 381 3500
www.rostock-port.de
VHF Ch 10
**Alter Strom** ✆+49 3815 1864
**Hohe Düne Yachthafen** ✆+49 0381 5040 8080
www.yachthafen-hohe-duene.de
www.rostock.de/en/holiday/tourist-information.html

### *General*

Warnemünde, a holiday resort and ferry terminal, still maintains an inshore fishing fleet which ties up with yachts in the Alter Strom alongside gabled houses. It lies at the entrance to the huge, commercial but ancient Hanseatic port of Rostock, whose docks and shipyards stretch for 15M due south from Warnemünde along the River Warnow.

Warnemünde is a good base from which to visit Rostock by train.

Warnemünde Alter Strom *Miranda Delmar-Morgan*

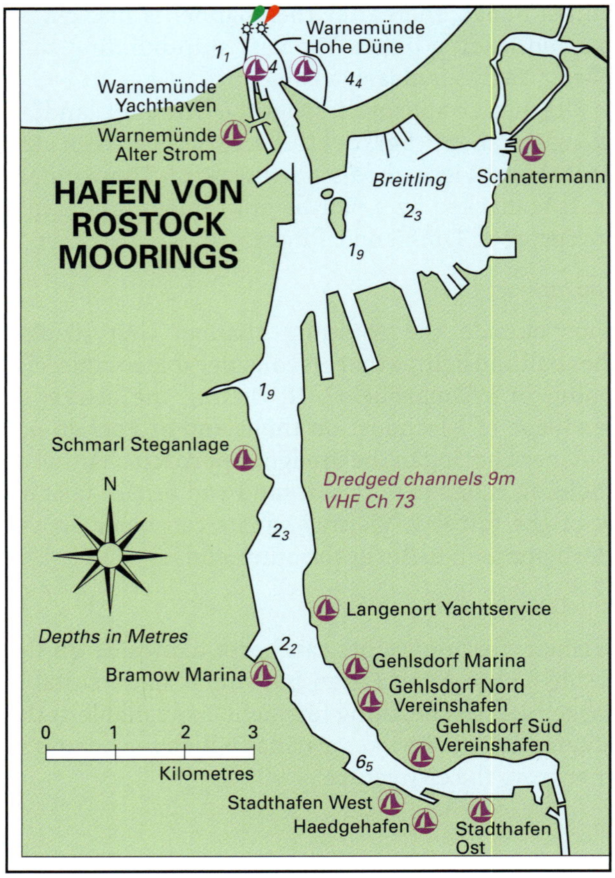


### *Approach & entrance*

54°13N 12°04'E

The harbour mouth is very obvious both by day and by night, and is equipped with powerful leading lights. There are no hazards outside the harbour, and a well-buoyed fairway extending some 7M out to the Rostock fairway buoy but beware of commercial traffic which must not be obstructed.

The harbour mouth is divided into two, the eastern side being the deep-water channel to the large and busy commercial port and to Rostock, whilst the western side leads to the yacht harbour and the fishing port. On the east side of the entrance the very grand Hohe Düne development has been built with its own large and well appointed marina. This has its own straightforward entrance as in the plan on page 43.

Immediately inside the western entrance of the main harbour there are again two channels, the eastern one leading past the entrance to the yacht harbour before rejoining the deep-water channel, and the western one being the Alter Strom, which is much used by fishing boats and tourist vessels. At night, beware several unlit dolphins at the seaward end of the dividing wall between the yacht harbour and the Alter Strom.

### *Anchorage*

Do not anchor in this busy waterway.

### *Berthing*

The Alter Strom, which is much the most picturesque and convenient area in which to berth, is now very congested with fishing boats and tourist vessels. Yachts

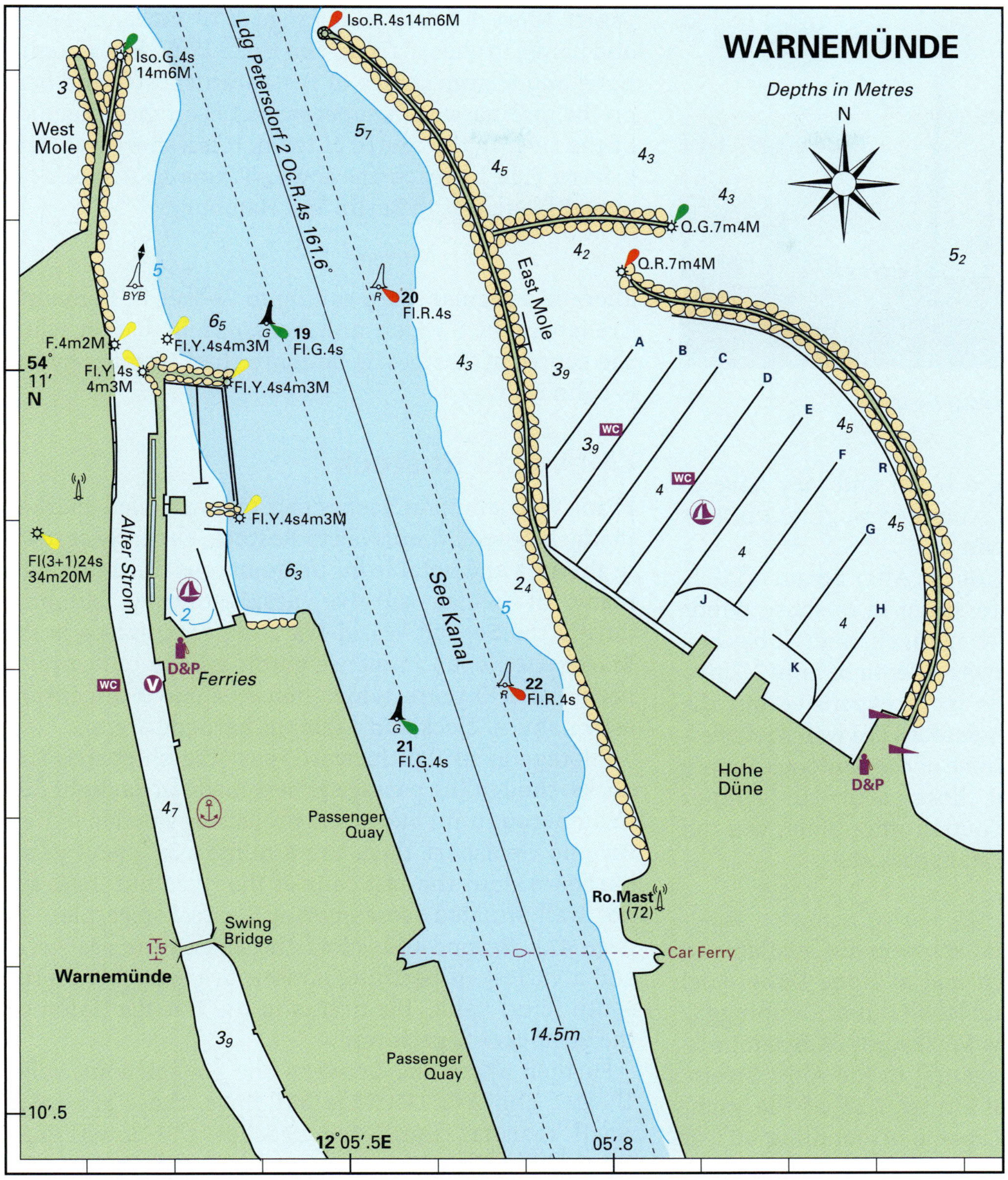

Warnemünde old harbour
*Miranda Delmar-Morgan*

Approach to Rostock *Miranda Delmar-Morgan*

may have difficulty finding a berth and may have to raft up to a fishing boat. Maximum draught 3.1m. It is uncomfortable in onshore winds.

The Yachthafen to the east of the Alter Strom is fairly convenient but is subject to surge in onshore winds and from ships passing in the main channel. It has box berths and the entrance carries a depth of only 2.2m.

The Hohe Düne marina is more expensive but the berths (box berths bows-to-pontoon) are well sheltered. There are toilet facilities on some of the pontoons. Empty pontoons may indicate that those particular facilities are not in use. If you arrive out of office hours you can collect a key card from the 5 star spa hotel.

### *Services*

Water, electricity, toilets and showers are available in the Alter Strom, Yachthafen and at Hohe Düne. Fuel berths in the Alter Strom and Hohe Düne. Campinggaz from Schiff Service Warnow Werkstatte Warnemünde (who are also Volvo Penta agents) in the Alter Strom. There is a crane capable of lifting 2.5T at the yacht harbour, and a larger one capable of handling 40T at Hohe Düne.

### *Facilities*

Provisions are available from nearby shops, and there are stalls selling pancakes, hot dogs and other forms of fast food on the Alter Strom. Since this is a holiday resort, there is a very wide range of restaurants, hotels and banks to choose from. The Hohe Düne has a luxury hotel and a large choice of restaurants, cafés and bars on the marina-side. A supermarket is on the other side of the river in the centre of town. It is a short walk and a ferry ride to reach the town. Trains to Rostock for onward journeys to Berlin and Hamburg.

### *Communications & travel*

There is a regular ferry sailing to Gedser in Denmark, Trelleborg in Sweden and Ventspils in Latvia while the centre of Rostock is no more than 10 mins by the S-bahn railway.

## Upriver to Rostock

From Warnemünde yachts can take the well-marked main channel 6M upriver to Rostock, the largest town in the area and notable for its numerous fine buildings, many of which survive despite heavy bombing during the Second World War. The centrepiece is the Marienkirche, an immense gothic edifice built over a period of 400 years, which houses a late 15th-century astronomical clock and a famous baroque organ.

Pilotage is straightforward, past the shipyards and docks, though the passage is best made in daylight due to numerous unlit buoys and projecting wooden jetties. Around Gehlsdorf there are a number of small yacht harbours along the east bank of the river, but these are not well situated for exploring Rostock (see plan on page 42). Beyond Gehlsdorf the river runs east/west and a variety of berthing options are available on the south (city) bank. The first is in the Haedge Hafen by the Rostocker Segelverein.

Further upstream, between the conspicuous Volks Theater and A.G. Getreide buildings, there are more small marinas until one reaches the town quay (Stadthafen Ost). This is separated from the town by a very busy main road but the town is worth a visit. The harbourmaster is in the ground floor of the local chandlery. Washing machines and good facilities.

All normal shopping facilities, hotels, banks and restaurants are available in the town centre, and

Statues in the centre of Rostock *Andy Beharrell*

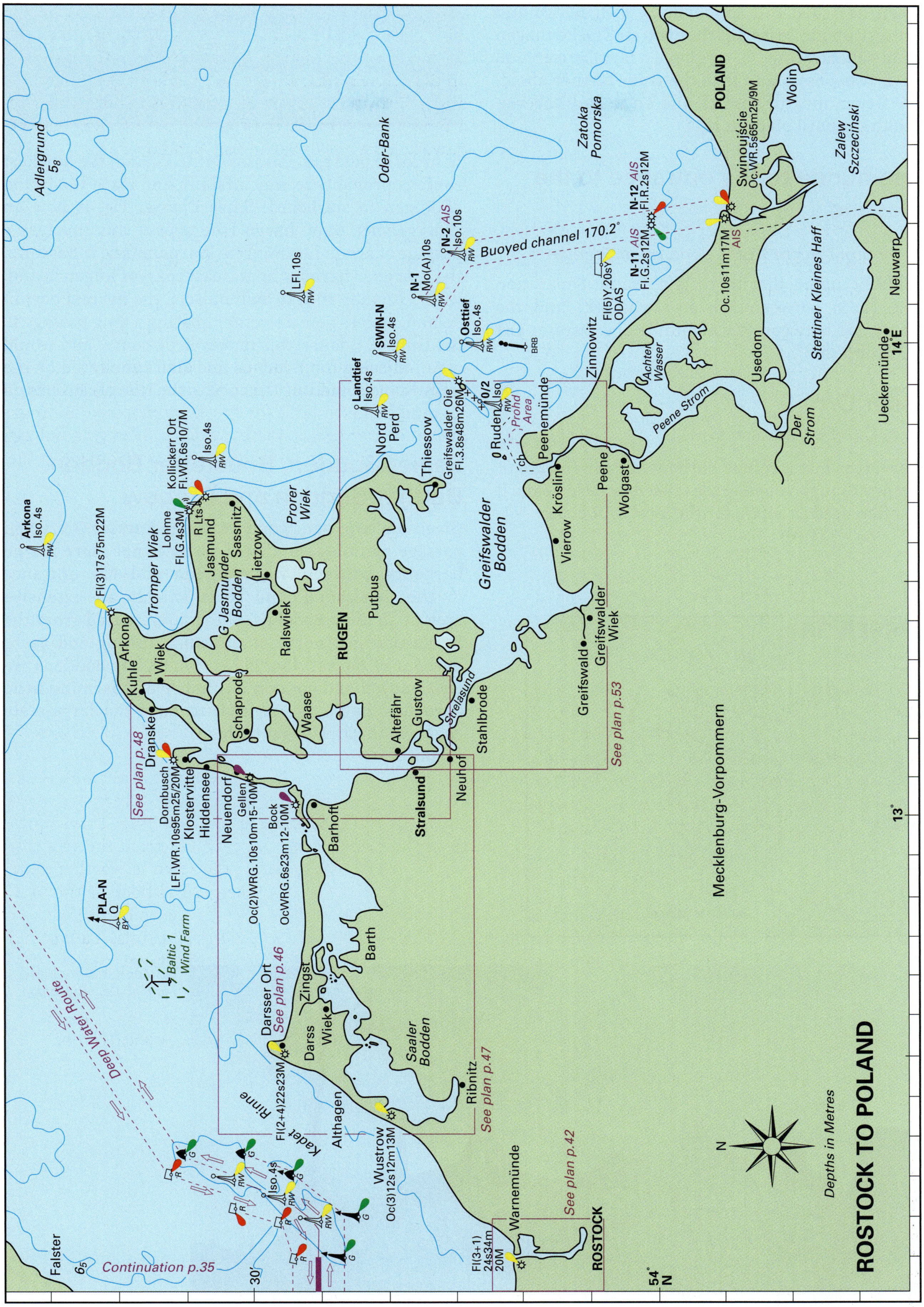
ROSTOCK TO POLAND
Depths in Metres
Mecklenburg-Vorpommern
RUGEN
POLAND
Adlergrund
Oder-Bank
Zatoka Pomorska
Arkona
Iso.4s
Tromper Wiek
Prorer Wiek
Greifswalder Bodden
Jasmund
Sassnitz
Lietzow
Ralswiek
Putbus
Thiessow
Stralsund
Strelasund
Stahlbrode
Greifswald
Greifswalder Wiek
Wolgast
Peene
Kröslin
Vierow
Peenemünde
Zinnowitz
Usedom
Achter Wasser
Peene Strom
Der Strom
Stettiner Kleines Haff
Zalew Szczeciński
Wolin
Swinoujście
Oc.WR.5s65m25/9M
Ueckermünde
Neuwarp
Buoyed channel 170.2°
Hiddensee
Kloster
Vitte
Neuendorf
Dranske
Kuhle
Wiek
Schaprode
Waase
Altefähr
Gustow
Neuhof
Barhoft
Barth
Zingst
Darss
Wiek
Darsser Ort
Saaler Bodden
Ribnitz
Althagen
Wustrow
Oc(3)12s12m13M
Kadet Rinne
Warnemünde
ROSTOCK
Falster
Deep Water Route
Baltic 1 Wind Farm
PLA-N
Landtief
SWIN-N
Osttief
Ruden
Greifswalder Oie
Fl.3.8s48m26M
N-1
N-2
N-11
N-12
See plan p.42
See plan p.46
See plan p.47
See plan p.48
See plan p.53
Continuation p.35
54° N
13°
14°E

the town has good rail connections with Berlin and Hamburg. Outside Rostock is the open air Klockenhagen Museum illustrating a regional farmhouse and farming. It is possible to take the train further afield, from Warnemünde to Rostock and on to Bad Doberan (see Kühlungsborn on page 41).

## Warnemünde to the entrance to the Strelasund

*Mecklenburger Bucht Traffic Separation Scheme*

It should be noted that there is a Traffic Separation Scheme (TSS) between Falster (Denmark) and the German coast between Warnemünde and Darsser Ort (see plan opposite).

## Darsser Ort

54°28'.3N 12°31'.5E (Harbour groyne)

Darsser Ort is just a refuge harbour for use in case of emergency though you may see it used by local boats. It is also often used as a base for the local SAR boat.

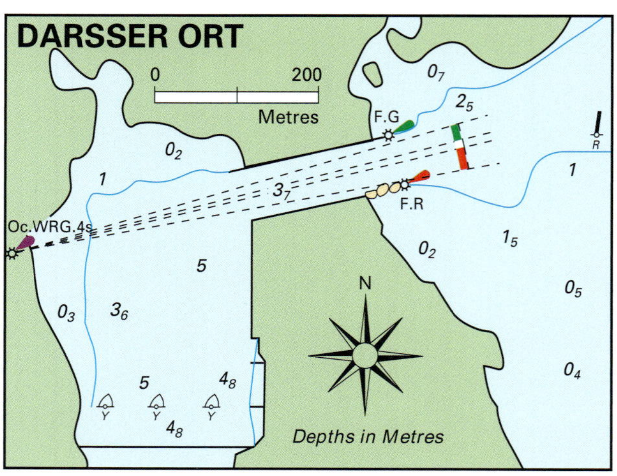


# 1C. DARSSER ORT TO THE POLISH BORDER

In order to get from Darsser Ort to Poland, the quickest route is probably to stay offshore and leave the island of Rügen to starboard. Since Darsser Ort is now an 'emergencies only' haven (see above) this involves a passage of around 100M from Warnemünde to Sassnitz, the first good harbour on the east coast of Rügen Island, with a further 40M to Świnoujście, the nearest port in Poland. Unless you are contemplating a long passage to the Gulf of Gdańsk this makes little sense, and would entail missing the Boddens and Haffs sheltered by the islands and sometimes likened to the Norfolk Broads on a grand scale.

## Saaler Bodden, Bodstetter Bodden, Barther Bodden and Grabow

Given the 'emergency only' access to Darsser Ort, when passage planning, one must assume that there are no harbours between Warnemünde and the entrance to the Strelasund. The coast shields an extensive area of shallow Boddens, which are entered from the Strelasund just north of the small fishing and yacht harbour of Barhöft (54°26'N 13°02'E). The Boddens are well buoyed and contain a number of charming little harbours, but it is essential to have the large-scale charts of the area to get to them.

Rostock main square
*Miranda Delmar-Morgan*

DARSS, ZINGST AND ADJACENT BODDENS
Darsser Ort/W Q(9)15s
Darsser Ort Fl(2+4)22s33m23M
Darsser Ort/O Q(3)10s
(May-Oct)
(May-Oct)
(May-Oct)
Darsser Ort
National Park
Prerow Bank
See plan p.46
Prerow
Darss
Born
Zingst
Bresewitz
Bodstedter Bodden
Bodstedt
Barther Bodden
Barth
Dabitz
Buoyed channels
Grabow
Pramort
Der Bock
Oc.WRG.6s 23m12-10M
Barhöft
Mast
Zarrenzin Oc.6s52m15M
Hiddensee
Gellen
Gellen Strom (buoyed)
Q.G
Strelasund
Buoyed
Prohner Wiek
STRALSUND
See plan p.48
Althagen
Wustrow
Saaler Boden
Buoyed channels
Oc(3) 12s12m13M
Dierhagen
Ribnitz
Q(9)15s
Depths in Metres
N
30′
25′
54° 20′ N
15′
30′
40′
50′
13°E

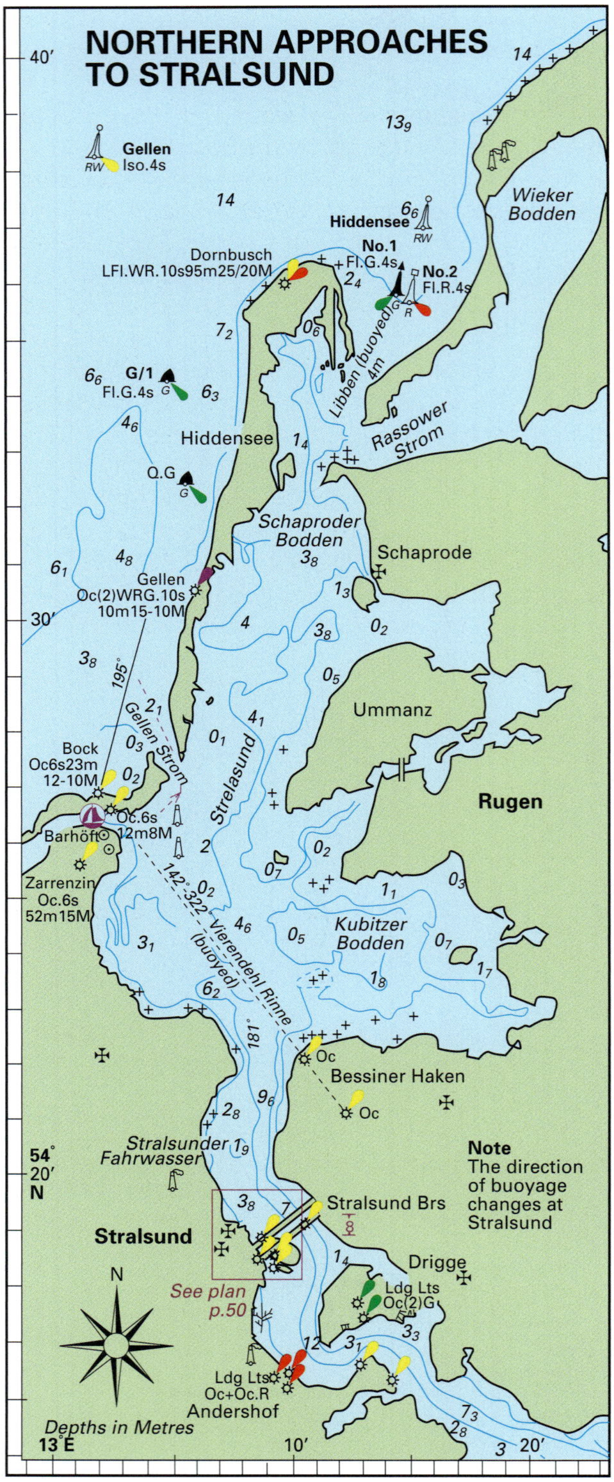


## Northern approaches to the Strelasund

The Strelasund offers the opportunity for yachtsmen to take an interesting route inside Rügen island, via Stralsund, to Greifswalder Bodden. This is a short-cut to the northern entrance of the Peenestrom channel which leads to the Stettiner Haff (Zalew Szczeciński).

The northern approach via the Gellenstrom west of Hiddensee island, starts at the Gellen Landfall Buoy (54°38'.4N 13°02'.6E) although from the west it is more practical to enter the channel at No. 1 G buoy (54°33'.9N 13°03'.4E) or in quiet conditions at No. 3/5 G buoy (54°32'.1N 13°03'.9E) in the western W sector of the Gellen Light (54°30'.5N 13°04'.5E Oc(2) WRG.10s10m15-10M white round metal tower, red top, stone base) although it would be unwise to attempt this approach to Stralsund in the dark as not all the channel buoys are lit.

The Gellen lighthouse is a 10m high white tower with red top, but the gap in the trees is usually easier to see than the lighthouse itself. Head towards the lighthouse to pick up the Gellenstrom channel buoys. The latter approach to No. 3/5 G buoy carries a minimum depth of 3m. There is a designated anchorage (Reede) between Barhöft and Bock near G buoy 29. In strong onshore winds it would be prudent to reach the Strelasund via the channels of the Schaproder Bodden in the lee of Hiddensee. These channels are well-marked and dredged to 2.5m and can be entered from the buoyed Libben channel to the northeast of Hiddensee at 54°36'N 13°10'.9E. Vitte and Kloster on Hiddensee are delightful.

Barhöft harbour *Andy Beharrell*

The view from Barhöft observation tower with Hiddensee island in the background *Andy Beharrell*

## STRALSUND

54°19'N 13°06'E

**Distances**
Warnemünde 51M, Świnoujście 50M, Szczecin 85M

**Lights**
**Approach**
**Darsser Ort** 54°28'.4N 12°30'.2E Fl(2+4)22s33m23M Round red tower, brown cupola and building 35m
**Zarrenzin Leading Lights** 195.1° *Front* 54°26'.9N 13°01'.4E Oc.WR.6s23m12M White framework tower, red lantern and gallery with white roof, grey stone base, white stripe 23m
*Rear* 1.3M from front Oc.6s52m15M White metal framework tower, red bands and lantern, white cupola 24m Visible on leading line only
**Kap Arkona** 54°40'.8N 13°25'.9E Fl(3)17s75m22M Red lantern on yellow round tower with two galleries 35m
**Channel**
**Bock Leading Lights** 322.1° *Front* 54°27'N 13°02'E Oc.6s12m8M White framework tower, red lantern and gallery with white roof, grey stone base, white stripe 13m
*Rear* 700m from front, as above. A back bearing on 322.1° can be used when heading south towards Stralsund

**Contacts**
**Stralsund North and Stralsund East Vessel Traffic Services** ✆+49 3831 25420, VHF Ch 16/67 (vessels must maintain a listening watch on VHF Ch 16 or 67 – broadcasts on VHF Ch 67 every 2hrs 0635–2235 and at 0235 LT). (Office hours 0700–2000 Mon–Fri, 0700–1300 and 1800–2000 LT weekends and holidays). **Port Ops** VHF Ch 11.
**City Marina harbour master** ✆+49 38 3144 4978
www.citymarina-stralsund.de
info@citymarina-stralsund.de

Stralsund was founded in 1209 and joined the Hanseatic League in 1293. Like Wismar, it was under Swedish control in the 17th and 18th centuries and came under Prussian control in 1815. It was very badly damaged in air raids during the Second World War. However, the fine Town Hall survived, and over its windows on the market side can be seen the arms of Hamburg, Lübeck, Wismar, Rostock, Stralsund and Greifswald.

The three parish churches of St Mary, St James (Jacobikirche) and St Nicholas demonstrate the prosperity of the town - especially the last, which was started in the 13th century and largely rebuilt after a fire in 1662. The award winning 'Ozeaneum' maritime museum has aquariums for the North and Baltic seas and the North Atlantic, and studies the life and biology of the Boddens.

The *Gorch Fock* (www.gorchfock1.de) is an obvious landmark in Stralsund harbour. She was built in 1933 at the Blohm and Voss yard in Hamburg and is a three-masted barque, named in honour of the German writer Johann Kinau who wrote under the pseudonym 'Gorch Fock'. She had a fairly chequered career as a ship. She started as a training vessel and then during the war became a stationary office ship in Stralsund. Oddly she was reactivated in April 1944, but on 1 May 1945, the crew scuttled her in shallow waters off Rügen in an attempt to avoid her capture by the Soviets.

The Soviets ordered a Stralsund-based company to raise and salvage her in 1947 at a cost of 800,000 Reichsmark (probably equivalent to around 3 million euros) and she was then restored between 1948 and 1950 and named *Tovarishch* (Russian for 'Comrade') in 1951 serving as a training vessel for the Russian navy out of Odessa. The end of the Soviet Union in 1991 meant the end of *Tovarishch* and she sailed under the Ukrainian flag for two years before being deactivated because of repairs being required. She returned to Stralsund as a museum ship in 2003 and was renamed the *Gorch Fock*. She has now been purchased by the town and around 10 million euros spent on her restoration in 2023.

This is an attractive port and holiday resort, full of old-world charm and with many historic buildings, cobbled streets and a lively open-air market. A vast amount of high-quality restoration work has been completed and more is being done. There are many good, modern shops. Direct trains to Berlin.

### *Approach*

The port lies on the west bank of the Strelasund, the narrow channel between the island of Rügen and the mainland, where the small island of Dänholm provided a convenient bridging point. Whether coming from the north or the south it is necessary to navigate through this channel, which is tortuous but very clearly marked and well lit. There is sometimes a small current in the Strelasund, with a direction and strength dependent on wind conditions over the southern Baltic.

The approach from the north is via the Gellenstrom (see above) and this leads eventually into the Strelasund via channels dredged to 4.5m. If intending to continue south to the Greifswalder Bodden, it will be necessary to enter Stralsund harbour to pass through the opening bridge, whether or not one stops at Stralsund itself. This bridge opens five times daily at 0520, 0820, 1220, 1720, 2130 but a check should be made at harbour offices or

Hiddensee, Vitte yacht harbour *Miranda Delmar-Morgan*

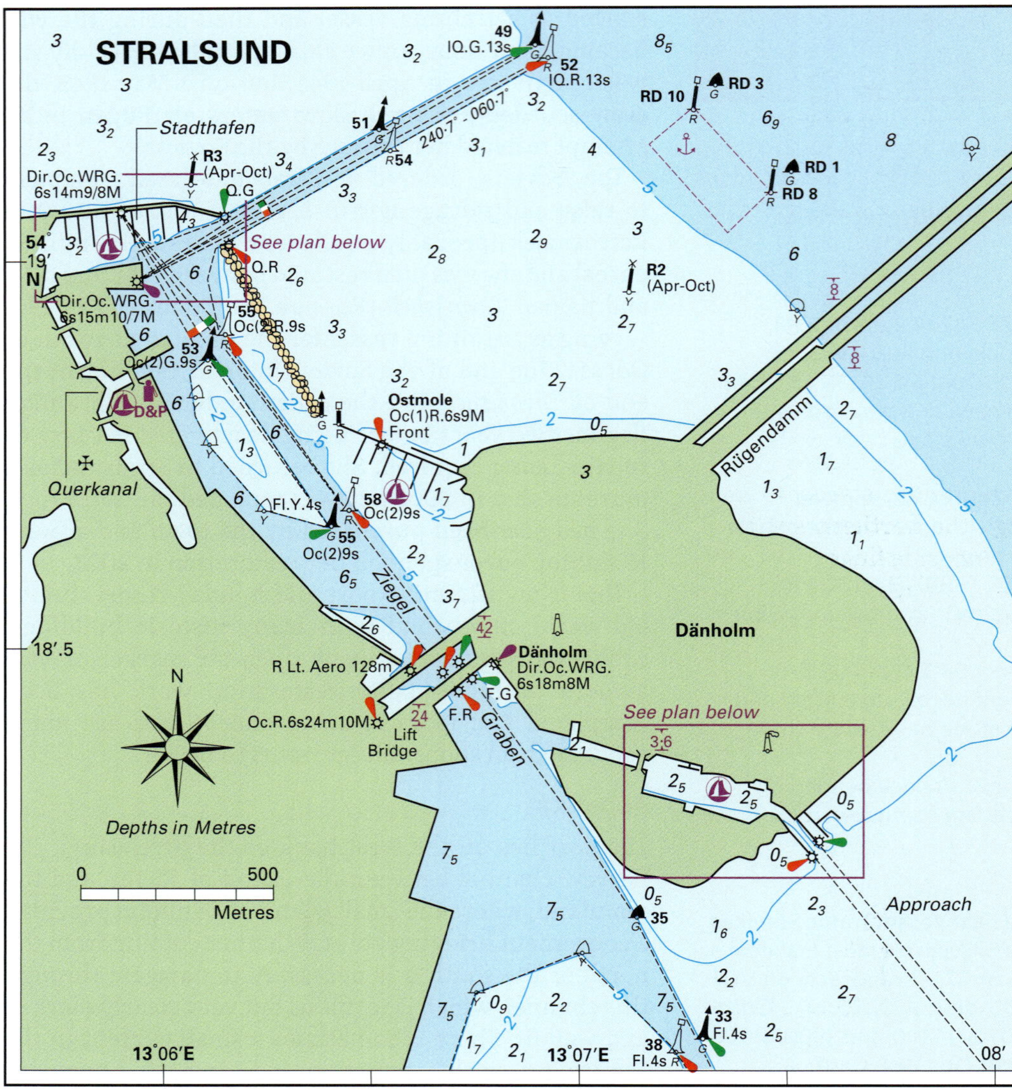


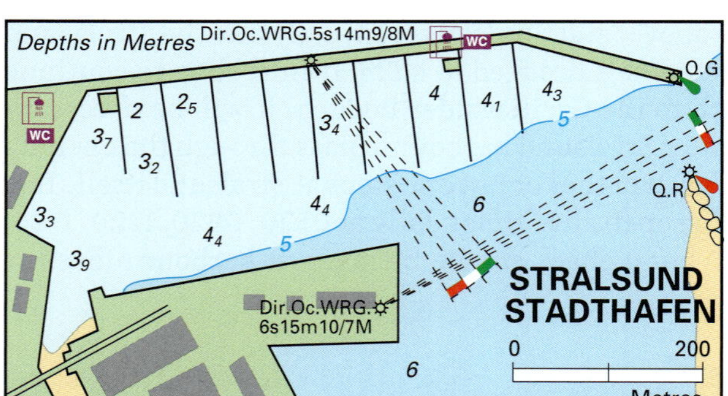

Stadthafen marina *Miranda Delmar-Morgan*

by calling *Stralsund Traffic* (VHF Ch 16/67). City Marina has a printout of the times.

Approaching from the south, the channel divides around the island of Dänholm (see plan page 50), the western fork (the Ziegel Graben) leading to the town through twin lifting road and rail bridges (see above for opening times). There are no shoreside waiting berths. The new fixed motorway bridge just north of the lifting bridge has a clearance of 40m. The longer part of the railway bridge connecting Dänholm to the larger island of Rügen does not open, and has a fixed height of 8m.

The direction of buoyage changes at the bridges.

### Berthing

Visiting yachts normally moor to pontoons in the Stadthafen which lies immediately to starboard after entering the harbour through the northern entrance. There are 240 berths, mostly alongside finger pontoons, but they are uncomfortable in southeasterly winds. Yachts may also be permitted to moor alongside the commercial quays midway between the north and south entrances, provided that no larger vessels are expected.

The basin at the south end of Dänholm island, which is accessed from the eastern fork (the main channel) of the Strelasund is quite small and usually full of local yachts. The yacht club at the northern end of Dänholm, to the north of the bridge might have berths, but it is quite exposed and both of these entail a long walk into the town centre. It is also possible to berth in the Querkanal close to the town centre but this has a depth of only 1.5m and has no facilities. Access is via an opening bridge which has fixed opening times.

The *Gorch Fock* – built in 1933 – now a museum ship in Stralsund *Andy Beharrell*

Stralsund, approach from north *Miranda Delmar-Morgan*

Stralsund aerial view with Rügen in the background *Miranda Delmar-Morgan*

### *Services*

Water, electricity and WiFi are available on the City Marina pontoons, with showers and toilets on Pontoon 8 and near the harbourmaster's office. Fuel is available at the Bunkerstation on the waterfront (Alter Schwedenkai).

### *Facilities*

There are floating fish restaurants on the harbourside walls but otherwise all shops, banks and restaurants are in the town centre, within easy walking distance from the Stadthafen. There is an Edeka supermarket southwest of the Rathaus, and various Nettos, Lidls and Aldis further out.

### *Communications & travel*

There are good train services to Berlin and Rostock from the Hauptbahnhof to the west of the town centre and from Rugendamn for onward passage to Mukran ferry port and Sweden.

## Rügen

For yachtsmen equipped with detailed German charts, Rügen offers numerous opportunities to discover a variety of small yacht harbours tucked away in the corners of the Bodden, on Hiddensee and the northern part of Rügen, all reached by closely buoyed and dredged channels. The main harbour though is Sassnitz on the east of the island. This is a good point to continue on either to Poland (Świnoujście) or to head north to Rønne on the west coast of Bornholm.

## SASSNITZ

54°30'.3N 13°38'.2E (east mole)

**Contacts**

**Port Authority** ✆+49 383 92 661 570, VHF Ch 69
**Marina Harbourmaster** ✆+49 162 23 70 864
www.stadthafen-sassnitz.de/marina
hafenbetrieb@stadthafen-sassnitz.de

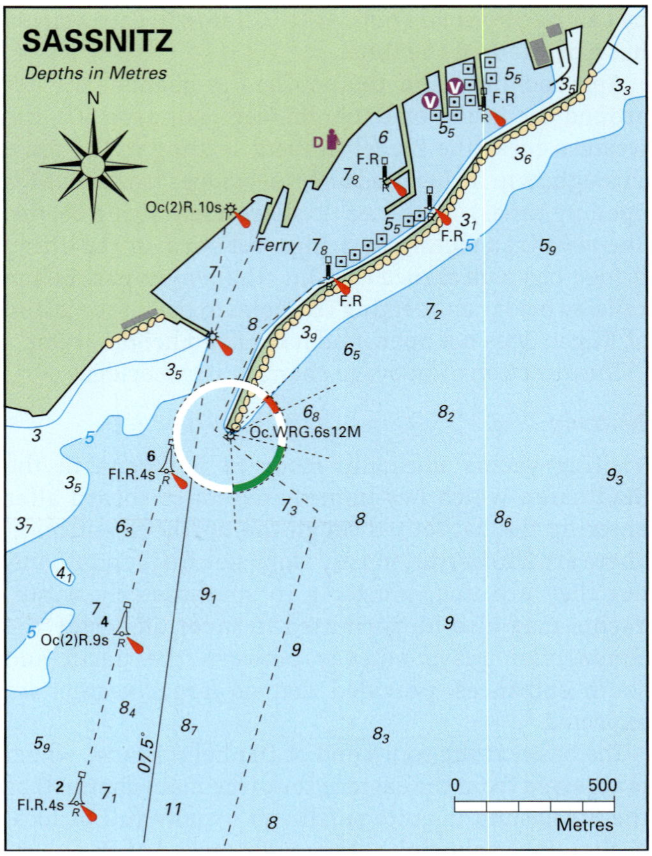

Sassnitz is a well-known seaside resort and port on Rügen, and is a gateway to the nearby Jasmund National Park *Andy Beharrell*

The only harbour of any consequence on the 'outside' of Rügen is Sassnitz, which lies on the east coast. Although still an active fishing port, the major ferry activity has now transferred to a new ferry port at Neu Mukran some 3M to the southwest. A small local ferry runs trips to Cap Arcona.

Sassnitz claims to have the longest harbour mole in Europe. Surprisingly, despite having such a long mole, the harbour is relatively open to the south-east and may be uncomfortable in such conditions. There are now moorings for yachts on the northwest side of the harbour. These consist of two jetties with posts, giving a total of 96 berths.

A slightly unusual tourist attraction is a former British submarine, HMS *Otus*. There are spectacular chalk cliffs along the coast just to the north of Sassnitz

An aerial view of Sassnitz harbour *Klugschnacker/Wikimedia Commons (https://commons.wikimedia.org/wiki/File:Sassnitz_(2011-05-21).JPG)*

The Rasender Roland (Racing Roland) narrow-guage steam train travels through the Rügen countryside between Putbus and Göhren *Andy Beharrell*

The Colossus of Prora – the longest hotel in the world is south of Sassnitz. Eight identical buildings, 4.5km in length. Started in 1936 as part of the Kraft durch Freude ('Strength through joy') programme, but never completely finished; it is now gradually being redeveloped *Ralf Roletschek / Roletschek.at / Wikimedia Commons (https://en.m.wikipedia.org/wiki/File:20-07-06-Prora-RalfR-DJI_0120.jpg)*

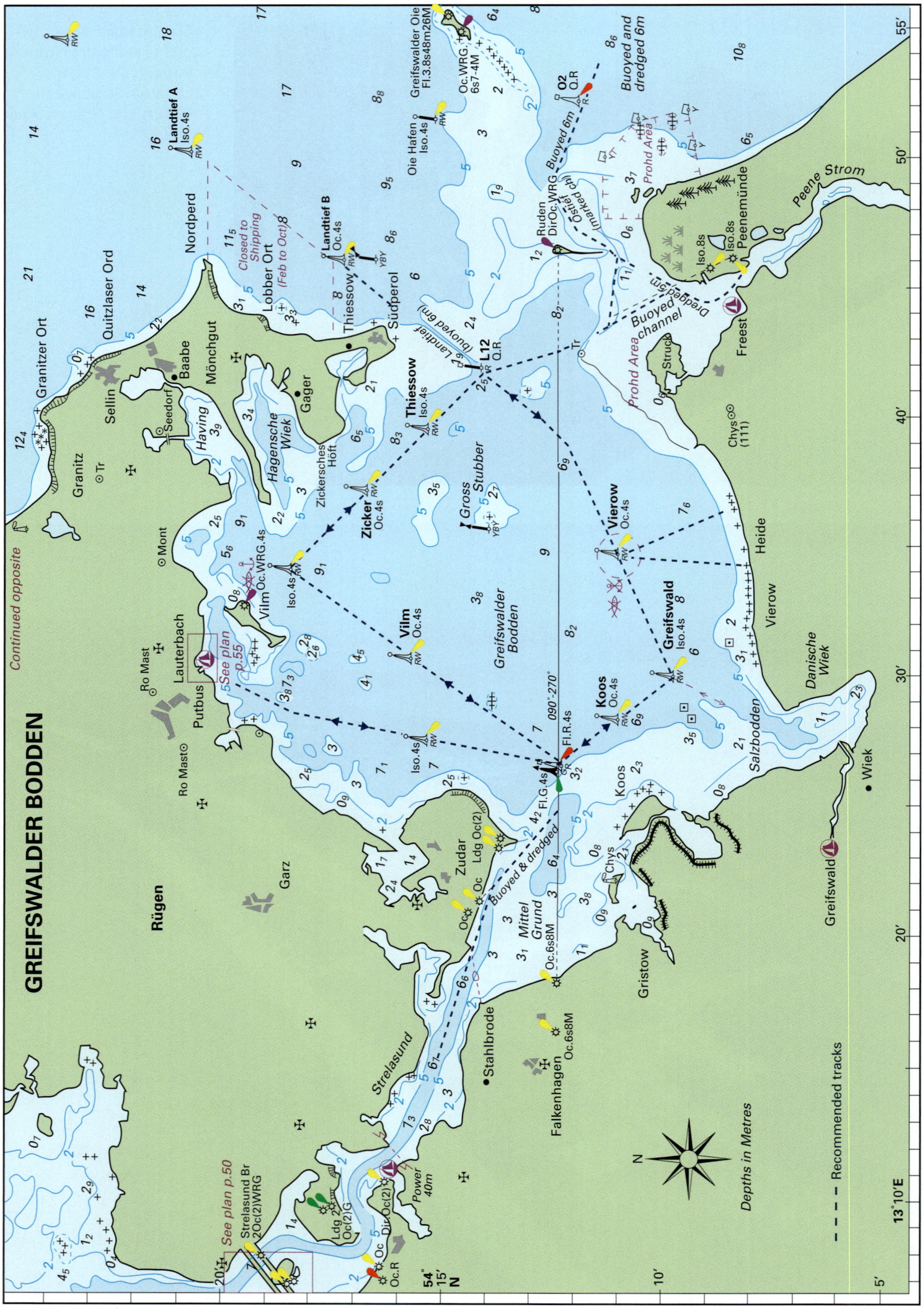
GREIFSWALDER BODDEN
Rügen
Greifswalder Bodden
Continued opposite
See plan p.55
See plan p.50
Depths in Metres
Recommended tracks

Jasmund National Park (near Sassnitz) is a nature reserve on the Jasmund peninsula, in the northeast of Rügen island. It is famous for containing the largest chalk cliffs in Germany *Andy Beharrell*

with many walking tracks through magnificent mature beech woods in the Jasmund National Park.

## Greifswalder Bodden

The southern end of the Strelasund leads into Greifswalder Bodden, a large body of mostly navigable water to the south of Rügen (see page 54).

From the eastern end of Greifswalder Bodden there are two alternatives:

- Via one of the two dredged channels through to the open Baltic, either northeast for Sweden and Bornholm or southeast for Świnoujście and the Polish coast;
- Or via the Peenestrom channel through to the Stettiner Haff (Zalew Szczeciński), a lake some 30M long straddling the German/Polish border from which there is access back into the Baltic.

## LAUTERBACH

54°20'.2N 13°30'.4E (south mole)

**Contacts**
Lauterbach Marina ✆+49 38 301 8090
www.im-jaich.de/hafen/heimathafen-lauterbach

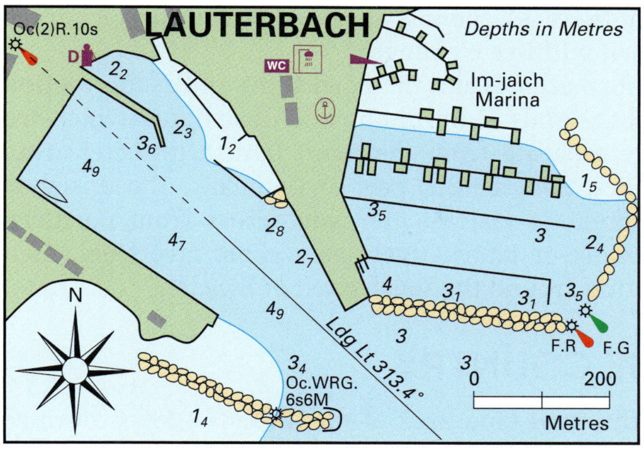


Lauterbach is on the north side of Greifswalder Bodden, on the south coast of Rügen island. The Im-jaich marina has 300 box berths on pontoons with 2.9 to 3.4m depths behind the eastern breakwaters. Beware narrow entrance and tight turns inside the breakwaters.

Fuel berth in the communal harbour where there are also some berths for visitors, WC €0.50, lovely walks and cycle rides. Putbus, about 1.5km inland, once a highly fashionable summer resort with a theatre, and Prince Putbus' palace are well worth a visit. Surviving from those days are a park and a circular terrace of fine houses. A narrow-guage steam train runs from beside the marina and will take you close to the palace (see Seedorf below). A supermarket and other shops will be found a short walk along the road to Putbus. There is a large charter fleet here, and it is also the home of Vilm Yachts.

## SEEDORF

54°21'N 13°39'E

Seedorf, also on the south coast of Rügen island, east of Lauterbach, is a beautiful natural harbour in unspoilt country, with some 40 berths amongst the reeds. It is approached by a buoyed channel with minimum depth of 2–6m. There are no facilities, but it is the harbour from which to visit the Jagdschloss, Prince Putbus' amazing hunting 'lodge' in the Granitz wood.

Although a 4km walk, the schloss is well worth the effort. There are spectacular views if you can brave the open sided spiral staircase! On the way one may also encounter the steam train which runs in a loop around this part of the island. There is an excellent fish shop with pickled herring rolls and fish brötchen. A travelling van visits with basic provisions, fresh bread rolls to order.

# DENMARK

Denmark lies on the doorstep of the Baltic and has much to offer the cruising yachtsman, both in its own right and as an interesting stop for those on their way to or from the Baltic proper. In this section we look at routes to the Baltic from the north of Denmark (either around the tip of Jutland or through the Limfjord) and include appropriate stops as you head over to western Sweden and also some appropriate stopovers if heading north from the Kiel Canal towards the west coast of Sweden.

Stopovers are chosen to allow for just day sailing from place to place. This is one of the joys of Baltic sailing - there is no need to do anything more than a day sail to get from harbour to harbour. While longer passages are straightforward (the further north you get the less night there is), there is always a harbour or anchorage to visit within easy range.

Information is also included at the end of this section on the islands of Bornholm and Christiansø which are quite separate from the main Danish cruising areas but are, nonetheless, part of Denmark. These islands are great to visit on the way across from northern Germany or alternatively as a short diversion when heading around the south coast of Sweden.

## THE COUNTRY

Of the total land area of 43,000km$^2$, 65% is devoted to farming with a further 12% used for forestry. Environmental considerations are given high priority. The countryside is generally flat with the highest point only 173m above sea level. Motorways connect the main cities by means of high-level bridges or tunnels between the major islands. Bridges to the smaller islands are either of sufficient clearance or open to allow the passage of yachts and other small boat traffic.

### The people, the church and the language

The Danes are friendly, tolerant and relaxed. They enjoy their pleasures and are happy to share them with visitors, but their harbours do become very busy during the main part of the sailing season.

Some 90% of the population of nearly 6 million are estimated to belong to the Lutheran Church which was established in 1536 and is the national church, under the direction of the state. Education has been compulsory since 1814 and there are several universities as well as various other institutions of higher education. A comprehensive social security system covers health, pensions, industrial accidents, unemployment and certain other hazards.

Danish is one of the Scandinavian languages and is most closely related to Norwegian and Swedish. The Danish alphabet is the same as the Norwegian, consisting of the 26 letters of the English alphabet plus æ, ø and å at the end. English is widely spoken, especially by the young and in the cities.

## PRACTICALITIES

### Yacht services & chandleries

There are chandlers in many of the main towns, although items sometimes have to be delivered from Copenhagen. There are several sailmakers, and yacht clubs or harbourmasters will be able to advise you where to get sails mended.

### Gas

Re-filling non-Danish gas cylinders is likely to be extremely difficult. However, camping gas cylinders are reasonably widely available (see 'Gas' section in main introduction, page 10).

### Diesel

Diesel can be obtained in many harbours but petrol is not so readily available and may have to be purchased at a filling station. Diesel at filling stations contains some bio fuel (see 'Fuel' section in main introduction, page 11, for further detail on the associated problems), so try to use marine outlets only.

### Shopping

Supermarkets in Denmark have a wide variety of foods. Prices are lower than Norway and Sweden but slightly higher than Germany, so if approaching Denmark via the Kiel Canal it is worth stocking up with non-perishable stores in Holtenau or other German ports.

Alcohol is widely available in supermarkets, without any of the restrictions on outlets that apply in Sweden or Finland. Alcohol prices are significantly lower than in Sweden, but higher than in Germany, and so, again, it pays to stock up before leaving Germany if possible.

Most shops, including hardware shops and some supermarkets, are closed on Saturday afternoons and many shops are closed on Sundays. However, bakeries are usually open on Sunday mornings, and these restrictions tend not to apply in tourist areas during the holiday season.

There some excellent fish shops or stalls to be found in many of the Danish harbours.

### Hotels & restaurants

There are many hotels and restaurants in the major towns, catering for all tastes and budgets, and modest restaurants and bars are to be found in most harbours during the season. The Danes have a more relaxed attitude to alcohol than the other Scandinavian countries, with a correspondingly lively nightlife.

### Laying up

There are a large number of boatyards where yachts can be laid up for the winter. Costs are generally reasonable but depend upon whether you require to be stored in a shed (heated or unheated) and other factors and you should seek local advice. Early booking is advised (see main introduction page 13 for further details).

## Berths

Danish harbours can be very busy during the peak summer months of July and August, as German and Swedish yachts join the ever-expanding fleet of Danish yachts and motor boats. This is exacerbated by the numerous festivals which take place during the summer season. Be prepared to raft up several boats deep if berthing alongside a quay. However, there is usually a friendly welcome and willingness to fit you in if at all possible, and the periods before and after the main holiday season are relatively quiet.

Berthing is usually in box berths with bow to a quay or jetty and the stern moored to a post on each quarter. Some berths are very narrow and the width between the posts may or may not be given (see Baltic mooring section in the main introduction, page 14). An unoccupied berth is marked by a green plaque at its head sometimes with the date on which its owner plans to return. A red plaque on the other hand indicates the berth is not to be used.

## Berthing charges

Fees are generally very reasonable. The harbour office is often unmanned and payment is usually by a machine which nearly always only take cards and not cash. The machine issues you with a sticker that must be displayed on the boat (harbourmaster/student will come round and check when they are on duty, often only for an hour a day). The machine will also dispense a card which gives you access to shower and washing facilities as well as electricity, and gives you the WiFi code.

Many marinas have *sejlerstuer* (sailors' lounges) accessible with the card and these offer free cooking and washing up facilities and sometimes a fridge as well as seating areas. Any money not spent on the card will usually be refunded when you return the card.

## Yacht clubs

Yacht clubs in Denmark are generally an association of local yachtsmen who are based in a particular yacht harbour. In many cases the club or association is responsible for the operation of the yacht harbour and the provision of the facilities. Visitors are usually offered temporary use of any club facilities during their stay.

## Danish harbour names

The following terms are commonly used:

| | |
|---|---|
| Lystbådehavn or Søsporthavn | yacht harbour or marina |
| Traffikhavn | commercial harbour |
| Fiskerihavn | fishing harbour |
| Gamle (Gammel) Havn | old port |
| Nordre Havn (Nordhavn) | north harbour/basin |
| Søndre Havn (Sydhavn) | south harbour/basin |
| Østre Havn (Østhavn) | eastern harbour/basin |
| Vestre Havn (Vesthavn) | western harbour/basin |

Møns Klint – a 6km stretch of limestone and chalk cliffs between Klintholm and Rødvig *Andy Beharrell*

# DENMARK KEY INFORMATION

## Rescue/Safety services

**Emergency** ☏ 112 (This is the emergency number for all EU countries).

VHF Ch 16 (24hrs 7 days a week)

**MRCC Lyngby Rescue Radio** monitors VHF Ch 16/70, DSC MMSI 002 191 000 (without prefix). Call Sign '**Lyngby Radio**' OXZ
☏+45 66 63 48 00.

## Charts and chart packs

UKHO Admiralty charts are excellent for the main channels around Denmark and for reaching all the passage harbours, and include details of the Traffic Separation Schemes, firing practice ranges, windfarms and other significant features both on the charts and in notes. Large-scale charts will be needed for exploration of the fjords and the Limfjord and for the approaches to Copenhagen.

Danish hydrographic charts give very good large-scale coverage (see **eng.dst.dk**) and details of the relevant chart are set out at the commencement of each harbour description below.

There are two excellent series of German chart packs (size A2) both of which are readily available in Denmark and internationally. They are published annually and come with electronic versions on CD and complementary pilot books and the relevant packs are as follows:

**NV Baltic Charts** (published by NV Charts):
Serie 1 Fünen – Kiel
Serie 2 Lübeck – Bornholm – København
Serie 3 Samsö – Sund – Kattegat
Serie 4 Rügen – Bodengewässer – Stettin
Serie 5 Schwedische Westküste

**Delius Klasing Charts** (published by Delius Klasing Verlag GmbH):
Satz 1 Kieler Bucht und Rund Fünen (includes the Kiel Canal)
Satz 2 Mecklenburg – Vorpommern – Bornholm
Satz 3 Westküste-Schweden
Satz 4 Grosser Belt bis Bornholm
Satz 5 Kattegat
Satz 6 Limfjord, Skagerrak, Danische Nordseeküste
Satz 11 Ostküste Schweden 1
Satz 12 Ostküste Schweden 2
The advantages of both these series are that one pack covers a large area and many harbour plans are included. They therefore represent very good value. The charts include a combination of large and small scales, which can take a little getting used to.

Navionics and other providers offer excellent, regularly updated electronic charts for plotters and iPads/tablets.
**UKHO charts** 2113, 2601, 2365, 2115, 902, 903, 2595, 2594, 2108, 2107, 426, 429, 894, 2591, 2592, 2532, 2596, 923, 938, 2597.

## Pilots and cruising guides

**In English**
*Germany and Denmark*, Nicholas Hill (Imray)
*Cruising Almanac* (Cruising Association/Imray)
*Komma's Havnelods, Aschehoug Dansk Forlag*.
Comprehensive harbour information in Danish but with easily understood symbols for facilities available. Published twice per year.

**In German**
*Dänemark I & 2*, Jan Werner (DK Edition Maritim)
*Hafenführer Dänemark* (DK Edition Maritim)
*Ankerplatz in Dänemark*, Gerti and Harm Claussen (DK Edition Maritim)
*Der Grosse NV Hafen Lotse*, Volumes 1, 2 and 3 (NV Charts) Complements Series 1, 2 and 3 of their charts.
*Hafenhandbuch Ostsee 1* covers all the harbours of Denmark apart from Jutland north of Grenå which are covered in the Nord See volume. Excellent harbour plans. (Delius, Klasing & Co). Complements DK chart series.

**In Danish/Swedish**
*Havneguiden Danmark og sydvestlige Sverige*, Per Hotvedt (Skaggerak Forlag), covers harbours and anchorages. Excellent drawings and aerial photos.
**www.harbourguide.com/en**

**Additional reading**
For more detail, Nicholas Hill's *Germany and Denmark* (Imray) is comprehensive. Another useful publication is Sejlerens Marina Guide newly published at the beginning of each season and available free at marinas. It is in Danish and German but has plans and aerial photos of marinas and easily understood symbols for the facilities available. Obtain a copy at the first Danish Marina you visit. Large scale charts are also essential.

## Time

Denmark uses UT+1 in winter and UT+2 in summer. Clocks change in line with the EU's daylight saving schedule, meaning that daylight saving time is observed from the last Sunday in March (0200 CET) to the last Sunday in October (0300 CEST).

## Kr Money

The unit of currency is the Danish krone (Dkr) divided into 100 øre. Although Denmark is a member of the EU, it voted not to join the Euro.

Cash points (ATMs) are numerous and all major credit cards are accepted in shops, at marinas and for fuel. In fact in many cases the credit card is the only method of payment.

## Formalities

**Customs**
There are limits on the quantity of alcohol, tobacco or other goods that may be imported, and these vary according to whether you are coming from another EU country.
Full details of the current restrictions and regulations can be found on www.skat.dk

**Embassies**
Royal Danish Embassy
55 Sloane Street, London SW1X 9SR,
☏+44 207 333 0200.
lonamb@um.dk, storbritannien.um.dk/en

British Embassy
Kastelvej 36/38/40, DK-2100 Copenhagen, ✆+45 35 44 52 00.
enquiry.Copenhagen@fcdo.gov.uk.

## Public holidays

Official public holidays in Denmark include: 1 Jan, Maundy Thursday, Good Friday, Easter Sunday, Great Prayer Day (May), Whit Sunday and Monday (May or June), 5 Jun (Constitution Day), 25–26 Dec.

## Communications

The country code for Denmark is 45. Dial 00 followed by the country code, area code (omitting any initial 0) and number. Mobile coverage is generally good throughout the country.

## Travel

Denmark can be reached very easily from most parts of Western Europe by air, rail and road.

There are **ferries** between Denmark and Norway, Sweden and Germany but no longer to the UK.

Low-cost airlines now operate to several **airports** including Esbjerg, Aarhus, Billund (in southern Jutland) and Copenhagen.

There is a large **train** network. When booking your train ticket do make sure to reserve a seat or you may have to stand! You can take bicycles onboard the trains. There are also many buses, especially useful in big towns.

If you have space, folding **bicycles** are very useful as there is excellent provision for cyclists with many cycle paths. Some towns and marinas have bicycles which you can pick up for a small deposit and either return or leave at another point (map on the bicycle).

## Websites

**www.sailbuddy.com** – Gives a short resume of harbour with plan and aerial photo plus contact details

**www.havneguide.dk/en** – An app with aerial photo and contact details

**www.MarinaBooking.dk** – A very useful website which enables you to book berths online in most of the main yacht harbours and marinas

**storbritannien.um.dk/en** – Danish Embassy in London.

**www.gov.uk/contact-consulate-copenhagen** – British Embassy in Copenhagen.

**www.visitdenmark.com** – Danish Tourist Board.

**www.visitcopenhagen.dk** – Copenhagen city website

**www.visitlolland-falster.com/tourist/index** – Tourist website for Lolland and Falster Islands

**www.sydsjaellandmoen.dk** – Tourist website for Møn Island

**www.visitfyn.com** – Tourist website for Fyn Island

**www.bornholminfo.dk** – Tourist website for Bornholm Island (includes harbour plans)

**www.dmi.dk** – Danmarks Meteorologiske Institut for weather forecasts and water levels

**Geodatastyrelsen,** the Danish Geodata Agency that produces official charts. They do not sell direct to the public. Corrections for Danish charts are available on their website **www.gst.dk/data-og-kort/soekort-og-marine-data/soekortrettelser**

**www.skat.dk** – Danish Customs. Not very user-friendly, but does give phone numbers for enquiries

**www.weilbach.dk** – Chart and nautical book suppliers, see under Copenhagen

## Radio communications & weather information

There are no regular **VHF** weather forecasts but Lyngby Radio is monitored 24/7 and can be contacted with request for weather information (see page ix for Lyngby Radio working channels). Gale warnings are however given in both Danish and English as well as navigational warnings on a very regular basis and the VHF coverage is excellent (they refer you to working channels, see page ix to get right channel for the area relevant to you).

Five-day forecasts in English are available on the **Danish Meteorological Institute** (dmi) website, **www.dmi.dk** and they also have a section on water levels **www.dmi.dk/vandstand** (*maalinger* are measurements and *vandstand* is water level). Most marinas/harbours will post daily weather forecasts from dmi during the season.

A very useful weather app from fcoo.dk is sejladsudsigt.dk which gives you 48-hr forecasts updated hourly.

In most harbours VHF is not used and any communication with harbourmasters is normally by telephone.

## Tidal streams and depths

There is little tide as such in the Baltic Sea areas of Denmark. The predominant current is north through the two Bælts and the Sound but the prevailing wind can vary this both in strength and direction to a marked degree, which makes it difficult to predict. The current is usually modest other than in the narrow parts of the channels of the two Bælts and the Sound north of Copenhagen. The NV chart packs include details of the prevailing north and south going currents.

Water levels can vary quite substantially by up to nearly 2m due to atmospheric and wind conditions. Strong offshore winds in particular can reduce the stated depth in the harbour. Depths generally are quite shallow and many of the harbours have depths around 2–2.5m so it is necessary to check charts and plan carefully before entering a new harbour. Mean level is used for chart datum. As a help Baltic sea levels are monitored every 30km in Denmark (see www.dmi.dk/vandstand for updated water level information).

When sailing in shallower water close to the coast look out for fishing flags and buoys and any implied hazards (nets and so on).

## Holding tanks

Holding tanks are not mandatory for foreign yachts but toilets must not be discharged within 2M of the shore nor in harbour. Shore facilities should be used whenever possible. Danish registered vessels built after 1 January 2000 with a fixed toilet now have to be fitted with holding tanks with the means of being discharged through a deck fitting.

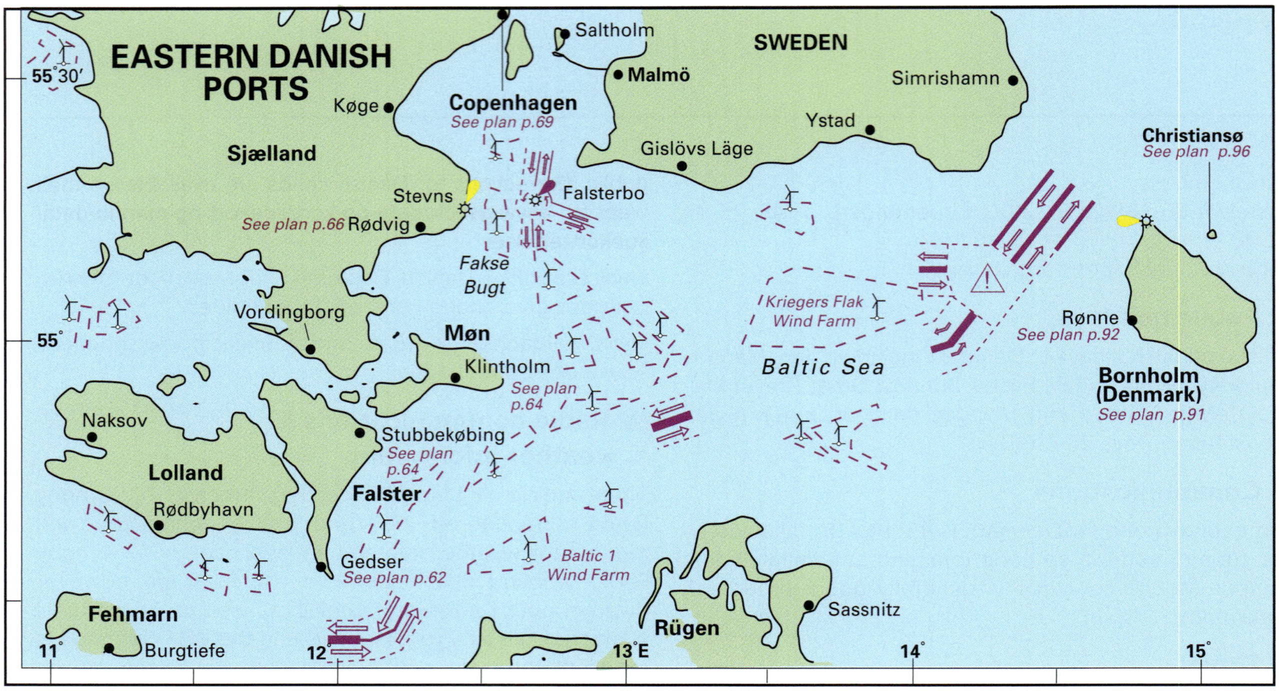


## 1D. EASTERN DANISH PORTS

These harbours are listed here as convenient harbours on the southern Danish islands on the quickest route from the Kiel Canal to Copenhagen or southern Sweden. They are chosen as being at approximately day sailing intervals. The route is relatively exposed and is closer to main shipping routes than in many other areas, but is a good way to head north towards Göteborg and the Bohuslän coast.

On leaving Kiel and heading towards Copenhagen or Sweden there are two main options – either to head east to Heiligenhafen (35M) and pass through Fehmarnsund (see Germany, page 34) before crossing the shipping channels and heading for the Gedser peninsula, or to head northeastwards to Denmark, either to Rødbyhavn (45M) or Gedser (70M). In either case close attention to shipping lanes, practice firing ranges and crossing ferries will be needed.

Rounding Gedser Rev (shoal) requires due care to navigate safely between the shallows off the land and the major turning point in the shipping lanes some 9M offshore. Once round Gedser Rev the route north or east is straightforward.

## RØDBYHAVN

54°39'N 11°20'E (starboard mole head)

### Distances

Kiel (Holtenau) 45M, Gedser 30M

### Lights

**Landfall buoy** 54°38'.3N 11°19'.4E RW LFl.10s
**Central pierhead leading lights** 045.2° *Front* 54°39'.2N 11°21'E Iso.R.2s17m6M Red triangle on red framework tower
*Rear* 300m from front, Iso.R.4s26m6M Red inverted triangle on grey framework tower
**West molehead** 54°39'.1N 11°20'.8E F.R.8m5M Red framework tower 5m
**East molehead** 54°39'N 11°20'.8E F.G.8m5M Green framework tower on hut 5m

### Contacts

**Harbourmaster** ✆+45 54 60 09 34
**Port Control** VHF Ch 74, havne@lolland.dk

*General*

Rødbyhavn, on the southwest coast of Lolland, is a busy port with a major ferry link to Germany. Access is straightforward with entry by day or night and, although not particularly yacht-friendly, it can be useful as a first stop in Denmark on passage from Kiel to Copenhagen or Sweden since it is just under 50M by the direct route. Otherwise it does not offer much appeal to the casual visitor. Ferries have priority when entering or leaving the harbour, and so caution is advised.

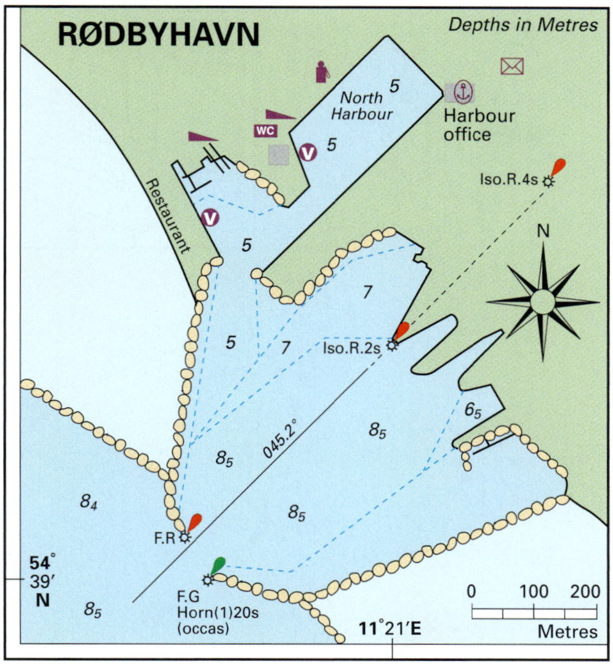


### Approach

From the landfall buoy follow the (lit) leading line on 045.2°. After passing between the breakwaters turn due north and head for the inner harbour.

### Berthing

Tie up alongside on the northwest side of the North Harbour or in one of the box berths (which are quite small) immediately to port when you enter North Harbour. There are also some box berths in West Harbour.

### Facilities

All main harbour facilities are available including restaurant and diesel, with petrol at 500m. Ferries to Puttgarden (Fehmarn). Train connections with Copenhagen and Hamburg.

## GEDSER YACHT HAVEN

54°34'.85N 11°55'.19E (starboard mole head)

### Distances

Kiel 70M, Rødbyhavn 30M, Stubbekøbing 30M, Klintholm 35M, Copenhagen 85M, Gislövs Läge (Sweden) 70M, Rønne (Bornholm) 100M

### Lights

**Gedser Odde** 54°33'.9N 11°57'.9E Fl(2)15s26m18M Racon (G) White hexagonal tower 20m

**Gedser Odde S end** 54°31'.7N 11°56'.2E Fl(3)R.10s13m10M Red pillar and lantern 14m Floodlit Horn(3)30s

**Leading Lights 350.5°** *Front* 54°34'.3N 11°55'.7E Iso.2s17m9M Red triangle on grey framework mast 15m *Rear* 376m from front Iso.2s26m9M Grey framework tower 30m

**Note** Buoyage in the entrance channel runs north to south (red buoys/lights to starboard on the approach from the South)

**Yacht harbour N mole** 54°34'.9N 11°55'.2E F.R.4m2M Grey post 2m

**Yacht harbour S mole** 54°34'.9N 11°55'.3E F.G.4m2M Grey post 2m

### Contacts

**Gedser Yacht Haven** ✆+45 54 17 92 45
gk@guldborgsund.dk
www.guldborgsund.dk/lystbaadehavne

### General

The Gedser peninsula on the south end of the island of Falster is about halfway between the Kiel Canal and Copenhagen or southern Sweden, with a major traffic separation zone some 9M offshore. It is a major ferry port but the yacht harbour is quite separate from the commercial harbour.

Gedser looking south-southeast *David Ridout*

### Approach

Approaching from the west, navigate to a position just east of the south cardinal buoy (54°30'.91N 11°50'.77E, unlit), keeping clear of the offshore wind farm. Approaching from the east, keep clear of the shoals which run some distance south-southeast from the tip of the peninsula.

As Gedser has a major ferry terminal, there is a buoyed and lit channel and a lit leading line – red buoys to starboard. Follow the channel until just before the entrance to the ferry harbour, then turn to port and follow the next part of the marked channel for about 0.75M, when the yacht harbour will be seen to starboard.

### Berthing

Berth in box berths or alongside on starboard side after entering the harbour, just before the fuel station. The southernmost berths carry a depth of 3m and the others 2.5m.

### Facilities

All basic facilities are available including a restaurant and a diesel berth. It is a 1km walk to the supermarket.

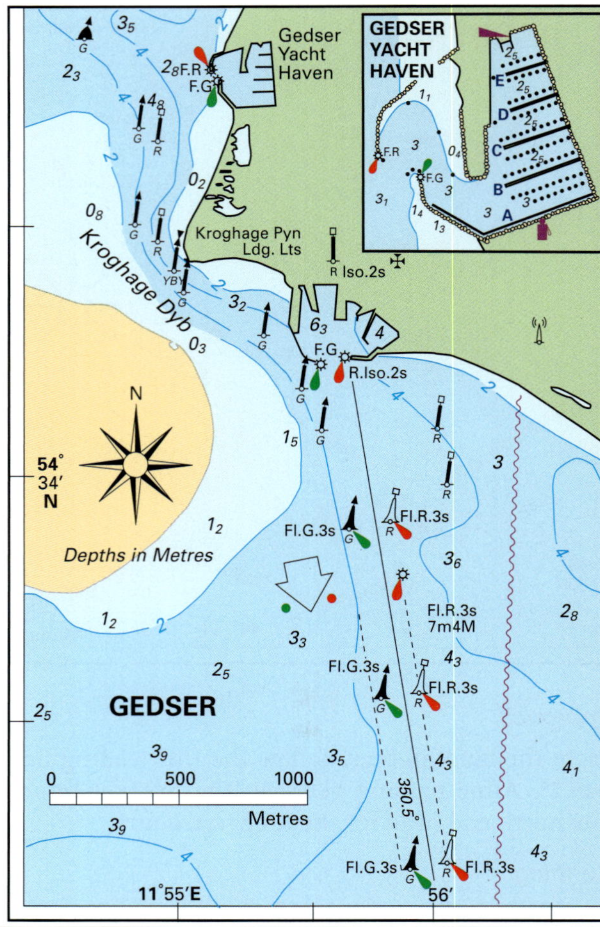


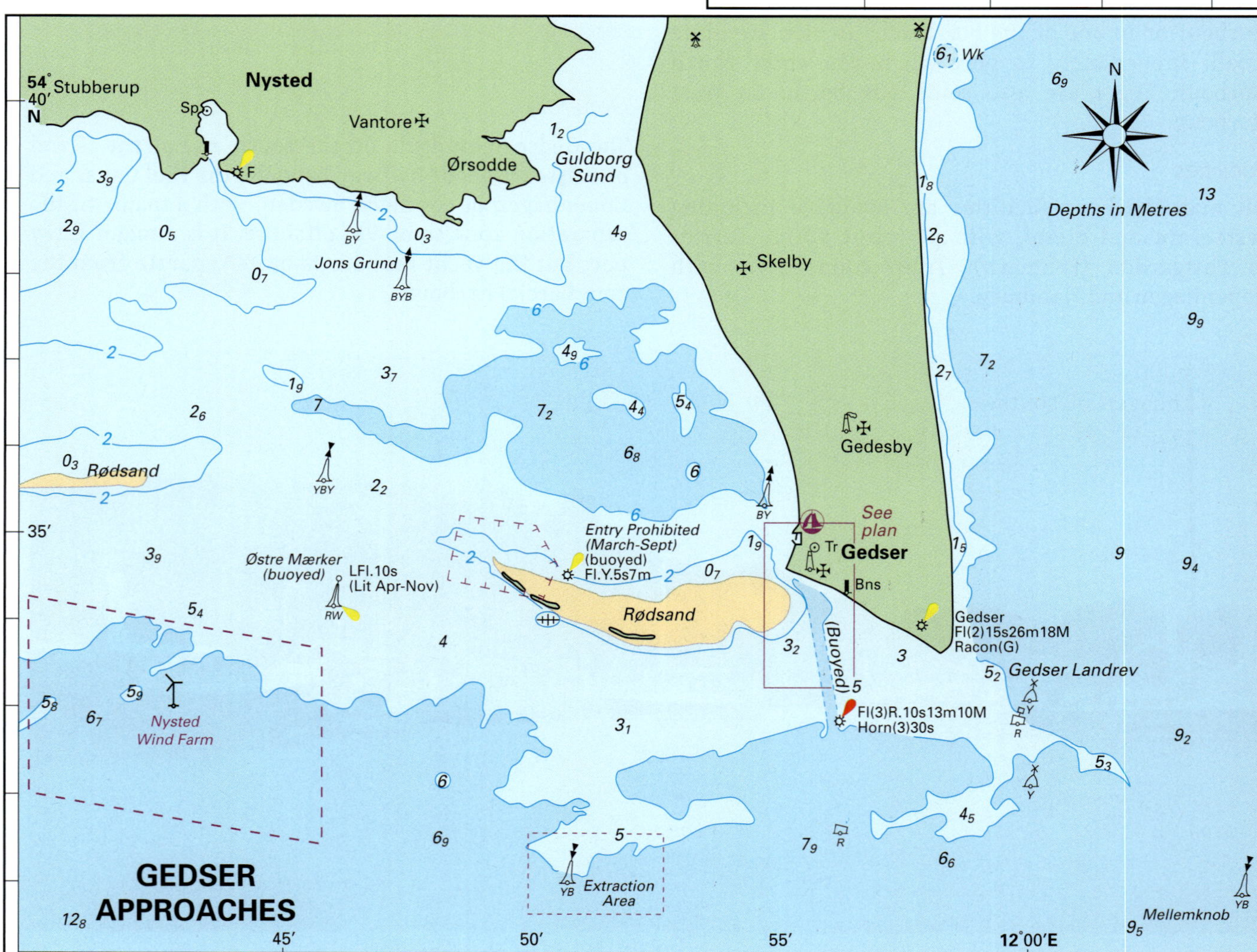

## STUBBEKØBING

54°53'.68N 12°02'.65E (east cardinal mark at entrance to channel into harbour)

### Distances

Kiel 95M, Gedser 30M, Klintholm 20M, Copenhagen 70M, Gislövs Läge 60M

### Lights

**Hestehoved** 54°50'.1N 12°09'.9E Oc(2)WRG.6s14m13–9M White house 4m
Red can buoy 54°49'.8N 12°11'.4E Fl(3)R.10s
Leading Lights 324° *Front* 54°53'N 12°07'.2E Iso.2s12m9M Red triangle on white tower 13m
**Skansepynt** *Rear* 520m from *front*, Iso.4s20m13M Red inverted triangle, white bands, on grey framework tower 19m
**Hårbølle** Pynt Leading Lights. 353.5° *Front* 54°53'N 12°08'.9E Iso.G.2s10m7M Red triangle, white bands on grey framework tower
*Rear* 480m from front. Iso.G.4s21m8M Red inverted triangle, white bands, on grey framework tower
**Borgsted** 54°54'.2N 12°06'.5E Oc.WRG.5s3m10–8M White house, red band.
**Hårbolle** 54°53'.3N 12°08'.2E Oc.WRG.10s6m12–9M Red triangle, white bands, on framework tower.
**Stubbekøbing** Leading Lights 176° *Front* W molehead 54°53'.5N 12°02'.7E F.G.3m Post. *Rear* 130m from front F.G.7m Grey framework tower
*Note* Buoyage in the main entrance channels runs northwest to southeast (red buoys/lights to starboard). Into the harbour, green buoys are to starboard

### Contacts

**Harbourmaster** ✆+45 51 74 01 09
stubhavn@guldborgsund.dk
www.guldborgsund.dk/lystbaadehavne
www.marinaguide.dk/stubbekoebing-havn/om-havnen

### *General*

Stubbekøbing is a useful stop on the way from Kiel to Copenhagen or southern Sweden especially if you choose to go through the Smålandsfarvandet. It is the largest town on the Grøsund and is a good place to get supplies. There is a recently extended marina, and a large commercial harbour with alongside berthing for yachts. It is also the ferry port for the island of Bogø which is directly north of the harbour. The ferry port is separate, west of the harbour, and out of bounds to yachts.

### *Approach*

54°49'.8N 12°11'.4E (red buoy Fl(3)R.10s marking the beginning of the buoyed channel)

The dredged and well-buoyed approach channel - red buoys to starboard - with leading lights, starts to the east of Hestehoved light. The initial course is 324° from near the red can buoy noted above, thereafter see plan, page 64. Leave the main channel opposite the harbour entrance and follow the buoyed channel southwards towards the commercial harbour. Just before the entrance turn eastwards to follow the breakwater round to the yacht harbour entrance. Do not cut the corner. A sign directs you to the Lystbådehavn where there is now a floating pontoon by the entrance which you leave to starboard before entering the yacht harbour.

### *Berthing*

The yacht harbour has box berths along the north mole with the first on your starboard side having a width of up to 5m and length 15m. These berths then become smaller and narrower as you head further into the harbour. Depths between 2.5–2.7m.

Alternatively you may tie up alongside in the main harbour. The fuel facility is also there. This harbour is council run.

### *Facilities*

All main harbour facilities are available including diesel, with petrol at 500m. There is a kiosk selling a limited selection of groceries and drinks beside the commercial harbour, and a shopping centre in the town some 500m further away, where there are the usual banks, restaurants and hotels, and a motor bike museum. Most types of repairs can be undertaken here. Bicycles can be borrowed from the harbourmaster.

Stubbekøbing aerial view *by kind permission of Stubbekøbing harbourmaster*

Stubbekøbing looking west with big box berths *David Ridout*

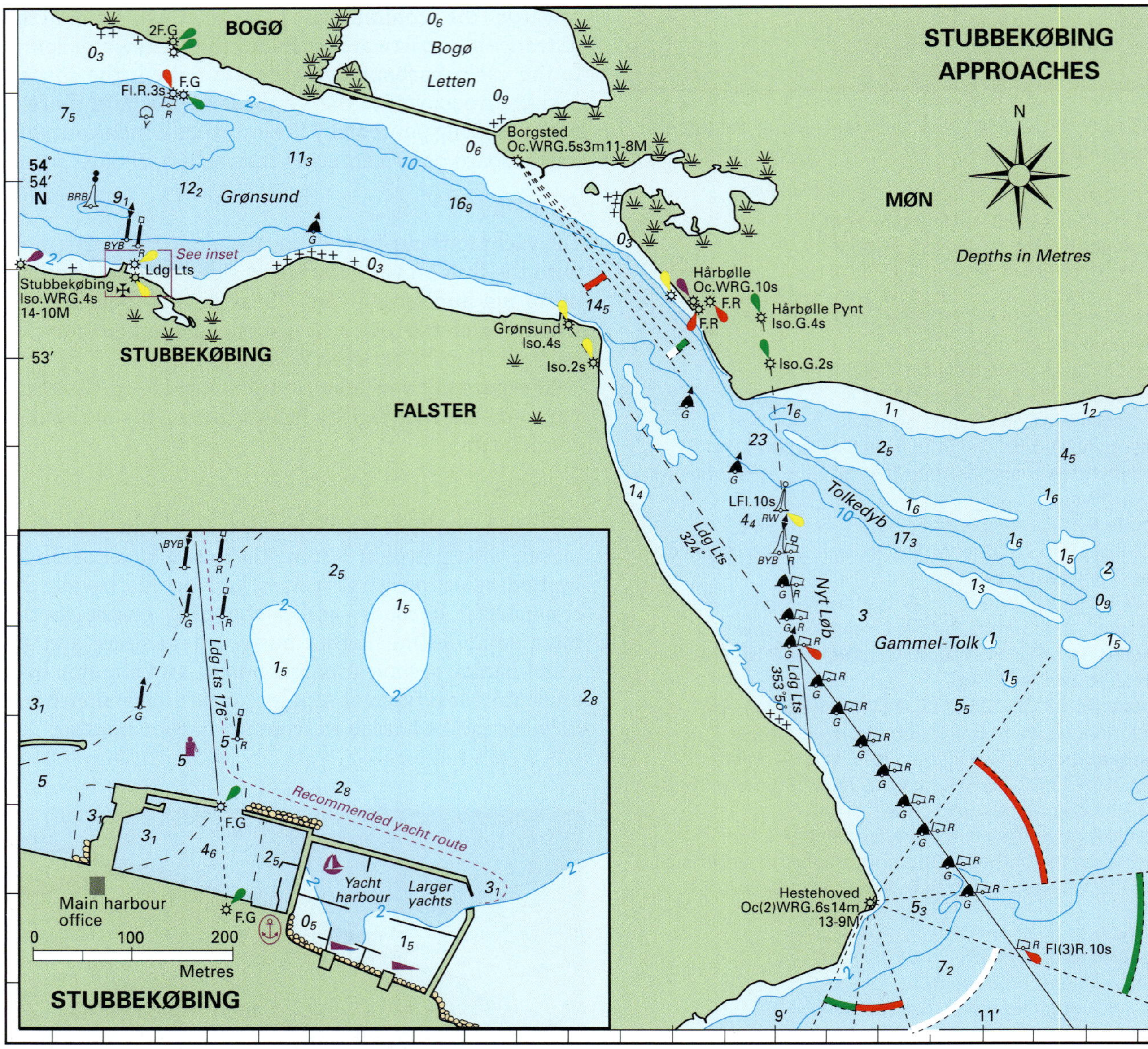


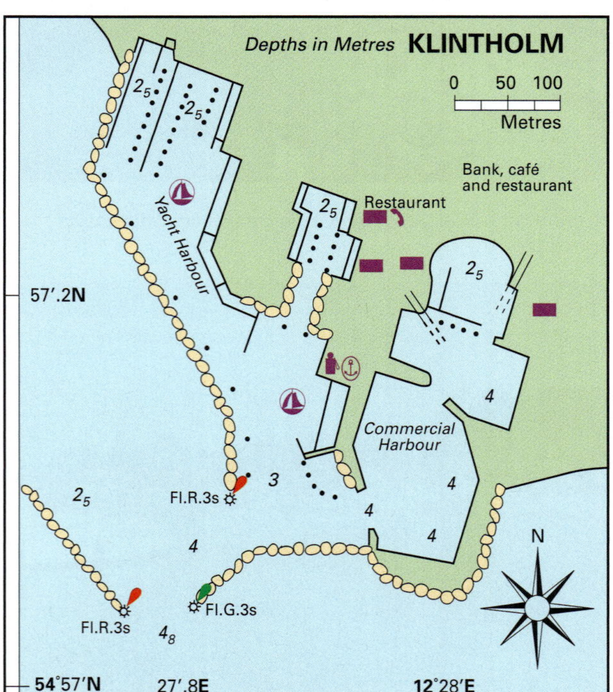


## KLINTHOLM

54°57'N 12°27'.79E (starboard mole head)

### Distances

Gedser 35M, Stubbekøbing 20M, Rødvig 25M, Copenhagen 55M, Gislövs Läge 40M

### Lights

**Møn SE Point** 54°56'.8N 12°32'.4E Fl(4)30s25m21M
Yellow square tower 13m

**North molehead** 54°57'.2N 12°27'.9E Fl.R.3s4m4M
Post

**South molehead** 54°57'.1N 12°27'.9E Fl.G.3s5m4M
White pedestal 3m

### Contacts

**Klintholm Harbourmaster** ✆+45 24 42 21 82
micl@vordingborg.dk
klintholm-havn.vordingborg.dk

Klintholm entrance *David Ridout*

### *General*

Klintholm is an attractive harbour with excellent facilities for yachts (havne.vordingborg.dk/havne/klintholm-havn/besejling). It is worth visiting in its own right, and also provides a good passage harbour as it is close to the direct route to Copenhagen and provides a good starting point for the leg to southern Sweden. It is the closest harbour for visiting Møns Klint and other attractions on the island (www.southzealand-mon.com/moen).

The focus of commercial activity here has moved away from fishing and large boat maintenance to a wind farm service centre and a modern marina. The fishing harbour to starboard as you enter is increasingly used for mooring especially by larger yachts, and the slipway and maintenance sheds have closed. A section of it is also designated for wind farm work boats that come and go throughout the day and night.

### *Approach*

The approach is straightforward with no hazards when coming from the south, but it is worth staying offshore as there are many gillnets set in the bay outside the harbour and they can be difficult to see against the cliffs on the shoreline. After passing between the breakwaters, bear to port for the yacht harbour.

### *Berthing*

Berth in box berths either in the smaller basin to the north of the entrance or in the larger basin to the northwest. Both carry 2.5m depth. Large yachts can moor alongside the W mole in the fishing harbour.

### *Facilities*

All main harbour facilities are available including diesel, with petrol at 200m. There is a small grocer's shop and restaurants nearby and two good beaches.

Guest moorings at Klintholm *Viv Fox*

## RØDVIG

55°15'N 12°22'E (starboard mole head)

**Distances**
Gedser 55M, Klintholm 25M, Copenhagen 35M

**Lights**
**Stevns** 55°17'.5N 12°27'.2E LFl.25s64m21M White round tower 26m
**Landfall buoy** 55°14'.1N 12°23'.6E LFl.10s Red and white pillar buoy
**East molehead** 55°15'.2N 12°22'.6E Fl.G.3s5m3M Red pedestal, white band
**West molehead** 55°15'.2N 12°22'.5E Fl.R.3s5m3M Grey conical concrete hut 3m

**Contacts**
**Rødvig Harbourmaster** ✆+45 56 50 69 54
www.roedvighavn.dk
havnekontor@roedvighavn.dk

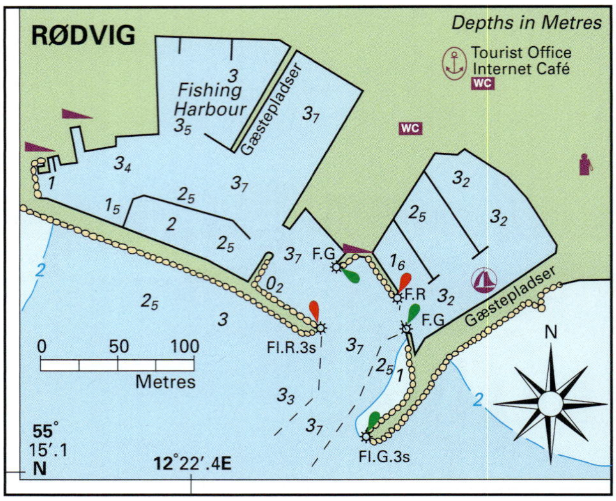


### General

Rødvig is a pleasant small harbour and a useful stop to break the journey from the south to Copenhagen. The yacht harbour to the northeast of the entrance is often congested. The fishing harbour to the west is relatively clear and has greater character, but no facilities. The passage between Klintholm and Rødvig takes you past the highest cliffs in Denmark - Mons Klint. From Rødvig you can also visit the Stevns Klint Cold War Museum (www.stevnsfortet.dk). This area was at the front line of the Scandinavian Cold War precautions and the museum is an interesting illustration of that preparedness.

### Approach

The harbour entrance should be approached in a north-northeasterly direction to avoid the many fishing stakes just offshore. Entry at night is not recommended on a first visit.

### Berthing

Berth in box berths in the yacht harbour to the north-northeast of the main entrance. The first two rows of berths carry a depth of 1.5m while the ones further in are deeper with 2.8m. If the yacht harbour is full there is alongside berthing for yachts in the fishing harbour to the northwest of the main entrance.

### Facilities

All main harbour facilities are available including diesel and petrol in the main harbour. WiFi.

The entrance to Rødvig *Andy Beharrell*

Guest moorings in Rødvig *Andy Beharrell*

Rødvig Flint Oven – a replica of a flint oven built in 1870
*Andy Beharrell*

# 1E. THE DANISH SIDE OF THE ØRESUND (THE SOUND)

*General notes*

The Sound is the most direct route to/from the Kattegat into the main part of the Baltic and, as such, is a major shipping route. It is also narrow, being only 3M wide at its narrowest point. There is a traffic separation scheme off Falsterborev, and another in the narrows between Helsingør and Helsingborg. The hazard is from the size of some vessels using this route (many of them are too large to use the Kiel Canal route out of the Baltic Sea), rather than the sheer numbers such as in the Straits of Dover, but nevertheless yachts crossing the sound should pay close attention to the normal rules for such schemes.

The waters between Copenhagen and Malmö are tortuous and shallow in places and crossed by the Øresund bridge, but there is a well-marked, dredged channel for large vessels. Currents in this area will vary with the wind in both strength and direction and can run up to 2kn in the narrower parts of the Sound. It therefore follows that close attention needs to be paid to navigation in this area.

All this may make the area sound hazardous but in practice it is far less so than, for example, the English Channel. It is an interesting cruising ground, home to large numbers of yachts on both the Danish and Swedish sides. There are several guest harbours on the Swedish shore (see chapter 2, page 109).

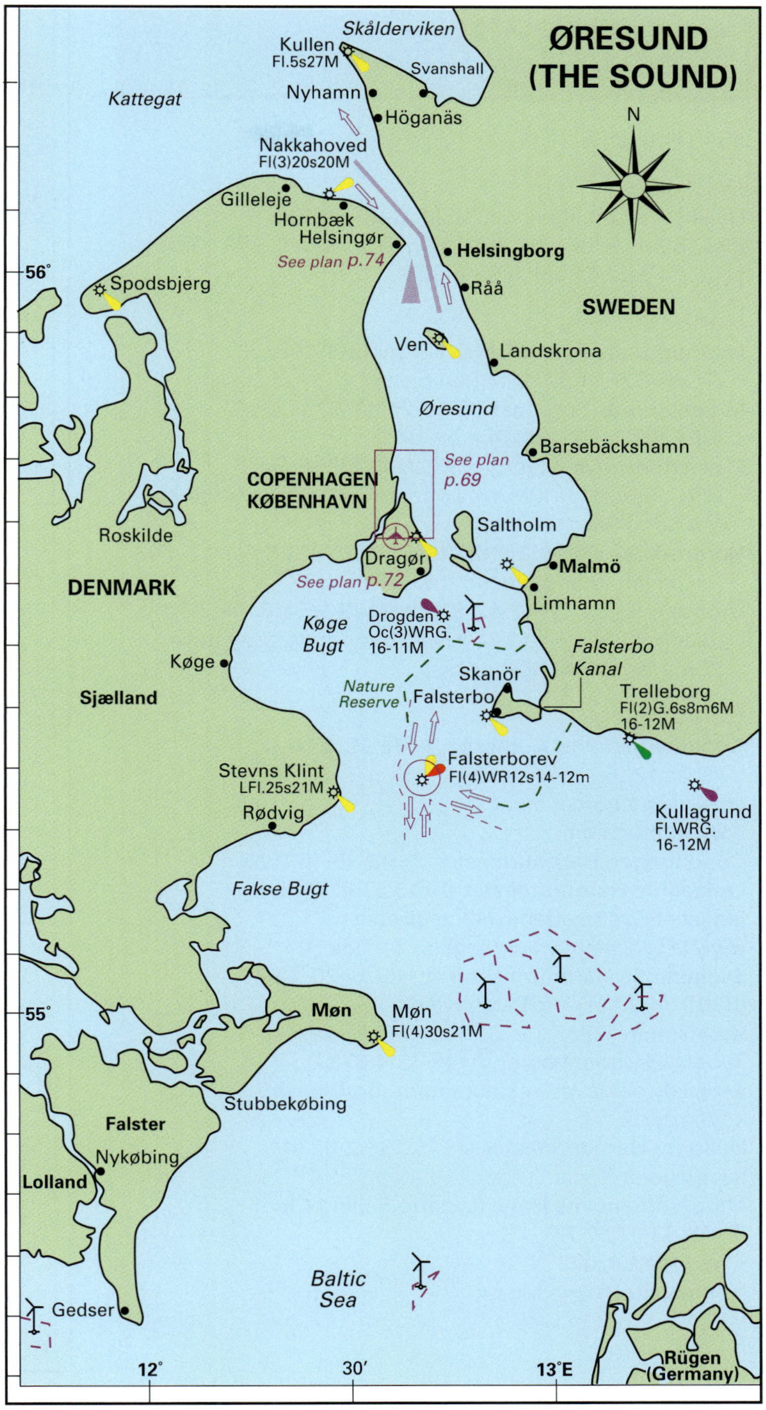

Lighthouses, Helsingør
*Arndale | Dreamstime.com*

## COPENHAGEN

55°41'N 12°36'E

### Distances

Helsingør 22M, Klintholm 55M, Gedser 85M, Kiel 150M, Stralsund 85M, Falsterbo Kanal 21M, Gislövs Läge (Sweden) 35M, Rønne 90M.

### Lights

**Middelgrunds Fort west** 55°43'.3N 12°39'.9E Oc.WRG.5s11m12–10M Red block

**Middelgrunds Fort east** 55°43'.2N 12°40'.1E Oc(2) WRG.12s11m12–10M Red block

**Prøvestenshavn oil jetty** 55°41'N 12°38'.3E Oc(3) WRG.15s10m13–10M White framework tower, white hut, red band 8m

**Nordre-Røse** 55°38'.2N 12°41'.3E Oc(2)WRG.6s14m17–13M Racon (M) Round granite tower 17m

**Drogden** 55°32'.2N 12°42'.8E Oc(3)WRG.15s18m18–13M Racon (X) White square tower, red bands, grey base 20m Horn Mo(U)30s (occas)

### Contacts

**Copenhagen Port Authority** ✆+45 35 46 11 11
VHF Ch 12/16
cmport@cmport.com
www.cmport.com

**Copenhagen Harbourmaster** ✆+45 35 46 11 38

**Langelinie Harbourmaster** ✆+45 2744 7545
langelinie.lystbaadehavn@gmail.com
www.langeliniehavn.dk/engelsk-forside

**Svanemølle Harbourmaster** ✆+45 39 20 22 21
(0900–1900 LT) info@smhavn.dk
www.smhavn.dk

**Tuborg Harbourmaster** ✆+45 3314 8787
www.kdy.dk/havne-restauranter/tuborg-havn/
kdy@kdy.dk

**Hellerup Harbourmaster** ✆+45 39 62 07 61
havn@gentofte.dk

**Margaretheholms Havn (Lynette Sailing Club)**
✆+45 32 57 57 78
www.lynetten.dk
havnekontor@lynetten.dk

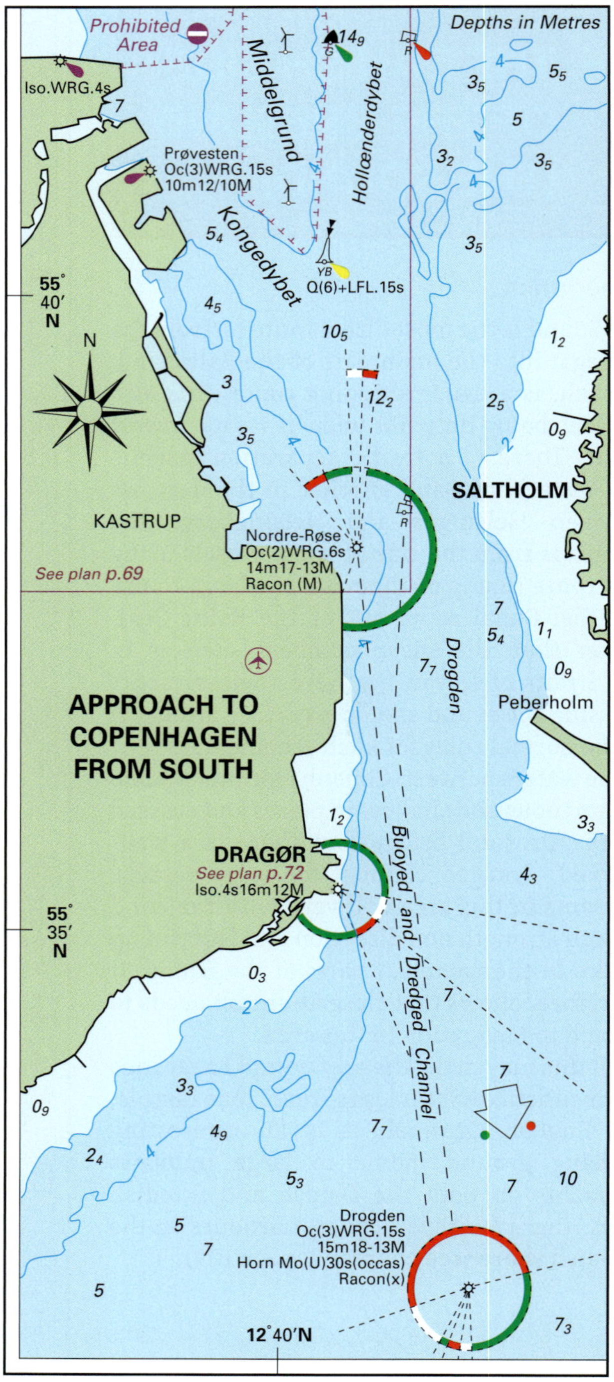


### *General*

Copenhagen is a friendly city with a strong feeling of history. There is much for the tourist, better described in one of the numerous shore-based guide books than here. Sightseeing in the centre of the city can be done on foot.

### *Approach*

The approaches to Copenhagen are well marked and lit but a large-scale chart is recommended. From the south - locate the red and green channel buoys just north of the Drogden lighthouse and follow the channel northwards but beware: RED buoys and lights are left to starboard.

To the northeast the Øresund Bridge to Sweden can be seen as it traverses Peberholm Island before entering a tunnel under the main shipping channel. After Nordre-Røse lighthouse is left to port, a branch of the channel (the Kongedybet) bears northwestwards on a leading line of 317.8° towards the city area and Trekroner light, leaving the pylons of the wind farm on Middelgrund to starboard.

By day and in poor visibility, care should be taken in the vicinity of the off-lying islands of Saltholm and Peberholm, which are surrounded by shoal water and are very low-lying; so much so that it is very easy to misjudge distances. From the north the approach is straightforward.

In 2021 the Danish parliament approved plans for the Lynetteholmen artificial island. This will be 3km$^2$ and eventually house 35,000 people and act as a flood protection barrier for Copenhagen. Foundations will be in place by 2035 and the project will be complete in 2070.

During the course of the works, entry into Copenhagen is through the main channel and is controlled by red

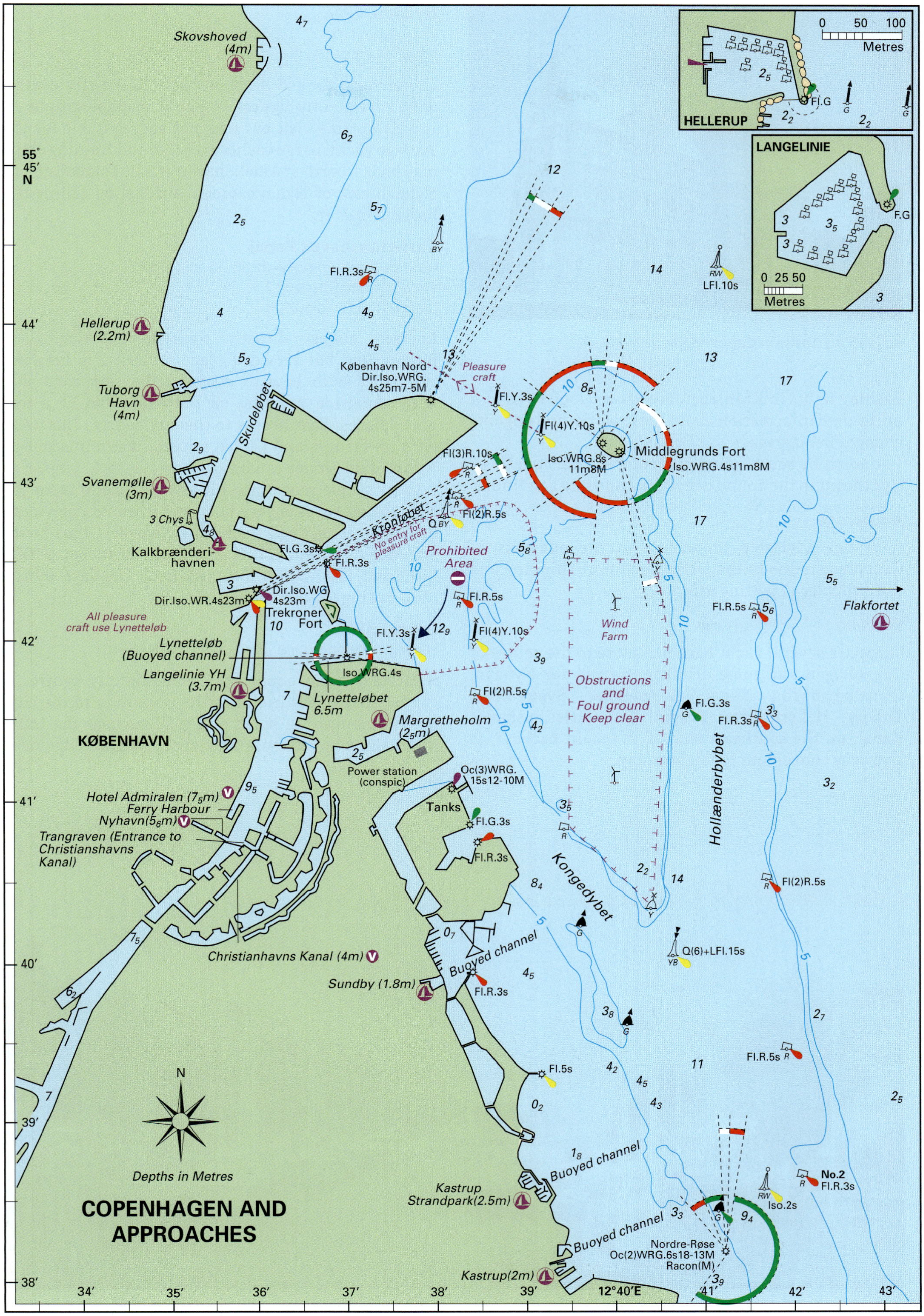

COPENHAGEN AND APPROACHES
Depths in Metres
HELLERUP
LANGELINIE
Skovshoved (4m)
Hellerup (2.2m)
Tuborg Havn (4m)
Svanemølle (3m)
3 Chys
Kalkbrænderi-havnen
Skudeløbet
København Nord Dir.Iso.WRG. 4s25m7-5M
Pleasure craft
Middlegrunds Fort
Iso.WRG.8s 11m8M
Iso.WRG.4s11m8M
Kronløbet
No entry for pleasure craft
Prohibited Area
Dir.Iso.WR.4s23m
Dir.Iso.WG 4s23m
Trekroner Fort
All pleasure craft use Lynetteløb
Lynetteløb (Buoyed channel)
Langelinie YH (3.7m)
Lynetteløbet 6.5m
Margretheholm (2₅m)
KØBENHAVN
Power station (conspic)
Oc(3)WRG. 15s12-10M
Tanks
Hotel Admiralen (7₅m)
Ferry Harbour
Nyhavn(5₆m)
Trangraven (Entrance to Christianshavns Kanal)
Christianhavns Kanal (4m)
Sundby (1.8m)
Buoyed channel
Wind Farm
Obstructions and Foul ground Keep clear
Kongedybet
Hollænderbybet
Flakfortet
Q(6)+LFl.15s
LFl.10s
Kastrup Strandpark(2.5m)
Kastrup(2m)
Nordre-Røse Oc(2)WRG.6s18-13M Racon(M)
No.2 Fl.R.3s
Iso.2s
12°40′E

Rosenborg Castle in Copenhagen *Andy Beharrell*

flashing lights in Kronløbet. See www.byoghavn.dk for up-to-date information about these works and ongoing changes in buoyage.

A north or south-going current can occasionally be significant in the Sound depending on wind conditions.

### *Anchorage*

It is not advisable to anchor in the environs of Copenhagen due to the large amount of shipping and the difficulty of getting ashore.

### *Berthing*

There are several yacht harbours close to the centre of Copenhagen and some details are given for Nyhavn, Christianshavns Kanal, Langelinie, Svanemølle, Tuborg, Hellerup and Dragør. The Christianshavns Kanal, on the southeast side of the main harbour, is also very convenient for sightseeing.

## Nyhavn

www.nyhavn.com
info@nyhavn.com

The picturesque old harbour, close to the city centre, which frequently figures in publicity photographs. It is well worth a visit but now not very suitable for the average yacht. Large yachts over 15m and training ships may book a berth at Amaliehaven at Sdr. Toldbod and in Nyhavn east of Nyhavnsbroen (bridge) by calling the harbourmaster.

## Christianshavns Kanal

Harbourmaster *mobile* ☽+45 40 96 37 72
www.marina.wilders.dk
marina@wildersplads.dk

Entered almost directly opposite Nyhavn, is a picturesque but crowded place. Mooring is between two poles with bow to quay on the starboard side with alongside mooring on port side and at a few other places. Easy access to the city centre. This area, with its bridges and gabled houses, is reminiscent of Amsterdam's inner canals.

Local people recommend it as the place to moor for sightseeing but it is very busy and it would pay you to book a place through the harbourmaster. Office hours are Mon–Fri 0800–1200 and 1600–1800, Sat 0900–1200 and 1600–1800, Sun and bank holidays 0900–1200 during the summer season.

## Langelinie

Harbourmaster *mobile* ☽+45 2744 7545

A circular basin about 1km from the city centre. It can be busy but is useful for its proximity to the city. It lies amongst the parks and gardens near the Little Mermaid, who sits on a rock at the water's edge near

Christianshavns Kanal berths *David Ridout*

Nyhavn in central Copenhagen *Andy Beharrell*

View of Frelsens Kirke Tower from Christianshavns Kanal *David Ridout*

Langelinie promenade. Mooring is bows to the quay with stern line to a buoy.

It is advisable to arrive at Langelinie early in the day to improve the chance of finding a vacant berth. There are basic facilities but no fuel is available. Payment is by card at the 'havnekontor'. Harbourmaster available Mon–Fri 1600–1700, Sat–Sun 1200–1300. You have to vacate your berth by 1400 on the day you are leaving.

## Svanemølle

✆+45 39 20 22 21
info@smhavn.dk

The largest of the Copenhagen yacht harbours and normally has space for visitors. It is approached in a southwesterly direction via a buoyed channel leading from the northern end of the dock complex. It is 4km from the main shopping centre, but the excellent public transport system makes travelling there easy. No fuel and rather tired facilities (fuel is available at Tuborg marina just to the north). Payment is by machine and the harbourmaster is only occasionally there.

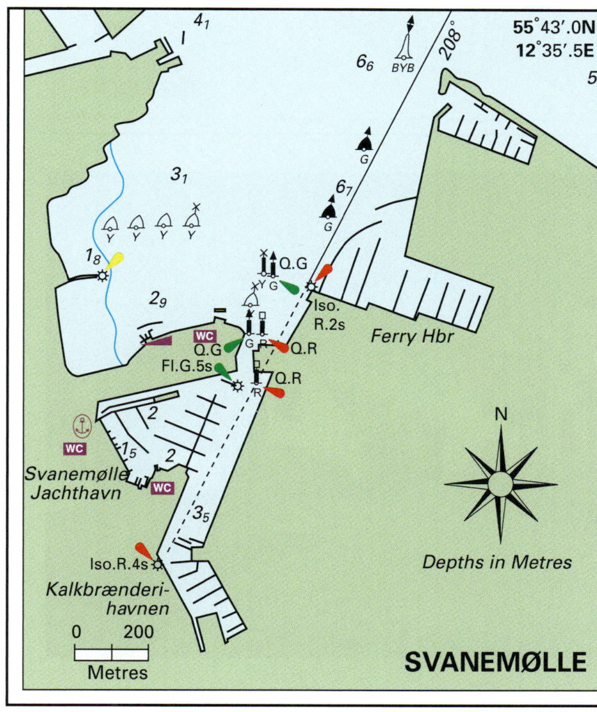

Approaches to Langelinie harbour *Andy Beharrell*

The Little Mermaid, close to Langelinie harbour *Andy Beharrell*

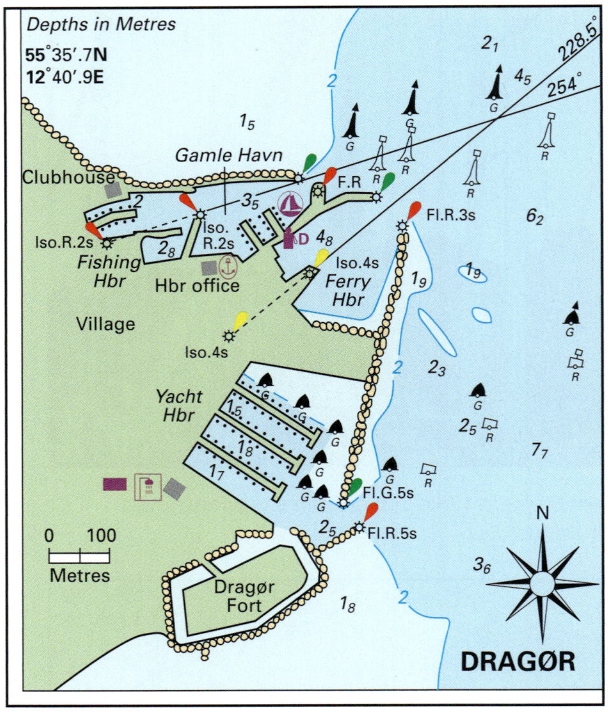


## Tuborg marina

☎+45 20 13 37 87, VHF Ch 13 (when manned)
kdy@kdy.dk

Lies just to the north of Svanemølle and has excellent modern facilities including water, electricity, showers, laundry, WiFi, diesel and petrol. Least depths 3m. It is the home of the Kongelige Danske Yacht Klub (Royal Danish YC). As with Svanemølle there is excellent public transport to the city.

## Hellerup

A small yacht harbour 6km from the city centre and 500m north of the Tuborg harbour. It is a small square basin flanked by trees and overlooked by the yacht club. There is an obvious buoyed channel leading to the south-facing harbour entrance. Mooring is bows-to with stern lines to posts. A new jetty to starboard before you enter the harbour offers additional mooring alongside when wind allows (not good in strong easterlies). Facilities include water and electricity on the quayside, toilets, showers and a sauna. There is no fuelling berth. The harbour office is on the port side as you enter the yacht basin and they will do their best to accommodate visitors. Hellerup shopping centre is about 300m away with a wide range of shops, banks, restaurants etc.

Houses around Dragør. The town was founded in the 12th century, and grew quickly as a fishing port *Andy Beharrell*

## Dragør

Harbourmaster VHF Ch 12/13/16 or ☎+45 3289 1570
www.dragoerhavn.com
havn@dragoer.dk

On the west side of the southern end of the Drogden channel (see plan page 68) is a pretty medieval fishing village developed by the Dutch. The town name derives from, Drag-, refers to dragging boats ashore while the ending -ør is common in Scandinavian placenames and means a beach covered in sand or gravel. There is easy access by bus into the city (30mins) and it is very convenient for the airport (15mins).

There is a marina on the south side of the harbour complex but it is shallow. The harbour area once used

Hellerup looking southeast *David Ridout*

for ferries is now available to yachts of more than 15m by prior arrangement with the harbourmaster and there is a diesel pump here. The Gamle Havn is where most people moor and depths here are 2.5–3.5m.

There are good facilities including laundry and WiFi and it is convenient for the little town with its excellent supermarket, as well as several cafés and restaurants. There is also a small boatyard.

### Services

There are several chandlers in Copenhagen, and most repairs can be arranged. There are a number of sailmakers in and around the city. Lyngby is 16km, 45mins by public transport, north of the Nyhavn, Copenhagen.

Danish, Swedish, German and British charts and pilot books may be bought from:

Weilbach A/S, Firskovvej 36,2800 Kgs. Lyngby, Denmark
☎+45 3334 3560
operations@weilbach.com
www.weilbach.dk
Customs: Toldskat København, Tagensvej 135, 2200 København N
☎+45 72 22 18 18

There is also a chandlery in Dragør to the south of Copenhagen.

Bue-Net, Søndre Tangvej 14, 2791 Dragør, Denmark
☎+45 32 53 42 76
bue@bue-net.dk
www.bue-net.dk

### Facilities

The city provides many restaurants and hotels. The main tourist information office is at Vesterbrogade 4A. Only Dragør and possibly Hellerup are close to shops for provisioning.

***Note*** The yacht harbours to the southwest of Copenhagen (such as Brøndby) also give easy access to the centre of Copenhagen by train, are near the airport and offer winter lay-up facilities which may be of interest.

Tourist information ☎+45 70 22 24 42
www.visitcopenhagen.dk

## HELSINGØR

56°02'N 12°37'.2E (south (port) pier head to main harbour)
56°02'.6N 12°37'.15E (PHE starboard mole head for marina)

### Distances

Gilleleje 12M, Copenhagen 22M, Halmstad 43M.

### Lights

**Kronborg** 56°02'.4N 12°37'.3E Oc(2)WRG.6s34m15–12M
NE tower of castle
**Leading Lights** 257.8° *Front* 56°02'N 12°37'.1E FW.13m6M
Grey mast. *Rear* 77m from front. FW.14m6M Square brick tower
**S pierhead** 56°02'.1N 12°37'.2E FR.7m6M
Red round metal tower
**N molehead** 56°02'.1N 12°37'.2E FG.7m6M
Green round tower

### Contacts

**Harbourmaster** ☎+45 49 28 10 80
nordhavnen@helsingor.dk
www.helsingor-havne.dk/lystsejlere/

### General

Overlooking the narrows, Shakespeare's Elsinore Castle (or to give it its correct name Kronborg Slot) dominates Helsingør. Originally built in the 15th century to enforce the collection of tolls from all ships sailing up or down the Øresund, it played a major part in the creation of Denmark's wealth. Helsingør has a large marina north of Kronberg Slot. The approach to the east facing entrance is straightforward. Tourist information is available at the harbour office.

### Berthing

#### Helsingør Marina, Nordhavn

56°02'.61N 12°37'15E Starboard mole head

There are visitor pontoons, as shown on the plan. These are stated to be for yachts 12–20m but the area can be used by other sized yachts if there is space. Elsewhere in the harbour the red/green availability notices apply. Depths are 2.5–3m.

Helsingør marina with Kronborg Slot in the background *Andy Beharrell*

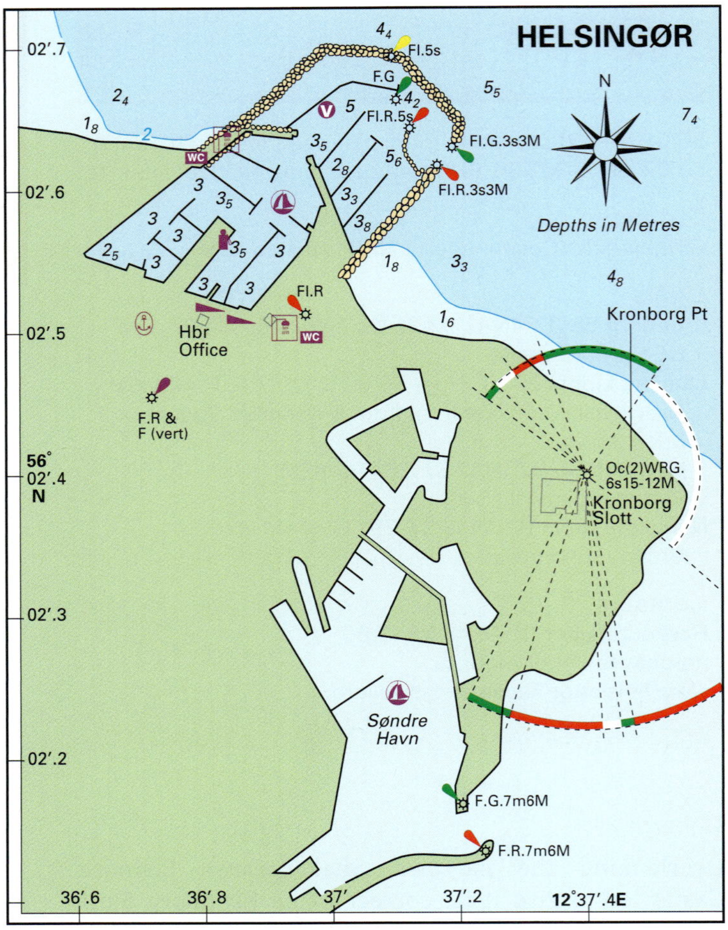


to the town centre and railway station with a splendid view of the castle. At the entrance it states that this is for yachts of over 15m but in practice smaller yachts are allowed.

### Facilities

All facilities are available including WiFi.

## GILLELEJE

56°08′N 12°19′E (starboard mole head)

### Distances

Grenå 50M, Anholt 50M, Lynaes 22M, Falkenberg 48M, Lynaes 22M, Helsingør 12M, Copenhagen 34M.

### Lights

**Nakkehoved** 56°07′.2N 12°20′.6E Fl(3)W.20s54m20M
White square tower

**W Molehead** 56°07′.8N 12°18′.7E Fl.G.3s7m4M
Green round tower

**E Molehead** 56°07′.8N 12°18′.7E Fl.R.3s7m4M
Red reflective post

### Contacts

**Harbourmaster** ✆+45 4016 6663
*mobile* +45 4021 1663
www.gillelejehavn.com/g-ster-geusts-gesten/besejling
gillelejehavn@gmail.com

### Søndre Havn

The marina office also administers berths in the main commercial harbour, Søndre Havn, southwest of the castle. Yacht berths are situated by the Kultur Værftet (a striking glass walled concert hall and theatre), just north of the ferry terminal. The approach to these is through the harbour entrance, then turn to starboard towards the Kultur Værftet.

There are three pontoons with electricity and water. Very large yachts can moor on the quay on the port-hand side. There is water and electricity but all other facilities are at the Nordhavn Marina some distance away. These harbour berths are, however, very close

### General

A busy fishing harbour, 12M to the northwest of Helsingør, which is gradually being taken over by yachts.

### Approach

The area to the north-northwest of the entrance, known as Gilleleje Flak, is littered with shoals which cause uncomfortable seas in onshore winds. It is marked by three cardinal buoys: north, east and south. The harbour entrance is approx. 500m SSE of the south cardinal mark. The harbour approach has one red and one green buoy. All these buoys are unlit but the mole heads are lit red and green (see above).

Kronborg Slot on approach to Helsingør with Nordhavn Marina entrance to its right, looking north *David Ridout*

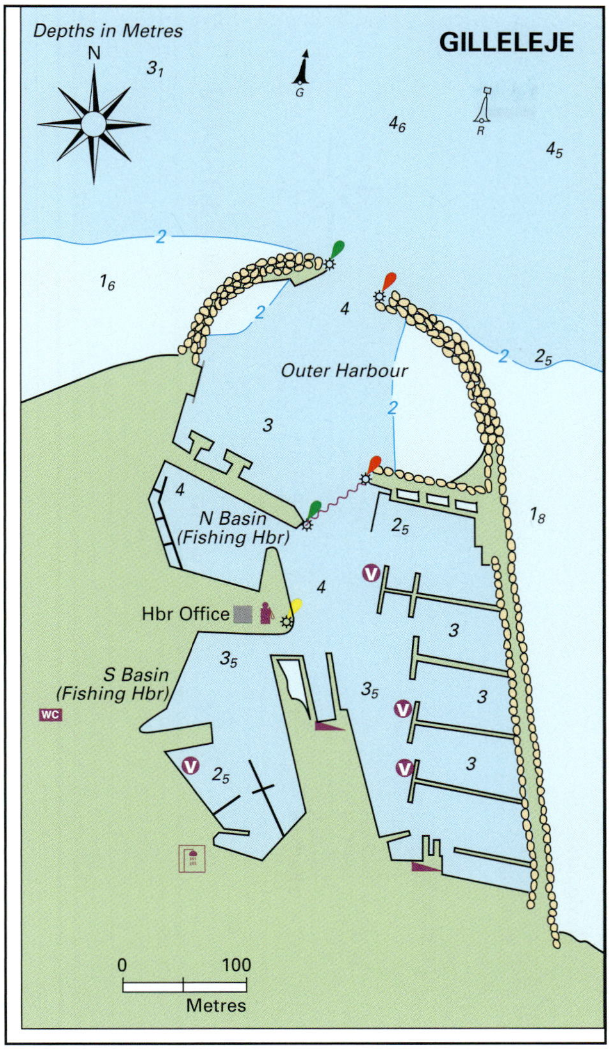


### Berthing

Berth in box berths at jetties running out from the east breakwater or alongside in the south fishing basin. Berth in any available space, but not in the North Basin which is reserved for fishing boats.

### Facilities

All facilities are available. WiFi. A variety of restaurants surround the harbour.

Fishing gear by the village green, Gilleleje *David Ridout*

Gilleleje looking northeast through entrance *David Ridout*

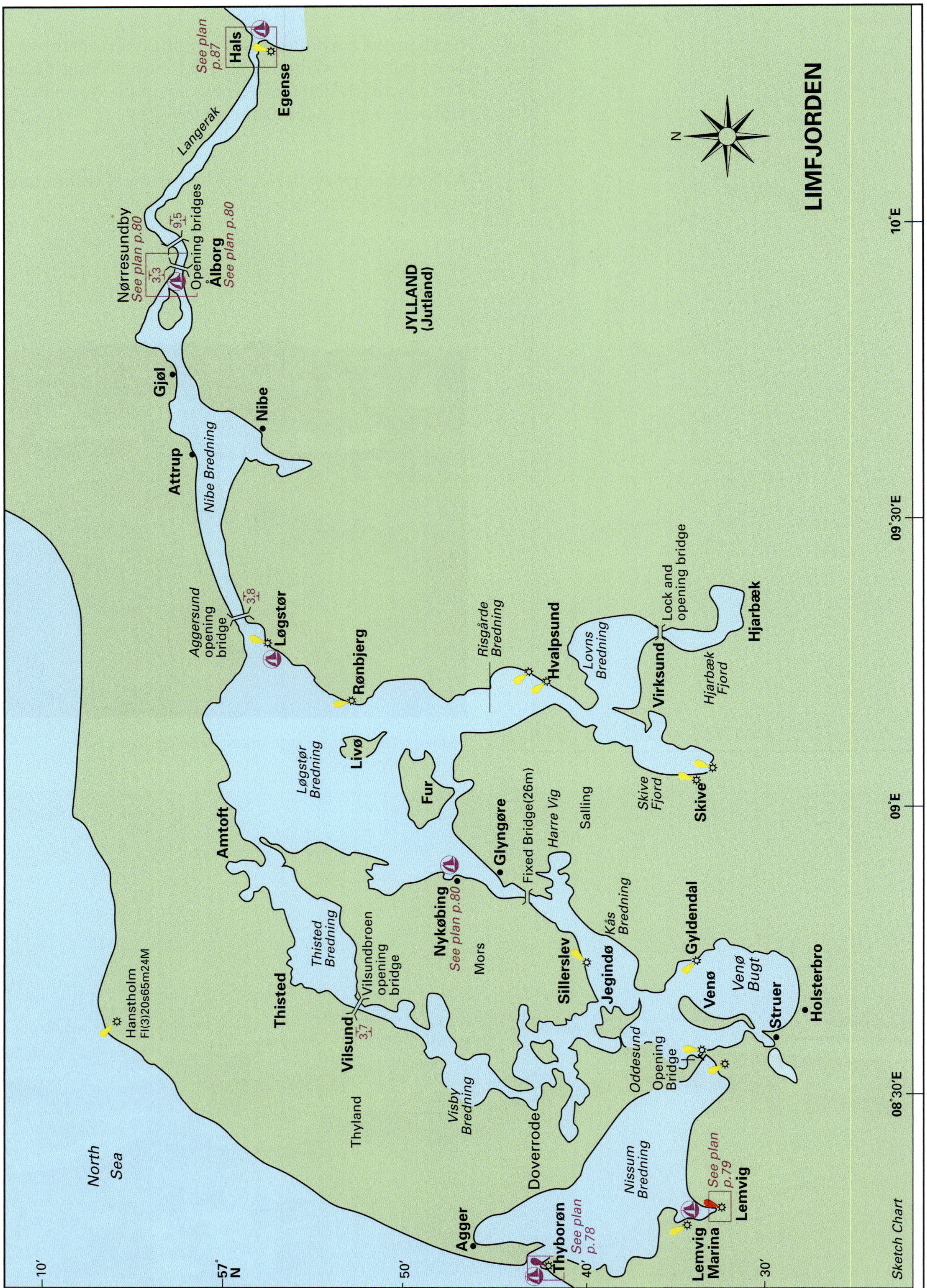
LIMFJORDEN
Sketch Chart
N
North Sea
JYLLAND (Jutland)
Hals
See plan p.87
Egense
Langerak
Nørresundby
See plan p.80
Opening bridges
Ålborg
See plan p.80
Gjøl
Nibe
Attrup
Nibe Bredning
Aggersund opening bridge
Løgstør
Rønbjerg
Løgstør Bredning
Livø
Fur
Risgårde Bredning
Hvalpsund
Lovns Bredning
Lock and opening bridge
Virksund
Hjarbæk
Hjarbæk Fjord
Skive Fjord
Skive
Salling
Harre Vig
Fixed Bridge(26m)
Glyngøre
Nykøbing
See plan p.80
Mors
Amtoft
Thisted
Thisted Bredning
Vilsundbroen opening bridge
Vilsund
Hanstholm
Fl(3)20s65m24M
Thyland
Visby Bredning
Doverrode
Sillerslev
Jegindø
Kås Bredning
Gyldendal
Venø
Venø Bugt
Struer
Holsterbro
Oddesund
Opening Bridge
Nissum Bredning
Lemvig
See plan p.79
Lemvig Marina
Agger
Thyborøn
See plan p.78
57° N
10'
50'
40'
30'
08°30'E
09°E
09°30'E
10°E

# 1F. APPROACH TO THE KATTEGAT THROUGH THE LIMFJORD

The Limfjord provides a very pleasant shortcut for yachts sailing to the Baltic from Scotland or further north. It saves the long sail round Skagen, where the seas can be unpleasant, and it provides sheltered sailing in beautiful surroundings in which to recover from the long passage across the North Sea. In fact one could spend a couple of weeks cruising in the area and still not see it all. Much of it is shallow but with a draught of less than 2m most of it is accessible. Minimum depth for the through route is 4m in the dredged channel west of Ålborg and maximum air draught 26m at the Sallingsund fixed bridge southeast of Nykøbing.

Unfortunately the approach to Thyborøn can be dangerous in onshore winds over Force 5, especially on the ebb when the current runs at up to 2kn (but this can increase up to 6kn in very strong winds). In which case diversion to Hanstholm, Hirtshals or round the Skagen may be necessary. If intending to enter the Limfjord via Thyborøn the two large scale Danish charts *108* and *109* or their German equivalents are essential.

Admiralty charts do not cover the Limfjord further west than Løgstør. It would be wise to source Danish charts before arrival. An alternative would be the German Chart *Set 6* published by Delius Klasing which covers the whole of the Danish North Sea coast, the whole Limfjord and some of the western Kattegat as well.

Lemvig. Yachts in the fishing basin *J. Parkinson*

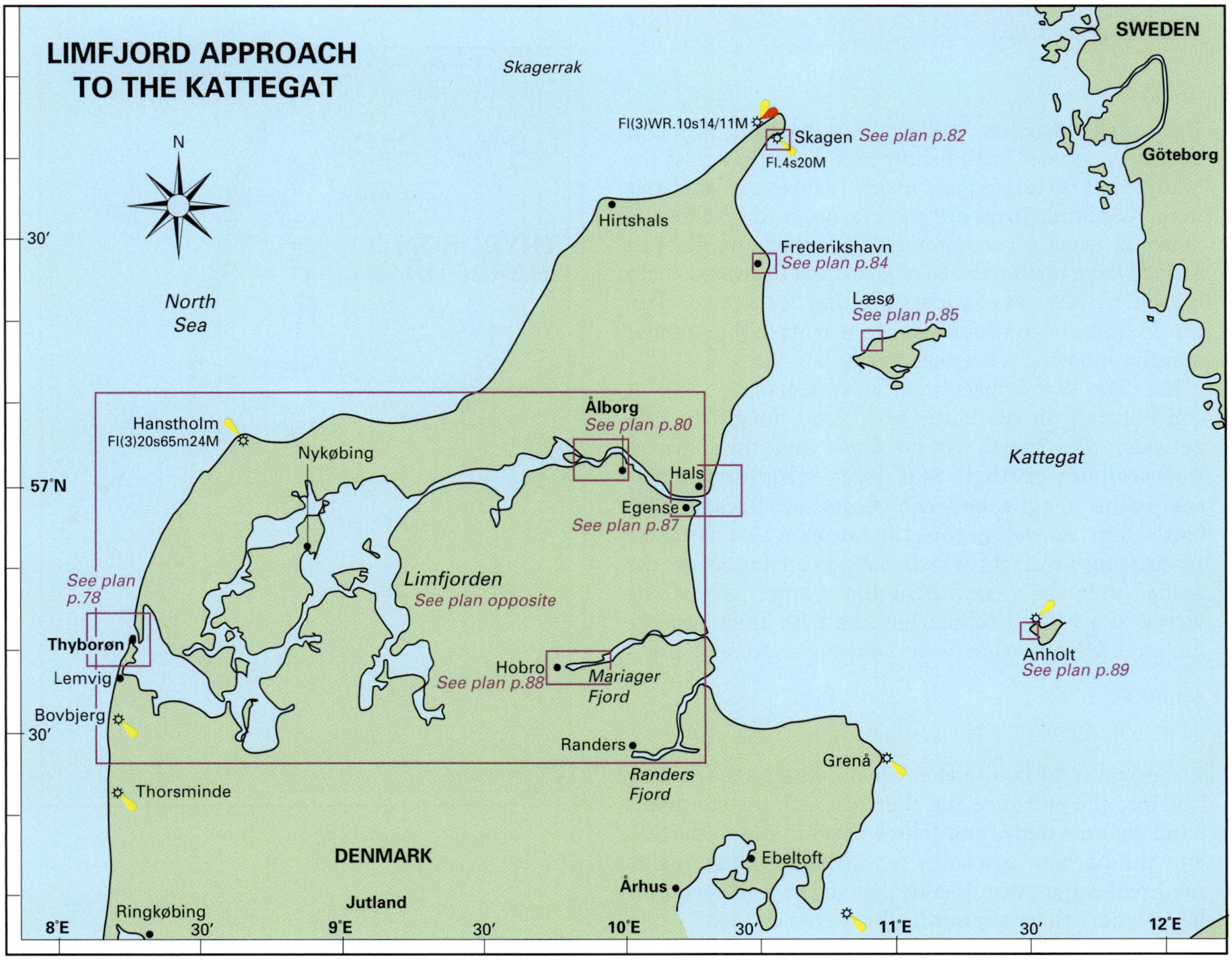

# THYBORØN

56°42'N 08°13'.52E (starboard or north mole head of harbour)

**Distances**
Edinburgh 400M, Den Helder 250M, Helgoland 170M, Ålborg 80M, Esbjerg 90M, Christiansand 85M

**Lights**
**Hanstholm** 57°06'.7N 08°36'E Fl(3)20s65m24M
**Lodbjerg** 56°49'.4N 08°15'.8E Fl(2)20s48m21M
**Løgstør Bredning** Fl(3)R10s
Leading Lights 082° *Front* 56°43'N 06°14'.1E Iso. WRG.4s8m10/8M *Rear* 0.5M behind front Iso.4s17m11M
**Landfall buoy** 56°42'.53N 08°08'.65E LFl.10s Red and white buoy
**Thyborøn** 56°42'.5N 8°12'.9E Fl(3)10s12M
**Bovbjerg** 56°31'.7N 8°07'.1E Fl(2)15s62m16M

**Tides**
HW Esjberg +0120 – +0230 ML 0.0

**Depths**
Least depth in approach from seaward about 6m and inside the bar 5–8m.

**Contacts**
**Harbourmaster** ✆+45 9690 0310
adm@thyboronport.dk
www.thyboronport.dk

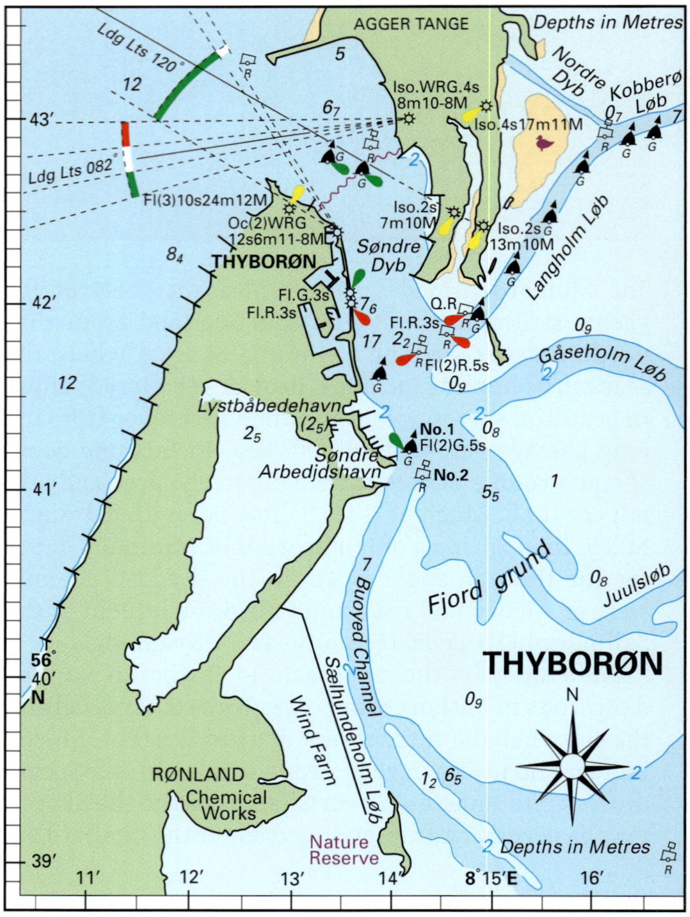


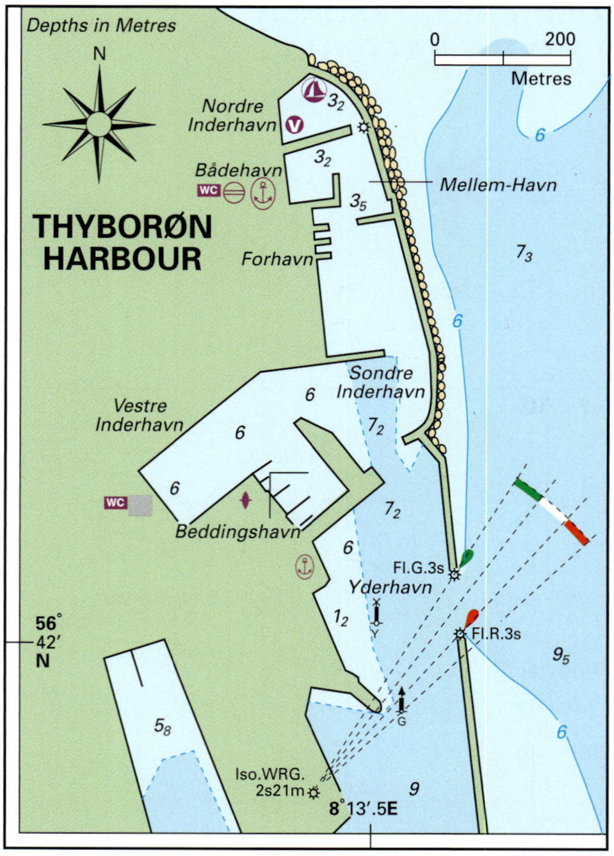


*General*

This small town has quite a large harbour which is mainly concerned with fishing and the ferry across the Limfjord. It is situated just inside the western entrance to the Limfjord. There are good facilities for yachts and it would make a good stopover whether one has just arrived from the North Sea or is waiting to depart. There is room for all sizes of yachts. Visiting boats can dock in Nordre Inderhavn which acts as a marina in the summer months. Mooring is between posts.

The Sea War Museum is well worth a visit. It concentrates on the battle of Jutland, fought in 1916 between the British Grand Fleet and the German Hochseeflotte or High Seas Fleet - the only major sea battle fought between fleets of Dreadnought battleships. As well as this, the museum also has some fascinating artefacts which have been found on the seabed over the years, including a large part of the wreck of a British submarine, the E50. Their website has an English version (www.seawarmuseum.dk/en).

*Approach*

56°42'53N 08°08'.65E (landfall buoy)

On arrival at the landfall buoy make 082° on the leading line into the entrance and there pick up the starboard hand channel buoys and follow them round to the SSE and the harbour entrance to starboard. Once inside the breakwater turn northwards to the northernmost basin where there are berths for yachts in 3.5m.

Thyborøn yacht harbour looking southeast *David Ridout*

The Oddesund lifting road and rail bridge across the Limfjord will open for yachts even at rush hour *E. Redfern*

The approach from the east involves picking up the narrow buoyed channel (some lit) which starts with a north cardinal mark at 56°37'.9N 08°17E and curves round northwards to join the main entrance channel past the harbour.

*Facilities*

All facilities are available including diesel which can be obtained from a barge in the main harbour.

## Lemvig

56°33'N 08°18'.33E (starboard mole head Lemvig Havn)

**Contacts**

Harbourmaster ✆+45 96 63 12 00

This is a small and attractive town in the creek on the south side of the westernmost lake of the Limfjord, the Nissum Bredning.

It is approached through a long buoyed channel which is dredged to 4.4m

The dredged channel leaves a marina to starboard but it is a long way from the town and it is better to continue further and berth in the main harbour either alongside one of the quays or in one of the many box berths which can accommodate quite large yachts. The harbour has been extended and has all facilities including diesel.

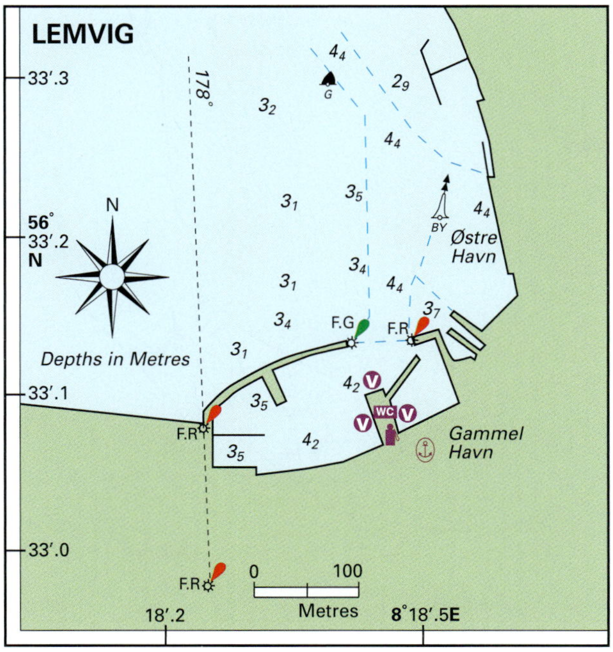


### Oddesund Bridge

56°34'.5N 08°32'.5E

**Contacts**

Bridge keeper ✆+45 97 87 50 55 or ✆+45 21 77 38 82
VHF Ch 16/12/13

This combined rail and road bridge opens on demand from 0600–1730 at a quarter to and quarter past the hour but remains closed for 15mins before a train is due. Contact the bridge keeper, hoist International Code Flag N in the rigging and wait.

Once through the bridge the more direct route to Ålborg and the Kattegat continues in a northeasterly direction but one can divert south into Venø Sund to visit Struer or take the northern route to Ålborg via a series of small lakes to Thisted Bredning and Thisted.

## Nykøbing

56°47'.53N 08°52'.13E (port mole at entrance to harbour)

**Contacts**

Harbourmaster ✆+45 2120 6260
www.msogm.dk/gaestesejler/regler-for-gaestesejlere
post@msogm.dk

Nykøbing is a useful stop on the direct route to Ålborg as it is 30M from Thyborøn and 35M from Ålborg. 2M southwest of the entrance channel is a fixed road bridge with a clearance of 26m.

Nykøbing is an old fisheries town with many museums. It is entered by a buoyed entrance channel dredged to 4.4m. It starts at the east cardinal mark just west of the point which forms the eastern side of the bay. Follow the buoyed channel on 345° with 2F.R lights in line bearing round on to 323.6° (2F.G Lights in line) through the harbour entrance. Then berth either at pontoons in the marina in 3m on the port hand (but observe the port hand buoy when entering and do not cut inside it) or continue into the Lystbådehavnen where there may be a box berth, or tie up along the quayside. All facilities are available and fuel may be possible in the Nordhavn where the fishing boats are moored but the pump is reported to be old.

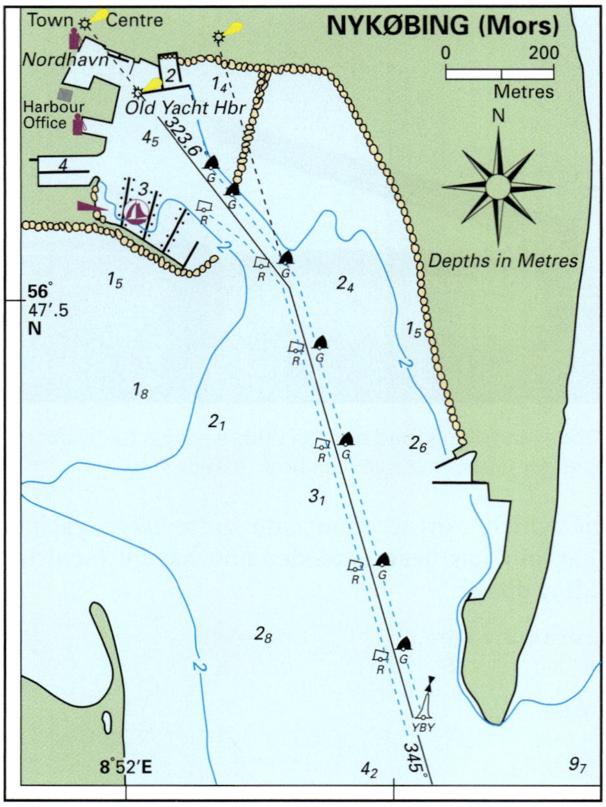


## Ålborg

57°03'N 09°55'E

**Contacts**

www.sejlklubbenlimfjorden.dk

Ålborg is the capital of the region, the centre of communications as well as being a university town. It now has major industries but its original wealth came from the herring fisheries. The old part of the town, the Østerågade, is attractive and interesting. It is well known for Ålborg Akvavit!

### *Approach*

The approach from the west by the Løgstør Bredning starts at the red port-hand mark some 26M west of Ålborg. Leading lights Iso.W.2s and 4s on 079.2° then lead up the channel to Løgstør where there is a marina with alongside berths in a canal which is entered just west of the main harbour.

The main channel to Ålborg then continues northeastward to the Aggersund Lifting Bridge, which opens on demand, in theory, but in practice seems to wait until there are a number of yachts waiting. At any bridge one can make one's wishes known by hoisting the N flag in the rigging and calling on VHF Ch 12/13.

The buoyed channel then continues for another 20M up to Ålborg. For the most part it is wide with depths over 4m but very narrow through the Drag Banke where it is dredged to 4m.

At Ålborg there is a choice of marinas but the most convenient ones for the shops and for a bus or train to the centre, are Ålborg Skudehavn (which has plenty of room both in box berths and alongside and now has a small wave barrier) and the Vestre Bådehavn (which is the last one on the south side before the railway bridge). It has restaurants and all facilities as well as an excellent chandlery but it is often crowded and a berth that is wide enough can sometimes be hard to find, especially as the channels between the box berths are very narrow.

There are two lifting bridges in Ålborg. The western one is a railway bridge which seems to stay in a closed

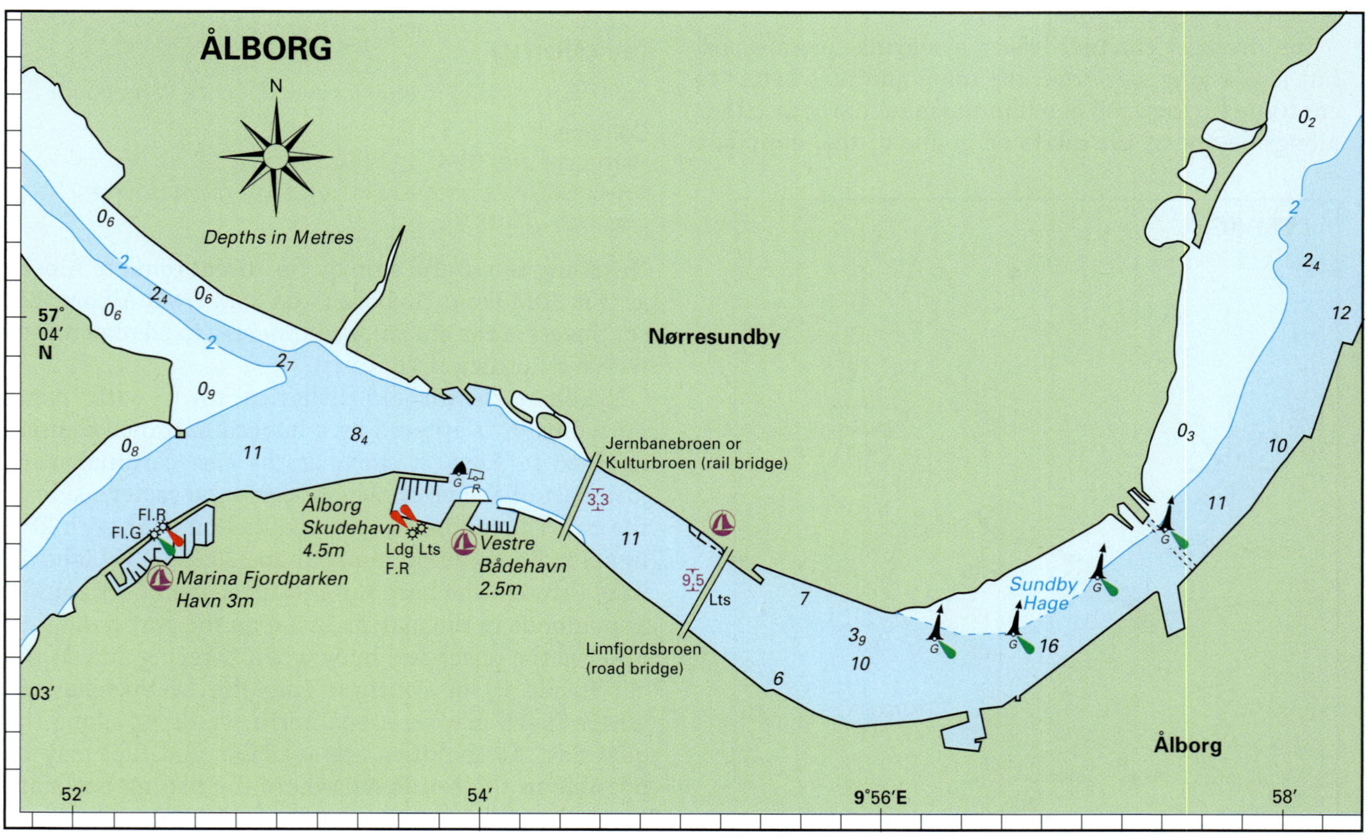

position most of the time. The bridge is operated by DSB and it is advisable to call up the bridge (VHF Ch 12/13/16) to find out opening times. The eastern bridge is the Limfjord Road Bridge which generally opens on the hour every hour, but this can change at busy times. Again contact on one of the aforementioned channels. Details of opening times and communication options for the bridges can be found on the Danish Harbour Pilot (www.danskehavnelods.dk). Simply click on each bridge on the map, though the results are in Danish. The route east from Ålborg to the sea at Hals and Egense is well buoyed and straightforward.

Ålborg Bridge with rail bridge beyond *J. Parkinson*

A view of the Limfjord in winter at its narrowest point with two bridges joining Ålborg and Nørresundby *Tomasz Sienicki/ Wikimedia Commons (https://commons.wikimedia.org/wiki/File:Limfjorden_zs_1_ubt.JPG)*

Ålborg, end of Tall Ships Race, taken from the road bridge *David Ridout*

Ålborg from the west with Ålborg Skudehaven – now with additional pontoon and wave barrier – and Vestre Bådehavn on south shore *Patrick Roach*

# 1G. DANISH HARBOURS AND ANCHORAGES OF THE KATTEGAT

## SKAGEN

57°42'.72N 10°36'E (outer pier south)

### Distances

Kristiansand 100M, Göteborg 47M, Edinburgh 500M, Fredrikshavn 20M, Copenhagen 145M

### Lights

**Skagen W** 57°44'.9N 10°35'.7E Fl(3)WR.10s31m14/11M White round tower
**Skagen Shoal buoy** 57°46'N 10°44'E NCM Q.Fl
**Skagen** 57°44'.1N 10°37'.8E Fl.4s44m20M Grey round tower
**Skagen outer mole N** 57°42'.92N 10°35'.92E Fl.G.3s5M
**Skagen outer mole S** 57°42'.72N 10°35'.99E Fl.R.3s5M
**Skagen inner pier N** 57°42'.87N 10°35'.65E Fl.G.5s3M
**Skagen inner pier S** 57°42'.84N 10°35'.55E Fl.R.5s3M
**Hirsholm** 57°29'.1N 10°37'.5E Fl(3).30s30m22M Round granite tower

### Contacts

**Port Authority** ✆+45 98 44 13 46, VHF Ch 12
**Lystbådehavn (Marina) Harbourmaster** ✆+45 98 44 33 41
lystbaadehavn@frederikshavn.dk
skagenlystbaadehavn.frederikshavn.dk/gaestesejlere
www.skagensejlklub.dk/gaestesejler

Skagen Lighthouse. Often known as Skagen Grey Lighthouse, it was brought into operation in 1858. When built it was near the centre of the Skagen Odde peninsula, but now due to coastal erosion it is on the Kattegat coast north of Skagen *Eyewave | Dreamstime.com*

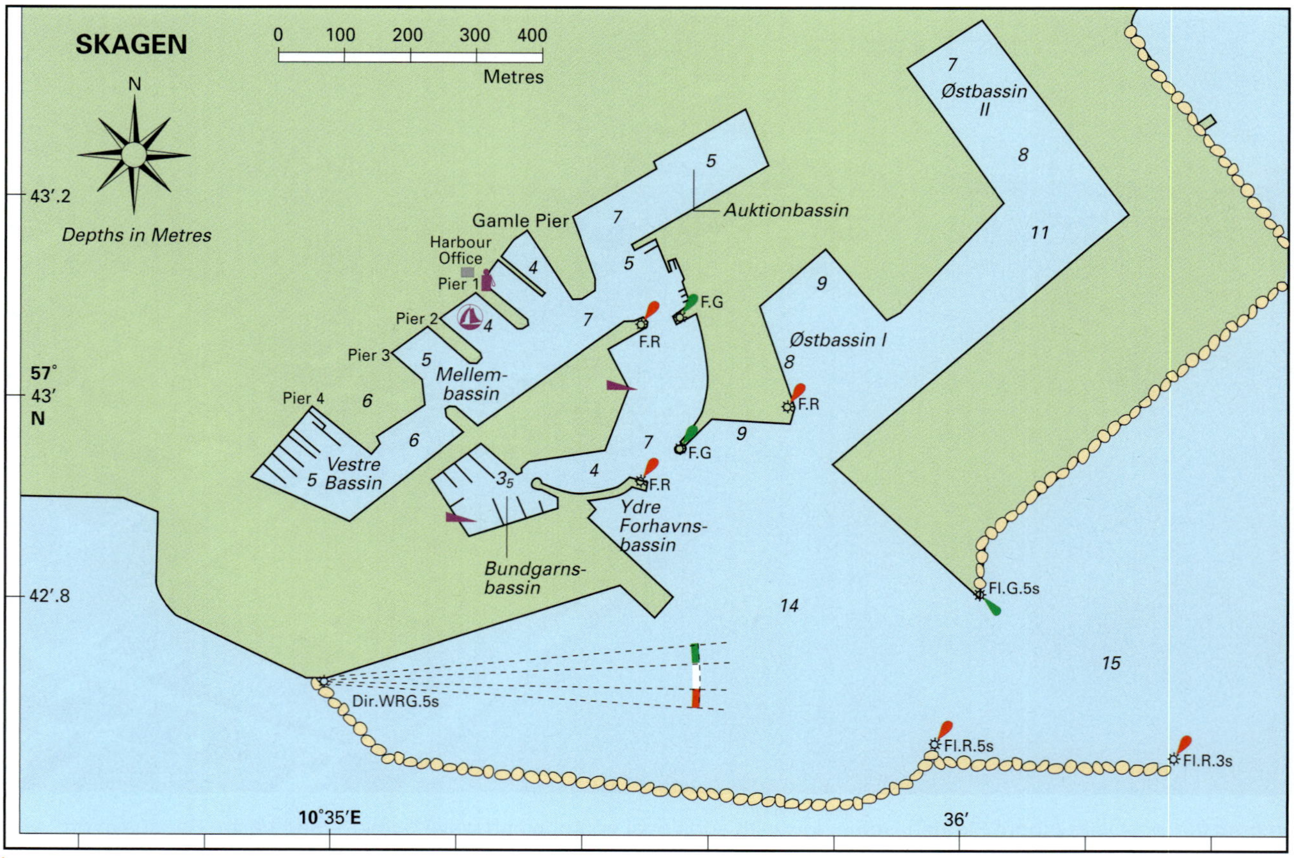

*General*

Skagen is a busy fishing harbour and a thriving holiday resort. The area is a favourite with Danish artists. The harbour provides good protection.

*Approach*

The flat Skagen headland with its two lighthouses is extended for 2M in an east-northeast direction by a shallow reef marked by a north cardinal mark. In strong west and northwesterly winds the seas can be heavy and in addition there is usually much commercial traffic rounding the headland. Once rounded, course can be set for Skagen harbour entrance giving the shallows off the point a reasonably wide berth.

New outer moles have been constructed (see Skagen lights opposite for details). From a position of approximately 57°42'·80N 10°36'·1E go on a heading of 280° to enter between these, aiming for the two inner pier heads marking the former outer harbour. Alter course to 335° for a short distance for next piers (fixed red and green) then head due north through the next harbour basin before turning to port for the marina.

*Berthing*

Berth in the marina on pontoons between Gamle Pier and Pier 1 or between Piers 1 and 2 in 4m depths. Should these two areas be completely full, the basin immediately northeast of Gamle Pier is sometimes opened up for mooring.

*Facilities*

All facilities including fuel.

## FREDERIKSHAVN

57°25'.61N 10°32'E (north marina mole)

**Distances**

Skagen 20M, Læsø Vesterø Havn 15M, Limfjord entrance 30M

**Lights**

**Hirsholm** 57°29'.1N 10°37'.5E Fl(3).30s30m22M Round granite tower Also FRW.30m
**Commercial Port NE Breakwater** Hd 57°26'N 10°33'.2E Fl.G.3s7m7M Metal post, green band
**Commercial Port Approach Light** 57°26'.2N 10°32'.5E Oc.WRG.10s14m9M
**Marina E Mole Hd** 57°25'.6N 10°32'E Fl.R.3s4m3M Mast
**Læsø Rende** 57°13'.1N 10°40'.3E Fl(2)10s27m6M White round concrete tower, black base

**Contacts**

**Marina harbourmaster** ✆+45 40 47 75 98
www.frederikshavnsejlklub.dk
frhmarina@mail.dk

*General*

Fredrikshavn Port is a very busy ferry and commercial harbour with ferries to Oslo, Larvik, Göteborg and Læsø. The Søsporthavn or marina is situated approximately 0.75M to the southwest of the entrance to the main port.

*Approach*

Approaching from the north the rocks and islands of Hirsholm, guarded by the Hirsholm Light, must be left to starboard and the shallows to the east of Fredrikshavn, which are marked by north and south

Aerial view of the Skagen peninsula from the south *Parrot of Doom/Wikimedia Commons (https://commons.wikimedia.org/wiki/File:Grenen_from_the_air.jpg)*

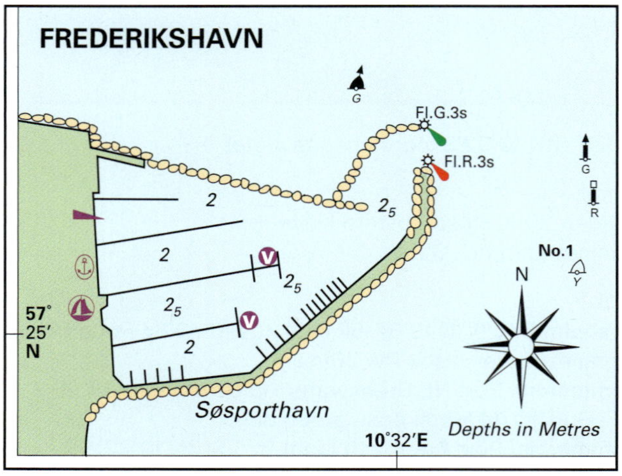

Frederickshavn, new berths to port soon after entering the marina *David Ridout*

cardinal marks and a green starboard hand buoy, must be skirted in the same way. Head for the marina which has a red and green buoy just before entering between the moles. Enter between the north and south mole (which is quite narrow) into the marina. From the south the approach is straightforward although fish traps may be a hazard close to the shore.

There are depths of 2.5m in buoyed entrance channel but subject to silting.

### *Berthing*

Moor in box berths with bows-to staging. There are several berths for large yachts on the south mole, some of them alongside.

### *Facilities*

All facilities are available but the marina is some way from the city centre. Local food shops nearby.

## SÆBY

57°19'.98N 10°32'.17E

### Lights

**Nordre Rønner** 57°21'.6N 10°55'.4E Fl.15s16m14M
Round granite tower

**Leading lights** 136.1° *Front* Outer E mole Head 57°17'.9N 10°55'.4E Iso.R.2s7m3M
Red triangle on red framework tower.
*Rear* 364m from front. Iso.R.4s14m3M
Red inverted triangle on framework tower

### Contacts

**Harbourmaster** ✆+45 98 46 10 59
saebyhavn.frederikshavn.dk
saebyhavn@frederikshavn.dk

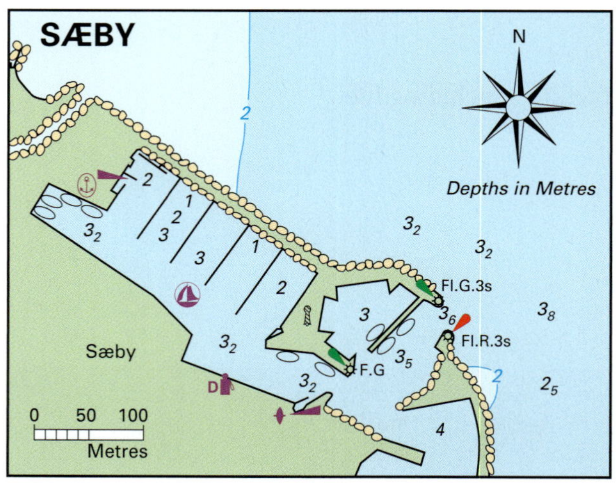

Entrance to Sæby harbour looking west *David Ridout*

## General

5.6M south of Frederikshavn, Sæby is a very charming harbour, which has recently been enlarged to accommodate many more yachts.

## Approach

This is straightforward but, as the waters are shallow, care should be taken in strong onshore winds. Once inside the harbour moles there are various mooring options. A large mosaic sculpture (Lady of the Sea) is prominent near the entrance.

## Berthing

Berthing is available alongside, immediately to starboard after entering between the moles. Alternatively, continue into the main section of the harbour with fuel to port and some alongside mooring to starboard. The first jetty on the starboard side has box berths. Look out as well for red/green availability markers. At the head of the harbour there are moorings close to the harbour office – pay by machine.

## Facilities

The harbour has all facilities, free WiFi, several restaurants and also a supermarket nearby.

There is a beautiful church with very old chalk paintings, restored between 2006–9. Beaches and a pretty park north of the harbour.

# VESTERØ – LÆSØ

57°17'.89N 10°55'.29E (starboard mole head)

**Distances**

Frederikshavn 15M, Skagen 27M, Limfjord Entrance 30M, Göteborg 45M

**Lights**

**Nordre Rønner** 57°21'.6N 10°55'.4E Fl.15s16m14M Round granite tower

**Leading lights** 136.1° *Front* Outer E mole Head 57°17'.9N 10°55'.4E Iso.R.2s7m3M Red triangle on red framework tower. *Rear* 364m from front. Iso.R.4s14m3M Red inverted triangle on framework tower

**Læsø buoy NW** Rev 57°15'.7N 10°45'.4E Fl(2)R.5s Red can buoy

**Læsø Rende** 57°13'.1N 10°40'.3E Fl(2).10s27m6M White round concrete tower, black base

**Contacts**

**Harbourmaster** ✆+45 98 49 92 22
www.havne.laesoe.dk
ar@laesoe.dk

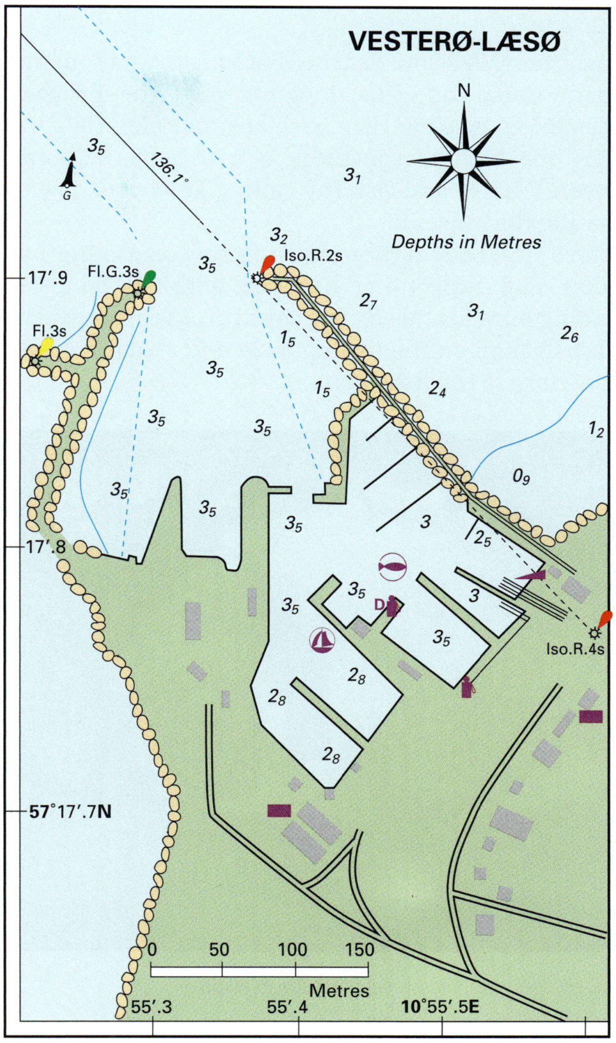


## General

Læsø is a quiet and attractive island with many sandy beaches. The island is unique in that it has several houses on which a thick layer of seaweed has been used for roofing. The main museum is one such and is well worth a visit. The island is popular with Swedish visitors as well as more local Danish boats.

## Approach

The leading line on 136.1° runs in from the northwest of the island with the Nordre Rønner reef with its light tower 2M to port and the northwest Læsø Reef (marked at its northwest corner by a red lightbuoy) 3.5M to starboard. The Nordre Rønner reef is extensively buoyed on the porthand but it is not until one is within 1M of the entrance that there are green starboard hand buoys. The entrance carries a depth of 3.4m.

## Berthing

The island has two harbours: Vesterø Havn on the northwest corner, 13M east-southeast from Sæby, and Østerby on the eastern end of the north coast.

Østerby harbour is particularly popular with the Swedes due to its proximity to Göteborg. In settled weather it is possible to anchor off in an area to the west of the harbour entrance.

The approaches to both these harbours are shallow and, given the long fetch from either Jutland or Sweden, strong swells can build up with onshore winds which will make the approaches to the harbours difficult if not dangerous.

*Facilities*

All facilities. Webcam. Beaches both north and south of harbour. Cafés and grills along the quay side. Brugsen supermarket nearby. Hire of bikes and electric cars. During the high season there is a free bus running between Vesterø and Østerby calling at various places including the museum.

Østerby Harbour at the eastern end of Læsø is another popular and welcoming harbour with all facilities including bicycle and electric car hire plus an excellent fresh fish shop on the fishing quay and a well-stocked grocer close to the fish shop.

Læsø, house with seaweed roof David Ridout

Læsø, Vesterø harbour looking northwest with entrance in the background David Ridout

## 1H. LIMFJORD APPROACH AND ENTRANCE

The main shipping channel for entry to the Limfjord begins 23M out in the Ålborg Bugt near the Svitringen South Light Tower but smaller craft can enter the channel much closer in, between the Hals Barre Light Tower and the twin Red and Green Light Towers marking the entrance (56°58'N 10°22'E).

## EGENSE AND HALS

56°58'N 10°21'.87E (Hals Barre north)

**Distances**

Fredrikshavn 30M, Vesterø 30M, Ålborg 15M, Mariager Fjord 20M, Anholt 42M, Grenå 45M

**Lights**

**Hals Barre** 56°57'.3N 10°25'.5E Iso.WRG.2s18m8M

**Svitringen Rende** S 56°51'N 10°36'.3E Fl.W.3s13m8M Red tower, white stripes marked SV S

**Korsholm Leading Lights Egense** N *Front* 294.3° 56°58'.4N 10°20'.1E Iso.G.2s5m9M Red 8-sided concrete tower Secondary light FlR3s5m3M

*Front* Iso.R.2s5m9M

*Rear* 1.2M from front Iso.W.2s20m15M Red inverted triangle on red framework tower.

All synchronised

**Contacts**

**Hals harbourmaster** ✆+45 51 52 66 24

info@halsbaadelaug.dk

www.halsbaadelaug.dk/gaester

Egense YH and Sail Club ✆+45 98 31 00 57

*Approach*

The channel continues with port and starboard hand buoys, some lit and some unlit, up to Ålborg. There is a succession of leading lights all the way up to Ålborg, 15M inland.

Hals, looking north *David Ridout*

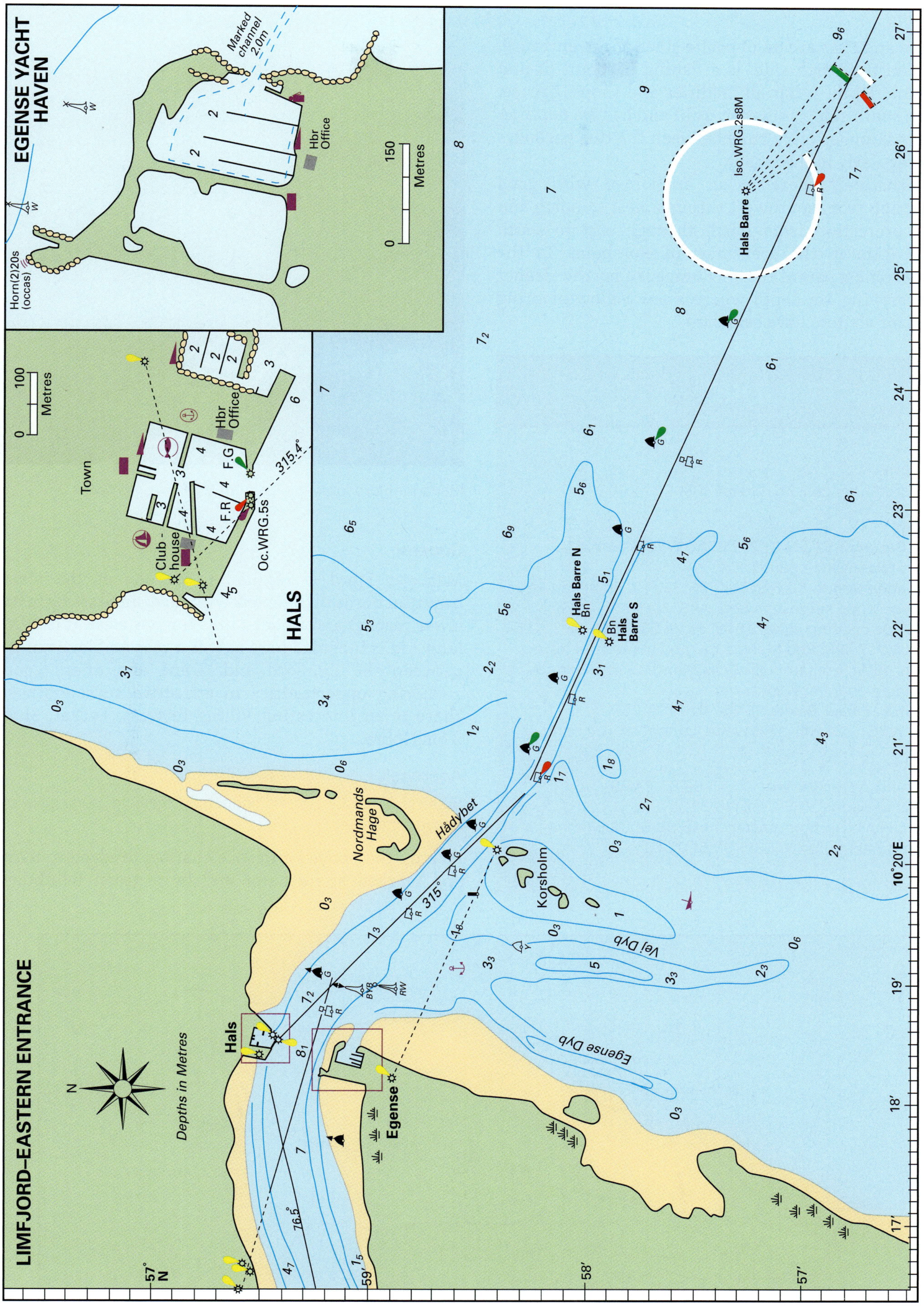
LIMFJORD–EASTERN ENTRANCE
Depths in Metres
N
Hals
Egense
Nordmands Hage
Hådybet
Korsholm
Vej Dyb
Egense Dyb
Hals Barre N Bn
Bn Hals Barre S
Hals Barre
Iso.WRG.2s8M
315°
76.5°
10°20'E
57° N
58'
59'
57'
17'
18'
19'
21'
22'
23'
24'
25'
26'
27'
HALS
Town
Club-house
Hbr Office
F.R
F.G
Oc.WRG.5s
315.4°
0 100 Metres
EGENSE YACHT HAVEN
Marked channel 2.0m
Hbr Office
Horn(2)20s (occas)
0 150 Metres

### *Berthing*

Egense and Hals are on opposite sides of the entrance. Hals, on the north side, is a fishing harbour, lit and with 3m depth. It has all facilities and shops. Egense, on the south side, is smaller, unlit and has 2m depth. A small passenger ferry runs between the two harbours very regularly in the season.

Alternatively there is an anchorage with good protection from southwest through west to north and some protection from north through east to south in 2.3–3.1m in the area west of Korsholm. In the southernmost part of the anchorage is a narrow deeper part carrying 4m depth where a few yellow mooring buoys for visitors have been laid.

## MARIAGER FJORD

### Distances

Limfjord Entrance 22M, Grenå 30M

### Lights

**Hals Barre** 56°57'.3N 10°25'.5E Iso.WRG.2s18m8M Red tower, white bands

**Svitringen Rende S** 56°51'N 10°36'.3E Fl.W.3s13m8M Red tower, white stripes marked SV S

**Als Odde Leading lights** 261.9° *Front* 56°42'.7N 10°20'.8E Iso.W.2s7m9M Red triangle on grey framework tower. *Rear* 1511m from front Iso.W.4s24m10M Red inverted triangle on framework tower

**Udbyhøj, Elkaer Bakke** 56°35'.4N 10°19'.2E Oc.WRG.5s33m15–12M White lighthouse, red band.

### Contacts

Hadsund Lystbådehaven ☎+45 98 57 24 39
Hadsund Bridge VHF Ch 12/16
**Hobro Havn Harbourmaster** ☎+45 98 51 02 67
Hobro Lystbådehavn ☎+45 98 51 07 70

Mariager Fjord looking east from Hobro *Patrick Roach*

### *General*

Mariager Fjord is reputed to be one of the most beautiful fjords in Denmark with reed-lined vistas in its lower reaches and wooded hills further west. It is 20M long and is included here as it is a reasonable distance between the Limfjord and Grenå and offers good anchoring opportunities in attractive surroundings. There is an interesting Viking fortress, Fyrkat, 3km from Hobro.

### *Approach*

56°43'N 10°25'.6E (green light buoy marking beginning of buoyed channel)

Pick up the buoyed entrance channel dredged to 5.7m and marked at its outer end by a green lightbuoy

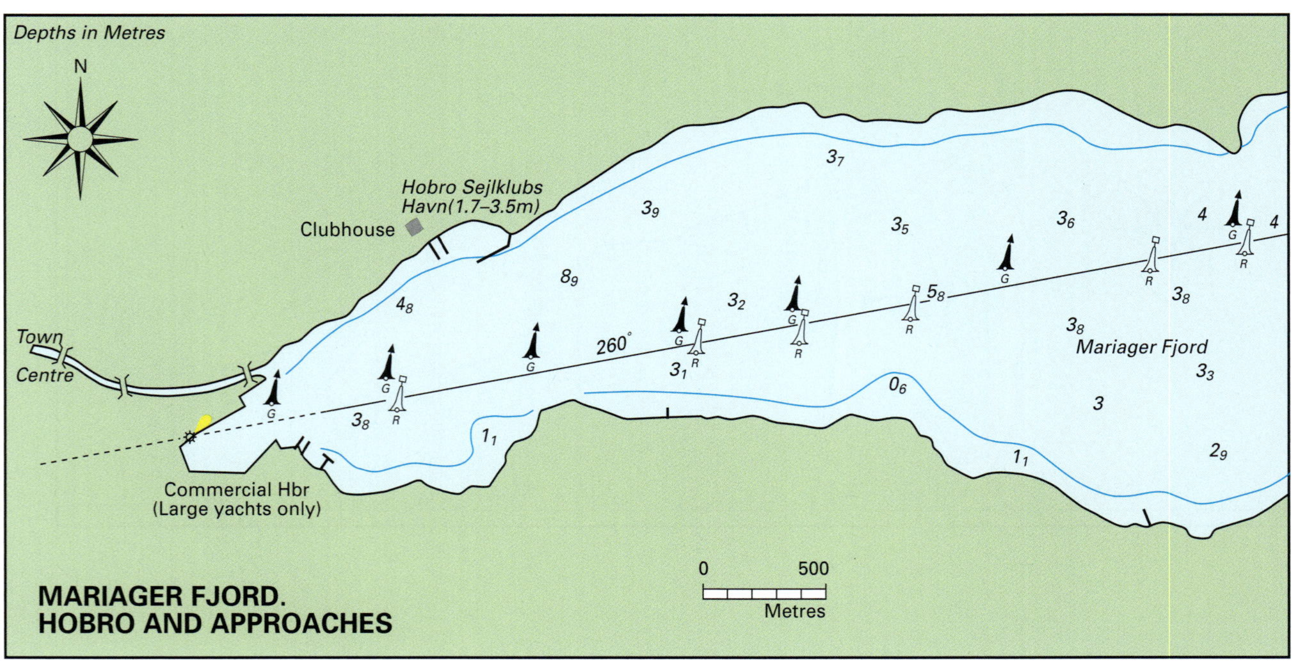


MARIAGER FJORD.
HOBRO AND APPROACHES

Fl(2)G.5s and make the approach on 262°. There can be a 2kn current in the entrance when entry and departure in strong easterlies can be very rough.

There is a lifting bridge at Hadsund, halfway down the fjord, which opens from sunrise to sunset every half an hour during the week, but at weekends there are occasional periods of an hour when the bridge does not open, and it is always advisable to telephone on approach (☎+45 98 57 12 14). Boats should wait at least 100m off the bridge and wait for the appropriate lights.

*Berthing*

Berth in Hadsund Harbour, Mariager Marina (midway along the south shore – www.mariager-sejlklub.dk), Hobro Havn or at one of the smaller marinas. Hobro Sailing Club (www.hobrosejlklub.dk) is adjacent to the marina at Hobro Havn and also has some berths.

## ANHOLT

56°42'.85N 11°30'.48E (starboard mole head)

**Distances**
Limfjord entrance 42M, Grenå 28M, Falkenberg 35M, Helsingør 55M

**Charts**
UKHO 2107, 2108
Danish 102, 124

**Lights**
**Anholt Near E end** 56°44'.2N 11°39'E Fl.15s40m14M White round tower with upper part red
**Anholt Harbour Outer N mole** head 56°42'.9N 11°30'.5E Fl.R.3s8m4M Post

**Contacts**
Harbourmaster ☎+45 86 31 90 08
*Mobile* +45 20 30 07 08
anholt@anholthavn.dk
www.anholthavn.dk

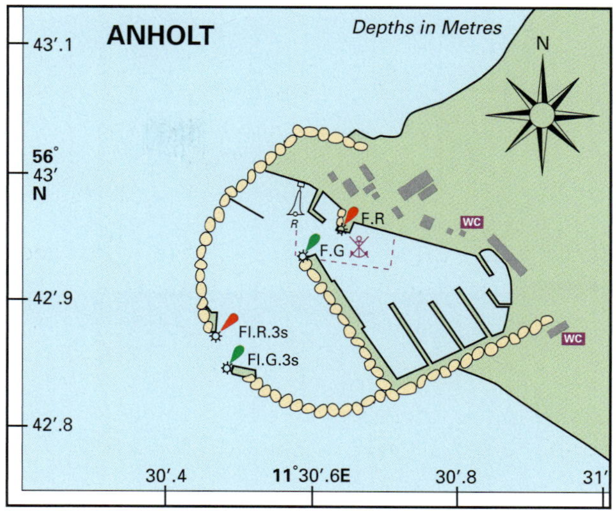


*General*

Anholt is a lovely little island 38M due east of Mariager Fjord. With good beaches, walking and cycling.

*Approach*

Easy approach from the west but the water is shallow for a long way out and is rough in onshore winds over Force 5. Beware shallow patches extending 3M northwest of the harbour and the 5M long Osterev Spit marked by an east cardinal mark extending from the eastern end of the island. The harbour entrance carries a depth of 3.5m.

*Berthing*

Berth bows-to pontoons with stern buoys. Notices warn that berthing alongside will be charged double. This is not surprising as the harbour is very crowded in season. Anchoring is possible in the outer harbour but make sure the channel is clear for the ferry from Grenå.

View over Anholt harbour, pre-season, looking west *David Ridout*

Deserted eastern beach on Anholt *David Ridout*

Mariager Fjord marina, half way between Hadsund and Hobro, looking northwest *David Ridout*

*Facilities*

All basic facilities and fuel. Anholt is famous for its nightlife and music-making so don't forget to take your earplugs!

## GRENÅ

56°24'.17N 10°55'.56E (port mole of marina)

Distances

Limfjord Entrance 42M, Mariager Fjord 30M, Anholt 28M, Ebeltoft 28M, Århus 38M

Lights

**Fornæs** 56°26'.6N 10°57'.4E Fl.20s32m21M Round stone tower

**Grenå Harbour N** approach 56°25'.07N 10°56'.12E Fl.G.3s10m5M Green mast 5m

**Grenå Harbour S** approach 56°24'.7N 10°55'.2E Fl.R.3s5m4M White pyramid, red top

**Lystbådehavn N** Breakwater Hd 56°24'.2N 10°55'.5E Fl.G.3s5m4M White pyramid green top. S Breakwater Hd Fl.R.3s5m4M White pyramid, red top

**Hesselø** 56°11'.8N 11°42'.6E Fl.15s40m13M White round tower

**Hjelm Summit** 56°08'N 10°48'.3E Iso.WRG.8s61m14–11M White round tower

**Sjælland Rev N** 56°06'N 11°12'.1E Iso.WRG.2s25m16–13M White colomn, red band, black pedestal

Contacts

Marina ✆+45 86 32 72 55
havn@grenaamarina.dk
www.grenaamarina.dk/en
www.youtube.com/watch?v=45uBTtAzUoo

*General*

Grenå marina is 1M south of the entrance to the commercial port from which ferries go to Varberg in Sweden and Anholt.

*Approach*

If approaching from the north leave the Kalkgrund north cardinal mark and south cardinal marks to starboard before turning west towards the marina entrance. From the south leave the Naveren East cardinal mark to port. There is 3.5m in the entrance and 2.5m just outside.

*Berthing*

Yachts over 13m berth alongside on the inside of the east mole in 3.2m and smaller yachts in box berths at the other jetties. These size restrictions are strictly enforced. The berths get smaller (and the water shallower) the further one proceeds into the harbour.

*Facilities*

All facilities are available including restaurants, WiFi and fuel. The marina is some way from the town centre but there are basic shops quite close. Also close to the marina is the Kattegat Centre Oceanarium which specialises in sharks. Grenå has a ferry to Varberg.

# 11. BORNHOLM AND CHRISTIANSØ

The islands of Bornholm and neighbouring Christiansø are both Danish, although geographically much closer to Sweden. Bornholm is sometimes referred to as 'the pearl of the Baltic', with white sandy beaches to the south, rolling hills and a claim to have the highest number of sunshine hours in the Baltic.

It occupies a strategic position at the entrance to the Baltic and has had an eventful history. Once a Viking stronghold, independent until the 10th century, it was then controlled by Sweden and then, in the 16th century, by Lübeck (a German Hanseatic League city). Awarded to Sweden by the Treaty of Roskilde in 1658, it was returned to Denmark in 1660. There are many historic buildings, including the famous 12th century round churches (fortress-churches) and the ruins of the imposing 13th century castle of Hammershus.

There are good connections from Rønne to Sweden by fast ferry to Ystad, with onward bus or rail connections from there to Copenhagen via the Øresund bridge. Currently there are also ferry services from Rønne to Sassnitz in Germany and Køge in Denmark, and from Kołobrzeg to Nexø. In addition, a ferry runs from Gudhjem to Christiansø.

All the harbours have a fairly straightforward approach, although there is usually an elaborate system of breakwaters once inside, to give protection to the inner basins. Access to some of the harbours on

the east coast and to Christiansø will be dependent on the weather, and significant currents can be generated round the island by strong winds. Some harbours have gates which close off the inner basin in bad weather.

It is a popular cycling destination, and bicycles can be hired at most of the harbours. There are bus services across the island, and cars can be hired in Rønne.

### *Traffic Separation Scheme*

If coming from Ystad or Simrishamn be aware that you will be crossing the main shipping lanes and associated TSS running through the Baltic. These pass about 5M northwest of Bornholm.

### *Firing practice areas*

Firing practice takes place in Danish waters, notably from the southwest coast of Bornholm at Raghammer Odde and off the south coast of Sweden (for more information see http://frv.dk/Sejladsinformation/Efterretninger).

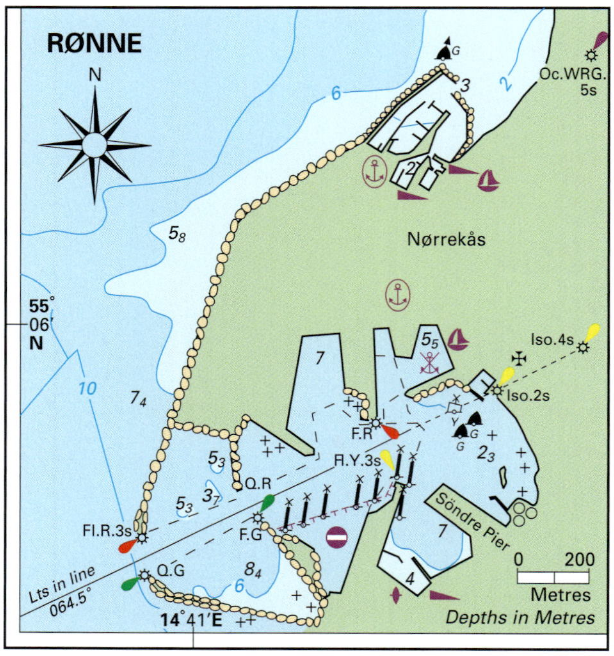


## RØNNE

55°06'N 14°41'E

### Distances

Gedser 100M, Copenhagen 90M, Sassnitz (Germany) 50M, Gislövs Läge (Sweden) 55M, Simrishavn (Sweden) 30M, Karlskrona (Sweden) 75M

### Lights

**Fairway buoy** 55°05'.1N 14°38'.6E LFl.10s
Red and white pillar buoy Whistle

**Leading lights** 064.5° *Front* 55°05'.9N 14°41'.8E
Iso.2s16m9M Framework tower 14m.
*Rear* 229m from front Iso.4s24m9M
Red mast 12m

**South shelter mole** 55°05'.6N 14°40'.9E Fl.G.3s11m7M
Horn20s (on request) Green tower 5m Floodlit

**East molehead** 55°05'.7N 14°40'.9E Fl.R.3s11m7M
Red framework tower 5m Floodlit

**Nørrekås** 55°06'.4N 14°42'E Oc.WRG.5s5m6–4M White hut, two red bands 3m

### Contacts

**Rønne Harbourmaster** ✆+45 56 95 06 78, VHF Ch 12/13/16 (0800–1600 LT)
roennehavn@roennehavn.dk
www.roennehavn.dk

**Nørrekås Harbourmaster** ✆+45 56 92 23 20 (0900–1000 and 1600–1700 LT)
yachtroenne@mail.dk
www.havneguide.dk/havn/roenne-lystbaadehavn-noerrekaas

### *General*

Yachts are expected to use the Nørrekås yacht harbour (to the north of the main harbour) and should only use the main harbour if the yacht harbour is full or weather conditions dictate.

### *Approach*

55°06'.4N 14°4'.7E (position of breakwater end)

Nørrekås should be approached on a bearing of approximately 100° in the white sector of the Nørrekås light. Leave the outer breakwater head with its green buoy to starboard. Beware the Hvidodde Reef 1M to the

Rønne *C.N. Hill*

St Nicolas's Church in Rønne *Andy Beharrell*

north marked by an East cardinal mark and a South cardinal mark. There is also an unmarked outlier on the south side of this reef with 3.7m over it, the Kasgaard Rev.

The approach to the main harbour is on 064.5° on the leading line.

### *Berthing*

Visitor berths are available on the first and second jetties as you enter the Nørrekås marina. These are finger berths with electricity and water. Depths are 3m at the outer berths and 2m or less further in. The berths in the two small basins to the south of the main marina may be more comfortable in onshore winds and carry 2m depth but the approach to them needs care.

If it is necessary to enter the main harbour there is the possibility of alongside berthing for yachts on the southern quay of the northern basin or the western wall of the southern basin.

### *Facilities*

All facilities are available at Nørrekås, including diesel.

As the main town on Bornholm, Rønne has all amenities including a tourist office, supermarket, bicycle hire, bus tours etc. WiFi. Ferries to Ystad, Køge and Świnoujście and an airport 5km away. However unless these features are required it is well worth considering one of the other smaller yacht harbours around the island, some of which are listed below.

## Other yacht harbours around Bornholm

## Hasle

55°11'N 14°42'E (on leading line close to breakwater)

**Contacts**

Harbourmaster ✆+45 56 92 23 22
haslehavn@brk.dk
www.marinaguide.dk/hasle-havn/om-havnen

This fishing and yachting harbour is 5M north of Rønne and makes a good alternative to it.

Approach the harbour mouth on a bearing of 097° in the white sector of Hasle light. Beware of a shallow patch with 3.7m just north of the leading line close to the harbour entrance.

Only Bassin IV is labelled clearly for guests, but Bassin III can also used. Mooring is alongside to fairly high stone quays. For electricity contact the harbourmaster.

There is a range of shops, restaurants in the town and buses to Rønne.

## Hammerhavn

55°16'.75N 14°48'.2E (between breakwaters of harbour entrance)

**Contacts**

Harbourmaster ✆+45 56 92 23 24
www.marinaguide.dk/hammer-havn/om-havnen

This bay on the northwest tip of the island is protected by breakwaters and makes a change from built-up areas. It is well placed for a visit to the ruins of Hammershus Castle or for walking in the Hammerknuden nature reserve. Approach the harbour mouth on a bearing of 075° in the white sector of Hammerhavn Light. Berth alongside the jetties of the inner harbour in 3m decreasing to 2m. The facilities are fairly basic but fuel is available. The nearest village with shops and restaurants is Sandvig 2km away.

A view of Hammerhavn looking north *Andy Beharrell*

Hammershus Castle – abandoned in the 1750s but still one of the largest medieval fortifications in Northern Europe
*Andy Beharrell*

The harbour at Tejn is very well sheltered and offers good facilities, although it is less picturesque than some on the island
*C.N. Hill*

## Allinge

55°16'.75N 14°48'.2E (leading line by harbour entrance)

**Contacts**
Harbourmaster ✆+45 56 92 23 28
www.marinaguide.dk/allinge-havn/om-havnen
allingehavn@brk.dk

Allinge is a classic Bornholm harbour and town and is very popular. It sits on the northeast coast and is very attractive and unspoiled. The harbour provides sheltered alongside berthing in 3.9m in the inner harbour with most facilities, but it may be closed by a shut gate between the outer and inner harbours in strong onshore winds. A black ball or three Vertical Red lights signal that the harbour is closed.

Approach the harbour mouth on 208.9° on the leading line though this may not be conspicuous at any distance. The entrance is not at all obvious from the approaches; there is a single green buoy near the harbour entrance which may be easier to find. The harbour should be approached with caution as there is little room for manoeuvre once inside. The harbour gets very crowded in the season, with much rafting up.

Fuel is no longer available except at petrol station. Shore power and showers available. There is free WiFi in café on quay. It is an easy passage to Christiansø (12M) and only 23M to Simrishamn in Sweden.

## Tejn

55°15'N 14°50'E (on leading line at harbour entrance)

**Contacts**
✆+45 56 92 23 32
www.marinaguide.dk/en/tejn-harbour/description
tejnhavn@brk.dk

This harbour is rather less picturesque than many of the others along the northern coast of Bornholm, but offers excellent shelter in bad weather. The entrance should also be straightforward even in poor conditions.

There is a basin for yachts, but this is rather cramped. Available places are marked with a green marker. Normally, yachts can tie alongside in the main basin. Fuel is available. A small supermarket is adjacent to the quay.

## Gudhjem South

55°12'.9N 14°58'.4E (on leading line close to harbour)

**Contacts**
Harbourmaster ✆+45 56 92 23 36
gudhjemhavn@brk.dk

Another pleasant harbour offering most facilities including diesel. However, access to the inner harbour is closed by a gate in onshore winds of more than 10m/s (20kn). This is signalled by a red ball hoisted on a flagpole or extinguished leading lights (F.R). Approach on 202°. Berth alongside or bow to quay with stern anchor in the inner harbour. Frequent ferries to Christiansø.

The tourist information office is located near the quay and will provide help and advice.

The harbour at Gudhjem on the northeast of Bornholm
*Viv Fox*

## Svaneke

55°08'.14N 15°08'.8E (leading line by north breakwater )

**Contacts**

Harbourmaster ✆+45 56 49 60 40
SvanekeHavn@brk.dk

A charming and well-preserved old market town with plenty going on and good bus connections to the rest of the island. Svaneke boasts Bornholm's largest fish smokery. The outer harbour gets rough in strong onshore winds and the inner harbour gate is closed in these conditions. Enter the bay on a course of 215° in the white sector of the sectored light at 55°08'.04N 15°08'.73E until the harbour mouth opens up and the leading line appears on 297°. Berth alongside or bow to quay with stern anchor in the inner harbour in 3.9m. All facilities available including diesel and a sailmaker.

## Nexø

55°03'.9N 15°08'.5E (on leading line by southern breakwater)

**Contacts**

Harbourmaster ✆+45 56 49 22 50
www.marinaguide.dk/nexoe-havn/om-havnen
www.nexohavn.dk

Nexø is a fishing and commercial port and has a summer ferry connection to Poland. It is an all-weather port and is a useful landfall if coming from Poland.

The town is one of the few that suffered during the Second World War, as it was bombed by Soviet aircraft while still being occupied by the Germans. The Russians moved in to replace the Germans at the end of the war and proved rather difficult to dislodge.

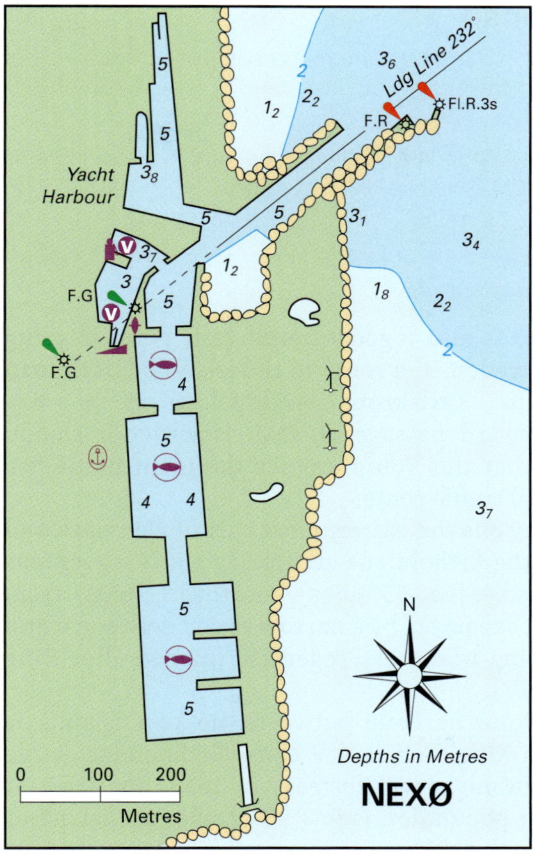


### *Approach*

Approach is straightforward. There are leading lines (F.G) on 232° (church spire in line with entrance), but in daylight it is probably easier to keep the church spire in line with the harbour entrance. As you come down between the pierheads, there is a commercial basin to starboard. Continue past this entrance. The masts of the local yachts can be clearly seen ahead, and you enter the yacht basin with a 90° turn to starboard.

Boats less than 10m in length can berth alongside or to stern buoys on the west quay of the old harbour (the second basin on the starboard side). Boats over 10m in length can use the next basin to the south. Moor to stern buoys. All facilities including fuel and WiFi. There are buses to other parts of the island.

The visitors' berths in the small basin to your starboard side as you enter Nexø harbour. You can tie alongside or use the stern buoys provided. Alternatively, turn to port and moor in the first basin, using stern buoys *C.N. Hill*

## Christiansø

55°19'.1N 15°11'.17E (on southern approach to harbour: east of Snarken red can buoy)

**Distances**

Rønne 27M, Allinge 14M, Gudhejm (the ferry to the island runs from here) 10M, Svaneke 11M, Nexø 17M

**Contacts**

Harbourmaster ✆+45 40 45 20 14
www.christiansoe.dk/en

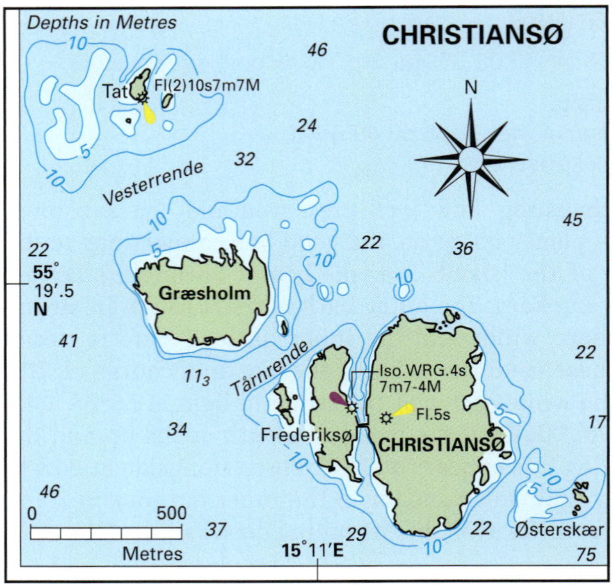


Christiansø is also a good jumping off point if going north to Sweden. The route to the island of Utklippan outside the Karlskrona Archipelago is a very straightforward passage of 41M. However it should be noted that this route crosses the main Baltic Sea commercial traffic route.

Christiansø is the easternmost part of Denmark and is part of the Ertholmene archipelago. It is a gorgeous small island – just 55 acres – northeast (10M) from Bornholm, separated by a narrow sound between it and the adjoining island of Frederiksø (named after King Frederick IV).

This unique harbour between the two islands is the reason King Christian V chose Ertholmene as the location for his naval fortress in 1635. The current permanent population is just 93 people. The island of Græsholm is just 27 acres in size and is 250m northwest of Frederiksø. It is uninhabited and is now a bird reserve, with large breeding colonies of common eider, red-breasted merganser, gulls, common murre and razorbill.

The sound between Christiansø and Frederiksø forms two harbours, separated by a swing footbridge which only opens by prior arrangement with the harbourmaster. The south harbour affords berths in 2–3m. The north harbour is occupied by fishing boats and has very limited, if any, space. It has been a fortress and naval harbour since the 1600s.

Approach the southern harbour from the west on the leading line on 103°, leaving the red can buoy (marking a dangerous rock, Snarken) to port until the harbour opens up and enter in the white sector of the light on Fredericksø. A black ball or three red lights signal that the harbour is closed either because of bad weather or because the harbour is full. Mooring is either alongside the main quay (which often involves rafting up) or by stern buoy on the west side (which is more exposed). Facilities are limited but diesel is available.

The harbour at Christiansø *Viv Fox*

The south entrance to the harbour at Christiansø *Viv Fox*

A view over Christiansø *Viv Fox*

SWEDEN
NORWAY
SWEDEN
FINLAND
Tornio
Luleå
Piteå
Oula
Skellefteå
Umeå
Vastra Kvarkven
Norra Kvarkven
Härnösand
Sundsvall
Gulf of Bothnia
Hudiksvall
Söderhamn
Gävle
Åland Islands
Turku
HELSINKI
OSLO
Uppsala
Lake Mälaren
Gulf of Finland
TALLINN
Lake Vänern
STOCKHOLM
Hiiumaa
Nynäshamn
ESTONIA
Saaremaa
Arkösund
Göta Kanal
Mem
Gotska Sandön
Pärnu
Trollhätte Kanal
Lake Vättern
Skagerrak
Göteborg
Gulf of Riga
Visby
Västervik
Gotland
Ventspils
Oskarshamn
Kattegat
LATVIA
RIGA
Kalmar
Öland
Skåne
Baltic Sea
DENMARK
Helsingør
Karlskrona
Helsingborg
Utklippan
LITHUANIA
Klaipėda
Malmö
COPENHAGEN
Simrishamn
Bornholm (Denmark)
Kaliningrad
RUSSIA
66°
65°N
64°
63°
62°
61°
60°N
59°
58°N
57°
56°
55°
10°
11°
12°
13°
14°
15°E
16°
17°
18°
19°
20°
21°
22°
23°
24°
25°E

# 2. SWEDEN

The Swedish coast is the longest and probably the most varied in the Baltic. The west coast runs north from the busy and heavily populated Øresund, passing the fertile shores north of Kullen until the Göteborg *Skärgård* is reached. After this come the wonderful cruising grounds of the Bohuslän coast before reaching the bare rocky foreshores backed by extensive forest towards the Norwegian border.

The southern coast is very different in nature. There are far fewer rocks, but instead long stretches of sandy beaches. Early in the season, some shoaling may occur in harbour entrances due to the shifting sand in winter storms. Rather than coming in close to the breakwaters, it is better to line up the entrance at least 200m out and follow the line in.

North and east of Simrishamn the geology begins to change to the more familiar rock-strewn coastline, with outlying archipelagos, or *skärgård*, of islands. The first major archipelago - the Blekinge archipelago - centres around Karlskrona.

The east coast from Kalmar to beyond Stockholm is largely a *skärgård* area. It demands careful navigation, but at the same time offers sheltered sailing in smooth waters dotted with hundreds of secluded anchorages and pretty visitors' harbours (*gästhamnar*). It is seldom crowded outside Midsummer but a fair proportion of those who visit the Baltic with the intention of exploring north and east become so entranced with this area that they never progress further. Indeed, the *Blå Kusten* (Blue Coast) and the *skärgård* surrounding Stockholm are immense cruising areas in themselves.

The Gulf of Bothnia has long been sailed by Swedes, Finns and Germans and is gaining in popularity with others. With yachting increasing in popularity in Poland, you are also likely to see larger numbers of Polish boats. A glance at the invaluable *Gästhamns Guiden* (see pilots and cruising guides, page 100) reveals many small harbours and marinas.

The season is necessarily shorter, with ice lingering into May, and those who venture north have the opportunity to experience an entirely different facet of Swedish cruising. This area includes the High Coast (*Höga Kusten*), which is a UNESCO World Heritage site. This can claim to be among the most beautiful of all the Baltic cruising areas.

Finally, in addition to its coastal waters, vast areas of central Sweden consist of interconnected lakes, many of them accessible to yachts with fixed masts. Lakes Vänern and Vättern are traversed by the hundreds of yachts which pass through the Trollhätte Kanal and Göta Kanal each year, but can be considered great cruising locations in their own right. Lake Mälaren, directly inland from the city of Stockholm, is also an extensive cruising ground and was cradle to some of the earliest Swedish civilisation and culture. It has many of Sweden's oldest buildings dotted around its shores.

## Key to section headings

# KEY INFORMATION

## Rescue/Safety services

**Emergency** ✆112 or VHF Ch 16

**MRCC Göteborg**, monitors VHF Ch 16/70, DSC MMSI 002 653 000, Call Sign '**Sweden Rescue**'
✆+46 31 699 080 or in emergency +46 31 699 050.

**Stockholm Radio**, VHF DSC MMSI 002652000
✆+46 86 017 906

Most emergencies will be referred to the Swedish Sea Rescue Society (SSRS). There are additional benefits if you join. See **www.sjoraddning.se/information-english**

## Charts and chart packs

Admiralty charts give good general coverage of the Swedish coast, quite sufficient for passage-making or cruise planning. However, for cruising the intricate Blå Kustens (Blue Coast) either side of Västervik, or Stockholm's superb *skärgård*, the Swedish publications are essential. These, produced by Sjöfartsverket, (the Swedish Maritime Administration), are divided into small-scale 'Coastal charts', medium-scale 'Archipelago charts' and large-scale 'Special and harbour charts' (more details will be found on their website **www.sjofartsverket.se**). The Swedish charts can be browsed online through their website **geokatalog.sjofartsverket.se/kartvisarefyren/**.

Of particular appeal to the yachtsman are the excellent Båtsportkort series of chart-packs, effectively a combination of 'Archipelago' and 'Special' charts, mostly at scales of 1:50,000 or 1:25,000. These have recently been revised and now come as 15 Spiral bound A3 sized booklets. However, the series does not cover the entire Swedish coast, and neither does it run in sequence.

There are also two useful series of German-published chart packs (size A2). They are published annually and come with electronic versions on CD and complementary pilot books. These are the NV Baltic Charts and the Delius Klasing charts.

## Chart datum

In 2005 a new national height system was introduced. Height references are now made from land-based marks and so, as the land rises the reference system also rises. As part of this change the Swedish will now use a datum called RH 2000 (Swedish National Height System 2000). All the EU countries around the Baltic will also use a common vertical chart datum known as Baltic Sea Chart Datum 2000 (BSCD 2000).

For Swedish charts the introduction of RH 2000 means that all charts and products will refer to a common chart datum. Traditionally depth information on Swedish charts has specified a mean sea level for a given year (usually the chart production year) resulting in a variety of reference. The Swedish Maritime Administration has therefore begun the process of adapting their databases and products to the new datum. This transition will be gradual and the aim is that it will be completed by the end of 2030. Care should therefore be taken to check the datum on any charts which you are using.

## Pilots and cruising guides

*Gästhamns Guiden* (in Swedish only) is free of charge and widely available at harbours, hotels and restaurants.
**www.svenskagasthamnar.se**

*Guest harbour guide – Gästhamns app* (in Swedish only) – an app-based guide to all the guest harbours in Sweden. The app can be downloaded from app.gasthamnsguiden.se. A useful guide to the extensive range of guest harbours available in Sweden.

*Harbour Guides (Hamnguiden)* – Books 5–8 cover Sweden as follows Hamnguiden 5, Göteborg – Svinesund, Havneguiden 6, Danmark og sydvestlige Sverige (mostly Denmark, but also covers southwest Sweden), Hamnguiden 7 Landsort – Skanör, Öland, Gotland & Bornholm, Hamnguiden 8, Arholma – Landsort. The printed books are available through **www.harbourguide.com** or annual subscriptions are available to access the harbours from all the books online (laptop/desktop or mobile devices). Annual subscriptions are around 50 euros.

*Arholma to Landsort* (Stockholm Archipelago). Norstedts Förlagsgrupp AB. No English version currently available

*Landsort to Skanor* Published in English by Norstedts Förlagsgrupp AB. Available from Imray.

*Norrlandskust* by Erik Nyström (Bilda Förlag). Available only in Sweden, with no English version. However, the excellent chartlets and photographs more than make up for this.

## Water stand (Havsvattenstånd)

The water level around Sweden is affected by atmospheric pressure and winds in both the North Sea and the Baltic. This will result in periodic oscillations in the water levels. Strong winds will force the water along the coast and water levels will be lower in some places and rise where the water is being pushed to. This effect can be quite significant if there are sustained periods of stronger winds. This process will affect both the water level and the currents. The Swedish Meteorological and Hydrological Institute (SMHI) publishes extensive data and forecasts for the water levels. This is available on **www.smhi.se/data/oceanografi/havsvattenstand**. It is worth browsing around this site and checking water level forecasts if heading into harbours where depth might be an issue.

## Currents

There are no permanent currents in the Baltic Sea. Fresh water flows from rivers into the sea and initially mixes as a thin layer above the salt water. This turns right with the rotation of the earth and gradually mixes. The southern coast of Sweden has a slow coastal current, but this is weakest in summer. The currents are strongest in the various sounds: the Northern Kvark, the Åland Sea, the Kalmar Sound and the Belt Sea. The Øresund and the Belt have the strongest currents as the main Baltic outflow to the North Sea is concentrated here. Forecasts for currents for the next 24hrs for much of the coast of Sweden can be accessed from **www.dmi.dk/strom**

## Time

Sweden uses UT+1 in winter and UT+2 in summer. Clocks change in line with the EU's daylight saving schedule, meaning that daylight saving time is observed from the last Sunday in March (0200 CET) to the last Sunday in October (0300 CEST).

## kr Money

The unit of currency is the Swedish krona (usually abbreviated to SEK, plural kronor and often spoken of as crown), divided into 100 öre.

Major credit and debit cards are universally accepted, both in payment for goods and services and by banks, nearly all of which have ATMs, known as *Bankomat*. All businesses (even taxis and public transport) now prefer card payment and it can be quite difficult to use cash, so many people like to get either pre-loaded cards or cards with zero or low charges for use overseas. It is worth spending some time researching card charges before going away as the situation tends to change frequently.

## Formalities

Sweden is a member of the EU and is part of the Schengen area (see main Introduction, page 8 for further details of Schengen requirements).

EU passport holders do not require visas. The British Embassy in Stockholm is located at Skarpögatan 6–8, Box 27819, 115 93 Stockholm, ✆+46 8 671 3000, info@britishembassy.se

EU citizens coming direct from another EU country do not need to seek customs or immigration clearance on arrival unless carrying items which must be declared.

For UK citizens wanting to spend more than the 90 days allowed under Schengen rules, you will need to apply for a visitor's permit. There are full details of this available on the Swedish Immigration Service website – **www.migrationsverket.se/English/Private-individuals/Visiting-Sweden/Visit-Sweden-for-more-than-90-days**. This permit can be for up to six months and, though issued by Swedish immigration, is valid in the whole Schengen area and not just Sweden. Time spent in the Schengen area under the permit is completely separate from Schengen time and so does not count towards the 90 day Schengen limit.

In 2025/6 the European Travel Information and Authorization System (ETIAS) system will be implemented. ETIAS will require citizens of approximately 60 countries who currently enjoy visa-free access to Europe's Schengen Area to obtain advanced authorization before travelling. This system is similar to the ESTA required for travelling to the USA. It is not a visa but advance security clearance for short-term visitors. There will be a transitional period for at least 6 months when people will be advised to get an ETIAS authorization, but it will not be a requirement. There will then be a 6 month grace period when ETIAS will be compulsory for most travellers, but first-time visitors since the end of the transitional period will still be granted entry. Application will be online and should be fairly quick and straightforward. The cost is expected to be €7 and this fee grants approved travellers three years of unlimited entries into the Schengen Area.

Alcohol and tobacco that has purchased elsewhere in the EU (duty paid) can be freely imported and it may be a good idea to stock up before arrival if possible.

## Overwintering with your boat in Sweden

Residents of non-EU countries are entitled to keep a boat in Sweden without clearing Customs for up to 18 months. If over-wintering you may leave your boat for winter storage and services to be rendered with a marine service company that is certified as a 'Bonded Warehouse', or 'Customs Warehouse', or as a company registered for 'inward processing' service activities on boats. If planning to overwinter, it is important to contact the boatyard where you are planning to leave the boat to ensure they meet these requirements. Boats with EU-VAT paid status (i.e. those in the EU at the time of transition) are not affected by this.

## Public holidays

Official public holidays in Sweden include:
1 Jan, 6 Jan (Epiphany), Good Friday, Easter Sunday and Monday, 1 May (Labour Day), Ascension Day (May), Whit Sunday and Monday (May or June), Midsummer's Eve and Day (close to the summer solstice), All Saints Day (a Saturday in late Oct/early Nov), 24–26 Dec and 31 Dec.

## Communications

It may be taken for granted nowadays that almost every Swede under 50 speaks fluent English.

UK mobile networks all have arrangements to allow UK phones to work in Sweden and coverage, even in the remotest island locations, is excellent. However, it is important to check the arrangements your contract provider has for charging as some will charge significant amounts for data and calls outside the UK.

Almost all marinas will have WiFi, as will many shops and cafes. It may be possible to get a Swedish SIM card for use while sailing in the country, but this is getting increasingly difficult without a Swedish address or residency. It is probably best to check in a mobile phone store as contracts and requirements change constantly.

## Travel

Sweden is well served by air, and some bus, rail and sea services from other parts of Europe.

Arlanda, approximately 42km from Stockholm, is the main international airport for the Stockholm region and places north. Gothenburg also has direct flights to the UK. Copenhagen is another alternative. It is also possible to drive direct from the UK using the Øresund bridge between Denmark and Sweden. Some budget airlines use Västerås airport.

If you are keeping a boat in Sweden and travelling with a lot of tools and/or equipment, it is possible to drive. One option is a ferry to the Netherlands and then drive to north Germany. Ferries run from Kiel – Gothenburg (overnight) or shorter crossings from Travemünde or Rostock to

Trelleborg. Alternatively, there are ferries from Puttgarden (Fehmarn island) to Rødby in Denmark or from Rostock to Gedser in Denmark.

If crossing by ferry to Denmark or driving all the way to Sweden, note that you will then need to pay the toll for crossing the Øresund Bridge. This is over £50 each way. See **www.oresundsbron.com/en/prices** for up to date information on prices.

Internal bus, train and air services are excellent. Some train services and ferry routes may offer discounts for senior citizens, so it is worth checking when making payment. Note that on many bus routes, the driver will not accept cash; tickets often need to be purchased in advance from a kiosk or elsewhere.

## Websites

Sites directly connected with charts, pilot books and cruising guides are shown under those headings. Sites for harbours are shown under the harbour. Many sites have English versions but often with only a summary of the content.

**sweden.se** – Describes itself as the 'Official Gateway to Sweden', with many useful links

**www.visitsweden.com** – The Swedish Travel and Tourism Council

**www.tullverket.se** – The Swedish Board of Customs. Includes regulations for 'Pleasure Boats' in English and links to other Swedish government sites

**www.gotakanal.se/en** – Göta Kanal Company's excellent and very informative website

**www.visitstockholm.com** – Lots of tips and ideas on what to do when visiting Stockholm

**www.skargardsstiftelsen.se/the-archipelago-foundation/** – Skärgårdsstiftelsen (the Archipelago Foundation) who own and manage many of the islands around the Stockholm Archipelago. The site also has an *Explore Archipelago* guide

**www.sjofartsverket.se/en/** – Lock opening times, bridge heights and bridge opening times (similar information for Stockholm at **www.portsofstockholm.com/stockholm/**)

**www.ksss.se** – The Kungl Svenska Segel Sällskapet (the Royal Swedish Yacht Club) have marinas at Saltsjöbaden and Sandhamn

**www.sxk.se** – The Svenska Kryssarklubben (Swedish Cruising Club or SXK). In Swedish only. The SXK also maintain mooring buoys in many archipelago locations for their members. It may be worth considering joining to be allowed to use these. Members are issued with an annual flag to fly when using the buoys to show they are entitled to use them but there is a weight limit on the buoys. They are all being regularly upgraded but check with the SXK for maximum weight

**www.gasthamnsguiden.se** – Useful details of guest harbours. It is in Swedish only, but Google translate is a very effective tool to help understand it

**www.smhi.se** – Provides shipping forecast for all Baltic areas in English as well as Swedish. Also provides details of the water stand, ice maps, the presence of algae (and an archive), environmental information and currents

**www.dockspot.com** – a site for booking spaces in a number of Swedish harbours in advance of arrival

**www.hamnsystem.se/en/** – a Swedish alternative to Dockspot for some harbours

## Radio communications & weather information

Weather forecasts in Swedish and English are broadcast at 0800 and 2000 Local Time on the working channels of all the many VHF stations remotely controlled from Stockholm – see page ix for details. Note that wind speeds are normally given in metres per second (m/s). As a very rough guide, halve this to get Beaufort; double it to get knots (kn).

## WC Holding tanks

Swedish law provides that no human waste, either solid or liquid, be discharged into Swedish waters – that is, within 12M of land. On-the-spot fines can be imposed. Although holding tanks are not compulsory, it will be very difficult to comply without a holding tank or some other method of avoiding discharge. The law also requires harbours to provide a pump out station for a holding tank, but compliance with this is not total. The Archipelago Foundation (Skärgårdsstiftelsen) often provides pump-out barges in remote locations.

Yachtsmen should take all possible steps to comply with these requirements. Most marinas and harbours will of course have toilet arrangements, but at nature harbours, or in the more remote harbours, it may be found that the only facilities are composting toilets.

Grey water tanks are not a requirement.

## Flying drones

Many people now sail with drones on board and, subject to flying them in a considerate and legal way, they can be a useful tool for pilotage and indeed for sharing pilotage information with other sailors. A Drone pilot licence is not needed for sub-250g drones (in the Open A1 category), but you do need to register it in Sweden and obtain a Swedish Operator's ID which you need to display on the drone. The UK Operator's ID is not recognised. You will need to fill out a form (available from **transportstyrelsen.se/en/aviation/aircraft/drones--unmanned-aircraft/**), print it out, sign it, rescan it, and email it to operatorsregistrering.dronare@transportstyrelsen.se along with a copy of your passport, all in PDF format. The cost is around £10 for a year, but this entitles you to fly the drone anywhere in the EU without any further documentation.

## THE COUNTRY

Sweden is a difficult country to summarise. The sheer variety of landscapes, culture and people gives a unique mix, meaning it is fascinating country to visit but also an intriguing country to research further. Historically it has played a pivotal part in Europe's development, but it has also played an important part culturally and economically. Here are some key facts about Sweden – some may surprise, many will probably not:

- The population of Sweden in 2024 was just over 10 million. This is 0.13% of the total world population and makes Sweden number 87 in the world by population
- Sweden is the fifth largest country in Europe with a total land area of 450,295km$^2$ and has one of the lowest population densities in Europe
- Two thirds of the country is covered by forest – a total area of 280,650km$^2$
- In the summer when populations are highest, there will be around 350,000 moose spread around the country, an average of 10–15 moose per 1,000ha. They are secretive animals though and the odds of seeing them are low
- Sweden has the highest number of McDonald's per capita in Europe
- Sweden has one of the highest recycling rates in the world, with over 99% of all household waste being either recycled or used for energy production
- Sweden is the country with the highest number of patents per capita in Europe
- Nicotine replacement gum was invented in Sweden
- Sweden is home to the Nobel Prize. They were instituted by Alfred Nobel, the Swedish chemist, engineer, and industrialist who invented dynamite, and are awarded in Stockholm each year

The varied nature of the cruising to be had around Sweden's coast is, to a large extent, a reflection of the country's geology. The country comprises four distinct zones, three of which are founded on ancient rocks. The northern two thirds of the country has mountains to the west, along the Norwegian border, while to the east it is boulder-strewn bare rock, with peat bogs and spruce, pine and birch stretching northwards until they are beaten by the climate. South of this the land slopes down to the central lowlands, which are more hospitable, with prosperous agriculture and deciduous trees among the conifers. Stockholm and Göteborg are in this region.

Southern Sweden has a central raised area with the same feel as the rocky north, bordered by coastal lowlands given over to agriculture and fishing. The fourth region, Skåne, in the extreme southwest, has the most recent rock, often covered with boulder clay, with beech and oak rather than conifers.

The coast from north of Stockholm down to Kalmar is fringed by tens of thousands of islands – some inhabited, some not, some rocky and desolate and others green and fertile. It is a seductive area and immensely popular with both Swedish and foreign yachtsmen. The southern part of the Swedish coast, from Kalmar round to Malmö, is attractive, with an undulating coastline and a number of interesting harbours. There is another, smaller, archipelago centred around Karlskrona.

A major resource is timber, which covers more than half of the country. North of Stockholm, paper mills are conspicuous by the clouds of steam they produce. Fishing is much reduced, and it is rare to see fishing boats out at sea.

Even the smallest islands in the archipelagos have holiday homes, and the owners need boats to visit them. It is estimated that there are around 900,000 leisure boats in Sweden and as a consequence, boat ownership in Sweden is higher than anywhere else in Europe.

### History

While the Danish and Norwegian Vikings headed west, Swedish Vikings went east and then south along the rivers of Russia to the Caspian and Black Seas, reaching Constantinople by 838. They settled Novgorod as a trading centre under their leader Rurik. By 900CE Rurik's successors had their capital in Kiev and ruled all the Slavic tribes from the Caspian and Black Seas to the Baltic in what was then called Kiev-Rus, the embryo Russia. ('Rus' was the Viking word for an oar or oarsman, probably because of their red hair.) Emperor Basil II of Constantinople, capital of the surviving eastern Roman Empire, even employed Rus Vikings as his 'Varangian guard', his personal and most trusted bodyguard, a tradition that lasted for four centuries.

During the Middle Ages, Sweden's south and west coasts were ruled by Denmark. Then in 1397 a royal marriage led to the Kalmar Union which united all the rest of Sweden and all of Norway under Denmark. To the Swedes the Union simply meant ever increasing taxes for the Danes to fund their wars in southern Jutland. Periodic Swedish rebellions were brutally suppressed.

Then came the Stockholm Massacre of 1520 when 80 Swedish nobles were arrested and publicly beheaded on a single day. The Swedes were so appalled that they united under Gustav Vasa to drive the Danes out of Sweden. Gustav Vasa was elected king of the newly independent Sweden (which still included Finland). During his reign, he consolidated the state and its treasury, laying the foundations for his later successor, Gustavus Adolphus.

Gustavus Adolphus (or Gustav II Adolf) was king from 1611 to 1632. He was both an enlightened ruler and an extraordinary military innovator. He was regarded as the founder of modern warfare by later generals such as Clausewitz, Bonaparte and Patten. During his reign he captured the whole of the Russian Baltic coast as well as Polish Livonia (i.e. most of modern Latvia and Estonia) where memory of his rule is still celebrated. He then fought with the German Protestant states in the Thirty Years War against the Holy Roman Emperor, reaching Bavaria before he was finally killed in battle. By the end of his reign, Sweden had become one of Europe's major powers, controlling nearly the entire Baltic coast and hence its trade as the main exporter of grain and shipbuilding materials to the rest of Europe.

Sweden was to remain a great power for the rest of the 17th century. Then in 1700 Denmark/Norway, Poland and Russia united to launch the Great Northern War to clip Sweden's wings. Charles XII of Sweden started well, but was routed when he tried to invade Russia and was later killed when he invaded Norway (still in union with Denmark). In the resulting peace treaty, Sweden kept most of Finland, but lost Karelia, in east Finland, and Estonia and Latvia to Russia, which, under Peter the Great, was now to become the latest nation to dominate the Baltic.

In the 18th century, Sweden, like most of Europe, settled down to the Enlightenment and improving democracy. Then at the end of the century came the French Revolution followed by the Napoleonic wars. Sweden initially sided with Napoleon, but fared badly, losing all of Finland to Russia in 1809. The Swedish parliament elected one of Napoleon's defecting generals, Jean-Baptiste Bernadotte, as their new king Charles XIV John. In 1813 Charles joined the allies against Napoleon and defeated Denmark, thereby gaining Norway for Sweden until 1905.

The impact of war had put an end to 18th century prosperity. About a million Swedes emigrated to America in the 19th century, although many returned bringing with them ideas about American industrial methods. Sweden's industrialisation was based on iron and steel, textiles and timber. The country had never had the deep class divisions that plagued other nations, and so was able to develop quietly as an economically successful liberal democracy with a model welfare state.

In World Wars I and II, Sweden remained neutral, although sometimes bowing to pressure from Germany. It continues to be a constitutional monarchy under King Carl XVI Gustav, is a member of the EU, but not the Eurozone, and has the 8th highest per capita income in the world.

The post-war period was one of comprehensive reform and put in place the building blocks for a period of social democratisation. There were new laws on old-age pensions, child allowances, health insurance, educational reforms, and the period marked a significant expansion of higher education institutions and research. In 1971 the old two-chamber Riksdag was replaced by a single chamber Riksdag with 350 members elected by proportional representation. This number was reduced to 349 members in 1975 to reduce the risk of a split vote!

In 1986, Prime Minister Olof Palme was assassinated. This was a shock to a country not used to political violence. Palme was replaced by Ingvar Carlsson, the deputy prime minister, but this event diminished Sweden's role in international politics.

In the 21st century Sweden emerged from the economic crisis which had dogged it at the end of the previous century. The 1990s had seen a profound change in the Swedish concept known as *folkhemmet* with economic responsibilities shifting from central government to the provinces and local municipalities and from the state to the individual. *Folkhemmet* is often referred to as 'the Swedish Middle Way', somewhere between capitalism and socialism. The vision of *folkhemmmet* is that society should be like a family, where everybody contributes, but also where everybody looks after one another. The concept is the basis of many social reforms which might otherwise be associated with socialist parties, such as universal healthcare and unemployment benefits.

In 2003 voters decided not to adopt the euro as the country's official currency and in 2009 same sex marriage was legalised. Sweden has long been a leading advocate for women's rights globally and emphasised how the inclusion and empowerment of women can help in peacebuilding, conflict resolution, and economic development.

## The people

Sweden has a population of just over ten million, and a political system which includes a hereditary monarchy and parliamentary democracy. The established national church is Lutheran – non-Lutherans (including 130,000 Roman Catholics) make up less than 1.5% of the population.

Early on in the modern period, attention was paid to the welfare of all sections of society, not just to the upper layers. Free education and poor relief started in 1807, old age pensions in 1890, employment injury insurance in 1901, and basic and disability pensions in 1914.

Further benefits were added until, by the 1990s, an income tax rate of 45% was required to fund them and social expenditure, including health and social assistance, comprised about a third of the gross national product. The education system is excellent, one result being a well-trained work force, another an appreciation of the arts, and a third, conveniently, widespread skill in the English language.

Friendly but sometimes formal, the Swedes have developed a regulated society which, from Gustav Vasa onwards, has looked after its environment and has avoided the worst squalors of industrialisation.

## PRACTICALITIES

### Shopping

The cost (and the standard) of living is higher than in much of Europe. All daily needs can be met with ease other than in some parts of the archipelagos – the *skärgårds* – where food stores may be few and far between. In supermarkets you can buy beers up to 3.5% in strength, but otherwise alcohol is relatively expensive and available only from Systembolaget, the state-owned chain of liquor stores (www.systembolaget.se).

The main supermarket chains are the Coop Konsum, ICA (pronounced *eeka*) and Axfood which trades under various names like Hemköp, Närlivs, Snabbgross and Willys.

### Health

In July and August mosquitoes can be an irritation, and the risks posed by tick-borne encephalitis should be taken seriously (see main Introduction, page 10 for further details and precautions).

### Alcohol

The blood alcohol concentration (BAC) limits are 20mg/100ml (0.02%) for drivers of boats over 10m or boats capable of over 15kn. For boats less than 10m and boats capable of less than 15kn, the BAC limit is 100mg/100ml. Penalties include fines or imprisonment, depending on the circumstances. The same requirements apply to visiting sailors and drivers, so if hiring a car, be sure to meet these requirements.

### Harbours and berthing

Visitors' marinas in Sweden are indicated by a gold anchor symbol on a blue background and the words *Gästhamn* or guest harbour.

Some harbours, especially those run by sailing clubs, are private, and although they will usually try to find you a berth, it is better to arrange this in advance rather than pitch up and hope for the best.

Harbours for visitors are called *gästhamnar*, or guest harbours. However, even within these, some of the berths will be private. It is considered bad form to take a private berth, even if empty – rather like parking in someone's driveway (the same is true in Finland). Having said that, some harbours or marinas also operate the red/green marker system – if you see a green, you may take the berth.

Usually there will be a set of moorings specifically set aside for visitors, and marked with the *gästhamn* sign (see illustration). The moorings can be stern buoys, booms, stern anchor, alongside or lazyline, or a mixture of any of these!

Many of the harbours, particularly the smaller ones and those north of Stockholm, may not have a harbourmaster available to take your mooring fee; instead, there may well be an 'honesty box' in which you can place your payment. This is an important reason to carry some cash (including small denominations), despite it being an almost cashless society.

It is often possible to book berths before arrival. This can be particularly useful during the busy holiday season. There are various websites offering this service including Dockspot (www.dockspot.com), Hamnsystem (www.hamnsystem.se/en/) and Go Marina (www.gomarina.com). We have referenced these throughout the text.

Electricity sockets are usually the marina type, although in remote harbours the two pin continental sockets may be found, and it is wise to carry an adaptor.

Diesel is readily obtainable, often at a berth at which a holding-tank can also be emptied. An increasing

When paying automatically at guest harbour, you will be issued with a mooring ticket *Viv Fox*

Guest harbours are clearly marked with a gästhamn sign *Andy Beharrell*

The Blå Kusten (Blue Coast) is an extremely attractive area, characterised by thousands of small islands *Andy Beharrell*

number of fuel points are only card operated, usually (but not always) with instructions in English and German in addition to Swedish.

Bottled gas may be a problem, with butane increasingly difficult to obtain as one progresses north. Campinggaz cylinders are increasingly difficult to replace anywhere in Sweden. There are reports of some places where they can be exchanged, but the situation changes quickly. It may be possible to get British propane cylinders (such as those manufactured by Calor gas) refilled, but a suitable regulator is likely to be required. If remaining in the Baltic for any length of time it may be worth buying one or more Swedish cylinders in the hope of reselling them on one's return south.

There are chandleries available all around Sweden. One of the main chains is SeaSea. They have branches throughout Sweden – see their website (www.seasea.se) for details of all the branches. Captains Chandlery (www.captains.se) in Stockholm is a good central location, but there are many other options around the coast. There are large independent chandleries in Ystad and Kalmar as well, but fellow sailors and/or harbourmasters will always point you in the right direction.

## Buoyage

Very many cardinal marks do not have topmarks and have to be identified only by their coloured stripes. This is not always straightforward, as the buoy may be silhouetted against the sun, or the paint may have become obscured or discoloured.

Similarly, red and green markers may be rather similar in shape, although their colours are usually more recognisable. Red and green markers will be found extensively in the channels through the archipelago, and they are almost invariably marking some particular hazard – a submerged rock or shoal. It is therefore even more important than usual to keep on the correct side.

Further north, and early in the season, it is possible to find buoys which have been moved out of position by the ice during the winter. Extra care should be taken if a buoy is not in the position indicated on your chart or chart plotter.

## Berthing fees

Berthing fees vary considerably depending on location and time of season. Some marinas charge a flat rate per boat, some by length, usually by range of lengths (e.g. 9–12m), and some by beam; some charge extra for showers, electricity or WiFi while others are inclusive. Saunas will often be an extra charge as well. Alongside berths are often charged at a higher rate.

Automatic vending machines are also on the increase, where you type in your boat details, insert a credit card, and are then issued with a sticker for your boat, together with relevant codes for the toilets, showers and other facilities.

## Nature harbours

The extensive chain of islands around the *skärgårds*, which in Stockholm's case extends up to 50M offshore, means there are an immense number of sheltered bays and inlets perfect for anchoring. These are known locally as 'nature harbours'. Many Swedish sailors tie up bow to the steep rocky shore with lines to convenient rocks/trees and secure the boat with a stern anchor. Alternatively, you can anchor in the middle of the bay and use a dinghy (but be careful not to obstruct the stern anchors of those who are rock mooring).

A miniature lighthouse in the intricate passage of the Blå Kusten (Blue Coast) *Andy Beharrell*

Facilities in these nature harbours are obviously very limited, but the point of them is to 'get away from it all'.

Extensive coverage of such harbours is beyond the scope of this book, but there are pilot books which can be purchased in local chandleries. Even if they are available only in Swedish, the aerial photographs and chartlets are invaluable.

## The Right of Public Access

Swedes are justly proud of their *Allemansrätten* (Right of Public Access) legislation. This is a unique right which gives people free access to the countryside, including the right to pick flowers, berries and mushrooms while appropriately respecting nature and property.

### RESTRICTED AREAS

Notwithstanding the above, there are various areas which are off limits for all or parts of the year, normally due to being either Military or Conservation Areas. Both are clearly indicated on Swedish charts.

The regulations controlling the former have been relaxed, so that it is no longer forbidden for foreigners to enter or cross them during peacetime. If there are smaller areas or installations within them where entrance is forbidden to all, they will be clearly marked on the ground.

At certain times of the year landing is not permitted on wildlife sanctuaries, and in some cases approach within 100m of the shore is forbidden. In addition to being marked on the chart a line of linked buoys will sometimes be used to close off an inlet or there may be a series of yellow signs setting out the dates when access is restricted, but even in their absence all restrictions should be rigorously observed.

From the yachtsman's point of view this means that a boat can be anchored anywhere (though not secured to a private jetty), and that one can then swim or go ashore, provided one respects the privacy of people's homes and does not enter gardens, trample growing crops, etc. Elsewhere one may walk across private land, pick berries, flowers or mushrooms (not those of protected species, of course), and even pitch a tent.

Naturally this freedom brings responsibilities. Disturbing wildlife – particularly nesting birds – leaving litter and lighting fires other than on purpose-built barbecues is not acceptable. Neither is driving or riding any motorised vehicle off the road, though pedal cycles (and horses) are fine. Fishing is limited to rod and line. Basically, show consideration for the enjoyment of others and one will not go far wrong.

## The Skärgårds

The archipelagos or *skärgårds* (pronounced *shair-gord*) are possibly the main attraction when cruising Sweden, with intricate passages through thousands of beautiful islands providing an absorbing and memorable experience. The Blue Coast, stretching from Oskarshamn to Arkösund, and the Stockholm Archipelago, as well as the Bohuslän coast on the west of the country, provide cruising grounds where one could wander for a month without ever repeating an anchorage, with rock mooring in remote corners an additional attraction (see further details of these areas on pages 130, 181 and 291).

However, when cruising in the *skärgårds* it is particularly important to take heed of the advice to carry adequate charts, and to be absolutely sure of your position at all times. You also need to be alert to the sudden appearance of huge ferries which can easily catch you unaware, especially in the Stockholm *skärgård*.

# WEST COAST OF SWEDEN

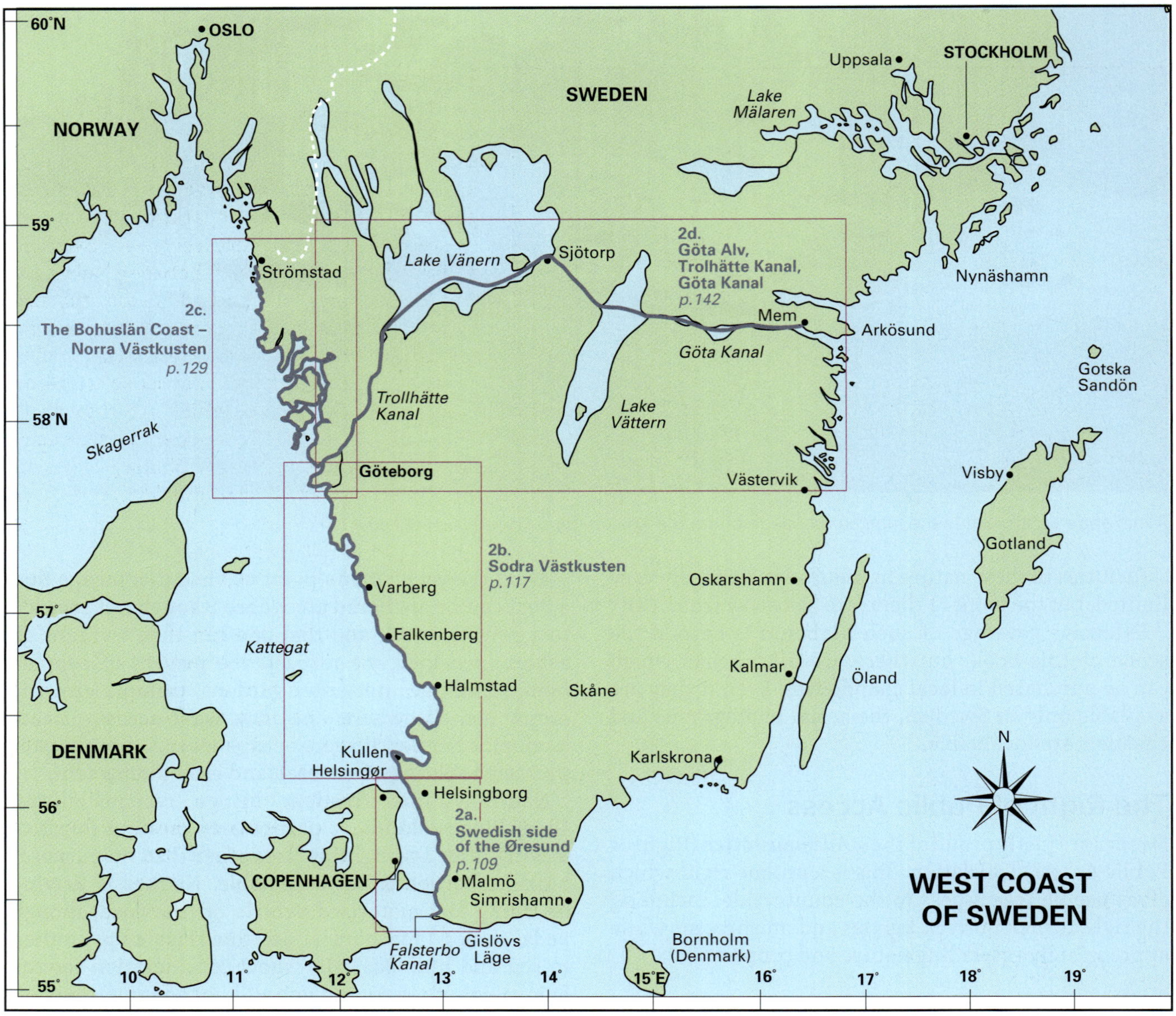

# 2A. THE SWEDISH SIDE OF THE ØRESUND

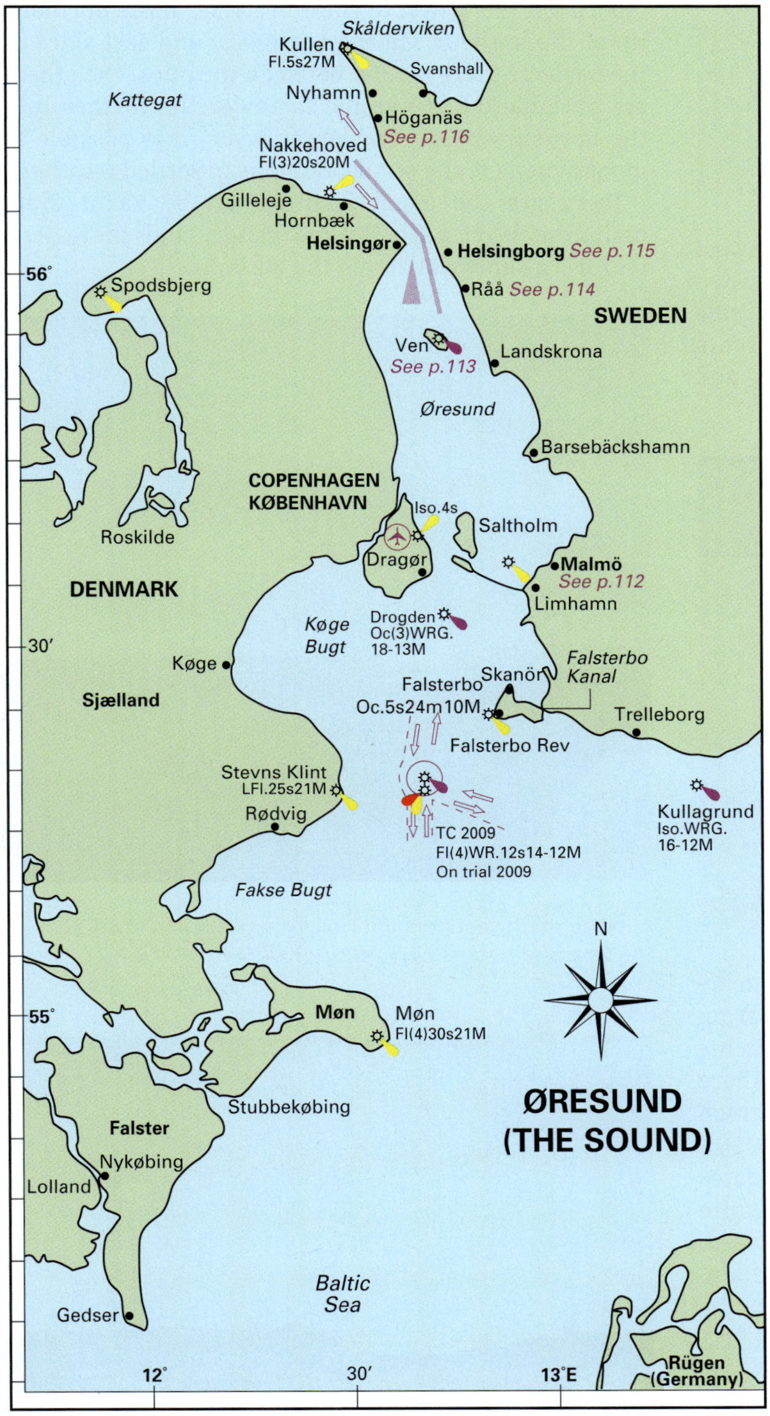


The Øresund (The Sound) is the most direct route from the Baltic into the main part of the Kattegat when coming from the east, and as such, is a major shipping route. It is also narrow, being only 3M wide at its narrowest point. There is a traffic separation scheme off Falsterbo Rev, the southwest corner of Sweden, and another in the narrows between Helsingør and Helsingborg. The hazard is from the size of some vessels using this route, rather than the sheer numbers, but nevertheless yachts crossing the sound should pay close attention to the TSS regulations, which are rigorously enforced. The waters between Copenhagen and Malmö are tortuous and shallow in places and crossed by the Øresund Bridge, but there is a well-marked dredged channel for large vessels. Currents in this area will vary with the wind in both strength and direction and can run at over 2kn in the narrower parts of the Sound. A 48hr forecast of the current is available from www.dmi.dk/strom. It therefore follows that close attention needs to be paid to navigation. However, you should not allow these warnings to put you off, since they are in no way unusual and it is a very interesting and rewarding cruising ground. It is home to large numbers of yachts on both the Swedish and Danish sides and there are many guest harbours listed on the Swedish shore alone.

It is perhaps worth noting that the Swedish laws relating to alcohol consumption by a yacht's crew have been known to be particularly actively enforced in this area.

The Øresund Bridge is a combined railway and motorway bridge across the strait between Denmark and Sweden. It is the second longest bridge in Europe *Antony Mcaulay/Dreamstime.com*

## SKANÖR

55°25'N 12°49'.66E (west mole head)

### Distances

Stralsund 68M, Rostock 78M, Travemünde 110M, Kiel 125M

### Contacts

✆+46 40 47 1188
www.skanorshamn.se
hamnkapten@skanorshamn.se

Skanör is a popular holiday spot on the southwest corner of Sweden. The harbour, which can be crowded at times, has box moorings with some space alongside a quay, and makes a useful stopping place on a route between the north German coast at Rügen and Copenhagen.

## FALSTERBO KANAL

55°24'.94N 12°55'.84E (east breakwater at beginning of canal, approaching from The Sound (northwest))
55°23'.56N 12°57'.98E (northeast breakwater at beginning of canal approaching from the east)

### Distances (north end)

Copenhagen 21M, Gislövs Läge 11M

### Contacts

✆+46 40 20 43 80
VHF Ch 11 (Falsterbo Canal)
www.falsterbokanalen.se

The mile-long Falsterbo Kanal (pronounced *Fahlstehr-boo Kah-naal*) provides a convenient short cut from Øresund to the Baltic, particularly useful to yachts coming from Copenhagen or beyond. Depth 4m. There are no locks, no dues and only one lifting bridge which opens every hour on the hour 0600–2200 (except 0800 and 1700) from 15 April to 30 Sept. Outside those dates it is open at 0630 and 1830. Signal light: fixed white and flashing red means stop, green means proceed. Both sailing and anchoring in the canal are forbidden. Access through the canal is only possible when the bridge is open.

### Höllviken

✆+46 40 45 34 92
hamnkontoret@falsterbokanalen.se

This is a small yacht harbour north of the bridge at the entrance to the Falsterbo canal. The northern section of the harbour where the guest berths are located is box moorings. The widest of these are 4.5m at the northern tip of the harbour. On the northwest and east sides of the harbour there is 3.8m between the piles. The others are variable but generally narrower the further into the harbour you go. For larger boats, it is possible to moor alongside the outer pontoons in settled weather.

There are the usual facilities at the Yacht Club, including WiFi with limited range, and there is a pizzeria a short walk from the harbour.

Looking northwest from the Höllviken gästhamn towards the Øresund bridge *Andy Beharrell*

The Höllviken gästhamn at the northern end of the Falsterbo canal *Andy Beharrell*

## MALMÖ

**Distances**
Copenhagen 13M, Göteborg 136M, Falsterbo Kanal 13M, Stralsund 80M

**Charts / harbour guides**
Swedish 921, 8141, 9211

**Contacts**
www.visitmalmo.se/en/

Malmö is Sweden's third largest city, and as such has every facility which would be expected, plus some cutting-edge architecture. It has excellent communications with the Øresund Bridge linking it to Denmark, as well as road, rail and air links to the rest of Scandinavia and beyond.

Three main yacht harbours serve the city.

### Malmö Dockan Marina

55°37'.1N 12°59'.19E (north mole head)

**Contacts**
☽+46 703 40 19 18
marinan@dockanmarina.se
www.dockan.se (go to 'Guest', click English flag)

The approach to the marina is deep water directly from harbour entrance. The Turning Torso skyscraper makes a good landmark from a distance when heading for Dockan. It is a neo-futurist skyscraper which was built in Malmö in 2005. When built, it was the tallest building in the Nordic region but Malmö was usurped by Göteborg in Sept 2022, when they built the Karlatornet. Moorings are boxes or fingers in 3.5m. Use a vacant mooring with green sign and pay at the machine. Most services are available including laundry, power, pump-out and fresh water. It is small with around 10 guest spaces, but it is well placed close to the centre of the city. Spaces can be booked in advance through Dockspot (www.dockspot.com/en/docks/105-dockan-marina-malmo).

### Malmö Lagunen

55°35'.9N 12°56'.26E (north mole head)

**Contacts**
Harbourmaster ☽+46 40 16 04 30
Office ☽+46 40 16 04 18
kansli@lagunen.nu
www.lagunen.nu

This marina is home to many local boats, with all the usual facilities, and is particularly suitable for families with a nearby playground, beach and open surrounding fields. It is, however, nearly 3km from the city centre, but the Bus 7 leaves from Limhamnsvägen every 10mins.

The approach is straightforward but with a well-marked reef, charted at 1.7m depth in places, just under 0.5M offshore. The entrance to the marina is unlit. Depth in the marina is 2.7m. There are no dedicated berths for visitors, but they are welcome to use any vacant berth with a green sign. Payment is at the marina office.

### Malmö Limhamn

55°34'.94N 12°54'.59E (west mole head)

**Contacts**
Vågbrytarevägen 216 12 Limhamn
☽+46 706 15 20 25
booking.smabatshamnen.se/en/

Just a couple of miles north of the Øresund bridge, this is the best prepared marina for visitors, with all the usual facilities available, including WiFi, but has the disadvantage of being some 5km from the city centre.

Malmö is the largest city in the Swedish county Skåne and the third-largest city in Sweden *Viv Fox*

MALMÖ
LIMHAMN-WEST AND LAGUNEN
YACHT HARBOURS (SWEDEN)
Fl(2)G.4s
Fl(2)G.4s
Fl.Y.6s
Oc.WRG.6s9M
Fl(2)G.4s
Iso.R.5s
Lagunen Yacht Harbour
Dockan Marina
Oil Tanks
Central Harbour
SWEDEN
South Harbour
096.5° Lts in line
F.R
F.R
Limhamn-West Yacht Harbour
Club - house
Club - house
092° Lts in line
2F.G
55° 35′.5 N
35′
12°54.5′E
56′.5
0 200 Metres
Depths in Metres
N

Approach is straightforward, with depth up to 3m, but beware of the pontoons on the east side, which shallow to 1m at the shore end. Use any vacant berth with a green sign and pay at harbour office.

If the harbour office is closed, ask for help at the Harbour Grill. Bikes can also be hired from here. There is a branch of the Hjertmans chandlery chain in Limhamn (Vågbrytarvägen, 21612 Limhamn) and there are buses to the city centre.

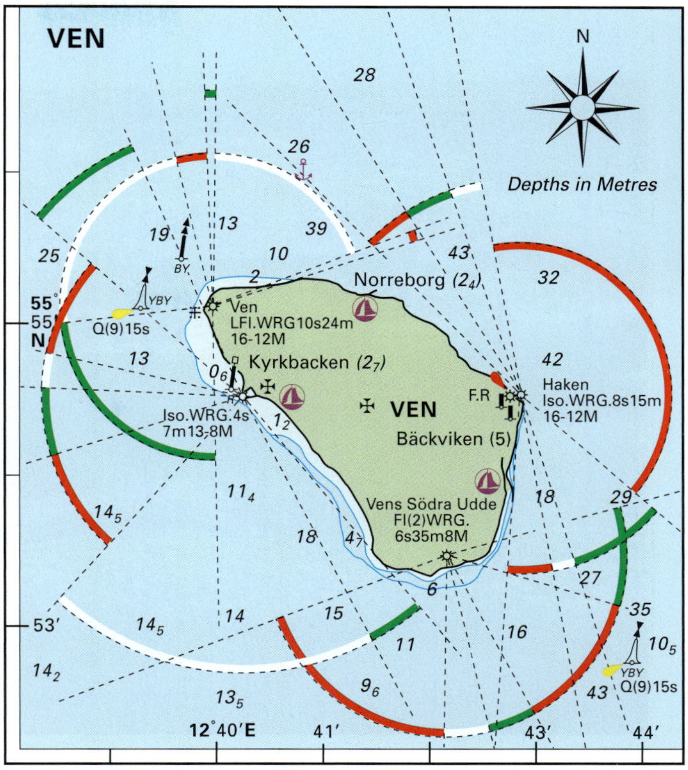


## Ven Island

Ven is a small Swedish island 3M from Landskrona and 4.5M off the Danish coast. It is a pleasant holiday island with two small and one slightly larger harbour. Ven is 2.3M long and 1.3M across, the highest spot being where Tycho Brahe built his castle, Uranienborg, 45m above sea-level. The island slopes from south to north, the new Western Lighthouse at the north western tip being 5m above the sea. Approach is simple from all directions, the only hazards being on the northwest corner of the island which are well-marked by cardinals.

### Kyrkbacken

55°54'.59N 12°.40'.26E (north mole head)

**Contacts**

✆+46 41872400

www.kyrkbacken.se

This is the best of the three harbours for visitors. Depth is 2.7m, and there are said to be 200 berths for visitors, both boxes and alongside, with usual facilities, including fuel. Harbour dues must be paid at the office, under penalty of an extra payment if they have to come to find you! The harbour is popular with Danish boats. There is a café and restaurant (Stures Krog – www.stureskrog.se) and also a small shop. You can rent bikes from the harbour and there is also a swimming beach and BBQ area close to the harbour.

### Norreborg

North coast. This is a small harbour, depth 2m, with minimal facilities and mooring head to quay, stern to a pile or anchor.

### Bäckviken

East coast. This is the main ferry harbour, which brings day visitors to the island from Landskrona. Depth is 2–5m and there are some box moorings, or alongside but the ferry berth must be kept clear. Power is available, but not much else.

Shore facilities include a convenience store and bicycle hire. The Tycho Brahe museum, which was in the past nominated for the 'European Museum of the Year Award', is a must. Here you can follow the famous scientist's life and how his research made Ven a scientific meeting place during the 16th century. There are several other interesting places to visit as well as a golf course and good beaches.

Anchorage is also possible almost anywhere off the island, depending on wind conditions. It may however be necessary to make a precipitate departure in the event of a sudden increase or shift of wind.

Kyrkbacken harbour on the island of Ven *Andy Beharrell*

Råå marina

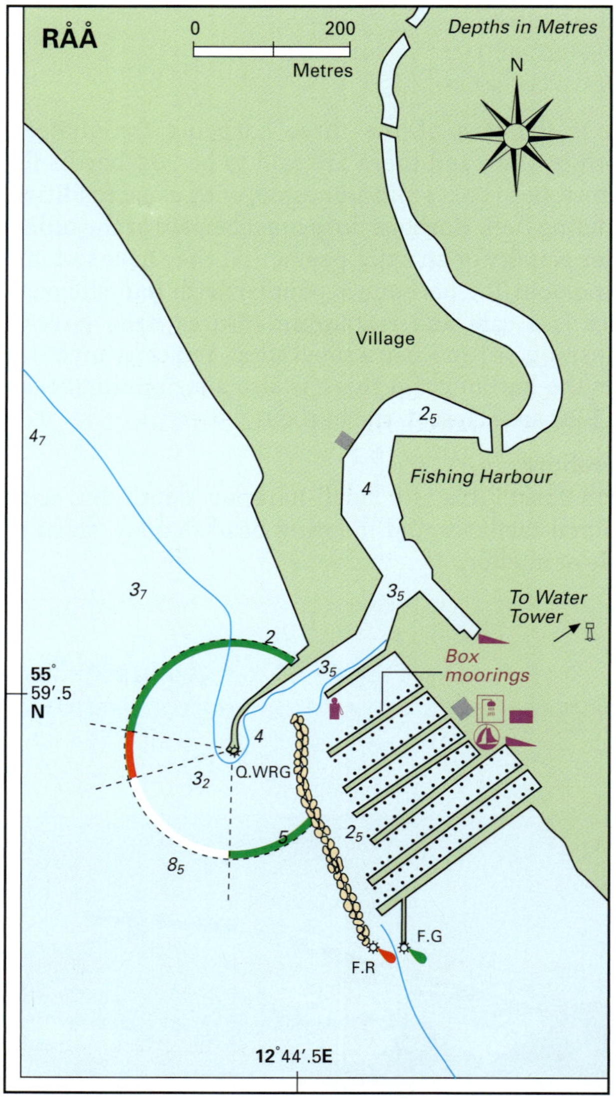


## RÅÅ

55°59'.44N 12°44'.45E (west mole head of northern entrance to marina)

### Distances

Copenhagen 22M, Malmö 29M, Falsterbo Kanal 40M, Stralsund 106M, Göteborg 103M

### Contacts

Råå Port Association
✆+46 42 26 16 35 0900–1300
raa.hamnforening@telia.com

This is an alternative yacht harbour for Helsingborg, about 3.5M south of the main port. Entrance is most easily made at the northern end, which is the mouth of the river Råå. Beware of possible strong currents in the entrance where depth is 3.5-4m and in the harbour is 2.5m. Berths are all between piles with bow to quay. Use any vacant berth, preferably with green tag. Harbour office in fishing harbour is manned 0900-1300.

Ashore it is a pleasant, if unremarkable, small town with a shopping centre close to the yacht haven. Also nearby is the fishing harbour with a fishery and shipping museum. There are several repair yards here and also a chandlery - Hjertmans (www.hjertmans.se/sv). Hjertmans are a sales agent for Elvstrom Sails and may be able to arrange repairs if needed.

## HELSINGBORG (NORRAHAMNEN)

56°03'N 12°41'E

**Distances**

Copenhagen 22M, Malmö 29M, Falsterbo Kanal 40M, Stralsund 106M, Göteborg 103M

**Contacts**

**Harbourmaster** ✆+46 42 21 13 21
www.hyc.se
hamnkapten@hyc.se

This large modern marina is 0.5M north of the main ferry entrance to Helsingborg and a distance of 2.5M across the Sound from Helsingør, and thus offers an alternative, should that popular harbour be overcrowded. All other Helsingborg harbour basins are closed to private yachts. There is an 8T limit on the pontoon berths, but within that limit you can use any vacant berth with a green tag. There are additional berths alongside the East Quay and at the northeast end of the harbour are stern buoys for mooring bows-to the jetty. Depth is stated to be 4m throughout, and maximum beam in the finger moorings is 4.2m. There are 400 guest berths, so you should always be able to find a space. Payment is through tallyweb.dk/norra-hamnen or via a machine outside the harbourmaster's office on the western side of the harbour. This will give access to the facilities in the HYC club building on the western side. Fuel is available from an automatic dispenser near the harbour entrance where there is also a pump-out for holding tanks. There is a good mechanic available in Råå who will come out to Helsingborg in the event of any engine work being required. His name is Patrik Swenson (Råå Marinmekano) ✆+46 70 243 3693.

Ashore, the 1km walk up to the ancient part of the city and the Karnän tower gives a good view over the area from the top. The Fredriksdal open-air museum and gardens are said to be worth a visit. The usual attributes of a major city are available, including a theatre and concert hall close to the marina.

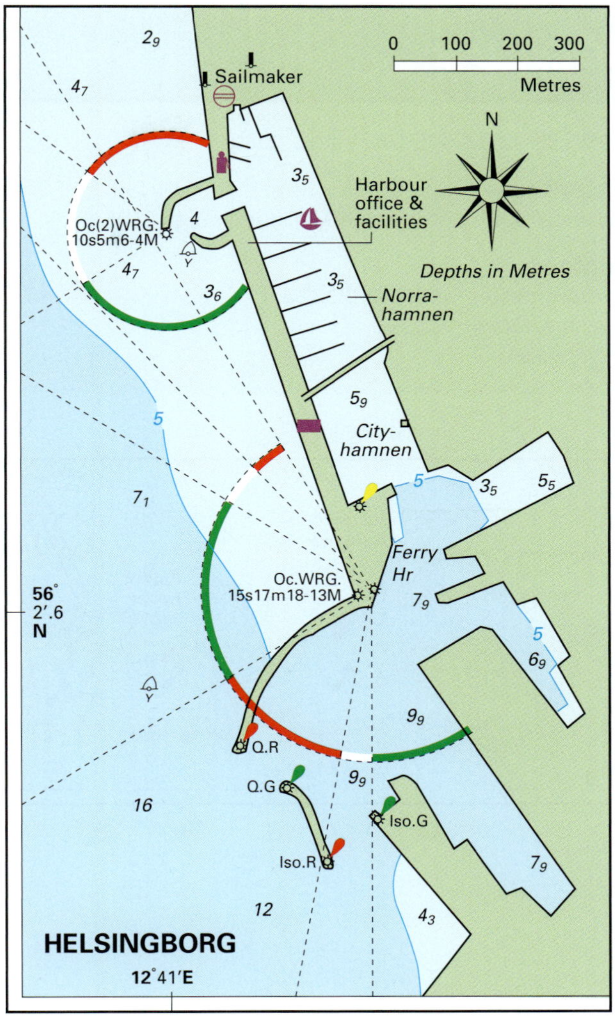

The view of Helsingborg gästhamn from the Karnän tower. Kronborg Slot (Elsinore Castle) is visible across the Sound in the background *Andy Beharrell*

Top: The Swedes at play in Helsingborg *Andy Beharrell*
Bottom: Helsingborg gästhamn looking north *Andy Beharrell*

## HÖGANÄS

56°11'.79N 12°32'.54E (west mole head)

**Distances**
Helsingør 10M, Göteborg 96M, Copenhagen 30M

**Contacts**
**Harbourmaster** ✆+46 42 133322
hamnmastare@hbs.se
www.hbs.se

Höganäs is 7M south-southeast of Kullen Västra Point, the northern entrance to The Sound; a pleasant small town in attractive surroundings with a marina with 2.5m depth and the usual facilities, including fuel and WiFi. Berthing is in box moorings. Use vacant berth with green tag. Öresundsmarin Boatyard has repair facilities. Shore facilities include good bathing close to the harbour, bicycle hire, and local museum. It is possible to fly from Ängelholm (Helsingborg) airport (20km) though one or two changes may be required for London and other destinations, so it may be easier to travel to Copenhagen via Malmö for more choice of direct flights.

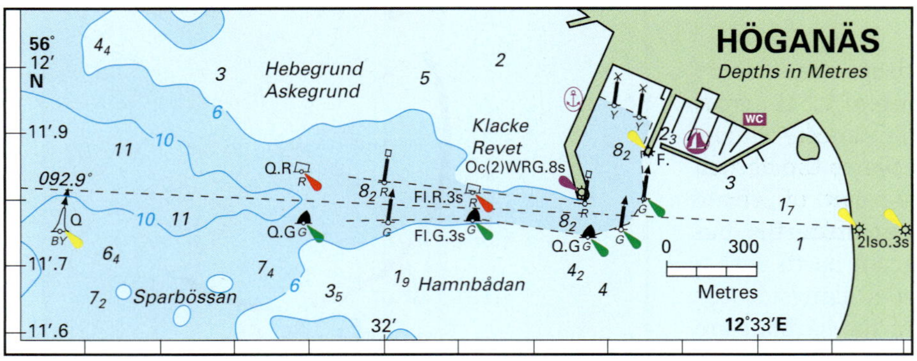

Höganäs harbour

# 2B. SOUTHWEST COAST

The coast between Kullen, at the north end of the Sound, to the frontier with Norway, has two different and distinct aspects. Starting from the south, the coast is low-lying and rather featureless. There is good agricultural land, beaches, golf courses and summer resorts.

The principal towns are Halmstad, the provincial capital of Halland with a population of around 65,000; Falkenberg with a population of around 20,000; and Varberg with a population of about 28,000. All three places are commercial ports.

Then about 25M south of Göteborg, the scenery begins to change from pastoral to rugged and the coast becomes broken and studded with the islands and rocks of the *skärgård* and this continues to the border. The principal geological feature is that of gneiss intermingled with granite which forms extensive rock slabs.

## Kullen to Göteborg

It is important to emphasise that the Kattegat is open water. The distance between the coast of Sweden and that of Jutland to the west varies from between 40–60M. A passage northwards is open to a very long fetch from the Skagerrak and likewise a southwards passage is subject to a long exposure to south or southwest winds. It follows that careful judgement must be made, particularly in unsettled conditions, as to when it is advisable to proceed.

In favourable conditions, a non-stop passage either way between Kullen and the sheltered waters of the *skärgård* south of Göteborg, a distance of some 80M, can be made with ease. But in strong onshore winds, bear in mind that the open coast is liable to be a lee shore and that the approach to some of the harbours may be hazardous. It is also advisable to contact the harbour or marina in advance to check the availability of berths during the busy holiday season.

Surface water travels from the Baltic Sea towards the North Sea but the rate is insignificant, being less than 1kn in the open sea. The tidal range is also of little account being not more than 0.3m in the North Kattegat decreasing towards the south. However, strong winds either from an easterly or a westerly direction may cause the sea level along this coast to fall or rise respectively by as much as 0.9m.

The climate in the Kattegat and more particularly in the Skagerrak can be affected by weather conditions prevailing in the North Atlantic.

Despite the caution given, it would be unreasonable to disregard the coast south of the *skärgård*. There are pleasant harbours for those wishing to break the journey and a selection of these is given below, proceeding from south to north.

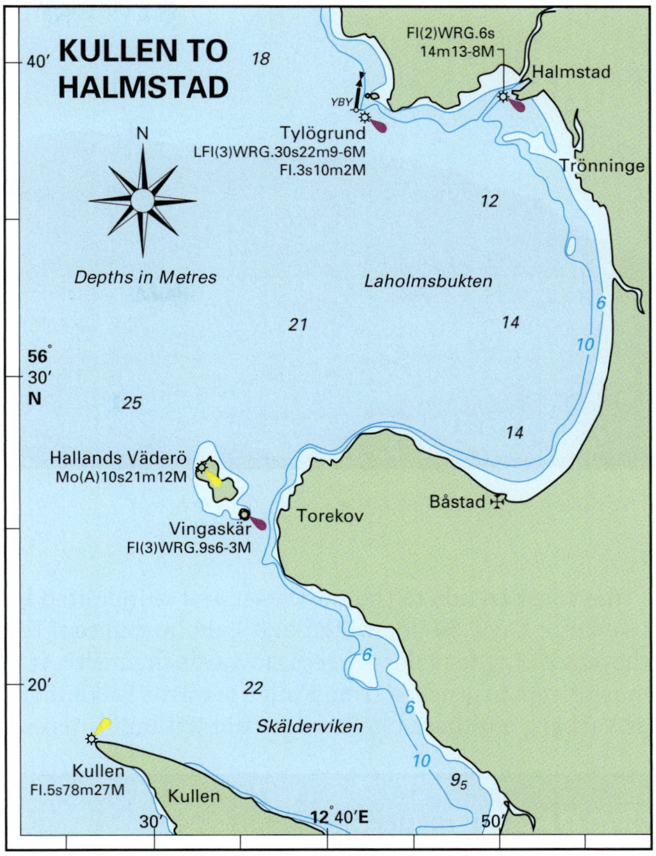

## 1. Kullen to Halmstad

Distance 25M

The promontory of Kullen is high and conspicuous. Approaching from the north it appears at first as an island until low-lying land to the east appears above the horizon. In 1941 the escape of the *Bismarck* from the Baltic was confirmed by the signalling station at Kullen.

The Kullen Peninsula from the south *Andy Beharrell*

Torekov harbour

The coast trends to the northeast and is indented by two large bays, Skälderviken and Laholmsbukten. For those wishing to make progress towards the north, it is more direct to proceed from Kullen towards Falkenberg or Varberg but these two bays are not without interest.

## TOREKOV

56°25'.74N 12°37'58E (north mole head)

**Contacts**
✆+46 431 363 534
info@torekovshamn.se
www.torekovshamn.se/en/

Torekov lies between the two bays and is a convenient place at which to stop, if going south, before rounding Kullen. When approaching the harbour the large white church can be seen from some way away. The harbour has around 20 guest berths. The north wall gives good shelter in box berths, but these are mostly private so you would need to check availability. Dedicated guest berths are in the western part of the harbour alongside the jetties. The northern side of the outermost pontoon is also guest berths (box mooring), but these may be subject to swell in north or northwesterly winds. Berths can be booked in advance through Dockspot on www.dockspot.com/en/docks/606-torekovs-gasthamn.

It is a pretty place but apt to be overcrowded. Diesel is available and there is a pump-out at the end of the jetty. The town has extensive facilities and good shopping. There is an ICA supermarket about 10mins walk from the harbour. Lying offshore is the only island in this part of the coast, Hallands Väderö, a nature reserve with shelter from westerly winds on its eastern side.

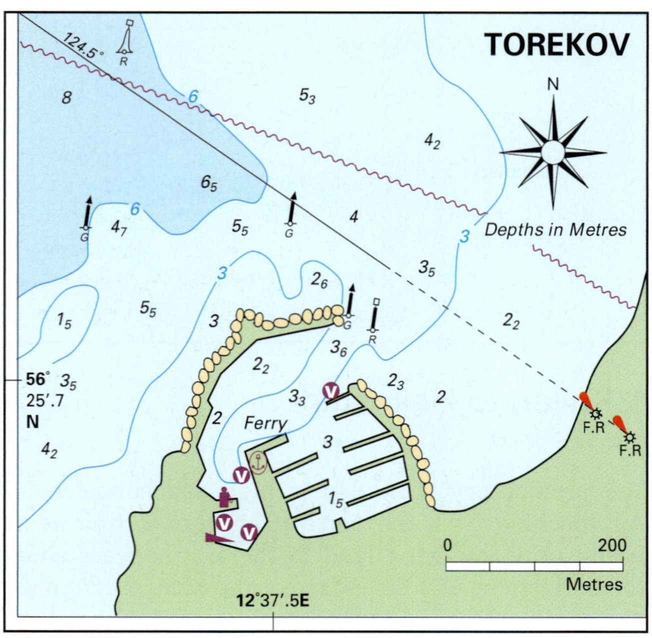


## HALMSTAD

56°38'.91N 12°50'.17E (outer breakwater head)

**Contacts**
Halmstad Segelsällskap
✆+46 760 26 8795
www.hss1910.se
info@hss1910.se
Halmstad Gästhamn
✆+46 70 205 7127
www.bknajaden.se
info@bknajaden.se

In the Middle Ages Halmstad was the largest town on the west coast and was a Danish town until the middle of the 17th century. It lies at the mouth of the River Nissan. The blue/yellow/grey grain silos (73m high) at the port make a conspicuous entrance marker from some way out. A buoyed channel leads into the river where there is shelter from all winds. The main berthing is the BK Najaden gästhamn to starboard on the River Nissan in pleasant surroundings and with good access to the town which has all the facilities expected of a provincial capital. There is some alongside berthing to starboard and after that there are some large Y-booms

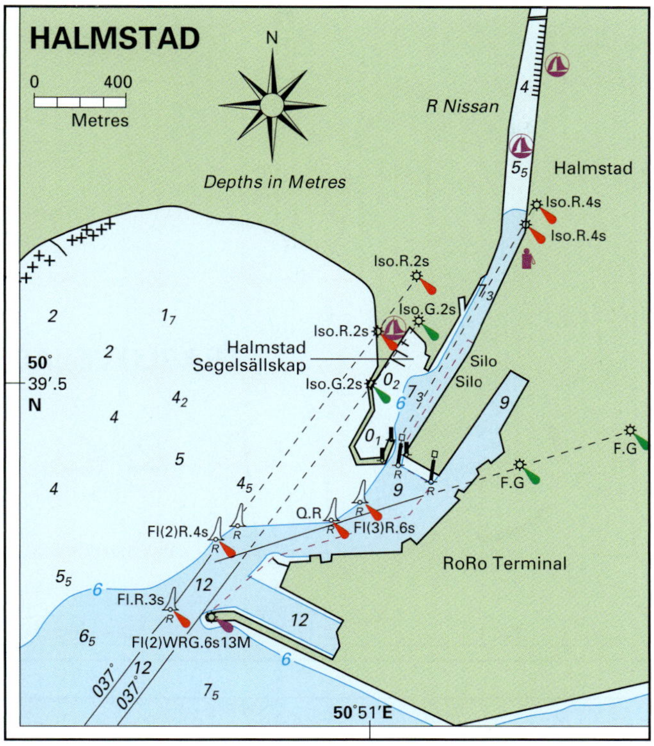


on a fairly high jetty. There may occasionally be some current in the river, so care may be required when berthing.

Payment is online through Tallyweb – tallyweb.dk/bknajaden. This will then give the details for the service building which has a kitchen area as well as showers and toilets.

The other possibility for berthing is Halmstad Segelsällskap port 1km from the city centre. This has 200 guest berths in 2-3m of water, nearly all box berths.

## 2. Halmstad to Varberg

Distance 38M

Leaving Halmstad and after passing Tylögrund lighthouse and the very popular resort of Tylösand, the coast trends in a north westerly direction. With shallow water extending some distance offshore it is advisable to give this stretch of coast a good offing.

## FALKENBERG (FALKENBERG'S BÅTSÄLLSKAP)

56°52'.89N 12°28'E (south breakwater head)

### Contacts

Sailing club ✆+46 34 68 41 24 (evenings only)
www.falkenbergs-batsallskap.se

Falkenberg is around 15M southeast of Varberg and 17M north of Halmstad and is a useful stopping place at the mouth of the river Atran. Protected by a series of moles and breakwaters there is good shelter and

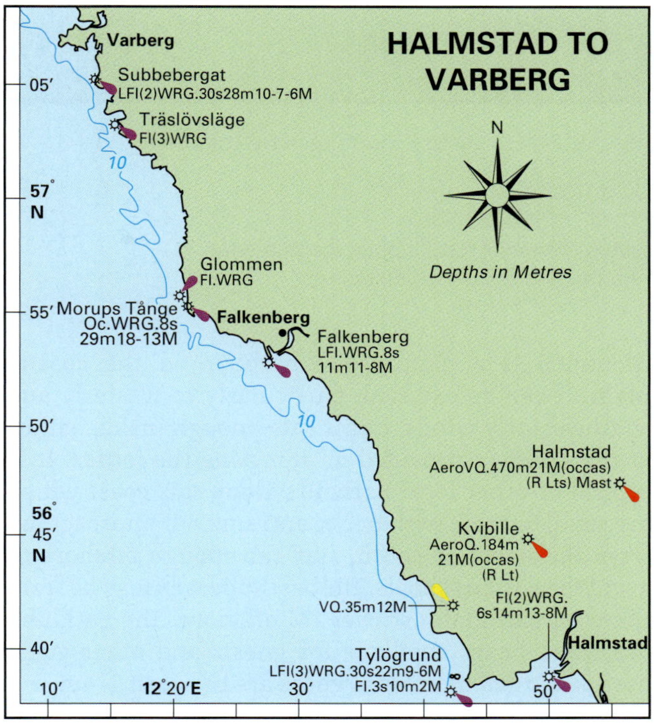


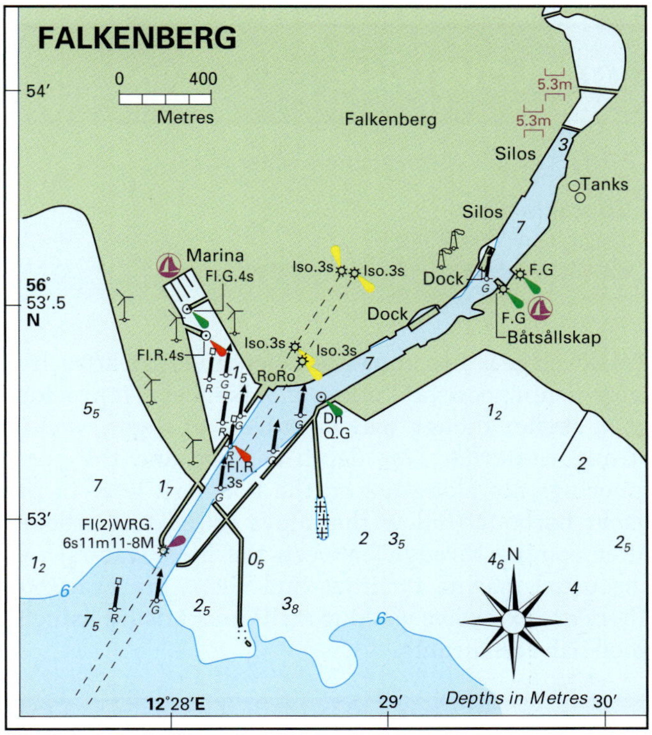


protection from any westerly swell caused by gales from the west or southwest. Berthing is available at Falkenberg's Båtsällskap in the river on the south side. There are 50 guest box berths in depths of 2.5m. There may be appreciable current from the river in certain conditions and it may be dangerous to approach or leave the port in the event of strong onshore winds.

Falkenberg is renowned as a food destination and has a vibrant restaurant scene. The tourist information office in town (Holgersgatan 7, 311 35 Falkenberg – www.falkenberg.se/en/) will be able to point you in the right direction.

## GLOMMEN

56°55'.74N 12°20'89E (north breakwater head)

**Contacts**
✆+46 07 9075 5725
www.glommensbatklubb.se/gasthamnen/
kontakt@glommensbatklubb.se

Glommen is a picturesque harbour on the coastal plain. It can be exposed, particularly to westerly and southwesterly winds, but is safe enough inside, either at the pontoon provided or alongside the jetties. It is typical of other local harbours along this coast which are small but safe with tricky entrances. If approaching from the north or south, stay far enough offshore to avoid the various shoals. The best approach may be from the west cardinal just over 1M offshore. The båtklubb has three boxes available for guests and other guest berths marked in green. Depths are between 2–4m.

Close to the harbour are cafés and restaurants with other facilities available if you walk into town.

## TRÄSLÖVSLÄGE

57°03'.43N 12°16'E (south breakwater head)

**Contacts**
Sailing club ✆+46 340 67 07 07
www.traslovslagesbatklubb.se/batgast

Träslövsläge is also known as Läjets and is an attractive large fishing port 14M north of Falkenberg. It provides good shelter though may be subject to slight swell in strong westerlies. The depth is 2·4m and the guest moorings are alongside on the northern jetty in the yacht harbour (follow the buoys round to starboard after coming through between the breakwaters). All the usual marina facilities and shops are available. There are extensive walking trails and, unsurprisingly, good fish restaurants.

## VARBERG

57°06'.47N 12°13'.9E (south outer breakwater head)

**Contacts**
Yacht club ✆+46 70 528 8529
www.varberg.se/trafikinfrastruktur/hamn/gasthamn
gasthamn@varberg.se
www.visitvarberg.se

This historic town and spa built in the 17th century and dominated by a medieval fortress, is worth a visit. It is charming and has a wide selection of shops plus a vibrant café life. It is one of the most important harbours in Sweden for the export of timber. There is a ferry connection to Grenå in Denmark. On entering, a marina lies to port on Getterön. This has little connection to the town so yachts wanting to visit Varberg town should go to the inner harbour (innerhamnen) on the starboard side (57°06'.7N, 12°14'.54E – mole head behind which is the visitors' harbour). The innerhamnen is a pleasant and often busy harbour with around 50 guest berths in

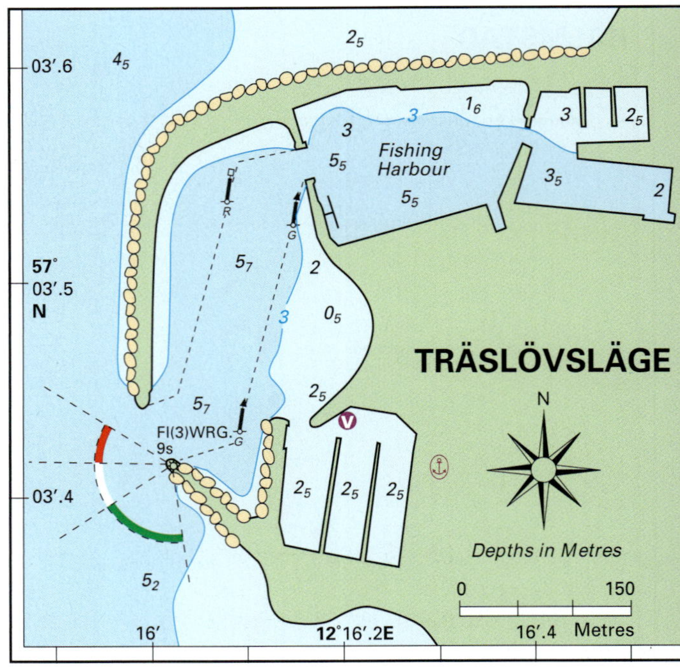


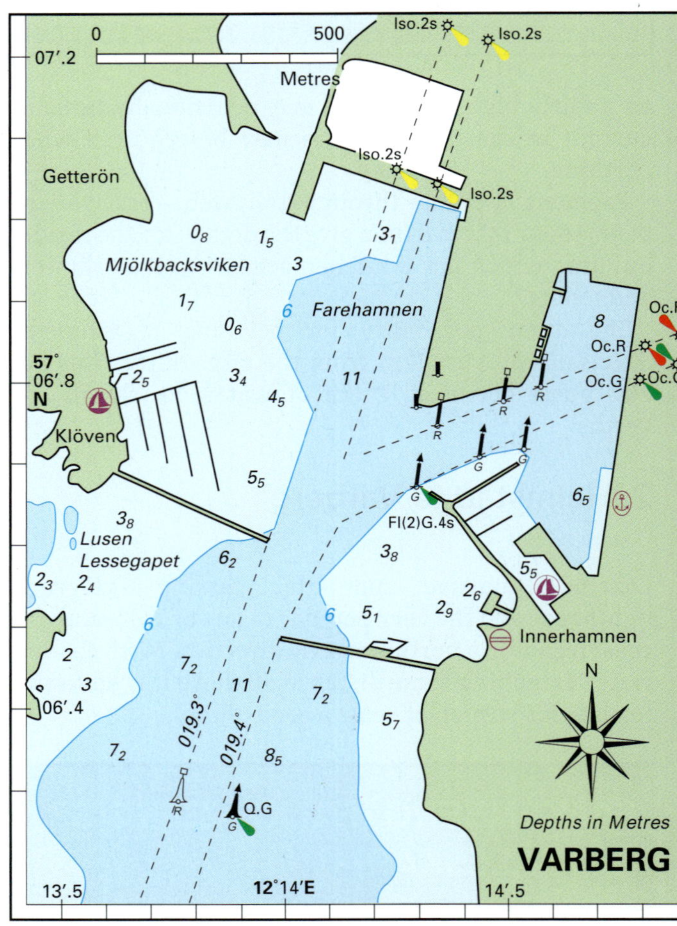

Varberg marina and innerhamnen, looking southeast

depths ranging between 3m and 5.5m. Most berthing here is alongside, but rafting up is likely to be required, particularly during unsettled weather when a number of yachts may be waiting to make a passage north or south. Some berths (green signs) may also be found inside the first mole protecting the inner harbour. Payment is made through a machine outside the harbour office. Varberg is arguably the best halfway house between the Sound and Göteborg. It is also a good landfall when crossing the Kattegat from the Limfjord (distance approximately 60M). In clear weather, the fortress is visible 15M from seaward and the Grimeton aero light tower can be seen from over 20M away.

Varberg Fortress was built between 1287–1300 and then expanded to include a castle in the 14th century. The fortress is now a museum and one of the more unusual exhibits is a lead-filled brass button that is claimed by some to be the projectile that killed Charles XII of Sweden.

## 3. Varberg to Göteborg (Långedrag)

Distance 40M

North of Varberg the character of the scenery begins to change and the first of many natural harbours is to be found. The channel proceeds northwards on a well-marked passage south of Malö and inside (east of) the lights at Lilleland (57°18'.37N 11°56'.62E), Hallands Svartskär (57°22'.42N 11°51'.35E) and Kungen (57°26'.93N 11°49'.88E). Abeam Tistlarna (57°30'.56N 11°43'.57E – position of the Lighthouse on Tistlarna), the *skärgård* is entered with protection from the west and in another 12M the main channel into the port of Göteborg is reached.

## Malö anchorages

For the north bound traveller, the bays just north of Malö will be the first experience of the scenery which will prevail in various forms thereafter. There are two possible anchorages. Skallahamn gives shelter in moderate depths apart from the risk of swell in strong south westerly winds. To the west of Skallahamn a snug anchorage is to be found between Hästholmen and Mönster. However, in these places, as generally on this coast, the quality of the holding ground cannot be relied upon.

The inner harbour at Varberg looking southeast *Andy Beharrell*

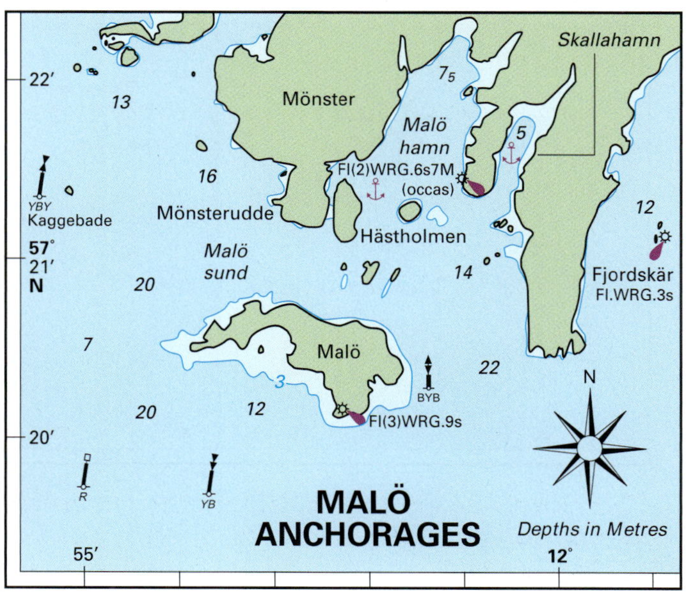

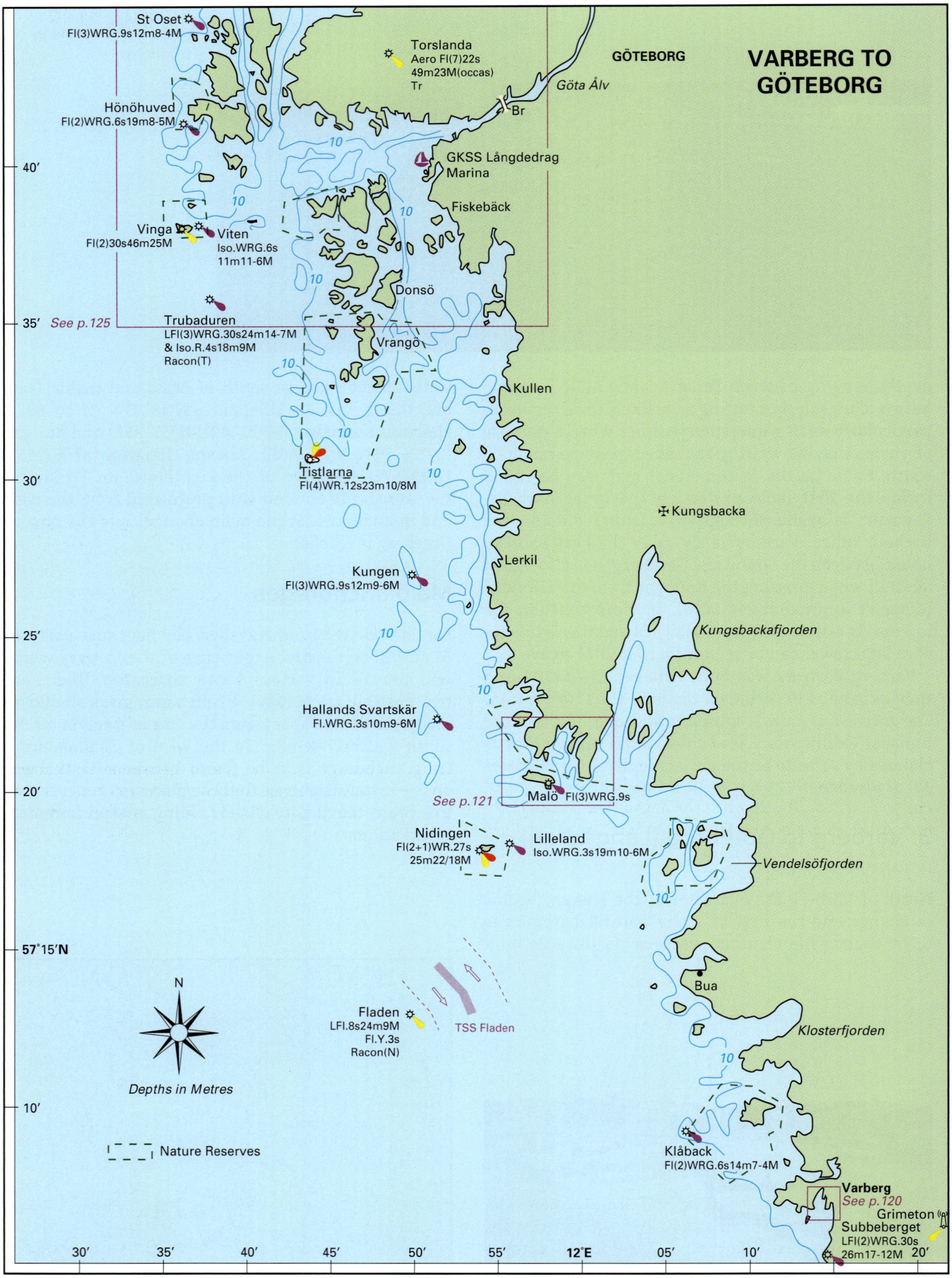
VARBERG TO GÖTEBORG
GÖTEBORG
Göta Älv
Br
St Oset
Fl(3)WRG.9s12m8-4M
Torslanda
Aero Fl(7)22s
49m23M(occas)
Tr
Hönöhuved
Fl(2)WRG.6s19m8-5M
GKSS Långdedrag
Marina
Fiskebäck
Vinga
Fl(2)30s46m25M
Viten
Iso.WRG.6s
11m11-6M
Donsö
Trubaduren
LFl(3)WRG.30s24m14-7M
& Iso.R.4s18m9M
Racon(T)
See p.125
Vrangö
Kullen
Tistlarna
Fl(4)WR.12s23m10/8M
Kungsbacka
Lerkil
Kungen
Fl(3)WRG.9s12m9-6M
Kungsbackafjorden
Hallands Svartskär
Fl.WRG.3s10m9-6M
See p.121
Malö
Fl(3)WRG.9s
Nidingen
Fl(2+1)WR.27s
25m22/18M
Lilleland
Iso.WRG.3s19m10-6M
Vendelsöfjorden
Bua
Fladen
LFl.8s24m9M
Fl.Y.3s
Racon(N)
TSS Fladen
Klosterfjorden
N
Depths in Metres
Nature Reserves
Klåback
Fl(2)WRG.6s14m7-4M
Varberg
See p.120
Grimeton
Subbeberget
LFl(2)WRG.30s
26m17-12M
40′
35′
30′
25′
20′
57°15′N
10′
30′
35′
40′
45′
50′
55′
12°E
05′
10′
20′

Lerkil marina

## LERKIL

57°27'.32N 11°54'.81E (outer mole head)

**Contacts**
**Harbourmaster** ✆+46 30 02 79 39
www.lerkil.net
hamnchef@lerkil.net

The last harbour before the shelter of the *skärgård*, Lerkil is a sizeable yacht harbour which gives good shelter, although the entrance may be difficult in strong north westerly winds. The depth at the harbour entrance is 4m and at the guest berths is between 2.5–3m. Berths are in Y-booms or alongside. There are reasonable facilities (water, electricity and toilets) and a pump-out on the end of the jetty as you enter the harbour.

There is a good bus service to Gothenburg from here.

## DONSÖ

57°36'.06N 11°47.51E

**Contacts**
**Harbourmaster** ✆+46 704 221 222
www.donsohamn.se
donso@donsohamn.se

Approach to Donsö is straightforward from the south. From the north an 8.6m bridge restricts access. On rounding the breakwater the gästhamn is three pontoons immediately to starboard. Berthing is alongside. A fourth pontoon is available on the east side just to the south of the ferry jetty. The harbour says that it can take 100 boats (but 50–70 may be more accurate in season) and it is possible to use other berths if marked in green. The depth throughout is 4.5–5m.

Donsö has around 1,500 permanent residents and while much of the island is housing, there are still nice walking areas particularly at the northern and southern extremities of the island. Fourteen shipping companies and a number of major fishing vessels are based on the island. The founder of the Stena ferry company – Sten A Olsson – grew up on the island.

The service house with toilets, showers, rubbish disposal and a washing machine (but no dryer) is at the southwest end of the harbour, just a short walk from the guest pontoons. There is also the Isbolaget. This was once the ice warehouse for the fishing fleet, but is now a restaurant and hotel. The island is car-free and most residents have small two-seater golf cart style vehicles.

Fuel is available on the western side of the entrance breakwater, level with the southern end of the harbour.

Donsö Island looking south. Guest berths to starboard on entering *John Sadd*

Aerial view of Donsö harbour, looking north. The guest berths are on the left furthest from the camera *Andy Beharrell*

## GÖTEBORG (GOTHENBURG)

57°41'N 11°50'E

### Distances

Arkosund 210M (390km) by inland waterway, Stockholm 350M (650km) by road, Copenhagen 130M

### Lights

**Trubaduren** 57°35'.7N 11°38'E LFl(3)WRG.30s24m14–7M Racon Helipad
Iso.R.18m9M Black tower, orange top, on grey base 25m
**Buskärs Knöte** 57°38'.3N 11°41'.1E Fl(3)WRG.9s12m7–4M Racon Orange tower 12m Floodlit
**Vasskärsgrund** 57°39'.2N 11°43'.4E VQ(8).WR.8s11m13–10M Racon Red tower, white top, red roof on grey plinth 12m
**Gäveskär** 57°39'.7N 11°46'.1E QR.10m4M White tower 10m Floodlit but obscured
**No. 29 Channel Marker** 57°40'.7N 11°48'.9E Fl(2)G.6s

### Contacts

Göteborg Port Control ✆+46 313 68 75 15,
VHF Ch 16; 12 (24hrs)
www.portgot.se
info@portgot.se
VTS Göteborg ✆+46 771 63 06 60,
VHF Ch 16; 13 (24hrs)
Marieholmsbron and Göta Älvbron bridges
VHF Ch 9 (24hrs)
Lilla Bommen Marina
**Harbourmaster** ✆+46 31 126667
info@goteborgsgasthamn.se
GKSS Långedrag Marina
✆+46 31 2990 40
hamnvakten@gkss.se
www.gkss.se/en

Among the islands of the *skärgård* are many harbours, both natural and artificial, particularly in the vicinity of Vrangö, Donsö, Styrsö and Brannö. It was in the roadstead north of these islands that a Royal Navy fleet, commanded by Admiral Sir James Saumarez in HMS *Victory*, was stationed for several years after 1808, guarding the British Baltic convoy system. The enterprising yachtsman can spend a leisurely time exploring the various nooks and crannies of the archipelago but, owing to the vicinity of Göteborg, the guest harbours are apt to be very busy. Apart from Vrangö, the islands mentioned above are within the commuter belt of Göteborg and frequent ferry traffic can create a disturbing wash.

## General

Göteborg is the second largest city in Sweden and is a working port with a wide and busy river – the Göta älv. The city is friendly and vibrant with much to offer both culturally and recreationally. Much of it is very attractive, with many fine buildings, canals and tree-lined avenues in the downtown area, good shops, and many excellent restaurants.

Overlooking the central (Lilla Bommen) marina is the impressive opera house and, a few hundred metres downriver, the aquarium and Göteborg Maritime Centre, whose moored museum ships are claimed to form the largest floating maritime museum in the world. The Natural History Museum is situated at Slottsskogen, and further out (about 25mins by tram from the city centre) are the Liseberg Amusement Park with its huge funfair and the nearby Universeum, an environmental museum.

Visitors generally use either Lilla Bommen Hamnen, referred to above, or the Royal Göteborg Yacht Club (Göteborgs Kungliga Segel Sällskap or GKSS) Långedrag marina some 5M further downstream on the southern shore.

The Port of Göteborg maintains an interesting website at www.portofgothenburg.com.

### *Approach & entrance*

From the sea the main approach channel from the southwest, leaving the Trubaduren tower to port, is wide, well buoyed and, where necessary, dredged. The charts note that small craft should avoid the north and south channels and use the small craft fairway to the south of the south channel. The main hazard for yachts is likely to be large commercial traffic. Other channels (all shown clearly on BA 858) lead in from northwest, west and south. All these channels converge south of the prominent Knippelholmen tower to continue up the Älvsborgsfjorden into the city centre. The Älvsborgsbron road bridge (clearance 45m), which lies some 2.5M east of the towers, is conspicuous from well out to sea. Sailing is forbidden east of the bridge, though motor-sailing is permitted, and all moored ships must be given at least 25m clearance.

The Lilla Bommen marina lies on the starboard hand about 250m short of the opening Hisingbron bridge

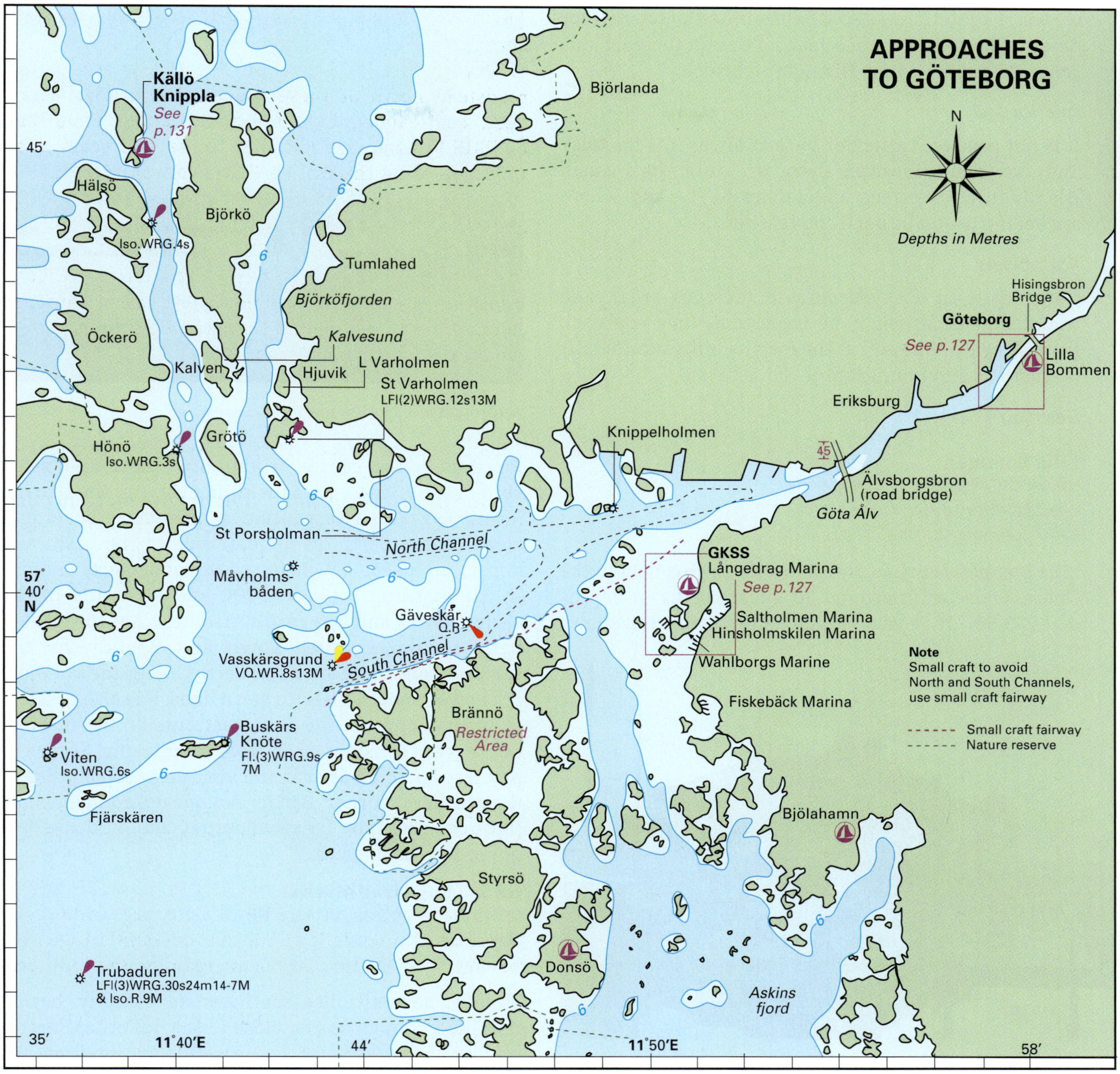


(closed 12m or 28m open), the entrance conveniently marked by a most distinctive red and white building (see photo on page 126). The square-rigged sailing ship *Viking* lies close by. It is now a hotel and restaurant.

If arriving from the canal system inland via the Göta Älv, the conurbation starts several miles upstream. Notice of imminent arrival is heralded by a rail bridge (swing bridge), the Marieholmsbron (clearance 5.9m). Opening times are displayed on a LED board. Just 1.3M further downstream is the massive Hisingbron bridge (vertical clearance, closed 12m, open 28m) which opens on request VHF Ch 9 or ✆+46 730 27 72 72. See

Nya Älvsborg Fortress on the north side of the approach channel to Göteborg shortly before the Älvsborgsbron bridge
*Andy Beharrell*

www.trafikgoteborg.se/sa-oppnas-broarna/ for further details. The Lilla Bommen marina lies on the port side some 250m beyond the Hisingbron bridge.

### *Anchorage*

It is not possible to anchor in Gota älv as it is too busy and crowded. However there are numerous small islands in the western approaches to the city where anchoring would be perfectly feasible.

### *Formalities*

Göteborg is in a skyddsområde (defence area), and yachts may occasionally be boarded as they approach from seaward. Enquire at the marina offices for details of Customs and Immigration.

Approach to Lilla Bommen *M. Lewin-Harris*

### *Berthing*

#### Lilla Bommen

☎+46 31 15 40 05
www.goteborgsgasthamn.se
info@goteborgsgasthamn.se

Lilla Bomnen is primarily a visitor's marina next to the Opera House with around 70 guest berths in depths of 1.2–3·5m. It is very popular due to its convenient location in the centre of the city. The four-masted ship – the *Viking* – helps with identifying the marina location. Enter with caution as passenger boats and small ferries berth on the east side of the basin and depart at speed. Movements are particularly intense in the morning between 0900 and 0930 and in the early evening and may result in some wash. The marina basin should be exited slowly and carefully for the same reason. There are a few berths alongside but most are bows to pontoons with stern lines. It is also possible to moor alongside the quay just outside the marina, but there is constant wash from river traffic. Secure in any free berth on arrival and visit the marina office at the southeast corner. Berths can be booked in advance through Dockspot (www.dockspot.com/en/docks/114-goteborgs-gasthamn).

GKSS Långedrag Marina *Nicholas Torsteinsrud-Smith*

#### GKSS Långedrag Marina

☎+46 703 39 93 98, VHF Ch 68
www.gkss.se
hamnvakten@gkss.se

Situated several miles southwest of the city, beside the GKSS clubhouse and close to several other, larger, private yacht harbours. Its peaceful surroundings are

GKSS Långedrag Marina – several miles southwest of Göteborg

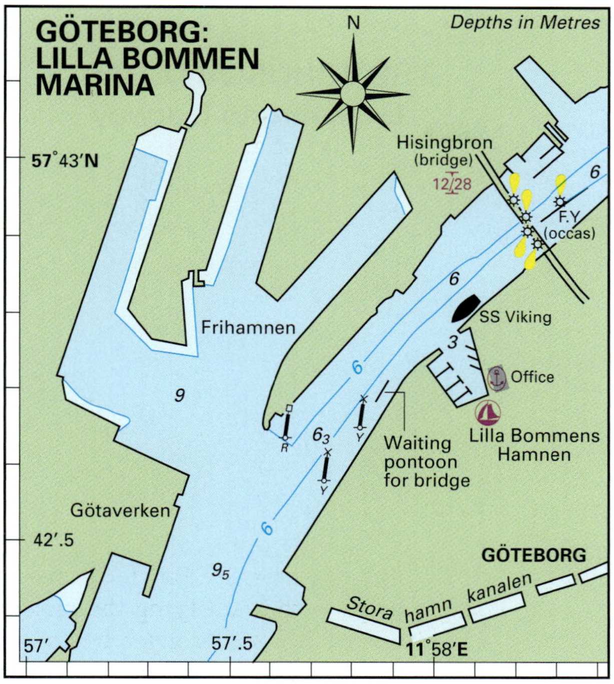


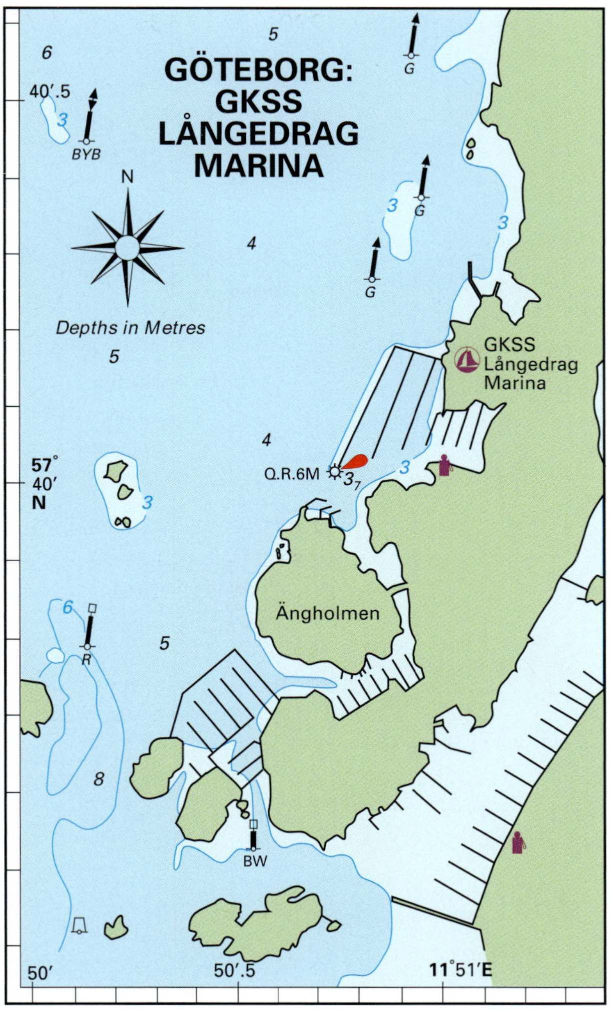


connected to the city by a 40min tram ride - interesting in itself. There are 550 permanent berths and although none are specifically reserved for visitors, there are green signs for berths which are available for visitors. Berthing is in boxes and the marina has 3-4m depth throughout. The berthing fee can be paid using the GoMarina app or using the automatic machine at the GKSS clubhouse.

### Services

The Lilla Bommen marina complex offers the usual showers, toilets and launderette, plus cafés, shops and a small chandlery in the office building. There is water and electricity to all berths.

The GKSS Långedrag marina has water and electricity to all berths, with laundry facilities at the GKSS clubhouse and a small shop close by. A weather forecast is updated daily. The yacht club is friendly, with a pleasant clubhouse and several good restaurants nearby.

Ask at Lilla Bommen marina office for the nearest available outlets of diesel, petrol and bottled gas. The nearest diesel pump to the GKSS Långedrag marina is at Wahlborgs Marine (open 0900-1700 weekdays, 1000-1400 weekends), on the south side of Saltholmen island. Bottled gas is available at the GKSS Långedrag marina, and both have facilities for emptying holding tanks.

There is a boatyard with travel-lift and engineers at the GKSS Långedrag marina. For electronic or radio repairs at either marina ✆+46 31 69 51 00 or 90 96 00, and for sail repairs ✆+46 31 29 00 21 or 29 11 52. Charts, sailing directions and books are available from Nautic AB, Fiskebäcks Hamn 35B, 426 58 Västra Frölunda (www.nautic-center.se), ✆+46 31 10 08 85.

### Facilities

From Lilla Bommen marina it is only a short distance to the Nordstan shopping mall with banks, supermarkets, delicatessen, bookshops, Systembolaget etc., with the city's train and bus terminals a short distance beyond. Cafés and restaurants abound, many with views out over the river. The Cityakuten hospital ✆+46 31 10 10 10, is about 1km away.

If moored at the GKSS Långedrag marina and intent on major shopping, ride two stops on the tram to the Konsum supermarket (open 0900-2200), with a bank with cash machine located about 400m beyond.

### Communications & travel

The proximity of Lilla Bommen marina to the city's bus and train stations makes it particularly convenient for crew arrival or departure. The Långedrag marina is served by trams, which run to the city centre (about 40mins). In addition, taxis or car hire are easily arranged. Göteborg's Landvetter International Airport is some 25km east of the city, while the City Airport is about 20km to the north, both with good bus connections. Passenger ferries from Denmark and Germany visit the port regularly.

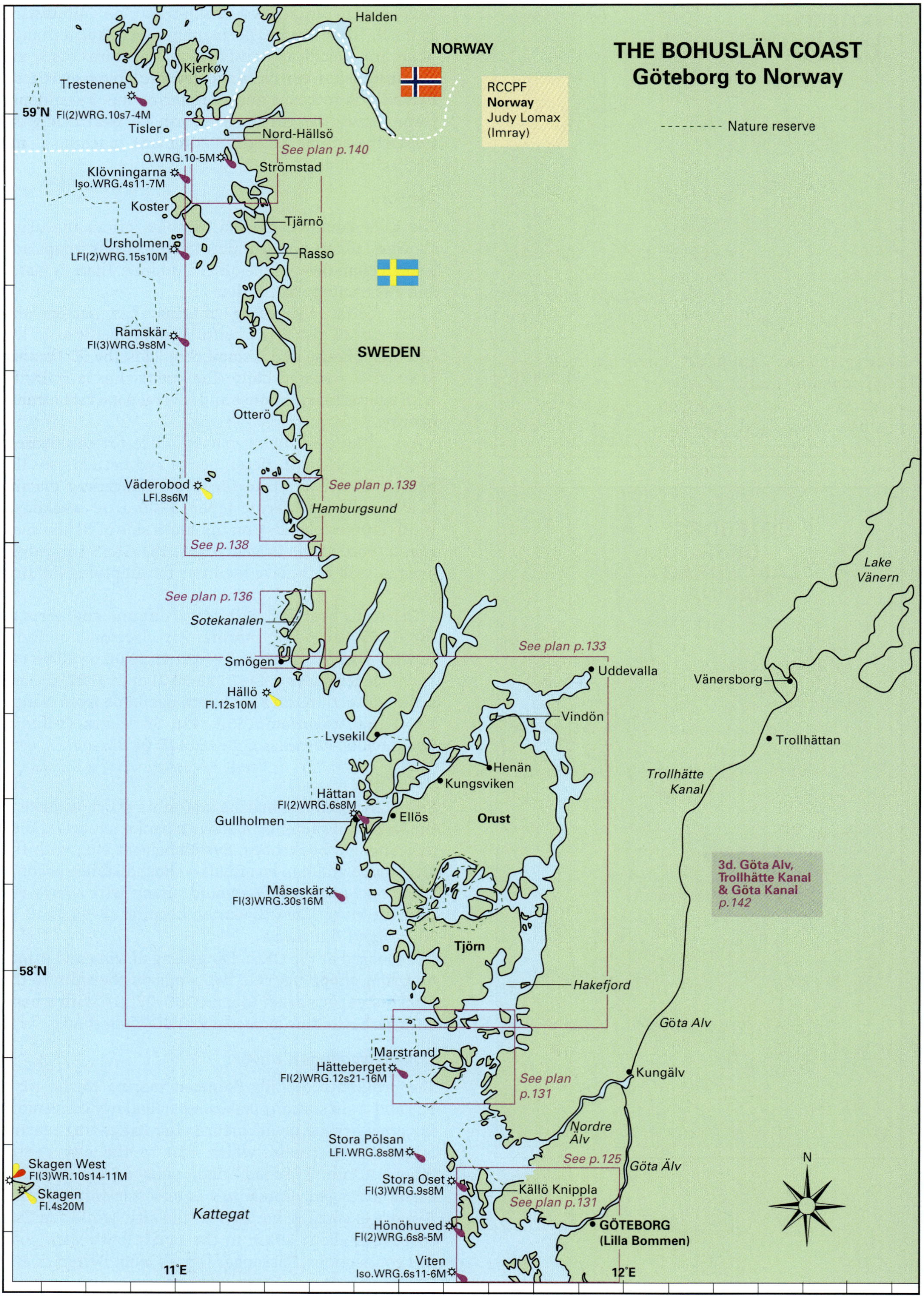
THE BOHUSLÄN COAST
Göteborg to Norway
RCCPF
Norway
Judy Lomax
(Imray)
Nature reserve
NORWAY
SWEDEN
Halden
Kjerkøy
Trestenene
Fl(2)WRG.10s7-4M
59°N
Tisler
Nord-Hällsö
See plan p.140
Q.WRG.10-5M
Strömstad
Klövningarna
Iso.WRG.4s11-7M
Koster
Tjärnö
Ursholmen
LFl(2)WRG.15s10M
Rasso
Ramskär
Fl(3)WRG.9s8M
Otterö
Väderobod
LFl.8s6M
See plan p.139
Hamburgsund
See p.138
See plan p.136
Sotekanalen
Smögen
See plan p.133
Uddevalla
Vänersborg
Lake Vänern
Hällö
Fl.12s10M
Vindön
Lysekil
Trollhättan
Henän
Kungsviken
Trollhätte Kanal
Hättan
Fl(2)WRG.6s8M
Gullholmen
Ellös
Orust
3d. Göta Alv, Trollhätte Kanal & Göta Kanal p.142
Måseskär
Fl(3)WRG.30s16M
Tjörn
58°N
Hakefjord
Göta Alv
Marstrand
Hätteberget
Fl(2)WRG.12s21-16M
See plan p.131
Kungälv
Nordre Älv
Stora Pölsan
LFl.WRG.8s8M
See p.125
Göta Älv
Skagen West
Fl(3)WR.10s14-11M
Skagen
Fl.4s20M
Stora Oset
Fl(3)WRG.9s8M
Källö Knippla
See plan p.131
N
Kattegat
Hönöhuved
Fl(2)WRG.6s8-5M
GÖTEBORG
(Lilla Bommen)
Viten
Iso.WRG.6s11-6M
11°E
12°E

# 2C. THE BOHUSLÄN COAST – NORTHWEST COAST

## Göteborg to the Norwegian border

This 80M stretch of coast between Göteborg and the Norwegian border, known as the Bohuslän Coast, is a highly attractive and interesting cruising ground. There are over 8,000 islands and skerries and the area also includes the Kosterhavet National Marine Park. The area is deservedly popular, especially for Norwegians sailing south or east from their bases in Oslofjorden or on the southeast coast. Although the Skagerrak can be very rough in strong southwesterly weather, virtually the whole distance can be sailed inside the relative shelter of the *skärgård*. In lighter weather winds can be fickle and a number of places are too narrow to sail.

It was originally settled by hunters and communication between settlements was by sea. Until the middle of the 17th century, it was part of Norway and this is reflected in place names and the local dialect. In time fishing became an important industry and fishing villages were settled up and down the coast. Fishing still has a significant role but many of the houses in picturesque places have become holiday homes. Religion has played an important part in local life, and was strongly influenced by the early 19th-century Calvinist clergyman Henric Schartau (who believed that closed curtains were a sign of sin within, with the result that many houses are still curtain free) and there are many beautiful and striking churches dating from the early 1800s to the early 20th century.

There are useful landfalls for those approaching from the North Sea across the Skagerrak. The coastline of pink Nordic granite is rather reminiscent of the Åland Islands, albeit a little higher, with the smattering of houses in the south slowly giving way to trees as one approaches Norway.

### *Coast & harbours*

The main towns, apart from Göteborg (population 637,000), are Uddevalla (population 57,000), Lysekil (population 7,300) and Strömstad (population 13,200). There are many sizeable villages or small towns of which the most notable is Marstrand, a well-known centre for sailing.

There are some 65 gästhamns listed in the *Gästhamns Guiden* and innumerable anchorages in the many fjords and sounds. To do justice to these would require a book on its own, so this one is confined to a few suggested places to allow a leisurely transit of the coast. It must be emphasised that the use of the largest available scale of chart is advisable for anything other than a purely offshore passage. Minimal tidal differences make for easy bows-to mooring or anchoring.

In season supplies and services are plentiful but before June and after the middle of August a little more planning is required as many of the smaller harbours may then close their facilities, particularly restaurants and fuel points.

During the season, and particularly at weekends, the coast (including the islands) is likely to be very crowded. This is a route south for Norwegians and Göteborg's maritime playground with thousands of holiday or weekend cottages all of which seem to have their own mooring or ready access to small marinas.

Typical Bohuslän fishermans' huts *Nicholas Torsteinsrud-Smith*

*Routes north*

To go north from Göteborg (see plan on page 125) there is a choice of routes, all clearly marked on both UKHO chart 858 and the Båtsportkort B. For the most direct and shortest route, leave the main ships' channel out of Göteborg after red channel buoy No. 20 and head on a northwest course leaving Skaddan to starboard with Måvholmnsskaren to port. Then pass south of Stora Porsholmen and between Stora Varholmen and Lilla Varholmen. This brings one to the Öckerö archipelago, and, if taking the passage on between Kalven and Grötö, beware of unmarked outlying rocks, some awash, particularly on the south side. The Kalvesund channel leading north-northwest is narrow, but clearly marked. This group of 10 notable islands and numerous islets is less than half an hour by car from the centre of Göteborg and readily accessible by all kinds of boats and ferry, so it is not surprising that in places there is no space for any more houses or boats. There are ten gästhamns many of which will still give you a feel for this wild and magnificent Bohus countryside. For the more adventurous, a detour some 8M west-southwest of Långedrag to Vinga, or 6M west to Fotö, may be considered. Each is typical in its way of the multitude of small island communities or uninhabited havens for which this part of the coast is renowned.

## Vinga

57°37'.89N 11°36'.6 (east breakwater head)

Vinga is a tiny, isolated harbour between two rocky islets. It is notable for its distinctive lighthouse and its associations with the celebrated Swedish singer/songwriter Evert Taube, who grew up here. Informal and popular concerts are held during the season – with consequent pressure on the limited available berths, so it may be worth checking for events in advance.

Narrow approaches from either east or west. Bows-to mooring on wooden quays or alongside stone pier. Basic facilities only. No provisions.

Fotö harbour *Nicholas Torsteinsrud-Smith*

## Fotö

57°39'.97N 11°39'.27E (outside harbour entrance)

Fotö is a typical small island harbour with guest berths for visiting yachts. It is connected by bridge to adjacent Hönö but retains a calm atmosphere and areas of barren rock to seaward. Mooring is on either side of the entrance alongside the mole or wooden pier. Limited facilities. The closest provisions are available c.3km away on Hönö.

## Källö-Knippla

57°44'.9N 11°39'.3E (southeast outer harbour limit)

**Contacts**
➁+46 70 656 3767
www.knippla.se/gasthamn
info@knipplahamn.se

Aerial view of Vinga *L.G.foto/Wikimedia Commons (https://commons.wikimedia.org/wiki/File:0523Vinga.jpg)*

Källö-Knippla harbour *Viv Fox*

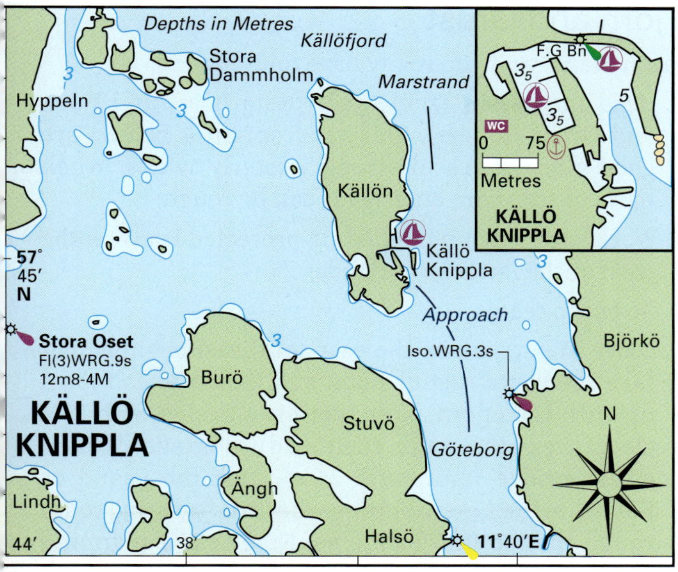


# MARSTRAND

57°53′N 11°35′.2E (off southern mole head)

**Contacts**

Harbour office ☎+46 70 346 9901
hamnkontoret@kungalv.se
www.marstrandsgasthamn.se/en

Typical gästhamn in Ökeröarna. There is an inner and outer basin to the gästhamn and guest berths are available in both. There are over 120 guest berths in depths of between 3.5–5m. Mooring is a mixture of stern buoys, and alongside the quay in the inner basin.

Just 14M from the Lilla Bommen marina or 9M from the GKSS. Easily entered on a leading line from the south and just off the main route from Göteborg to Marstrand. There are ample facilities for an overnight stop amid attractive, traditional Bohus houses. The village was originally built on the herring trade but is now a popular tourist spot.

This is a Mecca of west coast Swedish yachting, situated only 12M north of Källö-Knippla. The most attractive route is from the southeast through the narrow Albrektssunds kanal. Also there are well-buoyed entries from the open sea on the west and northwest. The town was founded in the 13th century and the harbour consists of two islands – Marstrandsön and Koön. The town hall in Marstrand dates from 1644 and is the oldest stone building in Bohuslän. The town hall in Marstrand dates from 1644 and is the oldest stone house in Bohuslän.

With winds in the south and southwest, it can get choppy in the harbour. Mooring is in finger berths, or bows-to with lazy lines. There are also a few Y-booms in some places and as most visitors will want to call here it can be very crowded even during the week. Spaces can be booked in advance online at www.marstrandsgasthamn.se/sv/bokning.

If Marstrand is very busy, it may be possible to anchor just under 0.5M to the southeast of Marstrand gästhamn, just east of Stenan.

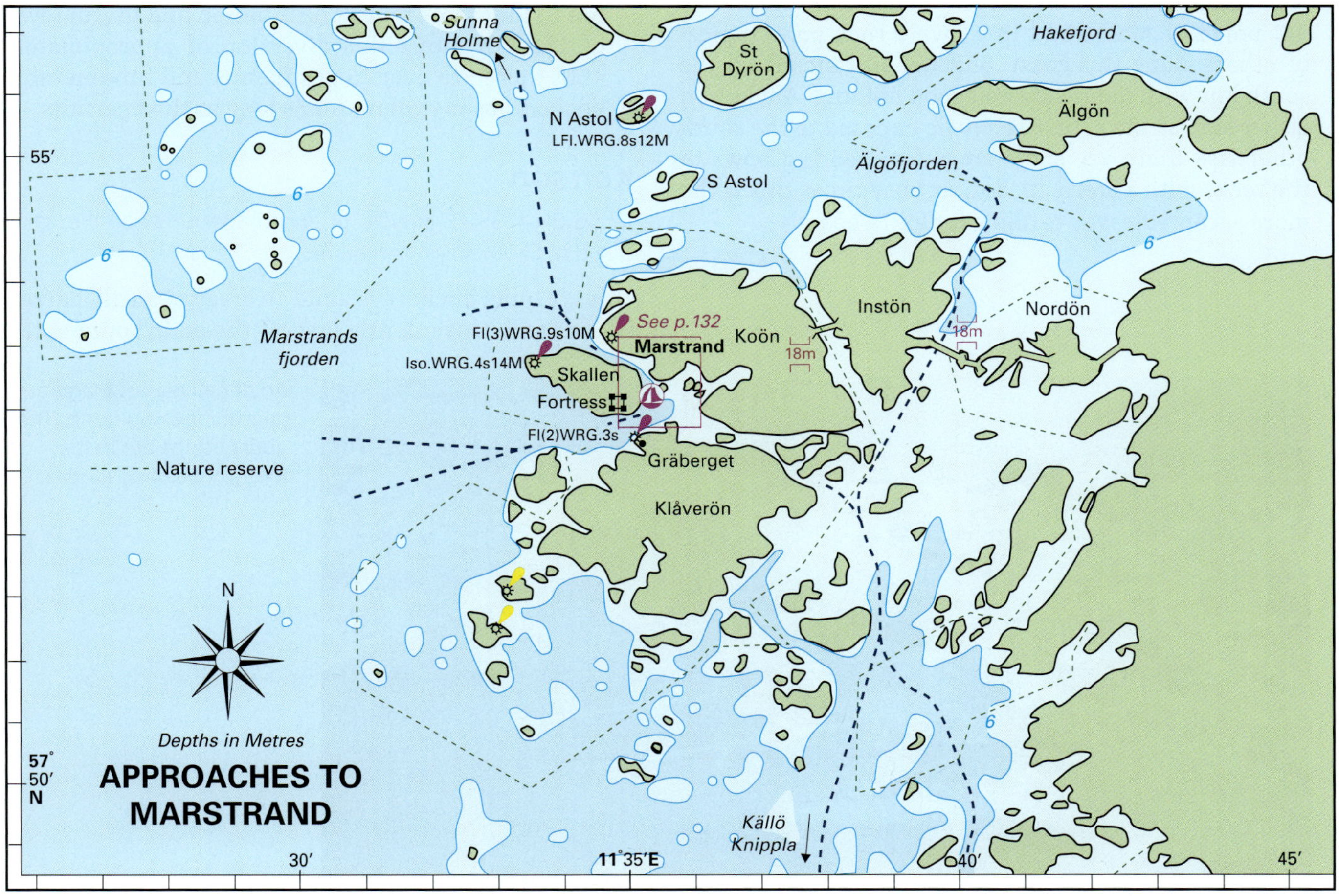

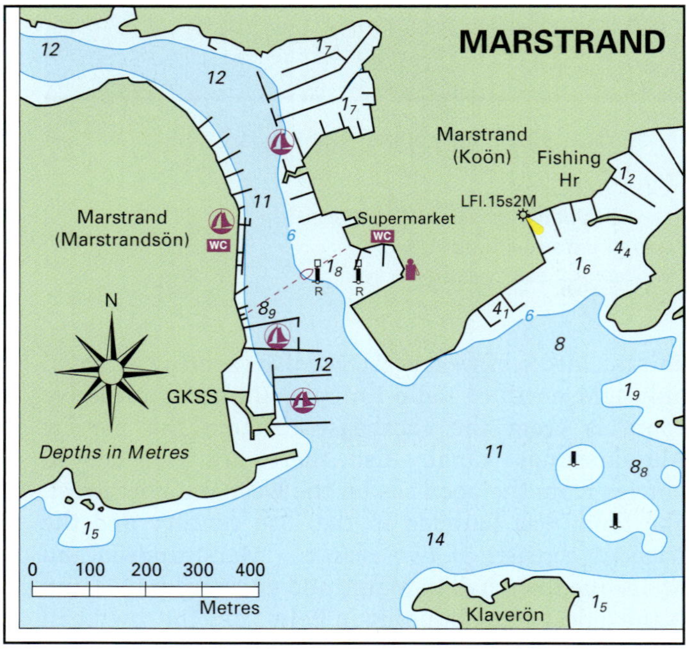


Good services, restaurants and supplies with extensive marine services available and a cash machine a short ferry ride away. Fuel is available from a self-service pontoon by the fishing harbour.

The harbour is dominated by the conspicuous Carlsten Fortress which is well worth a visit.

## Sunna Holme

58°00'.3N 11°31'.3E (middle of entrance between two small headlands)

A natural anchorage in beautiful surroundings, it lies 9M north of Marstrand in a lovely rock pool, typical of others along this coast. Shallow entrance from the south but with 6m inside and good holding. Anchor on either side as the centre is a little exposed to the south otherwise there are some rings for mooring bows to the rocks with a stern anchor. At busy times this is the more acceptable way to allow for extra boats.

## Tjörn and Orust

From Marstrand you really have four choices:

1. Head northeast (leaving Koön to starboard and Tjörn and Orust to port). This (and option 4 below) are good alternatives in strong westerly winds, when parts of the more open leads can be rough;
2. Work your way up the mainly protected leads on the west of the latter two islands;
3. Go out to sea;
4. Leave Marstrand by the east-southeast channel and take the route east of Koön and Inston which joins up with Hakefjord. Note there is a bridge with 18m clearance on this route. Then head up Hakefjord under either bridge (minimum 26m), past the island of Källön, to the Askeröfjorden where the twisting route round the top of Tjörn joins. Note that if planning to stop in Stenungssund for fuel or provisions, the bridge to Stenungsön appears deceivingly high, but has only 13m clearance. Larger yachts will need to round the island and approach the town from the north. Then north through Halsefjorden and the narrow 11M Svanesund to the top of Orust. Here in the Havstensfjord the important town of Uddevalla is found 4.5M to the northeast. If you turn to port just 3M to the west there is a very good boatyard near the Vindö bridge (Vindö Marin). They also offer winter storage and are registered with Customs as a Bonded Warehouse. There is excellent shopping at Henån only 5M further south. The route then heads southwest and through some narrow passages, passed Ellös to Gullholmen to the west or turn north 6M to the major tourist destination and useful town of Lysekil. Along this diversion of approximately 45M there are over 15 gästhamns and innumerable anchorages to explore for as long as time permits.

## Kärrsön

57°56'.2N 11°39'.7E (middle of anchorage between the small island of Skutholmen and Kärrsön)

This is a quiet anchorage amid an array of small, barren islands and conveniently just off the main route to the

An aerial view of Marstrand harbour looking north. The guest berths are in the foreground *Andy Beharrell*

east of Tjörn. Approach from the east and anchor either to the north of Skutholmen in the bay between Skutholmen, Kärrsön and Lilla Dyrön or head between Skutholmen and Bockholmen and anchor to the south of Skutholmen in the bay called Hättan Kärrsön. This latter option will be more sheltered in easterly winds. In winds from any other quarter, the anchorage should have good shelter.

## Mollösund

58°04'.3N 11°28'.2E (off fuelling pontoon)

**Contacts**

www.orust.se/uppleva-och-gora/gasthamnar/mollosunds-gasthamn

Mollösund is a delightful small village with a sheltered harbour, which can be very crowded in high season. There are lazy lines all round the harbour for bows-to berthing and the berths on the south side of the harbour can be booked on Dockspot (www.dockspot.com/en/docks/123-mollosund). Payment when berthed can be made through a GoMarina machine outside the service block. The service block is beside the Brygghuset café on the northwest corner of the harbour. Larger boats can berth on the jetty to port as you enter or a jetty to starboard inside the harbour.

Toilets, showers, washing machines, dryers and rubbish disposal are all available in the service house. There are cafes, ice cream shops and restaurants all around the harbour.

Fuel can easily be bought at jetties either side of the harbour entrance.

An aerial view of Mollösund looking north. The harbour is well sheltered from all directions *Andy Beharrell*

## Käringön

58°6'.86N 11°22'.02 (north cardinal buoy by harbour entrance)

**Contacts**

www.orust.se/uppleva-och-gora/gasthamnar/karingons-gasthamn

West of the partly narrow inner lead, this charming small island offers basic facilities (*Note* no fuel) mainly around the original fishing harbour. A few alongside berths can be found here, but the pontoons in the separate guest harbour to the west are the most likely option. Best approached from the east, keeping to the southern side of the bay to avoid shallow, unmarked rocks north of the guest harbour. Bows-to mooring

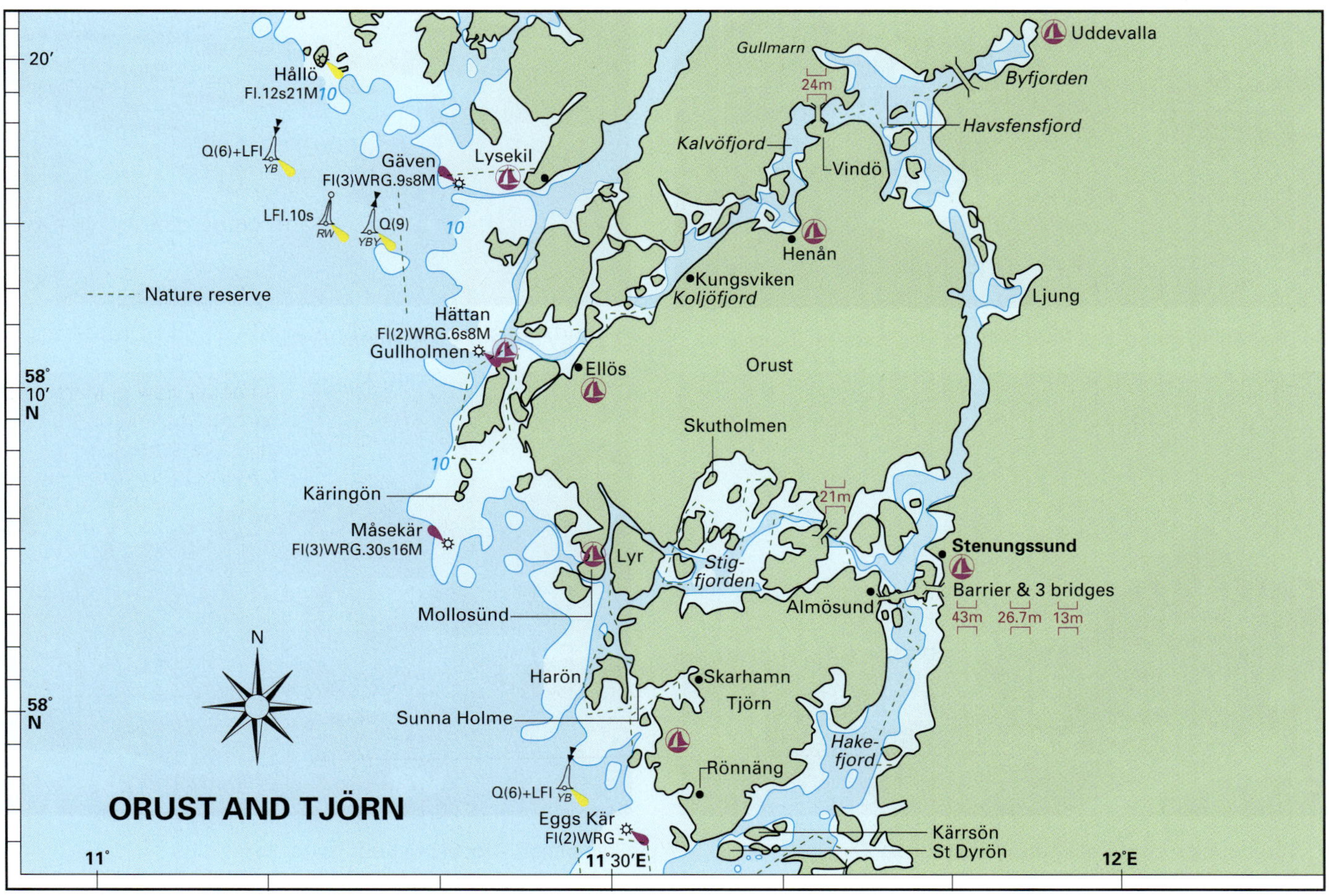

with stern buoys or alongside. Berths can be booked in advance through Dockspot (www.dockspot.com/en/docks/120-karingon-gasthamn). Facilities include a pump-out as well as toilets, showers and laundry. Berthing fees are paid using a GoMarina card machine.

Very popular in high season, particularly due to an excellent restaurant (Petersons Krog – www.petersonskrog.se/en) and numerous ad-hoc summer shops along paths to the rest of the sparsely populated island.

## GULLHOLMEN

58°10'.57N 11°24'.25E (southern entrance)
58°10'.69N 11°24'.34E (northern approx. mid entrance)

### Contacts

www.orust.se/uppleva-och-gora/gasthamnar/gullholmens-gasthamn

Gullholmen is a island gästhamn and holiday village. It is on the north of Härmanö and 3M west of Ellös on Orust. Well buoyed approaches from both north and south. The harbour lies between two islands and is completely sheltered. There are two entrances to guest harbour areas, the southern one has the gästhamn sign by it (yellow anchor on a blue sign). *Note* if approaching from the north, the first inlet you see between Gullholmen and Härmanö is not for visitors.

Moor alongside or bows-to with lazy lines. Good facilities including an ICA mini-market. Bracing walks to the top are rewarded with spectacular views. The permanent population mushrooms from 140 to about 4,000 in season when the harbour is also extremely crowded.

There is an alternative anchorage in the bay 1.4M south of Gullholmen on the eastern side of Härmanö. There are also several SXK (Swedish Cruising Association) buoys there for members.

## Henån

58°14'.5N 11°40.68E

### Contacts

Harbourmaster ✆+46 76 101 2069
www.orust.se/uppleva-och-gora/gasthamnar/henans-gasthamn
kommun@orust.se

The town has been known for shipbuilding and boatbuilding since the Middle Ages. Approach to Henån is straightforward from the north. It has a small gästhamn around 3.5M just west of south from Vindön. It has around 10 berths in boxes on the northernmost jetty in a depth of around 2.5m. It is sheltered from

The fishing harbour at Käringön *Nicholas Torsteinsrud-Smith*

Scenery around Gullholmen *Viv Fox*

The popular restaurant Petersons Krog at Käringön *Nicholas Torsteinsrud-Smith*

Gullholmen – local boat berths *Viv Fox*

The anchorage at Härmanö – just south of Gullholmen, looking south *Viv Fox*

The guest harbour at Henån looking north. The guest berths are the northernmost on the right. On the left-hand side is the Orust Yachtservice yard *Andy Beharrell*

most directions except the northwest. Facilities include water, electricity, washing, toilets, showers and rubbish disposal. Payment is made on arrival through the GoMarina app and once payment is made, the code to the facilities will be emailed.

On the western side of the harbour is Orust Yacht Service. They own Najad and they are also an Arcona and Bavaria service centre. Theirs is a full-service marina. They have space for around 250 boats for over-wintering and are also a Customs-bonded yard so will deal with all the necessary paperwork, eliminating the requirement for a bond. They have all yard facilities, but are particular specialists in dealing with groundings and keel issues. They have dealt with this on over 60 types of yacht and average around 40–50 a year. They can also do full restorations.

Henån is the main town on Orust and has a supermarket and Systembolaget just a couple of hundred metres from the gästhamn. Other shops and facilities are close by and with buses from here to Uddevalla and connections from there to Göteborg, this can be a good place for crew changes or leaving a boat for a while.

Typical narrow street at Fiskebäckskil *Nicholas Torsteinsrud-Smith*

## Fiskebäckskil

58°15'.08N 11°27'.78E (entrance to buoyed channel)

**Contacts**

www.lyckansslip.se/en/gasthamn

Just off the main coastal route, this attractive village offers most facilities for the visiting yachtsman at a well-run boatyard and marina at the end of the inlet. There is a fuelling berth, popular restaurant at the marina and a small supermarket within easy walking distance. There are about 40 guest berths and mooring is bows-to with lazy lines, vacant residents' fingers (green signs), or as directed by staff. Berths can be booked in advance through the gästhamn website (hamn.lyckansslip.se/en). A regular ferry runs from the northern tip of the village to the nearby town of Lysekil.

## Lysekil

58°16'.06N 11°26'.29E (by port hand buoy)

**Distances**

Marstrand 25M, Stromstad 48M

**Contacts**

www.lysekil.se/kultur-och-fritid/gasthamnar-och-husbilsparkeringar/gasthamnar.html
gasthamn@lysekil.se
Harbourmaster
✆+46 523 61 30 63

This is an old established resort town and as you approach, the skyline is dominated by the church with a tall spire. There are three possible guest harbours.

### Lysekil Havsbadets gästhamn

58°16'.06N 11°26'.37E

This harbour is on the east side of the Lysekil peninsula and just north of the small island of Släggö. The gästhamn has around 200 guest berths in depths of 2.2–4m. Mooring is a mixture of stern buoys, alongside and lazy lines. Berths can be booked in advance through hamn.lysekil.se/en/. The outdoor swimming area – Kallbadhuset – is just to the south of the guest harbour and next door is the Restaurant Havsbadet and the Havsbadsparken with Havshotellet, which has live concerts in the summer.

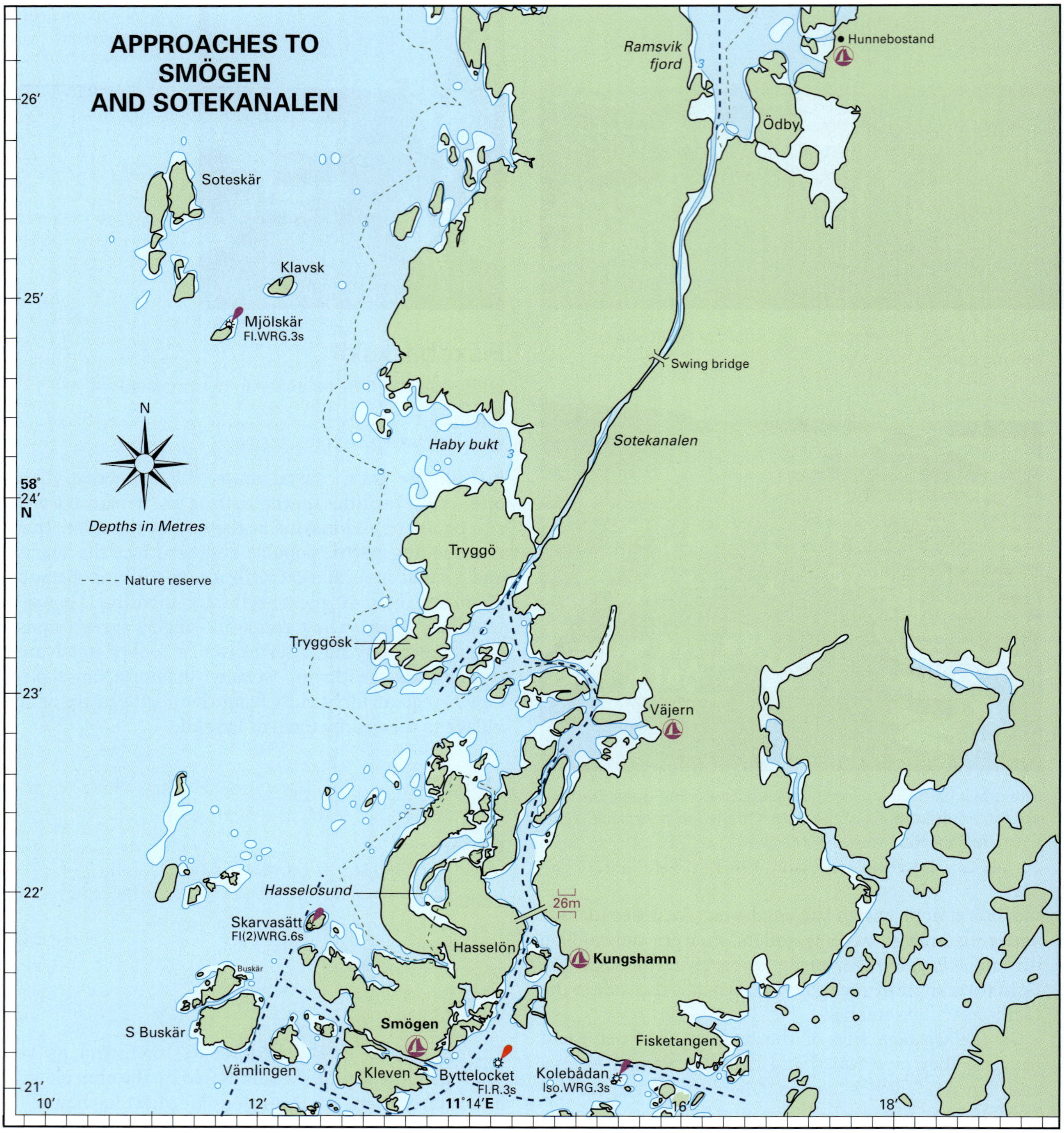


### Lysekil Gästhamn Fiskhamnen

58°16'.43N 11°26'.59E

The second possibility is the Lysekil fishing harbour. This has 40 guest berths, some alongside and some using lazy lines. The shelter behind the breakwater may be better in winds from the south than in the Havsbadet.

### Lysekil Gästhamn Norra Hamnen

58°16'.67N 11°25'.24E

The third possibility is on the western side of the peninsula. This gästhamn is called Norra Hamnen and is quite exposed to northerlies. It has 40 guest berths alongside and on lazy lines. The location is convenient for the old town (Gamla Stan) where many of the houses are up to 200 years old. There are extensive paths and it is a nice walk to the Stångehuvuds nature reserve at the end of the peninsula.

## Smögen

58°21'.16N 11°113'.79E (green buoy by entrance)

**Contacts**

www.vastsverige.com/sotenas/produkter/gasthamn-smogen/

Smögen is a lively tourist town and fishing port and can be very busy (and noisy) at the height of the season. However, it is also a fascinating place with extensive cafes and restaurants along with many tourist shops in the wooden houses overlooking the quay.

The summer town of Smögen *David Ridout*

Much prettier than Kungshamn 0.5M to its east, Smögen lies some 15m northwest of Orust and close to the open sea but exposed only to the east. There is a very long wooden quay called Smögens Gästhamn against which you moor or raft alongside and spaces at the western end can be booked in advance through Dockspot – www.dockspot.com/sv/docks/130-smogenbryggans-gasthamn.

There are good facilities but fuel is only available at nearby Kungshamn, an important fishing harbour with fish market and large processing factories. There is considerable modern development on its north side.

If time is short, it is only a day's sail of about 40M outside all the off lying islands and skerries to Strömstad, however that would be to miss much of the variety of this coast.

There are 16 gästhamns and countless anchorages between Smögen and Strömstad and various routes which may be taken, depending on your vessel's draught and air draught.

## Kungshamn

58°21'66N 11°14'80E (middle of central quay)

**Contacts**

www.kungshamn.nu/om/hamnar
hamnenkungshamn@sotenas.se
www.sotenas.se
Harbourmaster ✆+46 70 239 8323

Kungshamn is a useful alternative to Smögen, especially if the latter is full and is usually much quieter than Smögen. It is located on the outermost part of the Sotenäset peninsula and berthing is on the western side of the town in the old fishing harbour and on floating jetties to the south of it. On the jetties berthing is in Y-booms while in the old harbour, berths are either alongside or to a stern anchor. There are around 70 guest berths in 3-5m and some can be booked in advance through Dockspot – www.dockspot.com/sv/docks/119-kungshamn.

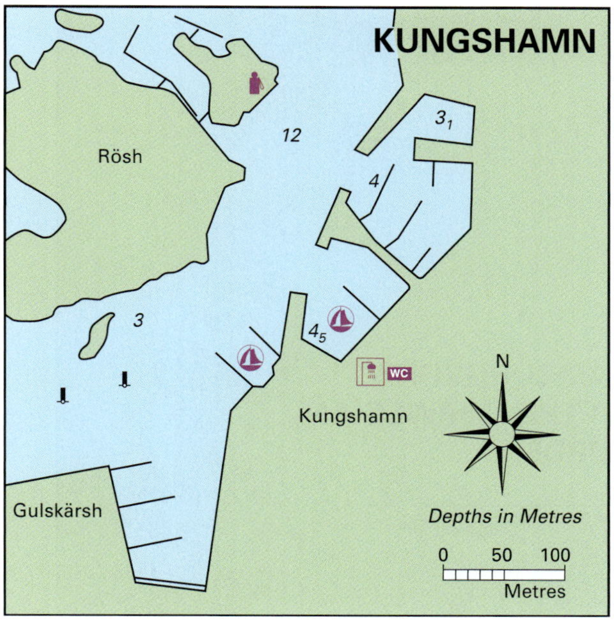


There is a small passenger ferry which operates between Kungshamn and Smögen. Details of the ferry are available on www.vastsverige.com/en/things-to-do/explore-the-west-coast-by-boat/ferry-lines/route-map-smogenkungshamn. There is also a ferry from Kungshamn to Hållö to visit the nature reserve there.

Sotekanalen with bridge in background *Nicholas Torsteinsrud-Smith*

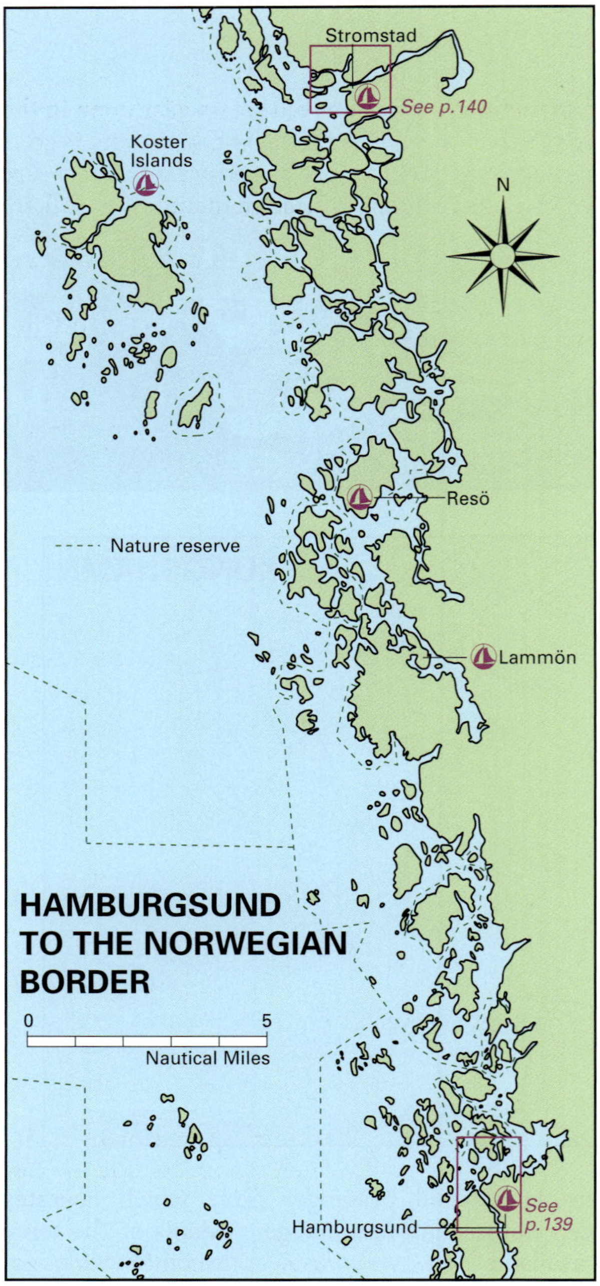


## Sotekanalen

58°23'.5N 11°14'.33E (southern entrance)

**Contacts**

kanaler.arnholm.nu/sotens.shtml

This partly artificial canal was opened in 1935 with the object of allowing local craft to avoid the exposed coast of the Sote peninsula which could be dangerous to small vessels in stormy southwest weather. Its length is just under 3M and passes through gentle Bohus countryside with a few houses and farms. Today it makes a convenient shortcut to the 200 berth gästhamn of Hunnebostrand and is used by some 50,000 vessels of all sizes each year, the limitation being a beam of 15m and draught of 4.5m. It has one opening bridge, which usually opens as you approach between 0600 and 2200 local time. There is no charge for transit, nor are there any suitable stopping places. Sailing is forbidden.

## Hunnebostrand

58°26'.52N 11°17'.58E (north of starboard pier into the visitors' harbour)

**Contacts**

hamnenhunnebostrand@sotenas.se
Harbourmaster ✆+46 70 588 7747

Hunnebostrand is one of the oldest of Bohuslän's fishing communities and is divided into two harbours. The northernmost one is for visitors but the southern one has several shipyards and repair facilities. Granite was exported from here and there is a stone mason museum in the small town. While still a centre of lobster fishing it is now a fairly genteel tourist and retirement town. It is the home of the Swedish Lobster Academy.

The guest harbour is sheltered by Sankt Göransö and Fiskholmen and has 200 guest berths in depths between 3-6m. There are buoys or lazy lines though on the westernmost jetty there are some Y-booms. Berths can be booked or paid for through Dockspot – www.dockspot.com/sv/docks/116-hunnebostrand-gasthamn.

Hunnebostrand, two harbours looking southwest *David Ridout*

View over Hamburgsund harbour *Viv Fox*

From here you can walk south along the Sote Canal and around the Ramsvikslandet nature reserve. By the harbour are many cafes and restaurants.

## Hamburgsund

58°33'N 11°16'.2E (south mole head)

**Contacts**

www.hamburgsund.com/om-hamburgsund/hamburgsunds-gasthamn/
www.hamburgsundsbokning.se/gasthamnar
info@turistenvast.se
Harbourmaster ✆+46 525 61188

The Hamburgsund sound is a natural waterway which, because of its totally sheltered position has been a centre of commerce and shipping for over 200 years. Sailing is forbidden and today its use is almost entirely leisure with some fishing activity which has attracted many holiday homes and boats. Despite this it is attractive, and there is much history to be found in the area by those so inclined. There is a well set up gästhamn in the centre which is popular in the season, and there is good basic shopping, including a supermarket. There are also good walks from the gästhamn including a walk up the hill to where Hornborg Castle once stood.

There are 50 guest spaces on both sides of the sound. Berths are alongside and a few on the eastern side have stern buoys. Spaces in the gästhamn can be booked in advance or paid for through Dockspot - www.dockspot.com/en/docks/115-hamburgsund.

There is a cable-operated vehicle ferry close to the marina which crosses at frequent intervals particularly at peak times and this needs care to pass safely.

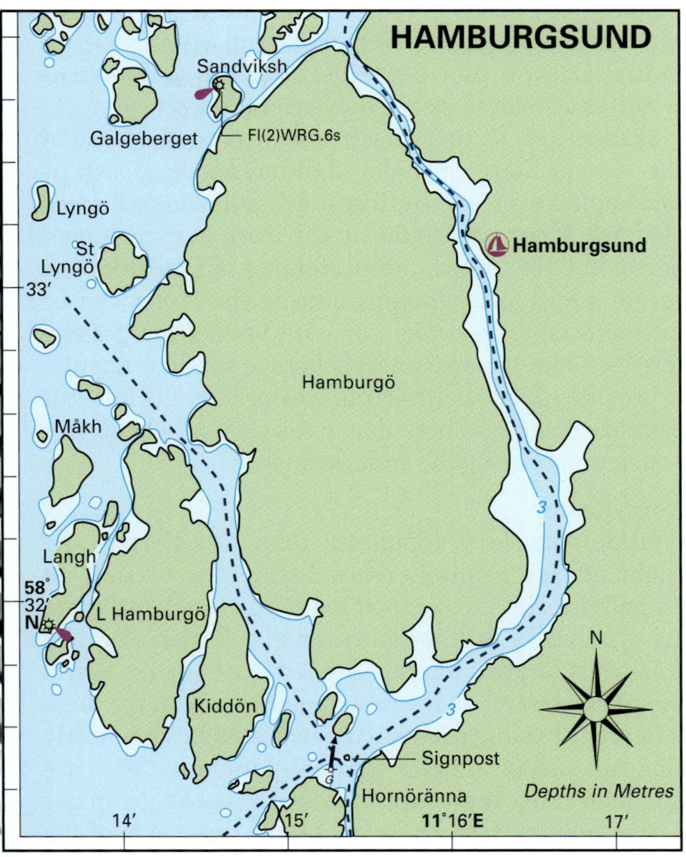


## Lammön

58°44'.38N 11°13'.13E (approach to main bay)

A perfectly sheltered natural anchorage some 2.5M southeast of the main inner lead. Although a detour, it offers peaceful surroundings, good holding and protection from all wind directions - particularly strong westerlies. Some possibilities for bows-to land mooring either side of southern approach to main bay when conditions allow.

## Resö

58°48'N 11°09'.7E

**Contacts**

www.reso.se/reso-gasthamn-2-2/
hamnen@reso.se
Harbourmaster ✆+46 727 07 85 54

A small, active fishing harbour, approximately 15M north of Hamburgsund, which makes its limited free spaces available to yachtsmen and is worth having a look at if time allows. The guest harbour has 40 spaces and is generally well protected with depths of 2-4m. Mooring bows-to by stern anchor on the northeast shore of Hamneholmen probably offers the best shelter, but it is also possible to go alongside the two jetties to the north of Hamneholmen. There are good facilities including pump-out, laundry, shops and cafes. There is a 10km trail right round the island.

## The Koster Islands

The southern approaches to Kosterfjorden can be subject to significant swell during prolonged periods of southerly or westerly winds. However, within a short distance further north, the Koster Islands (and the wealth of islets around them) provide sheltered waters onward towards Strömstad.

The two main islands, Nord-Koster and Syd-Koster are extremely popular summer tourist destinations, and the harbours are consequently very crowded in high season. There is a small cable ferry connecting Nord-Koster and Syd-Koster. This ferry is available to anyone between 1100 and 1630 every day. Locals have

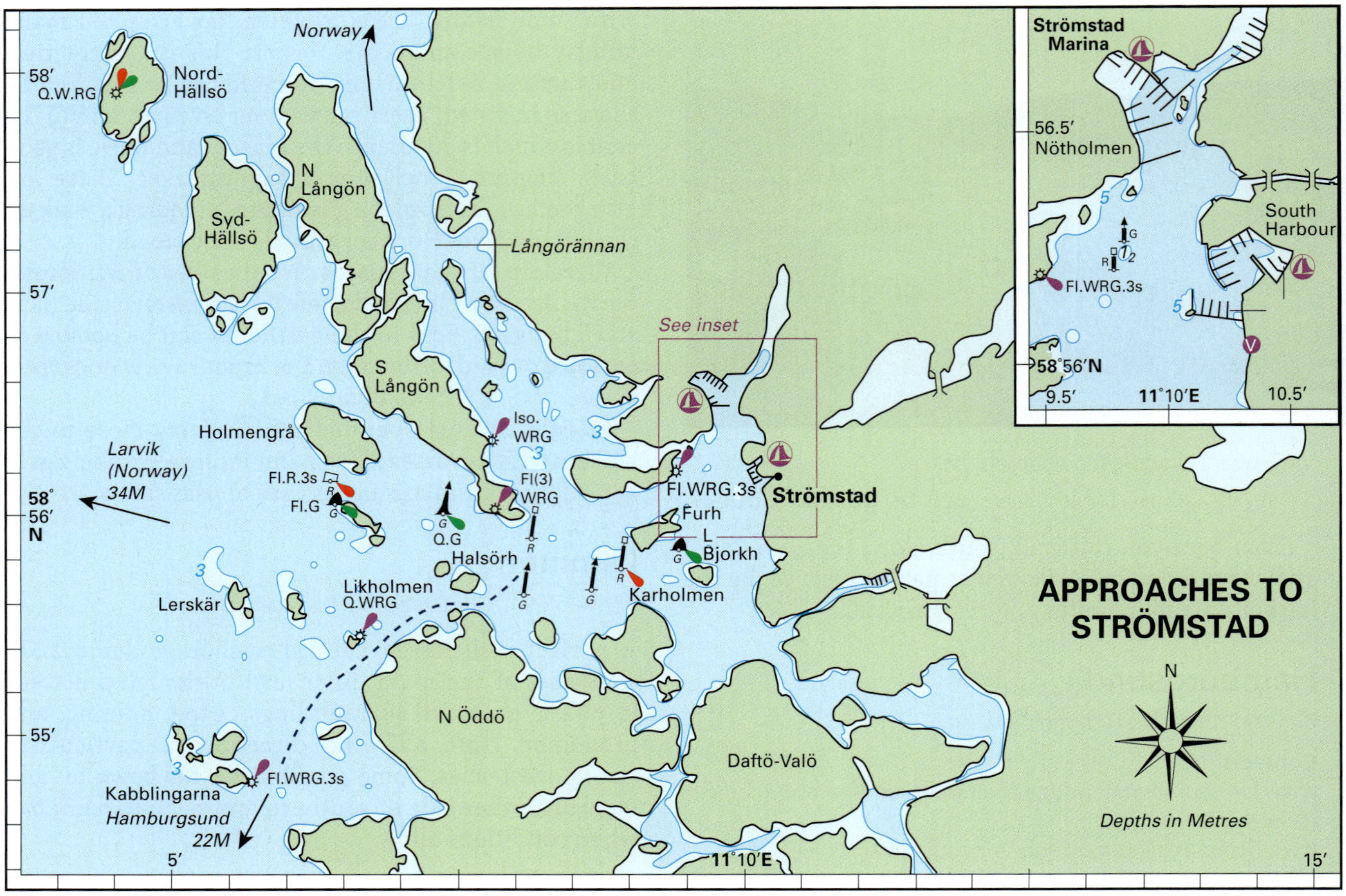


an access card to use it 24/7. There are also regular ferries between the islands and Strömstad.

The southernmost island of Ramsö on the other hand, has no ferry connection and it is therefore only the small harbour which becomes congested at peak times! Available space in the harbours considerably improves however by mid-August. Cars are prohibited on all the islands, which adds to the pleasure of exploring by foot or hired bicycle.

### Ramsö

Previously a small fishing community, the island is now home to a handful of summer residents and visiting yachts in the well-sheltered little harbour. There are no facilities (note this includes water) other than simple toilets, but the charm of the surroundings fully make up for this. Mooring is bows-to quay with stern anchor, or alongside. Additional berths alongside wooden quays at harbour entrance, although limited depth in places.

### Syd-Koster

This is the largest of the two main Koster islands and as such, has the most to offer in terms of services for visitors. The only shop for provisions (and fuel) is curiously situated at the crossroads in the centre of the island, although the walk to get there gives the opportunity to experience the essence of Koster life. A variety of small cafés and restaurants flourish in the summer, but many close in early August.

There are two main guest harbours adjacent to Kosterfjorden. Note that the small fishing harbour of Brevik is not recommended for visiting yachts as it requires precise navigation to approach through numerous unmarked shallows and rocks. Local knowledge is essential.

Kyrkosund on the southeastern coast is the quieter of the two guest harbours. The approach requires care and is best undertaken on a WSW course, just north of the Brattskär group of rocks. Turn on to a NW heading towards the harbour when abeam of the marker on L. Brattskär on your port side. Note the shallow area (1.8m) south-southeast of the harbour entrance.

Ekenäs lies further north and just to the east of the conspicuous Sneholm lighthouse. Approach is uncomplicated from south or north following a buoyed channel. Alongside berths on the main quay, or finger berths further south, are preferable if available. The recent additional pontoons outside the moles can be uncomfortable in a swell, or with wash from passing ferries. There is a spacious anchorage south of Ekenäs. It provides good shelter from westerly winds but it is a nature reserve so note that areas closest to land have restrictions during the summer months.

### Nord-Koster

Considerably less populated than Syd-Koster, the island offers a similarly relaxed atmosphere – only on a smaller scale. There is no food shop or fuel, but there are good walks to enjoy and a small selection of cafés/small restaurants. The main guest harbour by Västra Bryggan, is nevertheless as popular as any in the area. It lies in the sound between the two islands with mostly alongside berths on two separate pontoons. These are not bookable. There are also some bookable finger berths (with red/green lights) on the inner side of the

Strömstad Marina looking northwest *David Ridout*

easternmost pontoon. These can be booked through www.kosterhamn.se/en. The maximum beam is 4m.

The island's second harbour is at Vettnet on the eastern shore. This is much smaller, with roughly 15 guest spaces with bows-to mooring between fingers and booms, plus some alongside berths. Simple approach following the main leads and adequate depth for all but the largest of boats. All the usual basic facilities and a pleasant 1.5km walk to the relative liveliness of Västra Bryggan. Take a longer circuit to include visiting the double lighthouse towers along the way. This is the highest point of the Koster islands and offers excellent views to the open sea.

## STRÖMSTAD

58°56'.14N 11°09'.96E (north of the islet of Skurve)

### Contacts

Stromstad Marina ☏+46 526 13920
stromstadmarina.se
Southern Harbour ☏+46 526 19050
hamn.stromstad.se/en
gasthamn@stromstad.se

Barely 5M from the border with Norway, this is the northernmost town on the Swedish west coast and is a popular yachting centre.

It has very well buoyed approaches from the north and west for the regular ferry to Larvik. There are also approaches from the south but these have restrictions on headroom and draught which are only clear on the detailed Swedish charts. Most of the visitors' moorings are in the South Harbour which is approached by leaving the islet of Skurve, which is connected to the shore by marina berthing pontoons, to starboard. Berth on these (mainly alongside or some Y-booms) or continue into the inner harbour which is more convenient to the shore facilities if space is available there. Otherwise use any vacant 'box' with a green light. In total there are over 200 guest berths in depths of 1–8m.

The full facilities and services include an excellent SeaSea chandlery nearby (www.seasea.se). The community of 13,000 justify a first-class shopping centre and two large supermarkets plus a Systembolaget which does a brisk trade with the many visiting Norwegians. This is a 10min walk north of the marina.

South Harbour, Strömstad, looking northwest *Janny Bernays*

Mooring fees can be paid at the chandlery on the southern edge of the harbour or at the harbourmaster's office on the northern edge of the harbour. Booking in advance is also possible online on hamn.stromstad.se/en. Just beyond the harbourmaster's office there is an excellent tourist information office. Here one can obtain a ticket to operate the self-controlled cable ferry across to the marina lying to the northwest of the main town.

The northern marina, Strömstad Marina (gasthamn.stromstadmarina.se/en/), has a large chandlery and haul out facility up to 50T. It is a popular place for people leaving their boat and offers winter storage. It is necessary to ring the marina and book a place. There is the ferry connection referred to above and a free bus to town, but the Strömstad Southern Harbour is more convenient for a short visit and shopping.

## Strömstad to the Norwegian border

The route north to the Norwegian border is straightforward by way of the Långörännan channel giving access either up Oslo Fjord or towards Halden or Fredrikstad.

# 2D. GÖTA ÄLV, TROLLHÄTTE KANAL AND GÖTA KANAL

## THE GÖTA KANAL 'SWEDEN'S BLUE RIBBON'

Contacts
✆+46 141 20 20 50
info@gotakanal.se
www.gotakanal.se

The Berg flight of locks on the Göta Kanal *Viv Fox*

The term 'Göta Kanal' is often used to describe the entire 210M (390km) route between Göteborg on the west coast and Mem on the Baltic coast of Sweden, but this is not technically correct. The westernmost stretch is in fact a river, the Göta Älv, which is connected by the Trollhätte Kanal to Lake Vänern (the largest lake in Sweden and one of the largest lakes in Europe). Between Lake Vänern and the smaller Lake Vättern runs the 35M (65km) western section of the Göta Kanal proper, which includes the canal's highest point at almost 92m (302ft) above sea level. The eastern section between Lake Vättern and the Baltic Sea is some 50M (93km) in length. Thus only about half of the 'Göta Kanal' is actually canalised, and a good part of that is not the Göta Kanal at all.

In spite of its numerous bridges most yachts are able to pass through the entire system with masts in place, the minimum clearance being 22m at Norsholm on the eastern stretch. The maximum allowable length is 32m and the controlling width is 7.2m. Depths are nominally no less than 2.5m and currently advertised as 2.82m.

If taken slowly the passage offers plenty of variety: peace and quiet, but also plenty of interesting little towns and historical buildings to visit, not to mention several museums featuring the canal's own history. Many of the small guest harbours are surrounded by fields and open countryside, and children almost invariably enjoy the passage.

Here are some vital statistics about the canal:

- 190km of canal including 87km of excavated canal
- 6,000m of jetties and 6,800m of quays, piers and guide jetties
- 3,000,000 visitors every year
- 58 locks

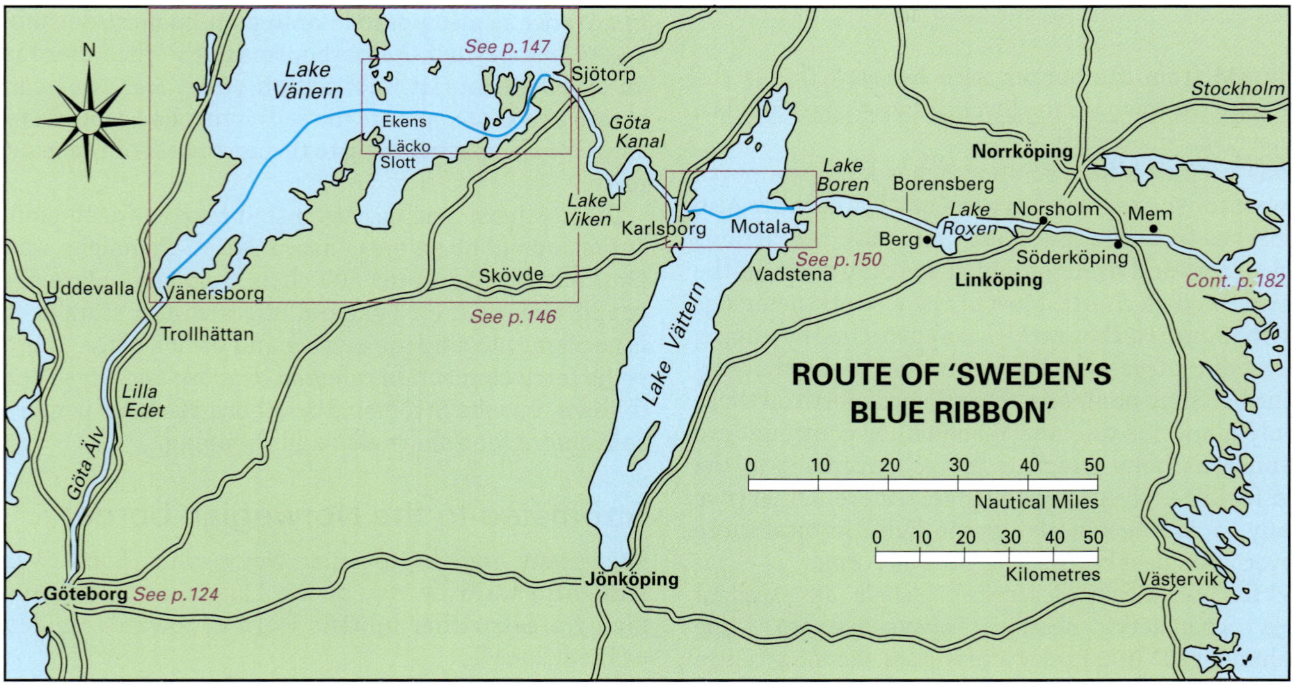

- 3,400,000m$^3$ of water in the excavated part of the canal
- 24 year-round employees and 100 lock keepers during the canal season

There is also a national bike trail running the length of the Göta Kanal, so if some of your crew want to cycle alongside you for some of the way, they can!

## History

The western part of the system was the first to be canalised, with the Trollhätte Kanal (bypassing the Trollhätte Falls) opening in 1800 to allow access for shipping to Lake Vänern. Work on the Göta Kanal section began in 1809, much of it dug using tin-clad wooden shovels, under the direction of Baron von Platen and the civil engineer Thomas Telford, and took 23 years to complete – around 84 million man hours. It was finally opened in 1832. However, commercial traffic decreased markedly after the mainline railway link across Sweden was opened in 1862, but the potential for tourism was soon recognised, with several passenger steamers plying its length. Now, the waterway is a popular holiday destination, and home to three historic vessels of the Göta Kanal Steamship Company in addition to many fleets of hire cruisers. Although originally in private hands, the Göta Kanal Company was registered in 1978 and the Swedish state took ownership of the canal company. The purchase price was 5.7 million Swedish Kroner. In 2016 they embarked on a renovation project titled Göta Kanal 2.0, the largest investment since the canal was built. 2022 was the 200th anniversary of the canal being built.

There are various historic sites related to the canal which can be visited. In Motala is the headquarters of the Göta Kanal Company. This building has been the office and archive for the company ever since the canal was built. Also in Motala is the grave of Baltzar von Platen. Baltzar wanted a simple funeral, but this was ignored by Charles XIV Johan. He arranged a funeral with appropriate pomp and ceremony. The body was carried to the grave next to the canal and saluted by 800 Grenadier soldiers. It is also said that Von Platen's horse was buried at the same time. In Vassabacken there is a post office – this is located where the canal met the old country road. The post office is now a museum run by the Moholm local history association and has an exhibition about the Göta Kanal and Vassbacken's postal history.

As you head along the canal, look out for the ell stones. These are large stones along the side of the canal and are the remains of an old compensation system – the more stones the drivers passed, the more they were owed. You may also spot some of the canal milestones.

### *Opening times*

The Trollhätte Kanal is regularly used by seagoing commercial ships of up to 4000T and is open all year round except at times in the winter when lock maintenance is being carried out or the flow of the water is affected by ice.

The Göta Kanal and the Eastern section are generally open from May to September inclusive with small variations from year to year. Advance booking is required for May and early June, and also from mid-August to the end of September (check website for precise dates each year). During these periods a convoy system is operated with boats moving together through the canal. In the intervening high season the canal operates between 0900 and 1800 daily and booking is not required but may be advisable as the volume of boats using the canal is tightly controlled.

### *Practicalities*

- Dues are payable in the upper lock of the Trollhätte Kanal. For the Göta Kanal they are paid at Sjötorp (if eastbound) or Mem (if westbound). It is worth booking your passage all the way through online as you receive a discount. You will be given a reference number which you present when entering the canal, and you will be issued with a package containing information and regulations.
- Fees for transiting the Göta Kanal include overnight stays at any of the 21 marinas along the Göta Kanal. There is a limit of five consecutive nights stay at any one marina. *Note* This arrangement does not cover

**Cross section of 'Sweden's blue ribbon'**

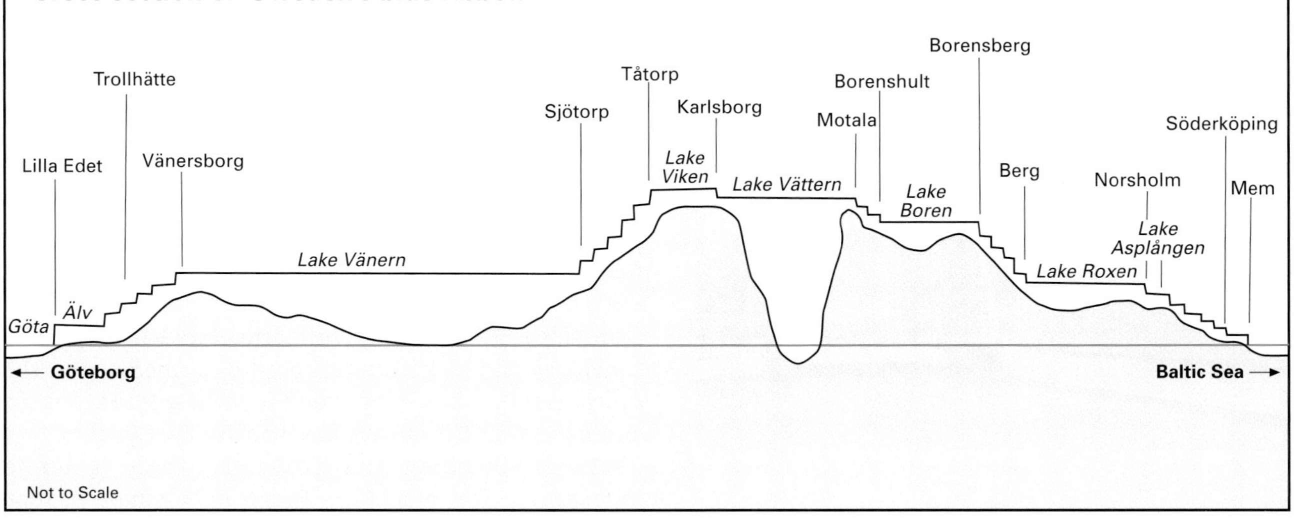

A passenger ferry across the Göta Kanal at Torreboda *Viv Fox*

Old Göta Kanal lock gates on show at Berg *Andy Beharrell*

A bridge over the Göta Kanal at Torreboda *Viv Fox*

A bridge over the Göta Kanal near Motala *Viv Fox*

the Trollhätte Kanal area or harbours/marinas on Lakes Vänern and Vättern.

- Heads may not be used at any time unless a holding tank is installed. There are now pump-out stations at most of the guest harbours.
- Take careful note of the safety regulations, especially relating to sound signals. While the regulations specify that a horn should be sounded when approaching locks and bridges and at entrances to narrow sections, many users will not do this. However, the cruise ships will sound a horn at narrow sections of the canal.
- Locks can be crowded in season and constant vigilance is required. In general, it is suggested that a minimum of three crew is desirable but for a vessel of moderate size two may suffice. Bear in mind that in the Göta Kanal lock keepers are no longer allowed to handle lines, so it is entirely down to yacht crews to do all line handling.
- Lifejackets are compulsory on the Göta Kanal.
- It is advisable to carry at least two lines of about 10m in length. Some of the older locks have uneven walls and an absolute minimum of four large fenders is recommended. A plank is also useful to hang outside the fenders.
- Delays can be expected at both locks and bridges, especially in the high season. The lifting road bridges at Töreboda, Karlsborg and Söderköping have fixed opening times, as do the railway bridges at Lyrestad, Töreboda, Motala and Norsholm, all listed in the information packs available on entering the canal. Other bridges on the Göta Kanal are remotely controlled and will normally open within 10mins of a yacht appearing. The lock keepers and bridge masters do not monitor VHF.
- There is a 5kn speed limit on both canals. With light traffic and an active crew it may be possible to complete the passage in five to seven days if in a hurry, but it is far more rewarding to allow more time. It can be very crowded during the Swedish holiday season which straddles the month of July and early August and there is much to be said for making the passage before or after that period. There is no obvious preferred direction of travel: the wind direction and strength can be significant when crossing the two lakes, and the current in the Göta Älv may be a factor after heavy rain.

## The Göta Älv and Trollhätte Kanal

The approach from the west is via the port of Göteborg, the first lock being encountered at Lilla Edet, 26M (49km) upstream. Below the first lock the stream in the Göta Älv can be strong, running at up to 3kn in the Göta gorge 2M below the lock. The average over the whole distance decreases from around 2kn in early summer to 1.5kn in the autumn.

On the Göta Älv and Trollhätte Kanal the approach to bridges and locks is monitored by cameras, and they will normally be opened when a yacht approaches, but commercial traffic always has priority over yachts.

Between Göteborg and Trollhätte, there is limited opportunity for mooring. There is a small harbour north of the lock at Lilla Edet but for scenic beauty and natural surroundings, it is better to proceed to the small marina at the top of the Trollhätten staircase.

This stretch of the system carries large (90m LOA) freighters, and movement by small craft after dark or in poor visibility is firmly discouraged. All six of its locks have a rise of between 6 to 8m, in contrast to the locks of the Göta Kanal the majority of which are 2.5m. In busy periods they may be filled by yachts wall-to-wall. Both sides of these large locks are fitted with small, recessed bollards some 3-4m apart vertically, so that those alongside can move lines up or down as the water level changes. Even easier is to secure to one of the ladders, generally against the south or southeast wall (the smoother of the two). Despite their impressive size, the locks are gentle in operation due to an unusual system of filling (or emptying) the chambers through gratings in their floors, which produces little turbulence. As one side of three of the locks is very rough you may find other yachts stacked against you. However, the water flow is so gentle that no turbulence is felt, hence there is little or no movement of yachts in the lock.

It can take between 45mins and 2.5hrs to pass through the four giant locks bypassing the Trollhättan falls – or more accurately the three locks, holding basin, and single upper lock – and if time permits it is well worth pausing in the guest harbour beside the upper lock to visit the Trollhätte Kanal Museum (open 1100–1900 daily) and explore the two flights of disused locks – the original 1800 flight, and larger replacements opened in 1844. Those currently in use date back to 1916. The final lock is at Brinkebergskulle, just short of Vänersborg where the canal merges with Lake Vänern, some 44M (82km) from the open sea.

There are five official guest harbours between Göteborg and Lake Vänern:

**Kungälv** About 10M upstream from the centre of Göteborg below the ramparts of the fortress of Bohus where there are a few berths approached by a narrow and tortuous channel.

**Lilla Edet** Just above and to starboard of the lock, depth quoted as 1.2—2m. No facilities except water.

**Åkerssjö** Immediately above the Trollhättan locks, with 15 berths.

**Spikön** Between Trollhättan's two bridges, the first lifting and the second a bascule, and close to the centre of the town: 25 berths with water and electricity, laundry facilities, showers and restaurant.

**Vänersborg** An unassuming but pleasant town with a wide range of shops in the pedestrian precinct. The marina is beside the railway station and 10-15mins from the shops and a large supermarket. It has most facilities including fuel, toilets, laundry and a good chandlery.

Travelling north there are two bridges. The first has been removed and in 2025 a new rail bridge was under construction. The road bridge (16.5m clearance) is opened on demand but expect a short delay whilst a queue of yachts develops.

A lock on the Trollhätte Kanal *Dick Beddoe*

Trollhätte Kanal lock. Moor or raft up on starboard wall (going up). Don't attempt mooring to the other side of the lock *John Sadd*

Lock gates on the Trollhätte Kanal *Viv Fox*

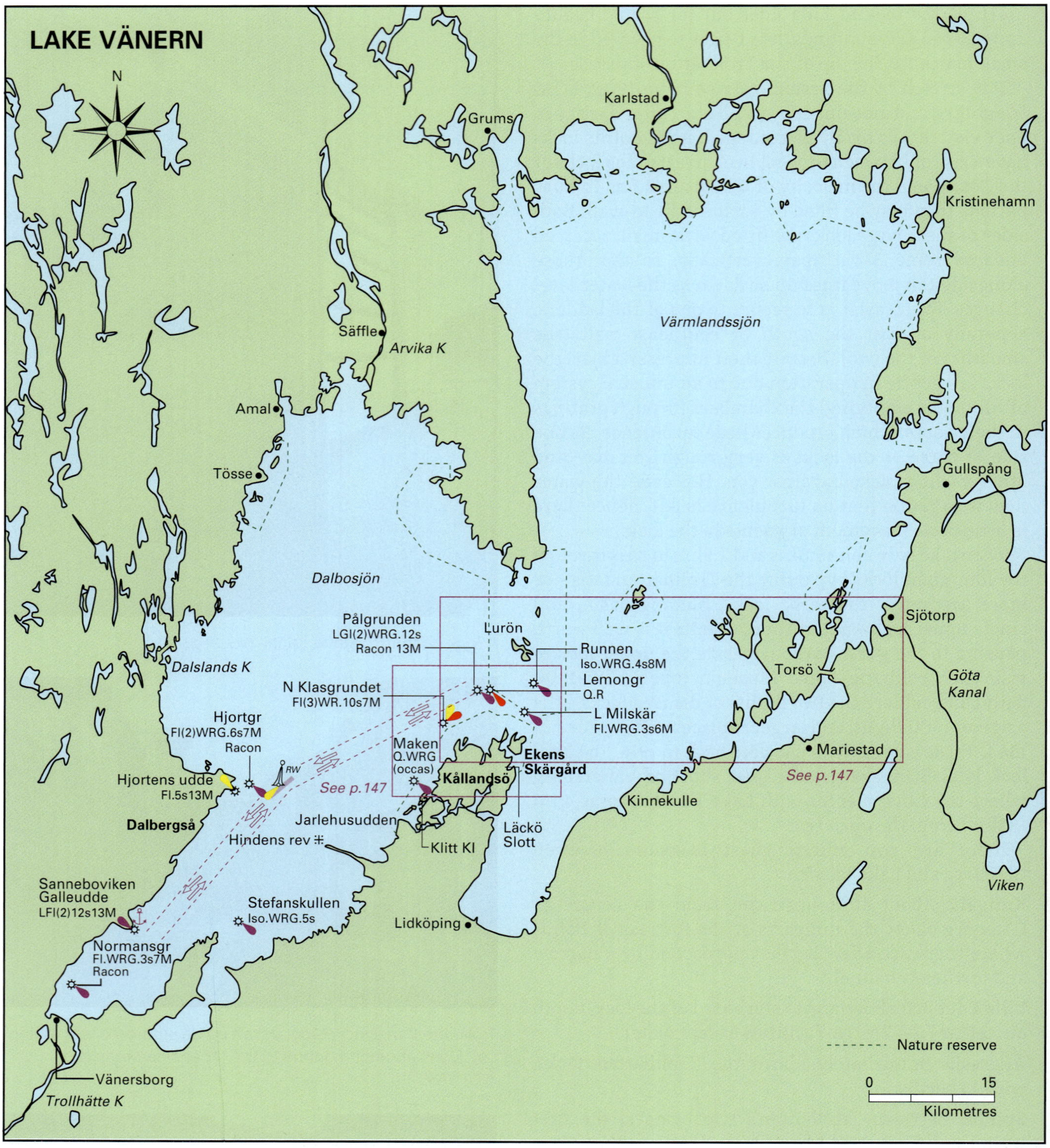


## Lake Vänern

### General information

Although the majority of yachts making their way across Sweden may be expected to take the direct route described below, Lake Vänern offers considerable scope for diversion. It is the largest expanse of fresh water in Sweden; from southwest to northeast is about 80M and from northwest to southeast is about 40M. The depths shown on the charts are subject to variation of up to one metre depending on the amount of melted snow and rain or the lack of either. There are wide stretches of open water where conditions can become very uncomfortable in bad weather. There can be short and steep seas in any winds greater than force 4. The shoreline is, however, much indented and provides many places of shelter in the right conditions.

The lake is conveniently divided by two promontories into sections, namely, Dalbosjön to the southwest and Värmlandssjön to the northeast. The channel between these peninsulas is restricted by the Lurö *skärgård* but the passage is well marked.

### Vänersborg – Sjötorp

From Vänersborg to the start of the Göta Kanal proper at Sjötorp, the course is initially in a northeasterly

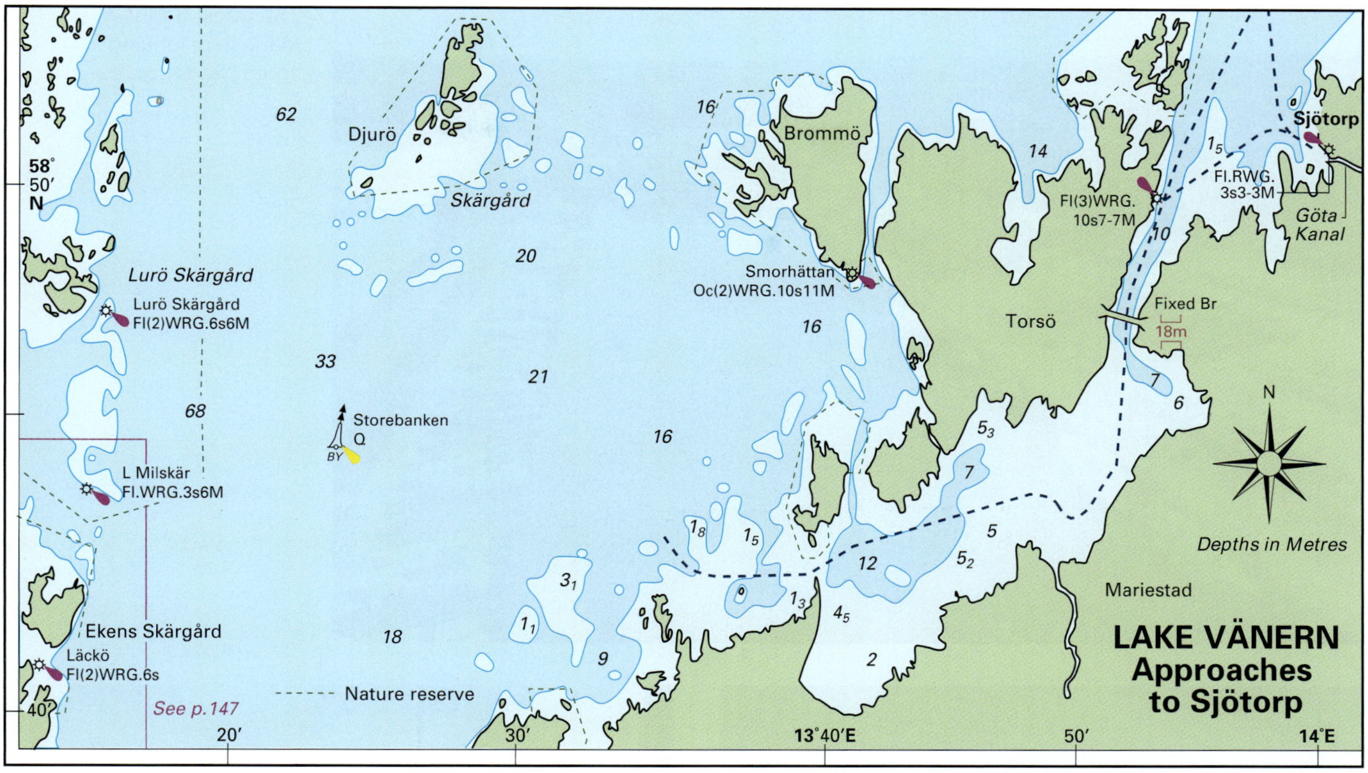

Vanersborg marina. The guest berths are in the foreground (lazy lines) or alongside the wavebreak, looking northeast *John Sadd*

The town hall in Lidköping *Viv Fox*

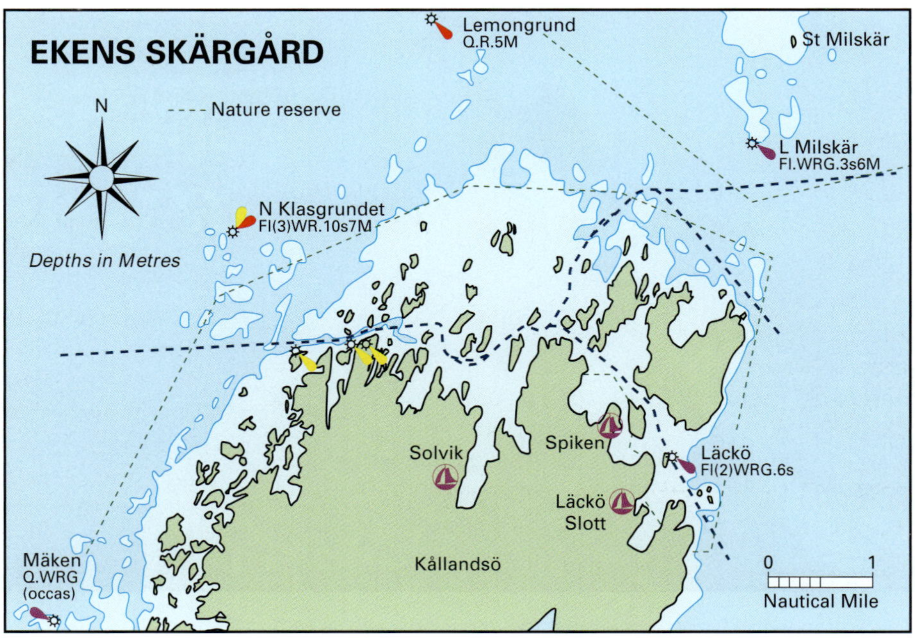


direction for just over 30M when the island of Kallandsö is reached. Passing through the Ekens *skärgård*, yachts proceed in an easterly direction for about 20M until Mariestad is abeam thereafter turning northwards under the bridge (clearance 17.8m) connecting the mainland with Torsö. For yachts with a greater air draught, it is possible to approach Sjötorp from the north by passing just south of Fällholmen. The land is generally low-lying, the principal landmark seen for many

The guest berths at Mariestad, looking south *John Sadd*

The small marina of Spiken on the way to the imposing medieval castle and grounds of Läckö *Viv Fox*

Concrete piles for guiding barges through the Ekens Skärgård *Dick Beddoe*

The entrance to Mariestad harbour, looking north *John Sadd*

Tåtorps Gästhamn *Viv Fox*

miles around being a table mountain, Kinnekulle (305m) (58°36'N 13°25'E) on the southeast shore. The lack of elevation means that care must be taken to sight the relevant buoys, specially the marks off the finger-like promontory of Hindens Rev and the marks at the approaches to the *skärgård*.

Between Vänersborg and Ekens *skärgård*, there are a number of inlets where shelter can be obtained. They include Sanneboviken (58°30'N 12°28'E), Dalbergsa (58°36'.4N 12°36'E), Jarlehusudden (58°37'N 13°1'E) and also in the bay to the east of Klitt island, a few miles north of Jarlehusudden. Within the *skärgård* itself there is a free choice of a number of anchorages in peaceful and beautiful surroundings.

The channel going from west to east divides in the middle of the passage through the *skärgård*, one branch heading north towards open water and the other proceeding between two lines of concrete blocks (once used for pulling through sailing vessels) in a south easterly direction. Both channels are very well marked. The southeast channel leads past the small marina of Spiken (58°41'.5N 13°12'E) to the imposing medieval castle and grounds of Läckö which is open to the public. There is a marina to the northwest of the castle and it is feasible to anchor in the bay to the east (see plan page 147).

A possible diversion is to Lidköping. This is a major town with over 40,000 inhabitants. There are various museums, gardens and galleries – one of which is at the former porcelain factory – and a museum about Lake Vänern. The town hall has become symbolic of the town itself and is said to have originally been Count Magnus Gabriel de la Gardie's hunting lodge. It was moved across the lake in the late 17th century to serve as the town hall when Count Magnus established the town.

The approach to Sjötorp passing Mariestad is by way of a winding buoyed channel which presents no difficulty provided a good lookout is maintained. The fine city of Mariestad has an early 17th-century cathedral said to be a copy of Stockholm Cathedral. Guest berths are to be found at the south end of the harbour. Full facilities are available and there is a main line railway connection. Boats which cannot go under the bridge with 18m clearance can go between Brommö and Fågelö, then northeast to find the way north of Sjötorps Svartskär before heading SE for Sjötorp.

At Sjötorp there is a marina in the outer harbour which is often crowded and is exposed to strong winds from the west and north. To avoid discomfort in strong westerly winds shelter may be obtained in the lee of the promontory to the west of the canal entrance.

### Two canals are found in the western region of Dalsland:

**Dalslands Kanal** starts at Köpmannebro (58°46'N 12°31'E) and ascends by way of 31 locks and a series of lakes almost to the Norwegian frontier. Passage is

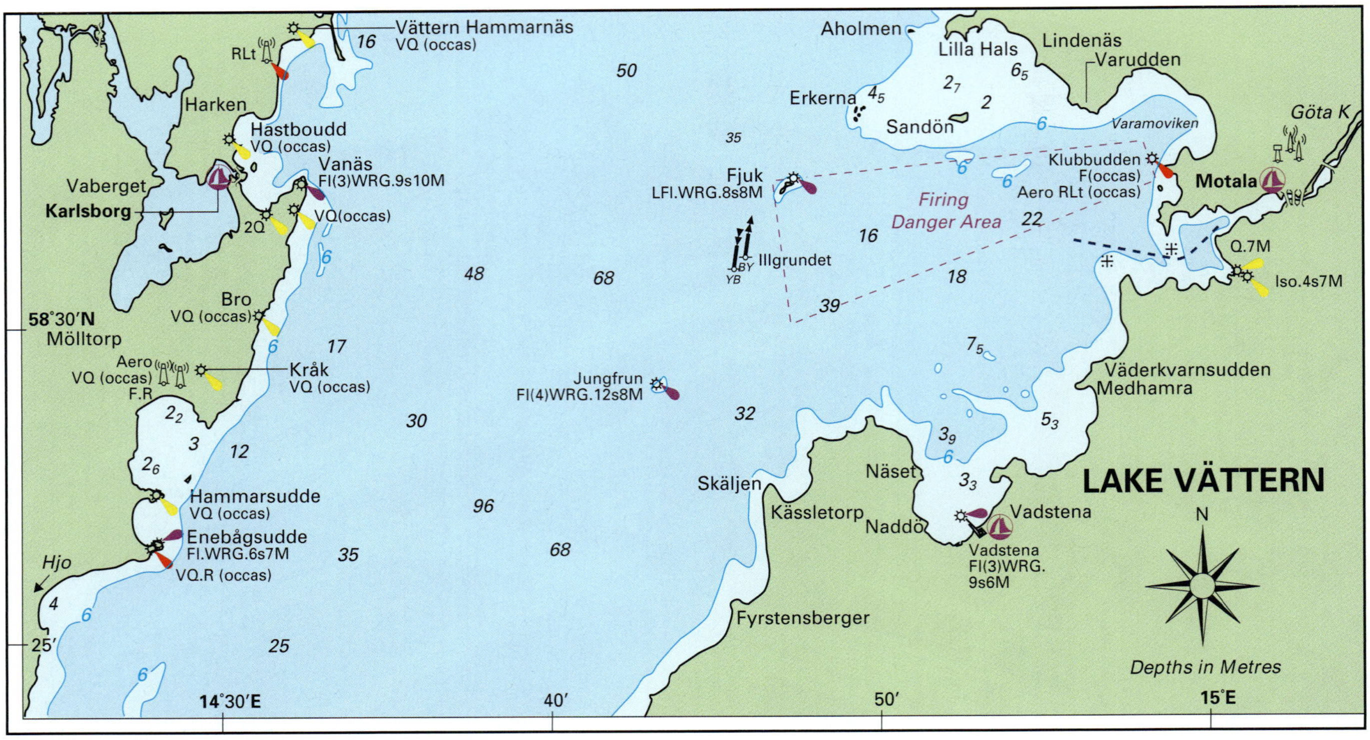


restricted to vessels drawing not more than 1.8m, not more than 22m in length, a maximum beam of 4.05m, and a masthead height of not more than 12m though this varies according to the parts of the canal which you wish to transit (see www.vastsverige.com/en/dalsland-canal/seafarer/dimensions-depth-and-speed/ for full details). Water depths in the canal may be less than quoted during a dry spell of weather. Check with the first lock keeper for current information concerning water depths further upstream.

**Arvika Kanal**, the longer of the two, leaves the lake just south of Säffle (59°08'N 12°55'E) and meanders north for about 40M through lakes and narrow channels. The maximum length, draught and masthead height are, respectively, 42m, 3m, and 16m. Maximum beam is 4.5m.

Both canals were formerly used for the transport of timber and other cargoes but this traffic has now ceased. They are used, when open in the summer, by pleasure craft and are of great scenic beauty.

The principal town in Dalsland is Åmål (population 12,800). This well laid out town, with a fine 17th-century church overlooking it, has a sheltered marina. A few miles to the south lies the Tösse *skärgård* with scenery resembling the islands of the Stockholm archipelago. The *skärgårds* of Djurö, Ekens and Brommö lying not far north of the direct route between Vanersborg and Sjötorp are also popular with those seeking natural surroundings, but during summer weekends and the holiday month of July, there is liable to be activity, sometimes noisy, and wash from fast power boats and the like.

At the north end of Värmlandssjon are two sizeable towns. The larger of these, Karlstad (population 80,000) is a commercial port and capital of the province of Värmland. There are all the facilities of a large town as well as a substantial guest harbour. In the northeast corner of the lake lies Kristinehamn where there is a small marina. Between the two towns and indeed along the entire north shore of Värmlandssjon the coast is much broken up and there are numerous sheltered anchorages.

Hjo church and square *Viv Fox*

## The Göta Kanal to Lake Vättern

This 35M section includes the route's highest point which is in the Berg Kanal. There is a small inlet with a pontoon for a few boats and an obelisk marks the point. This is a few miles before Tåtorp. The beautiful Lake Viken is almost 92m (302ft) above sea level. Eastbound vessels climb 20 locks in 9M to reach the angular lake, which accounts for some 11M of the section, then pass through their first descending lock just beyond its eastern exit. A further 15M through attractive

The gästhamn at Hjo *Viv Fox*

An aerial view of the gästhamn at Hjo *Viv Fox*

The guest moorings and castle at Vadstena *Andy Beharrell*

agricultural countryside without locks takes vessels through to Lake Vättern. There are eight guest harbours on the stretch between the two lakes – Sjötorp, Lyrestad, Hajstorp, Töreboda, Vassbacken, Tåtorp, Forsvik and Karlsborg – all with water, toilets and showers, but most without fuel pumps. Of the guest harbours mentioned above, Töreboda and Karlsborg are recommended for their facilities. Töreboda has supermarkets, a bank and is convenient for a crew change, being on the main line from Stockholm to Göteborg. The electricity supply for yachts is, however, limited with just six double sockets and a maximum of 6amps. Karlsborg has a fuel station and it also boasts an enormous citadel built in the early 19th century. There are guest harbours both in the canal and at Stenbryggen just below the fortress. A good museum is situated within the fortress.

The stretch between Lakes Vänern and Vättern is the wildest and most remote part of the canal – a landscape of lakes and fir trees, very different from further east where the waterway runs through lush pastures and carefully cultivated farmland. Lake Viken is particularly beautiful, with an abundance of possible anchorages in small bays and between islands. The lock at the west end of the lake is manually operated. At its eastern end is Forsvik Sluss (lock), which is both the highest (3.5m) and the oldest lock on the canal, and boasts the oldest iron bridge in Sweden. The walls of this lock are uneven, slope slightly inwards and vessels should beware of unexpected protrusions.

Motala guest harbour, looking west *John Sadd*

The entrance to Vadstena on Lake Vättern *Dick Beddoe*

## Lake Vättern

This lake is about 60M in length running approximately north to south. Vessels making the transit of the canal will normally proceed directly between Karlsborg and Motala. A possible diversion on the western shore of Lake Vättern is Hjo (www.visithjo.se) – around 20M south of Karlsborg. Hjo has some of the best-preserved

The Borensberg lock (sluss) *Viv Fox*

wooden houses from the 17th, 18th and 19th centuries. The town received its town charter in 1413 and grew as a port and trading centre. The gästhamn has 14 guest berths in 2–3.3m of water, though there may be other free berths marked green.

The 17M direct passage from Karlsborg to Motala is straightforward and the islet of Fjuk (58°32'.3N 14°47'.5E) provides a landmark two thirds of the way across the lake. A good lookout should be kept when approaching Motala from the west for the marks to the north of Käveröns showing the entrance to the channel. Note that the direction of buoyage is east to west here.

An alternative landfall is Vadstena, about 8M southwest of Motala. The 16th-century castle provides a conspicuous landmark. The guest harbour is in the castle moat and is approached by a narrow canal. It has

The staircase of locks at Berg on the Göta Kanal *Dick Beddoe*

15 berths in depths of 1.5–2.5m with a range of facilities, and additional berths in the approach canal. The castle is impressive as is the peaceful old town with its 13th-century convent and 15th-century abbey. Vadstena is easily accessibly by bus (20mins) from Motala.

Lake Vättern is long, deep and unindented for the most part and is noted for its sudden squalls. However, a group of islands at Djäknesundet, 10M north-northeast of Karlsborg (58°37'.5N 14°34'E) provides a number of attractive and sheltered anchorages. The archipelago and the channels at the north end of the lake consist of over 200 islands and for those with the time to spare is well worth a visit.

There are firing ranges on the lake and for information about firing times ✆+46 505 40460 or call "Lake patrol Karlsborg" on VHF Ch 14.

## Lake Vättern to the Baltic Sea

On the 50M stretch between Motala on the eastern shores of Lake Vättern and Mem, where yachts lock out into the Slätbaken, an inlet of the Baltic Sea, there are 37 locks, all 'downhill' if eastbound. The distance is served by six guest harbours - at Motala, Borensberg where the lock is manually operated, Berg, Norsholm, Söderköping and Mem itself. The guest harbour beside the canal entrance at Motala has 65 berths and most facilities, including a holding tank emptying station. The booms are mostly 3.7m wide and fairly short. The electricity supply is just 6 amps. The nearby canal museum includes a working model of a lock - much enjoyed by children of all ages. There is also a fascinating motor museum.

Less than 3M after leaving Motala, eastbound vessels reach a staircase of five locks at Borenshult. A wait of several hours may occur at this point. Lake Boren is 6M long and after Borensberg, a further 13M takes one through open agricultural country to Berg, where the canal descends four pairs of locks before reaching the small guest harbour, which has limited facilities but is handy for the small town's cafés and restaurants. Below the harbour basin is the spectacular Carl Johan flight - seven locks which lower the canal the 18.8m down to Lake Roxen. On summer days these locks are thronged with spectators who come to watch the yachts and river steamers pass up and down the flights. However waits can be long, and if one misses the 'traffic lights' it may be 2hrs or more before the direction of flow is reversed. At the bottom of the Carl Johan flight is the Lake Roxen/Carl Johan marina. The boom berths are 3.8m wide and there is a digital display of when the next 'locking up' time is. Wider boats can moor on the waiting jetty to the south though this is open to winds from the northeast round to the southeast. Both Lake Boren and the 13.5M Lake Roxen are very pretty, and offer unhurried travellers the opportunity to anchor in unspoilt surroundings and off the beaten track.

Norsholm is at the east end of Lake Roxen. The busy main railway line from southern Sweden to Stockholm passes over the Canal at this point. At the lock beside the railway bridge, hanging warps are provided as the rise is only 0.9m. From Norsholm onwards a further 15M of canal (broken by the small and rocky Lake Asplången) and 15 locks connect to the Baltic Sea at Mem. East of Norsholm the canal is at its most rural, meandering along between cow pastures and past pretty cottages and gardens.

By Söderköping east-going yachts are almost at their journey's end, and many are tempted to stay for a day or two before heading out into the Baltic. The town is a favourite with the Swedes, and in July an almost Mediterranean atmosphere develops as people stroll in the sunshine. The canal is lined with tourist shops and restaurants (including a famous ice cream restaurant) many with live music, and some yachtsmen will find the area both noisy and lacking in privacy. In compensation the town is most attractive with a fine 18th-century town hall and two medieval churches, both with beautiful interiors. Unlike Mem, Söderköping has many shops and is a good place for provisioning.

The guest harbour lies along the canal just above the town's lock and has 42 berths. The western end has boom berths which are a maximum of 4.6m wide. The maximum practical boat length is 42ft (13m). The middle jetty is reserved for the canal steamers though it can be used for visitors if no steamers are scheduled. The eastern end has booms which are 3.8m wide. If the town harbour is full it may be possible to stop at the quay to the west of the bridge upstream of the town. This is a 15min walk into town. The pump-out station is after the town lock when heading east.

There are quays at Mem on both sides of the lock, with a 125m quay on the Slätbaken (Baltic) side where vessels entering the canal system wait to enter the lock and while dealing with paperwork. This berth can be uncomfortable in east or southeast winds. Above the lock there is a second quay with depths of 2·5–3m and space for about 10 visiting boats, with a further 10 bows-to berths on the (single) guest harbour pontoon (small). Showers and toilets, telephone, café and restaurant are all to hand, but there is no town nearby. The warehouse just above the lock was the venue for the canal's official opening ceremony, carried out by King Karl XIV Johan in 1832. Today it houses a shop, café and youth hostel.

The upper guest harbour at Berg, looking west. The top of the Carl Johans flight of locks is in the lower right corner of the picture *John Sadd*

The top two locks of the Carl Johans flight. These locks lead into the Berg Upper pound with its guest harbour *John Sadd*

The guest moorings at Söderköping, looking east *John Sadd*

# SOUTH COAST OF SWEDEN

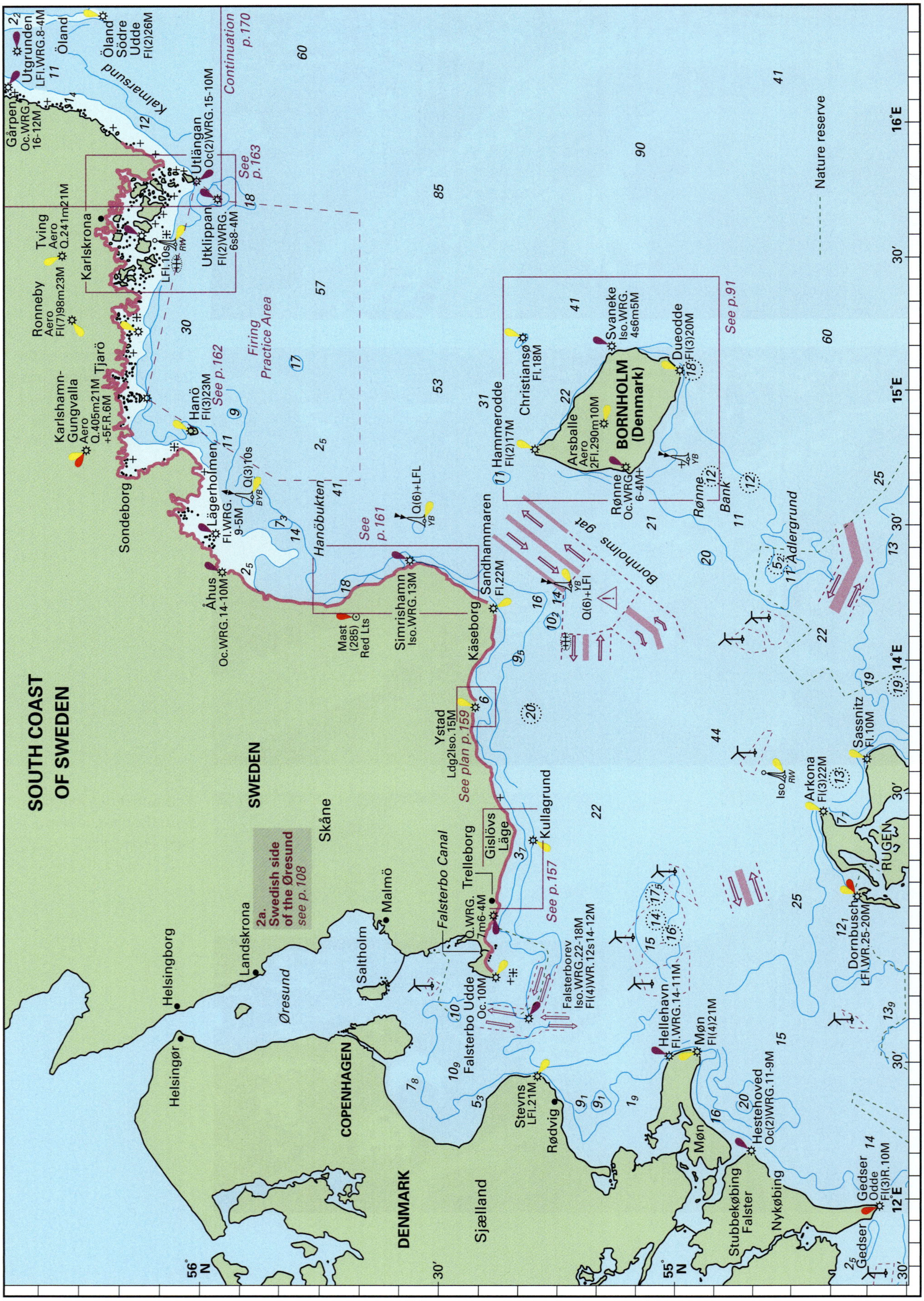

# 2E. SOUTH COAST OF SWEDEN

## GISLÖVS LÄGE TO UTKLIPPAN

The south coast of Sweden from Falsterbo as far as Simrishamn is largely low-lying, gentle, and with numerous sandy beaches. There are greater distances between significant harbours than on the rest of Sweden's coastline and the shore is open with few sheltered anchorages. Once past Simrishamn, the coastline starts to rise, and beyond Åhus it begins to assume the rocks and islands aspect, which is so typical of both the Kattegat and northeast coasts. There are firing ranges off this coast.

The entrance to Gislövs Läge marina *Andy Beharrell*

## GISLÖVS LÄGE

55°21'N 13°14'E

### Distances

Ystad 21M, Simrishamn 50M, Copenhagen 33M (by Falsterbo Kanal), Gedser (Denmark) 70M, Kiel 135M, Rønne (Bornholm) 55M

### Lights

**Kullagrund** 55°17'.9N 13°19'.5E Fl.WRG.3s18m16–12M
Red tower with black band, white lantern 20m Floodlit
**Trelleborg** 55°21'.4N 13°09'.1E Fl(2)G.6s8m6M

### Contacts

**Harbourmaster** ✆+46 410 73 33 77
**Marina office** ✆+46 704 807 692
VHF Ch 67 (Trelleborg commercial harbour)

Gislövs Läge (pronounced Yeece-leuvs Lair-ge) is a useful but somewhat featureless yacht harbour 3M east of the town of Trelleborg, itself a major ferry port and large commercial harbour but with no facilities for yachts. Several fishing boats and some traditional boats are based at Gislövs Läge, but the harbour is mainly reserved for yachts and is administered as one of the civic amenities of Trelleborg.

### *Approach*

On approach, the town of Trelleborg is very obvious from the sea, marked by the continual comings and goings of

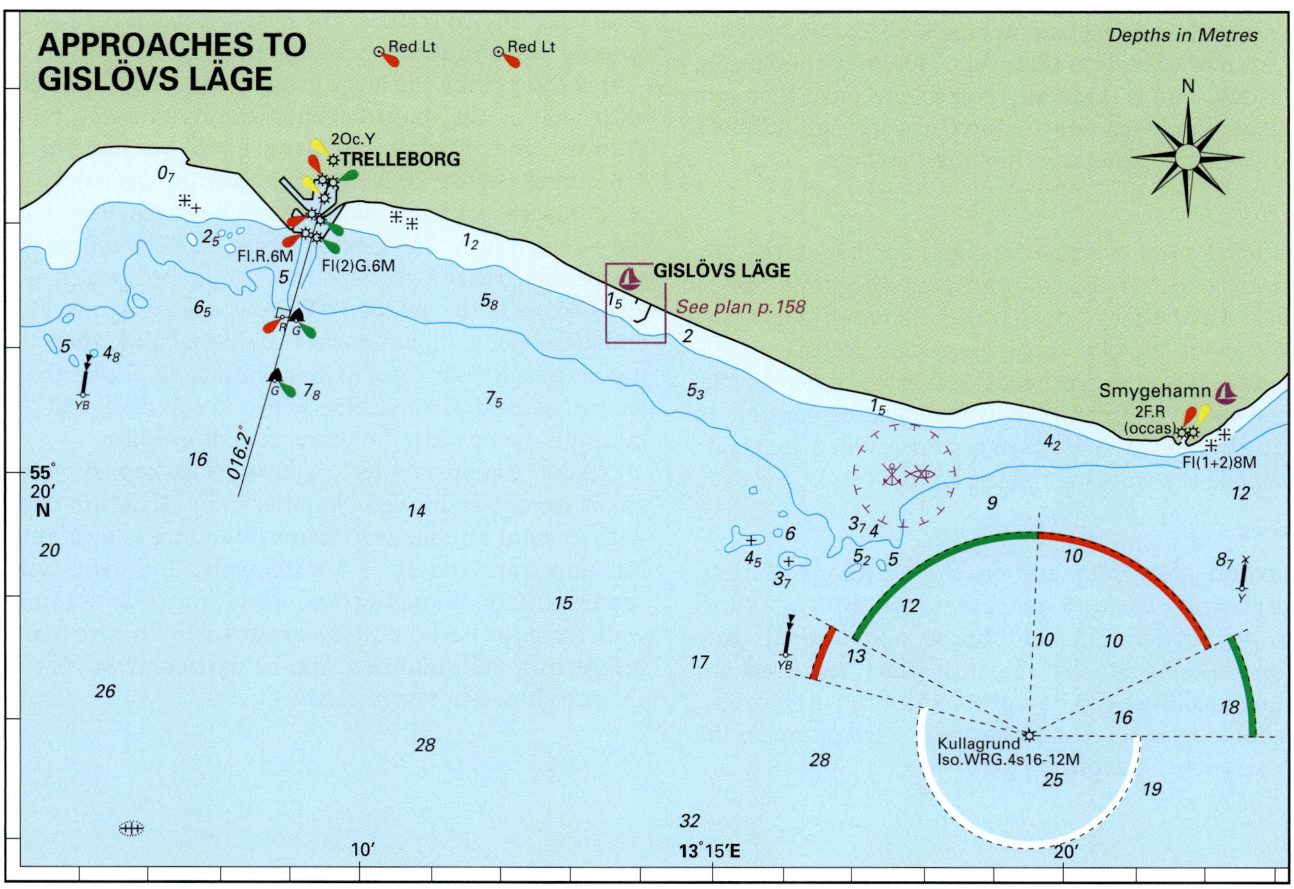

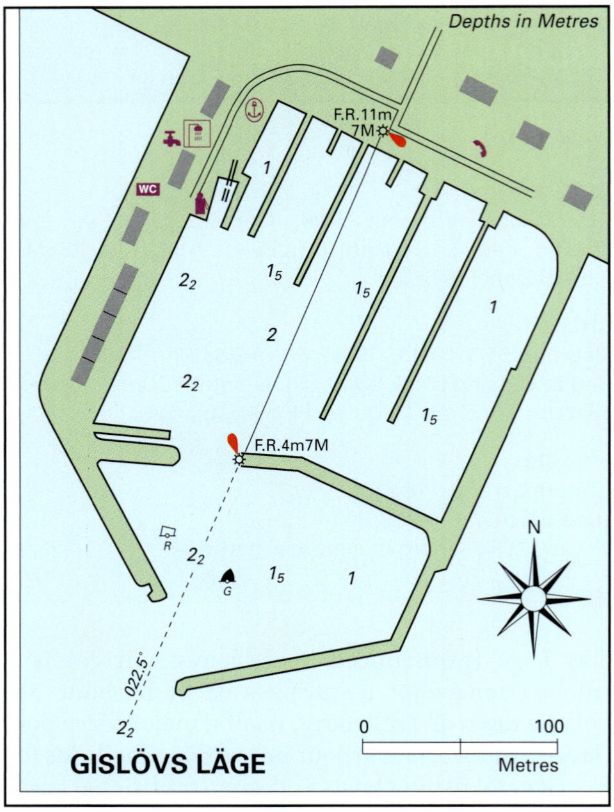


the ferries and other large vessels. Once within 3M of the coast, in normal visibility, the entrance to Gislövs Läge can be seen. Approach is on 022.5° with leading marks in line. There is a small outer harbour with small green and red buoys just inside the entrance showing the way to the inner harbour. The southwestern part of the inner harbour has depths of 2m or more, shoaling to the north and east and at times of low water have been known to be less than this. However the bottom is soft mud and it is usually possible to push through. Entrance should not be attempted in a strong southerly, when swell can penetrate the inner harbour.

### Berthing

There are a total of some 30 guest berths – eight box berths to port just inside the entrance with stern lines to posts, and a further 20 or so (rather narrow) slots at the outer ends of the two longer pontoons. Neither of the pontoons have hammerheads. Other available berths are marked by a green disc. It may also be possible to raft up alongside the western quay, provided yachts do not impede the working fishing boats.

### Services

Water and electricity are on the pontoons. Toilets, showers and washing machines are in two small buildings between the clubhouse and a small café (tokens bought at the marina office required for washing machines can be a problem). WiFi is free. Fuel is available from a self service credit card pump on the west quay (check depth).

### Facilities

Ashore, there is a small village, partly serving as a residential area for Trelleborg and partly as a quiet location for holiday homes, though there is a restaurant and a small grocery store about 10min walk up the road. Frequent buses go to Trelleborg which has all the attributes of a city.

## YSTAD

55°25'N 13°49'E

### Distances

Distances Gislövs Läge 21M, Simrishamn 28M, Copenhagen 58M

### Contacts

Marina office ✆+46 73 718 4613
www.ystad.se/fritid/smabatshamnar
ystadmarina@ystad.se

This is a busy ferry port for Bornholm in Denmark and Świnoujście in Poland with a separate yacht basin, depth 2.7m in entrance, to the west of the main harbour. These are protected from south to southeast by two outer breakwaters of rough boulders, the north one having been extended to provide improved shelter to the yacht harbour (which is generally well sheltered but susceptible to some surge in strong south westerlies). The yacht harbour entrance should be approached with caution in strong southwest to west weather and the approach is prone to shoaling with the sands shifting in storms. The best approach is to align yourself with the entrance about 200m off.

In the approach the large green grain elevator on the west side of the main harbour stands out well from seaward. The outlying shallows are well buoyed and lit.

Berthing (up to 30 berths for visiting yachts) is on walk ashore pontoons, with some alongside berths on the western jetty. The gästhamn can be very full in the season. Electricity is paid for with a Tallycard, which also gives access to the ablutions. There is a washing machine and diesel pontoon, but diesel is only available when the harbourmaster is present. It is not automatic. The berthing fee can be paid at a machine with a credit card, and the machine also provides Tallycards for late arrivals.

Ystad Skeppshandel (www.ystadskeppshandel.se) is an old-fashioned chandlery, an 'Aladdin's cave' with ancient and modern items. Bike hire is available. Bus and train station is 5 mins walk. The town with supermarkets, shopping and restaurants is a 15min walk from the harbour. It is a beautiful town with many interesting old buildings, and in particular St Mary's Church should not be missed.

Looking northeast from guest pontoons towards Ystad town
*Andy Beharrell*

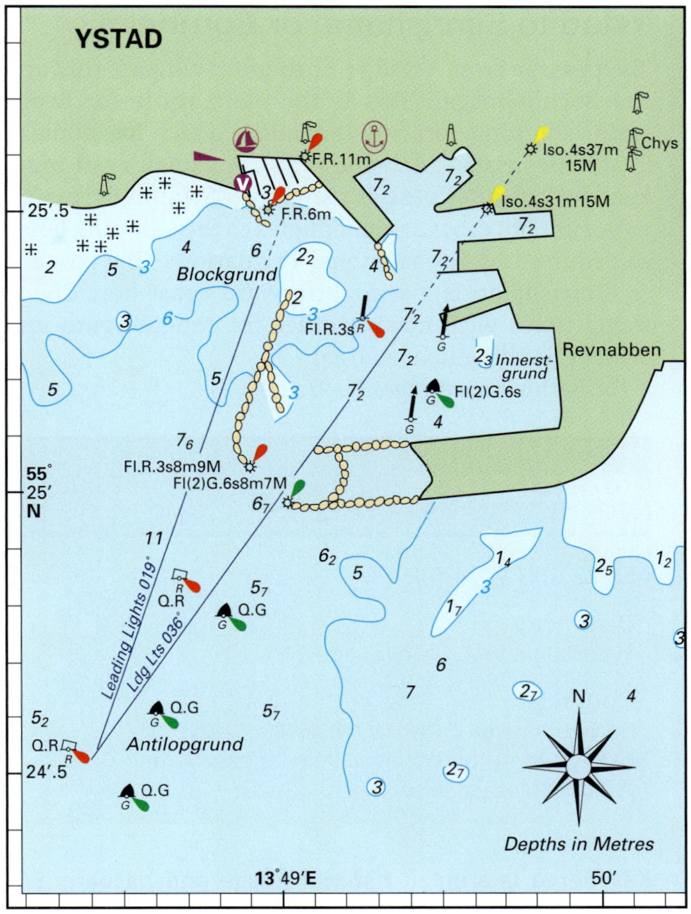

The harbour at Ystad looking northeast. The guest berths are on the jetty and the first pontoon from the left *Andy Beharrell*

## Ystad to Simrishamn or Bornholm

The passage from Ystad to Bornholm will pass through the Bornholmsgat. This is the main route for deep-water shipping entering the Baltic, which has a major Traffic Separation Scheme (TSS). All small craft must keep well clear of vessels using the TSS and if crossing to Bornholm, cross at right angles to the shipping lanes as required by international regulations. The passage to Simrishamn is a straightforward coast hop. Check firing times with marina office for ranges south and west of Sandhammaren light.

*For Bornholm see pages 91–97*

## KÅSEBERGA

55°22'.95N 14°04'.01E

**Distances**
Simrishamn 18M, Gislövs Läge 30M

**Contacts**
**Harbourmaster** ✆+46 73 718 4613
www.ystad.se/fritid/smabatshamnar/kaseberga/
ystadmarina@ystad.se

Kåseberga is a small fishing village and harbour 8M east of Ystad. It is managed by the harbour office at Ystad, so if you stop in Ystad, you can ask the Harbour Master there if you have any queries about Kåseberga harbour. There is 2–2.5m of water in the harbour and the guest berths are alongside on the south pier or the quayside. To the west of Kåseberga there is a firing range and warnings are broadcast on VHF.

Though it is a nice small harbour (and quieter alternative to Ystad), the main reason for a stay is to visit the Ales Stenar, also known as the Kåseberga Ship. This is the largest stone ship in Scandinavia and dates from around 600CE. Its purpose and function is much disputed, but human remains have been found there making it possible that it is a grave. Others believe that is might have astronomical functions. Either way, it is worth a visit!

An aerial view of *Ales Stenar* – a stone ship near Kåseberga *David Castor/Wikimedia Commons (https://commons.wikimedia.org/wiki/File:Ales_stenar_-_Ale%27s_Stones_-_2021_05_29.jpg)*

## SKILLINGE

55°28'.34N 14°17'.41E (start of entrance channel)

**Distances**
Hanö 38M, Rønne 27M, Ystad 23M

**Contacts**
**Harbourmaster** ✆+46 481 9217
www.skillinge.com

Skillinge is an alternative harbour to Simrishamn around 6M south and makes a good stop if heading across from Bornholm. The guest berths are in the southwest area of the harbour, more or less straight ahead as you go through the entrance. Mooring is between Y-booms or alongside the jetty. Depths are between 2-4m. The approach is relatively straightforward through a buoyed channel with a sharp turn around the breakwater into the harbour. Facilities include washing machines, showers, toilets and water and electricity and there are shops nearby.

The town has an interesting history and today is well known for its theatre. The traditional wooden houses are well-preserved and in the oldest part of town there are no roads but paths called Strädden. There is also a small maritime museum and many traditional boats have made the harbour their home, so there is plenty to do once you are moored.

## SIMRISHAMN

55°33'N 14°22'E

**Distances**
Gislövs Läge 50M, Rønne (Bornholm) 30M, Karlskrona 60M, Kalmar 100M

**Lights**
**Sandhammaren** 55°23'N 14°11'.8E Fl.5s31m22M Red metal tower, framework base 29m
**Simrishamn** 55°33'.5N 14°22'E Iso.WRG.6s16m13-9M White tower 15m
buoy **Långagrund** 55°32'.4N 14°30'.2E Q(6)+Fl.15s South cardinal pillar buoy, s topmark

**Contacts**
**Marina office** ✆+46 41 481 9217
hamnen@simrishamn.se
www.simrishamn.se/om-kommunen/hamnar
VHF Ch 11/16

Simrishamn (pronounced Sim-ris-hahmn) is a pleasant town with a busy commercial and fishing harbour, leading to a well-equipped yacht harbour. It is a convenient stopping place on the way to or from the Northern Baltic, though when the fishing fleet is active the harbour can be noisy and disturbed and particular

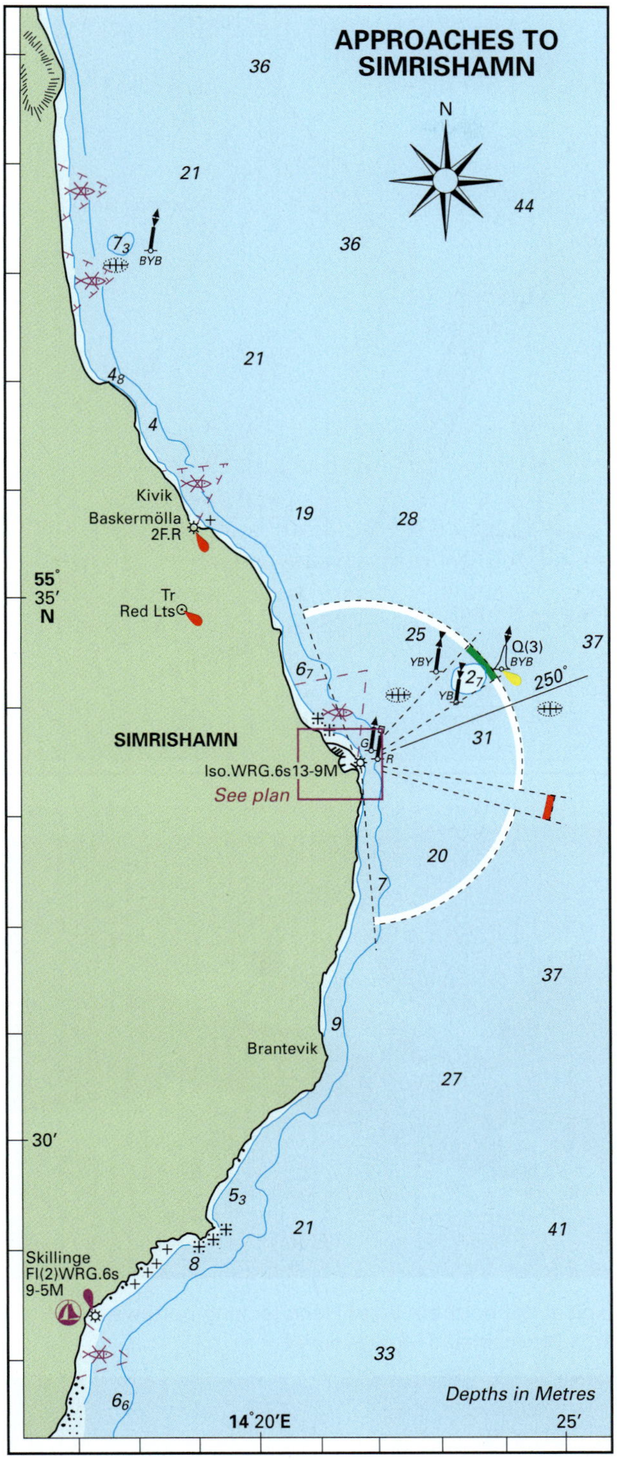


care must be taken on entry and departure. The largely 19th-century town has pretty cobbled streets, painted houses and open market, and the 12th-century St Nicolai Kyrka (church) is worth visiting.

### Approach

Both Simrishamn lighthouse and the gabled red-roofed church are good landmarks from offshore. When closer in, fluorescent orange leading marks will be seen on a bearing of 250°, keeping vessels well south of the 2.7m Nedjan shoal, itself marked by cardinal buoys. The harbour should only be approached with extreme caution in strong onshore winds, and unpredictable currents may be created both inside and outside the

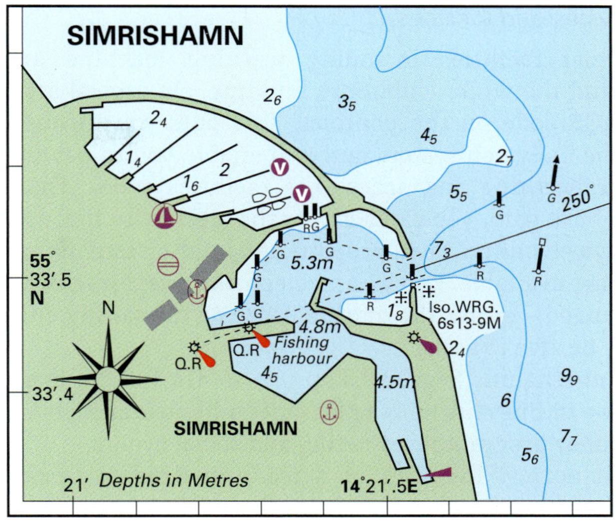


entrance by prolonged easterlies. The breakwaters are painted red and green on the ends making identification fairly straightforward on entry. The yacht marina with all facilities is immediately to starboard after entering the main harbour. The entrance to the marina is marked by buoys. Do not stray outside the marked channel.

### Berthing

The outer ends of the two southernmost jetties are reserved for visiting yachts, berths on the nearer jetty being alongside and reserved for those of more than 4m beam. The 26 visitors' berths on the second pontoon are step on pontoons, both depth and width being indicated on posts on the pontoon itself. Yachts which are too large to use the marina may be able to berth in the fishing or commercial harbours – contact the harbour office before arrival. With the decline in the fishing industry, there is reported to be more space in the fishing harbour for yachts.

The harbour at Simrishamn, looking east with the entrance on the right. The guest berths are on the outer end of both pontoons *Andy Beharrell*

*Services and facilities*

Normal facilities including washing machine are behind the white clubhouse building. On arrival scan the QR code on the pontoon. This puts you through to the Tallyweb system and will enable you to pay for your berthing and access the facilities codes. Once you have paid, you can activate the electricity through Tallyweb online. Fuel, propane and holding tank pump out are available. Engine and electronics repairs can be arranged - either the marina office or the sailing club may be able to assist.

Simrishamns Segelsällskap (✆+46 414 107 70) is an active sailing club with a pleasant clubhouse and a busy summer programme of racing and social events.

All normal facilities of a medium-sized town are available with the helpful tourist office close to the harbour. Bus and rail stations are within 0.5km of the marina.

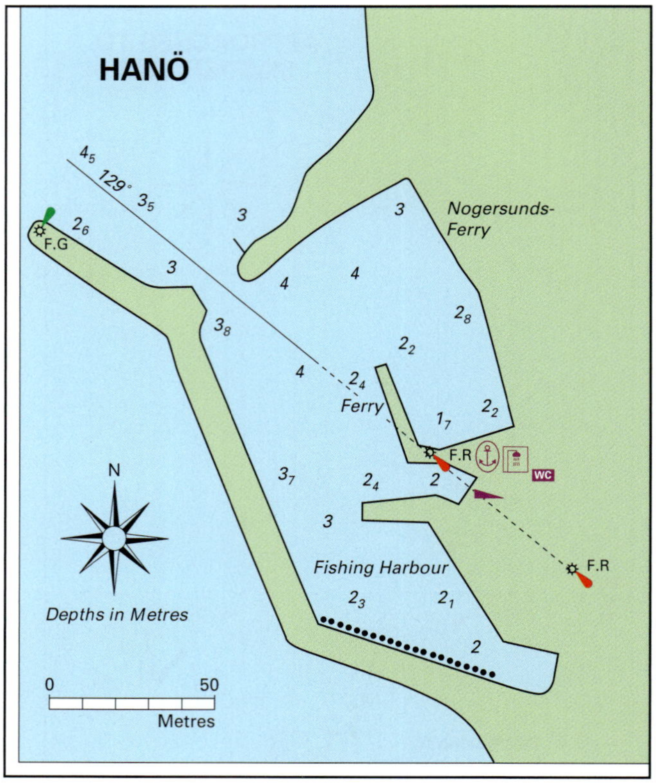


## HANÖ

56°01'N 14°50'E

**Distances**

Simrishamn 32M, Rønne (Bornholm) 55M, Karlskrona 28M, Utklippan29M

**Contacts**

Marina office ✆+46 456 53008, Mobile +46 768 993008
www.hano.nu
hanoharbourmaster@gmail.com

Hanö is a small artificial harbour on the west side of Hanö Island, and is a pleasant and convenient stopping place between Simrishamn and either Karlskrona or Utklippan. Approach is straightforward, but could be uncomfortable in northwest winds. Berthing alongside, or possibly rafting, particularly at weekends in the summer, where the harbourmaster will help. Depth is 2m anywhere, and 4m, alongside west or north piers. Basic marina facilities are available, also a shop and café.

There is an interesting walk up to the lighthouse and to the naval cemetery, where a cross was erected in 1973 in memory of the sailors of HMS *Victory*, who died there during the winter of 1810.

The spit at the northern tip of Hanö looking northwest towards the mainland *Andy Beharrell*

Hanö fyr (lighthouse). A lovely walk from the gästhamn. Look out for the herds of deer as you walk around the island *Andy Beharrell*

## The coast from Hanö to Karlskrona and beyond

It is only 8M north of Hanö that the east coast truly begins. This is an extraordinary coastline, consisting of thousands of islands with countless channels between them, many small harbours and myriad anchorages. Apart from Kalmarsund which runs inside the 70M-long island of Öland, the *skärgård* runs to about 100M north of Stockholm. This provides a fascinating cruising ground which can take many years to explore to the full. A book such as this can only scratch the surface of what is available, and safe navigation demands the presence of the most detailed charts available.

Sailing in the *skärgård* requires constant attention. The main channels are marked on the charts as a dashed line, indicating that these are safe for navigation. You may choose to take your own shortcuts, but you do so at your own peril. The channels are buoyed with red and green markers, which are usually there for a specific purpose, marking shoals or submerged rocks.

## TÄRNÖ

56°07'.39N 14°58'.32E

**Distances**
Utklippan 23M, Kalmar 29M

Tärnö is a good stop between Hanö and Karlskrona. The bay can be approached either from the east or west, but take care of offlying rocks and follow the charts carefully. Once in the bay, there are various mooring possibilities. The easiest may be the jetty on the eastern side of the bay. This has stern buoys for mooring bows-to the jetty. Alternatively you can anchor in the bay, or there is an SXK (Swedish Cruising Association) mooring buoy for members.

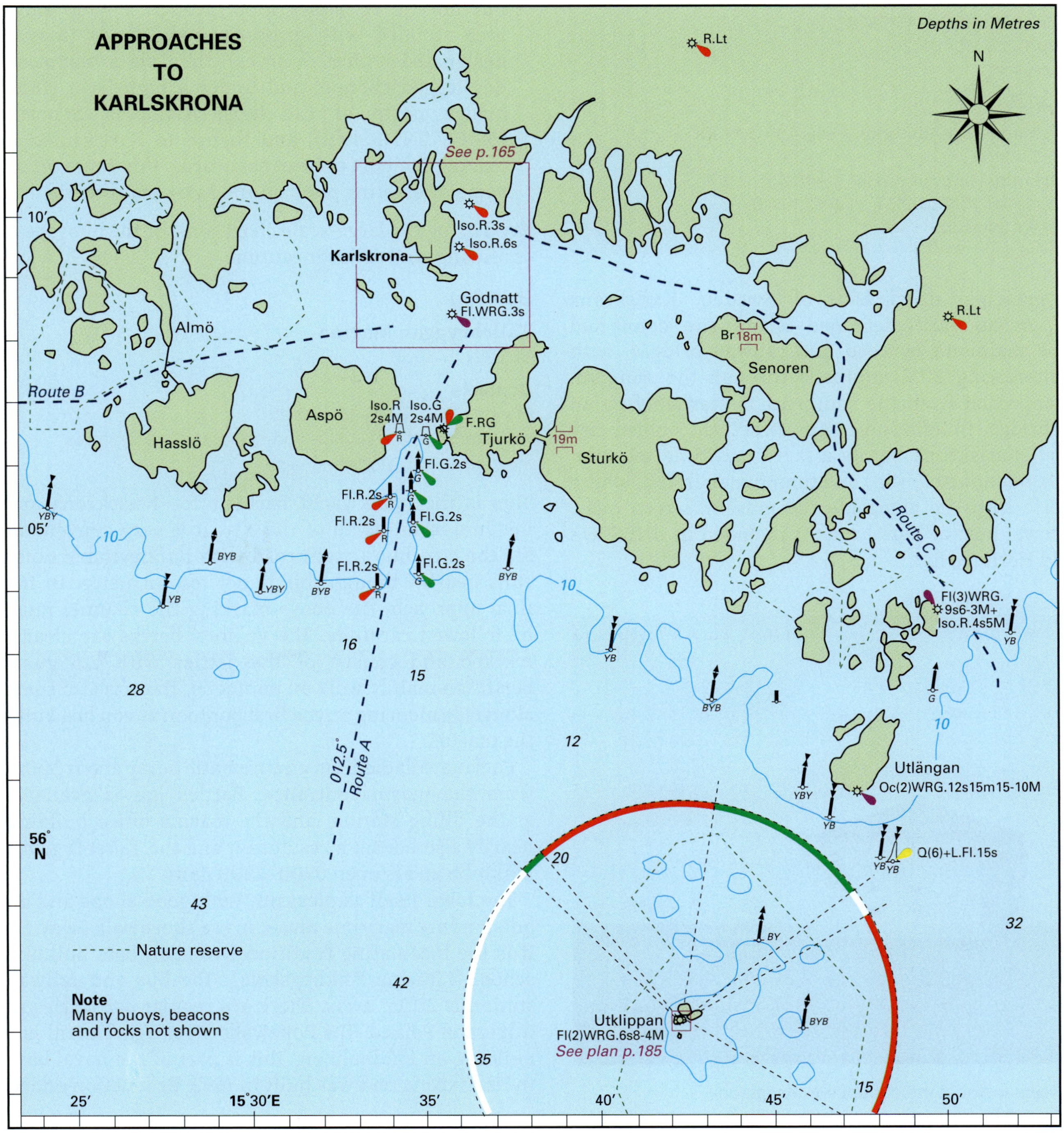

## KARLSKRONA

56°10'N 15°36'E

### Distances

Hanö 28M, Simrishamn 60M, Rønne 75M, Kalmar 50M, Utklippan, 13M

### Lights

**Utklippan south rock** 55°57'.2N 15°42'.2E Fl(2)WRG. 6s.31m W8/R5/G4M. Nov. to Mar. only.Red framework tower on old fort 30m

**Karlskrona Leading Lights 012.5°** *Front* Stumholmen, 56°09'.5N 15°36'E Iso.R.6s22m16M White round concrete tower 24m
Rear 0.7M from front Iso.R.3s37m16M White round concrete tower 15m

**Västra Försänkningen** 56°06'.5N 15°34'.5E Iso.R.2s6m6M Racon White and red dolphin Floodlit

**Godnatt** 56°08'.5N 15°35'.8E
Fl.WRG.3s20m11–7M
Grey fort

### Contacts

**Karlskrona Port Authority** ✆+46 455 303000, VHF Ch 14/16
**Karlskrona Harbourmaster** ✆+46 455 21871, Mobile +46 70 930 3151, VHF Ch 14/16
www.visitkarlskrona.se/en

The principal naval base of Sweden, Karlskrona occupies an easily-defended island site connected to the mainland by road and railway bridges, with an interesting 20M approach through the *skärgård*. The approach from the southeast is restricted by an 18m bridge. In addition to an attractive, cobbled city centre, Karlskrona boasts a large maritime museum (www.marinmuseum.se) on Stumholmen island, where historic ships lie alongside the museum's own quay. The naval port of Karlskrona is included in UNESCO's World Heritage list.

Defensive tower at the entrance to Karlskrona
*Andy Beharrell*

### *Approach & entrance*

There are three principal channels, all of which require large-scale charts:

A. The main channel, which leads between the large islands of Aspö and Tjurkö on a bearing of 012.5° and is well buoyed and lit.

B. The southwest channel, which is entered at the Hyperionsgrund buoy (56°06'.7N 15°22'E) and is buoyed but not lit. There is a swing bridge at Hasslöbron between Almö and Hasslö islands at 56°07'.7N 15°27'.7E. The bridge opens on the hour and remains open for 10mins. The bridge keeper's phone number is ✆+46 455 33 2240. Further details are given at: www.sjofartsverket.se/en/services/bridges-and-canals/hasslobron/

C. The southeast channel, which is entered east of Långören island at 56°03'.7N 15°50'E and is buoyed but not lit. It passes first through a wide shoal area studded with grass-covered islands (mostly designated nature reserves), then via a narrower, dog-legged channel and under a high level (18m) bridge north of the large island of Senoren (56°08'.2N 15°45'E), and thence to Karlskrona. If leaving the port to head eastwards, this route offers some interesting pilotage and saves many miles.

Even using the large-scale chart some of the buoyage is confusing, and calls for caution.

### *Berthing*

#### Tallebryggan Marina

56°10'N 15°35'.3E

**Contacts**

Marina office ✆+46 455 303150
www.karlskrona.se/kultur-fritid-och-turism/stadsmarina/
info@karlskronastadsmarina.se

This is the main yacht harbour for Karlskrona and lies in a basin north of the city. It is very convenient for the city, but a main road with its inevitable noise runs nearby, though this is not too intrusive. In the final approach, the buoys marking the channel must be followed carefully. The visitors' berths are clearly marked and consist of five jetties with 125 guest berths on mainly walk on pontoons. There is also some alongside mooring on the first pontoon as you head into the marina.

Fuel is available from an automatic pump about 200m from the marina entrance. Bottled gas is available at the filling station, and the marina office building nearby also houses a restaurant and the Tallebryggans Båtklubb and is open 0700–2200 daily.

The town itself is pleasant, with good shops and an outstanding maritime museum is a short walk away. By it is the fascinating traditional wooden boat building school (Litorina Folkhögskola). The bus and railway station is 200m away. There are regular car ferries to Gdynia in Poland. The Ropewalk (Repslagarbanan) is a building on Lindholmen. This is part of the naval base in Karlskrona and was built in 1692. Production ended

in 1960 but in 2006, after renovation, it was opened to the public and has a range of exhibitions as well as ropemaking demonstrations. At 300m, it is Sweden's longest wooden building.

### Dragsö Yacht Harbour

56°10'.4N 15°33'.9E

Marina office ✆+46 455 10596, Mobile +46 709 283788

Dragsö Yacht Harbour on Utkik island, administered by the Karlskrona Segelsällskap (sailing club), is quieter and much more scenic but is a long way from the city. Six of its 130 berths are reserved for visitors. A red/green system is used to indicate additional free berths.

From any of the approach channels, pass north of the conspicuous Godnatt tower and follow the buoyed channel south of Lindholmen island, south of the Arsenal and west of Saltö island. The small islet northwest of Saltö must also be left to starboard. Once past this islet a buoyed channel opens to the east. Follow it, and the marina's two pontoons will soon come into view to starboard beyond the clubhouse. Berthing is bows on, stern to a buoy, in depths of 2–2.5m, with visitors placed at the ends of the two outer (westernmost) pontoons. Swell may find its way in during strong northwesterly winds. The yacht harbour is in an almost enclosed lagoon surrounded by countryside, though some noise may penetrate from the nearby campsite. There is a children's play area and a barbecue area for the use of guests. There is water to all berths and electricity to most, with showers, sauna and laundry facilities ashore, a clubhouse with seasonal café, but no restaurant, shop or fuel. Slipway (with pressure hose and plenty of vacant cradles in summer) - enquire at the office. A diver is also available.

The Saltö Varv boatyard (www.saltovarv.se, ✆+46 455 15511), where minor repairs might be undertaken, is about 300m to the south (though further by water). They will be able to help locate other tradesmen. The harbour is not within walking distance of the city but is on a bus route and bicycles can be hired from the nearby campsite.

## FLAKSKÄR

56°03'.99N 15°43'.56E

**Distances**
Utklippan 7M, Kalmar 48M

Flakskär is a nice anchorage just to the east of Karlskrona. While it can be a bit exposed with winds from the west and northwest, it is possible to find shelter from most other wind directions and is particularly sheltered with winds from the south and east. There is a mooring buoy for SXK (Swedish Cruising Association) members.

The area is best known for the 'Whiskey on the rocks' incident. S-363 was a Soviet Navy Whiskey-class submarine. It ran aground near Flaskär (Torhamnaskär) on 27 October 1981 and rapidly turned into a major international diplomatic incident. In 2006 the vessel's political officer, Vasily Besedin, confirmed in an interview that there were nuclear weapons on board. He admitted that the crew had been ordered to destroy the boat if the Swedes tried to take over the submarine.

## UTKLIPPAN

55°57'N 15°42'E

**Distances**
Karlskrona 13M, Bergkvara 29M, Kalmar 48M, Visby (Gotland) 135M, Christiansø 42M

Utklippan provides an interesting and convenient overnight stop for yachts on passage along the Swedish coast. It consists of two small skerries situated 4.5M southwest of Utlängan, the nearest land. Four breakwaters nearly join the two skerries on their east and west sides, thus nearly enclosing the lagoon between them. In the north skerry a basin 90m x 40m was originally excavated for the use of the lighthouse tender, with two entrances, on the southeast and southwest sides (the southwest one is deeper). It is a delightful spot with perfect shelter and is capable - at a squeeze - of berthing up to 25 boats in 2.5-3m depths but be prepared to raft up. There is a lighthouse 30m high on the south skerry (you will need a dinghy to reach this) and an automatic foghorn. Shoals extend

The basin at Utklippan *Andy Beharrell*

The eastern entrance to the Utklippan basin *Andy Beharrell*

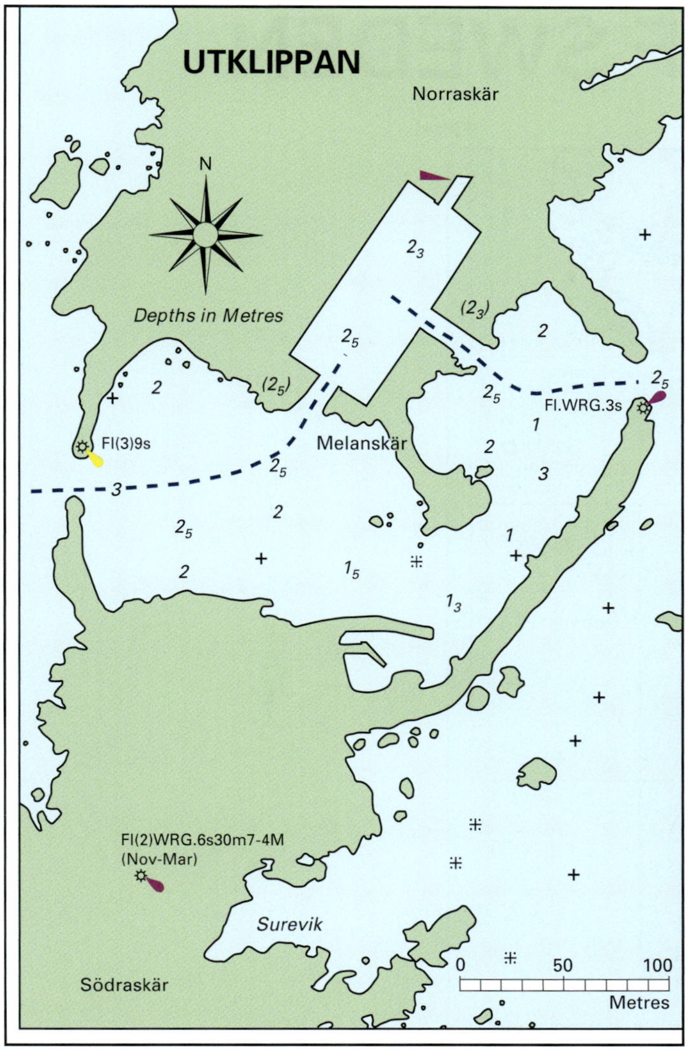


both north and south of the islands, which should be approached with care and a large-scale chart.

The final approach from either direction (favour the lee side) is via rock-fringed channels and thence between low moles, where strong currents can be encountered. At night, approach in the white sector of the Södraskär light from the northeast, or the green from the northwest. Facilities are limited to chemical toilets and refuse bins in season but the wild and attractive surroundings more than compensate. It is reported to be an outstanding spot for bird watching, though noisy in the nesting season when their young are vigorously defended. It is also a good spot for seal-spotting. The skerries out to the east will often have seals on them.

The basin at Utklippan looking south towards the lighthouse on the south island *Andy Beharrell*

Aerial view of Utklippan *L.G.foto/Wikimedia Commons (https://commons.wikimedia.org/wiki/File:Utklippan.jpg)*

# EAST COAST OF SWEDEN

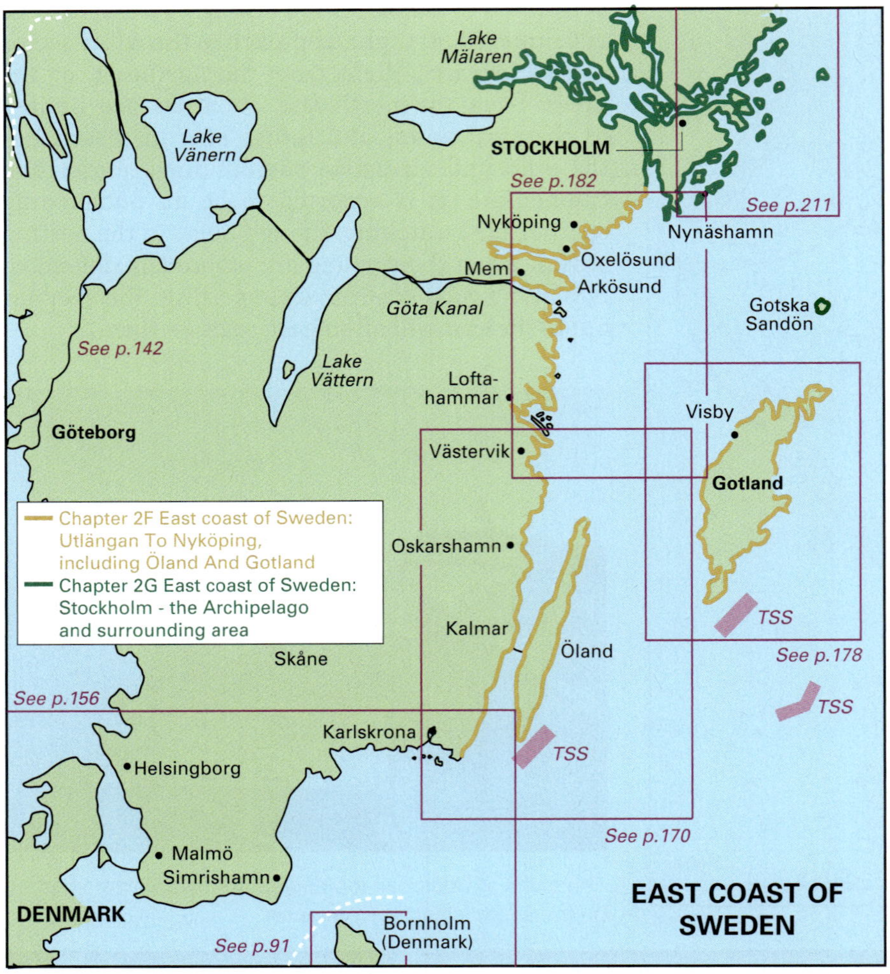


Sweden's east coast changes character as one moves north. For the first few miles it is open to the full width of the Baltic, and then comes under the influence of two major and one minor offshore islands. Öland, some 70M long is separated from the mainland by Kalmarsund, which is spanned by a bridge. Northeast of that lies Gotland, of similar length to Öland but wider, which is reputed to have some of the best summer weather in the Baltic. Visby is its principal harbour and is inclined to be busy during the peak months, but towards autumn the activity decreases and makes this an attractive time to visit. North of Gotland is the small island of Gotska Sandon which has no harbour, but is surrounded by superb sandy beaches off any of which one may anchor in suitable conditions.

North of Kalmarsund the *skärgård* begins with deep inlets and myriad offshore rocks and islands presenting a beautiful and interesting cruising area. The Göta Kanal meets the Baltic at Mem, some 70M north of Kalmarsund, and the *skärgård* continues to Stockholm which is set between the lake and islands of Mälaren to the west and the extensive Stockholm *skärgård* to the east and northeast.

There are firing practice areas on this coast.

## 2F. UTLÄNGAN TO NYKÖPING, INCLUDING ÖLAND AND GOTLAND

### Kalmarsund

The Baltic coast of Sweden north of Utklippan offers superb cruising in relatively sheltered waters among islands. The first 20M or so is open until the entrance to Kalmarsund, the strait which runs for 70M inside the island of Öland. It narrows from about 10M wide at either end to 4M at its narrowest, and it can funnel the wind to provide some brisk sailing. The town of Kalmar is immediately south of its narrowest point, where it is crossed by a high-level bridge with a clearance of 36m. The southern end of Gotland and Öland have a reputation for fog, but this tends to clear in summer as the sound is entered. There is a Traffic Separation Scheme off the southeast corner of Öland. There are numerous wind farms in Kalmarsund, and on Öland, not all of which are shown on the charts.

Kristianopel church – a beautiful example of early 17th century architecture *Andy Beharrell*

Kristianopel gästhamn *Andy Beharrell*

The entrance to Kristianopel gästhamn *Andy Beharrell*

Once north of Kalmar the *skärgård* begins to assert itself and the number of small harbours and anchorages increases far beyond the compass of this book. It is unwise to navigate anywhere on this coast without large scale (1:50,000 or greater) Swedish charts; from here northwards they should be regarded as essential. It is also wise to carry at least one of the local pilot books (see page 100) on board.

There are three relatively small harbours along the mainland before arriving at Kalmar. These are Sandhamn (not to be confused with the harbour of the same name in the Stockholm archipelago), Kristianopel and Bergkvara. The passage from either Utklippan or Karlskrona to Kalmar is quite lengthy, and any of these would be a comfortable overnight stop.

## KRISTIANOPEL

56°14'.78N 16°04'.09E

**Distances**
Utklippan 23M, Kalmar 29M

**Contacts**
www.kristianopelresort.se/gasthamn
info@kristianopelresort.se
✆+46 70 944 7220

Kristianopel is a good stop between either Karlskrona or Utklippan and Kalmar. Although it is possible to go up the Öland shore, Kristianopel makes a good alternative heading up the mainland shore. There are 70 guest berths in the gästhamn – mainly stern buoys, but it is possible to go alongside one of the outer jetties. The harbour is generally sheltered though there may be some set into the harbour in easterlies. In this case mooring against the inner side of the eastern jetty may be better. Depths are between 1.5–2.8m but closer to the latter in most of the harbour.

The harbour has all the services you might expect – toilets, showers and washing machines. There is also a pump-out station available. It is part of the Kristianopel Resort and harbour fees can be paid at the harbour office just by the main harbour jetty.

All around Kristianopel you can see remnants of the time when the border between Denmark and Sweden ran close to the town. The kilometre-long city wall protected the inhabitants, but also indicates the heavily fortified border between the countries from this era. The city was founded by the Danish King Christian IV in the early 1600s and is considered to be Scandinavia's first Renaissance city.

ÖLAND AND THE APPROACHES TO KALMAR
N
Depths in Metres
Västervik
See p.187
Kungsgrundet
LFl(2)WRG.9-6M
See p.182
Q(3)10s
Knoll's Ground
Kalmarsund
Q
Kråkelund
Ölands Norra Udde
Fl(4)15s14M
Tokenäsudde
LFl.WRG.12-8M
Stora Karlsö
LFl(2)WR.16/13M
Finnrevet
Fl(2)WRG.6s8M
Oskarshamn
See p.183
Blå Jungfrun
Byxelkrok
Högby
LFl(2)12M
Dämman
LFl.WRG.8s9-6M
Slottsbredan
Fl(2)WRG.6s
8-5M
Borgholm
Oc.WR.4s
5/3M
Kappeludden
LFl.12M
Ispeudde
LFl(2)WRG.
13-9M
Sillåsen
Fl(3)WRG.8s20m8-4M
Masknaggen
Q.WRG.14-10M
Berga
Aero F.R.71m22M
KALMAR
Färjestaden
See p.172
Öland
Mörbylånga
See p.156
Garpen
Oc.WRG.16-12M
Bergkvara
Utgrunden
LFl.WRG.8-4M
Segerstad
LFl(3)WRG.12-8M
Kristianopel
Grönhögen
Karlskrona
See p.165
Ölands Södra Udde
Fl(2)26M+F.WRG.
19-14M
Q(3)10s
Ölands Södra Grund
LFl.9M & 4.Q.3M
Kalmarsund
Traffic Separation Scheme
Nature reserve
Utlängan
Oc(2)WRG.15-10M
Utklippan
Fl(2)WRG.6s31m8-4M
30′
57° N
30′
56° N
16°E
30′
17°E
30′
18°E

# KALMAR

56°40'N 16°21'E

### Distances

Simrishamn 100M, Karlskrona 50M, Visby 95M, Västervik 65M

### Lights

**Southern approach**

**Ölands Södra** Udde 56°11'.8N 16°24'E Fl(2)30s41m26M
Round white stone tower, black band 42m Floodlit

**Utgrunden (north end of shoal)** 56°22'.5N 16°15'.7E LFl.
WRG.8s29m8–4M Racon
Black tower, white band and lantern, grey conical base 28m

**Skansgrundet** 56°39'.1N 16°22'.7E Oc(2)WRG.20s18m15–11M
Black tower, green band, grey conical base, white lantern 19m Floodlit

**Northern approach**

**Dämman** 57°03'.4N 16°41'.7E
LFl.WRG.8s9–6M
Orange tower, black band, grey base 21m

**Slottsbredan** 56°55'.7N 16°36'.3E Fl(2)WRG.6s20m8–4M
Black tower, green band and lantern, grey conical base 21m

**Krongrundet** 56°41'.4N 16°24'.5E Oc(2)WRG.8s10m15–10M
White tower, green and black stripe 11m

### Contacts

**VTS Oxelösund** ☎+46 480 10719, VHF Ch 9
**Kalmar Commercial Harbour** ☎+46 480 451450
VHF Ch 9, 12, 16
kalmar.hamn@kommun.kalmar.se
**Kalmar Guest Harbour** ☎+46 480 417700
☎+46 769 273199
gasthamn@ kalmar.com
www.kalmar.se (click on Tourism – Travel – Marinas)

Kalmar is one of Sweden's oldest towns, and the scene of the Union of Kalmar in 1397. It was originally a Viking stronghold, and became one of the major ports of the Hanseatic League. The present town, with a population of around 50,000, has many historic buildings dating back to the 17th century, a fine baroque cathedral and a picturesque and very interesting castle, which is a World Heritage Site, in a dominant position overlooking Kalmarsund. The castle museum has an outstanding exhibition of articles from the sunken 17th-century warship *Kronan*, while the maritime museum in the old quarter at the east end of the town is also worth visiting. Kalmar has a very good shopping centre which, like all these attractions is within easy walking distance of the harbour.

### *Approach & entrance*

From either direction, follow the main north-south shipping channel which passes close past the harbour. The entrance leads off it to the west at a point 1.2M south of the Öland bridge. Berthing is in the old northwest basin, the Ölandshamnen, which is approached through the Gamlahamnen, itself directly opposite the harbour entrance. Mooring is mainly with bows to the quay and stern to a buoy, though a few alongside berths may be found on the starboard hand near the entrance. There are also some booms in the far left-hand corner; the width of the berth is indicated on a sign at the end. Depths vary from 4.5m near the entrance to 2m at the head of the harbour. As the basin is entirely reserved for visitors, any free berth can be taken on arrival. There are some 120 berths; the office is in the tourist centre and the marina is fully operational May to October inclusive. Out of season arrangements can be made by telephone. Anchoring is not permitted in the vicinity of Kalmar harbour.

### *Services*

All the usual services are available including WiFi and sauna. Launderette time slots must be booked at the harbour office. Fuel (diesel and petrol) is on the north side of the marina entrance, though you may need to phone to get them to activate the pump (www.kalmarbatmack.se). There is a holding tank pump-out station. Kalmar is home to a particularly good

Kalmar castle viewed from the channel *Andy Beharrell*

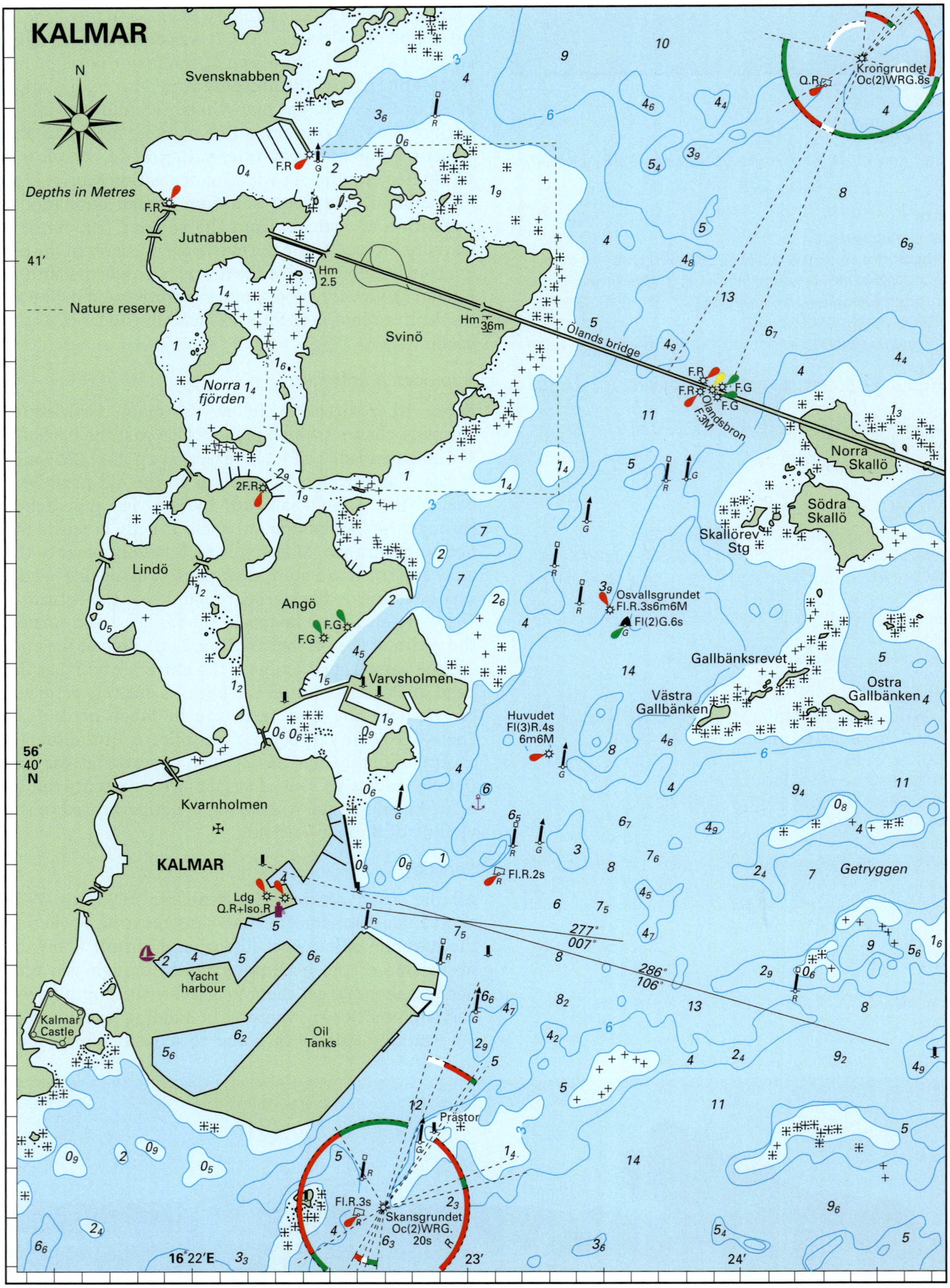
KALMAR
N
Depths in Metres
Nature reserve
Svensknabben
Jutnabben
Hm 2.5
Svinö
Hm 36m
Ölands bridge
Norra fjörden
Lindö
Angö
F.G
Varvsholmen
Kvarnholmen
KALMAR
Ldg Q.R+Iso.R
Yacht harbour
Oil Tanks
Kalmar Castle
Krongrundet Oc(2)WRG.8s
Q.R
F.R
2F.R
Ölandsbron F.3M
Norra Skallö
Södra Skallö
Skallörev Stg
Osvallsgrundet Fl.R.3s6m6M
Fl(2)G.6s
Gallbänksrevet
Västra Gallbänken
Ostra Gallbänken
Huvudet Fl(3)R.4s 6m6M
Fl.R.2s
Getryggen
277° 007°
286° 106°
Prästor
Fl.R.3s
Skansgrundet Oc(2)WRG. 20s
41′
56° 40′ N
16°22′E
23′
24′

Kalmar Castle – the site of the formation of the Kalmar Union in 1397 *Andy Beharrell*

chandlery, Baltic Skeppsfournering AB (☏+46 480 10600), across the road from the marina basin. Gas bottles, including Campinggaz and possibly Calor gas, plus German, Danish and Swedish makes can be refilled. Engine repairs can be arranged.

A company called Kalmar Marina (www.baltic.nu) offers winter storage and many other boatyard facilities, including a sailmaker (www.baltic.nu/en/sailmaking-and-rigging).

### *Facilities*

There is a very good shopping centre with excellent facilities adjacent to the harbour. A new and rather upmarket supermarket has opened here recently, and there is also a well stocked Clas Ohlsen hardware store. The town is well served with shops of all kinds.

The railway and coach stations are opposite the marina, providing easy access to the rest of the country. Car hire can be arranged by the chandlery. Taxis are readily available. The airport, a short distance inland, has several daily flights to Stockholm and Malmö. Altogether it is a good place for crew changes.

The entrance to Kalmar gästhamn *Andy Beharrell*

Sailing past Blå Jungfrun *Andy Beharrell*

## Blå Jungfrun (The Blue Maiden)

56°40'N 16°21'E

Blå Jungfrun is a National Park island in the northern part of Kalmarsund. The island has dramatic granite slopes and varied flora with an ancient stone maze on the south coast, and plays an important part in Swedish folklore. There are daytime anchorages at Sikhamn in the northwest and Lervik in the northeast, where summer students act as welcoming wardens. Alternatively, you can visit on a ferry from Oskarshamn and from Byxelkrok on Öland.

## Öland

Öland is the second largest island in Sweden (after Gotland) and is over 1,300km$^2$. It is separated from the mainland by the Kalmar Strait (Kalmarsund) and connected by the 3.5M Öland bridge from Kalmar to just north of Färjestaden. There is evidence that Öland was inhabited as early as 6000BCE and it remains very historically significant. Iron age burial grounds and ring forts are scattered across the island and the southern portion of the island is made up of small villages, stone walls and alvars. These are barren limestone terraces which led to the traditional agricultural landscape of southern Öland becoming a UNESCO World Heritage Site in 2000. The Stora Alvaret site actually covers some 260km$^2$, a fifth of the whole island and if you get a chance it is worth spending sometime exploring the landscape of the island. Cars can be hired from Borgholm, or perhaps even Kalmar.

As well as rune stones, iron age burial mounds and forts, Öland is well known for its windmills. In the middle of the 19th century there were over 2,000 mills though today there are around 350 left. Even though the numbers have fallen significantly, it is still quite easy if cycling around to visit them.

There are two small yacht harbours on the east coast of Öland at Kårehamn (56°95'N 16°88'E) and Böda (57°14'N 17°04'E). Depths are reported as just over 2m in outer parts. For harbours on the western side of the island see below.

The 10th century Karlevi Rune Stone *Andy Beharrell*

Windmills on Öland *Andy Beharrell*

Iron Age Burial *Andy Beharrell*

## GRÖNHÖGEN

56°15'.81N 16°23'.62E

**Distances**
Kristianopel 12M, Kalmar 25M

**Contacts**
visitoland.com/hamn/gronhogen
✆+46 70 276 9664

Grönhögen has around 20 guest berths. These are alongside berths in the western harbour. Depths should be around 2.5–3m and it is generally sheltered though can be a little exposed in strong southerlies. Entry is fairly straightforward with a single red and green marking the entrance channel. Leading marks (on a bearing of 054°) ashore give a visual approach between the moles and a sharp turn around the northern mole will bring you to the guest berths. The harbour has all the usual services including fuel, washing facilities and a pump-out station.

From Grönhögen it is a 5km walk out to the lighthouse Långe Jan on the southern tip of Öland. At 42m, the lighthouse is Sweden's highest and has a bird-watching centre as well as a visitor centre and café. Alternatively, bicycle rental is available to save a long walk.

## MÖRBYLÅNGA

56°32'.12N 16°21'.71E (start of entrance channel)

**Distances**
Grönhögen 17M, Kalmar 9M

**Contacts**
visitoland.com/en/hamn/morbylanga
✆+46 70 276 9664

Mörbylånga has around 10 guest berths alongside or on stern buoys. Entrance is from the north west through a well-marked channel with shallow areas either side of the channel. Leading marks bring you in on a bearing of 127°. The harbour offers good shelter, though there may be some set in strong westerlies.

The harbour has all the usual services and though a little industrial feeling, does have a good centre and shops. It is also a good starting point for a visit to the UNESCO World Heritage Site of Stora Alvaret and has bus connections to the southern tip of Öland, Kalmar and Borgholm.

## FÄRJESTADEN

56°39'.14N 16°26'.72E (just west of the start of entrance channel)

**Distances**
Kristianopel 29M, Kalmar 3M

**Contacts**
visitoland.com/hamn/farjestaden
✆+46 70 392 0700

Färjestaden is a sheltered harbour just south of the Öland bridge on the west coast of Öland almost directly opposite Kalmar. It offers a useful alternative to Kalmar if it is very busy and has around 40 guest berths on Y-booms and stern buoys. Ferries run every hour or so across to Kalmar (depending on the season). Depths are between 2–3.5m and the harbour is a modern one with good facilities. An extensive shopping centre is within walking distance of the harbour.

There is no fuel available, but there is a fuel jetty at Kalmar.

## BORGHOLM

56°52'.94N 16°37'.90E (just west of the southern entrance channel)

**Distances**
Byxelkrok 30M, Kalmar 17M

**Contacts**
strandborgholm.se/gasthamnen/
hamnkapten@strandborgholm.se
✆+46 70 758 2859

Borgholm is an excellent and very sheltered harbour 17M north of Kalmar. It is the main city of Öland, though it is one of Sweden's smallest cities. The first reference to the name Borgholm dates right back to the 1280s and Borg- refers to the ancient castle which stood there. The current Renaissance castle dates from 1684 and has been occupied by both the Danish and the Swedish at various times. In 1806 there was a fire which left it in its current ruined state.

Borgholm is also the site of Solliden Palace - the summer residence of the Swedish Royal Family and the personal private property of King Carl XVI Gustaf. It is possible to tour the gardens and is a nice walk from the guest harbour.

The guest harbour is part of the Strand Borgholm hotel and payment of the berthing fee allows use of the hotel facilities including the swimming pool and sauna. Other facilities include toilets, showers, waste disposal and laundry. A pump-out and fuel are available just to port as you come through the entrance.

There are two possible locations to moor - in the inner harbour, closest to the hotel, you can moor alongside against the jetty on the western side or bows-to the jetty from stern buoys on the eastern side. In the outer harbour you can moors bows to the pontoons from stern buoys. Depths vary but are around 2-4m depending exactly where you moor.

Entry to the harbour can be done from just north of west or from the northwest, but watch the buoyage carefully as it can be a little confusing as you approach. There are shallow patches directly to the west of the entrance and to the northwest, but both routes are well buoyed. There are two sets of leading marks for the southernmost of the two channels.

The town is a good place to stop for a while and stock up with extensive shopping and supermarkets in moderate walking distance. The tourist information is also very helpful if you are planning to tour the island at all. There is a good mini-golf course near the harbour.

Borgholm Castle – a useful landmark when heading along the Kalmar Strait *Andy Beharrell*

Aerial view of Borgholm harbour and entrance. Guest berths are on the right and in the inner harbour *Andy Beharrell*

The inner harbour at Borgholm next to the Strand Borgholm hotel *Andy Beharrell*

## BYXELKROK

57°19'.72N 16°59'.99E (the start of entrance channel)

**Distances**
Borgholm 30M, Kalmar 45M, Visby 45M

**Contacts**
visitoland.com/hamn/byxelkrok
✆+46 70 289 5259

Byxelkrok is a useful stop on Öland whether heading north or south, but is a particularly good jumping off port for crossing to Visby on Gotland which is just a 45M crossing. Byxelkrok is just 4M south of North Cape on Öland and was extensively redeveloped in 2020–22. It is a community-owned harbour and, as a result of the redevelopment now has a new southern breakwater giving much better shelter for the whole harbour. There are now 150 guest berths located both to port and starboard as you enter between the moles. To starboard are two jetties with stern buoys either side or it is possible to go alongside the north side of the southern mole. If you turn to port there are stern buoys onto the northern mole and a further jetty with stern buoys. Depths vary between 2–5m within the harbour.

From the middle of June to the end of July, the harbour is at its busiest, but they will generally find you a space. In an average year they cater for over 4,000 guest nights, most of these after Midsummer! Full services are available including laundry, showers and toilets, rubbish disposal and a pump-out station. Fuel is available from a local petrol station around 200m walk from the harbour.

A 30min walk north from the harbour brings you to the Neptune's Fields nature reserve. This is a long stretch of cobble beach covered with a plant called Viper's Bugloss which flowers in June and July, making the entire area appear blue. The cobble stone beach is made up of stones left during the last Ice Age which have been eroded by wave action. It was named by the well-known Swedish Naturalist Carl Linnaeus in 1741 when he visited the area. Just south of Neptune's Fields is the Forgalla Skepp, a Bronze Age ship shaped tumulus and a grave field. This has 32 small stone circles, nine 'cists', twelve round cairns, and one in the shape of a three pointed star.

An alternative harbour if crossing to Visby is Grankullaviken – the bay at the northern tip of Öland. There is a small jetty with stern buoys, depth is between 2–4m in most of the mooring area, though care should be taken as this is a relatively lightly used harbour. The jetty used to be where the ferries for Gotland left from, but is no longer used. There are nice walks from the jetty including to the lighthouse – Långe Erik on the northern tip of Öland.

Aerial view of Byxelkrok harbour. Guest berths are available throughout the harbour *Andy Beharrell*

GOTLAND AND THE
APPROACHES TO VISBY
Nature reserve
Depths in Metres
VISBY See plan p.179
Iso.WRG.12-8M
GOTLAND
FÅRÖ
Traffic
Separation
Scheme
Inshore Traffic Zone
Hoburgs
Bank

## VISBY (GOTLAND)

57°39′N 18°17′E

### Distances

Kalmar 95M, Västervik 55M, Arkösund 65M, Byxelkrok 45M

### Lights

**Follingbo** 57°35′.6N 19°22′.6E Aero VQ.243m21M. Mast
*Note* This light is 4M inland with obstructions
**Stora Karlsö**, west side 57°17′.5N 17°57′.8E LFl(2) WR.12s56m16–13M
White tower on dwelling 18m
**Visby, north breakwater** 57°38′.1N 18°16′.2E Q.R.9m9M
White tower, green band, 6m Floodlit
**Visby, south breakwater** 57°38′.1N 18°16′.4E Iso. WRG.4s11m12–8M
White tower, red band 8m Floodlit

### Contacts

**VTS Oxelösund** ☎+46 855 42 45 50, VHF Ch 9
**Visby pilots** ☎+46 498 21 01 38
**Visby Guest Harbour** ☎+46 498 21 51 90, Mobile +46 736 00 63 00
Guest Harbour VHF Ch 16/12 (0900–2100 LT)
info@visbygasthamn.se
www.visbygasthamn.se

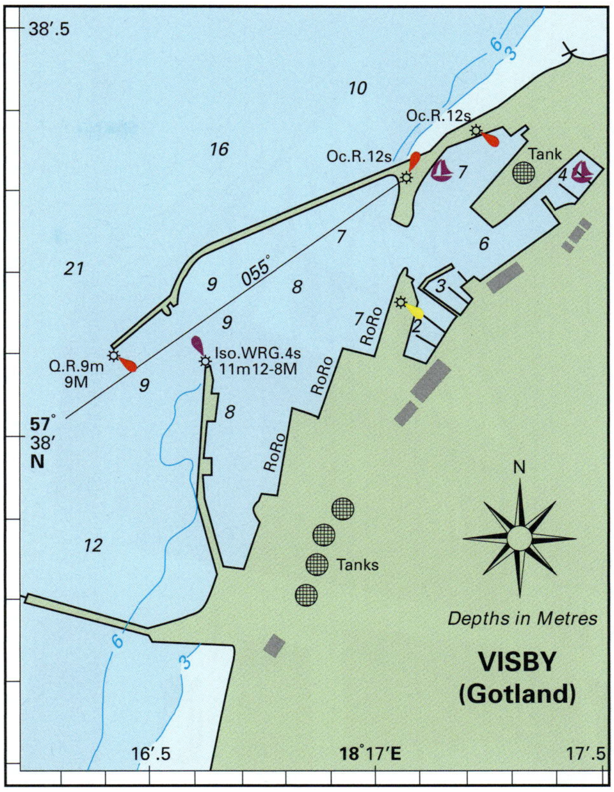


As will be seen from the distances above, getting to Visby from the mainland involves quite a lengthy journey. An alternative would be to stop for the night at a small harbour at the northern tip of Öland – Byxelkrok. From here to Visby is a distance of around 45M.

Visby (pronounced Vees-bu) is the only town of any size on Gotland, and is a beautiful mixture of old and new. It is arguably the best-preserved medieval city in Scandinavia and worth a visit if you have time. It has been on the UNESCO World Heritage List since 1995. Its position led to it becoming one of the most important trading centres of Europe in the 10th and 11th centuries, and later a principal depot of the Hanseatic League. This strategic position and wealth led to conflict, and the island of Gotland changed hands many times between the Swedes, the Danes and lastly the Russians, most recently in 1808. Visby's 13th-century towers and walls are a striking sight from the sea. They and ten early medieval churches stand witness to the city's former importance. A 'medieval week' is held in early August, particularly impressive on the Sundays at either end

The guest harbour at Visby *Andy Beharrell*

Medieval houses in Visby *Andy Beharrell*

when many local people wear period costume. There is also an excellent museum. The island's website can be found at www.gotland.se.

Visby's harbour is deservedly popular with both yachtsmen and tourists. It can become very crowded and noisy on warm summer nights – particularly during the various festivals – with sidewalk cafés, a quayside amusement park and other yachts hosting cockpit parties late into the night. Gotland is claimed to have the best summer climate in Sweden, with only half the average rainfall of the mainland, but the south and west coasts may be subject to fog, particularly in the Autumn.

### *Approach & entrance*

Both the water tower and the cathedral are conspicuous from offshore, as is the 343m Follingbo aero mast 4M southeast of the harbour. The entrance can be identified by the prominent oil tanks at its southern end, and often by the ferries berthed alongside. The outer harbour is large, with plenty of room to lower and stow sails once inside.

After dark, approach using the sectored light on the end of the south breakwater, transferring to the two occulting red leading lights on 055° for final entry. The main north/south shipping lane runs some 4M offshore to the west of Visby, carrying moderate to heavy traffic. A new pier and terminal for cruise liners has been built outside the harbour and when cruise ships are moored, it can be busy in town. Around 250 cruise ships moor at Visby each year.

### *Berthing*

Visiting yachts normally use the 200 berth marina in the extreme northeast of the harbour, where mooring is bows to a pontoon and stern to a buoy in depths of 3-6m, but it is crowded in the season. However, the harbourmaster is proud that they have not turned any yachts away since 2001 – they will always find you a space. At times they have fitted over 350 boats in! Local yachts have their own basin behind the ferry berth opposite the harbour mouth, but sometimes the harbourmaster will allow its use.

From Midsummer through to mid-August, you may well be met by a RIB which will direct you to a berth. When full, yachts have berthed against the northwest sea wall in the Inre Hamn but the walk to the harbourmaster's office and showers is longer. All berthing areas are administered from an office overlooking the northeast basin, open 0900–2100 in season. There are no suitable anchorages near Visby.

It is possible to book a berth in advance through www.dockspot.com. This is usually a premium of €10 over and above the usual berthing rate. There are 13 of these berths and they are on the northern side of the central pontoon. If your draft is greater than 3m the harbourmaster advises emailing them in advance.

### *Services*

The usual services and shops are available, including WiFi. Toilets and showers, crowded at times, plus a launderette, are near the marina office. Fuel (diesel and petrol with cash or credit card) is beside the slipway at the north end of the northwest basin. There are some excellent restaurants and a Systembolaget in town.

### *Communications & travel*

Cars and bicycles are available for hire. It is worth checking with the harbourmaster as close to the ferry

The small but well sheltered harbour at Lauterhorn on the island of Fårö *C.N. Hill*

terminal is a car hire company offering 'pre-loved cars'. This is considerably cheaper than the major car hire companies. The harbourmaster also offers a free car for 1hr if you want to go shopping. This can be booked in the harbourmaster's office. Frequent air and ferry connections with the mainland (the latter to/from Oskarshamn and Nynäshamn), and buses to all parts of Gotland.

## Other harbours on Gotland & Fårö

The northern tip of Gotland is a useful jumping off point for either the Stockholm archipelago or for Latvia in the Baltic States. There are three harbours within easy sailing distance of Visby. From these, it is around 60-70M to Nynäshamn at the southernmost part of the Stockholm archipelago. The harbours are Lickershamn, Kappelshamn and Lauterhorn on the island of Fårö, just to the northeast of Gotland. Of these, Lauterhorn is probably the most scenic. It lies in a bay which provides shelter from all directions and, in suitable weather conditions, would make a good anchorage.

Alternatively, it is possible to moor on the Öland side of the Fårösund in a small marina by the ferry port. Alternatively, there is the Fårösunds Båtklubb to the south or Fiskehamn to the north of the ferry. The Fiskehamn has alongside mooring or stern buoys in the Båtklubb. The depth in the Fiskehamn should be around 4-5m, but in the Båtklubb between 2-2.5m.

From here, it is 80-90M to Ventspils or Pavilosta in Latvia. The island of Fårö is worth a visit. This is easily done using the ferry. The island was the home of the famous film director Ingmar Bergman and is also scenically very beautiful. The nature reserve of Langhammars on the northwest coast of Fårö is where some of Gotland's most beautiful rock formations can be found. These are limestone rocks which have been weathered into characteristic karstic rock formations known as rauks. Fossils are abundant all around the area.

## Blå Kusten (The Blue Coast)

The Blå Kusten is an extremely attractive area, characterised by thousands of small islands, many with interesting harbours or anchorages which stretches some 60M from Oskarshamn in the south to Arkösund in the north. Whilst providing the main coastal conduit from the Southern Baltic to the northern cruising grounds, it also constitutes an attractive sailing area in its own right where one may linger in perfect shelter amongst the hundreds of wild islands, or venture up long leads to the several large and sophisticated towns.

The Blå Kusten is made up of a number of different archipelagos and nature reserves. Among the largest are the Gryt archipelago made up of four nature reserves: Gryt, Ängelholm, Ämtö and Väggö. This runs from just north of Valdemarsvik to north of Harstena. The Sankt (or Saint) Anna archipelago then runs up to just south of Arkösund.

The islands in the archipelago are made up of 1,900 million year old primary rock; mainly gneiss and granite. The landscape, however, was formed much more recently by the massive ice sheets that have periodically covered Sweden. The glacier ice polished the rocks making them generally smooth and round. The smoothest rocks will usually face to the northwest, the direction the ice came from, whereas to the southeast you may see steeper and rougher rock faces, often with loose rocks and stones.

Approaching the *skärgård* from the south through the wide and well-marked Kalmarsund, considerable mental adjustment is required before one gains confidence when sailing fast in flat water only yards from rocks, winding down leads which appear to be dead ends, and keeping check of one's position where the marks are unnamed. A cockpit-mounted chart plotter will prove to be invaluable when cruising around the *skärgård*. But these are the joys and skills of *skärgård* sailing, which can be safe and relaxing provided one obeys the rules. These are few and simple but absolutely vital – to have a detailed chart, to stay in the marked channels, and ALWAYS to know where you are. As so often, the key to safety and enjoyment lies in planning ahead. Decide where you are going and where you plan to stop. To explore the many delightful anchorages a copy of the Swedish book *Naturhamnar på Ostkusten* is invaluable and is available from the Svenska Kryssarklubben (Swedish Cruising Club or SXK) – see page 232. Membership of the SXK may also prove useful as they maintain a network of mooring buoys (8T limit at present) for their members and many of these are in out of the way bays and anchorages.

The Blue Coast is an important area for nesting birds, and many sites are out of bounds during the breeding season. These are marked both on the Swedish large-scale charts and on the water, where floating signs and yellow signs on the islands themselves give the dates of prohibition. These vary between February to August, and must be respected. Amongst the rich birdlife, you may see terns, oystercatchers, turnstones, razorbills and velvet scoters. On land in the pine forests, you

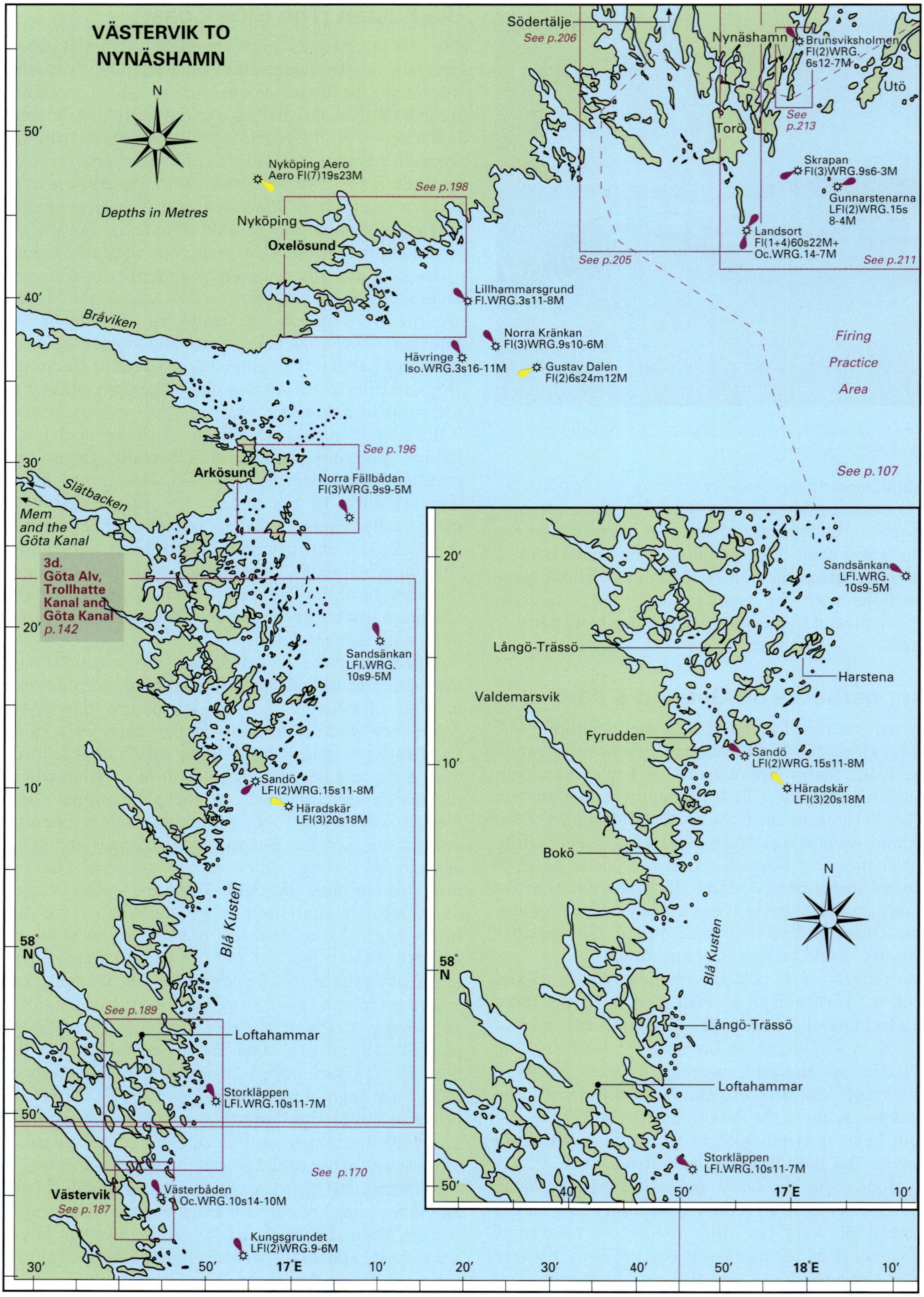
VÄSTERVIK TO NYNÄSHAMN
Depths in Metres
Södertälje
See p.206
Nynäshamn
Brunsviksholmen Fl(2)WRG. 6s12-7M
Utö
See p.213
Torö
Skrapan Fl(3)WRG.9s6-3M
Gunnarstenarna LFl(2)WRG.15s 8-4M
Landsort Fl(1+4)60s22M+ Oc.WRG.14-7M
See p.205
See p.211
Nyköping Aero Aero Fl(7)19s23M
See p.198
Nyköping
Oxelösund
Lillhammarsgrund Fl.WRG.3s11-8M
Bråviken
Norra Kränkan Fl(3)WRG.9s10-6M
Hävringe Iso.WRG.3s16-11M
Gustav Dalen Fl(2)6s24m12M
Firing Practice Area
See p.196
See p.107
Arkösund
Norra Fällbådan Fl(3)WRG.9s9-5M
Slätbacken
Mem and the Göta Kanal
3d. Göta Alv, Trollhatte Kanal and Göta Kanal p.142
Sandsänkan LFl.WRG. 10s9-5M
Sandö LFl(2)WRG.15s11-8M
Häradskär LFl(3)20s18M
Blå Kusten
See p.189
Loftahammar
Storkläppen LFl.WRG.10s11-7M
See p.170
Västervik
See p.187
Västerbåden Oc.WRG.10s14-10M
Kungsgrundet LFl(2)WRG.9-6M
Långö-Trässö
Harstena
Valdemarsvik
Fyrudden
Bokö
58° N
17°E
18°E

may encounter black woodpeckers, redstarts, thrush nightingales and whitethroats. You may also, however, encounter mosquitos when walking, so suitable protection against them is advised.

From the south, one enters the *skärgård* at Kråkelund. There are sheltered passages or leads running north from here for almost 60M. There are innumerable anchorages in sheltered bays. Fjords lead up to the towns of Blankaholm, Västervik and Loftahammar. At the northern end is the entrance to the Göta Kanal at Mem (see page 154).

While you may just be heading through the Blå Kusten on your way further north, it is well worth considering it as a stop in its own right. As a destination, it is often less crowded than the Stockholm and Finnish archipelagos, but is nevertheless certainly not a poor relation. With extensive anchorages and small attractive towns, it is worth spending some time here whether heading north or south. In this section we look at some possible places you may like to consider stopping. Some are anchorages, some towns and some just small jetties, but between them you should get a taste of what this section of coast has to offer. Think of it as the first course in a taster menu of archipelago sailing.

## OSKARSHAMN

57°15'.93N 16°27'.55E

**Distances**

Kalmar 36M, Västervik 30M, Visby (Gotland) 63M

**Contacts**

www.oskarshamn.se (click on Tourists – Marinas)

This is a busy, shipbuilding port but nevertheless pleasant, clean and tidy. Approach may be made from either the north or south of Finnrevet lighthouse which is 5M east by north of the harbour. The approaches are well marked, presenting no difficulty, even at night. However, beware of ferries in the narrow channels.

One of the more unusual sights in Oskarshamn is the Långa Soffan (literally this means the Long Sofa). It is a 72m long wooden park bench, located in the harbour area of Oskarshamn. It was used by the wives of sailors and fishermen to sit on while they waited for their husbands to return.

### Brädholmen Marina

✆+46 705 74 79 90

This is most visitors' preferred marina, at the head of the harbour, either side of the bridge to the island, mostly in 3m, bows-to with either a stern anchor or with stern buoys. Larger yachts can go alongside. This marina has all the usual services available. Diesel available on

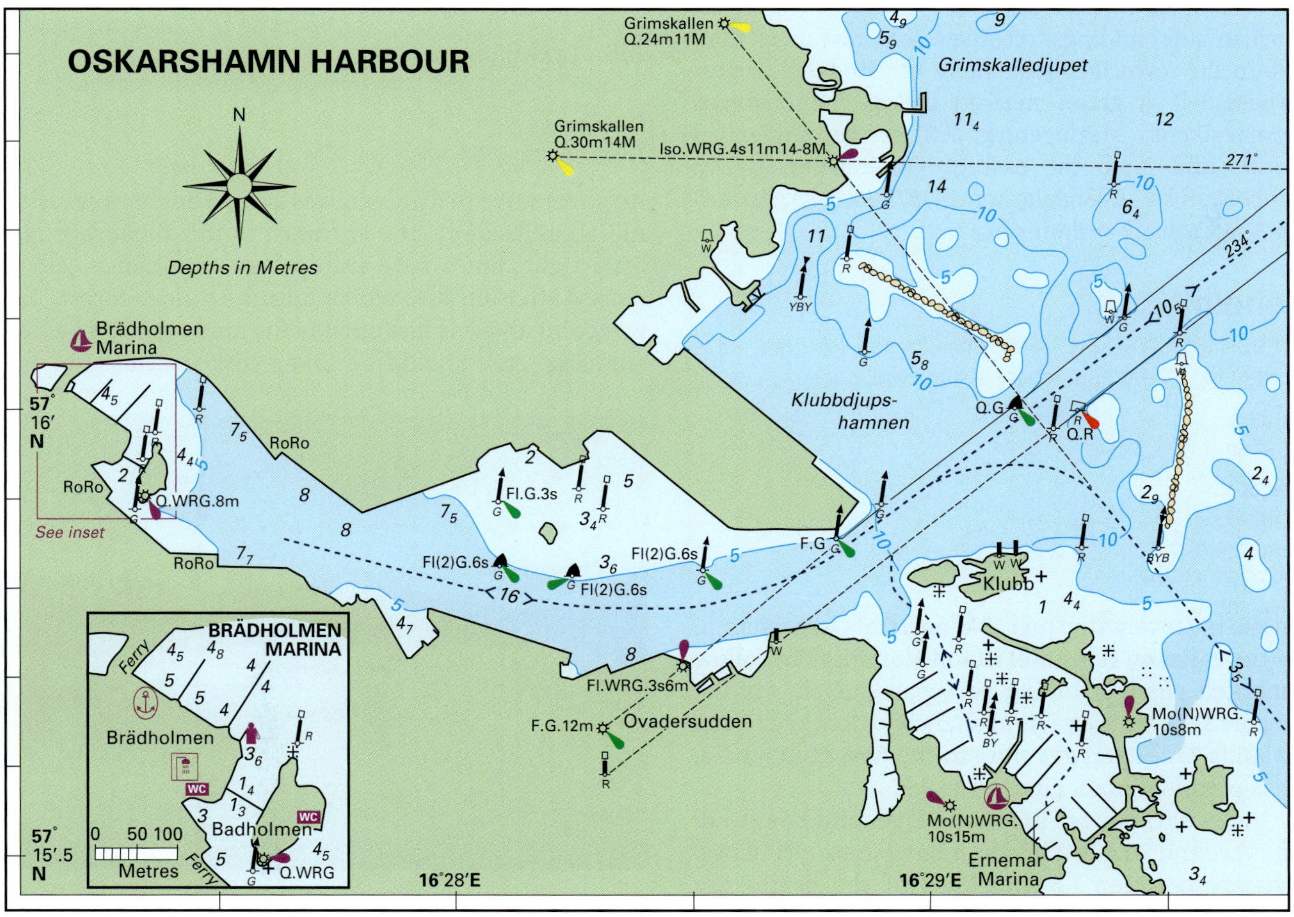

A foggy day in the Kalmar Strait *Andy Beharrell*

adjoining pontoon. There are all the shops and facilities of a fairly large town. The boatyard to the south of the main harbour has been recommended by locals. Berths can be booked in advance through Dockspot (www.dockspot.com/en/docks/530-oskarshamn-gasthamn).

### Ernemar Marina

57°15'.6N 16°29'.E

**Contacts**
✆+46 49 11 74 00
www.ernemarhamn.ernemar.se/guest-harbour

At the east end of the harbour. This is a quieter place with less urban surroundings, most services, but more than a mile to the town facilities. There are 10 guest berths, otherwise use a green marked space. The boatyard Ernermarvikens Marincenter AB is recommended by locals and is to the east of Oskarshamn (www.ernemarviken.se - Gröndalsgatan 37, 572 35 Oskarshamn) about 30mins walk or 5mins in a taxi.

## Figeholm

57°20'.95N 16°36'.76E (just east of the Hommeskär cairn – this is the start of the entrance channel into Figeholm)

**Distances**
Oskarshamn 10M, Västervik 32M

**Contacts**
www.fbk.nu
gasthamn@fbk.nu
✆+46 70 373 5446

Figeholm is a lovely stop just 10M north of Oskarshamn. From the cairn on the small island Hommeskär, follow the marked channel taking care particularly for the latter part as there are various shallow patches between the islands. Once you get close to the boat club jetties, there is plenty of manoeuvring space.

The guest harbour is run by the Figeholm Boat Club and has around 30 guest berths, mainly on stern buoys. Depths are between 1.5-4m. Most of the berths are around the boat club jetty, but it is also possible to go bows-to the jetty (Vasakajen) a couple of hundred metres to the northeast.

There is good walking around the local area including a nature reserve. The boat club does also have its own island Rågholmen, north of the entrance channel, about 0.7M east of the harbour. It may also be possible to moor here if you check with the club.

## Klintemåla

57°31'.08N 16°39'.09E

**Distances**
Oskarshamn 21M, Västervik 18M

**Contacts**
oskarshamn.com/product/klintemala-gasthamn
valborgs.i.klintemala@gmail.com
✆+46 70 731 7856

Klintemåla is a small and well protected harbour not far off the main north-south route through the Blå Kusten. Protection is good from most wind directions, though it may be a little exposed in easterlies. The route in is reasonably straightforward with all hazards fairly clearly marked, though if coming from the south don't turn west too quickly after the Vinökråkan light as there is an unmarked 1.5m shoal 0.4M from the light on a bearing of 325°. It is best to make the turn west once you are well clear of this shoal.

There are 12 guest berths on stern buoys and the depth should be at least 5m on both jetties, though the western jetty is just Y-booms for smaller motor boats. There is a small café, shop and fuel. Watch out for the jetty mooring chains when filling up.

### Älö - Lyckfjärden

57°32'.77N 16°41'.65E (Just outside entrance to anchorage)

**Distances**
Oskarshamn 23M, Västervik 16M

An alternative to Klintemåla is a small anchorage called Älö (Lyckfjärden). The entrance to the anchorage is a little tight, but a true archipelago experience. Älö is named after an "äle" which means an alder forest. The waypoint above is just outside the anchorage and when entering, care should be taken to keep closer to the

The jetty at Klintemåla *Andy Beharrell*

Anchored at Älö Lyckfjärden *Andy Beharrell*

south side to avoid a rock just 0.7m below the surface. Once past that simply keep central and you should have a minimum of 2.9m, though, as ever with the Baltic, do be aware of the current level of the waterstand.

Once inside the anchorage there is ample space to anchor in depths of around 4m in good holding.

## Idö

57°42'.24N 16°45'.83E

**Distances**

Oskarshamn 33M, Västervik 6M

**Contacts**

idoskargardskrog.se/gasthamn

✆+46 70 444 5708

On the route north to Västervik is an island called Idö and on the southern side of the island is a small guest harbour. Though exposed to the west, in quiet weather or for lunch, it would make a lovely stop on the way to Västervik. The direct route from the south through to Västervik runs through the very pretty channel between Grönö and Spårö and Idö is a short diversion to east – about 1.5M from Spårö. When approaching the guest harbour (particularly the eastern side of the jetty) be sure to keep the green buoy to starboard as there are rocks close by. Otherwise depths should be greater than 2m throughout and 4m at the outer end of the jetty. Room for manoeuvre can be limited in high season and it is worth taking care with the depth in the inner part of the harbour.

The island is an old pilot station and has a long history. Pilotage has been carried out from Idö since the 1600s and the pilot station was finally closed down in 1986. Generations of the same family often passed their pilotage skills on to each other and some families were pilots for up to nine generations. The pilot tower (Idö Lotsstuga) is a short walk from the guest harbour and was built in 1950. While quite functionalist in style, this is perhaps appropriate given its role. A climb up the stairs in the lookout tower is worth the effort and from the top, there is a lovely view of the surrounding archipelago. As you walk up the stairs there are pictures from the era of pilotage on the island. The café and restaurant is at the guest harbour and is a nice place to while away the time watching boats passing by.

Spårö båk lighthouse. If heading to Västervik the quickest route is to go between Spårö and Grönö. The lighthouse is on the top of Spårö *Viv Fox*

Boathouse on Idö *Viv Fox*

Idö guest harbour *Viv Fox*

## VÄSTERVIK

57°45'N 16°39'E

### Distances

Kalmar 65M, Visby 55M, Oskarsham 33M, Mem 50M, Arkösund 55M, Södertälje 95M, Nynäshamn 85M

### Lights

**Västerviks angöring** 57°44'.8N 16°55'.3E Q.Fl
North cardinal pillar buoy, n topmark
**Kungsgrundet** 57°41'.1N 16°54'.2E LFl(2)WRG.27m9–6M
Racon Black tower, red band, white lantern. Helipad
**Västerbåden** 57°44'.8N 16°44'.5E Oc.WRG.10s14m14–10M
Racon Red tower, black base 15m Floodlit
White lantern, red base
**Stickskär** Leading Lights 236°: 57°43'.3N 16°45'.3E
Front Fl.WRG.1.5s10m7–3M White tower
Rear Spårö 1M from front Iso.6s36m14M
White tower 8m

### Contacts

**Västervik Commercial Harbour** ☏+46 490 16920/10690 VHF Ch 12/16
**Notholmen Yacht Harbour** ☏+46 371 2385
**Västerviks Gästhamn** ☏+46 490 35066,
Västerviks Marina ☏+46 490 69800, Mobile +46 70 715 3200 (0800–1900 LT)

Västervik is a small industrial town with a modern harbour for small commercial vessels, many of them carrying timber. It is pleasant but unpretentious, with an attractive waterfront, some interesting old buildings and considerable charm. It has good shopping, including several large supermarkets and an open market, and a choice of three yacht harbours with several more in the approach. An outdoor song festival is held every July in the remains of Stegeholm Castle.

Västervik is an excellent base from which to explore the famous Blå Kustens archipelago to the north and south.

### *Approach & entrance*

The approach to Västervik involves the negotiation of intricate, rock-fringed channels and a large-scale chart is essential. From seaward there are two main approaches, both well marked on the chart:

A. From the east, pass close to Västerviks angöring north cardinal buoy, which lies some 4M north of Kungsgrundet light, and head west towards Västerbåden light. Turn south-southwest and follow the buoyed and lit channel, turning west across Lusärnafjärden entrance.

B. From the southeast head towards Idö Stängskär light on a bearing of 323° and pass close northeast of it. Head for the beacon on Spårö Island, and pass north through the Spårösund, to join the approach (A). Turn west and cross the broad entry to Lusärnafjärden, to reach the port of Västervik.

There are no restrictions on anchoring in the area. It is also possible to continue through the lifting bridge to the Gamlebyviken.

### *Berthing*

There are two yacht harbours on Lusärnafjärden both in quiet surroundings but at some distance from the town.

#### Solbergs Udde

☏+46 731 61 06 00 (preferably SMS message)
wss.nu/gasthamn

This is tucked behind a group of small islands on the south side close to the entrance. Around 20 of its berths are available for visitors, in depths of 2-5m, with a maximum beam of 3.5m and weight of 10T. The facilities are those of the nearby camping ground, restaurant and boatyard. Free spaces will be marked by green signs.

#### Gränsö Slott

☏+46 490 37080, Mobile +46 706 99 25 15

This is just north of Ekholmen Island, near the entrance to the Gränsö canal. It is run by the hotel and has 30 visitors berths in 1.5-2.3m, and has good basic services, plus use of the swimming pool and WiFi. It is a pleasant stop.

There are three yacht harbours near the town itself, which are reached by passing through the very well marked narrows close north of Lusärna island and

The narrow Spårösund which separates the islands of Grönö and Sparö on the southern approach to Västervik *C.N. Hill*

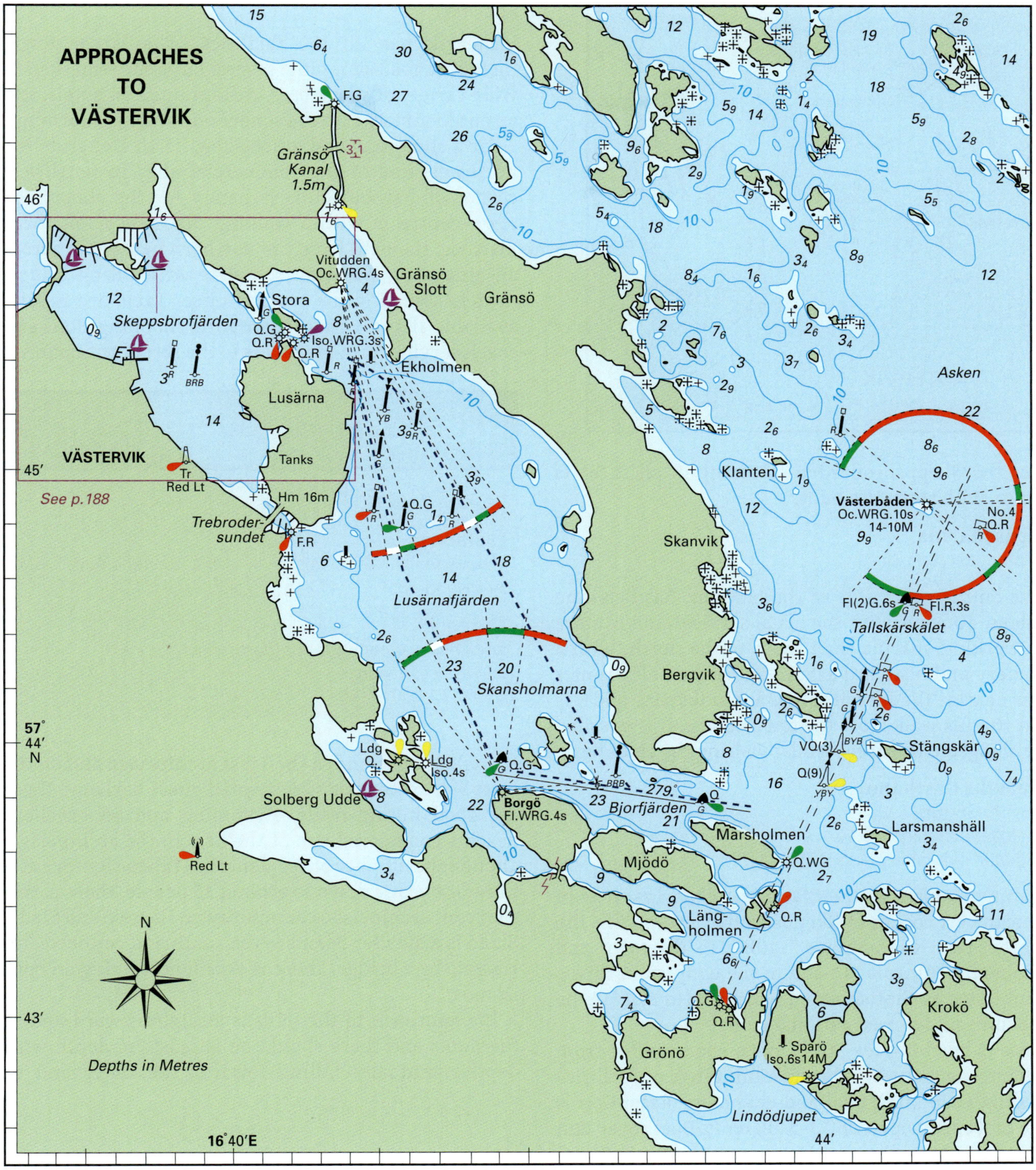

These posts mark the narrow but well marked passage between the Lusärnafjärden and Skeppsbrofjärden on the final approach to Västervik *C.N. Hill*

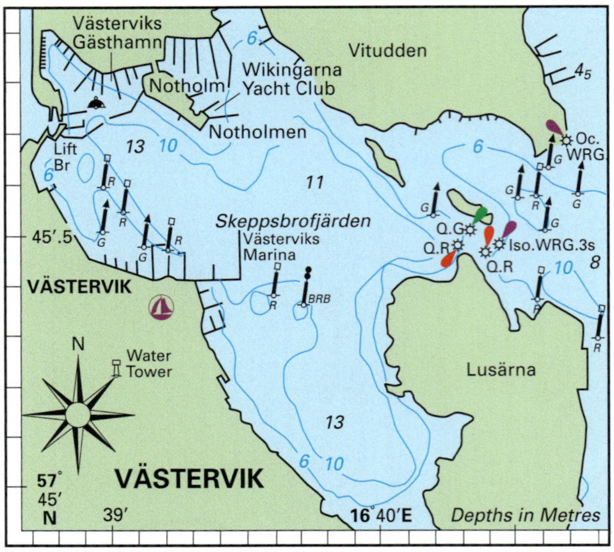


across the Skeppsbrofjärden. Mooring in all three is bows-to, with stern to a buoy.

### Pampas Marina

www.pampasvastervik.se

This is on the south side of the harbour, has berthing for about 40 boats with the usual services and is more of a 'working' marina than those to the north, with a chandlery and boatyard ashore and a good electronics dealer nearby. The surroundings are industrial, and it is about 10mins walk from the town centre. It is possible to lie alongside (for free) whilst visiting the chandlery.

### Västerviks Gästhamn

✆+46 490 35066
www.slottsholmenmarina.se
info@slottsholmenmarina.se

Sometimes known as the Blå Kustens marina, it is in the northwest corner of Skeppsbrofjärden and fills the space between the isthmus leading to the town and Notholmen peninsula. To add to the confusion, this is the one listed as 'Slottsholmen Marina Västervik' in the Gästhamnsguiden free national guide!

There is berthing for 500 yachts, good shelter from all but strong south winds and a full range of facilities including swimming pool and chandlery Reception is at the fuel berth, open 0800–1900 daily. Boats over 12m are requested to telephone in advance of arrival. There is a wide range of shops available close to the marina and this is a good place to stock up.

### Westerviks Segelsällskap Wikingarna Yacht Club

✆+46 490 12385
sekreterare@wikingarna.com
www.wikingarna.com

This marina is on the east side of the tip of the peninsula of Notholmen, east of Västerviks Gästhamn. Do not confuse it with a small boat marina to its north which does not take visitors. This friendly club has three pontoons, and keeps a few guest moorings on pontoons; much quieter than the town gästhamn and there is more chance of finding a berth. It is worth telephoning in advance of arrival to ensure a berth is available.

*Facilities*

Västervik has all the facilities of a larger town, including good shopping, several large supermarkets, a wide variety of snack bars, restaurants and hotels, and an outdoor market in the square on Saturday mornings.

For a short stay and quick shop, berth alongside the northwest end of the commercial quay in northwest corner of harbour. This is handy for the shops. The town centre is within walking distance of all three marinas, the path from the northern pair being across an attractive causeway complete with lifting bridge, next to which is the tourist office. Taxis are readily available if returning laden with shopping. Rail and coach services provide access to the rest of the country.

## HASSELÖ

57°49'.82N 16°43'.86E

**Distances**

Oskarshamn 41M, Västervik 10M, Loftahammar 8M, Arkosund 48M

**Contacts**

www.hasselo.com/boende/gasthamn
info@hasselo.com
✆+46 70 490 91130

Hasselö is an island in the Tjust archipelago and on the west side of the island is a small guest harbour. There are good hiking trails, swimming and an excellent beach – considered one of the best in the archipelago. Though the number of residents has fallen significantly in recent years, down to around 35 people, there is still a vibrant archipelago community on Hasselö and Sladö. Sladö is a smaller island to the south and connected to Hasselö by a bridge. There is excellent walking on both islands.

The approach to the jetty is straightforward and at the outer end there should be at least 7m depth with depths gradually falling towards the inner end of

Boat houses at Hasselö *Viv Fox*

the jetty. There are stern buoys for the main jetty, but mooring to the hammerhead is by stern anchor.

## LOFTAHAMMAR

57°54'.1N 16°41'.9E

**Distances**
Västervik 16M, Arkösund 43M

**Contacts**
Värd ✆+46 493 613 15
info@marincenter.se
www.marincenter.se/gasthamn

The buoyed entrance to the Loftahammar basin *Andy Beharrell*

Loftahammar is a large landlocked basin at the head of a long fjord; worth a visit being tranquil and picturesque. There are narrow, twisting and shallow routes from the west and east in addition to the main approach from the southeast. Loftahammar can also make a good departure point for Gotland; the passage to Visby is just over 50M.

The basin is approached by a very narrow buoyed channel between 2.5 and 3m deep. Make sure of staying in the channel to avoid a rock to port. If you stay fairly central there should be at least 3m through this channel. As you come out of the channel, the marina can clearly be seen to starboard and the guest pontoon is the third one along from the northwest end of the quay. There are stern buoys on the east side of the pontoon with double Y-booms on the west side. It has 50 guest berths with all facilities which are on a jetty marked with the guest harbour sign.

The marina has a range of services (though the toilet and shower facilities do require an access card) and an extensive workshop. A well stocked chandlery (seasea.se/butik/139/servicepoint-loftahammar), fuel dock (with both diesel and petrol and a minimum depth of 2.5m) and pump-out station on a separate floating pontoon are all available on entry to the marina. The surroundings are very scenic, and there is a useful tourist bureau in the town near the church. A well-stocked supermarket is close by.

The entrance to Loftahammar guest harbour. The guest pontoons are straight ahead through the entrance
*Andy Beharrell*

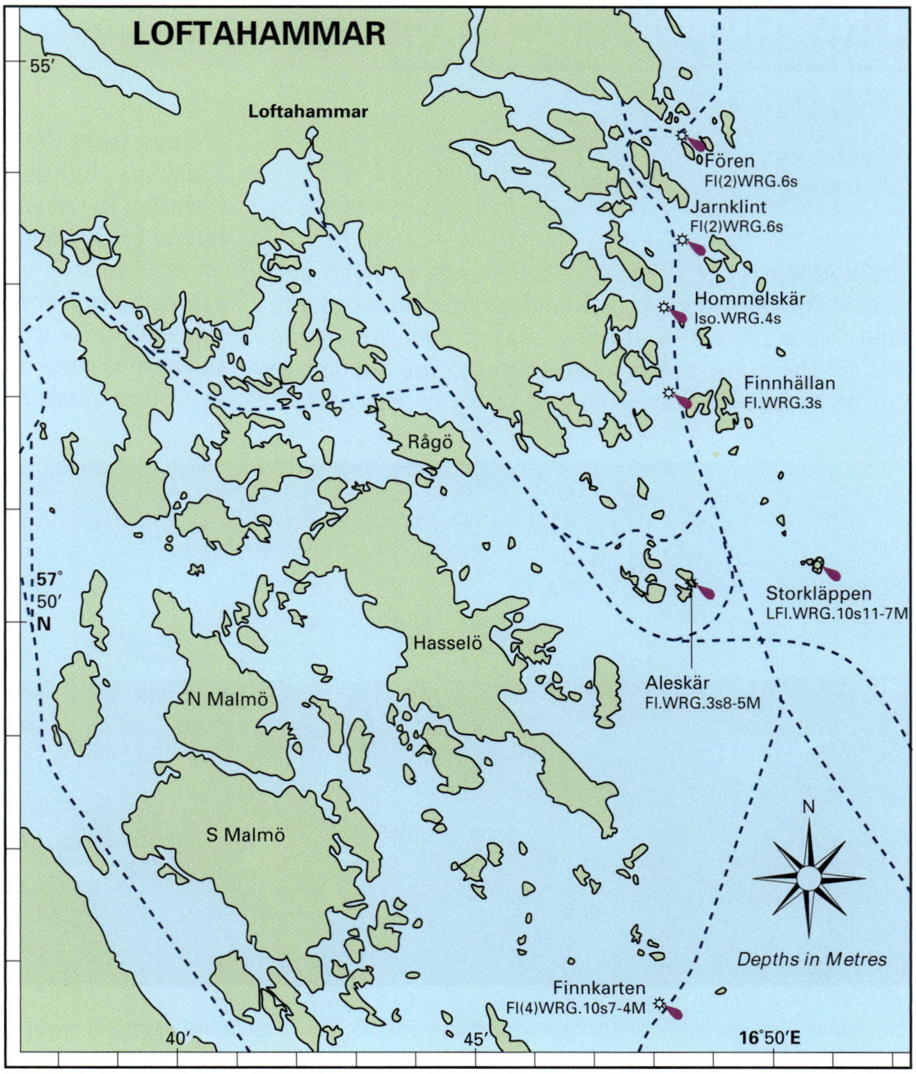

## LÅNGÖ-TRÄSSÖ

58°05'.87N 16°49'.45E

Distances
Västervik 19M, Loftahammar 11M, Arkösund 35M

Långö-Trässö is a useful anchorage about 19M north of Västervik in a beautiful part of the archipelago. There is a range of possibilities for anchoring or mooring to the rocks in the archipelago south of Stora Askö, but the bays between Häfsö, Långö and Trässö are perhaps some of the best. If coming along the main fairway head to the west opposite the gap between Jungfruskär and Tvarholmarna. Continue west between south Långholmen and Bredholmen and Röholmen. Stay a little closer to the northern tip of Trassö to avoid offlying rocks and then, depending on wind direction head south into the bay between Långö and Trassö to anchor in around 5m of water or keep heading west between Stora Bondklabben and Lilla Bondklabben to anchor between Häfsö and Långö. There is an SXK buoy in this bay for members, but plenty of space to anchor. It is a great area to explore by dinghy.

Anchored in the bay between Häfsö and Långö
*Andy Beharrell*

## LINDHOLMEN

58°05'.08N 16°49'.68E

Distances
Västervik 27M, Arkösund 27M

Lindholmen is an alternative anchorage to Bokö and just 1M further north. It is though a more secluded and sheltered anchorage and would make a good stop being just off the main north/south fairway. The anchorage can be entered either from the south or the east. If coming from the east you can head in just south of the Ljusklabb lighthouse and then enter through the gap between the northern tip of Grytsholmen and the small island of Grytshällen. Stay central to ensure sufficient water, but it is worth going slowly. Alternatively, you can come in from the south, but in this case ensure that you stay close to the western tip of Lindholmen. Once in there is good holding and plenty of space to anchor. It is often quieter here than around Bokö.

Panoramic view of all the anchorages in Långö-Trässö. The boat in the centre is moored in the bay between Häfsö and Långö
*Andy Beharrell*

The guest jetty at Bokö with the anchorage in the background *Andy Beharrell*

## BOKÖ

57°57'.31N 16°47'.5E

**Distances**
Västervik 29M, Loftahammar 21M, Arkösund 25M

Bokö is a good, sheltered and large anchorage about 29M north of Västervik. It is connected with Stora Ålö and large parts of both islands are nature reserves. Entry from the south or the north is fairly straightforward and the main hazard when entering the anchorage is a 1.7m shoal in the centre of the bay. Once past that, keeping fairly central will mean a minimum depth of 4m with good holding.

It is possible to find good shelter in winds from most directions, though winds slightly west of north may result in some slight set into the bay.

There is plenty of swinging room to anchor in the bay, but another option is to moor against the guest jetty on the eastern side of the bay. There is only space for a few boats rafted up on the jetty and it may be a little exposed in stronger westerlies or northerlies, but it is very secure and a good base to explore the island. There is an information point and compost toilet at the jetty and it is the starting point for a number of walks around the island. The island is farmed using traditional archipelago farming techniques with grazed woodlands and pastures as well as small fields and meadows.

## VALDEMARSVIK

58°12'.16N 16°36'.35E

**Distances**
Västervik 36M, Arkösund 34M

**Contacts**
Värd ✆+46 123 12200
turistbyran@tb.valdemarsvik.se
www.visitvaldemarsvik.se

Valdemarsvik is a bit off the beaten track, but if you have time or need a sheltered place for a break, it could be a good choice. It is around 10M from the main

Aerial view of Valdemarsvik gästhamn *Andy Beharrell*

fairway up a fjord which lies in a northwest/southeast plane. Coming north you turn off the main fairway just south of Stora Ålö or heading south you can make your way round the northern edge of Stora Ålö. Then simply head in a northwesterly direction. There are a couple of shallow patches where you need to pay close attention to the buoyage, but otherwise the pilotage is straightforward. There are a couple of shallow patches where you need to pay close attention to the buoyage but otherwise the pilotage is straightforward.

The gästhamn lies at the end of the fjord and there are around 75 guest berths, mostly between Y-booms, though there are a few alongside berths on the jetty on the southern shore. Toilets, showers, pump-out, laundry and all the usual facilities are available though for fuel you will need to stop at Båtaffären Marina AB on the north shore around 1M before the guest harbour (www.bataffaren.se).

The town's past industry was based around copper ore from Fångö and when the copper era ended in the 1870s a large tannery took its place. This is now all gone but many of the industrial buildings are still evident in town. There is a good walking trail around the town and up into the surrounding hills. Maps are available from the tourist office.

The town has convenient supermarkets,pharmacies and a Systembolaget so it is a good place to stock up on everything. There is also a range of restaurants.

You can book spaces in the gasthamn in advance online - www.stellpy.se/Valdemarsvik. Once booked the codes for the facilities will be texted to you. Alternatively you can pay in the tourist office in Sjöhuset - about 5mins walk from the gästhamn.

## FYRUDDEN

58°11'.47N 16°51'.23E

**Distances**
Västervik 34M, Loftahammar 26M, Arkösund 20M

**Contacts**
**Harbourmaster** ✆+46 760 14209
www.fyruddenshamn.se

This passage harbour is located 26M north from Loftahammar, making it a convenient stop for fuel, provisions and water. Mooring is either alongside or between Y-booms. There are wider berths available directly opposite the entrance though these are more prone to wash from the various tourist boats and water taxis coming in and out of the harbour.

Pump out and fuel is available on the jetty in the northwestern corner of the harbour. Water and electricity is available at all berths. There is a restaurant, pizzeria, a well-stocked shop and also local information available. It can be busy in high season, but recent developments have added a considerable amount of space and there are now around 65 guest berths with a depth of 4m. Payment is by machine and the receipt gives the codes for the facilities.

There is a boatyard and marine engineer around 10mins walk down the road - Gryts Motor and Mek. If the harbour is full, there is a good anchorage two bays to the north in Arsviken.

The guest harbour at Fyrudden *Andy Beharrell*

Aerial view of the anchorage at Håskö-Lisselön *Andy Beharrell*

## GUBBÖ KUPA

58°11'.78N 16°57'.15E

**Distances**
Västervik 34M, Loftahammar 27M, Arkösund 20M

If you want a peaceful and quiet anchorage on your way north as an alternative to Fyrudden, you may want to consider Gubbö Kupa. It is very sheltered from most wind directions apart from the north and northwest and with relatively steep rocks all around offers what should be a peaceful night anchored in 7–9m of water. There is a composting toilet, but little else apart from the delightful archipelago landscape.

## HÅSKÖ-LISSELÖN

58°15'.01N 16°54'.87E

**Distances**
Västervik 37M, Loftahammar 30M, Arkösund 16M

Håskö-Lisselön is a good sheltered anchorage just off the main fairway north. Entry is fairly straightforward. Coming from the south you come in between Bockholmen and Lisselön, keeping fairly central until you get to a small skerry on the northeast side of Bergholmen. Keep 10–15m off this skerry to avoid a 1.7m rock coming out of the shore of Bockholmen. This is well charted. Then turn into the bay and you can either moor bows-to the jetty with a stern anchor or simply anchor in the bay. If anchoring keep to the southern part of the bay to avoid an underwater cable. There is plenty of space for a number of boats.

Håskö has a long history as a pilot station from the 1500s and the last pilots left in 1895. Nowadays it is one of few places offering traditional archipelago agriculture – practices which are clearly visible as you walk around the island. There is a small shop here in season selling smoked fish, ice cream and other items, though this closes quite promptly at the end of the season, as with many places.

Aerial view of the anchorage at Harstena Flisfjärden *Andy Beharrell*

Aerial view of the jetty at Harstena village *Andy Beharrell*

## HARSTENA

58°15'.71N 17°01'.42E

**Distances**
Västervik 39M, Arkösund 16M

Harstena is one of the most popular islands in the Östergötland archipelago and is about 10M northeast of Fyrudden. It is arguably one of the most beautiful and sheltered stops on a passage north or south. There are several possible mooring options at Harstena, but perhaps the most reliable one is Flisfjärden. This is a good sized, but sheltered bay with various spots to moor on the rocks (according to the wind direction) and plenty of space for anchoring. With depths between 2.5-5m and good holding, it makes for a reliable stop in any part of the season.

The approach from the south is straightforward if you keep close to the north coast of Hasselön and then Harstena. There are a couple of well charted 2m shallows just northwest of the entrance but these are easily avoided by staying northeast of them. Heading south into Lilla Flisklabben there is plenty of depth. The approach shallows a little but even the narrowest part has a minimum depth of 3.5m.

Once anchored, it is an easy walk of around 1km to the village on the west side of the island where there is a shop, restaurant and 0.5km further on a bakery. By the bakery is a lake where rare red water lilies bloom in late July.

Alternatively it is possible to moor with a stern anchor to the jetty in the village itself - Lindholmsundet. This is a beautiful spot but can be very busy in high season when Flisfjärden may be a better bet.

### Risö – Grytsholmen

58°24'.67N 16°54'.04E

**Distances**
Västervik 47M, Arkösund 6M

Risö is about 5M south-southwest of Arkösund and makes a good alternative if you would prefer to avoid the town on your trip north or south. There are several possible anchorages on the eastern side of Risö. One of the prettiest is to the south of Grytsholmen.

This bay is easily entered from the east. Avoid the rocks marked by the east cardinal mark and then keep central to avoid an outlying rock on the north side of Verholmmsskären. Once in the bay you can anchor in 2.5-3m of water, though do check for a good set as there is quite a bit of vegetation on the bottom. You can also moor bows-to the rocks on the northern side of the western tip of Verholmmsskären.

Alternative anchorages are in the bay to the north of Grytsholmen or to the south of Verholmen by the small island of Högholm. There is a compost toilet on Verholmmsskären. All these anchorages are exposed in easterly winds.

Risö – Grytsholmen – an alternative anchorage about 5M south-southwest of Arkösund *Andy Beharrell*

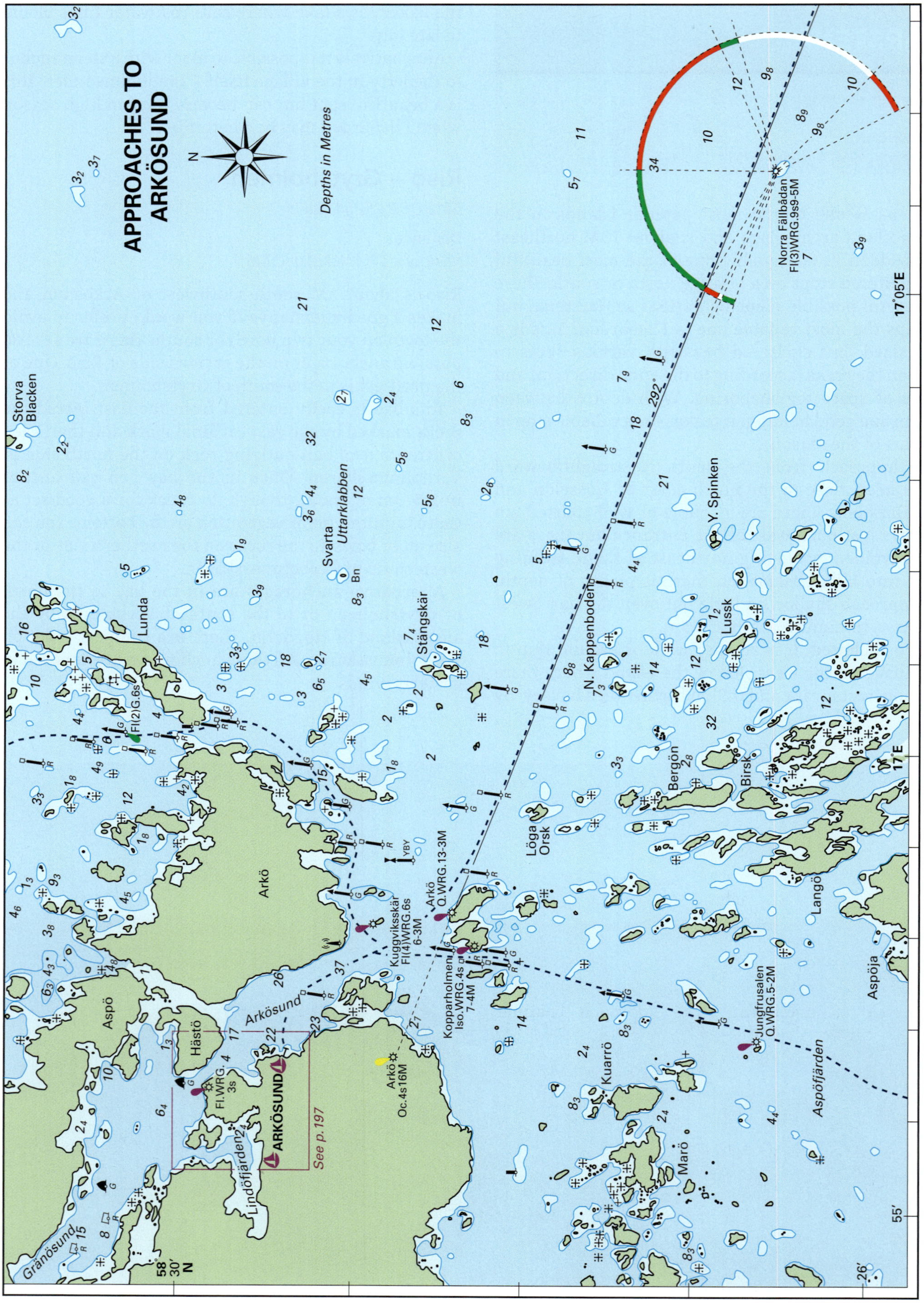
APPROACHES TO ARKÖSUND
Depths in Metres
N
Storva Blacken
Lunda
Svarta
Uttarklabben
Bn
Stängskär
Arkö
Aspö
Hästö
Arkösund
ARKÖSUND
See p.197
Lindöfjärden
Gränösund
Fl(2)G.6s
Fl.WRG. 4 3s
Arkö Oc.4s16M
Kuggviksskär Fl(4)WRG.6s 6-3M
Arkö Q.WRG.13-3M
Kopparholmen Iso.WRG.4s 7-4M
Jungfrusalen Q.WRG.5-2M
Norra Fällbådan Fl(3)WRG.9s9-5M
292°
YBY
Löga
Orsk
N. Kappenboden
Y. Spinken
Lussk
Bergön
Birsk
Langö
Kuarrö
Marö
Aspöja
Aspöfjärden
58° 30′ N
17°E
17°05′E
55′
26′

## The Göta Kanal

The eastern entrance to the Göta Kanal is at Mem (see page 154) which is reached through the Slätbacken. Allow a minimum of 4hrs for the attractive but tricky 21M from Arkösund to Mem if wanting to arrive at a particular time and be sure to allow sufficient time to combat the strong east-going currents which are sometimes encountered in the narrows at Ettersund and Stegeborg.

## ARKÖSUND

58°29'N 16°56'E

### Distances

Visby 65M, Västervik 55M, Mem 20M, Södertälje 60M, Nynäshamn 50M

### Lights

**Norra Fällbåden** 58°26'.5N 17°06'.2E Fl(3)WRG.9s16m9–5M
Black concrete tower, white top, yellow band, grey base 17m Wind generator
**Arkö, Östra Kopparholm Leading Lights 292°** Front 58°28'.4N 16°58'.4E Q.WRG.8m13–3M
White lantern, red rectangle, white stripe
**Kälebo** Rear 0.9M from front Iso.4s27m14M
White lantern, red column, white stripe
**Kuggviksskär** 58°28'.8N 16°58'.2E Fl(4)WRG.6s13m6–3M
White tower 12m

### Contacts

**Norrköpings Segelsällskap** ✆+46 125 20555
**Arkösund Quay** ✆+46 73 536 9884
**Badholmarna, Bäckmansviken and Nordanskog Yacht Harbours** ✆+46 125 20684, Mobile ✆+46 706 86 74 50

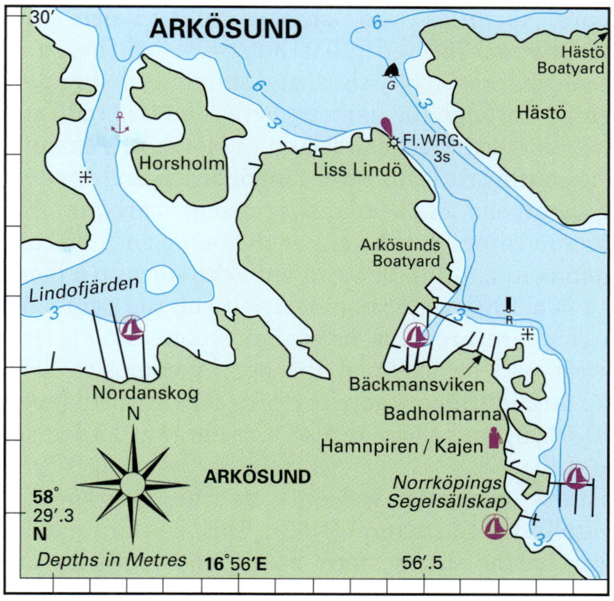


Arkösund is a popular yachting centre in an attractive rural setting.

### *Approach & entrance*

From the open sea, pass close north of Norra Fällbåden lighthouse to enter the Arkö approach channel, marked at intervals with spar buoys on either side, on a course of 292°. The channel is also indicated by the Arkö leading marks, but these are not easily visible. However, the buoyage is clear in daylight, and once the Arkö light is reached the entrance becomes obvious.

Entry is not recommended in the dark or in poor visibility. It is also possible to approach from the north, via one of several buoyed channels.

### *Berthing*

The Badholmarna Marina is private but there are two possibilities for visitors. The old quay was extended many years ago and three new jetties were built out from the quay, with lazy line mooring. This arrangement accommodates up to 200 visitors with depths ranging from 3m to 20m. During the low season there is usually space to moor alongside, but as it gets busier, you will need to use the lazy lines. During high season you will often be met by the harbour staff who will allocate berths.

The major drawback is that this area is very exposed to the southeast, and the outer berths would be very uncomfortable in a wind strength of more than around force 5. If possible, try to find a lee berth. The office is open from June to mid-August. It is possible to moor outside of these dates, but access to the facilities may not be available.

Northwest of the three small, low islands lies Bäckmansviken guest harbour – effectively four pontoons set in a rough square, with a single narrow entrance and some 20 berths inside in depths of 1.5–3m. It is unsuitable for vessels of more than about 11m (unless exceptionally manoeuvrable), but larger yachts may find a bows-to berth on the pontoon just beyond.

The guest harbours at Arkösund. The Norrköpings Segelsällskap Gästhamn (NSS) club harbour is in the foreground and the main guest harbour in the background *Andy Beharrell*

Shore facilities are shared with Kajen and Badholmarna. The red pillar buoy just off the guest harbour marks a rocky shoal and should be left to port on entry. Through the narrows between Liss Lindö and Hästö, and past the small island of Horshol, a channel to the southwest leads onto Lindöfjärden and the two long pontoons of Nordanskog yacht harbour. The 20 or so visitors' berths are at the outer ends of both pontoons in 2.5–3m, bows-to with the stern to a buoy. There is neither water nor electricity on the pontoons, though there are taps near their roots. Toilets and showers will be found at the nearby campsite Arkö Camp Strandgrillen where berthing fees are paid (open 0900–2100) and there is also a restaurant and small shop.

Visitors are also welcome at the Norrköpings Segelsällskap Gästhamn (NSS). This has around 20 visitor berths using stern buoys and facilities are available in the NSS clubhouse. Full details are available on nss.nu/nss-gasthamn/.

There are no restrictions on anchoring in this area. One recommended spot is west of Horsholm island.

### Services

There is a fuel berth near the root of the quay amongst the Hamnpiren/Kajen berths, the kiosk also contains a small shop. This will be open from 0800–2000 during the season, but the fuel berth is automatic outside of these hours. There are two boatyards in the area, the Arkösunds Båtvarv at Rökholmen on the Liss Lindö peninsula, and Hästö Båtvarv on the northern side of Hästö island. Arkösunds Båtvarv (✆+46 125 20053, open 0800–1630 weekdays only), can be reached on foot and has a 5.5T crane and a small engineering workshop. Hästö Båtvarv (✆+46 125 20073), is larger if less accessible, though several buoys are available for visitors. It has an 8T crane, open air and undercover storage, a diving service, large engineering workshop and GRP repair facilities.

### Facilities

Arkösund is a very popular tourist spot, with several cafés and restaurants and at least one large hotel. The tourist office (open 1000–1200 and 1400–2000) is within the hotel grounds. A supermarket is situated near the root of the Bäckmansviken pontoon. There is a regular bus service to Norrköping, connecting with the railway system and convenient if changing crews.

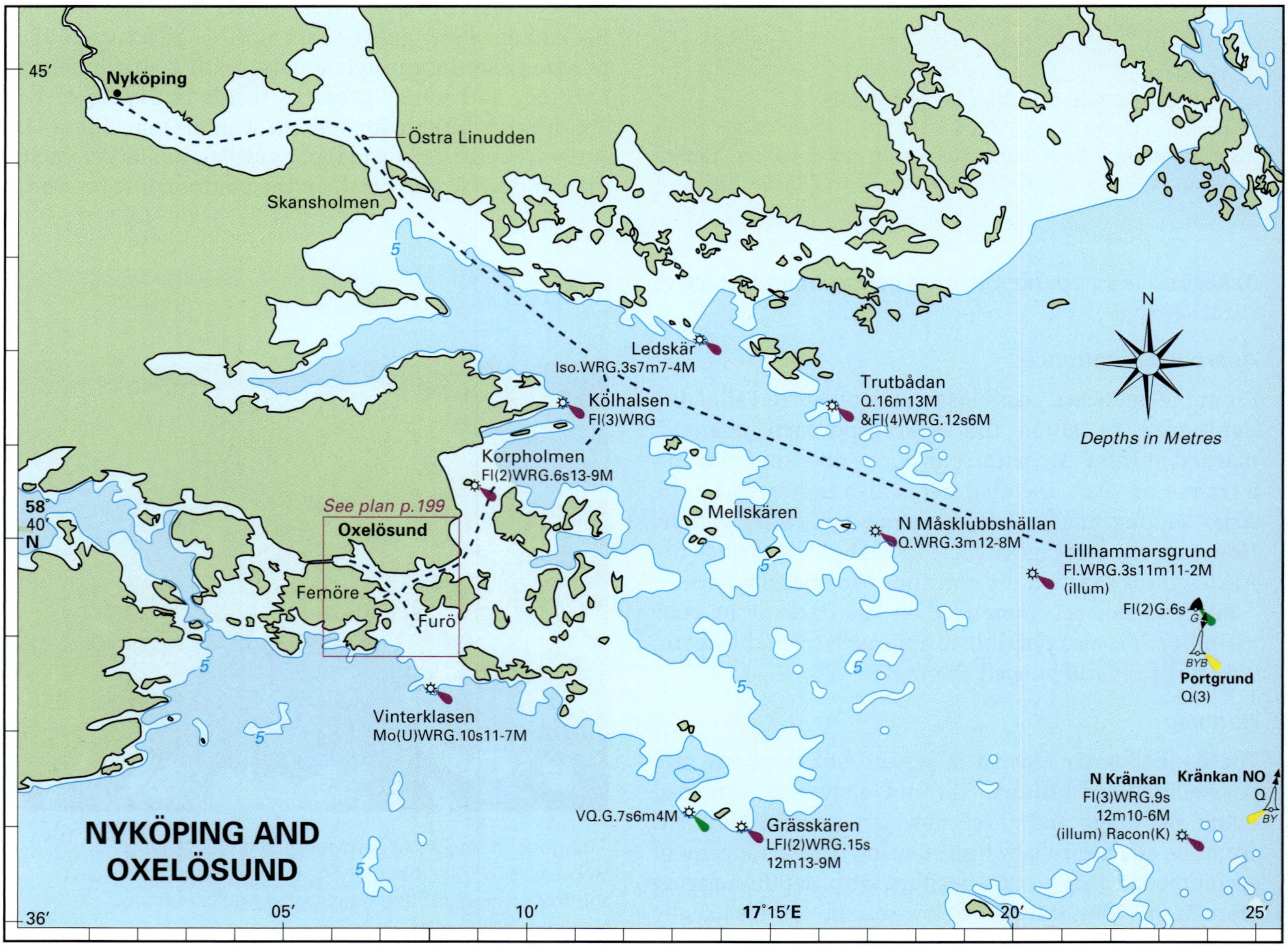

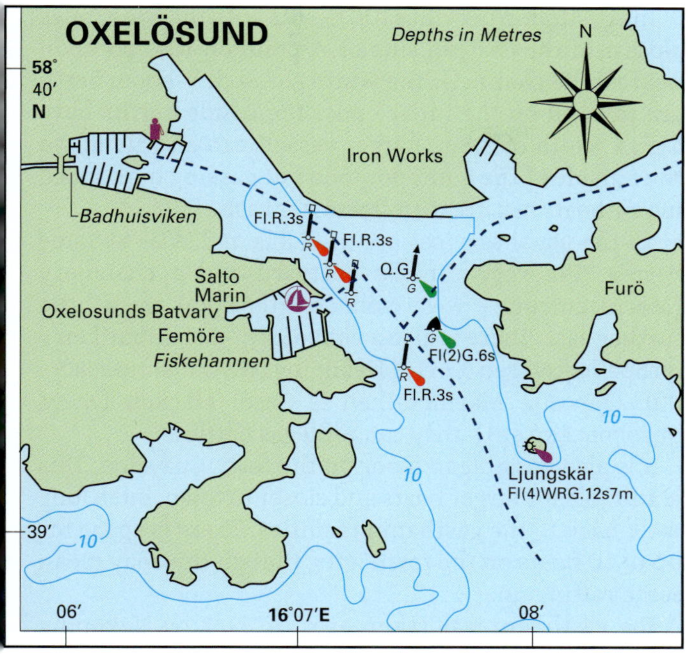


## OXELÖSUND

58°39′.3N 17°06′.1E

**Distances**
Arkösund 14M, Nyköping 10M

**Contacts**
Badhusviken:+46 76 868 14 20
oxelosundsgasthamn.se

A large town with a conspicuous ironworks to the east. While it is considered by some not to be the most attractive place, it is good for crew changes, stores and repairs. There are two major boat yards (Oxelösunds Båtvarv and Saltö Marin) offering all marine services and winter storage.

Gamla Oxelösund is an island museum of restored buildings and there are well displayed remains of Cold War defences to the south of the entrance. There are some nice walks around Femöre island.

### Approach & berthing

The prominent chimneys of the ironworks make a useful landmark, the entrance is very well buoyed and easy to follow to the two gästhamns.

First and to the south is the Fiskehamnen with 25 visitors' berths. Larger yachts will find greater depths of 2.5m–4.5m here. On the north side of the entrance to the Fiskehamnen is a restaurant – Restaurang Sailor and payment for the guest harbour can be made in the restaurant.

0.5M to the north and closest to the town is the well laid out Badhusviken marina with around 100 guest berths. This has three large jetties, with mooring using stern buoys. However, this is very open to strong winds from the southeast, and the jetties then offer little protection. If you can, find a berth on the jetty just inside the old harbour breakwater. Berths at Badhusviken can be booked using Dockspot (www.dockspot.com/en/docks/711-oxelosunds-gasthamn).

There is a good chandlery at Oxelösunds Båtvarv and both gästhamns have a full range of services. Fuel is only available at the Badhusviken marina.

### Facilities

There is an excellent children's playground at Badhusviken. The shopping precinct (around 15min walk from Badhusviken and 35min from the Fiskehamn) has good shops, a very good supermarket and Systembolaget. During the high season a free 'Tuf-Tuf' train, run by the local Rotary group, takes you the 1km up the hill to the

Aerial view of the Oxelösund Fiskehamn with the restaurant on the bottom right. The Badhusviken marina is in the background in line with the large grey shed *Andy Beharrell*

town centre and back every half hour otherwise bicycles are an advantage. There is a very modern church on the hill in town.

There is a One Sails sailmaker close to the Fiskehamn offering a full sailmaking and rigging service.

## NYKÖPING

58°44'.36N 17°01'.07E

**Distances**
Oxelösund 10M, Landsort 30M

**Contacts**
Värd ✆+46 155 248600
hamn.nykoping.se
nykopingsguiden.se
gasthamn@nykoping.se

An attractive small commercial and yachting harbour with the town marina on the west of the entrance and the large gästhamn and boatyard on the east.

The town was founded in 1187 and is one of the oldest in Sweden. It is divided by a river and has a medieval castle known as Nyköpingshus. Although it is some distance from the harbour, it is an attractive town with a good shopping centre, and well worth visiting.

Historically it is interesting as well and a visit to the castle museum is a good place to find out more about the bloody history. One part of this history is the Nyköping Banquet which took place in 1317. The three ruling brothers had fallen out, but in the name of reconciliation, Birger invited his two brothers Valdemar and Eric for Christmas. Presumably they had a nice Christmas dinner, at least hopefully they did because that was the last meal the dukes ever ate. When they headed for bed Birger's soldiers captured them and imprisoned them in the same dungeon which Birger had been imprisoned 10 years earlier. They were left to die from starvation. After five weeks in the dungeon they drew up their wills and these documents still survive in the Swedish archives today.

### *Approach & berthing*

There is a well-marked approach from the Lillhammarsgrund light (58°39'.7N 17°20'.3E) approx 4M off shore. This shoals to a 4m dredged channel at the Skansholmen Narrows, turns west at the Östra Linudden marker where it bears to port again and is too restricted to sail unless you are lucky enough to have a favourable wind.

The gästhamn provides 100 berths with the wider ones closest to the eastern side of A pontoon (the pontoon nearest the channel). The widths of each Y-boom berth are marked on the inner ends. The inside berths have a max width of 3.8m. Larger vessels can also tie up on the outside of the outer pontoon but passing high speed motor boats can create a tiresome wash.

All the usual services are available and WiFi at some berths. The very capable boatyard and a chandlery (Marincentrum – www.marincentrum.com) are a little further east. There is also a chandlery – Marinbutiken – on Spelhagsvägen 6, 611 31 Nyköping (www.marinbutiken.nu). Opposite Marinbutiken is Gasol Macken (www.gasolmacken.se) – they can refill gas bottles.

It is also possible to moor on the town quayside. This is suitable for larger boats and closer to town, but a long walk back to the gästhamn facilities. There is space for up to 20 boats on the town jetty, though this may mean some rafting up.

The gästhamn was taken over in 2023 by Nyköping Arena, part of the local municipality which also runs the canoe competition course which borders the gästhamn. The site offers all the usual facilities – laundry, toilets, showers and a sauna as well as chemical toilet emptying. Spaces can be booked in advance through the gästhamn website.

### *General*

There is a substantial supermarket situated conveniently opposite the Systembolaget, and several good restaurants in the middle of the town. The gästhamn is only 15mins by taxi from Skavsta airport though there are not currently any flights to/from the UK from there. However, it is only 1hr by train into the centre of Stockholm where you can transfer to Arlanda airport, so this is still a good place for crew changes or leaving one's boat.

Aerial view of Nyköping gästhamn looking east with the canoe course behind. Make sure you leave the cardinal at the bottom of the picture to port as you enter the gästhamn *Andy Beharrell*

# 2G. STOCKHOLM – THE ARCHIPELAGO AND SURROUNDING AREA

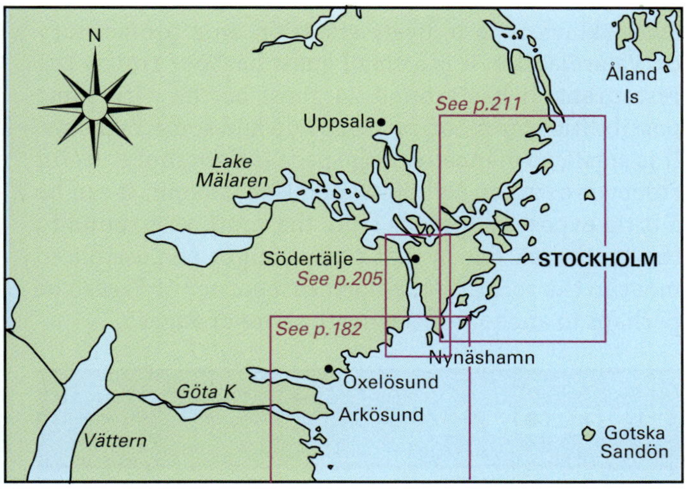


The Stockholm archipelago is perhaps considered the holy grail of archipelagos and many people will head north as quickly as possible to make the most of their time there. However, if you have the time, it is worth perhaps heading there a little slower. The much smaller archipelago between Nyköping and Nynäshamn makes a good introduction to archipelago navigation. If you have already come up through the Blå Kusten (Blue Coast) then you will be familiar with the techniques, but if you have made a longer passage to get north, it is worth considering slowing down as you close with the Stockholm archipelago.

Stockholm itself is hidden deep in the rock-strewn archipelago. The usual approach is from the south; the northern approach will be discussed later.

It is possible to sail from the northern tip of Gotland, but this may be a fairly lengthy passage of 60M or more. It is more likely that boats will be travelling from the neighbourhood of Arkösund or Oxelösund.

There are several possible routes from the south into Stockholm and its archipelago.

A. Stop at Oxelösund or Nyköping and then work your way through the archipelago between Nyköping and Landsort, cutting through to the north of Landsort and then on to Nynäshamn.

B. Sail inside Landsort, through the Södertälje Kanal, into Lake Mälaren and then to central Stockholm. This route has the advantage that it is more sheltered and quite scenic.

C. Pass east of Landsort, in which case the first obvious port of call is Nynäshamn. From Nynäshamn there are a variety of routes around the archipelago and into central Stockholm.

## A. OXELÖSUND TO LANDSORT

### ÄSPSKÄRSFLADEN

58°4'.51N 17°22'.49E

**Distances**
Nyköping 13M, Nynäshamn 25M

**Contacts**
www.naturumstendorren.se

In the 13th century the inshore route between Nyköping and Nynäshamn was often used to avoid the exposed coast at Landsort and the narrow section of this between the mainland and Krampö was known as Stendor Sound. This area is now the site of Stendörren Nature Reserve. Sten means 'rock' and dörren means 'door' so this is literally the 'stone door' through the archipelago. Heading through this sound from west to east brings you into the Tvären meteor crater. This is around 455 million years old.

Äspskärsfladen is a useful anchorage in the Stendörren reserve. You can enter the bay either from the south between Långa Uddsholmen and Äspskär or from the east between Långa Uddsholmen and Långa Udd. The southern entrance is the wider one, but both should have at least 4m depth. There are two blue mooring buoys for SXK (Swedish Cruising Club) members, but also plenty of anchoring space in 3-5m. Shelter is good, though winds from the south may bring a bit of a chop into the bay, so then anchor well to the east. Mooring to the rocks is possible in the northeast corner of the bay.

Aerial view of the anchorage at Äspskärsfladen, with Aspöfladen anchorage in the background
*Andy Beharrell*

The anchorage at Äspskärsfladen (Stendörren Nature Reserve) *Andy Beharrell*

There are several composting toilets around the bay. Landing on Långa Udd gives access to a series of marked walking trails which can take you all round the reserve. There is also a nature centre and observation tower for a different perspective on the reserve.

Bird life is plentiful. Look out for common tern, herring gull, eider ducks, oystercatchers and goosanders. If lucky, you might even see a white-tailed eagle.

Another alternative for anchoring is the bay Aspöfladen. This is just under 1M further on if heading from west to east towards Nynäshamn and is directly outside the Nature Reserve centre. However, this is much shallower with depths only just over 2m and a number of obstructions so care should be taken when anchoring.

## SVÄRDSKLOVA

58°43'.45N 17°14'.68E

**Distances**
Nyköping 8M, Nynäshamn 29M

Svärdsklova is in a lovely situation on a promontory on Vålarölandet. It is a small guest harbour run by the restaurant. It has around 24 guest berths with some possibilities for mooring alongside and some Y-booms. It is small, so manoeuvering space is tight, but a useful stopover between Nyköping and Nynäshamn. It can be a little exposed in winds from the southwest round to the southeast, but in that case it might be possible to moor to the rocks on the northeast corner of Fagerö or perhaps to anchor off the north shore of Fagerö.

## RINGSON

58°44'.36N 17°25'.94E

**Distances**
Nyköping 15M, Nynäshamn 25M

Ringson is a quiet, sheltered but very spacious anchorage. The only facilities are a couple of composting toilets. It makes an ideal stop between Oxelösund or Nyköping and Nynäshamn. There are two main possibilities for anchoring. The first of

Aerial view of Ringson Västerfjärden anchorage *Andy Beharrell*

Sävsundet – looking east *Andy Beharrell*

these is Västerfjärden. From a waypoint of 58°44'.28N 17°26'.23E head in on a course of 327°T. You should have a minimum of 3m through the channel in and it then opens up. There is good holding in 3-4m. You can land on the jetty at the south end of Västerfjärden and there are various walking routes around the island. There is a herd of deer which you may well spot grazing.

An alternative is to head from waypoint 58°44'.46N 17°26'.06E into Hummelviken – initially heading in just east of north and then turning sharply to just south of east to head into Hummelsvikfjärden. It is then possible to tuck into the bay to the east of Ärholmen to anchor, though look out for outlying rocks on the northeast tip of Ärholmen.

Leaving Ringson towards Nynäshamn you head through the narrow Sävsundet and from there you can head north towards Trosa or east to Landsort and Nynäshamn.

## FIFÅNG

58°43'.45N 17°14'.68E

**Distances**
Nyköping 8M, Nynäshamn 29M

Fifång is a useful stop between Nyköping and Nynäshamn as it is possible to ensure shelter from any wind direction. It is also a useful anchorage if you are planning to head up through the Södertälje Kanal into Lake Mälaren. The island has a bay in the north (Norrviken) which is sheltered from winds from the northwest round to the east and also a bay in the south (Sörviken) which offers good shelter for winds from the southwest round to the southeast (through north), so you will be well covered whatever the wind direction.

Both bays offer anchorages in 6-9m with plenty of space but in Sörviken there is also plenty of mooring to the rocks on the southern tip of the peninsula jutting out. In Norrviken there is rock mooring on the western side of the bay. Both these mooring areas have rings fixed into the rocks for attaching your shorelines.

In Sörviken the Södertälje Båtsällskap has some jetties in the northern part of the bay, but this is quite shallow, so it is probably better to anchor in the main bay.

## TROSA

58°54'.4N 17°33'.1E

**Distances**
Oxelsund 45M, Södertälje 25M

**Contacts**
Harbour office ✆+46 156 50 5200
www.trosanyagasthamn.se/
kontact@apelago.se

Trosa is an attractive old town with an interesting history. It dates right back to the 14th century and received its city privileges in 1454 from King Charles VIII of Sweden. Because of post-glacial rebound (the land rising after the Ice Age), the city centre was relocated in the 17th century to its current position by

Aerial view of the gästhamn at Trosa. It is possible to moor alongside the starboard jetty on the channel into town, but this can be more expensive *Andy Beharrell*

the estuary. The city was burnt down and plundered by the Russians in 1719 during the Russian Pillage of 1719–21 and was repeatedly attacked during the Great Northern War. When the Baltic fishery started to decline in the late 19th century the city turned to tourism and today it is one of the four wealthiest communities in Sweden. The tourist information office in the centre has a suggested walking tour (The Heritage Trail) which guides you around the key historical sites of the town.

The gästhamn is on the east side with 140 bows to with stern buoys or alongside berths in 2–2.2m. The stern buoys are dredged to 2.2m but watch out for depths due to silting. The end of the western side of the jetty is reserved for the skärgård ferry and the Göta Kanal cruise ships. There are also a limited number of berths up the canal towards the town. These have a maximum of 1.8m. Due to the limited depths in the harbour, it is worth checking the water stand (vattenstånd) before arrival. If the water level is a little low, anchoring at Fifång might be a suitable alternative.

The gästhamn has been extensively upgraded in recent years and the reception now offers some chandlery, canoe hire, bike hire as well as full services including laundry, toilets, showers and a sauna from 5pm all year round. There is a restaurant and café next door to the gästhamn building and this is open all year, though from September onwards the opening is at weekends only. Berths can be booked in advance through Dockspot (www.dockspot.com/en/docks/207-trosa-gasthamn).

Full services, including a chandlery and boatyard (Finessa Varvet – www.finessa.se) are available. The town facilities are a 10min walk from the gästhamn and include Coop and ICA supermarkets, a Systembolaget and a bookshop (Trosa Bökhandel – Torget 3) which stocks Swedish chart packs. A good anchorage may be found in Lagnnöviken bay to the southwest of the entrance channel.

## LANDSORT, ÖJA

58°46'.19N 17°51'.36E

Distances
Nyköping 29M, Nynäshamn 10M

If you have taken the archipelago route through from Nyköping to Nynäshamn, you will want to head through to the north of Landsort. You can enter the channel taking you round the north of Öja at a waypoint of 58°46'.27N 17°50'.54E. Head through between the red and green buoys and then turn north and follow the marked channel for 1M north and then back round to the east again. This is a good way to cut round to Nynäshamn.

A good stop on the way is the small harbour of Norrhamn, on the western side of Öja just after you come into the start of the channel before heading north. This harbour is exposed in westerlies, but has good shelter from the south and east. There are a few stern buoys, but otherwise moor bows-to with a stern anchor.

The island is still an active pilot station and from the jetty you can walk south to the Pilot Station, village and to see Landsort lighthouse. The distance to the lighthouse is about 3.5km. This is an important navigational mark. The original lighthouse was built in 1669, but most of the current characteristics date from a larger rebuild in 1870. The last lighthouse keeper left in 1963 when the lighthouse was fully automated.

The lighthouse at Landsort on the southern tip of Öja
*Andy Beharrell*

The small harbour on the western side of Öja
*Andy Beharrell*

## B. SÖDERTÄLJE AND THE SÖDERTÄLJE KANAL

59°12'N 17°38'E

### Distances

Västervik 95M, Arkösund 60M, Nynäshamn 40M, Lake Mälaren (from Mälarbron bridge) 5M

### Lights

**Landsorts Bredgrund** 58°43'.9N 17°51'.9E Iso. WRG.4s18m16–8M Racon. Orange tower. Floodlit
**Landsort, south point** 58°44'.4N 17°52'.1E White tower, red top 25m
**Asenskallen** 58°47'N 17°42'.1E Fl.WRG.3s12m8–5M White tower, green band 9m
**Granklubben** 58°47'.9N 17°44'.9E Fl(4)WRG.12s13m13-9M White lantern

### Contacts

**Södertälje Kanal** ☏+46 771 630 655
*Canal Control Centre* VHF Ch 14/68
**Södertälje Guest Harbour (Lilla Gästhamnen)** ☏+46 70 68 72 699
www.lillagasthamnen.se/
lillagasthamnen@gmail.com
**Järnvägs and Motorvägsbroarna bridges** VHF Ch 16/68
**Slussbron lock and bridge** VHF Ch 14
**Mälarbron bridge** VHF Ch 14/16/68
☏+46 771 630655
**Southern Canal information ( Södertälje canal)** – www.sjofartsverket.se/sv/tjanster/kanaler-slussar-broar/sodertalje-kanal
**Northern Canal information (Mälar Bridge and lock)** – www.sjofartsverket.se/sv/tjanster/kanaler-slussar-broar/sodertalje-malarbron/

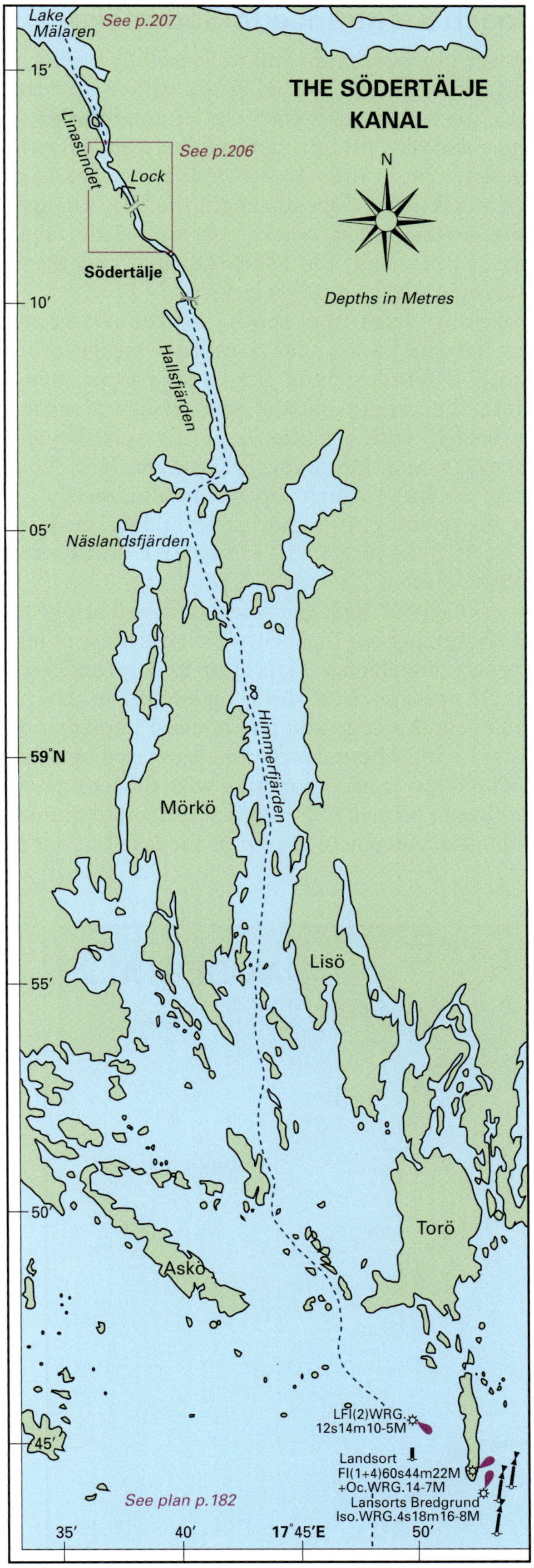


Södertälje grew up by the strait that at that time connected Lake Mälaren and Saltsjön. This was the fastest route by sea to Lake Mälaren from the south. By the Viking Age, however, the land uplift resulting from the ice age had made the route impassable and the only way the Vikings could get their boats to Helgö, Birka and other trading posts in Lake Mälaren was to pull the boats on logs across the isthmus. It was not until 1820 that the canal and lock was built. Södertälje (pronounced Seu-dehr-tehl-je) is a commercial port and town of about 25,000 inhabitants. A surprising tonnage of commercial traffic still uses the Södertälje Kanal each year but it is also very convenient as a route into Stockholm.

If heading northwards from the Nyköping area, the *skärgård* is entered at the Landsort light, where a lumpy sea can build. In such conditions, the well sheltered and interesting approach to Stockholm offered by the Södertälje Kanal may prove a real boon. The canal then takes you into Lake Mälaren.

However, depending on where you have come from, it is a fair way to get to Landsort, and Södertälje is a further 35M from there. The harbour at Trosa is a good place at which to break the journey.

## Approach & entrance to Södertälje

The entrance to the channel up to Södertälje begins at Landsort, and the first few miles are rather intricate and rock strewn. It leads into the Himmerfjärden, a long and relatively straight fjord which trends north-northwest for more than 30M before it reaches Lake Mälaren at Viksberg. Over its length the fjord changes its name several times before reaching Södertälje's two sections of canal, the Södra Kanalen and Norra Kanalen, separated by a single lock.

Approaching from the south, as the waterway narrows, vessels pass under a railway bridge (40m clearance), before reaching the canal proper. Some 0.3M into the canal's narrow section lies a second railway bridge, with a motorway bridge just beyond (the Järnvägs and Motorvägsbroarna bridges, both clearance 25.9m), which open simultaneously. A request for opening, if required, should be made to Södertäjle VTS ✆+46 771 630 675 or VHF Ch 68, who will advise times.

The guest harbour, lock and associated road bridge lie about 0.5M further on. The lock, which has a rise of less than 1m, accommodates vessels of up to 120m and 5.5m draught. It operates 0815–2115, opening southbound at 15mins past the hour and northbound immediately following the southbound lock, and is crossed by a low bridge which opens in conjunction with the lock gates. Payment has to be made by card if southbound but not if northbound; you pay to get out of the lake but not to go in.

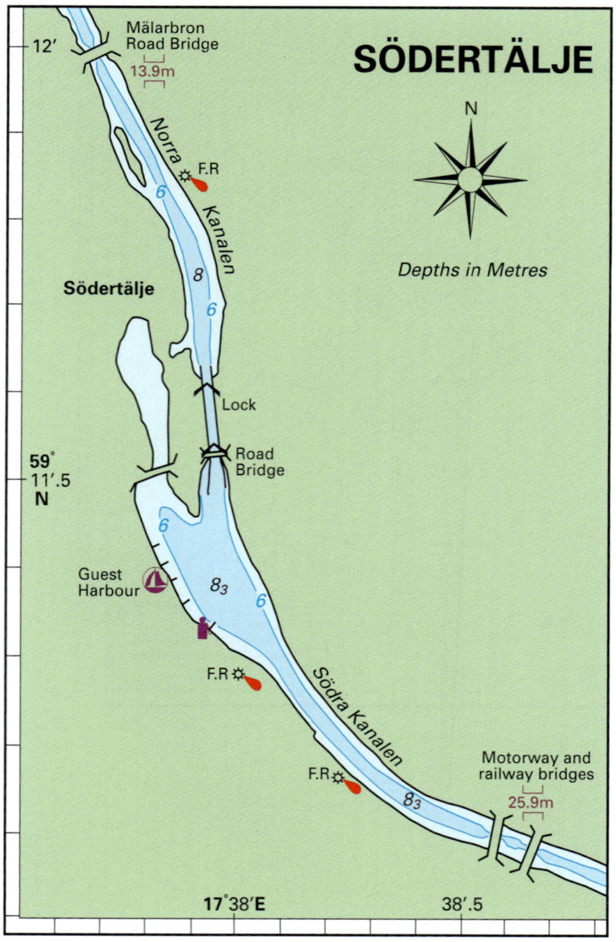


A third road bridge, the Mälarbron bridge, is encountered some 0.4M beyond the lock, close to the northern end of the canal. This bridge (clearance 13.9m) opens at 0900, 1100, 1300, 1500, 1800, 1900 and 2100 Mon–Thurs; 0900, 1100, 1300, 1500, 1800, 1900, 2000 and 2100 Friday; and hourly 0800–2100 weekends. Full details are available on www.sjofartsverket.se/en/services/bridges-and-canals/sodertalje-malarbron/.

It is advisable to check the opening times of the lock and the bridge if you are heading north, otherwise you might find you have to wait up to 90mins in a 0.5M length of canal with nowhere to tie up. It is possible to contact the lock and bridge on VHF Ch 14 to request an opening of the bridge soon after the lock.

From the Mälarbron bridge it is only a few miles further into Lake Mälaren (see page 207) which is an extensive cruising area in itself. The passage from Lake Mälaren to central Stockholm is quite straightforward.

### *Regulations*

Sailing in the canal is forbidden between the south end of the Södra Kanalen and Linasundet to the north, and commercial shipping takes precedence over leisure craft at all times. It is recommended, but not mandatory, that small craft monitor VHF Ch 16/68 whilst in the canal section. There is no space for even a small yacht to pass a ship in the canal or lock, so all vessels must obey the light signals situated on the east bank at each end of the canal and at the lock – 2 Iso.R.3s signifies STOP or DO NOT ENTER. Yachts may not pass through the lock at the same time as commercial vessels – permission to enter is given on VHF Ch 68 or by loudspeaker.

### *Berthing*

There are waiting berths (to starboard on approaching) both below and above the lock, but for a longer stay use the guest harbour on the west side of the channel just south of the lock. This has 90 visitors' berths in 2–8m depths, mostly bows-to between booms and step off pontoons. Enter any berth on arrival unless actually marked 'private' or 'reserved'. The harbour office, open 0730–2200 in summer, is situated in the café/shop about 50m south of the pontoons.

### *Services*

Water and electricity are provided on the pontoons, with showers and launderette ashore. Fuelling berth (diesel and petrol), near the café and shop.

### *Facilities*

Södertälje is a quite industrial town and is the base for the truck manufacturer Scania and the pharmaceutical company Astra Zeneca. This means that it has all the facilities of a good-sized town with an excellent shopping centre within walking distance, with the bonus of an excellent swimming pool complex. The railway station, which has a quick, frequent service to Stockholm central station, is only 5mins walk from the harbour.

## Södertälje to Stockholm

To reach Stockholm from the Södertälje canal is a journey of around 25–30M, although having come this far, most visitors would probably prefer to spend some time exploring Lake Mälaren.

From the canal head due east into the city. There are various bridges, one of which is high (26m) and fixed, as well as four lifting bridges and a lock. Payment has to be made at the lock by card if leaving the lake, but not if you are entering it. Just past the final bridge, the channel leads into the main waterway in the centre of Stockholm, and it is just a short journey from here to the Wasahamnen in the centre of the city.

In sequence from west to east (i.e. from Lake Mälaren to Stockholm. Reverse this if going out of Stockholm), you encounter the following:

**Grondalsbron** (fixed road bridge, clearance 25.2m)
**Lilljeholmen** (lifting road bridge, clearance 14·7m closed; fixed span 15·5m)
 ✆+46 8 670 28 10, VHF Ch 12, 16, 68
**Årstabron north** (fixed rail bridge, clearance 20m)
**Årstabron south** (fixed rail bridge, clearance 26m).
**Johanneshovsbron** (motorway bridge, clearance 32m)
**Hammarbyslussen** (lock)
 ✆+46 8 670 2815, VHF Ch 12, 16
**Skansbron** (lifting rail bridge, clearance 11.4m closed)
 ✆+46 8 670 28 15, +46 8 670 28 10, VHF Ch 12
**Danviksbron** (lifting rail bridge, clearance 11.8m closed)
 ✆+46 8 508 279 11 or +46 8 670 28 10, VHF Ch 12, 16

Please note that these clearances are given as 'vertical clearance'. This is the height at high water plus the expected maximum swell. The Port of Stockholm website (portsofstockholm.com/stockholm/bridges/) also gives the 'free height'. This is the height at 'mean water level'.

## Lake Mälaren

Lake Mälaren, the third-largest lake in Sweden, stretches for some 70M to the west of Stockholm and provides a fine sailing ground in beautiful surroundings. Much of its charm lies in the fact that it is not one great sheet of water but is broken up by many large and small islands, forming a variety of channels through which to explore.

Water levels in Lake Mälaren are less than a metre above those in the Baltic, and it can be entered from the south via the Södertälje Kanal (see page 206) or from the east via the Hammarbyleden, just south of Stockholm. Prehistorically it was continuous with the sea. With the thawing of the ice sheet in the north of Scandinavia the whole country gradually rose, until the medieval settlements were cut off from the sea by the rapids which now separate Stockholm's Gamla Stan (old town) from the Södermalm.

### *Local interest*

The lake is home to or visited by large numbers of wildfowl and other birds. You would be unlucky not to see at least one Osprey or Sea Eagle most days. Though not as many sailing yachts are to be seen on Lake Mälaren as in Swedish coastal waters it is nevertheless a very popular cruising ground. There are nearly 30 yacht harbours on the lake itself and another dozen or so on its various extensions, as well as limitless possibilities for anchoring. However, the surrounding land rises to more than 30m in places and is well wooded, sometimes making the wind flukey or non-existent.

There are many interesting and historic places on Lake Mälaren's shores, and a month or more could easily be spent visiting them all. A selection of the most well-known follows.

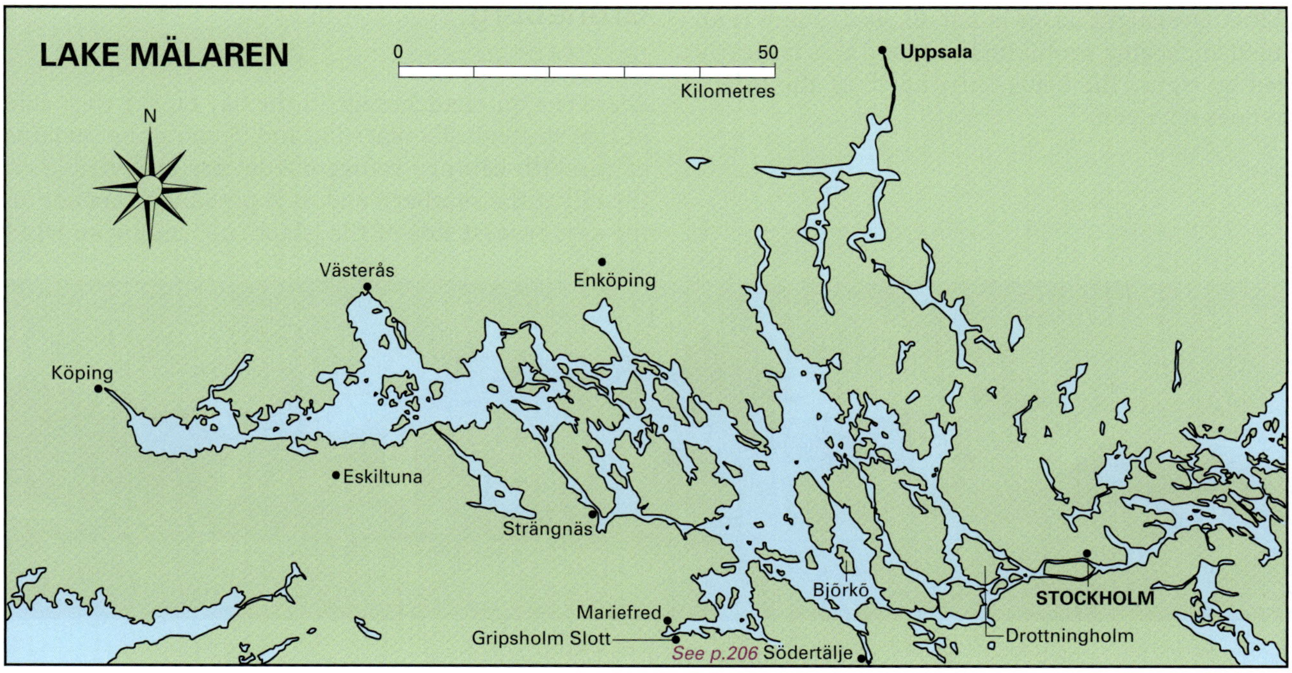

## Rastaholm

59°17'.62N 017°38'.78E

**Contacts**
✆+46 8 560 230 70

The visitors berths at Rastaholm are on the northwest side of the first pontoon and has 5-6m of water. Mooring is bows-to with stern buoys, alongside or it is possible to anchor.

The harbour is open from May to September. Facilities include power, water, toilets, showers, sauna, pump-out and a restaurant (only open during the main season). There are nice walks and the sunsets are particularly beautiful to watch from here.

The guest jetty at Björkö *Robin Matthews*

## Björkö

59°19'.87N 017°32'.42E

Birka on this small island was the ancient Viking capital of Sweden and is now a World Heritage site. There are some supplies, an excellent museum, a good restaurant, lovely walks around the burial mounds and some reconstructed buildings. A fairly basic gästhamn with 40 visitors' berths (bows-to with stern buoys) can become very busy during the season. If it is quieter mooring alongside may also be available, but be careful as you may be charged double. It can be quite exposed in strong westerlies. A new pontoon was built in 2023 with power and water available and the depth at pontoon is 2.5m.

## Drottningholm

59°19'.5N 17°53'.5E

Home of the Swedish royal family. The palace and gardens are well worth a visit as is the unique wooden 18th-century royal theatre. Anchoring is now prohibited outside Drottningholm Palace. Instead, the authorities have installed approximately 25 mooring buoys. These are free of charge but can only be used between 0600 and 2200. Overnight usage is not allowed. There is an extended anchoring prohibited area and this is clearly marked by signs. The bridge just north of the palace (1.3m) does not open.

Anchored off Drottningholm Palace. Please note that since this photo was taken anchoring here has been prohibited. There are now mooring buoys for use *Robin Matthews*

## Gröneborg

59°32'7N 17°06'E

There is a quiet anchorage in the bay on the west side of this strategically placed island. Some stone remains of the 13th-century refuge citadel are still visible on the hill at the southern end. It is possible to anchor on the east or west side of the island, depending on wind

Drottningholm Palace – the private residence of the Swedish Royal Family *Andy Beharrell*

The fuel berth and moorings at Mariefred *Andy Beharrell*

direction, but it is exposed to the north and south. Beware of the shoals at the north and south ends of the island. There is a small beach for dinghies on the east side of island and a picnic area on the southwest tip.

## Mariefred

59°15'.4N 17°13'.5E
www.mariefredsmarina.se
info@mariefredsmarina.se
✆+46 73 663 3301

The beautiful Gripsholm Slott, which houses the National Portrait Gallery, is within easy walking distance of the gästhamn and is certainly worth a visit. Limited depths but all facilities and 40 visitors' berths (some stern buoys with bows to jetty and some Y-booms) and good facilities. A delightful little town with a variety of shops and a Systembolaget, which became established to service the royal castle.

Berthed opposite Gripsholm Slott *Andy Beharrell*

Aerial view of the berths at Mariefred and Gripsholm Slott *Andy Beharrell*

## Strängnäs

59°22'.7N 17°02'.5E

**Contacts**

www.strangnashamn.se
strangnashamn@gmail.com
✆+46 73 256 1934

Although touristy this is a charming little Episcopal seat with a striking red brick cathedral. All the usual facilities are available at the 40 berth gästhamn (with stern buoys) just northwest of the Tosterbron swing bridge. A new high level bridge (26.4m clearance) 'Nya Strangnasbron' has been constructed to the northwest of the town. The Stallarholmsbron (closed 3.1m) now opens 20-30mins past each hour and the Tosterbron (closed 2.8m) 10mins after uneven hours.

Berths can be booked in advance through Dockspot (www.dockspot.com/en/docks/133-strangnas).

## Kungsängen

59°28'.59N 017°45'.45E

**Contacts**

www.kungsangensbatsallskap.se
✆+46 70 699 3240

Kungsängen is a members' boat club, but has a gästhamn. The approach is uncomplicated from the bay. The gästhamn is sheltered from the west, north and east, but exposed to the south. Surges against the jetty may sometimes be a problem. Depth around the jetty is 3-4m. Mooring is bows-to with stern buoys and power, water, toilets, showers, laundry and rubbish disposal are all available. There is a supermarket, restaurants, cafés and library in the town centre which is 10mins walk away. Regular trains to Stockholm are less than 10mins walk from marina. It is possible to sail all the way to Uppsala provided air draft is less than 15m to clear a bridge at Stäket.

## Uppsala

59°51'.5N 17°55'E

There are 20 visitors' berths at the gästhamn but with restricted facilities although all services can be obtained nearby. There is a height restriction (15m) for accessing Uppsala, so check charts and air draft carefully. This is Sweden's most famous university town and it also boasts the country's largest cathedral. See the Linnaeus Botanical Garden.

## Västerås

59°36'.09N 016°32'.70E
www.vasterasgasthamn.se
✆+46 70 699 3240

Said to be Sweden's largest freshwater port. With many miles of cycle paths it is ideal for a cycling break. It has a 13th-century cathedral and is close to Västerås airport, though there are not as many flights from Västerås as from the main airport for Stockholm – Arlanda. There are 30 visitors' berths at the gästhamn which is about 800m from the shopping centre. There is only one small guest pontoon to starboard from the entrance and the depth is 2m at the outside end. The stern buoy berths along the southwest side of pontoon are small, and there is some kind of obstruction at about 2m depth on the northeast side. Anundshög Viking site 8km to the northeast of the city is worth a visit.

Many passenger boats ply the routes around Lake Mälaren, most notably the Mariefred which has been steaming between Stockholm and Mariefred continuously since 1903.

Aerial view of Strägnäs gästhamn *Andy Beharrell*

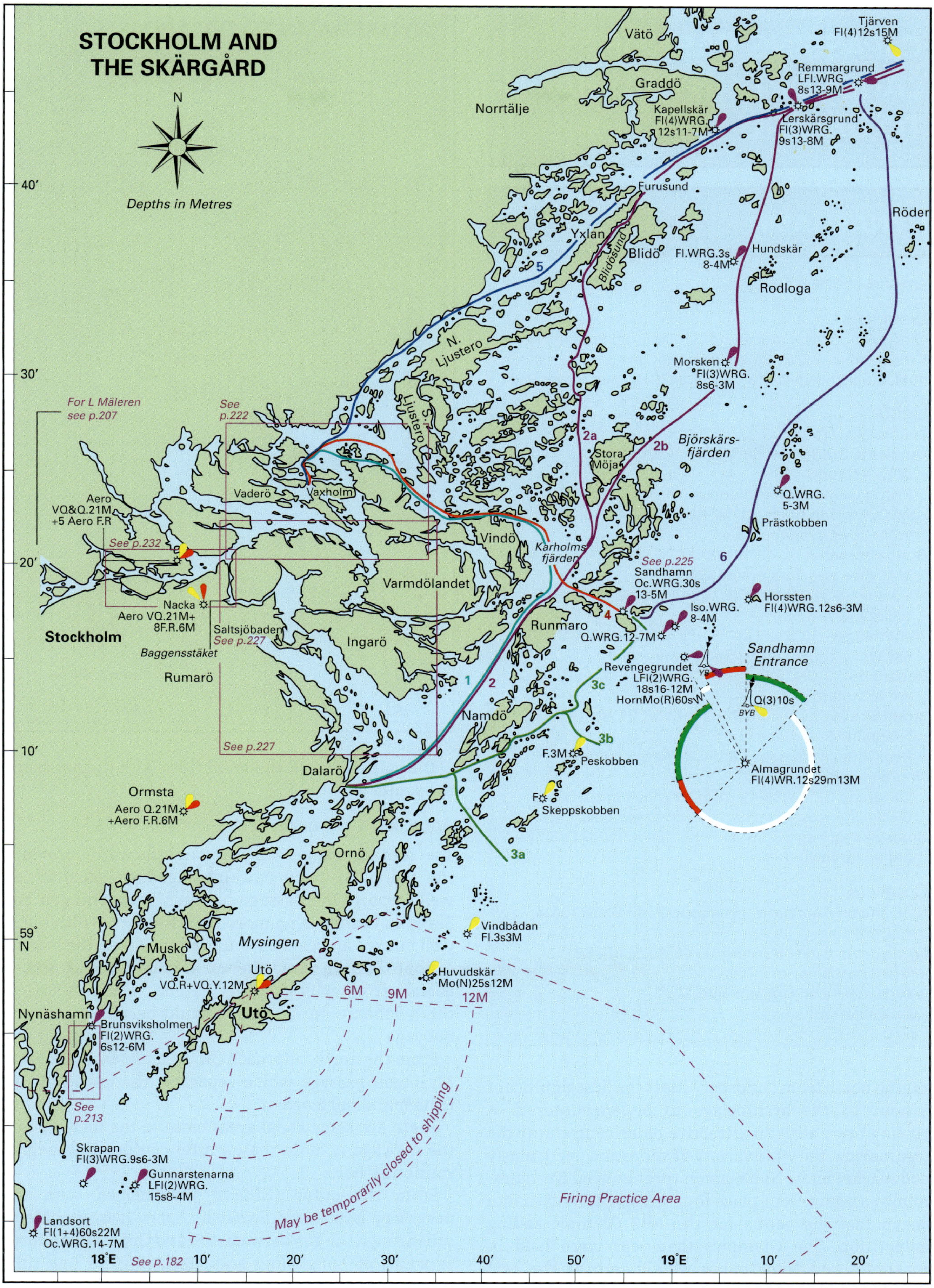
STOCKHOLM AND THE SKÄRGÅRD
N
Depths in Metres
Vätö
Graddö
Norrtälje
Kapellskär
Fl(4)WRG.
12s11-7M
Tjärven
Fl(4)12s15M
Remmargrund
LFl.WRG.
8s13-9M
Lerskärsgrund
Fl(3)WRG.
9s13-8M
Furusund
Yxlan
Blidösund
Blidö
Fl.WRG.3s
8-4M
Hundskär
Rodloga
Röder
N. Ljustero
S. Ljustero
Morsken
Fl(3)WRG.
8s6-3M
2a
2b
Björskärs-
fjärden
Stora Möja
Q.WRG.
5-3M
Prästkobben
6
For L Mälaren
see p.207
See
p.222
Vaderö
Vaxholm
Aero
VQ&Q.21M
+5 Aero F.R
See p.232
Vindö
Karholms
fjärden
See p.225
Sandhamn
Oc.WRG.30s
13-5M
Horssten
Fl(4)WRG.12s6-3M
Varmdölandet
Nacka
Aero VQ.21M+
8F.R.6M
Stockholm
Saltsjöbaden
See p.227
Baggensstäket
Ingarö
4
Iso.WRG.
8-4M
Runmaro
Q.WRG.12-7M
Sandhamn
Entrance
Revengegrundet
LFl(2)WRG.
18s16-12M
HornMo(R)60s
Q(3)10s
BYB
YB
Rumarö
1
2
3c
Namdö
3b
See p.227
F.3M
Peskobben
Almagrundet
Fl(4)WR.12s29m13M
Dalarö
Ormsta
Aero Q.21M
+Aero F.R.6M
F
Skeppskobben
3a
Ornö
5
Vindbådan
Fl.3s3M
Mysingen
Musko
Utö
VQ.R+VQ.Y.12M
Huvudskär
Mo(N)25s12M
6M
9M
12M
Nynäshamn
Brunsviksholmen
Fl(2)WRG.
6s12-6M
See
p.213
May be temporarily closed to shipping
Skrapan
Fl(3)WRG.9s6-3M
Gunnarstenarna
LFl(2)WRG.
15s8-4M
Firing Practice Area
Landsort
Fl(1+4)60s22M
Oc.WRG.14-7M
40′
30′
20′
10′
59°
N
18°E
See p.182
10′
20′
30′
40′
50′
19°E
10′
20′

# C. PASSING EAST OF LANDSORT – NYNÄSHAMN TO DALARÖ

## NYNÄSHAMN

58°54'N 17°57'E

### Distances

Västervik 85M, Arkösund 50M, Södertälje 40M, Saltsjöbaden 35M, Stockholm (via the Baggensstäket) 45M, Stockholm (via the skärgård) 70+M, Sandhamn 45M

### Lights

*Southern approach*

**Landsorts Bredgrund** 58°43'.9N 17°52'.5E Iso. WRG.4s18m16–8M
Racon Orange tower Floodlit

**Landsort, south point** 58°44'.4N 17°52'.1E
White tower, red top 25m

**Gunnarstenarna** 58°46'.5N 18°03'.3E LFl(2)WRG.15s14m8–4M White structure on red base

**Måsknuv** 58°51'.4N 18°01'.1E Mo(A)WRG.8s13m13–7M
White tower 10m

**Trehörningen** 58°53'.5N 17°56'.8E VQ(6).WRG.6s8m10–5M White square metal framework tower

**Bedarö** 58°53'.8N 17°56'.6E
White lantern

**Strathmos** Lights in Line 315° Front 58°54'.8N 17°57'.7E F.R.8m2M Red g on pillar
Rear 100m from front F.R.11m2M Red g on pillar

*Northern approach*

**Örngrund** 58°53'.8N 18°01'.5E Q.WRG.10m10–5M
Black GRP tower, red band on concrete base

**Brunsviksholmen** 58°55'.1N 17°58'.7E Fl(2)WRG.6s8m12–6M White tower 8m

### Contacts

**Nynäshamn Commercial Harbour** ✆+46 8520 10615
VHF Ch 11/16

**Nynäshamn Guest Harbour** ✆+46 8520 68888
info@Nynäshamn.se
www.Nynäshamn.se/gasthamn
www.visitNynäshamn.se

Coming north from Landsort, this is the first significant harbour of the archipelago to be encountered. A growing town with an attractive older centre near the large marina, the wide variety of shops and particularly good market make Nynäshamn (pronounced Nu-nairs-hahmn) a convenient place for storing up. Nynäshamn was in fact the venue for the 1912 Olympic sailing competition. The Olympics that year were held in Stockholm and Nynäshamn was chosen as the best place for the sailing (above Göteborg/Gothenburg). The classes were 6m, 8m, 10m and 12m. You may not see as many of them around now, but it is still a lovely sailing area.

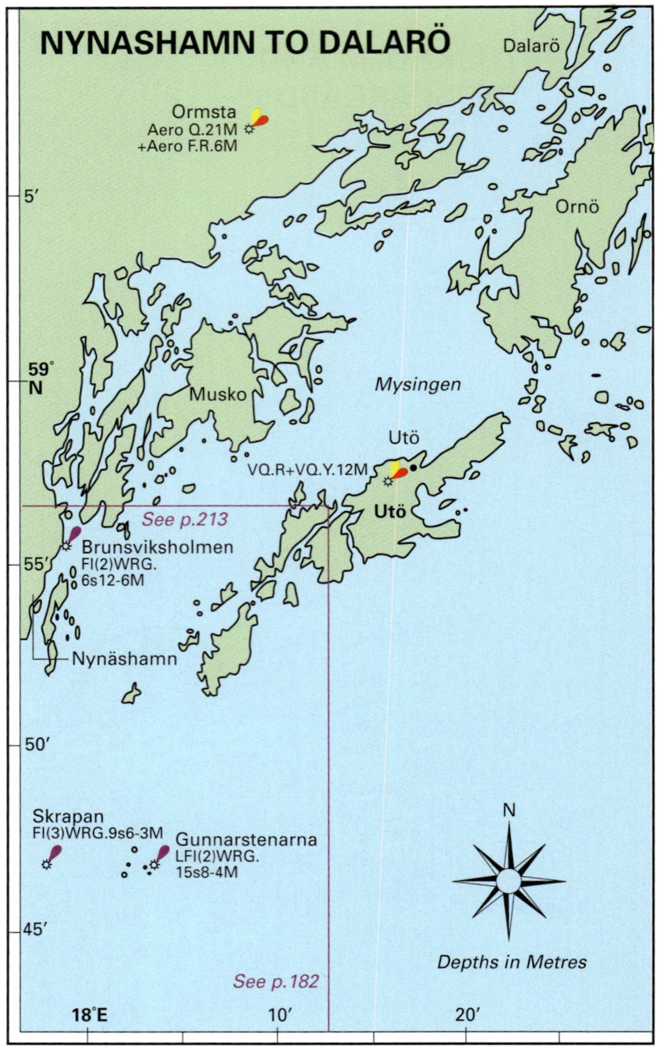


The marina is well sheltered from both the north and the south.

### Approach & entrance

The southern approach is straightforward, provided the red pillar buoy marking Pigbåden shoal is left well to port. The passage between Trehörningen and Skrapan islands is no more than 100m in width but is well buoyed and carries a minimum of 4m. The marina is approached around the north end of Trehörningen island, from which shoals extend nearly 400m to the northeast. No liberties should be taken with the buoyage.

From the north, approach can be made from the wide Mysingen passage which separates the island of Utö from mainland Sweden.

There are some shoal areas close to the marina, and the buoyage is more than a little confusing. Navigate cautiously here.

From the outer *skärgård*, and armed with the necessary large-scale Swedish charts, it is possible to sail through the gap between Utö and Ornö, either north or south of Långbäling and Marbäling. At one time closed to yachts entirely, some restrictions remain and anchoring, scuba diving and fishing are still forbidden in the area. There is a firing range to the southeast of Utö which extends up to 12M offshore and this area

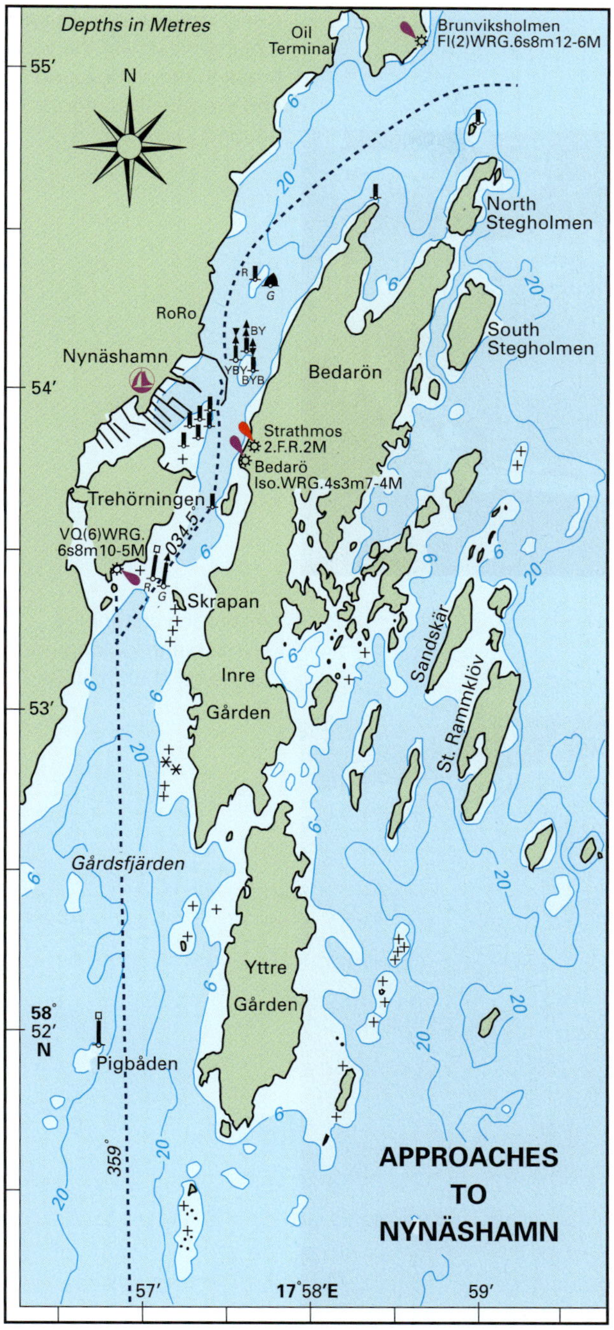


may be temporarily closed to navigation. For details call Utö skjufält VHF Ch 16, call ✆+46 10 823 3000 or email exp-amf1@mil.se.

### Anchorage

There is too much traffic to anchor off Nynäshamn itself, with commercial ships including cruise liners and ferries berthing north of the marina, but plenty of possibilities exist amongst the nearby islands.

### Berthing

Nynäshamn Gasthamn is a large marina with some 300–500 visitors' berths in 4–10m depths. There is a very long jetty and wavebreak to the north of the marina. Berthing on this jetty is alongside on the inside. Berthing on the outside is not recommended due to wash from passing vessels and ferries. Berthing elsewhere in the harbour is a mixture of booms and stern buoys. All berths, other than those very close to the shore and the southern pontoons, are available to visitors. Berthing fees are calculated by reference to beam and are in the middle band, but halve if the yacht is not occupied. This makes Nynäshamn a good place to leave a boat if you are heading home for a while. Even if only leaving the boat for a few days, it will be worth asking the cost of a weekly contract as this is substantially discounted. Berths can be booked in advance through Dockspot (www.dockspot.com/en/docks/126-Nynäshamn).

### Services

Most, though not all, berths have access to water and electricity, with showers, a sauna and laundry facilities ashore. Fuel (diesel and petrol) from the fuel jetty close north of the marina which is self-service and open 24/7. There is also a pump-out and a separate fuel jetty. As with many Swedish marinas, there is now also a boat wash in the gästhamn.

### Facilities

The marina office also doubles as the town's tourist office. There are all the usual facilities of a

Nynäs Havsbad – the Hotel Spa and Conference Centre just south of Nynäshamn *Andy Beharrell*

Aerial view of Nynäshamn looking west with the wave break in the foreground and the guest pontoons beyond *John Sadd*

Approach channel to Nynäshamn looking north to the gästhamn *Andy Beharrell*

Aerial view of Nynäshamn gästhamn *Andy Beharrell*

medium-sized town, including good shopping, the aforementioned market and a Systembolaget liquor store. Many pavement cafés and restaurants near the waterfront, including several in the marina itself. There is an excellent and famous fish smokery on the quay, and a van delivers fresh bread each morning. A new chandlery opened in 2024, called All At Sea and is located at Centralgatan 7a, Nynäshamn. (✆+46 9 664 4638, www.allatsea.se, info@allatsea.se)

*Communications & travel*

The marina is immediately adjacent to the railway station with a direct and inexpensive line to Stockholm (about 1hr), making it a convenient spot for crew changes or from which to explore the capital. This line is part of the main Stockholm commuter system, so a single ticket will last 75mins from when you start using it. This is usually enough to get into the centre and perhaps even a few stops on the Stockholm metro.

Ferries run to Gdansk, Rostock and Gotland in Finland from the ferry terminal to the north of the marina. There is also a regular ferry running to the Gotska Sandön National Park about 40M north of Gotland during the season, weather permitting, and a ferry to Utö and the islands to its south (Nåttarö, Rånö and Ålö).

The marina office is happy to hold mail for visiting yachts (Nynäshamns Gästhamn, Fiskargränd 5, 14930 Nynäshamn, Sweden). There is WiFi at the marina.

## Nåttarö Kvarnviken

58°52'.93N 18°06'.58E
www.explorearchipelago.com/sthlm/southern-archipelago/nattaro

Nåttarö Kvarnviken is a small harbour on the west coast of the island of Nåttarö. It can be a little exposed to the north and the west, but access is fairly straightforward – keep the two green lateral marks to starboard on entry and you should then have more than 6m of water in the approach to the jetty. There are stern buoys with more than 3m of water but it shoals rapidly towards the shore, so the outermost buoys on the eastern pier (ferry jetty) are the deepest. Avoid the pier end as the ferry uses this.

If the water is warm enough there is a snorkelling trail with underwater signage to find out more about what there is under the Baltic! There is also a shop, restaurant, and some nice walks around the island.

## Nåttarö Östermarsfladen

58°53'.46N 18°08'.4E
www.explorearchipelago.com/sthlm/southern-archipelago/nattaro

Nåttarö Östermarsfladen is an alternative to Kvarnviken on the north coast of Nåttarö. It is a large bay so may have some fetch in stronger northerly or northeasterly winds, but surrounded by islands as it is, this is unlikely to be too significant and the shelter in winds from the west round to the east through south is very good. The Archipelago Foundation (*Skärgårds* Stiftelsen) has laid some buoys in the bay and there is also a small jetty to moor to by stern anchor, but many people choose to anchor in the bay. The holding is good, but if anchoring here be aware of some old military cables left on the sea bed.

Aerial view of the jetties at Nåttarö Kvarnviken *Andy Beharrell*

Aerial view of the northern part of Nåttarö. The anchorage at Östermarsfladen can be seen top right *Andy Beharrell*

The approach can be either from the east or the west. The western approach can be useful if coming from the outer archipelago by sea and the strait just to the north of St Vallringen should have a minimum depth of 4m. From the east there are two possible straits - one to the west of Oxholmen and one to the east. The eastern one is more straightforward as there are isolated rocks to be avoided on the western entrance which involve an almost S-shaped entry. There are also shoals off the north of Oxholmen which you should be careful to avoid. Otherwise entry is reasonably straightforward.

The gästhamn at Utö Gruvbryggan, looking west *John Sadd*

## Utö

Utö is an island on the edge of the *skärgård* with a popular harbour of the same name on its northwest coast at 58°58'3N 18°19'6E. The harbour (Utö Gruvbryggan) is approximately 15M from Nynäshamn. Come in close to the west cardinal to avoid a 1.1m shallow patch and pick up the narrow buoyed channel - also with leading marks. The gästhamn mooring is with a stern anchor to the jetties north and south of the harbour, though avoid the ferry jetty. The final approach needs to be made with care, and there is a narrow but well buoyed entrance with conspicuous leading lines. Out of season, there may be room to tie alongside, but mooring at busier times is by stern anchor.

Facilities include a bakery, small supermarket, craft shops and cafes, fuel jetty and a separate pump-out barge on the northern side of the harbour. There is a nice view from the windmill.

There is a sheltered anchorage at Utö Kyrkvik (58°57'72N 18°17'68E). There are two SXK (Swedish Cruising Club) moorings in Kyrkviken but also

The anchorage at Utö Kyrkvik *Andy Beharrell*

swinging space for several boats near the jetty on the western side. Approach the mooring round the north of Skomakarskär island and turn in as the entrance opens up. There should be a minimum depth of around 4m in inlet. Ferries come in and out so anchor well clear of the fairway. There is a lovely church with a beautiful votive ship from 1730. Nice walking around the island as well.

The island is popular for its unspoiled nature, though it has a history of mining. The mines date from the 1100s and more than 2 million tonnes of iron ore has been mined and processed. There is still evidence of this history all over the island with deep lakes where mining was done and a mining museum on the island. There are several attractive anchorages among the islands to the south (Nåttarö, Ränö and Ålö) with the popular Båtshaket fish restaurant on the latter.

## Ornö

www.orno.se

Ornö is a large island to the south of Dalarö and can make a good stop on the way to the *skärgård*. If heading through to Stockholm via the Baggenstaket there are various anchorages on the western side of Ornö, or if heading through to the main archipelago, harbours on the east may be more appropriate. From these, you can head north to Namdö and Runmarö and on into the main archipelago.

### Ornö – Kolnäsviken

59°04'.85N 18°23'.09E

Ornö Kolnäsviken is an anchorage on the western side of the island around halfway up the western side. Entry is from the north and the channel is to the east of the small island off Bjurviksudd. This should have at least 2.5m in depth, but take care to stay central and keep clear of the rocks on either side. Once in there is a small, but very sheltered anchorage with 4–6m of water. There is a compost toilet on the north shore of the bay, where it is also possible to moor to the rocks.

### Ornö – Kyrkviken

59°03'.1N 18°26'.01E
www.orno.se/service/

Ornö Kyrkviken is a small guest harbour on the eastern side of Ornö. Entrance is fairly straightforward and there is a short buoyed channel to bring you through to the jetties where you can moor by stern anchor in over 4m of water. There is a restaurant, bakery, toilets and showers. The mini supermarket takes the marina fees and there is electricity but no water. Kayak hire is available.

A 5min walk from the gästhamn is a small museum about life on the island in the late 19th and early 20th century. This is housed in an 18th century school house. About 15mins walk away is evidence of the mining history on Ornö. At the end of the 19th century they started mining feldspar for the porcelain industry among others and the mines provided jobs for up to 20 people at times. Mining continued through to the 1960s, but now, all that remains is the quarry and various abandoned bits of equipment

## Dalarö

59°07'.65N 18°23'.69E (around 0.2M off southwest tip of Dalarö peninsula)

**Distances**

Nynäshamn 21M, Saltsjöbaden 14M, Stockholm (via the Baggensstäket) 24M

This can be a useful jumping off point for the *skärgård* when coming from the south. Dalarö is historically very significant and has a long history as a customs station. The name of Dalarö appears in the 13th century in Danish King Valdermar's sailing route, a description of the route from Utlängan in southern Sweden to Tallinn, Estonia. As a result of its important strategic position the waters around Dalarö have many well-preserved shipwrecks dating as far back as the 17th century and the area is popular with divers. One of these wrecks – the *Resande Man* (the Travelling Man) is featured in the Vrak Museum of Wrecks in Stockholm. She started from Dalarö and foundered in bad weather when she dragged her anchor near Landsort (www.vrak.se/en/wrecks-and-remains/resande-man/).

There are two guest harbours, the Hotellbryggan and the Askfatshamnen. The Hotelbryggan has neither water nor electricity, and is distinctly exposed, not only to weather but to the wash of passing motorboats

Kyrkviken guest pontoon on Ornö, looking northwest *John Sadd*

Dalarö Skans fortress – dates from 1683 *Andy Beharrell*

The gästhamn at Dalarö Askfatshamnen. Take care to stay inside the two red buoys off the gästhamn as the channel shallows rapidly *Andy Beharrell*

and ferries. However, it is the closest to the centre of Dalarö and is free for up to 4hrs if you want a quick visit in calmer weather.

The other harbour is Askfatshamnen, not far away. One jetty with around 30 guest berth is reserved for visitors. This has quite widely spaced booms. During the peak season, the gästhamn, like many, is manned by students who will direct you to a berth. There are the usual good quality services. The harbour is directly next to the entrance to the Dalarö Canal (only usable by motorboats – a 2.5m fixed bridge) and so there can be some wash in high season, but this is not too intrusive and it is completely quiet at night. It is only a 5min walk into town up the hill and there are shops and good restaurants in town.

A final alternative spot to moor is Dalarö Skans. The fortress was built in 1683 to replace an old structure from 1623 and was to defend the southern approaches to Stockholm. However, it was never actually used in anger and even the Russians avoided it during the Russian pillages of 1719. Today it is a restaurant and wedding venue, but also has a jetty with lazy lines for mooring. This makes a nice lunchtime or evening stop in more settled weather, but could get quite exposed in winds from the west to north.

## Grönskärsfladen

59°07'.93N 18°39'.62E (on the track of the first set of leading lines)

**Distances**

Nynäshamn 27M, Saltsjöbaden 15M, Stockholm (via the Baggensstäket) 25M

Grönskärsfladen (in between Grönskär, Grenskär and Jungfruskär) is a beautiful, sheltered anchorage. The entrance can be a little daunting, but with care is fairly straightforward and well-marked. Starting from the waypoint, follow the leading lines on Kuggmaren, all the time watching to the north for the leading lines on Klinten (Grönskär) to line up. Once you are on that track turn to the north and once close to the shore at Klinten (Grönskär) follow the island shore into the anchorage. The islands are managed by the Archipelago Foundation and protected as a nature reserve. Once in the bay there is plenty of space to anchor in around 5–6m of water or alternatively, there are a couple of places to moor on the rocks. The north shore of Kuggmaren is well protected from southerlies, or in westerlies, the eastern shore of Grönskär has a few spots to moor against the rocks. There are compost toilets on both Kuggmaren and Grönskär.

Moored to the rocks at Grönskärsfladen. There is also plenty of space in the bay to anchor *Andy Beharrell*

# STOCKHOLM AND ITS ARCHIPELAGO

## The Skärgård

The Stockholm Archipelago or *skärgård* (pronounced shair-gord) is a vast area of islands stretching from Landsort in the southwest to Tjärven, on the edge of the Åland Sea, in the northeast. It is quite heavily populated, particularly during the summer, and is very popular with Swedish yachtsmen but, nevertheless, offers a most attractive cruising ground (see page 107). It is also attractive to Swedish residents who, around midsummer, flock to their second homes around the archipelago.

In this section we look at various routes through the archipelago for those who are cruising to Stockholm or perhaps on to the Gulf of Bothnia, the Åland Islands and the Finnish Archipelago. We also examine the *skärgård* itself and look at various destinations within it. The archipelago can be split into the inner *skärgård*, and the outer *skärgård*, but none of the distances are huge and the channels are generally sheltered.

The inner *skärgård* is dotted with small guest harbours, though there are few marinas of any size other than those at Stavsnäs, Sandhamn and Bullandö. The outer archipelago however, to the north and east of Sandhamn, presents a wild and challenging cruising ground. This area is well charted, though

The houses you will see around the archipelago are often second homes, but all are immaculately maintained *Alex Beharrell*

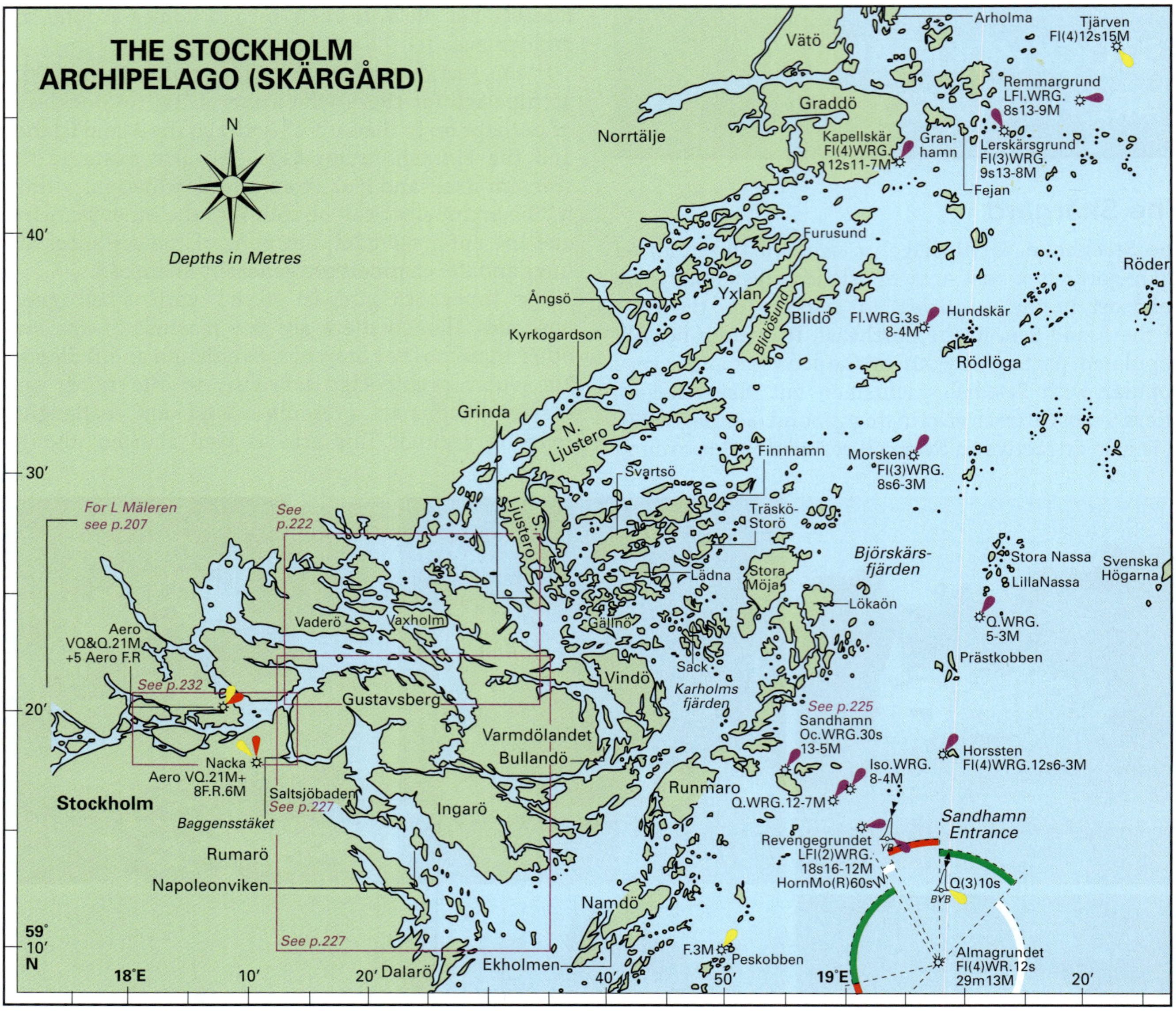


largely devoid of navigation marks and quite heavily rock-encumbered, but with care can be navigated in safety to reach some of the most beautiful and remote anchorages in the whole of the Baltic. In the *skärgård*, as elsewhere on the Swedish coast, ensuring that one keeps a constant and accurate track of one's position among the numerous reefs and islands is vital. If following the well-charted routes, you should have few problems but if you go 'off piste' take particular care. Cruising in the archipelago can involve navigating within metres of rocks. Strong winds can blow up quite suddenly, kicking up short seas. A complete set of current, large-scale Swedish charts is essential.

A further potential hazard is posed by the large modern ferries and cruise liners which weave their way through the tortuous passages which characterise much of the inner approaches to Stockholm. At times a ferry's upperworks may be visible behind a nearby island, looking like a moving block of flats. It cannot be stressed too often that these ferries have absolute right of way AT ALL TIMES. Some of the 'pinch points' are so narrow that they do not allow room for a ferry to pass even a small yacht, and the vast difference in speeds should be taken into account whenever one of these gaps is approached – not forgetting to look astern as well as ahead!

## Routes within the skärgård

Since the various routes through both inner and outer *skärgårds* are effectively limitless, the following brief descriptions barely scratch the surface of what is possible. The plan on page 211 outlines the routes being described. These are only suggestions, and there are innumerable variations.

Routes 1–3 are the routes which can be taken if coming from the south – Nynäshamn or Utö. These routes diverge at Dalarö. Sandhamn is another entry point for the *skärgård* (the small island group at Huvudskär (58°58'N 18°34'E) is a useful stopping off point if heading to/from Sandhamn).

Route 1 Dalarö to Vaxholm (the inner *skärgård*)

Route 2 Nynäshamn to Tjärven at the northern end of the archipelago

Route 3 From the southwest into the *skärgård* and Sandhamn

Route 4 Sandhamn to Vaxholm

Route 5 Tjärven (at the northern end of the archipelago) to Vaxholm

These routes are all outlined on the plan on page 211. The Swedish chart, Arholma-Landsort *Skärgårdskort*, provides a very useful overview of the *skägård* and makes passage planning among the islands much easier.

## Route 1 Dalarö to Vaxholm (the inner *skärgård*)

This route, the latter parts of which are much used by both international and inter-island ferries, leads northeastwards up the main channel inside the islands of Nämdö (59°12'N 18°42'E), and Runmarö (59°16'N 18°44'E) before swinging west along the north coast of Vindö (59°21'N 18°41'E). It branches to pass either north or south of Kavlön and Västerholmen – via the Grindafjärden to the north or the Sandöfjärden to the south – but the two rejoin at the narrows south of Vårholma (59°25'N 18°29'E).

It then continues west-northwest via the Lindalssundet to the tiny island of Brödstycket (59°25'N 18°24'E), where larger vessels turn southwest to follow the main channel to Stockholm. Smaller craft – though including some sizeable inter-island ferries – continue west towards Hästholmen (59°25'N 18°21'.5E) to take the very narrow passage between Hästholmen, Resarö and the small islands which lie between, to approach Vaxholm from the north. The entire passage measures some 35M, and for much of its distance follows major shipping channels, well buoyed and lit (for details of Vaxholm itself, see page 234).

There is a possible diversion from this route which takes one south of Djüro, passing under a fixed road bridge (20m) and then heads northwards up the very beautiful Älgöfjärd to rejoin the main route. This takes you past the Bullandö marina which purports to be the largest marina in the Baltic (see details on page 225).

## Route 2 Nynäshamn to Tjärven at the northern end of the archipelago

From Nynäshamn northeastwards through the Stockholm *skärgård* to Tjärven where the Åland Sea begins, there is a choice of route. The early stages of both follow Route 1, diverging where that heads west around Vindö island. There is then a choice between inner and outer passages:

A. The inner route continues northeast across the Kanholmsfjärden to pass west of Södermöja (59°24'N 18°51'.5E) and Stora Möja (59°25'.5N 18°53'E), then north via an intricate but well-marked 8M passage between smaller islands to reach the south end of Blidösund (59°35'N 18°51'E), which separates Yxlan and Blidö islands. The north end of Blidösund gives onto the main Stockholm–Åland channel, known as the Söderarm. This route measures some 50M in total and includes some very attractive stretches, especially that between Stora Möja and Blidösund. It is well buoyed, but is not lit between Stora Möja and the northern end of Blidösund.

B. The outer route follows that above as far as the south end of Södermöja, but passes east of both it and Stora Möja. It then continues northeastwards through a more open passage than that of 2A, past Morsken (59°30'.9N 19°05'.4E) and Hundskärsknuv (59°35'.9N 19°07'.5E) light structures, and rejoins the above in the vicinity of 59°43'.5N 19°10'.5E. The total distance is some 52M, and it is well buoyed and lit throughout.

## Route 3 from the southwest into the *skärgård* and Sandhamn

The outer *skärgård* is in many ways more interesting than the inner part, with deciduous trees – birch and oak scrub – which makes a change from the fir trees which are prevalent further inshore. However, the pilotage is more challenging and demands great care. There are few floating marks – instead there are stone cairns, wooden triangles and marks painted on the rocks – but these are not always shown on the charts and their significance is not always apparent.

The best routes eastward to the outer *skärgård* are as follows:

A. Via the sound south of Gillinge (59°06'.5N 18°39'E).

B. South of Mörtöklubb (59°09'N 18°37'E) a high, conspicuous islet south of the larger Mörtö, and then in a general east-northeast direction passing south of Orrön (59°10'.5N 18°42'E) and north of Måsskär (59°11'.7N 18°48'E), after which turn southeast and south.

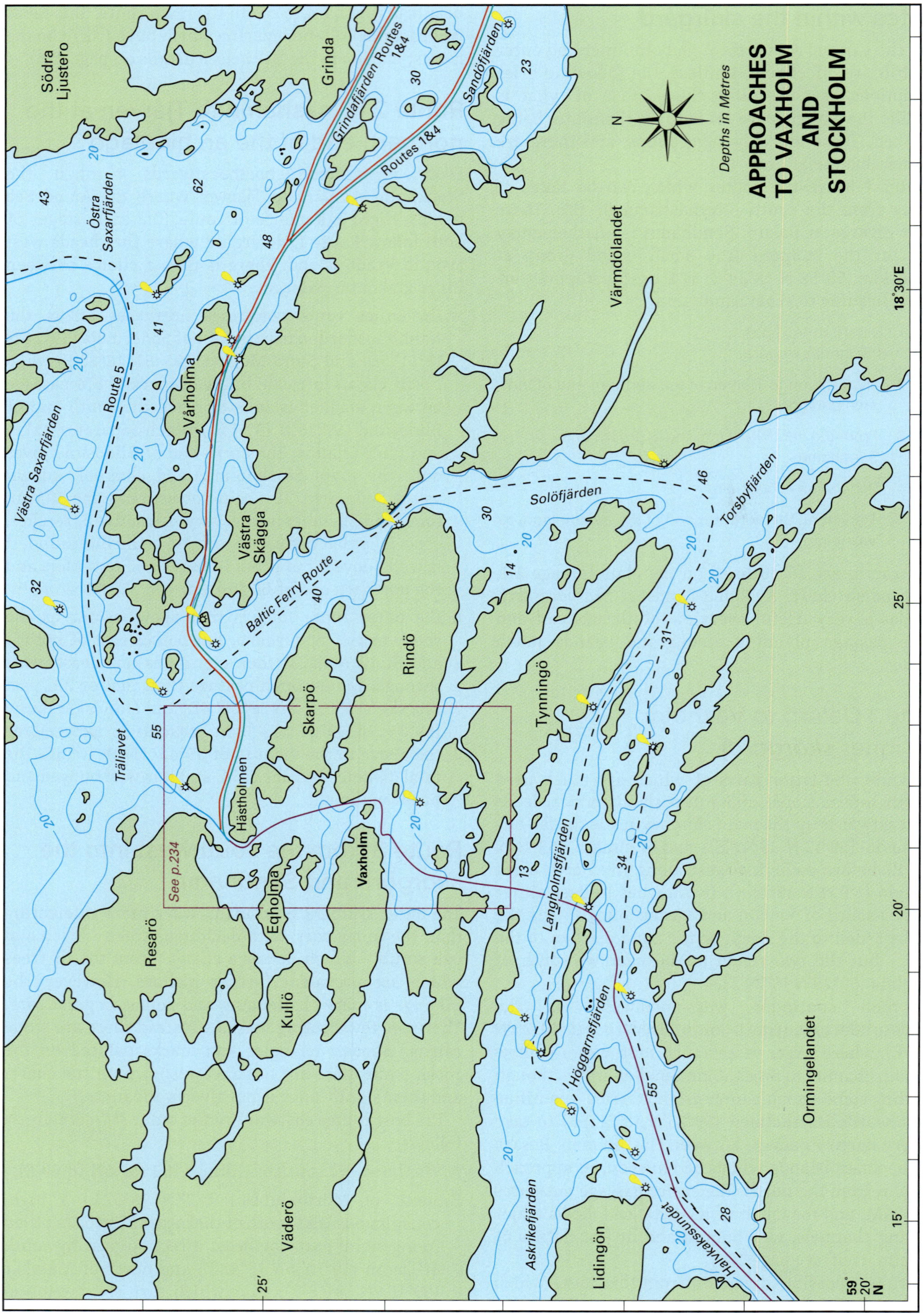
APPROACHES TO VAXHOLM AND STOCKHOLM
Depths in Metres
N
Södra Ljustero
Grinda
Grindafjärden Routes 1&4
Sandöfjärden
Routes 1&4
Östra Saxarfjärden
Västra Saxarfjärden
Route 5
Vårholma
Västra Skägga
Baltic Ferry Route
Solöfjärden
Torsbyfjärden
Värmdölandet
Rindö
Skarpö
Hästholmen
Vaxholm
Eqholma
Trälavet
Tynningö
Langholmsfjärden
Höggarnsfjärden
Resarö
Kullö
Väderö
Askrikefjärden
Lidingön
Halvkakssundet
Ormingelandet
See p.234
18°30′E
25′
20′
15′
59° 20′ N

The sights and sounds you encounter around the Stockholm Archipelago are varied and sometimes eclectic *Alex Beharrell*

C. To reach Sandhamn (see page 225 for details of this major sailing centre) follow the above route as far as Måsskär, continuing northeast to pass close east of Stora and Lilla Melskär (59°12'.5N 18°49'.5E). The route then leads northwest for a short distance, and then northeast again to pass west of the very conspicuous Algkobb (59°14'N 18°53'E). It then continues northeast up the Stora *Skärgården* between Hötterskär and Stora Hästskär, past Osterskär light (59°15'.5N 18°57'E), and finally approaches Sandhamn via the southeast entrance between Sandön and Korsö.

## Route 4 Sandhamn to Vaxholm

Leaving Sandhamn by its narrow northwest entrance, this relatively straightforward route heads northwest between Getholmen (59°15'N 18°52'.5E) and Smörasken (59°15'N 18°52'.2E) and south of Hasselkobben to emerge into the Kanholmsfjärden north of Runmarö, where it joins Route 1 towards Vaxholm. The total distance is approximately 22M.

## Route 5 Tjärven (at the northern end of the archipelago) to Vaxholm

The main approach to Vaxholm from the northeast follows the main channel used by the Åland and Helsinki ferries, which are likely to pose a considerably greater challenge to the average yacht than the navigation. From the Tjärven light structure (59°47'.5N 19°22'.2E) the channels runs southwest and narrows to pass between Furusund and the north end of Yxlan island. It then splits either side of a group of small islands at 59°36'N 18°47'E, leaves the Södra Växlet shoal to the north, and continues southwest parallel to the mainland shore, north of the small islands of Långh (59°32'.2N 18°34'.4E), Huvön and beyond en route to the Trälhavet and Hästholmen (59°25'N 18°21'.5E) where it joins Route 1 for Vaxholm.

The scenery is less varied than that further south, consisting of long straight fjords fringed by long islands covered with fir trees, and there are fewer of the snug anchorages which are such a feature of the other routes. From Tjärven to Vaxholm is just over 40M.

# CRUISING AROUND THE SKÄRGÅRD

## Ägnö, Napoleonviken

59°14'.22N 18°24'.03E

**Distances**
Nynäshamn 29M, Stockholm (via the Baggensstäket) 16M

Napoleonviken is a convenient and sheltered anchorage on the route through from Dalarö, or the outer southern archipelago, to Stockholm via Saltsjöbaden and through the Baggenstaket. The anchorage is on Ägnö and there should be a minimum of 4m in the entrance channel. It is narrow, but if you stay in the middle to avoid outlying rocks, you should be fine. It may even be worth keeping slightly to the western side of the entrance past Brandholmen to avoid the shallows on the east side.

Once past these, the bay slowly opens up into a large bay for anchoring. There is good shelter from most wind directions if tucked into the eastern or western arm.

You can anchor in around 7m of water or there are various places to moor against the rocks, particularly on the eastern shore of the northern arm of the bay. Watch out for the outlying rocks on the northern shore.

An alternative is to head up Kalvfjärden to the west of Ägnö to Tyresö. There are stern buoys onto the jetty at Fiskarholmen (59°13'.09N 18°19'.21E ) and you are moored close to Tyresö Slott (castle). This castle was completed in 1636 and is the site of the first English Garden in Sweden. Today the Nordiska museet (Nordic Museum) owns the palace and it is open for guided tours during the summer. This is a very secure berth and if you are expecting bad weather, it may be a good place to wait it out (www.cafenotholmen.se).

## Nämdö

59°12'N 18°45'E

**Distances**
Vaxholm 23M, Nynäshamn 32M, Sandhamn 9M

**Contacts**
www.explorearchipelago.com/sv/sthlm/mellersta-skargarden/namdo

Nämdö is a convenient stop on the way north from Nynäshamn and Dalarö to the inner and outer *skärgård*. There are several possible anchorages, but one of the best is at the north of the island, an anchorage called Skärvassa.

The approach from the northwest is fairly straightforward though there is a 2.9m shoal in the channel off the southern tip of Käckskär. Once past that you can head into the anchorage either side of Långvikskobben and anchor in around 5m in the bay. Be aware of recently laid underwater cables running through the middle of the bay from southwest to northeast. Bows-to mooring to the rocks is possible on the western side of the bay. There is a sauna on the eastern side. It can be exposed in northeasterlies, but is well protected in other wind directions.

There are various alternative anchorages in the south of the island as well. Norrviken Bay on Uvön offers good shelter or the next bay to the southeast opposite Nämdö (Dalsundet) are both other possibilities. In the event of northerly winds the bay between Alkläppen and Ängsholmen would make a good alternative.

The eastern arm of the anchorage at Napoleonviken, looking towards the east *Andy Beharrell*

## Bullandö

59°17'9N 18°39'1E

**Contacts**

✆+46 8571 45210
www.bullandomarina.se
kundservice@bullandomarina.se

This large marina lies just a short distance off Route 1 detailed above. The approach from the east passes under a fixed road bridge with 20m clearance, but from the north there are no obstructions.

It has 75 visitors berths on lazy lines adjoining the harbour office and restaurant with a few more alongside a pontoon and some stern buoys, but the harbour office can normally find you a space. Berths can be booked in advance through Dockspot (www.dockspot.com/en/docks/650-bullando-gasthamn).

Water, electricity and WiFi are available along with excellent showers, sauna and laundry. For such a large marina it has quite a small but well stocked food shop which also has a limited supply of chandlery (including Campingaz), and a popular restaurant. There is a large boatyard which can handle any kind of repair and has extensive laying up facilities. The bus stop is just outside the gates with a direct bus service to Stockholm.

## SANDHAMN

9°17'N 18°55'E

**Distances**

Nynäshamn 45M, Saltsjöbaden 25M, Vaxholm 20M, Stockholm 30M

**Contacts**

**KSSS marinas** ✆+46 857 15 32 85, Mobile +46 702 13 20 68, VHF Ch 68
ksss@ksss.se
www.ksss.se
**KSSS Lökholmen** ✆+46 857 15 31 03, Mobile +46 702 13 20 68, VHF Ch 20, 68

Sometimes described as the 'Cowes of Sweden', Sandhamn has been the offshore home of the Royal Swedish Yacht Club, the Kungl Svenska Segel Sällskapet (KSSS) for more than a century. Additional berthing space on the adjacent island of Lökholmen was acquired in 1946. The whole area becomes very crowded in high summer, particularly in July at the time of the annual Round Gotland Race, which regularly attracts up to 500 yachts. It can, not surprisingly, be very noisy at night, particularly at weekends.

The island of Sandön is picturesque in the extreme, with clapboard houses, sand roads and several good beaches. There is a permanent population of about 100 which increases vastly in summer, and a hotel/restaurant, the Sandhamns Värdshus, which is said to have been open throughout the year ever since 1672. The old yacht club building adjoining the marina is now a hotel with good facilities.

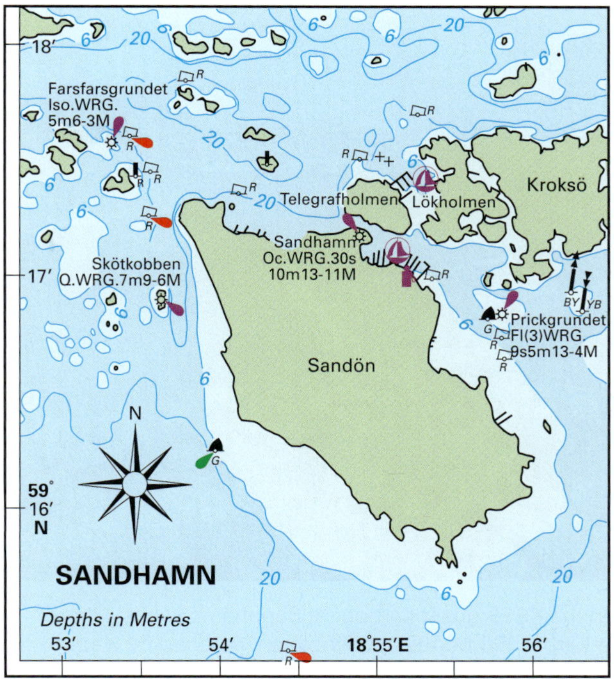

Sandhamn attracts a variety of visitors *Andy Beharrell*

Moored alongside at the KSSS harbour in Sandhamn. In high season, mooring is bows-to with lazy lines *Andy Beharrell*

When the KSSS guest harbour at Sandhamn is busy, there are a further 150 berths at Lökholmen, reached by water taxi *Andy Beharrell*

### Approach & entrance

See Routes 3 and 4 on page 221 and 223.

### Berthing

Although in theory three separate marinas – the Västerhamn, the KSSS and the Österhamn – all are administered by the KSSS and share common shore facilities. Around 200 visitors berths are available on Sandhamn, in 2.5m or more, with a further 150 at Lökholmen, reached by water taxi. Berthing on one of the three marinas' six pontoons is mainly bows-to with a lazyline astern, preferably as directed by one of the KSSS staff.

Water and electricity is available at most berths, with showers and other facilities ashore (the ablutions are distinctly inadequate for a marina of this size), and fuel from a jetty near the southeast end of the marina where holding tanks can also be emptied. Both mechanical and sail repairs can be carried out, but there would almost certainly be a considerable delay in high season. There is a boatyard on the west side of Lökholmen but no chandlery on either island, the nearest (and that small) being close to the ferry berth at Stavsnäs. Berths at Sandhamn can be booked in advance through Dockspot (www.dockspot.com/en/docks/128-sandhamn-gasthamn).

There is also a new guest harbour – Telegrafholmen – on the north side of the island Telegrafholmen. This is also operated by KSSS with approximately 80 berths. A ferry operates to Sandhamn. The approximate position is 59°17'.54N 18°55'.13E (✆+46 571 532 85).

### Facilities

The island has adequate food shopping from two small supermarkets, a post office, numerous cafés, restaurants and small shops. There is an excellent, if expensive, bakery on the waterfront.

Aerial view of the KSSS harbour in Sandhamn. The fuel jetty is visible before the last marina section *Andy Beharrell*

## SALTSJÖBADEN AND THE BAGGENSSTÄKET

59°16'N 18°19'E

### Distances

Nynäshamn 35M, Stockholm (via the Baggensstäket) 10M, Sandhamn 25M

### Lights

**Fjärdhällan** 59°09'.3N 18°33'.3E
White round tower, black base 7m
**Grönö** 59°12'.5N 18°34'E Iso.WRG.4s7m5–3M
Red tower, white top 8m
**Boo** 59°18'.6N 18°17'.8E Fl(2)6s2m6M White hut, green band
**Kingshamn** 59°20'.1N 18°12'.6E Fl.WRG.3s6m6-3M
White lantern

### Contacts

**KSSS Marina** ✆+46 70 678 4186
marinam@ksss.se www.ksss.se
**Pålnäsviken Mobile** ✆+46 72 201 2803
hamnoland@saltsjobadensbatklubb.se
www.saltsjobadensbatklubb.se/gastplatser

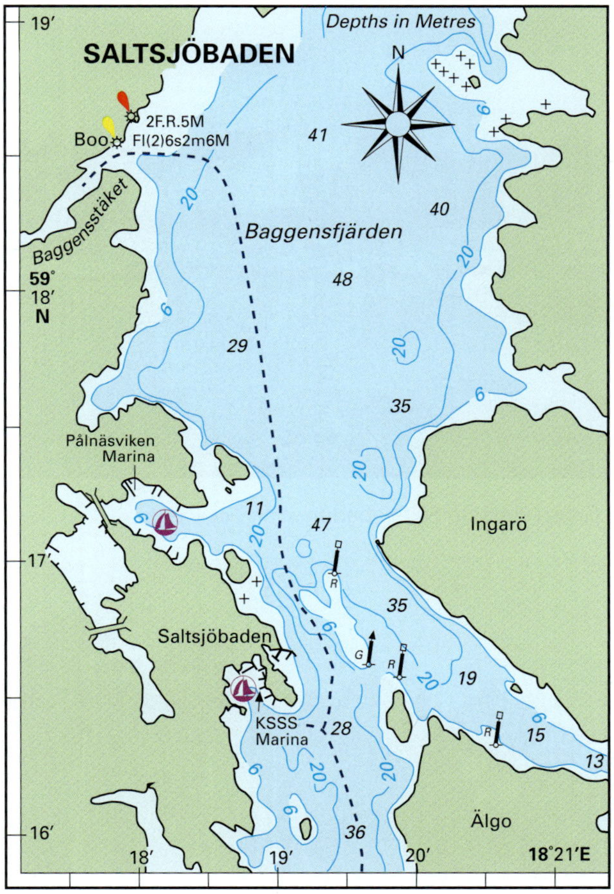


Saltsjöbaden (pronounced Sahlt-sheu-bahd-ehn) has long been a popular spa and summer holiday resort, surrounded by attractive countryside and only half an hour by rail from Stockholm. It is the mainland headquarters of the Kungliga Svenska Segel Sällskapet (Royal Swedish Yacht Club, better known as KSSS), whose extremely helpful staff also administer one of the two marinas. The narrow Baggensstäket (pronounced Bahggehns- stairck-eht) forms the southeastern - and smaller - of Stockholm's two 'back entrances'.

### *Approach & entrance*

The approach up the wide Ingaröfjärden, giving onto the Ägnöfjärden and the Baggensfjärden, is largely unbuoyed, but quite straightforward. Saltsjöbaden lies at the south end of the Baggensfjärden and 2M short of the narrow entrance to the Baggensstäket and the Skurusundet - a long, winding but very attractive gorge which runs for 5M between high wooded banks to Kungshamn, less than 4M from the city centre. Depths in the Baggensstäket are least at its southeastern end, with under 3m in some sections. The channel has no locks and is crossed by a single bridge with 30m clearance.

### *Berthing*

The best harbour in Saltsjöbaden is the KSSS gästhamn. They reserve around 30 berths for visitors (green stern buoys with green signs on the jetty) in depths of 2.5-12m, though it has on occasion fitted in many more visitors. Although the marina has several different sections, visitors should pass south of the small central island when the pontoons will be seen to starboard. Mooring is, as usual, bows-to with a buoy astern. The berths are close to a popular but quite noisy restaurant.

The marina is not obvious when you are coming up from the south, as it is concealed by the small island. However, the Grand Hotel is a very obvious landmark, and you head for that, leaving the island to starboard. You should take care here, as, unusually for Sweden, there are many mooring buoys in the bay with attached yachts. The visitors' moorings are very clearly marked.

The Pålnäsviken marina (Saltsjöbadens båtklubb) also has three places for visiting boats. The visitors moorings are blue and in front of the clubhouse, next to the mast crane. Payment can be made online at saltsjobadensbatklubb.se/produkt-kategori/hamnen/. Once payment is made you will receive codes for the toilets and showers.

### *Services*

Water and electricity are provided on the KSSS pontoons, with a card phone, toilets, showers and launderette near the marina office. There is a small engineering workshop at their clubhouse, and the very helpful staff can assist in organising any other work which needs to be done. They will also advise regarding possible yards in which to lay up ashore. Fuel is available at the Pålnäsviken marina, east of the central island, and there are a number of boatyards in the area.

### *Facilities*

Surprisingly, there are no food shops or stores within walking distance. A 20min walk inland or three stops on the train (ask for directions at the marina office) takes one to the large shopping mall at Tippen, which also has a post office, Systembolaget and much more.

The imposing Grand Hotel overlooks the harbour and has 135 hotel rooms, three bars & restaurants, a café, 9 conference rooms, ballroom, pool and spa. Fast trains run every 20mins to the centre of Stockholm - an attractive and interesting ride in itself which takes about half an hour. The station is only a few minutes' walk from the harbour.

The Grand Hotel at Saltsjöbaden *Andy Beharrell*

The KSSS moorings at Saltsjöbaden *Andy Beharrell*

The western entrance to the Baggenstäket channel *Andy Beharrell*

A narrow section towards the eastern end of the Baggenstäket channel *Andy Beharrell*

## Gustavsberg

59°19'.49N 18°22'.51E (just off gästhamn)

**Distances**

Nynäshamn 36M, Stockholm (via the Baggensstäket) 12M

**Contacts**

www.gustavsberggasthamn.se
info@gustavsberggasthamn.se
✆+46 8 120 57790

Gustavsberg is an alternative stop to Saltsjöbaden on the way to Stockholm through the Baggensstäket. The harbour is fairly new and was redeveloped in 2018. The major constraint is a 22m fixed bridge and 24m powerlines.

The gästhamn has 45 places and three of these can be booked through Dockspot (www.dockspot.com/en/docks/177-gustavsbergs-gasthamn). There are various options for berthing; Y-booms, stern buoys and mooring lines. Depths are between 2.5–10m. The facilities are excellent and all can be organized through the harbour office. There is a sauna for rent, toilets, showers, two washing machines and dryers. There is also boat rental from the harbour; motor boats, cruisers, SUPs and kayaks can all be rented from here.

Services based in the marina mean that this could be a good stop if any work is required. The harbour has a good boatyard and if mechanical work is required, there is a large Mercury dealer, apparently the largest in Sweden. Outdoor winter storage is possible. The yard has a crane lift with a maximum weight of 14T.

The approaches to Wasahamnen are full of sights to draw your attention *Alex Beharrell*

## APPROACHES TO STOCKHOLM

Most yachtsmen working their way north along the east coast of Sweden will want to visit Stockholm, one of the most beautiful cities of Northern Europe and offering a huge amount for all tastes. In particular, the incomparable Wasa Museum must not be missed.

The Wasahamnen marina is well located in the centre of the city. In the height of the season, it may be rather crowded but berths can be booked on-line through Dockspot (www.dockspot.com/en/docks/140-wasahamnen). There is also a fair amount of wash from the small and large ferries which are used by local commuters.

It is certainly worth going into the centre by boat, but there are also a number of harbours some way out which have good rail access to the centre. Two possibilities are Nynäshamn (1hr by train) and Saltsjöbaden (*c*.45mins by train). Tickets can be booked in advance from Swedish Railways (SJ) - www.sj.se/en.

There are a variety of different routes which lead to the city, the one through the offlying archipelago or *skärgård* being further subdivided into two major channels with potentially innumerable variations. The most southerly approach is the 'back entrance' via the Södertälje Kanal (see page 205). The southeasterly approach via the narrow Baggensstäket (see page 227) departs just north of Saltsjöbaden to emerge at Kungshamn less than 4M east of the city centre. The *skärgård* routes from the Baltic twist through a myriad of possible channels to pass close to Vaxholm and enter the city from the northeast.

# STOCKHOLM

59°20'N 18°04'E

### Distances

Vaxholm 10M, Nynäshamn (via the Baggensstäket) 45M, Sandhamn 30M, Mariehamn 70M, Öregrund 85M

### Contacts

**Stockholm Port Authority** ✆+46 867 02600
VHF Ch 9/12/16
info@portsofstockholm.com
www.portsofstockholm.com
**VTS Stockholm** ✆+46 867 02810
VHF Ch 16/73 (yachts have no obligation to report but should maintain a listening watch on VHF Ch 73)
btc@portsofstockholm.com
**Wasahamnen Marina** ✆+46 8 661 9187
info@wasahamnen.se
www.wasahamnen.se

Stockholm, established where access to Lake Mälaren could be controlled, was founded as a town by Birger Jarl in 1250, and was especially concerned with the metalwork industry which had developed inland. It was an important trading centre during Hanseatic times, when half the population was German. The old town and royal palace remain on the central island, the Gamla Stan, which has medieval and renaissance street plans. Modern Stockholm, with a population now approaching two million, has spread across the waterways to the mainland. It is a friendly, relaxing city with tree lined squares and beautiful waterfronts blended with modern architecture, all intersected by busy waterways.

Stockholm has many places of cultural interest, including outstanding museums, palaces and churches. However, for those of a nautical bent, pride of place must go to the 17th-century man-of-war *Wasa*, raised in 1961 after 333 years on the seabed – seemingly almost undamaged – from the spot where she filled and sank within minutes of setting out on her maiden voyage. The ship, together with the display of artefacts which surround her, are without equal anywhere in the world. In the coming years the museum will be spending nearly £12m to build a new support structure for the ship as cracks are starting to emerge at stress points where the ship is supported in the original steel cradle from 1964.

The tourist office website can be found at www.visitstockholm.com. The slightly more formal City of Stockholm website (also with an English version) is at www.stockholm.se.

### *Approaches*

The three main approaches to Stockholm are detailed on pages 219–223.

### *Berthing*

There are several large yacht harbours in the Stockholm area, but only one is convenient for the city and accepts visitors. There is also a public quay, normally used only by large yachts, with facilities geared to the requirements of sizeable vessels – contact the port authority before arrival.

Visiting yachts of normal size use the Wasahamnen marina, sandwiched between the Vasa museum, the aquarium and the nearby Tivoli Gröna Lund. Wasahamnen is on Djurgården island, on the north side of the channel and well within walking distance of the city centre. As might be expected, they become very full during the holiday season and it is best to arrive early or reserve a berth in advance by telephone or through Dockspot (www.dockspot.com/en/docks/140-wasahamnen) preferably on an inner pontoon, as the outer berths can be uncomfortable due to wash or strong winds.

### Wasahamnen Marina

✆+46 8 661 9187 (0800–1600),
info@wasahamnen.se www.wasahamnen.se

Wasahamnen has around 100 visitors berths in 2–6m, arranged on two long pontoons lying parallel to the shore. Most berthing is walk on pontoons one side with a boom on the other. Some of the Dockspot berths are to stern buoys onto the main jetty by the Harbour Office, but there are others on the outside pontoon. The

A wide angle aerial view of Wasahamnen marina in Central Stockholm, looking west
*Wasahamnen Marina*

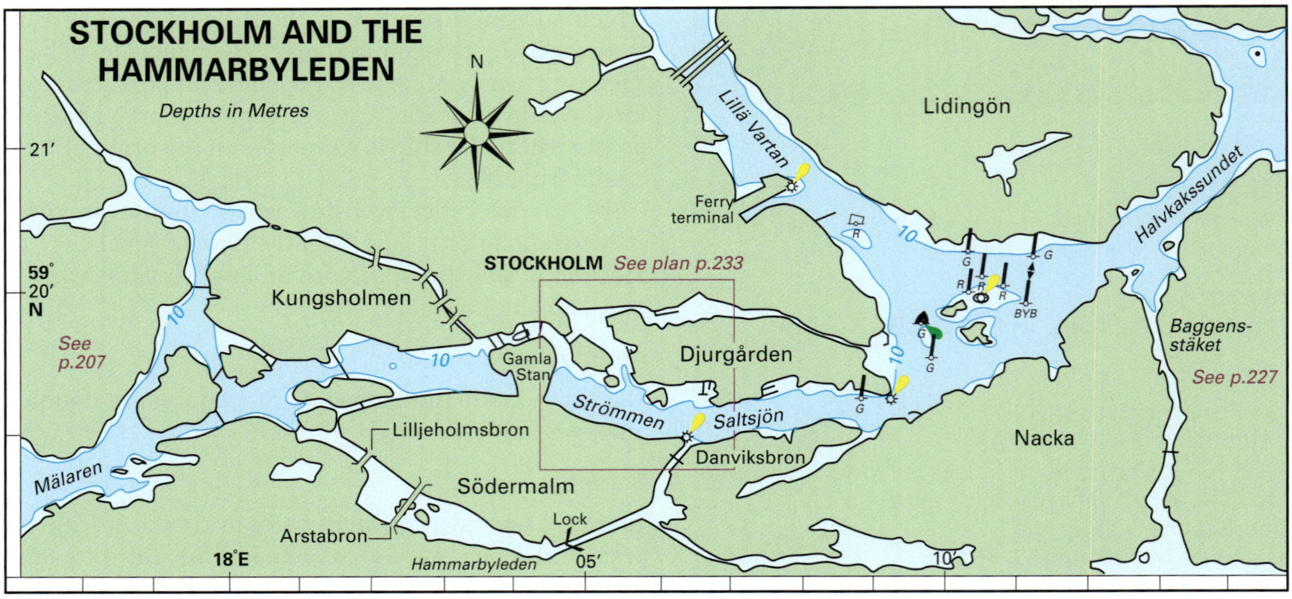


maximum size for boats inside the marina is 13.5m and a maximum length of 20m on the outside Dockspot berths. On arrival, take any vacant space and report as soon as convenient to the harbour office on the inner pontoon.

### *Services*

The Wasahamnen marina has electricity and water throughout, with toilets, showers and laundry facilities (included in the mooring fee - you need to book the time you want to use them on the list in the laundry) ashore. WiFi is available in most berths. There are many cafés and restaurants nearby. About 5mins walk from Wasahamnen is a well-stocked convenience store. Turn right out of the marina and walk past the Abba Museum down Djurgårdsvägen. The shop is further down on the right past the Djurgårdskyrkan. Alternatively, walk across Djurgårdsbron into town and there are various supermarkets.

Wasahamnen marina does not sell fuel - the nearest yacht fuel is at the guest harbour of Fjäderholmarine 2–3M east of Wasahamnen, Vaxholm and at the north end of the Baggensskäket route. Weather forecasts are usually displayed at the marina office, and in addition a forecast is available, in English, on request from Stockholm Radio (MMSI 002652000).

There is a very well-equipped chandlery called Captains at Kommendörsgaten 26, 114 48 Stockholm (about 10mins walk north of Djurgården). This was formerly part of the Watski chain but is now independent (✆+46 8 663 7777 www.captains.se).

More general charts are available from Kartbutiken at Mäster Samuelsgatan 54.

Staff at the Svenska Kryssarklubben (Swedish Cruising Club) headquarters, at Augustendalsvägen 54, S-13127 Nacka Strand, ✆+46 8 448 2880, info@sxk.se, www.sxk.se, are very helpful and the club has a good range of yachting publications and charts on sale.

### *Facilities*

Stockholm has all the shopping opportunities one might expect of a major European capital, including many familiar British names, and top-quality goods of all types can be bought - at a price. There is a particularly helpful tourist office on the Hamngatan.

A view of the waterfront at Stockholm *Andy Beharrell*

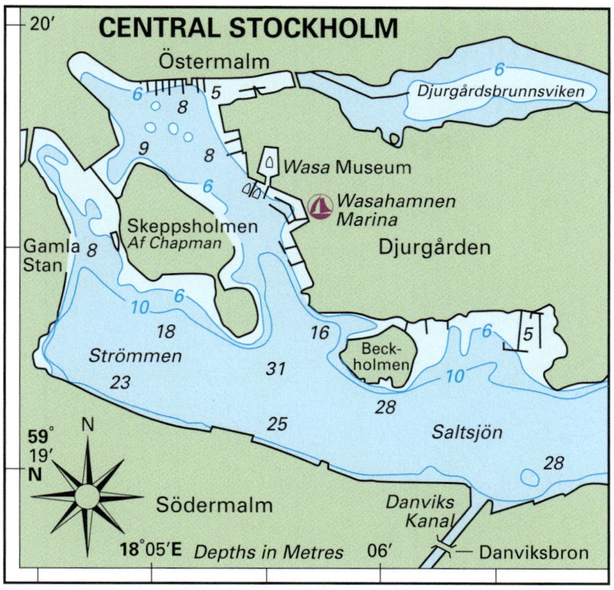

Traditional boats near Wasahamnen *Andy Beharrell*

### *Communications & travel*

Travel within the city centre is made easy – even enjoyable – by the frequent buses and modern underground system or one can get a ferry across to the old town. You can either purchase a travel card or use contactless payment on all public transport. Alternatively, as Stockholm is largely flat and appears to breed singularly considerate drivers, bicycles are a very practical way to get around. All three international airports can easily be reached by bus or train (but note that the main airport Arlanda is some 30M north of the city). Frequent rail, coach and ferry services run between Stockholm and other parts of Europe.

## Vaxholm

59°24'N 18°21'E

**Contacts**

Guest harbour ✆+46 8 541 32200
www.waxholmshamn.se
info@waxholmshamn.se
www.destinationvaxholm.se/en

The *skärgård* approach to Stockholm contains innumerable possible routes, but all come together northeast of Vaxholm. The main shipping channel passes east of Rindö, but most yachts will take the very narrow passage between Hästholmen, Resarö and the small islands which lie between. On approaching Vaxholm from the north, yachts are directed to pass east of the forbidding castle – which occupies an island in the centre of the channel – so leaving the western channel for the inter-island ferries.

There is a guest harbour at the southeast corner of Vaxholm island which has some 100 visitors berths in depths ranging from 0.5–6m. Mooring is by lazyline. The narrow entrance faces east and is well protected, but considerable wash rolls in from all the ferry and motorboats outside. Not surprisingly the harbour becomes very crowded and is very noisy in high summer, particularly at weekends. Berths can be booked in advance through Dockspot (www.dockspot.com/en/docks/141-waxholms-hamn). Boats over 15m in length should ring to book in advance. The marina has all the usual services, and has a washing machine and two dryers. Book your slot at the harbour office. Fuel is available at a jetty by the marina entrance or at a pontoon to the west of the castle which must be approached from the north. See page 232 for details of fuel outlets in or closer to Stockholm.

The inner courtyard at Vaxholm Fortress *Andy Beharrell*

The main gästhamn jetty at Vaxholm *Andy Beharrell*

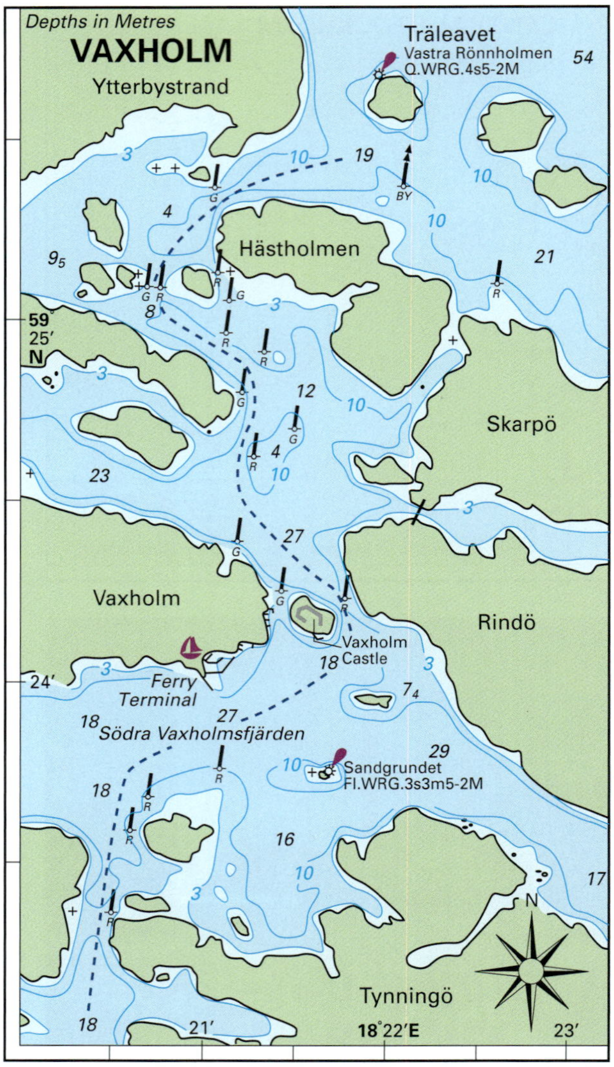


There is good shopping close to the harbour, including one of the few Systembolagets in the *skärgård*, a well-stocked SeaSea chandlers (Hamngatan 10, 185 32 Vaxholm), and a good Coop supermarket. Frequent ferries run into central Stockholm or, for variety, take the bus over the bridges which link the island with mainland Sweden.

The fortress at Vaxholm sits on the island of Vaxholmen between Vaxholm and Rindö and dates back to the 16th century when King Gustav Vasa ordered the island to be fortified to defend the approaches to Stockholm. The current fortress was completed in 1863 having taken 30 years to build. However, the architects hadn't allowed for developments in military technology and when a rotating shell from a rifled barrel was fired at the walls in 1872, it went straight through! That spelled the end of the fortress's defensive role.

A view of Vaxholm from the fortress. To the right is the fuel jetty and to the left (behind the building) is the gästhamn *Andy Beharrell*

An aerial view of Vikingarnas Segelsällskap harbour at Ekholmen *Andy Beharrell*

## Ekholmen

59°26'.85N 18°28'.95E

**Distances**
Vaxholm 6M, Nynäshamn 48M, Furusund 20M

Ekholmen is a delightful small island with a small guest harbour owned and run by the Vikingarnas Segelsällskap (Viking Yacht Club). The club was founded in 1899 and they bought Ekholmen in 1936. It is now run as a secondary base for the club with a lovely clubhouse on the hill and a wood-fired sauna. They use the base for their Midsummer celebrations and are happy to host guests. There are a few stern buoys, but otherwise moor against the jetties with a stern anchor.

If you are visiting around Midsummer there is a tradition of serenading the ferry as it goes past the north of the island in the evening, though serenading may be too grand a phrase as they basically bang anything that makes a noise - pots, pans or anything else!

The jetties at Ekholmen – an island owned by Vikingarnas Segelsällskap *Andy Beharrell*

## Grinda

59°24'.85N 18°33'.16E

**Distances**
Vaxholm 8M, Nynäshamn 45M, Furusund 22M

**Contacts**
www.grinda.se/hamn-mack/gasthamn/
gasthamn@grinda.se
✆+46 70 245 5774

Grinda is a small island to the south of Södra Ljusterö and on the western side of the island is a gästhamn called Värdshusviken. There is space for 140 boats in depths ranging from 2 to 6m. There are stern buoys to the hammerhead of the T-jetty, while on the inner part of the jetty there are lazylines. Alongside berthing may be possible if it is not busy. There can be some swell from passing ferries.

The City of Stockholm bought the island in the 1940s, but it is now owned by the Archipelago Foundation. In high season staff will often greet boats and guide them to berths. It can be a busy, lively (and noisy) spot in peak season and is exposed to westerlies, but is a beautiful island. There are all the facilities you would expect from a medium-sized guest harbour - toilets, showers, pump-out and even a sauna. The restaurant is popular and is also a hotel, so there are a lot of day visitors coming in on the ferry. Berths can be booked in advance through Dockspot (www.dockspot.com/en/docks/110-grinda).

If you would prefer a quieter spot there is a good anchorage to the south of Grinda in between the island and Hästholmen. Hästholmensundet can be approached from east or west but if coming in from the east, watch out for some rocks in the middle of the channel - coming past these rocks to the south is the best approach. You can also moor bows-to the rocks on the northern side of Hästholmen. From the beach it is a short walk to the hotel at Hemviken.

Värdshusviken gästhamn at Grinda *Andy Beharrell*

An aerial view of the anchorage at Gällnö Hemfladen *Andy Beharrell*

Aerial view of the anchorage at Säck Krokholmsviken *Andy Beharrell*

## Gällnö

59°23'.79N 18°36'.99E
Distances
Vaxholm 8M, Nynäshamn 45M, Furusund 22M

**Contacts**
www.gallno.se
info@gallno.se

Gällnö is a popular anchorage a couple of miles to the east of Grinda. There are several possible anchorages but the main one is in the bay on the western side of the island known as Hemfladen. Approach is fairly straightforward and if you head south of the islands of Lammskär and Högh the main bay will open up ahead of you. You can anchor in the southern portion of the bay and this will put you closest to the shop and café. The holding is good in around 4-5m. Alternatively, if this area is too busy, you can head into the northern section of the bay and anchor there in 4-7m. However, be careful of an outlying 0.6m rock to the north of Idskäret.

Another alternative is Norra Gränholmsviken. This bay is very sheltered and is on the northernmost tip of Gällnö. In the middle of the entrance is a rock, so either stay close to the Björkholmen shore or the Gränholmen side. Once in you can anchor either in the western or eastern side of the bay in 4-7m.

## Lådna

59°25'.59N 18°41'.73E (entrance to Lådna)

**Distances**
Vaxholm 13M, Sandhamn 24M, Furusund 12M

The island of Lådna has a good bay on the south side of the island called Hemviken. The bay offers shelter from all wind directions and approach is fairly straightforward - simply stay in the middle of the channel. Depending on wind direction, it is possible to anchor either in the western part of the bay or the eastern part. The eastern bay may offer more possibilities to find shelter and there is good holding in 4-6m of water.

## Säck

59°23'.8N 18°47'.91E

**Distances**

Vaxholm 17M, Nynäshamn 42M, Furusund 20M

Säck is a small bay in between the islands of Säck and Krokholm. It is sheltered in most conditions and can be very popular with Swedish visitors (particularly motorboats) during the high season, but, as with many destinations, they prefer to moor to the rocks, so there is usually plenty of space to anchor. Entry is narrow, but there should be a minimum of 2.4m throughout if you stay central. Once in, there is plenty of space to anchor in 8-9m. Care is needed when anchoring in the northeastern corner of the bay as there is an underwater cable. The signs for these may not precisely match the charted position, so keeping well clear is advised.

## Träskö-Storö

59°26'.51N 18°46'.53E

**Distances**

Vaxholm 16M, Nynäshamn 45M, Stockholm 29M

Träskö-Storö is a beautiful anchorage in the heart of the archipelago. It has two separate anchorages - east and west. The western anchorage can be accessed from the fairway to the north of Träskö-Storö. You can enter either between Inspektoren and Bryggvedsholmen with a depth of around 6m or between Långraden and Bryggvedsholmen with well over 10m. Well-sheltered anchorages are available in the bays at Lindholmen and Flakholmen (with a compost toilet available on the northwest tip of Flakholmen) or between Flakholmen and Träskö-Storö. Both anchorages are between 4-6m depth with good holding.

The larger anchoring area is in the eastern section of the bay. Enter between Bryggvedsholmen and Långraden and then anchor either in the bay between Högholmen and Grytholmen or leave Grytholmen to the north and anchor in the bay formed by Träskö-Storö. There are composting toilets all round the bay.

If you are feeling adventurous it is possible to go alongside the rocks on the western edge of Grytsholskobben but take care of the rocks on the northwest tip of the island. Bows-to the rocks is possible on various parts of the bay.

The harbour can be busy in high season, but there is generally space to swing at anchor. There is also a sauna in the bay between Högholmen and Grytholmen and a nature trail around the island.

## Svartsö (Alsvik)

59°26'.30N 18°39'.35E

**Distances**

Vaxholm 12M, Nynäshamn 45M, Stockholm 22M

**Contacts**

✆+46 8 542 473 25

Svartsö is a small marina and local ferry stop. The approach is uncomplicated from the southwest and east, taking care to avoid visible rocks between marina and Björkh island. The shelter is good from the north, but somewhat exposed to the east and west. Some

Aerial view of the anchorage at Träskö-Storö *Andy Beharrell*

shelter from the south is provided by Björkh island. Berthing is bows-to with stern buoys or stern anchor, Y-booms (but very narrow), otherwise alongside (if not busy). There is about 5m of water at the end of the pontoon but less further in.

There is a well-stocked grocery store. It is a good starting point for pleasant walks around Svartsö and short distances to the restaurant (Svartsö Krog, 10min walk) and Bistro Sågen - a 30min walk. There is a hotel on the north side of the island. Bikes are available for hire at the grocery store.

## Finnhamn (Djupfladden) – Paradiset

59°28'.3N 18°48'.49E (just off southern entrance to Djupfladen)

**Distances**

Vaxholm 17M, Nynäshamn 47M, Stockholm 27M

Any harbour that calls itself 'Paradise' has to be good, however immodest the naming is and Finnhamn Paradiset lives up to its name. Given this reputation it can be very busy though in high season, but either end of the season, it is a beautiful place to stop with good facilities. It can be approached from both the north and south. From the south there should be a minimum of 6m in the approach channel, but if coming in from the east be aware of an unmarked 1.6m rock 0.1M just south of east from the entrance.

The northern entry is quite narrow and a little convoluted but you should have a minimum of 4m through the tightest part entering the bay. From the north approach between the small islands of Malinskobbe and Tärnskäret and then after Malinskobbe turn to a bit east of south to make your way through the northern entrance.

Once you are in the bay there are just a couple of small shoals to take care of off the eastern side of the small island Mor Annaskobbe and just off the beach at the northern end of the bay. Other than those, the bay is quite spacious and has lots of potential mooring options - anchoring in the main bay, bows-to the rocks (particularly on the western edge of Stora Jolpan) or stern buoys to the jetty on the northeastern side of the bay. There are rings in the rocks in some places to moor to, but not universally.

There are compost toilets around the bay and rubbish disposal at the jetty along with electricity, though you will need to get this activated when you pay. You can pay at the Youth Hostel on the other side of the island (where there is also a restaurant) or they will come round each evening for payment to save you a walk. The walking around the island is excellent.

If possible try and anchor with reasonable clearance from the small island of Annaskobbe as this is private and the residents have occasionally let boats know that verbally!

## Lökaön – Österviken

59°24'.27N 18°58'.02E

**Distances**

Vaxholm 24M, Sandhamn 8M, Furusund 18M

Lökaön Österviken is part of the *Möjaskärgården* nature reserve in the outer archipelago. Much of the area is managed by the Archipelago Foundation. This bay is one of the most secure anchorages in the outer archipelago and offers a range of mooring possibilities. There is plenty of space to anchor either in the northern or southern part of the bay in around 4m of water.

A view of the jetty at Finnhamn Djupfladen *Andy Beharrell*

Coming through the northern entrance into Finnhamn Djupfladen *Andy Beharrell*

An aerial view of the Gubben anchorage at Stora Nassa. The channel heading northeast between Bäckskäret and Jungfruskäret into Jungfrusundet is clearly visible *Andy Beharrell*

Alternatively, you can moor to the rocks on the eastern side of the peninsula coming down from the north in 2.5–3.5m of water or there are other possibilities on the northern edge of Betsdelen, though take care of outlying rocks in some places.

While there are not that many facilities apart from compost toilets, Österviken is a secure anchorage in most wind directions. There may be some set into the bay in easterlies, but even then it may be possible to tuck further into the northern or southern bays for protection.

## Storra Nassa

59°26'.72N 19°12'.85E (Gubben anchorage)

**Distances**

Vaxholm 30M, Sandhamn 14M, Furusund 18M

**Contacts**

www.storanassa.com

Storra Nassa (Greater Nassa) *skärgård* is arguably one of the beautiful areas in the outer archipelago. There are many possible anchorages here and careful examination of the chart may find you a sheltered space in various parts of this island group. We have picked one of the anchorages here – Storra Nassa Gubben. This lies fairly central in the island group and is best approached from Nassafjärden. Head between Västerkobben and Stora Bonden, staying fairly central for the deepest water and then turn northeast between Bäckskäret and Jungfruskäret into Jungfrusundet. From there you can turn round the small island of Pojkaskobb into the Gubben anchorage, though beware of off-lying rocks off the western shore of Kalvkobben.

It is possible to approach the anchorage from the north as well, but this area is a protected bird reserve so the approach between Stora Bonden and Jungfruskäret is preferred.

This anchorage is quite tight to swing in so it is also possible to anchor in Jungfrusundet itself in around 6–8m.

It is also possible to moor bows-to the rocks on the northwestern tip of Gubben where the rocks are fairly steep to apart from one central small section, so take care when approaching.

## Lilla Nassa

59°23'.28N 19°11'.18E (waypoint to enter from the south)

**Distances**

Vaxholm 30M, Sandhamn 11M, Furusund 21M

If Stora (Greater) Nassa is too big for you, then you may like to try Lilla (or smaller) Nassa. This group of islands is just over 2M south of Storra Nassa and, while it cannot accommodate as many boats, is just as beautiful – a true outer archipelago experience.

The moorings are best approached from the south, approaching to the east of Rödskäret. If you stay central there should be plenty of water and you can head straight into the bay called Lilla Nassa Fladen. This is a bay on the southern side of Sprickopp and while it is possible to anchor here in around 4-6m there are also lots of possibilities for mooring to the rocks. On the western side of Lilla Nassa Fladen there are even mooring rings to save using your own pitons.

Another alternative (depending on the wind direction) is to navigate round to the western side of Sprickopp and in the bay there are plenty of rock mooring rings.

## Svenska Högarna

59°23'.28N 19°11'.18E (waypoint to enter from the south)

**Distances**
Vaxholm 40M, Sandhamn 21M, Furusund 24M

Svenska Högarna (the "Swedish Hills") is the outer, outer, outer archipelago! It is about as far east in the archipelago as you can get and is best visited in fair weather. There are some fairly open stretches of water to get there, so choosing appropriate weather is important, but, once there, the relatively higher islands should give better shelter than some of the lower level skerries.

There are two SXK (Swedish Cruising Club) moorings there and the other main mooring option is bows-to the rocks on the eastern side of Getryggen (part of Storön). There is also a guest jetty, but this is really just for smaller boats. The whole area is quite shallow, so a draft of 2m or over may make this challenging and it is important to check the water stand level before heading out there.

The approach is from the west via Högfjärden. Once close aim for Manskär and then turn south towards the strait between Storön and Skrubban. Take care of various offlying rocks on the northeastern side of Storön. Once past those, head carefully down between Getryggen and Västermanskobben to assess the various mooring options.

The lighthouse of Svenska Högarna is an iconic Swedish lighthouse. It is 18m tall was built in 1874. In 1966 the lighthouse keepers left and it was automated.

## Rödlöga

59°35'.97N 19°09'.02E (western entrance to Rödlöga)

**Distances**
Vaxholm 30M, Sandhamn 21M, Furusund 9M

There are two possible harbours on Rödlöga, but the best is probably the bay between Rödlöga and Megelskär. At Seglarberget (on Rödlöga directly opposite the southwest corner of Högskar) you can moor directly to the rocks with several rings mounted for mooring lines. Alternatively, much of the south shore of Megelskär can be used for rock mooring. There is room to swing at anchor in around 6-7m of water in the bay between Rödlöga, Högskar and Megelskär.

There is also an SXK buoy in Rödlöga Byfladen to the east, but anchoring there is more difficult and the ferry jetty and around must be kept clear.

Aerial view of Rödlöga Byfladen *Andy Beharrell*

Aerial view of the western anchorage at Rödlöga – the bay between Rödlöga and Megelskär *Andy Beharrell*

Entry to Rödlöga is easiest from the west. From Kudoxafjärden enter from between Rödkobbsgrundet and Lönnskar staying a little north towards Rödkobbsgrundet to avoid a 2.8m shallow patch. Turn south to enter the bay between Lönnskar and Megelskär. From Seglarberget there is a well-marked path across to the island shop (Rödlögaboden) and a small café - Café Truten. Alternatively, a short row in the dinghy will get you there by water.

There is a pump-out jetty on the Megelskär shore.

## Blidö – Stämmarsund

59°38'.17N 18°55'.17E

**Distances**

Vaxholm 24M, Nynäshamn 58M, Mariehamn (West) 42M

**Contacts**

www.blidobryggabistro.se/g-sthamn

The main channel (used by ferries and commercial traffic) goes to the north of Norra Ljusterö and Yxlan. While this is a direct route, it can be busy and so, if heading north or east, it can be nice to use the channel between Yxlan and Blidö. This tends to be quieter and perhaps more scenic than the main channel. A good stopping point along this route is Blidö Stämmarsund. If heading for the Åland Islands, this may also be a good jumping off point with Mariehamn (West) around an 8–10hr sail from Blidö. There are closer setting off points, but Blidö is convenient if coming out from Vaxholm or Stockholm.

The gästhamn at Stämmarsund is straightforward to approach and mooring is with lazy lines or stern buoys. Stern anchors are not allowed as there are various cables on the bottom. Depths throughout should be a minimum of 2m and generally closer to 6m.

At Blidö there is a restored sand barge - a classic Roslag boat called Sandkilen Helmi. This is used for charter trips.

## Kyrkogårdsön (Siaröfortet)

59°33'.2N 18°37'.46E

**Distances**

Vaxholm 13M, Sandhamn 24M, Furusund 12M

**Contacts**

www.blidobryggabistro.se/g-sthamn

If you are heading along the main channel out of Stockholm, Kyrkogårdsön can make a nice stop. It is a small island and given its strategic location on the main channel, it is hardly surprising that they built a fort there. It was built around 1916 but not finished until 1924. The fort is built into the rock of the island and it is called Siaröfortet as it was originally meant to be on the island of Siarö next door. In fact, it is located confusingly on the island of Kyrkogårdsön - so called because there is a cemetery for cholera victims on the

The jetty at the south end of Kyrkogårdsön (Siaröfortet)
*Andy Beharrell*

The anchorage at Ängsö Norrviken *Andy Beharrell*

island. The fort is covered with concrete to a thickness of around 4-6m and was designed for around 250 soldiers to man it. However, it was never really manned properly in peace time as it was considered too damp to be habitable. By the time the Second World War broke out, it was out of date anyway, and, while it as used occasionally for military exercises until the 1960s, it gradually fell into disrepair until taken over by the State Property Agency.

It is though, an interesting museum and on the southern end of the island is a small gästhamn with space for around 15 boats. The approach is straightforward from the main channel and you can head either side of Kyrkogårdsön to approach the jetties. As long as you are moored bows-to the jetty, you should find plenty of water. There are stern buoys on the eastern side, or it is possible to go alongside the western jetty. Siaröfortet can be a little exposed if the wind is in the south. In that case, one of the islands to the north of the main channel, like Ängsö may be a better choice.

## Ängsö

59°37'.7N 18°45'.5E (Norrviken)
59°37'.75N 18°46'.24E (Svartviken)

**Distances**

Vaxholm 13M, Sandhamn 24M, Furusund 12M

Ängsö is a good alternative to Siaröfortet if the wind is in the south. There are several possibilities on Ängsö. To the north are two possible bays to anchor - Norrviken and Svartviken. Both are sheltered in most wind directions apart from north and northeasterlies. In Svartviken you can anchor in around 5-8m, similarly in Norrviken.

Ängsö is a National Park and, if you are visiting in May, it is worth walking to see the Adam and Eve orchids in bloom.

## Furusund

59°39'.4N 18°55'E

**Distances**

Vaxholm 24M, Nynäshamn 60M, Mariehamn (West) 41M

**Contacts**

www.furusundshamnkrog.se
info@furusndshamnkrog.se
✆+46 8 263835

For centuries Furusund has been known as a good natural harbour for seafarers on their way to the Åland Islands and it is now on the main ferry route from Stockholm through to Mariehamn and ports in Finland. The harbour probably dates from the 17th century, but seafarers have clearly been using it for a lot longer as on the rocks above the guest harbour is a rock carving which is thought to date from 1463 and is a compass rose (Kompassrosen). It is the oldest such carving in the Nordic region, though due to land uplift, it is now well above sea level.

Furusund has also been the site of a pilot station, a quarantine hospital and an optical telegraph. The optical telegraph is at the top of Telegrafberget Hill and was built in 1837. It was able to send a message to Stockholm in 7mins using ten rotating panels which enabled 1,024 different combinations. Relay stations would pass the message on.

The approach to the guest harbour is straightforward and mooring is by stern buoy. There is space for approximately 150 boats in depths ranging from 2-3m. It has a fuel dock and all the facilities you would expect - toilets, showers, pump-out and a sauna. There is also an excellent restaurant.

## Granhamn

59°44'.01N 19°07'.68E

**Distances**

Vaxholm 32M, Mariehamn (West) 34M, Furusund 8M

Granhamn is a small island just to the south of Tjockö and just off the main channel coming out from Stockholm. It is a bit under 2M to the east of the ferry port of Kapellskär and sheltered in most winds apart from easterlies. There is space to moor to the rocks on the north shore of Granhamn or space for a few boats to anchor in between Granhamn and Granhamnsören. Approach is from the east and is straightforward. Once in the bay, you should be able to anchor in around 4m of water.

Granhamn was apparently a popular harbour for ancient sailing ships - indeed the rocks are covered in carvings made by sailors, presumably while they were waiting for a fair wind. One carving dates from 1811 when the island was defended against Napoleon's privateers. The harbour used to be so well frequented that there was an inn here until the end of the 19th century - the foundations are still visible behind the toilets!

The anchorage makes a convenient departure point if you are heading from Stockholm to the Åland Islands and on to Finland with Mariehamn West a reasonable day sail away.

## Fejan

59°44'.63N 19°10'.07E

**Distances**

Vaxholm 34M, Mariehamn (West) 32M, Furusund 10M

**Contacts**

www.fejan.com

Fejan is a good alternative to Granhamn if you are heading to or from the Åland Islands. The small gästhamn is well sheltered from the usual southerly and southwesterly winds, but is very exposed to the north and east. Mooring is by lazy line, but take care of the depths on the inshore jetty as there are some shallow patches.

The island has a long history as a quarantine station. During the cholera outbreak of the 1890s ships had to wait for a period of quarantine at Fejan. At times there could have been up to 200 ships waiting and the worst-affected were taken ashore to a hospital. The hospital and quarantine facility are now a hostel and conference facility run by the Archipelago Foundation.

The anchorage at Granhamn – a good setting off point for crossing to the Åland Islands *Andy Beharrell*

## Arholma Österhamn

59°50'.61N 19°07'.41E

**Distances**
Vaxholm 39M, Mariehamn (West) 30M, Furusund 15M

**Contacts**
www.arholma.nu

Arholma is an excellent stop on the way north, south or east. Heading north, Arholma to Öregrund is 38M and this is a good next stop for the Gulf of Bothnia. Alternatively, Arholma to Stockholm can also be done in a day. East to Mariehamn on the Åland Islands is a similar distance.

Österhamn is the main anchorage and you can either moor bows-to on a jetty on the southwest corner of the bay or there is plenty of swinging space for a large number of boats. It can be busy in the high season, but it could rarely be considered full.

If coming in from the east (Mariehamn for example), you can head north of the island of Ovanskär (though be careful of the rocks - Dämban - lying off the northern tip) and then turn to the south along the eastern shore of Arholma. You can then follow the island round into Österhamn. Coming from the south, you will need to keep to the east of Isskär, Käringön and Hummelön to stay in the deep water, but the channel is straightforward and wide. As you come in from the west be careful of a 2.6m shoal to the northwest of Bärören, but otherwise there are not too many obstacles.

Österhamn also has a very convenient pump-out barge moored close to the jetty and so can be an ideal place to empty holding tanks.

Arholma itself is a very attractive island and popular summer residence. If you head ashore, it is a lovely walk to the church and windmill. If you then carry on to the western shore and follows signs to the lighthouse, you can make your way up to the highest point of the island where the lighthouse is built. This was built in 1768 and is partly built from stones retrieved from the ruins of Lidö Castle, which was destroyed in the Russian Pillage of 1719-21. The lighthouse is now a listed building and in the summer is used as an art gallery.

From the lighthouse you can head a little further north to the main jetty and restaurant - a vibrant spot in high season. If you keep walking to the northern tip of the island you can visit the Arholma Battery (or Fort) which was decommissioned in the 1990s and is now a museum.

An alternative anchorage on Arholma is just to the north of the main ferry jetty on the western side of the island. The bay here is called Ahlmansviken, named after the pilot Mathias Ahlman. A jetty here has space for around 20 boats to stern anchors, but it is completely exposed to westerly winds.

Aerial view of the excellent anchorage at Arholma Österhamn *Andy Beharrell*

Arholma lighthouse – built in 1768 *Andy Beharrell*

# THE GULF OF BOTHNIA

Note that many more lights, buoys and beacons exist than are shown on the plans which accompany this section.

During the winter, storms and ice can cause considerable damage to buoys which are sometimes not replaced in the early part of the season. Buoys can also be moved out of place by the ice.

Guides to this part of the world are few. By far the best is Norrlandskust by Erik Nyström (Bilda Förlag). This is in Swedish without an English translation, but the many small charts and aerial photographs are invaluable. Google translate through the phone camera can help with this, but even a small smattering of Swedish would go a long way to understanding much of the text. Unfortunately, the book is not available in the UK, but it is easily found in Sweden.

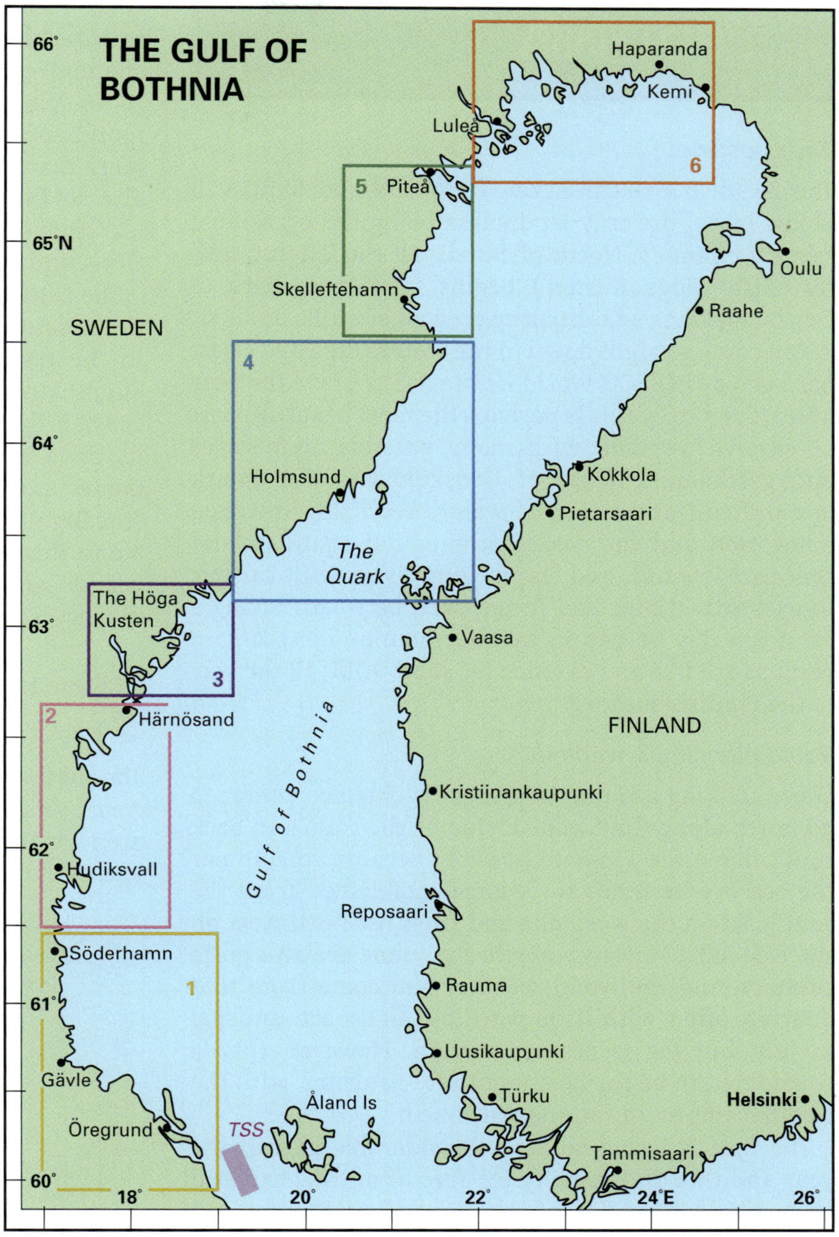


## General

The Gulf stretches northeast for some 350M with the Swedish/Finnish border neatly bisecting its closed end. Commercial shipping carries mainly paper, timber and iron ore. There is little commercial fishing activity. There is considerable local yachting all along the coast, particularly in the vicinity of the main towns of Hudiksvall, Sundsvall, Harnösand, Umeå, Skellefteå and Luleå, but though the area is popular with German and Finnish yachtsmen it has been less frequently visited by cruisers of other nationalities. However, for those who wish to get away from the beaten track, the Gulf of Bothnia provides excellent sailing, often in *skärgårds*, and even in July when the southern cruising grounds are crowded, one can still enjoy a solitary night at anchor in the most idyllic surroundings.

For many it is natural to want to reach the top of the Gulf. However, it is impossible for most cruising yachts to visit Haparanda on the Swedish side of the Tornio river because of the rock strewn approaches and fixed bridges, but the sheltered harbour at Haparandahamn is 18km southeast and is connected by bus. The northernmost point by water is at Töre, a little further west, which can be reached with care and detailed charts.

Many of the smaller harbours will not have a harbourmaster or anyone else to come to collect your mooring fee, but instead have an 'honesty box' into which you drop an envelope with your payment in cash.

1. Svartklubben to Söderhamn
2. Hudiksvall to Härnösand
3. The Höga Kusten
4. Husum to Bjuröklubb
5. Skelleftehamn to Luleå
6. Luleå to Haparanda

# 2H. THE SWEDISH COAST OF THE GULF OF BOTHNIA

*The coastline*

The Swedish coast between Öregrund and Sundsvall is low lying, the only landmarks being the occasional factory chimney. North of Sundsvall the 'High Coast' (Swedish 'Höga Kusten') begins, and from here to Örnsköldsvik is a fascinating area where hills of about 250m come straight down to the water. The High Coast has been a UNESCO World Heritage Site since the year 2000. Scenically this is perhaps the most beautiful part of eastern Sweden, with many possible anchorages and gästhamns. North of Örnsköldsvik, The Quark is a difficult area of shoal waters requiring intricate navigation and the coast becomes flat again. Inland there are low hills and fast flowing rivers with various tourist attractions, and it may well be worth hiring a car for a day or two if weather-bound. The *skärgård* restarts at Piteå and extends for some 90M, all the way to the Finnish border.

*Route planning & weather*

When making a round trip, most yachtsmen prefer to go north along the Swedish side of the Gulf and back south down the Finnish, possibly because in summer the sea breeze tends to become established from the southeast on the west side and from the northwest on the east side. However northerly winds are also quite common and the worst weather can come from that quarter, often with little warning. Gales are unusual in July, but fog is not uncommon. However, this is considered to be the best month for cruising, with the weather improving as one sails north.

The Gulf is icebound for a considerable part of the year and though normally ice-free after May can still be very cold in June. It is fed by rivers from Sweden and Lapland, giving the Gulf as a whole very low salinity. There is no tide, but there are some local currents and the water level is subject both to wind direction and to changes in atmospheric pressure, so it is important to check the water stand level before entering any relatively shallow harbours. Many harbours are very shallow and all are becoming more so due to continuing land rise since the Ice Age.

## Stockholm archipelago to Öregrund

The Väddö Canal, which provides a convenient shortcut if coming from the Stockholm *skärgård*, has has a fixed bridge with 17m clearance at approximately 60°03'N. There are also two opening bridges. Bagghusbron, at the southern end of the canal, and Älmstabron at the northern end (see www.sjofartsverket.se/en/services/bridges-and-canals/).

If leaving from the Stockholm archipelago, a good jumping off point is Gräddö, near Norrtäljie, or from one of the small harbours around Arholma (see Arholma Österhamn on page 244). From there, the route runs parallel to the coast and clear of the TSS to enter the channel which runs up to Öregrund. The channel can be entered at Svartklubben (60°10'.6N 18°48'.7E), but a more straightforward passage can be found approximately 2M north of this. It is not much more than 40M from Gräddö to Öregrund. Indeed, it is also not far to Mariehamn in the Åland islands (slightly less than 40M from Gräddö), and from Mariehamn to Öregrund is also an easy day's passage.

The coastline between Furuvik (just south of Gävle) in the south and Ragvaldsnäs (just south of Sundsvall) in the north is known as the Jungfrukusten (www.jungfrukusten.nu) or the 'Virgin Coast'. Gävle, on this coast, is the oldest city in Northern Sweden. It received its town charter in 1496. The Virgin Coast is partly named after the island Storjungfrun (this translates as "the Big Virgin"), but also partly after the virgin nature along this section of coast. This area has over 4,500 islands and some lovely sandy beaches and fishing villages, so can be worth taking some time to explore.

### 1. Svartklubben to Söderhamn

Distance 90M

The southwest gateway to the gulf and Gävleborg coast. Apart from the infrequent mill chimney, landmarks are rare and you will come across progressively fewer yachts outside the main centres.

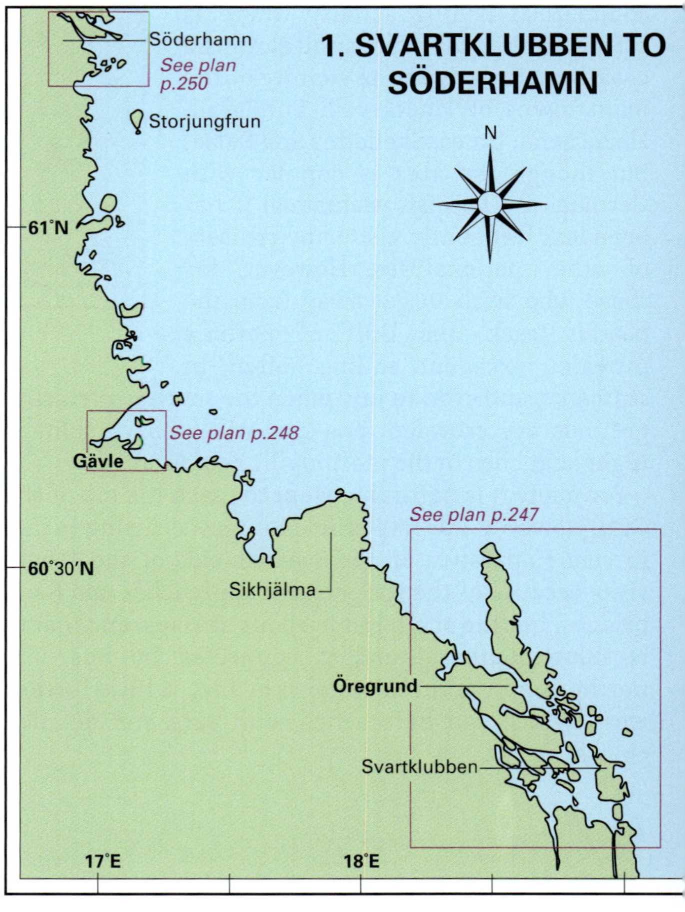

Aerial view of the gästhamn at Öregrund *Andy Beharrell*

## Öregrund

60°20'.5N 18°26'.8E
www.oregrundshamnen.se

The southeast approach to Öregrund (pronounced Uhr-e-gruhnd) is via the well-buoyed, sheltered and straightforward *skärgård* route. From the northwest it is relatively easy through the Öregrunds Grepen.

A busy harbour, particularly in season, with 80 guest berths ranging from 3–7m depth. There is a long jetty at the harbour entrance, and the more sheltered berths are on the inner side. Mooring is by lazy line. There are some stern buoys on the outer side. The not unusual north winds can make the harbour uncomfortable when it is best to cross 1M to anchor, in clay, in the sheltered Kullbådaviken from where there is a nearby ferry back to town.

All the usual facilities are available from the gästhamn (laundry, rubbish disposal, water, WiFi, electricity, toilets, pump-out). Öregrunds Båtvarv ✆+46 173 30423 is less than 1M to the south offering general boatyard engineering and lay up. Market on the quay, good shopping which includes a supermarket, Systembolaget and bookshop for Swedish charts. Wide selection of restaurants, interesting church and maritime museum.

There are bus connections to Stockholm.

There are few guest harbours between Öregrund and Gävle, although there are several nature harbours and anchorages. One possibility is Sikhjälma (60°34'.5N 17°49'E), which is a small holiday village 30M from Öregrund. There are very limited facilities and only four guest berths bows-to wooden staging with a stern anchor in 2.5m.

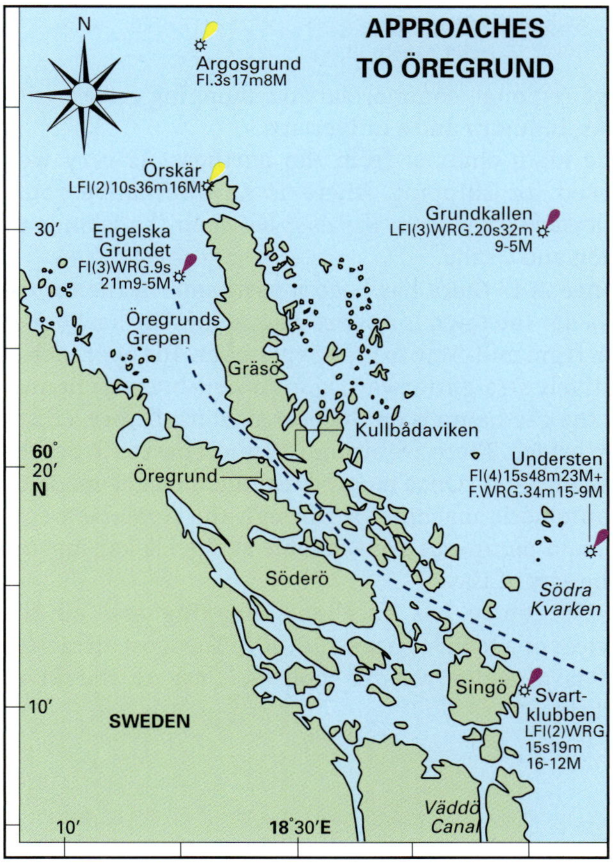

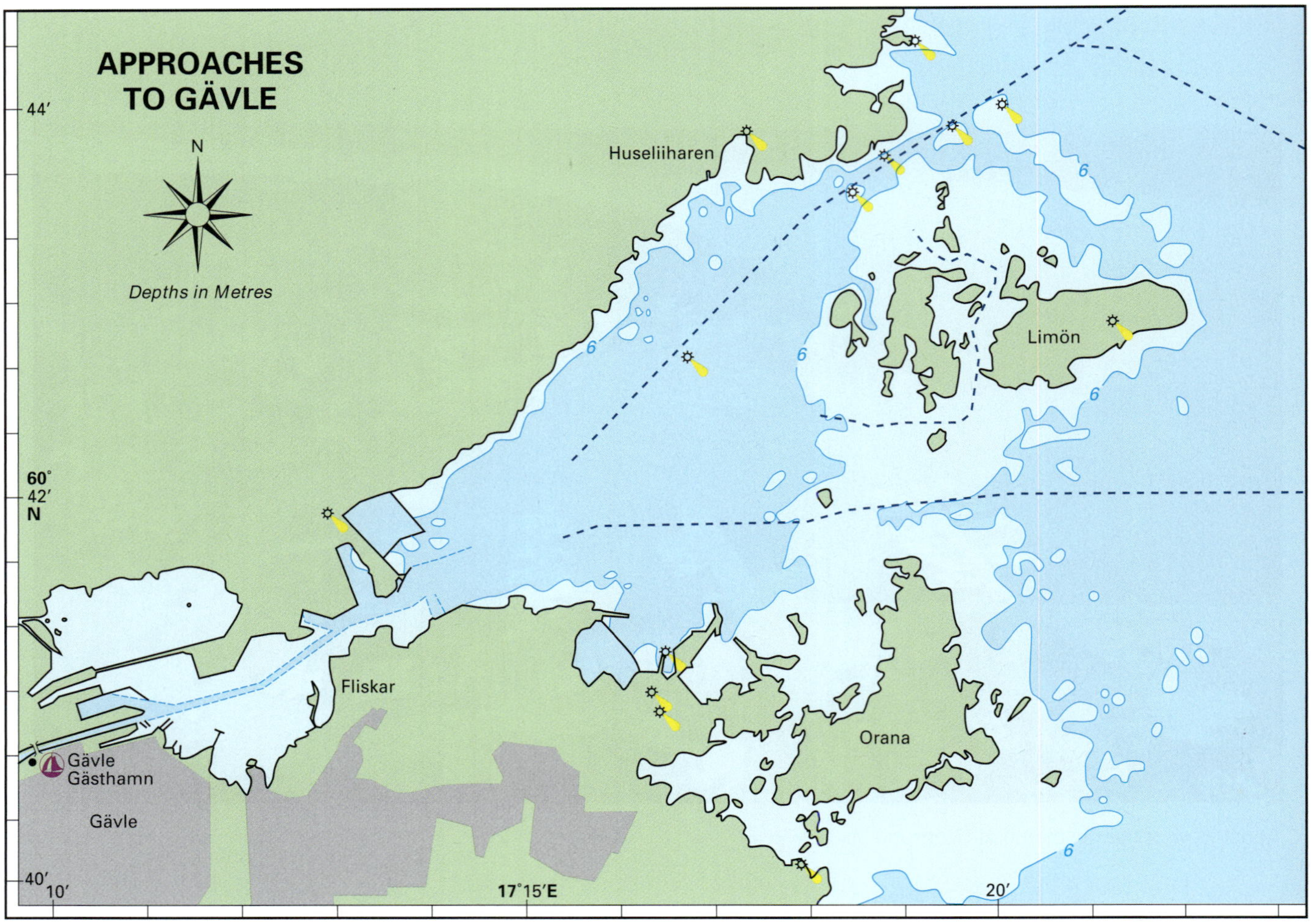


## Gävle

(pronounced Yairv-leh)
60°40'.70N 17°09'.88E
www.visitgavle.se
www.gavle.se/gavle-gasthamn

Large regional, commercial and shopping centre with docks, industry and a university.

The main channel from the northeast is very well marked for shipping. There is an alternative route for leisure craft from the east between the islands of Limön and Orana.

Since 2017 there has been a gästhamn in the centre of Gävle. The town is a short walk away. The harbour is open from mid-May to mid-September. The approach is relatively straightforward along a well-buoyed channel and the gästhamn is on the port side just before a fixed 2.4m bridge. There are around 30 guest berths in depths between 3–5m. Once moored, payment can be made by an automatic machine or through the GoMarina app. Fuel and pump-out are available at the Fliskar marina to the east of Gävle.

Gävle centre has excellent shopping and all the services of a town of nearly 70,000. The most attractive part is of older wooden houses, close to the River Gavleän.

The berths at Gävle gästhamn *Andy Beharrell*

## Norrsundet

60°57'.8N 17°15'.0E
www.nmk-boat.se

This lies a few miles north of Gävle, and the harbour is a few miles down an inlet. Once past the now disused commercial quay, the channel narrows, and although the approach is straightforward, care needs to be taken. There are six stern buoys to a wooden staging, a small clubhouse with the usual facilities and a supermarket 200m away. A bus service to Gävle is available.

The harbour should be sheltered even in the worst weathers.

Heading north, there is an extensive archipelago containing several anchorages and natural harbours behind the island of Kusör.

The guest moorings at Norrsundet *Andy Beharrell*

## Axmar

61°02'.9N 17°09'.6E
www.axmarbrygga.se/gasthamn

The approach to Axmar is at least 3m at the shallowest, but although the channel is well buoyed, it is somewhat complicated, and needs to be taken with caution.

There is a restaurant with a long section of staging, stern buoys provided. Keep to the section of staging where there are buoys – on the southern end of the staging there is a submerged rock! There are no warning signs.

The restaurant is busy in the season with around 50,000 visitors each year, and there are the usual facilities of ablutions, electricity and water, but apart from that, this is a very remote and beautiful spot.

Aerial view of the guest moorings at Norrsundet *Andy Beharrell*

## Storjungfrun

61°10'.1N 17°20'.3E
www.visitsoderhamn.se/sv/storjungfrun-gasthamn
info@visitsoderhamn.se
skargardsenheten@soderhamnn.se

Take care to avoid the well-marked Storgrundet shoal 2M to the east of the prominent black and white lighthouse just above the small gästhamn. Once you have arrived, you can pay through Dockspot (www.dockspot.com/en/docks/426-storjungfrun-gasthamn). The gästhamn has a composting toilet, sauna and bbq areas. There is also a 12V solar-powered charging station for mobiles in the sauna building.

Mooring is by stern buoy to the inside of the breakwater wall in 2.4m, but it can be crowded at weekends and in season. The harbour can be uncomfortable in a southeasterly but is nonetheless much more attractive than the mainland gästhamns at Vallvik or Ljusne. Excellent walks to the west side.

Here there are the first clear signs of rising land. The seaward side of the island is strewn with lichen covered, rounded rocks or large stones. Wood plank pathways have been laid to picturesque wooden houses and the delightful old chapel.

Aerial view of the guest moorings in front of Axmar Brygga
*Andy Beharrell*

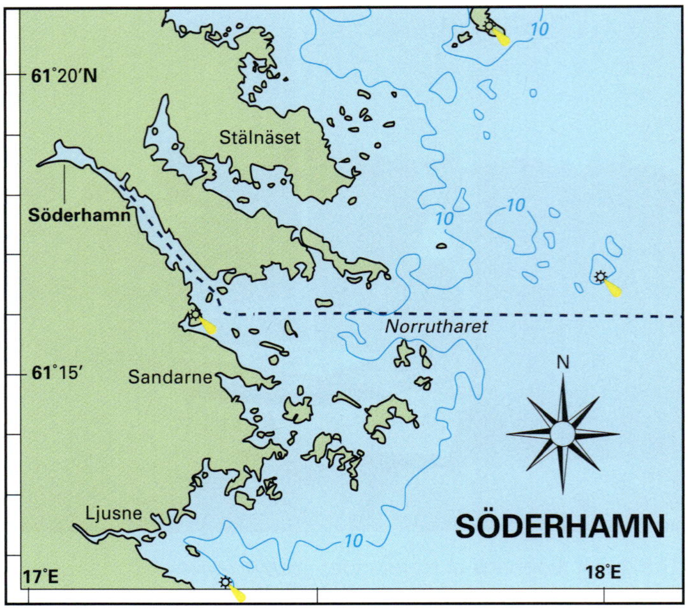


## Agön

61°34′.2N 17°18′.2E

This small island is almost bisected by a deep inlet which runs from the south northwards. The islands of Agön and Kråkön have the remains of large number of fishing villages, but as the coast has risen over time (due to glacial uplift), many of the associated harbours have become too shallow and the fishermen moved elsewhere. If you take the dinghy across to Drakön, it is possible to see the remains of a medieval harbour. There is also a nice walk from the jetty at Agön across to the old harbour of Agö. It is possible either to anchor or to tie up against a small jetty using a stern anchor. It is a picturesque and well sheltered spot. There is a compost toilet and bbq spot at the end of the guest jetty.

There is a good chance of seeing a range of birds including velvet scoter, eider duck, arctic tern and if you are lucky, white-tailed eagles. On Tihallan opposite the entrance to the bay, you may well also see grey seals.

## Söderhamn

61°17′.6N 17°04′.7E

www.visitsoderhamn.se/en/soderhamn-guest-harbour

A gästhamn in the centre of town with eight bows-to berths from stern buoys in 2m. Well serviced with all the facilities of a municipal centre nearby. The gästhamn has restaurants and other facilities close by and the centre of town is around 20mins walk away. The main railway and E4 highway pass through town. The gästhamn is at the *Skärgårdsterminalen* – this is where the M/S Moa (a traditional ferry/ice-breaker built in 1904) sets off for trips around the Söderhamn archipelago. She is operated by a non-profit association. There is a pump-out on the pierhead and electricity available at the berths. There are bars and restaurants close by.

The guest jetty at Agön *Andy Beharrell*

The guest berths at Söderhamn with stern buoys to the jetty *Andy Beharrell*

Söderhamn town centre *Andy Beharrell*

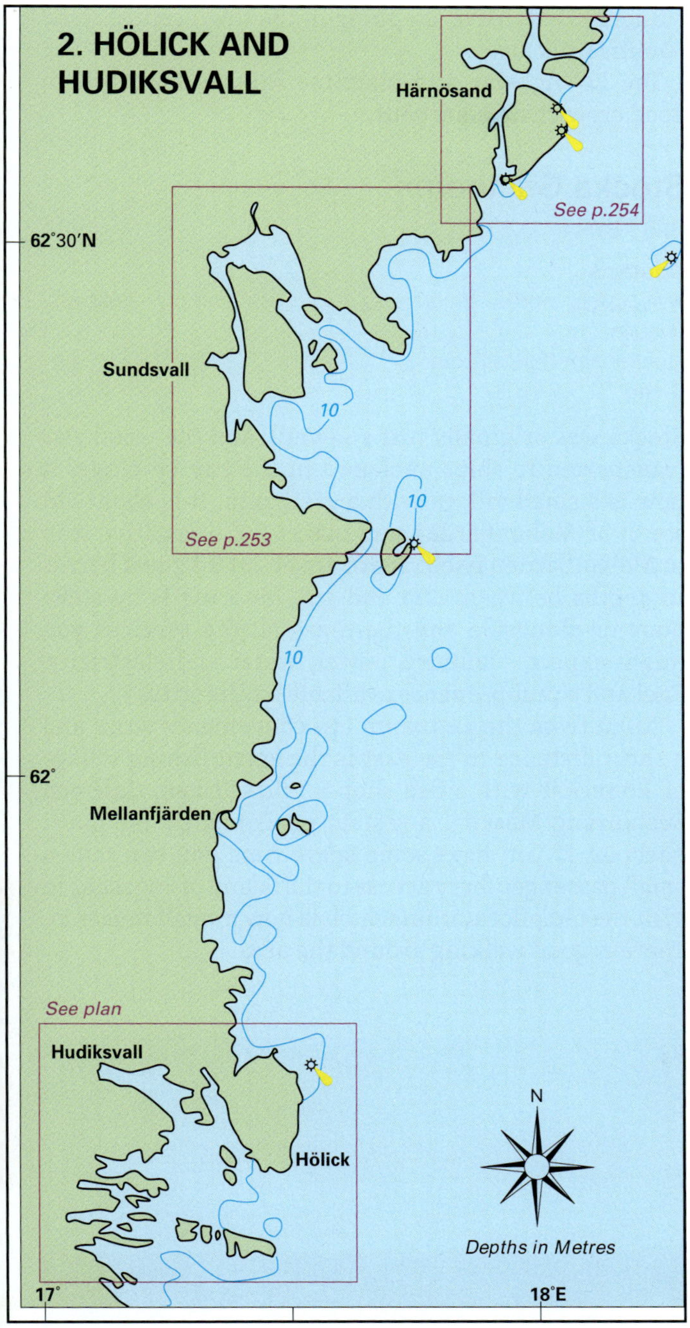


## 2. Hudiksvall to Härnösand

**Distance** 85M

This section covers the coast north from the Hornslandet peninsula to the start of the 'Höga Kusten' (High Coast).

There are a series of small fishing villages along the north Hälsingland and Medelpad coasts. The wide Sundsvallbukten leads into Sweden's largest river delta. There are useful anchorages in addition to the 20 gästhamns covering this area, mainly around Hudiksvall and Sundsvall. As you sail north the land starts to rise where the High Coast begins between Sundsvall and Härnösand.

## Hölick

61°37'.5N 17°26'.1E

**Contacts**

www.holickshamn.se

This comprises a small harbour and holiday camp.

Having passed either side of the Olofsgrund shoal 1M north of Ago, Hölick is in an old fishing harbour on the southwest corner of Hornslandet 3M further north. Be sure to enter between the approach buoys outside the harbour breakwaters to the west of the lighthouse. Mooring is in Y-booms in the berths marked 2-11, and larger yachts might not fit in.

The harbour is generally sheltered but can be exposed in westerlies. There are few services apart from a café/restaurant across the harbour, as most facilities are 500m away at the camp site though there are composting toilets and rubbish disposal behind the car park opposite the harbour. There is a very attractive small chapel high on the rocks above the village and excellent marked walking trails around the nature reserve.

Road access only to Hudiksvall 30km away.

Aerial view of Hölick gästhamn. The guest berths are on the right hand pontoon at the outer end *Andy Beharrell*

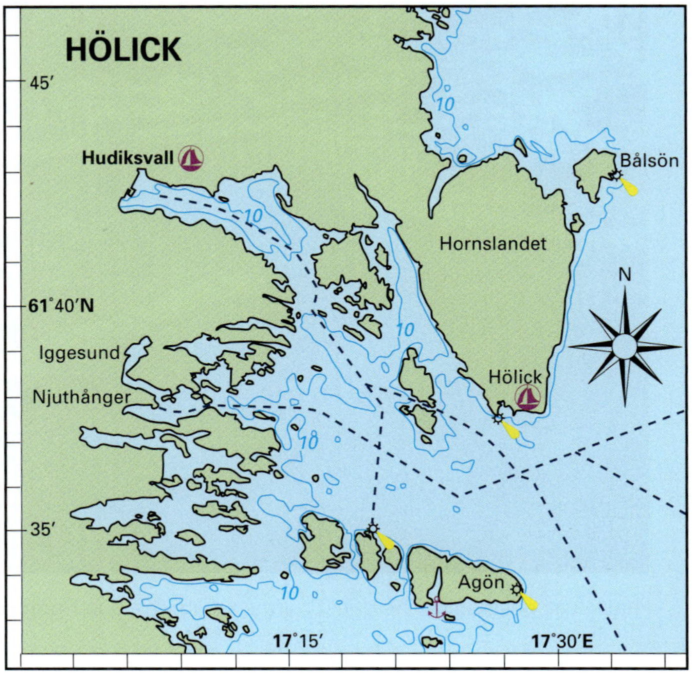

## Hudiksvall

61°43'.5N 17°07'.1E

**Contacts**
www.visitgladahudik.se
www.hsss.se
info@hsss.se
✆+46 650 94165

Large municipal centre with docks and deep-water berths. The main harbour lies 15M from the sea along well marked channels from the open sea but with some shipping. As you enter there is a large marina to starboard. The 12 guest berths are on the southernmost pontoon with Y-booms or stern buoys in 3.5-7m. It is possible to go alongside but this would be exposed in winds from the south or east as there is some fetch in the inlet from the east.

### Strandpiren Gästhamn Hudiksvall

**Contacts**
www.strandpiren.se/gasthamn-marina
info@strandpiren.se
✆+46 650 10444

An alternative mooring place would be at Strandpiren Gästhamn Hudiksvall, just before the town marina to starboard on arrival. There are 30 guest berths in 5m of water on Y-booms, stern buoys and alongside. There are showers, electricity, water and WiFi as might be expected. The facilities are in the hotel which also has a restaurant. You can also hire SUPs and jet-skis (!).

There is extensive shopping in the town centre some 10mins walk away.

The E4 highway and mainline railway make this a good crew change harbour.

## Stocka Gästhamn

61°53'.57N 17°21'.57E

**Contacts**
www.upplevnordanstig.se/sv/stocka-gasthamn-och-stallplats-husbilar
stockahamn@gmail.com
✆+46 70 581 7826

Stocka was originally just a sawmill and the wood was transported to ships anchored in the bay by barge. It now is a small village with a gästhamn. It is about 5M south of Mellanfjärden and makes an alternative stop to Mellanfjärden itself. There are about 20 guest berths in depths between 1.7m and 4m. Mooring is by stern buoy or alongside and there are all the services you might expect – laundry, power, water and electricity. Fuel and a pump-out are available on the jetty.

700m from the gästhamn is a convenience store and a short distance to the east is the small fishing village of Rönnskär with a fish shop – Vilda Fisken. Café och Restaurang Måsen – a restaurant is just by the guest harbour. If you have some spare time you can take a small passenger ferry across to the island of Ingaskär to visit the old pilot station which is now a small museum. There is good walking around the area.

Hudiksvall gästhamn. The guest berths are on the outer pontoon *Andy Beharrell*

## Mellanfjärden

61°57'.4N 17°20'.5E
www.upplevnordanstig.se/sv/boende/gasthamnar

Mellanfjärden is an attractive old fishing village. The easiest approach is from the south of Jättholmarna 5M to the east. There is a lit leading line and then unlit buoys to the gästhamn just past a local boat marina to port. It is well sheltered with 20 berths, bows-to a wooden quay from stern buoys. The wooden quay has the Sjömarket restaurant (www.mellanfjarden.se) on it. There is large almost enclosed bay just to the east. This makes a good anchorage as an alternative to the guest harbour. The entrance to the bay is quite obvious, but there are also leading lines in the distant trees.

Village-style facilities serve this attractive collection of red-painted wooden houses with a hotel on the quay.

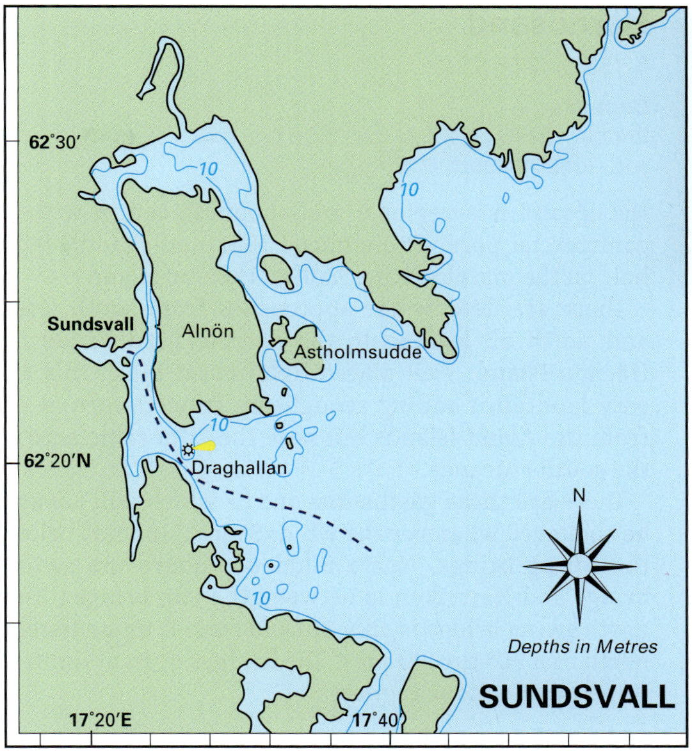


## Sundsvall

62°23'.37N 17°19'.38E

**Contacts**
www.sundsvall.se/gasthamn
hamnkiosken@gmail.com
☎+46 70 686 4021

Rebuilt deep-water marina in a neo-Renaissance town. The town was first chartered in 1621 and has burned down and been rebuilt four times. The first time was in 1721 when it was set on fire by the Russian army during the Russian Pillage of 1719–21. In 1888 both Umeå and Sundsvall caught fire (probably caused by a spark from a steamship) and the Sundsvall fire was the largest in Sweden's history. After the fire (unlike Umeå) the town decided to rebuild using stone. As a result Sundsvall's centre was nicknamed Stenstaden (the stone city). Situated at the head of its own fjord, the town has some richly ornamental buildings and nearby beaches.

Follow the deep-water channel under the motorway bridge – with clearance of 32m, this should provide no problems for yachts.

The gästhamn is more or less straight ahead after you come under the bridge and has 25 berths in 3–12m mostly to stern buoys but it is exposed to the east in stronger breezes. There is a clubhouse with washing machine, dryer, cooking and dining area, television, all provided with the mooring fee, and there are all the facilities expected of a town of nearly 50,000, including a large chandlery. The chandlery is called Hjertmans Båtillbehör (www.hjertmans.se, info@hjertmans.se, ☎+46 60 64 1700) and is about 40mins walk from the gästhamn.

Sundsvall is well served by the mainline rail network and E4 highway.

The boathouses and restaurant at Mellanfjärden *Andy Beharrell*

## Härnösand

62°38'.1N 17°56'.2E

**Contacts**

Bridges ✆+46 611 15687 (pre 1600 hrs) or ✆ +46 601 20184 (post 1600 hrs)

Härnösand is a regional and shopping centre with a commercial port. (Pronounced Hair-neu-sahnd). It is half on the mainland and half on Härnön Island.

There are deep water approaches from south, east and north all leading to the narrow fjord inside of Härnön Island. Well placed lighthouses make this an easy landfall if sailing straight up from Öregrund or from the Åland Islands but note the 20m cable across the south entrance.

There are three gästhamns one of which will always be sheltered whatever the wind. Södra Sundet is below the lifting bridge, Norra Sundet is above the swing bridge and Nattviken is between the two bridges. The north swing bridge is only 8m wide and is immediately north of a 90° turn to port. The bridges open at limited times by telephone request.

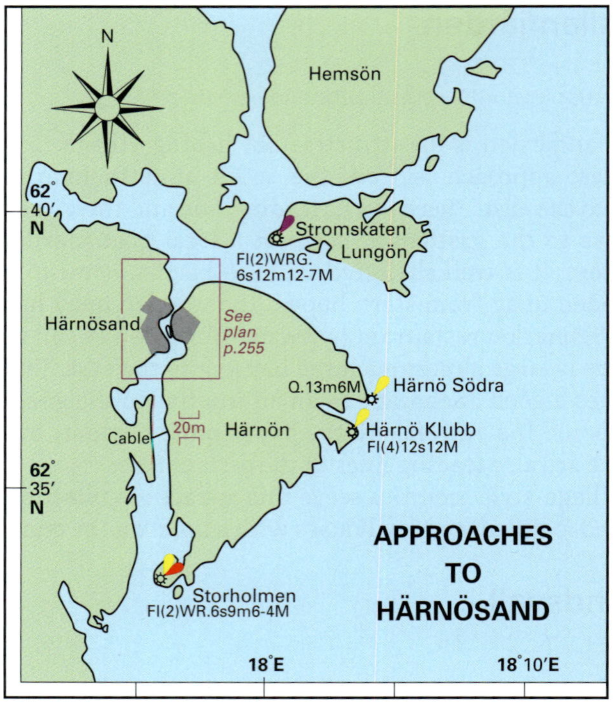


### Södra Sundet gästhamn

62°37'.58N 17°56'.4E

www.harnosand.se/gasthamnar

**Contacts**

gasthamn@harnosand.se

✆+46 611 348278

Södra Sundet gästhamn has 30 berths in around 3m of water. These are mostly on Y-booms, but it is possible to go alongside the main jetty as well. The gästhamn is well situated for the town centre, which is only a short walk through the old town. If leaving a boat for a while, this would probably be the best location. Once you have paid the harbour fee, this is valid for all the marinas in Härnösand.

### Nattviken gästhamn

62°37'.93N 17°55'.92E

**Contacts**

www.harnosand.se/gasthamnar

gasthamn@harnosand.se

✆+46 611 348578

Nattviken is the smallest of the guest harbours and is in the pool in between the bridges on the way through Härnösand. It is very sheltered and has around 10 guest berths on stern buoys bows-to on the north shore of the pool.

Aerial view of Södra Sundet gästhamn – Härnösand south *Andy Beharrell*

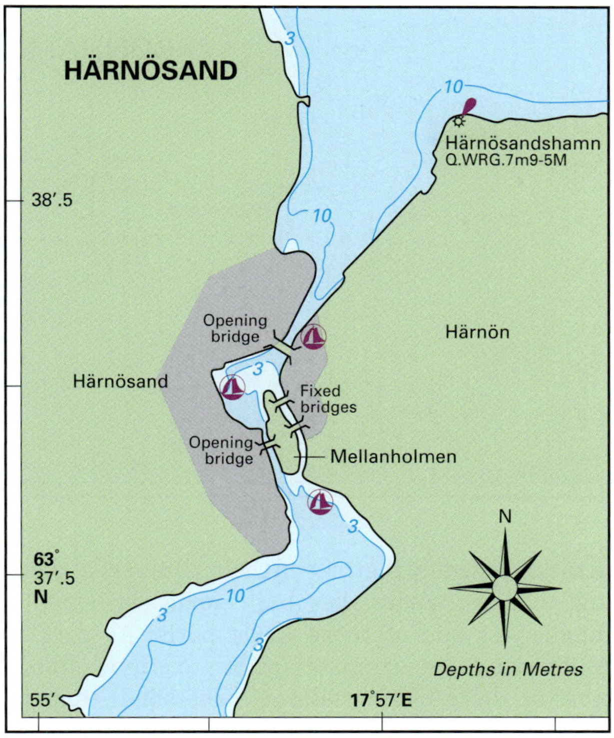


## 3. The Höga Kusten

Distance 45M

In the centre of Västernorrland this is, in many ways, the most attractive part of the whole of the Gulf of Bothnia. UNESCO World Heritage Site status recognises the Höga Kusten (High Coast) as something special. Even if you are short of time, don't miss this area if possible.

During the last Ice Age 3km of ice depressed the region by 800m. In the last 10,000 years the land has risen by over 400m and remains the fastest rising coast around the world. Currently rising at 9mm per annum it is expected to continue its upward trend for another 5,000 years. It is not unlike the west coast of Scotland but is lower and less austere. The steep tree clad hillsides stretch down to the water which is often fringed with pink Nordic granite among the red houses with white windows.

This makes for an ideal cruising ground with 20 gästhamns and many anchorages dotted along the 45M from Härnösand to Örnsköldsvik.

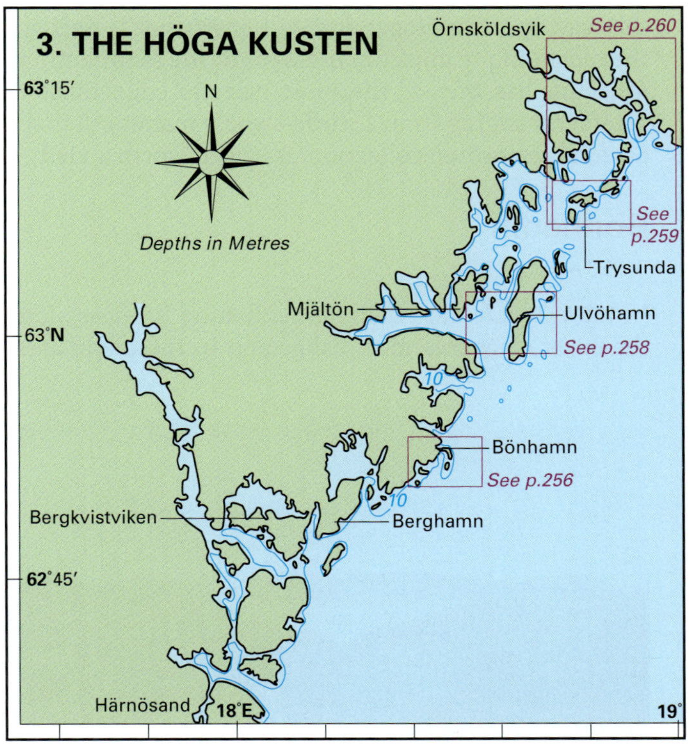


### Norra Sundet gästhamn

62°38'.06N 17°56'.25E

**Contacts**

www.harnosand.se/gasthamnar
gasthamn@harnosand.se
☽+46 611 348278

Norra Sundet is just to the north of the northerly bridge in Härnösand. There are 25 guest berths to stern buoys on the eastern side of the channel.

Each of the gästhamns has the usual facilities although fuel is perhaps most easily obtained from the fuel station on the mainland north of Norra Sundet. There is a helpful boatyard Dahlman Marin (www.dahlmans.nu, info@dahlmans.nu, ☽+46 611 556666) 500m across the bay from Södra Sundet Gästhamn.

There is a large shopping centre spread across both banks of the fjord, a university, multi-faith cathedral and various museums including Härnösand's Car Museum on Djuphamnsvägen which has 220 cars dating from 1899 to 1990.

The gästhamn at Härnösand north. The guest berths are on the right *Andy Beharrell*

## Häggvik

62°54'.58N 18°17'.53E

**Contacts**
www.haggviksgasthamn.com
✆+46 76 781 4030

Häggvik is a delightful and very sheltered stop on the High Coast. It is well worth a stop. The approach is relatively straightforward from the south - keep central as you go through the narrow entrance gorge 0.5M before Holmen and then, as you get close to Holmen, you will pick up the buoyage to round the island towards the gästhamn. It may be possible to go alongside, but most berths are stern buoys with around 30 berths available in depths of over 3m. The facilities are much as might be expected - sauna, showers, toilets, laundry etc. There is also a nice kitchen and dining area with a book swap and local information. Under a marquee there is an outdoor eating area.

When visiting Häggvik, it is worth taking the time to walk up Stortorget. This local viewpoint gives an excellent view of the harbour and is a nice walk. On the way up to Stortoget you will pass what is perhaps the most unique museum in Sweden. The Mannaminne Museum has one of the most eclectic collections of artefacts ranging from a stuffed wooly mammoth to the Swedish accordion collection. It is well worth a visit.

## Bönhamn

62°53'N 18°27'.2E

In 1557, Gustav Vasa distributed fishing licences along the coast of Norrland to fishermen in the Gävle area.

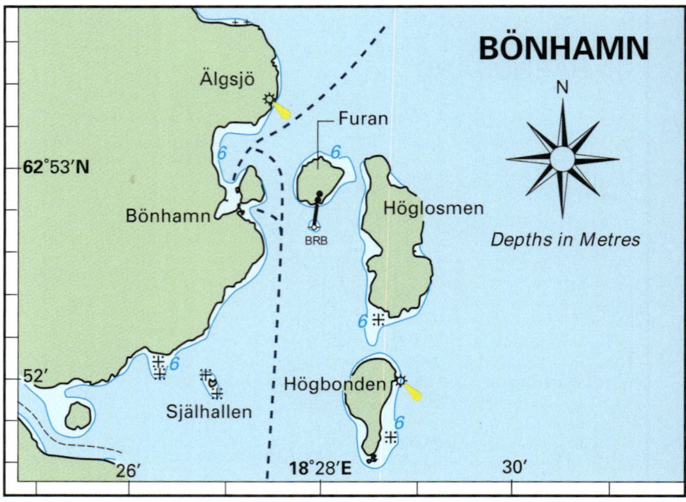


The fishermen would then spend their summers at these fishing villages, where they built small settlements. Bönhamn was one of these Gävle ports. As part of their lifestyle there was an obligation to attend church so most of these fishing villages have small chapels. Bönhamn's fisherman's chapel dates from 1659 and is worth a visit. This makes Bönhamn a very pretty old fishing and holiday village, not to be missed.

The harbour is 1M inside the prominent Högbonden light (62°52'N 18°28'.8E) and the narrow southeast entrance is less easy than that from the north. It is difficult to argue with their claim to be the 'best kept gästhamn on this coast'. In total there are around 35 spaces, but the berths off the new starboard breakwater are very shallow. It is possible to take a boat from Bönhamn to the Högbonden lighthouse to visit.

A view of the jetty at Häggvik from Stortorget. The gästhamn can be seen on the right. The impact of glacial land uplift is clear – the lake used to be connected to the main inlet *Andy Beharrell*

The lighthouse is now a youth hostel and is the second-highest lighthouse in Sweden as well as being one of the most powerful.

Out of season it may be possible to moor alongside, but the harbour is usually crowded in season, especially at weekends when mooring bows-to from stern anchors can produce crossed lines. Water, power, showers etc at the harbour. There is a café, kiosk, restaurant and art gallery in season. Good walks both north and south of the village giving wonderful views.

## Norrfällsviken

62°58'.5N 18°31'.3E

**Contacts**

www.norrfallsvikencamping.com
info@norrfallsvikencamping.com
✆+46 613 21382

Approach is through a fairly narrow channel which opens out into a large bay. At the end of the bay there is a campsite with moorings for visitors, either alongside, bows-to with a stern anchor or in booms (for smaller boats). Depths range between 3–7m. The campsite has a range of facilities including kayak hire, bike hire, a small grocery store and sauna.

The small gästhamn at Bönhamn looking east *Andy Beharrell*

Aerial view of the harbour and guest jetty at Norrfällsviken *Andy Beharrell*

## Ulvöhamn

63°01'.4N 18°39'.6E

**Contacts**
www.ulvohotell.se

Between the islands of north and south Ulvö lies the generally sheltered Ulvösund. Entry via the shallow and twisting southwest route is enlivened by the regular Ulvö ferry which has little respect for other vessels! The northeast and southwest entrances are more straightforward. Very deep water in the sound makes anchoring off difficult but there are three gästhamns with bows-to mooring from stern buoys or anchors and some rock moorings near the southwest entrance.

One of the gästhamns is called Kommunkajen. This is on the western side of Ulvöhamn. You can moor bows-to with a stern anchor, but the bottom gets rapidly deeper as you move away from the jetty, so allow for plenty of stern anchor warp. The bay is quite open, so in winds from southwest anticlockwise through to easterly, it can be a little exposed if the breeze gets up.

The easternmost of the guest harbours is called Hotelbryggan. Along the jetty there are various mooring options including stern buoys and bows-to with a stern anchor. In lower season, it might be possible to moor alongside the hotel jetty.

The large and attractive village has a permanent population, shop, pharmacy, hotel and restaurants. The usual facilities and fuel are available. Try to see the ancient wooden chapel with painted interior and taste the local fermented herring speciality of Surströmming. Ulvö Hamnkrog used to be a fermented herring salting plant, and was actually the very first place to package Surströmming in tin cans. The harbour is very popular in season but well worth a visit.

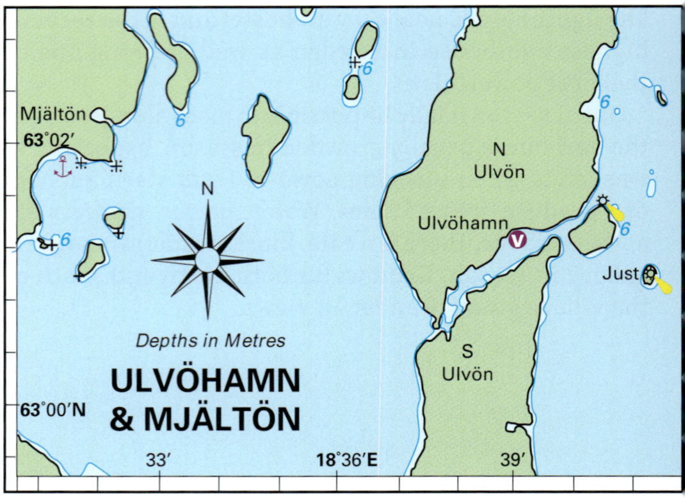

The jetties at Mjältön Baggviken *Andy Beharrell*

## Mjältön

63°02'.3N 18°32'.3E

Mjältön is a natural lagoon. The narrow and shallow entrance reveals itself on the southeast side of the island. Totally protected and deep in the centre. Limited

A view of the Hotelbryggan at Ulvöhamn from Lotsberget hill observation point *Andy Beharrell*

bows-to mooring to basic pontoons on the northeast side. If anchoring off, a trip line may be wise following extensive logging on the south side. Barbecue areas on the beach and composting toilet. There are good walks into the nature reserve.

You can even try and set a new record by walking to the top of Sweden's highest island peak! Bastutoberger is about a 2km walk and reaches 236m above sea level, increasing at 9mm per annum. There is a local tradition that you take a stone from sea level and add it to the cairn on the top of Bastutoberger.

## Docksta

63°03'.06N 18°19'.75E

**Contacts**

www.dockstahavet.se
dockstahavet@gmail.com
✆+46 76 313 6628

Docksta is a great stop on the High Coast. It is particularly good for visiting the Skuleskogen National Park or for walking up the local peak – Skuleberget. The approach to the harbour is relatively straightforward. There is plenty of water up the Dockstafjärden and the gästhamn is on the western side at the head of the inlet.

Mooring is mostly to Y-booms with 10 booms and some spaces alongside. The marina is open from mid-May to the end of August and can accommodate boats up to 60' on the guest pier. It can be a little exposed in strong southerlies, but otherwise is generally sheltered. There are toilets, showers, laundry and a very well-kept lounge with coffee. On arrival, you will usually be met by the hosts and they will allocate you a berth.

This is an ideal place for a crew change as well. The marina also has a guest house suitable for a family which can be booked through AirBNB and further accommodation in one of the old boat houses, so crew can even wait for you to arrive in luxury. There are buses to Härnösand where you can connect with trains. It is best to book bus and train tickets together on sj.se/en. The main E4 north/south road also goes straight past the gästhamn.

There is a bus service to the Skuleskogen National Park (established in 1984) which runs from around the start of July to early August, but out of this season, the Docksta hosts will often be able to give you a lift. However, it is possible to walk directly from the gästhamn to the peak of Skuleberget. The alternative is to take the chairlift to the top, but however you get there, from the peak you can muse on the fact that, had you been there 10,000 years ago there would have been a peak of around 10m above sea level.

Now Skuleberget stands 295m above sea level and is still rising, so each time you visit, you can claim a record. The glacial land uplift continues in the High Coast area at about 8–9mm each year, so while the land is getting higher, bear in mind that the water is getting shallower!

If you don't want to walk that far, you can rent DragonForce 65 model yachts from the harbour and run races with friends or other visiting boats.

## Trysunda

63°08'.4N 18°47'.4E

The name Trysunda is a reflection of the history of the island. Trysunda means three sounds and in the days when it was a fishing port for Gävle there were three entrances to the island. Land uplift has resulted in two of those being closed, so there is now just one entrance from the south.

Trysunda is now an enchanting holiday village in a nature reserve. Entrance is easy from the southwest and mooring is bows-to a substantial jetty from stern buoys in 3–7m. It may be exposed to the south when it may be possible to anchor on the north of the island. There is power, water, washroom etc at the gästhamn.

This former fishing village is now almost entirely holiday homes with very few permanent residents. It is beautifully maintained but very little is open before Midsummer when a small shop and restaurants appear for the season. Interesting wooden seamen's chapel dating from 1654 with a painted interior. Excellent walks around the island.

Aerial view of the gästhamn at Docksta *Andy Beharrell*

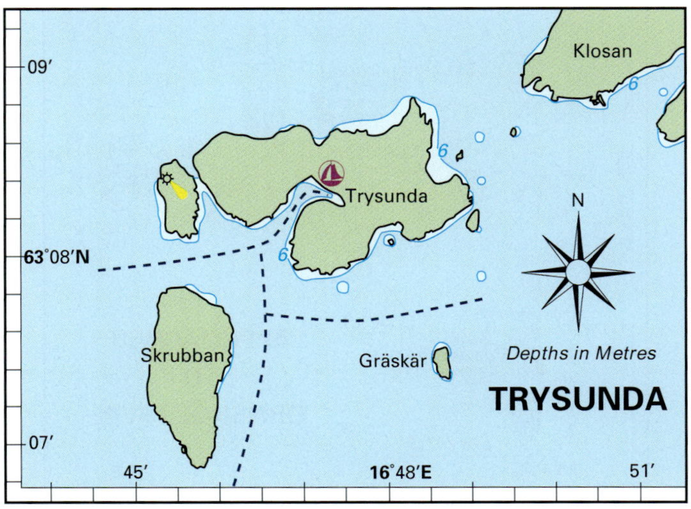

## Örnsköldsvik

63°17'.16N 18°42'.67E

**Contacts**

☏+46 660 222166

Örnsköldsvik (pronounced Urn-sheulds-veek) is a regional centre and commercial port which marks the northern end of the High Coast. From the open sea the Skagsudde light (63°11'.3N 19°01'.4E) marks the start of a deep-water channel. After 4M this joins with the coastal route from the southwest from inside Trysunda. A sharp turn to port precedes 5M of well-marked and lit channel right up to the extreme northwest corner of the harbour.

The gästhamn of 35 berths in 3m is very central to the town and offers boom, stern buoy or alongside moorings with all the usual services. The services are in a servicehus located in the restaurant directly next to the gästhamn. There are many nearby anchorages from which to choose but all are well away from town.

The large and modern town centre provides extensive shopping and services. The town is also Sweden's Ice Hockey centre. It is well served by the E4 highway and buses but with no immediate rail link.

The gästhamn at Örnsköldsvik. The gästhamn are the moorings on the left by the service building *Andy Beharrell*

## 4. Husum to Bjuröklubb

Distance 110M

The Västerbotten and Quark coastline is well served by the E4 highway which links most of the dozen gästhamns. However at sea there are quite shallow areas along this coast, some of which extend well offshore. While signs of current or past industrial activities are spread along the coastline, the island of Holmön just offshore claims to be Sweden's sunniest.

## Husum

63°19'.8N 19°08'.5E

**Contacts**

www.husumsbatklubb.se/sida/1083/gasthamn

☏+46 70 578 0163

Husum is a safe harbour and commercial centre. It has a well-lit and buoyed entrance towards a dominating pulp mill.

The guest berths at Husums Båtklubb *Andy Beharrell*

An aerial view of the Järnäs-Udden peninsula with the old pilot station at Järnäsklubb on the right *Andy Beharrell*

This is a convenient first stop north of the Höga Kusten but the gästhamn is 3km away from the town. There are seven berths for alongside or bows-to from stern anchor moorings in 2–4m. The facilities are fairly basic as most services are in town, but there are toilets, showers, shore power and water available with pump-out facilities as well. Bikes are available for loan and there is a BBQ with a wood store for guest use.

The E4 highway is within 3km.

## Järnäsklubb

63°26'.3N 19°40'.7E

Järnäsklubb is an old pilot station. The harbour is situated 3M northeast of the Störbaden light (63°24'.5N 19°30'.36), which should be given a good offing. There is a leading line, but it is not easy to find. The narrow entrance opens out into a much larger bay, and the harbour itself cannot be seen until you are well inside the bay. There is alongside mooring for five rafted in 1–3m. To accommodate the claimed 10 boats all would have to be less than 7m LOA. There is a small cafe with toilets, showers and limited electricity points.

If the harbour is full, it is possible to anchor in the bay outside. Shelter in here should be good.

## Norrbyskär

63°33'.8N 19°52'.5E

A fascinating island, the site of an abandoned sawmill. The small gastbrygga at Kalmarn on the northern end has space for no more than three alongside unless rafting. Take great care to avoid the sunken timbers at either end. Basic facilities and a 1km walk down to the village. Here there are 20 bows-to visitors' moorings from stern anchors with better facilities but close to the ferry quay from Norrbyn and exposed to the east.

In the 19th century this became the largest sawmill company in Europe and was set up as a model society. The management and workers' houses lining the street are now holiday homes. There are remains of its previous use all over the island and a miniature reproduction of the mill draws many day visitors from the mainland.

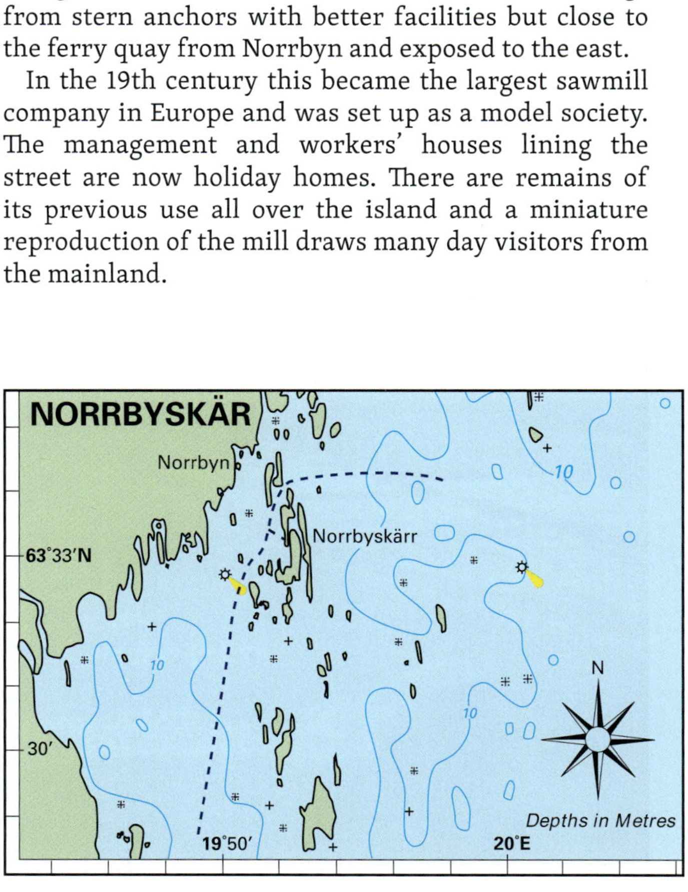

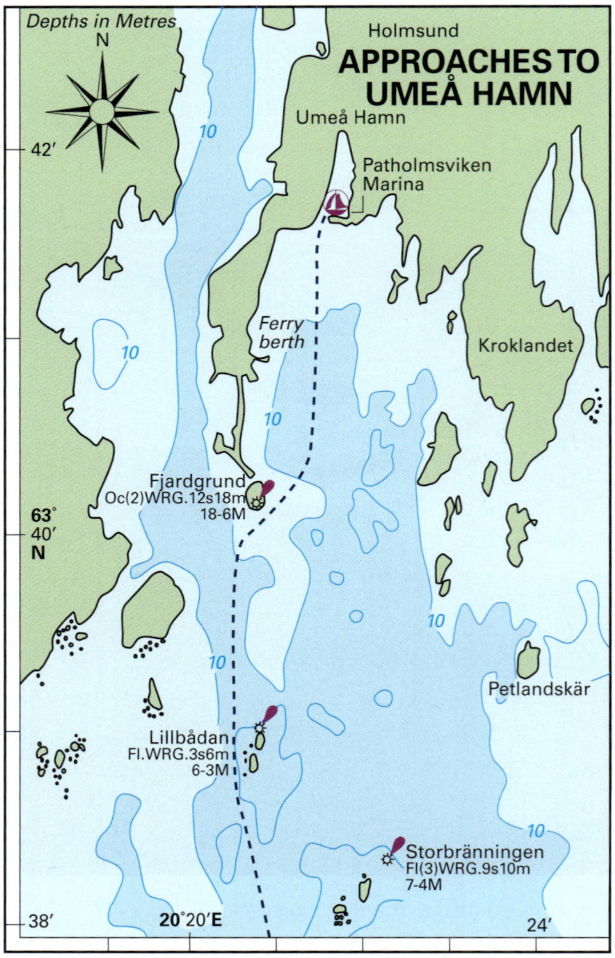


## Holmsund, Umeå

63°49'N 20°16'E

**Contacts**
www.pvbk.net
info@pvbk.net

Umeå is a provincial capital, ferry port and yacht club marina.

The main entrance north-northeast from the Vaktaren light (63°36'.9N 20°25'.4E) is well buoyed and lit for the ferries to Finland. From the Lillbådan light (63°38'.9N 20°20'.8E) there is a straightforward deep water route to the north-northeast of the long Fjardgrund peninsula. This leads past the docks to starboard at Umeå Hamn but is then blocked by a 3.8m fixed bridge before going all the way 18km inland to Umeå.

Visiting yachts usually berth at the Holmsund, Patholmsviken Yacht Club and gästhamn to the east of Fjardgrund and north of the ferry terminal. However, north of the Lillbådan light can be very confusing with conflicting buoyage for different channels.

There are 20 bows-to moorings from stern buoys in 3–5m, water and power on the pontoon, washing machines, toilets, showers and a sauna at the yacht club. You can also borrow bikes from the club.

There are adequate shopping and services at Holmsund 1km north and full services in a large shopping centre with a hospital and two universities 15km to the north by No. 124 bus at Umeå. The Great Fire of Umeå was in 1888 and it destroyed most of the city. As part of the rebuild they planted birch trees along the streets, resulting in Umeå being known as 'The City of Birches'.

Lift out and lay up services are available from the nearby yard making this potentially a good place to leave a boat for the winter or even for a shorter period while heading home. The E4 highway, rail services and a busy local airport make this a good place to change crew.

## Byviken

63°48'.4N 20°52'.5E

Small guest and ferry harbour on the north of Holmön Island.

A straightforward entrance from the north to moor bows-to from stern buoys behind the east breakwater. There is 3m near the fairway but quickly shoaling towards the shore. You need to turn immediately to port on entering, and watch the depth sounder carefully. Water and power on the quay with basic facilities nearby.

An aerial view of the Patholmsvikens båtklubb (yacht club) at Umeå *Andy Beharrell*

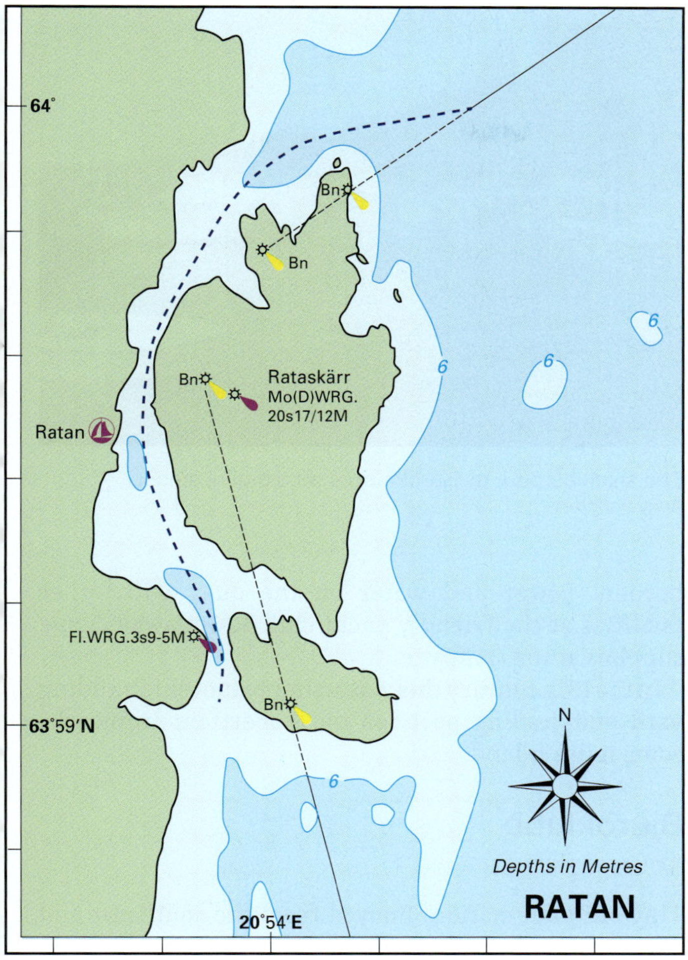


In season there are a café, kiosk, restaurant and excellent boat museum between the ferry and prominent lighthouse on the west of the harbour. Small shop, chemist and Systembolaget 2km to the south.

Lying 6M offshore this is a popular weekend destination and good jumping off place for Finland just 45M to the east.

## Ratan

63°59'.5N 20°53'.7E

### Contacts

www.ratan.se/boende/bo-som-besokare

The best natural harbour on this coast. Easy deep-water entrance from the southeast but more care is needed for the shallow north entrance. Mooring in 4.5m alongside or bows-to from stern anchors if crowded. Power, water and fuel on the quay with other facilities within 300m. Can be exposed to strong southeast winds when it might be preferable to anchor in the lee of Rataskär Island.

Ratan was an important customs port and the site of a 'land uplift' experiment by Celsius and Linnaeus in the 19th century. The small building for their mareograph still stands. The excellent restaurant at Tullgårdens Gärtgifueri (www.tullgardens.se) was previously a holiday home for worn-out housewives but originally built for the Customs Chief Officer. Scene of a major battle with the Russians in 1809.

You can cross by dinghy for good walks on Rataskär.

The guest jetty at Ratan *Andy Beharrell*

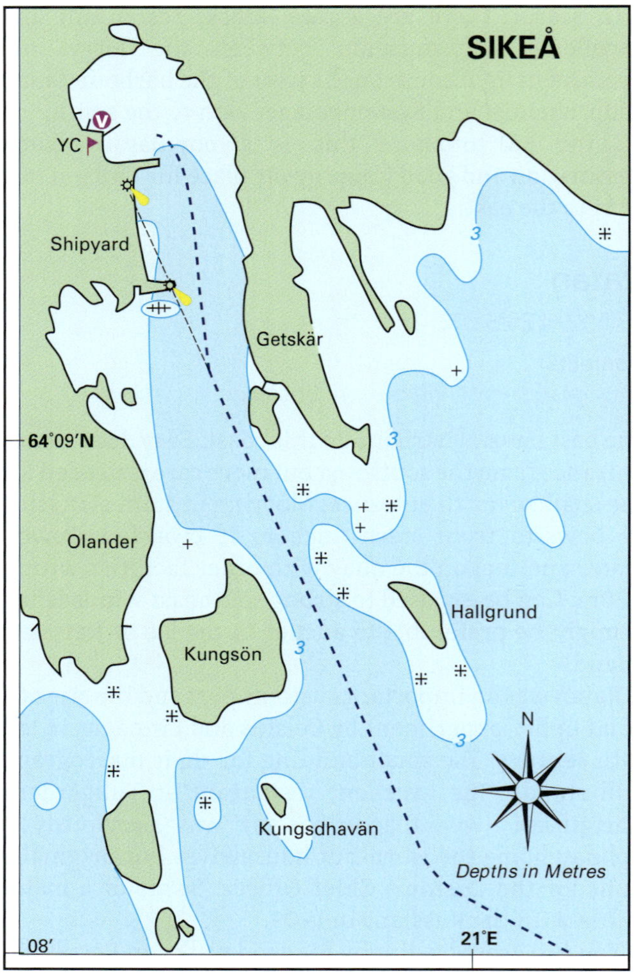

The small harbour at Bjuröklubb – an old pilot station *Andy Beharrell*

## Sikeå

64°09'.6N 20°58'.7E

Sikeå is an abandoned shipbuilding yard and port for ironworks, now a holiday camp.

It is a straightforward, well-marked entrance from the southeast. Moor in 2·5m bows-to from stern buoys at the end of the quay in the photo but it is shallow beyond. Power and water on the quay with other facilities at the friendly yacht club 300m away. Some supplies at the campsite.

In the 18th century this was an important shipbuilding yard and trading port for the Robertfors Ironworks some miles inland.

## Bjuröklubb

64°19'.8N 21°22'.5E

Tiny old pilot station. Buoyed from the southeast and easy approach from the north to inside of Bjuron point. Unless there are small boats moored bows-to there is alongside berthing for four in 1–4m. There have been reports of shoaling, and so care should be taken entering the harbour. In settled weather it is also possible to anchor off.

Basic facilities with a barbecue and free sauna but the invigorating walk up to the lighthouse is well worth the effort for spectacular views and the sunset.

In season there is a café near the lighthouse and fish for sale from a boat in the harbour.

Aerial view of the berths at Sikeå gästhamn *Andy Beharrell*

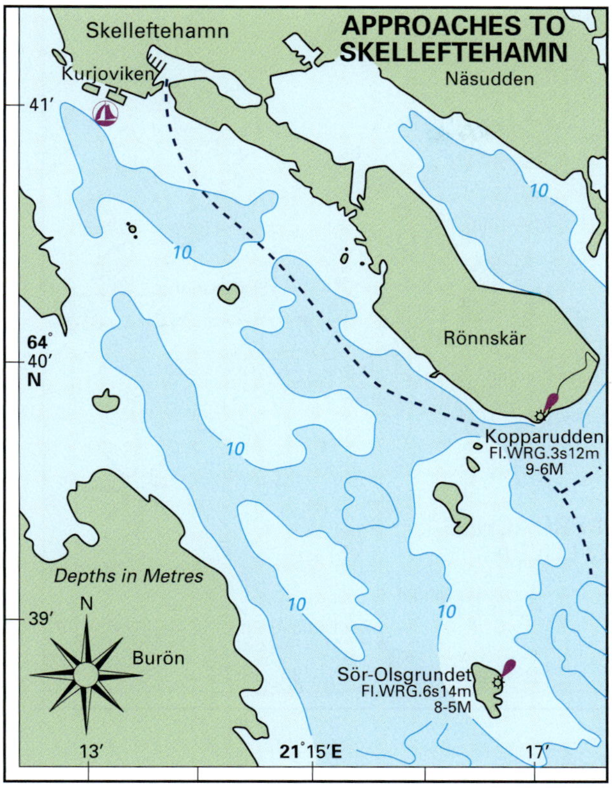


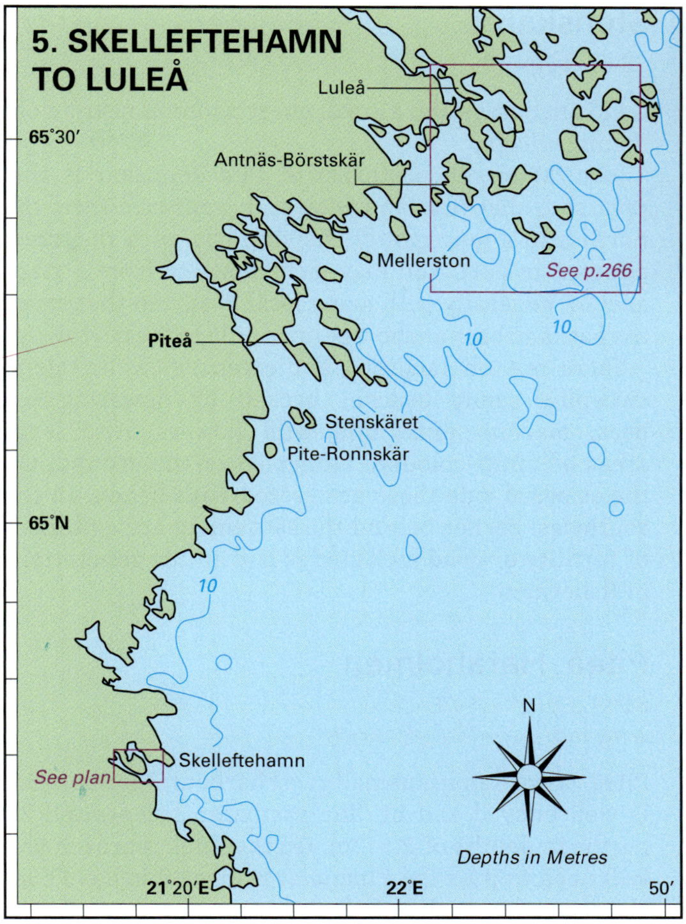


## 5. Skelleftehamn to Luleå

Distance 70M

### Norbotten and the North Skärgård

www.bottenviken.se/en/places

The waters are often shallower but the islands become more frequent throughout this area which becomes progressively more attractive. Gästhamns are less common and usually smaller but the opportunities to anchor increase.

### Skelleftehamn, Kurjoviken

64°41'.2N 21°13'.7E
www.bottenviken.se/en/kurjoviken-skelleftea-en

Sailing Club marina and guest harbour.

Like Umeå, the town of Skellefteå is some 18km inland and cannot be approached by sailing yachts due to several low fixed bridges. Visiting yachts normally berth at the friendly Ursvikens Sailing Club at Kurjoviken.

From the south pass either side of Skötgrönnan beacon (64°35'.9N 21°30'E). From the north leave Gäsören light (64°39'.8N 21°19'.3E) to starboard. Then join the main buoyed channel just north of the Rakan light (64°38'.8N 21°18'E) and steer northwest to pass south and west of the prominent foundry on Rönnskär. Continue northwest approximately 2M through the buoys until the narrow entrance to Kurjoviken opens on the starboard beam. There is a leading line through this 2.7m channel to the marina which could be tricky in a strong onshore wind. A new gästhamn pontoon is immediately to port with bows-to mooring from stern buoys or anchors.

Water and power on this pontoon and all the usual facilities at the nearby clubhouse.

There is adequate shopping and some services within 2km and frequent buses to a large shopping centre in town. Boatyard, lift out services and lay up facilities at the marina. Pleasant walks around Kurjoviken.

### Pite-Rönnskär

65°03'.2N 21°33'.4E
www.bottenviken.se/en/piteronnskar-skelleftea-en

A prominent red lighthouse overlooks this old pilot station.

This little island lies 3.5M west of the Nygrån light (65°01'N 22°41'.5E). Even with a large scale chart the entrance looks unfriendly but round the buoy to it's north to pick up the leading line and creep into this spectacular spot. A small ferry from Piteå claims the immediate alongside berth leaving just enough space for six boats to moor bows-to from their own stern anchors in 2.5m. During the season and at weekends more than 10m LOA is likely to be too large. By July long weeds stream to the surface.

An ideal lunch stop with few facilities. Most of the wooden houses are now holiday homes handed down through the generations. Fishing nets used to be stored for the winter in the small wooden chapel. It is worth seeking out a guide to climb the unusual iron lighthouse for panoramic views.

## Stenskäret

65°07'N 21°43'E

Good anchorage and a small guest pontoon near an old fishing village.

Just 7M to the northeast of Pite-Rönnskär is this reverse L-shaped island. However, approach from the north into a long gently shelving bay with the guest pontoon to port. You may moor bows-to from a stern anchor, generally with many local boats but the rest of the bay is an easy anchorage open only to the northwest.

There are no facilities but extensive walks along sweeping sandy beaches backed by flowering sea peas, marram grass and wild flowers. Also large areas of multi-coloured stones cover the ground. On the seaward side these are coated with lichen. In the southwest corner behind the settlement are a number of fertility or good luck circles laid out by generations of fishermen.

## Piteå, Haraholmen

65°18'.33N 21°27'.47E
www.vastrakajen.se/gasthamn/

Piteå Västra Kajen is a small guest harbour. The approach is well buoyed and lit. The gästhamn has around 20 berths in depths of 2.5–3m. On the final approach you will need to pass the Pitsundet bridge. This has 13.5m clearance when closed (for opening ✆+46 70 256 10 51). Nearby sandy beaches at Pitsundet seem to attract many Norwegians for their holidays. The gästhamns on the north side of this peninsula are only suitable for boats drawing less than 1.2m and 1.5m.

During the 1970s the summer water temperatures around Piteå were reported for three consecutive years to be Sweden's warmest and as a result the beach at Pite Havsbad became known as "Norrbotten's Riviera".

## Mellerston

65°11'N 21°47'.4E

Mellerston is a possible lunch time anchorage. Another 7M north and to the east of Bondön is the large island of Mellerston. On its north shore are several anchorages the westerly of which has a small and shallow guest pontoon.

There are no facilities but this is a useful lunch time anchorage in 1.5–2m open only to the northwest.

## Antnäs-Börstskär

65°25'.7N 22°06'.5E
www.bottenviken.se/en/antnasborstskar-lulea-en

Small guest pontoon and anchorage by a friendly village. There is an easy relatively deep-water entrance from the northwest. The pontoon for 10 bows-to berths has some stern buoys in 2m and is straight ahead. Anchor in deeper water in the bay which is exposed only to the northwest.

The few facilities include a free sauna and wood barbeque provided by the commune but please use the axes provided to split replacement wood.

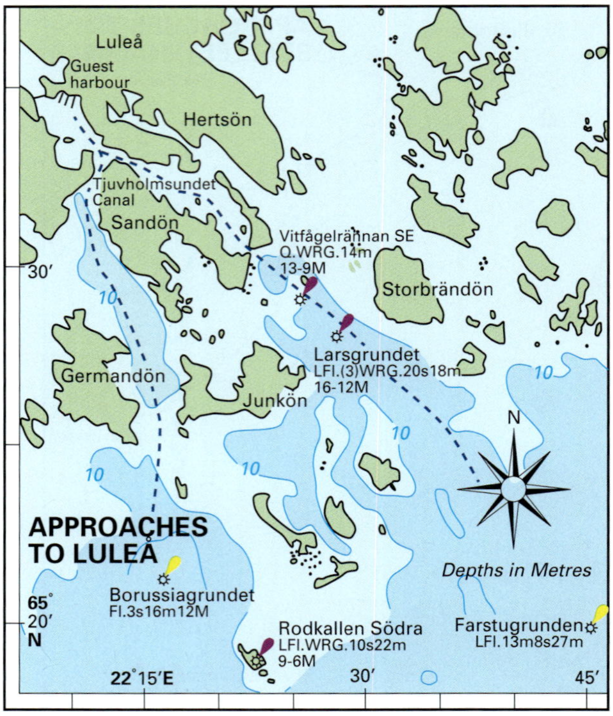


## Luleå

65°34'.8N 22°09'.7E

**Contacts**

www.bottenviken.se/en/ettan-lulea-en
www.visitlulea.se/en/destinations/lulea-tourist-center

Regional capital, industrial, commercial, shopping and yachting centre.

The 1M long, dredged Tjuvholmsundet canal is convenient for leisure boats coming from the south. The very well-buoyed commercial route from the open sea starts just north of the Farstugrunden whistle buoy (65°19'.8N 22°45'E). After 16M to the northwest the narrows at Likskarët (65°31'N 22°22'E) are reached.

These two routes meet just north of Sandön 5M later but still 2.5M short of the marina. Pass the impressive icebreaker fleet to starboard and head for the west end of the marina for the Ettans Båthamn gästhamn. The marina has 590 berths of which 50 are guest berths which are bows-to the jetty between booms in 3.5m. Larger vessels can moor alongside further west on the town quay.

The gästhamn is fully equipped with good facilities and all the usual boatyard services. Dues are paid at the comprehensive Granek chandlers (Småbåtsgatan 2, 972 35 Luleå) behind and there is a restaurant attached. The nearby major shopping centre will meet all needs.

This town of nearly 75,000 is well served by road, rail and air communications to make it a first-class crew change base.

The World Heritage site at Gammelstad Church Village 10km to the northwest is well worth a visit for its interesting history and good restaurants. Luleå is also an excellent place from which to hire a car for a short break to drive into the Arctic Circle, Lapland and even Norway. Don't miss the spectacular Storforsen Falls en route.

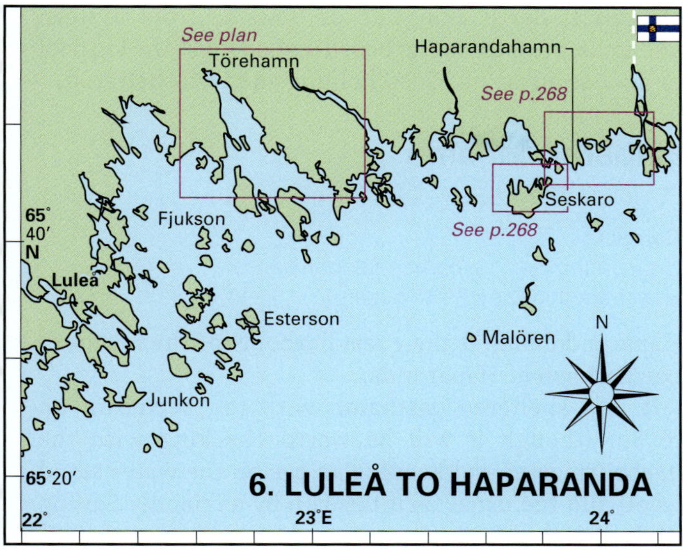


## 6. Luleå to Haparanda

**Distance**
65M

The top of the Gulf is border country. The *skärgård* which started around Piteå continues all the way round to the Finnish border. In places it is shallow but there are enough gästhamns, anchorages and deep water to make this an attractive cruising area in its own right. Don't expect to find many visiting yachts but this leaves space for abundant wildlife and waterfowl.

### Junkon

65°27'.4N 22°24'.3E
www.bottenviken.se/en/junkon-lulea-en

Restored harbour with windmill and walks. The harbour at Junkon is on the northeast side of the island. The approach is straightforward from either the west around Örnudden (keeping north of the northerly cardinal off the point) or from the main channel from the east though make sure to stay east of the shallow patch just to the south of Orrskärsudden. There are 20 berths for alongside, bows-to from stern anchors or between booms in 1.9–2.5m. Services include wood-burning saunas, barbecue areas with firewood, café, showers, toilets, electricity (15 out of the 20 berths), an archipelago museum and rubbish disposal.

Since being declassified as a defence area the harbour and buildings have benefited from a make-over financed by the EU. There are a small café, museum, windmill and good walks on the island which is visited by a day trip boat from Luleå. It is sometimes possible to buy fish from a local fisherman.

### Esterson

65°32'.9N 22°47'.5E

Quiet natural anchorage. Enter either end of the channel between the two islands Esterső n and Saxskäret. From the southeast stay south of the rocky shallows and mind the regular fishing nets. There is an overnight anchorage just west of the house in good holding. Exposed to the northwest and east.

### Fjukson

65°40'.9N 22°37'.3E

Well placed overnight anchorage. Approach from the west and it is simple to anchor in 8m just west of the house on the north shore. Good mud holding but exposed to the west. Well positioned if visiting Töre 15M further north.

### Törehamn

65°54'.1N 22°39'E
www.bottenviken.se/en/tore-kalix-en

Gästhamn at the top of the gulf.

Follow the transits and well-buoyed channel past Törefors to the grain silos. There are six guest berths in 1.9m in the gästhamn or go alongside in deeper water outside. There are few facilities but a café serves the nearby campsite.

This is the most northerly point in the Baltic Sea so it may be quite busy in season. Close by is a large yellow buoy with a letter box on its side. If you fill in the form provided you will receive a certificate recording that you have reached this landmark.

The yellow buoy at Törehamn – the most northerly possible point of navigation *Fiona Slay*

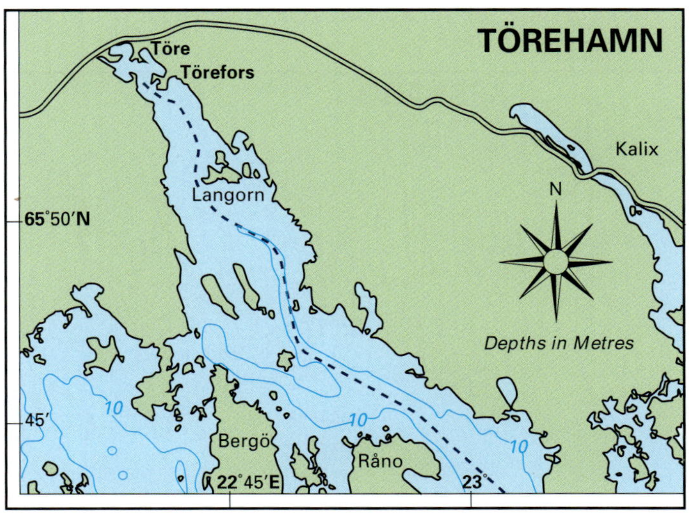

## Malören

65°31'.6N 22°33'.5E

Remote lighthouse island. A bow shaped island with two lights and a Racon beacon. Enter from the south and anchor southwest of the pier but because of land uplift do not expect to find more than 1.5m. Exposed but safe in all winds except from the southwest. This is a convenient but shallow stop if crossing the top of the gulf. Popular at the weekends during the season.

## Sandskär

65°33'.605N 23°44'.73E (approach)

The approach is a simply marked channel (though possibly not on charts) and leading lines, though these are not clear. An excellent new floating jetty showed recent investment but otherwise it is back to basics – a composting toilet and a murky water well, and (of course) a sauna.

Sandskär is lovely, important for nature, and often used for netting and ringing migrating birds. Moose are "occasional visitors" – they can swim, or walk across the sea ice.

The fishermen's church had previously served as Tornio's granary before relocation. A long sandy spit forms the northern part of the island and is fringed with beaches.

## Seskaro, Leppäniemikajen

65°44'.56N, 23°44'.57E

Seskaro is a small guest harbour on an attractive agricultural island. There is a jetty for fishing vessels and pontoon for smaller boats. Services include power and water outlets, toilets, shower and a sauna. Leppäniemikajen is a good alternative to Haparandahamn in the event of a draft of 2m or more. There is a frequent bus (Line 322) from there into Haparanda/Tornio.

The entrance is from the west of Seskarö, round the top and then SE into Leppäniemikajen harbour, following the buoyed fairway. Most yachts will have to enter from the northwest as entrance from the east is not possible for yachts due to a low bridge with 11.5m clearance. Berth alongside or bows-to from a stern anchor at the jetty to starboard just north of the log pool or anchor off in 7m. Good holding and well sheltered.

## Haparandahamn

65°46'.3N 23°54'.5E

**Contacts**

www.bottenviken.se/en/haparandahamn-en
www.bkbothnia.se/gaster-guests

Haparandahamn is the guest harbour for the northern border town of Haparanda.

It is a sheltered gästhamn with ten berths in up to 3m (though it will be worth checking with the harbourmaster and keeping an eye on the water stand level) and the usual facilities run by a friendly Sailing Club. Not the most interesting spot but convenient if visiting Haparanda some 18km to the northeast, access to which is restricted by rocky shallows and fixed bridges. Haparanda lies on the Swedish side of the River Tornio and is best visited by bus.

## Båtskärsnäs

65°47'.12N 23°25'.35E

**Contacts**

www.norrkustmarina.se/english
butik@norrkustmarina.se
✆+46 923 67 02 72

Norrkust Marina claims to be the largest boatyard in the Bay of Bothnia, with an 80T crane. It is situated on east side of peninsular southeast of Karlsborg and there is a gästhamn with 40 visitors berths in 2–6m with fuel, toilets, showers, a kitchen, rubbish disposal and WiFi though there is no public transport. The yard offers winter storage in a heated hall (1000M²), cold storage (7000M²) or outside. Authorised dealers for Volvo and Yanmar, so they can offer winterisation services. They are also agents for liferaft and lifejacket servicing. The marina is close to the Norwegian border and can provide contact details of transport companies who may be able to transport boats by road (size dependent) to Narvik, Norway. A Rustler 36 successfully made the reverse journey from Narvik to Norrkust Marina in August 2023. Their claim to fame is as the northernmost marina in Sweden.

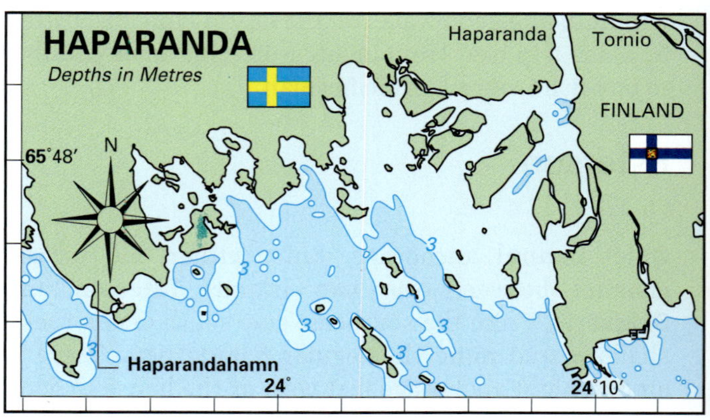

Tre Kronor – built in 2005 *Andy Beharrell*

A Viking ship replica off Nynäshamn *Andy Beharrell*

An island in the main Stockholm channel taken over by cormorants *Andy Beharrell*

Tranquil archipelago mooring *Andy Beharrell*

Swedish toilet art *Andy Beharrell*

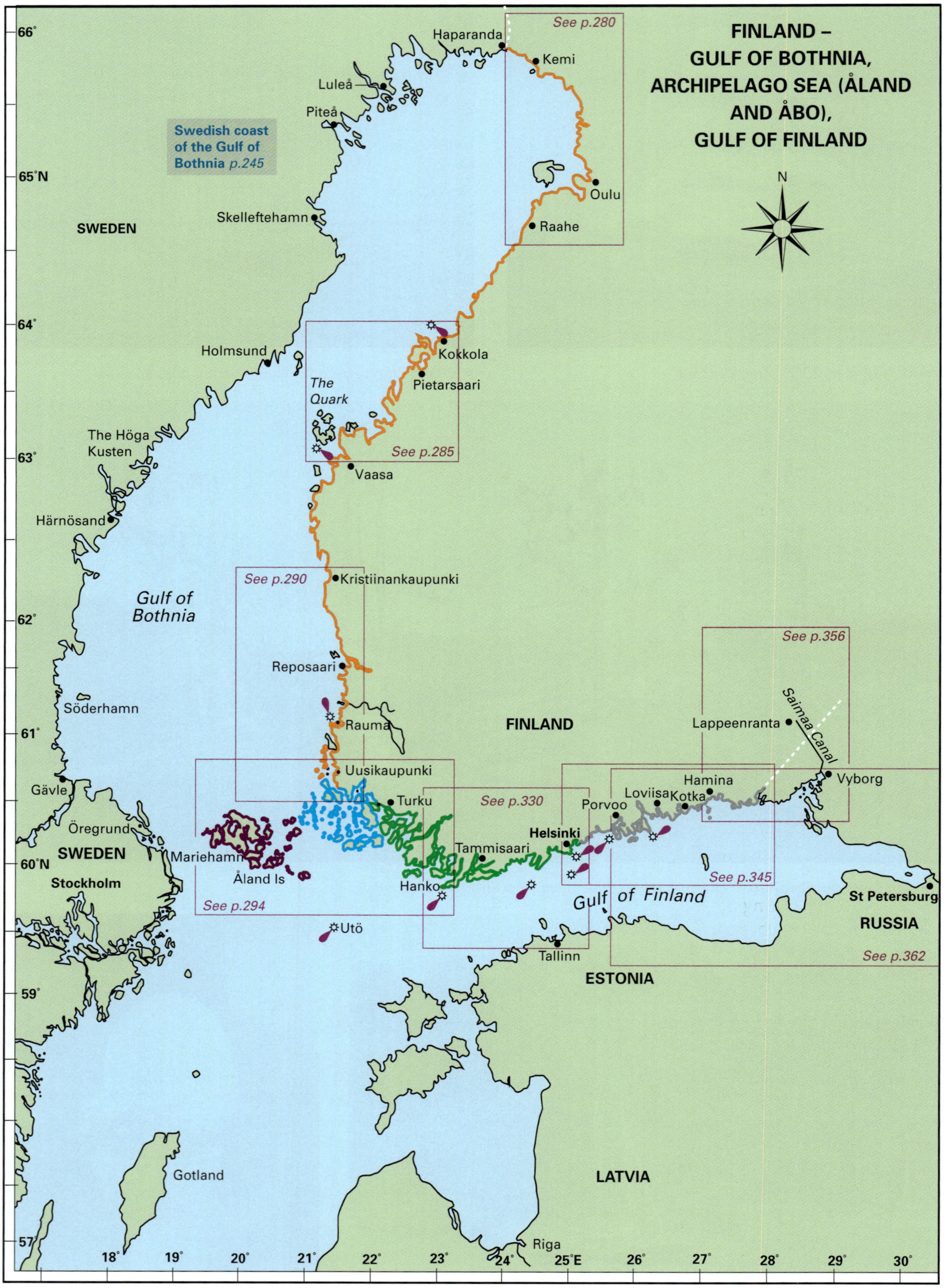
FINLAND –
GULF OF BOTHNIA,
ARCHIPELAGO SEA (ÅLAND
AND ÅBO),
GULF OF FINLAND
N
See p.280
Haparanda
Kemi
Luleå
Piteå
Swedish coast of the Gulf of Bothnia p.245
Oulu
Raahe
Skelleftehamn
SWEDEN
Kokkola
Holmsund
Pietarsaari
The Quark
The Höga Kusten
See p.285
Vaasa
Härnösand
See p.290
Kristiinankaupunki
Gulf of Bothnia
Reposaari
See p.356
Söderhamn
Rauma
FINLAND
Saimaa Canal
Lappeenranta
Uusikaupunki
Hamina
Vyborg
Gävle
Turku
See p.330
Loviisa
Kotka
Porvoo
Öregrund
Helsinki
SWEDEN
Mariehamn
Tammisaari
Stockholm
Åland Is
See p.345
Hanko
Gulf of Finland
St Petersburg
See p.294
Utö
RUSSIA
Tallinn
See p.362
ESTONIA
Gotland
LATVIA
Riga
66°
65°N
64°
63°
62°
61°
60°N
59°
57°
18°
19°
20°
21°
22°
23°
24°
25°E
26°
27°
28°
29°
30°

# 3. FINLAND

Cruising in Finland means meandering amid tree-clad islands, with clear, tideless and sheltered waters, colourful villages, well-run marinas, secluded anchorages, warm summer days, rich and fertile land, and fragrant forests carpeted with pine needles.

Finland ranks as the world's happiest country based on the 2023 World Happiness index. They scored 7.8 out of a total possible score of 10 and were closely followed by Denmark. These levels of happiness are thought to come from Finland's strength of communal support and mutual trust. Finns feel strongly that they are free to make their own choices, and there is almost no suspicion of government corruption. All these factors help make the people extremely friendly.

The animal life seems happy as well (!) and wildlife abounds – wild whooper swans, eider, white-tailed eagles, deer, sea trout, turbot and many other species. There is a special satisfaction in being able to navigate in complete confidence through myriad channels between the islands, often only a matter of feet from the rocks, with the use of the Finnish charts. In complex areas where each island looks much like its neighbour, a small, removable adhesive marker may be found useful to keep track of one's position on the chart. Electronic charting is very helpful in this regard.

To the north, the Gulf of Bothnia extends almost to the Arctic Circle. The further north one goes, the less it is populated and the trees predominate.

The Åland Islands, a favourite cruising ground for yachtsmen from Sweden and Finland – not to mention further afield – are of particular interest, not only because of their beauty, but also because of their connection with the sailing traders. The Åland Sea, the stretch of water that separates Sweden from the Åland Islands is only about 19M wide if measured between the easternmost Swedish *skärgård* and the westernmost Finnish one and forms a well trodden path for yachts and ferries during the summer months but is not to be taken lightly in poor weather.

The boundary between the Åland Islands and the rest of Finland is marked by the Kihti (Skiftet), a long, narrow sound only 0.9M wide in its northern part becoming 20M wide in the south. It runs north-south on longitude 21°09'E. West of this boundary the language spoken is almost entirely Swedish. East of it Finnish speakers and Finnish place names gradually become more frequent. The waters between the western Åland Islands and Hanko are said to be the densest archipelago in the world.

From the Åland Islands to Hamina, just short of the border with Russia, the coast is a saaristo or *skärgård* coast, that is to say there is a sheltered route in smooth water behind the fringe of islands. It is difficult to convey the fascination of this kind of sailing to those who have never experienced it. One sails for hundreds of miles in smooth water through a vast forest or rock garden, stopping almost at will.

At first the pilotage may seem difficult, especially if it is blowing hard, but the waters are excellently marked by buoys, lighthouses and stone cairns, and by pairs of wooden transits on shore. These cairns, or kummel are the oldest marks in the islands, and very skilfully sited. They show the general direction of the route but not, of course, every isolated danger.

Yachtsmen who are new to these waters often expend a great deal of nervous energy looking for 'the next mark'. It should be borne in mind, however, that if there are no rocks there will be no marks, sometimes for several miles. Therefore, as a general rule, one is better off if one cannot see a mark than if one can – provided one is in the fairway, which means on the correct side of the relevant island. There are exceptions, of course...

An entirely separate cruising ground is the Saimaa Lake area, an immense landlocked complex of lakes entered through the Saimaa Canal. The Canal starts near Vyborg (see page 367), and runs through territory secured by the Russians in 1944 and leased back to the Finns in 1963 in return for the latter undertaking the upkeep of the canal. The Saimaa lakes are a favourite cruising ground for local yachtsmen, especially at the time of the Savonlinna Opera Festival in July, but are little visited by foreign yachts.

The Board of Management of the Saimaa Canal issues a well-produced booklet of instructions for small-boat traffic in the Saimaa Canal, it is also available online (https://vayla.fi/en/transport-network/waterways/canals-and-bridges/the-saimaa-canal). At the time of writing, because of the ongoing conflict between Russia and Ukraine and the need to go through Russian territory to access the canal, it is no longer accessible, but the guidance has been left in the pilot in the hope that this situation changes during the life of this edition.

There are many beautiful and interesting harbours in Finland and it is only possible in this guide to mention a small selection of them.

# KEY INFORMATION

## Rescue/Safety services

**Emergency** ✆ 112 (no area code required). Applicable to all emergencies. Calls answered in English as well as Finnish or Swedish.

**Maritime rescue alarm** ✆+358 294 1000

**International distress frequencies:**
VHF-DSC Ch 70
**MRCC Turku Rescue Radio** and **MRCC Helsinki Rescue Radio** monitor VHF Ch 16/70, MF DSC 2187.5kHz. Call Sign '**Rescue Centre Turku**' or '**Helsinki**'.

In Finland, the Border Guard is the lead SAR authority and responsible for coordinating all SAR activity. Finland's Search and Rescue Region (SRR) extends beyond Finland's territorial waters into international waters bordering the SRRs of Sweden, Russia and Estonia.

The SRR is divided into two so-called Search and Rescue Sub-Regions (SRS). The West Finland Coast Guard is responsible for maritime SAR operations in the West Finland Search and Rescue Sub-Region, with missions coordinated by the Turku Maritime Rescue Coordination Centre (MRCC), under the command of the Coast Guard Headquarters. The Gulf of Finland Coast Guard District is responsible for the Gulf of Finland Rescue Sub-Region (RSR), with missions coordinated by the Helsinki Maritime Rescue Sub-Centre (MRSC Helsinki).

In Finland, MRCCs receive distress messages by telephone and via the Global Maritime Distress Safety System (GMDSS). Contact between the MRCCs and both vessels in distress or danger and the subsidiary and maritime SAR units operating at sea takes place via the marine VHF radio distress and working channels, and digital selective calling (DSC).

Finland's Maritime Search and Rescue: **raja.fi/en/maritime-search-and-rescue**

## Charts and chart packs

UKHO Admiralty charts are useful for passage planning and offshore navigation, but the large-scale official Finnish charts are essential in order to enjoy the delights of cruising inside the archipelago. Details of Finnish charts are available at **www.traficom.fi/en/finnish-nautical-charts-portfolio**.

**Finnish small-scale charts with a scale of 1:100 000 to 1:500 000 for Sea Areas around Finland**
Gulf of Bothnia: 958 (Bay of Bothnia), 957 (Kvarken), 955 (Southern Sea of Bothnia), 956 (Northern Sea of Bothnia)
Archipelago Sea: 953, 935 (Sea of Åland).
Western Gulf of Finland: 952.
Eastern Gulf of Finland: 951.

**Coastal charts at 1:50 000 scale**
Gulf of Bothnia (chart numbers: 40–60)
Archipelago Sea (chart numbers: 23–37)
Gulf of Finland (chart numbers: 13–22)

**Chart folios**
Packs with 25 pages, at 1:50 000 scale. These are also known as *Merikattasarjo* (Finnish) or *Sjörtsserie* (Swedish) and are less expensive than coastal charts. These are strongly recommended. Chart folios are updated approximately every 4 or 5 years according to a schedule. Besides the normal 1:50 000 chart sheets, there are many special charts included in the series. These are essential for navigation in the labyrinthine archipelagos.

The chart folios have letters:
A Vyborg – Helsinki
B Helsinki – Parainen
C Åland Islands
D Turku Archipelago
E Sea of Bothnia
F The Kvarken
G Bay of Bothnia
S Saimaa Canal
L Lappeenranta – Savonlinna
(Lake Saimaa)
M Savonlinna – Kuopio (Lake Saimaa)

## Pilots and cruising guides

*Suuri Satamakirja (Stora Hamnboken)* series in four volumes, shows over 450 anchorages and all the major and minor harbours. Much of the text is in Finnish/Swedish but the book is still valuable because of the good chart drawings and photographs. Only one book is in English/German: *The Great Harbour Book IV*.
**www.satamakirja.fi**

**SH1**: Numbered harbours in *Vol 1 Turun Saaristo (Åbo Skägård)*

**SH2**: Numbered harbours in *Vol 2 Ahvenanmaa (Åland)*

**SH3**: Numbered harbours in *Vol 3 Suomenlahti (Finska Viken)* (Gulf of Finland)

**SH Bottenhavet**: Numbered harbours in *Pohjanlahti (Bottenhavet)* (Gulf of Bothnia, Sweden and Finland)

**GHB**: Numbered harbours in *The Great Harbour Book IV*. 145 natural and guest harbours from Sweden, Finland and Estonia published in English and German

**FMA**: Numbered harbours in *Käyntisatamat-Besökshamnar*. Published yearly in mid May, it gives accurate, up-to-date information on all the harbours along the Finnish coastline (including the Archipelago Sea) and their services, presenting them in an easy-to-use, symbol-based format, which can be read in English, Finnish, Swedish and German. The numbers of the harbours in the packs correlate to the numbers on the charts in the chart folios, increasing from east to west, making route planning and refuge seeking fast, easy and convenient. Distance diagrams of all the chart series are shown to help planning schedules and routes

**SKS**: Numbered harbours in the *Saaiman Käyntisatamat Besökshamnar*, published yearly. It has the same format as above and covers the Saimaa Lake. It also gives instructions for small boat traffic in the Saimaa Canal in several languages including English

*Åland Gasthafen*, is available in Swedish, Finnish and German. It has excellent aerial photos and plans of most of the harbours and anchorages in the Åland Islands. It is widely available for sale in most information offices and harbours and is very popular with the locals.

## Time

Clocks change in line with the EU's daylight saving schedule, meaning that daylight saving time is observed from the last Sunday in March (0200 CET) to the last Sunday in October (0300 CET).

## € Money

Finland uses the Euro. Major credit and debit cards are universally accepted. Finland is close to being a cashless society although nearly all banks have ATMs.

## Formalities

Finland is a member of the EU and is part of the Schengen area, so if you have already cleared in there are no further formalities (see page 9 for further details of the Schengen requirements). Visas are not required for EU passport holders.

The Frontier Guard (Finnish *Rajavartiolaitos*, Swedish *Gränsbevakningsväsendet*) is the national security agency which is responsible for border crossings and passport control. For current regulations on formalities such as clearance, immigration, customs and restrictions visit
**raja.fi/en/guidelines-for-travellers**

A yacht coming directly from another Schengen country need not report to a passport control point nor is it required to sail within the official channels to the nearest Passport Control station.

All crew members must carry their passport or national ID card. A crew list signed by the captain is required if transiting the Saimaa Canal.

Foreign yachts arriving in Finland from a non-Schengen country must keep to the official Customs routes, and report to the nearest coastguard station or Port of Entry along the channel. The passport control station should be alerted by VHF Ch 68/16 or by telephone, approximately one hour before arrival.

When sailing between Finland and a non-Schengen country (e.g. Russia), a yacht always has to go to the passport control point and file a Customs declaration. A clearance declaration is issued on completion of formalities and this must be shown to the authorities at the port of departure.

Visas are required for visitors from and to Russia (also Kaliningrad).

Finnish Customs ✆+358 9 6141
**www.tulli.fi**

The Finnish Embassy in London is at 38 Chesham Place, London SW1X 8HW, ✆+44 20 7838 6200. Visas by appointment only: appointment.lon@formin.fi

Since 2015, all Schengen visa applicants will be requested to submit their biometric data, including fingerprints and a digital photograph.
sanomat.lon@formin.fi
www.finemb.org.uk/en

The **British Embassy** in Helsinki is located at Itäinen Puistotie 17, 00140 Helsinki, ✆+358 9 2286 5100.
**www.gov.uk/world/organisations/british-embassy-helsinki**
info.helsinki@fcdo.gov.uk

In addition there are **Honorary British Consuls** in a number of the larger towns and cities, including Mariehamn (now a Consulate General), Turku, Kotka and Vaasa, Tampere, Rovaniemi, Oulu, Kuopio.

Finnish Border Guard
✆+358 295 420000
**raja.fi/en**
(for Border crossing points information and telephone numbers)

For EU boats, proof of VAT status is required and also the Ship's Radio Licence. One member of the crew must have a radio operator's certificate of competence. An EU-registered boat on which VAT has been paid can be kept in Finland indefinitely. A non-EU registered boat can stay in the country for up to 18 months, but a bond may be payable whilst over-wintering and Customs should be notified before the yacht comes ashore.

The yacht is expected to carry standard safety equipment, but as of 2010 there is no requirement for the skipper to hold the International Certificate of Competence or any other formal qualification.

Sailing whilst under the influence of alcohol is an offence under Finnish law, and the authorities can (and do) stop a vessel at sea to check the alcohol levels of both the skipper and whoever is at the helm.

The Finnish flag is white with a blue Scandinavian cross; the Åland flag blue with a red cross on a yellow cross. Although the Åland Islands are administered by Finland they value their separate identity and the 'border' between the Åland islands and the rest of Finland is marked by the *Kihti* (Swedish *Skiftet*), a deep channel running north-south approximately along longitude 21°07'E. The Åland flag should be flown in Finnish waters west of this line and the Finnish flag in the rest of Finland. Never fly the two flags together.

## Public holidays

Official public holidays in Finland include:
1 Jan, 6 Jan (Epiphany), Good Friday, Easter Sunday and Monday, 1 May (May Day), Ascension Day (May), Midsummer's Eve and Day (third weekend in June), 1 Nov (All Saints' Day), All Saints' Day (Saturday between 31 Oct and 6 Nov), 6 Dec (Independence Day), 24–26 Dec (Christmas).

Local festivals and other events are held in many towns throughout the summer, listed in the Finland Festivals booklet and on line at **www.festivals.fi**

## ✆ Communications

The telephone country code for Finland is +358, and if dialling from abroad the initial 0 of the area code is not required.

The Finnish telephone system is excellent with extensive mobile coverage. Most telephone kiosks have been removed. For international calls dial +, followed by the country code, area code (omitting any initial 0) and number.

Internet access is widespread, with free terminals in almost every public library and excellent mobile coverage for data purposes. Other options are included in the text for each harbour. It is essential to quote the correct postcode when addressing mail to Finland.

### ✈ Travel

Helsinki has good communications by **air** with all parts of Europe, and Mariehamn and Turku can be reached from Stockholm and Helsinki. There are many daily **ferry** services linking Helsinki with Turku, Mariehamn, Stockholm and other destinations, including Tallinn in Estonia. The rail/ferry and coach/ferry services to Europe are good, as is the rail service within Finland.

A **train** service links Helsinki to St Petersburg, for which **coaches** also depart several times each day. There are also five sailings weekly by **ferry** to St Petersburg and travelling this way there is no need for a Russian visa for up to a 48hr visit. At the time of writing of this edition, visits to Russia (and the Finnish Saimaa lakes region via the Saimaa Canal) are not viable due to the ongoing conflict with Ukraine, but advice and information has been left in the pilot, in the event that circumstances change during the life of this edition.

### Websites

Seemingly everyone in Finland has their own website, and this is certainly true of nearly all companies and government organisations. The following are just the tip of the iceberg and even brief use of an internet search engine will uncover hundreds more.

The following websites are of particular interest to sailors visiting Finland:

**www.visitsaaristo.net** – The harbour plans and numbers are the same as in the Käyntisatamat-Besökshamnar (see above)

**www.ymparisto.fi/en/nature-waters-and-seas/recreational-use-nature** – Everyman's right

**www.nationalparks.fi/en** – Information on National Parks

**www.sail-in-finland.info** – About sailing in Finland

**www.ilmatieteenlaitos.fi** – The website of the Finnish Meteorological Institute, containing everything from today's weather forecast to long term climate statistics

**www.visitfinland.com/en/** – The homepage of the Finnish Tourist Board

**www.finland-tourism.com** – The Official Online Travel Guide to Finland, maintained by the Finnish Tourist Board and containing much of direct relevance to visitors, including travel information and many useful links

**www.festivals.fi** – The website of the Finland Festivals organisation, with details of thousands of local festivals and events, all with relevant email and/or website addresses

**www.visitaland.com** – The official Åland tourist gateway website

**www.visitparainen.fi** – A well-constructed website covering the Turku archipelago (the Turunmaan saaristo or Åbolands skärgård) effectively those islands east of the Kihti (Skiftet)

**www.yachtclub.com/europe/scandinavianyc.html** – A useful site providing links to the homepages of most yacht clubs in Scandinavia and beyond

### WC Holding tanks

In Finnish waters, the discharge of untreated sewage is prohibited at a distance of less than 12M from the nearest land i.e. within their territorial waters. Although holding tanks are not compulsory for non-Finnish flagged yachts, it will be difficult to comply without this or some other method of avoiding discharge.

The availability of pump-out facilities compares well with other countries, and they can be found in most guest harbours and some anchorages.
**www.roopekartta.fi/map**

### Radio communications

Finland's VHF coast radio stations are extremely well organised and convenient to use, and all parts of the coastline have excellent coverage. All VHF stations are remotely controlled from Turku (see map page ix).

### ❄ Weather information

Weather bulletins are broadcast in English at 0633 and 1833 UT on Turku Radio on VHF Ch 70. Gale warnings are broadcast on receipt and at 0233, 0633, 1033, 1433, 1833 and 2233 UT. See **www.fintraffic.fi/en/maritime_traffic/maritime-traffic-services/maritime-safety-radio** for full details including all the working channels.

### RESTRICTED AREAS

There are 17 Restricted Areas in Finnish waters, some of which contain smaller Military Areas and all of which are marked on current Finnish charts. They range in size from a single island to an area west of Helsinki measuring, at its extremes, some 29 by 30·5km. Although movement within Restricted Areas is no longer forbidden or even limited, certain activities are, in particular scuba diving and bottom fishing (though use of a rod or a towed line appears quite acceptable). Pleasure craft under 24m can anchor where they wish. No Military Area may be approached within 100m unless within a marked fairway. These regulations apply to all, regardless of nationality. Further details can be found on the Finnish Defence Forces website at **www.mil.fi**

In addition to the Restricted Areas, there are Conservation Areas – most often to ensure that breeding birds remain undisturbed – where limitations on movement and/or anchoring may be in force for part of the year. Like the Restricted Areas they are clearly marked on the Finnish charts and should be rigorously observed.

## THE COUNTRY

Finland is a varied country culturally and historically. Some key facts (some useful and some not!) about Finland:

- Finland has a population of just over 5.5 million and 1.3 million of them live in Helsinki. It is the most sparsely populated country in Europe
- Finns consumes 12kg of coffee per year per person- the second-highest consumption per capita in the world, so you can always find a good coffee
- Finland has 187,888 lakes which are larger than 500m$^2$. 57,000 of them have an area larger than 10,000m$^2$
- The Moomins are Finnish. Author Tove Jansson (1914–2001)was also a well-known Finnish artist and illustrator and lived every summer on the island of Klovharun in the Porvoo archipelago with her partner Tuulikki Pietilä. Fans of the Moomins can visit Moominworld at Naantali
- The Finns are sauna-mad – there are an estimated 3.3 million saunas for a population of 5.6 million
- Finland has nearly 87,000 square miles of forest – this is 74% of the land in Finland
- The Finns love heavy metal, they have more heavy metal bands per capita than any other country in the world

It is also a beautiful country known by the Finns as *Suomi*, 'the land of lakes and fens'. It has a narrow coastal plain, which supports most of the population and farming. Further inland there is a rocky, forested plateau some 100m above sea level where the wildlife is largely undisturbed. The plateau, also known as the Finnish Lakeland, contains about 188,000 lakes, which drain westwards into the Gulf of Bothnia and south into the Gulf of Finland. Lake Saimaa is the fourth largest lake in Europe.

The Lappi uplands of the far north comprise a third of the total country. Life in Lapland is difficult to sustain because most of it is boggy in the summer and extremely cold in the winter. Reindeer herding and tourism support a limited population.

The highly indented Baltic coastline is fringed with thousands of islands, including the remarkable Archipelago Sea, between continental Finland and the main island of Åland, and also the Kvarken (Quark(en)) which stretch more than halfway across the Gulf of Bothnia towards Sweden. All together there are 75,818 islands with an area of over 0.5km$^2$ in Finland. If you take into account all the other smaller islands, the total number is 178,947. 549 of these are permanently inhabited and have no road connection to mainland.

As with north Sweden, much of the geography of Finland can be explained by the Ice Age. The glaciers were thicker and lasted longer in this part of Europe. Having been compressed under the enormous weight of the glaciers, the land is still rising about 9mm a year in the Kvarken area and 4mm in the south of Finland due to 'post-glacial rebound'. In fact, the surface area of Finland is expanding by about 7km$^2$ annually.

The Moominhouse at Moomin World – Naantali near Turku
*Andy Beharrell*

Finland is a parliamentary republic with a central government based in the capital, Helsinki.

Since its independence from Russia in 1917, Finland has developed into a Nordic-style welfare state, resulting in widespread prosperity. It has one of the highest per capita incomes in the world.

Finland today is a top performer in education, economic competitiveness, civil liberties, quality of life and human development. In 2023 Finland was ranked fifth in the World Press Freedom Index and sixth in the Human Capital Index. According to the 2023 Fragile States Index it was just above Iceland and Norway making it the third most stable country in the world.

The largest sector in the economy is services (69.1%), followed by manufacturing (28.2%). Within this electronics, machinery, vehicles and other engineered metal products make up 21%, the forest industry 13% and chemicals 11%. Forests play a key role in the country's economy, making it one of the world's leading wood producers and providing raw materials for the crucial wood-processing industries.

## The people, the church & the language

Finnish and Swedish are the official languages in Finland.

Finland is home to several distinct ethnic groups and at least three major languages. The majority of Finns speak Finnish as their native tongue while Swedish is spoken in some coastal areas and mostly in the autonomous region of Åland. The Sami language is the official language in northern Lapland. In many places road signs, as well as names on street maps, will be in more than one language.

Finnish is an agglutinative language, part of the Uralic language family, related to Hungarian and very difficult to master. Lacking the common Latin or Teutonic origins of the majority of European languages it appears totally alien to most visitors – almost no words can be guessed, even when seen written. Fortunately, the excellent Finnish educational system means that almost everyone, from marina staff through to bus drivers, speaks passable and often fluent English (and often German and/or French as well).

Swedish is somewhat easier to understand and, again, almost all Swedish-speaking Finns also speak excellent English. Although the national percentage is relatively small, a disproportionate number of Finnish yachtsmen come from this group and several of the major yacht clubs consider a good command of Swedish to be an essential requirement for membership. Even so, the visitor should be aware that Swedish-speaking Finns are very definitely Finns and not Swedes, even in the Åland Islands where Swedish is the official language, spoken by up to 90% of the population.

The Samis (Lapps) live in the northern part of the country so are unlikely to be encountered by cruising yachtsmen unless travelling inland. The Lappish language (which has several distinct variants) is related to Finnish, as is their culture. Although the Samis of Finland now number no more than 7,000, they maintain close links with those resident in Norway, Sweden and Russia.

There are two national churches, Lutheran and Eastern Orthodox, with 75% of Finns belonging to the former.

## History

The earliest inhabitants of Finland are the Sami people, previously called Laplanders, who are believed to have been living in the Arctic regions of Norway, Finland and Russia since the end of the Ice Age at around 10000BCE. They continue to maintain their traditional way of life as fishermen or by herding reindeer, as much as modern civilisation will allow.

They arrived around 3000BCE and for much of their history had little contact with their Germanic or Slavic neighbours. By the Middle Ages, the huge areas of forest, lakes and marshlands kept them living as farmers in small self-regulating communities. There was no central power-base to coordinate the country as a whole.

Remote anchoring *T. Fooks*

Contact with Sweden had been growing since Viking times, as southern Finland was on the Viking's route through Russia to Constantinople. Christianity started to arrive in the 11th century and was consolidated in the Catholic Northern Crusades by the Swedes and Dominican monks who arrived in 1249. Many Swedes came to settle in Finland. Turku in the southwest became a larger Swedish city than any in Sweden itself. Meanwhile Russian Novgorod established its influence and its Orthodox church in Karelia in eastern Finland.

Finland was increasingly seen as a part of Sweden, and this was formally established in 1362 when Finnish representatives were invited to help elect a new Swedish king. In the following centuries, Finns paid Swedish taxes, provided soldiers for Swedish armies and became Lutheran when Sweden did. Many new cities were built, notably Helsinki in 1550 under the name Helsingfors.

During the 17th century Sweden encouraged settlement of the empty wilderness of central Finland which came at the expense of the Sami nomads. The Lutheran requirement that everyone should be able to read the bible greatly increased literacy and education. The 18th century saw improved Finnish farming, increased trade and greater prosperity for most Finnish peasants.

Then in 1809 Sweden lost a war with Russia who took Finland as a Grand Duchy under the Tsar until the Russian Revolution of 1917. It was only under the Russians that Finns began to think of themselves as a nation, spurred on by the Tsar's 'Russification' policy. In 1835 the poem Kalevala was published and became the national epic, and by 1900 Sibelius had written Finlandia. The piece of music was a covert protest against Russian censorship and so initially had to be performed under alternative names at concerts. It was sometimes called *Happy Feelings at the awakening of Finnish Spring*, and sometimes *A Scandinavian Choral March*. But Russia also provided a market for Finland's developing industry and training for Finland's soldiers.

Following the 1917 Russian revolution, Finland declared its independence and this was accepted by the Bolsheviks. A substantial number of rural and industrial workers wanted Finland to follow Russia's socialist ideals, however, and there followed a bitter civil war that lasted a year before the 'Whites', proponents of a Finnish democratic mixed economy, prevailed.

Between the World Wars there were a number of reforms to make Finland more egalitarian. By the 1930s Stalin had clearly changed his mind about Finnish independence. In 1939 the secret Molotov-Ribbentrop pact between Russia and Germany put Finland and the Baltic states under the Russian 'sphere of influence'. Stalin wanted to station troops in Finland. Marshal Mannerheim refused and led Finland in a heroic defence in the 1939–40 Winter War. Then Hitler offered to help. Mannerheim succeeded in walking the very narrow path required to keep the Russians out without being overrun by Germany or becoming involved in any of Hitler's other objectives. In 1944 Germany was clearly losing in Europe, and Mannerheim fought the Lapland War to remove the remaining German troops from north Finland. Then as president he negotiated the peace with the USSR, giving as little away as possible while still maintaining trading relations.

In the 1990s Mannerheim was voted the greatest Finn ever. He was also a fastidious gourmet and inventor of the Marskyn Ryyppy (Marshal's tipple) – aquavit, gin and Noilly Pratt, filling the glass to 1mm below the rim and to be drunk in three gulps without toasts or spillage!

Finland joined the EU in 1995 and in 2002 the Euro replaced the Finnish markka. For a long time Finland remained resolutely outside NATO and in a 2016 poll 61% of Finns preferred not to join the NATO alliance. However, the balance of opinion changed rapidly with the Russian invasion of Ukraine in 2022. In April 2023 Finland became the 31st member of NATO. The uneasy relationship with Russia has led to increased tensions around Baltic waters and in November 2023 Finland temporarily closed its entire border with Russia.

The beauty of remote anchorages *John Langdon*

# CRUISING AND GENERAL INFORMATION

## Yacht services & chandleries

Throughout Finland, visitors' marinas are indicated by a white anchor on a blue background and the words 'Vierassatama', 'Gästhamn' or 'Guest Harbour' - or occasionally all three. There are numerous good boatyards and a chandlery at most harbours of any size, though probably the largest and best-stocked ones are to be found at Uusikaupunki, Mariehamn, Turku, Hanko and, of course, Helsinki.

## Gas

Propane gas (LPG) is the most widely available. Some suppliers will also have butane gas. International Campinggaz (ICG) cylinders can be exchanged at Mariehamn East (at STI fuel station near harbour), at Hanko, at the NJK harbour in Helsinki and at HSK Lauttassaari, Helsinki (www.hoski.fi). The main problem that you will encounter is that Sweden, Norway and Finland all have different connectors. Swedish cylinders can be exchanged for Finnish cylinders at the STI fuel station in Mariehamn East, and at the NJK in Helsinki. It is virtually impossible to refill non-Finnish cylinders but OY Interenergy, near Lohja, might be worth a try(www.pressocenter.com)

## Diesel

Diesel is obtainable at nearly all marinas, often together with a station at which a holding-tank can be emptied. There is a bio component additive of 12% on all diesel (for marine or road use). The original biofuels obligation in Finland called for 19.5% for the bio component, but this was reduced to 12% in 2022 with the sharp rise in fuel prices.

## Shopping

There are many well-stocked supermarkets as well as small local shops throughout the coastal area of Finland. Prices are generally higher than in England.

## Alcohol

Beer with an alcohol content of less than 4.8% is available in supermarkets and other shops, but full-strength beer (4.9–8%), wines and spirits can only be purchased at branches of ALKO, the national alcoholic beverage retailing monopoly in Finland, which are generally only found in the main towns. The location of all the ALKO stores is available on www.alko.fi/en/shops-services. In both supermarkets and ALKO stores, prices are higher than in the UK.

## Yacht clubs

The principal club is the Nylandska Jaktklubben (NJK - www.njk.fi/klubben/briefly-in-english), which has a fine clubhouse in Helsinki including a marina which welcomes visiting yachts. It also owns a number of islands and anchorages where its members enjoy their privacy.

The Finnish Cruising Club (Merikarhut, or Sea Bears - www.merikarhut.fi/english-page) also owns islands and anchorages for the exclusive use of its members.

## The cruising season

Finland has an even shorter cruising season than Sweden, and it should be noted that some services are only provided between mid-June and mid-August, if that. The numbers of Finnish cruising yachts are already falling off by the third week of July and decreases markedly by early August. By late August most local yachts are sailing in local home waters or already laid up ashore.

## Private islands

Most smaller islands in Finland and Åland are privately owned, many sporting one single house and most likely a sauna, and although anchoring off seems to cause no problems it is polite to do so out of sight of the house (and sauna). The owners of islands guard their privacy jealously and using a private jetty is not allowed.

It is important that you adhere to the Everyman's Right basic rules, which grant you the right to roam in the countryside. A very good article on anchoring and landing restrictions in Finland has been published online (www.sail-in-finland.info/2015/01/anchoring-landing-restrictions-finland/).

Even on private land, you do not need the landowner's permission, and there is no charge. However, you must not damage the environment or disturb others while exercising public access rights. For more information on the Everyman's Right have a look at the advice on the Visit Finland website (www.visitfinland.com/en/articles/finnish-everyman-rights-the-right-to-roam/).

## Online information

The website Visit Saaristo (www.visitsaaristo.net/en) has information on most of the harbours in Finland and is worth researching for each of the locations listed in this section. The left-hand side of the page lists all the harbours, or simply scroll around the map and click on the harbour you are looking at.

For tourist information the Visit Finland website (www.visitfinland.com/en) is an excellent reference source for many towns in Finland and towns will often have their own tourist information site.

# 3A. THE FINNISH COAST OF THE GULF OF BOTHNIA

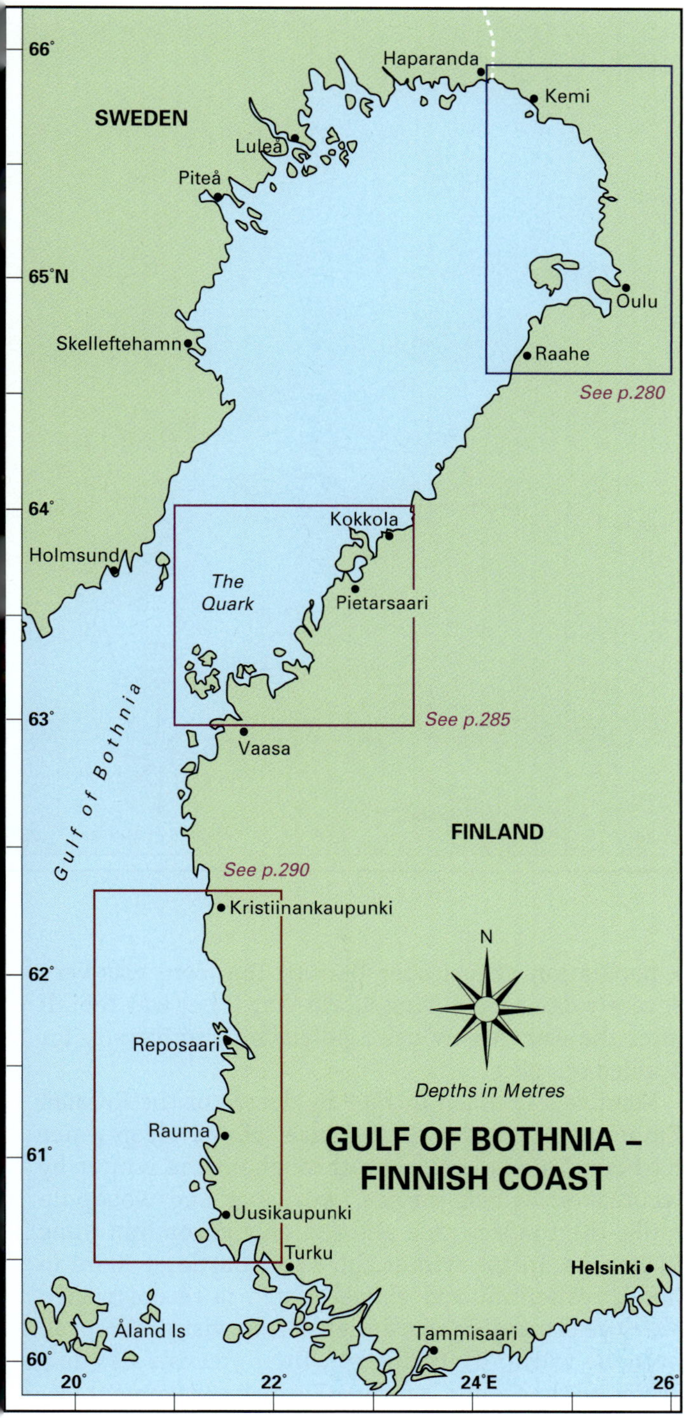


The following section has been arranged from north to south, assuming that most yachts in the Gulf of Bothnia will have sailed north along the Swedish coast. The Gulf of Bothnia on the Finnish side is divided into three areas:

1. Bottenviken or Bay of Bothnia to the north between Tornio and Kalajoki
2. Kvarken or (Quark(en)) between Kalajoki and Kaskinen
3. Bottenhavet or the Sea of Bothnia in the south between Kaskinen and Uusikaupunki.

Heading south from Tornio there are many small harbours or *gästhamns* and several important towns of interest: Kemi, Oulu and Raahe in the north; Kokkola, Pietarsaari (home of Nautor and Baltic yachts) and Vaasa in the Kvarken; Kristiinankaupunki, Pori (with its world famous jazz festival), Rauma and Uusikaupunki further south. The coastline is mostly flat with shallow water necessitating careful passage-making at a considerable distance from the coast. There are many small skerries dotted around the northern part of the Gulf of Bothnia (Bottenviken) between Tornio and Kemi, around Oulu and Raahe.

In the Kvarken, extensive skerries reach almost all the way across to the Swedish coast. Many of them are nature reserves. Further south in the Bottenhavet, the skerries are close to the shore. These areas do not necessarily provide good shelter.

### *Navigational charts & harbour guides*

*Note* Many harbours described in this section have a reference number labelled (xxx) which corresponds to the harbour guides below. However, some of the numbers may change over time.

**Planning charts (1:250,000)**
F958 (Perämeri) Bay of Bothnia
F957 (Merenkurkku) The Quark
F955 (Southern Sea of Bothnia)
F956 (Northern Sea of Bothnia)

**Chart folios (1:50,000)**
E-Selkämeri/Bottenhavet (Sea of Bothnia)
F-Merenkurkku/Kvarken (The Quark)
G-Perämeri/Bottenviken (Bay of Bothnia)

**Harbour guides**
*The Great Harbour Book – Bottenhavet* (**GHB** *xxx*)

*Käyntisatamat/Besökshamnar* guide to 511 harbours on the Finnish coast (the numbers of the harbours in the book correspond with the numbers on the charts, **FMA** *xxx*).

### *Lights*

**Kokkolan Majakka** 63°59'.8N 22°51'.7E, Fl(2)WRG.10s23m12M (Racon T)
**Vaasan Majakka light** 63° 14'.35N 20° 55'.6E, Fl(2)WRG.10s, Racon (T)

## 1. BAY OF BOTHNIA: TORNIO TO RAAHE

**Distance**
Tornio to Raahe: 120M

**Charts / harbour guides**
Merikarttasarja–G Perämeri/Bottenviken
Rannikkokartat 59, 58, 57, 56, 55

The northeast (Finnish) corner of the Bay of Bothnia is a shallow area which can be inhospitable in bad weather. Extensive shoals often call for long diversions. However, this coast is very well charted and recommended routes are shown, along with the minimum depth to be expected. The many transits and buoys make navigation straightforward. Care should also be taken with the water depth in this area which is affected by the currents flowing between the North Sea and the Baltic Sea, atmospheric pressure and wind direction. Depending on the direction and strength of the wind, depths can vary by up to 2m. The strongest variations in water levels in the Baltic Sea are to be found in the Gulf of Bothnia and the Gulf of Finland.

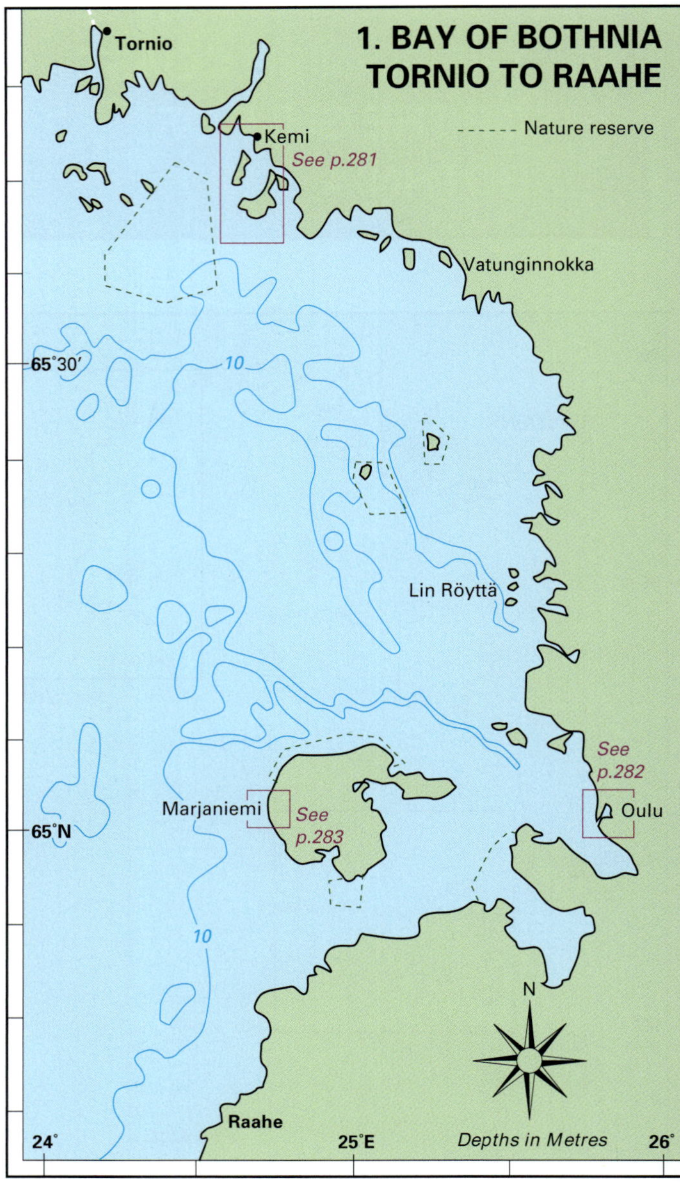


## KOIVULUODONLETTO

65°45.9N 24°13'.7E (south mole)

**Charts / harbour guides**
**GHB** *117*

This is the first small harbour to the east of Tornio (the border between Sweden and Finland) deep enough for sailing boats up to 3.5m draught. There are pontoons with water and electricity; six bows-to spaces from stern buoys and four finger pontoons in 3-3.5m; pumpout station and sauna. There are walks through the woods and marshlands.

Approach from the southeast on the transit at Kiuasletto to avoid a rock awash 0.2M southeast of the harbour entrance.

## KEMI

65°43'.7N 24°33'.2E (south mole)

**Distance**
Tornio 20M

**Charts / harbour guides**
**GHB** *116* **FMA** *1964*

**Contacts**
www.visitkemi.fi
www.kemi.fi
www.kemi.fi/vapaa-aika-ja-kulttuuri/matkailu/vierassatama

Kemi is a town near the city of Tornio in the Lapland region. It is at the mouth of the river Kemijoki and has a population of just over 19,000. The town was very severely damaged during World War II but was rebuilt after the war. It now has a polytechnic university for applied sciences.

Kemi was founded in 1869 by decree of the Russian Emperor Alexander II because of its deep-water harbour. This is kept open throughout the winter by icebreakers which service two paper and woodpulp mills, the timber trade and the only chromium mine in Europe. In the winter the Snow Castle of Kemi (a hotel, restaurant and chapel which is reconstructed every year to a different design) draws visitors from all over the world. If visiting in winter you can also do a cruise on the Sampo, a former Finnish government ice-breaker that offers cruises on the Gulf of Bothnia. This is probably better than trying the same on your own boat!

The commercial and ferry port is on the peninsula of Ajos 6.5km to the south.

Kemi can be approached from the west following the transit (083°) between Selkäsaari to the south and Kojukallio to the north (2.4m). If approaching from the

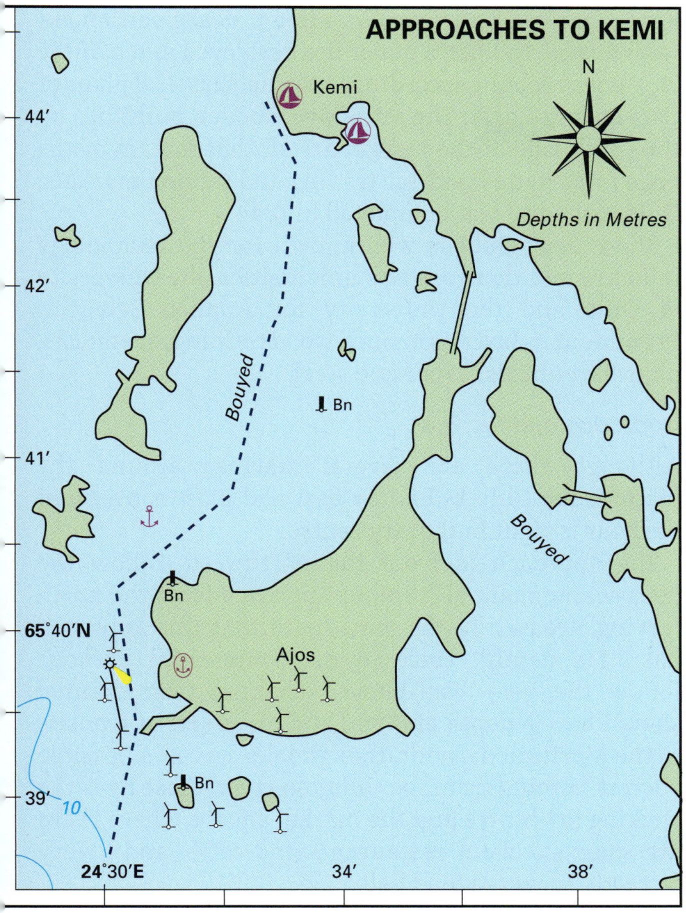


south (10m deep water channel) past the commercial harbour to the west of the Ajos peninsula, follow the well-buoyed channel towards the marina. The final approach (011°) has a transit (church spire and Mansikkanokka light). The well-sheltered *gästhamn* provides 20 berths, some bows-to and some with stern buoys in 2.4m which are ahead of you when you enter the harbour. The water is slightly deeper around the berths with stern buoys.

The local yacht clubs with their restaurants, saunas and other services provide visitors with every facility during the high season.

Waste disposal, pump out station, electricity, mast crane, boat ramp, liquid gas, fuel (only diesel), recycling, toilets, sauna, showers, drinking water, laundry room, restaurant, cafeteria, playground, campfire pits, guiding services.

Many more shops and restaurants are to be found in the town centre about 1km away. It is about a twenty-minute walk to the train station (stop on the Helsinki-Lapland line). Trains to Rovaniemi, to Arktikum Museum, Pilke (Forestry Museum), and Korundi (Art Gallery). A discounted ticket for all three is available.

## VATUNGINNOKKA

65°33′N 25°06′.7E (south mole)

**Distance**
Kemi 26M

**Charts / harbour guides**
**GHB** *109* **FMA** *1938*
www.ii.fi

This is a safe harbour on an exposed coast, and is easily identified by the surrounding wind turbines. Straightforward entrance from the west-southwest with a lit transit (78°).

Approach from the west, leaving Samulinmatala to the south. Beware of the fish farms in the area. The channel leading to the marina has a depth of 2.2m.

The small harbour has 10 finger pontoons in 2–4m, with good facilities, provided by the power company Vapo, and shared with the caravan site. There is a café and good walks around the area. It may be possible to buy fish from the fish farm on the south side. Fuel is available and there are showers, sauna, washing machine, water and electricity.

Sunset from Kemi marina *Robin Matthews*

Approaching Kemi *Robin Matthews*

The visitors berth at Röyttä *Fiona Slay*

## Röyttä

65°16'.2N 25°13'E (south mole)

**Distance**

Vatunginnokka 22M, Marjaniemi 32M

**Charts / harbour guides**

**GHB** *108* **FMA** *1927*

Röyttä is a popular excursion island and nature reserve. The substantial stone walls give excellent shelter in all winds. The island is looked after by the Finnish Forest and Parks Service and is part of a preservation area.

Röyttä was a loading port for the timber trade until 1960 and has also been an important base for fishing and a pilot station. The deepest approach is from the west, between Satakari and Röyttä through a well-buoyed channel. The marina has 40 visitor berths in 2–3m with stern buoys. Water and electricity on the pontoon. Several yacht clubhouses, one of which offers a sauna. There are limited facilities and no supplies but good walks on a very attractive island. It can become very crowded during Midsummer and harvest festivals.

There is a narrow-gauge track along the top of the southeast wall which is now used to trolley luggage to the many holiday homes.

## OULU (ULEÅBORG)

65°00'.9N 25°27'.5E (harbour mole, Market Square (Meritulli))

**Distance**

Röyttä 20M

**Charts / harbour guides**

**GHB** *99* **FMA** *1914*

Oulu, the capital of Northern Finland, is the fifth biggest town in Finland and the largest town in the region with a population of 200,000. It was founded in 1605, by King Charles IX of Sweden, after a peace settlement with Russia. In 1822, a major fire destroyed much of the city. It was rebuilt according to the neoclassical plans of Carl Ludvig Engel. The attractive wooden buildings on the south side of the market are all that remain of the once important wood-tar trading and salmon markets. Oulu cathedral was completed in 1844.

These days Oulu is well-known for the technology industry and there are two universities, the University of Oulu and the University for Applied Sciences. Prominent industries include wood refining, chemicals, pharmaceuticals, paper and steel.

### *Approach and facilities*

Although there are several marinas around the picturesque Oulu Delta, the best and most convenient harbour is right in the city centre.

The approach is from the northwest. Follow the deep-water channel (10m) or approach from the north leaving Kraaseli to the west (note that this approach has 1.8m depth). Once in the commercial harbour follow the very well-buoyed channel (the channel should have a depth of 3.3m) and three sets of transits to the Meritulli harbour, though take care of a possible current coming from the Oulujoki river. Close by is the striking art centre and the market square where there are some excellent restaurants and cafés, and a very attractive covered food hall.

There are 11 bows-to berths from stern buoys in 2.3m. Water and electricity on the pontoons. The showers, sauna, toilet facilities and washing machine are in a café at the corner of the Market Square, the Kahvilamakasiini (red granary), where you collect the key (against a deposit of €20). Convenient diesel pump (24h) on the quay (credit cards only). Pump out station.

Airport with several flights a day to Helsinki.

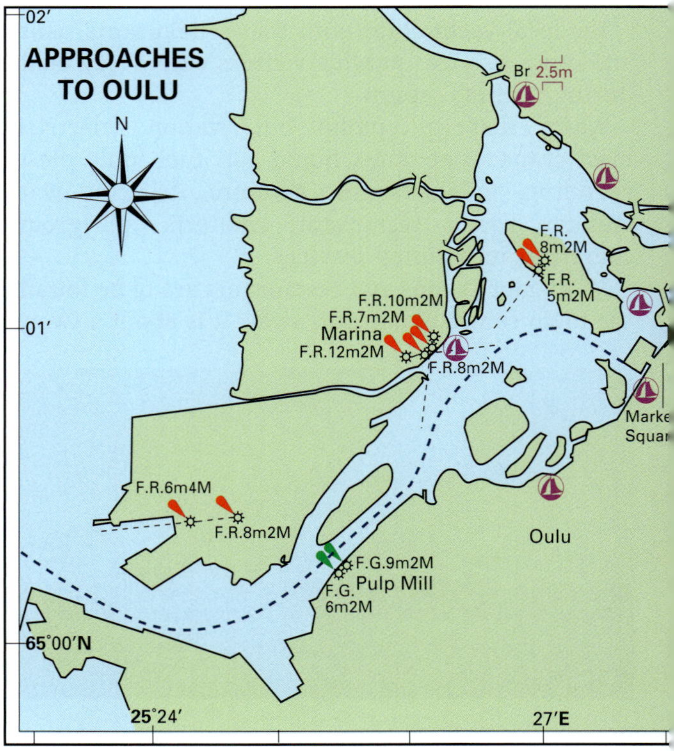

## MARJANIEMI, HAILUOTO

65°02'.4N 24°32'.8E (south mole, Hailuoto)

**Distance**
Oulu 33M, Kemi 58M, Röyttä 32M

**Charts / harbour guides**
**GHB** *94* **FMA** *1900*

**Contacts**
www.majakkapiha.fi/en/guest-harbor

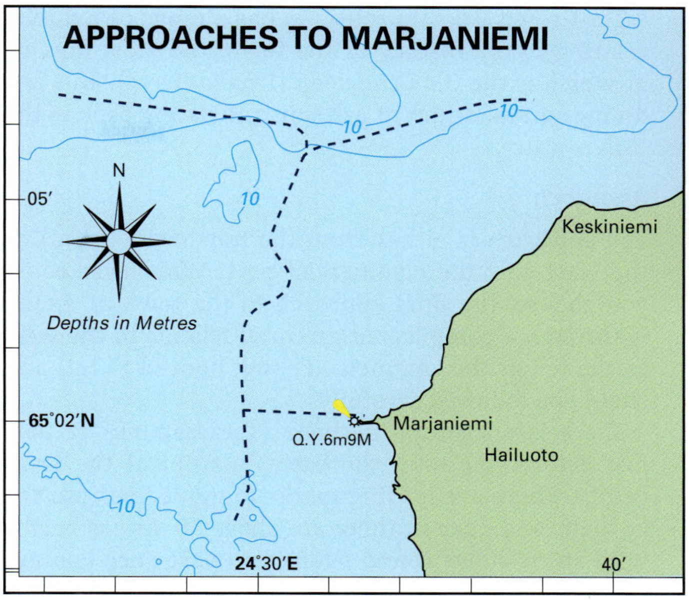


A safe harbour, protected by a mole, on the west coast of Hailuoto island, west of Oulu, this is the largest island in the Bay of Bothnia. The island was formed by post-glacial rebound (the land rising once the ice sheet melted) and is now the third largest island in Finland. It is getting slightly larger every year thanks to continuing land uplift.

The island is a popular holiday destination known for its extensive sandy beaches and attractive walks through the dunes and pine forests. The prominent lighthouse (25m high) and pilot station on Marjaniemi were built in 1871. Three wind turbines on the southern mole are visible from a long way off.

Marjaniemi is now a small fishing harbour with an active pilot station, campsite and *gästhamn* of up to 50 berths. The approach from the north is a winding route following designated fairways, including one very narrow channel between two buoys - don't attempt to take shortcuts. The approach is straightforward from the north-south coastal channel 4.2m past the island.

Moor bows-to from stern buoys or alongside pontoons in 4.1m. The Arctic Lighthouse Hotel, Cafe Kaija and Cafe Helmi are all nearby. Berthing fees are collected at Cafe Kaija near the marina. Water and power are available on the pontoons. It is sometimes possible to buy fish from the local processing shed.

The lighthouse at Marjaniemi *Fiona Slay*

There are good walks along the foreshore but the turnstones will protest if you stray a little too close to their nesting grounds. This is an excellent departure point if heading back west to the Swedish coast of the Gulf of Bothnia. Piteå, for example, is just under 80M and Bjuröklubb (further south) is just under 85M.

## RAAHE (BRAHESTAD)

64°41'.1N 24°27'.7E (south mole Terässatama guest harbour)

**Distance**
Oulu 41M, Marjaniemi 26M

**Charts / harbour guides**
**GHB** *91, 92* **FMA** *1876, 1868*

**Contacts**
www.visitraahe.fi
www.visitraahe.fi/museonrannan-vierasvenepaikat

Raahe has a great maritime history. Count Per Brahe, Queen Kristina's governor general in Finland, discovered Raahe harbour and founded the town with the name Salo in 1649. In the year of 1652 the name was changed to Brahestad and later to Raahe. Like many other wooden towns, Raahe was devastated by fire in 1810, and was rebuilt to new design principles with a rectilinear town plan featuring an unusual central square (known as Pekkatori). The British Navy then bombarded the harbour and burned down the shipyard during the Crimean War in 1854.

In the 1860s and 1870s, Raahe was the largest shipping town in Finland for about ten years. The wealth of that era has helped make the Old Town of Raahe one of the best-preserved wooden towns in Finland. Trade and shipping continued to be the main sources of income before the establishment of Rautaruukki steelworks in early 1960s.

The Crown Granary museum has a range of exhibits relating to the history of the town, the most famous of which is the *Old Gentleman* (*Wanha Herra*). This is a diving suit made out of calfskin and dating back to the 18th century.

### *Approach*

The approach is either from the northwest (2.4m) or the west past the commercial port. Whichever route you choose, the final approach to the town of Raahe is through a complicated group of islands to the west of the town. The channels are well buoyed (2.1m) and should be followed carefully.

There is a visitors' harbour (Terässatama) to port just before you enter the basin in front of the town centre. There are leading marks to guide you into the harbour and once in there are about 20 visitor berths with stern buoys round slightly to port once you are through the breakwaters, just after the first two jetties with Y-booms (for locals). Depths in the harbour are around 2.5m. It is a 3km walk to the town. Services include a 5T fixed harbour crane. The other harbour is the Ruiskuhuone pier at the Museum Quay, right in front of the town.

Alternatively you can moor alongside the town quay (Museonlaituri) near the Pakkahuoneen museum (www.visitraahe.fi/museonrannan-vierasvenepaikat). There are around 10 visitor berths here in a minimum of 2.5m of water. In quieter times it may be possible to go alongside the jetty. Services available include water, electricity, showers, supermarket, restaurants and a pharmacy.

Count Per Brahe, founder of many towns in Finland
*Robin Matthews*

## 2. THE KVARKEN: KOKKOLA TO VAASA

**Distances**
Raahe to Kokkola 75M, Kokkola to Vaasa 75M

**Charts / harbour guides**
Merikarttasarjat – F, Merenkurkku, Kvarken
Rannikkokartat 48 to 54

### The Finnish side of the Kvarken (Quark(en))

This covers a vast archipelago of 5,600 attractive islands stretching from Kokkola (Karleby) to Kaskinen (Kasko). The archipelago is characterized by unusual ridged washboard moraines. These are called 'De Geer moraines' and were formed when the continental ice sheet melted between 10,000 and 24,000 years ago.

This relatively narrower section of the Gulf of Bothnia separates the Bay of Bothnia (Bottenviken) in the north and the Sea of Bothnia (Bottenhavet) in the south. At its narrowest, the minimum distance from the outermost islands in the archipelago to the Swedish mainland is 25M and the depth is only 25m.

The Kvarken archipelago is a UNESCO World Heritage Site. The archipelago is continuously rising from the sea in a process of rapid glacio-isostatic uplift, whereby the land, previously weighed down under the weight of a glacier, lifts at rates that are among the highest in the world. As a consequence islands appear and unite, peninsulas expand, and lakes evolve from bays and develop into marshes and peat fens (whc.unesco.org/en/list/898/).

There are well-buoyed routes inshore of many of the islands. These, together with their minimum associated depths, are all well marked on the chart. Excellent transit marks make this much easier to cover than the charts might suggest.

### MAAKALLA

64°18'.87N 23°30'.96E (west mole)

**Distances**
Kokkola (Mustakari) 31M

**Contacts**
visitkalajoki.fi/en/be-active/in-the-wild/maakalla/

Maakalla is an attractive small island 30M north northeast of Kokkola. Anchoring is not recommended as the bottom is very rocky, but it is possible to moor on the jetty on the southeastern corner of the island. The jetties on the west are private for the local fishermen, but it may be possible to buy smoked fish from them. The jetty is used by the ferries bringing visitors during the day, but it is possible to berth between 1500 and

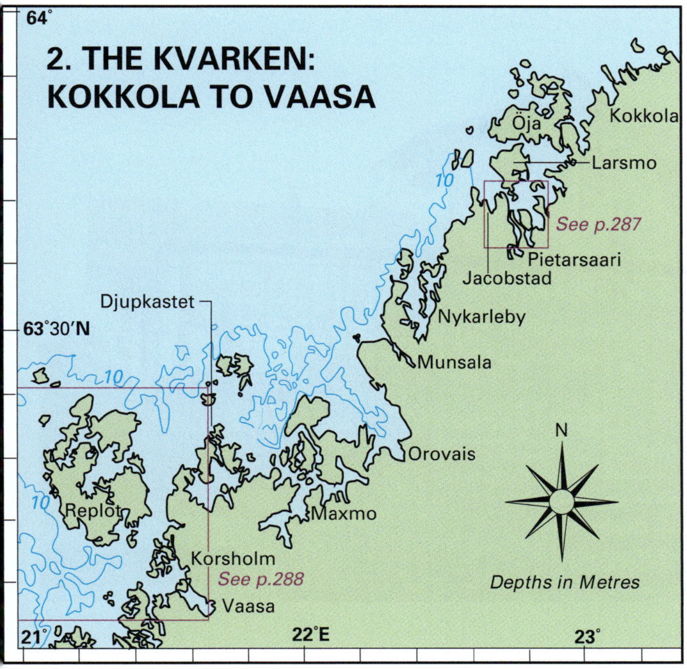


0930 the next morning. Approach carefully to avoid the rocks at the southern end of the jetty. The berths are hidden behind the rocky peninsula until the last moment of the approach.

## TANKAR

63°56'.9N 22°51'.1E (west mole)

**Distances**
Kokkola (Mustakari) 9M Loht

**Charts / harbour guides**
**GHB** *78* **FMA** *1752*

**Contacts**
www.visitkokkola.fi/en/the-lighthouse-island-of-tankar/the-guest-harbour/
www.tankar.fi
✆+358 41 545 3432

The church on Maakalla *Fiona Slay*

Tankar is a very attractive small island 9M northwest of Kokkola. It is a popular holiday destination, with a very prominent lighthouse, built in 1888, which is 27.5m high. The light element originally came from Henry Lepautre's factory in Paris and was the most powerful of its time (13M). Today it is still one of the brightest lighthouses in Finland and still has a pilot station.

It is worth visiting the sealing museum, which describes Tankar's historic way of life. The tiny church is booked throughout the summer for the celebration of weddings. The café and restaurant offers very good fresh food. There are fish-smoking boxes near the pontoon and a sauna.

Leave the charted route which passes very close to the eastern shore of the island when the entrance bears 252°. Make sure that you leave the E-cardinal buoy to port. There are 8–10 visitors moorings in 3m of water, bows-to from stern anchor or buoys. Berths can be booked in advance through www.satamapaikka.com (satamapaikka.com/?portfolio=tankar-vierassatama).

The lighthouse on Maakalla *Fiona Slay*

The lighthouse on Tankar *Fiona Slay*

The Gamlakarleby Segelförening clubhouse, Mustakari *Robin Matthews*

## KOKKOLA, MUSTAKARI

63°51'.8N 23°06'.8E (south mole)

**Distances**
Raahe 66M, Pietarsaari 28M

**Charts / harbour guides**
**GHB** *77* **FMA** *1768*

**Contacts**
www.kokkola.fi
www.mustakari.fi/8920/gasthamnen
www.visitkokkola.fi/en/

This is the largest harbour for visitors on the stretch of coast between Raahe and Pietarsaari. The island's name - Mustakari - literally translates as "Black Rock" and dates from the era when it was a shipyard. Remnants of tar can still occasionally be seen on the shore.

Mustakari lies in the northeastern corner of Kokkola. It is home to one of the oldest sailing clubs in the Gulf of Bothnia, the Gamlakarleby Segelförening (GSF) (www.mustakari.fi) founded in 1871. There is a very good restaurant in the beautifully-maintained wooden clubhouse which dates from 1908. There are moorings for visiting yachts in the southern part of the marina. The approach can be tricky in onshore winds. Facilities include showers, sauna, washing machine, pump out station, fuel. The town is around 3km away - a 30min walk.

### *Approach*

From the Kokkola light (Kokkolan Majakka 63°59'.8N 22°51'.7E) follow the main buoyed channel southeast towards the chimneys of the town before branching east just before reaching the island of Repskär (fairway buoys K8 and K9) towards the northern tip of Trullevi (63°55'N 23°04'.3E) to join the channel parallel to the Trullevi peninsula (three sets of transits) that leads southeast towards Mustakari. The channel is very shallow (2.5m) and great care is needed. Mustakari *gästhamn* has 50 berths bows-to from stern buoys in 2.5m.

During the Crimean War Kokkola was involved in a fight known as the 'Skirmish of Halkokari' in 1854, during which the Royal Marines from HMS Vulture and HMS Odin tried to come ashore and were repelled by the local population supported by Finnish troops and Russian military. One of the British gunboats fell into the hands of the local defenders. This boat can still be seen in Kokkola's English Park. The British Treasury pays for the maintenance of the graves of the nine Royal Marines who lost their lives.

Neristan is the old part of town with picturesque wooden houses and their 'gossip mirrors' - worth a look.

## PIETARSAARI

63°41'.4N 22°41'.5E (north quay, Smultrongrundet SSJ YC)

**Distances**
Kokkola 28M, Vaasa 70M

**Charts / harbour guides**
**GHB** *67, 68* **FMA** *1700, 1704*

**Contacts**
www.ssj.nu/en
✆+358 44 723 7940

Pietarsaari lies 28M southwest of Kokkola, inside a very dense and at times shallow archipelago. There are two recommended routes through the skerries.

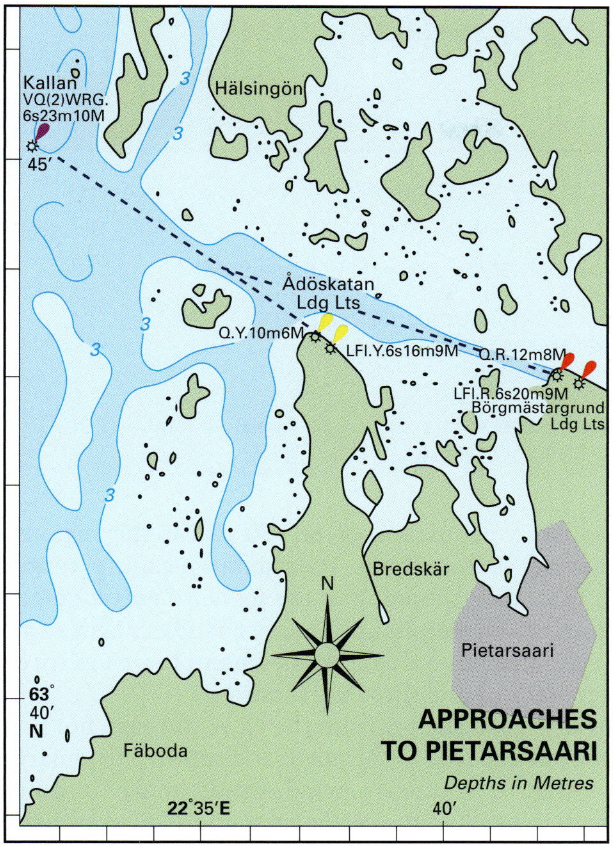


The main channel from the west (9m) leads from Pietarsaaren Majakka light (63°44'.6N 22° 31'.8E, Fl) to the commercial port of Alholmen Leppäluoto. The alternative approach towards the commercial port is to leave the coastal channel (3m) 9M north of Alholmen and follow the inner lead (1.8m) through the archipelago north of Pietarsaari.

From Alholmen, the channel leading to the town is shallow (1.8–3m) and narrow. It leads directly to the SSJ, Segelsällskapet i Jakobstad yacht club where there are 30 bows-to moorings with stern buoys in 1.8–3m. This visitor harbour is only open from 15 June–15 August. All these routes are very well buoyed.

All the usual services are on hand and the yacht club has a good restaurant but it is 1km north of the town.

Although there are still many old wooden houses around the city centre, considerable late 20th-century development has transformed the shopping area where every facility is available.

Pietarsaari is well known amongst sailing enthusiasts for being home of Nautor Swan and Baltic Yachts.

## MIKKELINSAARET / MICKELSÖRARNA, KUMMELSKÄRET

63°27'.6N 21°46'.4E (south mole, Mickelsörarna)
63°27'.61N; 021°46'.41E (Kummelskär)

**Distance**
Vaasa 25M

**Charts / harbour guides**
**GHB** *59* **FMA** *1608*

**Contacts**
www.kvarkenguide.org

If you intend to explore some of the many islands of the Kvarken, there is a route that leads around the Mickelsörarna archipelago which is made up of almost 300 islands, reefs and islets. Large and small forested islands are surrounded by relatively deep water with fewer underwater rocks than in many other parts of the Kvarken area, as well as rocky reefs and heath-covered islands. The many ancient ruins bear witness to the fact that humans have roamed these islands for a long time. The former coastguard station at Kummelskäret now serves as a harbour for excursions and also houses a nature centre (kvarkenguide.org). It has 10 moorings, bow-to from stern anchor or buoys, or alongside. Most of the islands south of Kummelskäret are nature reserves.

The circular route leaves the main coastal channel and heads north, east of the Krokskäret/Villskär archipelago (3m). It leads to Kummelskäret harbour. The western route leads between the Krokskäret archipelago to the east and the Mickelsörarna archipelago to the west, a well-buoyed route (2.4m) which joins the main channel in the south. You can also approach Kummelskäret from the west and the open sea.

Kummelskäret is an old pilot station with lookout tower, known as the 'Gateway to the Kvarken'. There is a small guest harbour with compost toilets, sauna, restaurant and nature centre in season. A barbecue is also available and there are nice walks around the area. The approach is a few metres off the main buoyed fairway in about 4m of water. The harbour is sheltered from north and south but a little exposed to the southeast and west. There are several stern buoys to the outer side of the pontoon and limited alongside berths on the inner side. Beware of a reputed rock in middle of the inner harbour.

Mooring is a pontoon and concrete jetties with no power or water. Note that the harbour layout has changed from that shown in many books and guides - the outer floating pontoon has been moved from the western jetty to the eastern.

The harbourmaster may allow you to climb to the top of the pilot watch tower to have a magnificent view out over the Kvarken and to watch the sunset.

## DJUPKASTET

63°18'.2N 21°37'.7E (transit on land)

**Distance**
Kokkola 62M, Pietarsaari 47M

Excellent safe anchorage just 0.7M off the main channel. Approach from the west, leaving Kvargrund Island to port.

The entrance is well marked with buoys and a transit. Good holding.

There is a small pontoon with stern buoys, which can be used with prior agreement from the WSF (Vaasa sailing club, see Vaasa). Floating pump out station in the middle of the anchorage.

## VAASA (VASA), VASKILUOTO (WSF)

63°05'.7N 21°35'.2E (north mole, Wasa Segelförening)

**Distances**
Pietarsaari 65M, Kristiinankaupunki 80M

**Charts / harbour guides**
**GHB** *46* **FMA** *1536* (Vaskiluoto)

**Contacts**
www.wasasegelforening.fi/guest-harbour.html
✆+358 44 277 8456

Vaasa has a population of 66,960 and is the regional capital of Ostrobothnia. It is a busy sailing centre with first-class shopping in the Remell Centre, hotels, restaurants, museums and Fantoy chandlers 1km away. Heavy industries provide employment; there are three power stations and three universities.

There is good shelter from the west and east, but it is somewhat exposed to the north and south, particularly the latter. A southerly wind would make it quite difficult to berth in the *gästhamn* section. It is a modern industrial town, and from the 17th century tar was the most important export. The city's wealth grew as the export trade expanded.

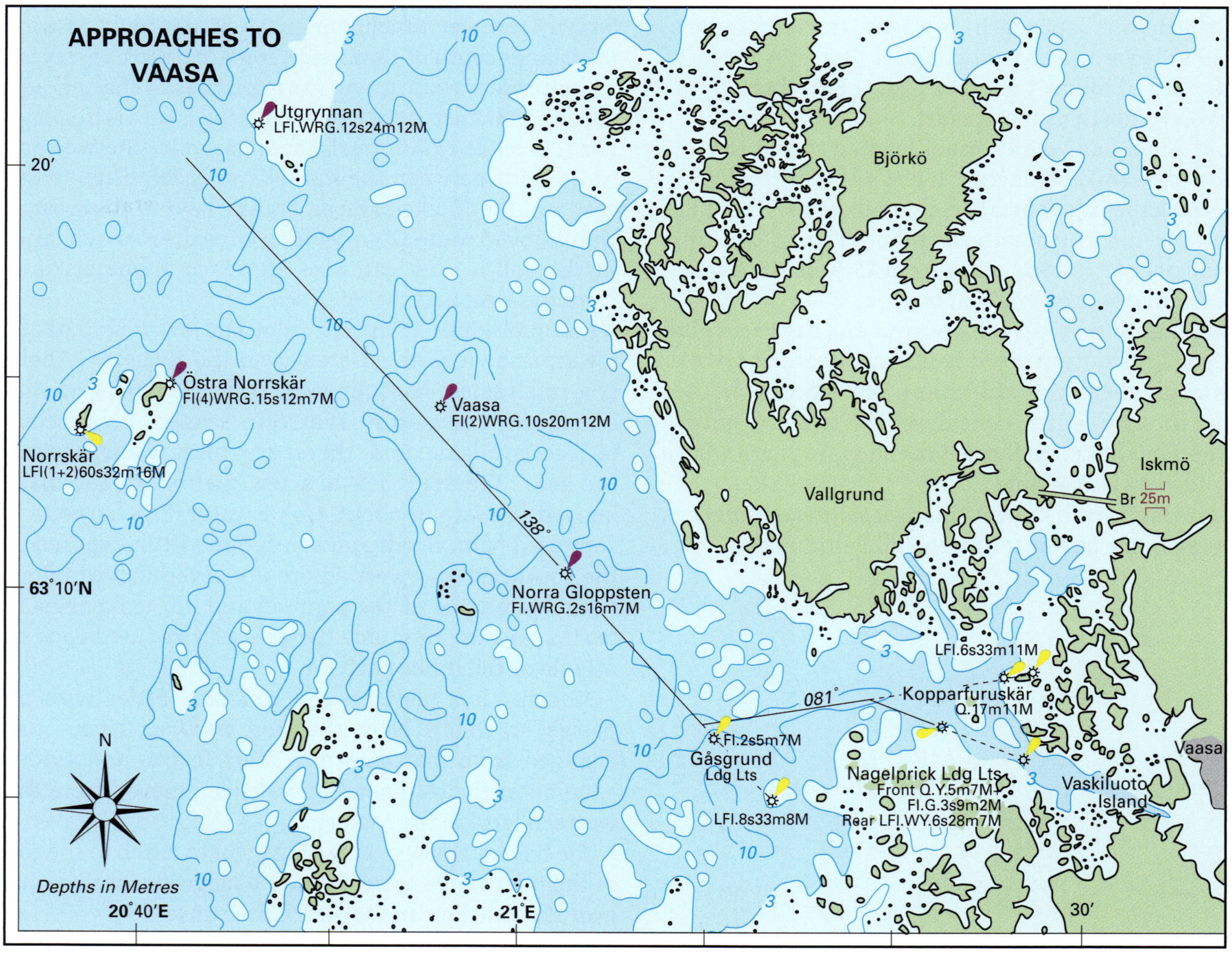

The old Customs House in Vaasa *Robin Matthews*

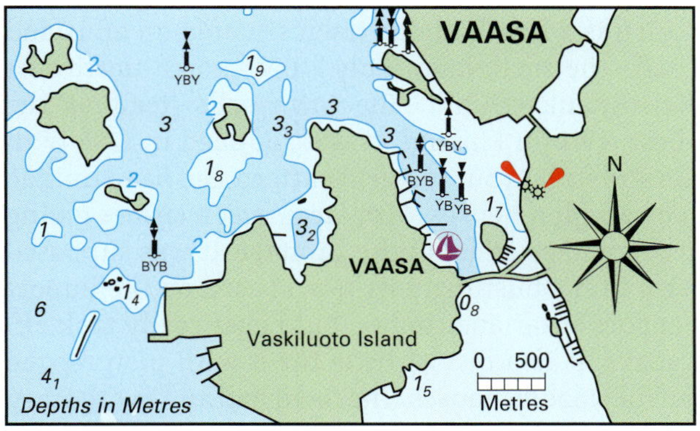


There are various well-charted and buoyed routes from the Vaasan Majakka light (63°14'.35N 20°55'.6E) west of Vallgrund island towards Vaasa. This is the main approach from the open sea when crossing from Sweden. The shipping channel leads straight to the commercial harbour on the western shore of Vaskiluoto/Vasklot island. There are three marinas next to each other on the northeastern side of the island, which is connected to the city via a low bridge (about a 20-minute walk). The Wasa Segelförening Yacht Club (WSF), the southernmost marina, is a Swedish-speaking club.

It is well run with good facilities and a very good restaurant in the handsome wooden clubhouse. Bicycles can be borrowed from the yacht club for shopping. There are also buses into town. Fuel is available from the jetty between the yacht clubs but it has only 2m of water alongside. There are 20 visitor moorings on the north side of the pontoon bows-to from stern buoys in 3-3.5m.

It is possible to anchor off or berth alongside the town quay which is convenient for shopping but short of facilities.

### *Approach*

You can only approach the eastern side of Vaskiluoto island and Vaasa from the northwest as the south side of the island is blocked by two low bridges. New pylons have been installed which now give 30m clearance - ample for most yachts so there is now sufficient water and air draft to head directly to the marinas.

## BERGÖ

62°56'.74N 021°10'.87E

### Distances

Pietarsaari 70M, Kristiinankaupunki 51M

This is a single pontoon with five berths, suitable for an overnight stay. From the main fairway, take the smaller fairway north until the south cardinal buoy, then turn to port. The pontoon is not immediately obvious until the derelict ferry pier is passed. There is about 2.5m depth at the outside end of the pontoon. There are toilets and showers, but these are rather dilapidated. The harbour fee is voluntary. There is a pleasant outlook and a village with two shops, a service station, café, sauna, etc. about 3km away.

The visitors pontoon at Bergö *Robin Matthews*

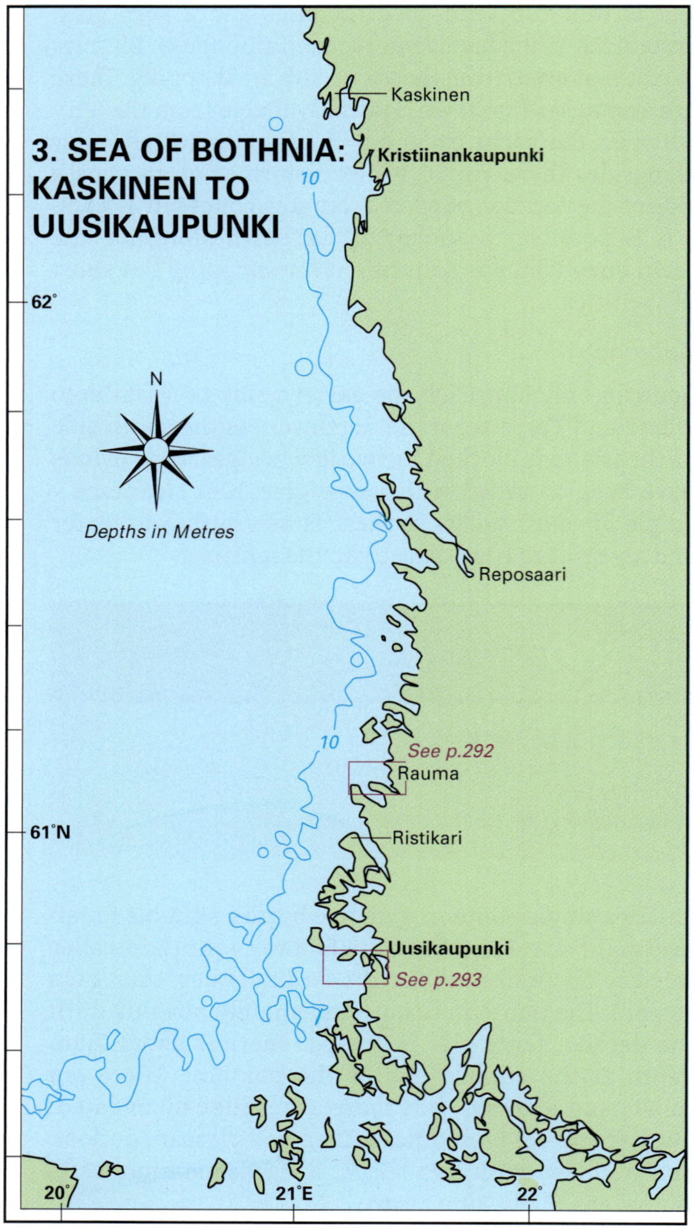


## KASKINEN (KASKÖ)

62° 23'.1N 21° 13'.2E (pier)

**Distances**
Vaasa 62M, Kristiinankaupunki (Kristinestad) 14M, Reposaari 53M

**Charts / harbour guides**
**GHB** *31, 32* **FMA** *1440*

**Contacts**
www.visitkaskinen.fi/en

Kaskinen is a small, idyllic town situated on an island just off the mainland only 10M north-northwest of Kristiinankaupunki. The town sells itself as the smallest town in Finland. It was founded in 1785 with all the streets laid out in a grid pattern and has a unique plan of wooden houses with large green spaces giving a garden village effect in the summer. It was supposed to grow into a bustling port town based on the import and export of tar and timber, but never really took off. Nowadays, it is a quaint little town with picturesque colourful wooden houses. The town hall and apothecary are impressive. All eateries are closed on Mondays except for a mobile takeaway van in the square.

There are two possible ways to approach the town, either from the north via an approach channel (3.4m), through the Järvöfjärden or from the south following the shipping channel (9m) past the commercial harbour. Kaskinen is also an entry port. There have been reports of missing buoys in the entrance channel so care is required. Once in, moor at the town quay. There are 50 spaces alongside or bows-to from stern buoys in 3.5m. Facilities include water, electricity, showers, washing machine, sauna and all the other amenities of a town of 1,400 inhabitants.

Wooden house in Kaskinen *Robin Matthews*

## 3. SEA OF BOTHNIA: KASKINEN (KASKÖ) TO UUSIKAUPUNKI (NYSTAD)

**Distances**
Vaasa to Kaskinen (Kaskö) 62M
Vaasa to Kristiinankaupunki 76M
Kristiinanaupunki to Uusikaupunki 127M

**Charts / harbour guides**
Merikarttasajat – E / F and Rannikkokarten 40 to 44

Once you leave the vast archipelago of the Finnish Kvarken (Quark(en)), the coast south of Vaasa becomes progressively more exposed to the west and the shoreline shallower. There are not many harbours and anchorages to choose from. Kaskinen (Kaskö), Kristiinankaupunki (Kristinestad), Reposaari, Rauma and Uusikaupunki (Nystad) are larger harbours that are deep enough for most sailing boats.

City quay in Kristiinankaupunki *Robin Matthews*

## KRISTIINANKAUPUNKI (KRISTINESTAD)

62°16'.3N 21°23'.1E (pier)

**Distances**
Vaasa 76M, Merikarvia (Sastmola) 31M, Reposaari 54M, Uusikaupunki (Nystad) 127M

**Charts / harbour guides**
**GHB** *27, 28* **FMA** *1432, 1433*

**Contacts**
www.visitkristinestad.fi

Kristiinankaupunki on the island of Koppö was founded in 1649 by Count Per Brahe who noted the excellent conditions for a port. Kristiinankaupunki has a centuries old tradition as a marketing and trading town, and a distinguished history of ship and boatbuilding. The beautiful town hall was built in 1856 and the town is now one of Scandinavia's best-preserved wooden towns. The authentic and picturesque buildings with their wooden fences stem from the 18th and 19th centuries.

Today the centre of the little town of 8,000 inhabitants has changed its face somewhat, but in the narrow alleys you can travel back hundreds of years in time.

The only approach to the town is from the south, either cutting through the skerries south of Furuviken (1.8m) following the buoyed channel (Chart 812.2) or taking the deeper approach which involves leaving the main coastal channel (4-5m) 4M south of Kristiinankaupunki and turning north at Härkmeri island. The approach channel is well buoyed (5m) all the way to Östra Sidan, the commercial harbour. Stay in the middle until you have passed the fountain to port and reached Hotel Kristina to starboard. There are 30 spaces bows-to from stern buoys in 3m at the *gästhamn* to the east side, and ten further spaces at the town centre on the west side in around 3m depth. For the latter, stay strictly within the buoyed channel. Note that the buoys for the last 0.5M (approx.) are not lit at night. Fees for the gästhamn are payable at the hotel and include showers and sauna, and for the town centre moorings at the Tourist Information Centre in front of the quay.

Facilities include water, electricity, sauna, showers, washing machine, fuel and all amenities associated with a town of this size.

Ulrika Eleonara church has a wooden-tiled roof and a crooked spire reputedly caused by Russian soldiers unsuccessfully trying to pull it down.

Kristiinankaupunki was the first 'Cittaslow' town in Finland with the aim of slowing down the pace of city life, focusing on food quality, optimal use of space, reduced traffic flow, and opposing cultural standardisation.

## KILEN

62°02'.3N 21°18'.44E

**Distances**
Kristiinankaupunki (Kristinestad) 15M, Uusikaupunki (Nystad) 85M

Kilen gästhamn is part of a larger resort built around a former fishing harbour and sawmill. It is sheltered from the east and south and although a long breakwater provides some shelter against swell from the north and west, it can still be exposed in strong winds. The approach is from the northwest through a buoyed channel beginning at the Kyrkoskär 1 west cardinal buoy (Waypoint 62°04'.14N; 21°14'.12E) and has a minimum depth 2.5 m. From the south, start from the Arvio west cardinal buoy (Waypoint 62°00'.57N; 21°15'.43E), heading northeast until the Kiili 1 buoy is reached (62°02'.82N 21°17'.49E), then joining the northern route. The depth in harbour is 2.5-3m and mooring is bows-to with stern buoys. Mooring alongside may be possible, but the water is shallow near the jetty.

There is power, water, toilets and a shower (you can get the key from the museum office which is open 0900-1600) available. The open-air Kilens Hembygdsgård museum nearby preserves the culture of the Swedish-speaking Finns in the area, and has a collection of fishermen's and farm houses. The café is open during office hours.

## REPOSAARI (RÄFSÖ)

61°37'N 21°26'.6E

**Distances**
Kristiinankaupunki 54M, Uusikaupunki 73M

**Charts / harbour guides**
**GHB** *17* **FMA** *1362*

Reposaari is the deep-water harbour for Pori (Björneborg). It is situated on an island connected to the mainland by many bridges and railway lines. The whole area is industrial mainly to the southeast of Reposaari at Mäntyluoto and the northwest at Tahkoluoto. The tanks, chimneys and wind turbines can be seen from a distance. Yet Reposaari is a good, sheltered stopover.

The approach is straightforward. Leave the main coastal channel (3.4m) and approach the harbour through the commercial shipping channel (10m) towards the industrial harbour. Once through the breakwaters, turn to port following the transit and buoys (3.6m) that lead to the northwestern side of Reposaari and to the 60-berth visitor harbour. Moor alongside or bows-to from stern buoys in 2–2.5m. Good shelter. There is a wide range of facilities available. While the municipal centre of Pori, 22km away, can be reached by dredged channel (1.5m) it is probably best visited by bus or rail.

## RAUMA (RAUMO)

61°08'.1N 21°28'.1.4E (Syväraumanlahti, northwest tip)

**Distances**
Reposaari 37M, Uusikaupunki 36M

**Charts / harbour guides**
**GHB** *4, 5, 6* **FMA** *1327, 1331, 1333*

**Contacts**
www.rauma.fi
www.poroholma.fi/vierasvenesatama

Rauma is a World Heritage Site and shipbuilding centre. It is also an entry port for customs and immigration.

Rauma is one of the oldest harbours in Finland. Built around a Franciscan monastery, where the mid-15th-century Holy Cross Church still stands, it is an outstanding example of an old Nordic city constructed in wood. Although ravaged by fire in the late 17th century, it has preserved its ancient vernacular architecture. The very well-preserved wooden houses have been sensitively adapted for modern use and merit the World Heritage Site status which is bringing tourism and new prosperity to the town (whc.unesco.org/en/list/582). Cycling is a good way to get about. The Maritime Museum on Kalliokatu is worth a visit to learn about the local

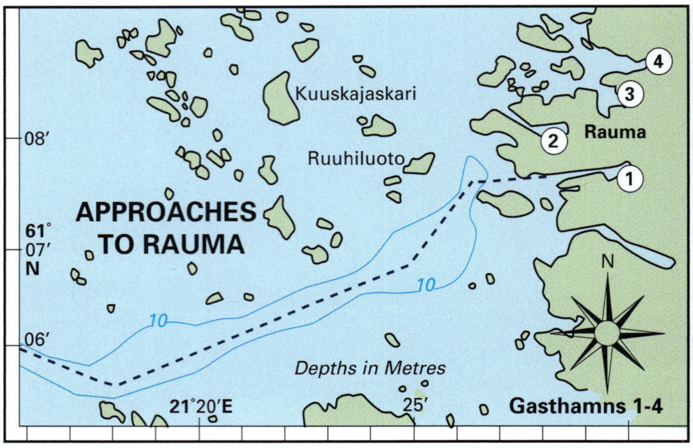


history of Rauma as a major shipping centre, internment of Finnish sailors on the Isle of Man in WW2 and even boasts a simulator to try your hand at navigating your fishing trawler into Rauma harbour! Dotted around the town are quirky wooden figures by Kerttu Horila, a local sculptor.

The very well-marked main deep-water channels from the northwest and southwest (amongst other shallower ones) lead to the commercial harbour of Ulko-Petäjäs. From here you can access a service harbour and two visitor harbours. Careful study of the large scale chart (804.1) is necessary before entering these harbours.

Petäjäs (61°07'.9N 21°27'.4E) is a fully-serviced shipyard with fuel, chandlery, boat ramp, engine and other services (not for overnight staying) with 5 berths in 2m. Two visitor harbours are located on the north side of the town: Poroholma (61°08'.1N 21°28'.1E) with 15 berths bows-to from stern buoys in 1.9m, and Syväraumanlahti (61°08'.4N 21°28'.4E) with a visitor pontoon at the entrance to the 400-berth marina. Entry to both marinas is by either a southern route (south of Iso-Sauko island) with a minimum depth of 1.2m, or a northern route (north of Pöllä and Kaskinen islands) with a minimum depth of 3.4m. For most yachts, therefore, the slightly longer northern route is preferable. The two routes divide at the Petäjäs 1 and 2 cardinal buoys. Both marinas are around 2.5km from the town centre. Most facilities are available nearby but fuel and chandlery only at the Petäjäs shipyard.

Marela Museum, Rauma *Robin Matthews*

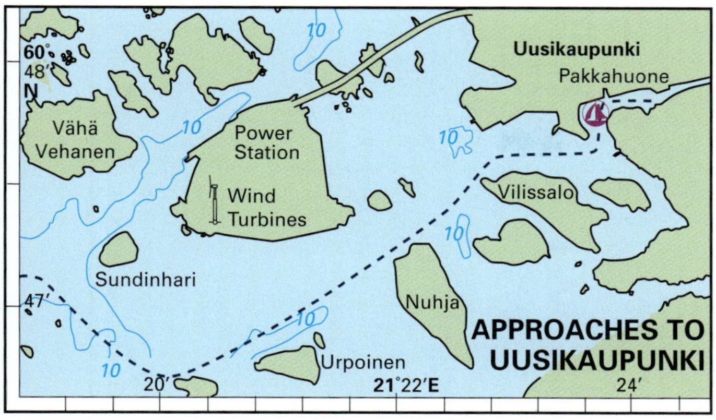


## UUSIKAUPUNKI (NYSTAD)

60°47'.9N 21°24'.3E (Pakkahuone)

**Distances**
Rauma 36M, Turku 55M approx.

**Charts / harbour guides**
**SH1** *126* **FMA** *1060, 1072*

**Contacts**
www.uusikaupunki.fi
www.karilla.fi/vierasvenesatama
www.visituusikaupunki.fi/en

Situated between the Sea of Bothnia and the Archipelago Sea, Uusikaupunki is a major sailing centre and attractive but large and industrialised town. Like most towns up and down the Gulf of Bothnia and the Turku Archipelago, Uusikaupunki also has some very well-preserved wooden houses from the 17th and 18th centuries.

There are three main approach channels: from north, west and south, all of which are well marked and converge just northwest of Urpoinen island at 60°46'.8N 21°20'E (see chart 802.1). Then follow the fairway (and transit) south of the fertiliser plant and wind turbines on the island of Hanko and turn to starboard northwest of Vilissalo island and enter the very narrow (2.5m) channel which leads northwards to the inner harbour. After a sharp turn to starboard the fully-sheltered and award-winning Pakkahuone *gästhamn* with up to 80 berths from stern buoys lies ahead and to port.

Up to 3m is claimed but this shoals to 1.5m beyond the café. Very good facilities and two chandlers, boatyards, extensive shopping and services. Fuel available from a prominent jetty to port. Salmeri is a very good service harbour to the south east of Sorvakko (60°47'.6N 21°23'.9E), which can deal with any repairs and engine troubles. However, it is about a 30-minute walk to the town centre.

Bus and rail services are good to Turku International Airport, about 40km to the southeast, this makes Uusikaupunki useful for crew changes.

## ISOKARI/ENSKÄR

60°43'.18N 21°01'.99E (Start of entrance channel)

**Distances**
Seglinge 34M, Uusikaupunki 15M approx.

**Contacts**
www.isokari.fi/satama
www.visituusikaupunki.fi/en/sea-and-nature/isokari-lighthouse-island

Isokari is a small island 12M to the southwest of Uusikaupunki. It has a prominent red/white lighthouse on the west side, built by the Russians in 1838. It has been a pilot station since the 17th century and is still currently in use. The small harbour is on the east side of the island near the pilot station and is open to winds from the north and east.

Approach from the main fairway until Isokarinportti 1 (red) and 2 (green) buoys are reached (waypoint: 60°43'.17N 021°01'.99E), then follow the narrow buoyed channel and turn hard to port into the harbour. Beware of the rock marked by a small buoy in the middle of the harbour – stay close to the jetty to avoid it. Mooring is alongside in 1.5–3 m water.

There are very few facilities, but there is a barbeque, a small open-air café (open during the summer) and a toilet next to the café. The island is a nature reserve, but can get busy during summer. Tours of the lighthouse can be arranged.

The Russian lighthouse on Isokari *Robin Matthews*

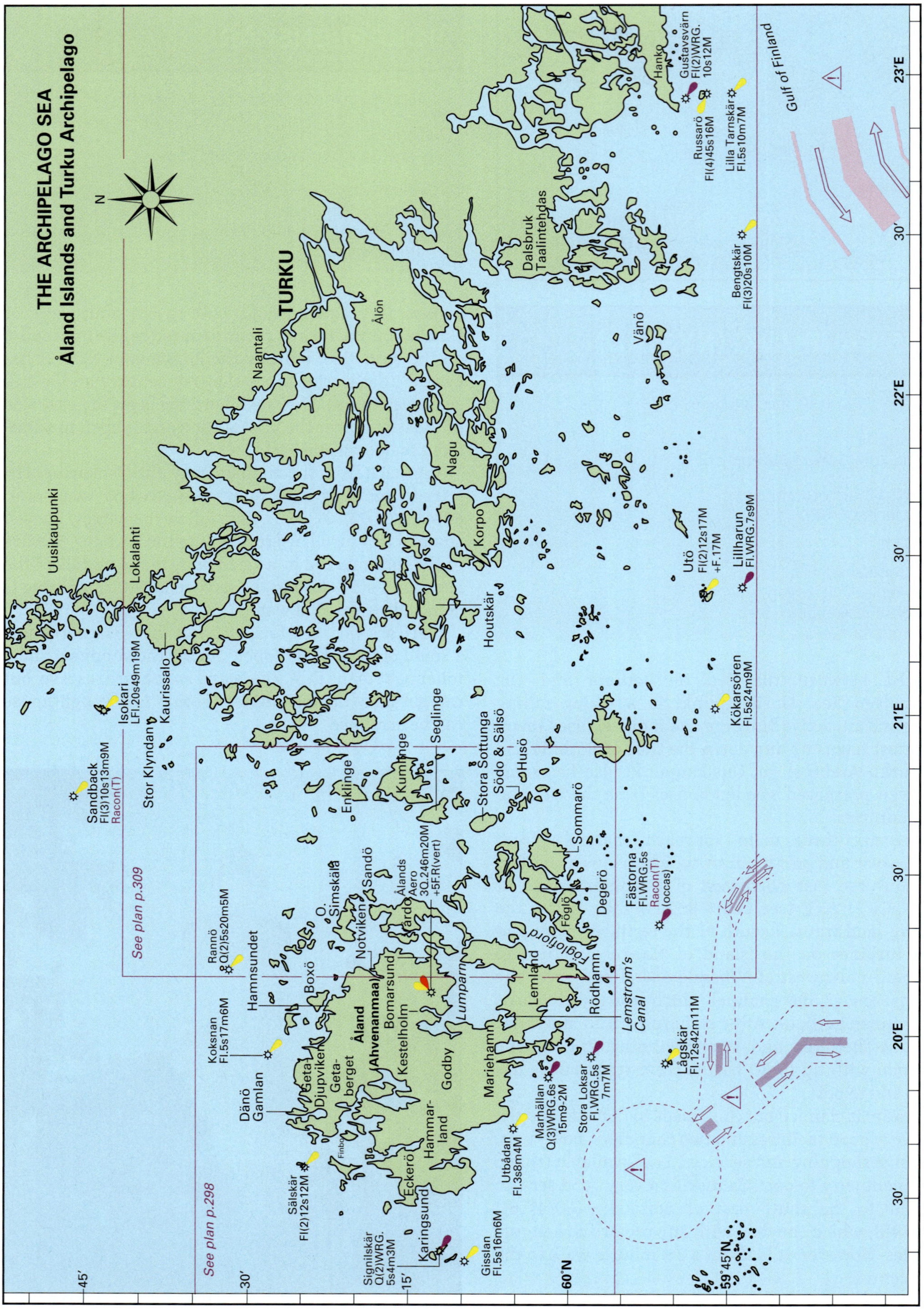
THE ARCHIPELAGO SEA
Åland Islands and Turku Archipelago
N
TURKU
Naantali
Uusikaupunki
Lokalahti
Kaurissalo
Isokari
LFl.20s49m19M
Stor Klyndan
Sandback
Fl(3)10s13m9M
Racon(T)
See plan p.309
See plan p.298
Rannö
Q(2)5s20m5M
Hamnsundet
Koksnan
Fl.5s17m6M
Dänö
Gamlan
Sälskär
Fl(2)12s12M
Signilskär
Q(2)WRG.
5s4m3M
Gisslan
Fl.5s16m6M
Utbådan
Fl.3s8m4M
Marhällan
Q(3)WRG.6s
15m9-2M
Stora Loksar
Fl.WRG.5s
7m7M
Lemstrom's
Canal
Lågskär
Fl.12s42m11M
Fästorna
Fl.WRG.5s
Racon(T)
(occas)
Kökarsören
Fl.5s24m9M
Utö
Fl(2)12s17M
+F.17M
Lillharun
Fl.WRG.7s9M
Bengtskär
Fl(3)20s10M
Lilla Tarnskär
Fl.5s10m7M
Russarö
Fl(4)45s16M
Gustavsvärn
Fl(2)WRG.
10s12M
Hanko
Gulf of Finland
Dalsbruk
Taalintehdas
Vänö
Ålön
Nagu
Korpo
Houtskär
Seglinge
Kumlinge
Enklinge
Stora Sottunga
Södo & Sälsö
Husö
Sommarö
Degerö
Föglö
Föglöfjord
Rödhamn
Lemland
Lumparn
Mariehamn
Godby
Kastelholm
Bomarsund
Vårdö
Ålands
Aero
3Q.246m20M
+5F.R(vert)
Notviken
Sandö
Ö.
Simskäla
Boxö
Åland
Ahvenanmaa
Geta
Getaberget
Djupviken
Finby
Hammarland
Eckerö
Karingsund
45'
30'
15'
60°N
59°45'N
30'
20°E
30'
21°E
30'
22°E
30'
23°E

# 3B. THE SEA OF ÅLAND AND THE ARCHIPELAGO SEA: ÅLAND ISLANDS AND TURKU ARCHIPELAGO

The following section covers the complex area which includes the Åland Islands (Ahvenanmaa in Finnish and Åland in Swedish) and the Turku Archipelago (Turun Saaristo in Finnish and Åbo Skärgård in Swedish), also known as Southwest Finland. The combined areas of the Sea of Åland and the Archipelago Sea, covers around 3,205M$^2$ of sea and islands.

Most yachts sailing from Sweden towards Finland would probably cross from the Stockholm archipelago to the Åland Islands, particularly if they are short of time. The crossing from Arholma Österhamn (see page 244) to Mariehamn West is 30M.

This section is therefore structured to reflect travel from west to east, from Åland to Hanko, leading to the Gulf of Finland.

The shipping lanes between Finland, the Åland Islands and Sweden are very busy with ferry traffic. Mariehamn is a centre for ferry traffic *Andy Beharrell*

Åland flag *Andy Beharrell*

## INTRODUCTION

The Archipelago Sea (Saaristomeri in Finnish, *Skärgårdshavet* in Swedish) is part of the Baltic Sea between the Gulf of Bothnia, the Gulf of Finland and the Sea of Åland, within Finnish territorial waters. By some definitions it is the largest archipelago in the world by the number of islands (6,700 islands), although many of these are very small and close together. The main ports in this area are Turku on the mainland and Mariehamn (West and East) on the Åland Islands.

The islands are divided between the region of Southwest Finland and the autonomous region of Åland. The border between the regions runs along the Skiftet (*Kihti* in Finnish), a long and narrow sound, only a mile wide in the northern part of the Archipelago Sea but relatively open in the south, which runs north-south roughly along longitude 21°07'E.

The larger islands are inhabited and are linked by ferries and bridges. The Åland Islands, the largest islands in the region, form an autonomous area within Finland. Although the Åland Islands are within the EU they remain outside its tax area. This exception allows for maintained tax-free sales on the ferries between Sweden and Finland, provided they stop at Mariehamn or Långnäs, and at the airport. It also means that Åland is a different tax-zone, which means that tariffs may be levied on goods brought to the islands. The Åland Islands flag is a red cross on a broader yellow cross on a blue background. This flag reflects that fact that the majority of the population is of Swedish origin. The colours are those of the Åland Islands coat of arms – a a golden red deer on a blue field and the coat of arms of Finland – a crowned golden lion on a red field. The islands print their own stamps, register their own ships and are a member of the Nordic Council. They therefore enjoy a large measure of autonomy. It is legally a demilitarized zone, and its citizens are therefore exempt from military service.

The autonomy in Åland means that the government can pass laws in various areas; traffic, healthcare, education and business among others. In recent years there has been positive population growth as people have moved to the islands from various places. The population is around 30,000, of whom 12,000 live in Mariehamn.

The Archipelago Sea covers a roughly triangular area with the cities of Mariehamn (60°06'N 19°57'E), Uusikaupunki (60°47'.9N 21°24'.3E), and Hanko (59°49'.1N 22°58'.1E) at the corners. The archipelago can be divided into inner and outer archipelagos, with the outer archipelago consisting mainly of smaller, uninhabited islands. The total surface area is 8,300km$^2$, of which 2,000km$^2$ is land.

The islands east of the Skiftet are part of the province of Southwest Finland.

There are 257 larger islands of over one square kilometer within the Archipelago Sea and about 17,700 smaller islets. A good estimate of the smallest uninhabitable rocks and skerries is about 50,000. It would require an entire summer to explore the whole archipelago and a lifetime to sample all the secluded anchorages or 'natural harbours', so it is worth dedicating plenty of time in your cruising plans.

The islands began to emerge from the sea shortly after the last Ice Age 10,000 years ago. Due to post-glacial rebound the process is still going on with new skerries and islands being slowly created and old ones growing and even merging. The current rate of rebound is about 4mm a year. Because the islands are made of mainly granite and gneiss, two very hard types of rock, erosion is slow and due to its southerly location, the effect of post-glacial rebound is smaller than for example in the Kvarken (about 9mm) further north in the Gulf of Bothnia.

The sea area is shallow and most of the channels are not navigable for large ships.

## Administration, demographics and culture

Based on the languages spoken the archipelago can be divided into three parts. The Åland Archipelago in the west is almost completely Swedish speaking, the Åboland archipelago in the south is mostly Swedish speaking and the northern archipelago is Finnish speaking. In many cases, place names are shown on the chart in both languages - usage here following that of the Merikarttasarjat chartbook series.

There are a number of small 'private' islands in the Archipelago Sea and although these are not shown as such on the chart, the owners normally fly a national flag when at home. It is polite to recognise their privacy by not anchoring within sight of buildings or venturing ashore uninvited. Visiting yachts are strongly recommended to follow the 'everyman's right'. www.nationalparks.fi/hikinginfinland/visitorguidelines

The number of permanent residents on the islands is roughly 60,000, with 27,000 of them living in Åland.

Many Finns have summer residences on the islands in the area, known for its natural beauty. Due to this, the population of many islands can double or more during the summer.

The Archipelago Sea is a paradise for sailing with children. The innumerable islands are surrounded by waters which are sheltered and crystal clear. A short day sail will bring fresh adventures with each new anchorage.

Because Christianity spread to the islands before reaching the mainland, the churches on the major islands are relatively old; dating from the 13th, 14th and 15th centuries, with the oldest ones in Åland. About 75% of Finns are members of the Evangelical Lutheran Church of Finland, and this proportion is even higher in the archipelago.

One of the local sports is disc golf. There are a total of 18 disc golf courses around the islands, many of them in beautiful locations with great sea views. Disc golf is pretty much like golf except that you use a frisbee, or in fact several. The 'hole' is a basket with chains around it to help the disc drop into a metal tray. Different discs are used for different throws, so you might have a driver disc, a mid-range disc and a putter. Packs of discs can be bought very reasonably in many of the shops in Mariehamn and it is worth having a go. If nothing else, it is a great excuse for a walk around to see the scenery. Details of all the courses are available on www.discgolf.ax.

The national flower of the Åland Islands is the cowslip.

## Useful information

When phoning the Åland Islands, first dial the country code (+358) and then the local code (18), i.e. ✆+358 18...

Emergency number (as with the rest of Finland) ✆ 112

Åland Central Hospital ✆+358 185355, 24hr duty ✆+358 18 538500, 24 hour dentist ✆+358 18 14600

Coastguard ✆+358 295 420 000

West Finland Coastguard ✆+358 295 427 000

Åland Sea Rescue Society (Ålands Sjöräddningssällskap) ✆+358 18 19475 www.sjoraddningen.ax

Finnish Border Guard www.raja.fi/en/

Taxis ✆+358 18 26000, ✆+358 18 22100

Sailmaker Jouni Lahdenperä ✆+358 40 54 86 226

Divers Jerry Wilhelsson ✆+358 457 3798 907, Jan Lönnqvist ✆+358 457 3135 856, Jan-Ola Karlsson ✆+358 40 584 5122

Åland Tourist Information ✆+358 18 24000, www.visitaland.com/en

## Communications

The islands are linked by bridges and ferries, also called *lossi* in Finnish and *färja* in Swedish. Pedestrians travel free on the numerous inter-island ferries. There are also large commercially-operated cruise ferries connecting the Finnish cities of Turku and Helsinki to Åland and Sweden. There is an airport in Mariehamn and a grass strip on Kumlinge.

During cold winters official ice roads are established between some islands and it is sometimes possible to drive across the ice from the mainland.

**Acknowledgement**

Partly adapted from: Wikipedia®

Ferries of various sizes ply the routes around the Åland Islands *Andy Beharrell*

## Websites

Online information about the Åland Islands is extensive. The following websites are worth browsing if you are planning a visit:

- www.visitaland.com/en
- www.visitsaaristo.net/en (very useful - details of all harbours throughout Finland)
- www.mariehamn.ax
- www.visitfinland.com/en/articles/top-things-to-do-in-aland

*Navigational charts & Harbour guides*

### Chart folios

C-Ahvenanmaa/Åland, D-Turunmaan saaristo/Åbolands skärgård (scale 1:50,000)

### Harbour guides

*Stora Hamnboken Vol.1 Turun Saaristo/Åbo Skärgård* (**SH1** *xxx*) and *Stora Hamnboken Vol.2 Ahvenanmaa/Åland* (**SH2** *xxx*)

*Käyntisatamat/Besökshamnar* guide to 511 harbours on the Finnish coast (the numbers of the harbours in the book correlate with the numbers in the chart folios - **FMA** *xxx*).

*Åland (Gästhamnar, Farleder, Ankarplatser)*, Anders Hellberg, Peter Bergström and Ben Johans - available throughout the Åland Islands.

### See also

Navigational charts - Finland and Åland and Harbour books and literature page 272 (general introduction to Finland).

## Suggested cruising routes

Cruising through the Archipelago Sea can take any number of routes, criss-crossing the Archipelago Sea depending on time constraints, final destination and personal interest. The suggested routes in this chapter, together with the harbours and anchorages listed below are just that - suggestions. Finnish charts are excellent and if the recommended routes in the chart folios (which also indicate the minimum depth that could be encountered along them) are followed closely, the danger of hitting a rock or running aground are minimised. Of course, one can wander between them too - at your own risk. It is also possible to sail from Mariehamn direct to Hanko without stopping, but then one would be missing some of the best *skärgård* sailing in the entire Baltic.

Ice road between Oulunsalo and Hailuoto. This is the longest ice road in Finland *Estormiz/Wikimedia Commons (https://commons.wikimedia.org/wiki/File:Hailuoto_Ice_Road_20130113_05.JPG)*

## ROUTE 1 CIRCUMNAVIGATION OF THE MAIN ISLANDS OF ÅLAND, RÖDHAMN AND DEGERBY

A cruise around the main island of Åland is strongly recommended for anyone who does not have the time to venture further east. There are many beautiful, peaceful and remarkably unfrequented anchorages to be discovered, together with a cross-section of cultural and historical sights. A fair insight into Åland will be gained even with this limited visit. The route begins in Eckerö, heads southeast towards Mariehamn, enters Lumparn through the Lemström's Canal, exits Lumparn via the Prästösundet, and finally skirts the northeast and northwest coasts of Åland before returning to Eckerö.

Eckerö Post and Customs House - built by the Russians in 1828 *Andy Beharrell*

## KÄRINGSUND (KÄRINGSUNDET), ECKERÖ

60°14'.05N 19°32'.15E (Käringsundet lighthouse)

**Charts / harbour guides**

**SH2** 35 **FMA** 1275

**Contacts**

www.karingsund.ax
www.karingsundsgasthamn.ax

This is a landlocked fishing harbour on the west coast of Eckerö accessed through a very narrow entrance which presents no difficulty in ordinary weather. A small lighthouse with a sector light (Q.WRG) is located on the southern headland at the entrance to the pool. Inside the harbour there is a patch of rocks just above water. Pass north of these rocks, and then turn starboard towards the wooden jetty. Alternatively after entering the pool immediately turn to starboard between the rocks to port and close to the headland.

There is a large jetty to the east of the village, with room for about 50 yachts, bows-to from stern buoys. It is also possible to anchor between the rocks and the jetty. Käringsund has been developed as a summer

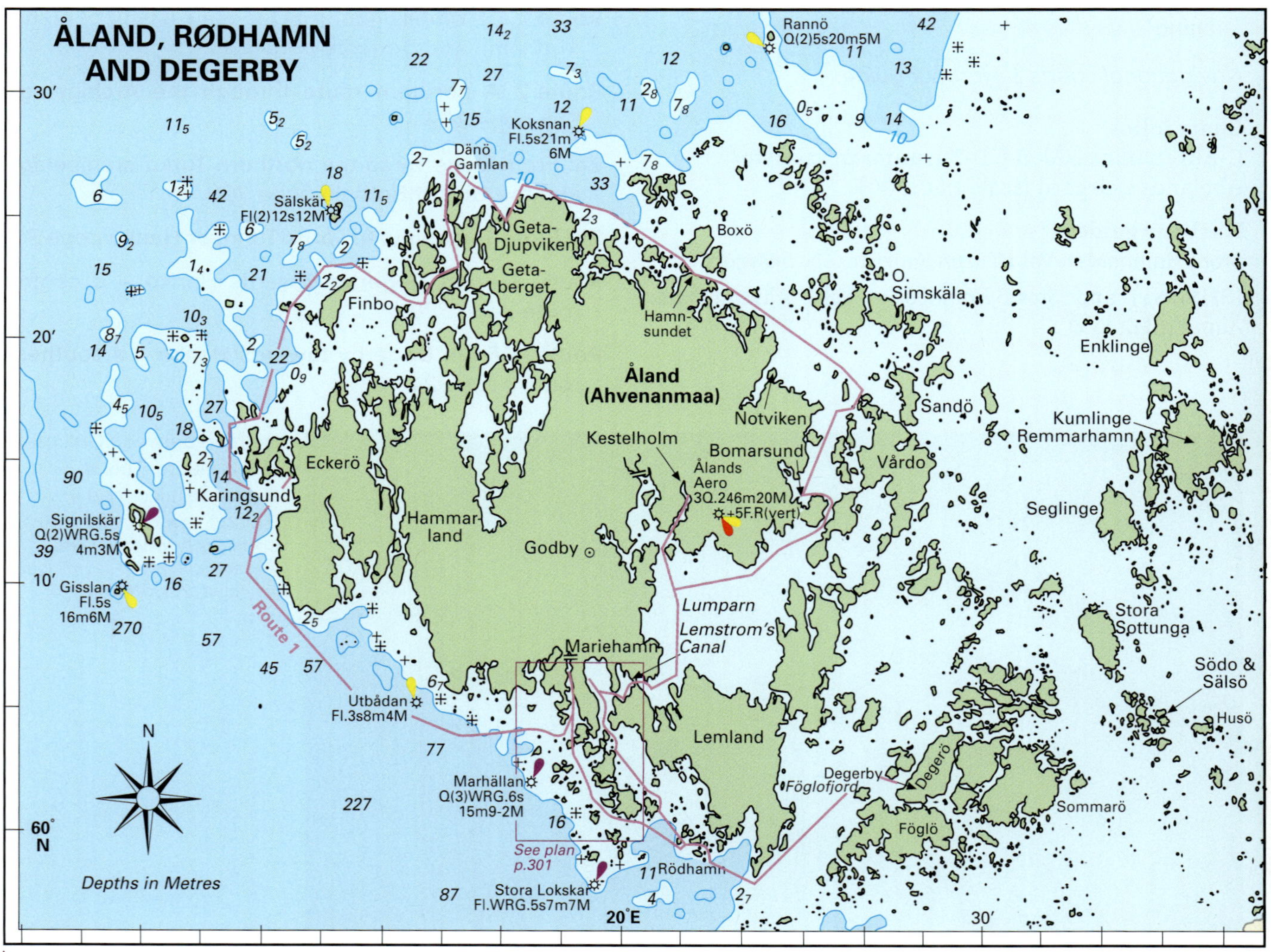

Archipelago boats outside the hunting and fishing museum at Eckerö
*Andy Beharrell*

resort and can become crowded but it is still attractive and comfortable. A large former post house is located about a mile south of the harbour entrance and is very conspicuous.

It is only 25M to Arholma (Sweden) and the entrance to the Stockholm archipelago. Therefore it is a handy port of departure to and from Sweden. A ferry to Sweden departs from the L-shaped quay about 10mins walk from the yacht harbour, making Käringsund a convenient place for crew changes. Facilities include fuel, showers, sauna, restaurant, WiFi, electricity, water (20m), pump-out station.

There is an interesting museum as well which tells the story of life in the archipelago and the fishing and hunting culture of the islands (www.jaktfiskemuseum.ax). About 20mins walk to the south (past the ferry terminal) is the Eckerö Post and Customs House (Eckerö Post & Tullhus). This grand building was built in 1828 and was the westernmost extremity of the Russian Empire at the time. It was deliberately built as a building that was far too large for its purpose as a visual demonstration of Russian supremacy.

Aerial view of Eckerö (Käringsund) harbour *Andy Beharrell*

# MARIEHAMN (MAARIANHAMINA)

60°06'N 19°56'E (Länsisatama)

### Distances
Stockholm 70M, Hanko 105M, Turku 75M

### Lights
**Marhällan** 60°01'.9N 19°52'.5E Q(3)WRG.6s15-9M
Round red tower, black bands. Floodlit
**Tvibenan** 60°02'.4N 19°53'.3E Q.WRG.6m4M
White rectangle
**Leading Lights 052°** *Rear* 100m from front, LFl.G.6s21m11M 046°-vis-058° Red rectangle, yellow stripe
**Korsö** *Common front* 60°02'.4N 19°54'E Iso.WRG.7m8M
Racon Red rectangle, yellow stripe
**Leading Lights 066°** *Rear* 180m from front, LFl.6s17m8M 062°-vis-070° Red rectangle, yellow stripe
**Granö** 60°03'.5N 19°55'.7E Q(2)WRG.5s6mW6M
Orange tower, white lantern
**Lotsberget Leading Lights 028°** *Front* 60°05'N 19°56'.2E Iso.Y.2s31m10M 023°-vis-033°
Red rectangle, yellow stripe, on metal framework tower, white lantern
*Rear* 457m from front Iso.6s57m10M
Red rectangle, yellow stripe, on metal framework tower
**Nyhamn light** 59°57'.5N 19°57'.3E sector light, Iso.R.2s, occas
**Rödko light** 60°09'.6N 20°04'E, Fl.WRG.3s

### Contacts
**First Port of Entry**
Mariehamn Port Call Centre ☎+358 18 5310
info@hamnen.ax
VHF Ch 12, 16 (call *Mariehamn Port*)
www.mariehamnshamn.ax/en/
www.noonsite.com

Mariehamn has a year-round population of just under 11,500, though some 1.5 million tourists are estimated to pass through each year. It is the capital of the region of Åland.

It stands on a tongue of land separating two arms of the sea and has two yacht harbours, West Harbour (Västrahamnen) and East Harbour (Östrahamnen). Although less than a mile separates the two harbours by land, by sea it involves a detour of some 15M for yachts so that when coming from the south the decision as to which to head for must be made before passing Nyhamn light (59°57'·5N 19°57'·3E, sector light, Iso.R.2s, occas) see plan on page 267 (Åland, Rödhamn and Degerby, Route 1). Some motor yachts may be able to shorten this detour by passing under the 5.3m bridge between Styrsö and Nåtö.

The massive wind turbines around Nyhamn will be spotted a long way off. West Harbour is the deeper one and more easily reached by visiting yachts unfamiliar with the area, but is rather less sheltered than the East Harbour which is slightly closer to the town centre.

The four-masted barque *Pommern*. Now a museum ship
*Andy Beharrell*

Old wooden houses in Södragatan fringe wide tree-lined avenues, pedestrian areas full of small cafés, and a good shopping centre in this relaxed and spacious town.

Mariehamn is of particular interest as the last home of square-rigged ships, and having been the port of registry for Captain Gustaf Erikson's famous 'Flying P' line. The four-masted barque Pommern, which last sailed commercially in 1939, is now a museum ship in the West Harbour and is well worth a visit, as is the nearby Åland Maritime Museum (note the North Atlantic chart on display, published by James Imray & Son in 1864).

The Maritime Quarter including museums, historic vessels and boatbuilding sheds can be found near the East Harbour and is worth a visit. Mariehamn is the centre for many events (see www.visitaland.com/en/events-in-aland/) including the annual Rockoff Festival held at the end of July.

### *Approach & entrance*

Coming from Sweden and heading for the West Harbour, Mariehamn is usually approached either from the southwest or south.

Crossing from the Stockholm archipelago the most straightforward route will lead to the Marhällan light (60°01'.9N 19°52'.3E) which can be left to port or starboard. Two leading lights (marks), one in the white sector and the other in the green sector of Korsö light (60°01'.9N 19°53'.8E) will lead directly into the approach channel (leading lights on Lotsberget-028.1°) towards Mariehamn West Harbour. The marina lies to the north of the ferry docks and the barque *Pommern*.

There is also a well-buoyed (unlit) approach channel from the west, which provides a convenient short cut for yachts coming from the west coast of Åland. It enters the archipelago in the vicinity of 60°04'N 19°47'E and joins the two main routes 4M further east at 60°04'N 19°55'E.

Several other routes are possible (south or southeast), however, when approaching from the open sea

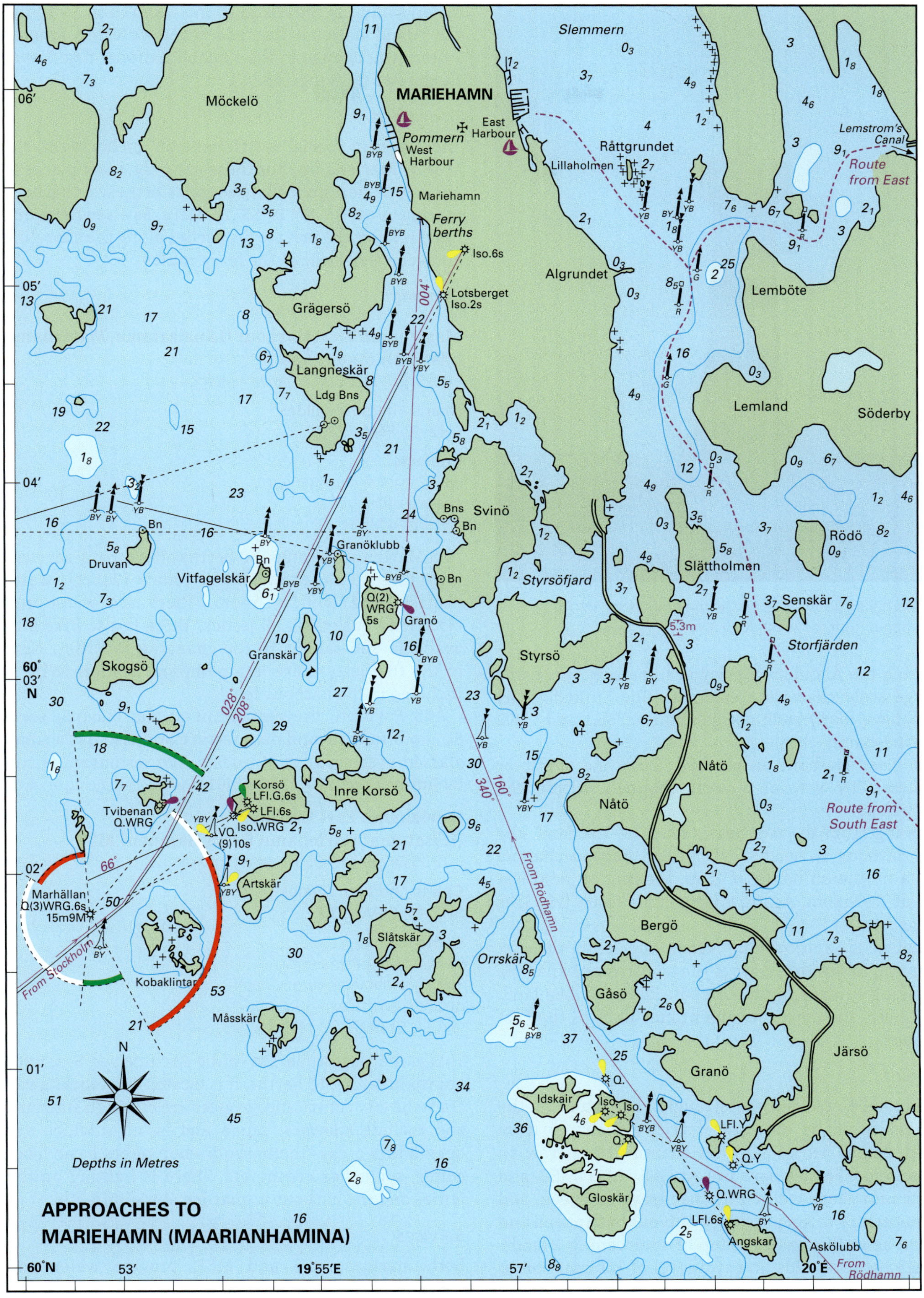

APPROACHES TO MARIEHAMN (MAARIANHAMINA)
MARIEHAMN
Möckelö
Pommern
West Harbour
East Harbour
Mariehamn
Ferry berths
Iso.6s
Lotsberget Iso.2s
Slemmern
Råttgrundet
Lillaholmen
Lemstrom's Canal
Route from East
Grägersö
Langneskär
Ldg Bns
Algrundet
Lemböte
Lemland
Söderby
Svinö
Bns
Bn
Granöklubb
Vitfagelskär
Druvan
Styrsöfjard
Slättholmen
Rödö
Senskär
Storfjärden
Granö
Q(2) WRG 5s
Granskär
Skogsö
Styrsö
Nåtö
Korsö LFl.G.6s
LFl.6s
Iso.WRG
VQ.(9)10s
Inre Korsö
Tvibenan Q.WRG
Artskär
Marhällan Q(3)WRG.6s 15m9M
From Stockholm
Kobaklintar
Måsskär
Slåtskär
Orrskär
From Rödhamn
Route from South East
Bergö
Gåsö
Järsö
Idskair
Gloskär
Angskar
Askölubb
LFl.Y
Q.Y
Q.WRG
LFl.6s
Depths in Metres
60°N
53′
19°55′E
57′
20°E

The Marhällan lighthouse on the main entrance into Mariehamn from the west *Andy Beharrell*

entering the Åland archipelago can be very confusing – large scale charts are essential. The Finnish chart folios have many such special charts, 756.1 and 756.2 for Mariehamn.

The East Harbour is reached from the south or southeast, by way of several channels within the archipelago.

Coming from the southeast, south of Lemland, the East Harbour is reached via a well buoyed channel with a minimum depth of 3.7m, starting at Järsö just west of Rödhamn. Again, a large-scale chart (756.1) is a necessity.

Finally, if approaching from the east through Lumparn, follow the buoys to the Lemströms Kanal, via the swing bridge, round Lemböte north of Lemland. From here, the most convenient marina is in the East Harbour.

### Caution

It cannot be stressed too strongly that many of the channels used by the large ferries which ply from Stockholm to Turku via Mariehamn are narrow in the extreme. Ferries have priority AT ALL TIMES, and yachts must keep well clear. They travel at speed, and it is necessary to keep a sharp look-out both ahead and behind as well as over the top of intervening islands. An AIS receiver adds an extra level of information to help increase awareness of the ferry movements.

### Formalities

See page 273 for details.

When sailing in the Åland Island waters you fly (only) the Åland national flag and when entering Finnish waters you change to the Finland national flag. Never fly the two flags together.

### Anchorage

There are no special restrictions on anchoring in the area of Mariehamn, but there are only a few places to anchor including one that lies opposite the west harbour marina at 60°05'.8N 19°55'.1E. Here, as elsewhere, one must respect the private properties along the shoreline and keep well clear of the ferry routes.

### Berthing

#### Mariehamn West Harbour (Länsisatama, Mariehamn Västra Hamnen) ÅSS

60°05'.8N 19°55'.4E (marina entrance)

**Charts / harbour guides**
**SH2** *46* **FMA** *1220*

**Contacts**
www.segel.ax/ass-marina/
gasthamn@segel.ax
☏+358 18 13610

ÅSS Marina with some 160 berths offers many services including sauna, showers and toilets (24hrs), waste disposal and laundry room. There are water and electricity outlets on all jetties. There is also bike hire available and saunas in the changing facilities. Next to the fuel jetty there is a pump-out station. WiFi is included in the harbour fee.

ÅSS Pavilion, the restaurant at the marina, seats 80, both indoors and on a terrace and also has a small glassed-over area for 35 guests. The restaurant is run by Jimmy Ström (☏+358 18 19141 www.paviljongen.ax).

#### Mariehamn East Harbour (Itäsatama/Mariehamn Östra Hamnen) MSF

60° 05'.9N 19° 56'.9E (southern mole)

**Charts / harbour guides**
**SH2** *45* **FMA** *1230*

**Contacts**
www.msf.ax/gasthamnen/
www.gasthamn.ax/sv/gasthamn
gasthamn@msf.ax
☏+358 18 19979

This is the largest marina in the Archipelago Sea, with approximately 340 berths. It is located two blocks away from the city centre and services are of a high standard and include showers, sauna and laundry which are open 24hrs a day. The harbour shop offers basic food, coffee, sodas, ice cream, etc. There is lighting on the jetties and the harbour is guarded at night in July.

### Services

Both marinas, ÅSS and MSF, provide water and electricity, and there are showers, sauna, laundry and toilet facilities ashore. There are diesel pontoons (West Harbour: 24hrs, card payment, East Harbour: 24 hhrs, card payment) where holding tanks can be emptied.

The MSF marina at Mariehamn east. Most berthing is in box berths *Andy Beharrell*

Finnish and some Swedish propane bottles can be exchanged at both marinas and Campinggaz is available at the STI fuel station near East Harbour.

There are small shops, cafés and restaurants near both marinas, plus a daily delivery of fresh bread to the harbour office every morning at around 0800 in high season.

Sail repairs can be arranged at the West Harbour ✆+358 4054 86226.

The Wemarin chandlery, is situated at Skarpansvägen 20, 22100 Mariehamn, on the eastern side of the peninsula (✆+358 18 12990, www.wemarin.com, info@wemarin.com).

A few local charts are on sale at the West Harbour marina office, but for a full range of Swedish and Finnish charts and guides visit Mariehamns Bokhandel, Torggatan 14, Mariehamn (✆+358 18 19745, www.bokhandel.ax, bokhandel@mb.ax)

### *Facilities*

The main shopping centre lies on the east side of the peninsula, close to the East Harbour. Mariehamn offers all the facilities of a medium-sized town, including food stores, Alko, banks, restaurants and hotels, together with an excellent tourist information office (8 Storagatan, Mariehamn 22100) and library. Parents with children aboard are recommended to visit the latter, which has an excellent children's area and play section with toys, books, CDs in English, storytelling and craft activities during July.

### *Communications & travel*

Mail can be sent to both marinas – c/o ÅSS Marina, Strandpromenaden, Postbox 135, 22101 Mariehamn, Åland, Finland or c/o Mariehamns Seglarförening, Postbox 155, 22101 Mariehamn, Åland, Finland.

There are regular flights and ferries from Mariehamn to Stockholm, Turku and Helsinki. An inter-island ferry serves the archipelago, and all the islands can be reached from Mariehamn without difficulty.

Car hire is readily available if you want to explore the island further. Try Rundbergs (1B Strandgatan, Mariehamn 22100 ✆+358 18 15222) garage in the north of the peninsula. However, Mariehamn itself might have been designed for the cyclist, having almost no hills and little traffic. Bicycles can be hired from both

The ÅSS Marina in Mariehamn West Harbour looking south *John Sadd*

The eastern entrance to the Lemstroms Canal. The bridge has a vertical clearance of 3.3m when closed *Andy Beharrell*

The guest harbour at Kastelholm looking north with Kastelholm Castle in the background *Andy Beharrell*

marinas, with a wider choice including tandems and children's bicycles available from a store opposite the ferry dock on the west side of the peninsular.

If you do have access to a car then the Stallhagen brewery is a very nice place to eat and, if not driving, sample their various brews (including one called the Pommern). There is also a shop selling their various beers (www.stallhagen.com/en).

## Lemströmin Kanava (Lemströms Kanal)

60°05'.8N 20°01'E

The canal was built in 1880 to facilitate traffic between Lumparn and Slemmern (eastern Mariehamn).

The Lemströms Kanal is in a beautiful setting, built in red granite and with a swing-bridge. This bridge is opened every full hour on the hour for a period of 10mins, though the precise hours depend on the season. In low season the hours are usually 1100–1800, while in high season, the hours extend to 0900–2200. For full detail check www.visitaland.com/en/practical-info/lemstrom-canal/. One needs to be at or near the bridge, visible to the guard/control building, before the full hour. Note: it opens 10mins **before** the hour for the final opening of the day. It will be opened at other times, on payment of a fee (in 2025 this was €90), by contacting the operator on ✆+358 18 33731.

## KASTELHOLM

60°13'.4N 20°05'.07E (deep pool opposite golf club)
Marina (N 60°13'.7N 20°04'.8E)

**Charts / harbour guides**
**SH2** *27* **FMA** *1250*

**Contacts**
www.kastelholm.ax
kastelholmsmarina.melina@gmail.com

Situated on the main island of Åland, Kastelholm lies only 12.5M northeast of Mariehamn. The southerly approach is from Lumparn, a relatively deep area between Åland, Lemland and Lumparland. From Rödko light (60°09'.6N 20°04'E) follow the buoyed channel northwards to west of Tingön island. Holmsudden is the narrow sound that opens up to the northeast of Tingön. The river setting, with cows and sheep grazing down to the water's edge, is a contrast to the rocky coast. The overhead cable has a clearance of 22m. The large marina is quite near the castle. Facilities include water, electricity, pump out station, fuel, showers and sauna. There is a small but well-stocked shop and café on site and fresh bread and rolls are available from the café. Bikes can be rented

Kastelholm Castle at sunrise *Hugh Rayment-Pickard*

Aerial view of the jetty at Bomarsund looking just east of north *Andy Beharrell*

Aerial view of the jetty at Bomarsund looking south with Prästötornet (part of the fortress remains) in the foreground *Andy Beharrell*

from the harbour. Anchoring is possible opposite the marina in 3-4m. Anchoring in the pool at the end of the channel near the castle is now forbidden.

Kastelholm Castle is the only medieval castle on the Åland Islands and was built in 1380. The Swedish King Gustav Wasa visited there and his son Erik XIV was imprisoned there. Today it is described as a carefully restored ruin (open 1000-1700). On the same site is also the Jan Karlsgården open-air museum and the Vita Björn prison museum. Close by is the Smakbyn restaurant which opened in 2013, with master chef Michael Bjorklund and is very popular (reservations ✆+358 18 43 666, www.smakbyn.ax).

There is a golf course with two rounds of 18 holes and a 9 hole disc golf course.

This is an excellent place to spend Midsummer and watch the ceremony of raising the pole. All the locals are dressed in national costume.

The Åland Distillery is the only distillery on the islands and is close to the harbour at Kastelholm. They offer distillery tours and have a good restaurant on the site as well. Unfortunately, because of local licensing rules, you cannot purchase their gins from the distillery, but they offer an excellent tasting tour (www.alanddistillery.com, restaurant@alanddistillery.com, ✆+358 457 345 8249).

## BOMARSUND

60°13'.1N 20°13'.9E (jetty)

**Charts / harbour guides**

**SH2** *3* **FMA** *1190*

**Contacts**

www.bomarsund.ax
en.wikipedia.org/wiki/Battle_of_Bomarsund
www.puttescamping.ax

The bridge between Bomarsund and the island of Prästö has a clearance of only 3m and therefore you can only access Bomarsund from the north. From Lumparn sail anticlockwise around Prästö leaving the islet of Slätskär to port before entering the small bay of Notviken. Bomarsund/Notviken offers good anchorage secure from all winds except northerlies. There are 26 spaces, bows-to from stern buoys (or anchor) to the wooden quay on the east side (1.9-3m). In the middle of the bay the water is deep (9m). At Puttes Camping, 200m away, showers, toilets and a café are available. Puttes Camping charge a fee for the use of this jetty which also provides electricity.

Moored at the jetty at Bomarsund managed by Puttes Camping *Fiona Ferguson*

The view from Prästötornet looking just west of north towards Storholmen *Andy Beharrell*

This anchorage was a favourite of Tsar Alexander III; there are Russian characters to be seen on the cliffs at the entrance. It is possible to berth alongside the cliff face for climbers to ascend.

The ruins of the Bomarsund Fortress, bombarded and captured by the Anglo-French fleet during the Crimean War in 1854, are still plainly visible. A 800m walk through the campsite leads to the fortifications or there is a 4.2km walk around all the various fortress ruins with excellent views over the islands

There is a large visitor centre near the bridge, www.museum.ax for details of all the Åland museums and their opening times.

Havsvidden marina and entrance *Robin Matthews*

## Delvik

60°14'.8N 20°12'.8E

The anchorage in Delvik, north of Storholm (around 1.5M just west of north from Bomarsund) is a good alternative in northerly winds.

Anchor at the head of the bay or in good holding in the inlet to the northeast (3–5m). This bay combines scenery with solitude.

## Hamnsundet

60°22'.5N 20°05'.2E (pontoon)

**Charts / harbour guides**
**SH2** *18* **FMA** *1180*

**Contacts**
www.marinahamnsundet.ax/en/
info@marinahamnsundet.ax
✆+358 18 49408

Conveniently situated in the sound, between the islands of Boxö, Boxö-ön and Åland, on the remote northern shore, Hamnsundet lies just off the main route around Fasta Åland. It is a small service harbour and coastguard station offering good shelter except from the northeast and east. There are 20 visitors' berths, bows-to pontoons from stern buoys (or anchor) and alongside the quay. Facilities include all normal guest harbour services including fuel. Power is only available with a 100m lead and water can be found on the fuel berth. There is a kiosk during the short sailing season.

## Boxö

60°23'.04N 20°06'.17E

*Anchorage*

The north entrance is straightforward with plenty of water and no known hazards provided you keep in the middle of the bay. The southerly entrance is more complicated with shoals of 1.2m. From the north, anchor in 3-4m to the east of Lillören. From the south, anchor in 4m to the east of Stengrundet. Some charts (but not all) show an underwater cable. On the west side of the northern entrance is the 'Russian Jetty' from where it is possible to view Russian fortifications from the First World War.

## Havsvidden, Geta

60° 25'.3N 19° 54'.7E (harbour mole)

**Charts / harbour guides**
**SH2** 19 **FMA** 1263

**Contacts**
www.havsvidden.com/sv/havsvidden-gasthamn
info@havsvidden.com
✆+358 18 49408

This is a small and rather shallow marina attached to the Havsvidden hotel and conference centre, located on the exposed and remote northern shore of Åland called Geta. There are many submerged rocks towards the northwest of the small inlet and the approach has to be from the east-northeast, very close to the eastern shore to avoid rocks in the middle of the bay. Follow the transit marks and proceed along the seaward side of the breakwater until the end, then turn hard to port, keeping within the marker buoys. Keep an eye out for any boats coming out, as there is very little room for two boats to pass. Also watch out for the suspended line marking the bathing area. The water depth on the outer part of the pier is 2.8m though the advertised depths are between 1.5-2.5m. There can be a severe swell in strong north winds. There are 25 places on the pontoon, bows-to from stern buoys.

Power, water, fuel and pump-out facilities are all available. The resort facilities (toilets, showers, swimming pool, 3 saunas, etc.) are also included in the marina fee and there is a good restaurant. It tends to become crowded in the summer, so a reservation might be advisable. Berths can be booked in advance through Dockspot (www.dockspot.com/en/docks/156-havsvidden).

## Djupviken, Geta

60°24'N 19°50'E (anchorage)

**Charts / harbour guides**
**SH2** 9

A long narrow inlet with an excellent anchorage in about 3m at its head. Very good shelter, even from the north. From this anchorage it is possible to climb along a marked path to the second highest hill Geta Berget in Åland (275m). There is a wooden tower at the top from which a good view can be obtained on a fine day – where there also is a coffee shop. An excellent place to appreciate the natural beauty of Åland.

There is a circular hike (around 6km) which will take you up to the Soltuna Restaurant and Café (www.soltuna.ax) and a disc golf course at Soltuna.

## Heading east from Mariehamn

Most of the vessels and ferry traffic between Mariehamn and Helsinki passes this way.

The route starts in Mariehamn, heads southeast into Rödhamnsfjärden and then north of Ledskär (59°58'N 20°10'E) to Degerby (60°02'N 20°23'E).

A stone labyrinth on Rödhamn. You can find these throughout the Baltic and it is thought that the fishermen would walk these before setting out to ensure favorable winds, plentiful catches, and confuse the smägubbar (meddling trolls)
*Andy Beharrell*

## RÖDHAMN

59°59'.1N 20°06'.1E (marina)

**Charts / harbour guides**
**SH2** *51* **FMA** *1205*

**Contacts**
www.segel.ax/gasthamnar/rodhamn/

An excellent landlocked harbour, which is a good place to wait for a fair wind for Sweden. Enter from the northwest or southeast.

The beautiful old harbour of Rödhamn ('red harbour') was an important anchorage for sailing ships en route from Sweden to Finland, as ships would sometimes lie for weeks waiting for favourable winds to carry them across the Sea of Åland. A pilot station was built in 1818 and remained in use until the 1920s. In the late 1980s the building was recreated using building plans from 1858. There is also a small museum depicting the history of the radio beacon, in use from 1937 until 1970.

In addition to the *gästhamn*, the Åland Yacht Club (ÅSS) has a marina and premises on the island including a café offering fresh bread and cinnamon buns (delivered to the boat first thing in the morning), freshly smoked fish and various cakes and snacks. On the northwest side of the island is a wood-fired sauna which can be booked through the café.

There is a pump-out station moored in the harbour.

Aerial view of the jetties at Rödhamn *Andy Beharrell*

Jetties on Rödhamn. The furthest jetties (near the cottages) are reserved for ÅSS members *Andy Beharrell*

## DEGERBY

60° 01'.8N 20° 23'.2E (pontoon Degerby Lotsudden)

**Charts / harbour guides**
**SH2** *8* **FMA** *1155, 1160*

**Contacts**
www.degerbygasthamn.ax
✆+358 457 245 6629

Degerby lies on the west coast of Degerö island. It is considered to be the central point of the Föglö archipelago. There are two gästhamns with good facilities and fuel, and shops and restaurants are within walking distance. At the gästhamn there is a small supermarket, post office, telephone, showers, sauna and laundry. Both gästhamns are open from the southwest through northwest to the northeast. Degerby Gästhamn to the northeast of the ferry jetty is more sheltered from the southwest due to the ferry quay and has 30 places on a pontoon pier, bows-to from stern buoys.

Degerby Föglö marina, Lotsudden (60°01'·8N, 20°23'E), is just 0·3M south of the ferry landing. This jetty has 45 places, bows-to from stern buoys. Seagrams Restaurant and Hotel (www.seagram.ax/) is next to the harbour. When approaching be sure to stay to the north of the green buoy about 500m off the end of the jetty before starting your approach. There are a couple of underwater rocks about 400m off the jetty to the southwest. The harbourmaster is based on a small powerboat in the inner harbour and payment can be made directly to him.

Aerial view of Degerby. Degerby Föglö marina is in the foreground and the other gästhamn is on the left by the ferry jetty *Andy Beharrell*

# ROUTE 2
# A NORTHERN ROUTE THROUGH THE ARCHIPELAGO SEA

## Route 2a Leading to the northern Turku archipelago and the Gulf of Bothnia

The northeastern part of the Åland archipelago has some of the most fascinating and least frequented waters, not least because they are off the beaten track from Mariehamn to Hanko and Helsinki. These northern waters can be approached from the west, from Vårdö (east of Åland) after crossing Lumparn or from the southwest, from Degerby. The northern route wanders northeast through the communities of Kumlinge and Brändö, which comprise many small islands and skerries. It also leads towards the northern part of the Turku archipelago, Uusikaupunki and the Gulf of Bothnia through the Kihti (Skiftet), the sound that separates the Åland Islands from Southwest Finland.

### Seglinge E, Finnhälla

60°12'.7N 20°42'.5E (wooden pontoon)

**Charts / harbour guides**
**SH2** *52* **FMA** *1120*

**Contacts**
www.seglinge.ax/sv/seglingehamnen
✆+358 40 506 1299

This is a quiet and secluded harbour on the east side of the island of Seglinge, in the narrow sound between the islands of Synderstö and Snäckö, and Seglinge. Coming from the northwest or southeast, follow the leading marks to enter the harbour, passing just north of two north cardinal buoys. Enter the pool in mid-channel, between Seglinge and Yttre Holmen. There is a frequent cable ferry between the south point of Snäckö and Seglinge. Moor alongside in 2.2–4m to a wooden jetty 200m past the ferry landing stage or further along, bows-to from stern buoys (30 spaces). Very rural with old fishing huts and boathouses.

There is a well-stocked small shop 500m up the road. Water is available from a pump at the top of the track on the right and there is electricity on the jetties. Forest walking trails lead to a disused windmill (2km) and the famous Stangnäs cauldrons – deep hollows in the rocks where it is said that offerings were made for better fishing – with excellent views of surrounding islands. There is also a disc golf course.

### Remmarhamn, Kumlinge

60°15'.4N 20°44'.2E (concrete jetty)

**Charts / harbour guides**
**SH2** *50* **FMA** *1115*

Remmarhamn is located just 2.5M further north in the sound from Seglinge, following the west shore of Snäckö. This is the largest guest harbour on the island. It is exposed to the southwest and there can be a strong current from under the road bridge to the east.

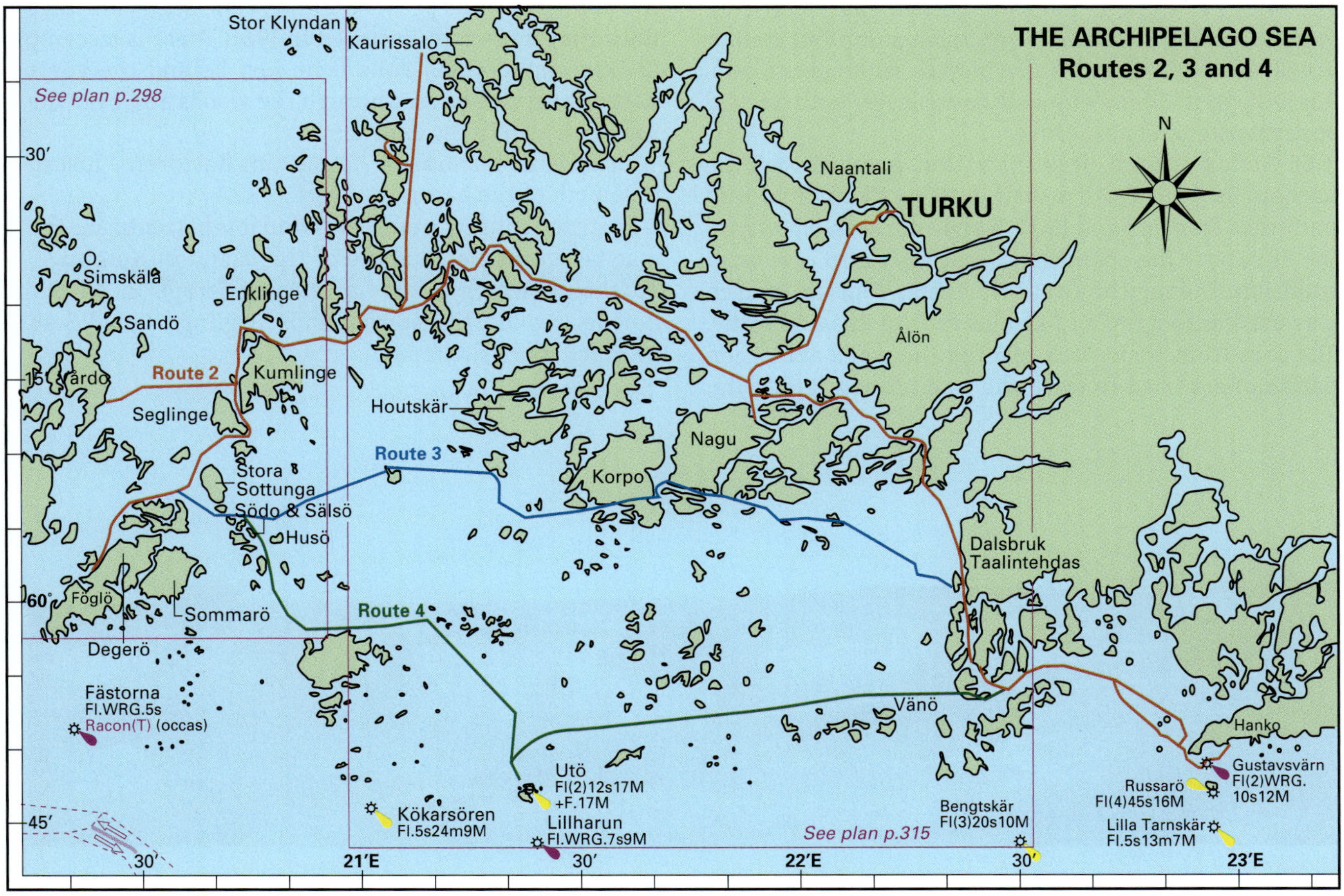

Aerial view of the jetty at Remmarhamn, Kumlinge. The road on the left runs south to the ferry from Snäckö to Seglinge
*Andy Beharrell*

The guest harbour is situated in the bay south of Ljugarsholm (Näset). Moor bows-to from stern buoys (2.5–4m) (45 spaces). Fuel and bottled gas, electricity, water, laundry, showers, sauna and a pump-out station are all available. There is also bicycle rental at the café. The village is 3km away and has a large well-stocked supermarket and post office.

St Anna's church, less than 4km northeast of the harbour is well worth a visit with its distinctive wall paintings from around 1500, a style not seen elsewhere in Finland. The paintings are in the Franciscan tradition. During the Great Northern War the church was used as lodging and stables for the Russian Army. The soot from their fires covered the walls and when parishioners tried to wash the soot off at a later date, this also removed many of the paintings, so they decided to whitewash the walls instead to preserve the paintings. This preserved the Franciscan paintings until they were fully restored in 1961. There is a scenic (3.6km) walk which runs from just behind the guest harbour service house through the woods and over the rocky plateau to the church.

There is a restaurant – Restaurant Kastören – just to the north of the harbour.

In strong southwest to west wind it is better to use the marina on the north shore of the island in Kumlinge, Torsholm, which is also a safe anchorage in all but northerly to northeasterly winds. Seglinge would then be much more sheltered.

Scenery on the walk from Kumlinge jetty to St.Anna's church *Andy Beharrell*

The northern jetty at Lappo at sunrise *Hugh Rayment-Pickard*

## Bärö

60º18'.2N 20° 44'.6E (northern mole)

**Charts / harbour guides**
**SH2** *7* **FMA** *1105*

**Contacts**
www.gladalaxen.com/en/services/guest-harbor
✆+358 18 55 304

Bärö is an island to the northwest of Kumlinge. The small harbour, a former coastguard station is situated on its north shore close to the southern tip of Enklinge island. It is open from the north to northeast. The former coastguard station has been leased and transformed into a very good restaurant, Glada Laxen (www.gladalaxen.com), open only in the summer from mid-June through August. Reservations ✆+358 18 55304.

There are 20 spaces alongside or bows-to from buoys or anchor in 2.5-3m.

There are not many paths on the island because it essentially consists of rocks, but climbing up the 40m high watch tower gives a magnificent view of the archipelago.

## Skaftfjärden, Bärö

60°17'.24N 020°44'.72E

*Anchorage*

From waypoint 60°16'.6068N; 020°43'.7005E, keep clear of the Skaftkudden promontory, then turn north and keep midway between the low-lying rocks to port and the eastern shore to starboard. The minimum depth is 5.5m in entrance. Anchor in 5m water. The anchorage is reasonably sheltered, but the surrounding land is not high. There are no facilities.

## Lappo

60°18'.9N 20°59'.7E (pontoon)

**Charts / harbour guides**
**SH2** *40* **FMA** *1000*

**Contacts**
www.lappo.ax/gasthamn/
✆+358 45 1255 516

This picturesque guest harbour is open to the east and so can be exposed from the north through east to the southeast. It is surrounded by traditional boathouses and has good facilities nearby. Approach from the northeast, following the transit, leaving the small island of Bastholm to port. There are two main jetties and the northern jetty is significantly deeper. Depths on the southern jetty are around 1.5-2m. You can moor bows-to from stern buoys or tie alongside to the pontoons (1·5–4m) (90 spaces).

There are several good walks leading to a sandy beach and a bird reserve west of the jetty. The Archipelago Museum is open in high season and contains fine examples of traditional boats. Lappo also has good services, a sauna (with excellent views), washing machine, water, electricity, supermarket, pump-out station, fuel, a fishmonger, a restaurant, harbour café and a disc golf course.

## Jurmo

60°30'.9N 21°04'.5E

**Charts / harbour guides**
**SH2** *26* **FMA** *1025*

**Contacts**
jurmo.ax (click on guest harbour in top menu)
www.nationalparks.fi/archipelagonp

The island of Jurmo, in the northeastern part of the Åland Islands can be reached either from the southeast coming from the Skiftet or directly from Kumlinge or Bärö from the west, sailing in a northeasterly direction. This western route through the archipelago is a very scenic and intricate one (see charts 738 and 737) but can only be attempted by yachts with a draught of not more than 2.1m.

An aerial view of Lappo gästhamn in the Åland Islands looking north *John Sadd*

The Jurmo guest harbour is located to the south of the island and is exposed to the west, southwest and east. The final approach is from the south, between Mjöholm and Tällholmen following transits and fairway buoys. Moor bows-to from stern anchor to the pontoon (2.4m) or alternatively anchor off the village (7–12m) with a line ashore on Tällholmen.

Jurmo is a very pretty guest harbour with many traditional wooden houses and boat sheds. Facilities include recently refurbished toilets and showers, water, electricity, fuel, sauna, washing machine, fuel, shop, restaurant and pump-out. The harbour fee can be paid in the café and shop. There are several very interesting forest walks on the island. Jurmo prides itself for raising a herd of Highland cattle and for bringing Icelandic horses onto the island for the summer. You can buy the beef in the summer shop on the island!

## Gullvivan, Björnholma

60°25'.88N 21°3'.15E

**Contacts**

www.hotellgullvivan.com/archipelago-hotel-restaurant-gullvivan/

Gullvivan is a small marina belonging to the nearby Archipelago Hotel. There is space for about 14 boats moored bows-to with stern buoy, and 2-3 more moored alongside the pontoon. The depth of water around the pontoon is about 4m and it is sheltered from the north, but open to the east and south.

Approach is from the east between the north and south cardinal buoys (waypoint: 60°25'.9157N 21°03'.6174E), turning to the north at the second south cardinal buoy. Entrance is straightforward with no known hazards. Power, water and rubbish disposal is available at the pontoon, and toilet, showers, restaurant and a sauna ashore.

## Route 2b From Lappo or Torsholma towards Turku or Hanko

To sail towards Turku or Hanko taking the northern route through the Finnish archipelago, leave Torsholma or Lappo and head east across the Skiftet (Kihti) sound. (See plan page 315.)

## Iniö

60°23'.8N 21°23'.4E (Norrby)

**Charts / harbour guides**
**SH1** *43* **FMA** *958, 954*

**Charts / harbour guides**
www.norrbyhamn.fi

Norrby lies to the east of the island of Iniö in a sheltered basin formed by a cluster of islands, Iniö, Kolko, Hepmo and Jumo. Approach either from the southwest, leaving the main channel (3.5m) and entering between Kupmo and Iniö or the southeast from Perkala fjärden leaving Kolko to starboard and the islets of Bergholm, Grisselholm, Hästholm and Jeppörarna to port. Kolko

The guest jetty at Gullvivan *Robin Matthews*

sound is well marked by cardinal buoys. Turn sharp around Jeppörarna to enter the approach channel (2.4m) that leads to the landing following the transit on Likholmen.

There are two harbours on Iniö:

### Norrby

Norrby is close to the village but is very shallow and cramped (1·5–2m). There is a post office.

### Bruddalsviken

www.bjorklundbatslip.fi/eng/Guestharbour.html
✆+358 2463 5343

Only 0.5M further to the northwest (60°24'·3N 21°22'·6E), although further away from the village, has more space and is deeper (2·5–3m). Both have water (for an extra charge), electricity, showers, sauna, restaurant and shop. There is boat storage and an engineering and general marine workshop called Björklund Båtslip (www.bjorklundbatslip.fi) here as well.

## Pähkinäinen

60°19'.7N 21°41'.7E

**Charts / harbour guides**
**SH1** *96* **FMA** *858*

**Contacts**
www.pahkinainen.fi

This is an almost landlocked small guest harbour and anchorage on the island of Pähkinäinen. Enter the lagoon from the east, leaving the islets of Mäntykari, Kalliokari, and Pikku Viljakari to port, and the shoals and Mustaluoto to starboard. There are two pontoons with 50 spaces 1·5M from the entrance to port. Mooring here is bows-to from stern buoys (or anchor). The pontoon on the right-hand side is private or reserved for the ferry. The facilities are very limited. There is a floating pump-out station to the east of the pontoon. Space is available to anchor in the lagoon, as far as the southwest corner at Varsalahti (60°19'·8N 21°40'·8E), but beware of the submerged rock to the north of Varsalahti. This is a very popular weekend destination and owned by the city of Turku.

## Näsby, Houtskär

60°13'.5N 21°22'.0E

**Charts / harbour guides**
**FMA** *970*

Näsby harbour is located on the northern part of Houtskär. Approach from the west along the 3m route between Houtskär and Benskär. At Roslaxnäs turn starboard and westwards into the bay. Alternatively, you can approach from the east through a buoyed channel between the islands of Kivimo and Roslax. This channel can be approached from either the north or the west and the first green buoy in this channel is at 60°14'.048N 21°19'.590E. Moor bows-to from stern buoys at the pontoon with places for 50 boats. There is electricity, water, fuel, a restaurant, sauna, shower, toilet, WiFi and washing machine.

Näsby village is 200m inland. There you find a well-stocked supermarket and café. The wooden well-preserved church is from 1703. A culture path with 10 stops describes the history of the island and there is also the Houtskär Archipelago Museum (Houtskärs Skärgårdsmuseum) just around the corner from the guest jetty. This has various buildings showing archipelago life.

Bruddalsviken looking south. The guest berths are to starboard on entry. Björklund Båtslip boatyard is in the background *John Sadd*

Aerial view of Näsby jetty looking towards the east *Andy Beharrell*

Boathouses at Näsby on Houtskär *Andy Beharrell*

## Nagu, Kyrkbacken

60°11'.6N 21°54'.6.E

**Charts / harbour guides**
**SH1** *79* **FMA** *746*

**Contacts**
www.naguhamn.fi
✆+358 40 055 2923

A naturally sheltered bay, fringed by sand and pine trees on the northeast coast of the island of Nagu. This has become the attractive setting for a marina. The approach channels from the northwest and the east are well marked. Enter the harbour from the northeast, leaving two east cardinal buoys to starboard. There are 120 berths on pontoons, some finger pontoons, some bows-to with stern buoys, and some spaces alongside. There is a pump-out point on the fuel jetty. The toilets, sauna and laundry block are all to a very high standard.

The marina is the most popular in the archipelago and gets very crowded during the summer, particularly during Midsummer. It is possible to pre-book berths through the website. The marina and associated shops also offer kayak hire, SUP hire and bike hire - both standard bikes and e-fat bikes. There is a swimming beach close to the marina and mini-golf. The ferry to Själö (Seili) goes from next door to the marina and from there, another ferry to Rymättylä (Hankö) gives road access on to Naantali and Turku on the mainland.

The St. Olav fieldstone church dates from the 1440s and is worth a visit - it has Finland's oldest bible in the church.

There are fish and bread shops in separate little wooden cabins along the beach: the wonderful hot-smoked rainbow trout is not to be missed - smoked on site behind the kiosk. There are also very good restaurants, cafés and hotels and a range of shops along the front near the marina. A fuel station, post office, pharmacy and supermarket are only a short walk away. This is a very useful stop to provision and fuel up. It is usually very quiet; night silence 2300-0700 is observed, apart from Midsummer!

An aerial view of Nagu gästhamn looking just south of west *Andy Beharrell*

## TURKU (ÅBO)

60°25'.9N 22°13'.6E (mouth of the Aura river)

### Distances
Mariehamn 75M, Hanko 65M

### Lights
**Lillharun** 59°43'.6N 21°24'.2E Fl.WRG.7s17m8M
Racon Black concrete tower Wind generator
**Utö** 59°46'.9N 21°22'.3E Fl(2)12s40m18M
Auxiliary F.38m10M Square white granite tower, red stripes 24m. In centre of island
**Bokullankivi** 59°50'.8N 21°25'.4E Fl.WRG.5s9m9M
Racon White tower, black band Wind generator
**Lövskär** 60°13'.2N 21°43'.6E VQ(5)WRG.6s7m7M
Frame¬work tower
**Petäis** 60°14'.3N 21°48'.1E Fl.WRG.3s6m4M
Black concrete base, white lantern
**Orhisaari** 60°16'.5N 22°00'E Q(2)WRG.6s18m10M
White metal framework tower, concrete base
**Rajakari** 60°22'.7N 22°06'E Fl.WRG.4s13m11M
Red and white round concrete tower
**Kalkkiniemi** Oc.WRG.3s

### Contacts
**Turku Port Authority** ✆+358 02 2674 122
VHF Ch 12/16/71 (call Turku Port Control)
turkuport@port.turku.fi
www.visitturku.fi

Turku is worth the detour from the open sea. It was the capital of Finland until the early 19th century and is the country's sixth largest city, with a population of more than 190,000. It is also one of the most important ports in Finland, handling oil, containers and other freight, together with frequent ferry services to Stockholm and Mariehamn. Its shipyards construct some of the biggest cruise liners including the Icon of the Seas, delivered to Royal Caribbean in November 2023, which was, at the time, the world's largest at 365 metres in length with a gross tonnage of 248,655T. She runs on liquefied natural gas, utilises fuel cell technology and carries 7,600 passengers with 2,350 crew members.

The modern city, built on a grid pattern, was rebuilt in 1827 after the old town was virtually wiped out by fire. The 13th-century cathedral, gutted by the fire, has been completely restored. Turku Castle, which stands near the mouth of the Aura river, dates back to the 13th century and now houses an interesting museum. There is an excellent maritime museum, the Forum Marinum, with exhibits both ashore and afloat. It is the National Museum for Maritime History and also the Finnish Navy Museum (www.forum-marinum.fi).

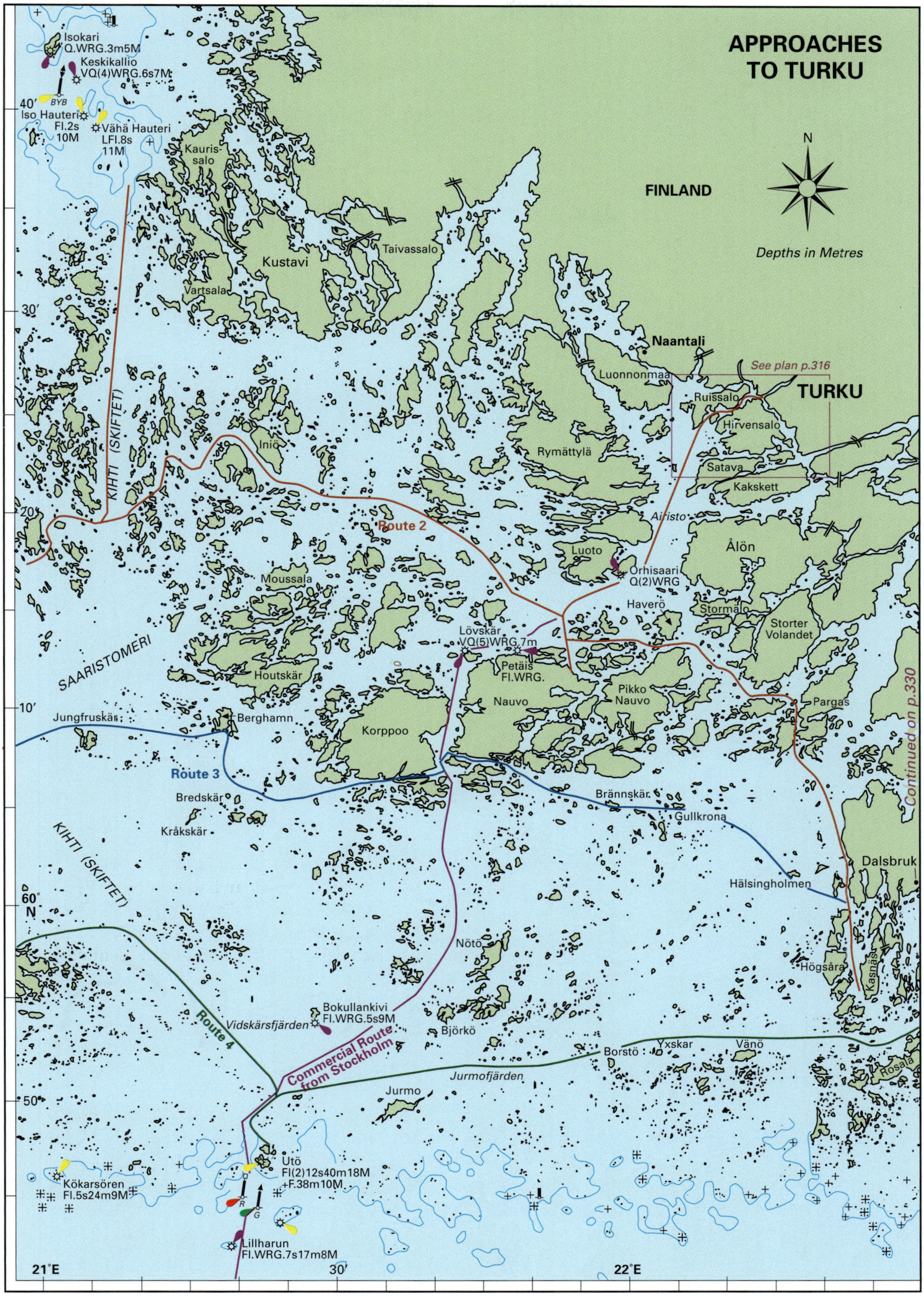
APPROACHES TO TURKU
N
FINLAND
Depths in Metres
Isokari
Q.WRG.3m5M
Keskikallio
VQ(4)WRG.6s7M
BYB
Iso Hauteri
Fl.2s
10M
Vähä Hauteri
LFl.8s
11M
Kauris-salo
Kustavi
Taivassalo
Vartsala
Naantali
See plan p.316
Luonnonmaa
TURKU
Ruissalo
Hirvensalo
Satava
Kakskett
Rymättylä
Iniö
KIHTI (SKIFTET)
Route 2
Airisto
Ålön
Luoto
Orhisaari
Q(2)WRG
Moussala
Haverö
Stormälö
Storter Volandet
Lövskär
VQ(5)WRG.7m
Petäis
Fl.WRG.
SAARISTOMERI
Houtskär
Nauvo
Pikko Nauvo
Pargas
Jungfruskär
Berghamn
Korppoo
Continued on p.330
Route 3
Brännskär
Bredskär
Gullkrona
Kråkskär
KIHTI (SKIFTET)
Dalsbruk
Hälsingholmen
Nötö
Högsåra
Kasnäs
Bokullankivi
Fl.WRG.5s9M
Vidskärsfjärden
Route 4
Björkö
Commercial Route from Stockholm
Borstö
Yxskar
Vänö
Rosala
Jurmofjärden
Jurmo
Utö
Fl(2)12s40m18M
+F.38m10M
Kökarsören
Fl.5s24m9M
Lillharun
Fl.WRG.7s17m8M
40′
30′
20′
10′
60° N
50′
21°E
30′
22°E

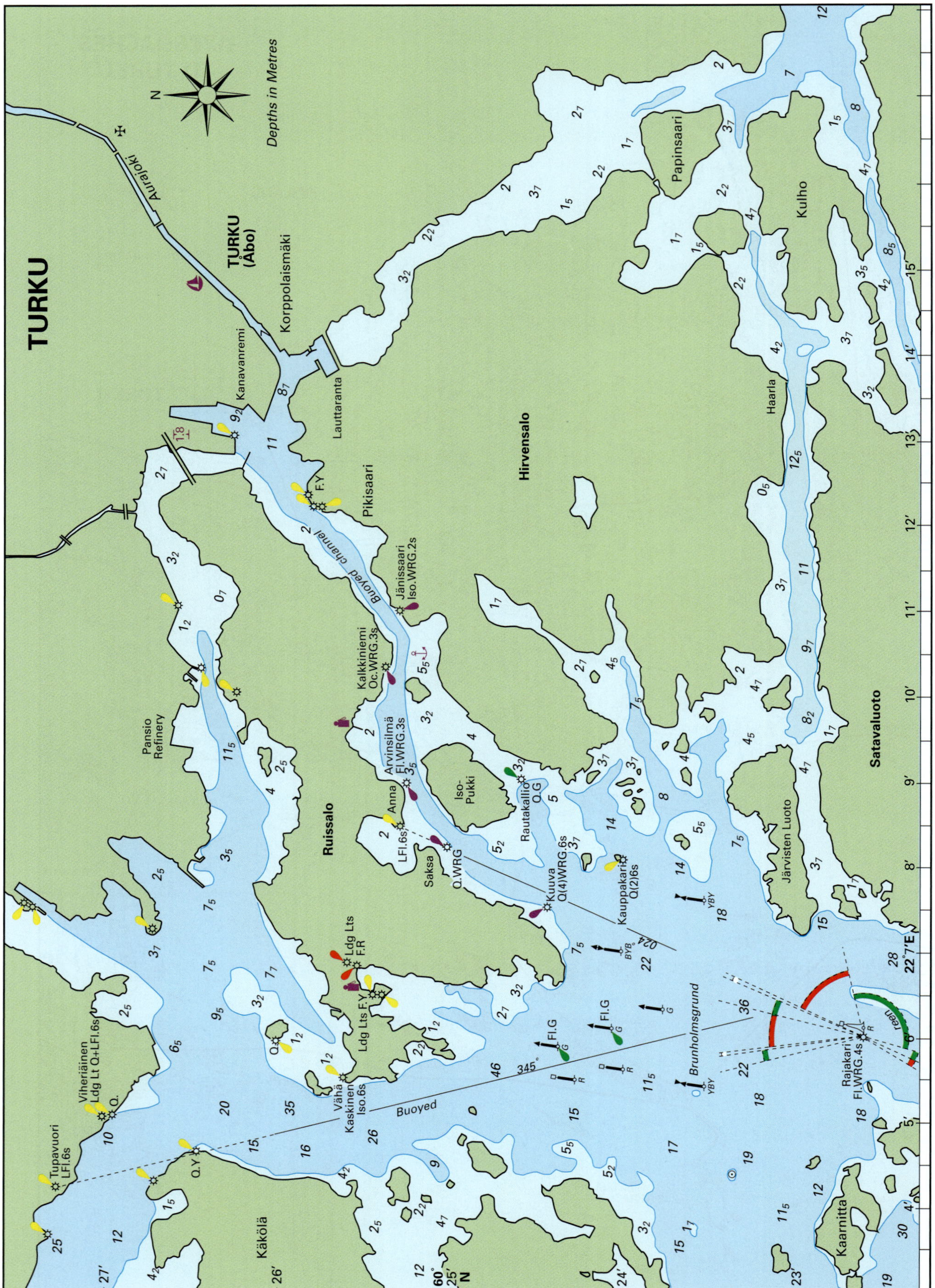
TURKU
TURKU (Åbo)
Aurajoki
Korppolaismäki
Kanavanremi
Lauttaranta
Pikisaari
Hirvensalo
Papinsaari
Kulho
Haarla
Satavaluoto
Järvisten Luoto
Ruissalo
Pansio Refinery
Buoyed channel
Depths in Metres
Jänissaari Iso.WRG.2s
Kalkkiniemi Oc.WRG.3s
Arvinsilmä Fl.WRG.3s
Anna LFl.6s
Saksa
Q.WRG
Iso-Pukki
Rautakallio Q.G
Kuuva Q(4)WRG.6s
Kauppakari Q(2)6s
Ldg Lts F.R
Ldg Lts F.Y
Vähä Kaskinen Iso.6s
Viheriäinen Ldg Lt Q+LFl.6s
Tupavuori LFl.6s
Käkölä
Brunholmsgrund
Buoyed
Rajakari Fl.WRG.4s
Kaarnitta
F.Y
Q.Y
Fl.G
YBY
BYB
345°
024°
60° 25′ N
22°7′E

Box berths at Turku guest harbour. The marina office is by the black restaurant in the background
*Andy Beharrell*

### *Approach & entrance*

The approach is from the southwest through the main commercial shipping channel (13m). Change course to approximately 021° when you reach Rajakari lighthouse (60°22'.6N 22°05'.8E). This leads straight into the narrow, well-buoyed and deep approach channel towards Turku, between Ruissalo and Iso-Pukki, regularly used by large ships. There is an alternative channel to the east of Iso-Pukki (3m). Both channels join at Kalkkiniemi. Follow the channel to Turku docks, turn to starboard past the passenger and commercial port, and then to port up the Aura river past the shipbuilding yards and the three-masted Suomen Joutsen.

### *Berthing*

www.turunvierasvenesatama.fi/en
www.youtube.com/watch?v=sL-ppXdNzww
info@turunvierasvenesatama.fi
✆+358 400 536 613

There are several well-equipped marinas outside Turku, but visiting yachts will undoubtedly find it most convenient to moor at the city-run guest harbour, Aura å västra (**FMA** *688*), situated on the west bank of the Aura river, just downstream from the foot ferry. The marina office (open 0800–2200 in season) doubles as a café, both occupying a small black kiosk.

Among the 70 berths are several suitable for yachts of up to 3.5m beam and 2m draught, with larger yachts (up

The Suomen Joutsen (Swan of Finland) was built in 1902. From 1961 she was the seamen's school for the Finnish Merchant Navy and in 1991 she was donated to the city of Turku as a museum ship
*Andy Beharrell*

to 5m beam) berthing further downstream. Berthing is between posts, so check the width! During the season marina staff will usually help you in. Considerable disturbance is caused by wash from the many passing tourist boats. If there is no room on the west side, there are spaces alongside the quay on the east bank, below the foot ferry.

The guest harbour is often full to capacity from mid-June to the end of July, but it may be possible to lie alongside one of the charter vessels moored along the quayside. Check with marina staff. Berths can be booked in advance through the marina website and through Satamapaikka (www.satamapaikka.com/).

Masted yachts are prevented from continuing up the river by a fixed bridge (4.1m), but there are several public quays and landing places further up the river where a dinghy might be secured for short periods.

*Services*

The guest harbour has water and electricity on the pontoons (though washing boats down with fresh water is forbidden) with good quality toilets, showers, sauna and laundry facilities in a block just across the road.

The marina office can give you a phone number for the delivery of fuel from a small road tanker.

The nearest chandlery is Meredin-Ulkoiluaitta at Marina Pargas Ab – Meredin, Tervsundintie 70, 21600 Parainen. This is around 45min drive away, but is a well-stocked chandlery and, if you are heading on to Helsinki, is an easy stop at Pargas (around 27M sailing).

✆+358 2 275 275
meredin@meredin.fi

Boat repairs at Satavan Venepalvelu
✆+358 20 735 1414
svp@satavanvenepalvelu.fi
www.satavanvenepalvelu.fi

Sailmaker and repairs at Purjeneulomo Niiniranta Oy
✆+358 2 275 3059
www.northsails.com/en-uk/pages/sailloft-helsinki-finland

*Facilities*

The yacht harbour is about 20mins walk along the riverside to the town centre, where all normal shopping needs can be met. There is a K-market supermarket almost opposite the guest harbour via the foot ferry which is very convenient for stocking up. There are also excellent outdoor and covered markets and various supermarkets, including one in the basement of a shopping mall. There is the usual range of cafés, restaurants and hotels, many overlooking the water and some on historic vessels moored on the river itself.

Several enormous out-of-town shopping centres lie to the north of the town on the bus route to Naantali. There is a ferry service to Naantali which is a lovely town and, while it is accessible by yacht, there is a 15m bridge which will limit the ability of many to get there. Naantali is also the location of Moominworld!

*Communications & travel*

There is a bus stop behind the marina, one way leading to the maritime museum, castle and docks, the other to the city centre and the airport. Ferries leave the docks daily for Stockholm and Mariehamn.

Helsinki airport is easily reached by train, bus or plane. The connections make Turku an excellent stop for crew changes.

## Airisto, Stormälö

60°15'.1N 22°06'.4E (pier)

**Charts / harbour guides**
**SH1** *3* **FMA** *738*

**Contacts**
www.airistomarina.fi/en/
info@airistomarina.fi
✆+358 40 594 7961

This old harbour was used in the 19th century by the Tsarist navy with deep water all around the bay. There is a marina situated on the west side of the island of Stormälö. It is part of a holiday hotel development and can accommodate 100 boats. Yachts moor bows-

Airisto marina *M. Strobel*

to from stern buoys, alongside or in berths. There is space for several larger yachts alongside the outer pontoon. The marina has water, electricity, fuel, gas, WiFi connection and a pump-out station. The marina charge includes showers, toilet and sauna. Berths can be booked in advance through the marina website (www.airistomarina.fi/make-a-booking/).

There is also a restaurant and a kiosk selling smoked fish and fresh vegetables.

## Paraisten Portti

60°09'N 22° 17'.1E (pier)

**Charts / harbour guides**
**SH1** *88* **FMA** *638*

**Contacts**
www.pargasport.fi/fi/Satama
myynti@paraistenportti.fi
✆+358 44 975 8806

Located on the southern peninsula of the larger island of Jermo, Paraisten Portti is a convenient service harbour in the sound between the islands of Attu, Jermo, Tammo and Sorpo. However, it is exposed to the north and to wash from passing boats. It has room for 30 boats in 2–2.3m, bows-to from stern buoys. It has a good restaurant and the facilities include fuel, electricity, shop and pump-out station. There is also a sauna and jacuzzi available for rental.

An alternative in northerly winds is a good anchorage, just 1M further north, in 10m in a large bay east of Dirholmen (Digerholm) (60°10'N 22°16'.6E) at the north end of Sorpo (Käringholm). It is open to the east and southeast.

## Hamnholmen

60°01'N 22°21'.4E

**Charts / harbour guides**
**SH1** *31*

The anchorage of Hamnholmen lies within the Archipelago National Park and therefore care should be taken to respect the rules and regulations. It is located west of Purunpää and north of Noströ and Högsåra with a good sheltered anchorage on the eastern side of the island. Access is easy from the main channel (4.2m). Approach either from the south, leaving all the islets and rocks at the entrance to port or from the north rounding the east cardinal buoy just off Judasholm. Anchor in the north or south (3.5m) part of the pool. Note that there are many submerged rocks around Dömmaskärsgrunden south of Gåshalsen (see chartlet 702.4).

## Kejsarhamnen, Högsåra

59°57'.7N 22°21'9E

**Charts / harbour guides**
**SH1** *54* **FMA** *620*

**Contacts**
www.visitsaaristo.net/en/location/hogsara-kejsarhamnen-kemionsaari-8019

Kejsarhamnen is a bay on the north side of the island of Högsåra on the west side of Jungfrusund. It affords excellent anchorage for large and small yachts. The bay can be entered from the north, between Nämanön and North and South Furuholm or from the east. The latter can be easily identified by the white cairn on the northern tip of Killingholm. The holding ground in the southern part of the bay is not good. However, there is a guest pontoon with electricity on the south shore just off Killingholm with 30 spaces, bows-to from stern anchor. There is a floating pump-out station just off the pontoon. Limited facilities ashore include a shower, sauna and a kiosk. The guest pontoon is open to north winds.

The bay is called after Tsar Alexander III who used to anchor here in the royal yacht Standart. The nearby beach makes this a popular harbour for boats with young families. Fuel is obtainable at the village of Högsåra. An alternative well-sheltered anchorage with muddy bottom is located half a mile further north in Norrfladan off Nämanön, tucked behind the islands of North and South Furuholm. Anchor in 4m towards the northwestern end of the lagoon.

## Byviken, Högsåra

59° 57'.23N 22° 22'.15E

**Charts / harbour guides**
**SH1** *41* **FMA** *597*

This harbour on the island of Högsara, situated on the west side of the Jungfrusund, has a long history of providing pilotage services: as far back as the 16th century its tenant farmers piloted ships owned by the Swedish Royal Navy through the island's rocky waters. The island's pilotage services continued right up to 1985, and a visit to the local museum in the main harbour (Byviken) is worthwhile. The resident population has dwindled from about 100 in the 1950s to about 40 today, and the remaining inhabitants now depend on tourism and forestry for their living. The island's main employer is the Maritime Administration's shipping route station. The island has two places for guests to berth. Byviken gästhamn is on the southern side of the bay and can accommodate up to 40 boats, bows-to from stern buoys. The village is famous for Farmors (Granny's) Café which sells mouth-watering pastries, snacks, coffee and bread. Lunch and dinner are also available. The café also has a small guest harbour with space for around 20 boats called Cafébryggan and spaces can be reserved here in advance through their website – www.farmorscafe.fi/en/vierasvenesatama. A small ferry from Svartnäs calls in at the harbour, meaning that the pontoon is sometimes susceptible to passing wash. It is also open to the east.

# ROUTE 3
# A CENTRAL ROUTE THROUGH THE ARCHIPELAGO SEA LEADING FROM DEGERBY TOWARDS HANKO

*Lights*

**Enskär lighthouse** (60°07'.4N 20°34'.9E, Fl.WRG.3s)
**Tjurgrund light** (60°06'.56N 20°41'.8E, Q(2)WRG.6s)

From Degerby follow the main northeasterly route as for Route 2 until you reach Skarpskär (60°06'.7N 20°28'.4E). From there, follow the transits eastwards until you have reached Enskär lighthouse (60°07'.4N 20°34'.9E). The central route leads in a southeasterly direction past Sottunga and eastwards through the Archipelago Sea. From Sottunga, the central route continues past Husö, Jungfruskär, south of the large island of Korppoo (Korpo), then north of Ängsö and Bergö. From there it continues east-southeast and passes south of Brännskär and close south of Gullkrona. The final leg is southeasterly via Helsingholmen and through the Jungfrusund, between Högsåra and Kasnäslandet where the central and northern routes meet to join the southern route north of Rosala (see plan page 309).

Alternatively, starting from Degerby in the northeasterly direction, at Sandön (60°04'.1N 20° 26'.3E) turn eastwards on the route with the name Ämbarsunden. Note the minimum depth of 1.8m! This route is beautiful, narrow at places and you can see a lot of wildlife. The route ends at Sälsö, just east of Husö, to join the central route.

West of Hanko the routes meander through the Archipelago National Park which is home to a range of wildlife and many bird species. This national park extends from Jungfruskär in the northwest to south of Korpoström across to Högland in the east. Then it goes south just to the west of Kasnäs right down to the outer edges of the archipelago at Bengtskär and then back across taking in Jurmo and Utö. Full details, including maps are available on the National Park website luontoon.fi/en.

## Sottunga/Sottungalandet

60°06'.5N 20°40'9E (pier)

**Charts / harbour guides**
**SH2** *56* **FMA** *1165*

**Contacts**
www.sottungagasthamn.fi
✆+358 40500 8015

Sottunga is a small service harbour open from the beginning of June until September. It is at the southern end of the island, north of the islets of Hamnklobb, Snackö and Hamnö. Tjurgrund light (60°06'.56N 20°41'.8E ) has three white sectors from the west, south and southeast for the approach to the harbour; there is a transit as well. There are 40 spaces on a single pontoon (though they often manage to fit more boats in in high season), bows-to from stern buoys (or anchor) to the pontoon near the ferry landing (2.5–3m) or alongside at the quay. Water and fuel are available in the inner harbour with a shop at the centre of the island. Bikes are available from the guest harbour to cycle to the

Jurmo – part of the Archipelago (Kansallispuisto) National Park *Anne Fleck*

Mary Magdalene church at Sottunga *Andy Beharrell*

Aerial view of the guest jetty at Sottunga. The restaurant and inner harbour are just out of the picture on the right *Andy Beharrell*

Bänö-ön anchorage looking northeast *Andy Beharrell*

shop. The Restaurant Salteriet operates throughout the season near the guest harbour. Berthing fees can be paid there. There are toilets, showers and a sauna along with a pump-out station on the jetty.

Sottunga is the smallest municipality in Finland and the island has a population of just 100 and is a typical traditional agricultural landscape with small cultivated areas surrounded by deciduous forest – hazel and thick pine forest. The island's wind turbine supplies all their power needs and is called 'Oskar'.

The small ferries to Snäckö, Föglö, Galtby and Långnäs berth just west of the harbour. There is a beautiful 18th century wooden church built in 1728 and dedicated to Mary Magdalene, 300m down the road, and several interesting walks around the island.

## Bänö-ön

60°04'.8N 20°35'.4E

### *Anchorage*

A large and much indented bay affording anchorage sheltered from all winds. Enter between Bänö-ön and Gåsholm, the island east of it, or between Gåsholm and the two small skerries northwest of it to port and Bänö/Söderön to starboard. Anchor at the mouth of the Bänö-ön eastern (Söderklobba) bay with good holding, or in easterly winds in the bay on west side of Gåsholm (clay bottom); or in the bay Ålviken between Bänö and the islands immediately west of it. There are various opportunities to moor to the shore, bows-to from stern anchor. Popular and very pleasant, remote and big enough to feel deserted.

## Jungfruskär

60°08'.3N 21°04'.2E (pontoon)

**Charts / harbour guides**
**SH2** *25* **FMA** *995*

This is a beautiful inhabited group of islands, the largest ones being Jungfruskär, Nölstö and Hamnö. They are situated in the centre of the Archipelago Sea, remote from civilisation, softer and more tranquil than one might expect from their appearance at some distance. Enter from the north or the southwest and anchor anywhere in the sound between Hamnö and Jungfruskär, taking care to avoid the submerged rock close to the northeastern tip of Hamnö and the submerged power cable close by. Alternatively you might prefer to moor bows-to with a stern anchor to the small guest pontoon on Jungfruskär (2–2.8m at the end of the pontoon) or bows-to with stern anchor to the shore just south of the pontoon. The other piers are private. Jungfruskär is open to the north.

Jungfruskär *Anne Fleck*

## Berghamn, Storlandet

60°09'N 21°19'E

**Charts / harbour guides**
**SH1** *8*

*Anchorage*

A perfect landlocked harbour, wilder and grander than Jungfruskär, and secure from all winds. It is approached through two narrow channels, one from the south, between Röstholm and Hamnholm, the other from the southwest, through the Hamnholms sound between Hamnholm and Berghamn. Anchor anywhere in the middle of the lagoon, south of the west cardinal buoy, in order to keep clear of the two small ferry piers on the south tip of Berghamn and Lukholm. Alternatively, moor bows-to the shore with a stern anchor on the east side of Hamnholmen immediately to port after the Röstholm and Hamnholm entrance.

## Verkan

60°10'.44N 21°33'.32E

**Charts / harbour guides**
**SH1** *136*

**Contacts**
www.verkan.fi

The approach to Verkan does require some careful navigation through the various shallows, but the buoyage is very clear. Approach in a minimum of 3.5m can be made from the south between Lempersö and Elvsö, taking care to stay the right side of the cardinals. Keep following north and just after the small island of Järm you will pick up a buoyed channel and then a series of cardinals. At the last northerly cardinal, you will see the gästhamn of Verkan in front of you.

Heading in from the north, pick up the day mark on the western tip of Brändholm and just to the south are buoys (initially lateral and then cardinal) to guide you into Verkan.

The guest pontoon is just after the ferry jetty and beyond that is a fuel and pump-out jetty which is straightforward to berth at. There is space for around 60 boats on stern buoys bows-to the pontoon, though there have apparently been up to 140 boats in high season. Five of the stern buoys can be booked in advance through the website – www.ravintolabuffalo.fi/varaa-satamapaikka/.

Facilities are good and include saunas, toilets, rubbish disposal, showers, washing machines, restaurant (Ravintola Buffalo) and some shops, though for any major shopping you will need to head into the village of Korpo, about 25mins walk away where there is a K-market. The *gästhamn* can rent bikes to make the journey easier, or to explore the island further. Kayak and SUP hire through the shop.

Aerial view of Verkan gästhamn *Andy Beharrell*

The main guest jetty at Verkan looking southwest *Andy Beharrell*

The guest jetty at Korpoström *Andy Beharrell*

## KORPOSTRÖM

60°06'.6N 21°36'E

**Charts / harbour guides**
**SH1** *60* **FMA** *838*

**Contacts**
www.skargardscentrum.fi/hamn/
visit@skargardscentrum.fi
✆+358 40 139 1218

The guest harbour is situated to the south of the large island of Korpo in the narrow strait between the main island and the offshore island of Kait. It has two visitors' pontoons with 70 spaces, bows-to from stern buoys just east of the fuel pontoon (1.5–2m). The marina has a smart hotel and wooden promenade with a high-class restaurant overlooking the harbour. Services include fuel, pump-out station, water, electricity, showers, sauna, washing machine, bike hire, store, restaurant, café and tourist office. Various events and exhibitions take place at the Archipelago centre which runs the harbour, so it is worth checking their website – www.skargardscentrum.fi.

Korpoström is known for the big naval battle between the Swedes and the Russians in 1743 that took place in the narrow strait and ended with the defeat of the Swedish navy.

As an alternative, a good anchorage in the channel is located 1.5M to the east (Norrsund) with private homes and a public jetty at Rumar (60°06'.7N 21°38'.7E) in 2.5–3m.

### Stenskär and Birsskär

60°04'.3N 22°02'.9E and 60°04'.3N 22°02'.7E

**Charts / harbour guides**
**SH1** *109* **FMA** *762, 766*

**Contacts**
www.stenskar.fi/sv/gaestbrygga

The guest berths at Helsingholm looking northwest from the other side of Hemviken bay *Anne Fleck*

A well-protected, landlocked harbour between Stenskär, Birsskär and Gråsö. A wonderfully scenic and sheltered anchorage, just south of Gullkrona. Enter from the north or southwest, following the buoyed channel. Berth either bows-to jetty with stern buoy in east corner (Stenskär 15 places), or alongside the pier running east from Birsskär Island (25 places). There is also a good anchorage between the islands. Both guest harbours provide electricity, water, waste disposal, toilet, shower, sauna, nature trail, and fresh fish for sale. The blue buoys are private.

### Helsingholm

60°01'.8N 22°16'.9E

**Charts / harbour guides**
**SH1** *30* **FMA** *626*

**Contacts**
www.helsingholm.fi

Anchor in the open bay to the north of the island or moor bows to wooden jetty (40 places, depth 1.5–2.5m). Protected from the south with very attractive view to the north. There is a sand bar between Helsingholm and Sandö, but a buoyed channel across it. Helsingholm is very popular, partly because of its beautiful location but also due to the warm welcome afforded by the host family Andersson. There is a sauna which can be booked and the harbour offers electricity, composting toilets and showers. Smoked fish available in season.

Looking out from Helsingholm *Anne Fleck*

## ROUTE 4
## A SOUTHERN ROUTE THROUGH THE ARCHIPELAGO SEA LEADING FROM DEGERBY TOWARDS HANKO

*Lights*

**Enskär lighthouse** 60°07'.4N 20°34'.9E, Fl.WRG.3s

From Degerby follow the main northeasterly route as for routes 2 and 3 until you reach Skarpskär (60°06'.7N 20°28'.4E). From there, follow the transits eastwards until you reach Enskär lighthouse (60°07'.4N 20°34'.9E). The southern route leads in a southeasterly direction past Sottunga (see page 320) and continues southwards to Husö and Kyrkogårdsö, passing north of Kökar before heading southeast towards Utö.

From Utö, Route 4 continues eastwards to Jurmo and Borstö (possibly with a diversion north to visit Björkö and Nötö in the Archipelago Sea National Park), east past Yxskär to Vänö, and finally north of Rosala and Hiittinen (Hitis) for the final leg southeast to Hanko (see plan page 309).

The total distance from Mariehamn's West Harbour to Hanko's East Harbour by Routes 3 and 4 is approximately 122M.

## Husö

60°03'.9N 20°48'.2E

*Anchorage*

A small anchorage in the southwest corner of the island. Enter from the southeast, between Varpskär and Husö Södra Näset making sure to leave the east cardinal buoy, and shortly after that a rock awash (marked by an iron post) to port. Anchor in the pool east of Södholm. The small ferry to other Åland destinations runs from the southern point of the island. It has many holiday cottages and is worth a visit. Very attractive rock formations and good bird watching.

A biological station is situated on Husö which is a part of the Environmental and Marine Biology Department at Turku Akademi University. The station functions as the base for aquatic studies, but also botanical, mycological and entomological studies are conducted. The station provides space and equipment for experimental aquatic ecology, laboratory analysis, biological sampling as well as field investigations of coastal areas and lakes.

## Kökar

59°57'N 20°54'E (northern approach)

Kökar comprises Karlby, Finnö and Helsö villages, and is both Åland and Finland's most southerly community.

### Sandvik, Kökar

59°56'.3N 20°53'E

**Charts / harbour guides**
Chart C741, 27, 28
**SH2** *39* **FMA** *1140*

**Contacts**
www.sandvik.ax
☏+358 457 342 9242

This is one of the most interesting of the Åland villages. Sandvik is the best of the three yacht harbours for visitors – an excellent natural harbour on the north coast of Karlbylandet, affording secure shelter from all winds. The approaches are well marked by transits as well as by buoys. There are several rocks in the harbour

The fishing boat at Sandvik (Kökar) is an obvious landmark as you approach the jetty *Andy Beharrell*

Left: St Anna's church on Hamnö. A nice walk from Sandvik guest harbour on Kökar *Andy Beharrell*

Right: Sandvik guest harbour has a café and small grocery store *Andy Beharrell*

marked with unlit blue poles, but keep well clear as the rocks extend some way around the poles. The guest harbour is situated on the south side of Hamnösund, the deep bay to the southeast of Hamnö. Berth bows-to from stern buoys; 50 spaces in 2–3m. Except for the buoys across the end of the pontoon, these are too close to the pontoons for any yacht much over 40', but there is also good anchoring in the middle of the bay. The service house has showers, toilets, a laundry, a kitchen and dining room. There is a fuel boat run by the harbourmaster. He may be able to come alongside to refill tanks.

The shop at the end of the marina stocks food essentials and also bakes delicious cinnamon buns and fresh bread. There are bikes available for hire to explore Kökar where everywhere is within a 10km distance.

Take a walk and visit the church of St. Anna, a distance of around 2km. There is a nice path through the woods which avoids the road. The path turns off just after the bridge across to Hamnö. St. Anna's is a 17th-century church built on the site of an old Franciscan monastery, founded in Hamnö in the 15th century and a Bronze Age settlement. The church and grounds are very beautiful and in the church is a baptismal font made of Gotland limestone from the 13th century. It is possible to change crew by using the ferry. This takes approximately 2.5hrs to/from Långnäs on mainland Åland or from Galtby in the Turku Archipelago.

Aerial view of Sandvik gästhamn and camp site looking north. St Anna's church can be seen on the left *Andy Beharrell*

### Karlby, Kökar

59°55'.6N 20°54'.7E

**Charts / harbour guides**
**SH2** *37* **FMA** *1145*

**Contacts**
www.brudhall.com/harbour-on-kokar/
✆+358 18 55926
✆+358 18 55955

This is the principal village in the Kökar group of islands. It is all fairly shallow and yachts with more than 1.8m draught should take great care. The approach is from the southern tip of Kökar. The entrance to the very narrow and rocky passage is from the west side of Karlbylandet, between Klobbkläppen (on which there is a cairn) and Inre Jusskär (see charts C743 and C741.2). It is easily identifiable by a disused pilot station on the island of Aspskär, to the east of Inre Jusskär. Pass between Bässkär (which has a cairn on top) to port and Utterskär (which also has a cairn at its tip) to starboard. Follow three pairs of white transits bearing roughly southeast, east and northeast. When close to the third pair (on Amborsö) turn north-northwest and pass through a narrow gap between the two islands of Stenholm and Halsholm; there is a cairn on Halsholm and another white transit. The depth in this gap is about 2.5m. When past the narrows, turn to port and follow the buoyed channel to the marina at the head of the inlet (see plan **SH2** *37*).

Berth bows to the quay from posts, stern anchors or alongside (2–2.5m). The marina services include toilets and showers, laundry, sauna (and also a private sauna and jacuzzi for hire), pump-out and fuel. The harbour is surrounded by traditional painted red houses and the hotel and restaurant overlook the harbour. Small grocery store.

### Helsö, Kökar

59°57'N 20°55'.4E

**Charts / harbour guides**
**SH2** *36* **FMA** *1135*

**Contacts**
www.havspaviljongen.ax/en/guest-harbour
info@havspaviljongen.ax

Northeast of the island of Kökar. A small marina (50 spaces) with saunas and showers, fuel jetty and an excellent restaurant with a lovely 360° view (www.havspaviljongen.ax/en/). Water and electricity are available. The marina gets very crowded in the season but when busy it may be possible to drop a stern anchor and run to the end of the pontoon (3m).

There are bikes available for hire and it is 6km to Karlby.

## Utö

59°46'.9N 21°22'.2E (end of the pier)

**Charts / harbour guides**
**SH2** *63* **SH1** *127* **FMA** *797, 798*

**Contacts**
www.utohannashorisont.fi/vierasvenesatama
www.uto.fi
www.utohotel.fi/en/home/

Utö is a pilot station affording good shelter in any weather conditions. There are 45 permanent residents on the island. Although the military left in 2005, there are still military installations on the island. The main harbour is well protected by the surrounding islands and is almost landlocked. The approach from the northwest is intricate but very well marked as it is the main approach channel from the Gulf of Finland

Boat houses by the main harbour in Utö *Andy Beharrell*

Aerial view of the Utö Havshotel jetty with the western entrance to the island *Andy Beharrell*

to the Archipelago Sea. Pass between Finnskär and Ormskär. Alternatively, if coming from the open sea, there is a shortcut through a very narrow entrance between Finnskär and Utö (3m). Follow the buoyed approach channel closely as the harbour tends to shoal very quickly towards the east. Anchor in the bay or moor bows-to with a stern anchor to the eastern side of the main pontoon (the western side is reserved for local fishing boats, a ferry and the pilot boat). There is electricity available, composting toilets and rubbish disposal. A sauna is available to book. Water, however, is scarce on the island as it is all produced from a desalination plant. The harbour has space for around 30 boats. You can see the current situation in the harbour from the Utö webcam (www.uto.fi/webcam).

The alternative mooring option is at the Havshotel. This small jetty will accommodate around 12 boats in 4m of water with stern buoys to moor bows-to the jetty. Toilets and showers are available, but the showers are an extra charge, given the water situation on Utö.

Utö itself is isolated and barren but has rather interesting scenery with bare rocks and low-lying vegetation. There are various restrictions for nesting birds during spring and autumn migrations. The landscape is littered with bunkers and all sorts of remnants of its military and Russian history. The military installations are out of bounds. The lighthouse on Utö (Utön Lisäloisto, F.W.) is the oldest working lighthouse in Finland; the original tower was built in 1753 and the current tower in 1814. The lighthouse is painted as the signal flag H (Hotel) because of the pilot station. The light signal matches this with four short flashes (....) as Morse code letter 'H'. It has a chapel just below the light and this can be visited with a guided tour of the lighthouse. Basic facilities on the island include two small shops and a café, but fuel is not available. At the Havshotel jetty is also a pizzeria. There is a ferry to Naugo year-round.

## Jurmo

59°49'.6N 21°34'.9E (southern breakwater)

**Charts / harbour guides**
**SH1** *48* **FMA** *802*

**Contacts**
www.jurmo.ax
✆+358 40 506 4777

Jurmo is an interesting deserted low-lying and exposed island, geologically different from the others. Much of it is a bird sanctuary but there are walking trails and a small church of interest. The island is known for its stone circles and mazes, some of which may date back to the Bronze Age. Their original purpose is unknown, but may be related to various rituals – perhaps fishermen wanting to ensure good catches. One possible explanation (or urban myth?) for their use (in both Finland and Sweden) was that a young virgin maiden stood in the middle of the labyrinth. Young suitors would try to win her hand by getting to the centre of the labyrinth first. This was known as the Jungfrudans or virgin dance game.

There is a very attractive anchorage in 4m just west of the leading line and a well-marked approach into the marina. Alternatively, moor bow-to from stern buoys in the small harbour (1.8–3.8m). Manoeuvring in a strong southwesterly wind can be very tricky in the confined marina. There are basic shopping facilities but no fuel.

## Björkö

59°54'.5N 21°40'.8E

**Charts / harbour guides**
**SH1** *13* **FMA** *806*

Björkö is a beautiful bay on the southwestern side of the island. Enter between the southwest tip of Björkö and the high rocky skerry of Yngerskär (the local pilot books suggest a depth in the entrance of 1.8m, but anecdotal reports suggest nearer 3m though do watch the water stand level). The passage is marked by a west cardinal buoy which you need to be careful to round appropriately. After that, the bay is relatively clear and you can anchor in 5–7m at the head of the bay. The water elsewhere is deeper and would require significantly more scope. Alternatively moor bows to the shore with a stern anchor.

This is a highly recommended anchorage for swimming in the beautiful pool on the western side of the island and for the view over the surrounding islands. It is very popular with the Finns, especially on weekends. There are no facilities but there is a pump-out barge moored in the bay.

Looking south from Björkö. The two yachts in the distance have just come in through the entrance *Andy Beharrell*

Looking east at the bay on Björkö *Fiona Ferguson*

Looking north towards the swimming lake on Björkö with yachts moored in the bay to the right *Fiona Ferguson*

Looking south at the bay on Björkö *Fiona Ferguson*

The guest jetty at Borstö *Jukka/Wikimedia Commons (https://commons.wikimedia.org/wiki/File:Borst%C3%B601.jpg)*

## Nötö

59°57'.2N 21°45'.4E

**Charts / harbour guides**
**FMA** *794*

Nötö is located in the southern archipelago of Nagu, and it is one of the largest islands in the Archipelago National Park. In the centre of the village there is a windmill, and a few minutes away from the village harbour a chapel, inaugurated in 1757. During the summer season, a cafeteria opens in the old primary school building, where various art and other exhibitions are held.

The shop sells groceries, fuel, drinking water and gas. Shower, sauna and laundry facilities can be reserved. The approach to the harbour is well-marked. There is a pontoon with stern buoys with 10 spaces, or alternatively anchor in the small bay just west of the pontoon.

## Borstö

59°51'.6N 21°58'.1E

**Charts / harbour guides**
**SH1** *16* **FMA** *782*

This sheltered harbour is on the southeast side of the island surrounded by skerries. Approach from a position about one mile northeast of the island and identify the transit boards on the islet of Bredskär (southeast of Borstö). Turn to starboard once you have passed Basskär and follow the next transit (west-southwest) on the southern tip of Borstö. Anchor off the jetty or moor bows-to from stern buoys to the guest pontoon (2.5–3m). A delightful fishing hamlet with a special variety of flat fish which is smoked in a shed by the harbour. Walk to the Borstö Gumma (Borstö Lady), an old ship's figurehead on the hill.

## Vänö

59°52'.1N 22°11'.5E

**Charts / harbour guides**
**SH1** *132* **FMA** *608*

An interesting island, very beautiful in fine weather. The easiest approach is from the northeast, between Inre Bosskär and Hemören following the transit marks on Ölonskär and then to a second set of transit marks on Skinnarskär. The final approach is from the southeast. It is also possible to approach from the northwest, but this is not recommended unless familiar with the skerries.

Moor bows-to from stern buoys (2.7–3.6m) to the pontoon (30–40 spaces). There is a small grocery shop and an indoor/outdoor cafe on the waterfront. There are ruins of an old seafarer's chapel dating back to the 1600s and the new chapel, built as a replica of this in 1975 is a pleasant 1.5km walk. Facilities include water, electricity, sauna, pump-out station and a fishmonger.

## Rosala

59°51'.76N 22°25'.11E

**Charts / harbour guides**
**FMA** *579*

**Contacts**
✆+358 400 829 184

Rosala guest harbour is in a bay on the northwest side of the island. The bay is fairly sheltered though could be a little exposed in northerlies. There is space to anchor or the guest harbour has a long jetty with stern buoys for visitors. The main jetty has 3–7m depth though other jetties are a little shallower.

The village is walking distance (just over 2km) and in the village is the Rosala Viking Centre (www.rosala.fi/en/) which holds various events and exhibitions during the season.

The guest jetty at Rosala *Fiona Ferguson*

## All routes

### Kasnäs

59°55'.3N 22°24'.6E

**Charts / harbour guides**
**FMA** *591*

**Contacts**
www.kasnas.com/enwww.kasnas.com/en/harbour/guest-harbour
port@kasnas.com
☎+358 2 5210 117
☎+358 40 55 87 293

Kasnäs is located on the mainland at a crossroads. The routes north and northwest, west and east meet at Kasnäs. A large marina well protected from all winds with places for 100 boats.

Kasnäs offers a sheltered guest harbour, spa, sauna, laundry and childcare room. Berths can be booked in advance through Dockspot (www.dockspot.com/en/docks/259-kasnas-gasthamn). There is also a restaurant, local shop and a summer marketplace, fuel, electricity, water and WiFi.

The Nature Centre Blåmusslan and geological nature path will be of interest to all age groups. An excellent place for crew changes with bus connections to Turku and Helsinki.

# 3C. GULF OF FINLAND – WESTERN PART

## Routes between Hanko and Helsinki

There are two main routes along the southern coast of Finland from Hanko towards Helsinki. They converge in several places and, therefore, it is possible to 'mix and match' along the way. Up-to-date, large-scale Finnish charts are a necessity when cruising this area. East of Hanko the routes meander through a national park, the Ekenäs *Skärgårds* Nationalpark (Tammisaaren Saariston Kansallispuisto) which is home to elk, white-tailed deer and many bird species.

Between 23°20'E and 23°45'E the northern route passes north of Skärlandet, Torsö and Växär. This is a pretty, peaceful, easily followed route with some summer houses and many places to anchor. Fuel is available at several points. In rough weather it provides a welcome alternative to the more interesting, though exposed, southern route. The southern route passes south of Älgö and north of Busö, has some beautiful anchorages and is certainly the more popular of the two. Both converge at 59°55'N 23°45'.5E.

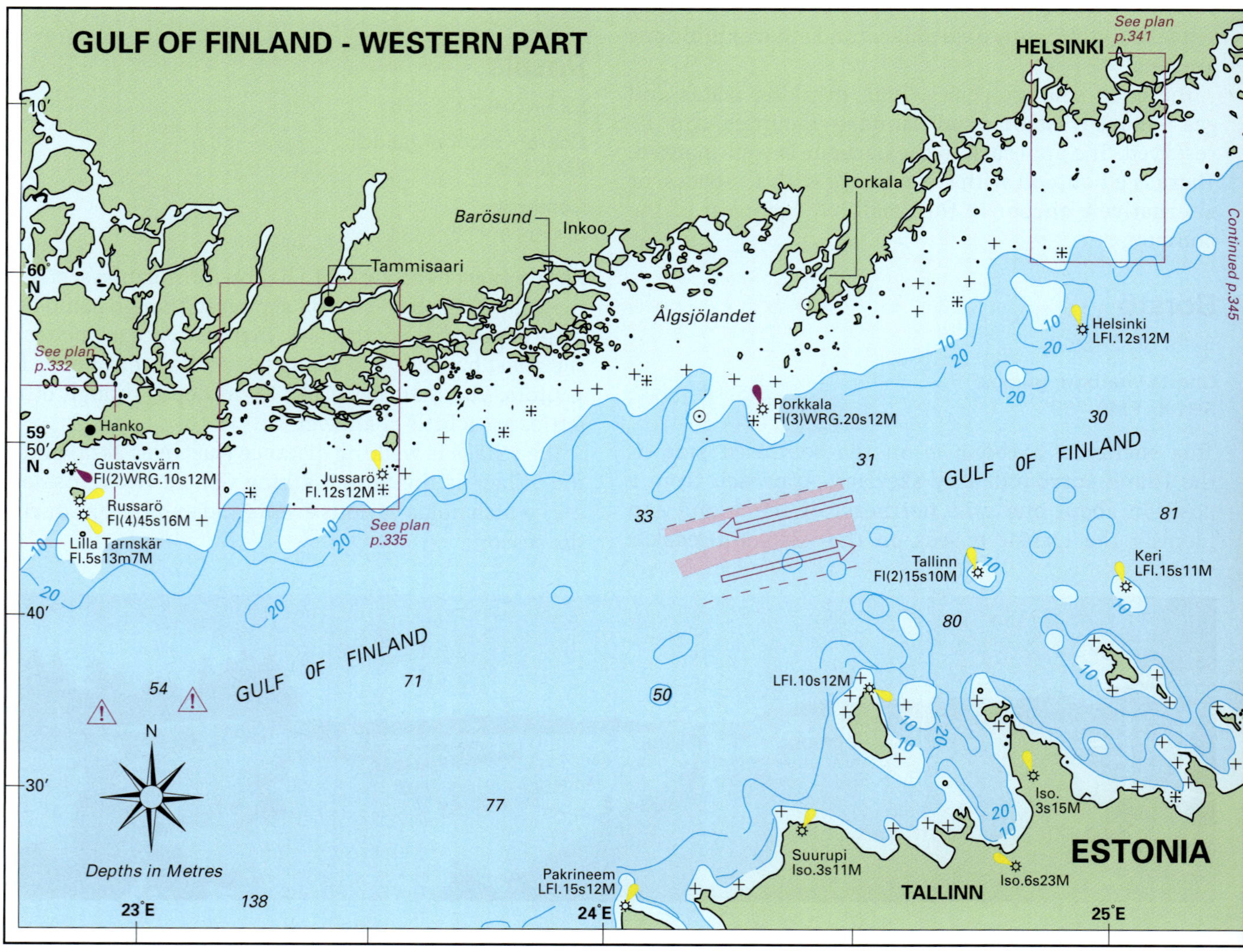

Between 23°45'E and 24°24'E the northern route leads through Barösund, a relatively straight, well buoyed and lit sound between Orslandet and Barölandet.

The southern route winds and twists between many small islands, and is sometimes open to the Gulf of Finland in the south. It is very enjoyable from both the pilotage and scenic points of view. Both channels cross the Porkalafjärden (Porkkalanselkä) and converge just off Porkkala.

From here, the coastal route which is usually followed presents no difficulty. It can be exposed to swell in places.

*Navigational charts – harbour guides*

### Planning chart

F952 (Gulf of Finland - West, 1:250,000)

### Chart folios

B-Helsinki-Parainen/Helsingfors-Pargas (scale 1:50,000)

### Harbour guides

*Stora Hamnboken Vol.3 -Suomenlahti/Finska Viken* (**SH3** xxx)

*Käyntisatamat/Besökshamnar* guide to 511 harbours on the Finnish coast (the numbers of the harbours in the book correlate with the numbers on the charts - **FMA** xxx).

### See also

Navigational charts - Finland and Åland, and harbour books and literature page 272 (general introduction to Finland).

Uusimaa Recreation Area Association has local information on many of the place on this route. It might be worth browsing their website prior to a visit (www.uuvi.fi/fi/kohteet/).

The midsummer pole on the beach at Hanko *Andy Beharrell*

## HANKO (HANGÖ)

59°48'36N 22°57'E

### Distances

Turku 65M, Mariehamn 105M, Lehtma 50M, Haapsalu 55M, Tallinn 60M, Helsinki 70M

### Lights

**Fläckgrund** 59°52'.4N 22°50'.4E Q(2)WRG.3s6m9M Red rectangle, yellow stripe

**Bengtskär** 59°43'.4N 22°30'.1E Fl(3)20s51m10M Round granite tower and building 46m Wind generator

**Hanko** No.1 59°44'.1N 23°02'.6E VQ(3)5s12m6M e on black beacon, yellow band

**Russarö** 59°46'N 22°57'.1E Fl(4)45s34m16M Red octagonal tower 21m

**Djubkobben Leading Lights** 327° *Front* 59°48'.4N 22°58'.2E Fl.3s8m11M Red rectangle, yellow stripe, on framework tower
*Rear* 59°49'.1N 22°57'.2E Iso.12s22m14M Red rectangle, yellow stripe, on framework tower

**Hankoniemi Pohjoinen Leading Lights** 319° *Front* 59°49'.3N 22°55'.6E FFl.Y.1s16m7M 315°-vis-323° Red rectangle, yellow stripe, on framework tower
*Rear* 59°49'.4N 22°55'.4E FIFl.Y.6s26m9M 315°-vis-323° Red rectangle, yellow stripe, on framework tower

### Contacts

**Hanko Port Authority** ✆+358 19 2203 801
VHF Ch 12, 13, 14, 16, port@hanko.fi
www.visitsaaristo.net for Itämeren Portti Marina
www.itamerenportti.fi
www.hanko.fi

The pleasant bilingual town of Hanko, population 8,100, was founded in 1874 and quickly developed as a spa town popular with the Russian ruling classes. A number of majestic 19th-century Finnish/Russian-style wooden villas are located to the northeast of the harbour amidst parks and tennis courts.

It has always been a useful destination, known to sailors since the 15th century and its continued prosperity has been mainly due to the fact that its commercial port - the West Harbour - is closed by ice for shorter periods than most other Finnish ports. For some 50 years around the beginning of the 20th century Hanko was a major point of embarkation for Finns leaving their native country for new lives in the USA and Canada - up to 370,000 by some estimates. In the Moscow Peace Treaty in 1940, Hanko was leased to the Soviet Union as a military base. This role was replaced by Porkkala after the armistice between Finland and the Soviet Union in 1944. It was returned to Finland in 1956.

Today Hanko remains popular as a holiday resort and tourist centre with two marinas in its East Harbour, both of which welcome visiting yachts. From the cruiser's point of view Hanko is a convenient port of call since it involves practically no detour from the main coastal fairway. Nowadays the Hanko Regatta is

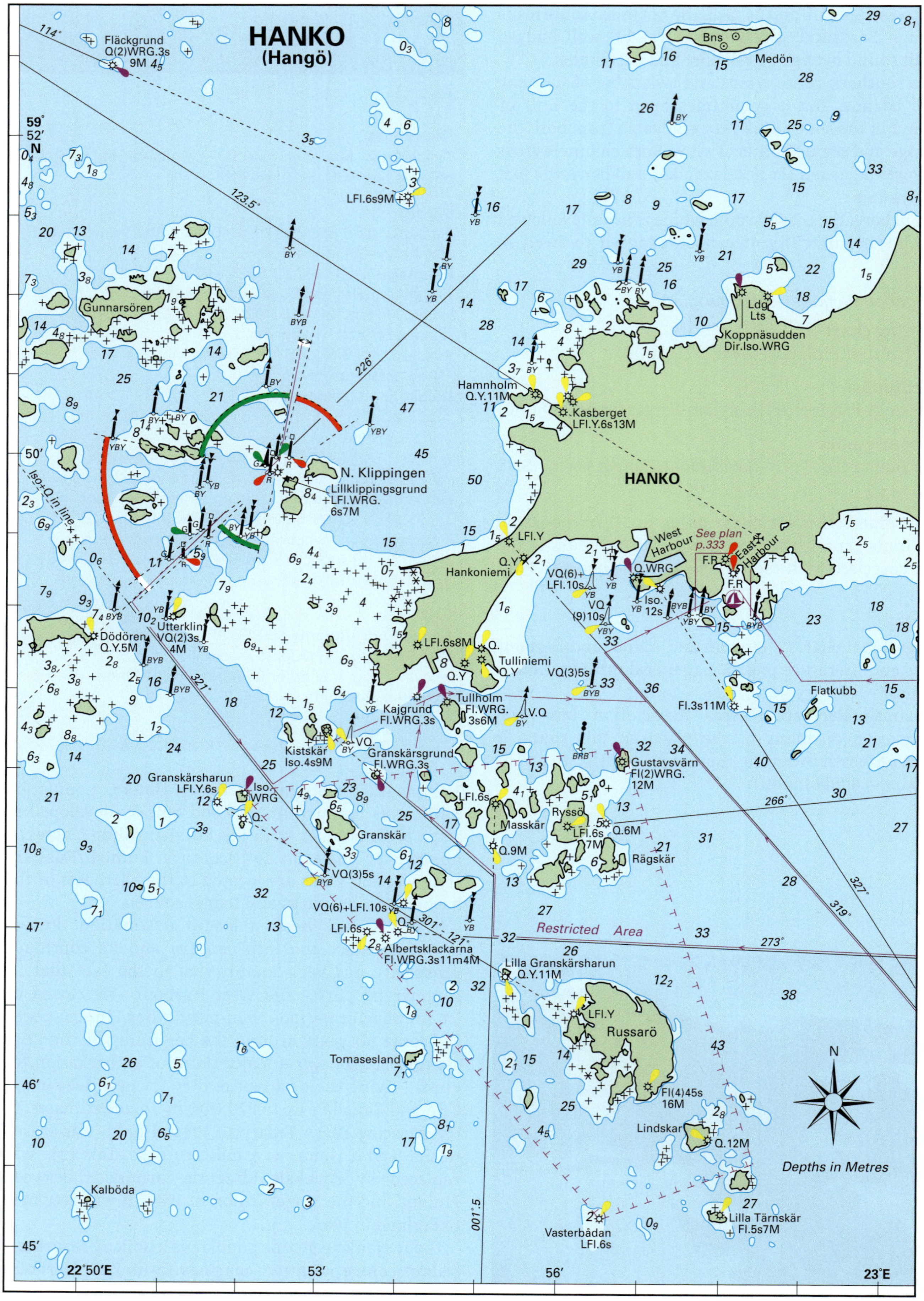

HANKO
(Hangö)
Fläckgrund
Q(2)WRG.3s
9M
LFl.6s9M
Bns
Medön
Gunnarsören
Ldg
Lts
Koppnäsudden
Dir.Iso.WRG
Hamnholm
Q.Y.11M
Kasberget
LFl.Y.6s13M
N. Klippingen
Lillklippingsgrund
LFl.WRG.
6s7M
HANKO
Iso+Q in line
LFl.Y
Q.Y
Hankoniemi
West
Harbour
See plan
p.333
East
Harbour
F.R
Q.WRG
VQ(6)+
LFl.10s
VQ
(9)10s
Iso.
12s
Dödören
Q.Y.5M
Utterklin
VQ(2)3s
4M
LFl.6s8M
Q.
Tulliniemi
Q.Y
VQ(3)5s
Fl.3s11M
Flatkubb
Kajgrund
Fl.WRG.3s
Tullholm
Fl.WRG.
3s6M
V.Q
Kistskär
Iso.4s9M
VQ.
Granskärsgrund
Fl.WRG.3s
Gustavsvärn
Fl(2)WRG.
12M
Granskärsharun
LFl.Y.6s
Iso.
WRG
Q.
LFl.6s
Masskär
Ryssö
LFl.6s
7M
Q.6M
Rägskär
Granskär
Q.9M
VQ(3)5s
VQ(6)+LFl.10s
LFl.6s
Albertsklackarna
Fl.WRG.3s11m4M
Restricted Area
Lilla Granskärsharun
Q.Y.11M
LFl.Y
Russarö
Tomasesland
Fl(4)45s
16M
Lindskar
Q.12M
Depths in Metres
Kalböda
Vasterbådan
LFl.6s
Lilla Tärnskär
Fl.5s7M
59°
52′
N
50′
47′
46′
45′
22°50′E
53′
56′
23°E
114°
123.5°
226°
321°
301°
121°
266°
273°
327°
319°
001°.5

Aerial view of Hanko port. East harbour marina is visible on the far right
*Hansny/Wikimedia Commons (https://commons.wikimedia.org/wiki/File:20070809_1594_korr.jpg)*

one of the major summer fixtures in the national and international sailing calendar. However, as with all these social events, it also attracts crowds of young people who come to party and drink.

Facilities for children are particularly good with playgrounds, beaches and plenty of open areas of rocks and short springy grass. Some visitors have likened the smooth, pinkish rocks to parts of northern Brittany.

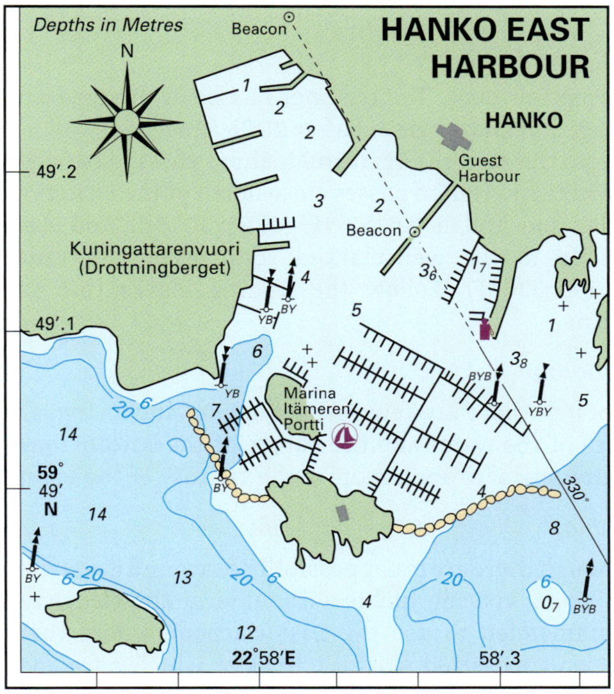


## *Approach & entrance*

The waters surrounding Hanko contain many hazards. However, the area is well marked with transits, buoys and beacons. Using a large-scale chart, navigation in daylight is a great deal easier than appears at first sight. Entry by night should not be attempted unless familiar with the area.

From the northwest, coming from the Archipelago Sea (see Routes 2, 3 and 4, plan 309 and page 315), the route leading to Hanko either follows an open yet rocky channel (2.5m) through the national park between Finnharugrundet (59°53′.7N 22°42′.8E) and south of Uddskatan (59°48′.5N 22°53′.4E). This should not be attempted in rough weather or poor visibility. Alternatively, pass close south of Fläckgrund lighthouse (59°52′.4N 22°50′.2E) and follow a somewhat circuitous path through a number of well-marked deep commercial channels around the western end of the Hanko peninsula. Approach the harbour passing north of Högskär (see chart plan 637.1). Continue in a northeasterly direction to the harbour entrance (see chart plan 637.1A).

Light tower on the approaches to Hanko from the west. On the southern end of the peninsula opposite Tullholmen
*Andy Beharrell*

From the southeast and the open sea, approach from Hanko No. 1 east cardinal buoy (59°44′.1N 23°02′.4E). The channel is wide and all hazards are well marked.

In the vicinity of 59°48′.7N 22°56′.4E, head east-northeast towards the marina. Enter the harbour from the southwest, immediately south of the Kuningattarenvuori (Drottningberget) peninsula. Although very narrow, the entrance is well marked by cardinal marks. Incoming vessels may be met by

Hanko looking south *Anne Fleck*

a reception boat. The channel has been dredged and changed. A chart printed after 2005 is needed.

From the east, the beautiful inshore passage between Helsinki and Hanko passes close north of the islands of Mulan and Andalskär (59°48'.5N 23°00'.8E), and leads directly to the well-marked southeastern entrance (course 330°T). Follow the leading marks into the marina.

### *Anchorage*

Although there are few restrictions on anchoring, the depth of the water and the nature of the bottom make it impractical to anchor off in the vicinity of the town.

### *Berthing*

Although there are other possibilities around the Hanko peninsula, visiting yachts without local knowledge are recommended to use the East Harbour where there are two good-sized marinas, both of which have good facilities and excellent shelter.

#### Hanko Östra hamnen

www.hsfmarine.fi
info@hsfmarine.fi
✆+358 19 232 770

Hanko (Itäsatama/Hangö) Östra hamnen (59°49'.1N 22°58'.1E), open to the southwest, is located on the east side of the harbour basin and has some 220 visitors berths in depths of up to 3m. Mooring is bows-to from stern buoys, finger pontoons or alongside. However, the depth shoals quickly towards the shore (1.5m or less). If not met by a reception boat on arrival, take any suitable vacant berth and visit the marina office (open 0800–2400 in high season) as soon as possible. Berths can be booked in advance through the marina website (www.hsfmarine.fi/sv/hamnen).

#### Hanko Itämeren Portti

www.itamerenportti.fi/eng/
office@itamerenportti.fi
✆+358 400 544 164

Hanko, Itämeren Portti (Gateway to the Baltic), Smultrongrundet (59°49'.1N 22°58'E) just opposite, welcomes visiting yachts. It is built astride several small islands in the southwestern part of the harbour and has a further 150 berths, most equipped with finger pontoons. Depths range from 2–3.5m or more.

A regular ferry (free to berth-holders) runs between the marina and the shore.

### *Services*

Both marinas have water and electricity on the pontoons with toilets, showers, saunas, laundry facilities and restaurants ashore.

There is a fuelling point at the end of the eastern mole which forms the starboard side of the southeast entrance where holding tanks can be emptied, and bottled gas (Finnish and Swedish cylinders only) and a few charts are available. It may be worth refuelling on arrival if there is no queue, as there can be a long wait on summer mornings. There is a Volvo Penta service centre nearby.

There is no boatyard at the East Harbour itself, but there are several in the wider Hanko area including

Ranmarina Oy, Ranmarinantie 120 , 25500 Perniö, Finland (www.ranmarina.fi, telakka@ranmarina.fi) is located at 60°07'.7N 23°01'.6E.

✆+358 2 732 2124

Finnish charts (together with some English paperbacks) are stocked by Tias Bok at Vuorikatu 10 Berggatan, some 600m north of the harbour.

✆+358 40 628 0924
tiankirja.tiasbok@gmail.com

### *Facilities*

General provisions may be bought from a small mobile shop at the Itäsatamat (open 0800–2100 weekdays, 0900–1900 weekends) or from the wide variety of shops and supermarkets in the town centre, approximately 1km away, where there is also an outdoor market. In addition, the town centre has the usual post office, tourist office (www.visithanko.fi/en), hotels and restaurants. Shopping trolleys can be borrowed from the guest harbour office against a deposit and bicycles can be hired.

### *Communications & travel*

Hanko is a very suitable place to leave a yacht whilst returning home or changing crew. There are good rail connections in Hanko, and international air travel is possible via Helsinki or Turku. Car ferries run to Rostock in Germany. For more local exploration, bicycles can be hired from several places around the harbour, including the fuel pontoon.

## TAMMISAARI (EKENÄS)

59°58'.6N 23°25'.6E

**Charts / harbour guides**
**SH3** *122* **FMA** *453*

**Contacts**
www.visitraseborg.com/en/
www.ekenasport.fi
info@ekenasport.fi
☎+358 19 241 1790

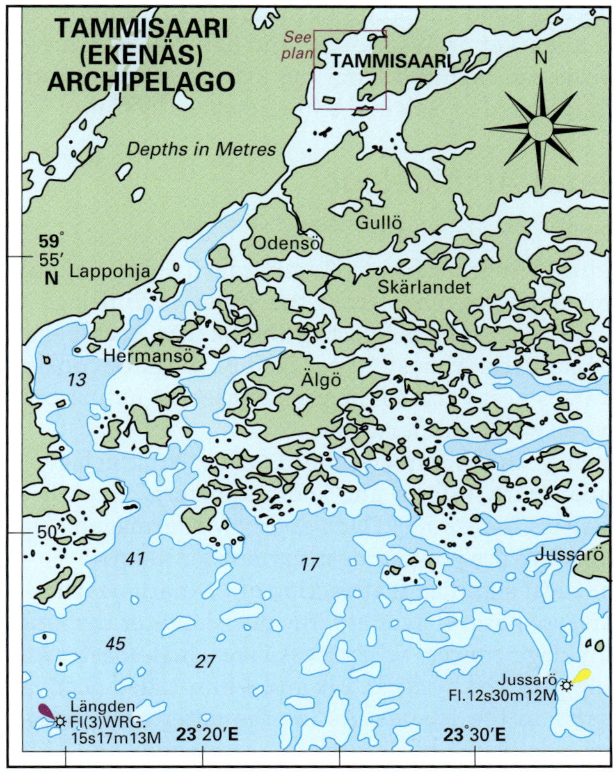


Tammisaari, population 15,000, is a delightful, leafy town with many traditional wooden houses and a small guest harbour able to take around 120 yachts. There is a particularly appealing beach just south of the marina, backed by a children's playground, making Tammisaari an excellent port of call for those with young aboard.

Although the channel leading to the town is 12M from the Gulf of Finland, the approach is deep, well marked and presents no difficulty. On reaching the guest harbour, near the road bridge (H3.1m), it is impossible to miss the ornate building which houses the Knipan restaurant – built on stilts in the harbour at a time when only one licensed premises was permitted 'on the soil of the town' (www.knipan.fi).

Visitors' berths are on the east side of the main jetty (to which the restaurant is attached). The pontoons either side of the fuel berth (1.6m) are private, though if the owner is away a green sign may be left at the berth to show it is free. Depths shoal quickly towards the land to 1.5m. There are 100 spaces bows-to from stern buoys, piles or you can anchor in the bay nearby. The marina office occupies a small building near the fuel berth which doubles as a café.

Berths on the main quay have access to water and electricity (though some berths require long hoses and leads), and there are toilets, showers, sauna and laundry facilities ashore. A weather forecast (in Finnish and Swedish) is posted at the marina office and is updated daily.

Directly across the bay, and clearly visible from the marina, is a large boatyard, Oy Eke – Marin Ab (www.eke-marin.fi/en), which also stocks a wide range of chandlery. Although it mostly deals with motorboats, the yard can handle yachts of up to 20T and 13.5m LOA and undertake repairs in all materials. There are engineers and electricians on site and extensive undercover storage. This would be a definite possibility for over-wintering if booked well in advance.
☎+358 400 473 364 or ☎+358 400 490 672,
telakka@eke-marin.fi

Guest harbour at Tammisaari (Ekenäs) *Andy Beharrell*

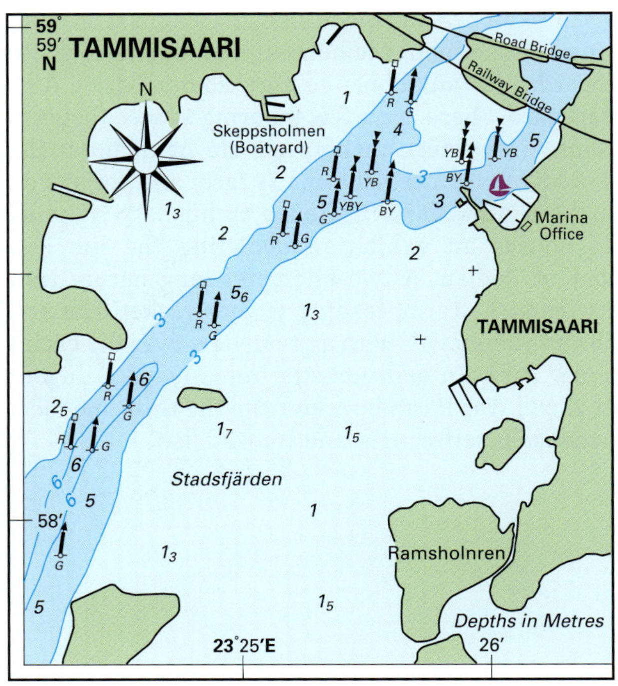

There is good shopping of all kinds in Tammisaari, with a market on Wednesday and Saturday mornings. Bicycles can be hired from the marina office, and the town is linked to Helsinki and elsewhere by rail.

## Ekenäs Archipelago

www.nationalparks.fi/en/ekenasarchipelagonp

Heading south from Tammisaari, the Ekenäs archipelago stretches from the inner archipelago to the open sea. It forms part of the Ekenäs Archipelago National Park. Almost 90 per cent of the park consists of watery areas and so the park conserves nature both above as well as underwater.

During the summer, the Ekenäs archipelago is popular with sailors and motor boaters, as well as canoeists. The islands Fladalandet, Modermagan, Älgö and Jussarö are popular destinations for hikers.

The most significant attraction of the national park is its diverse natural habitats. The big islands of the inner archipelago conceal wilderness lakes, lush forests and beaches backed by cliffs. Elk and white-tailed deer can be seen on the islands. As for the outer archipelago, thousands of sea birds such as scaup, gulls and eider duck nest on the islets. In the southern parts of the park you can even see grey and ringed seals.

In the Ekenäs Archipelago National Park, visiting yachts can stay overnight in Modermagan, Fladalandet, Rödjan in Älgö, and Jussarö provided visitors follow the 'everyman's rights'.

luontoon.fi/en

## Älgö, Rödjan

59°51'.8N 23°23'.4E (Älgö, Rödjan) (southwestern entrance)

**Charts / harbour guides**
**SH3** *103* **FMA** *483* (Ålgö, Rödjan 486k Norrklobbarna)

The safest approach is from the channel that cuts across the southern Ekenäs archipelago south of Älgö. Approach from the southeast. Pass between Långskärsklobben and Modermagan (see chart B635.3), leaving Horsholmen, Mejholmen and all the rocks to starboard, and Fanklobben to port. Rödjan lies on Älgö to starboard. There are a few mooring spaces (bows to the shore with a stern anchor) in 1–2m, or anchor in the pool. Rödjan's former fisherman's farm and cottage on Älgö, the largest island in Ekenäs Archipelago National Park, houses an exhibition depicting the life and history of Rödjan. A two-kilometer-long nature trail starts from the farm, leading to Storträsket lake and an observation tower with a great view over the entire National Park. In addition, the remains of a dugout from World War II can be seen from the trail. The farm manager sells self-caught and smoked fish.

## Älgö, Norrklobbarna

59° 51'.7N 23° 22'.9E

### *Anchorage*

When you reach the southwestern tip of Skedö (Västerudden) from the southwest, look out for leading marks on Norrklobbarna. These will lead you towards a very narrow passage between Norrklobbarna and Skedö. Once inside the pool, turn to port. Take care to avoid the rock at the northwestern tip of the islet to starboard. Anchor anywhere in the pool (2–10m). This is a very beautiful spot with a spectacular entrance. If it's crowded, there is an alternative secluded anchorage in Skedöfladan, a kilometer-long lagoon approached from the east, south of Fanklobben, opposite Horsholmen. The tall stands of birch and conifer give protection from all quarters. Anchor in 12m (or less, depending on the wind direction). Note that the soundings in Fanklobben are approximate and are highlighted in red on Finnish charts.

## Groplandet, Gropen

59°51'.5N 23°25'.8E

**Charts / harbour guides**
**FMA** *480*

### *Anchorage*

Approach between Långskärsklobben and Modermagan (see chart B635.3), leaving Horsholmen to port. Sail into the pool to starboard, leaving the private north cardinal buoy/marker to starboard. The Gropen pool provides excellent anchorage (5–9m) in all winds. It is possible to moor to the shore in the southwest corner of the Gropen pool. On the north shore is a Merikarhut/ Sea Bears private harbour (for members only).

## Jussarö

59°49'.8N 23°34'.3E

**Charts / harbour guides**
**SH3** *39* **FMA** *445*

**Contacts**
www.jussaro.net/en/
www.jussaro.net/en/guest-marina/
info@jussaro.net
✆+358 40 505 3422

This small harbour lies to the north of the island between Lilla Jussarö and Jussarö. There are transits to guide you into the harbour. The single pontoon can accommodate up to 20 boats in 2.5–5.5m, bows-to from stern buoys. It is open to the northwest. There is a useful bathymetric image giving all the harbour depths on the website.

The island, in the Ekenäs Archipelago National Park, lies right at the edge of the open sea. It has been well-known to seafarers for more than 700 years. Jussarö's history is one of mining, fishing, seafaring and the defence of the Gulf of Finland. The island was under

The guest jetty at Barösund showing the fuel jetty in the foreground *Andy Beharrell*

the control of the Finnish Defence Forces until 2005. Today it is open to the public.

There is a café (Café Ön) next to the guest marina. There is also a barbecue area and sauna. For swimming, head out to the Iron Beach that lies amongst red rocks. You can learn about the fascinating history of the island on guided walks.

From Lotssuberget tower, where pilots once kept a lookout for ships, and the old disused lighthouse towards the southeast end of the island, there are spectacular views of the open sea.

Limited facilities include water, electricity, sauna and a floating pump-out station.

## Långön

59°56'.4N 23°43'.7E

**Charts / harbour guides**
**SH3** *71*

### *Anchorage*

This useful anchorage is 1.8M north of Fjärdskär lighthouse on the narrow northern route between Hanko and Helsinki. It lies opposite the small harbour of Sandnäsudd (**SH3** 99, **FMA** 434), where there is a small shop and fuel. Anchor very close to the southwestern shore of the island of Långön in 2.5m or around the corner on the southeastern tip in 1.5–2.5m. The anchorage is open to the south.

## Flakholmen

59°55'.76N 23°46'.8E

**Charts / harbour guides**
**SH3** *22*

### *Anchorage*

On the northern route leading towards Barösund there is a good small natural harbour at Flakholm. Anchor in the bay on the eastern side or moor to the shore. An alternative is to anchor north of Flakholm, a perfect landlocked pool secure from all winds. Anchor anywhere in the middle of the lagoon. Along the north shore there are many private summer houses.

## Barösund

59°58'.6N 23°52'.8E (Orslandet)

**Charts / harbour guides**
**SH3** *4* **FMA** *422, 425*

**Contacts**
www.barosund.fi
www.ravintola-scola.fi/vierassatama

The Finns are justly proud of Barösund, with its narrow and high rocky sides. It boasts a small shop, one of the few between Hanko and Helsinki not to involve a considerable detour, together with many summer homes and hence a lot of small motorboat traffic.

The guest berths and jetty at Älgsjö, Elisaari. There are excellent walks from the guest harbour around Älgsjölandet
*Fiona Ferguson*

There is a good, strong jetty on the south side of the route to tie up to, a small supermarket with most essentials including fuel and post office, in Barösund, Orslandet.

Barösund, Barölandet, on the opposite (north) side, is a service harbour with a fuel pump and not much else. There are limited facilities and the pontoon is exposed to the wash from the intense summer traffic of motorboats, the wind and the current in the sound. Alternatively, anchor north or northwest of Sparrholm (0.6M) towards the northeast end of the sound. Mörholmen island is private.

## Älgsjö, Elisaari

59°58'.7N 23°54'.6E

**Charts / harbour guides**
**SH3** *133* **FMA** *419*

**Contacts**
www.elisaari.fi/satama
info@elisaari.fi
✆+358 40 701 6301

An outstanding City of Helsinki Island Park marina, only 40km west of the capital. The entrance is at the northeastern corner of Mörholmen through a 20' wide channel running south between Mörholmen and Bråtaholmen. Its depth is 2.2–3m. The charted depth of 1m is incorrect, as are soundings further along the sound which has a minimum depth of 2.3m between Älgsjölandet and Orslandet. It does at times get narrow between the reeds, but keep going. Moor to the solid wooden staging, bows-to from stern buoys, anchor or lie alongside (130 spaces).

It gets very crowded on Midsummer's Night. There is a beautiful nature trail, campground, a small kiosk and two classic wood-fired saunas. Facilities include a restaurant, electricity, water and a pump-out station.

## Vormö

60°00'.4N 24°11'.5E (Hamnholmen)

**Charts / harbour guides**
**SH3** *131* **FMA** *408s* Stickellandet

*Anchorage*

Between Barösund and Porkkala, the coast becomes exposed with no good sheltered harbours or anchorages.

Anchor off the village on Vormö at the southwest end of the island in 4m between the southeastern side of Hamnholmen and Vormö, or secure to a tree with a stern anchor (good holding). The easiest way in is from the northwest, between Hamnholmen and Furuholmen. If entering from the north, hug the west coast of Vormö and beware of the submerged rocks in mid-channel just south of the northwest tip of Vormö (see charts B, **SH3** 131). It is open to the southwest. An attractive spot amidst many summer houses.

Stickellandet (60°01'N 24°14'E) is considered to be an emergency anchorage which can be used in bad weather, depending on the direction of the wind. It is located just inside the firing exercise danger area of Porkkala (see notes page 274 on restricted areas in the general introduction to Finland). The anchorage is protected from the southwest but open to the northwest and north. It lies directly on the northern coastal channel. Enter from the north, close to the shore of the small islet to the northeast of Vormö, Stickellandet. Anchor in 2–3m or bows-to from stern anchor to the northern tip of the islet.

## Porkkala, Dragesviken

59°59'N 24°25'.4E

**Charts / harbour guides**
**SH3** *88* **FMA** *403*

**Contacts**
www.porkkalanmarina.com/in-english
info@porkkalanmarina.fi
✆+358 40 159 1779

Porkkala is a peninsula in the Gulf of Finland situated just 20M west-southwest of Helsinki. It has always had great military strategic value. At the end of the Second

World War the Soviet Union leased and established a naval base in Porkkala, thus replacing it with the one they occupied until the end of the Second World War in Hanko and returning it to Finland in 1956.

From the coastal route, the approach channel is very short and straightforward. Enter the very narrow sound through a well buoyed channel passing east of Högholmen (2.4m) or pass west and north of Högholmen (1.5m). There are several places to moor or anchor. Berth alongside the eastern jetty of the customs and coastguard station on Tullandet in 4m (in an emergency only or if clearing customs). In strong easterlies there is a good anchorage 300m to the east by Kyrkogårdsön Island, shallow but sheltered and with good holding.

Porkkala, Dragesviken in the northeastern corner (59°59'N 24°25'.4E) is the guest marina. Follow the narrow sound between Tullandet and Kyrkogårdsön, actual depth in channel is 2.1m. If approaching from the southeast leave the coastal channel at 59°58'.2N 24°26'E, turn northwestwards, leaving south cardinal and west cardinal buoys to starboard before turning north to enter the well-marked entrance to the basin. Moor to the northern side of the first pontoon. The third pontoon is a fuel dock. Facilities include fuel, water, electricity, shop, restaurant, washing machine, sauna and pump-out station.

A fine anchorage with good holding can be found north of the marina at the head of the basin.

This is a popular birdwatching area, particularly during the migration of Arctic geese and other waterfowl. It is a useful place to leave for Tallinn which is only 34M away to the south.

## Stora Brändö

60°02'.6N 24°35'.6E

**Charts / harbour guides**
**SH3** 108

The south shore of Stora Brändö together with the outlying islets form part of a bird sanctuary where landing is prohibited between 1 April and 31 July. It is best approached from the southwest by way of the main coastal channel. There is a transit for commercial shipping on the islets south of Stora Brändö. Leave the channel following the transit and approach the west shore of Stora Brändö. Fairway markers guide you in. There are several possibilities for anchoring or to secure a boat to the shore with a stern anchor. The western shore is open to the west and southwest. There are a few mooring buoys on the northeastern side of the island as well. However, it is strewn with rocks and care must be taken in approaching these and the pontoon ashore (1.8m).

The coast around Porkkala, Dragesviken *Andy Beharrell*

# HELSINKI (HELSINGFORS)

60°08'7N 24°58'.1E

## Distances
Hanko 70M, Tallinn 45M, Porvoo 35M, Loviisa 60M, Kotka 75M, Haapasaari Island 80M, Vyborg 130M, St Petersburg 175M

## Charts and guides
UKHO 2218, 2248, 3818
Finnish A+B626, 18; (**SH3** *35* **FMA** *356, 336, 324, 325, 345, 289, 307, 339*)
Merikarttasarja A: Viipuri - Helsinki/Viborg - Helsingfors
Merikarttasarja B: Helsinki - Parainen/Helsingbois - Pargas
Stora Hamnboken Vol.3

## Lights
**Helsinki** 59°56'.9N 24°55'.7E LFl.12s25m12M Racon White round tower, upper part red, three galleries, aluminium lantern 25m. Helipad
**Gråskärsbådan** 60°02'.2N 24°53'.6E Fl.WRG.3s12m7M Red concrete column
**Flathällgrundet** 60°05'N 24°58'.1E VQ(3)5s12m4M Black diamond on black metal structure, yellow band, on piles (East cardinal)
**Harmaja Leading Lights** 007° *Front* 60°06'.3N 24°58'.7E Racon Red round tower, white band, square base
**Suomenlinna Church** *Rear*, 60°08'.9N 24°59'.4E (2.6M from front) Fl(4)15s54m20M Racon Cupola on church tower
**Särkkä** 60°09'.1N 24°58'.2E Fl.WRG.2s2m6M White lantern, red band
**Valkosaari (Luoto) Leading Lights 356.5°** *Front* 60°09'.6N 24°58'.2E Q.R.2m6M White lantern, red band
**Valkosaari** Rear 240m from *front*, Iso.WRG.4s7m7M White lantern, red band
**Rysäkivi** (VQ(3)Y.3s)

## Principal harbours
**Helsingfors Segelklubb** (HSK), Lauttasaari (www.hoski.fi/in-english/marina/ satama@hoski.fi ✆+358 40 032 9955)
**Blekholmen**, NJK www.njk.fi
**Pohjoissatama/Helsingfors**, Norra hamnen (Helsingin Moottorivenekerho (HMVK)
**Katajanokka/Skatudden** (en.marinabay.fi info@marinabay.fi ✆+358 50 544 8008)
Liuskasaari/Skifferholmen (Helsingfors Segelsällskap (HSS) www.helsinkisailing.com/satama hss@helsinkisailing.com ✆+358 40 9 633 637)
**Suomenlinna/Sveaborg** (www.suomenlinna.fi/en/visitor/other-services/guest-harbour/)

## Contacts
**Helsinki Port Authority** ✆+358 207 641000
port.helsinki@hel.fi
www.portofhelsinki.fi
**Helsinki Vessel Traffic Service** www.fintraffic.fi/en/vts/masters-guide
Use relevant VHF channel according to sector (all vessels more than 24m in length must maintain a listening watch on the relevant VTS channel). From east to west:
VTS Sector 1: VHF Ch 71
VTS Sector 2: VHF Ch 9
Helsinki VTS, Master's Guide:
www.fintraffic.fi/en/maritime_traffic/fintraffics-vessel-traffic-services-brief
www.visithelsinki.fi

Helsinki, the capital of Finland, has a population of over 1.3 million. It is Finland's major political, educational, financial, cultural and research centre as well as one of northern Europe's major cities.

It was founded in 1550 by the Swedish King Gustav Vasa and became the Finnish capital in 1812, taking over from Turku at a time of Russian domination. It is a prosperous and pleasant city with the relaxed and friendly atmosphere typical of most major Scandinavian capitals. Nearly everyone speaks English and the standard of living is high.

The historic buildings, in particular both the Lutheran and Russian Orthodox (Uspenski) cathedrals and the university in the old part of the city, are important aesthetic and historic landmarks.

The South Harbour (Eteläsatama/Södra Hamnen), the main harbour for passenger ships and yachts (Blekholmen (NJK), see website above), is conveniently close to the city centre.

The offshore fortress of Suomenlinna (Sveaborg) or 'Fortress of Finland', built in the mid-18th century, lies just 1.5M to the southeast of the South Harbour. It is a UNESCO World Heritage Site on five connected islands and is well worth a visit for its museum, galleries, heavily-built stone walls and beautiful buildings. It has a small guest harbour and can be reached by ferry from Helsinki's South Harbour.

### *Approach & entrance*
Helsinki is surrounded by water on three sides, and there are many possible approaches through the hundreds of nearby islands. However, although local yachtsmen appear to sail where they wish, the visitor is advised to use only the main routes indicated, at least until familiar with local hazards (of which there are many). Whichever approach is used, it is essential to be equipped with detailed charts.

### *Approach from the south*
This is the main approach from the open sea and is heavily used by shipping, including cruise liners and fast ferries. A good watch must therefore be kept at all times. From Helsinki light (white round tower, upper part red, three galleries, aluminium lantern, 50°56'.95N 24°55'.6E), the channel runs slightly east of north with Harmaja lighthouse (60°06'.3N 24°58'.5E) in line with Suomenlinnan Kirkko (church) light (60°08'.87N 24°59'.2E). It passes close east of Harmaja light, but

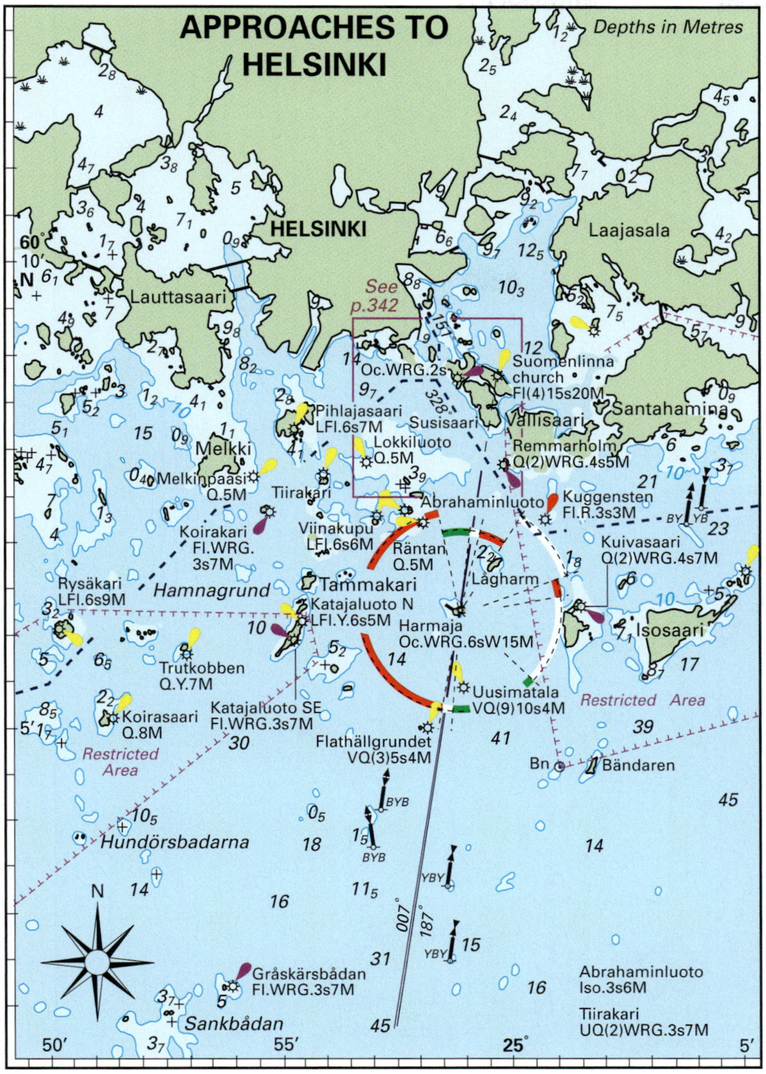

The fleet of ice-breakers at Helsinki waiting for the winter *Andy Beharrell*

Helsinki Cathedral *Andy Beharrell*

yachts should leave the main shipping channel before it continues northeast between the islands of Susisaari and Vallisaari.

Yachts are better advised to keep west of Susisaari island and to enter the South Harbour by the southern entrance, between the islands of Särkkä Långören and Länsi Mustasaari, the northwestern island that forms part of Suomenlinna.

### Approach from the southwest

The inshore passage through the islands from the southwest passes between Rysäkari island (60°06′N 24°50′E) and Rysäkivi light, following three sets of transits and the well-buoyed channels in a northeasterly direction to converge with the southern approach west of Länsi Mustasaari. It is clearly marked, but it is easy to become confused by the plethora of beacons, lights and leading marks. It is advisable to consult chart B626.1 carefully. The tower of Suomenlinna church is a useful landmark throughout.

### Approach from the east

The deep-water channel for vessels using the inshore route from the east passes south of the islands of Santahamina and Vallisaari and joins the main channel from the south approximately 1M north of the Harmaja light. However, a slightly shorter but more interesting route, that carries 2.4m, passes north of Santahamina (see chart 626.2) through the swing bridge at Hevossalmi, operating at HR+00 and HR-30.

### Anchorage

Although there are few official restrictions on anchoring in the Helsinki area, in practice it is almost impossible to find a spot which does not involve landing on private property.

### Berthing

There are at least 15 yacht harbours and clubs in the immediate vicinity of Helsinki, but the visitor will normally find it most convenient to use one of the marinas near the city centre. All the websites for these marinas (including contacts, services and information) are listed at www.visitsaaristo.net.

If heading for the Helsingfors Segelsällskap (HSS), Liuskasaari marina (**FMA** 345), turn sharp to port north of Särkkä island. It lies further away from the city centre – though it is near a tram route – but its berths are undoubtedly quieter than those at the NJK.

Alternatively, continue to the Nylandska Jaktklubben (NJK) (**FMA** 336) pontoons on Blekholmen (Valkosaari) island following the buoyed channel west of Luoto island into the South Harbour.

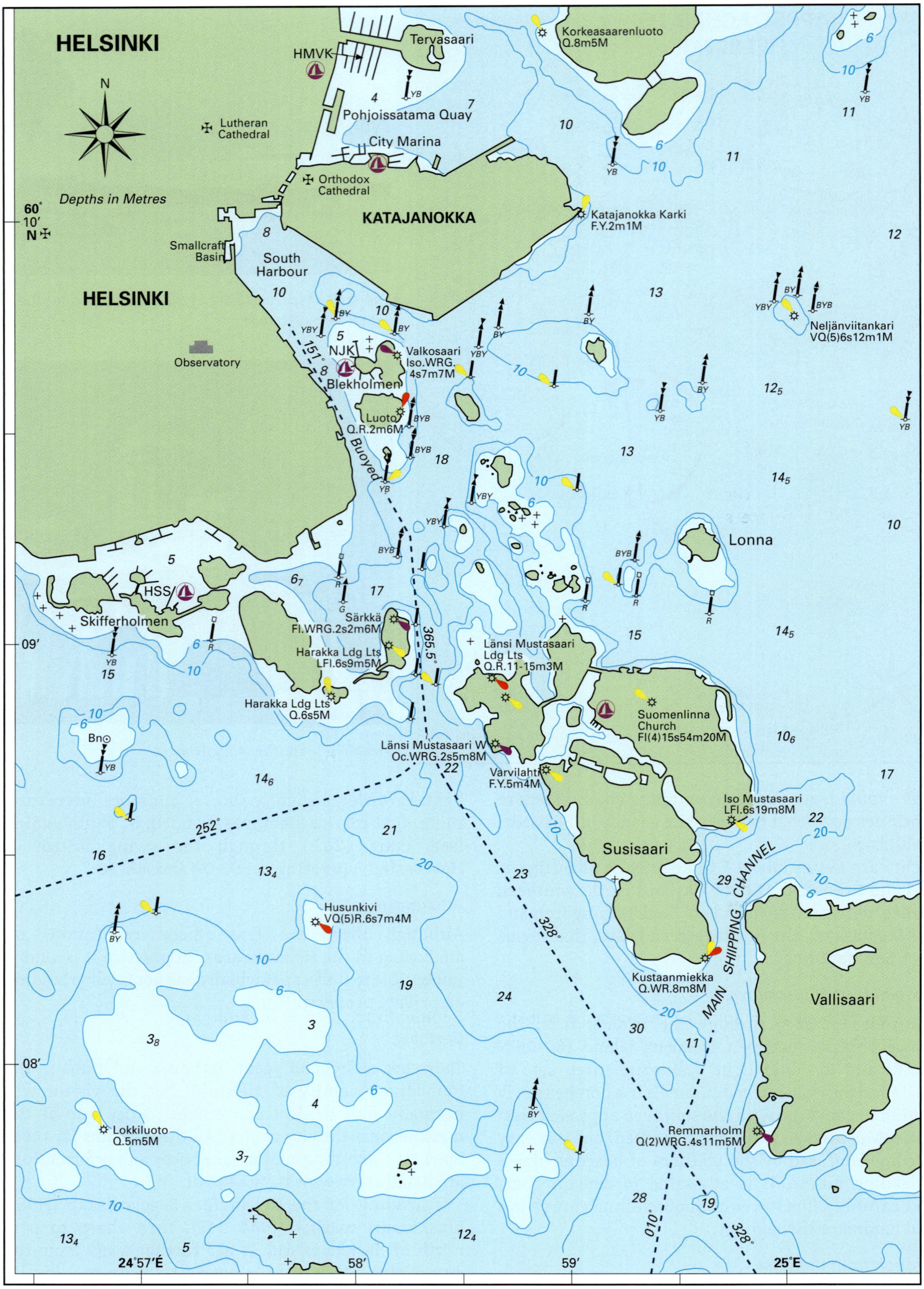
HELSINKI
HMVK
Tervasaari
Korkeasaarenluoto
Q.8m5M
Pohjoissatama Quay
Lutheran Cathedral
City Marina
Orthodox Cathedral
Depths in Metres
KATAJANOKKA
Katajanokka Karki
F.Y.2m1M
Smallcraft Basin
South Harbour
HELSINKI
Observatory
NJK
Valkosaari
Iso.WRG.
4s7m7M
Blekholmen
Luoto
Q.R.2m6M
Buoyed
151°
Neljänviitankari
VQ(5)6s12m1M
Lonna
HSS
Skifferholmen
Särkkä
Fl.WRG.2s2m6M
Harakka Ldg Lts
LFl.6s9m5M
Harakka Ldg Lts
Q.6s5M
365.5°
Länsi Mustasaari
Ldg Lts
Q.R.11-15m3M
Suomenlinna Church
Fl(4)15s54m20M
Länsi Mustasaari W
Oc.WRG.2s5m8M
Varvilahti
F.Y.5m4M
Iso Mustasaari
LFl.6s19m8M
Bn
252°
Susisaari
MAIN SHIPPING CHANNEL
Husunkivi
VQ(5)R.6s7m4M
328°
Kustaanmiekka
Q.WR.8m8M
Vallisaari
Lokkiluoto
Q.5m5M
Remmarholm
Q(2)WRG.4s11m5M
010°
60° 10′ N
09′
08′
24°57′E
58′
59′
25°E

The dry docks in Suomenlinna. Many of the traditional boats are laid up here for the winter *Fiona Slay*

The NJK is the oldest yacht club in Finland and has an imposing and beautiful clubhouse on Blekholmen island, though the sailing activities of the club are now situated some distance from the city centre on the island of Koivusaari, Björkholmen (60°09'.7N 24°51'E). At Blekholmen there are some 25 visitors' berths in 3m depth. All moorings are bows-to from stern buoys. Berths marked 'P' are available for visitors.

The surroundings are very scenic and visitors are made most welcome, but it is not particularly peaceful since large ferries pass and dock very close by. A two-minute ferry journey (every 20mins from 0800 until late in the evening) connects Blekholmen with the shore, from where it is only a short walk into the city centre.

For any of the marinas north of the Katajanokka peninsula adjacent to the downtown area, Katajanokka or Pohjoisranta marinas, pass between Luoto and Ryssänsaari.

The city-run Katajanokka marina (**FMA** 325) on the north side of the Katajanokka peninsula (the site of the magnificent Orthodox cathedral) is the closest to the city of all Helsinki's marinas. They can be contacted on VHF Ch 68. It occupies the westernmost pontoon on the north side of the Katajanokka peninsula - the two to the east are private - and offers berthing for 120 yachts in depths of 4m or more, some alongside, some on finger pontoons and some with stern buoys. Berths can be booked in advance through the website - en.marinabay.fi/venepaikka and there is also a map of the marina on their site (en.marinabay.fi). There is little wash to contend with, and security is good, but there is continuous noise from the nearby road.

Helsingin Moottorivenekerho (HMVK) (**FMA** 324), Pohjoisranta-Tervasaari (www.pohjoisrantaharbour.fi, meriurheuli@hmvk.fi, ✆+358 40 508 8344) just to the north on the south side of the causeway to Tervasaari island, north of Katajanokka, has around 400 berths, all of them box moorings (some of which are rather narrow) in 2-4.5m. The visitors' pontoon is the one nearest to the shore; alongside mooring is mostly for bigger boats. There are a few boxes 15m by 5m and more boxes 13m by 4m. Berths can be booked in advance through the website (www.venekerhot.fi/hmvk/booking).

Berths are often available in July and the first half of August if permanent berth holders are away. The marina is peaceful and secure, if rather less picturesque than the two island marinas, and is convenient for the city.

Larger, traditional yachts may find a welcome alongside the Pohjoissatama quay between the Katajanokka and HMVK marinas, but should contact the Port Authority before arrival. The marina on the north side of the Tervasaari causeway does not accept visitors. There is a small boat pool close to the covered market in the northwest corner of South Harbour where a yacht or dinghy might be left during a shopping trip (subject to the two-hour time limit).

A slightly different option for berthing is the guest harbour on Suomenlinna. The harbour is in the bay between five islands (Länsi-Mustasaari, Pikku Mustasaari, Iso Mustasaari, Susisaari and Susiluoto) and the approach is through a straightforward buoyed channel. At the end of the channel, turn 90° to starboard for the guest berths which are on the south side of the bay. There are 40 berths in 2-4m of water and a regular ferry from the northern shore of Mustasaari to Kauppatori in Helsinki centre. The Foundry café next door to the guest jetty offers food and guest facilities (www.valimo.org).

Suomenlinna is known by the Swedish as Sveaborg (Castle of the Swedes). It was renamed in Finnish to Suomenlinna (Castle of Finland) in 1918 for obvious reasons! The fortress was started in 1748 as protection against Russian expansionism, but the Swedes ended up surrendering it to the Russians in 1808. The islands were used as the base for the Russian Baltic fleet during the First World War. On the southeast tip of Susisaari is the submarine Vesikko which is now a museum ship. After the ceasefire with the Allies in 1944, Vesikko was retired and Finland was banned from operating submarines after the war, so Vessiko became a museum. Suomenlinna was listed as a UNESCO World Heritage Site in 1991.

### *Services*

All four marinas have water and electricity at their berths with toilets and showers ashore and a pump-out station. The Blekholmen (NJK), Liuskasaari (HSS)

The guest berths at Suomenlinna looking from the northern side of the harbour to the south *Andy Beharrell*

The *Vessiko* saw service in the Winter War and Continuation War. She is now a museum ship in Suomenlinna *Andy Beharrell*

and Pohjoissatama (HMVK) marinas provide laundry facilities, while the NJK and HSS also have saunas on their islands, as well as first-class restaurants. Fuel is available at the HSS and HMVK, but not at the Katajanokka or NJK marinas. It might be possible to exchange propane gas cylinders at these clubs.

Helsinki and its surrounding area has many boatyards able to carry out work of almost any description, in addition to winter lay-up. The advice of a club secretary or marina manager should be sought as to which to approach first.

For a very wide range of chandlery it is worth taking the bus to Lauttasaari island towards the west of the city, where three good-sized chandleries stand close together on Veneentekijäntie, near to the Helsingfors Segelklubb (HSK) (**FMA** 356).

The largest of these is Maritim Oy (Veneentekijäntie 1, 00210 Helsinki), which stocks an enormous range of paint, hardware, electronics, pilot books and charts.
☎+358 10 2740 310
info@maritimshop.fi
www.maritim.fi

Nearby are other chandleries:
Marinekauppa (Veneentekijiantie 3, 00210 Helsinki (Lauttasaari)
www.marinekauppa.com/fi
kaskapalvelu@marinekauppa.com
☎+358 10 5485605

Captain's Shop (Veneentekijäntie 11, 00210 Helsinki)
www.captainsshop.fi
lauttasaari@captainsshop.fi
☎+358 9 682 2512

For sailmakers there are various options:
One Sails (Lauttasaari) (Veneentekijäntie 1, 00210 Helsinki)
www.onesails.com/lofts/finland-helsinki/
info@onesails.fi
☎+358 40 013 1371

UK Sailmakers (Finland) (Suomenlinna B 14, 00140 Helsinki)
www.uksails.fi
myynti@uksails.fi
☎+358 9 668 311

North Sails (Veneentekijäntie 12, 00210 Helsinki)
www.purjeneulomoniiniranta.fi
fin@northsails.com
☎+358 2 2753059

### *Facilities*

Helsinki has excellent shops of all kinds, as expected in a capital city.

The open-air and covered markets overlooking South Harbour are well worth a visit, mainly for their wide variety of fish, fresh vegetables and fruit. The small delicatessens in the covered market – the 'Vanha Kauppahalli' or 'Gamla Saluhallen' – to the west are particularly tempting but far from cheap.

There are many large supermarkets in the main shopping centre, a few minutes' walk from the harbour, and there are others beneath the main railway station. The large Akateeminen Kirjakauppa bookshop on Pohjoisesplanadi 39 stocks books, magazines and newspapers in many languages including English.

There is a tourist information office near the harbour (www.myhelsinki.fi/en/info/tourist-information), and many excellent restaurants in addition to those at the Nylandska Jaktklubben and the Helsingfors Segelsällskap.

### *Communications & travel*

There are good rail, air and coach services between Helsinki and all major European cities, plus regular ferries to Tallin and Stockholm, the latter via Mariehamn.

Temppeliaukio Church in Helsinki is built directly into solid rock. It is also known as the Church of the Rock *Fiona Slay*

# 3D. GULF OF FINLAND – EASTERN PART

Heading east from Helsinki, the choice of routes diminishes as you approach the Russian border. The skerries become less dense. The main northern route hugs the mainland and passes close to the bigger towns and harbours such as Porvoo, Loviisa, Kotka, Hamina, ending in Virolahti on the border with Russia. The approach to these towns is still quite a long way inland from the main route. The southern route passes south of Emäsalo/Emsalö, Suur-Pellinki/Stor-Pellinge, Kejvsalö islands and comes closer and closer to the main route near Kotka, where the routes branch out again. If heading to St Petersburg, take the route southeast towards Haapasaari island, the border control point near the Russian border. The northern route continues eastwards and passes close to Santio island, the second border control point with Russia. If heading towards Vyborg/Viipuri and the Saimaa Canal and lakes, you have to clear customs and border formalities at Santio (see chapter 3 page 357), though at the time of publication of this edition, this route is not open due to the ongoing conflict in Ukraine.

*Navigational charts – Harbour guides*

**Planning chart**
F951 (Gulf of Finland - East, 1:250,000)

**Chart folio**
A-Viipuri-Helsinki/Viborg-Helsingfors (scale 1:50,000)

Stora Hamnboken Vol.3 - Suomenlahti/Finska Viken (**SH3** *xxx*)

**See also**
Navigational charts - Finland and Åland, and harbour books and literature page 272 (general introduction to Finland).

## Havsudden, Emsalö

60°13'N 25°36'.9E
**SH3** *34*

*Anchorage*

Situated at the southern end of the island of Emäsalo/Emsalö, just off the main commercial channel when approaching from the open sea and heading towards the oil refinery at Sköldvik and Porvoo, Havsudden is a small bay on the southwest coast of Emsalö.

A delightful anchorage in the southeast corner of the bay in 6m. Well sheltered except from north to northwest. Surrounded by trees and a few summer houses. There are two private pontoons on either side at Neste and Meriniemi and a few private moorings. Keep clear of these.

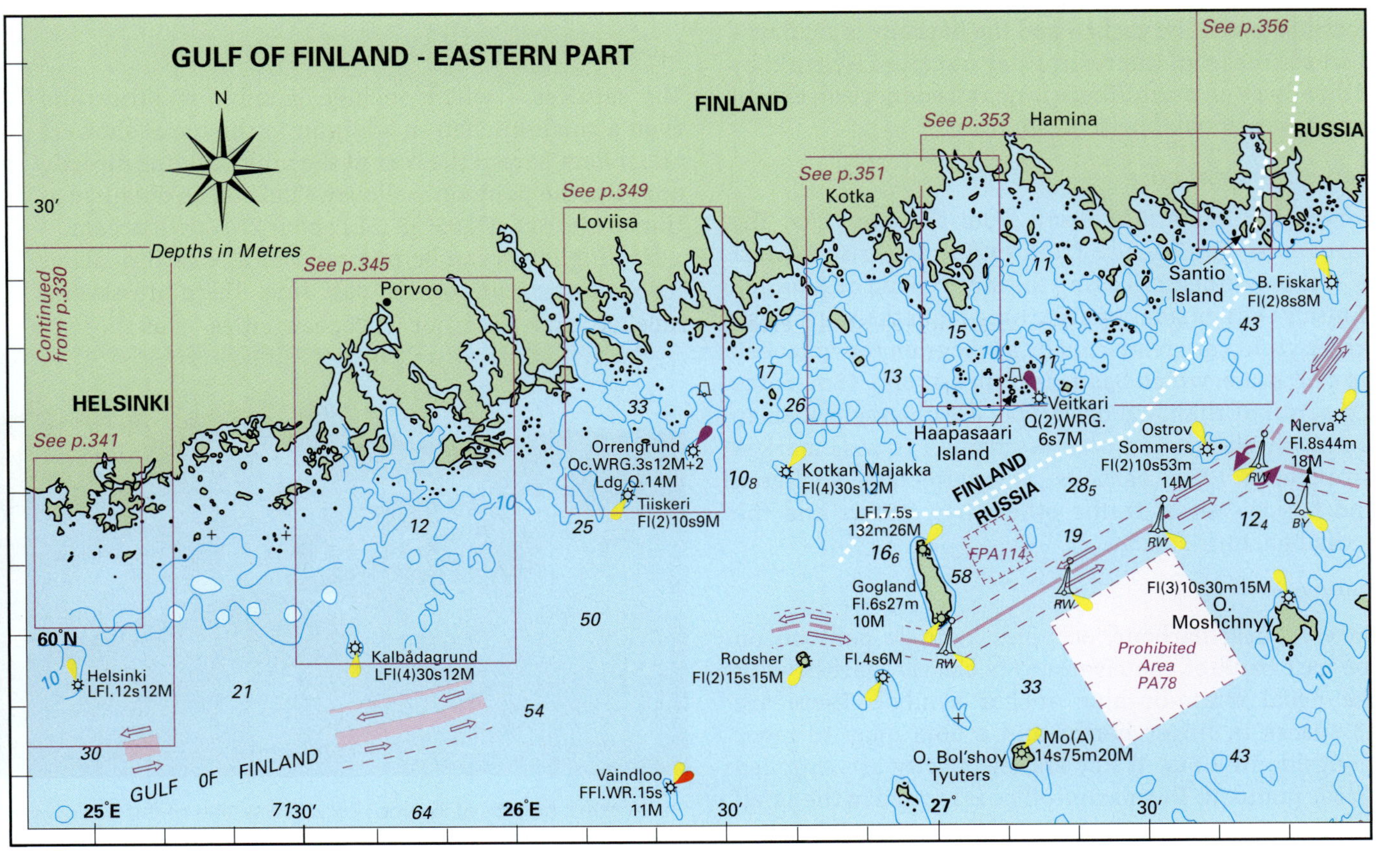

# PORVOO

60°23'.3N 25°39'.9E

## Charts / harbour guides

**SH3** *89* **FMA** *250*
Merikarttasarja A: Viipuri – Helsinki/Viborg – Helsingfors
Stora Hamnboken Vol.3

## Lights

**Kalbådgrund** 59°59'.1N 25°36'.1E LFl(4)30s27m12M
Racon Red concrete tower, white stripe 25m Helipad
**Porvoon Majakka Leading Lights 016°** *Front* 60°05'.6N 25°36'E Fl.WRG.2s10m6M
Racon Red tower, black band 10m
*Rear* **Larsskär** 60°08'.7N 25°37'.8E LFl.8s36m9M
Red rectangle, yellow stripe
**Havsudden Leading Lights 012°** *Front* 310m *from rear*, Q.R.18m10M
Red rectangle, yellow stripe
**Varlaxudden Leading Lights 340.5°** *Front* 1570m *from rear*, Q.Y.15m12M
Red rectangle, yellow stripe
*Common rear* 60°12'.9N 25°37'.1E Q.R.28m12M
Red rectangle, yellow stripe

## Harbour contacts

**Porvoo Guest Harbour** ✆+358 19 584 727
www.visitporvoo.fi/en/
cafejokiranta@gmail.com

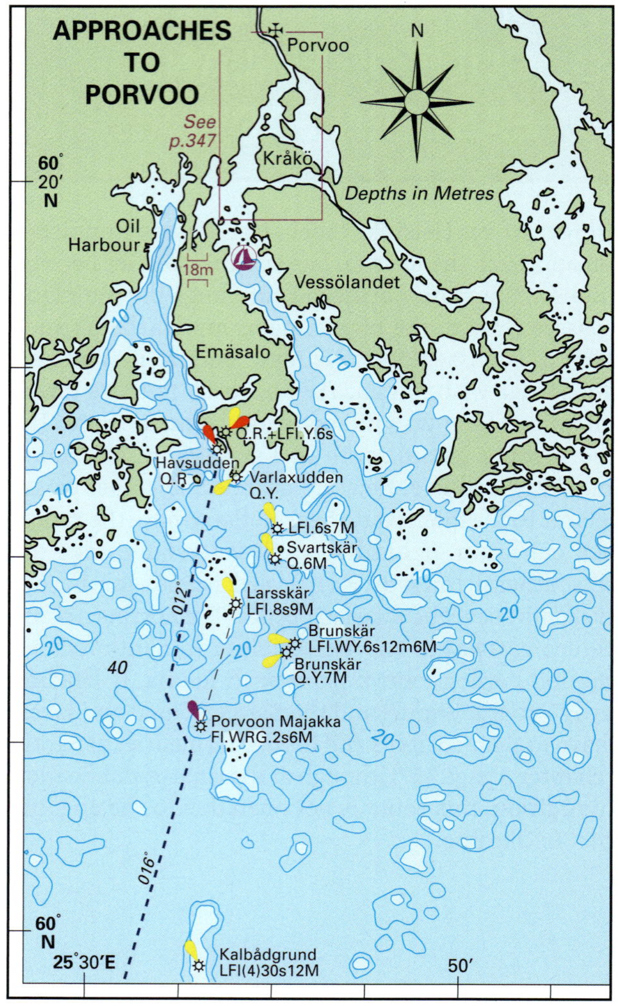


Porvoo is the second oldest town in Finland, established in 1346. Its 15th-century cathedral overlooks the town, and there are numerous museums and art galleries. It is worth rowing upriver beyond the bridge to admire a most attractive row of fishermens' houses. If it is not possible to visit by yacht – and the harbour is shallow – it would make an interesting day out from Helsinki by either ferry or coach. There is no rail connection except for an occasional tourist steam train.

### *Approach & entrance*

Porvoo lies some 12M north from the open sea. The harbour is approached from either south-southwest or south-southeast, leaving the large island of Emäsalo (Emsalö) either side. Approaching from the southwest, larger yachts are restricted by a bridge on the northern tip of Emsalö, which has a clearance of only 18m. Some 4M south of the town of Porvoo, the channel shoals to (1.9m) in places. The narrow channel is well marked throughout. The harbour is completely sheltered and has no vessel traffic other than yachts and the occasional tourist boat.

### *Berthing*

Porvoo guest harbour, occupies a single pontoon on the east bank of the river and is clearly marked with the usual white-on-blue anchor symbol. There are 23 spaces in finger berths and a 66m quay to moor alongside in 2.5m. Water and electricity are supplied on the pontoon. The marina office is located in the small blue café slightly upstream. Berths can be booked in advance through Satamapaikka (www.satamapaikka.com).

### *Services*

The services – which include laundry facilities and even a small kitchen in addition to the usual showers and toilets – are at the rear of the pink building directly opposite the pontoon walkway. Fuel can be obtained at Hamari (60°21'.4N 25°38'.5E) about 2M downstream.

Holding tanks can be pumped out at a facility about 0.5M downstream on the east side. There are several

Fishermen's houses at Porvoo. Porvoo was one of the six medieval towns of Finland *Andy Beharrell*

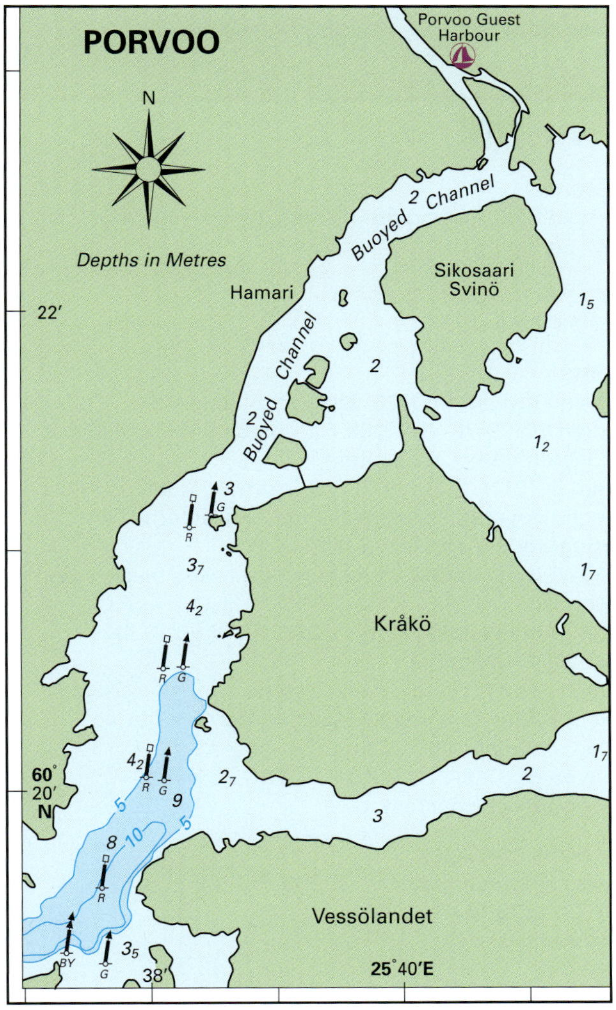


boatyards in the vicinity where repairs can be carried out and where it might be possible to lay-up. There is a variety of marine engineers and other services: the marina office produces a useful booklet detailing local services, in Finnish and Swedish only.

### *Facilities*

Porvoo has good shopping, including a small outdoor market, within a short walk of the guest harbour.

### *Communications & travel*

Porvoo is linked to Helsinki by bus and the occasional tourist train.

## Sandholmsudden, Pellinki

60°14'.1N 25°52'.2E

**Charts / harbour guides**
**SH3** *98* **FMA** *232*

**Contacts**
www.benitascafe.fi/en

In the northern coastal channel (3m) that runs north of the island of Pellinki, 1.1M west of Sunisundet is Benitas Café and a pontoon harbour with 15 places. A good mooring in southwesterly winds when Sunisundet is quite windy. There is a nice café with some food and fuel sales.

## Suninsalmi (Sunisundet)

60°14'.7N 25°53'.8E

**Charts / harbour guides**
**SH3** *114* **FMA** *229*

The northern coastal channel (3m) that runs north of the island of Pellinki passes through Sunisundet, the sound between Tirmo on the mainland and the island of Sundön. West from the ferry that connects Sundön with the mainland is the guest harbour of Sunnisund. It is open to the southwest and west. There are 30 spaces, bows-to from stern buoys, on finger pontoons or alongside in 1.8–2.5m. This is the main shopping point for the Pellinki group of islands with a convenient jetty and a modest supermarket. Fuel (only 1.5m at the fuel jetty), gas and provisions can also be purchased here. There is a good anchorage with excellent holding in the bay on the opposite side of the channel.

Northeast from the harbour (1.5M) there is a good fish shop with a jetty – Nyholms Fisk – at Fölisöudden (60°15'.5N 25°56'.0E) (**FMA** *228*) – easily approached from the main coastal channel.

## Bockholmen

60°12'N 25°54'.8E
Charts / harbour guides

**SH3** *7*

### *Anchorage*

Just off the southern route between Helsinki and Kotka (9m), Bockholmen is a well sheltered and attractive anchorage surrounded by islands and almost landlocked. Good holding ground. Approach from the south, leaving Bockholmen lighthouse to starboard. Turn east as soon as you reach the lagoon and pass north of Tällholmen island. The anchorage is situated on the eastern side of Tällholmen in 4–5m. Beware of the rock awash 0.1M to the northeast of Tällholmen.

Bockholmen anchorage *M. Strobel*

## Bockhamn (Byön)

60°16'.07N 25°59'.53E

**Charts / harbour guides**
**SH3** *6* **FMA** *217*

The island of Byön, south of Sarvisalo lies just off the northern route (2.4m) towards Loviisa. The lagoon is situated to the southeast of the island. It is owned by Nylands Outdoor Association (Föreningen Nylands Friluftsområden) and open to everyone. Enter from the southeast just over a cable east of a white stone cairn off the buoyed channel. Keep to the centre of the very narrow entrance channel (2.7m). Anchor in the center of the lagoon (clay bottom) or bows-to from a stern buoy or anchor either east or west of the entrance to the pool (15-20 spaces) in 2m. The anchorage is almost landlocked and safe in all winds. There are just a few small summer houses and a farm nearby. It can get very crowded during high summer.

## Sävtäktet

60°17'.1N 26°08'.3E

**Charts / harbour guides**
**SH3** *119*

### *Anchorage*

Very attractive anchorage between Helsinki and Kotka. It lies amidst a cluster of islands in Grundfjärden to the east of the island of Hästön. Situated roughly equidistant from the northern and the southern routes, it can be approached either from the south or the northeast.

### *From the south*

From the south cardinal buoy south of Risholmen leading mark, head towards the west of Risholmen island, past the narrow entrance between Skogshället, Lilla Risholmen to port and Risholmen to starboard. The archipelago widens at this point. Continue in a northerly direction (0.4M) until you have passed between Stora Andholmen (with a cairn) to starboard and Träskesholmen to port and anchor in the pool (7-8m). There are three red fairway buoys to guide you in.

### *From the north*

Leave the main channel at the top of Kejvsalö island and head southwards entering the pool at the southeastern corner of Våtskär island.

Sävtäktet, looking east *M. Strobel*

## LOVIISA

60°27'N 26°14'E

### Distances
Helsinki 55M, Porvoo 40M, Kotka 35M, Haapasaari Island 40M, Santio 56M

### Charts / harbour guides
**SH3** *68* **FMA** *200, 201*

### Lights
**Loviisan Kivi light** 60°26'.23N 26°15'.7E, Q.WRG
**Tiiskeri** 60°09'.7N 26°15'.8E Fl(2)10s16m9M Racon Black concrete tower and lantern
**Tainio** 60°012'.7N 26°24'.7E VQ(5)6s17m6M Racon White round concrete tower, black top, red lantern 17m
**Orrengrund, W end** 60°16'.4N 26°26'.3E Oc.WRG.3s13m12M White concrete tower, black lantern. Floodlit
**Orrengrund Leading Lights 023.1°** *Front* 60°16'.4N 26°27'.1E Q.13m13M
Racon Red rectangle, yellow stripe
*Rear* 520m *from front* LFl.6s25m14M
Red rectangle, yellow stripe
**Skarven** 60°17'.8N 26°20'.91E Fl.WRG.3s7m4M Racon Black concrete tower

### Harbour contacts
**Loviisa Harbourmaster** ✆+358 19 515 163
VHF Ch 12/13/14/16
www.visitloviisa.fi

Loviisa is a small and interesting town at the head of a long, peaceful inlet. It has a population of around 16,000. Loviisa is best known for its fortifications, the wooden houses of its old town and the Strömfors Iron Works. It was a thriving port during the 19th century and a resort town for the Russian nobility prior to 1914. Overlooking the guest harbour is the Museum of Seafaring (www.merenkulkumuseo.fi) which has a fine collection of model ships and old photographs.

Finland's greatest composer, Jean Sibelius, spent his childhood summers in Loviisa and the house, just beyond the church, is open during the tourist season. A Sibelius Festival is held in the town each summer.

About 4.5M to the south, on the narrow approach to the town, stands the fortified island of Svartholm. It is well worth visiting (www.visitsvartholm.fi).

### *Approach & entrance*

Loviisa is situated some 12M north from the open sea. The nuclear power station on Hästholmen (60°22'N 26°21'E) is a conspicuous landmark from afar. The approach from the southeast is straightforward, leaving Lilla Hudö and Hudö to port and Yttre Täktarn to starboard. Though narrow where it passes between Hudö and some offlying islets, the channel is well marked with transits, beacons and buoys. This is the approach route for the industrial port at Valko. Further north, past the industrial docks, the channel shoals progressively to 2.7m and widens before reaching the

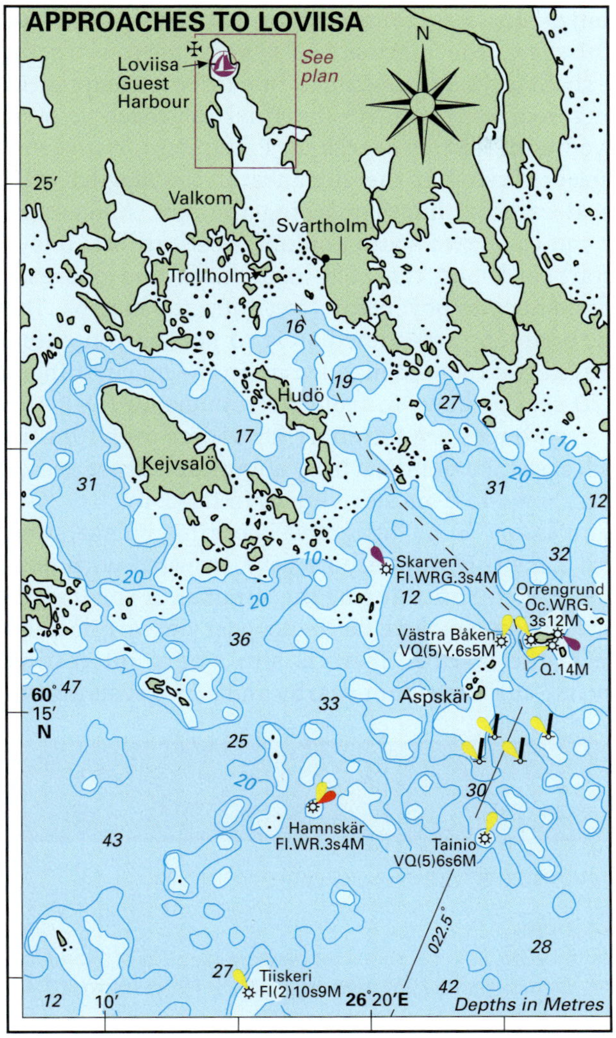


town. The final stretch is well marked with lateral buoys and Loviisan Kivi light (60°26′.23N 26°15′.7E).

Approaching from the west, there is a shortcut that passes through the skerries north of Stor Hudö and joins the main shipping channel south of Svartholmen.

### *Berthing*

#### Loviisa Laivasilta (Skeppsbron) marina

☎+358 40 740 7308 (Harbourmaster)
Laivasilta 1, 07900 Loviisa
www.visitkotkahamina.fi/en/places/loviisa-laivasilta-service-marina/
www.youtube.com/watch?v=tQAWzaszksM

Loviisa Laivasilta (Skeppsbron) marina (**FMA** *201*) lies southeast of the town centre amid pleasant, park-like surroundings. There is a visitors pontoon, bows-to from stern buoys in 2–2.5m. It is the longest pontoon as you approach the harbour.

The harbour office at Laivasilta occupies a small kiosk near the fuel berth.

#### Loviisa Tullisilta

Deeper yachts can moor to a jetty at Tullisilta, about 0.4M further south, where there is a single pontoon with 5 berths in up to 3m (on the outside). It lies directly on the fairway, is subject to swell from passing boats and lies some distance from the town centre.

At Tullisilta harbour dues are paid at the tourist information office.

### *Services*

The guest harbour has all the usual facilities including showers, toilets, sauna and launderette, with cafés and restaurants nearby. Fuel is available at the service dock close south of the long visitors pontoon, where holding tanks can also be pumped out. The jetty at Tullisilta has toilets, showers and a small shop.

There are several boatyards in the area, and mechanical and other work can be carried out by a variety of local companies - seek advice at the marina office. M-Yachts is a large boatyard to the south of Loviisa. They offer winter storage and most boatyard services.

www.m-yachts.fi
info@m-yachts.fi
☎+358 40 6304243

Within the boatyard is also a Doyle Sails loft for sailmaking services.

www.doylesails.com/lofts-loviisa
martin.rosenstedt@m-yachts.fi
☎+358 40 5118501

### *Facilities*

All normal shopping needs can be met in Loviisa town centre, a pleasant 750m walk from the guest harbour, where there are also the usual cafés, restaurants, etc.

### *Communications & travel*

Loviisa is on the railway network, though travelling to Helsinki would require several changes. Buses run to Helsinki and Helsinki-Vantaa international airport.

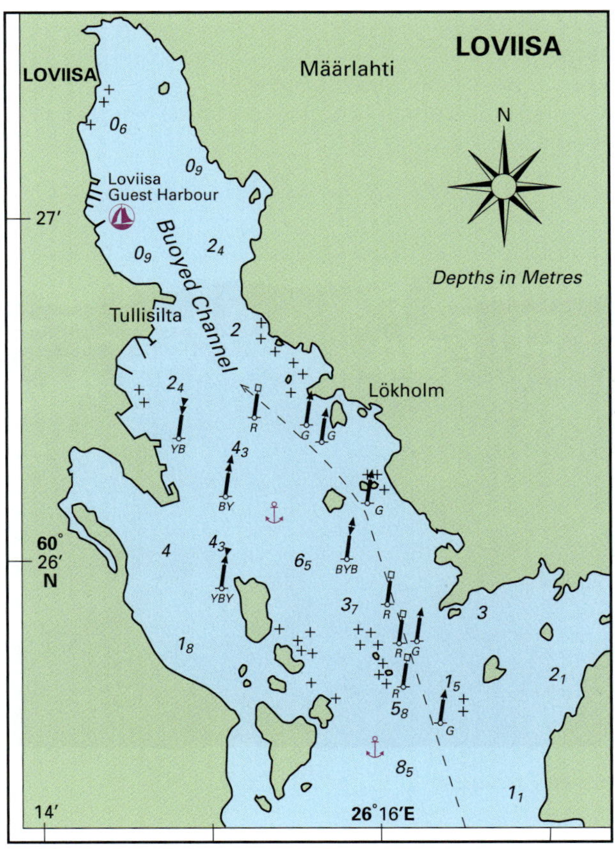

## Svartholm

60°22'.8N 26°18'1E

**Charts / harbour guides**
**SH3** 117 **FMA** 194

**Contacts**
www.cafesvartholm.fi/
www.visitsvartholm.fi

Approach from the east from the fairway leading to Loviisa. Follow the marked fairway towards the service dock, located on the northern bank, or to the guest pontoons located on the northeastern corner of the island. Pontoons with stern buoys (4m). The guest harbour is on the northeast side of the island with depths between 1–4m and is open to the southeast and northwest-north winds.

Svartholm Castle and island is a great destination for the whole family. In the castle there is an exhibition, which introduces the island's history. The fortress is a bastion fortress and was started in 1748, but the Swedish era ended in 1808 when they surrendered to the Russians. It played an important role and was bombarded by the British fleet during the Crimean War. Since the 1960s it has been gradually renovated. There are also guided walks that can be arranged and adventures for children.

There is a tourist boat going from Loviisa to Svartholm several times a day. This is a convenient way to do some shopping and sightseeing and return later in the day to Svartholm where you have left your yacht.

## Kaunissaari/Pyttis Fagerö

60°20'.6N 26°46'.5E (south mole)

**Charts / harbour guides**
**SH3** 47 **FMA** 172

**Contacts**
www.kaunissaari.fi/kaunissaaren-satama/
www.visitkotkahamina.fi/en/places/pyhtaa-kaunissaari-service-marina/

Kaunissaari *M. Strobel*

Situated on the southern tip of the island of Kaunissaari, the marina has a very narrow, rocky, and shallow (2.5m) entrance not to be attempted in strong southerly winds. The final approach is well buoyed with leading marks on Piktäniemi, but seems rather confusing at the entrance of the marina with several cardinal buoys marking the spit. Make sure that you leave two south and one west cardinal buoys to starboard, and the port-hand mark and one east cardinal buoy to port before you enter the marina. The guest pontoons are immediately to port as you enter. There is little room to manoeuvre in the marina. There are 20 spaces, bows-to from stern buoys in 1·9–2·4m. The stern buoys are too short for yachts over 10m (in which case take the stern buoy alongside). There are 20 spaces, bows-to from stern buoys in 1.9–2.4m.

Kaunissaari is an attractive working village, well worth a visit. It can become very crowded with day-trippers from Kotka during the summer. A small well-stocked shop, smoked fish, and post box are located close to the marina. There is also a very interesting maritime curio museum nearby and a nice restaurant.

## KOTKA

60°27'.5N 26°57'.2E (Sapokanlahti)

### Distances

Helsinki 75M, Loviisa 35M, Haapasaari Island 15M, Hamina 20M, Santio Island 30M, Vyborg 65M, St Petersburg 110M

### Charts / harbour guides

**SH3** *55* **FMA** *149, 146*

### Lights

**Kotkan Majakka** 60°10'.3N 26°39'.2E Fl(4)30s23m12M Racon Yellow metal column, blue band Helipad
**Luppi** 60°14'.3N 27°01'.8E Fl.WRG.3s8m6M
**Rankin Kivikari (Patricia)** 60°21'.2N 26°57'.4E UQ(5)6s10m3M Racon White metal post, red band
**Rankki** 60°21'.9N 26°58'.3E Fl(3)WRG.10s11m6M Black round concrete tower on reef
**Lelleri** 60°24'N 26°58'.5E Fl(2)WRG.5s5m7M Yellow round tower, black top
**Pirköyri** 60°27'.5N 26°58'.6E Fl.WRG.3s6m5M Red lantern on white concrete base

### Contacts

**Kotka Port Authority** ✆+358 20 790 8800
*VHF* Ch 16, 11, 13, 14
**Kotka Vessel Traffic Service** ✆+358 204 485 391
*VHF* Ch 67 (all vessels more than 12m in length must maintain a listening watch while in the fairways of the Kotka pilotage area)
**Kotka Guest Harbour** ✆+358 44 239 9915
**New Port Kotka** ✆+358 5 225 0074
www.kotkanpursiseura.fi (for Sapokanlahti Yacht Club KPS)
www.kotka.fi
www.haminakotka.com

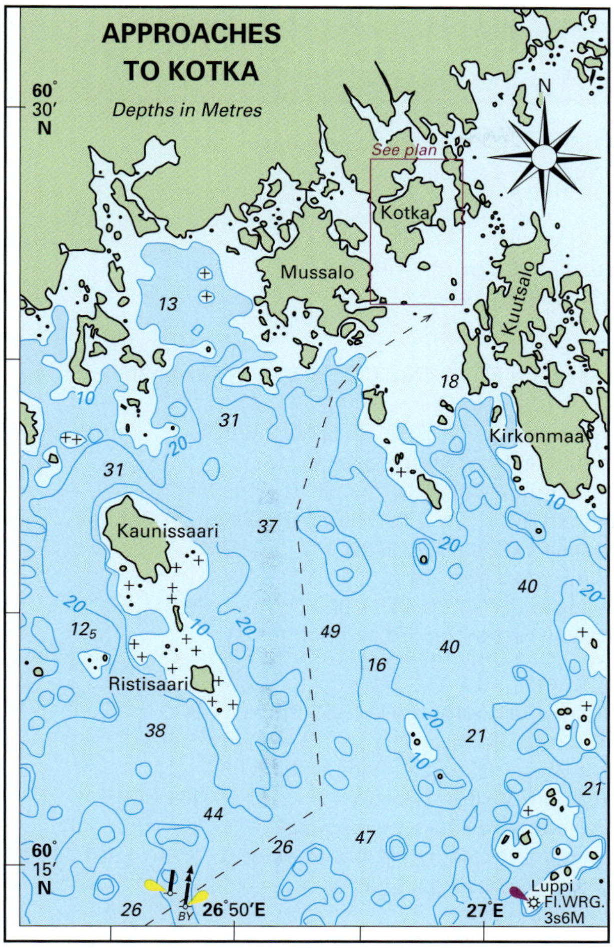


With a population of more than 50,000, Kotka is the largest city between Helsinki and the Russian border, and is an important port mostly handling timber, paper and forest products. Originally it occupied only the island of Kotkansaari but over the years has spread inland and to the adjacent islands. Another reason for coming to Kotka is to visit the fishing lodge, built in 1889 for Tsar Alexander III. It lies by the rapids at Langinkoski about 5km northwest of the town and is easily reached by bus. It is intriguing and well worth visiting.

The Kotka Maritime Festival is held annually in early August – details on the Kotka city website (see page 350).

The stunning Maritime Museum of Finland and Maritime Centre Vellamo (www.kansallismuseo.fi/en/suomenmerimuseo), is situated near the docks on the north side of the island.

On the northwest side of Kotkansaari Island, north of the pontoons, is the Maretarium (aquarium) and an impressive water garden with pleasant walks.

### *Approach & entrance*

www.youtube.com/watch?v=0gdwEOhAxYg

From the open sea, Kotka (Finnish for 'eagle') lies 6M to the north. The approach channel from Helsinki passes north of the island of Kaunissaari, follows three sets of leading marks to pass between Mussalo, the commencial port of Kotka and Viikarinsaari island, between Varissaari island and Kukouri fort, and finally northwest to the harbour entrance.

Approaching from the southeast, one of several approaches is between the islands of Kirkonmaa to starboard and Rankki to port towards Lelleri light (60°24′.02N 26°58′.32E), leaving Lehmäsaari to starboard, where the route joins the main approach.

### *Berthing*

Kotka, Sapokanlahti on Meriniemi has 50 berths and is situated on the southeast shore of the Kotkansaari peninsula. It is run by the city's yacht club – the Kotkan Pursiseura KPS/KSS. The Marina Café Laituri (Winger) manages guest boat services (www.marinacafelaituri.fi). The Yacht Club also has a very good restaurant, the Ravintola Meriniemi in a stunning wooden building overlooking the harbour.

Visitors are normally berthed on the second pontoon on the left after entering the harbour (clearly identified with the usual white-on-blue anchor), which can take yachts up to 14m, bows-to from stern buoys in 2.5–5m.

Larger yachts may be able to berth north of the town at Kotka City Marina, a service harbour (see below), beyond the old icebreaker Tarmo (built in Newcastle in 1907 and now a museum ship). It is operated by Kotka Yacht Store Oy. It is a large modern marina, which can take up to 30 visitors (4m), alongside or on finger pontoons. Most of the spaces are reserved for

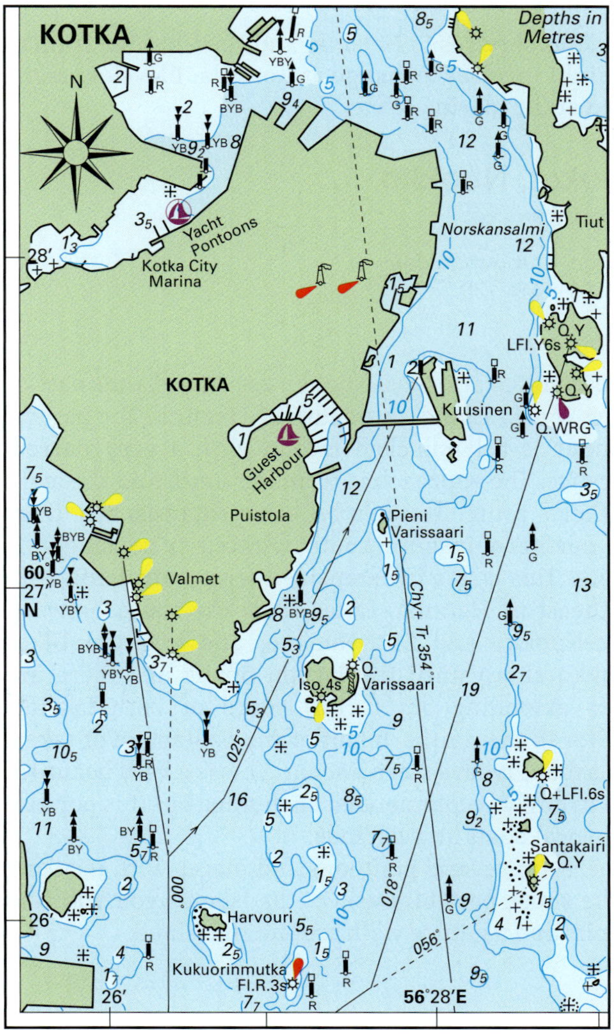

permanent berth holders and it would be wise to phone in advance (see details below). The area is a former passenger wharf and the water is deep.

### *Services*

Sapokanlahti (KPS/KSS) has water and electricity on the pontoon, with toilets and showers ashore. Laundry facilities are located in the marina yacht club building. The fuelling berth (where holding tanks can also be emptied) is at the end of the long, tree-shaded central mole, and also sells charts and a small amount of chandlery. Finnish propane gas cylinders can be exchanged there.

Kotka Yacht Store Oy (www.kotkayachtstoremarina.fi, hello@kotkayachtstore.com, ✆+358 105 177111), located in New Port Kotka, has a very large undercover facility and specialises in the laying-up and storage of boats. Other services include servicing, refitting and yacht transport. Veleiro Oy (www.veleiro.fi, info@veleiro.fi ✆+358 52 109 555), just north of Kotkansaari, in the Puolanlaituri district past the docks, also offers winter storage and all kinds of boat repairs (including Volvo Penta spare parts) and a chandlery.

### *Facilities*

The shopping centre is about 15min walk from the yacht harbour. There is also an outdoor market, as well as banks, restaurants and hotels in the town.

### *Communications & travel*

Good bus services to Helsinki and Hamina. The train to Helsinki involves a change at Kouvola. Bicycles can be hired at the marina office.

## Nuokot, Nuokko

60°27'N 27°13'4E

**Charts / harbour guides**
**SH3** *80* **FMA** *128*

### *Anchorage*

Ulko-Nuokko and Sisä-Nuokko are two islands east of Suuri-Musta island, due south of Hamina. The natural harbour is a landlocked lagoon with a very narrow entrance. The approach is from the south and the main southern route. It can't be easily approached from the northern inshore route without a considerable detour. This is due to extensive skerries stretching 8M southeast of Hamina. Enter from the south between Ulko-Nuokko and Sisä-Nuokko, and hug the Ulko-Nuokko shore until the lagoon opens up. There are rocks extending out (0.1M) south of both islands. Anchor in the southern half of the pool in 5m or take a line ashore from a stern anchor. This is a very beautiful and strongly recommended anchorage but it is popular with local boats at weekends.

There are several pontoons and places with mooring to the shore possibilities. On the islands you will find firepits and a nature walk around the island.

## HAMINA (FREDRIKSHAMN)

60°33'.4N 27°10'.9E (Rampsinkari (south))

### Distances
Kotka 20M, Haapasaari Island 15M, Santio Island 20M

### Charts / harbour guides
**SH3** *32* **FMA** *137, 138*

### Lights
**Haapasaari** 60°17'.4N 27°12'.3E VQ(10)Y.6s4m3M
Grey round tower
**Kivikari** 60°17'.5N 27°12'.5E Q.WRG.8m7M
White lantern, white base
**Kaurakari** 60°30'.8N 27°10'.5E VQ(5)6s4m4M
**Ulkokari** 60°31'.5N 27°11'.3E VQ(2)Y.3s4m2M Column
**Norskari** 60°31'.8N 27°11'.5E VQ.6s5m3M
White post, red band
**Suviluoto** 60°32'.3N 27°11'.8E Fl.WRG.3s3m5M
Yellow rectangle, red stripe, on post

### Contacts
**Hamina Port Authority** ✆+358 20 790 8800
VHF Ch 12, 13, 16
office@haminakotka.fi (Rampsinkari)
**Tervasaari Visitors' Harbour** ✆+358 40 075 6005
www.rampsi.fi/vierasvenesatama
**Haminan Pursiseura Harbourmaster** ✆+358 44 981 7740
haminanpursiseura@gmail.com
www.visithamina.fi
www.haminakotka.com

Just 40km west of the Russian border, Hamina is a pretty, spacious town with an unusual ground plan. Eight roads radiate from the old town centre, with others forming concentric circles around them so that, from the air, it resembles a giant spider's web. Designed to fit inside a vast rampart, Hamina has been

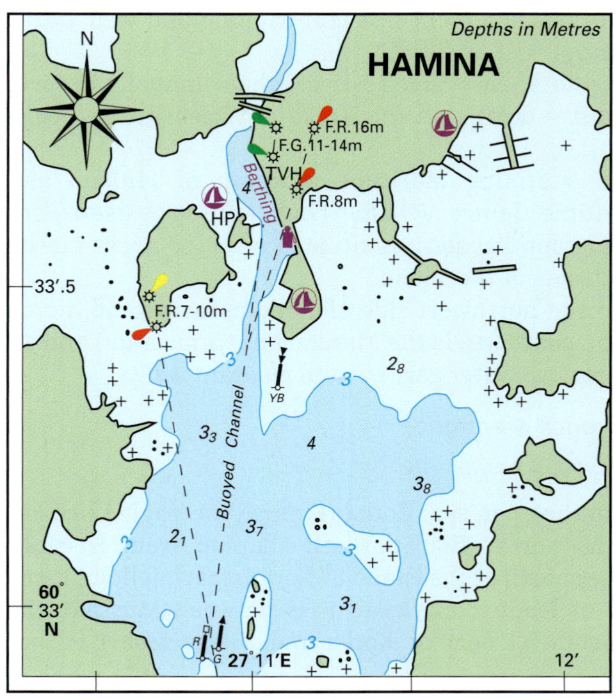

## APPROACHES TO HAMINA, INCLUDING HAAPASAARI AND SANTIO ISLANDS

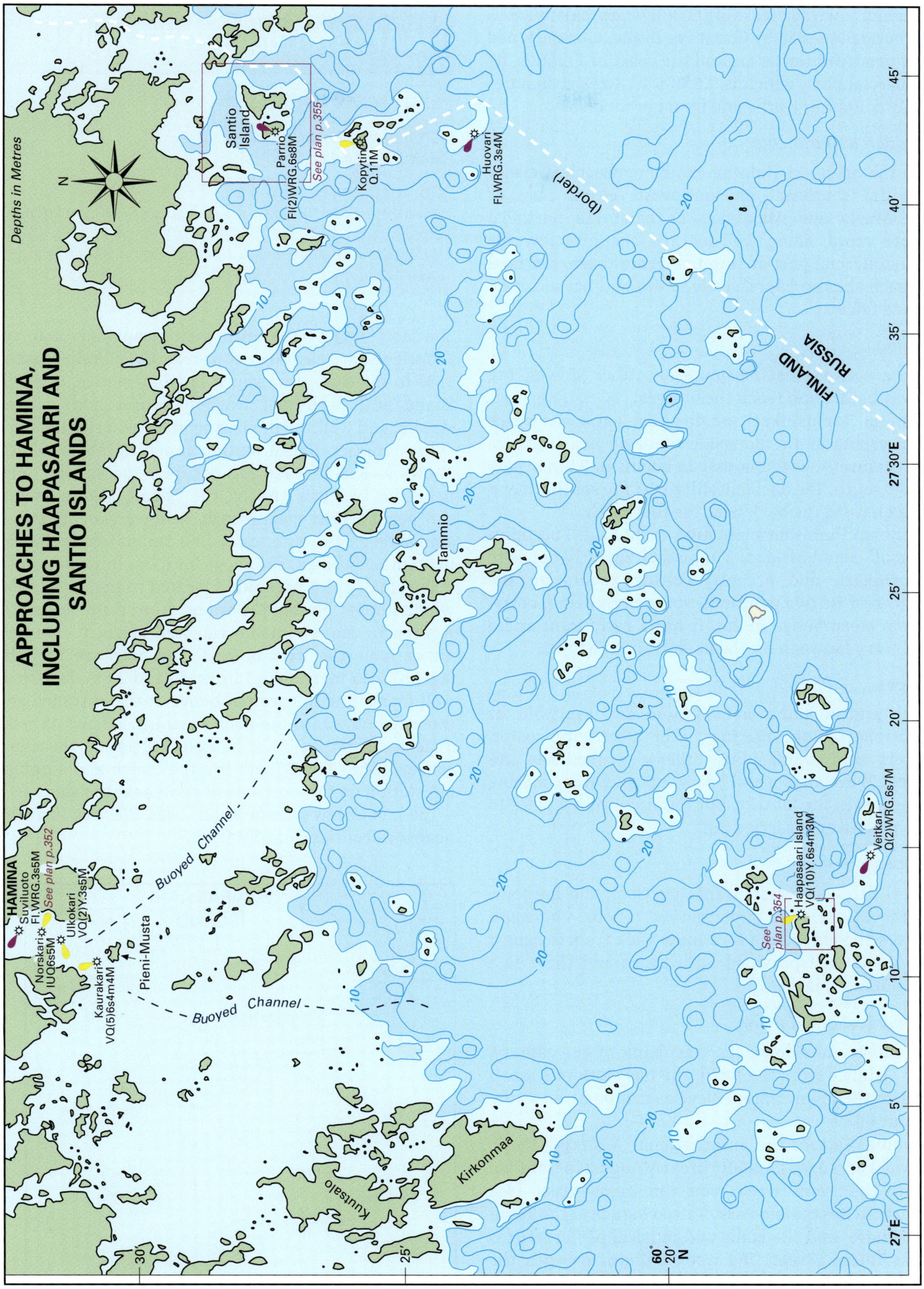

a garrison town for most of its 360 years' existence. It was founded in 1653 by Count Per Brahe, who designed many beautiful towns around the coast of Finland. Its commercial port, which is 2.5M downstream, handles mainly container traffic and forest products.

### *Approach & entrance*

From the open sea Hamina can be approached either from the southeast or southwest, either side of Suuri-Musta and Majasaari, or from the northern inshore route, along well-marked channels towards the commercial port of Hamina. From there, the final approach shoals progressively to 4m and has a clearly marked fairway.

### *Berthing*

There are two guest harbours on either side of the fairway before you reach the bridges.

Hamina Rampsinkari, on the east bank has space for 35 yachts in 4m alongside the quay near the café and restaurant, with another 15 berths in 2.2m or less further south. The harbour office is at the southern end of the quay (in the bar), near the fuel berth.

Haminan Pursiseura (Hamina Yacht Club), occupies the small island of Pieni Vuohisaari, directly opposite Rampsinkari, and accepts visiting yachts on the southern of its two pontoons, space permitting, bows-to from stern buoys in 2m. It has a restaurant and a small ferry between the yacht club and the town.

### *Services*

Diesel and a pump-out station are available at Rampsinkari. Both marinas offer electricity, water, showers and sauna, but otherwise facilities are limited. There are several boatyards and other marine businesses in the locality, but Hamina is not a place to have major works carried out.

### *Facilities*

Several cafés and restaurants overlook the harbour, and there is a good supermarket nearby. The town centre, which is about a 15-minute walk from the guest harbour, is well provided with shops and there is a large outdoor market.

### *Communications & travel*

The railway runs down the west bank of the estuary, some distance from the town; the bus station is much closer to the town centre. Bicycles can be hired at the harbour office.

Hamina Tattoo, the International Military Music Festival is arranged annually in early August in Hamina. During the event week, you can enjoy great free concerts in Kesäpuisto Park, Tattoo Parade at the Town Hall Square, and the stalls and musical performances of the Tattoo Street. The week culminates with the March Shows in the event arena Hamina Bastion.

## HAAPASAARI/ASPÖ ISLAND

60°17'.3N 27°11'.7E

**Charts / harbour guides**
**SH3** *29* **FMA** *134*

**Contacts**
www.raja.fi/en/guidelines-for-travellers-at-border-crossings
www.raja.fi/en/guidelines-for-boaters-at-border-crossings
www.tulli.fi/en

The most obvious reason to visit Haapasaari is to get Frontier Guard clearance to or from St Petersburg some 95M to the east. However, it is an attractive, unspoilt island with well-kept wooden houses and cobbled streets, and well worth visiting in its own right.

The Frontier Guard station (opening hours 0800–2200) ☏+358 295 426 130 occupies the smaller inlet near the western end of the island, where yachts can berth whilst clearance is being arranged, either alongside on the outer quay in 4.5m on inside the bay in 2.5m as directed. See above for more information.

The small guest harbour is located in the larger inlet which almost bisects the island from south to north. Approach can be made via well-marked channels either from the west or east. The entrance into the lagoon is no more than 12m wide and 3.5m deep. It is well marked with cardinal buoys at the entrance and fairway buoys into the pool. Berthing is bows-to with a stern anchor onto the pontoon in the northeastern corner in 1.5–2.2m. There is a fuel berth and a pump-out station on the west side of pool, near the shop.

The island ferry from Kotka uses the western pier near the Frontier Guard station.

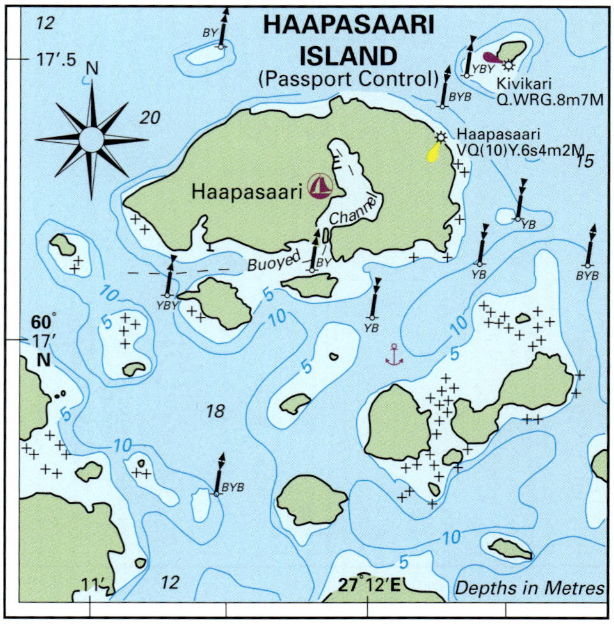

## Ulko-Tammio

60°21'N 27°27'.2E

**Charts / harbour guides**
**SH3** *127* **FMA** *122*

The deep-water commercial channel going east-west, turn southeast (130°) at approx 60°23'.5N 27°19'.5E. Pass east of Lammasaari and Rääntiö to the north west bay of Ulko-Tammio. A pontoon is located on the south shore.

Ulko-Tammio is the pearl of the national park of the Gulf of Finland. Its harsh cliffs and lush groves are both beautiful and impressive. Ulko-Tammio is an excellent destination for birdwatchers. The museum with its cannons and the cave, which was part of the fortification of the area during the Second World War is an interesting place to visit. Ulko-Tammio claims to be the world's first phone-free tourist island, following an initiative in 2023 to encourage visitors to enjoy a digital detox whilst on the island.

## Lapurinsalmi

60°28'.3N 27°35'.1E

**Charts / harbour guides**
**SH3** *65*

### *Anchorage*

This is a small natural harbour only a few miles away from Santio Frontier Guard station situated on the southwestern shore of Siikasaari, between Lapuri island and the mainland. Approach from the west. Anchor in 9m in the first third of the pool. The water becomes shallow after that and there are some rocks on the north side. This could be a good anchorage in which to wait before or after clearing immigration at Santio, though it is open to the east and west.

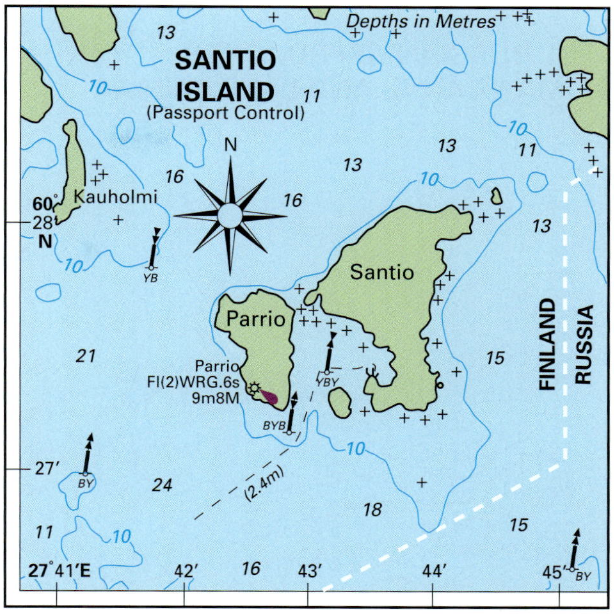


## SANTIO ISLAND

60°27'.4N 27°43'.2E

**Charts / harbour guides**
**SH3** *101*

**Contacts**
raja.fi/en/border-checks-of-pleasure-craft-in-the-saimaa-canal

Santio is a Frontier Guard station (see above) right on the border with Russia. Heading to or from Vyborg, or to the Saimaa Canal and Lakes, you must check in and out of Finnish/Russian waters at Santio Island. Vyborg and the Saimaa Canal are some 40M to the northeast. The formalities and how to approach the Saimaa Canal will be described in the next section. Moor to the solid pontoon (2–4m) (the inner side is well sheltered in strong winds) and yachts may be allowed to lie alongside overnight before a dawn departure – lie alongside the pontoon and await attention. There is no fuel available and no facilities other than rubbish bins, toilets and a barbecue, and though the island appears attractive, visitors are not permitted to leave the harbour area.

See 3E. Russian Approaches, Saimaa Canal and Lake Saimaa for Frontier Guard station and crossing procedures.

The harbour at Santio Island *John Sadd*

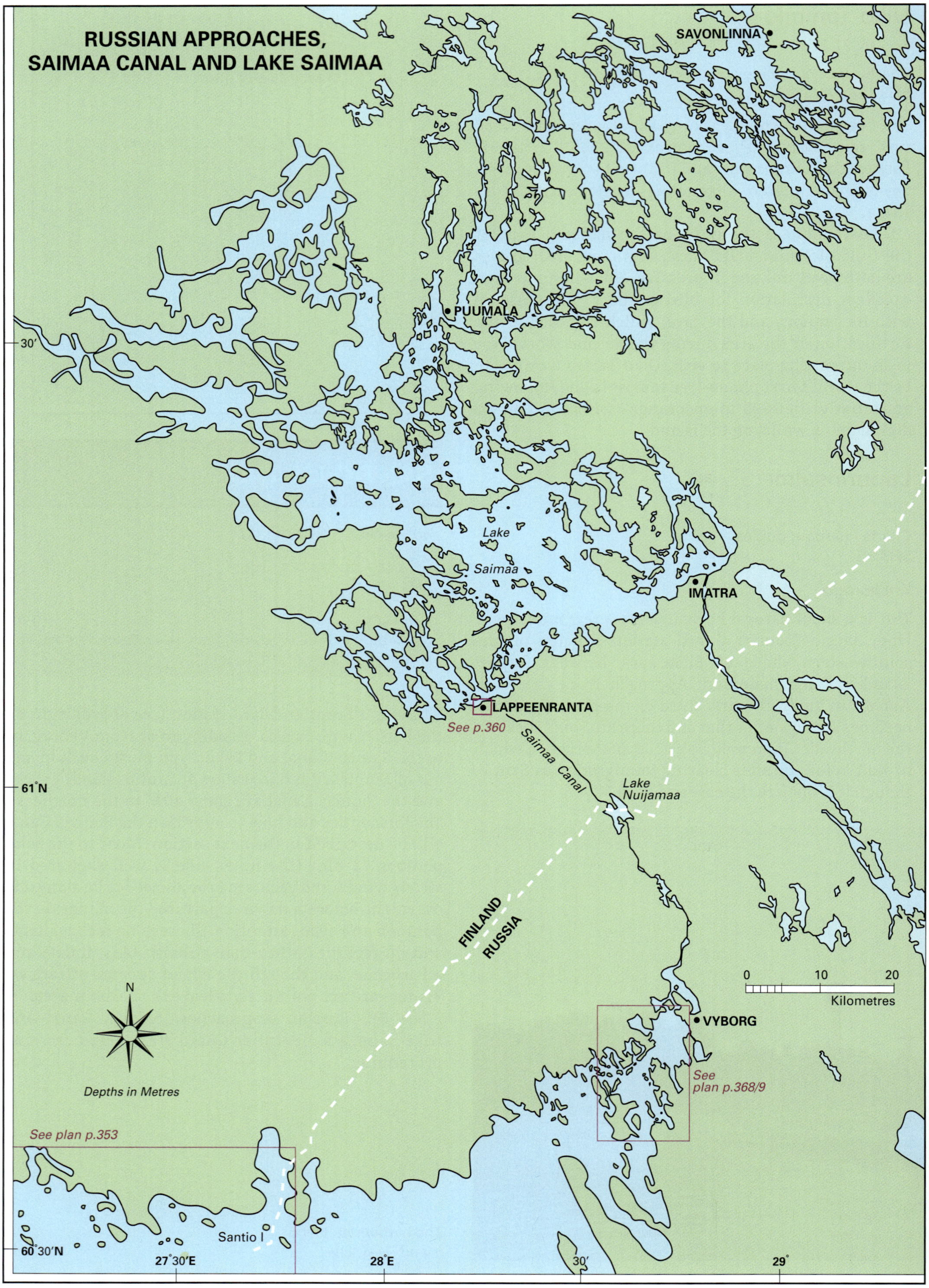
RUSSIAN APPROACHES,
SAIMAA CANAL AND LAKE SAIMAA
SAVONLINNA
PUUMALA
Lake
Saimaa
IMATRA
LAPPEENRANTA
See p.360
Saimaa Canal
Lake
Nuijamaa
FINLAND
RUSSIA
0
10
20
Kilometres
N
VYBORG
See
plan p.368/9
Depths in Metres
See plan p.353
Santio I
30′
61°N
60°30′N
27°30′E
28°E
30′
29°

# 3E. RUSSIAN APPROACHES, SAIMAA CANAL AND LAKE SAIMAA

At the time of preparation of this new edition access to the Saimaa Lakes via the Saimaa Canal and indeed all Russian territory was closed to yachts due to the ongoing conflict between Russia and Ukraine. We have left all the information about the area here in the event of a change in the political situation, but it seems likely to be some years before this is the case.

The Saimaa Lakes area is beautiful and so an alternative would be to hire a car from Kotka or perhaps take the train from Helsinki to Lappeenranta (just over 2 hrs) or Savonlinna (around 4.5hrs). See www.vr.fi/en for details and ticket prices.

The beautiful Saimaa Lake area is normally reached via the 23M (43km) Saimaa Canal.

Inaugurated in 1856, at the time when Finland was part of Russia as an autonomous Grand Duchy, the Saimaa Canal connected the enormous area of inland waterways, comprising more than 120 lakes in the south-central part of Finland, to the sea. The canal was built between Lappeenranta and Vyborg (now part of Russia).

When Finland became independent in 1917 the Karelian Isthmus, the stretch of land between the Gulf of Finland and Lake Ladoga, remained Finnish.

After the Winter War, fought between the Soviet Union and Finland between 1939 and 1940 which left many thousands of soldiers dead during an attempted invasion of Finland, the Saimaa Lake was effectively cut off from the Gulf of Finland. During this conflict, the Soviet Union sought to claim parts of Finnish territory, demanding – amongst other concessions – that Finland cede substantial border territories in exchange for land elsewhere, claiming security reasons and the defense of the approaches to Leningrad (St Petersburg). When the Moscow Treaty was signed in 1940, some parts of Finland were ceded to the Soviet Union, including the southeastern Karelian Isthmus, including Vyborg and its approaches. In 1963, the USSR leased the Soviet section of the Saimaa Canal and its approach channel to Finland for 50 years. In 2008 negotiations took place to secure the lease for another 50 years starting in 2013 (with a rent of €1.22 million a year).

### *Approach*

The shortest way to reach the Saimaa Canal is from the Frontier Guard station at Santio Island (see page 355) through the relatively narrow regulated passage leased from Russia by the Finns, leading through Russian waters. When travelling to and from the Saimaa Canal, provided that you conform to all the rules and regulations governing this passage you do not require a visa for Russia. Not having a valid visa restricts you to keeping strictly to this channel until you have reached the Finnish Border in Nuijamaa (50M), half way through the Saimaa Canal. The total distance between Santio Island and the entrance of the Lake Saimaa is 62.5M.

It is imperative that you read the information issued by the Finnish Ministry of Transport and Communications in the Saimaa Canal Pleasure Craft Guide and that you consult the Finnish Maritime Agency website before you leave.

www.traficom.fi/en/transport/maritime
www.vayla.fi/en/transport-network/waterways/canals-and-bridges/the-saimaa-canal

The Finnish Maritime Agency lists the forms required for the border crossings, which can be downloaded from their website. From these you will find all the necessary contact details, procedures to follow, papers required, forms to complete and formalities to observe at the border crossings.

Ship making passage along the Saimaa Canal *Viv Fox*

Pleasure craft have been exempt from fees for use of the Saimaa Canal since the beginning of 2012. It may all look very complicated and you might even wonder whether it is worth the effort but if you follow everything to the letter, your passage to and from the Saimaa Lake should be smooth and truly enjoyable.

One piece of advice: it would be wise to keep your original registration documents on board but make sure you have copies for the border guards in Russia. This might speed up the clearance procedure considerably.

Outward clearance from Finland must be obtained at the Frontier Guard station at either Haapasaari or Santio islands, although Santio might be the more straightforward option. When arriving at Santio or Haapasaari, the boat must follow the official navigational fairways, or the so-called customs fairway. The master of the boat must report to the border crossing point one hour before arrival. To Santio calls are made by VHF 68 or ✆+358 295 426 110, and to Haapasaari by VHF 68 or ✆+358 295 426 130.

At the inspection, the skipper hands in the 'Vessel's Report' form and makes a 'leisure boat inspection notification' to the customs. All leisure cruising through the Saimaa Canal is regarded as traffic across the EU's external borders in respect of border inspections.

Finnish entry/exit checks on leisure craft arriving at Lake Saimaa from the sea through the canal or leaving Lake Saimaa are carried out at the customs quay in Nuijamaa, the border crossing in the canal. Leisure boats not exceeding 24m in length may sail without a pilot, provided that there is a VHF radio telephone on board, tuned to VHF 11 for the duration of the entire passage; the skipper has a document certifying that he/she owns the boat and/or has the right to navigate it; and that there is a person on board with English or Russian skills to take care of communications.

In the territorial waters of Russia near Santio, a Russian guard vessel often keeps watch from a nearby buoy. When approaching or leaving Santio, leisure boats are requested to navigate close to the Russian guard vessel and to slow down so that the identification marks of the boat can be seen. Signals given by a guard vessel must be observed at all times.

The Russian border officials have the right to check that the documents of a boat and its crew are in order. Leisure boats may sail only during daylight hours, between 0800 and 2000 Moscow (UTC+3) time. If you leave Santio Island at 0600 (summer time), you might just make it to the Finnish border at Nuijamaa by 1800. Once in the canal, the locks and opening of the bridges operate like clockwork. Eight locks – at Brusnitchnoe, Iskrovka, Cvetotchnoe, Ilistoe, Pälli, Soskua, Mustola and Mälkiä – handle 76m difference in water level between the Baltic and Saimaa Lake.

Each lock is 85m long and 13.2m wide. There are also seven opening bridges and six fixed ones (minimum clearance 24.5m), and transit normally takes between 6 and 8hrs.

Some fuel might be available on the Russian section of the canal – i.e. before reaching Lappeenranta – but skippers would be wise to ensure that they have plenty for the transit.

Provided you maintain a steady speed, the passage through the locks will be very smooth. The cruising speed limit in the canal is set at 6.5kn (12km/h) for pleasure craft. Russian Customs control is at Brusnitčnoe (lock No. 1) and passport control is at Pälli (lock No. 5). If the voyage has already begun and delays occur during it (such as an engine failure), the authorities must be notified of this in order to avoid unnecessary searches and enquiries. You should inform, for example, the coastguard or Saimaa VTS, and they will forward the notification. If necessary, you can ask the Russian authorities to forward your notification to the Finnish authorities.

If you have a visa for a later visit to St Petersburg or Kaliningrad, ensure that it is not stamped in the Canal.

Charts 600A and 600B (1:100,000) of the chart folio A – Vyborg – Helsinki show the regulated passage permitted for vessels in accordance with the treaties on Saimaa Canal. More detailed Russian large-scale charts of the area surrounding Vyborg are recommended (see below). There are two approach channels, one to the town of Vyborg (not part of the treaties on the Saimaa Canal, so a visa is required) and the regulated passage to the canal. Large-scale charts will avoid confusion.

Both plans on pages 368 and 369 in the Russia chapter illustrate this.

*Navigational charts & harbour guides*

#### Planning chart

F951 (Gulf of Finland – East, 1:250,000)

#### Chart folios

A Viipuri-Helsinki/Viborg-Helsongfors (scale 1:50,000)
S Saimaan kanava (1:10,000)
L Lappeenranta – Savonlinna (1:40,000)
M Savonlinna – Kuopio (1:20,000)
V Savonlinna – Joensuu (1:40,000)

#### Russian charts

28007 (INT 1257) (1:25,000)
Approaches to Vysotsk and Vyborg
28008 (INT 1258 (1:10,000)
Povorotnyy Lighthouse to Ostrov Malyy Vysotskiy
28010 (INT 1259) (1:12,500)
Dubovyy Light-Beacon to Ostrov Lavola

#### Harbour guide

*Saimaan Käyntisatamat, ja kanavat*, published annually, also give instructions for small boat traffic in the Saimaa Canal in several languages, including English. The numbers of the harbours in the book correlate with the numbers on the charts (**SKS** xxx).

## Lake Saimaa

Charts F921 (1:250,000)
Folios Merikarttasarja L, M and V (1:40,000)
www.gosaimaa.com/en

Glacial melting at the end of the last Ice Age formed the south-central lakes of Finland, including the Saimaa

Mustola lock (Mustolan sulku) on the route into the Saimaa Lakes *Viv Fox*

Lake. Major towns on its shores include Lappeenranta, Imatra, Savonlinna, Joensuu and Kuopio. The deep channels covering some 500M are mainly used to transport commercial goods such as wood, minerals, metals and pulp. Both lakes and canal are major transport routes for the forest products trade. Log rafts, consisting of felled timber piled on the ice during the winter and cleared from the south as the ice melts are frequently encountered as they are moved under tow at an unstoppable 1-2kn. A yacht may encounter random logs floating in the water and even in the canal.

It is hard to describe the fascination of sailing in the fourth largest natural freshwater lake in Europe. The lake is navigable for deep-draught yachts with max air draft masts for some 200M, as far as Joensuu (62°35'N 29°45'E) (Chart folio V/ Savonlinna-Joensuu) and Kuopio (62°50'N 27°40'E) (Chart folio M/ Savonlinna-Kuopio). The channels described locally as 'deep' are at least 4·2m, the 'main' channels at least 2·4m.

The water is very clean throughout and it warms very quickly to a swimming temperature of +20°C. It is strictly forbidden to drop any waste or empty holding tanks into the lake and therefore all harbours are equipped with pump-out stations. Winds are light and die at night. Due to the long hours of daylight during the summer, it is possible to navigate day and night.

People using the waterways may anchor, or moor and go ashore, under 'everyman's right' except where it is expressly prohibited, for example nature reserves during the nesting season (www.nationalparks.fi/en/hikinginfinland/).

The Saimaa Lake is dotted with 14,000 islands and narrow passages, which divide the lake into many parts - it feels like sailing through a forest maze. There is good sailing on the larger bodies of water and there are many sheltered but often tortuous channels. Like everywhere else in Finnish waters, the routes through the Saimaa Lake are very well marked with transits and buoys, and the charts are as detailed as the coastal ones (chart folios L, M and V). For planning purposes, the small scale planning chart (1:300,000) at the beginning of each chart folio shows the general area plan with all possible cruising routes including minimum depth, and clearance of bridges and overhead cables. When choosing a route, make sure that you check all the bridges and overhead cables beforehand.

For the scope of this pilot book, only the harbours of Lappeenranta, Imatra, Puumala and Savonlinna will be described. There are about 100 further harbours and anchorages classified in the Saimaan Käyntisatamat harbour guide and on the website.

www.gosaimaa.com

If you intend to sail towards Joensuu or Kuopio, which mark the limit of the navigable waterways for yachts with max air draft, consult chart folios:
M – Savonlinna – Kuopio (1:20,000) and
V Savonlinna – Joensuu (1:40,000)

### Distances

Joensuu – Lappeenranta 153M
Joensuu – Savonlinna 75M
Kuopio – Lappeenranta 164M
Kuopio – Savonlinna 90M

## LAPPEENRANTA

61°04'.1N 28°11'.2E (north mole, Rapasaari)

### Distances

Imatra 22M, Puumala 40M, Savonlinna 78M

### Charts / harbour guides

**SKS** *4030*

### Contacts

www.satamapaikka.com
(marina spaces can be booked in advance)
www.gosaimaa.com
www.visitlappeenranta.fi
www.lappeenranta.fi

Following completion of the Saimaa Canal in 1856, Lappeenranta became the largest inland port in Finland. It remains a centre for the timber processing industry and is a thriving city with some 72,000 inhabitants. The cosmopolitan university has 15,000 students. It is a friendly town, popular with both Finnish and Russian tourists. The large paper mill is a prominent landmark on the approach from the canal with large wood ponds either side of the fairway. The old military area of Linnoitus on a hill overlooking the harbour has a good museum. It was successively a Swedish, then a Russian fortification and finally has been a Finnish prison and barracks since 1809. Lappeenranta also boasts the largest sand castle in Finland. It is built yearly and is open from June to September.

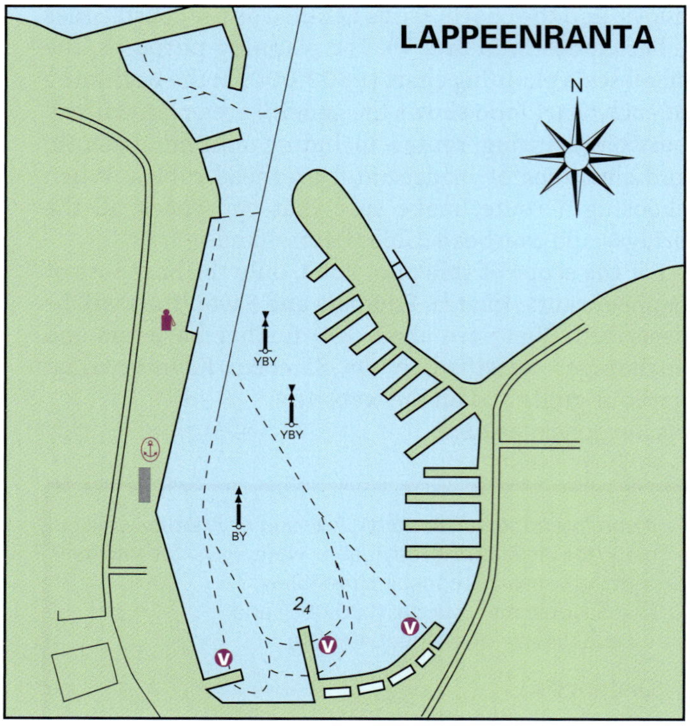


### *Approach & entrance*

Lappeenranta lies to the west of the canal entrance. Pass between Hyötiönsaari and the mainland, under a bridge with 24.5m clearance. This leads into the extensive wood processing area, with log ponds and a timber wharf.

Further west, when you have reached the northwestern tip of Pappilanniemi, providing your clearance is less than 18m, turn sharp southwest between the Pappilanniemi and Akkasaari E, underneath the power cable. If not sure, it is safer to make a detour (1M) in a northwesterly direction to go around the island of Pieni Kaijansaari. The way into the marina is very well buoyed with plenty of cardinal buoys (though these can be confusing).

### *Berthing*

Guest harbours in the Lappeenranta area are all located near the town centre. Guest harbours in Linnoitusniemi and Kasinonranta are suitable for small and medium-sized boats. Vessels over 15m long can be moored at the fortification quay.

**Linnoitusniemi** sometimes referred to as Rapasaari, offers 20 visitors berths on the west side of the bay near the entrance, all bows-to from stern buoys.

**Linnoituksen laituri**, a little further south is a new facility, a 220m long quay intended for boats of more than 15m.

**Maalaistenlaituri**, in the southwest corner of the bay, has 10 visitors berths and some additional space for short (maximum four-hour) visits, particularly convenient as it is the closest to the shopping centre.

**Kasinonranta**, in the southeast corner, is the largest facility with 50 visitors berths, some alongside and some bows-to from stern buoys, in 2.5m.

### *Services*

All three berthing areas have water and electricity, with toilets, showers and sauna ashore. Fuel is available at Linnoitusniemi, where holding tanks can be emptied and there is also a small chandlery and a grocery store.

### *Facilities*

Good shopping and several lively markets in the town centre as well as cafés at Linnoitusniemi and several good restaurants. There are also two 'boat restaurants' at Maalaistenlaituri.

### *Communications & travel*

The airport lies about 3km outside the city, while mainline trains and express coaches run to Helsinki and elsewhere.

## Imatra

61°12'.6N 28°43'.3E

**Charts / harbour guides**
**SKS** *4081*

**Contacts**
www.gosaimaa.com

Imatra is a small town about 20M east-northeast of Lappeenranta. The town centre is on the west bank of the Vuoski River, the only river which flows from the southern Saimaa Lake into Lake Ladoga, over the border in Russia, which is only 13km away. The Vuoski River was a major defensive line against the Soviet advance during the Winter War (1939–1940). Before the Karelian Isthmus became part of Russia, it had been an important route for trade. There are spectacular rapids south of the town and the hydroelectric station built in 1929 helps control the lake levels.

There is a well-protected visitors marina on the west side of Imatra, between Lammassaari island and the mainland, owned by the nearby Imatra Spa Hotel. Mooring is bows-to from stern buoys in 4m. All berths have water and electricity, with toilets and showers in the hotel, where fees are also paid.

Basic food items are available at the hotel shop, otherwise the town can provide for most needs. Fuel is available at the marina at the south end of the bay. The marina lies 8km from the town centre. Bus No. 3 runs between the central station and the hotel.

Distance to Lappeenranta airport is 37km.

## Puumala

61°31'.2N 28°10'.6E

**Charts / harbour guides**
**SKS** *4407*

**Contacts**
www.visitsaaristo.net
www.puumala.fi

Puumala, 40M north of Lappeenranta, lies half way between Lappeenranta and Savonlinna. It is an attractive small town on the northern bank of the narrows through which larger traffic must pass en route from the southern and northern sections of the lake. A road bridge spans the channel (28.5m).

There is a municipal quay, also used by cruise and tourist boats, plus a guest harbour with all the usual facilities including fuel, both close to the bridge in 3m or more. A good supermarket is situated 5mins walk up the hill, where there is also a bank and other small shops. It is a convenient stop on the way north.

## SAVONLINNA

61°52'N 28°54'E

**Charts / harbour guides**
**SKS** *4528, 4529, 4536*

**Contacts**
www.visitsavonlinna.fi/en/

Savonlinna is situated 80M to the northeast of the canal entrance. It is a town of 36,000 inhabitants and is very popular with tourists. It is world famous for its opera festival, held in July each year in the imposing setting of the Olavinlinna Castle.

Olavinlinna (also known as also known as St Olaf's Castle) was built on a small island in 1475 to protect and control the border between the Kingdom of Sweden and Russia. The town itself straddles several islands and literally forms a bridge across the Saimaa Lake.

Savonlinna is also home to many old steam boats still in use today and they lend a certain grace to the scene.

### *Approach & entrance*

Savonlinna lies on one of the lakes' deep (4.2m) channels and the southerly approach is straightforward. If your intention is to continue sailing north, you have to have one railway and two road bridges opened. You need to announce your intention in advance and get an estimated time of opening for the bridges, which do not necessarily open at the same time. The telephone number to call to arrange the opening is displayed on the bank as you approach the railway bridge.

### *Berthing*

There are three possibilities for mooring on the south side of Savonlinna that don't require the opening of bridges. There are two on either side of Haislahti, straight ahead as you approach the town from the south. Haislahti läntinen (west) (61°52'N 28°52'.3E) has 20–25 mooring spaces and limited facilities. However it is very conveniently situated for the Citymarket shopping centre. V-S Marin (61°52'N 28°52'.4E), just across the water to the east, is near the town centre. Fuel is available and holding tanks can be emptied there. The boatyard has a ramp, can service engines and carry out some repairs. It also has 15 mooring spaces. Facilities include a café, small chandlery, showers and sauna, water and electricity. It is located very near the Kauppalinna shopping mall.

The biggest and most peaceful guest marina is Törninpyörä (61°51'.8N 28°53'.4E) with 60 guest spaces, bows-to from stern buoys. There is water and electricity on the pontoons but, apart from that, facilities are rather limited. The pontoons belong to the Perhehotelli Hospitz, just across the park. There you can have a shower and a sauna. The hotel has a nice veranda and a restaurant.

### *Communications & travel*

Savonlinna has an airport that connects it to Helsinki (335km). There are also good train and express coach services to the capital, making Savonlinna by far the best city in the northern lake area for crew changes. There is also a regular ferry to Lappeenranta.

Olavinlinna (also known as St Olaf's) Castle in Savonlinna. The castle was originally built in 1495 *Viv Fox*

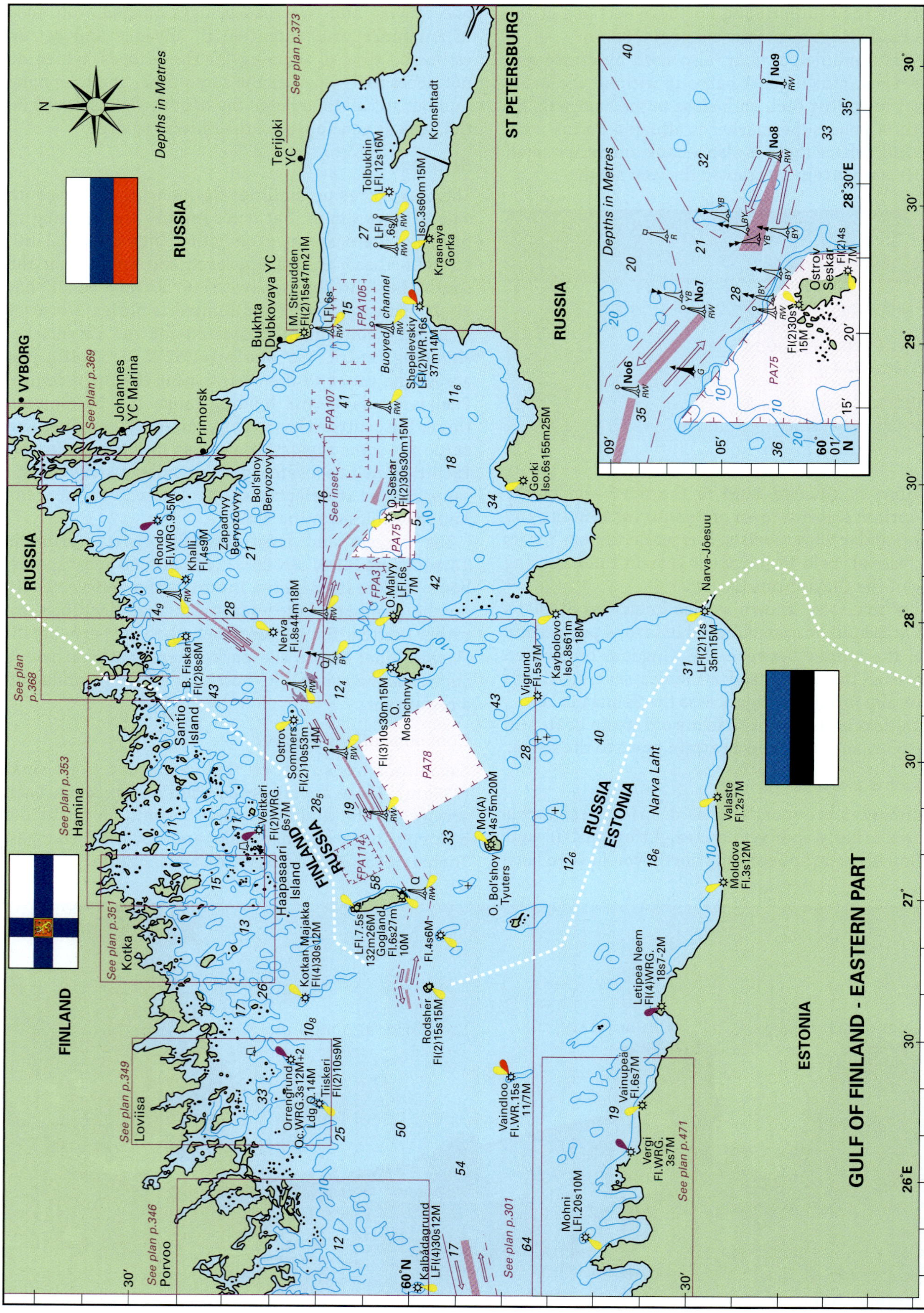
GULF OF FINLAND - EASTERN PART
Depths in Metres
FINLAND
RUSSIA
ESTONIA
ST PETERSBURG
VYBORG
See plan p.369
Johannes YC Marina
Primorsk
Bukhta Dubkovaya YC
M. Stirsudden Fl(2)15s47m21M
Terijoki YC
See plan p.373
Tolbukhin LFl.12s16M
Kronshtadt
Krasnaya Gorka Iso.3s60m15M
Shepelevskiy LFl(2)WR.16s 37m14M
Buoyed channel
FPA105
FPA107
See inset
O.Seskar Fl(2)30s30m15M
PA75
Gorki Iso.6s155m25M
Rondo Fl.WRG.9-5M
Khalli Fl.4s9M
Zapadnyy Beryozovyy
Bol'shoy Beryozovyy
Nerva Fl.8s44m18M
O.Malyy LFl.6s 7M
FPA3
Kaybolovo Iso.8s61m 18M
Narva-Jõesuu
LFl(2)12s 35m15M
B. Fiskar Fl(2)8s8M
See plan p.368
Santio Island
Ostrov Sommers Fl(2)10s53m 14M
O. Moshchnyy Fl(3)10s30m15M
PA78
Vigrund Fl.5s7M
Narva Laht
Valaste Fl.2s7M
Moldova Fl.3s12M
See plan p.353
Hamina
Veitkari Fl(2)WRG. 6s7M
Haapasaari Island
FPA114
Mo(A) 14s75m20M
O. Bol'shoy Tyuters
Gogland LFl.7.5s 132m26M
Fl.6s27m 10M
Fl.4s6M
See plan p.351
Kotka
Kotkan Majakka Fl(4)30s12M
Rodsher Fl(2)15s15M
Letipea Neem Fl(4)WRG. 18s7-2M
See plan p.349
Loviisa
Orrengrund Oc.WRG.3s12M+2 Ldg.Q.14M
Tiiskeri Fl(2)10s9M
Vaindloo Fl.WR.15s 11/7M
Vainupeä Fl.6s7M
Vergi Fl.WRG. 3s7M
See plan p.471
See plan p.346
Porvoo
Kalbådagrund LFl(4)30s12M
See plan p.301
Mohni LFl.20s10M
60°N
26°E
27°
28°
29°
30°
No6
No7
No8
No9
Ostrov Seskar
Fl(2)30s 15M
Fl(2)4s 7M
28°30'E
60° 01' N

# 4. RUSSIA

At the time of publication of this new edition the Saimaa Lakes and all Russian territory, including Kaliningrad, was closed to yachts due to the ongoing conflict between Russia and Ukraine. We have left all the information about the area here in the event of a change in the political situation, but it seems likely to be some years before this is the case. Prior to making any decision about visiting, it would be best to check the up to date Foreign, Commonwealth and Development Office (FCDO) advice. This is available online at: www.gov.uk/foreign-travel-advice/russia

Foreign yachts have been made welcome in Russia since the break-up of the Soviet Union in 1991 and have visited in ever increasing numbers, even though the formalities are complex and facilities for yachts are still somewhat limited by western standards. Although there are continuing uncertainties as to Russia's relationship with the West, the general consensus is that it remains a very rewarding destination, and that facilities are likely to continue to improve.

That part of Russia which borders the far east of the Baltic Sea is almost entirely low-lying and backed by extensive marshes and lakes. The delta of the River Neva was an uninhabited swamp until the founding of St Petersburg in the early 18th century, and little of the city stands more than 5m above sea level. The 200m contour lies several hundred kilometres inland.

The seas in the eastern part of the Gulf of Finland are as shallow as the land is low, with the 10m contour running well to the northwest of Kronshtadt and much of the Nevskaya Guba has depths 5m or less, other than where dredged. This may partly explain Russia's desire to retain Vyborg, close to the Finnish border, the approaches to which carry considerably greater depths.

Despite this, St Petersburg is home to a wide range of major industries – steel works, shipbuilding, mechanical equipment and heavy electrical engineering – as well as lighter industry such as timber processing, textiles and electrical goods. With minor exceptions, its only local fuel is some oil shale and peat, and its only mineral bauxite. The surrounding land grows timber and flax and not much else – nearly all fuel, food and other raw materials have to be brought in from outside.

## History

Russia as a nation was founded in the 9th century by Swedish Vikings who traded along its rivers to the Black Sea and Constantinople (or Byzantium, now Istanbul). *Rus* is thought to be the Viking word for an oar or oarsman. The Viking leader Rurik founded a base at Novgorod near the Baltic coast in 862CE. Oleg, his successor, moved their capital to Kiev further south, and came to rule a huge Slavic area known then as Kiev-Rus. It was strongly modelled on Constantinople, the capital of the surviving eastern Roman Empire. In 998 Kiev-Rus converted from paganism to Orthodox Christianity, which until 1057 still included the Roman Church.

Between 1223 and 1240 Ghengis Khan's Mongol Horde conquered all of Kiev-Rus up to Novgorod, which was now part of the Hanseatic League. It was still the Golden Age of Islamic civilisation and, as was the Moslem custom, once the ferocious fighting was over, the Mongols educated, and delegated much administrative power, to local rulers of their vassal states. The Russian Prince Alexander Nevsky was thus allowed to recruit an army to halt the Catholic Northern Crusades into Russia. (Rome now saw pagans and Orthodox Christians as equally legitimate targets.)

The centre of Russian power had been pushed northwards from Kiev to Moscow. During the 14th century, when Mongol control of eastern Europe began to decline, Moscow regained more and more of its earlier territory, particularly under Ivan III the Great. His son Ivan IV the Terrible consolidated this autocratic control and declared himself the first Tsar (Caesar) of all the Russians.

The death of Ivan's childless son in 1598 finally brought Rurik's dynasty to an end. There followed a leaderless 'Time of Troubles' when the Polish-Lithuanian Commonwealth from the east and Swedish Gustavus Adolphus from the north made huge inroads into Russian territory. Then in 1613 an assembly of Russian cities elected Michael Romanov, son of the Patriarch of Moscow, to become Tsar, thereby starting the second and final Russian dynasty, which lasted until the Revolution of 1917.

During the 17th century the Romanovs steadily regained much lost ground in the west and new territory in the east. By the beginning of Peter the Great's reign (1672–1725), Russian territory reached the Pacific Ocean, making Russia the largest country in the world, although much of it was unproductive and very under-populated. Russia's only port in the west, however, was Archangel in the Arctic. Peter made a secret alliance with Poland-Lithuania and Denmark to start the Northern War against Sweden, which still controlled most of the Baltic coasts. The outcome was to give Peter both the east and the south of the Gulf of Finland. Russia now replaced Sweden as the dominant power in the Baltic. Peter built St Petersburg as his new capital on the marshes of the Neva River, modelling it on the canals of Amsterdam.

On Peter's death, a series of Tsars and Tsarinas down to Catherine II the Great (1762–96) allowed a degree of liberalism to the nobles and gentry, but the lives of serfs became even worse. Catherine was regarded as an enlightened despot, enthusiastically promoting the

# KEY INFORMATION

## Rescue/Safety services

**Emergency** ✆ 112

**Rescue at sea**

**St Petersburg Rescue Coordination Centre** monitors VHF Ch 16 and 71/72. Call Sign '**St Petersburg Rescue Coordination Centre**'
✆ +7 812 3274147, +7 812 4958995, +7 812 7188995

## Charts and pilot books

British Admiralty and Russian charts cover the area, the latter more detailed and in many cases to a larger scale. Russian charts are essential if planning to take any short cuts across the Nevskaya Guba between Kronshtadt and St Petersburg.

*The Baltic Pilot Volume II* (NP 19) More suited to the needs of ships than of yachts.

*Cruising Guide to Baltic Russia*, Vladimir Ivankiv, Graham and Fay Cattell. Available from the Cruising Association and major suppliers in Scandinavia.

## Time

St Petersburg and its environs are on Moscow time - UT+3 all year round.

## ₽ Money

The Russian currency is the rouble (divided into 100 kopeks), the only legal tender even though Euro and US dollars are highly popular.

Banks and other authorised exchange offices (in hotels, restaurants and some shops) are widespread, and cash advances can also be drawn on most major credit cards, though subject to the usual commission. Roubles can be obtained from ATMs.

## Public holidays

Public holidays are flexible, but may occur on:
1 January, 7 January (Russian Orthodox Christmas), 23 February (Defenders of the Motherland, or Men's Day), 8 March (International Women's Day), Easter Sunday (note that Orthodox Easter may not be on the same date as Easter in the West), 1–2 May (International Labour Day), 9 May (Victory Day 1945), 27 May (City Day – St Petersburg only), 12 June (Russian Independence Day), the last 10 days of June (St Petersburg's White Nights – a festival rather than a public holiday), 7 November (Russian Unity Day), 12 December (Russian Constitution Day), 31 December.

## Communications

The Russian telephone system is generally good, and mobile phone coverage very good in the St Petersburg area though charges are high. Internet access in the city is available at the Central Telephone Office, as well as at practically all hotels, restaurants and cybercafés.

Card telephones with international dialling are now widely available in St Petersburg. All accept prepaid cards, which can be bought locally, and some also accept Visa or Mastercard.

International calls can usually be made during office hours from the two major yacht clubs, or from the tourist hotels though at much greater cost. To obtain an international line dial 8, wait for the dial tone, then dial 10 followed by the country code, area code (omitting any initial 0) and number.

The country code for Russia is 7, the city code for St Petersburg and the surrounding area, including Vyborg, is 812 (if dialling from abroad the initial 0 should be omitted).

## Travel

**St Petersburg** and its environs are well served by air, train, coach and ship.

St Petersburg's airport is known as Pulkovo and handles both international and domestic flights. It is located some 17km south of the city. There are direct flights to/from many European cities, including London.

A mainline **railway** connects St Petersburg with Helsinki four times daily using Allegro train taking 3½hrs. Coaches depart several times each day. There is also a direct coach service to Tallinn, Estonia, with four or five departures daily.

**Taxis** are available everywhere, but taxi drivers are well attuned to the presence of foreign tourists and for major journeys it is as well to arrange a taxi through the yacht club to avoid being charged excessive prices.

## Websites

**www.saint-petersburg.com**
**www.vyborg.ru** Very professional Vyborg city homepage

## Radio communications

**VHF** radio is much used for marine communications. See details of requirements under sections on approach and individual harbours.

## Weather information

Radio Navtex broadcast from Tallinn (identification Station U) is the most reliable means of getting weather information.

No weather bulletins or navigational warnings are currently broadcast for the area via VHF. However it may be possible to obtain a forecast for the St Petersburg Harbour area from the pilot station on VHF Ch 16, 09 and 20.

Church on the Spilled Blood, St Petersburg *V. Ivankiv*

arts, the sciences and her liking for handsome young guardsmen, while further restricting the power and wealth of the Orthodox Church and the freedoms of the serfs. In the Wars of Partition, Russia, Austria and Prussia destroyed the huge state of Poland-Lithuania. Russia gained much of central Europe while both Poland and Lithuania ceased to be independent states for over a century.

During the Napoleonic wars Tsar Alexander I changed sides four times. In the process he gained all of Finland from Sweden in 1809. Then after Napoleon's invasion of 1812 he drove Napoleon from Moscow, right back to Paris. Russia was now seen as the Saviour of Europe.

As the 19th century industrial revolution got under way in the rest of Europe, Russia was clearly falling badly behind. There were some reforms, notably the abolition of serfdom in 1861, but any attempt to speed up the process was ruthlessly crushed, leaving bureaucracy and incompetent leadership everywhere. Then in 1917 the communist revolution replaced the old order with one where all the means of production were to be managed by the state on behalf of everybody. The Russian Empire was now the Union of Soviet Socialist Republics. For all its high ideals, however, communism proved no more effective than the tsars, and perhaps for the same reasons.

In Second World War Hitler replayed Napoleon's 1812 invasion with the same outcome. The Nazi war machine was defeated in the east by Soviet troops, while the allies in the west defeated the rest. As the main victor, Russia now imposed communism on the nine subject countries in eastern Europe that it had captured, with corresponding damage to their economies. The whole Soviet communist system finally collapsed in 1991 and the Soviet Union was dissolved.

## The people, the church & the language

Within the borders of what is now Russia there are many groups with customs, habits and languages quite different from those of the northwestern Russian. The Russian Federation contains, for instance, sixteen autonomous republics, five autonomous regions and ten autonomous areas, all based on ethnic differences. St Petersburg in particular is a cosmopolitan city where members of these groups may be encountered at any time, together with nationals of republics lying outside the Russian Federation.

With the abolition of communism as the state orthodoxy, the Russian Orthodox Church has enjoyed a major revival and now has more than 17,000 priests and 450 monasteries throughout the country as a whole. Churches and cathedrals are amongst the finest buildings in all Russia's Baltic cities, though many suffered vandalism during the Soviet era.

The Winter Palace, St Petersburg *V. Ivankiv*

## CRUISING INFORMATION

The attractions of a cruise to Baltic Russia have traditionally been principally concerned with St Petersburg, but there are several other possibilities, particularly since foreign vessels are now permitted to visit specified harbours on the north coast of the Gulf of Finland, albeit under strict conditions. The major condition is that checking in and out of Russia is permitted only at Vyborg, St Petersburg and, for those wishing to visit the Saimaa Lakes, at Brusnitchnoe. If wishing to visit any of the seven harbours on the way east to St Petersburg, the yacht must have checked in at Vyborg on the way. To visit on the way back west, do not check out when leaving St Petersburg but do so at Vyborg after visiting the harbours. In all cases ensure that the Russian Coast Guard is fully aware of intentions. Note that yachts are not permitted to stop at any harbours other than those listed.

### Caution

When sailing in the eastern Baltic, and particularly the shallow Nevskaya Guba, it is important to be aware that although the area has no daily tidal rise and fall, depths can vary considerably from those charted as a result of sustained strong winds from west or east. Changes of more than a metre in a few hours are not unusual. In addition to this, prolonged high pressure may result in a further decrease of up to 0.5m on charted depths.

### Yacht services & chandleries

In St Petersburg there are several chandleries, sail lofts and workshops where general repairs can be carried out. The Central River Yacht Club in St Petersburg (CRYC) has facilities for sailmaking and general repairs (though electronic skills are limited); there is also a chandlers, mostly selling imported equipment.

### Holding tanks

As yet there are no requirements for holding tanks and there are no pump out stations.

### Gas

Gas bottles are unobtainable and refilling is also not possible.

### Diesel

Diesel is available at CRYC very much cheaper than elsewhere in the Baltic.

### Shopping

Current EU sanctions have strongly affected what is available in the shops. Imported goods including food are scarce or non existent and local producers have raised their prices.

Many shops now accept credit cards, though this should never be assumed. Shopping falls into several categories:

- Western shops, though only a few are actually run by Western companies. Almost anything is available, though prices are expensive in line with Scandinavia as a whole. Credit cards are generally welcome.
- Local super (and hyper-) markets which carry good quality food at reasonable prices, clothes shops and boutiques and European-type hardware stores sometimes with a chandlery section. Most still accept cash (roubles) only, though an increasing number accept credit cards. All hypermarkets and most supermarkets accept credit cards as well as cash (roubles only) but some checkouts may not have card terminals available so check before choosing a particular checkout.
- Kiosks by the thousand, with tempting prices but often poor quality (check for sell-by dates). Alcohol in particular should NEVER be bought at a kiosk. However, if looking for a souvenir, the selection of nesting matryoshka dolls is immense and some bartering is generally acceptable.
- Markets sell meat, fruit, vegetables etc, usually of acceptable quality. Prices are often adjusted upwards when foreigners appear, so again it may be possible to bargain – always assuming that the language barrier can be overcome. Bags may not be provided.

There are several large DIY chains where tools and general hardware items can be purchased.

### Alcohol

Alcohol is easily available in shops and supermarkets. The alcohol limit for those in charge of a leisure craft is 16mg.

### Yacht clubs

In Russia most clubs remain owned by organisations such as town councils, local business enterprises, trade unions or the military, though others are being privatised. They employ full-time staff for administrative and technical work, frequently have their own boatyard facilities including sailmaking, and often have round the clock security.

## Approach to Russia

Baltic Russia can be reached from Estonia or from Finland.

### If coming from or returning to Estonia

Because Russian rules dictate that vessels sailing from Estonia must join the shipping lane which starts south east of Gogland Island, this route is less favoured. It also means that there is no point in sailing further east along the Estonian coast than Vergi. However, it is recommended to clear out at either Tallinn (No 12 border post) or Vergi. These posts are not permanently manned so arrangements for clearance need to be made in advance – it is recommended to call the Estonian Police and Border Guard helpdesk on ✆+372 612 3000 or +372 637 7440.

### If coming from or returning to Finland

Here there is a choice of routes – from Helsinki, Haapasaari or Santio:

***From Helsinki*** clear out with Customs and Immigration, follow the coastline and join the shipping lane south of Gogland Island.

From Haapasaari, clear out with the Finnish Border Guards, cross the buoyed border between buoys 15 and 16, go south of Sommers Island to join the shipping lane.

***From Santio*** (most useful if visiting Vyborg and the other harbours and/or wishing to sail via Bjorkesund). Cross the border between Kozlinyj and Kopytin Islands to join the Saimaa Channel. For Vyborg, continue with the Saimaa Channel. For St Petersburg leave the Viipuriin Light to port and head for Bjorkesund. Leaving Bjorkesund head for the main shipping lane and proceed to Kronshtadt. Contact Primorsk Traffic on VHF Ch 68 when entering and leaving Bjorkesund.

## VYBORG (FINNISH: VIIPURI)

60°42'.58N 28°43'.73E (centre of final approach channel)

### Distances

Helsinki 130M, Kotka 65M, Haapasaari Island 60M, Santio Island 40M, Kronshtadt 95M, St Petersburg 110M

### Lights

**Ostrov Khalli** 60°24'.2N 28°08'.3E Fl.4s16m9M
Red metal framework tower, concrete base 12m

**Ostrov Rondo** 60°27'.4N 28°21'.6E Fl.WRG.1.5s14m9–5M
White rectangle, black stripe, on red framework tower 10m

**Vyborgskiy** 60°31'.6N 28°22'.7E Fl(2)8s14m10M Whis
White octagonal tower, red bands 10m

**Lotsmanskiy lightbuoy** 60°34'.5N 27°24'.5E LFl.6s Red and white pillar buoy, b topmark

**Povorotnyy, N point** 60°34'.5N 28°25'.6E
Fl.WRG.1.5s18m7–2M
White octagonal tower, red lantern 13m

**Ostrov Igrivyy buoy** 60°35'N 28°28'.75E Q(6)+LFl.15s
South cardinal lightbuoy Yellow and black pillar

**Vysotskiy-Yuzhnyy breakwater head** 60°36'.7N 28°33'.2E
Fl(2)6.5s8m3M Green tower, white band

**Leading lights** Five sets of leading lights plus many lit buoys guide a vessel through the Vysotsk narrows into the Vyborgskiy Morskoy Kanal, the buoyed channel leading to the junction of the Saimaa canal approach with the Vyborg final approach (see plan page 369)

**Dybovyy** 60°40'.2N 28°38'.9E
Fl.G.2s6m2M Green column 3m

**Saymenskiy** 60°41'.9N 28°42'.8E Iso.Y.2s8m3M White column, red stripe 4m

**Vyborg Severnyy** 60°42'.6N 28°44'.1E Oc.R.3s23m4M White rectangle, red stripe, on white round concrete tower 9m

Many more lights and lit buoys exist in the approaches and harbour area.

### Contacts

Vyborg VTS Controller ✆+7 812 789 3244
VHF Ch 12 (call *Vyborg Radio 5*)

Vyborg Pilot Service ✆+7 812 783 3449/93266
VHF Ch 10/74 (call *Vyborg Pilots*)

Vyborg Harbourmaster ✆+7 812 782 0477/789 9650
VHF Ch 12/16

Vyborg Radio VHF Ch 2/16/24

Vyborg Favorit YC with Customs Quay in background *Vladimir Ivankiv*

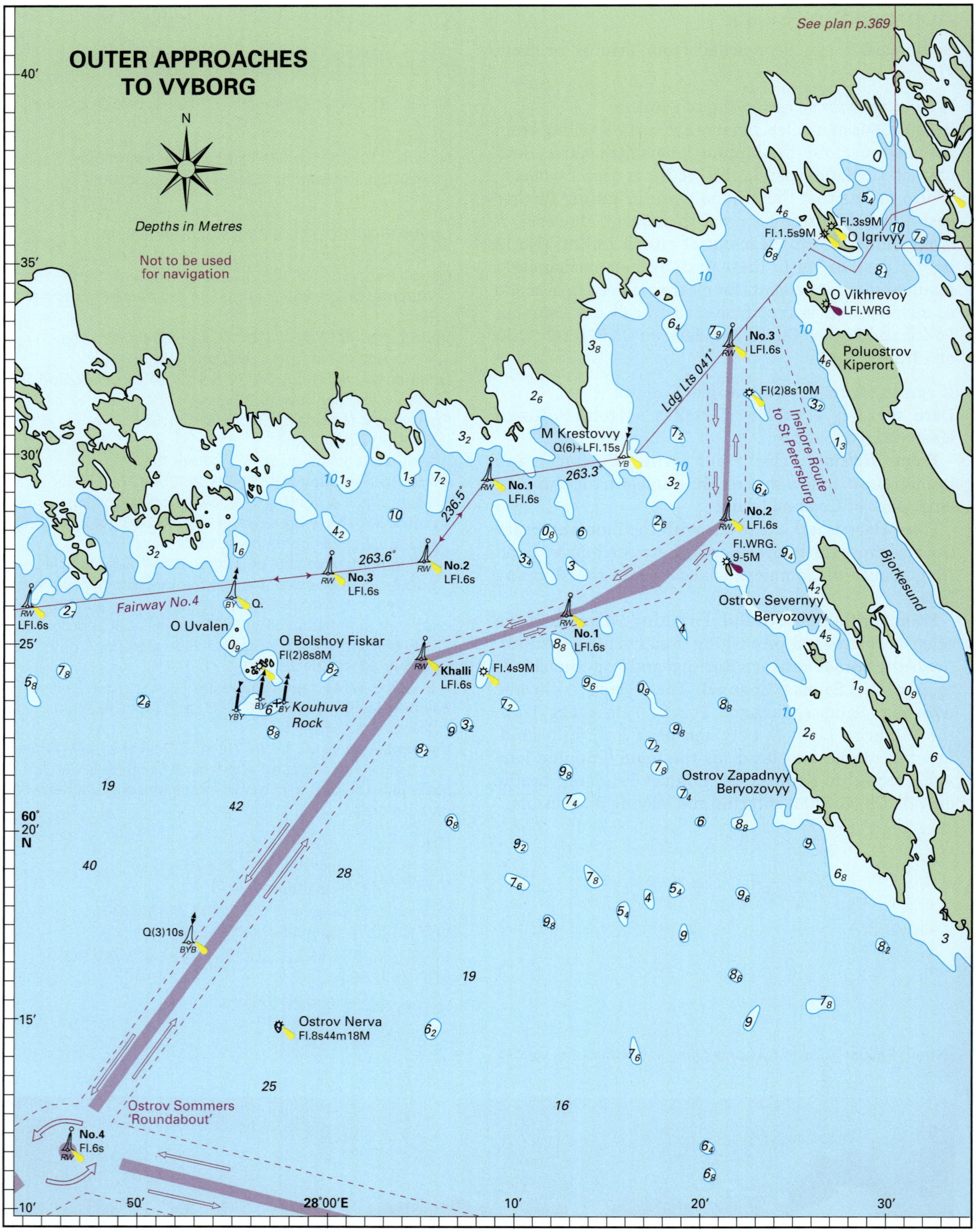
OUTER APPROACHES TO VYBORG
N
Depths in Metres
Not to be used for navigation
See plan p.369
O Igrivyy
Fl.3s9M
Fl.1.5s9M
O Vikhrevoy
LFl.WRG
Poluostrov Kiperort
No.3
LFl.6s
Fl(2)8s10M
Ldg Lts 041°
Inshore Route to St Petersburg
M Krestovvy
Q(6)+LFl.15s
263.3°
No.1
LFl.6s
236.5°
No.2
LFl.6s
263.6°
No.3
LFl.6s
Fairway No.4
Q.
LFl.6s
O Uvalen
O Bolshoy Fiskar
Fl(2)8s8M
Kouhuva Rock
Khalli
LFl.6s
Fl.4s9M
No.1
LFl.6s
No.2
LFl.6s
Fl.WRG.
9-5M
Ostrov Severnyy Beryozovyy
Bjorkesund
Ostrov Zapadnyy Beryozovyy
Q(3)10s
Ostrov Nerva
Fl.8s44m18M
Ostrov Sommers 'Roundabout'
No.4
Fl.6s
40′
35′
30′
25′
60° 20′ N
15′
10′
50′
28°00′E
10′
20′
30′

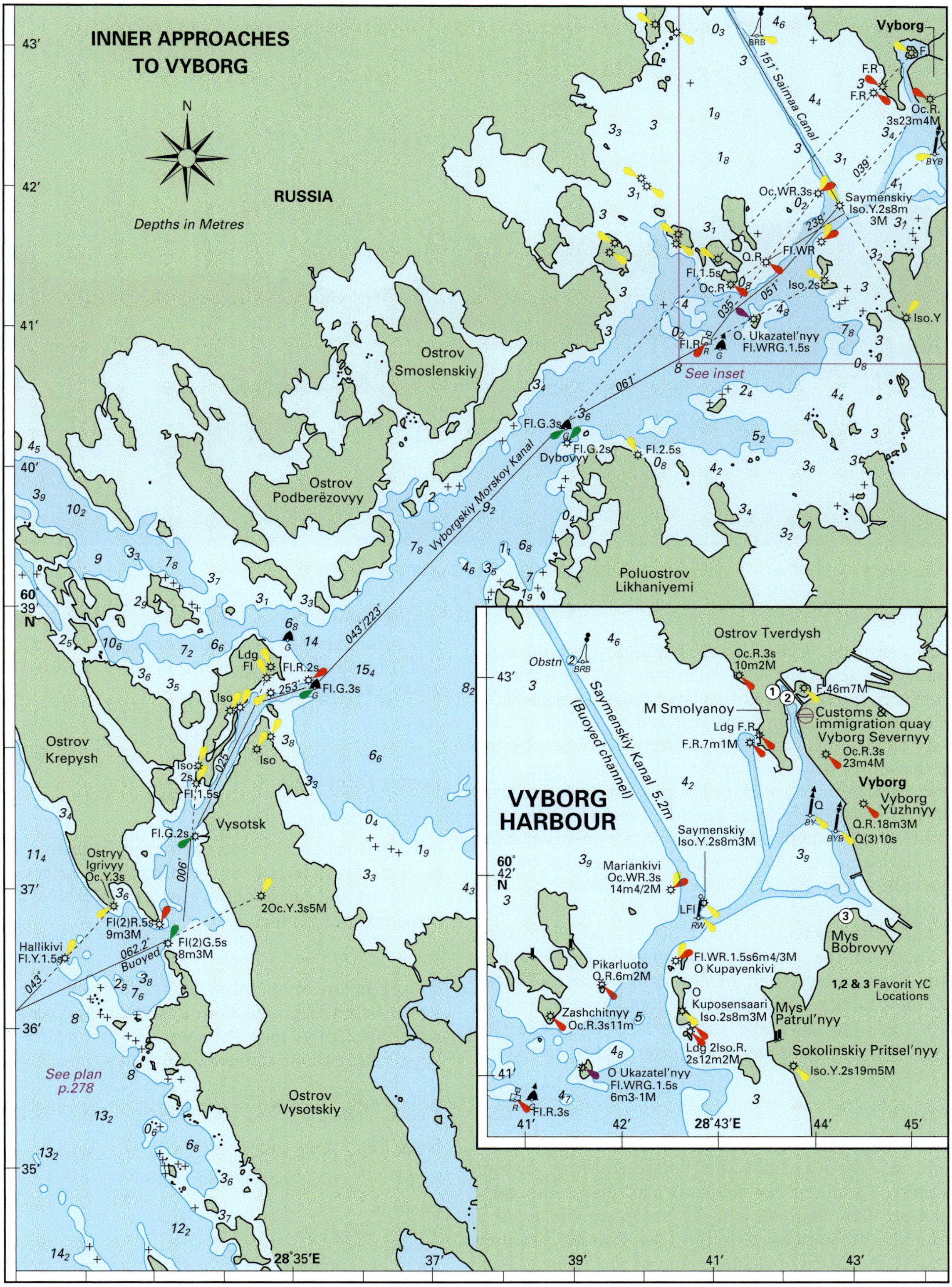
INNER APPROACHES
TO VYBORG
N
RUSSIA
Depths in Metres
Vyborg
151° Saimaa Canal
Saymenskiy
Iso.Y.2s8m
3M
Oc.WR.3s
Q.R
Fl.WR
Fl.1.5s
Oc.R
Iso.2s
Iso.Y
O. Ukazatel'nyy
Fl.WRG.1.5s
Fl.R
See inset
F.R
Oc.R.
3s23m4M
Ostrov
Smoslenskiy
Ostrov
Podberëzovyy
Fl.G.3s
Fl.G.2s
Dybovyy
Fl.2.5s
Vyborgskiy Morskoy Kanal
Poluostrov
Likhaniyemi
043°/223°
Ldg
Fl
Fl.R.2s
Fl.G.3s
Iso
Ostrov
Krepysh
Iso
2s
Fl.1.5s
Fl.G.2s
Vysotsk
Ostryy
Igrivyy
Oc.Y.3s
Fl(2)R.5s
9m3M
Fl(2)G.5s
8m3M
2Oc.Y.3s5M
Hallikivi
Fl.Y.1.5s
Buoyed
See plan
p.278
Ostrov
Vysotskiy
28°35'E
37'
39'
41'
43'
60°
39'
N
VYBORG
HARBOUR
Ostrov Tverdysh
Obstn
Saymenskiy Kanal 5.2m
(Buoyed channel)
Oc.R.3s
10m2M
F.46m7M
M Smolyanoy
Customs &
immigration quay
Vyborg Severnyy
Ldg F.R.
F.R.7m1M
Oc.R.3s
23m4M
Vyborg
Vyborg
Yuzhnyy
Q.R.18m3M
Q(3)10s
Saymenskiy
Iso.Y.2s8m3M
Mariankivi
Oc.WR.3s
14m4/2M
LFl
Mys
Bobrovyy
Fl.WR.1.5s6m4/3M
O Kupayenkivi
Pikarluoto
Q.R.6m2M
O
Kuposensaari
Iso.2s8m3M
Mys
Patrul'nyy
1,2 & 3 Favorit YC
Locations
Zashchitnyy
Oc.R.3s11m
Ldg 2Iso.R.
2s12m2M
Sokolinskiy Pritsel'nyy
Iso.Y.2s19m5M
O Ukazatel'nyy
Fl.WRG.1.5s
6m3-1M
Fl.R.3s
28°43'E
42'
44'
45'

Vyborg, 2 Favorit YC left, Customs Quay middle, and 1 Favorit YC right *Vladimir Ivankiv*

### *General*

For centuries Vyborg was Finland's second most important town and cultural centre. Already a trading centre in the 12th century, it later became a port of the Hanseatic League and was attacked by Russia at least four times during the 14th and 15th centuries. By the 18th century it was held by Peter the Great as part of his programme to consolidate his grip on St Petersburg. In 1812 it became part of Finland, then under Russian control, and benefited greatly from the opening of the Saimaa Canal in 1856. The port still handles timber, agricultural products, minerals and ironware.

Vyborg reverted to Russia following fierce fighting – and major damage – during the Second World War. Almost all the Finnish population were evacuated and the city resettled by Russians from elsewhere in the country, with a current population of around 80,000. Both the castle and the large and attractive Park Monrepo Reserve, beyond the bridge, are worth exploring.

### *Approach*

All foreign vessels, including yachts, are required to inform Vyborg at least 2hrs before entering Russian waters. Details of the necessary telephone numbers and/or VHF channels should be obtainable from a number of sources including the Finnish Frontier Guard, the Board of Management of the Saimaa Canal (see page 357). Russian visas are not required if only visiting the Saimaa Lakes but are required for a visit to Vyborg. Leaving the Saimaa Channel the final approach is via the main Vyborg fairway on course 24.8° turning to port to enter the port and proceed towards the castle. It is recommended to use the engine. The Immigration and Customs control berth is quay 2 (60°42'.79N 28°43'.67E).

### *Berthing*

There are three possibilities in Vyborg all with the Favorit Yacht Club.

### *General facilities*

Vyborg is reported to have several restaurants where good meals can be had for very reasonable prices. Maps of the city and surrounding area are available from the bookstore at Pr Lenina 6.

### *Communications & travel*

Vyborg is on the mainline railway between Helsinki and St Petersburg, and also on the principal coach and bus route. Trains to St Petersburg depart nearly every hour, taking about 3hrs for the journey.

## 1 & 2. Favorit YC (formerly the Vyborg Sea Yacht Club)

60°42'.90N 28°43'.62E (general location of moorings)

**Contacts**

✆+7 813 782 4536

There are mooring places both to port and starboard within the harbour (berthing 1 and 2). The starboard moorings below the castle are nearest to the city but have less facilities and security. Berthing reservation required.

Lavola *Vladimir Ivankiv*

## 3. Favorit YC (Mys Bobovyy)

60°41'.85N 28°44'.17E (yacht moorings)

**Contacts**
+7 813 789 9708

This is an exposed pontoon, some 2km from the city thus less attractive to visitors. Berthing reservation required.

## Lavola Yacht Club Harbour

60°46'.33N 28°41'.97E

**Contacts**
+7 931 210 3832

This harbour is of most use for anyone going to check out in the Saimaa Canal. It is not possible to check in or out at Lavola – this harbour cannot be visited unless the yacht is already checked into Russia.

# PERMITTED HARBOURS BETWEEN VYBORG AND ST PETERSBURG

## Johannes Marina

60°31'.53N 28°39'.34E

**Contacts**
Harbourmaster *mobile* +7 911 000 7531
Watchman +7 911 923 7330
johannes-port.ru/maps/23--johannes-info-map.html

It is necessary to call up the harbourmaster or watchman before arrival. A modern development close to the town of Sovetskij and reached by a circuitous route from Bjorkesund.

## Primorsk Yacht Pier 29a

60°21'.81N 28°36'.64E

**Contacts**
+7 911 119 0287 or +7 911 002 2092

*Caution* 2m draught limitation at the yacht berths. It is necessary to call in advance.

Approaching Primorsk Yacht Pier *Vladimir Ivankiv*

Approaching Bukhta Dubkovaya *Vladimir Ivankiv*

## Bukhta Dubkovaya Yacht Club

60°14'.07N 28°59'.66E

**Contacts**

Harbourmaster ☎+7 911 928 0868

Berth reservation is required well in advance. Also call up when approaching the harbour. If the harbourmaster is not available call the hotel (☎+7 901 300 4560). Modern development with usual facilities and restaurant.

## Terijoki Yacht Club

60°11'.21N 29°42'.17E

**Contacts**

☎+7 812 611 0300 or +7 921 942 3845
VHF Ch 16/72
www.yct.ru

Terijoki is the Finnish name for the town now called Zelenogorsk.

Vessels are required to be under engine in both approach channel and harbour.

On approach contact the harbourmaster on VHF Ch 16/72 for permission to enter harbour. Usual facilities and access to fitness centre. Culture park with cafés, restaurants.

Terijoki Yacht Club *Vladimir Ivankiv*

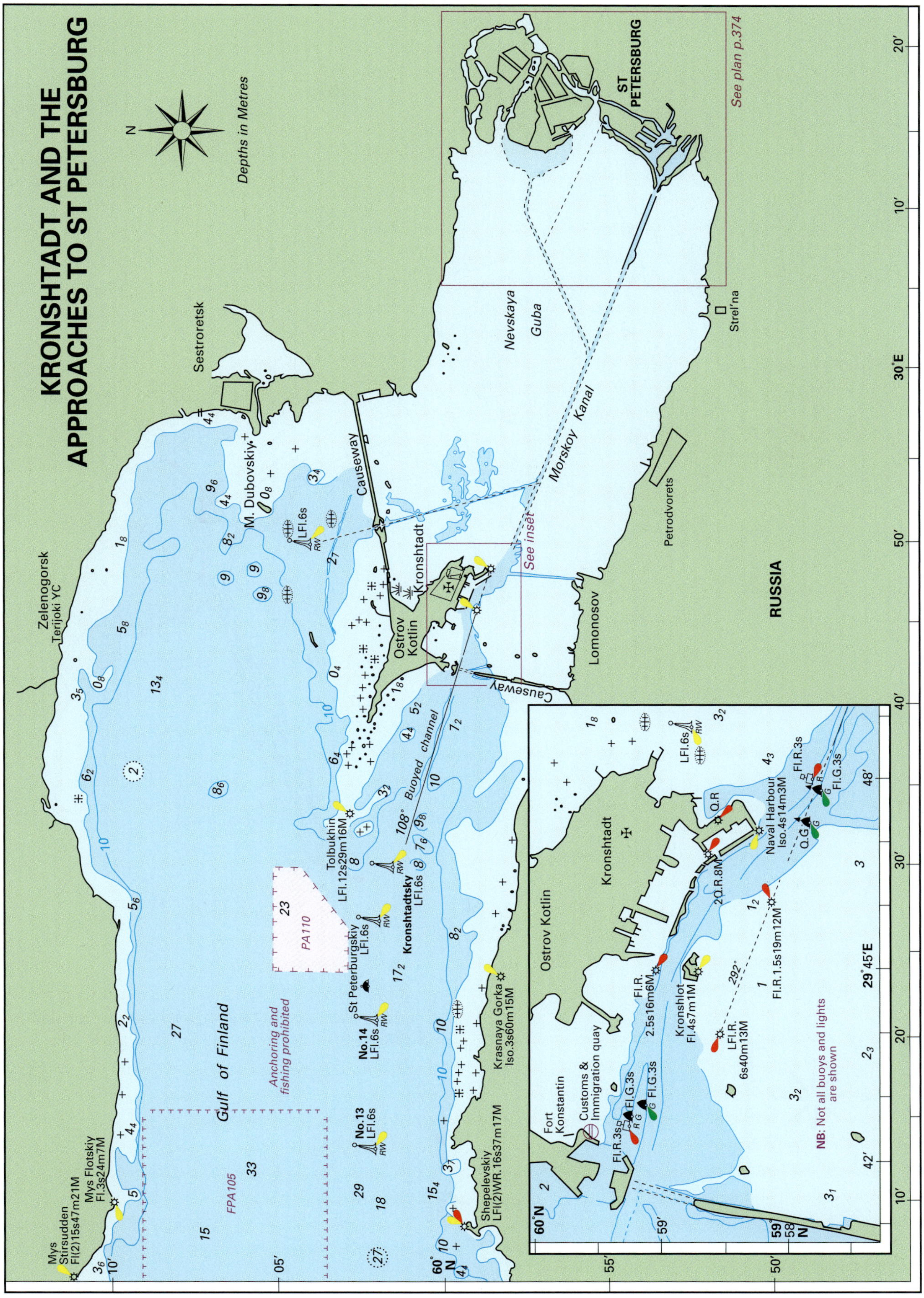
KRONSHTADT AND THE APPROACHES TO ST PETERSBURG
Depths in Metres
Gulf of Finland
Anchoring and fishing prohibited
FPA105
PA110
Zelenogorsk
Terijoki YC
Sestroretsk
M. Dubovskiy
Causeway
Ostrov Kotlin
Kronshtadt
See inset
Morskoy Kanal
Nevskaya Guba
See plan p.374
ST PETERSBURG
Strel'na
Petrodvorets
Lomonosov
RUSSIA
108° Buoyed channel
Tolbukhin LFl.12s29m16M
St Peterburgskiy LFl.6s
Kronshtadtsky LFl.6s
No.14 LFl.6s
No.13 LFl.6s
Mys Stirsudden Fl(2)15s47m21M
Mys Flotskiy Fl.3s24m7M
Shepelevskiy LFl(2)WR.16s37m17M
Krasnaya Gorka Iso.3s60m15M
Ostrov Kotlin
Kronshtadt
Fort Konstantin
Customs & Immigration quay
Fl.R.3s
Fl.G.3s
Fl.R. 2.5s16m6M
Kronshlot Fl.4s7m1M
LFl.R. 6s40m13M
2Q.R.8M
Q.R
Naval Harbour Iso.4s14m3M
Q.G
Fl.R.3s
Fl.G.3s
Fl.R.1.5s19m12M
292°
NB: Not all buoys and lights are shown
29°45'E
60°N
59°58'N
30°E
60° N

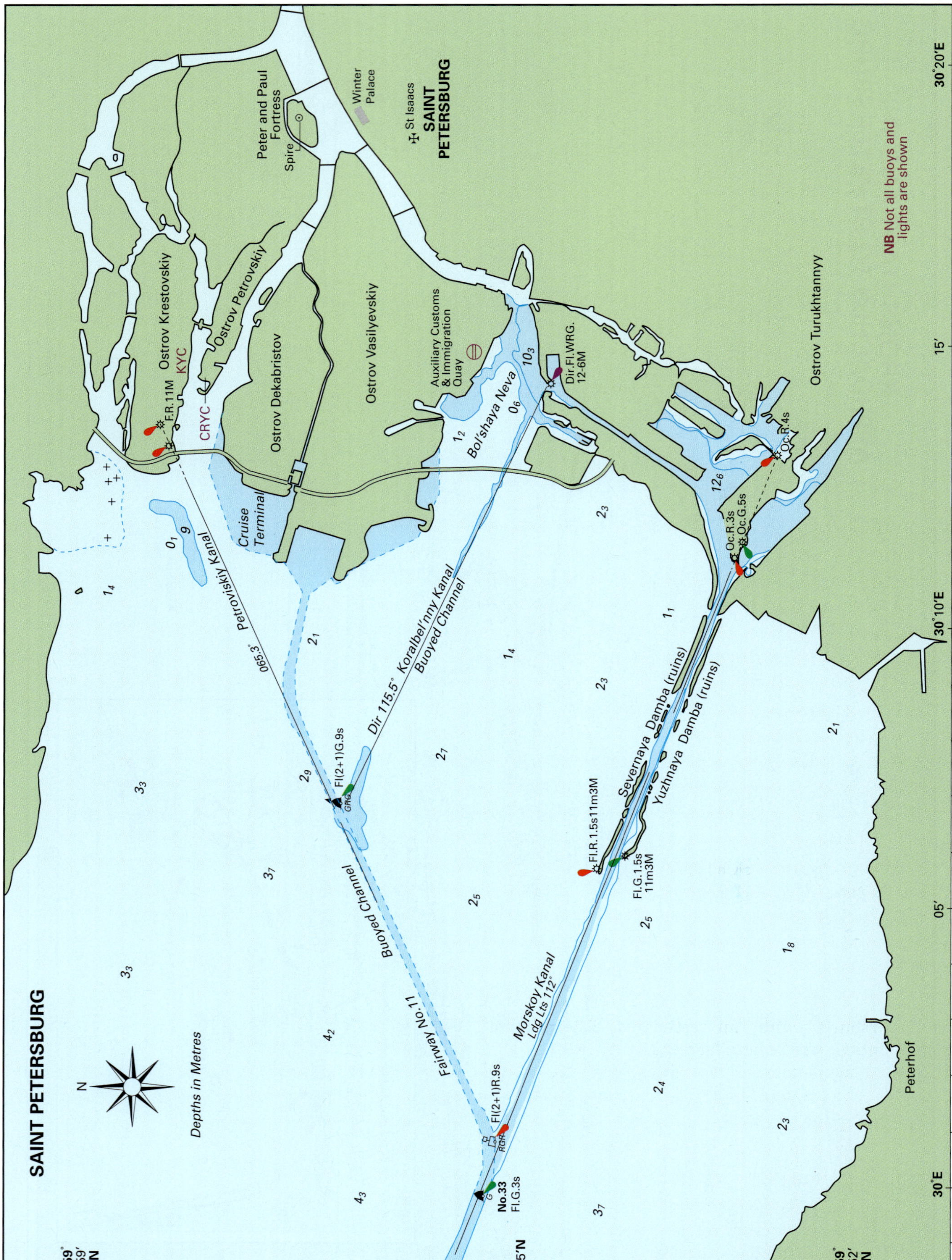
SAINT PETERSBURG
Depths in Metres
N
NB Not all buoys and lights are shown
Ostrov Krestovskiy
KYC
CRYC
F.R.11M
Ostrov Petrovskiy
Ostrov Dekabristov
Ostrov Vasilyevskiy
Peter and Paul Fortress
Spire
Winter Palace
St Isaacs
SAINT PETERSBURG
Auxiliary Customs & Immigration Quay
Cruise Terminal
Bol'shaya Neva
Dir.Fl.WRG. 12-6M
Ostrov Turukhtannyy
Oc.R.4s
Oc.R.3s
Oc.G.5s
Petroviskiy Kanal
065.3°
Dir 115.5° Koralbel'nny Kanal
Buoyed Channel
Fl(2+1)G.9s
GRG
Buoyed Channel
Fairway No.11
Severnaya Damba (ruins)
Yuzhnaya Damba (ruins)
Fl.R.1.5s11m3M
Fl.G.1.5s 11m3M
Morskoy Kanal
Ldg Lts 112°
Fl(2+1)R.9s
RGR
No.33
Fl.G.3s
Peterhof
59° 59′ N
55′N
59° 52′ N
30°E
05′
30°10′E
15′
30°20′E

## ST PETERSBURG

59°59'.55N 29°41'.33E (centre of entrance through causeway at Fort Konstantin)

### Distances

Helsinki 175M, Tallinn 185M, Haapasaari Island 95M, Santio Island 85M, Vyborg 110M

### Lights

**Shepelevskiy** 59°59'.5N 29°08'E LFl(2)WR.16s37m14M Round white stone tower, red bands.

**Krasnaya Gorka** 59°58'.4N 29°23'.2E Iso.3s60m15M Red rectangle, white stripe on red metal framework tower 38m

**Buoy Sankt Peterburgskiy** 60°01'.5N 29°29'.8E LFl.6s Red and white pillar buoy, B topmark

**Tolbukhin** 60°02'.5N 29°32'.7E LFl.12s29m16M Round white stone tower and building.

**Kronshtadt Naval Harbour, south elbow** 59°58'.2N 29°47'.3E Iso.4s14m3M Red framework tower 12m

**Severnaya Damba (north breakwater)** 59°54'.3N 30°05'.7E Fl.R.1.5s11m3M White column, red bands, on base 9m

**Yuzhnaya Damba (south breakwater)** 59°54'.1N 30°05'.9E Fl.G.1.5s11m3M White column, red bands, on base 9m. There are Leading Lts on 108° through the barrier at Kronstadt

Many more lights and lit buoys exist in the approaches and harbour area

### Contacts

**St Petersburg Port Traffic Control Centre**
☎+7 812 251 0290, VHF Ch 9

**St Petersburg Radar Guidance System (RASKAT)**
VHF Ch 12

**St Petersburg Vessel Movements Control System**
VHF Ch 16/78

**St Petersburg Customs and Border Control**
VHF Ch 6 (call *Granit*). Call when in the vicinity of the Sankt Peterburgskiy lightbuoy, giving ETA
St Petersburg

**St Petersburg Port Authority** ☎+7 812 118 8951
VHF Ch 9/16/26

### *General*

St Petersburg, with an estimated 5.2 million inhabitants, is the second largest city in Russia. It is built on a complex of waterways, and is a grand and spacious city. It is justifiably recognised as the cultural capital of Russia – few cities in the world have art galleries, concert halls, museums and theatres which can compare with those of St Petersburg.

No visitor should miss the Hermitage (the Winter Palace), which undoubtedly contains one of the world's greatest collections of art treasures, nor the Russian Museum, actually an art gallery. The Peter and Paul Fortress, the cruiser Aurora, St Isaac's Cathedral, the Admiralty, Chesma Church, Kazanski Cathedral, Smolny Cathedral, the St Petersburg Philharmonia and the Kirov Theatre, to name a few, are very special and deserve a visit. A pocket guidebook such as St Petersburg in the Lonely Planet series will prove invaluable. A few miles outside the city are the resplendent Peterhof summer palace with its wonderful fountains and gilded statuary and Tsarskoye Selo, Catherine's Palace with its world famous Amber Room.

Peterhof can be reached by hydrofoil from behind the Hermitage while Tsarskoye Selo can be reached either by local train from Vitebski Station or by shuttle buses 342, 287, 347a from 'Moskovskaya' Metro Station (Blue Line).

Foreign yachtsmen, especially yachtsmen from Western Europe, are still few and far between. In consequence they receive a warm welcome, and the facilities at the Central River Yacht Club are now much improved.

### *Approach & entrance*

Approach from the Gulf of Finland, either via Bjorkesund or the main shipping channel (for route via Bjorkesund see Approach to Russia page 367).

For approach via the main shipping channel – approach south of Ostrov Gogland via the Sommers big ship channel 'roundabout' at 60°11'.5N 27°46'.00E and Ostrov Seskar 60°04'.00N 28°20'.00E observing traffic separation lanes throughout (see plan page 362). A well-buoyed channel leads past the Sankt Peterburgskiy Landfall buoy and thence south of Ostrov Kotlin, at the eastern end of which lies the city of Kronshtadt. The route is fringed by various prohibited and restricted areas, and care should be taken to remain within the buoyed channel.

When approaching Kronshtadt yachts should contact the local Coastguard Post on VHF Ch 6, callsign *Granit* (pronounced Graneeet), to inform them of the name of the boat and the destination, St Petersburg, even though the boat's agent will have already informed the coastguard.

A pilot vessel, St Petersburg, is often stationed off the Sankt Peterburgskiy lightbuoy but Port Regulations do not require yachts to take a pilot at any stage of the approach detailed here.

Customs and Immigration procedures are carried out at Fort Konstantin on Kotlin Island. The naval port city of Kronshtadt is also located on Kotlin Island.

Kotlin Island lies just off the entrance to the Nevskaya Guba which could be described as a large bay with St Petersburg situated at its head. The island is now joined to the mainland by two causeways which, with the island, form a protective barrier to the city. There is only one entrance through the causeway, close to Fort Konstantin (see plan page 373).

Note that the Customs and Immigration post at the Passenger Terminal is now regarded as an auxiliary post for yachts and can be used if the authorities so decide. However, unless instructed to go elsewhere, all yachts should report to Fort Konstantin.

After clearance, it is possible to berth in the harbour at Fort Konstantin if wishing to explore Kronshtadt.
In theory, yachts are permitted to berth at any of the St Petersburg yacht clubs but in practice many are not suitable due to their location distant from the sights,

The Central River Yacht Club entrance *T. Gunnersen*

inaccessibility to masted craft because of bridges or possible lack of facilities. Central River Yacht Club (CRYC) and Krestovski Yacht Club (KYC) are considered the most suitable and most visiting yachts berth at one or the other.

### *From Kronshtadt to CRYC and KYC*

Once past Kronshtadt take the Deep Sea Channel (Morskoy Kanal) to buoy 33 at 59°55'.17 30°00'.60E, then change course to 65.3° (two fixed red Leading Lights in line) to the GRG buoy at 59°56'.7N 30°06'.6E. Continue on the same course to the end of the fairway when a direct course can be set along the more northerly buoyed channel for the north-facing entrance of the CRYC avoiding the sandbanks created by the Neva

Central River Yacht Club *V. Ivankiv*

Krestovski YC, Central River YC in background *V. Ivankiv*

River. Alternatively, head for the KYC which is located on the opposite bank of the Malaya Neva.

### *Anchorage*

Anchoring is not prohibited outside the port area, the buoyed channels and the military areas around Kronshtadt. However there are no viable anchorages.

### *Berthing*

## Central River Yacht Club (CRYC)

59°57'.96N 30°14'.27E (centre of entrance)

**Contacts**

Petrovskaya Kosa 9, St Petersburg 197110
✆+7 812 235 6636
yachtclubspb@gmail.com
spbryc.ru (in Russian, open with Google Translate)

Situated on the western part of Ostrov Petrovskiy. The CRYC is largest yacht club in St Petersburg and one of the largest in Russia, with seven pontoons of up to 50m in length in its main harbour, a southern work harbour, and a separate guest harbour at the western tip of the island, next to which stands the easily identified clubhouse. The approach is straightforward. Depths are normally around 3m, and the guest harbour pontoons have water and electricity, with toilets and showers ashore, plus a kiosk and restaurant. There is good access to the city, including a nearby trolleybus which runs directly to the Nevsky Prospekt, and a metro station within about a 20 minute walk.

## Krestovski Yacht Club (KYC)

59°57'.97N 30°14'.78E (yacht moorings)

This yacht club is located east of CRYC on the opposite bank of the Malaya Neva. Good facilities. Restaurants within a short walk. Access to the city by metro – nearest metro station about 10mins walk. Only disadvantage is the nearby disco club which can be rather vibrant. Berth reservation required, particularly for craft over 20m long.

Visitors are recommended not to drink tap water without boiling it first – arrive with tanks full of Finnish or Estonian water, or buy bottled. This also applies to tooth brushing.

### *General facilities*

St Petersburg offers cafés and restaurants at all levels, as well as street stalls selling blinis (pancakes) and all kinds of breads and pastries. City tours and guided visits to the many museums, art galleries and churches can usually be arranged for modest fees through the yacht clubs. Tickets for the Kirov Theatre are extremely difficult to obtain through official channels, but are often obtainable outside the theatre immediately before the performance. Performances at the famous Philharmonia and other concert halls can usually be booked at the box office.

For medical care try:
American Medical Centre ✆+7 495 933 7700
American Cardiovascular Centre ✆+7 812 558 8797
Euromed Clinic ✆+7 812 327 0301
International Clinic ✆+7 812 320 3870

# 5. POLAND

The Polish coastline, which stretches for some 180M, is largely low lying with few features but there are harbours suitable for yachts every 30 to 50M and the unspoilt country is interesting. There are two regions of particular appeal to the cruising yachtsman – the inland 'Zalew Szczeciński' area between Świnoujście, Szczecin and Dziwnów, adjacent to the German border, and the Gdańsk/Gdynia area in the extreme east, just short of the border with Russian Kaliningrad.

The inland seas between and around Świnoujście and Szczecin provide areas of sheltered-water sailing. There are a number of attractive fishing harbours and several yacht harbours, many of which have been considerably upgraded. It is possible to cross the border from (or into) Germany via the Peenestrom.

In contrast, Gdynia is a major city and container port and has a well-equipped yacht harbour with some of the best facilities – and certainly the best chandleries – in Poland. Between these two areas lie some half dozen small harbours, several of which have either fully-fledged marinas or at least some provision for visiting yachts. The jewel in the crown, however, is Gdańsk. Nothing can beat berthing in the centre of this lovely UNESCO city beneath the impressive black crane, having wound your way down the canals of the 'Solidarnosc' shipyards.

There has been massive investment in infrastructure and Poland can now lay claim to being a Baltic cruising ground with excellent marinas in its own right rather than simply a curiosity for a few intrepid yachtsmen. German, Scandinavians, and occasionally British yachtsmen are cruising in Poland in increasing numbers and the facilities and infrastructure are improving accordingly. The Poles themselves have started to embrace yachting and indeed have begun to fill their own marinas with local boats, which can leave visitors short of space.

However, it remains a tricky coastline. Several ports have very narrow entrances which have been channelled through the adjacent beach and are prone to silting. Surprisingly large ships can suddenly emerge in these narrow canal entrances and therefore calling the port on the VHF prior to entry is not only advised but is sometimes obligatory.

Winds above Force 4 with any northing in them can make some entrances untenable and phoning ahead to local harbourmasters can sometimes be helpful to elicit local knowledge about the entrance. Strong cross winds can also make some of these artificial entrances tricky with a strong set across the entrance for which navigators must make allowance.

Breakwaters have been extended and marinas much improved, but surge and groundswell can still be a major issue, both at the entrance and in the marinas. You should be prepared to divert if necessary. Rønne on Bornholm is the Polish sailors' favoured port for diversion. The ubiquitous and jolly 'pirate ships' which take day trippers out to sea in clement conditions are a useful indicator that the entrance is tenable.

On looking at charts of the north coast one sees quite large areas of inland water adjacent to the coast but all of them apart from the Zalew Szczeciński are too shallow for vessels drawing more than 0.5m.

There are military firing ranges along the coast, as well as offshore exercise areas which are restricted when in use – dates and times are broadcast on VHF and are also available from the local harbour authorities.

## THE COUNTRY

Poland is a fascinating country both culturally and historically. Key facts about Poland include:

- Poland is one of the most religious countries in the world – over 90% of the population claim to be believers. 89% are Roman Catholic
- Poland is the eighth largest country in Europe – larger than both the UK and Italy
- Europe's heaviest animals are resident in Poland – the European Bison lives in the 380,000-acre Białowieża Primeval Forest. This is Europe's last ancient forest and home to 800 bison
- Poland has its own unique version of Valentine's Day. This is known as Kupała or Wianki and is celebrated on 21 June – the 'Feast of St John the Baptist' day. Men jump over bonfires and, women hope to receive wreaths. Wreaths with candles are floated on the water and if you get one you will be lucky in love
- The population of Poland is 38.5 million making it the eighth largest in Europe
- National holidays include 3 May in honour of the introduction in 1791 of the first democratic constitution, and 11 Nov, remembering Poland regaining its independence in 1918

From the quiet anchorages and small marinas of the Bay of Pomerania in the west to the Amber Coast and Bay of Gdańsk in the east, the shoreline is mainly low-lying with few features. This terrain is the result of the last glacial period when much clay, sand and other small debris was deposited, and is characterised by beaches, national parks and small protected harbours. The national parks have preserved large forested regions, though agricultural land begins not far inland, much of it growing cereals and still in the hands of small farmers.

There are extensive inland lakes and several shallow inland seas, including two major routes to Berlin. The eastern coastal area is known as the Amber Coast due to the large quantities of amber (petrified tree resin from some 40 million years ago) which are still washed onto the beaches following winter's northwesterly gales. There are some quite extensive national parks along the coast and any restrictions should always be taken account of.

Poland's major industries include coal, copper and steel production, engineering, chemicals, shipbuilding, fishing and forestry. Almost all the previously state-owned industries have been privatised, and the most recent investments in Poland have centred on technology, automotive and industrial equipment, manufacturing, electronics, computers and banking. In addition to being a major hub of shipbuilders and repairers, Poland is one of Europe's biggest moulders of GRP yacht hulls. The Poles also have skilled metal workers and produce high quality steel and aluminium yacht hulls.

### Language

Polish words are often difficult to pronounce because of unfamiliar consonant groups. However, people in Poland are helpful and friendly to foreigners and language is seldom a problem. At most shops, hotels, customs offices and marinas some of the staff will be able to assist with at least basic English. English is now taught in schools instead of Russian so, for asking directions in the street for instance, a young person is likely to be more helpful than someone older. The older members of the population are more likely to have learnt Russian at school.

In the west, especially near Świnoujście or Szczecin, both German and English are likely to be understood since there are many visiting German yachts. As always, slow, careful pronunciation and basic vocabulary will aid communication. If not, the use of Google Translate can be helpful when trying to communicate with harbourmasters and others.

Some useful phrases are: *dzień dobry* pronounced 'jin-dobry' (good morning); *dziękuję* pronounced 'jin-ku-yea' (thank you); *prosze* pronounced 'pro-sheh' (please); *przepraszam* pronounced 'pseh-pra-sham' (excuse me); *tak* (yes), *nie* (no), and *toaleta* (toilet). (One point regarding the latter is that the symbols WC and a circle indicate women, with a triangle for men. Showers use the international visual symbol or the words *natryski* or *prysznice*.) At harbours, the word port is used, the harbourmaster is the *kapitan* working in the harbour office or *kapitanat*. The marina manager is the *bosman* (from the English bo's'un).

### History

Poland is historically a land of transition between east and west, where different peoples and cultures have existed side by side. The Slavs, including the Polanians who gave the country their name, migrated north to the region which was then inhabited by the Balts and the Finns. These earliest cultures formed city-states with regional leaders, thus establishing from the 9th century onwards the dynasties which were to rule Poland.

From the 10th century the Catholic religion provided a further unifying force. In the 14th century the Piast dynasty united the Polish city-states, codified the common law, established the university in Kraków, built roads and fortified castles. The Golden Age continued following the Polish victory over the Teutonic Order in 1410.

During the Jagiellonian dynasty (1382–1572) the crowns of Poland and Lithuania were combined and the economy flourished, while intellectual and artistic growth were exemplified by the contributions to astronomy of Nicolaus Copernicus. At the end of the 18th century three successive partitions by Russia, Prussia, and Austria imposed outside rule on the country, but although foreign political rule dominated the geographical region, the Polish culture strengthened internally giving rise to figures such

# KEY INFORMATION

## Rescue/Safety services

**Emergency** ✆ 112 (this is the emergency number for all EU countries)

**MRCC Polish Rescue Radio** monitors VHF Ch 16, DSC MMSI 002618102. Call Sign **'Polish Rescue Radio (SPL)'** ✆+48 58 661 01 97, ✆+48 58 620 55 51,
Mobile ✆+48 505 050 971
**www.sar.gov.pl/en**

## Charts, pilots and cruising guides

UKHO and Polish charts cover the coast adequately for passage making but it will be necessary to obtain Polish or German charts for detailed coverage of the smaller harbours.

UKHO charts may be obtained from Smart Co Ltd, ✆+48 91 488 33 79, Gdynia & Szczecin offices. Szczecin@smart.gda.pl, **www.smart.gda.pl**

Polish charts and other nautical publications can be obtained from Biuro Hydrograficzne Marynarki Wojennej in Gdynia (Jana z Kolna 8, 81–301 Gdynia). ✆+48 58 626 3283 bhmw@ron.mil.pl **bhmw.gov.pl/en/**

Guides to various parts of the Baltic can be purchased from **www.wydawnictwonautica.pl/baltyk.pl** including *Polskie Wybrzeże Bałtyku* – a guide to the Polish Baltic Coast. This is in Polish, but may nevertheless be useful. Fellow Polish yachtsmen will always be happy to help translate.

*Mapa Zeglarska* (full name Mapa Zeglarska Zalewu Szczecińskiego, Kamienskiego i J Dabie) – a useful and detailed chart on a scale of 1:85,000 which covers western Polish waters as far east as Dziwnów. Also contains information on customs and immigration, buoyage, VHF channels and telephone numbers, plus some photographs. In Polish, with English and German translations

*Baltic Pilot Volume II* (NP 19) – the British Admiralty pilot book for this area in English, but written with big ships in mind rather than yachts

*Cruising Guide to Poland 2025* (Cruising Association)

*Küstenhandbuch Polen und Litauen* by Jörn Heindrich, (Delius Klasing)

*Hafenhandbuch Polen*, DSV, (Delius Klasing)

*The Cruising Almanac* Imray/Cruising Association
**www.imray.com**

## Time

Poland uses UT+1 in winter and UT+2 in summer (from the last Sunday in March until the Saturday before the last Sunday in September).

## zł Money

The Polish unit of currency is the złoty, divided into 100 groszy. Currency can be readily exchanged at most banks or at bureaux de change (kantor in Polish) within the major shopping areas, and ATMs (cash dispensers) are also widely available.

## Formalities

Poland is a member of the EU and of the Schengen Area (see main Introduction page 9 for details of Schengen requirements).

Visas are not required for UK or EU passport holders, nor for citizens of the USA.

Yachts coming from a non-Schengen area country (or if there are people on board who hold non-EU passports) should report to a passport office. In practice this means only the larger ports which have ferry services from other Baltic countries. Arriving yachts may be hailed by an official asking for their last port of call.

As a result of no longer being part of the EU UK boats must now check out of the UK using form C1331 and then check into the EU/Schengen area at an Official Port of Entry. British Citizens arriving through airports or on ferries will need to get stamped into the EU/Schengen area. Schengen rules mean that you are allowed to stay in the Schengen area for a maximum of 90 days in each of the previous 180 days. The 180-day period is a rolling window, so you must count back 180 days from each day of your stay. To help with this, there is a Schengen visit calculator on **www.ec.europa.eu/assets/home/visa-calculator/calculator.htm?lang=en**

In late-2025 the European Travel Information and Authorization System (ETIAS) system will be implemented. ETIAS will require citizens of approximately 60 countries who currently enjoy visa-free access to Europe's Schengen Area to obtain advanced authorization before traveling. This system is similar to the ESTA required for travelling to the USA. It is not a visa but advance security clearance for short-term visitors. There will be a transitional period for at least 6 months from late-2025 when people will be advised to get an ETIAS authorization, but it will not be a requirement. There will then be a 6-month grace period when ETIAS will be compulsory for most travellers, but first-time visitors since the end of the transitional period will still be granted entry. Application will be online and should be fairly quick and straightforward. The cost is expected to be €7 with a validity of three years.

The yachts registration papers, radio licence, insurance documents, and International Certificate of Competence (or equivalent) are required.

The Polish flag is equal parts of white over red.

Polish Embassy, London
47 Portland Place, London W1B 1JH
✆+44 207 291 3520
londyn@msz.gov.pl
**www.gov.pl/web/unitedkingdom/embassy-london**

Polish Helpdesk
Informacja Celna-Ministerstwo Finansów
ul. Świętokrzyska 12, 00–916, Warszawa, Poland ✆+48 22 6943194,6943091 celina@helpdesk.mofnet.gov.pl
The Polish Visa Section, 10 Bouverie Street, London EC4Y 8AX, ✆+44 207 8228 900

The British Embassy in Warsaw can be contacted on ✆+48 22 311 0000
**www.gov.uk/government/world/poland**

## ☼ Public holidays

1 Jan, Easter Monday, 1 May (Labour Day), 3 May (Constitution Day), Ascension Day, Corpus Christi (60 days after Easter), 15 Aug (Assumption Day), 1 Nov (All Saints Day), 11 Nov (Independence Day), 25–26 Dec (Christmas Day and Boxing Day)

Peak summer holiday time is July to mid-August

## Communications

The country's telephone code is +48. 5G mobile coverage is good around major towns and cities, elsewhere it may revert to 3G or 4G. To obtain an international line, dial 00 followed by the country code, area code (omitting any initial 0) and number. When dialling within Poland all calls require the 2-digit area code.

Marinas often prefer mobile phones for communication since VHF certificates are expensive for staff to acquire.

## Travel

Major **airports** serve Warsaw, Gdańsk and Kraków, with smaller airports near Poznan, Szczecin, Katowice and Wrocław. Wizz Air and Ryanair have cheap direct flights to the coast, LOT and BA use Warsaw. Easyjet fly to Krakow. Gdańsk airport is 30mins by taxi from the marina in Gdańsk city centre.

**Railways** connect most cities and towns. Schedules are posted on large boards showing times, express services and track numbers. Some journeys need reservations, book at the station. The national Polish Railway Company – Polskie Koleje Państwowe (PKP) – is made up of two separate companies, PKP Intercity (**www.intercity.pl**) for long-distance trains and Przewozy Regionalne (Polregio) (**polregio.pl**) for regional trains. You can book Polish domestic train services through **www.intercity.pl**. SKM commuter trains run between the three cities of Gdańsk, Gdynia and Sopot.

**Bus** and **tram** tickets can be purchased in advance at a newsagent (Ruch kiosk) which you then validate in the machine on the bus and tram. Contactless payment is becoming more widely available on buses and trams.

## Websites

Many harbours and marinas now have their own websites which are listed under the communications section of each harbour. Some sites are available with an English translation (look for an English flag at the top of the website), but if not Google Translate usually offers a reasonable quality translation. If you go to translate.google.com and click on the 'websites' button, you can enter the appropriate website to get a translation.

**www.poland.pl** – The official Polish website, with some useful links.

**bhmw.gov.pl/en/** – The official website of the Polish Hydrographic Office.

**baltyk.imgw.pl** – Baltic sea areas forecast

**southcoastbaltic.eu/en/ports** – An online EU-funded website with all the ports and harbours from Ribnitz-Damgarten (Germany) in the west to Klaipėda (Lithuania) in the east. The guide also covers Bornholm as well as the entire Polish coast.

**www.saj.org.pl/mapa-przystani/** – A useful map of marinas on the Polish Baltic coast.

**www.wladyslawowo.pl** – Website of the Władysławowo region, which encompasses some eight towns and villages. Interesting, but very little about the harbour.

**www.gdynia.pl** – Gdynia city website, including brief information about the yacht harbour in the tourism section.

**visitgdansk.com** – Gdańsk tourist website. Click top right for the English version of the website.

**www.noonsite.com/Countries/Poland** – Tips on Poland for cruising sailors by cruising sailors.

**www.polandforvisitors.com**

**www.lonelyplanet.com/poland**

## Radio communications

**VHF**

VHF Ch 16 for SAR and VHF Ch 11 is their working channel. VHF Ch 6/10 are the preferred Ship to Ship channels for yachts (VHF Ch 6 should not be used in Gdańsk Bay, and VHF Ch 10 should not be used around Władysławowo and Hel as these are used for port operations)

*VHF stations*

Świnoujście VHF Ch 25; Kołowo VHF Ch 24; Barzowice VHF Ch 25; Rozewie VHF Ch 24; Kyrnica Morska VHF Ch 25; Grzywacz VHF Ch 26, Kołobrzeg VHF Ch 24; Rowokol VHF Ch 26; Oksywie VHF Ch 26.

## ❄ Weather information

Sea areas are: Western, Southern, South-eastern, Central, Northern Baltic and Polish coastal waters. Wind speed is given as m/sec (metres per second) – to convert (approximately) to knots, double the reading, and to convert to Beaufort halve the reading. Weather forecasts in Polish and English are broadcast by Witowo (pronounced vitovo) Radio on VHF Ch 24/25/26 first announced on VHF Ch 16. The English version is transmitted at 0133, 0733, 0933 1333, 1933 UTC. Witovo Radio can be contacted on MMSI 002610210. In the of Gulf of Gdańsk weather bulletins and navigational warnings in English are announced by VTS-Zakota (MMSI 0026 11400) on VHF Ch 16/71 and then transmitted on VHF Ch 66 at 0105, 0805, 1405 and 2005 LT.

Weather Bulletins for all sea areas in the Baltic are transmitted on Navtex twice daily.

Meteorological information can also be obtained by telephoning offices at Gdynia ✆+48 58 620 5493 (24hr) or Szczecin ✆+48 91 434 2012 (24hr).

Gdańsk pirate ship *Miranda Delmar-Morgan*

as the composer Frederic Chopin. As a legacy of her diverse history, the cruising yachtsman can detect Pomeranian influence in the western port of Szczecin, admire the medieval fortifications in Kołobrzeg, and see the Prussian influence most clearly within the restored old city of Gdańsk.

Following the end of World War I in 1918 Poland regained her freedom, but in 1939 the invasion of the country by Germany, in co-operation with the USSR, signalled the beginning of World War II. Following the end of the war Poland came under the influence of the Soviet Union, and during the post-war period a Communist regime was imposed. The Polish people were frustrated by the government, the economy deteriorated, and strikes became increasingly frequent. This led to the founding of the independent trade union Solidarity (Solidarność).

With Solidarity, hope for democratic reforms strengthened. Another new factor for the regime was the increased influence of the Catholic Church headed by Polish Pope John Paul II. Unrest continued and the persistence of Polish citizens eventually forced the Soviets to negotiate in 1989. Following this meeting, democratic elections were held in Poland and Solidarity won 99% of the seats in the Senate. Changes following the election quickly re-established a free-market economy and social reform. This transition, although painful, has been fairly rapid. Poland has experienced economic growth since 1989, sometimes in partnership with foreign investors, and is receptive to new ideas. Poland joined NATO in 1999 and became a member of the European Union in 2004.

In 2011 Poland took over the rotating Presidency of the EU for the first time since accession and Prime Minister Donald Tusk's centre-right Civic Platform party won the parliamentary elections of that year. In 2014 Poland asked Nato to station 10,000 troops there, to show the NATO Alliance's resolve to defend all its members after Russia seized Crimea and later that year Donald Tusk resigned to take up the post of president of the European Council. The new government was a much more populist government and in December 2023 the situation reverted when the Law and Justice (PiS) party got the majority of the votes. Donald Tusk became the new Prime Minister succeeding Morawiecki, leading a coalition of three parliamentary groups made up of Civic Coalition, Third Way, and The Left.

Funding from several sources has been used to upgrade wharfs, roads and rail networks, to build new marinas and repair ancient buildings. Poland is being transformed and has excellent facilities for visiting sailors.

# PRACTICALITIES

## Shopping

Every town has its shopping area, usually in the centre where rows of shops offer a variety of goods. Large supermarkets are located at the edges of the towns, and there are also many open markets where fresh food and other products are available at prices lower than those in the shops. Bakery goods can be bought at a *piekarnia*, sweet rolls and cakes from a *cukiernia* – try *sernik* (cheese cake).

## Hotels & restaurants

Most towns, especially seaside tourist resorts, have a range of hotels varying widely in quality and price.

Restaurants are similarly diverse, from high-priced speciality restaurants to pavement cafés and fast food outlets. If visiting one of those serving Polish food consider sampling *barszcz* (beetroot soup), *bigos* (a stew made with sauerkraut and a variety of meats,) or *pierogi* (large dumplings usually stuffed with white cheese and potatoes, meat or fruit). In summer open air snack bars spring up selling grilled fish, sausage or other kinds of meat served with fresh bread and pickles – and of course there are the ubiquitous American burger and pizza chains.

Cafés (*kawiarnia*) serve rich desserts and a variety of drinks. Tea, Turkish, expresso and even iced coffee are popular, Polish beer is good (try Bosman, Xywiec or Warka) and imported wine plentiful. Vodka can be bought in a variety of forms and flavours including *wioniówka* (sweet or dry cherry) and *Xubrówka* (flavoured with bison grass found only in one region of the country). Polish cognac is known as *winiak*. *Miód* (mead) is a delicious liqueur made from honey.

## Medical matters

To get medically necessary state healthcare in Poland, you need a Global Health Insurance Card (GHIC) or a European Health Insurance Card (EHIC). For information on applying for a GHIC card, look at the NHS webpage www.nhs.uk/using-the-nhs/healthcare-abroad/apply-for-a-free-uk-global-health-insurance-card-ghic/ However, cruisers would still be well advised to have travel insurance covering health. The Polish National Health Fund is marked as NFZ. Clinics operate a normal 5-day week, otherwise go to the nearest hospital. For an ambulance dial 999 from a landline or 112 from a mobile phone. NFZ registered dentists offer basic care (www.nfz.gov.pl).

Fruit stall Władysławowo *Miranda Delmar-Morgan*

## Yacht services & chandleries

Drinking water is always readily available as are showers and toilets. However, an electrical connection may be some distance away and require a long lead and not always with the 3-pin EU connector. A continental 2-pin adaptor can be useful.

Fuelling berths are becoming more frequent but in an emergency a nearby filling station selling diesel can generally be found (a few 20ltr containers may prove useful). The fuel sold for yachts is the same as that sold for cars and this contains up to 7% bio-additives.

Polish propane gas bottles can sometimes be exchanged or refilled at the larger filling stations such as Shell and BP, but Calor gas is not available and Campinggaz is rare. It is prudent to stock up before entering the country.

The widest selection of chandlery is available in Gdynia (see page 406), with more limited stocks at Świnoujście, Szczecin, Kołobrzeg, Władysławowo and Gdańsk. Elsewhere chandleries can be a bit thin on the ground. In the Szczecin area facilities for yachts are improving with marinas, boatyards, sailmakers and chandleries.

There are reasonable boatyards at Szczecin, Kołobrzeg, Łeba and Górki, and it is possible to lay up ashore in Gdynia, Górki, Łeba, Kołobrzeg and Szczecin though obtaining a cradle could be a problem. A lot of yacht building takes place at Górki, where there are overwintering facilities and six yacht clubs, but little transport and no shops.

## Firing ranges

The plan on page 384 shows details of the firing ranges along the Polish Coast. The coast between Darłowo and Ustka (Area 6) and less so off the Hel peninsula (Areas 10 and 11) are the most difficult to navigate when they are active. There are also three small areas where navigation is forbidden at any time (Areas 3, and 15 north of Gdynia and Area 14 west of Hel).

Firing times are broadcast by Witowo Radio VHF Ch 24/25/26 at 0133, 0533, 0933, 1333, 1733, 2133 UT along with the weather forecast and other navigational warnings, after first being announced on VHF Ch 16. Słupsk Radio maintains a 24hr watch on VHF Ch 16, and 2182kHz, and issues warnings and weather on VHF Ch 71 at 0715, 1245, and 1845 LT.

Up-to-date information can be obtained by phoning the Polish Navy 8th Coastal Defence Flotilla Operations Officer ✆+48 661 417 339. Firing times and other navigational warnings for the northwest coast are also broadcast by Słupsk Radio on VHF Ch 71 at 0715, 1245, and 1845 LT after first being announced on VHF Ch 16 or ✆+48 59 814 4889 (H24).

See also the plan on page 415 and note on page 418 about Regulated Area 117.

Gdańsk waterfront
*Miranda Delmar-Morgan*

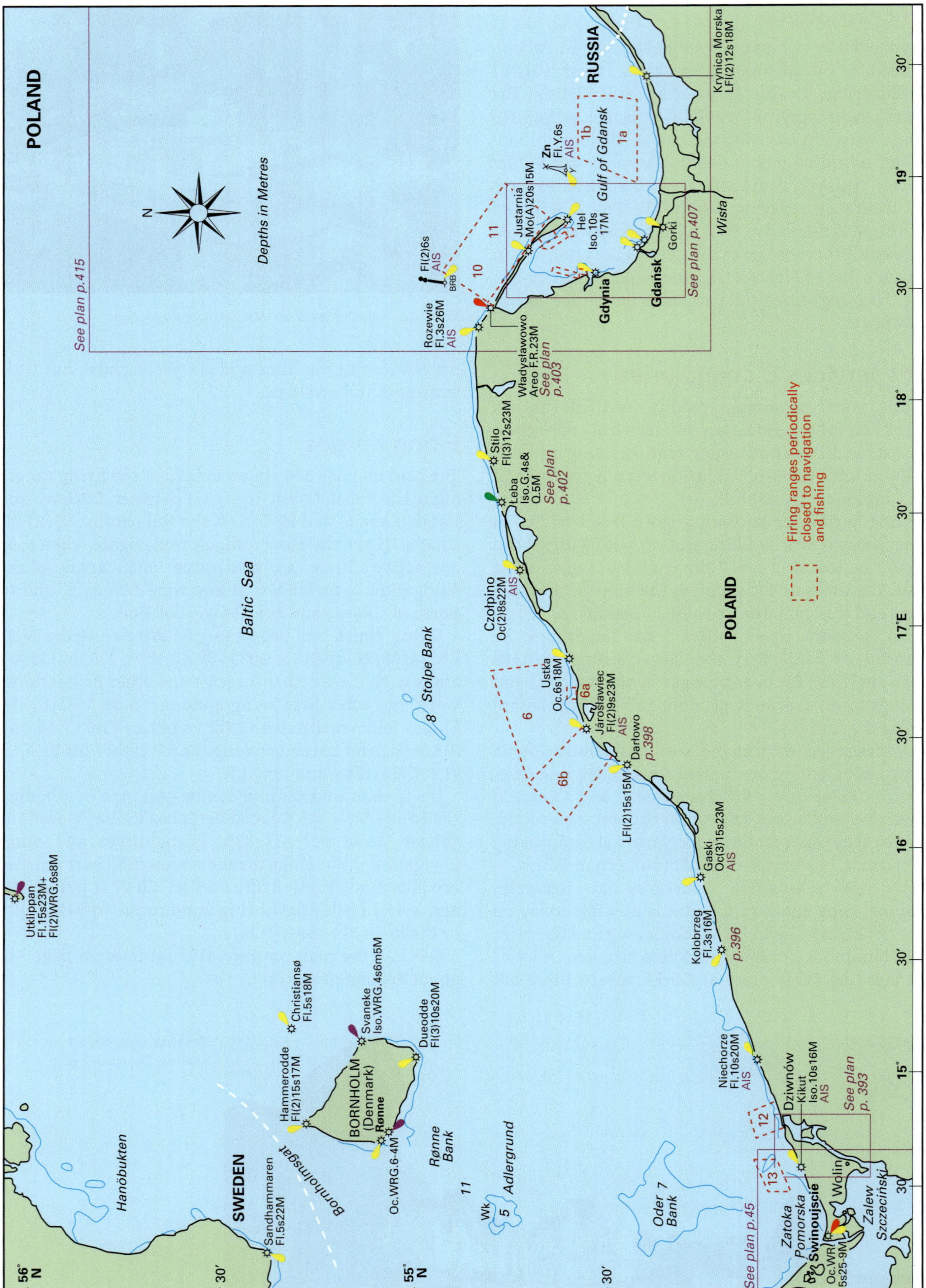
POLAND
Depths in Metres
See plan p.415
Baltic Sea
Stolpe Bank
SWEDEN
Hanöbukten
Sandhammaren
Fl.5s22M
Bornholmsgat
Hammerodde
Fl(2)15s17M
BORNHOLM
(Denmark)
Rønne
Oc.WRG.6-4M
Christiansø
Fl.5s18M
Svaneke
Iso.WRG.4s6m5M
Dueodde
Fl(3)10s20M
Utklippan
Fl.15s23M+
Fl(2)WRG.6s8M
Rønne Bank
Adlergrund
Oder Bank
Zatoka Pomorska
Zalew Szczeciński
Świnoujście
Oc.WR
.5s25-9M
Wolin
See plan p.45
Dziwnów
Kikut
Iso.10s16M
AIS
See plan p. 393
Niechorze
Fl.10s20M
AIS
Kolobrzeg
Fl.3s16M
p.396
Gaski
Oc(3)15s23M
AIS
LFl(2)15s15M
Darłowo
p.398
Jarosławiec
Fl(2)9s23M
AIS
Ustka
Oc.6s18M
Czołpino
Oc(2)8s22M
AIS
Leba
Iso.G.4s&
Q.5M
See plan
p.402
Stilo
Fl(3)12s23M
Władysławowo
Areo F.R.23M
See plan
p.403
Rozewie
Fl.3s26M
AIS
Fl(2)6s
AIS
BRB
Justarnia
Mo(A)20s15M
Hel
Iso.10s
17M
Gdynia
Gdańsk
Gorki
See plan p.407
Wisła
Zn
Fl.Y.6s
AIS
Gulf of Gdansk
RUSSIA
Krynica Morska
LFl(2)12s18M
Firing ranges periodically
closed to navigation
and fishing
56° N
55° N
15°
16°
17°E
18°
19°
30'

# 5A. ZALEW SZCZECIŃSKI TO BERLIN

## ŚWINOUJŚCIE

53°55'N 14°17'E

### Distances

Stralsund 50M, Rønne 72M, Trzebież 15M, Szczecin 35M, Dziwnów 20M, Gdynia 190M

### Lights

**Świnoujście** 53°55'N 14°17'.1E
Oc.WR.5s65m25/9M Yellow round tower on red building 65m
**Landfall buoy** 54°14'.7N 14°11'E Iso.10s Red and white pillar buoy
**Kikut** 53°59'N 14°34'.9E Iso.10s91m16M Grey round stone tower, white lantern 18m
**Outer Leading Lights 170.2°** *Front* Mlyny (west breakwater) 53°55'.6N 14°16'.6E Oc.10s11m17M White beacon resembling windmill 11m
*Rear* **Galeriowa** 520m from front, Oc.10s23m17M White triangle on white round tower, three galleries 24m
**East breakwater** 53°55'.9N 14°16'.8E Oc.WR.6s13m2M Red tower

### Contacts

Świnoujście Harbourmaster ✆+48 91 440 3571 (24hr)
Świnoujście Port Control and VTS ✆+48 91 321 6203 VHF Ch 12/16/71/18
Basen Stoczniowy (Basen Pólnocny) Marina
✆+48 91 321 9177, VHF Ch 74
*Mobile* +48 537 200814 www.osir.swinoujscie.pl
marina.bosmanat@osir.swinoujscie.pl

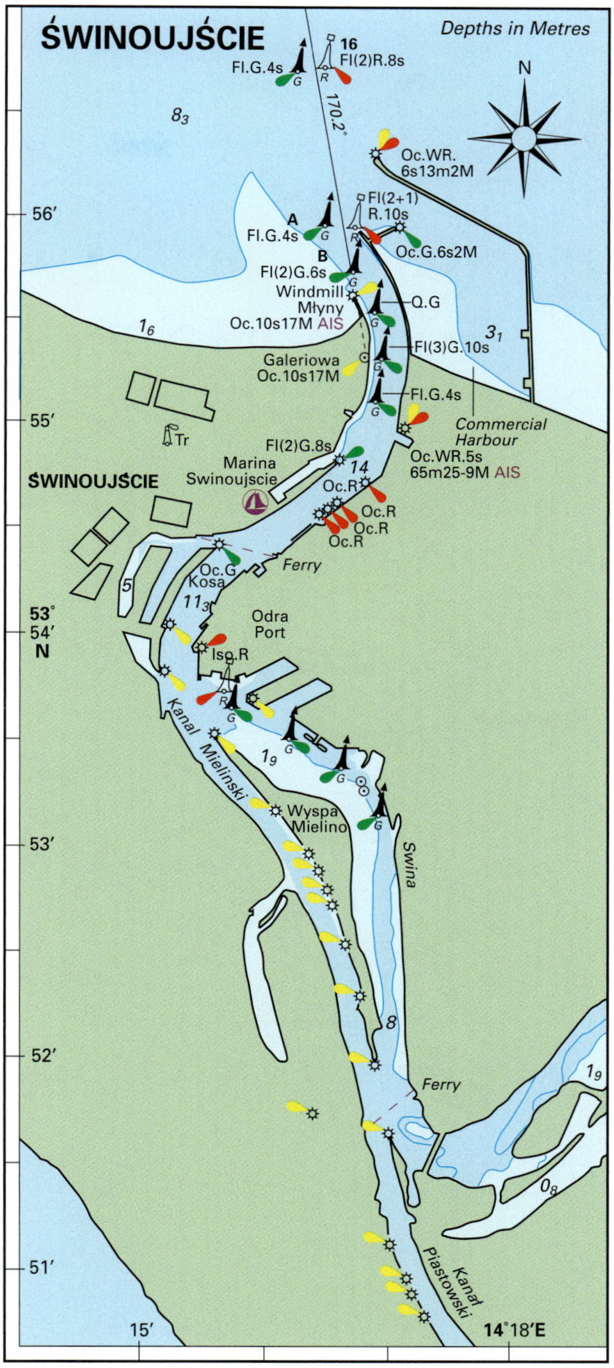


*General*

Świnoujście (pronounced *Sfeen-o-weesh-chey*) is the outer port of Szczecin. It lies at the mouth of the Odra River, which separates Usedom and Wolin islands, just east of the Polish/German border. It is a holiday resort with an esplanade and a blue flag beach as well as a commercial, fishing and naval harbour. A considerable amount of commercial traffic passes through the harbour en route to Szczecin, via the Odra River.

*Approach & entrance*

53°56'.2N 14°16'.8E (north mole)

The main shipping channel is 14m deep and is well buoyed on a bearing of 170° from the landfall buoy (some 20M offshore) to the breakwaters. Yachts can safely take their own route but avoiding a shoal which extends 1M offshore close west of the entrance. There is a large breakwater on the eastern side which protects ships associated with a gas terminal. Take care at night and in poor visibility not to confuse the entrance to the gas port with the main port entrance.

The inner eastern breakwater, the lighthouse, and the harbour control tower are all conspicuous from well offshore. The entrance itself is obvious, well-marked and free from obstructions. There can be currents across and into the entrance of up to 2kn or an outflow current of up to 4kn depending on the strength and direction of the wind.

Świnoujście can also be approached from the south via the Kanals Piastowski and Mielenski from the Zalew Szczeciński.

*Anchorage*

There is no anchorage within Świnoujście itself – continue some 10M southeast to the lake and island area of Zalew Szczeciński.

Zatoka Pomorska
ZALEW SZCZECIŃSKI
Depths in Metres
Buoyed Channel
Oc.WR. 6s2M
Oc.G.6s2M
Młyny
Oc.Or10s11m17M
AIS
Galeriowa
Oc.Or.10s23m17M
Oc.5s68m 25/9M AIS
Swinoujście
WOLIN ISLAND
USEDOM
Kanał Mielinski
Jezioro Wicko Wielkie
Lubin
Stara Swina
Marked channel
See plan p.385
Kanał Piastowski
(border marked by buoys)
Stettiner Haff
Iso.2s7M & Oc(2)R.8s3M
GERMANY
Haff Iso.4s
Q(6)+LFI
Fl.G
Zalew Szczeciński
Buoyed channel
Buoyed channel
Buoyed channel
Wolin
Dziwna
Wolińska Mielizna
See plan p.393
Zatoka Skozewska
Fl.WRG.4s6M
Fl(2)8s25m13M Fl.WRG.4s6M
141.3°-321.3°
Altwarp
Nowe Warpno
Jezioro Nowowarpieńskie
Fl(3)8s26m13M +Fl.WRG.4s6-4M
Fl(3)8s26m13M + Fl.WRG.4s6-4M
Oc(2)R.8s3M
Oc(2)R. 8s3M
Oc(2)R. 8s3M
Gbsierzyno
Trzebież
See plan p.388
Odra (buoyed)
Stepnica
Q.R
Q.G
168°-348°
GERMANY
POLAND
Kielpiński Ostrów
To Szczecin
See continuation p.389
Police
14°20'E

Świnoujście approach *Miranda Delmar-Morgan*

*Berthing*

The municipal marina (Marina Świnoujście) in Basen Północny (Stoczniowy) is on the west side of the harbour 1M south of the entrance. The brick water tower beyond the southwest end of the basin is conspicuous and there is a SAR centre at the marina entrance. It is safe, comfortable and has good facilities. It is about 1km from the town centre.

Limited berthing may also be available alongside in the town centre by arrangement with the harbourmaster, but there are no facilities and there can be wash from passing traffic.

*Facilities*

Basen Północny has been greatly improved. Facilities are good with showers and toilets now on both sides of the basin, new pontoons, and alongside berthing in 3m depths. Fuel is available from 0900–1800 from Port Petro Serwis Grzegorz Kaska (ul. Jachtowa 1, 72-600 Świnoujście, ✆ +48 601 77 88 98, prokaska@wp.pl). Water and electricity are available via a card system. There is also a bar/café, laundry and WiFi if you are within range.

Bus, train and ferry services to Szczecin are available where there are connections to Poznan and Berlin. Regular ferry services to Sweden via Rønne on Bornholm and to Copenhagen or to Trelleborg and Ystad on the south coast of Sweden.

## THE KANAŁ MIELEŃSKI AND ZALEW SZCZECIŃSKI

Leading southeast from Świnoujście is the Kanał Mieleński, which then becomes the Kanal Piastowski before opening into the wide Zalew Szczeciński. Both the canal and the buoyed channel across the Zalew Szczeciński are dredged to 10m, and there are 5m depths across most of the remainder of the area. The main channel is well buoyed and lit, with 25m towers at 2M intervals.

The surrounding area is heavily forested and offers many quiet and scenic anchorages, though yachts venturing outside the fairway should keep a sharp watch for the many fishing nets, marked by stakes with red and white diamonds; the red side indicating danger and the white pointing to safe passage.

The Zalew Szczeciński can also be accessed from both west and east – the former from Stralsund through the Greifswalder Bodden and the Peenestrom (see pages 54–5), and the latter from the Baltic east of Świnoujście via Dziwnów, Kamień Pomorski and Wolin (see page 394).

Outer leading mark at end of western breakwater at Świnoujście *Andy Beharrell*

Aerial view of the Port jachtowy Basen Północny in Świnoujście *Andy Beharrell*

# TRZEBIEŻ

53°40'N 14°31'E

### Distances

Świnoujście 17M, Szczecin 15M, Ueckermünde 20M, Karnin (at S end of Peenestrom) 26M

### Lights

**From northwest:**

**Brama Tower No. 3** 53°39'.92N 14°32'E Iso.2s25m7M Red tower with two galleries

**Brama Tower No. 4** 53°39'.83N 14°31'.83E Iso.2s25m7M Green tower with two galleries

**North Landfall Buoy TN-A** 53°40'.85N 14°29'.85E Fl.G.2s G buoy

**Leading Lights 150.2°** *Front* 53°39'.6N 14°31'.1E Oc.4s11m7M Red oblong shape on white framework tower

*Rear* 433m from front Oc.4s22m7M Red oblong shape on framework tower

**From southeast:**

**Leading Lights 301.2°** *Front* 53°39'.8N 14°30'.9E Oc.Y.4s11m4M Yellow square shape on white framework tower

*Rear* 380m from front Oc.Y.4s18m4M Orange inverted triangle on white framework tower

### Contacts

**Port w Trzebieży**
53°40'.00N 14°31'.02E
**Harbourmaster** ☎+48 91 312 83 46
VHF Ch 71
btrzebiez@ums.gov.pl

**Marina Trzebież**
53°39'.52N 14°31'.15E
**Harbourmaster** ☎+48 789 327 991
bosmanat@marinatrzebiez.pl
www.marinatrzebiez.pl

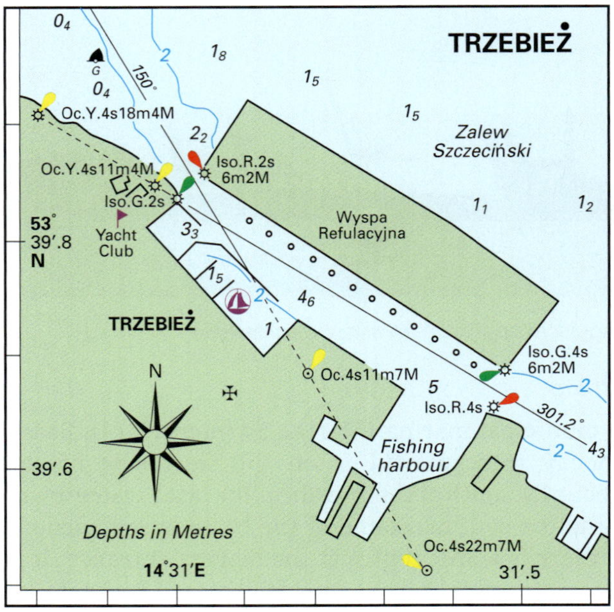


### General

At the southern neck of the Zalew Szczeciński, on the western shore, lies Trzebież (pronounced *Cheh-byeh*). The main berthing possibility is the Marina Trzebież. This is just a short distance to the northwest of the port. The marina has depths of 2–5m but it is quite shallow on the innermost wall. It can be approached either from the north or the south by buoyed channels off the main channel to Szczecin. Both channels have leading lights. A plan of the marina is available on www.marinatrzebiez.pl/wp-content/uploads/2020/03/PlanPortu.jpg.

### Facilities

Facilities include water, diesel, electricity, showers, WCs, and a café/bar but limited shopping. There is a Customs office. The marina is the headquarters of the Polish Sailing Association and the café/bar serves as a club when the fleet is in. There is a 30T hoist and some maintenance services. Yachts are also welcomed at alongside berths in the more sheltered fishing harbour where there are facilities similar to the yacht harbour. Both harbours are subject to surge from onshore winds and passing ships. Train to Szczecin.

Trzebież harbour *Miranda Delmar-Morgan*

## SZCZECIN

53°25′N 14°33′E

### Distances
Stralsund via the Peenestrom 85M, Świnoujście 35M, Trzebież 15M

### Lights
Night approach not recommended – the latter part is narrow and unlit.

### Contacts
**Szczecin Harbourmaster** ☎+48 91 433 6657/440 3596 (0830–1500 LT Mon–Fri)

**Szczecin Port Control and VTS** ☎+48 91 433 0697/ 440 3510, VHF Ch 16/69

**Szczecin Customs** ☎+48 91 440 6500

**NorthEast Marina Szczecin** ☎+48 91 311 15 21, VHF Ch 65
*Mobile* +48 539 924 222
www.northeast-marina.pl
marina@zstw.szczecin.pl

**Marina Gocław**
*Mobile* ☎+49 73 002 3666
marinagoclaw@o2.pl

**Pogon Marina**
☎+48 91 462 4657 or +48 602 808 280
sejk@fr.pl
www.marinapogon.pl

**Marina Club** ☎+48 601 938 289
or +48 601 984 897
www.marina-club.pl
i.look@marina-club.pl

**Yacht Club AZS Szczecin** (Academic Yacht Club)
☎+48 91 461 2734
www.jkazs.szn.pl
Jkazs.szn@gmail.com

**Centrum Zeglarski** ☎+48 91 460 0844
www.zentrumzeglarskie.pl
biuro@centrumzeglarskie.pl

**Camping Marina** ☎+48 91 460 11 65
www.campingmarina.pl
campingmarina@campingmarina.pl

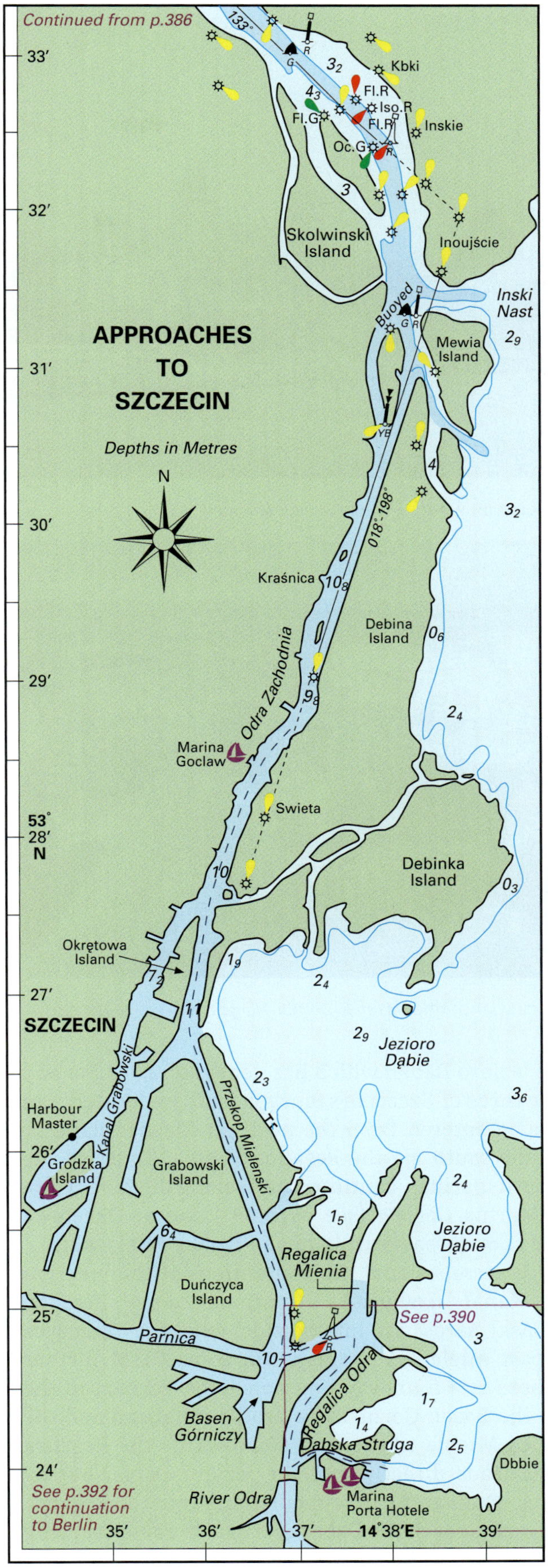


### *General*
Szczecin (pronounced *Sheh-chen-chin*) was a Slavic fishing and trading port from the 9th century, and today is the seventh largest city in Poland. In spite of its distance from the sea it remains one of Poland's major ports and is an important shipbuilding and ship repair centre. It has extensive waterways bordered by trees and fields and there are historic monuments dating from the 14th century, although the city was very severely damaged during the Second World War.

### *Approach*
Waypoint 53°42′N 14°29′.1E

From the Zalew Szczeciński and Trzebież the ship channel follows the Odra River south to Szczecin. It is clearly marked and dredged to a minimum of 10m. Although some areas outside the fairway have adequate depths, shoal areas also exist just close to the main channel.

Szczecin city wharf *Miranda Delmar-Morgan*

Szczecin panorama *Miranda Delmar-Morgan*

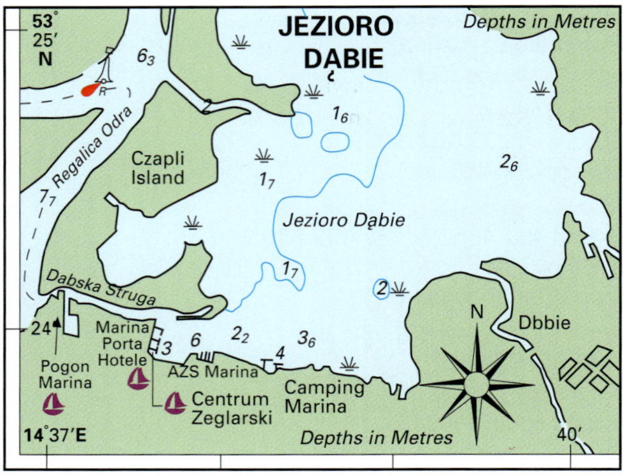


The Jezioro Dąbie, which has depths of 2.3–3.5m and where three of Szczecin's four marinas are located, can either be entered from the north at Mewia Island or from the south via the Regalica Mienia. To reach the southern marinas, continue south along the River Odra past Marina Gocław (see page 391) and at Okrętowa island take the eastern channel, Przekop Mieleński.

Large vessels signal their intentions at the junction with Kanał Grabowski. Continue along Przekop Mieleński across its intersection with the Dunczyca and past Mielenski island until, some 0.8M further on, there is a four-way junction – the Parnica to the west, the Basen Górniczy (a dead end) ahead and the Regalica Mienia to the east. Northwards the Regalica Mienia leads directly into the Jezioro Dąbie, but by turning south at the first opportunity into the Regalica Odra yachts reach the Dąbska Struga, the canal serving Pogon Marina, Marina Porta Hotele, the Centrum Zeglarski and the AZS Yacht Club (see page 391).

The entrance to the canal is distinctively marked on the starboard hand by the bridge superstructure of a large ship set on dry land but beware the long spit which extends 20m into the river on the northern side of the entrance.

### *Berthing*

All of the marinas listed below are at the southern end of the Dąbie Lake and can be approached via the lake, but it is littered with stakes and very shallow, so the canals provide the main access. They are some distance from town but well served by buses.

### NorthEast Marina Szczecin

53°25'.6N 14°34'.2E

This marina is on Grodzka island, opposite the town, just below the fixed bridge. This is much more handy than the more established marinas and is closer to town than those in the Dąbie Lake.

Depths of 2.5–5m depths. There is a bus service into town and a great view of the city. The marina has WiFi and most facilities in place including a pump-out station, but no diesel – that is 1km away. There are just over 25 visitors' berths and 50 residents.

The town quayside has excellent shower, toilet and laundry facilities behind the Tourist Office. The quayside is quite busy with ferry traffic which causes wash.

Gocław Marina, Szczecin *Miranda Delmar-Morgan*

## Marina Gocław
53°28'.45N 14°36'E

A pleasant yacht harbour situated at Gocław, on the west bank of the main channel about 2M north of the city centre and 20mins away by bus or tram. Mooring is bows to the quayside and stern to a buoy in about 4m.

The marina is quiet and totally sheltered and facilities are reasonable. Some food is available in the hotel, part of the marina complex, and there is a small shop across the road. Water and electricity on the quayside and showers ashore. It is possible to arrange for diesel to be delivered in containers and the garage is around 1km away. It has a mast crane, much used by German yachts exiting or entering the German canal system. There is a boatyard (with no marina facilities) a short distance to the south.

## Pogoń Marina
53°24'N 14°37'.2E

Pogoń Marina lies on the south side of the Dąbska Struga near its junction with the Regalica Odra and about 500m west of the Marina Porta Hotele. It is not as large as its neighbour, with fewer facilities but in equally pleasant surroundings, and is better suited to smaller yachts. There are around 20 guest berths and 240 residents.

## Marina Club
54°24'N 14°37'.2E

This marina is the most expensive and is situated in pleasant surroundings at the southern end of the Jezioro Dąbie. It is reached via the Dębska Struga, passing the Pogon Marina en route. New pontoons, with approx depths of 2.5–4m. Marina Club has all facilities and a fuel berth. There is a mast crane.

## Jacht Klub AZS Marina
A most welcoming marina in the two basins adjacent to Marina Club. Depths are 2–2.5m in the northern basin and 1.5–2m in the southern one, though the inshore side of both basins is quite shallow, so take care the further you head in. Berths outside the basins carry depths of 3–5m.

### *Services for yachts*
Centrum Żeglarskie has an enormous Dornier Flying Boat hanger dating from the 1920s which provides winter storage, and slippage and craneage. There is a sailmaker and a well-stocked chandlery (Sail Store, Przestrzenna 3, 70-800 Szczecin – www.sailstore.pl).

Pogon Marina has the usual facilities, sells Campinggaz and has a marine electronics outlet.

AZS Marina (Academic Yacht Club) has the usual facilities as well as a Taverna type bar/restaurant.

Camping Marina allows sailors from adjacent marinas to use their laundry facilities. Berths are exposed to the fetch of the Dąbie Lake.

For charts there is a Smart chandlery and Aquarius Marine Services in Szczecin.

### *General facilities*
Szczecin has all the facilities of a major city, including some good shops, banks and restaurants. The Marina Club has a restaurant, and there is a good supermarket in Dąbie, a short (2km) bus ride east of the marina.

### *Communications & travel*
Transport to the city centre, about 4km by road, involves a change from bus to tram at Basen Górniczy where tickets for both the bus and the tram are sold. There are good train services to all parts of Poland and, via Berlin, to the rest of Europe.

The airport for Szczecin is at Goleniów, 45km north. Direct flights from UK with Wizz Air, Ryanair, and LOT.

### *Caution*
Within the port area, yachts and other small craft must always yield to ship movements. *The Baltic Pilot Volume II* (NP 19) includes extensive instructions for these areas and the ship turning basins.

Gocław Marina entrance *Miranda Delmar-Morgan*

# RIVER AND CANAL PASSAGE SZCZECIN TO BERLIN

NV Map/guides cover the passage. These are obtainable from Imray www.imray.com, www.hansenautic.de or www.sail-ho.pl at Gdynia

Many German yachts unstep their masts to make this trip twice a year, between their winter moorings near Berlin and their summer sailing ground of the Baltic. The usual route is by the West Oder and the Oder-Havel Kanal which then gives access to the German canal system.

### *Pilotage notes*

***Draught*** Passage may be made by either the West Oder (Odra) or the East Oder. The West Odra has much less current, and its recommended draught is officially 1.8m, though up to 2m is thought to be safe. There is a connection between the two rivers about 25M south of Sczcecin which can provide a compromise, as the limiting section of the West Oder is the dredged section approaching the locks at Oder-Havel Kanal. There may be more depth in the East Oder, which is the main river, but as such is faster flowing and more subject to depth/current variations according to the weather further inland.

Advice should be sought before leaving Sczcecin. There is lock access to the canal from either Oder.

***Air draught*** The official recommendation is 4m, but a motor yacht with an air draught of 4.2m is known to have made safe passage in August 2019, reporting a minimum clearance of 30cm. This is despite markings of 3.45m and 3.75m on the first two bridges in central Sczcecin, which is thought to refer to winter flood conditions. Any vessel contemplating passage should check the current conditions with the Sczcecin harbourmaster before departure. There is a relatively new shiplift at Niederfinow, clearance is 4.4m.

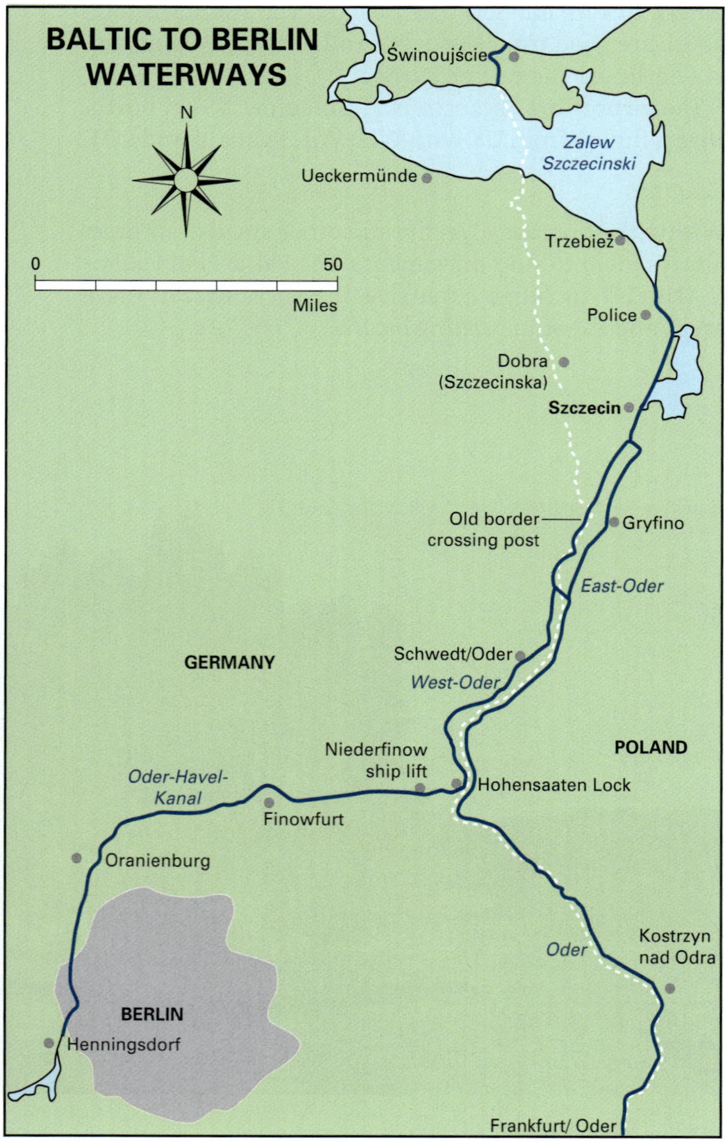


### *Distance & time*

106M (GPS distance) should take about four days cruising at 5.5–6kn.

### *Formalities*

None, both countries being part of the Schengen area. 10M south of Szczecin is the now abandoned Polish/German border crossing where it is possible to stop overnight. There are no facilities.

### *Moorings & facilities*

Hohensaaten Lock is 35M from Szczecin where you leave the West Oder River and join the Oder-Havel Kanal.

4M past the lock is Marina Oderberg ✆+49 33369 75540 www.marina-oderberg.de. Draught is restricted to 1.8m. Full facilities including a good restaurant. The town of Oderberg is 1.5M further on, with basic shops and small supermarket.

66M beyond the marina are the ship lifts at Niederfinow. This huge piece of canal engineering, built to replace a series of four conventional locks, is one of the biggest in Europe, lifting vessels something over 30m. Air draught is 4.4m with little prospect of ever increasing. Shortly after this there is a one-way section of canal which changes traffic direction at set times during the day. Leisure craft do not appear to be required to comply, the canal being wide enough to permit a yacht to pass an on-coming barge with care.

Near the town of Oranienburg there is an anchorage in the lake immediately south of the Schleuse Lehnitz lock in 3.5m. This is suitable for an overnight stop. The lake near Oranienburg has been dredged for sand. The bottom outside the marked channel is very uneven and shelves steeply.

Leave the Oder-Havel canal after Henningsdorf and enter the lake area west of Berlin. One lock, then via a short canal to the River Spree. There is a wide choice of places to moor, some free, in and around Berlin. The central ones, though free and convenient, have no facilities and are subject to continual disturbance from passing river traffic. Generally more remote places are preferable, and most have readily available public transport to the city centre.

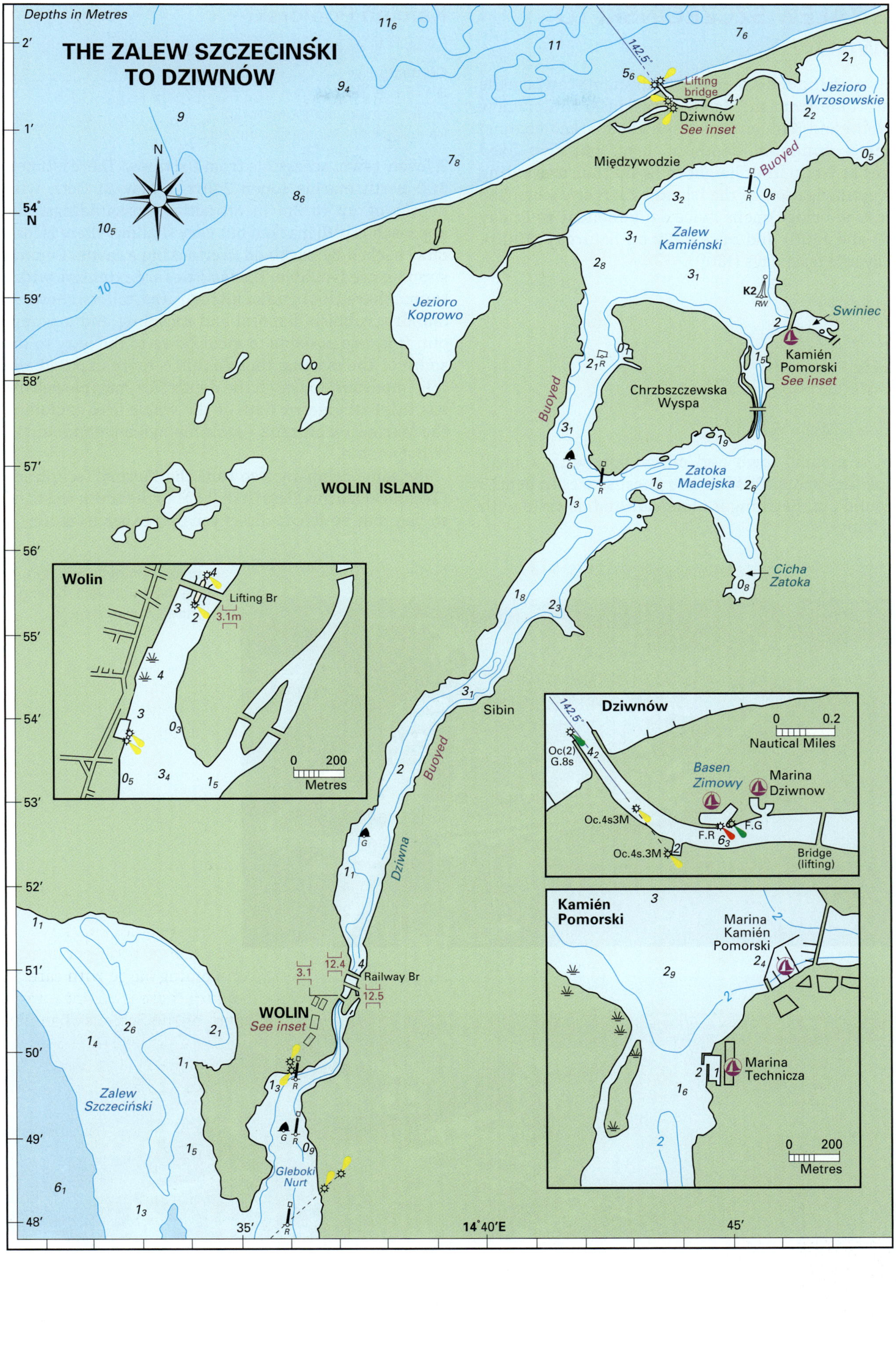
Depths in Metres
THE ZALEW SZCZECIŃSKI TO DZIWNÓW
Lifting bridge
Dziwnów
See inset
Jezioro Wrzosowskie
Międzywodzie
Buoyed
Zalew Kamiénski
K2
RW
Swiniec
Kamién Pomorski
See inset
Jezioro Koprowo
Chrzbszczewska Wyspa
Zatoka Madejska
Cicha Zatoka
WOLIN ISLAND
Sibin
Dziwna
Railway Br
WOLIN
See inset
Zalew Szczeciński
Gleboki Nurt
14°40′E
Wolin
Lifting Br
3.1m
Metres
Dziwnów
Nautical Miles
Oc(2) G.8s
Basen Zimowy
Marina Dziwnow
Oc.4s3M
F.R
F.G
Oc.4s.3M
Bridge (lifting)
Kamién Pomorski
Marina Kamién Pomorski
Marina Techniczna
Metres

## THE ZALEW SZCZECIŃSKI TO DZIWNÓW

Yachts with limited water and air draughts can take the inland route from the Zalew Szczeciński to Dziwnów via Wolin and Kamień Pomorski. The marked channel carries a minimum depth of 1.7m, but two fixed bridges at Wolin limit height to 12.4m thus preventing a circumnavigation of the island by larger yachts. The lower road bridge opens twice daily Monday to Friday (0900 and 1600) and once daily on Saturday (1000), Sunday and feast days (1300).

### Wolin

53°51'N 14°37'E

**Contacts**

✆+48 530 102 602
www.gminawolin.pl
dyrektor.ckis@gminawolin.pl

Wolin is a small town and minor port with a small marina for yachts. This has five guest spaces in depths of around 2m. Berthing is alongside and bows-to with stern buoys.

### Kamień Pomorski

53°58'N 14°46'E

**Contacts**

✆+48 661 213 391
www.marinakamienpomorski.pl
kontakt@marinakamienpomorski.pl

A lovely town, accessible from Dziwnów. There is a new 300 berth marina (open 24hrs, 1 May–31 Oct), with depths of up to 2m in attractive surroundings. The approach is well marked but very shallow. There is long quay backed by parkland overlooking a castle. General supplies are available. The facilities are extensive with a sauna, shared lounge and kitchen area, toilets, showers, laundry, rubbish disposal and recycling and a pump-out. It is also possible to moor bows-to the jetty to the south of the marina, though this is more exposed and it is important to watch the depth. The marina website has full bathymetric data of the whole area including the Marina Techniczna – www.marinakamienpomorski.pl/batymetria.

The same company also runs the Marina Techniczna (Technical marina) less than 0.5M to the south west and so they may be able to direct you to free berths there.

Kamień Pomorski marina from the southwest looking northeast *Andy Beharrell*

The Marina Techniczna from the southwest. Kamień Pomorski marina can be seen in the background *Andy Beharrell*

# 5B. COAST OF POLAND

## DZIWNÓW

54°01'N 14°44'E

**Distances**
Świnoujście 20M, Kołobrzeg 30M

**Lights**
**Świnoujście** 53°55'N 14°17'.1E
Oc.WR.5s65m25/9M
Yellow round tower on red building 65m
**Kikut** 53°59'N 14°34'.9E Iso.10s91m16M
Grey round stone tower, white lantern 18m
**Niechorze** 54°05'.8N 15°03'.9E Fl.10s63m20M Grey octagonal tower and red building
**Leading Lights 142.5°** *Front* 54°01'.2N 14°43'.8E
Oc.4s8m3M White diamond on white metal framework tower
*Rear* 130m from front, Oc.4s13m3M
White rectangle on red and white framework tower
**West breakwater** 54°01'.4N 14°43'.5E Oc(2)G.8s10m7M Column
**East breakwater** 54°01'.5N 14°43'.6E Oc(2)R.8s10m7M Column Horn Mo(A)60s

**Contacts**
**Dziwnów Harbourmaster** ✆+48 91 3813 340
VHF Ch 10
**Dziwnów Port Control** ✆+48 91 381 3754/3642
VHF Ch 10/16
**Opening bridge** ✆+48 6912 90865, VHF Ch 10
**Marina Bosman** ✆+48 501 958 836
**Marina Dziwnów**
www.port.dziwnow.pl
marinadziwnow@gmail.com
✆+48 91 38 11 235

### General

Dziwnów (pronounced *Jiv-noof*) set amongst trees, is an attractive small fishing and holiday resort at the mouth of the Dziwnów River, which links to the Jezioro Wrzosowskie and Zalew Kamieński lakes and thence to the Zalew Szczeciński. To the west lies Wolin island and to the east the Polish mainland.

### Approach

54°01'.4N 14°43'.5E western molehead

The coastline on either side consists of low forested hills and sandy beaches, with no off-lying dangers. Entrance is straightforward using the 142.5° leading line although the leading marks can be difficult to see because of trees. Depths are 4.2m in the entrance and 5m inside.

***Warning*** In winds over Force 5 from the west or northwest the entrance can be dangerous and should not be attempted. About 0.6M inside the entrance (beyond the yacht berths) lies an opening bridge (with 2.2m air draught when closed) which operates on request.

### Berthing

The Dziwnów Marina, with depths of 3.5m, on the north side of the channel has good shelter. It has finger pontoons but space is quite tight, and it soon fills up. Yachts can raft onto the outside moles up to about three deep but after that, and for yachts over 12m it may be best to go through the bridge and try the Kamień Pomorski or Techniczna marinas.

The bridge (VHF Ch 10) opens on demand on the even hours. Call with estimated time of arrival (24hrs). It remains closed in winds of Force 6 and above.

An alternative for smaller boats might be the pontoons 1M to the east of the bridge. There is space here for 30 guests in over 3m on small finger pontoons. There is a café and restaurant here as well.

### Facilities

Dziwnów marina has a clubhouse with bar, laundry facilities and WiFi. Very helpful staff will organize bike hire. There is a bunker station to port beyond the bridge. General shopping, banks and small restaurants are available in the town. There is a supermarket 200m away.

An aerial view of Dziwnów marina *Andy Beharrell*

# KOŁOBRZEG

54°11'N 15°33'E (east mole head)

## Distances

Świnoujście 50M, Dziwnów 30M, Darłowo 30M

## Lights

**Niechorze** 54°05'.8N 15°03'.9E Fl.10s63m20M
Grey octagonal tower and red building
**Dźwirzyno** 54°09'.6N 15°23'.4E Oc.R.4s7m6M
Red post
**Kołobrzeg** 54°11'.3N 15°33'.4E Fl.3s36m16M
Red round tower, black cupola
**Koł light buoy** 54°13'.5N 15°30'.6E LFl.10s
Red and white pillar buoy, b topmark
**West breakwater** 54°11'.4N 15°33'.2E Oc.G.4s11m7M
Green round column, two galleries
**East breakwater** 54°11'.5N 15°33'.2E Oc.R.4s
Red round column, two galleries Horn Mo(K)60s
**Gaski** 54°14'.7N 15°52'.5E Oc(3)15s50m23M Red round tower, gallery and cupola

## Contacts

Kołobrzeg harbourmaster ☎+48 94 352 2703 (0730–1530 LT Monday–Friday)
Port Control ☎+48 94 352 2799, VHF Ch 12/16
Solna Marina *Mobile* ☎+48 785 882 842
www.zpmkolobrzeg.pl
sekretariat@zpmkolobrzeg.pl

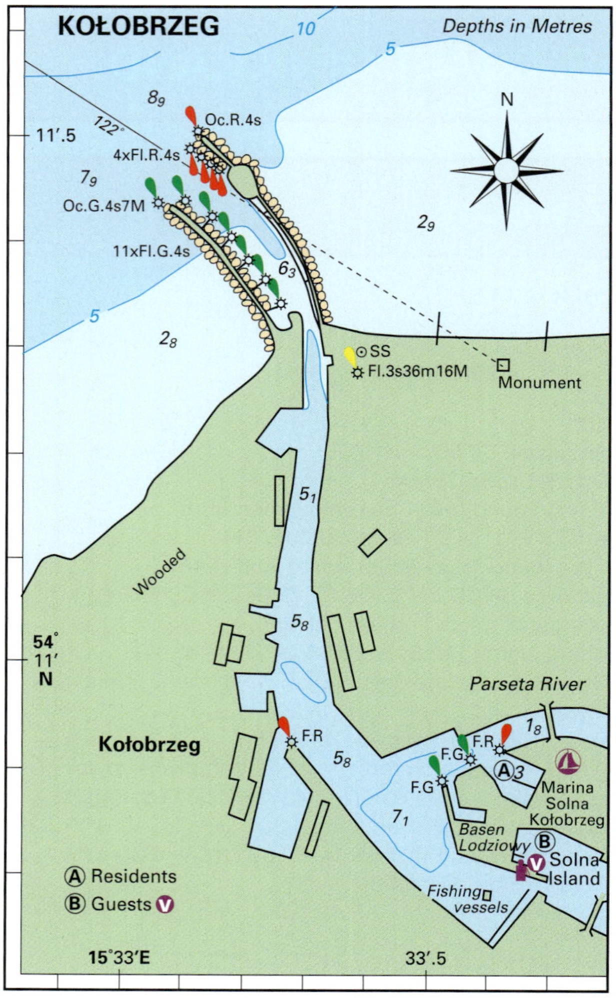

An aerial view of Kołobrzeg marina. The basin for visitors is on the right and Solna marina can be seen on the left by the bridge. This is for residents only *Andy Beharrell*

The entrance channel to Kołobrzeg

*General*

Kołobrzeg (pronounced *Co-wob-jeck*) is a tourist resort and commercial and fishing harbour, the largest on the long stretch of coast between Świnoujście and Gdynia. The harbour entrance has a boardwalk, popular with tourists who gather to watch the maritime activities, and a long seafront promenade with shops and cafés. Near the marina stand parts of the walls of a fort built in 1774, where there is now a café and bar and music is played on summer evenings. It is a busy place with an industrial port. Rail links to Szczecin. Customs point.

*Approach*

The approach channel lies on a bearing of 148° from the Koł landfall buoy, though the surrounding coast is clear of off-lying hazards. Two curved concrete moles extend from the entrance, the red structure on the port hand one being particularly prominent. Keep the needle-like monument 'Marriage to the Sea' on a bearing of 122° and when the eastern molehead is abeam you can turn into the port. The large brick lighthouse can also be seen from well offshore.

Vessels up to 85m use the port and the channel is very narrow, so it is essential to call Port Control (VHF Ch 12) in advance. The entrance itself is narrow and is subject to swell from west through northwest. It can also be affected by strong cross-currents, depending on wind strength and direction. Extensive alterations and bright yellow baffles have been added to the moles to improve safety. Depths are 5-6m in the entrance and harbour, decreasing to 3m in the marina basin.

Do not confuse the illuminated pleasure pier 800m to the east with the entrance.

Beware of tourist 'pirate ships' which are busy in summer and also fishing nets anywhere along the adjacent coast where there are small fishing villages. They can be found well out at sea.

***Warning*** In west or northwest winds over Force 5 the entrance can be dangerous and should not be attempted.

*Berthing*

Kołobrzeg Marina (Marina Solna) lies 0.6M inside the entrance at the northwest end of Solna island. It is for residents only. A basin with 250 visitor berths has been excavated to the south of Marina Solna and small signs labeled *'goście'* (guests) direct you onwards to the new basin. Yachts requiring depths greater than 3m can lie on the outside of the Basen Lodziowy quay.

*Facilities*

Facilities in Marina Solna are excellent and available to all visitors, and the staff are multi-lingual. It has its own Harbourmaster office and ablutions. Finger pontoons are quite long and well-spaced. There is a bar/restaurant at Marina Solna and in the Redoubt. The attractive town is a short distance away and has open air cafes and good shops. There is a sailmaker and yachts can be slipped and repairs carried out. Diesel is available 0900-1300.

## DARŁOWO

54°26'.5N 16°22'.5E (west mole head)

### Distances
Kołobrzeg 32M, Ustka 22M

### Lights
**Gaski** 54°14'.7N 15°52'.5E Oc(3)15s50m23M
Red round tower with gallery and cupola
**E. Mole near root** 54°26'.4N 16°22'.7E LFl(2)15s20m15M
Red square tower with white gallery and dome
**Jaroslawiec** 54°32'.3N 16°32'.6E Fl(2)9s50m23M
Red round tower with white dome

### Contacts
Harbourmaster ☎+48 94 314 2683 or +48 94 314 2485 VHF Ch 12
Marina Manager ☎ *Mobile* +48 509 462 214 www.marina.darlowo.pl/en
Opening Bridge ☎+48 94 314 2976 VHF Ch 12
SAR VHF Ch 11/16 ☎+48 505 050 975

### *General*
Darłowo port is a 10 minute ferry ride from the town, which is attractive, with well-preserved historical sites, and well worth a visit. King Erik, who was the last king of Scandinavia, was married to a daughter of Henry V of England and made Darłowo his base for piratical raids on Scandinavia after he was deposed and banished, hence all the pirate ships. It is a popular holiday resort with an outdoor sea pool and lots of restaurants.

### *Approach*
In fair conditions the approach is straightforward, but the entrance itself is narrow and curved. Depths are around 4m, but an uncomfortable surge can enter in strong winds from between west and north.

A retracting bridge 0.5M inside the entrance opens on the hour (24hrs) when craft are waiting, and by special arrangement. Commercial ships use this port and the canal is very narrow. Permission to enter or leave must be sought on VHF Ch 12. Yachts awaiting a bridge opening can lie on the seaward wharfside but will be uncomfortable in onshore winds when a bad scend will build.

***Warnings*** The entrance is dangerous in onshore winds over Force 5 and susceptible to cross currents. There are firing ranges, Areas 6, 6a, 6b and 6c between Darłowo and Ustka (see under Ustka, page 400, for details). It is possible to call the harbourmaster on VHF Ch 12 before entering to check on conditions at the entrance.

### *Berthing*
Darłowo has marina facilities and a clubhouse, with finger pontoons in the Basen Rybacki, which was the fishing harbour. In severe conditions if a scend is entering the marina then lying alongside up the river may provide more shelter but there are no facilities here.

Basen Zimowy on the west side of the canal has pontoons and has electricity, toilets, showers and laundry.

### *Facilities*
The clubhouse has excellent facilities (including WiFi), but there is no fuel. Strong winds might carry dust and grit from the shipyard across the marina. Very nice staff who will greet you late at night. The marina is popular with local boats and is busy in high season.

A local garage (Orlen BP on the west side of the river) about 2km away in town will refill gas bottles if given notice. Basic supplies can be obtained in the port area and across the foot bridge. The interesting town can be reached by the ferry or the riverside walk and has plenty of shops and hardware stores.

Retracting bridge at Darłowo *Miranda Delmar-Morgan*

Darłowo marina – looking out from the clubhouse *Darłowo harbourmaster*

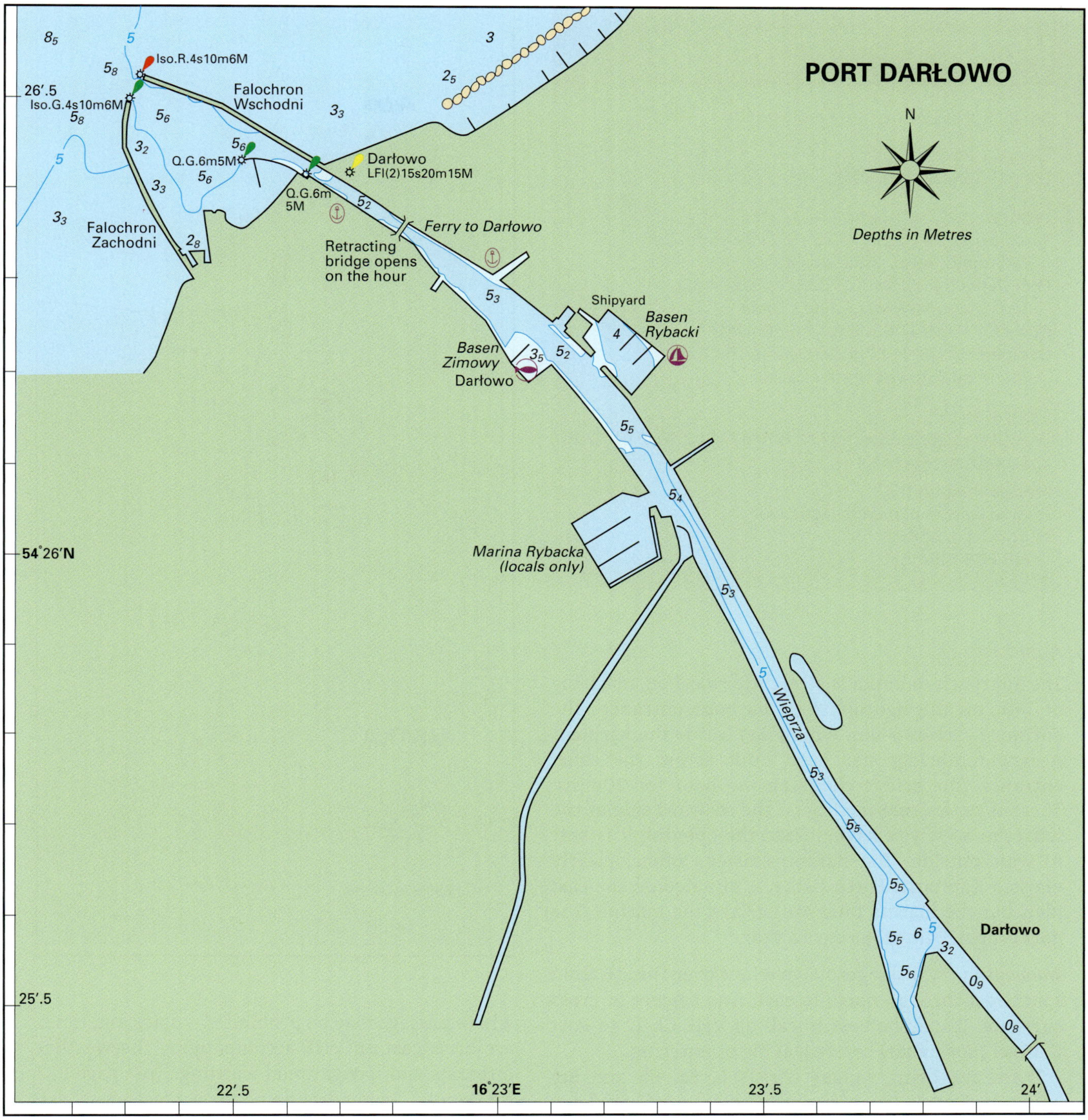

The clubhouse at Darłowo marina and the guest pontoons
*Darłowo harbourmaster*

# USTKA

54°35'.50N 16°51'.0E (west mole head)

**Distances**
Daryowo 20M, Leba 30M

**Lights**
**Jaroslawiec** 54°32'.3N 16°32'.6E Fl(2)9s50m23M
Red round tower, white dome
**Port Ustka** 54°35'.3N 16°51'.3E Oc.6s22m8M
Red octagonal tower, white cupola.
**Rowy** 54°40'.1N 17°03'.1E Iso.Y.6s10m2M
**Czołpino** 54°43'.1N 17°14'.5E Oc(2)8s75m22M
Round brick tower, black cupola

**Contacts**
Port Control (Bosmanat) ✆+48 660 477 563, VHF Ch 12/16
kpustka@umgdy.gov.pl
Medical help ✆ 112
www.ustkaport.pl/marina-jachtowa/
biuro@ustka.port.pl
✆+48 885 515415

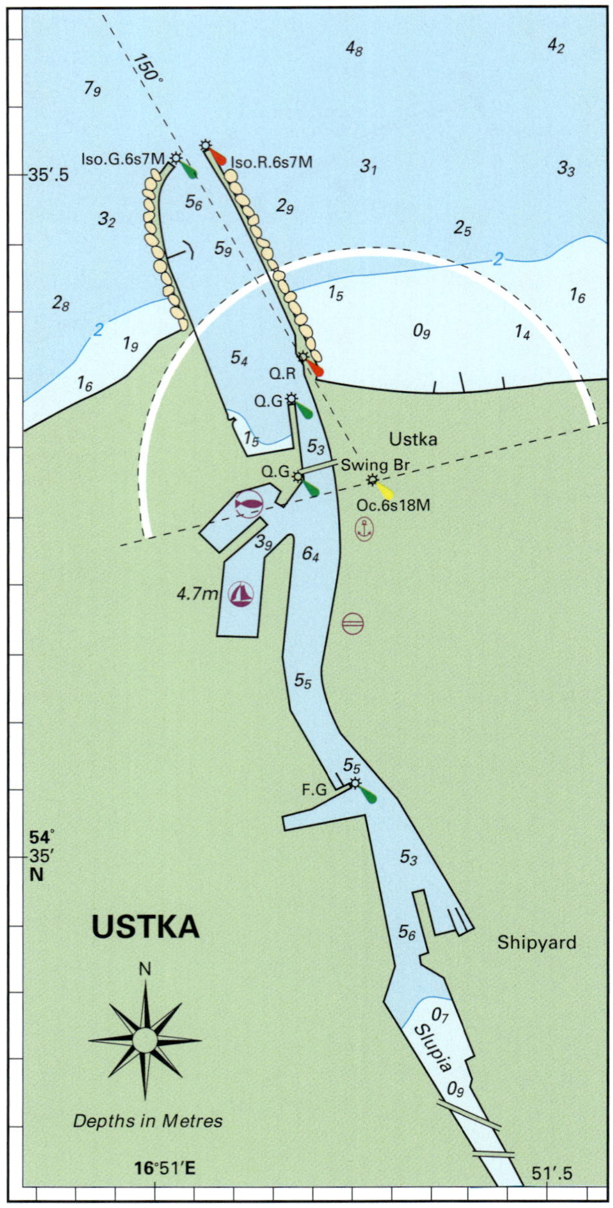


*Approach*

The approach to Ustka is straightforward on a bearing of 150° on the lighthouse or harbour entrance. The entrance carries 5-6m, with 4-5m inside the harbour. A new footbridge has been built across the canal entrance. The bridge closes on the hour for 20mins. There is no waiting facility on the seaward side of the wharves, so if you have missed the opening it is best to wait outside. The harbourmaster's office, clearly marked Kapitanat Portu Ustka, is situated on the east pier, but the marina dues are paid at the marina. The port is open 24hrs, 365 days a year.

*Warnings* Entry is dangerous in winds over Force 6 from southwest through north to east. And beware of cross currents. It may be best to call on VHF Ch 12 to Port Control (Bosmanat) before leaving or entering.

There are firing ranges (Areas 6, 6a, 6b and 6c) between Ustka (pronounced *Oostka*) and Darłowo where passage may be prohibited – dates and times are broadcast on VHF accompanying the weather forecasts and navigational warnings (see page 383 for details). In general firing takes place every day

Aerial view of the yacht harbour at Ustka looking south *Andy Beharrell*

The footbridge at Ustka. The bridge closes on the hour for 20mins *Andy Beharrell*

0500–0200 the next day (except Sun, Mon and public holidays). It may be necessary to make a long diversion out to sea. Patrol craft are in attendance.

### *Berth*

The harbour is mainly devoted to fishing, with some commercial traffic, and is also a popular holiday resort. There are two basins immediately beyond the bridge to starboard. The northern one is for fishing vessels and the southern one has been developed as a marina for yachts up to 12m. The pontoon fingers are quite small and soon fill with local yachts but it is possible to lie alongside the quays.

Larger yachts can also berth alongside on the quay on the east side of the harbour clear of a crane and the SAR vessel. Swell may enter the harbour in strong northerlies and the canal and basins are subject to severe surge in adverse conditions. Call the harbour authorities during the day to check if conditions are better on the quay and you may be able to move from the marina to the quay.

### *Facilities*

Showers and toilets are in a block resembling a portacabin, for use by sailors and fishermen. There is a good selection of shops in town.

Aerial view of the footbridge at Ustka looking northeast over the fishing basin *Andy Beharrell*

## ŁEBA

54°47'.11N 17°33'.80E (safe water RW buoy)

### Distances

Kołobrzeg 85M, Darłowo 55M, Ustka 30M, Władysławowo 30M, Gdynia 65M

### Lights

**Czołpino** 54°43'.3N 17°14'.6E Oc(2)8s75m22M
Round brick tower, black cupola 25m
**Dir Lt 203°** 54°46'.1N 17°33'E Dir.WRG.7m8–6M
**GW buoy Łeba** 54°47'.2N 17°32'.5E LFl.10s Red and white pillar buoy, b topmark
**West breakwater** 54°46'.2N 17°33'E Q.10m5M
**Marina breakwater** 54°45'.9N 17°33'E F.G.
**Stilo** 54°47'.3N 17°44'.2E Fl(3)12s75m23M
Red, white and black banded tower 33m

### Contacts

Łeba Harbourmaster ☎+48 59 866 2973 (0730–1530 LT)

Łeba Port Control (Bosmanat) ☎+48 59 866 1530/8
VHF Ch 12

Łeba Marina ☎+48 59 866 1735
*Mobile* +48 605 668 427, VHF Ch 12/16/17
www.port.leba.eu/pl/port

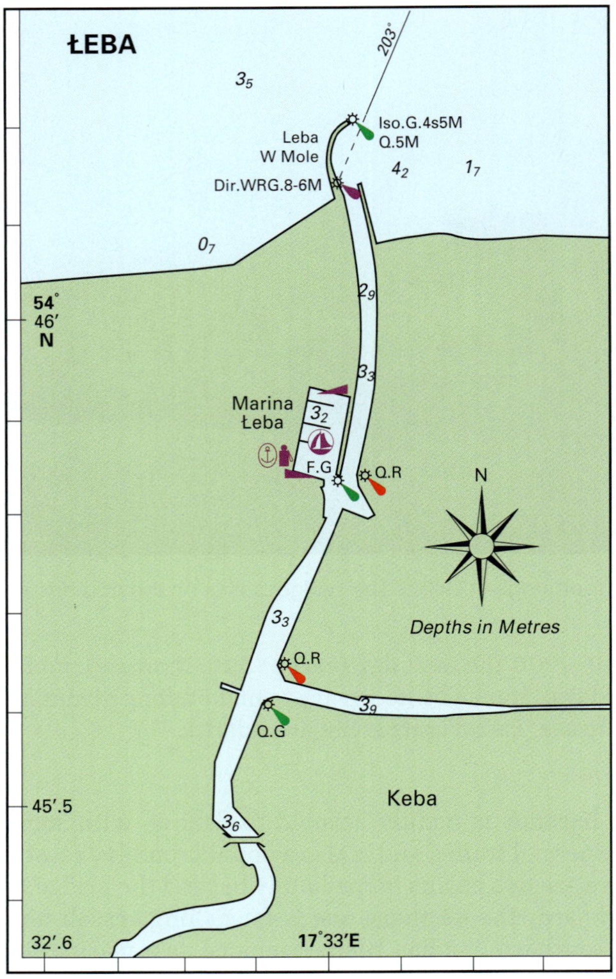

Aerial view of Łeba Marina looking north *Andy Beharrell*

### General

Łeba (pronounced *Weh-ba*) is a popular tourist resort with a small commercial and fishing harbour. The relatively new yacht marina with all facilities is on the starboard hand just inside the entrance. Łeba is close to the Slowinski National Park, a UNESCO Biosphere Reserve with forests, lakes and beautiful shimmering sand dunes.

### Approach

Between Ustka and Łeba the Traffic Separation Scheme (TSS) Słupska Bank East has an inshore traffic zone for vessels less than 20m. Czołpino lighthouse to the west is obscured by trees apart from the lantern.

The suggested approach is made on a bearing of 203° from the Łeba light buoy, heading for the leading light tower which is on a white column on the west mole. Whilst there are no offlying hazards the adjacent depths are very shoal. There is a very tall white column on the east mole supporting radar.

Entry is made between two curved concrete breakwaters – it is both shallow (2.5m to sometimes as little as 1-1.5m after storms) and narrow. Call on VHF Ch 12 before entering to check the depth. A signal mast is on the port hand close to the entrance and shows Traffic Safety Signals.

The Port Control Office is on the eastern side in a bungalow. Request permission to enter or leave from Port Control on VHF Ch 12. Port Control will provide guidance in poor visibility.

*Warning* The entrance shoals and although it gets dredged regularly it is dangerous in winds over Force 5 from west to northeast through north. Also beware of cross currents and there can be an outflow of up to 2kn from Lake Łebsko.

### Berthing

The marina is just beyond it to starboard and needs a sharp starboard turn to enter. Łeba Marina has 120 berths inside a long eastern wall which blocks swell entering from the main harbour entrance, however it still suffers from surge. Mooring is alongside thin finger pontoons and yachts of up to 24–26m can be accommodated in depths of 2.3–3m, though there is up to 4m in a few places and it can be as shallow as 1.5m. Berths towards the north side of the marina appear to be silting and are shallower. Larger yachts berth in the southwest corner. The marina office is clearly marked in English and staff will assist with mooring.

### *Facilities*

Water and electricity on the marina pontoons, with showers, and laundry facilities. WiFi. Diesel berth in the marina. There is a boatyard nearby, and a winter storage facility is planned for the marina site, but as yet no chandlery. The marina and its facilities are notably well maintained and the staff, who speak English and German, will assist with information about the harbour and town.

There is a bar/restaurant in the marina complex, and some overnight accommodation on the upper floor. Shopping is to be found in the town. There is an ATM 500m to the south near the bridge and a Polo supermarket across the bridge. Bicycles can be hired for exploration of the National Park.

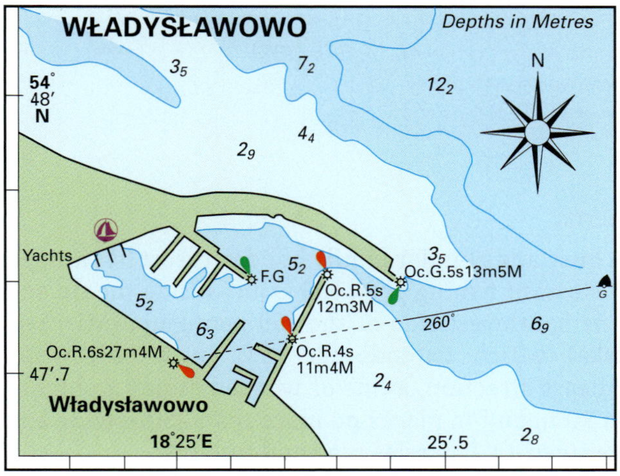


## WŁADYSŁAWOWO

58°47'.87N 18°26'.53E (safe water mark)

### Distances

Kołobrzeg 115M, Ustka 60M, Łeba 30M, Hel 22M, Gdynia 30M, Gdańsk 32M

### Lights

**Rozewie** 54°49'.8N 18°20'.2E Fl.3s83m26M
Red round tower, red top, two galleries
**Landfall buoy** 54°47'.8N 18°26'.5E LFl.10sRW buoy
**Leading Lights** 260° *Front* E Breakwater 54°47'.7N 18°25'.2E Oc.R.6s14m4M Yellow framework tower
*Rear* Ldg Lt 245m from front Oc.R.6s22m4M
On roof of building
**Jastarnia** 54°42'N 18°40'.9E Mo(A)20s22m15M
White round tower, red bands, gallery

### Contacts

**Harbourmaster** ✆+48 58 674 0486
Bosmanat ✆+48 355 33 56 (Ring for information on firing ranges)
Marina ✆+48 501 417 937
**Port Control** ✆+48 58 674 0066, VHF Ch 10/16
www.szkuner.pl

### *General*

Władysławowo (pronounced *Vwah-dih-swa-vo-vo*) is an artificial harbour near the root of the Mierzeja Helska (Hel peninsula) and some 4M southeast of Rozewie Point, a prominent headland which forms Poland's northern most extremity. This is Poland's largest fishing port, landing between 25–35,000T of fish annually, but it has some facilities for a small number of yachts. It is also a popular holiday resort.

Aerial view of Władysławowo port looking west with the yacht berths in the background

### Approach

Just to the north west of Rozewie Lighthouse is an area marked as 'entry forbidden' on the chart for reasons unknown, and although there are no physical marks it is best to comply.

Straightforward approach and entrance on 260° from the landfall buoy with the front leading mark, which is a column on the east breakwater, 100m back from the east molehead, in line with the tall Dom Rybaka tower (see plan page 403) though care must be taken not to stray north of the approach line on closing the north breakwater. Keep an eye on the depth sounder during the approach as the sandbanks shift. There is a small green unlit buoy on the approach, and a red pillar buoy 300m east of the eastern end of the breakwater.

*Warnings* The approach is dangerous in winds over Force 5 from the north and east because of sandbanks.

Between Władysławowo and the eastern end of the Hel peninsula are two firing ranges (Areas 10 and 11) firing up to 10M out to sea. Firing times will need to be checked (see under firing ranges and navigational warnings on page 383).

### Berth

Berth on the yacht pontoons with fingers and stern buoys in the extreme west of the harbour clearly marked 'For Yachts Only'. Yachts can also lie on the southwest harbour wall, against tyres. The harbour carries a depth of 4m almost throughout.

### Facilities

There is water/electricity on the pontoons. Independently run showers/toilets near the shipyard/marina entrance opposite the harbourmaster's office.

There are shops/restaurants in town 1km to northwest of shipyard gate and also a shipyard with mechanical and electronic workshops. Trains to Hel, Gdynia and Gdańsk.

The yacht berths in Władysławowo harbour. The large fishing fleet can be seen in the background *Andy Beharrell*

## HEL

54°36'N 18°48'E

**Distances**

Łeba 52M, Władysławowo 22M, Gdynia 10M, Gdańsk 15M, Kaliningrad 30M, Klaipėda 105M

**Lights**

**Jastarnia** 54°42'N 18°40'.2E Mo(A)20s22m15M White round tower, red bands and gallery

**HL-S SCM** 54°35'.3N 18°48'E Q(6)+LFl.15s

**Hel** 54°36'N 18°48'.75E Iso.10s39m17M Red octagonal masonry tower with gallery vis 151°-102°

**Contacts**

Marina ✆+48 58 675 01 50

Port office ✆+48 58 675 08 08
porthel@home.pl
www.porthel.home.pl

Harbourmaster ✆+48 58 675 0618

Port Control ✆+48 58 675 0624, VHF Ch 10/16/71

Marina Manager ✆+48 58 675 0618
www.hel-miasto.pl
www.hel.pl

### General

This busy and popular family holiday resort has a small and pleasant fishing port. Hel is just inside the tip and on the southwest side of the Hel peninsula (Mierzeja Helska) which extends for 18M in a northwest/southeast direction, a line of wooded dunes no higher than 30m, and in places no more than 250m wide and quite steep-to. It carries road and rail links.

*Warning* Between the eastern end of the Hel Peninsula and Władysławowo are two firing ranges (Areas 10 and 11) firing up to 10M out to sea. Firing times will need to be checked (see page 383).

### Approach

54°35'.97N 18°47'.98E (west mole)
54°35'.30N 18°47'.90E (HL-S south cardinal buoy)

Approach from the south is straightforward but do not confuse the entrance with that of the naval harbour 1M to the northwest where entry is prohibited.

Approach from the north involves rounding the South cardinal mark at the end of a very shallow spit running out from the tip of the peninsula. Unlit nets are a real menace over the whole area, on both sides.

Commercial shipping in the area is moderately heavy, but yachts using the inshore traffic zone to Gdynia remain clear of the major separation scheme for the ports of Gdynia and Gdańsk.

### Berth

In the yacht basin on the west side of the harbour. Moor to pontoons or alongside in depths from 4-8m. Good shelter in north and westerlies, but subject to surge in

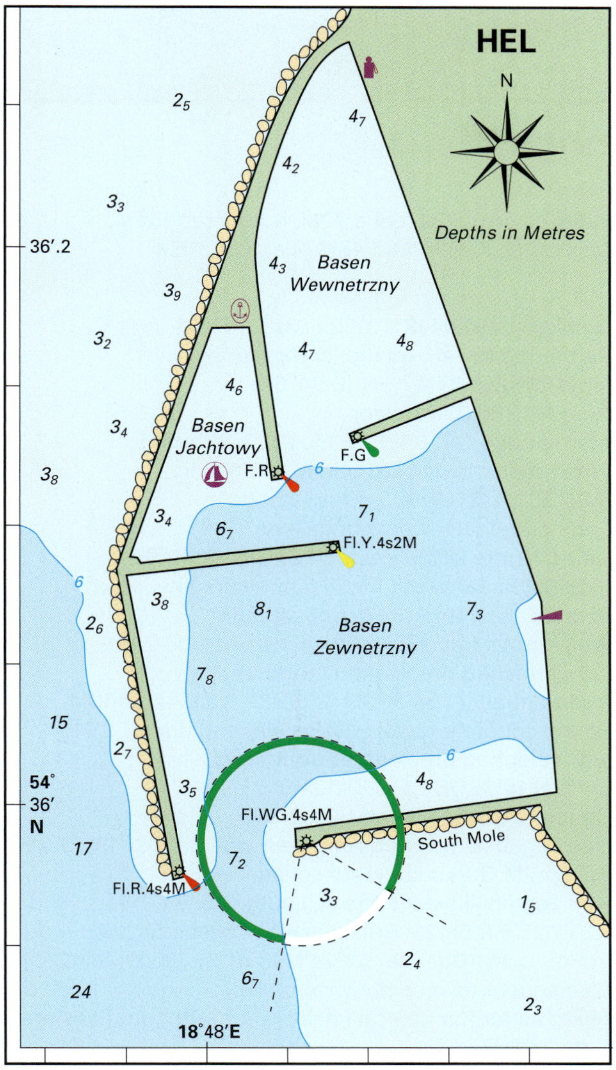


strong winds with southing in them, and pontoons can be noisy chafing against the piles.

### *Facilities*

Water on the quay and electricity on the pontoon. Showers/toilets are in the onion domed building on the breakwater. Diesel in the fishing harbour. Workshops and mobile crane on harbourside.

Shops and restaurants (including an 'Admiral Nelson' and a 'Captain Morgan' where there are menus in English) in the main street close to the harbour. Maritime Museum and a Baltic Seal aquarium. Trains to Gdynia and Gdańsk.

The onion-shaped marina office at Hel *Andy Beharrell*

Yacht berths at Hel *Andy Beharrell*

## JASTARNIA

54°40'.94N 18°40'.42E

**Distances**
Łeba 61M, Władysławowo 30M, Gdynia 11M

**Contacts**
Marina ☎+48 798 675 458, VHF Ch 10 (call *Bosman port Jastarnia* or *Bosman marina*)
mzp@jastarnia.pl
jastarnia.pl

*General*

Jastarnia is a convenient stop around halfway along the southern side of the Hel peninsula. There are 126 spaces in the marina overall including space amongst these for around 30 guests. There is around 5-6m of water throughout the harbour and plenty of space for manoeuvring.

The facilities are good with water, electricity, toilets, showers, laundry and a drier. The approach is straightforward with a well-buoyed channel, though it could be a little exposed in strong southerlies.

There is a slipway and travel lift which can handle boats up to 68T. Winter storage is also available for yachts up to 20m. There is a sailing school as well.

Aerial view of Jastarnia marina looking north across the Hel peninsula *Andy Beharrell*

## GDYNIA

54°32'N 18°33'E

**Distances**
Władysławowo 35M, Leba 70M, Kołobrzeg 155M, Gdańsk 10M, Kaliningrad 45M, Klaipėda 115M

**Lights**
**Rozewie** 54°49'.9N 18°20'.3E Fl.3s83m26M
Red round tower, red top, two galleries
**Władysławowo** 57°47'.8N 18°24'.6E
Aero F.R.78m23M Tower
**Jastarnia** 54°42'N 18°40'.9E Mo(A)20s22m15M
White round tower, red bands and gallery
**Hel** 54°36'.1N 18°48'.9E Iso.10s39m17M
Red octagonal tower with gallery
**Leading Lights 271.5°** *Front* 54°32'.2N 18°32'.9E
Oc.Y.5s15m8M White metal framework tower 15m
*Rear* 0.57M from front Oc.Y.5s30m8M
White metal framework tower, black stripe 24m
**South detached breakwater, north end**
(main entrance) 54°32'.1N 18°34'.8E Iso.R.4s15m10M
Round concrete tower with gallery and dome
**South detached breakwater, south end**
54°31'N 18°33'.7E Oc.G.10s12m9M
Concrete tower with glass cupola
**Basen żeglarski (yacht basin), east wall** 54°31'N 18°33'.2E
F.G.6m2M Green concrete column
**Basen żeglarski (yacht basin), south wall** 54°31'N
18°33'.2E F.R.5m2M Red concrete column on hut
**Port Północny (Gdańsk)** 54°24'N 18°41'.8E Fl(3)9s61m25M
Blue square tower with white gallery
***Note*** Lights for the central (main) and north entrances are not described

**Contacts**
Gdynia Harbourmaster ☎+48 58 621 0705/7983
VHF Ch 12

Gdynia Port Control ☎+48 58 621 6636, VHF Ch 12/16 (Yachts are required to monitor VHF Ch 12 and request permission to leave or enter the marina)

Gdynia Marina *Mobile* +48 785 174 719
VHF Ch 12 www.gdyniasport.pl/pl/obiekty/marina-gdynia
marina@gdyniasport.pl

Gdynia Yacht Club Marina *Mobile* +48 785 557 777
VHF Ch 12 www.marinayachtpark.pl
office@marinayachtpark.pl
Gdynia tourist information www.gdynia.pl/turystyczna-en

*General*

The Gulf of Gdańsk has two Traffic Separation Schemes running across it from the Hel Peninsula to the Gdynia and Gdańsk approaches. There are two prohibited areas to the north of Gdynia and several yellow buoys marking one of them. It also has further nets to avoid, and numerous sailing clubs with yachts, dinghies and frequent regattas. It is a very busy place. Gdynia (pronounced *Guh-din-ya*) is a major commercial and shipbuilding port. Most container traffic for Poland

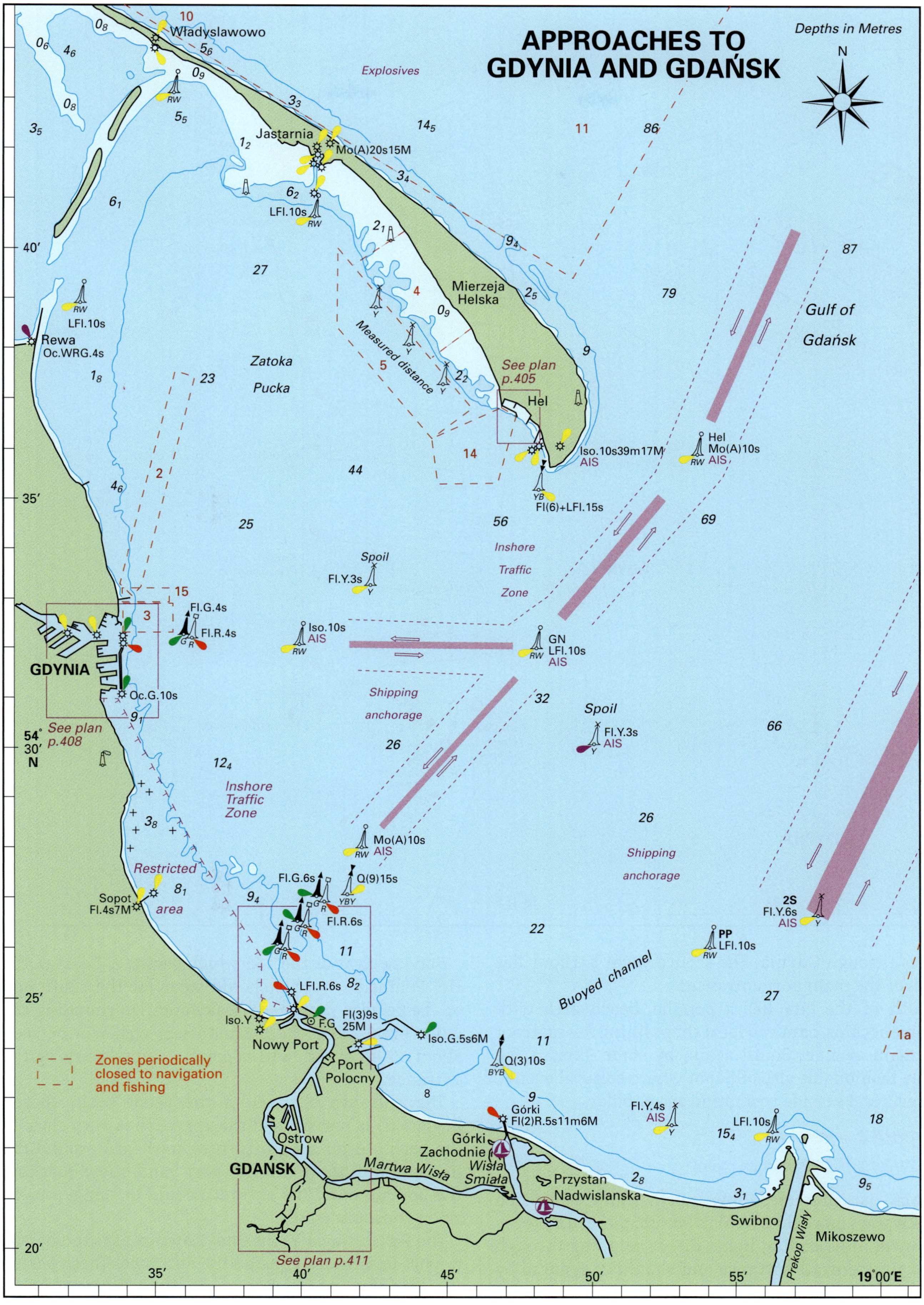

APPROACHES TO GDYNIA AND GDAŃSK
Depths in Metres
N
Władysławowo
Explosives
Jastarnia
Mo(A)20s15M
LFl.10s
Mierzeja Helska
Measured distance
See plan p.405
Hel
Iso.10s39m17M AIS
Hel Mo(A)10s AIS
Fl(6)+LFl.15s
Gulf of Gdańsk
Rewa
Oc.WRG.4s
Zatoka Pucka
Inshore Traffic Zone
Spoil
Fl.Y.3s
Fl.G.4s
Fl.R.4s
Iso.10s AIS
GN LFl.10s AIS
GDYNIA
Oc.G.10s
See plan p.408
54° 30′ N
Shipping anchorage
Fl.Y.3s AIS
Restricted area
Sopot Fl.4s7M
Mo(A)10s AIS
Fl.G.6s
Q(9)15s
Fl.R.6s
2S Fl.Y.6s AIS
PP LFl.10s
Buoyed channel
LFl.R.6s
Iso.Y
F.G
Fl(3)9s 25M
Iso.G.5s6M
Q(3)10s
Nowy Port
Port Polocny
Zones periodically closed to navigation and fishing
Górki Fl(2)R.5s11m6M
Fl.Y.4s AIS
LFl.10s
Górki Zachodnie
Wisła Śmiała
Przystan Nadwislanska
Ostrow
GDAŃSK
Martwa Wisła
Swibno
Mikoszewo
Prekop Wisły
See plan p.411
40′
35′
25′
20′
45′
50′
55′
19°00′E

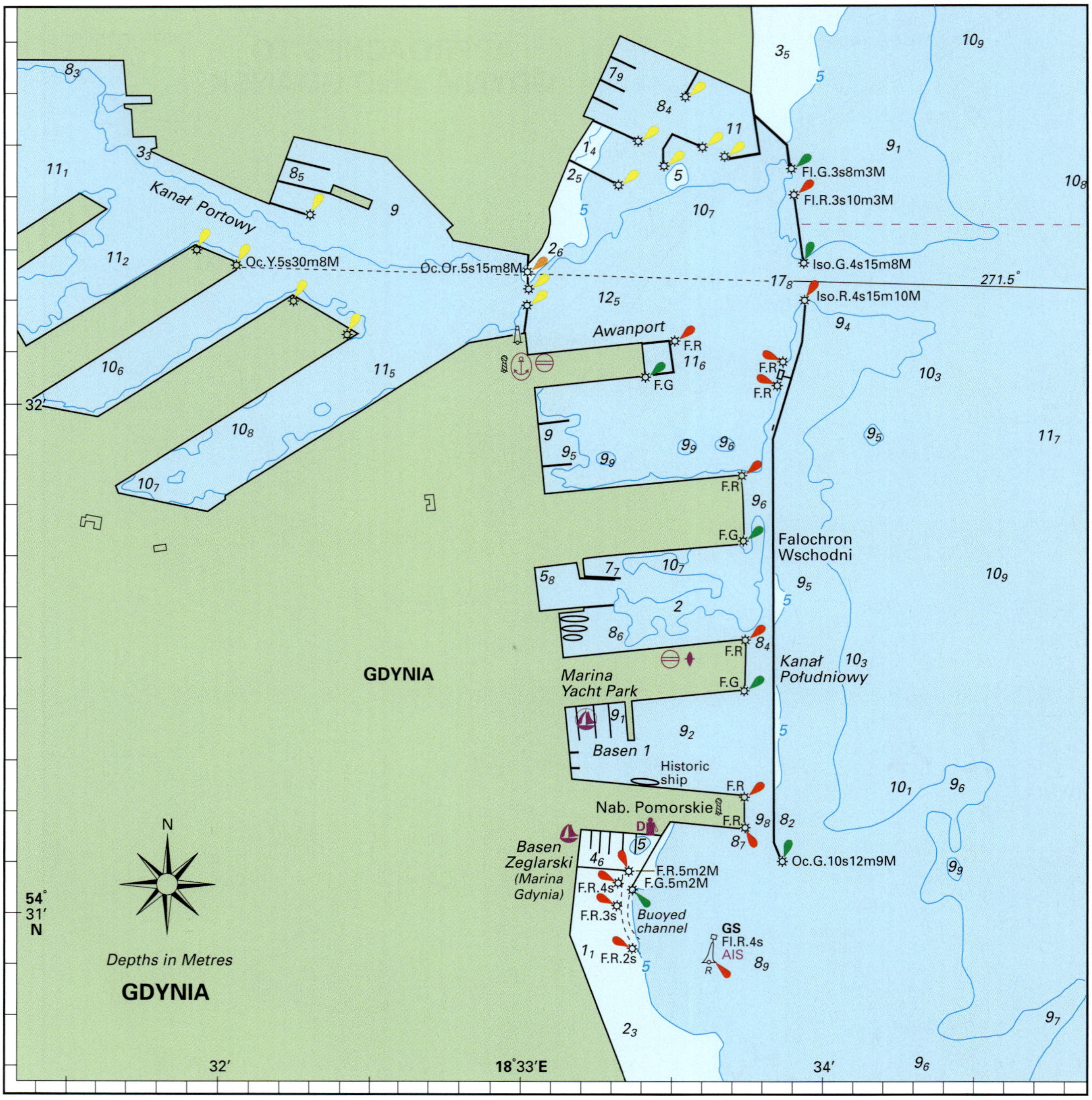


passes through Gdynia. The secure yacht harbour lies south of the main port entrance.

South of the city lies a popular beach area with pavement cafés, bars and local shops lining the seafront and main avenue. South again, by some 9km, is the highly fashionable city of Sopot where cultural events, concerts and seaside recreation are popular.

### *Approach & entrance*

54°30'.95N 18°33'.20E (south mole)

Gdynia is protected by north-south detached breakwaters more than 1.5M in length, pierced by three entrances. The leading lights direct shipping through the main (central) entrance and should be ignored by yachts.

Staying clear of the TSS which begins 2M east of the Hel Peninsula, yachts should steer for the south end of the eastern detached breakwater. On rounding the outer breakwater the marina's east wall will be seen about 550m ahead, with a green column marking the entrance.

The entrance channel to the yacht basin (Basen Zeglarski) is narrow and the approach is very close to the beach. After a tight turn to starboard around the harbour wall there are two port hand buoys marking the 2m contour. This entrance could be dangerous in strong onshore winds.

The Polish Naval Yacht Club Kotwica uses the berths to port immediately inside the entrance. These berths use long floating polypropylene lines. Visiting yachts should call in advance on VHF Ch 12 for permission to enter and leave, and to ensure/request a berth. The *Dar Pomorza* square rigger is conspicuous on an adjacent quay.

Alternatively, particularly for larger yachts, it may be possible to berth in the Marina Yacht Park. This is in the next basin to the north of Basen Zeglarski and means rounding the southern end of the outer breakwater.

It should be noted that a restricted area extends southwards from a point approximately 100m south of this, due east of Orłowo.

### Berthing

For Marina Gdynia, the marina master's office is at the marina entrance and staff will direct an incoming yacht to a vacant berth. The marina is run by the town and there are about 30-40 visitors' berths. Maximum length is 20m and there is a maximum draught of 3.2m in the entrance. Guest berths depend on availability. It is not possible to book ahead and in season berths are often in short supply, particularly if there are yachting events taking place. Showers are extra - payment by card or coin.

There is a slipway which will handle up to 2.7T for launching

For larger yachts the Marina Yacht Park may have some free berths for guests depending on resident's movements. They can handle yachts of up to 20m alongside and a maximum of 14m on the pontoons. The depth is 8-9m throughout. There are toilets, showers (extra charge), electricity, water and laundry.

### Facilities

Fuel is available in the eastern corner of the Basen Zeglarski.

Gdynia undoubtedly has the best chandleries in Poland. They include SMART, an Admiralty chart agent and an agent for Imray, NV Charts and Delius Klasing publications.

There is a 3T crane for masts and small craft and a larger one can be arranged if required. Engineers and boatbuilders are also available. The nearest sailmaker is at Gdańsk. Winter storage outside can be arranged although a cradle may be difficult to find. There is free WiFi throughout the city.

Good shopping is available on the main avenue leading from the marina with further shops, including smaller speciality shops, along the main walkway. An open-air market is located adjacent to the multi-level Batory shopping centre, about 10mins walk up the avenue. For major provisioning it may be worth visiting the major Real superstore development approximately 20mins by taxi west of the city centre.

The railway station is about 15mins walk from the marina. There is a frequent service to Gdańsk, 20km and about 25mins to the southeast, and good links with Szczecin and Berlin.

Aerial view of Gdynia marina looking west

## SOPOT

54°26'.80N 13°34'.76E (outer mole, south eastern end)

### Distances
Gdańsk 3.3M, Gdynia 4.5M, Hel 12.5M

### Lights
**Safe water RW buoy** 54°26'.7N 18°34'.8E LFl.10s
**South end of outer mole, stbd hand** 54°26'.8N 18°34'.7E Fl.G.6s4M
**Northeast tip of pier** 54°26'.9N 18°34'.7E Fl.Y.5s4M
**Northeast tip of inner mole** 54°26'.8N 18°34'.7E Fl.R.6s4M

### Contacts
✆+48 500 696 588, VHF Ch 63
www.marina-sopot.com.pl/
bosman@marina.sopot.pl

Sopot is set at the foot of the long pier which lies halfway between Gdynia and Gdańsk. It is an interesting and highly fashionable resort with all the associated entertainments, shops and restaurants. Good facilities with electricity, water, toilets and showers. The marina has over 100 spaces (though many of these are residents) and can be exposed to southeasterlies.

Aerial view of Sopot marina looking north

## GDAŃSK

54°21'N 18°39'E

### Distances
Łeba 80M, Gdynia 10M, Kaliningrad 45M, Klaipėda 110M

### Lights
**Hel** 54°36'.1N 18°48'.9E Iso.10s39m17M 130°-vis-080° F.R Red octagonal tower with gallery
**Port Północny** 54°24'N 18°41'.8E Fl(3)9s61m25M Blue square tower with white gallery
**Outer Leading Lights 196°** *Front* 54°24'.5N 18°38'.4E Iso.Y.5s23m13M White triangle with red border, on white metal framework tower 24m
*Rear* 330m from front Iso.Y.5s31m13M Triangle on black metal framework tower 36m
**Inner Leading Lights 147.7°** *Front* 54°24'.6N 18°39'.8E Oc.G.5s23m8M Two white triangles with red borders, on white beacon 20m
*Rear* 370m from front, Oc.G.5s35m8M Black triangle on dark grey beacon 32m
**East breakwater** 54°25'N 18°39'.5E LFl.R.6s13m7M Red tower 13m
**West molehead** 54°24'.7N 18°39'.6E LFl.G.6s13m7M Green framework tower
**Górki** 54°22'.5N 18°46'.9N Fl(2)R.5s11m6M Red round tower with gallery
**Krynica Morska** 54°23'.1N 19°27'E LFl(2)12s53m18M Red round tower, white lantern

### Contacts
**Gdańsk Harbourmaster** ✆+48 58 343 0610
VHF Ch 14

**Gdańsk Port Control** ✆+48 58 343 0710
VHF Ch 14/16

**Gdańsk Marina** *Mobile* +48 695 56 48 48
www.marinagdansk.pl

### *General*
The historic city of Gdańsk (pronounced *Guh-dansk*), and the Nowy (pronounced *Novv-I*) Port is situated at the mouth of the Wisła River, the largest river in Poland. The city has a population of around one million people and is at a strategic location on the old Amber Road.

Gdańsk entrance *Miranda Delmar-Morgan*

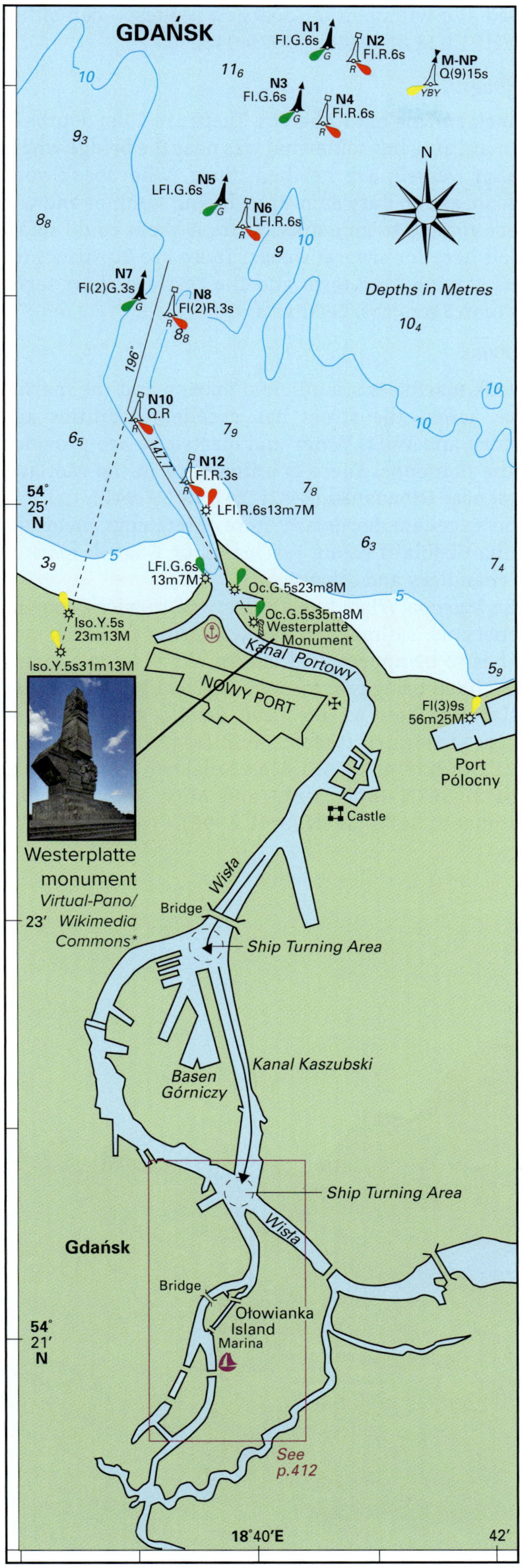


*(https://commons.wikimedia.org/wiki/File:0579_Westerplatte_monument_SW.jpg)

The city has long been a fortified trading settlement and was a stronghold of the Teutonic Knights, then later a formidable member of the Hanseatic League. A strong Prussian influence is seen in the old waterfront buildings, especially the Crane Gate, constructed in 1440, claimed to be the largest goods lift of the 15th century.

The Stare Miasto (old town), originally built with much Dutch influence, has been carefully restored since the Second World War when 80% of the city was destroyed.

There are many attractions, cultural events and outdoor festivals as well as numerous shops and cafés. It is worth allowing plenty of time here to see everything.

The three week festival of St Dominic's Fair takes place in late July/early August and claims to be the largest trade and cultural event in Europe, attracting large numbers of visitors.

Amber is available from local artisans, and the National Museum houses an excellent collection of art, including Polish and Flemish paintings, relief panels and sculpture.

The local shipyards were the birthplace of Solidarity (Solidarność), the union movement which eventually led to the demise of Soviet control in Poland, and are now a World Heritage Site. The shipbuilding and bulk-shipping areas are to the north and east of the old town.

### *Approach & entrance*

The approach from within the Gulf of Gdańsk is straightforward and can be taken in all but the severest of onshore weather conditions. Yachts should stay well clear of the TSS which begins 2M east of the tip of the Hel peninsula. The outer and inner leading lines can be followed, although yachts can safely cut the corner and head directly for the eastern (outer) breakwater head.

Permission to enter (or leave) must be sought from Gdańsk Nowy Port Control on VHF Ch 14.

Just inside the entrance, on the east side, there is a large monument commemorating the men who died when the first shots of the Second World War were fired, by a German battleship, at the barracks on Westerplatte. It is customary to hold one's ensign at the dip when passing it.

The channel follows the Kanal Portowy and Wisła River for 3.7M through the commercial port and shipyards. At the ship turning area, north of Basen Gorniczy (54°23′N) follow the eastern channel, the Kanal Kaszubski. At the next ship turning area (54°21′.7N 18°40′E) follow the small channel directly ahead – the Motława River – which leads to the marina in the heart of the old city directly opposite the historic Crane Gate (54°21′N 18°39′E).

In 2018 a small pedestrian bridge was built for pedestrians to cross from the mainland to the island of Ołowianka. This bridge is at 54°21′·217N 18°39′.627E and in the high season it opens for boats at 30mins past the hour and closes on the hour. Off season it's mostly

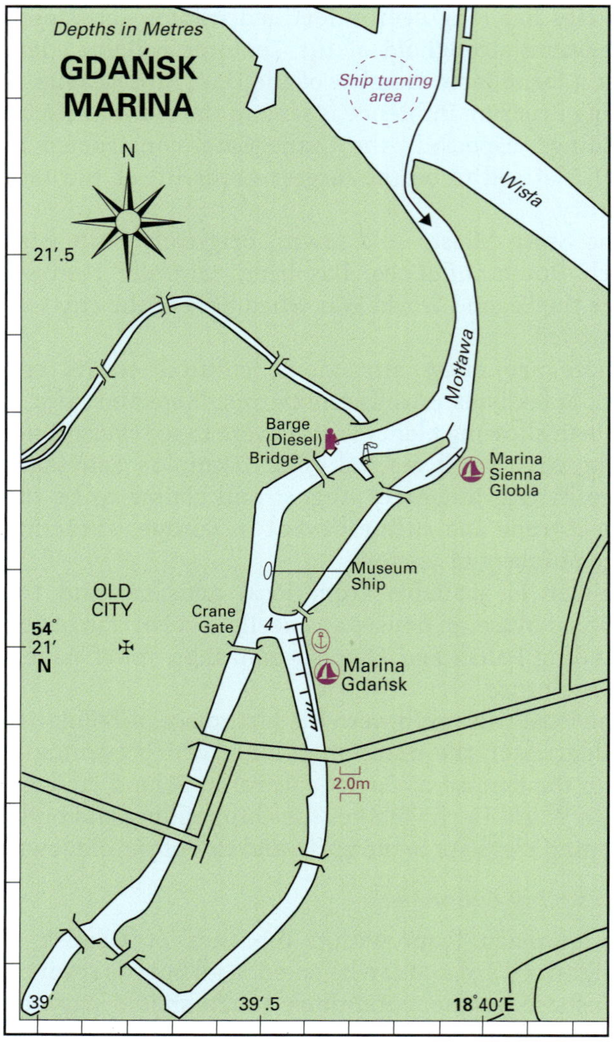


closed and will open for boats on request - call either on VHF Ch 14 or ✆+48 516 970 048.

### Berthing

Gdańsk marina has 67 berths. There are 2.8m depths in the main area but somewhat less near the bridge where smaller vessels are berthed. Staff, who speak good English, are on duty 8am-8pm during summer and will direct visitors to an empty berth. A yacht could safely be left here for several weeks. There are 30 spaces for boats staying long-term and the rest are short-term, less than 3 months, berths.

### Facilities

Gdańsk marina is a municipal marina and the marina office across the street has excellent facilities and laundry and WiFi. Water and electricity are provided on the pontoons. There is a fuel jetty in the Motława Canal near Ołowianka (54°21′.26N 18°39′.94E).

The excellent hardware store, Metalzbyt, near the Sienna Grobla II basin, just north of Gdańsk marina, has chandlery and other goods.

The Martwa Wisła has a variety of services, marine electricians, sailmakers, overwintering facilities etc., but has to be approached via the Wisła Smiala owing to the fixed bridges across the Martwa Wisła. Martwa Wisła translates as *The Dead Vistula* and the fixed bridges are located at Most Siennicki (7.5m clearance at 54°21′.305N 18°40′.633E), Most Kolejowy (8m clearance at 54°21′.363N 18°41′.518E) and Most Wantowy (9m clearance at 54°21′.394N 18°41′.639E).

A pirate ship off the historic Crane Gate *Andy Beharrell*

Gdańsk marina looking north from the bridge *Andy Beharrell*

The *General Zaruski* tall ship moored in Gdańsk. She is used as a sail training vessel for Polish students *Andy Beharrell*

Gdańsk has all the facilities of a long-established city. Restaurants, cafés and small shops will be found along the waterfront and in the Stare Miasto (old town) area. There is a small grocery store near the marina, but it is necessary to travel further for major shopping.

*Transport*

Gdańsk Airport has international and national connections, and there are also good train services to Szczecin and Berlin. Marina staff can assist in arranging taxis to the airport or station if requested.

## GÓRKI ZACHODNIE

54°21'.445N 18°47'.011E (just outside entrance)

**Contacts**
☎+48 58 307 31 15
www.jsg.com.pl
biuro@jsg.com.pl

The harbour of Górki (pronounced Gor-key) is located 5M to the east of the main entrance of Gdańsk, at the mouth of one of the channels which form the Wisła delta (see plan on page 360). The entrance is protected by breakwaters but they are on a shoal area of sand. There is no internal route from Gdańsk owing to the fixed bridges.

*Warning* Sandbanks make the approach particularly dangerous in onshore winds and it is probably best not entered in onshore winds over Force 5.

This a major centre for yacht building and home to around six yacht clubs, including the National Sailing Centre. There are several big yards here: Alu International specialise in aluminium; the Conrad Shipyard built the *Malcolm Miller*; Galeon shipyard has a 200T travel lift. Dehler Yachts, and a Yamaha agent are also here.

Overwinter storage is available and there is a good choice for yacht and ship repairs and good boatyard facilities, but there is not much in the way of shops or transport. SAR is located here.

There are various berthing options although these have changed considerably in recent years. The Gdańsk municipality now runs five marinas (including Gdańsk marina in the centre).

Górki Zachodnie municipal yacht harbour is named after Captain Krystyna Chojnowska - Liskiewicz. She was a Polish naval engineer and sailor and was the first woman to sail single-handed around the world, completing her trip in 1978. The harbour was previously know as Jachtklub Stoczni Gdańskiej (Gdansk Shipyard Yachtclub), but changed to Górki Zachodnie when taken over by the municipality.

The marina is located on the west bank of the Wisła Śmiała river, 0.5M from the entrance to the Gulf of Gdańsk. It was refurbished using EU money and opened in May 2023. There are over 180 guest berths available and facilities include water, electricity, rubbish disposal and other facilities. The public transport line 111 allows access to the city. It runs from Górki Zachodnie - Nowotna - Academy of Music - Main Railway Station.

## PRZYSTAŃ NADWIŚLAŃSKA

54°20'.742N 18°48'.758E (just outside entrance)

**Contacts**
☎+48 516 284 853
www.sportgdansk.pl/obiekty/przystan-nadwislanska/

This harbour has around 75 spaces, and while none are specifically for guests, they will usually manage to find a small number of guests a space.

Aerial view of Górki Zachodnie marina looking south

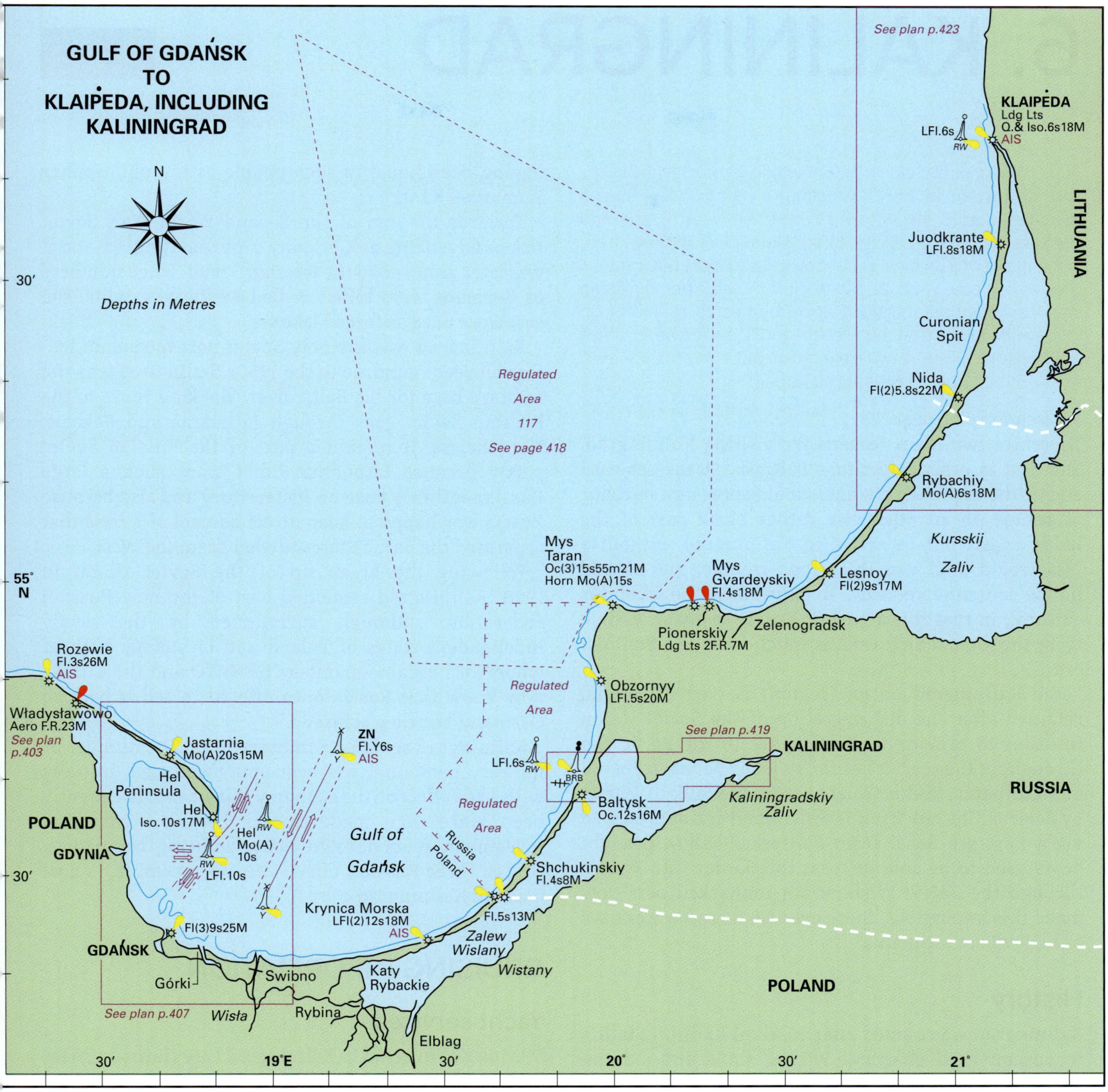
GULF OF GDAŃSK
TO
KLAIPĖDA, INCLUDING
KALININGRAD
N
Depths in Metres
See plan p.423
KLAIPĖDA
Ldg Lts
Q.& Iso.6s18M
AIS
LFl.6s
RW
LITHUANIA
Juodkrante
LFl.8s18M
Curonian
Spit
Nida
Fl(2)5.8s22M
Rybachiy
Mo(A)6s18M
Kursskij
Zaliv
Lesnoy
Fl(2)9s17M
Zelenogradsk
Mys
Gvardeyskiy
Fl.4s18M
Pionerskiy
Ldg Lts 2F.R.7M
Mys
Taran
Oc(3)15s55m21M
Horn Mo(A)15s
Regulated
Area
117
See page 418
Obzornyy
LFl.5s20M
Regulated
Area
See plan p.419
KALININGRAD
LFl.6s
RW
BRB
Baltysk
Oc.12s16M
Kaliningradskiy
Zaliv
RUSSIA
Regulated
Area
Russia
Poland
Shchukinskiy
Fl.4s8M
Fl.5s13M
Zalew
Wislany
Wistany
POLAND
Krynica Morska
LFl(2)12s18M
AIS
Katy
Rybackie
Elblag
Rybina
Swibno
Wisła
Górki
See plan p.407
GDAŃSK
Fl(3)9s25M
Gulf of
Gdańsk
ZN
Fl.Y6s
AIS
Y
Hel
Mo(A)
10s
RW
LFl.10s
Hel
Iso.10s17M
GDYNIA
POLAND
Hel
Peninsula
Jastarnia
Mo(A)20s15M
Władysławowo
Aero F.R.23M
See plan
p.403
Rozewie
Fl.3s26M
AIS
55°
N
30′
30′
30′
19°E
30′
20°
30′
21°

# 6. KALININGRAD

At the time of publication of this new edition the Saimaa Lakes and all Russian territory, including Kaliningrad, was closed to yachts due to the ongoing conflict between Russia and Ukraine. We have left all the information about the area here in the event of a change in the political situation, but it seems likely to be some years before this is the case. Prior to making any decision about visiting, it would be best to check the up to date Foreign, Commonwealth and Development Office (FCDO) advice. This is available online at: www.gov.uk/foreign-travel-advice/russia

*See location plan page 378*

There are two main reasons for visiting Kaliningrad. The first is practical in that Baltiysk, at the seaward end of the approach channel, could serve as a harbour of refuge on an otherwise rather bleak part of the Baltic coast( but to arrive in Kaliningrad without a visa would land you in serious trouble, and should not be contemplated save 'in extremis'). The second is cultural, in that it is a part of Russia easily accessible from the west which retains much from the Stalinist era.

The Kaliningrad oblast (region) is part of Russia, retained after the disintegration of the Soviet Union in order to provide ice-free access to the Baltic Sea throughout the year. It lies sandwiched between Poland and Lithuania, and is isolated from the bulk of Russia by Belarus. The city itself is well inland and approached via a long sea canal from Baltiysk. Shallow-draught boats used to be able to cross the border into Poland through the Zalew Wislany but unmarked nets now make this impossible. There are also inland waterways to Klaipzda in Lithuania.

## History

Kaliningrad was named after Mikhail Kalinin, Stalin's inconsequential chairman of the USSR Praesidium, when the area was captured at the end of the Second World War. The whole Kaliningrad *oblast*, or region, is only 120km by 300km, with its capital in Kaliningrad City, formerly Königsberg.

In the Middle Ages Kaliningrad was part of east Prussia, northeast of Poland. Prussia still consisted of pagan tribal lands that Poland had failed to subdue, so in 1226 they invited the Teutonic Knights to conquer and convert the area to Christianity. Although nominally a Polish fiefdom, after much slaughter Prussia became populated by immigrant Germans who owned the land while the locals had to work as serfs. Then in the Reformation, the Knights' Grand Master secularised the order and made Prussia a Grand Duchy, building Königsberg (now Kaliningrad city) as its capital.

As Prussia expanded, Berlin became its new capital, but Königsberg continued to be a major German cultural centre until the end of the Second World War, having been home to such people as the philosopher Immanuel Kant.

Towards the end of the Second World War, Soviet troops advancing on Germany captured the area and it was later annexed to the Russian Soviet. Huge numbers of Germans were killed or fled westwards, while the rest were used as forced labour.

Kaliningrad was the only Soviet port to remain ice-free all year round, so in the 1950s Stalin used it as the military base for his Baltic fleet. The land route to the Russian Soviet goes through Lithuania and Belarus. Nonetheless, it remained part of the Russian Soviet partly because Lithuania didn't want such a large Russian military base on its territory and also because Russia was happy to keep direct control of a base that separated the Baltic States further from the West.

Following the break up of the Soviet Union in 1990, Kaliningrad remained part of the new Russian Federation, although surrounded by the newly independent states of Poland and Lithuania, both of whom also became members of NATO and the EU. We now know that Russia once offered to sell it back to Germany, but they refused.

Kaliningrad remains a military base. The number of military personnel has been much reduced, initially with a bad effect on the economy, but it has subsequently been more than made up for by tax breaks and investment from foreign manufacturing companies. One in three Russian televisions, for example, is now made in Kaliningrad.

## CRUISING INFORMATION

### Yacht services

Marina Kaliningrad in Kaliningrad City Harbour offers basic yacht services (see below under Kaliningrad for details).

Kaliningrad Yacht Club Harbour has very limited services.

### Chandlery

Seek advice from Marina Kaliningrad.

### Holding tanks

There are no laws requiring holding tanks and there are no pump out facilities.

### Gas

It is most unlikely that bottles can be refilled and visitors would be advised to carry sufficient for the duration of their visit.

# KEY INFORMATION

## Rescue/Safety services

**Emergency** ✆ 112
**MRCC Kalingrad Rescue Radio** (GMDSS Area A1) monitors VHF Ch 16/70, Ch 3/7). Call Sign **'Kalingrad-1'**.
✆ +7 4012 538 470

## Charts and pilot books

Russian charts

*Baltic Pilot Volume II* (NP 19)

*Cruising Guide to Baltic Russia*, Vladimir Ivankiv, Graham and Fay Cattell available from the Cruising Association and chart agents in Scandinavia

## Time

Kaliningrad is on UT+2 all year.

## ₽ Money

The rouble (divided into 100 kopecks) is the official currency. ATMs accepting credit cards can be found in the city centre where there are also exchange offices. Tips should always be made in roubles.

## Formalities

Formalities are as described in the section on Russia.

Notice of arrival must be submitted to the Customs Post at Kaliningrad at least 72 hours prior to the yacht's arrival by the host yacht club or agent. Passport Control and Customs are located at the furthest north-eastern corner of Basin No 3 (Quay 81). Working hours are generally between 0800 and 2000 only so arrival and departure have to be timed accordingly. Inward and outward clearance are both mandatory and both may take several hours.

As in St Petersburg persons staying in the country more than a week + an extra weekend (i.e. 9 days) should register visas with the immigration department. In practice this is not strictly enforced as far as those arriving and departing by yacht are concerned. It does however apply to those leaving by other means of transport e.g. plane, train or ferry.

## Public holidays

As for Russia – see page 364.

## Communications

Public call boxes, either coin or card operated, are widespread. To obtain an international line dial 8, wait for the dial tone, then 10 followed by the country code, area code (omitting any initial 0) and number. If dialling from abroad the country code for Russia is 7 and the area code for Baltiysk and Kaliningrad is 4012.

VHF Ch 16/74 (preferably dual watch) should be monitored on approach.

## Travel

There are road and rail links to the surrounding countries, and ferry services to Gdynia with the Polish line Zegluga Gdańsk and to St Petersburg. Kaliningrad airport lies some 18km distant with regular flights to Moscow, Copenhagen and destinations in Germany. Taxis are inexpensive and readily available for the journey from yacht harbour to city centre.

## Websites

**marinakaliningrad.ru/engservices.html**
Marina Kaliningrad website (in English) with charts and advice on navigation and formalities.

**www.inyourpocket.com/kaliningrad** Tourist information

## Radio communications

VHF Ch 16 should be monitored at all times.

Baltiysk Traffic VHF Ch 16/74 call sign 'Baltiysk Traffic'

Kaliningrad Port Control VHF Ch 67 call sign 'Kaliningrad Port Control'

Border Guard VHF Ch 74 call sign 'Impuls'

Customs Control VHF Ch 74 call sign 'Mech'

Pilots VHF Ch 67 call 'Kaliningrad 11'

See also detail regarding reporting in Formalities above.

## Weather information

Navtex and the internet are the best way of obtaining weather information .

Kaliningrad Radio broadcasts warnings and weather forecasts, in Russian, on VHF Ch 07 on receipt and at 0533 and 1333 UT.

## Diesel

Available at Marina Kaliningrad.

## Shopping

All supplies can be obtained.

## Alcohol

As in the rest of Russia, alcohol supplies are unrestricted.

## Caution

The situation in all Russian ports is always subject to change and every effort should be made to check current requirements while the cruise is still at the planning stage.

The security of both yacht and crew is plainly of great importance and all sensible precautions should be taken.

## KALININGRAD

54°38'.88N 19°52'.02E (centre of harbour entrance)

**Distances**
Gdynia 45M, Gdańsk 45M, Klaipzda 80M

**Lights**
**Shchukinskiy** 54°31'.6N 19°44'.5E Fl.4s50m8M Black and white metal framework tower 29m
**Baltiysk Fairway** rear light, 54°38'.4N 19°53'.7E Oc.12s30m16M Round white tower, red top, two galleries 32m
**Obzornyy** 54°49'.7N 19°57'.3E LFl.5s54m20M Triangle on orange round tower, white bands 22m
**Mys Taran** 54°57'.6N 19°58'.9E Oc(3)15s55m21M Emergency light Iso.4s13M Red octagonal tower on building 30m Horn Mo(A)15s13m Red metal mast 4m120m NW of light
**Baltiysk Fairway Leading Lights 122.1°** *Front* 54°38'.6N 19°53'.1E Oc.12s12m12M
Two white rectangles with black stripes on red metal framework tower 21m
*Rear* 770m from front Oc.12s30m16M
**Fairway No.1 buoy** 54°41'.3N 19°45'.1E LFl.6s Red and white pillar buoy
**North mole** 54°39'N 19°52'.3E Fl.R.2.5s3M
**South mole** 54°38'.8N 19°52'.1E Fl.G.4s1M
Many more lights and lit buoys mark the Kaliningradskiy Morskoy Kanal

**Contacts**
See Key information section above.

### *Approach & entrance*

Beware of the Navy firing ranges to the north and northwest of the port of Baltiysk and the cape of Taran.

Particular attention should be paid to Regulated Area 117 (see plan on page 415). It is important to monitor VHF Ch 16 when sailing in or close to Russian waters so as to be able to respond to instructions as all vessels will be on their radar.

Approach is made from the Gulf of Gdańsk (see plan page 415). Though depths are generally good within 1M of the coast it would nevertheless be wise to keep well offshore until able to approach via the designated channel on 122°, passing Fairway Buoy No. 1 en route.

Contact should be made with Baltiysk Traffic (land based border guard call sign 'Vyshka' or coast guard ship call sign 'Velbot'). Required information is name of vessel, last port, port of arrival, purpose of entering territorial waters, number of persons on board. Reporting is mandatory, and contact should be made when more than 7M (or 1hr) from the entrance. An escort vessel may approach the yacht to check credentials and escort her in. Night approach should be avoided as immigration and customs working hours are generally 0800–2000.

Final entry is straightforward, with the Passport Control and Customs berth on the north side of the channel 2M from the entrance in the northeast corner of Basin No. 3 (quay 81) (54°38'.19N 19°55'.29E). From Baltiysk the well-buoyed Kaliningradskiy Morskoy Kanal runs some 22M (41km) between low-lying banks to the commercial port and city of Kaliningrad. Depths are dredged to a nominal 9m throughout its length, but shoal steeply on either side.

For Marina Kaliningrad follow the Morskoy Kanal all the way into the city. Marina Kaliningrad is situated on the northern bank of the River Pregolya just before the railway bridge which cannot be passed by masted craft.

For the Kaliningrad Yacht Club harbour in the southeastern corner of the Kaliningradskiy Zaliv (the large inland sea traversed by the Kaliningradskiy Morskoy Kanal) the main channel is followed as far as light beacon No. 30 (54°41'.40N 20°22'.40E). From there a course of 235° is followed for 1M, before swinging

Kaliningrad Marina Channel and berthing, showing industrial backdrop *Photos kindly supplied by Marina Kaliningrad*

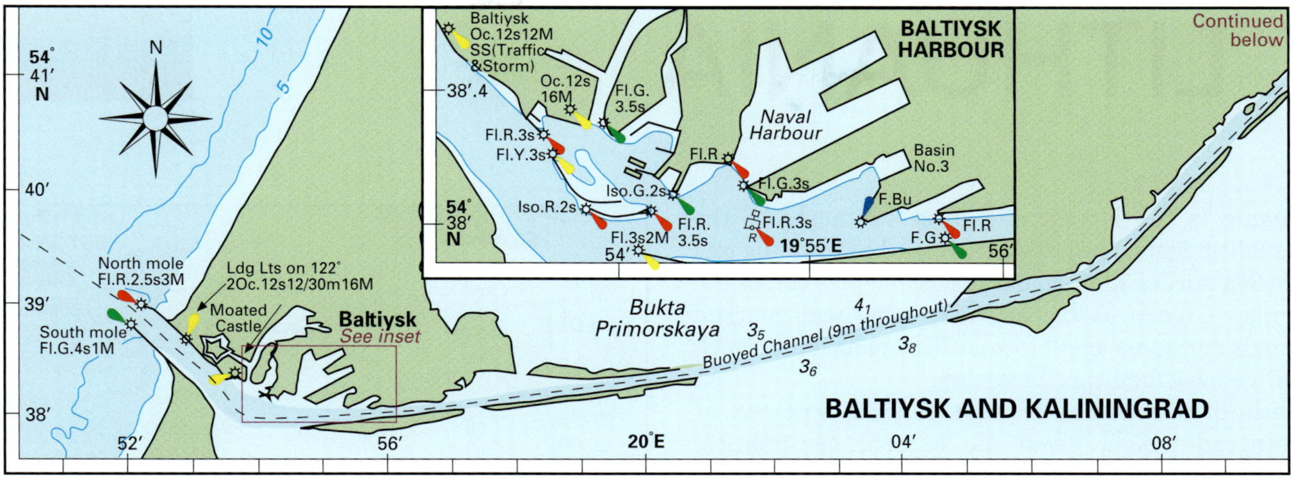


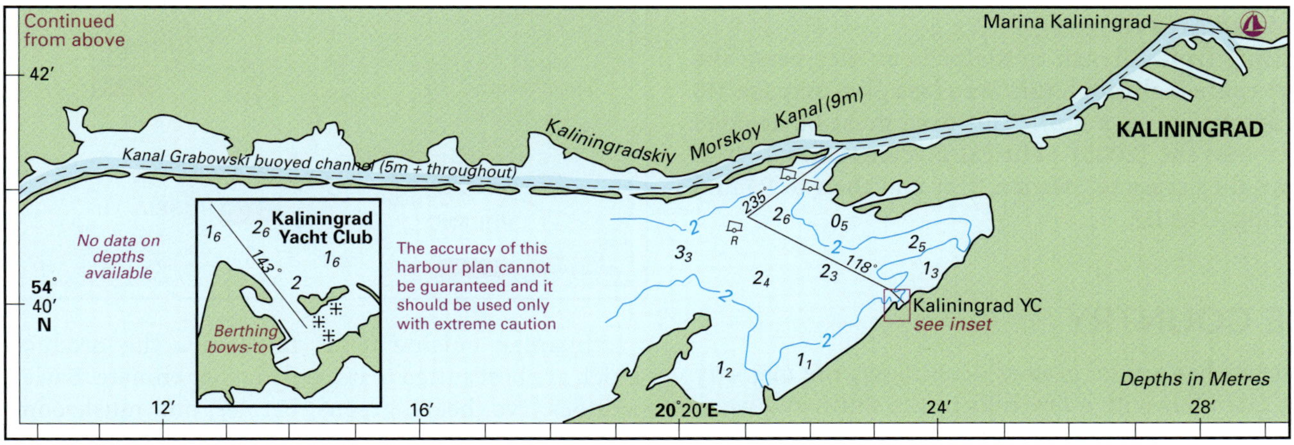


onto 118° towards the harbour and buildings of the Kaliningrad Yacht Club and 143° for the final approach. Parts of the route are shallow – less than 2m – though the bottom is soft. Do not stray as there are unmarked fishing nets and wrecks in the Kaliningradskiy Zaliv.

At least 4hrs should be allowed between the Passport Control berth and the yacht harbour.

### *Berthing*

#### Baltiysk

Although there is a yacht harbour within the Naval Base area this is not available for foreign leisure craft.

#### Marina Kaliningrad

54°42'.28N 20°28'.76E (yacht moorings)
Anton Pavloski ☏+7 921 269 52 16 (24hrs), +7 4012 523 362
http://marinakaliningrad.ru/engservices.html

Developed in Kaliningrad City harbour and currently the best option for visiting yachts. Foreign visitors are welcome but advance reservation of a berth is recommended, as most berths are occupied by locals. Contact Anton Pavlovski (website in English with charts and advice on navigation and formalities).

Facilities include finger pontoons, water (not drinking quality) and electricity, one toilet and one shower (both in containers), fuel, repairs, crane, etc. The marina and boat yard has a 24hr security guard. The managers speak English, but the guards do not. The marina is just 1.5km from the city centre. Nearest bus stop is about 1km. No shops or restaurants nearby. During the day there is some wash from excursion boats on the river.

#### Kaliningrad Yacht Club

54°39'.93N 20°23'.26E
☏+7 4012 466 331

Located on the southeast coast of the Kaliningradskiy Zaliv has berthing for about 10 visiting yachts moored bows-to in 2.5m depth. Its members are most welcoming to visitors. Public transport 1.5km. City centre 15km.

Yachts with a draught of over 2m should berth at Marina Kaliningrad.

*Note* Pionerskiy has been omitted from this edition as it is now closed to yachts.

# 7. LITHUANIA

Lithuania is the largest and most southerly of the three Baltic States, but despite this it has only the one Baltic Sea port of Klaipėda. It is possible to explore the Curonian Lagoon as far as Nida, using well-marked channels and some small former fishing harbours such as Mingė have facilities for yachts.

South of Lithuania lies the Russian enclave of Kaliningrad which, given the current geo-political situation is off-limits for yachts.

### Regulated Area 117

**If sailing from Gdansk to Klaipėda or vice versa the direct route is through this area (see plan on page 415 and details on page 418). This area must be avoided under current (2025) political circumstances. It is essential to cross to Sweden first and then to Poland avoiding Area 117.**

## THE COUNTRY

Lithuania has a total area of 65,300km$^2$, the majority a flat plain but with a few hills in the south and west. To the east and southeast the Baltic Highlands rise, the highest point being Mount Juoapine at 292m. There are many lakes, particularly in the northeast, and meandering rivers. Marshes and swamps are prevalent. The 99km coastline has sandy beaches backed by sand dunes and pine forest, while in the southwest the long Curonian sand spit almost encloses the Curonian Lagoon. South of Klaipėda lie the famous amber mines.

Lithuania's economy became one of the fastest growing in Europe post independence and was the largest economy of the Baltic States. Industry accounts for 28% of GDP, oil transit activity between Russia and Europe 12% and services 68%. Petroleum refining, food processing, energy supplies. chemicals, furniture, wood products, textile and clothing are the main industries.

Main foreign trade is with Latvia, Poland and Germany. About 50% of land is arable though the agricultural sector now employs only 9% of the workforce. Mineral oils and fuels, furniture, plastics, machinery, vehicles and their parts, electrical machinery and wood form the major exports.

Lithuanians are a lively people. They like to think of themselves as the literal centre of Europe and indeed in 1989 the National Geographic Institute of France estimated that the exact geographic midpoint of the continent is the village of Purnuškės, just north of the Lithuanian capital Vilnius. Hardly definite evidence given that many countries lay claim to the title, but it is enough for the Lithuanians to party hard and often!

Lithuanian cuisine tends to feature the products which are best suited to its cool norther climate. Barley, potatoes, rye, beets, greens, berries, and mushrooms are locally grown, and dairy products tend to feature heavily. In coastal areas, as with much of the Baltic, fish dishes are popular. One speciality is grey *cepelinai*, which literally translates as Zeppelins. These slightly glutinous potato dumplings are possibly the most mis-named of foods: they are far from their light and airy namesakes, but far more likely to weigh you down for a considerable time afterwards. They were originally named didžkukuliai or dumbbells, but in 1900 they were renamed in honour of Count Ferdinand von Zeppelin, the pioneer of the airship.

Lithuania even has a national scent made up of wildflowers, raspberry, ginger, sandalwood and musk aromas. The scent was designed to overcome the perception that Lithuania lacked a well-known identity. You will often find it used by local tourist offices but even the government are fans. The Prime Minister's chief of staff once apparently sent a bottle to every foreign minister in Vilnius!

In terms of sport, Lithuanians seem to be much better at sports where you throw things rather than kick them. Their national basketball team has won three bronze medals at the Olympics and many Lithuanian players have made it to the NBA's Hall of Fame.

### Highlights

The Curonian Spit is a UNESCO World Heritage Site.

# KEY INFORMATION

## Rescue/Safety services

**Emergency** ✆ 112

**MRCC Klaipėda Rescue Radio** monitors VHF Ch 16/70, DSC MMSI 002770330. Call Sign **'Klaipėda'.** ✆+370 46 391257 or +370 46 391258. *Email* mrcc@mil.lt. Within 6M from shore it is possible to call 112 and ask to be connected to SAR.

## Charts and pilot books

British Admiralty and Lithuanian Maritime Safety Administration charts cover the coast.

*Lithuanian Maritime Safety Administration* 7 sheet charts covering the coast in the approaches to Klaipėda.

*Lithuanian Inland Waterways Authority* Curonian Lagoon and the Nemunas Delta.

*Latvian chart 1253*

*Baltic Pilot Volume II* (NP 19)

## Time

Lithuania is in the Eastern European time zone (UT+2 in winter/UT+3 in summer). Summer time starts and ends on the same dates as the rest of the EU.

## € Money

Lithuania adopted the Euro in 2015. Credit cards are widely accepted.

## Formalities

Lithuania is a member of the EU and the Schengen Area (see Main Introduction page 9 for details of Schengen formalities). EU passport holders do not require visas. If a visa is needed contact the Lithuanian Consulate at Lithuania House, 2 Bessborough Gardens, London SW1V 2JE ✆+44 207 592 2840, amb.uk@urm.lt **http://uk.mfa.lt**. The British Embassy in Vilnius can be contacted on ✆+370 5 246 2900, **be-vilnius@britain.lt**, **www.gov.uk/government/world/lithuania**

Formal reporting is not required for passages between Lithuania and another Schengen country. Klaipėda Port Immigration/Coastguard may call up yachts on VHF Ch 73 when about 6M off to enquire as to last port of call and number of persons aboard. Alternatively Immigration may visit to check boats after arrival.

To prevent possible difficulties entering harbour at the same time as a large cargo vessel is moving, it is recommended to call VTS on VHF Ch 9 call sign *Radio 5* when approaching the harbour entrance. When departing it is similarly advisable to call the Coastguard on VHF Ch 9 call sign *Impuls 3* to report flag state, number of persons aboard, nationality, previous port and port of destination.

Although nationals are required to have a boat driving licence, this does not apply to skippers of foreign flagged vessels. In practice, skippers and crew would be advised to carry any certificates of competence wherever they are sailing.

All craft, regardless of flag state, are required to carry pyrotechnics appropriate to the category of vessel.

## Public holidays

Major public holidays occur on:
1 Jan, 16 Feb (Independence Day), 11 March (Restoration of Independence), Easter Sunday and Monday,1 May (Labour Day), 24 June (St John's Day), 6 July (Statehood Day), 15 Aug (Feast of the Assumption), 1 Nov, 24–26 Dec.

There are also many 'commemorative days' on which most shops and offices remain open.

## Communications

There are efficient telephone and mail systems and full coverage of mobile phone networks. Internet access is widely available with many free WiFi points.

The country code for Lithuania is +370.

## Travel

Taxis and minibuses provide local transport, and Klaipėda is served by international bus and rail networks.

There are international **airports** at Vilnius, Kaunas and Palanga. Palanga is more suitably located for crew changes in Klaipėda. Airline services change frequently so it is best to check availability when required.

Comprehensive **bus** and **rail** network with trains running from Vilnius to Warsaw, Berlin, Budapest, Prague and Sofia. **Ferries** run from Klaipėda to Germany and Sweden.

## Websites

**www.portofklaipeda.lt/the-port-of-klaipeda**
Port of Klaipėda

**www.yacht.lt/** Klaipėda Old Castle Harbour

## Radio communications

Navigational and other information is broadcast on request by Klaipėda Radio 5 on VHF Ch 9.

## Weather information

**www.meteo.lt**
Also call Klaipėda VTS on VHF Ch 9, call sign 'Klaipėda Radion 5'.

The Curonian Spit looking northeast over Nida *E. Redfern*

## The people, the church & the language

Of a total population of some 2.95 million, 84.2% are Lithuanians, 6.6% are Poles and 5.8% are Russians. The remaining 3.4% is made up of small numbers from Belarus, Ukraine, Germany and Latvia. 67% of the population is urban. Visitors to Lithuania can be assured of a warm and friendly welcome.

The majority of believers (approximately 77%) follow the Catholic faith, but there are also large numbers of Russian Orthodox, Evangelical Lutherans and Baptists.

The national language is Lithuanian, in modern times similar only to Latvian but also said to bear a resemblance to ancient Sanskrit. It is one of the officially recognized languages of the European Union. There is still a strong Polish influence in much of the country – the capital, Vilnius, was a Polish city for many centuries – and the language is widely understood. The generations educated in Soviet times tend to speak Russian whereas younger generations will have learnt English in school.

## History

The Lithuanian people together with the Latvians are descended from the Balts, the earliest Indo-European settlers still living in the Baltic. They seem to have been peaceful people and by the Middle Ages were being raided first by Vikings and then by Russians from Kiev-Rus and Novgorod.

From the mid 12th century, however, the main tribes were becoming united and started to fight back. Duke Mindaugas of Lithuania eventually quashed his rivals, converted to Christianity to get the Teutonic Knights on side, captured much of Russian Novgorod and was crowned King of Lithuania in 1253. Subsequent rulers had the title of Grand Duke, however, and by 1560 had reverted to paganism to keep the support of the Samogitian tribe.

In the course of the 13th and 14th centuries Lithuania continued to make territorial gains in Russia, while fighting off the Teutonic Knights from Prussia and Latvia. The disruption caused by Ghengis Khan's armies helped Lithuania to win more and more Russian territory, sometimes helped and sometimes opposed by the Mongols.

By the end of the 14th century, Lithuania was one of the largest countries in Europe and included present-day Belarus, Ukraine, and parts of Poland and Russia, so in 1377 when Jogailla became Grand Duke, he ruled most of modern Belarus and Ukraine. Lithuania relied heavily on its Russian territories for resources and manpower. They were allowed to keep their old administrative structures and their Orthodox Christian religion, now regarded by Rome as heresy.

Lithuania itself was a mixture of pagans and Orthodox, as well as Jews and some Muslims. There were clear advantages in joining Catholic Western Europe. So in 1386 Jogailla converted to Catholicism and married the young Queen of Poland, thereby starting the highly successful union with Poland that was to last for four centuries.

Towards the end of the 18th century, the huge extent of Poland-Lithuania's territory lead to the Wars of Partition, at the end of which 90% of Lithuania was controlled by Tsarina Catherine the Great and the rest became part of Prussia.

During the 19th century there was a period of intense "Russification" of Lithuania by Tsar Alexander, but this only intensified the growing nationalist movement defined by the Lithuanian language and its traditions from before the union with Poland.

During the First World War, Lithuania was occupied by Germany until its defeat in the west in 1918. Then the newly formed Red Army tried to take both Lithuania and Poland. It was not until 1924, when Klaipėda was retaken from Germany, as Lithuania's only Baltic port, that all fighting ended and Lithuania could start to build a united independent nation.

During the Second World War Lithuania was occupied first by the Soviet Union, then Germany, and then by the Soviet Union again. After the war Lithuania was made a Soviet within the USSR. Soviet Union rule was fiercely resisted and more Lithuanians were killed in the years following the war than during it. Then eventually in 1990, following Gorbachev's reforms, Lithuania became the first Soviet to declare its independence. USSR troops promptly captured the Vilnius broadcasting tower, killing 14 civilians and wounding many more, but amateur radio operators were able to broadcast to the world what was going on. Then, when the coup in

Moscow against Gorbachev failed, the Soviet system collapsed and Soviet troops withdrew. Lithuania became a member of the UN in 1991, of the EU and NATO in 2004 and signed the Schengen agreement at the end of 2007.

In 2018, Lithuania officially joined the OECD and in a milestone for the country, Dalia Grybauskaitė was the first female President of Lithuania. She served from 2009–19 and was the first to be re-elected for a second consecutive term. On 24 February 2022, Lithuania declared a state of emergency in response to the 2022 Russian invasion of Ukraine and the 2023 NATO Summit was held in Vilnius.

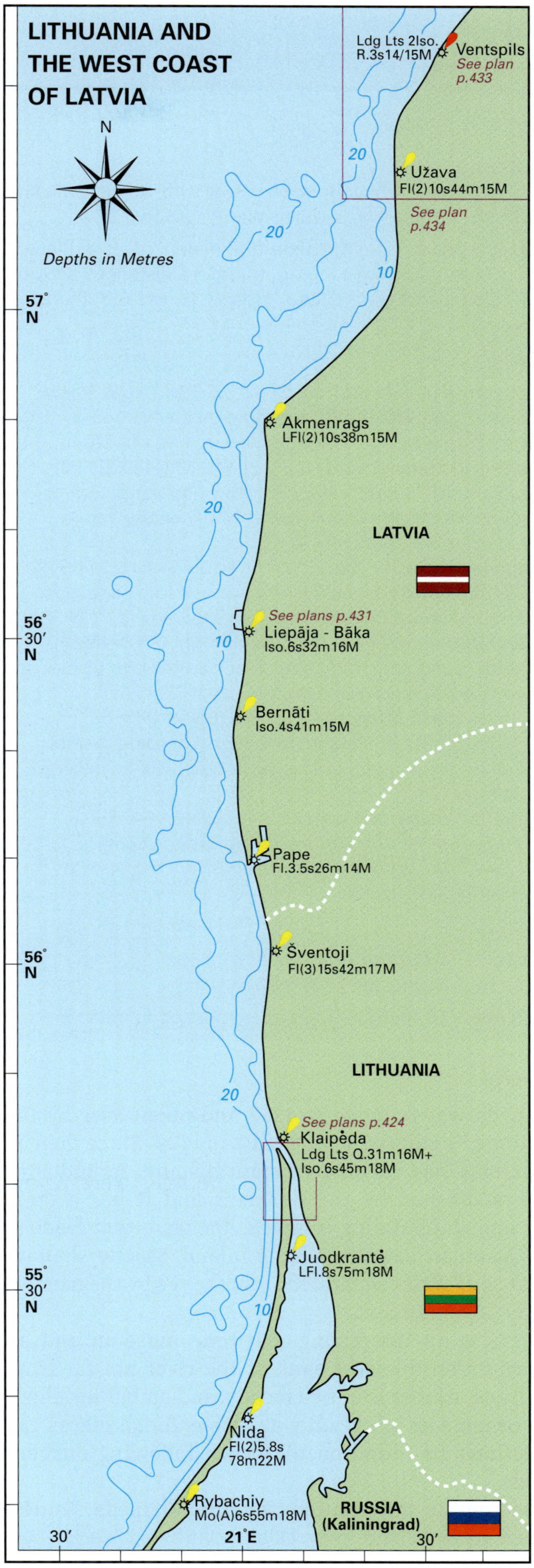


## CRUISING INFORMATION

### Yacht services

See under Klaipėda, page 424.

Sailing is popular both at Klaipėda and on the inland lakes. Although many yachts are privately owned, some still belong to yacht clubs. The Lithuanian Yachting Union is very active and organises training and regattas.

### Chandlery

Most local yachtsmen buy from online chandlers. Winter storage and repairs are possible.

### Holding tanks

See main introduction page 10 for general information. Holding tanks are not yet mandatory although desirable.

### Gas

See main introduction page 10 for general information. Exchange Campinggaz cylinders are not available.

### Diesel

See main introduction page 11 for general information. All diesel contains a 6% bio component There is a fuelling berth at Klaipėda.

### Shopping

Well stocked shops and supermarkets can be found in Klaipėda and other towns.

### Alcohol

Alcohol can be purchased from shops and supermarkets without restriction.

The alcohol limit at sea for leisure boats is 0.4/ml but in case of an accident charges may be brought even if under this limit.

## KLAIPĖDA

55°43'.6N 21°04'.5E

### Distance

Liepāja 50M, Fårösund 145M, Southern tip of Gotland 124M, southern tip of Öland to Władysławowo 110M

NOTE: If sailing from Klaipėda to Poland, it is essential to avoid Area 117 off Kaliningrad, therefore distances shown are to Gotland and Öland thence to Poland thereby avoiding Area 117.

### Lights

**Juodkrantė (if coming from S)** 55°33'.39N 21°06'.9sla5E LFl.W.8s75m18M White rectangle on black square metal framework tower with viewing platform 20m

**Šventoji (if coming from N)** 56°01'.51N 21°04'.93E Fl(3) W.15s42m17M Red rectangle with white band on red square metal framework tower with balcony and lantern room 39m

**Klaipėda Leading Lights 092.5°** *Front* 55°43'.67N 21°05'.47E Q.W.31m16M White rectangle with black stripe and white diamond above on red metal framework tower 29m *Rear* 285m from front Iso.W.6s45m18M 000° -vis-180° White round concrete tower, black bands and black stripe with balcony and lantern room 37m

**Klaipėda North breakwater** 55°43'.76N 21°04'.65E Fl.R.3s16m5M White square with red borders marked '2 B' on black metal cylindrical column with a viewing platform 12m

**Klaipėda South breakwater** 55°43'.62N 21°04'.61E Fl.G.3s16m5M White triangle with green borders marked '1 B' on black metal cylindrical column with viewing platform 16m

### Contacts

**Klaipėda Port Control** ✆+370 46 499 799
Yacht Harbourmaster ✆+370 46 490 975
**Klaipėda VTS** VHF Ch 9/16 call sign *Klaipėda Radio 5*

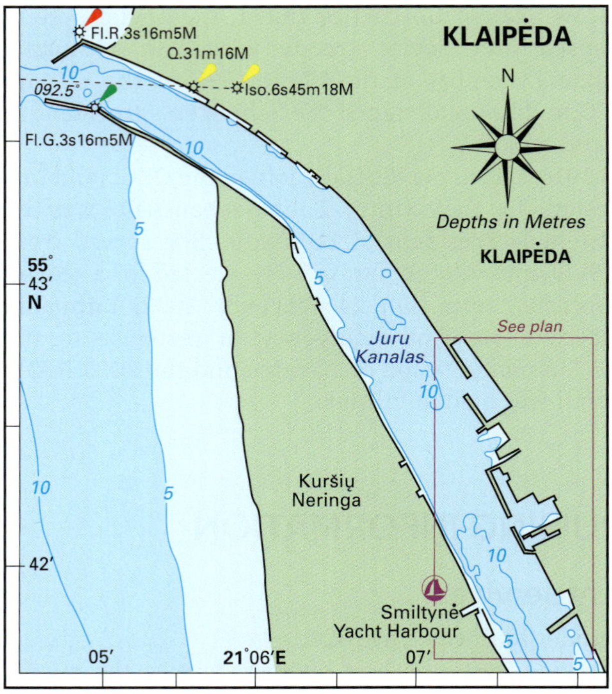


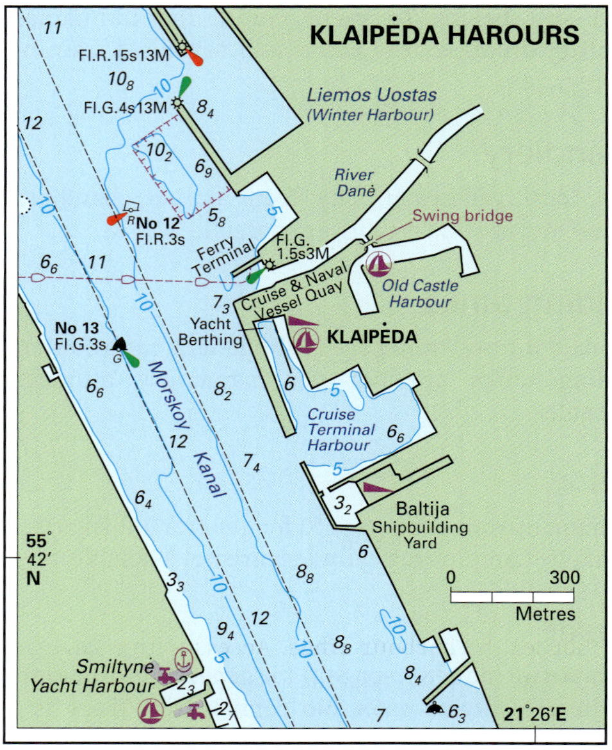


### *General*

Klaipėda was founded in 1252 and taken over by the Teutonic Knights who fortified it in 1404. Since then its ownership has been in constant dispute. Its industry was established by the Germans and it has a large port and shipbuilding complex. The waterway leads to the Curonian Lagoon, a large inland, mostly shallow, expanse of water separated from the sea by the narrow, sandy Curonian Spit.

There is an interesting maritime museum and an aquarium on the west bank of the river not far from Smiltynė. Amber is mined locally, and amber jewellery and ornaments are readily available. Small pieces can sometimes be found on the beach following onshore winds.

For tourist information see the Klaipėda Tourist Information website (www.klaipedatravel.lt/en/).

### *Approach & entry*

The town and the harbour entrance are clearly visible from seaward and the entrance, heavily used by commercial shipping, is well marked for entry at any

A quiet summer evening in Klaipeda *Mantas Volungevicius/ Wikimedia Commons (https://commons.wikimedia.org/wiki/File:Quite_summer_evening_in_the_port_city_Klaipeda.jpg)*

Smiltynė yacht harbour *Derbrauni/ Wikimedia Commons (https://commons. wikimedia.org/wiki/ File:Smiltyn%C4%97s_ yacht_harbor.jpg)*

time, though it would become hazardous for small craft in strong onshore (westerly) winds.

From the safe water light buoy No. 1 (55°43'.82N 20°59'.63E) follow the leading line on 092.5°.

### *Berthing*

Visitors should berth in Old Castle Harbour on the town side of the Curonian Lagoon - the Harbourmaster uses every endeavour to find space for all visitors although on occasion it may be necessary to tie up alongside in the entrance to the River Danė. The bridge swings every hour and stays open for 15mins for traffic. Access to Old Castle Harbour is via an opening bridge from the River Danė. This harbour offers good shelter and facilities. It is also convenient for the town. The Cruise Terminal Harbour is usually reserved for residents. On the opposite side of the Curonian Lagoon there is a further reconstructed facility for yachts at Smiltynė - see below for more information.

Klaipėda Harbour is a commercial waterway and anchoring is not permitted.

### Old Castle Harbour and Cruise Terminal Harbour

55°42'.35N 21°07'.32E (centre of entrance to Danė river)
55°42'.14N 21°07'.42E (centre of entrance to Cruise Terminal Harbour for fuel berth)
www.yacht.lt/en/

Water and electricity are available in both harbours with toilets and showers in a facilities building which also houses the harbour office. Access with a keycard. Washing and drying machines also available as well as a fuel berth. Good repair and craning facilities.

### Smiltynė Yacht Harbour

55°41'.85N 21°07'.27E (yacht harbour entrance, midway between moles)
www.smiltynesjachtklubas.lt/en

Water and electricity are available on the quay, with toilets and showers in the club building. Repairs and craning can be organised through the harbour captain, but the availability of parts and equipment is likely to be limited. Facilities and spares would be better at the Old Castle Harbour side. This harbour has two basins and is well equipped.

Whilst the Smiltynė harbour is thought to be safe in all weathers, strong onshore winds can send enough swell along the 2M of river to make the berths uncomfortable.

### *General facilities*

The town centre is very close to Old Castle and the Cruise Terminal harbours but on the opposite side of the river from Smiltynė (ferry a short walk from the harbour). Shops are well stocked and there is a good indoor/outdoor market. There are several restaurants in the town.

## Nida

55°18'.11N 21°00'.65E (yacht harbour entrance, midway between moles)

Nida, some 30M from Klaipėda, is set among attractive surroundings on the sandspit which separates the Curonian Lagoon from the Baltic Sea. Nida is accessible by bus or taxi as well as water. The harbour consists of two basins. The northern one is just for fishing boats and the southern one is for guests. Mooring is bows-to from stern buoys and there is water and electricity available.

*Note* Passage through the Curonian Lagoon should be made only within the marked channel. The minimum depth in the Lagoon channel is 2.1m but this does depend on the water level in the lagoon and may fluctuate by up to 0.3m. Outside the channel the waters are very shallow.

Midsummer celebrations in Nida *Derbrauni/Wikimedia Commons (https://en.m.wikipedia.org/wiki/File:Midsummer_in_Nida_03.jpg)*

Traditional houses in Nida *Zairon/Wikimedia Commons (https:// commons.wikimedia.org/wiki/File:Kurische_Nehrung_Wimpel_der_ Kurenfischer_in_Nida_1.JPG)*

# 8. LATVIA

The Latvian coastline stretches from Ainaži in the eastern part of the Gulf of Rīga to Pape on the Baltic Sea coast. It provides an attractive cruising ground with a combination of interesting harbours and places of great historic interest. Visiting yachtsmen can be sure of a warm welcome.

Particular care should be taken when transiting the Irbensky Strait due to extensive shoals outside the buoyed channels.

## THE COUNTRY

The name *Latvija* is derived from the name of the ancient Latgalians, an ancient Baltic tribe (along with the *Curonians*, *Selonians* and *Semigallians*). They form the ethnic core of modern Latvians along with the Finnic Livonians.

Latvia's total area of 64,589km$^2$ consists mostly of a low lying plain, though to the east the country becomes hilly. The land is crossed by a number of rivers, many of which drain into the Gulf of Rīga. The largest of these is the Daugava which rises in Russia. There are also numerous lakes, streams, marshes and bogs. Forest covers 43% of the country and peat bogs account for a further 10%. Nearly half the land is agricultural, with small farms and fields often tucked away in forest clearings. The

# KEY INFORMATION

### Rescue/Safety services

**Emergency** ☎ 112

**MRCC Rīga Rescue Radio** monitor MF 2182 kHz, VHF Ch 16, DSC MMSI number 002750100 on MF 2187.5 kHz and VHF Ch 70. Call sign **'Rīga Rescue Radio'** **www.mrcc.lv**

**Coast Guard** Emergency phone ☎+371 67 323 103, +371 29 476 101, +371 67 082 070

### Charts, pilot books & cruising guides

UKHO Admiralty and Latvian Hydrographic Service charts cover the coast. UKHO Admiralty charts are useful for passage planning but for detailed navigation the Latvian charts must be used.

The Folio of Charts of Latvia for Yachts is recommended (covering the coast from just south of Klaipėda (Lithuania) to the southern end of Moon Sound including southern coast of Saaremaa (Estonia). This also includes detailed harbour charts for all Latvian ports). Charts are available through **https://lja.lv/en**. Queries can be sent to mapshop@lja.lv or ☎+371 6706 2101.

Baltic Pilot Volume II (NP 19) Pilot of Baltic Sea, Latvian Coast. Maritime Administration of Latvia. Updated by Notices to Mariners at **www.lja.lv/en/ATONLV/getNMList/current**

### Time

Latvia is in the Eastern European time zone (UT+2 in winter/UT+3 in summer). Summer time starts and ends on the same dates as the rest of the EU.

### € Money

The Euro. All major currencies can be readily exchanged at banks or exchange booths, and cash is easily obtained from ATMs. Credit cards are widely used.

### Formalities

Latvia is a member of the EU and of the Schengen Area (see Main Introduction page 9 for details of Schengen formalities). EU passport holders do not require a visa. The website of the **Latvian Embassy https://www.mfa.gov.lv/en/** lists countries whose citizens do not need visas.

If a visa is needed contact the Consular Office of the Latvian Embassy at Grove House, 248A Marylebone Road NW1 6JZ, consulate.uk@mfa.gov.lv

**The British Embassy** in Rīga can be contacted on ☎+371 6777 4700, britishembassy.riga@fcdo.gov.uk, **www.gov.uk/government/world/latvia**

Formal reporting is not required for passages between Latvia and another Schengen country.

Within the country, it is a requirement for yachts to report arrival and departures to the coastguard at each port visited. Calls should be made on VHF Ch 16 giving name of vessel, number of persons on board, intended destination and flag state. This is not an immigration formality but a matter of maritime safety. In practice most reporting is done by the harbour office.

Latvian Border guards are on duty in some harbours and perform a role as coastguards. In some harbours (Pāvilosta and Liepāja) a yacht declaration form (essentially a crew list) has to be completed at the harbour office and this information is subsequently forwarded to the border guards.

Although nationals are required to have a 'boat driving licence', this does not apply to skippers of foreign flagged vessels. In practice, skippers and crew would be advised to carry any certificates of competence wherever they are sailing.

### Public holidays

Public holidays:
1 Jan, Good Friday, Easter Sunday and Monday, 1 May (Labour Day), 4 May (Declaration of Independence), the second Sunday in May (Mothers' Day), 23 June (Līgo, the midsummer festival), 24 June (St John's Day), 18 Nov (Independence or National Day), 25–26 Dec, 31 Dec. There are, in addition, Remembrance Days on which some services may not be open.

### Communications

Mobile phones and the mail system all function efficiently. WiFi and internet access is available in most ports in Latvia. Access to high-speed internet in Latvia is among the best in the European Union, according to data published by Eurostat.

To ring abroad from Latvia dial 00 followed by the country code, area code (omitting any initial 0) and number.

The country code for Latvia is 371 followed by the 8 digits which comprise Latvian telephone numbers (this includes the area code).

Mobile numbers begin with a 2 and landlines with a 6.

### Travel

Rīga has an international **airport** with direct flights to many European and Scandinavian cities. Rīga can be reached by bus and train from cities all across Europe. There is also a good internal network for **bus** travel.

**Ferries** sail from Liepāja to Travemünde (Germany), from Ventspils to Nynäshamn (Sweden). At time of writing, in 2025 there are no ferries to or from Rīga. However, routes and operating companies change frequently and the current situation should be checked before any plans are made. Useful website for ferry information www.directferries.com

### Websites

**www.inyourpocket.com** – The homepage of inyourpocket – search for Latvia

**www.rigathisweek.lv** – The homepage of the Rīga This Week guide

**www.lja.lv/en/** – The Maritime Administration of Latvia, including the Latvian Hydrographic Service and current chart catalogue

**www.latvia.travel/en** – Tourist information about Latvia.

### Radio communications

VHF Ch 16 should be monitored while on passage. The coastguard at Pape and Kolka lights may call up passing craft including yachts. Details of VHF channels and call signs will be found under each harbour heading.

### Weather information

Weather forecasts and navigational warnings are broadcast in the Liepāja area on VHF Ch 11 at 0805 and 2005 LT, by Rīga Rescue Radio (MRCC Rīga) on VHF Ch 71 at 0703 and 1503 LT. Rīga Traffic and Ventspils Traffic give weather information on request.

Weather information is available online on **marine.meteo.lv** and **videscentrs.lvgmc.lv**.

coastline extends some 500km along the Baltic Sea and the Gulf of Rīga, and is lined with sandy beaches, mostly backed by dunes and pine forest.

Latvia's harbours all lie in river mouths and in former times served fishing fleets and canning factories. With the demise of the Soviet Union the market for processed fish disappeared. At the same time fish stocks diminished and EU quotas came into force, all contributing to a loss of work for the fishing fleets. This has given some of the harbours opportunities to develop facilities for yachting. The major harbours Liepāja, Ventspils (which also has an oil terminal) and Rīga are ice-free ports and have commercial import/export trade.

Services account for 74% of GDP and industry for about 22%. Major products are synthetic fibres, textiles, electronics, processed foods, timber, processed wood products, processed metals, pharmaceuticals, railroad cars. Agriculture is now of lesser importance but, combined with forestry, still provides about 8% of employment compared with 24% for industry and 68% for services. Forestry provides important exports such as sawn timber, and both major and minor harbours export timber in all its forms. Approximately 50% of trade is with the EU and major exports comprise foodstuffs, wood and wood products, metals, machinery and textiles.

Latvia is an intriguing country - here's a few facts which you may not know about Latvia:

- The inventor of Levis jeans was actually a Latvian tailor called Jākobs Jufess. He was backed financially to produce them by Levi Strauss. The rest is history!
- On 23 August 1989, 2 million people from Estonia, Latvia and Lithuania joined hands in protest against Soviet occupation. They formed a massive human chain spanning 690km through the capitals of all three nations. It united people from the Baltic States in their pursuit of freedom and is now is included in the UNESCO Memory of the World Register
- The first Christmas tree was decorated in Riga in 1510 - something which has now become a global phenomenon. The Brotherhood of Blackheads (which existed in Riga from about 1334 until 1939) recorded detailed information in their archives. The

tree was apparently decorated with bouquets of ribbons, dried flowers, straw dolls, weave and fruits

- The artist Mark Rothko was born in Daugavpils in southeast Latvia. He then moved and became best-known in the US. His No. 6 (Violet, green and red) became one of the priciest paintings of all time when it sold for 140 million euros in 2014. The Daugavpils Fortress has a Mark Rothko art centre where you can learn more about the artist who could be considered the founder of abstract expressionism
- Ice Hockey is Latvia's most popular sport with a number of players going on to play in the USA for NHL teams. The second most popular sport in the country is basketball
- The Latvian flag is considered to be the oldest national flag in the world still in use. It was first documented in the *Rhymed Chronicle of Livonia* which covers the period from 1180 to 1343

### Highlights

Rīga Old Town. Villas from Tsarist times and beach at Majori, Jūrmala. Rundales and Mežotne Palaces. Europe's widest waterfall – the Rumba at Kuldiga. Sigulda and the cable car crossing the Gauja river.

## The people, the church & the language

The total population of some 1.88 million is made up of 62% Latvians and 24% Russians, the remainder comprising mainly Belorussians and Ukrainians. 84% of the population have the status of 'citizen', which is dependent upon both residency and proficiency in Latvian.

The majority of Christians are Lutherans, but many follow the Orthodox faith and in the east of the country there is a predominance of Catholics. The national language is Latvian. Some of the ethnic Russian population speak only Russian. The generations educated in Soviet times have fluent Russian, whereas younger generations have fluent English.

## History

The Latvian people, like the Lithuanians, are descended from the Balts, Indo-European tribes who arrived around 3,000BCE. The Daugava River through Rīga had been one of the trading routes of the Amber Road to the Mediterranean and Black seas since ancient times. In the 12th century, the Hanseatic League set up a trading centre on the river near modern Rīga.

Present day Latvia evolved from the major tribes whose names live on in the regions - Kurzeme, Zemgale, Vidzeme and Latgale. The Couronians in the west were fighting folk, known as Baltic Vikings, while the tribes to the south and east were prosperous and peaceful farmers. In between, around the Gulf of Rīga, were Livonian fishermen and traders.

Latvian peoples were still mainly pagan, although some were members of the Russian Orthodox Church. Then the Pope declared the Northern Crusade. Bishop Albrecht arrived in Rīga in 1202 with 300 boatloads of soldiers, the 'Livonian Brothers of the Sword', to convert everybody. The Livonian Order made steady progress conquering much of Latvia and then southern Estonia, but was routed when they attacked Lithuania in 1236. The Pope assigned the survivors to the Teutonic Order, a more disciplined and even more ruthless crusading army, brought in by Poland to subjugate pagan Prussia to the southwest.

Once Latvia and southern Estonia were defeated, German immigrants formed a ruling elite of landowners and merchants, while the local people were reduced to serfs. The name 'Livonia' was used to describe the whole conquered area, which later included all the rest of Estonia as well.

Over the coming years Livonia was fought over by Denmark, Sweden, Russia and the Polish-Lithuanian Commonwealth. By the end of the 16th century Livonia was a Duchy within Poland-Lithuania. Then Gustavus Adolphus of Sweden won it in 1621. Under his control, serfs were liberated and offered education and large private estates were broken up.

In 1700 came the Great Northern War, when Denmark, Poland-Lithuania and Russia sought to break up the huge Swedish empire in the Baltic. In 1710 Peter the Great secured Swedish Livonia for Russia. Then at the end of the century, a similar alliance broke up Poland-Lithuania, and Russia gained the rest of Livonia. Gustavus Adolphus's reforms were reversed as Russia used the German landowners of Livonia to run the Duchy.

In the 19th century Latvian nationalism developed, centred on the Latvian language, just as similar movements in Estonia and Lithuania centred on their respective languages. Tsar Alexander III's efforts to Russify all three were correspondingly counter-productive. Poverty led to a growth of socialist revolutionary movements. During the attempted Russian revolution of 1905, a thousand armed conflicts were registered in Latvia, between peasants and the German nobility.

During the First World War, Germany occupied Latvia until 1918 when Latvia declared itself an independent democracy within its current ethnographic borders. There were three more years of fighting before Latvia had cleared both German and Soviet forces. Land reforms were then introduced whereby traditional landlords were allowed only fifty hectares, the rest being shared amongst the Latvian peasantry. Soon more land was under cultivation than ever before and Latvian prosperity continued to grow until the Second World War.

During the Second World War Latvia suffered the same fate as Estonia and Lithuania: first Soviet occupation, then Nazi and then Soviet again.

After the war Latvia was made a Soviet within the Soviet Union, with large numbers being deported to Siberia and replaced by Russians. The Soviet authorities did, however, see the potential of Latvia and set up some of its most advanced chemical and manufacturing facilities alongside the existing farming and food processing. As in the other Baltic States, passive resistance grew in the later 1980s. On 23 August 1989, to mark 50th anniversary of the signing of the infamous Molotov-Ribbentrop Pact, two million Lithuanians, Latvians and Estonians formed the 'Baltic Way', a human chain 690km long that linked their three capital cities. Independence at last returned with the collapse of the Soviet Union in 1991.

Latvia is now a democratic member of NATO, the UN, the EU and signed the Schengen Agreement in 2007. They joined the Eurozone in 2014 and adopted the euro as their currency. In the same year Riga was the European Capital of Culture and Latvian Valdis Dombrovskis was named vice-president of the European Commission. In 2015 they held the presidency of Council of the European Union. In May 2023, the parliament elected Edgars Rinkēvičs as new President of Latvia, making him the European Union's first openly gay head of state.

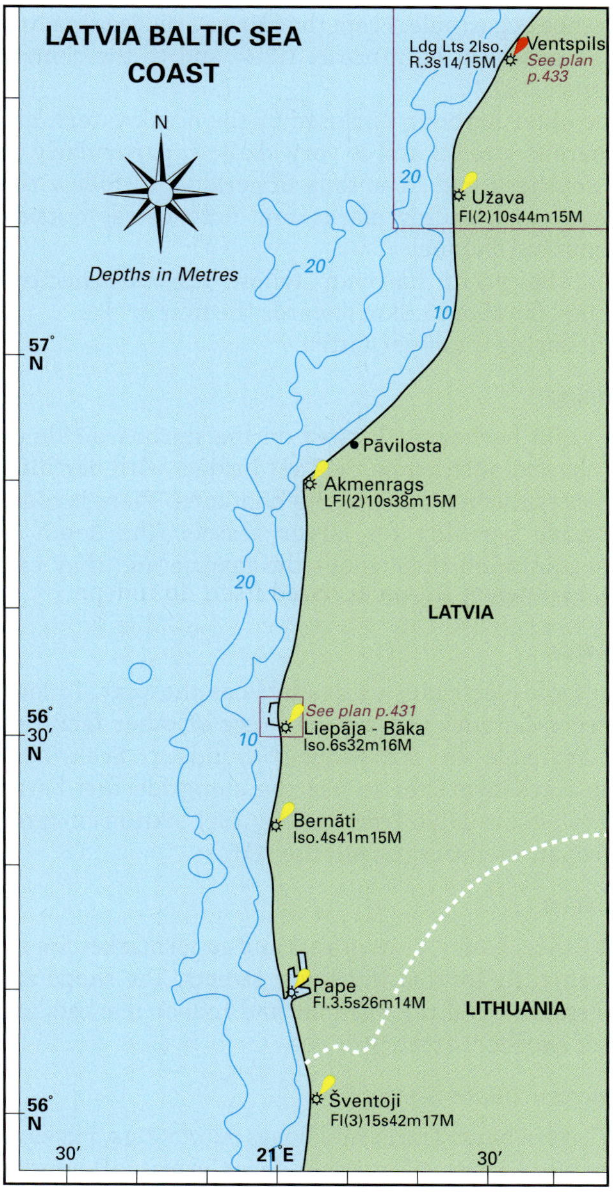


## CRUISING INFORMATION

### Yacht services

Advice regarding craning and repair facilities should be sought from the local yacht club or harbour captain, but other than in Liepāja, Ventspils and Rīga the availability of parts and equipment is likely to be limited.

Local yachts are taken ashore during winter and some foreign yachts overwinter. Anyone planning to overwinter should check the options early in the season and ensure that their insurers are agreeable. There may be a problem finding suitable cradles although it is sometimes possible to have a local cradle adapted. Twin keeled craft can easily be accommodated. There are over-wintering facilities on both banks of the river at Pāvilosta.

Yachts clubs are run as businesses and own a number of yachts but private yacht ownership continues to increase.

### Chandlery

The major cities of Liepāja, Ventspils and Rīga offer the best opportunities of obtaining chandlery. Spare parts may be available elsewhere and advice should be sought from the harbourmaster. Most local boatowners make purchases online.

### Holding tanks

Holding tanks are not yet mandatory although desirable. Pump out facilities provided in some larger ports.

### Gas

Regate, the chandlers at Kipsala, Rīga, stock exchange Campinggaz cylinders.

### Diesel

Latvian diesel contains 5% bio component. There are fuelling berths at Liepāja, in the River Daugava 5M north of Rīga (57°02'.30N 24°03'.74E), and at Pāvilosta. Non-masted craft can also obtain fuel beyond the bridges in the Daugava River. Elsewhere fuel can generally be obtained either through special delivery organised by a yacht club or harbour captain, or by cans carried from the nearest filling station.

### Shopping

Well stocked shops and supermarkets can be found in all towns.

### Alcohol

Alcohol can be purchased from shops and supermarkets without restriction.

There is a blood-alcohol limit of 0.5/ml in inland waterways. At sea this applies to professional seamen on commercial ships but it is considered that the same regulation could be applied to leisure sailors in the case of an accident.

# 8A. BALTIC SEA COAST LATVIA

## LIEPĀJA

56°30'.76N 21°00'.74E (yacht moorings)

### Distances
Klaipėda 50M, South Gotland 80M, Ventspils 55M

### Lights
**Bernati** 56°22'.9N 20°58'.9E Iso.W.4s41m15M Red planking on metal framework tower 21m
**Liepāja-Baka** 56°31'.0N 20°59'.5E Iso.W.6s32m16M Round tower, red and white bands 30m
**Akmenrags** 56°49'.9N 21°03'.4E LFl(2)W.10s38m15M Red round stone tower 37m
**Central entrance, Leading Lights 067.7°** *Front* 56°32'.7N 20°59'.9E Iso.R.3s21m12M White rectangle, black vertical stripe on white framework tower 20m
*Rear*, 984m from front, Iso.R.3s33m14M
Red trapezium, white vertical stripe on red framework tower 30m
**Central entrance, north side** 56°32'.3N 20°57'.9E Iso.R.4s10m3M Red round column with platform 5m
**Central entrance, south side** 56°32'.2N 20°57'.9E Iso.G.4s15m2M Green round column with platform 5m
**South entrance, Leading Lights 112.4°** *Front* 56°31'.4N 20°59'.7E Iso.G.2s33m9M White rectangle, black stripe on framework tower 30m
*Rear* 422m from front Iso.G.2s49m9M White rectangle, black stripe on framework tower 45m Both lights visible on leading line only
**South entrance, north side** 56°31'.8N 20°58'.1E Iso.R.2s9m3M Red round column with platform 5m
**South entrance, south side** 56°31'.7N 20°58'.1E Iso.G.2s11m2M Green round column with platform 5m

### Contacts
**Liepāja** VTS VHF Ch 11/16. Call sign **'Liepāja Radio 1'**
**Harbour** ✆+371 2615 5882
www.liepaja-sez.lv/en/liepaja-marina/
info@liepajamarina.lv

*Liepāja lighthouse and port* *Alvals/Wikimedia Commons (https://commons.wikimedia.org/wiki/File:Liepaja_lighthouse_and_port.JPG)*

Liepāja (pronounced *Leea-pie-ya*) is known throughout Latvia as the *"City where the wind is born"* thanks to the constant sea breeze. A song with the same name (In Latvian: *"Pilsētā, kurā piedzimst vējš"*) was composed by Imants Kalniņš. This is now the city's anthem. Its reputation as the windiest city in Latvia was reinforced by the largest wind farm in the country (33 Enercon wind turbines) being built nearby. The name is derived from the Livonian word *Liiv*, which means "sand".

Liepāja is Latvia's third major port, handling mainly grain and timber but also with a shipyard, naval base and fishing harbour. Liepāja is a developing commercial centre. The town centre, which has been refurbished, straddles the canal which connects Lake Liepāja to the Baltic Sea.

For further information about the town, see www.liepaja.travel/en/

### Approach & entry

56°30'.39N 20°49'.78E (safe water buoy)

The approaches to Liepāja harbour are shallow and should be regarded as unsafe in bad weather. Either the southern or the central entrances should be used, although there have been reports that the northern entrance is passable. From the fairway the leading line to the southern entrance is 112.4° and to the central entrance 067.7°.

The outer harbour, enclosed by the breakwaters, has numerous wrecks and is very shallow, particularly at the southern end. It is thus imperative to follow the buoyage and leading marks, and not to stray outside the marked channel.

For the yacht harbour, follow the Tirdzniecības channel for about 1.5km towards the first bridge.

Anchoring is not permitted.

### Berthing

The yacht harbour is located on the starboard side of the channel just below the first bridge, with berthing (finger pontoons) on two long pontoons. There is some alongside berthing for larger vessels. The depth is 4.5m minimum throughout the marina and they can accommodate boats up to 60m.

### Services

Water and electricity are available on the quay. Toilets, showers, laundry and a wide range of other facilities are available in the harbour building. Seek help from Harbourmaster to use the alongside fuel berth otherwise available from nearby fuel station in cans. For repair facilities consult the HM.

### Facilities

Post Office, banks, restaurants and supermarket are all conveniently located in nearby streets. The shops are well stocked and the open air and indoor markets are full of excellent fresh produce.

### Communications & travel

WiFi at harbour. Trains and buses run to Rīga, buses to Ventspils. Ferries to Travemünde in Germany. Domestic airport at Liepāja (see Travel, page 427).

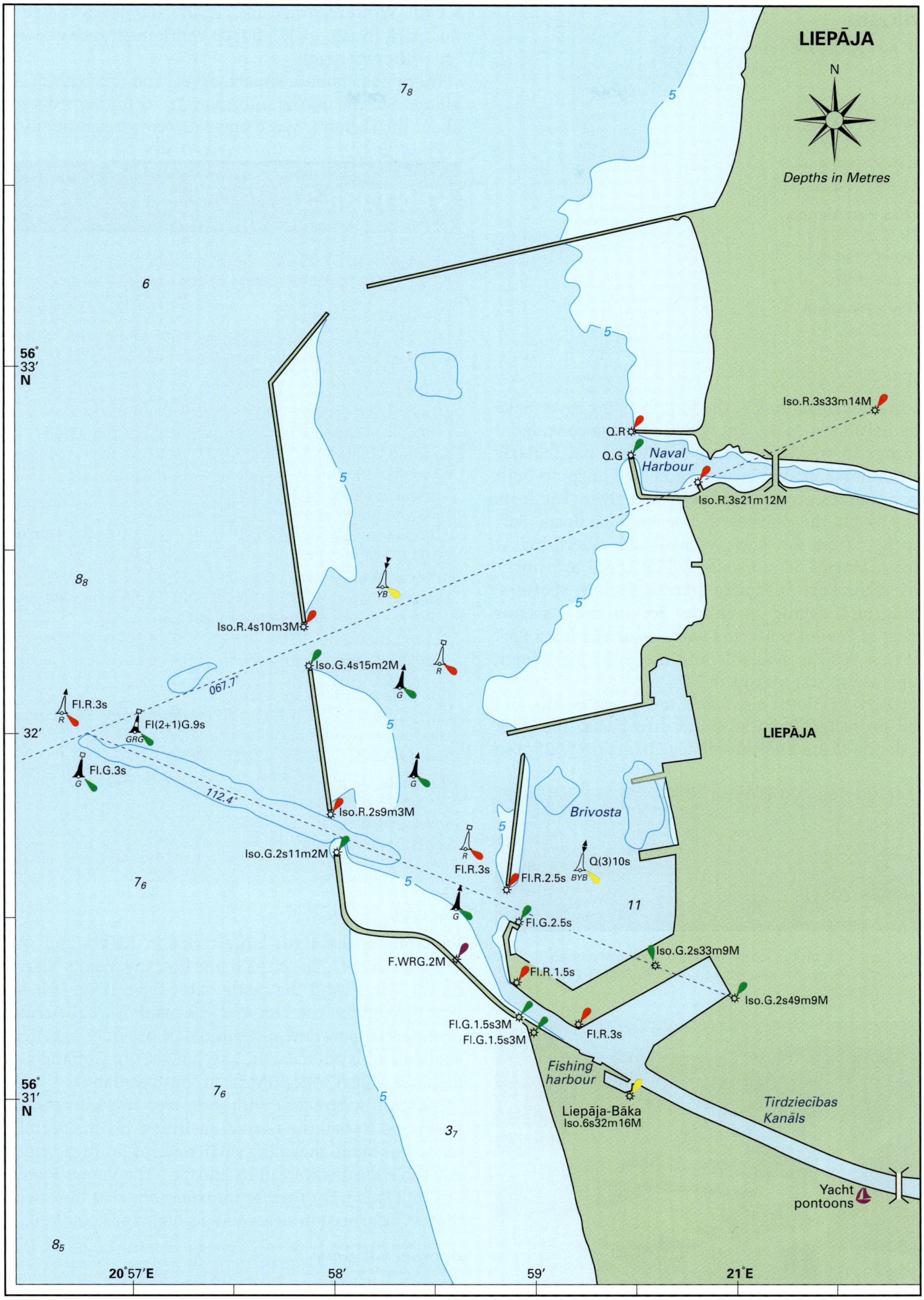
LIEPĀJA
N
Depths in Metres
Iso.R.3s33m14M
Q.R
Q.G
Naval Harbour
Iso.R.3s21m12M
Iso.R.4s10m3M
YB
Iso.G.4s15m2M
R
G
067.7°
Fl.R.3s
R
Fl(2+1)G.9s
GRG
Fl.G.3s
G
112.4°
Iso.R.2s9m3M
Brivosta
LIEPĀJA
Iso.G.2s11m2M
Fl.R.3s
Fl.R.2.5s
Q(3)10s
BYB
Fl.G.2.5s
Iso.G.2s33m9M
F.WRG.2M
Fl.R.1.5s
Iso.G.2s49m9M
Fl.G.1.5s3M
Fl.G.1.5s3M
Fl.R.3s
Fishing harbour
Liepāja-Bāka
Iso.6s32m16M
Tirdziecības Kanāls
Yacht pontoons
56° 33′ N
32′
56° 31′ N
20°57′E
58′
59′
21°E

## Pāvilosta

56°54'.34N 21°08'.94E (safe water buoy)
56°53'.53N 21°10'.03E (centre of harbour entrance)

**Contacts**

**Pāvilosta Marina**
✆+371 2912 5521
www.pavilostamarina.lv
pavilosta@pavilostamarina.lv

**Pāvilosta Port Marina**
✆+371 2912 5521
www.pavilostaport.lv
info@pavilostaport.lv

**Boat Park Pāvilosta**
✆+371 2927 4532
www.boatpark.lv
info@boatpark.lv

Pāvilosta is a small port at the mouth of the River Saka on the Baltic Sea coast. Entry and exit are considered dangerous in winds over Force 5 (20kn) particularly from the north or northwest. There are purpose built yacht harbours on both sides of the river. Pāvilosta Marina is on the starboard side and Pāvilosta Port Authority is on the port (village) side. Berthing at Pāvilosta Marina is alongside while there are finger berths at the Port Authority marina. Toilets, showers, washing and drying machines are in the harbour building at Pāvilosta Marina and also at Pāvilosta Port Authority. WiFi is available and there is a fuel berth just upriver on starboard side.

Boat Park Pāvilosta also has a few guest berths and is well protected from all wind directions. The park has a depth of 3m and can manage boats up to 25m in length. Winter storage and repairs are also available at Boatpark (boatpark.lv – but do check insurance validity for winter storage).

There is a small supermarket and restaurant in village. See the tourist information site for more details about the region (www.dienvidkurzeme.travel/home/).

Pāvilosta harbour moles *Laima Gūtmane (simka)/Wikimedia Commons (https://commons.wikimedia.org/wiki/File:P%C4%81vilosta_-_panoramio_(13).jpg)*

Pāvilosta harbour *Kārlis Volkovskis/Wikimedia Commons (https://commons.wikimedia.org/wiki/File:P%C4%81vilosta,_Dienvidkurzeme_(125).jpg)*

## VENTSPILS

57°24'.40N 21°31'.53E (centre of harbour entrance)
57°23'.73N 21°32'.38E (centre of entrance to Fish Dock)

### Distances

Liepāja 55M, South Gotland 95M, Fårösund 85M, Roomassaare 65M, Roja 70M, Rīga 115M

### Lights

**Užava** 57°12'.6N 21°24'.9E Fl(2)W.10s44m15M
Racon White round stone tower with balcony 19m
**Leading Lights 143.7°** *Front* 57°23'.7N 21°32'.5E
Iso.R.3s28m14M Red rectangle, white stripe, on framework tower 25m
*Rear* 0.5M from front, Iso.R.3s45m15M
Red rectangle, white stripe, on framework tower 35m
**Oviši** 57°34'.1N 21°43'.0E LFl.W.7.5s38m15M
Racon White round stone tower 37m
**North breakwater** 57°24'.5N 21°31'.6E Fl(2)R.3s14m4M
White round concrete tower, red lantern 11m
**South breakwater** 57°24'.3N 21°31'.5E Fl(2)G.3s14m3M
White round concrete tower, green lantern 11m

### Contacts

**Port Control** VHF Ch 9/16 call *Ventspils Traffic Service* for clearance on entry or departure
**Yacht Harbour** *Mobile* +371 283 11919

**Ventspils Marina**
✆+371 2831 1919
www.ventspilsmarina.lv/eng/
ventspilsmarina@nym.lv

### *General*

Ventspils is the sixth largest city in Latvia and was founded in 1343. The city's name literally means "Castle on the Venta" and the castle dates from 1290. It is ice free throughout the year and as a result is a substantial commercial port and oil terminal. It provides excellent shelter and is the nearest Latvian port to Gotland at a distance of just over 90M from south Gotland.

The town is attractive with wide, tree-lined streets and parks and has all the normal facilities. If time permits take a bus to the charming small town of Kuldiga, which has the widest waterfall in Europe – the *Ventas Rumba* or *Venta Rapid*. For further information, visit the town's tourist information site: www.visitventspils.com/en/.

### *Approach & entry*

From north: 57°28'.52N 21°25'.91E (fairway buoy)
From south: 57°26'.28N 21°24'.67E (fairway buoy)

The approach is via a straight, buoyed channel to the harbour entrance. It would be unwise to stray from the channel due to a number of dangerous wrecks in the

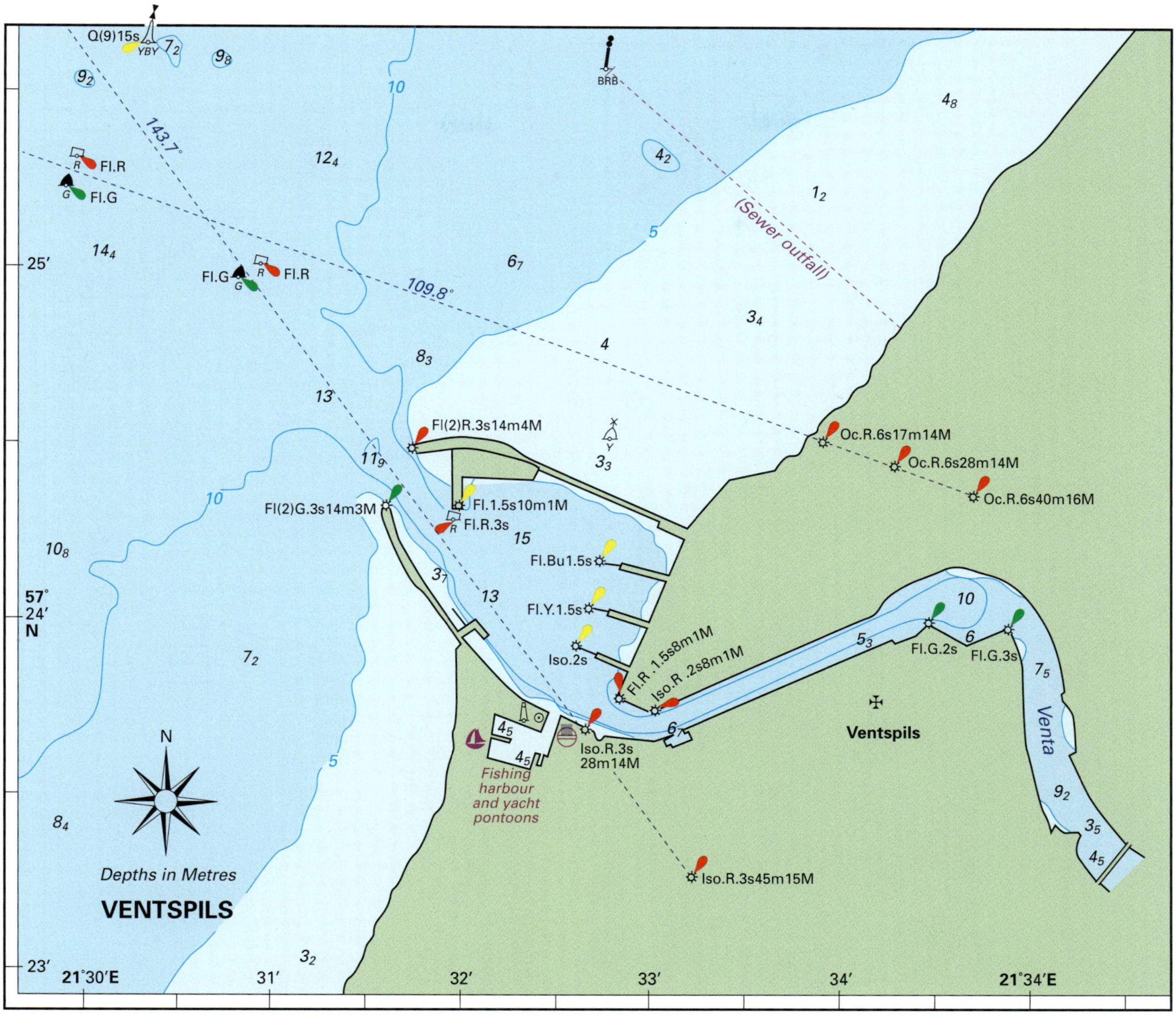

Ventspils harbour *Edgars Šulcs/Wikimedia Commons (https://commons.wikimedia.org/wiki/File:Ventspils_viduslaiku_pils_4.jpg)*

vicinity. Prior to entry (and departure) all boats should call VHF Ch 9/16 *Ventspils Traffic Service* for clearance. Entry is straightforward by day or night, although a detailed chart is necessary for the latter.

### Berthing

Yachts berth at the western end of the fish dock. Keep to the starboard side of the harbour, and head for a large grey/white building. Turn to starboard just before the building and moor at the head of the basin in front of the harbour office building, bows-to staging and stern to a buoy. Recent developments include an extension to the western side of the basin with finger berths. The depth should be a minimum of 3.5m throughout though the water level may vary by up to 0.3m above or below the mean. Anchoring is not permitted.

### Services

Electricity and water is available on the quayside and showers, sauna and laundry facilities in harbour building. Fuel can be delivered in cans by arrangement with the harbour office. The harbour staff may also be able to assist with limited repair facilities.

### Facilities

Bar available. Small general store outside the dock gates. For shops, banks and restaurants, plus indoor and open air markets, it is necessary to go into the town some 2.5km away.

### Communications & travel

WiFi at the harbour. From Ventspils it is possible to travel by bus or train all over Latvia, or across Europe, via Rīga. Car hire can be arranged via the harbour office. Ferries to Nynäshamn (Sweden).

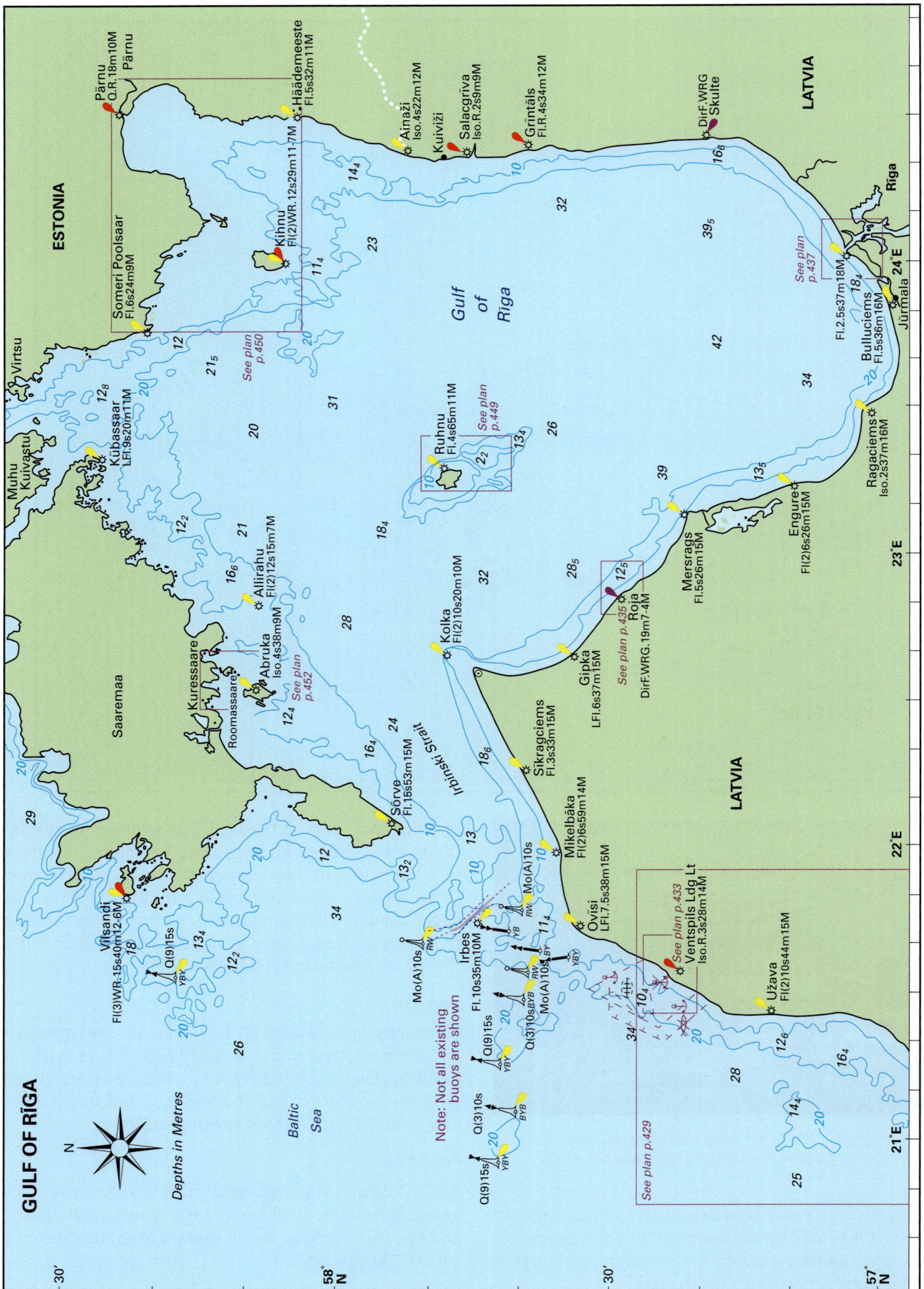
GULF OF RĪGA
Depths in Metres
N
Baltic Sea
Note: Not all existing buoys are shown
ESTONIA
LATVIA
Saaremaa
Gulf of Riga
Irbinski Strait
Pärnu Q.R.18m10M
Pärnu
Häädemeeste Fl.5s32m11M
Kihnu Fl(2)WR.12s29m11-7M
Someri Poolsaar Fl.6s24m9M
Virtsu
Kübassaar LFl.9s20m11M
Muhu
Kuivastu
Allirahu Fl(2)12s15m7M
Abruka Iso.4s38m9M
Kuressaare
Roomassaare
Sõrve Fl.15s53m15M
Vilsandi Fl(3)WR.15s40m12-6M
Ruhnu Fl.4s65m11M
Kolka Fl(2)10s20m10M
Ainaži Iso.4s22m12M
Kuiviži
Salacgriva Iso.R.2s9m9M
Grīntāls Fl.R.4s34m12M
DirF.WRG Skulte
Riga
Fl.2.5s37m18M
Bulluciems Fl.5s36m16M
Jūrmala
Ragaciems Iso.2s37m16M
Engure Fl(2)6s26m15M
Mersrags Fl.5s26m15M
Roja DirF.WRG.19m7-4M
Gipka LFl.6s37m15M
Sikragciems Fl.3s33m15M
Mikelbāka Fl(2)6s59m14M
Ovīsi LFl.7.5s38m15M
Irbes Fl.10s35m10M
Mo(A)10s
Q(9)15s
Q(3)10s
Ventspils Ldg Lt Iso.R.3s28m14M
Užava Fl(2)10s44m15M
See plan p.450
See plan p.449
See plan p.452
See plan p.435
See plan p.437
See plan p.433
See plan p.429
58° N
57° N
21°E
22°E
23°E
24°E

# 8B. THE GULF OF RĪGA

## ROJA

57°30'.64N 22°48'.79E (centre of entrance to outer harbour)

### Distances

Ventspils 70M, Roomassaare 45M, Rīga 50M, Pärnu 75M

### Lights

**Kolka** 57°48'.0N 22°38'.0E Fl(2)10s20m10M
Red round tower with balcony and lantern room 21m
Racon (K)

**Gipka** 57°34'.2N 22°39'.5E LFl.W.6s37m15M
Two red rectangles over white square on metal framework tower 30m

**Dir Lt. 215°** 57°30'.5N 22°48'.6E F Sectored DirF. WRG.19m7-4M Red triangular tower 19.5m

**Northwest mole** 57°30'.7N 22°48'.7E Fl.G.3s6m2M
White round column 3m

**Southeast mole** 57°30'.6N 22°48'.8E Fl.R.3s6m2M
Red round column 3m

### Contacts

**Rojas Osta (Port Authority)** ✆+371 264 34813
VHF Ch 10/16, Call *Roja 1*

**Roja Port**
✆+371 2643 4813
www.rojaport.lv/jahtam
rojasosta@apollo.lv

A commercial and fishing harbour (pronounced *Roy ya*) in the entrance to the Roja River with facilities for yachts. Its location makes it useful if on passage between Ventspils and Rīga, or Rīga and Ruhnu or Saaremaa. The town is small but has adequate facilities.

Roja church *M.Strīķis/Wikimedia Commons (https://commons.wikimedia.org/wiki/File:Rojas_eva%C5%86%C4%A3%C4%93liski_luterisk%C4%81_bazn%C4%ABca,_Rojas_kapi,_Roja,_Rojas_novads,_Latvia_-_panoramio.jpg)*

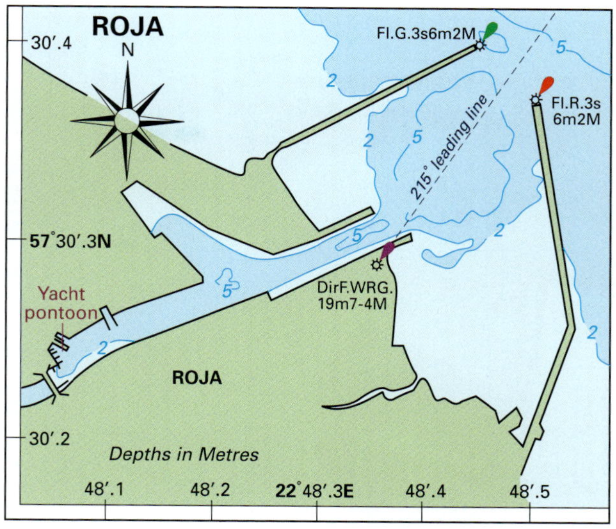


### Approach & entry

Follow the sectored light F.WRG on leading line 215°. Once inside the outer harbour it is essential to keep to the marked channel, as depths outside it shoal rapidly. Pass between the inner moles and continue past the fishing vessel berths to the yacht pontoons at the head of harbour on the starboard side.

### Berthing

Yachts berth to finger pontoons and a jetty just below the road bridge. The minimum depth is 3.5m and they can handle yachts up to 20m. There are 40 berths available. A pedestrian bridge connects the two sides of the river. Anchoring is not permitted.

### Services

Electricity and water on the pontoons. Showers and toilets in facilities building or hotel. Diesel can be supplied by arrangement with the harbour captain, whose advice should be sought for any matters relating to repairs etc.

### Facilities

Adequate food and general shops within a short distance of the harbour. Bars and restaurants at the Roja and Mare hotels.

### Communications & travel

WiFi at harbour. Bus services to Rīga and elsewhere.

## Mērsrags

57°20'.95N 23°11'.92E (safe water buoy)
Approach via lateral red/green buoyed channel.
57°20'.08N 23°08'.47E (centre of harbour entrance)
57°20'.09N 23°07'.57E (yacht moorings)

**Contacts**

**Mērsrags Yacht Centre**
✆+371 2940 9290
mer_kur@inbox.lv

**Yacht Club Kurland**
✆+371 2659 7371
Kurland.projects@gmail.com

Engures Ezers, lake behind Mērsrags *J. Sedols/Wikimedia Commons (https://commons.wikimedia.org/wiki/File:Engures_ezers_pie_Dzedriem.jpg)*

A commercial/fishing port on the western shore of the Gulf of Rīga, open to the east. Entrance is straightforward. There are yacht berths either side of the river at head of harbour before the road bridge with a minimum depth of 3m. Shops and cafés will be found ashore and WiFi is available at the harbour.

## Engure

57°09'.75N 23°13'.93E

**Contacts**

Engure Marina
✆+371 2917 2323
marineengure@gmail.com

With the removal of the floating clubhouse berthing facilities have been expanded both on the west and the south side of the harbour. The approach channel is subject to shifting sands and skippers are advised to seek information from the harbourmaster before attempting entry. Once inside there around approximately 50 berths in a minimum depth of 3.5m

## Jūrmala

56°59'.56N 23°55'.33

Jūrmala is the collective name for a number of famous holiday resorts/health spas situated along a narrow strip of land between the Lielupe River and the Gulf of Rīga. The river entrance from the Gulf of Rīga in 2024 was silted and unusable. Access is available only to unmasted craft via the River Bullupe from the River Daugava. Anchoring in the river may be possible. Contact the Harbour Authority for up to date information (✆+371 26 613 344 or osta@jurmala.lv).

A number of small private marinas and yacht clubs lie on the bank of the River Lielupe.

## RĪGA

56° 57'.20N 24°05'.30E (yacht moorings Rīga City Marina)

### Distances

Roja 50M, Roomassaare 85M, Salacgrīva 45M, Pärnu 80M

### Lights

**Ragaciems** 57°02'.1N 23°29'.2E Iso.W.2s37m16M Red slatted daymark and skeletal mast on square framework tower 30m

**Bulluciems** 56°59'.6N 23°53'.2E Fl.W.5s36m16M Red and white planking on a framework tower 28m

**Daugavgrīva** 57°03'.6N 24°01'.3E Fl.W.2.5s37m18M Racon Round white concrete tower, black bands, balcony 35m

**Leading Lights 141°** *Front* 57°03'.6N 24°01'.3E Iso.R.5s20m11M White daymark, red stripe, on red framework tower 15m
*Rear* 549m from front Iso.R.5s29m11M White rectangle, red stripe, on square red metal framework 26m. Both lights visible on leading line only

**West breakwater** 57°03'.9N 24°00'.6E Fl.G.3s11m2M White concrete tower 7m

**East breakwater** 57°04'.1N 24°00'.9E Fl.R.3s11m4M Round red metal tower with balcony 11.5m

### Contacts

**Rīga Traffic** VHF Ch 9/16 ✆+371 67030800

Rīga City Yacht Club
✆+371 2919 6943
www.pilsetasjahtklubs.lv/en/city-yacht-club-marina/
pilsetasjahtklubs@gmail.com

Rīga Sport Sailing Centre
✆+371 2917 1615
✆+371 2658 7222
stala@inbox.lv
VHF Ch 13

Jahtas Marina and Boatyard
✆+371 2837 2837
armands@jahtas.eu (Armands Kirilovs)
www.jahtas.eu

Auda Marina
✆+371 2948 6273
oto@kompozits.lv

Rīga is the capital city of Latvia, with a population of about 800,000, and lies on the River Daugava about 8M from the sea. There is a busy port along the banks of the river between the city centre and the sea and a considerable amount of industry outside the central area. The Old Town is a UNESCO listed World Heritage site and extremely picturesque. You will find a range of buildings and architectural styles; from Romanesque to Gothic and Baroque. A walk through the streets of the Old Town should not be missed when visiting Rīga.

The newer city centre is spaciously laid out with tree-lined streets and parks. For further information, visit www.latvia.travel/en/city/riga or www.liveriga.com/en/visit.

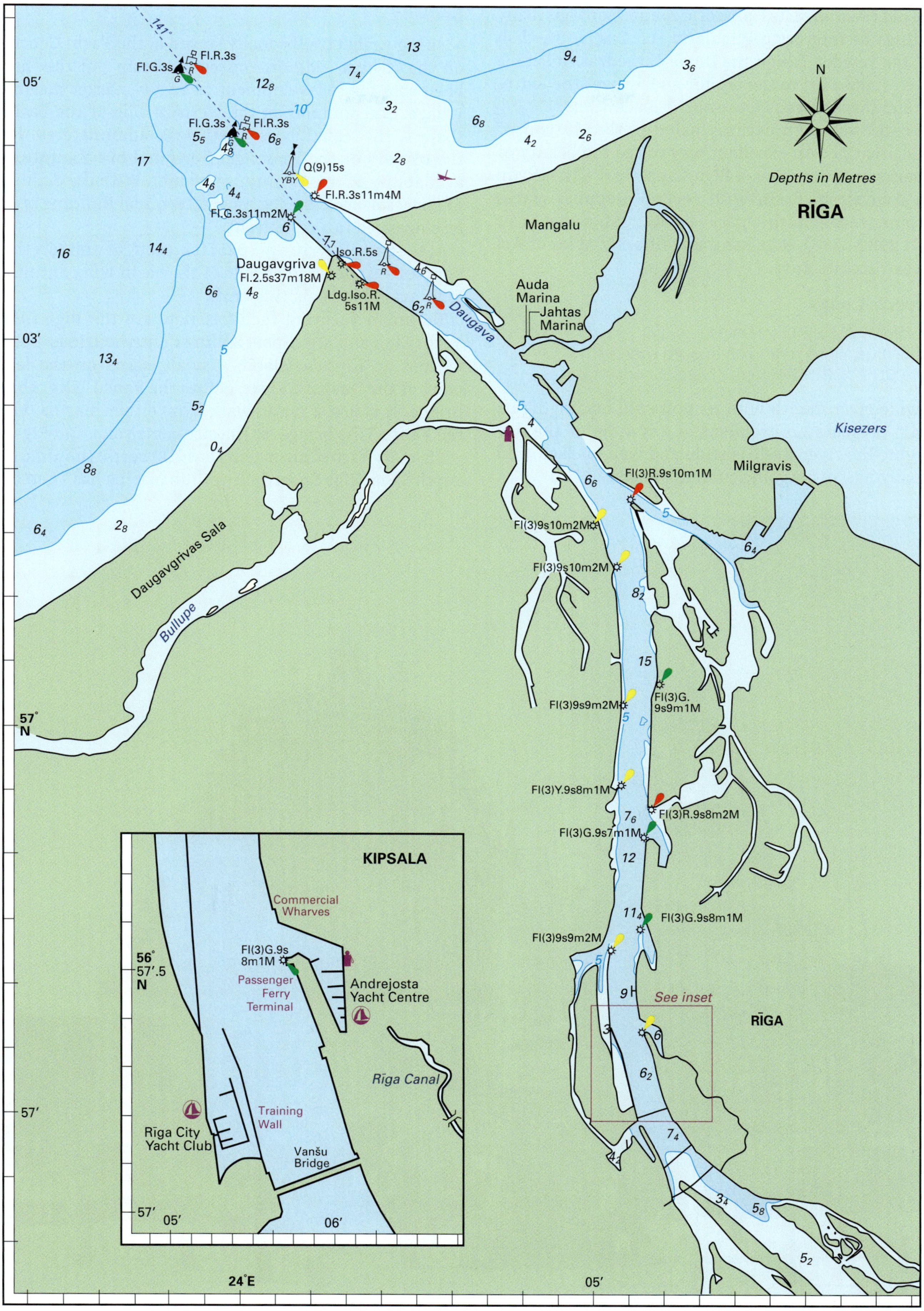

RĪGA
Depths in Metres
N
Fl.R.3s
Fl.G.3s
Q(9)15s
YBY
Fl.R.3s11m4M
Fl.G.3s11m2M
Daugavgriva
Fl.2.5s37m18M
Iso.R.5s
Ldg.Iso.R.
5s11M
Mangalu
Auda
Marina
Jahtas
Marina
Daugava
Kisezers
Milgravis
Fl(3)R.9s10m1M
Fl(3)9s10m2M
Fl(3)9s10m2M
Daugavgrivas Sala
Bullupe
Fl(3)G.
9s9m1M
Fl(3)9s9m2M
Fl(3)Y.9s8m1M
Fl(3)R.9s8m2M
Fl(3)G.9s7m1M
Fl(3)G.9s8m1M
Fl(3)9s9m2M
See inset
RĪGA
KIPSALA
Commercial
Wharves
Fl(3)G.9s
8m1M
Passenger
Ferry
Terminal
Andrejosta
Yacht Centre
Rīga Canal
Training
Wall
Rīga City
Yacht Club
Vanšu
Bridge
56°
57′.5
N
57′
05′
06′
05′
03′
57°
N
57′
24°E
05′

The old town with its Hanseatic connections has many buildings of interest particularly the Castle, Swedish Gate, the Powder Tower, the Dome Cathedral, St Peter's Church (take a lift to the top for a view over the entire city) and the restored House of the Blackheads.

There are various museums including the Museum of the Occupation. An excellent way to see the beauty of the parks and city is via a Rīga Canal Boat – these run from Andrejosta Basin with several stopping places en route through the park (www.rigabycanal.lv or ✆+371 2980 2388). Rīga has many fine examples of Art Nouveau architecture.

### Approach & entry

57°06'.50N 23° 56'.94E (safe water buoy)
Approach via lateral red/green buoyed channel
57°04'.02N 24°00'.76E (centre of harbour entrance)

The wide river mouth with its powerful leading lights on 141° presents no problems at any time of the day or night. The river itself is wide and well marked, and normally has an outgoing current of around 2kn.

### Berthing

Visiting yachts traditionally stayed at the Yacht Centre on the eastern side of Andrejosta Basin but this has been sold for redevelopment as an up-market marina village. The pontoon on the western side of the basin (before the canal boat berths) is administered by the owners of the Passenger Terminal but the future availability of this facility is in doubt. With the demise of ferry services, the Passenger Terminal Building is to be converted to a restaurant.

At the time of writing (2025) it is thought unlikely the pontoon on the western side of the basin will continue to be available to visiting craft.

The main yachting facilities now are the Rīga City Yacht Club and Rīga Sport Sailing Centre marinas, both located on Ķīpsala Island, a small island on the left bank of the Duagava River, before the Vanšu Tilts cable bridge. It is just a 15min walk from either marina, via the Vanšu Tilts bridge, to the city centre and 'Old Rīga'.

Rīga City Yacht Club marina has 200 berths, minimum depth 3.8m. Rīga Sport Sailing Club marina has 7 berths

House of the Blackheads – a building in the old town of Riga *Diego Delso/Wikimedia Commons (https://commons.wikimedia.org/wiki/File:Plaza_del_Ayuntamiento,_Riga,_Letonia,_2012-08-07,_DD_10.JPG) Creative Commons Attribution-Share Alike 3.0 Unported license*

A view over Riga from St Peter's Church *Diego Delso/Wikimedia Commons (https://commons.wikimedia.org/wiki/File:Vistas_desde_la_iglesia_de_San_Pedro,_Riga,_Letonia,_2012-08-07,_DD_12.JPG) Creative Commons Attribution-Share Alike 3.0 Unported license*

An aerial view of Riga City Marina *Robin Matthews*

minimum depth 4m. A full bathymetric map of the marina depths is available through their website.

Other possible facilities include Jahtas Marina and Auda Marina. These are located on the east bank of the Daugava River and are much further from the centre of Rīga, but could be a convenient first stop when sailing from elsewhere. Jahtas have a 30m concrete pontoon equipped with drinking water, electricity and lighting. This jetty is intended for guests and so is kept free and accessible 24hrs, 7 days a week. It is the first accessible berth when sailing from the Gulf of Rīga and travelling along the Daugava to the mouth of the Vecdaugava. Jahtas also offer full boatyard services including a temporary lift-out, should any works be required. Minimum depth is 6.5m and they can cope with boats up to 20m.

Auda Marina is just after Jahtas Marina on the east side of the river. The minimum depth should be 3.5m.

### *Services*

At both Rīga City Yacht Club and the Rīga Sport Sailing Centre water and electricity are provided on the pontoons. Toilets, showers and washing machines are available in service buildings. There is a fuel berth at Latvijas Jahta (Pildne) about 5M down river. For repairs seek advice of the Harbourmaster. Campinggaz bottles can be exchanged at Regate, the chandlers at Kipsala. Pump out facility at Rīga City Marina.

The Jana Seta Map Shop is the largest chart supplier in the country and will dispatch orders abroad. Most major credit cards are accepted.

85a Elizabetes iela, Rīga LV-1050, ✆+371 6724 0894 and +371 2700 0062, veikals@karsuveikals.lv or www.mapshop.lv/en/

### *Facilities*

Rīga itself has all the facilities of a major city - many shops, a choice of restaurants, banks, post office etc. The market, which takes place in four ex-Zeppelin hangars, is one of the largest in Europe, open 7 days a week and can provide almost anything edible and much more besides!

### *Communications & travel*

WiFi at harbours. There is an international airport and railway and bus services within Latvia and to cities all over Europe. Taxis and hire cars are available from the city.

## Skulte

57°19'.20N 24°21'.81E (safe water buoy)
Sectored approach light flashing W/R/G.
57°19'.02N 24°23'.97E (centre of harbour entrance)
57°19'.06N 24°24'.68E (yacht moorings)

A small commercial harbour on the eastern shore of the Gulf of Rīga, open to the west. A pontoon with finger berths has been established well into the harbour giving good shelter. Water and electricity and other services are available and the minimum depth is 3.9m. There is a small general store close by but little else.

## SALACGRĪVA

57°45'.35N 24°21'.49E (yacht moorings)

### Distances

Rīga 45M, Roomassaare 65M, Pärnu 40M

### Lights

**Leading Lights 072.3°** *Front* 57°45'.4N 24°21'.2E
Iso.R.2s9m9M White rectangle, black stripe, on framework tower. 6.4m Visible on leading line only
*Rear* 207m from front Iso.R.4s24m9M
White rectangle, black stripe, on framework tower 18m

### Contacts

**Salacgrīva 52 (Port Authority)** VHF Ch 12/16 call *Port control* ✆+371 2925 6812

**Salacgrīva Port**
✆+371 2925 6812
port@salacgrivaport.lv
www.salacgrivaport.lv/en

A small commercial port conveniently located midway between Rīga and Pärnu.

### *Approach & entry*

57°44'.80N 24°17'.78E (safe water buoy)
Approach via lateral red/green buoyed channel
57°45'.26N 24°20'.40E (centre of harbour entrance)

The harbour entrance is well marked with buoys and leading marks on 072.3°, but becomes rough in onshore (westerly) winds.

### *Berthing*

There is a small pontoon for yachts with stern buoys. Anchoring is not permitted.

Salacgrīva yacht moorings looking south *Robin Matthews*

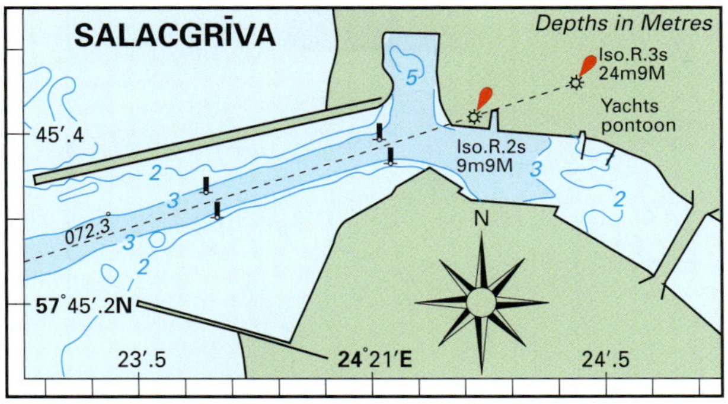


### Services

There are toilets and showers in the facilities building and shops and restaurants are available in the village. Water and electricity. Pontoon protected by security coded gate.

### Facilities

Bar and restaurant at the harbour, with shops and cafés in the nearby village. WiFi at harbour.

### Communications & travel

Buses to Rīga and north to Estonia.

## Kuiviži

57°47'.34N 24°20'.57E (centre of harbour entrance)
57°47'.29N 24°21'.03E (yacht moorings)

**Contacts**

**Kuiviži Marina**
✆+371 2562 3500
info@kapteinuosta.lv
www.kapteinuosta.lv/en-gb
www.salacgrivaport.lv/en/uznemejdarbiba/technical-data-of-the-kuivizi-port/yacht-tourism-leisure

Kuiviži is a redeveloped fishing harbour with separate and well sheltered facilities for yachts. Shallow and narrow entrance recommended to enter only in daylight with good visibility but not in strong onshore winds. The harbourmaster stresses that entering and leaving Kuiviži port must be done following the leading line of the floating mark because there are fishing nets and creels placed close to the channel. The details of the floating mark is as follows vertical red-white at 57°46'.95N 24°17'.10E. The light characteristic is Mo(A) B.10.2s.

There is a small shop and WiFi at the harbour hotel. There is a restaurant (www.kapteinuosta.lv/en-gb/restaurant), toilets, showers and a sauna.

WESTERN
ESTONIA - MAINLAND
& ISLANDS
Depths in Metres
N
Gulf of Finland
Bengtskär
Fl(3)20s51m10M
Russarö
Fl(4)45s34m16M
Jussarö
Fl.12s31m12M
See plan p.471
Tallinnamadal
Fl(2)15s29m10M
See plan p.466
Naissaar
LFl.10s48m12M
Viimsi
Suurupi
Tallinn
Pakrineem
LFl.15s73m12M
Lohusalu
See plan p. 464
Osmussaar
Fl(2)18s39m11M
See plan p.463
Dirhami
ESTONIA
Tahkuna
LFl(2)15s43m12M
Kardla
See plan p.459
Ristna
LFl.WR.15s37m
12-8M
Kõpu
Fl(2)10s
102m26M
HIIUMAA
Norrby
Iso.2s19m12M
VORMSI
Haapsalu
See plan p.461
See plan p.458
Heltermaa
Muhu
Väin
(Moon Sound)
Baltic
Sea
Sõru
Kassaare Laht
Soela Väin
59°N
Åland Is
Turku
Helsinki
60°N
Mariehamn
Hanko
Gulf of Finland
Tallinn
Hiiumaa
ESTONIA
Pärnu
Saaremaa
Gulf of
Rīga
Ventspils
57°N
LATVIA
Rīga
Liepāja
LITHUANIA
20°E
Klaipėda
25°E
MUHU
Kuivastu
See plan p.456
See plan p.434
Kübassaar
LFl.9s20m11M
See plan p. 450
Pärnu
Sõmeri
Vilsandi
FFl(3)WR.15s
40m12-6M
SAAREMAA
Kuressaare
Roomassaare
Abruka
Iso.4s38m9M
Allirahu
Fl(2)12s15m7M
See plan p. 452
Kihnu
Fl(2)WR.12s29m
11-7M
Häädemeeste
Fl.5s32m11M
58°N
Sõrve
Fl.15s53m15M
1
RW
Mo(A)10s
Kolka
Fl(2)10s20m10M
Ruhnu
Fl.4s65m11M
See plan p.449
Ainazi
Iso.4s22m12M
Salacgriva
Iso.R.2s9m9M
Irbes
Fl.10s35m
10M
Gulf
of
Riga
Sikraguciems
Fl.3s33m15M
Grīntāls
Fl.R.4s34m12M
Mikelbāka
Fl(2)6s59m14M
Gipka
LFl.6s37m15M
Ovisi
LFl.7·5s38m15M
Roja
DirF.WRG.20m4M
LATVIA
LATVIA
22°E
24°E

# 9. ESTONIA

Estonia is a most attractive destination for the cruising yachtsman, with good facilities and interesting towns and cities, as well as some intricate pilotage.

The Estonian Maritime Authority has encouraged the building of new yacht harbours as well as improvements to existing harbours. These new or improved harbours vary in size some being very small and shallow while others are purpose-built modern facilities.

The most popular route for visiting yachts on passage between the Gulf of Rīga and the north coast of Estonia or Gulf of Finland is via Moon Sound, which runs between the mainland and the larger Estonian islands. Notwithstanding Arthur Ransome's well known 1923 voyage from Rīga to Helsinki described in *Racundra's First Cruise*, passage through Moon Sound should not be attempted without large-scale local charts, as in places the navigable channels are narrow and the waters on either side are shallow and rock strewn. This applies particularly to the northern part of the passage between Vormsi and the mainland.

The route is well marked with transit beacons and buoys where necessary, but it is dangerous to venture outside the channel. Since the establishment of good harbours at Heltermaa and Kärdla on Hiiumaa, the route between Vormsi and Hiiumaa is increasingly used particularly for yachts transiting to or from the Hanko peninsula in Finland. The complete coastline is covered by Estonian sheet charts but there are three small craft portfolios which cover the whole of Estonia and these are ideally suited for the cruising yachtsman.

Other than the major ports, caution should be exercised if approaching in darkness.

## THE COUNTRY

The territory of Estonia (officially known as the Republic of Estonia) consists of the mainland, the larger islands of Saaremaa and Hiiumaa, and over 2,300 other islands and islets. In total the country covers an area of 45,335km$^2$. With a population of just over 1.3 million, Estonia has one of the lowest population densities in the world: just 31 per km$^2$. This places it 188th in the world.

The country consists for the most part of a low lying plain with higher ground towards the east. There are numerous streams and lakes including one of Europe's largest, Lake Peipsi, lying on the border with Russia. The coast is also low lying and, particularly to the west, is fringed by the many islands they are famous for. These make up nearly 10% of Estonian land. The surrounding seas to the south and west are shallow. About a quarter of the country is forested.

Like the Lithuanians, the Estonians regard their country as the geographical centre of Europe and one study put the island of Saaremaa as that point. It doesn't mention whether the study was funded by the Estonian tourist authority! Nevertheless, the island of Saarema was the site of a significant meteorite strike. The Kaali craters are a group of 9 craters caused by a meteorite strike somewhere between 1530–1450BCE – a time known as the *Holocene* period. They are well worth a visit if you have a chance.

Estonia is a go-ahead modern country with a strong online presence and good internet connections and innovation is a key part of their digital identity.

Sorve Lighthouse, Saaremaa *Ilme Parik/Wikimedia Commons (https://commons.wikimedia.org/wiki/File:S%C3%B5rve_tuletorn.JPG)*

However, traditions are still important to them. Here are some facts about Estonia which you may or may not know:

- Estonia ranks third in having the most business start-ups per capita. One of the best-known Estonian start-ups is Bolt – the mobility app and car/scooter hire company. They now have more than 150 million users across 45 countries
- Estonia has the highest number of supermodels per capita (a claim which is difficult to verify!)
- At 99.9% of the population, Estonia has one of the highest rates of adult literacy in the world. The only country higher is North Korea with 100% – again, a claim that is difficult to verify!
- Tallinn is one of the best-preserved medieval cities in Europe
- The Estonian national flag, the blue, black and white tricolour, allegedly represents the sky, the soil and the Estonians' pursuit of light and happiness
- Estonians are one of the best countries in the world at wife-carrying – a sport with its own category in the Guinness Book of Records. The name is something of a misnomer though as it doesn't specify that it has to be your own wife…

Tourist information is available online for most places, but a good starting point is www.visitestonia.com/en.

### Highlights

Haapsalu castle, Kuressaare Castle, two Swedish churches on Ruhnu, Kaali crater on Saaremaa, Tallinn old town

Above: A view of the Estonia monument from Tahkuna lighthouse. The ferry Estonia sank while on overnight passage from Tallin to Stockholm on 28 September 1994 *HendrixEesti/Wikimedia Commons (https://commons.wikimedia.org/wiki/File:Tahkuna_stone_labyrinth_2008.jpg)*

A memorial in Tallinn to the ferry Estonia which sank in 1994 *Liilia Moroz/ Wikimedia Commons (https://commons.wikimedia.org/wiki/File:Estonia_memorial.jpg)*

## The people, the church & the language

Estonians are of the same race as the Finns and share a similar language. In the 20th century great numbers of the native population emigrated, and today Estonia has a total population of just over 1.3 million and an ethnic mix of which about 68% are Estonian and 22% Russian, the balance being made up of Ukrainians, Belorussians, Finns and Latvians. About 70% live in urban areas, nearly 30% (about 408,000) live in Tallinn alone.

The official language is Estonian – a Finno-Ugric language – but most speak or understand Russian. Finnish and German are commonly understood and many people are delighted to communicate in excellent English. Estonia suffered badly from the Soviet policy of 'Russification', and since independence the government has introduced laws concerning not only citizenship requirements but also language ability for employment. Some of the ethnic Russian population speak only Russian. The generations educated in Soviet times have fluent Russian, whereas younger generations have fluent English. German is a good alternative with the older generation.

Estonians often describe themselves as pagan. Forcibly converted to Christianity by the Teutonic Knights, the majority of those still practising are split between the Lutheran and Orthodox churches with a smaller number adhering to the Catholic faith.

Visitors, whether they come by sea, air or land, can be assured of a warm welcome.

## History

Estonia's border with Latvia is now set by language. The Estonian language, like Finnish, is part of the Finno-Ungrian family, while Latvian is Indo-European. Nonetheless, both countries have shared much of their history over the past few centuries.

In the late Middle Ages, Estonia was made up of eight 'counties', but still had no central ruler. Raids and counter raids with its neighbours were graduating into battles and invasions as the evolving nations of Denmark, Sweden, Russia, Prussia and Poland recognised the strategic importance of Estonia's coast.

In 1193 Pope Celestine declared the Northern Crusades, thereby telling the foreign invaders that they now had God on their side – except the Russian Christians, now that Rome had broken with the Orthodox Church. By 1227 the Danes had conquered north Estonia by sea, while the south was defeated by the Brothers of the Sword following their conquest of Latvia. Reval (now Tallinn) became a Hanseatic port. A century and a half later, the Danish king decided to move out of Estonia

# KEY INFORMATION

## Rescue/Safety services

**Emergency** ✆ 112
**MRCC Tallinn Rescue Radio** monitors VHF Ch 16/69, DSC MMSI 00 276 0100. Call Sign **'Tallinn Rescue'.**
**www.rescue.ee/en**
jrcc@politsei.ee

## Charts and pilot books

British UKHO Admiralty and Estonian charts cover the coast. British UKHO Admiralty charts are useful for passage planning but for detailed navigation the Estonian charts should be used. The Estonian chart folios are as follows:

*Charts of Estonia Vol. 1* Gulf of Finland – Suurupi Peninsula to Narva

*Charts of Estonia Vol. 2* Vainameri – Suurupi Peninsula to Saaremaa.

*Charts of Estonia Vol. 3* From Saaremaa to Ruhnu

Some harbours are also shown on the following Latvian charts 1251, 1011, 1013

*Baltic Pilot Volume II & III* (NP 19)

## Time

Estonia is in the Eastern European time zone (UT+2 in winter/UT+3 in summer). Summertime starts and ends on the same dates as the rest of the EU.

## € Money

The Euro. Cash is easily obtained from ATMs. Credit and debit cards are widely accepted.

## Formalities

Estonia is a member of the EU and of the Schengen Area (see main Introduction page 9 for details of Schengen formalities). EU passport holders do not require visas. The website of the Foreign Ministry (**www.vm.ee/en**) lists countries whose citizens do not need visas. If a visa is needed, contact the Estonian Consulate at 44 Queens Gate Terrace, London SW7 5PJ ✆+44 207 838 5388, london@mfa.ee, **https://london.mfa.ee**

The British Embassy in Tallinn can be contacted on ✆+372 667 4700, infotallinn@fco.gov.uk, **www.gov.uk/government/world/estonia**

According to the Estonian regulation Requirements for Operating Recreational Craft skippers of recreational craft flying the Estonian flag (and skippers of foreign flagged craft whose flag state requires such) require a registration certificate and a certificate of a skipper of a recreational craft. For British-flagged craft there is no legal requirement to have such certificates when sailing in Estonian waters as there is no requirement for such under British law. In practice, skippers and crew would be advised to carry any certificates of competence wherever they are sailing.

## Public holidays

Public holidays:
1 Jan, 24 Feb (Independence Day), Good Friday, Easter Sunday, 1 May (May Day), Pentecost, 23 June (Victory Day), 24 June (St John's Day), 20 Aug (Restoration of Independence Day) and 24, 25, 26 Dec.

## Communications

There are efficient telephone and mail systems and full coverage of mobile phone networks. Internet access is widely available with many free WiFi points.

To obtain an international line, dial 00 followed by the country code, area code (omitting any initial 0) and number. Dialling within Estonia only the 7 digit number is required. There are no longer area codes nor an initial 0. All mobile numbers start with 5. The country code for Estonia is 372.

## ✈ Travel

Tallinn has an international **airport** only 3km from the city centre, with domestic airports at Pärnu and on the islands of Hiiumaa (Kärdla) and Saaremaa (Roomassaare). The country is served by a network of **buses** and **trains**, while **Eurolines** provides a link to cities in most European countries.

Tallinn has **ferries** to Helsinki and Stockholm. Other international ferries run from Paldiski to Kapellskär (Sweden). Internal ferries run between Rohuküla and Heltermaa (Hiiumaa) and Vormsi island; between Virtsu and Kuivastu (Muhu) and thence to Saaremaa; between Triigi (Saaremaa) and Sõru (Hiiumaa); between Munalaid and Kihnu and between Roomassaare (Saaremaa) and the small offlying island of Abruka.

## Websites

A great deal of information about Estonia is available on the internet, much of it in English. However, it should be remembered that not all sites are updated regularly.

**www.inyourpocket.com/estonia** – a useful guide to sights with additional tourist information

**www.visitestonia.com** – the main tourist information site for Estonia.

**www.vta.ee** – The Estonian Maritime Administration

## Radio communications

VHF radio is much used for marine communications – details of channels and call signs will be found under most harbours.

VHF Ch 16 should be monitored while on passage e.g. the coastguard station at Paldiski may call up passing craft including yachts.

## Weather information

Weather bulletins and navigational warnings are broadcast at 0633 and 1533 LT on VHF Ch 1/3/5/7/20/26/27 by Tallinn Radio, in English and Estonian.

Meteorite crater at Kaali, Saaremaa *Robin Matthews*

and sold his part to the Teutonic Knights, who now included the Brothers of the Sword, to add to Livonia, as they called their conquered territories. The whole of Estonia and Latvia were now managed by immigrant German landlords and merchants.

During the Reformation the Grand Master of the Teutonic Knights became a Lutheran and Livonia did the same. To meet the Lutheran rule that everyone should be able to read the Bible in their own language, literacy and education were now provided to the locals.

Later in the 16th century, the rivalries between Denmark, Sweden, Ivan the Terrible's Russia and the Polish-Lithuanian Union lead to the Livonian War. In 1561, Sweden took over north Estonia, while southern Estonia and north Latvia became Polish Livonia in the 1580s. Then Gustavus Adolphus became king of Sweden. He conquered most of the Baltic coastal regions and in 1625 Livonia became Swedish. Gustavus Adolphus did much to improve the lot of the indigenous peasantry, but then came the Great Northern War to destroy the Swedish Empire. Under the Treaty of Nystad in 1710, Estonia became part of the Russian Empire, which ruled them through their existing Germanic authorities. As in Latvia and Lithuania, pride in their language and traditions began to develop, particularly during the 19th century.

With the 1917 Russian Revolution, the Bolsheviks allowed north and south Estonia to unite, and the modern borders between Estonia and Latvia were more or less established. Both countries still had to fight for their independence, however, as first Germany and then the Red Army tried to re-assert control. At last in 1920 the Soviet Union accepted Estonia's independence.

During the interwar years, the large estates were broken up and redistributed, the Estonian language replaced German and Russian in schools and Estonian art began to flourish.

Then came the Second World War with invasion by first the Soviets, then the Nazis and then the Soviets again. Despite fierce resistance, Estonia became one of Stalin's Soviets. Huge numbers of Estonians were executed or deported, being replaced by Russians as the new elite.

Hope was kept alive across the nation through traditional Estonian songs. Since Stalin's days the authorities had tried to hijack the national singing festival by making everyone sing songs about the joys of Soviet communism. 1969 was the centenary of the festival, so the authorities brought in several extra brass bands to drown out any attempts to sing nationalist songs, but to no avail.

Restrictions began to ease from 1985 under Gorbachev's reforms. Estonians were able to watch Finnish TV to see how the rest of the world was living and to hear the news without any Soviet bias. Then in 1988 passive resistance turned into the 'Singing Revolution'. A series of public concerts were lead with patriotic songs by Estonian rock bands, with up to 300,000 Estonians participating – a quarter of the population. The old Estonian three coloured flags had been banned so they flew them in three separate pieces. More and more of the Estonian authorities began to support them, or at least to bow to the inevitable. Estonia finally regained its independence on 20 August 1991, with full recognition by Yeltsin's Russia.

Estonia is now well established as a free-market democracy, a member of both the EU and the Eurozone.

In the years since independence the pace of change has been fast, progress rapid and Estonia has made great strides towards updating facilities and services.

Estonia orientates itself firmly towards the West and joined both the EU and NATO in 2004, signing the Schengen agreement in 2007. In 2011 they adopted the euro and they were the first ex-Soviet republic to do so. Following a new government in 2021, Estonia became the only country in the world led by elected women as the head of state and as the head of government: the president, Kersti Kaljulaid, and the prime minister, Kaja Kallas. In her cabinet Kaja Kallas also had several women in other key positions. In 2023 Prime Minister Kallas of the Reform Party won the parliamentary election, taking 31.4% of the vote and formed her third government.

## CRUISING INFORMATION

### Yacht services

Yachting, both sail and motor, has become increasingly popular with Estonians. Many harbours have a yacht club but these are mostly owned by groups of businessmen and run as businesses, often with a hotel and restaurant open for tourists or conferences as part of the complex. The clubs may own a small fleet of racing yachts but many boats - including expensive motor yachts - are privately owned.

### Chandlery

Chandlery and charts can be obtained at some harbours, but it is wise to obtain charts before arrival as stocks may be limited. For further information, see the website of the Republic of Estonia Transport Administration (www.transpordiamet.ee/en/mobility-and-transportation/navigational-information/navigational-charts).

Although some chandlers still exist, most Estonian yachtsmen make purchases online.

### Holding tanks

Holding tanks are obligatory for new Estonian boats. Although not obligatory for others, it is illegal to discharge toilets or grey water within 5M of the coast. It is intended that Estonian harbours provide pump-out facilities but so far only the more modern or reconstructed harbours have such facilities alongside.

### Gas

Campinggaz is available in Pärnu and Tallinn.
www.campingaz.com

### Diesel

Fuelling berths are available in Pärnu, Roomassaare, Kuressaare, Kuivastu, Kärdla, Haapsalu, Dirhami, Lohusalu, Tallinn (Haven Kakumäe, Pirita and Old City Marina). Elsewhere fuel can usually be obtained by arrangement with the yacht club or Harbourmaster. There is a bio-component added.

### Shopping

Well stocked shops and supermarkets can be found in all towns.

### Alcohol

Alcohol can be purchased from shops and supermarkets without restriction. There are large alcohol outlets adjoining the ferry terminal in Tallinn.

The alcohol limit at sea for leisure boats is 0.5mg alcohol in 1g of blood (i.e. 0.5/ml) or 0.25mg alcohol in 1l of breath.

### Direction of travel

The general direction of travel in Estonia in this chapter is from south to north, starting with the island of Ruhnu and proceeding via Kihnu to Pärnu thence to the island of Saaremaa, through Moon Sound and the islands of Hiiumaa and Vormsi, returning to the mainland at Haapsalu. The direction follows the coast northwards and eastwards to Tallinn, Hara and Vergi including some islands as appropriate.

Windmills at Angla, Saaremaa *Fry72, Karel Frydrýšek/ Wikimedia Commons (https://commons.wikimedia.org/wiki/File:Angla_tuulikum%C3%A4gi_,_Angla,_Ostrov_Saaremaa,_Estonsko_02.jpg)*

## RUHNU

57°46'.90N 23°16'.20E (yacht moorings)
57°46'.80N 23°16'.32E (centre of harbour entrance)
57°46'.62N 23°17'.39E (safe water buoy: normally on station May–Oct)

### Lights

**Ruhnu Lighthouse** 57°48'.08N 23°15'.6E Fl.W.4s65m11M
Dark brown metal tower with supporting pillars, balcony and lantern 40m

### Contacts

**Ruhnu (Ringsu) Marina**
✆+372 509 6239
www.slmarinas.ee/en/ports/ruhnu-marina/
renno@saarteliinid.ee

Ruhnu is a small island in the Gulf of Rīga with a population of just 60. Before 1944, it was for centuries populated by ethnic Swedes and traditional Swedish law was used. Ringsu harbour on the southeast point provides good shelter (in the inner portion) with individual finger berths. Additional alongside berthing inside the west mole in the outer harbour has less shelter from south and east and becomes untenable in strong southeasterly weather. The harbour has space for around 65 boats and has a minimum depth of 2.7m.

The village is about 3km distant and it has limited shopping, post office, bar and museum. There are no banks but most currencies accepted by harbour office. The leading line for approach is 286.6°. Entry is recommended in good visibility and moderate weather only. Ruhnu is a useful and convenient staging point on passages between Latvia and Estonia.

When moored there it is worth visiting St Madeline's Church which is the oldest standing wooden building in Estonia. The Ruhnu lighthouse and museum are also worth a visit. The most unusual visitor though was in 2006 when a 330lb brown bear arrived. It is thought to have come via an ice floe across the Gulf of Riga from Latvia, some 25M away. The bear's arrival became a media sensation in Estonia and Latvia. It evaded capture for many months though tourists hoping to catch a glimpse of it outnumbered permanent residents for some time. It is believed to have headed back to Latvia now, but...

Aerial views of Ringsu Harbour on Ruhnu *Robin Matthews*

## Kihnu

58°08'.49N 24°01'.17E (yacht moorings)
58°08'.50N 24°02'.76E (safe water buoy)

### Contacts

**Kihnu Marina**
✆+372 446 9932
www.slmarinas.ee/en/ports/kihnu-marina/
kihnu@saarteliinid.ee

Kihnu is a small island in the approaches to Pärnu surrounded by shoals up to 2M offshore. If approaching from the south keep at least 2M offshore leaving east cardinal mark to port and on reaching leading line sail in on 273° (see *Estonian Small Craft Chart Vol. 3*). If approaching from north or east, well-buoyed channels lead in to join the leading line.

There is a fishing/ferry harbour with pontoons and stern buoys for yachts. The minimum depth is 3.5m and there are around 40 berths. Facilities include bars and a shop. The island has a very small permanent population. See www.visitkihnu.ee/en for tourist information about the island which they call Treasure Island. There are ferries to Munalaid (and thence to Pärnu by coach).

Aerial view of Kihnu harbour *Robin Matthews*

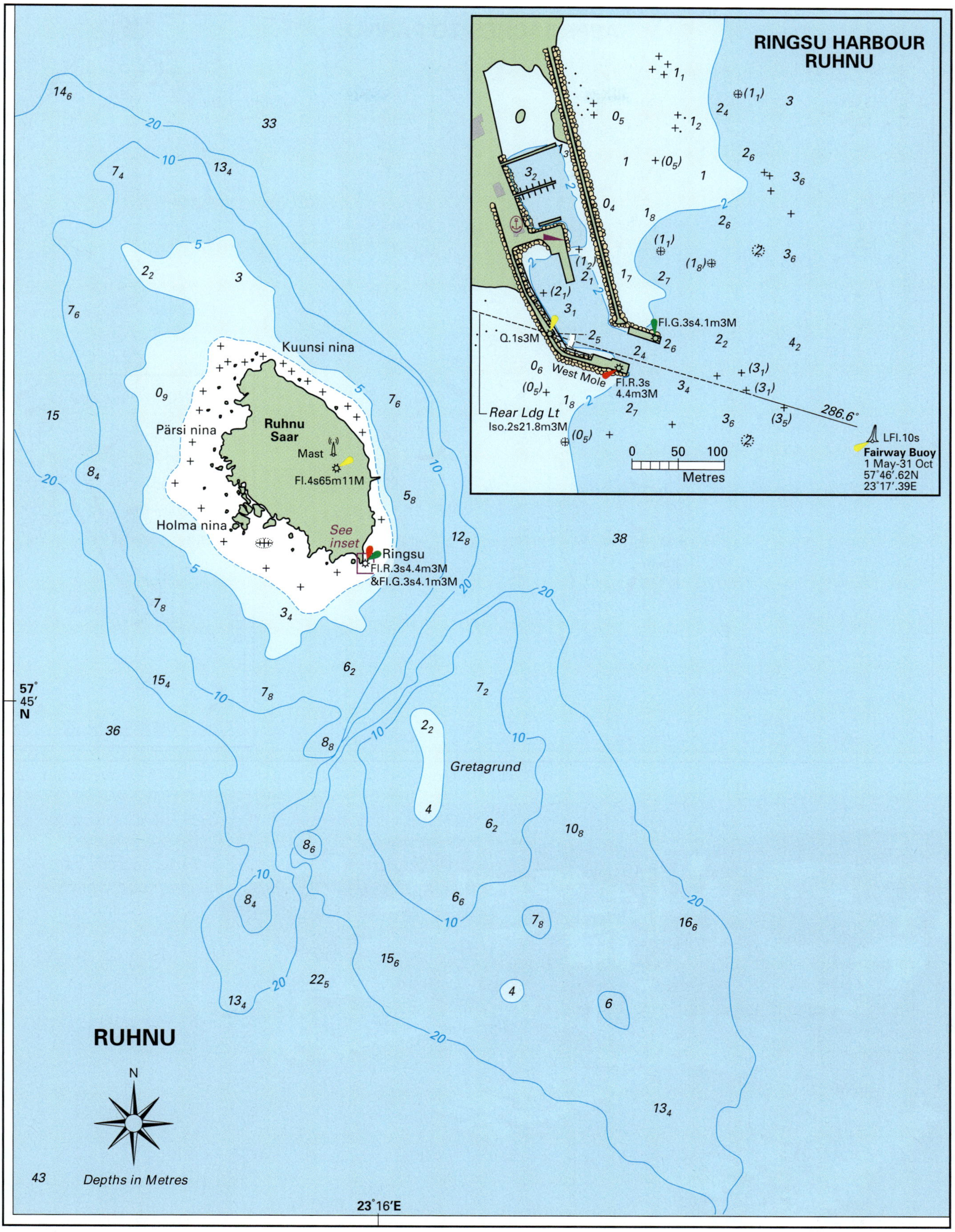
RINGSU HARBOUR
RUHNU
West Mole
Q.1s3M
Fl.G.3s4.1m3M
Fl.R.3s
4.4m3M
Rear Ldg Lt
Iso.2s21.8m3M
286.6°
LFl.10s
Fairway Buoy
1 May-31 Oct
57°46'.62N
23°17'.39E
Metres
Kuunsi nina
Ruhnu
Saar
Mast
Fl.4s65m11M
Pärsi nina
Holma nina
See inset
Ringsu
Fl.R.3s4.4m3M
&Fl.G.3s4.1m3M
Gretagrund
57° 45' N
23°16'E
RUHNU
N
Depths in Metres

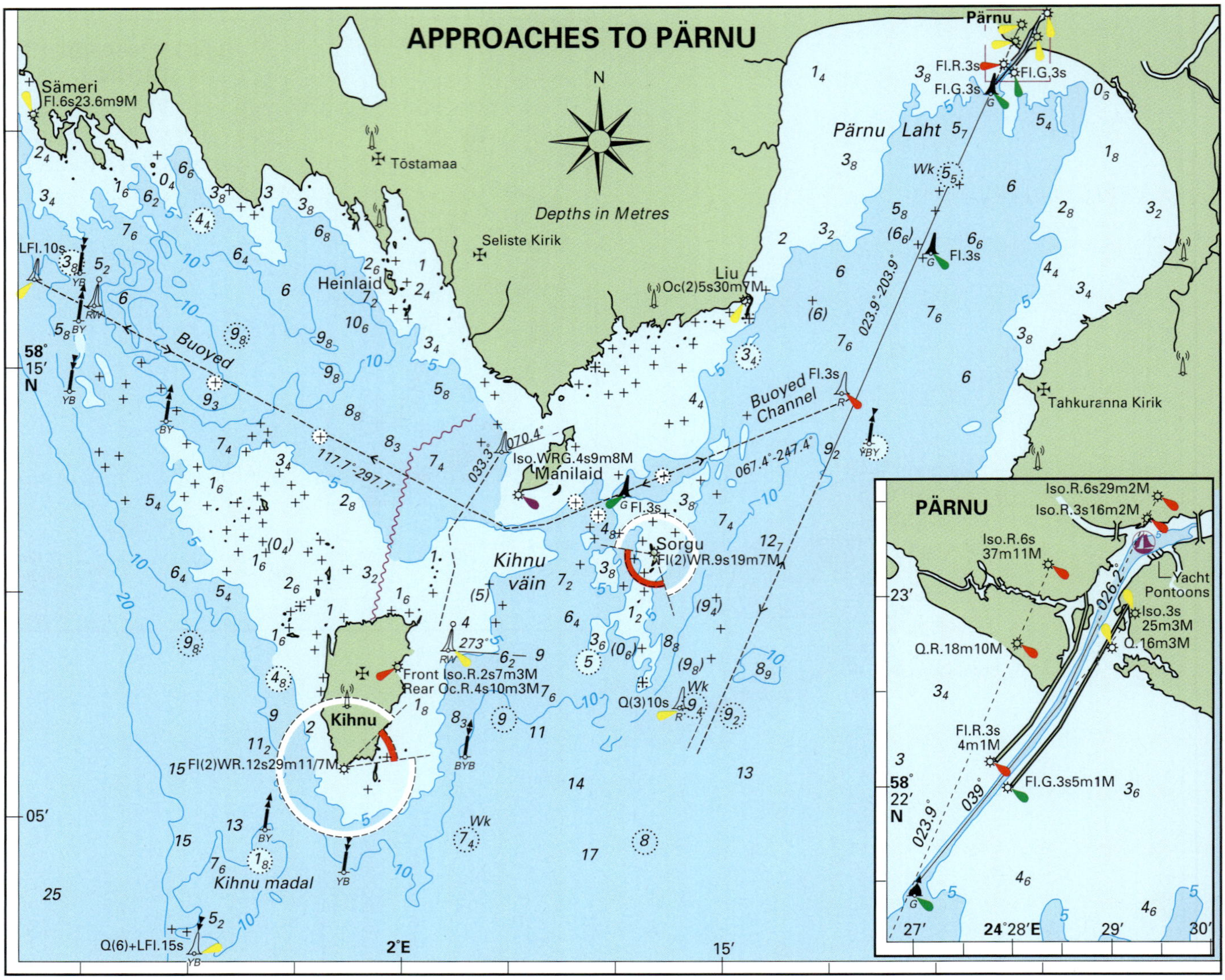

Pärnu Yacht Club moorings looking south towards the entrance breakwaters *Robin Matthews*

## PÄRNU

58°23'.17N 24°29'.22E

### Distances

Rīga 80M, Salacgrīva 40M, Roomassaare 75M, Virtsu (inside Kihnu) 50M, Virtsu (outside Kihnu) 60M

### Lights

**Kihnu** 58°05'.8N 23°58'.3E Fl(2)W.R.12s29m11–7M
Round white metal tower with balcony 28m
**Häädemeeste** 58°04'.4N 24°29'.2E Fl.W.5s32m11M
White square metal framework tower 28m
**Sorgu Saar** 58°10'.7N 24°12'.00E Fl(2)WR.9s19m7M
Round red brick tower with balcony 16m
**Liu Light Beacon** 58°16'.6N 24°15'.9E Oc(2)5s30m7M
White planking on metal framework tower 28m
**Pärnu Leading Lights 023.9°** *Front* 58°22'.7N 24°27'.9E
Q.R.17.6m10M White rectangle, black stripe, on red round metal tower 22m. Visible on leading line only
*Rear* 821m from front, Iso.R.6s37m11M White rectangle, black stripe, on metal framework tower 34m
**East breakwater** 58°22'N 24°28'E Fl.G.3s5m1M White metal column, green band, concrete base 3m
**West breakwater** 58°22'.1N 24°27'.7E Fl.R.3s4m1M White metal column, red band, on concrete base 3m

### Contacts

**Pärnu Yacht Club Marina**
☎+372 5307 8777
www.jahtklubi.ee/yacht-marina
info@jahtklubi.ee
VHF Ch 16, call "Parnu sadam"

Pärnu, the fourth largest city in Estonia, is a holiday resort in the extreme northeast corner of the Gulf of Rīga and is known as Estonia's Summer Capital. Timber is exported and there is a small amount of fishing. It is surrounded by beautiful sandy beaches – one of which is reserved for women only.

Pärnu is also known for its stone wall. The wall was built between 1863 and 1864 on top of the remains of a 17th-century seawall, constructed under the orders of Catherine the Great of Russia. She inherited control of the town after the Russians took it from the Swedish in 1710. According to legend, if a couple holds hands while walking along the wall and kisses at its endpoint they will stay together forever.

St Catherine's Church is a Russian Orthodox church and is also worth visiting. It was built in 1764 and named after Catherine the Great, who presented the church to the city after a visit in 1764. For full tourist information, see www.visitparnu.com/en/.

### *Approach & entry*

58°22.04N 24°27.76E (centre of harbour entrance)

Straightforward approach on 023.9°, following the leading marks.

### *Berthing*

Berth at Pärnu Yacht Club on the east bank of the river just round a bend. Mooring is bows-to a pontoon with a stern line to a buoy in 2.5-3m depths in reasonable shelter. Visitors should use the first pontoon (marked as A pontoon) if possible, or otherwise tie up where space allows and seek advice at the yacht club. See www.jahtklubi.ee/yacht-marina/entrnace (*Note* this is not a typo) for a plan of the marina and also links to useful YouTube videos showing the entrance and the marina. It claims to be the biggest marina in Estonia, though Tallinn Noblessner Marina and Tallinn Kalev Yacht Club have been extended and may now be larger!

Anchoring is not advised as the waterway is used by commercial shipping.

### *Services*

Water and electricity on the pontoons, showers and toilets at the yacht club (which also has a bar and a restaurant). There is a fuel berth beyond the yacht club pontoons and a chandlery.

### *Facilities*

The small town is about a mile from the yacht club and has all facilities including shops, post office, banks and restaurants.

### *Communications & travel*

Buses to Tallinn, Rīga and elsewhere. Airport for domestic flights. Ferries to Ruhnu and Kihnu (via coach to Munalaid thence by ferry).

WiFi is available at the sailing club.

## MÕNTU (SAAREMAA)

57°56'.58N 22°07'.27E

### Distances

Fårösund 105M, Ventspils 38M

### Contacts

**Mõntu Marina**
☎+372 502 3860
www.montusadam.ee/en/home/
info@montusadam.ee

Mõntu is a very small port on the southern peninsula of Saarema island. While it is exposed to winds from the north through to the east, it is reasonably sheltered from other quarters. However, as with other small harbours care should be taken to ensure appropriate conditions will remain during any stay. It may make a suitable landfall in appropriate conditions when coming from Gotland or perhaps heading north from Ventspils.

### *Berthing*

Approach to the harbour is on a leading line 298.5°. The leading lines are white rectangles with black stripes (Q W 1s – Iso W 4s). The end of the breakwater has a Fl R beacon for entering at night. Berthing in the harbour is on pontoon berths and there are around 20 in total in a minimum depth of 3m.

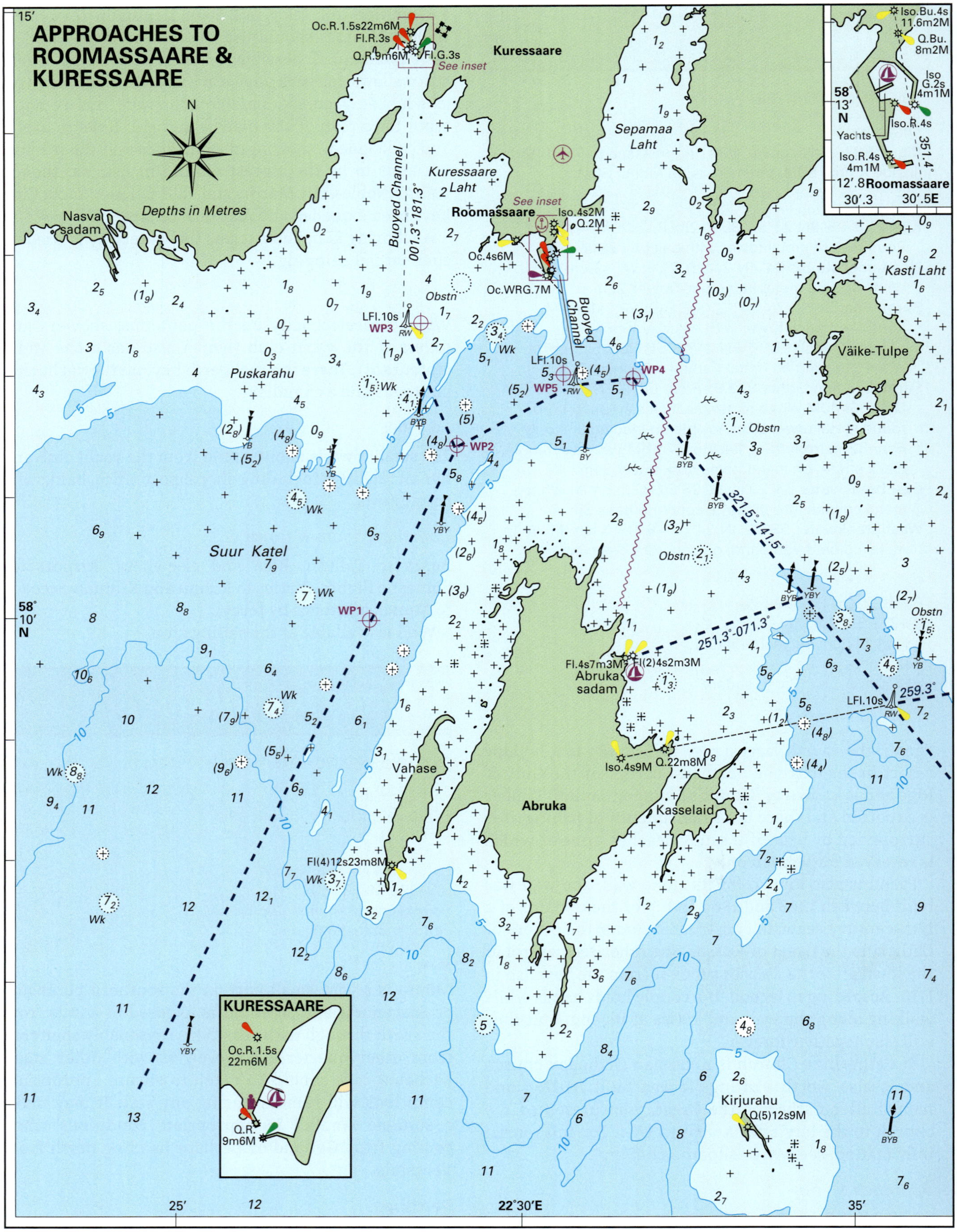
APPROACHES TO ROOMASSAARE & KURESSAARE
Depths in Metres
Kuressaare
Roomassaare
Kuressaare Laht
Sepamaa Laht
Kasti Laht
Väike-Tulpe
Nasva sadam
Puskarahu
Suur Katel
Abruka
Abruka sadam
Vahase
Kasselaid
Kirjurahu
Buoyed Channel
001.3°-181.3°
Buoyed Channel
321.5°-141.5°
251.3°-071.3°
259.3°
WP1
WP2
WP3
WP4
WP5
See inset
Oc.R.1.5s22m6M
Fl.R.3s
Q.R.9m6M
Fl.G.3s
Iso.4s2M
Q.2M
Oc.4s6M
Oc.WRG.7M
LFl.10s
Fl.4s7m3M
Fl(2)4s2m3M
Iso.4s9M
Q.22m8M
Fl(4)12s23m8M
Q(5)12s9M
KURESSAARE
Oc.R.1.5s 22m6M
Q.R. 9m6M
Iso.Bu.4s 11.6m2M
Q.Bu. 8m2M
Iso G.2s 4m1M
Iso.R.4s
Yachts
Iso.R.4s 4m1M
351.4°
58° 13′ N
12′.8
Roomassaare
30′.3
30′.5E
58° 10′ N
15′
25′
22°30′E
35′

## ABRUKA

58°09'45N 22°31'43E

### Contacts

**Abruka Marina**
✆+372 5332 8096
www.slmarinas.ee/en/ports/abruka-marina/
abruka@slmarinas.ee

Abruka is a small island between Mõntu and Kuressaare. The village has a population of just over 30 people but it is a holiday destination for Estonians with various guesthouses and other accommodation available. The island is forested with wooded meadows and alvar environments. These have a rich diversity of species.

There are various nature trails beginning at the harbour taking you through parts of the Abruka Nature Conservation Area. The trails vary in length but are mainly between 4-5km. At the northern end of the island, there is apparently a peculiarly chiming magic rock. If you can find it and knock on it, you will be granted a wish...

#### *Berthing*

Approach to the harbour starts at a safe water mark and from there you follow a leading line on 321.5° / 141.5°. The breakwaters are marked with red and green lights/beacons (Fl G 3s, Fl R 3s). Berthing in the harbour is on pontoon berths and there are around 30 in total in a minimum depth of 2.5m.

Facilities at Abruka include water, electricity (additional charge), laundry (additional charge), toilets and showers and a sauna which needs to be pre-booked and is charged separately.

Aerial view of Kuressaare *Hiiumaamudeliklubi/Wikimedia Commons (https://commons.wikimedia.org/wiki/File:Kuressaare_linn_ja_sadam_2015.jpg)*

## KURESSAARE (SAAREMAA)

58°13'.02N 22°30'.34E (yacht moorings)
58°14'.63N 22°28'.32E (centre of harbour entrance)

### Distances

Ventspils 65M, Roja 45M, Rīga 85M, Kuivastu 50M, Pärnu 75M

### Lights

**Abruka safe water buoy** 58°09'.34N 22°35'.58E
LFl.10s3M
**Abruka** 58°08'.9N 22°31'.5E
Iso.W.4s38m9M White round concrete tower, black bands 36m
**Allirahu** 58°09'.7N 22°47'.2E
Fl(2)W.12s14.9m7M Metal framework tower with orange planking on all sides 9.8m
**Kuressaare Fairway buoy** 58°12'.5N 22°28'.14E
LFl.W.10s3M
**Kuressaare Leading Lights** 1.3° *Front*
58°14'.65N22°28'.23E Q.R.9m6M White rectangle with red stripe on red metal cylinder 7m
*Rear* 240m from front Oc.R.1.5s22m6M
White rectangle with red strip on building – height above building 3m

### Contacts

**Kuressaare City Harbour**
✆+372 503 1953
✆+372 453 3450
www.kuressaarejahisadam.ee/en/port/
info@kuressaarejahisadam.ee
VHF Ch 11/16, call "Tori Sadam"

The harbours of Kuressaare and Roomassaare on the southern shore of the island of Saaremaa are close together and both in Kuressaare. Kuressaare harbour has the advantage of being within the town whereas Roomassaare, which has the advantage of a better location for onward passages, is some 4km to the east.

In the middle of the 19th century, Kuressaare became a spa town when large reserves of 'healing mud' were found close to the town and as a result, the first mud spa was built in 1840. It is the capital of Saaremaa, the largest of the Estonian islands and the second largest island in the entire Baltic Sea. The island has one of the highest standards of living in Estonia and is highly popular with tourists. Kuressaare has many attractive buildings and a superb moated castle complete with large museum (it is claimed that the castle is the best-preserved medieval fortress in the Baltic) plus good shops, several large supermarkets and many cafés and restaurants. Other places of interest on Saaremaa include Panga Pank, the windmills at Angla and the meteorite crater at Kaali. Full tourist information is available through their website on www.visitsaaremaa.ee/en/.

*Approach & entry*

### Approaching from southwest in Suur Katel bay

From SW
Waypoint 1 58°10'.00N 22°27'.00E
Waypoint 2 58°11'.90N 22°29'.40E
Waypoint 3 Kuressaare safe water buoy 58°12'.5N 22°28'.14E to join leading line of 01.3°

### Approaching from southeast (east of Abruka)

Head for the Abruka safe water buoy 58°09'.34N 22°35'.58E. Follow the outer leading line for Roomassaare 321.5° until Waypoint 4 (58°11'.90N 22°31'.70E) is reached then proceed to Roomassaare safe water buoy Waypoint 5 (58°11'.97N 22°30'.78E) then follow a course to Waypoints 2 and 3 as above.

The approach is by a long, buoyed and dredged channel on a leading line of 001.3° from the fairway buoy. The channel is said to be dredged to 2.5m but weed can give false depth readings.

*Berthing*

Kuressaare City Harbour is located very close to the town. Berthing is to stern buoys and bows to pontoons with limited alongside berthing. The minimum depth is 2.3m and the total number of berths is over 130. There is no shelter to be obtained outside the harbour and the water is shallow outside the channel so anchoring off is not possible. Anchoring within the harbour would not be permitted.

*Services*

Water and electricity is available on the pontoons and toilets, showers, sauna and laundry facilities in the harbour office building. There is also a fuel berth and holding tank pump-out facilities. For repairs etc seek the advice of the Harbourmaster.

*Facilities*

There is a restaurant at the harbour (www.hafen.ee). Charts are available for sale at the harbour office and all facilities - shops, banks, post office, restaurants, outdoor market, car hire and tourist office are on offer in the town.

*Communications & travel*

Buses and ferries to Tallinn are available and there is an airport for domestic flights at Roomassaare (4km distant). WiFi available.

## ROOMASSAARE (SAAREMAA)

58°12'.80N 22°30'.60E (yacht moorings)
See plan on page 452

### Distances

Ventspils 65M, Roja 45M, Rīga 85M, Kuivastu 50M, Pärnu 75M

### Lights

**Abruka** 58°08'.9N 22°31'.5E Iso.W.4s38m9M
White round concrete tower, black bands 36m
**Allirahu** 58°09'.7N 22°47'.2E Fl(2)W.12s14.9.8m7M
Metal framework tower with orange planking on all sides 8m
**Outer Leading Lights 321.5°** *Front* 58°12'.82N
Black rectangle, white stripe, on red framework tower 12m
*Rear* 721m from front Oc.W.4s33m6M
Black rectangle, white stripe, on metal framework tower 30m
**Fairway buoy** 58°11'.97N 22°30'.78E LFl.W.10s3M
**Inner Leading Lights 351.1°** *Front* 58°13'.17N 22°30'.43E
Q.Bu.8m2M Black rectangle, white stripe, on red metal post 7m
*Rear* 107m from front, Iso.Bu.4s11.2M Black rectangle, white stripe, on red metal post 9.7m
**Yacht harbour West mole** 58°12'.97N 22°30'.42E
Iso.R.4s4m1M Red metal post 2m
**Yacht harbour East mole** 58°12'.96N 22°30'.48E
Iso.G.2s4m1M Green metal post 2m

### Contacts

**Roomassaare City Harbour**
✆+372 5335 8313
www.slmarinas.ee/en/ports/roomassaare-marina/
roomassaare@slmarinas.ee
VHF Ch 14, call sign "Roomassaare Sadam"

*Approach & entry*

### Approaching from southwest in Suur Katel bay

Waypoint 1 58°10'.00N 22°27'.00E
Waypoint 2 58°11'.90N 22°29'.40E
Waypoint 5 (Roomassaare safe water buoy) 58°11'.97N 22°30'.78E to join leading line 351.4° to enter harbour

### Approaching from southeast (east of Abruka)

58°12'.97N 22°30'.45E centre of harbour entrance

Head for the Abruka safe water buoy (58°09'.34N 22°35'.58E). Follow the outer leading line on a course of 321.5° until Waypoint 4 (58°11'.90N 22°31'.70E) is reached then follow a course to Waypoint 5 Roomassaare safe water buoy (58°11'.97N 22°30'.78E) to join leading line 351.4° to enter harbour.

Aerial view of Roomassaare harbour *Hiiumaamudeliklubi/Wikimedia Commons (https://commons.wikimedia.org/wiki/File:Roomassaare_sadam_2015.jpg)*

*Berthing*

Roomassaare has a small modern marina in the inner basin, beyond the commercial harbour. Berths are alongside individual finger pontoons in 2.5–4.5m. There is no shelter to be obtained outside the harbour, so anchoring off is not possible.

*Services*

Water and electricity on pontoon, toilets, showers and sauna in the harbour office building. Fuel berth which also has holding tank pump-out facilities. For repairs etc seek the advice of the Harbourmaster.

*Facilities*

Bar, restaurant and small shop in the harbour area. All facilities – shops, banks, post office, restaurants, outdoor market, car hire and tourist office – in Kuressaare.

*Communications & travel*

There is a bus to Kuressaare from outside the marina, and thence bus and ferry to Tallinn etc. The island also has an airport handling domestic flights.

## LÕUNARANNA

58°32.46′N 23°19.16′E

**Lõunaranna Marina**

☎+372 503 6640

www.lounaranna.ee/avaleht/eng/

olaf@lounaranna.ee

Lõunaranna is a small and slightly shallow harbour on the island of Muhu and would make a possible stop when heading to Kuivastu or perhaps further north on to Hiiumaa. See the local tourist information site for further details about the island www.muhu.info/en/home.

*Berthing*

Approach to the harbour starts at a safe water mark (58°31'.28N 23°19'.38E). From there hold a course of 360° along the channel which is marked with mid-channel buoys. Then follow the lateral buoys to enter the harbour. Berthing in the harbour is on pontoon berths and there are around 30 in total in a minimum depth of 2.3m.

## KUIVASTU

58°34'.36N 23°23'.58E (yacht moorings)

### Distances

Roomassaare 50M, Pärnu (inside Kihnu) 50M, Pärnu (outside Kihnu) 60M, Haapsalu 30M

### Lights

**Kübassaare** 58°25'.70N 23°17'.99E LFl.W.9s20m11M
Round concrete tower, black upper white lower with balcony and lantern 18m

**Pöörilaid** 58°27'.68N 23°37'.78E Fl(4)WRG.18s14m7M
White round concrete tower with balcony and lantern 13m

**Viirelaid** 58°32'.69N 23°26'.58E Fl.WR.8s15m9–7M
Red round concrete tower with balcony and lantern 11m

**Virtsu** 58°34'.03N 23°30'.10E Fl.W.5s19m11M Red upper and white lower – square concrete tower 18m

**Kuivastu Leading Lights 267.7°** *Front* 58°34'.42N 23°23'.39E Q.W.11m6M W White rectangle, red stripe, on red metal framework 8m
*Rear* 320m from front Iso.W.3s17m6M
White rectangle, red stripe, on red metal framework 12m

**Kuivastu Yacht Harbour Light beacon** 58°34'.32N 23°23'.58E Fl.G.5s4m3M Green concrete column 3m

**Kuivastu Pier Light beacon** 58°34'.42N 23°23'.79E Q.R.8m2M Red concrete column with balcony 5m

### Contacts

**Kuivastu Marina**
✆+372 5342 8555
www.slmarinas.ee/en/ports/kuivastu-marina/
valdur@saarteliinid.ee
VHF Ch 14, call "Kuivastu harbour"

Kuivastu is the harbour for ferries between the Estonian mainland and Muhu (for Saaremaa) and has a purpose-built yacht harbour adjacent to the ferry terminal. There is no town but Kuivastu offers an excellent stopover on the journey through Moon Sound. The 'Old Russian Inn' visited by Arthur Ransome is a short distance along the road, but sadly is no longer an inn!

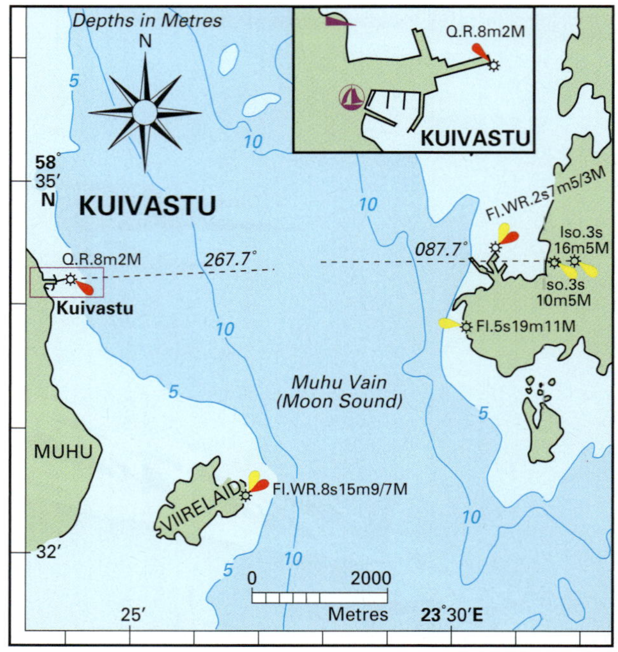


### Approach & entry

58°34'.33N 23°23'.57E (centre of harbour entrance)

Approach on leading line used by ferries 267.7° / 87.7° (front beacon Q.W, rear Iso.W.3s) towards ferry quay to enter dredged entrance channel south of ferry quay between a pair of lateral buoys. Turn to starboard at final port hand buoy.

### Berthing

Berthing is on finger pontoons and there is space for up to 50 boats in a minimum depth of 2.9m. Larger vessels lie alongside quays.

### Services & facilities

There is water and electricity on pontoons. Toilets, showers, sauna and washing facilities are available in the harbour building. The fuel berth is on the breakwater immediately to port as you enter. There is a small shop and restaurant and WiFi.

### Communications & travel

Buses to Saaremaa and Estonian mainland (for Tallinn). Car hire via HM office.

Kuivastu harbour with the ferry terminal in the foreground *Robin Matthews*

Aerial view of Kuivastu harbour *Robin Matthews*

Aerial view of Sõru harbour *Hiiumaamudeliklubi/Wikimedia Commons (https://commons.wikimedia.org/wiki/File:S%C3%B5ru_sadama_panoraam.jpg)*

## Sõru (Hiiumaa)

58°41'.45N 22°31'.33E (centre of harbour entrance)
Approach waypoint 58°41'.30N 22°31'.30E in dredged channel

**Sõru Port Marina**
☎+372 527 2865
www.slmarinas.ee/en/ports/soru-port-marina/
soru@saarteliinid.ee

***Note*** It is important to follow the channels marked on the chart as the area is very shallow.

The harbour is used by ferries from Triigi (Saaremaa) but has good shelter for yachts in the inner harbour. Berthing is alongside to port as you enter with a minimum depth of around 2.3m. There are limited facilities ashore.

Orjaku harbour *Hiiumaa Development Centre & Ivo Panasjuk*

## TRIIGI

58°35.52'N 22°43.17'E
Triigi Marina
☎+372 504 6819
www.slmarinas.ee/en/ports/triigi-marina/
mati.pold@saarteliinid.ee

Triigi marina is a small harbour on the northern side of Saaremaa in the rural municipality of Leisi. From there it is possible to access Tuhkana beach which is said to be one of the best beaches on Saaremaa. However, you may want to get a taxi across there as it is nearly 20km.

### *Berthing*

Approach to the harbour is on the Triigi leading line 228.6° / 48.6°. The leading line is orange triangles with a black stripe. Berthing in the harbour is on pontoon berths and there are around 40 in total in a minimum depth of 3m.

## ORJAKU (HIIUMAA)

58°47.19'N 22°46.15'E
Orjaku Harbour
☎+372 5345 5059
www.hiiumaasadamad.ee/en/orjaku/
sadamad@hiiumaa.ee

Orjaku harbour is a small fishing harbour close to a nature reserve. In 1912, the Russian government started to turn the harbour into a naval base for the mine laying fleet of the Imperial Russian Navy and the long breakwaters are evidence of this activity. For tourist information on Hiiumaa see www.hiiumaa.ee/en/.

### *Berthing*

Approach to the harbour is initially on a leading line 003.7° / 183.7°. The fairway begins at the Orjaku buoy "E". After a point of 58°47.00′ N 22°46.22′ E follow a course of 342.5° / 162.5° and enter around the east breakwater. Berthing in the harbour is on pontoon berths, y-booms and stern buoys to the jetty. There are around 40 berths in total in a minimum depth of 2.7m.

# HELTERMAA (HIIUMAA)

58°51'.99N 23°02'.69E (yacht moorings)

## Distances

Roomassaare 72M, Kärdla 24M, Haapsalu 17M

## Lights

**Heltermaa Leading Lights 254.7°** *Front* 58°51'.93N 23°02'.86E Q.R.8m10M White diamond with black stripe on metal framework 12m
*Rear* 315m from front, Oc.R.4s19m10M
White diamond with black stripe on metal framework 18m

**Heltermaa Pier Lt beacon** 58°52'.02N 23°02'.97E F.W.5m4M grey metal column 3m

## Contacts

**Heltermaa Marina**
✆+372 523 7633
www.slmarinas.ee/en/ports/heltermaa/
heltermaa@saarteliinid.ee
VHF Ch 9/16, call "Heltermaa harbour"

Heltermaa is the harbour for ferries between the Estonian mainland at Rohukula and Hiiumaa and has a purpose-built yacht harbour close to the ferry terminal. There is no town. For tourist information on Hiiumaa see www.hiiumaa.ee/en/.

### *Approach & entry*

58°51'.99N 23°02'.78E (centre of harbour entrance)
Approach on leading line 254.8° and turn to starboard before reaching the ferry quay. The yacht harbour is west of the ferry quay.

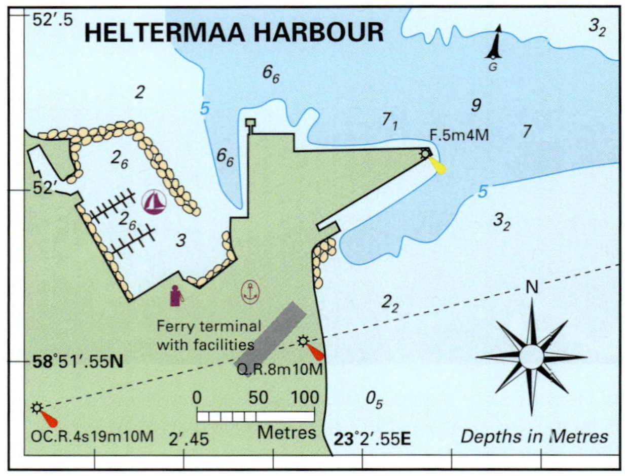


### *Berthing*

Berthing is on finger pontoons and there is a total of 42 berths in a minimum depth of 2.6m.

### *Services & facilities*

Water and electricity is available on the pontoons. Toilets, showers and a sauna are in the passenger terminal building. The fuel berth is on the southern side of the harbour.

### *Communications & travel*

WiFi. Buses around the island. Ferry to mainland thence bus to Tallinn etc. Domestic airport at Kärdla.

Aerial view of Heltermaa harbour from the southeast *Robin Matthews*

## KÄRDLA (HIIUMAA)

59°00'.56N 22°45'.19E (yacht moorings)

### Distances

Roomassaare 89M, Heltermaa 24M, Haapsalu 30M

### Lights

**Kõpu lighthouse** 58°54'.96N 22°11'.98E Fl(2)10s102m26M
White square stone tower, balcony, red lantern 36m

**Takhuna lighthouse** 59°05'.48N 22°35'.17E
LFl(2)15s43m12M White conical metal tower, balcony, lantern 43m

**Kärdla Leading Lights 162.2°** *Front* 59°00'.62N 22°45'.26E Fl.WG.2s5/2M
White rectangle with green stripe on green metal cylinder 5m
*Rear* 556m from front Fl.2s5M
White rectangle with green stripe on grey metal framework 17m

**East mole Lt beacon** Fl(2)R.4s2M
Red metal cylinder 2.7m

North mole beacon is Kärdla Front Ldg Lt 162.2°

### Contacts

**Kärdla Marina**
☎+372 5666 2514
www.hiiumaasadamad.ee/en/kardla/
sadamad@hiiumaa.ee
VHF Ch 16, call "Kärdla Marina"

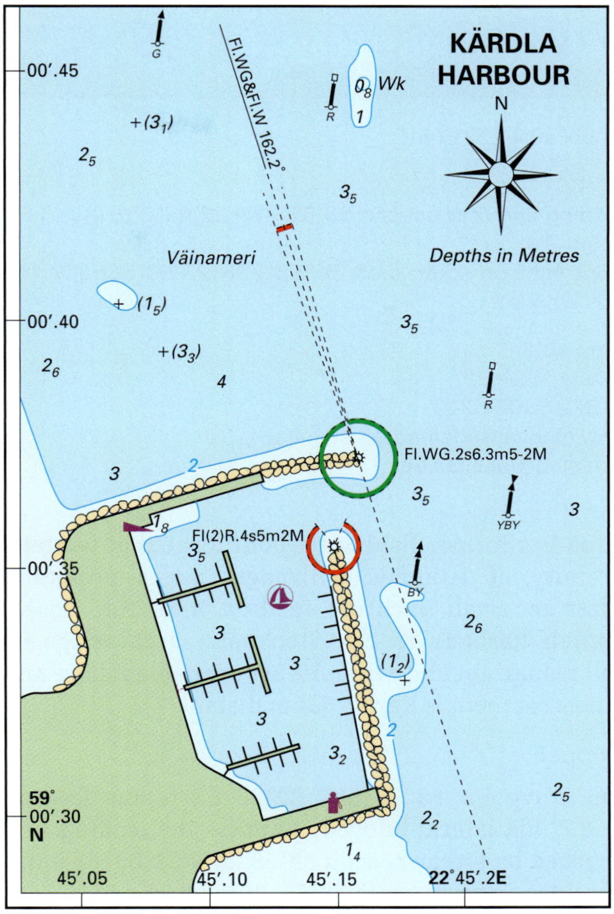


Kärdla is the capital of Hiiumaa and the main small town on the island. The name possibly derives from the Swedish *Kärrdal* meaning "marsh valley". This would make sense as the town is located in a lowlands valley. The yacht harbour is purpose-built on site of former small fishing/commercial harbour. Hiiumaa harbours have made a video about the island and their harbours – see www.hiiumaasadamad.ee/en/news/video-story-about-our-harbours/.

### *Approach & entry*

Main Fairway : From Waypoint 1 (59°03'.7N 22°43'.4E) steer to Waypoint 2 (59°00'.7N 22°45'.2E) then to Waypoint 3 (59°00'.6N 22°45'.3E)

**Approach from east through Püssirahu passage:**

Waypoint 1 (59°02'.2N 22°55'E) Proceed on course 244° to pass Waypoint 2 a south cardinal buoy Voirahu (59°01'.3N 22°51'.6E)

Change to course 268° to Waypoint 3 Fairway Buoy Vissulaiu (59°01'.2N 22°47'.9E)

Change to course 248° to join a laterally buoyed channel at Waypoint 4 buoys Vissulaiu 1 and 2 (59°01'.1N 22°47'.3E)

Continue on course 248° to Waypoint 5 buoys Vissulaiu 5 and 6 (59°00'.8N 22°46'.1E)

Change course to 237° to Waypoint 6 buoys Vissulaiu 7 and 8 (59°00'.7N 22°45'.8E)

Change course to 252° to enter harbour. 59°00'.6N 22°45'.3E (centre of harbour entrance)

It is dangerous to enter or leave the harbour in strong north to easterly winds

### *Berthing*

Berthing is on finger pontoons and there are 80 berths available in a minimum depth of 3.2m. Shelter is good but avoid first line of pontoon berths in strong north to easterly winds.

### *Services & facilities*

Water and electricity is available on pontoons and the toilets, showers, sauna and washing facilities are in the harbour building. There is a fuel berth and pump out facility at the southern end of the harbour. A small shop and two restaurants are close by. Winter storage. Banks, shops in Kärdla about 1km distant.

### *Communications & travel*

WiFi. Buses around island. Bus to Selver supermarket in season. Ferry to mainland from Heltermaa. Domestic airport.

Kärdla harbour *Hiiumaa Development Centre & Ivo Panasjuk.*

## KALANA (HIIUMAA)

58°55'.30N 22°03'.51E

### Lights

**Leading line rear beacon** 58°55'.37N 22°03'.68E (Iso (1) R 2s 9m 2M)
**Front light on south mole** 58°55'.28N 22°03'.66E (Oc (1) R 4s 3m 2M)

### Contacts

Kalana Marina
✆+372 5300 6343
www.hiiumaasadamad.ee/en/kalana/
sadamad@hiiumaa.ee

Kalana is a former fishing harbour located at western extremity of Hiiumaa with new moles providing shelter to small yachting facility. It is the closest Estonian harbour to the Stockholm archipelago. A small restaurant and camp site are available ashore and the nearest town is Kärdla 33km distant.

*Approach*

From Waypoint 58°55'.01N 22°03'.6E follow leading line 6.7° via lateral buoyed channel. The leading line is marked by a rear beacon 58°55'.37N 22°03'.68E and front light on south mole 58°55'.28N 22°03'.66E.

During strong winds from the southwest a heavy swell builds up in the approach to the bay. With winds in excess of Force 5 (10 m/s) it may be considered unsafe to try to enter the harbour.

*Berthing*

Berthing is on finger pontoons and the minimum depth is 2.5m.

## Sviby (Vormsi)

58°58'.20N 23°18'.70E

**Contacts**

Sviby Marina (Vormsi)
✆+372 509 7267
www.slmarinas.ee/en/ports/sviby/
sviby@saarteliinid.ee

Sviby is the harbour for ferries from Rohuküla on the mainland. There is berthing for yachts on the northwest side of the jetty with limited facilities. Berthing is on finger pontoons with a minimum depth of 2.4m.The island is interesting as there are many remains from the time when it was inhabited by Swedes. Most of the Swedes moved to Sweden prior to the Soviet Occupation of Estonia. Since independence in 1992, some Swedish families have started to return to the island and rebuild their former estates, though they are generally just summer visitors.

## HAAPSALU

58°57'.50N 23°31'.61E (yacht harbours)

### Distances

Kuivastu 30M, Kardla 30M, Hanko 55M, Lohusalu 45M, Tallinn 65M

### Lights

**Paralepa Leading Lights 152.7°** *Front* 58°56'.04N 23°28'.97E Q.15.5m6M White round concrete tower with balcony and lantern 16m
*Rear* 800m from front, Iso.4s38m6M Round white tower, black bands on upper part. Balcony, black lantern 34m
**Kajakarahu Leading Lights 094.2°** *Front* 58°57'.19N 23°30'.83E Q.R.7m2M Orange triangle, yellow stripe, on metal column 8m
*Rear* 600m from front Iso.R.3s12m2M
Orange triangle, yellow stripe, on metal framework yellow
disk on top 13m
**Holmi Leading Lights 073.2°** *Front* 58°57'.59N 23°30'.67E Q.G.8m2M White rectangle, black stripe on metal framework 7m
*Rear* 390m from front Iso.G.3s14m2M White rectangle, black stripe on metal framework 12m
**Tahu (now unlit) Daymarks only in Line 049.8°** *Front* 58°58'.40N 23°32'.14E White rectangle, black stripe on metal framework 6m
*Rear* 233m from front White rectangle, black stripe on concrete post 9m
***Note*** All three pairs of lights visible on leading lines only

### Contacts

Haapsalu Grand Holm Marina
✆+372 520 7656
✆+372 472 9880
www.grandholmmarina.ee
valdo.kivi@grandholmmarina.ee
VHF Ch 12, call "Grand Holm"

Haapsalu Veskiviigi
✆+372 520 7656
✆+372 472 9880
www.veskiviigi.ee/en/
valdo.kivi@grandholmmarina.ee
VHF Ch 12, call "Grand Holm"

Westmeri Yacht Marina
✆+372 5303 9129
www.westmeri.ee/en/port/
info@westmeri.ee
VHF Ch 11, call "Westmer"

Haapsalu lies on a small peninsula, on which also stand the ruins of an old castle with a high tower. It is a pleasant old town of about 15,000 inhabitants with medieval roots. At the end of the 19th century it was a popular resort for the wealthy of St Petersburg and their grand wooden villas dominate the scenery – it is still a health spa famous for mud baths. There are several museums, including the restored railway station which is now a museum and tourist office. A

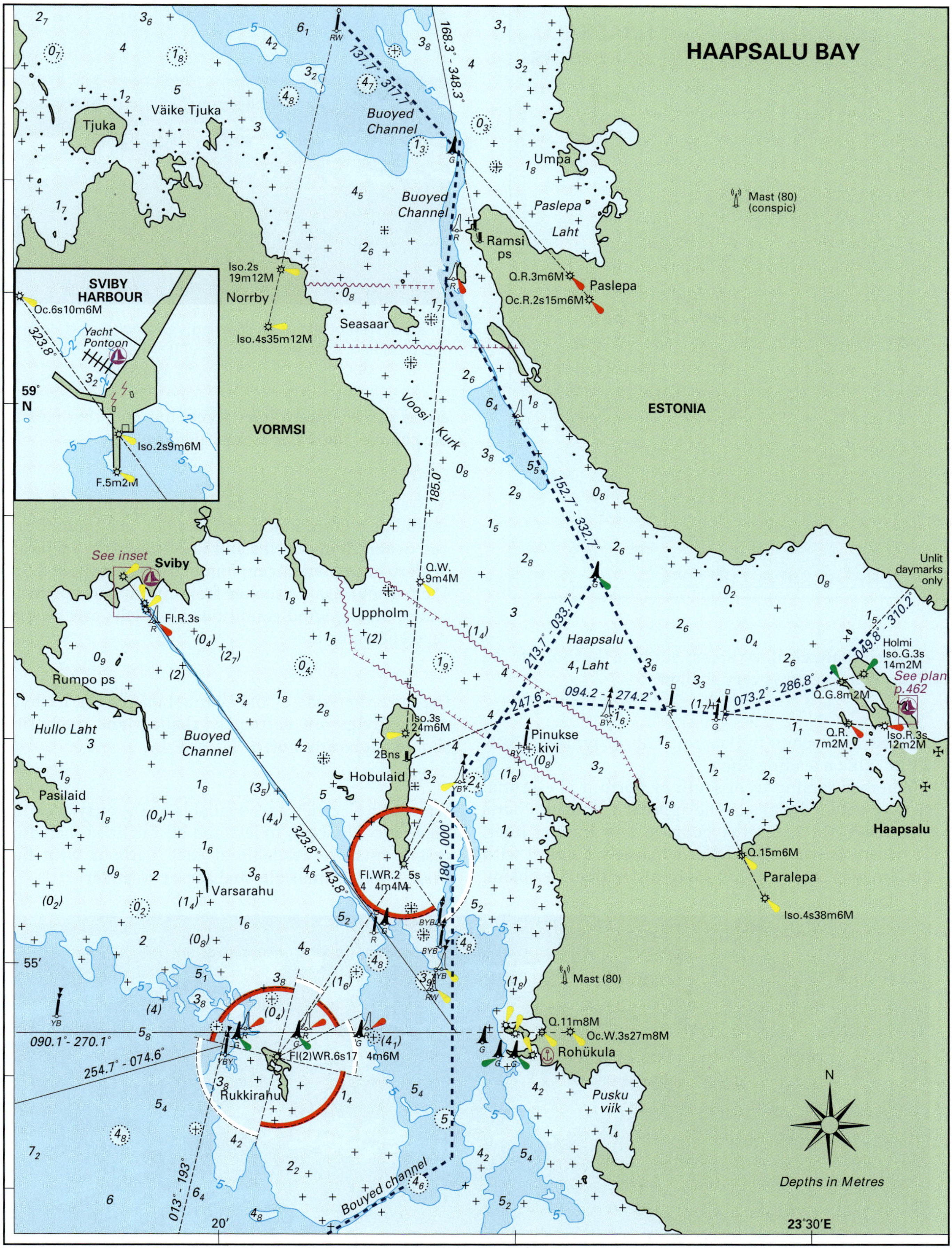
HAAPSALU BAY
SVIBY HARBOUR
Yacht Pontoon
Oc.6s10m6M
Iso.2s9m6M
F.5m2M
59° N
See inset
Sviby
Fl.R.3s
Väike Tjuka
Tjuka
Buoyed Channel
Umpa
Paslepa Laht
Paslepa
Ramsi ps
Q.R.3m6M
Oc.R.2s15m6M
Mast (80) (conspic)
Iso.2s 19m12M
Norrby
Iso.4s35m12M
Seasaar
VORMSI
Voosi Kurk
ESTONIA
Q.W. 9m4M
Uppholm
Haapsalu Laht
Unlit daymarks only
Holmi Iso.G.3s 14m2M
See plan p.462
Q.G.8m2M
Q.R. 7m2M
Iso.R.3s 12m2M
Haapsalu
Rumpo ps
Hullo Laht
Pasilaid
Iso.3s 24m6M
2Bns
Hobulaid
Pinukse kivi
Fl.WR.2 5s 4 4m4M
Varsarahu
Q.15m6M
Paralepa
Iso.4s38m6M
Mast (80)
Q.11m8M
Oc.W.3s27m8M
Rohükula
Fl(2)WR.6s17 4m6M
Rukkirahu
Pusku viik
Bouyed channel
Depths in Metres
090.1° - 270.1°
254.7° - 074.6°
013° - 193°
323.8° - 143.8°
185.0°
180° - 000°
137.7° - 317.7°
168.3° - 348.3°
152.7° - 332.7°
213.7° - 033.7°
094.2 - 274.2°
073.2° - 286.8°
049.8° - 310.2°
247.6
55′
20′
23°30′E
N

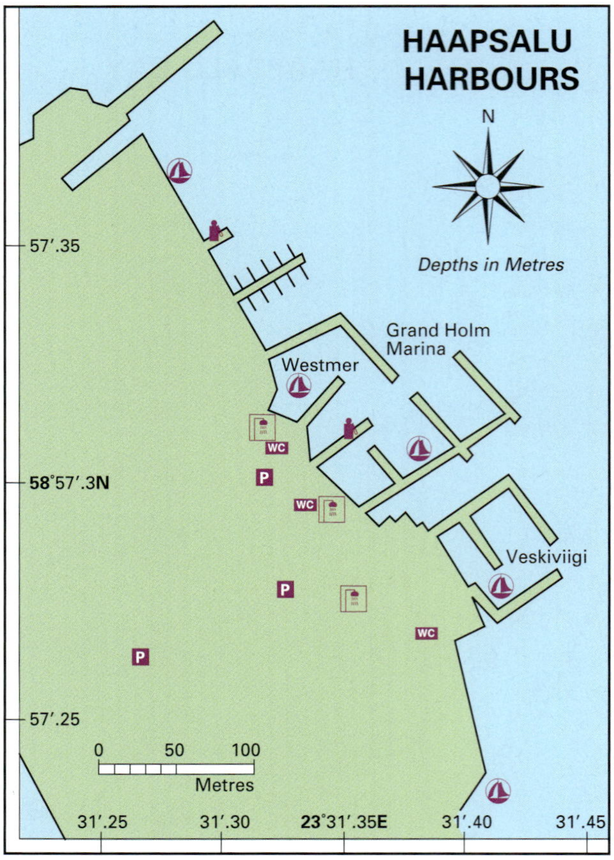


dredged channel allows access but note that outside the channel the water is very shallow.

### *Approach & entry*

Approach waypoint in Haapsalu Laht (Bay) 58°57'.30N 23°27'.70E on leading line.

Whether coming from south or north it is essential to have detailed plans of the approach. Consult *Charts of Estonia, Vol 2*; for the buoyage and leading lines. Provided the latter are followed closely a vessel with 2m draught can approach Haapsalu without problem.

An aerial view of Haapsalu showing Veskiviigi, Grand Holm and Westmeri *Robin Matthews*

A dredged channel allows access but note that outside the channel the water is very shallow.

### *Berthing*

At Westmeri mooring is to finger pontoons and there should be a minimum depth of 2.5m, maximum beam 4m. Grand Holm Marina and Veskiviigi have a mixture of stern buoys and finger pontoons with depths of 2.5m. The harbour has no shelter from the east or northeast and in strong wind conditions all berths can become very uncomfortable.

### *Anchoring*

Depths either side of the channel and in the harbour surroundings are extremely shallow and anchoring should not be attempted.

### *Services*

Water and electricity are available on the quay or on the pontoons. Showers, toilets and all facilities including restaurants are available at each harbour with fuel available at Grand Holm and also at Westmeri.

An aerial view of Haapsalu showing Westmer in the foreground *Robin Matthews*

Aerial view of the harbour at Dirhami *Robin Matthews*

For repair facilities, sailmaker etc, enquire with the harbourmaster where berthed.

### *Facilities*

The harbour is located about 2.5km from the town. Take the bus from the end of the short lane leading from the yacht club gate. Haapsalu has all the usual facilities of a major town; post office, shops, restaurants etc.

### *Communications & travel*

WiFi. Regular bus service to Tallinn and other Estonian towns, but no rail connection. Hire cars can be arranged at the harbour or at the tourist office. See the tourist information website on www.visithaapsalu.com/en/ for further details.

## Dirhami

59°12'.58N 23°29'.97E (yacht moorings)

**Contacts**

**Dirhami Marina**
☏+372 479 7221
☏+372 5623 4523
www.dirhami.ee/en/
www.dirhami.ee/en/port/
info@dirhami.ee

A commercial/fishing harbour with dedicated berthing facilities for yachts on pontoons or alongside the pier. Entry/exit dangerous in strong northerlies or northeasterlies but it is sheltered inside the harbour. Dirhami is a useful point of arrival/departure for Finland. Toilets and showers available along with a fuel berth. There is a small shop nearby and a café. Tables can be booked through the website. Internet is available at the harbour office.

The marina can also offer winter storage.

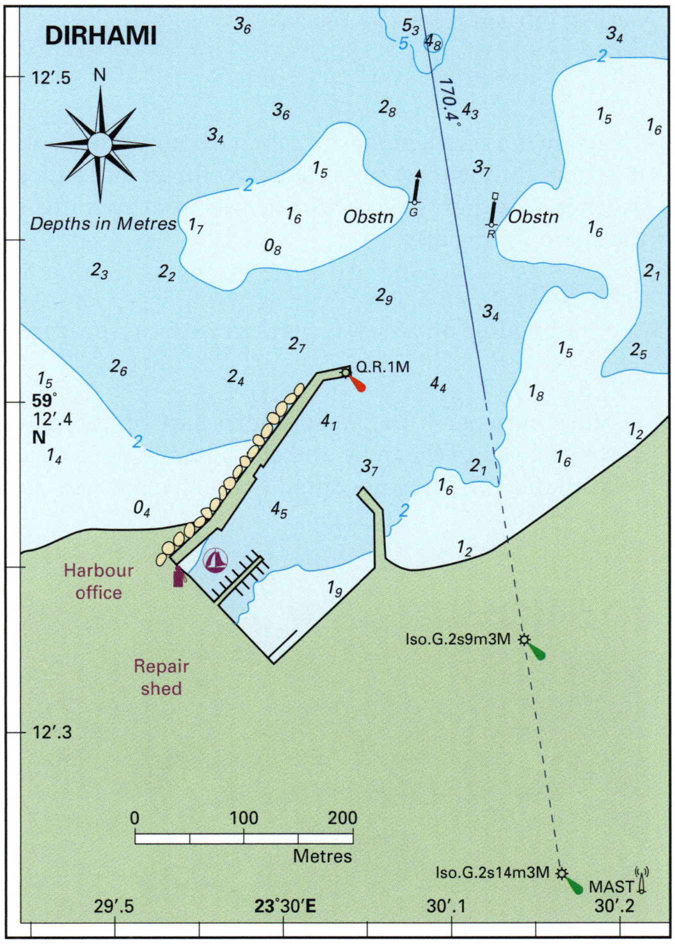

## LOHUSALU

59°24'.16N 24°12'.28E (yacht moorings)

### Distances
Kärdla 52M, Haapsalu 45M, Hanko 45M, Tallinn 25M

### Lights
**Pakri Lighthouse** 59°23'.24N 24°02'.26E
LFl.W.15s73m12M Red round brick tower with balcony 52m
**Suurupi** 59°27'.81N 24°22'.82E Oc(2)15s68m12M
White round stone tower with balcony and black lantern 22m
**Leading Lights 233.3°** *Front* 59°24'.15N 24°12'.39E
Iso.R.2s5m6M White rectangle, red stripe on metal post 3.5m
*Rear* 134m from front, Iso.R.4s8m6M White rectangle, red stripe on white metal post 5m

### Contacts
**Lohusalu Marina**
✆+372 5340 9442
www.lohusalu.ee/en/
lohusalu@lohusalu.ee
VHF Ch 10, call "Lohusalu marina"

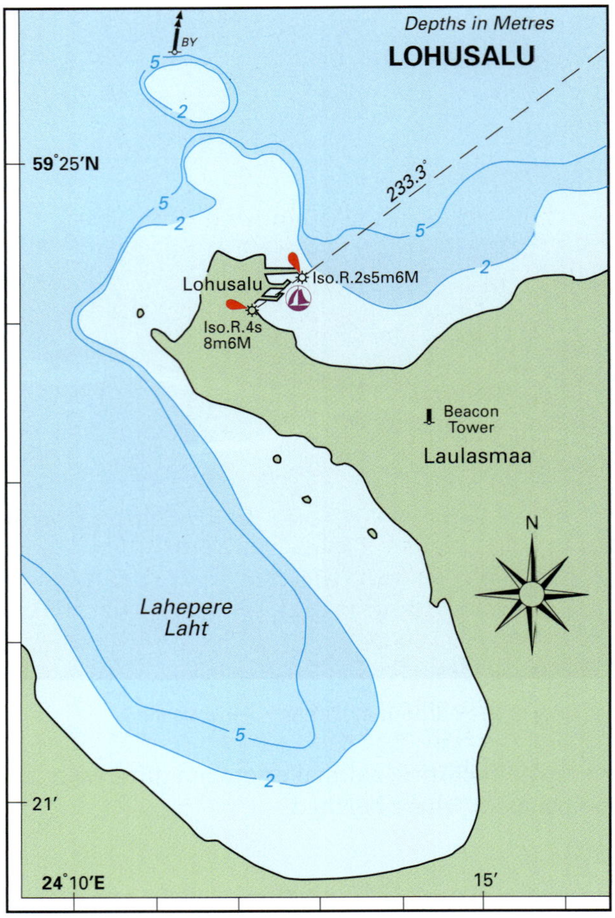


Lohusalu is a small, modern yacht harbour with around 15 spaces for visitors, surrounded by forest and superb beaches. See their website for details of attractions in the surrounding area.

### Approach & entry
The leading line on 233.3° is marked with two beacons.

### Berthing
Visitors may berth in the southern part of the main harbour bows to the quay and stern to a buoy if space is available. Anchoring outside the harbour is not advised, due to fishing nets and lack of shelter. See www.lohusalu.ee/en/contact-us/plan/ for a plan of the harbour.

### Services
Water, electricity, showers, toilets, sauna, laundry facilities and pump out facilities are all available, though the fuel berth at the head of the harbour has only 1.5m depth. For other services seek advice at the harbour office.

An aerial view of Lohusala harbour, looking west *Robin Matthews*

### *Facilities*

Restaurant at the yacht club, plus a small rural café in season. Shops in the town of Laulasmaa, about 5km distant.

### *Communications & travel*

WiFi at harbour. Buses to Tallinn and elsewhere.

## Naissaare

59°33'.43N 24°33'.22E (yacht moorings)

Naissaare Marina
✆+372 5345 0651
www.slmarinas.ee/en/ports/naissaare/
naissaar@saarteliinid.ee

Naissaare is an island lying northwest of Tallinn Bay and is a convenient stopover when sailing between Tallinn and Finland or worth a visit for its own interest. It was formerly inhabited by people of Swedish descent and the whole island is a nature conservation area. For details of the nature conservation area and walking trails, go to www.rmk.ee/en/exploring-nature/where-to-go/ and under 'Choose Nature Reserve', select 'Naissaare Nature Reserve'. The island was later a source of aggregate and a store and workshop for mines during Soviet times.

### *Berthing*

Berthing is on finger berths or alongside and there is a total of 29 berths available. The minimum depth is 3.5m. The harbour has the usual facilities with toilets, showers, water and electricity. The ferry from Tallinn uses this harbour for regular scheduled services, as well as excursions.

## Tallinn

**Distances**

Haapsalu 65M, Lohusalu 25M, Hanko 60M, Helsinki 45M, Vergi 55M

Tallinn, the capital of Estonia, has about 408,000 inhabitants and is a busy commercial harbour and industrial centre. It was part of the Hanseatic league from the 13th century and has the oldest surviving Gothic town hall in northern Europe. The city was fought over and badly damaged by both the Russians and the Germans but the old town in particular has been skilfully and tastefully restored. There are several possibilities for berthing based on Tallinn (Haven Kakumäe, Old City Marina, Noblessner/Lennusadam and Pirita). Haven Kakumäe is located west of Tallinn in Kopli Laht. Old City Marina is located beside the city and is, therefore, the most convenient for sightseeing, public transport etc. Noblessner/Lennusadam is a short distance to the northwest by bus or walking and located in a former submarine dock. Pirita is 6km east of the city, built for the yachting Olympics in 1980 and subsequently became Tallinn's main centre for yachting.

Tallinn has an international airport, frequent ferries to Stockholm and Helsinki, and rail and bus links throughout Estonia and to many cities in Europe via Eurolines.

Naissaare Harbour, looking northwest *Robin Matthews*

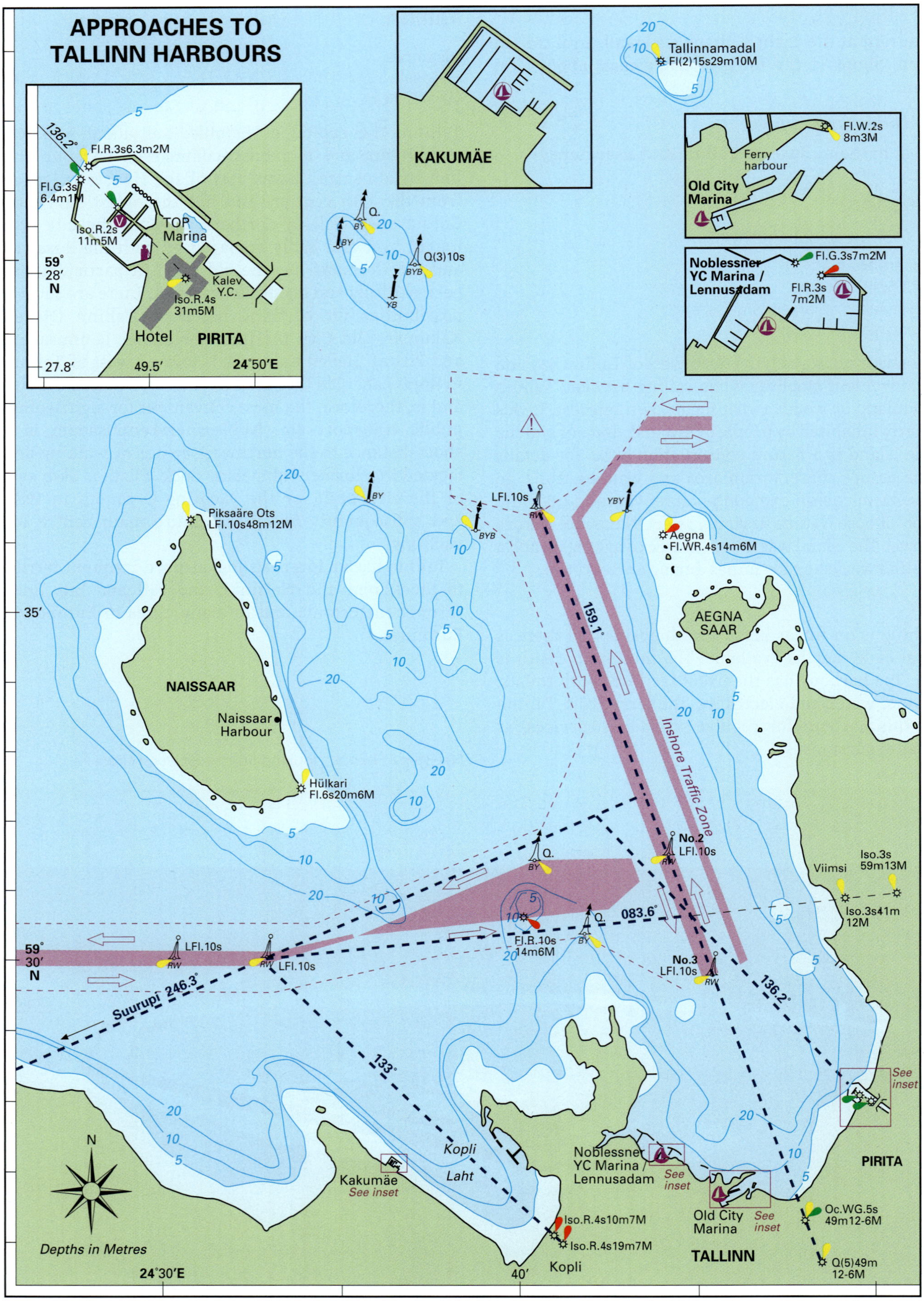
APPROACHES TO
TALLINN HARBOURS
136.2°
Fl.R.3s6.3m2M
Fl.G.3s
6.4m1M
Iso.R.2s
11m5M
TOP
Marina
59°
28′
N
Kalev
Y.C.
Iso.R.4s
31m5M
Hotel
PIRITA
27.8′
49.5′
24°50′E
KAKUMÄE
Tallinnamadal
Fl(2)15s29m10M
Fl.W.2s
8m3M
Ferry
harbour
Old City
Marina
Noblessner
YC Marina /
Lennusadam
Fl.G.3s7m2M
Fl.R.3s
7m2M
Q.
BY
YB
BYB
Q(3)10s
LFl.10s
RW
YBY
Aegna
Fl.WR.4s14m6M
AEGNA
SAAR
159.1°
Inshore Traffic Zone
Piksaäre Ots
LFl.10s48m12M
35′
NAISSAAR
Naissaar
Harbour
Hülkari
Fl.6s20m6M
No.2
LFl.10s
Viimsi
Iso.3s
59m13M
Iso.3s41m
12M
083.6°
Fl.R.10s
14m6M
59°
30′
N
LFl.10s
No.3
LFl.10s
136.2°
Suurupi 246.3°
133°
See
inset
PIRITA
Kopli
Laht
Kakumäe
See inset
Noblessner
YC Marina /
Lennusadam
See
inset
Old City
Marina
See
inset
Oc.WG.5s
49m12-6M
Iso.R.4s10m7M
Iso.R.4s19m7M
Q(5)49m
12-6M
TALLINN
Kopli
40′
24°30′E
Depths in Metres
N

## TALLINN HAVEN KAKUMÄE

59° 27'.05N 24° 36'.21E

### Lights

**Suurupi 3 safe water buoy** 59°29'.99N 24°32'.65E RW LFI (1) W 10s

**Kopli Front light beacon** (ISO R 4s) and Kopli Rear light beacon (Iso.R.4s)

### Contacts

**Kakumäe Marina**

✆+372 677 7444
www.havenk.com/en/
marina@havenk.com
VHF Ch 10, call "Haven Kakumäe"

Kakumäe marina is situated in Kopli Laht on the site of a former fishing harbour and is a large purpose-built marina. It is further away from Tallinn city centre than the other berthing options, but the city is easily accessible from there by public transport. It is ranked as a five-star harbour, so has all the facilities you might expect.

*Approach & entry*

Approach Kopli Laht (bay) from the Suurupi 3 safe water buoy 59°29'.99N 24°32'.65E and follow the leading line 133°- 313°T until the outer breakwater of Haven Kakumäe is abeam to starboard. Then head for waypoint 59°27'.10N 24°36'.65E to turn to starboard to enter the harbour.

*Berthing*

There is good all round shelter within the marina. Berthing is mostly to long finger pontoons with a maximum depth of 4m.

*Services*

Water and electricity is available on pontoons and toilets, showers, sauna, launderette, pump out facility, fuel berth and some chandlery are located by the Harbourmaster's office. Also available are lift out facilities, engine servicing and most other maintenance services. Winter storage and all services are provided by Yachts Service www.yachts-service.ee/en/. Their lifting capacity 130T.

*Facilities*

There is WiFi and restaurants onsite and shops, banks and other facilities are available in Tallinn. A bus service to Tallinn is available from Kakumäe.

## TALLINN NOBLESSNER/ LENNUSADAM (SEAPLANE HARBOUR)

59°27'.21N 24°43'.88E (yacht moorings)

### Lights

**Naissaar Lighthouse** 59°36'.22N 24°30'.64E LFl.W.10s48m12M Octagonal white conical concrete tower, red top and balcony 45m

**Aegna** 59°36'.04N 24°43'.8E Fl.WR.4s14m6M Yellow rectangle on red metal post 12m

**Vahemadal** 59°30'.61N 24°39'.97E Fl.R.10s14m6M Octagonal truncated pyramid with white upper and red lower part 13m

**Tallinnamadal** 59°42'.72N 24°43'.89E Fl(2)W.15s29m10M Racon Red round metal tower, yellow top, black base, with three galleries 31m

**Noblessner/Lennusadam East mole Lt beacon** 59°27'.31N 24°44'.22E Fl.R.3s7m2M Red metal column with balcony 5m

**Noblessner/Lennusadam West mole Lt beacon** 59°27'.34N 24°44'.12E Fl.G.3s7m2M Green metal column 3m

### Contacts

**Lennusadam (Tallinn Seaplane Harbour)**

✆+372 502 2877
www.meremuuseum.ee
sadam@lennusadam.eu
VHF Ch 9, call "Port Noblessner"

**Noblessner Yacht Marina**

✆+372 5688 8825
www.noblessner.ee/en/noblessner-marina/
port@noblessner.ee
VHF Ch 9, call "Port Noblessner"

Lennusadam and Noblessner marinas in Tallinn. Noblessner is the marina on the right
*Robin Matthews*

These are two harbours side by side sharing the same entrance. Lennusadam, also known as Tallinn Seaplane Harbour is, not surprisingly from the name, a former seaplane harbour and Noblessner has historical links although has been subject to a massive redevelopment.

### Approach & entry

Located in Peetri harbour. This is a straightforward approach from Tallinn Bay.

### Berthing

Berthing is on finger pontoons but do note that some are reserved for resident yachts. Caveat: although work has been carried out on the outer breakwater, strong onshore winds and washes from passing ferries still cause disturbance making the berths in both harbours uncomfortable at times. The seaplane harbour is slightly deeper with a minimum depth of 6m, but you should have 4.5m in Noblessner yacht marina.

### Services

Both marinas are modern and have all the facilities that you might expect - water and electricity on the pontoons, toilets, showers, sauna and washing facilities.

### Facilities

There are a number of restaurants and cafés at the harbour and it is not far into town for anything else. The Seaplane Harbour Maritime Museum is worth a visit. Other facilities as for Old City Marina.

### Communications & travel

WiFi. Tallinn city centre can be reached by bus no. 3 from Noblessner and bus no. 73 from Lennusadam to Tallinn centre.

## TALLINN OLD CITY MARINA

59°26'.54N 24°45'.50E (yacht moorings)

### Lights

**Naissaar Lighthouse** 59°36'.22N 24°30'.64E LFl.W.10s48m12M Octagonal white conical concrete tower, red top and balcony 45m

**Aegna** 59°36'.04N 24°43'.8E Fl.WR.4s14m6M Yellow rectangle on red metal post 12m

**Vahemadal** 59°30'.61N 24°39'.97E Fl.R.10s14m6M Octagonal truncated pyramid with white upper and red lower part 13m

**Tallinnamadal** 59°42'.72N 24°43'.89E Fl(2)W.15s29m10M Racon Red round metal tower, yellow top, black base, with three galleries 31m

**Tallinna Leading Lights 159.1°** *Front* 59°26'.24N 24°47'.91E Oc.WG.5s49m12/6M Red conical tower on a house 18m
*Rear* 1.1km from front Q(5)W.5s80m12M White round stone tower, black top with balcony and lantern 40m

**Vanasadam North mole Lt beacon** 59°26'.95N 24°46'.54E Fl.W.2s8m3M Green metal construction 5m

### Contacts

**Tallinn Old City Marina**
✆+372 510 3360
www.ts.ee/en/old-city-marina/
marina@portoftallinn.com
VHF Ch 14, Call sign 'Tallinn Radio 5' before entry

### Approach & entry

Tallinn Old City Marina is located in the old Admiralty Basin. It is a straightforward approach from Tallinn Bay, but, when just over 0.5M from the northwestern breakwater, it is essential to call Port Control on VHF Ch 14 (Call sign 'Tallinn Radio 5') or to telephone on ✆+372 631 8588 for permission to enter. This is because of the close proximity of the ferry port and associated traffic.

### Berthing

Berthing in the marina is on individual finger pontoons with a minimum depth of 4.3m. The marina can tend to get very full during the holiday season and at weekends, but the friendly staff make every effort to find a space.

An aerial view of Old City Harbour *Port of Tallinn / Tallinna Sadam/Wikimedia Commons (https://commons.wikimedia.org/wiki/File:Old_City_Harbour,_Tallinn.jpg)*

The Tallinn skyline from the harbour *Dennis Dolkens / Dreamstime.com*

The City of Tallinn at sunrise *Tomas1111 / Dreamstime.com*

### Services

Water and electricity are available at all berths and toilets are beside the security gate. Showers and sauna are in yacht club. A pump out station is available with the fuel berth to starboard as you enter the marina.

### Facilities

All facilities - banks, post office, restaurants, tourist office available in Tallinn.

### Communications & travel

WiFi. Local, national and international buses and also local trams will transport you where you want around the area and there is an airport for domestic and international flights.

## TALLINN (PIRITA) TOP MARINA AND KALEV YACHT CLUB

59°28'.22N 24°49'.07E (centre of harbour entrance)

### Lights

**Naissaar Lighthouse** 59°36'.22N 24°30'.64E
LFl.10s48m12M Octagonal white conical concrete tower, red top and balcony 45m
**Aegna** 59°36'.04N 24°43'.8E Fl.WR.4s14m6M
Yellow rectangle on red metal post 12m
**Vahemadal** 59°30'.61N 24°39'.97E Fl.R.10s14m6M
Octagonal truncated pyramid with white upper and red lower part 13m
**Tallinnamadal** 59°42'.72N 24°43'.89E Fl(2)W.15s29m10M
Racon Red round metal tower, yellow top, black base, with three galleries 31m
**Tallinna Leading Lights 159.1°** *Front* 59°26'.24N 24°47'.91E Oc.WG.5s49m12/6M
Red conical tower on a house 18m
*Rear* 1.1km from front Q(5)W.5s80m12M
White round stone tower, black top with balcony and lantern 40m
**Pirita Leading Lights 136.2°** *Front* 59°28'.13N 24°49'.24E
Iso.R.2s11m5M Orange round concrete tower, three white balconies 9m
*Rear* 400m from front Iso.R.4s31m5M White square concrete tower 28m
**Pirita northeast breakwater** 59°28'.23N 24°49'.10E
Fl.R.3s7m2M Orange metal cylinder with balcony 5m
**Pirita southwest breakwater** 59°28'.20N 24°49'.05E
Fl.G.3s7m1M Green metal column with balcony 5m

### Contacts

**Tallinn-Pirita TOP Marina**
✆+372 508 2837
www.piritatop.ee/?lang=en
toomas@piritatop.ee

**Kalev Yacht Club**
✆+372 5301 0450
www.kjk.ee/en/
sadam@kjk.ee
VHF Ch 11, call "Kalev Marina"

### Approach & entry

The approach is straightforward, with the television tower visible from many miles offshore and the gable end of the convent ruins coming into view on closer approach. The harbour entrance with its double breakwater is conspicuous and there are no offlying hazards.

### Berthing

Yachts may berth at either TOP Marina or further in at the Kalev Yacht Club. For the TOP visitors' area, on entering harbour turn to starboard and berth in the area bounded by the first two quays. TOP should have a minimum depth of 3.5m. Berthing at Kalev Yacht Club is limited but if space is available, access is by turning to port on entering the harbour and proceeding towards the road bridge. Kalev Yacht Club is on the starboard side before the bridge. Kalev Yacht Club marina should have a minimum depth of 3m.

### Services

Water and electricity is available at all berths and there is rubbish disposal, toilets and showers at both TOP Marina and Kalev Yacht Club.

The fuel berth close to the museum ships at the head of the western basin, where the pump out station is situated.

There is a boatyard beside the marina and the Kalev Yacht Club has skilled shipwrights and well-equipped workshops where repairs can be carried out, as well as a small sail-loft. There is a chandlery within the complex.

### Facilities

There is a good restaurant at the Club. Other facilities, including an ATM are in the foyer of the Pirita TOP Spa Hotel.

The large Selver supermarket (on the opposite side of the main road a few hundred metres southwest), stocks most items, and there are other shops and kiosks in the vicinity. Facilities, including post office, restaurants and tourist office, are available in Tallinn itself.

There is a good beach beyond the river east of the harbour, with the impressive and well-preserved ruins of St Birgitta's convent just inland.

### Communications & travel

WiFi is available in the area of the harbour but does not extend to the visitors' area.

Local buses run along the main road behind the harbour. It is necessary to purchase tickets in the local kiosk before boarding.

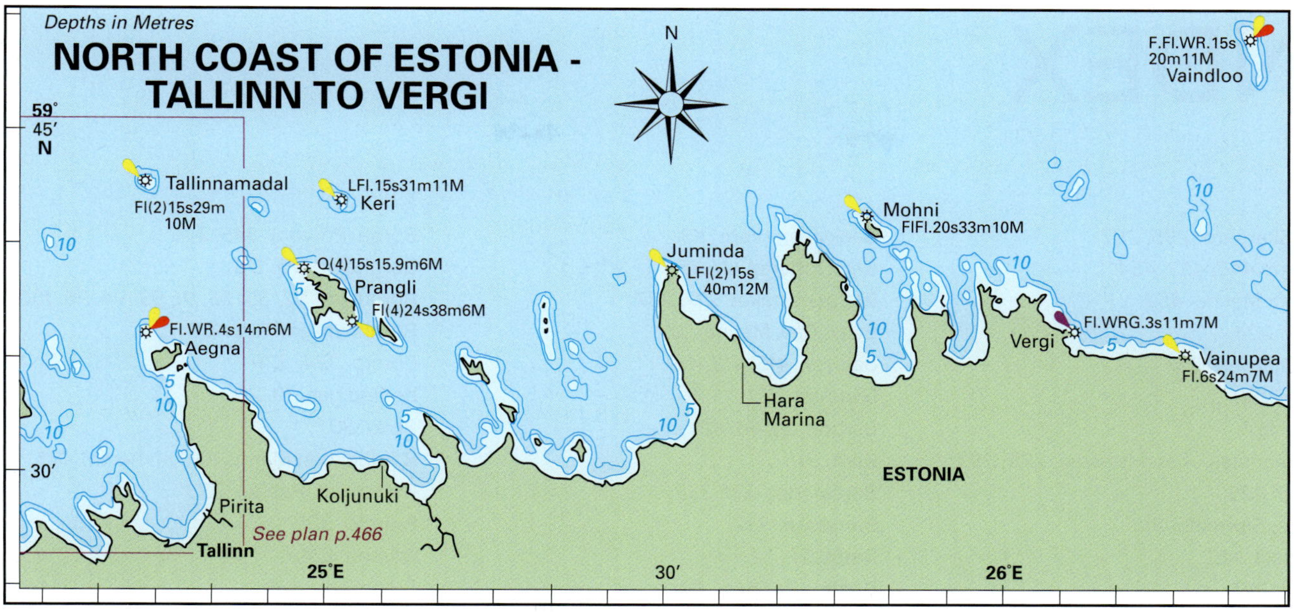


## Prangli (Kelnase harbour)

59°38'.23N 25°00'.75E (yacht moorings)

**Contacts**

Kelnase Marina
☎+372 5191 9167
www.kelnase.viimsi.ee/en
www.visitharju.ee/en/port-of-kelnase-on-prangli/ (there are some useful photos on this page of the marina)
info@prangli.ee

Prangli is a small island off Muuga Bay, northeast of Tallinn, with approximately 100 inhabitants. It is the most northerly island in Estonia with year-round inhabitants. For tourist information about the island visit www.visittallinn.ee/eng/visitor/see-do/things-to-do/marinas/181183/kelnase-harbour-on-prangli-island. The harbour is used by the passenger ferry to Leppneeme. There are dangerous rocks in the approach so it is essential to use good charts. The approach and entry should be made only in daylight and calm conditions. Berthing is partly alongside and also stern buoys to the pontoon. The facilities include electricity, water and toilets.

## Koljunuki Marina

59°30'.18N 25°05'.29E
☎+372 523 5000
www.koljunuki.ee/?lang=en
sadam@koljunuki.ee

An alternative to Prangli on the mainland is Koljunuki marina. It is a small marina but well sheltered from all directions. Entry is straightforward through a channel well-marked with lateral buoys. The guest berths are bows-to the pontoon from a stern buoy and there should be a minimum depth of 2.5m.

## Hara Marina

59° 35'.25N 25° 36'.77E
☎+372 5690 0433
www.harasadam.ee/vaikelaevasadam/
sadam@harasadam.ee

Hara is a former Soviet submarine base built between 1956 and 1958. The base was apparently used to demagnetize the hulls of the Soviet submarines. It is a deep water harbour with excellent all-round protection provided by both the offlying island of Hara and huge breakwaters. Easy entry in deep water but recommended in daylight only.

### *Berthing*

The berths are bows-to a pontoon with small finger pontoons for the area which they call Külaliskai guest harbour (the northerly pontoon). There are also berths on the other pontoon slightly to the south which are bows-to the pontoon with stern buoys. This section is called Jahtkai yacht harbour (see www.harasadam.ee/vaikelaevasadam/#Ala-kaart). There are approximately 24 berths with a minimum depth of 6m. Electricity and water on the pontoon.

### *Facilities*

There is a modern restaurant (www.harasadam.ee/restoran/) and shore facilities including toilets, showers, WiFi, washing facilities and a pump-out. The nearest shopping is at Loksa. There is a bus stop at the far end of the lane.

# INDEX

# AIG AN OIR

# Aig an Oir

## At the Edge – Scotland's Atlantic Oakwoods

*Text by Robert Burton*

THE SOCIETY OF WILDLIFE ARTISTS
LANGFORD PRESS · 2005

Langford Press, 10 New Road, Langtoft,
Peterborough, PE6 9LE
Telephone/Fax 01778 341132
www.langford-press.co.uk
Email sales@langford-press.co.uk

Designed and typeset in Arepo, Cycles and Frutiger
by Nye Hughes, Dalrymple, Edinburgh
Printed and bound in Singapore under the supervision
of MRM Graphics Ltd, Winslow
Photography by Chris Christenson of Coldwells Art
Company Limited, Dalkeith
Eadar-theangachadh bho Bheurla le Uilleam MacNeacail
Gaelic Translation by William Nicolson

A CIP Record for this book is available from the
British Library

ISBN 1-904078-18-4



Half-title: Carl Ellis *Brown trout*
Frontispiece: Louise Oppenheimer *Seasons at Barnluasgan,* handwoven wool wallhanging
Below: John Paige *Golden-ringed dragonfly emerging*
Opposite: John Paige *Midges*
Contents: Jane Smith *Oak leaf print*
Forewords: Carry Akroyd *Sessile* (p.8) *and pedunculate* (p. 9) *oak leaf studies*

## ACKNOWLEDGEMENTS

The artists, author and publisher would all like to express their heartfelt gratitude to Moira Baptie and Roland Stiven for administering the Aig an Oir project so expertly and for their help in this publication. Without their hard work and dedication the project would not have been such a great success. Thanks also to Forest Enterprise Scotland staff Margaret MacCallum, Jamie McIntyre and Chris Marsh for showing Robert Burton around the study areas and for their part in organising the artists' residencies.

The project partners would like to thank Allan MacColl and Moira Hunter for kindly granting their permission to reproduce part of their father Donald MacColl's poem, *Beside Loch Shiel*. Our thanks also to Michael Schmidt of Carcanet Press for granting us licence to reproduce part of *Woods of Raasay* by Sorley MacLean.

# Contents

# Forewords

By the nature of what they do, artists who take wildlife and the natural world as their starting point spend hours on their own. It might be out in the field, head down, hunched over a sketchpad or at an easel, often with a telescope or binoculars, trying to realize their observations or record sensations. Or else it's in the studio, working to shape ideas and raw material from the field into some kind of meaningful creative end.

Occasionally, however, there are opportunities to work alongside other artists and as a group share a focus on a specific place or kind of habitat. This adds an air of excitement and collective enthusiasm, as experiences are compared, observations contrasted, and sometimes new techniques acquired or working materials swapped. Someone finds a great spot for butterflies on the wing; another is absorbed by the plants; one artist tells of a good site for singing warblers; or two or three together are inspired by the same aspect of the wider landscape. Someone has an interesting range of papers to work on, and another artist has brought their woodcutting materials.

It was exactly these kinds of individual and shared experiences that lay at the heart of the Aig an Oir project. Three groups of eight artists – SWLA members and artists from the local community – gathered for a week in each of the project areas, and through the year there were further visits by SWLA members, local artists and bursary winners, who visited the sites either on their own or in groups of two or three.

Whatever the nature and timing of the artists' visits, their output was prolific and incisive, and a varied selection graces the pages of this book. The result is a beautiful and powerful portrait of the oakwoods, which, together with the text, reveals their essential character and also brings to life broader concepts and principles, such as biodiversity, ecology, habitat management and sustainability, as well as their historical and cultural heritage, all of which are fundamental to understanding and appreciating the woods.

I would like to thank all the artists who volunteered to participate and enthusiastically contributed their creativity and time. Their effort was skillfully managed and sensitively administered by Moira Baptie of FCS and Roland Stiven, the overall project manager, and we are extremely grateful to both of them. The artists are also very grateful to all the FCS staff and rangers from the three project areas, who offered so much advice and local knowledge. From the very beginning, Hugh Insley, Chief Executive, Forest Enterprise Scotland, was determined to see the Aig an Oir project happen. Now that it is successfully concluded we would like to thank him particularly.

It is said that a work of art is never finished, it just stops in interesting places. In a sense, that is also true of the native Atlantic oakwoods and the story of their restoration – a work in progress with a wealth of interesting places to stop and observe their natural history and understand their place in the economic and cultural history of the west coast of Scotland, and places to just simply appreciate their beauty.

**Bruce Pearson**
*Vice President, Society of Wildlife Artists*

The Atlantic Woodlands, scattered along the extreme western fringe of the continent, are one of the most important and scarce habitats in Europe. Scotland can be considered very fortunate in having the largest and most intact share of this unique ecosystem, and yet, among the general population, knowledge of the presence and significance of these relicts is abysmally low. This magnificent book and accompanying exhibition will undoubtedly help raise awareness and appreciation of these national treasures, as well as generating concern for their continued survival.

Throughout the country 'the rainforest' appears to be an essential part of the curriculum in virtually every primary school. As a result we have raised a generation of young people who know more about the tropical forests of the Amazon basin or Borneo than they do of the woodlands in their own country. When I tell audiences that Scotland has its own rainforests, I am treated to scepticism or disbelief. Yet ecologists recognise the Atlantic Woodlands as part of the Temperate Rainforest Biome, which spreads from New Zealand to Chile, and is even more fragmented and threatened than its tropical equivalent.

If scientists have yet to convince us of the value of our Atlantic Woodlands perhaps artists will succeed? Artists, with their intuitive sympathy for atmosphere, nuance and detail, seem to have the ability to connect closely with this intricate and intensely complex environment of weather-shaped trees and blankets of bryophytes. In the eighties, in a parallel project to Aig an Or, a group of Canadian artists, under the auspices of the Western Canada Wilderness Society, produced an exhibition and book on the Carmanah temperate rainforest of Vancouver Island that changed the hearts and minds of the local population and eventually led to the creation of a new Provincial Park. In the same area, scientists had been struggling for years to get the authorities to listen to their arguments for protecting biodiversity.

Now, in Scotland, we finally have an exhibition and publication – the result of an exemplary level of community involvement – that does justice to our beautiful Atlantic Woodlands in all their many guises. Without doubt it will have a similar impact in strengthening our commitment, at all levels, to protecting these scarce remnants from any further degradation and encourage the regeneration of former forested areas on the West Coast.

The Royal Botanic Garden Edinburgh, with its deep commitment to both Scotland's natural heritage and the study of biodiversity, especially among the less well-known mosses, liverworts and lichens that thrive in the Atlantic Woodlands, is keen to raise awareness of conservation issues among all levels of society. Our experience has also been that a combination of art and science can be a powerful medium. In the recent past we have been involved in a number of successful projects in this area, including the Scottish Rare Plants project and the Millennium Forest exhibition Return of the Natives. We are equally proud to be associated with Aig an Or and congratulate the team that turned this exciting vision into a reality through hard work and dedication. I would now encourage you, while enjoying the many beautiful images in this publication, to take the underlying message concerning the future of these precious places into your heart.

**Ian D. Edwards**
*Royal Botanic Garden Edinburgh*

Tha an leabhar tha seo a toirt taghadh dh'en ealain a chruthaich buill comunn nam Fiadh-Bheatha, agus a ghabh pàirt 'sa phrosceit seo 'Aig an Oir' 'sa bhliadhna 2004.

'S ann ri linn 'Aig an Oir' a dh'eirich an iarrtas air fiosrachadh fhaotainn air obair Coimmisean na Coille, comhla ris na coimhearsnachan a's na sgirean a leanas mar

tha Ceannloch san eilean Sgitheanach, Sunart, A' Mhorairne agus Cnàpadal, na tri ma dheireadh an Earra-Ghaidheal.

Chaidh an sgrùdadh seo air adhart gus ath-bheothachadh thoirt air doireachan daraich an taobh siar.

Than a coilltean seo prìseal airson an cumadh, is mar a tha iad sgaoilte fosgailte air a' ghrùnnd, a leigeal le solus na greine cead fàs thoirt air fluraichean beaga nadurach, is eile mar cròtal is corcuir. Tha an cuspair seo air fhoillseachadh gu ealanta air na làrich chaidh ainmeachadh.

Ged a bhuineas na craobhan dhan àite, se glé bheag a tha nàdurach mu'n timchioll.

Dh'eirich an suidheachadh seo mar thorradh air cleachaidhean, agus feumalachd muintir na sgìre fad linntean, mar a tha Rob Burton ga mhineachadh sa leabhar.

Tha gu leor 'sa làtha ann a faotinn coire dh'an phoileasaidh a bha ann nuair nach robh am beachd an riaghladh ach fàs math a thoirt air fiodh ann an aithgearrachd, agus canaidh moran gu robh e cearr craobhan coigreach a' chur as ùr fo sgàil na seann deidhinn, ach 's math gu robh an seann stòc calma fallainn, chos a nis gun gabh car a chur 'sa ghnothach.

Tha e na adhbhar molaidh gu bheil na coilltean iomallach seo, chaidh air di-chuimhne, a nis a' faotinn taic bho na coimhearsnachan airson an cumail beò, agus dochas gu 'm bi e chum buanachd do'n linn ri teachd.

Tha eachdraidh na coilltean seo a' dearbhadh cho cugallach sa bha iad, coltach ris an tuath bha nabachd riuthe. 'S en gealltanas is fhearr againn gum mair agus gu meudaich na craobhan seo, an dòchas gum bi sin chum math muintir na sgìrean 'sa bheil iad air oir a h-Alba.

Chaneil sinn idir a deanamh leisgeul iomradh a' thoirt ann an Gàidhlig air a leabhar agus air a phroiseact. Tha an canain coltach ris na doireachan, an cunnart a dhol a bith. Chunnaic mise na craobhan seo an toiseach air latha briagha samhraidh san Og- Mhios sa bhliadhna 1972. Air an t-slighe tilleadh a Ard na Murchan, stad mi feòrach do dhuine nach do thuig mo chainnt, ach stiùir an nighean aige mi air an rathad cheart gu aiseig Chorrain Ard Ghobhar.

'Se taic chaich chur am proseict seo air adhart, gu araidh na fir seo:

Rob Livingston-Hi Arts, Bruce Pearson agus Chris Rose, le cheile a Fiadh Beatha nan Ealain. Cheart cho feumail bha an taic airgiod a fhuaradh bho Iomart Lochaber, Whelk Eorpach, North Highland Leader + 2000–2006 Programme. 'Se n uidh a bh'aig na coimhearsnachan, agus luchd ealain fad às, comhla ri feadhainn faisg air laimh san tri coimhearsnachan, gun a shoirbhich cho math leis a ghnothach. Chuidich e gun d'fhuair sinn cead feum a dheanamh dhe'n na tallaichean agus na cailearaidhean, ach chan fheum sinn di-chuimhne dheanamh air oifeagearan na proseict agus sgiobean a Chomisean fhein.

Bha luchd ealainn a sealltainn torradh an cuid obrach aig An Tuireann am Portrigh, Taigh Tasgaidh Cille Mhàrtainn faisg air Cnàpadal, Studio Resipol Suinart agus Taigh Bàn Lochalin 'sa Mhorairne (aite bithidh).

Bha na cruinnichean bha sin air leth taitneach agus cairdeil; chur sluagh an àite eolas air urrachan a Chomumm Ealain. Chord sin ris na h-uile. Bithidh an taisbeanadh ri fhaicinn anns na Botanics an Dun Eidean san t-Sultain 2005 far am bi Rob Burton fhein a bha uaireigen a fuireach an Earra-Ghaidheal. Ma tha buanachd re tighinn an cois na h-obrach seo, bithidh duil gun cuidich e na coimhearsnachan ri tìde.

**Uisdean Insley**
*Ard Runaire, Iomart Coilltearachd na h-Alba*

THIS BOOK BRINGS TOGETHER A selection of the art created by members of the Society of Wildlife Artists who took part in the Aig an Oir (At the Edge) project during 2004.

Aig an Oir grew out of a desire to gain recognition for the work of Forestry Commission Scotland and its partners, including the local communities on Skye, in Sunart and Morven, and at Knapdale, to restore the native Atlantic oakwoods in the west of Scotland.

These woods have a magical quality, which derives from the shape and distribution of the trees, their open ground flora, the epiphytes that cover the trees and, most of all, the special light within them. The essence of this has been captured brilliantly by the Society's artists during the three Aig an Oir residencies.

Although they are native woodlands, little about them is natural. The very quality that everyone appreciates has been created by man's intervention over the centuries, as Robert Burton describes in this book.

Leaving these woods alone and trying to preserve them is not an option. This approach will surely lead to their eventual extinction. And yet our past attempts to regenerate them have produced something very different to the desired end product. Open space allows a thick tangle of many species, few of which are oak trees. This brings a realisation that the future management of these woods and the re-creation of these attractive open woodlands with their almost lawn-like ground flora is going to take time, patience and probably the use of techniques with which foresters have lost familiarity, such as controlled grazing.

With the wisdom of hindsight everyone now recognises that the overzealous pursuit of wood production under earlier forestry policies was a mistake. Native woodlands such as these never should have been underplanted with exotic conifers, and it is lucky that they have been robust enough to survive sufficiently well for us to be able to reverse the process.

The project has been a celebration of these remote and often overlooked woods and of those individuals and communities who have contributed not only to their survival and return from the brink but also to ensuring that they are secured for future generations.

The history of these woods has proved to be as fragile, and yet at the same time as enduring, as the communities living among them. The strongest guarantee for their future existence is that they contribute to, and are understood to be of value to, the communities of these places at the edge of Scotland.

We make no apology for promoting Gaelic through this project and book. As the native language of the area, it is even more threatened than the oakwoods. The first time I saw these beautiful woods was on one of those special west-coast days in June 1972, when sun from a cloudless day shone through the freshly opened leaves. Returning from a visit to Ardnamurchan Point, I stopped at an isolated house to ask the way back to Corran Ferry. The old man working in his garden looked at me, shook his head, and went indoors to find his daughter, who was more comfortable speaking English.

Aig an Oir would not have happened if it hadn't been for the support and help from our partners, Robert Livingston of HI~ARTS and Bruce Pearson and Chris Rose from the Society of Wildlife Artists, and, importantly, the funding received from Lochaber Enterprise and the European WHELK and North Highland LEADER+ 2000–2006 Programmes. However, it is the enthusiasm of the local communities, the artists from far afield and from within the three communities, the local studios and art galleries, the Project Officers, and the local Forestry Commission teams that has really made it truly special.

The evening 'hangings' when the Society's artists presented the initial results of their work at the An Tuireann Arts Centre on Skye, Kilmartin Museum near Knapdale, Resipole Studios in Sunart and Whitehouse Restaurant in Lochaline were exciting, vibrant and happy occasions, bringing the nation's top wildlife artists into direct contact with communities seldom in the limelight. That alone was a huge reward and success.

The exhibition at the Royal Botanic Gardens in Edinburgh in September 2005 and this book, skilfully penned by Robert Burton, himself once a resident of rural Argyll, continue this success. As products of Aig an Oir, all of these outputs will help to secure the future of both Scotland's Atlantic oakwoods and the communities who care for and depend upon them.

**Hugh Insley**
*Chief Executive, Forest Enterprise Scotland*

1

# At the edge

*Bi gach creutair d'a laigead*
*Dol le suigeart do 'n choill*

*There's no creature so feeble*
*But goes with joy to the woods*

FROM THE SONG OF SUMMER
BY ALEXANDER MACDONALD

If you drive into the western Highlands of Scotland, turning off and heading west from Loch Ness perhaps, or coming up directly from the south via Loch Lomond, you enter one of the wildest and most remote parts of Britain. The human population is small and scattered, and you can go for miles without seeing a building or another human. The landscape is breathtaking, but although the steep, rugged hills impart a grandeur to the scene, they are bare. Along the valley below, the terrain is softer. It is clothed with patches of deciduous, broadleaved woodland: a few acres here and there, perhaps a larger spread covering miles of the valley floor, or just a ribbon of trees following a burn up the hillside.

These woods go unremarked; they are not what visitors come to the Highlands to see. Yet they are part of the once-great Caledonian Forest, which is better known for its stands of dramatic ancient Scots pines, familiar to visitors to Speyside in the central Highlands. They are the remains of a special habitat known as the Atlantic oakwoods. Within the Highlands, the oakwoods range from Sutherland in the north to Loch Lomond in the south. Elsewhere, they can be found along the length of the Atlantic seaboard: in south-west Scotland, the west coast of Ireland, the English Lake District, West Wales and Cornwall, and thence to Brittany in France and Galicia in Spain.

With good reason the Atlantic oakwoods are sometimes described as a temperate rainforest. The Highlands are famous for their wet climate, and with nearly 2000 mm of rain falling every year on Fort William, this is well within the range of rainfall in tropical rainforests. We think of tropical rainforests as thronging with life: monkeys, hummingbirds, bizarre insects and garish orchids. We are told that saving rainforests is vital for preserving 'biodiversity'. We know this from television programmes and books, but the rainforest on our doorstep has been woefully neglected. It turns out that 'the Celtic rainforest' is unexpectedly rich in animal and plant species, with thirty-four species regarded as priorities for conservation in a British context. They are not so dramatic as the flamboyant wildlife of the tropics, but the remnants of their woodland home are national treasures and are worthy of preservation for their own sakes.

Thirty years ago, I lived in Argyll. It was the time when the Forestry Commission was planting vast tracts of country on the west coast with exotic conifers. Rows of fast-growing Sitka spruce were sprouting all over open moors, and, to my distress, they were also being planted under the native oaks and birches. The oaks and birches initially acted as sheltering nurses but would later be crowded out as the conifers overtook them. How silent and barren would be the new forests when they crowded out the native vegetation! Exotic conifers were not the only problem. On land that was still farmed, I noticed that nothing grew under stands of deciduous trees except a sward of grass. The sheep were eating out any tree seedlings that tried to sprout. What would be left after the current stands of trees died, I wondered.

In the years since, there has been a serious change of heart, and the native woods are being restored. The Atlantic oakwoods have been identified as a

Matt Underwood
*Across the sound from Kinloch woods, Skye (detail)*
gouache · 84 x 55 cm

threatened habitat in a European context, and Forestry Commission Scotland, together with private woodland owners, is making strenuous efforts to save them. The future of the woods is now much more secure. Restoration of existing woods by natural regeneration bolstered by new plantings, although a slow process, is bringing back the woods' former ecological structure and diversity, and will make them safer and more viable in the future. Hand in hand with woodland restoration goes the conservation of the rare and endangered species that are restricted to the Atlantic oakwood ecosystem.

In 2004, Forestry Commission Scotland arranged for members of the Society of Wildlife Artists to visit the western Highlands and record their impressions of the oakwoods as part of a campaign to draw attention to the importance of the woods and the efforts to preserve them. Through the medium of the artists' work, which is shown on these pages, it is hoped that the beauty and wildlife values of the oakwood habitat will be better appreciated. The project was dubbed *Aig an Oir*.

We were particularly interested in the concept of these woods being 'at the edge' – *aig an oir* in Gaelic. The Atlantic oakwoods are at the edge in several important ways. Geographically, they are at the edge of Europe (and those of the west Highlands are on the edge of Scotland), and they are at the edge of the land, where it meets the sea. The wet but mild 'oceanic' climate generated by the Gulf Stream sweeping in from the Atlantic is the key to the woods' unique ecological value. The woodland is also at the edge because it was nearly destroyed by centuries of climate change, grazing by domestic stock, timber extraction and, more recently, the planting of conifer trees and the spread of other exotics such as rhododendron. Today the once-wide sweep of woods across the Highlands is represented

1

2

by no more than scattered scraps.

We visited three places: the Kinloch Hills on Skye, Ardnamurchan and Morvern on each side of Loch Sunart, and Knapdale and Taynish in mid-Argyll. They contain some of the largest and best-preserved areas of Atlantic oakwood and they are home for a number of rare species. All three areas are designated as Special Areas of Conservation (SAC). SACs form a network of large protected areas across the European Union called 'Natura 2000', which is designed to conserve the most important sites for habitat and species conservation across Europe.

If you have not been to the Atlantic oakwoods before, and even if you are familiar with the natural history of woods elsewhere, I urge you to take advantage of any guided tours on offer or at least acquire a colour leaflet. Otherwise you will miss some of the fascinating features they have to offer.

1. Paul Henery *Atlantic oak, Leitir Fura, Skye*
   mixed media · 96 x 116 cm

   *I spent all day painting a windswept oak on the shore below Leitir Fura. The trunk was covered in lichens, which appeared ancient, while the newly emerged oak leaves were bright and fresh. I stood next to an otter holt and looked across to Knoydart, watching the great black-backed gulls patrolling the coastline constantly.*

2. Darren Rees *Loch Sunart from Ceol na Mara*
   acrylic · 26.5 x 35.5 cm
3. Darren Rees *Rubha an Daimh, Loch Sunart*
   watercolour · 26.5 x 35.5 cm
4. Darren Rees *West along Loch Sunart*
   acrylic · 29 x 39 cm

3

4

1

4

1. Darren Rees *Resting heron*
   acrylic · 25 x 36 cm
2. John Davis *Common Seals, Faery Isles*
   watercolour · 15 x 22 cm
3. Robert Greenhalf *Sheep on the beach, Kentra Bay*
   watercolour · 28 x 38 cm
4. John Busby *Resting seals*
   watercolour · 19 x 27 cm
5. Dafila Scott *Seals hauled out, Loch Sunart*
   oil on paper · 38 x 51 cm
6. Robert Greenhalf *Herons – Rubna an Daimh*
   watercolour · 28 x 38 cm

Dafila Scott *Seals hauled out, Loch Sunart*

*The upper reaches of Loch Sunart feel quite landlocked, so it was somehow surprising to find the seals hauled out on the rocks at Garbh Eilean. They looked so comfortable! Being dry in parts and wet in parts, they caught the morning light in different ways, and it made interesting effects on their coats. Sometimes it wasn't obvious where seal ended and rock or weed began.*

Robert Greenhalf *Sheep on the beach, Kentra Bay*

*At low tide, Kentra Bay becomes a wide expanse of sand and mud, with only a shallow river meandering to the sea. There are a few small islands – little more than rocks topped by grasses and other salt-tolerant plants – and there are areas of saltings around the head of the bay. The local sheep moved with the tides, visiting the islands and saltings at low water and retreating to the higher areas with the turning tide.*

2

3

5

6

Pascale Rentsch *Sound of Mull, Sunart*
emulsion and acrylic · 20.5 x 48.5 cm

1

1. Martin Ridley *The bait digger, Taynish*
   oils · 30 x 60 cm
2. Martin Ridley *Two crows later I, Loch Sunart*
   oils · 39.5 x 48 cm
3. Martin Ridley *Two crows later II, Loch Sunart*
   oils · 39.5 x 48 cm

Martin Ridley *Two crows later*

*I wanted a title to suggest a brief passage of time, the time it takes for an autumn squall to blow through. Frequent showers funnelling down the loch is one of the ingredients that make the Sunart oakwoods so special. The vista is ever changing, often dramatically, and sorties of hooded crows seemed to mark the passing showers perfectly.*

2

3

1

2

1. Greg Poole *Across from Kinloch Woods*
acrylic on paper · 75 x 55 cm

*Across from Kinloch woods I get the long view. A small oak perched below me on a rocky outcrop, sweetshop-coloured with thrift and orange lichen circles. Great black-backed gull stands guard on an islet. Oystercatchers are only temporarily alarmed when an otter climbs ashore, lollops, poking around before seamlessly taking to water again.*

2. Greg Poole *Burn meets the shore , Kinloch Woods*
charcoal · 73 x 59 cm

*Where the burn leaves the shelter of the woods to cut across the rocky shore, I made two charcoal sketches in pouring rain. Redstart singing right at the top of the aged ash overhead, invisible.*

*The ash a worn grey bark, its upturned branches sleeved with lichens, ending in feathered, yellow spearlet clusters of new leaves. The burn has carved itself a channel with sides softened with moss, wood sorrel, creeping yellow pimpernel, ferns and water avens.*

3. Greg Poole *Tattooed oak*
acrylic on paper · 78 x 55 cm

*Oak with newly opened, translucent, yellow-ochre leaves against the light. Trunk crusted and tattooed with lichens. Looking through to sound and mountains beyond, a rent in the cloud gleams silver in the royal-blue waters.*

3

1

2

1. Carry Akroyd *Faery Isles*
aquatint · 60 x 20 cm

*I walked around the area, climbing up on to rocks and peering through branches to get a sense of the whole magical place. Very still, quiet and secret, full of birds coming and going. Fox, squirrel, deer and signs of an otter restaurant, with footprints.*

2. Carry Akroyd *A walk at Taynish*
aquatint · 60 x 20 cm

*This is the walk, on reserve footpaths, from the shore of Loch Sween up to the top of Barr Mòr (bald top). It includes many dragonflies, the old mill and waterfall, the bog, the gatehouse, and the charcoal platforms with plantation oaks, then twisty oaks and birch opening to the bracken summit.*

3. Peter Partington *Disputing territory – grey herons, Sunart*
watercolour · 49 x 37 cm

3

1

1. Paul Henery *Cuillins from Kinloch woods, Skye*
watercolour · 43 x 56 cm

*The bluebells have gone,*
*Shadows are faint,*
*Treecreepers search alone,*
*Only the dark, skeletal oaks remain.*
*Above the woods, above the loch,*
*First snows have covered the Cuillins,*
*A buzzard passes over,*
*Woodland colours are rich.*

2

3

2. Anna Kirk-Smith *After the rain, Taynish*
acrylic on canvas · 61 x 152 cm

*The cold winter light filtering through an old oak overgrown with ivy and lichens.*

3. Anna Kirk-Smith *Fleeting light, Taynish*
acrylic · 27 x 96 cm

*A brief break in the clouds allowed the waters of Linne Mhuirich to silver through winter trees. The light and hues change fast: glassy and clear here, grey and rain-soaked within minutes.*

1

1. Carry Akroyd *Knapdale skyline*
   watercolour · 48 x 76 cm

   *This is a condensed impression of the northern escarpment, showing the characteristic knaps and dales. It is from an imagined viewpoint, and the information for it was gathered from Crinan Ferry, the road to Islandadd Bridge, and along the canal from the swing-bridge. The painting shows areas where plantation spruce has been cleared, and the vestigial border oaks and pioneer birch are encroaching on the bare slopes.*

2. Carry Akroyd *By Crinan*
   watercolour · 60 x 60 cm

   *I made a number of sketches from Crinan woods, hanging on to my drawing book through wind and rain. Looking down, the road and canal squeeze between the estuary and the abrupt rise of Knapdale. Cleared hillsides contrast with plantations, and the oak and birch persist in inaccessible corners, ready to come back. Ravens honk and float about.*

2

Peter McDermott *Ancient oak – dappled light, Kinloch*
watercolour · 26.5 x 65 cm

*Like some aged grandfather surrounded by younger members of the family, this old retainer silently bears testimony to new generations of seed and sapling.*

2

# Looking around the woods

The narrow roads that wind through the western Highlands are often uncomfortably wedged between sea and hillside. The water on one side holds the attention of passengers in the cars and buses that pick their way around the bends. There are boats, seabirds, seals and perhaps even dolphins to exclaim at; and the trees pass in a blur. Even with footpaths and signs as guides, I suspect few visitors, or even residents, will find the time to go beyond the special observation points and take a walk through the woods. Even those that do may not realise that they are in a treasure house of natural wonders, laced with relics that point to human occupation through distant centuries.

I am lucky because I have been shown around some of the best examples of the Atlantic oakwoods by people who know them well. I have seen things that I would never have noticed or appreciated if I had been on my own. My guides interpreted the broad canvas – the ecology of the woods and the history of management that has determined how the woods look as they do – and the fine detail – the presence of a moss or an insect. Armed with these introductions to the woods, I went out to observe for myself. So I wandered among the trees, taking pleasure in simply being there and looking for anything of interest. I would pause to watch and record, and then try to explain to myself what I was seeing. Sometimes I accompanied the artists, and I found that our ways of working were not dissimilar.

John Busby *A maze of oak branches, Salen woods, Sunart*
conté drawing and watercolour
38 x 27.5 cm

*I was intrigued by the way the oak branches twisted back on each other and formed an intricate pattern against the hillside and loch. First leaves showing as delicate warm yellows.*

My first visit was to Ariundle, a National Nature Reserve in Strontian Glen, and my guide was Eilidh-Ann Madden, the local ranger, born locally and delighted to have found such a job near home. Ariundle comes from the Gaelic *Àirigh Fhionndail*, meaning 'shieling of the white meadow'. A shieling was a hill pasture. The Norse name for Strontian Glen is more appropriate: Egadale – oak valley.

The outstanding impression on entering Ariundle, and other Atlantic oakwoods, is a feeling of space among tall trees set in a sea of mosses. The mosses blanket the woodland floor, smother boulders, climb the tree trunks and spread out to festoon the branches in many shades of green. The outlines of the woodland floor are softened and rounded by the thick layer of moss. Large boulders make comfortable seats with 15-cm cushions of soft, springy greenery. Ancient stone walls look like closely trimmed hedges.

The lush growth of mosses is one of the signs of the environmental basis of the Atlantic oakwoods. There is an unusually high degree of 'oceanicity' – a combination of high humidity, frequent rain, cloud cover and mild climate, which comes from the proximity of the Gulf Stream. Only the west coast of Ireland has a greater oceanicity than this part of western Scotland. Once you are aware of the mosses, you will be struck by the exuberance of their growth wherever you look. The moss carpet absorbs huge amounts of rainwater, which evaporates slowly during dry spells, maintaining the level of humidity and the growth of other lower plants – the liverworts and ferns, and the many-hued lichens. The mosses are at their best in darker parts of the woods, on northern slopes and under a dense canopy. In lighter situations, on sunny slopes and along the edges of the woods, there are patchworks of tree lungwort and other lichens, which are one of

SMEÒRACH CHLANN RAGHNUILL

*Eòin bhuchullach, bhreac na coille,*
*Le 'n òrganan òrdail mar-ruinn,*
*'S feadag ghlan am beul gach coilich*
*'S bìnn feadail air geugan barraich.*
*'S mise 'n t-eanan beag le m' f'headan,*
*Am madainn-dhriùchd am bàrr gach badain,*
*Sheinneadh na puirt ghrinn gun sgreadan –*
*'S ionmhuinn m' fheadan feadh gach lagain.*

THE MAVIS OF CLANRANALD

*The spotted woodland birds their lay*
*With their well tuned organs play;*
*The cock's loud clarion, shrill and clear,*
*On high-tapped boughs is sweet to hear.*
*A little bird with my reed I rove,*
*Each dewy morn from grove to grove;*
*I sing not harshly my sweet song,*
*Strains that to lowly dells belong.*

BY ALEXANDER MACDONALD

the glories of these woods. Eilidh-Ann also showed me the fern called polypody, which grows along the branches of the trees. It relies on continual dampness, and she told me that a frazzling of its fronds is an indicator of a dry summer.

## THE OAKWOODS

Some woods, although classified as 'Atlantic oakwood' habitat, have precious few, if any, oak trees. Oaks may be replaced by birches, both downy birch and silver birch, which are pioneering species that quickly colonise open ground where the trees have been cleared. Where the soil is alkaline, often in damp hollows, ash and wych elm form the canopy, and there may be a ground layer with dog's mercury, enchanter's nightshade and ramsons – the strong-smelling wild garlic. Alder and goat willow also like wet places, and they spring from mats of *Sphagnum* bogmosses in places where it is too soggy to walk. Here, too, are yellow flag iris, meadowsweet and angelica. There may be some exotic trees planted among the natives, but no one knows if the Scots pines in Ariundle are naturally occurring or planted.

The oaks in these woods are mostly sessile oaks

1

*Quercus petraea*, which are more characteristic of the thin, acid soils of highland Britain, but there may be pedunculate oaks *Quercus robur*, which are the dominant oaks in the richer soils of lowland Britain. The sessile oak is so named because its flowers and acorns do not have stalks like the pedunculate oak. The leaves are the other way round and the sessile oak is the one with stalked leaves. Just to confuse matters the two species hybridise, so identification can be a matter for the expert.

The ecosystem of an oakwood, at its simplest, consists of three layers. The main storey consists of large trees of oak and birch, and sometimes elm and ash, which provide a canopy of branches and leaves. The understorey consists of smaller trees, especially hazel but also holly, rowan, gean, juniper and hawthorn. The ground layer is made up of grasses, bracken and other ferns, blaeberry and heather, mosses and many kinds of flowers. But this simple scheme is infinitely variable. The details of the composition of species and the height of the layers vary according to soil, exposure and wetness. Shade is important for the lower layers. A dense canopy shuts out the light, stifling the ground layer and preventing the growth of a new generation of trees. When an old tree falls, light is let in and seedlings sprout from dormant seeds around it.

1. Nik Pollard *Path through Barnluasgan III*
acrylic on board · 30 x 122 cm

2. Matt Underwood
*Linear study*
conté · 58 x 41 cm

*I passed this oak tree every day and admired the lichen all over the trunk, up into the lower branches; its tattooed appearance made it visible within the wood from the shore.*

2

1

2

1. Dafila Scott *Oak trunk with epiphytes*
oil on paper · 38 x 25.5 cm

*This was a particularly spectacular oak, with strongly orange and reddish lichens growing on it, as well as lots of moss, liverworts and ferns, going way up in to the canopy.*

2. Dafila Scott *Oakwood and bluebells*
oil on paper · 25.5 x 38 cm

*Going into the woods at Ariundle was like going into a magical ancient woodland, even though most of the trees are not that old. For me the most striking thing was the moss everywhere – on the ground, on the boulders and up the trees. It reminded me of all sorts of stories from childhood and gave me a feeling of being enclosed, at first comfortably so but later rather less comfortably so.*

1

1. Carry Akroyd *A gannet glimpsed through oaks and ferns*
   pencil sketch · 29 x 21 cm
2. Carry Akroyd *Rain passing Barnluasgan ridge*
   watercolour · 40 x 57 cm
3. Carry Akroyd *From Barnluasgan to the Paps*
   watercolour · 40 x 57 cm

2

3

1

2

1. John Cox *Mossy hummocks and bluebells*
pastel, crayon and watercolour · 59 x 41 cm
2. John Cox *A well-lichened oak*
watercolour and gouache · 40 x 30 cm
3. John Cox *Raven family over Leitir Fura*
watercolour · 41 x 28 cm

*Even when we were first shown round the ruins of Leiter Fura in the pouring rain, the place was fascinating. When I went back, the rugged, bleak and desolate atmosphere had gone. The sun was blazing down. A couple of adders were sunning themselves on the broken-down rocky walls, and a family of ravens played around in the air as I painted; but it was the ruins themselves and their history that really interested me.*

Following spread

4. Nik Pollard *Path through Barnluasgan I*
acrylic on board · 30 x 122 cm
5. Nik Pollard *Path through Barnluasgan II*
acrylic on board · 30 x 122 cm

3

4

5

1

1. David Guy Measures *Oaks amidst the boulders with great mossy boles*
watercolour · 38 x 28.5 cm

2. David Guy Measures *An isolated oak on the shore of Loch Sunart*
watercolour · 28.5 x 22 cm

*Because of morning rain, I set up to paint from the back window of the caravan, whereupon the rain ceased and the sun appeared.*

2

1

2

3

## SPRING FLOWERS

Spring is the best time to visit these woods, just before the foliage of the trees unfurls into the pale green tracery overhead and the midges put in an appearance. The flowers are at their brightest and the bracken has yet to spread its fronds and smother the woodland floor. Some of the flowers can be found in any deciduous wood, as their names suggest: wood sorrel and wood anemone. I saw blue bugle and violet, yellow celandine, cow-wheat and yellow pimpernel, and many more. When I visited Ariundle in late May, it was primrose time; on later visits, there were eye-catching swards of bluebells, and a careful search revealed common spotted and other orchids. At Knapdale there is rare narrow-leaved helleborine. This orchid is found on calcareous soils, in open woods where it gets plenty of sunlight. The decline of woodland management and the replacement of the old woods by dense conifers have led to shading, which has driven the helleborine out of many of its old haunts (although recent restoration work and removal of conifers are allowing it to spread again).

On sunny days, the interest of woodland flowers is doubled by the butterflies, bees and other insects visiting them for nectar to sip and places to lay their eggs. Violets attract pearl-bordered, small pearl-bordered and dark green fritillaries; lady's smock is the food plant of orange tips; and the various grasses that make up much of the ground layer are important for speckled woods and chequered skippers. The chequered skipper is a speciality of these woods. It has been in decline for half a century and is now extinct in England. Its British stronghold is about fifty sites in the western woods of Scotland. It needs damp glades with good growths of purple moor grass, its favourite caterpillar food plant, and bugle, marsh thistle and bluebells to provide nectar for the adults. Long swathes of suitable habitat are created by the clearings under power lines, which makes it easy to find good places to search for this butterfly!

4

1. Alastair Proud *Conifer stump and bugle*
   watercolour · 30.5 x 39.5 cm
2. Alastair Proud *Basil thyme growing amongst grasses and brambles*
   watercolour · 18 x 24 cm
3. Alastair Proud *Wood sorrel, Kinloch woods*
   watercolour · 18 x 24 cm
4. Jane Leycester Paige *Narrow-leaved helleborine,* Cephalanthera longifolia
   watercolour · 31 x 24 cm

1

2

3

1,2 Jane Leycester Paige *Marsh cinquefoil,* Potentilla palustris, *and heath spotted orchid,* Dactylorhiza maculata
watercolour studies · 31 x 24 cm

*Both of these flowers are found around Loch Barnluasgan. The heath spotted orchid is easily recognised, when compared with the common spotted orchid, by the wide, frilly labellum and small 'tooth', giving the flower a 'crinoline lady' look.*

3. Keith Brockie *Grass of Parnassus*
watercolour · 19 x 9 cm

4. Darren Woodhead *Butterfly studies I*
watercolour · 28 x 38 cm

5. Darren Woodhead *Butterfly studies II*
watercolour · 28 x 38 cm

*After a brief warm spell days before we arrived, chequered skipper and speckled wood butterflies were out in their droves. Often feeding on bugle and bluebells, the skippers were always defensive of their territories, darting off at the sight of other passing insects.*

4

5

1. Richard Tratt *Chequered skipper butterfly*
oil sketch · 15 x 20.5 cm
2. Richard Tratt *Small pearl-bordered fritillary*
watercolour · 15 x 20 cm
3. John Cox *Green hairstreak*
watercolour · 12 x 10 cm
4. Richard Tratt *Chequered skippers*
oil on board · 25.5 x 25.5 cm

1

2

3

4

When the leaves are still not fully spread, it is easy to spot small birds flitting and perching in the canopy as they sing. A few weeks later, they will be disembodied voices and shadowy figures flitting among the leaves, so focusing binoculars to match the bird with the song will not be easy. Yet birdwatching visits should not be too early in the year because some of the best birds associated with oakwoods are migrants and reach the Highlands about a month after they appear in the south of England. They, like the resident species, subsist on the insects living on tree leaves, and successful nesting for some birds depends on the abundance of caterpillars. By July, nesting and song are over, but even in winter a wood may suddenly become alive with a band of birds passing by through the trees. Mostly they are tits, often with goldcrests and treecreepers, and occasionally great spotted woodpeckers, foraging together.

The most abundant birds are chaffinches, robins and blue tits, but the woods can be surprisingly devoid of birds where there are stands of single-age oak and little understorey. This habitat lacks variety and may not contain the succession of abundant food supplies needed for rearing broods of baby birds. There may also be a shortage of nesting places. Young trees do not have the holes required by tits and redstarts, while blackbirds and robins do not like open woods without an understorey.

The melancholy song of the willow warbler is, for me, the most distinctive sound of these woods. At times their incessant complaining songs seem to be everywhere. The visually almost identical, but vocally very distinct, chiffchaff is nothing like as common as it is in the south; but the bird that got the most attention from the artists, as well as me, was the wood warbler. We liked it because it sang from low perches, where it was easy to watch and paint. We could sit comfortably in one place while the bird performed in a circuit around us, singing from one perch, then a few minutes later flying, still singing, to another perch and so on. A poet has described the song as 'little waves of pearls dropped and scattered and shivered on a shore of pearls'. More prosaically, the song starts with a stuttering *tip-tip-tip*, which accelerates into a trill, but confusingly the trills are mixed with bursts of plaintive notes, so it sounds as if there are two birds singing.

1

Three other songbirds are typical of western oakwoods, and two of these are frequently met in the Highlands. I watched a pair of tree pipits carrying food for their young, but I must have been too near the nest because they flew from perch to perch, refusing to deliver to the waiting nestlings, so I moved on. The redstart nests in holes in trunks and stumps, and has eye-catching plumage. The name is Old English for 'red tail' and the Gaelic is, contrarily and oddly, *cean-dearg* – 'red head'! We did not find any of the third species, the pied flycatcher. It is common in the west of England and Wales but something of a rarity in western Scottish woods. Nestboxes have been put up in several woods to encourage it, with some success.

Elusive woodland birds to look for include treecreepers swarming jerkily up tree trunks and spotted flycatchers darting out from perches to snap up insects (but watch out for chaffinches, which also do this), but the woodcock is the prize. You may catch sight of it flying away silently through the trees when it is disturbed, but it draws attention to itself in the long summer evenings by flying up and down woodland edges, uttering a very distinctive croaking. This is its territorial display, called 'roding'.

2

3

1. Robert Greenhalf *Redstart and wood warbler*
four-colour woodcut · 16 x 39 cm

*The oakwoods along the north shore of Loch Sunart were alive with the 'ticking and trilling' of wood warblers. Hyperactive and sticking to the canopy, where the yellows and greens of their plumage echoed those of the oak leaves, they were initially difficult to locate. By climbing the steep, boulder-and-moss-strewn hillside, I found that I could often get level with, or even above, the birds in the trees at the foot of the hill. From this vantage point I looked down through a mosaic of lemons and greens, light and shade, often with a glimpse of dark blue sea beyond. Redstarts were much less numerous and surprisingly elusive, allowing only a few tantalising glimpses.*

2. Barry W. Van Dusen *Chaffinch studies, Loch Sunart*
watercolour · 30 x 39.5 cm

3. Michael Warren *Woodcock*
watercolour · 40 x 40 cm

Darren Woodhead *Singing male redstart, Sunart, 31 May.*
watercolour · 38 x 58 cm

*Males were elusive in these woodlands, singing from perches high in the crown of tall oaks.*

warren 05

2

3

1. Michael Warren *Coal tit, goldcrests and waxwings*
   graphite and watercolour · 52.5 x 35 cm

   *The woods were very quiet. Then a group of birds appeared, a coal tit with a small party of goldcrests. As I sat painting and sketching, I heard waxwings. A party of about thirty flew low overhead. There was a large irruption of this species into Scotland in autumn.*

2. Michael Warren *Bullfinches*
   graphite and watercolour · 35 x 47.5 cm

3. Andrea Rich *Bearded*
   woodcut on Hosho paper · 40 x 51 cm

   *I have named this print after the tree. I believe it was an old birch, almost completely covered in moss and lichen. I was in Knapdale and hiking on the Faery Isles on an overcast and drizzling morning. The sky would clear and the sun would shine through from time to time. When the light reached this beauty, its bark shone violet and the moss glistened. I remember thinking that the isles could have been named for this tree alone. It looked enchanted. It was late in the year and I hadn't seen many birds, but these robins were curious and obliging and made fine ornaments in the branches.*

1

2

1. Paul Henery *Sunlit treecreeper*
watercolour · 27 x 33 cm

*As the treecreepers search the trunks and branches, broken sunlight casts oak leaf shadows, against a backdrop of bluebells.*

2. Paul Henery *Treecreeper sketches*
watercolour · 29 x 21 cm

3. William Neill *Coal tit*
watercolour · 41.5 x 51 cm

*Some of these old oaks have suffered impressive damage during their lives, huge branches broken off, no doubt in winter gales. These are sometimes still bedded in the tree, but more often, as in this case, the branch lies below and becomes the source of new life. Despite the damage there is always evidence of the ability to resurrect and grow again from the ruin. On a warm summer's day, this seemed almost as prolific as any tropical rainforest.*

4. William Neill *Great spotted woodpecker*
watercolour · 35.5 x 41 cm

*When I found this nest there was much activity, with the adults coming and going regularly. Both birds were happy once I had settled down some distance away with my telescope, and their hard work was non-stop. It was extraordinary just how much food they could find and how quickly they could find it. This was not so surprising when I returned the next day and found that the birds had flown. Fledged chicks must be quite demanding!*

3

4

5

6

5. Darren Woodhead *Singing wood warbler*
watercolour · 28 x 38 cm

*Lemon-yellow oakwoods hold a variety of singing birds and none more vocal than trilling wood warblers. This male held a territory in a shallow bowl on the lee side of a hill. He sang continuously until midday, with a short break before his afternoon activities began, performing song flights and vociferously proclaiming his territory.*

6. Dafila Scott *Wood warbler, Ariundle*
oil on paper · 25.5 x 20.5 cm

*During an afternoon and a morning at Ariundle in mid-May, it was impossible to walk in the woodland without seeing and hearing wood warblers. From underneath, the yellow throat was well set off by the early leaves of the oaks.*

RAVINES

The hillsides above the oakwoods are drained by burns that, over the millennia, have cut their way into the underlying rock. The channels where they now flow are damp, dark reservoirs of humidity, where the vegetation has escaped the ravages of grazing animals and is lush even by the standards of the west coast. Where a footpath crosses a ravine by a bridge, stop to look up and down, or, even better, find a larger stream which has cut a wide gorge and walk up between the vertical faces. You enter a place that is the nearest thing in these woods to the rainforest of popular imagination.

At Resipole, I picked my way up an amazing ravine that is famous for its epiphytic growths. The ravine is deep, steep-sided and, entering it, you are cut off from the outside. It is a 'lost world', very different from the airy woods and pastures beyond the rim. Stepping gingerly over boulders and skirting still pools linked by shallow riffles and cascades, my route was sometimes barred by eroded, bare skeletons of trees that had toppled into the ravine long ago. Their gnarled successors still hung over the rim on each side, intermingled with smaller hazels and hollies. On the flat bottom of the ravine, green islands are dotted with primroses and violets, water avens and yellow pimpernel, and arrays of freshly unfurled ferns.

The biggest interest was the rock faces on each side of the ravine. There are swards of thick moss growing on the walls, wringing wet with water dripping off the tips. Liverworts cover the flat rock faces, with tiny ferns, wood rush and a few flowers nestling in cracks. Tangled ropes of honeysuckle hang down like lianas, heightening the rainforest effect. Sometimes I thought I had spotted a plant I had not seen before, only to find it was only a large, ebullient version of something common growing in a particularly favourable niche of dampness, light or fertility. In this ravine, there is one lichen, *Parmentaria chilensis*, that is found nowhere else on the mainland of Britain but is widely distributed in Central and South America. I would have liked to find it because a photograph shows that it lives up to the description of 'blackberries floating in custard'.

1

2

3

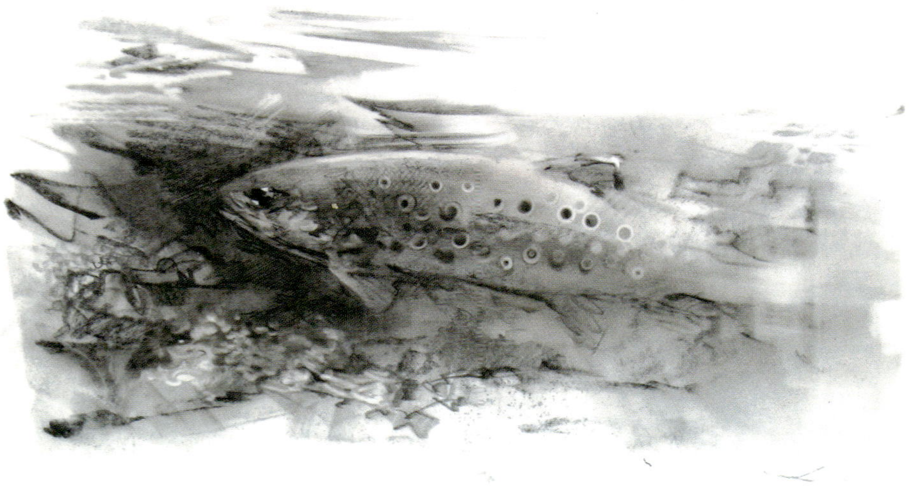

1. Peter Partington *The Glen Pool, Sunart*
   watercolour · 31.5 x 49 cm
2. Carl Ellis *Barnluasgan stream (field study)*
   pastel on paper · 20 x 29.5 cm

   *Every bend in the stream is dressed with autumn leaves fashioned by nature... Even the trout are in this season's colours!*
3. Carl Ellis *Trout*
   pencil on film · 14 x 20 cm
4. Bruce Pearson *Oakwood gorge, behind Resipole Studios, Sunart*
   mixed media · 82 x 48 cm

4

## WOOD ANTS

Where there is plenty of sunlight, the woods swarm with wood ants. You sit down and become aware that there are ants all around you. They are running along the ground, climbing over boulders, and swarming up trees. At about 1 cm long, they are obvious once you notice them, especially when they are streaming along a trail leading to the nest. There is a two-way traffic of ants passing and repassing, heading out empty-handed and returning with prey and building materials.

Look for a gang of ants dragging a beetle, caterpillar or even a wasp to the nest. They are rather uncoordinated but each ant has an idea of which way to head and the victim moves slowly in the right direction. Some ants appear to be returning empty-handed but they probably have a stomach full of honeydew. They will have visited aphids in the tree canopy to collect the sugar-rich honeydew that the aphids secrete when concentrating and digesting the sap on which they feed.

On one hand, wood ants prey on the caterpillars of pine looper moths and other insect pests; on the other hand they protect and encourage aphids, which also cause significant damage to trees. However, it is not known whether wood ants have a significant impact on the populations of any of these pests, but they are an important link in the forest ecosystem. In their turn, they are food for squirrels, woodpeckers and other birds. They also help to disperse the seeds of common cow-wheat, violet and wood anemone.

1

The nest is a mound of pine needles, twigs and other bits of plant debris and, on a warm day, is a seething mass of ants. Although apparently just a 'heap', the nest has a structure. The surface is carefully tended to make a rainproof thatch and inside there are galleries where the queens (note the plural; there are several in a nest) lay their eggs and the workers tend the larvae and pupae. The interior temperature is carefully controlled by opening and closing the entrance holes. In spring, the ants behave as a living 'solar heater'. Masses of workers come out to sunbathe, and then they go back inside, where their body heat warms the galleries.

The species most likely to be found in the oakwoods is the Scottish wood ant *Formica aquilonia*, one of six British species. It is classed as 'nationally scarce' and its numbers have declined sufficiently for it to be the subject of a UK Biodiversity Action Plan (as have the other species of wood ant). It needs undisturbed, open woodland where there is plenty of sun to warm the nest, so glades and clearings are good places to find nests. Forestry practices have driven out wood ants – dense commercial forests are too shaded, and clear felling ruins their habitat – but wood ants are safe in the old oakwoods. They could be called nature's woodland managers, and Forestry Commission Scotland has issued guidelines for their protection. For instance, clumps of trees are left around nests during felling operations.

INSECT-EATING PLANTS

Scatterings of pretty violet-blue flowers are a common sight in glades and along the edges of tracks where the ground is wet. They could be mistaken for real violets but for the rosette of pale green, glistening leaves pressed to the ground like a many-armed starfish. They are butterwort, an insectivorous plant which flourishes in poor, acidic soil. Look closely at the leaves and you may see tiny insects stuck to the surface. Through a magnifying glass, the glistening is resolved into tiny droplets of a sticky substance. They trap small flies, ants or sometimes even a butterfly, while special glands pour out a digestive juice that pools around the insect. The proteins in its body are digested and absorbed into the plant's tissues.

Much less conspicuous, but sometimes given away by a head of tiny white flowers, is sundew, another insectivore. Its rosette of round, reddish leaves nestles among cushions of *Sphagnum* bogmosses. Each leaf is covered with a pile of sticky-tipped hairs that act as an active flypaper. As the insect attempts to pull clear of one hair, nearby hairs bend over and stick to it until its struggles are subdued. Over the next few hours the leaf curls over the insect like a grasping hand and digestion starts.

Neither butterwort nor sundew needs insects to survive but they produce more flowers and set more seed if they can catch some insects to provide nutrients that are in short supply in poor soils.

3

2

1. Brin Edwards *Wood ant nest at Mudalach*
   watercolour and gouache · 29 x 22 cm
2. John Cox *Sundew*
   watercolour · 8 x 8 cm
3. Brin Edwards *Butterworts*
   watercolour · 30 x 20 cm

   *These small insectivorous plants grow along the wet tracks and banks at Kinloch woods. They give the impression of scattered stars against the mud and stones.*

1

2

3

1. Greg Poole *Insectivorous carpet*
acrylic on paper · 75 x 55 cm

*I lay out on my mac to get a close look at the plant life in one of the damp patches below the lichen-bearded hazels. Through the magnifying glass I gradually enter another world. A red ant makes its way through a forest of moss, avoiding the sticky dewdrop tentacles of the sundew. Purple butterwort flowers rise out of a whorl of their insect-trapping leaves. Dark-spotted leaves of marsh orchid and glaucous spikes of young iris. Tormentil creeps and hugs the mossy hummocks.*

2. Jane Smith *First signs of spring (toad)*
monotype · 40 x 19 cm

*I first sat down to draw the bog trees, with their glowing mossy coats, and after sitting still for a while, the wood resumed its life around me. I suddenly realised that a chiffchaff had been singing for a while – spring had started without me noticing. There were channels through the new, crazy-green waterweed, where an otter had been hunting. I caught a movement from the corner of my eye and realised what the otters had been after – the toads had started to emerge.*

3. Jane Smith *High summer (dragonflies)*
monotype · 72 x 28 cm

*I'd never tried to identify dragons and damsels before this summer, but once I'd started, it became an obsession. Looking at them closely, it's hard to imagine how something so delicate can withstand the stresses of such vigorous flight. That a larva can crawl out of the bottom of a ditch and transform itself into a highly engineered flying machine, more manoeuvrable than a helicopter and more beautiful than a jewel, is breathtaking.*

Bruce Pearson *Oakwoods, June 1st, Ardnamurchan*
monotype · 64 x 92 cm

1

1. David Guy Measures *A glade in Ariundle Forest*
   watercolour · 20 x 28 cm
2. David Guy Measures *Oaks standing deep in moss*
   watercolour · 28 x 23 cm

2

1

1. Carl Ellis *Autumn alders (field study), River Add, Knapdale*
pastel on paper · 28.5 x 18 cm

*It was a chill morning – I had already been soaked up to the knees in a muddy ditch and carelessly tripped over barbed wire. As I stumbled across a shallow, pebbled stretch of the river, the thought of cleaning some of the mud off my hands seemed like a good idea. As I sat back down to drink some coffee, this unremarkable scene suddenly burst into life as the sun's first rays illuminated the river bed. Before my eyes the pebbles and stone seemed to be heated up, like molten rock!*

2. Andrew Stock *Looking south across Caol Scotnish*
oil on board · 91 x 60 cm

*A still, dank morning in November. Rain was threatening and I worked quickly on a watercolour sketch. There was no movement until the lone herring gull purposefully crossed my view. I painted this picture back in my studio in Dorset.*

2

# 3 Living in the woods

The castles that dot the Highland landscape are part of the cultural heritage of Scotland but the woods once played as vital a role in the lives of the Highland people. Castles were the setting for the deeds of the great and powerful, as recounted in story and song; the woods were the setting of the untold, unsung, everyday lives of the common people. Both castles and woods are testaments to a vanished way of life.

Walking through these woods is like visiting one of Scotland's archaeological or historical treasures: Skara Brae or Melrose Abbey perhaps. Their ruins open a window on the past and help the imagination conjure up the continuity of past generations who lived and died there. But even with a ruin, you need a guide or guidebook to get the full meaning of what you are looking at. This is even more true of the historical significance of an oakwood, which would go unnoticed unless you are already aware that even a wood can be shaped by history.

The woods that fringe the west coast of Scotland are the remnants of a vast forest – the Wildwood or Greenwood – that once covered much of Britain. The appearance of this forest is not known but it was not a continuous mass of trees, dark under a dense canopy, as was once believed. It was more likely to have been a mosaic of open woodlands and areas of heath, moor and meadow. The open nature was maintained by large herbivorous mammals. As well as today's red and roe deer, there would have been elk, wild boar and beaver, which no longer live in Britain, and extinct tarpan (wild horse) and aurochs (wild cattle).

The composition of the woodland was dynamic, and the dominant types of trees changed as the climate got wetter or drier, colder or milder. It also depended on the soils and exposure. In the Mesolithic period, about 6,000 years ago, western Britain was, it is believed, largely an oakwood habitat, but much of the western Highlands north of Loch Linnhe was still birch and hazel. Even when the forest was at its greatest extent, about 5,000 years ago, perhaps only 85 per cent of the Highlands was covered with trees. Thereafter, the forest began to retreat. This was partly due to climate change; cool, damp summers and mild winters favoured peat bogs over woodlands.

Woods have existed on the sites of present-day woods since trees invaded the land after the last Ice Age, but no natural woodland survives and there has been none for centuries. People came spreading up from the south, hard on the heels of the trees, and their activities, barely perceptible at first, modified the structure of the woods where they dwelled. There is no truly natural woodland left in the British Isles, and ecologists refer to 'semi-natural woods', which are those that have existed, unbroken but modified by Man, since primeval times. They could be called 'cultural woods' to emphasise the importance of human influence.

Change started with the arrival of the superior Neolithic (New Stone Age) people, who brought agriculture as they spread across Europe from the Near East. A greater scale of change came with people wielding bronze implements. With the grazing of their flocks and herds and by clearing spaces for agriculture, Bronze Age people began to make a significant impact on the woods. Then,

John Davis *Roe deer in Arichonan (detail)*
watercolour · 35 x 51 cm

O CHOILLE GU BEARRADH

*Coille na greine*
*'s i éibhneach is mireagach:*
*a' choille ioma-ghaothach,*
*an leug fhaodail dhrithleannach;*
*coille na sgàile*
*'s i tàmhach neo-dhribheagach:*
*coille a' chrònain*
*'s oranach luinneagach.*

*Os cionn no coille beithe 's calltuinn,*
*Caoruinn agus feàrna,*
*'S os cionn nam bruthaichean uaine*
*Far a bheil an fhraineach òg*
*'S am fiar òg 'nam brat-làir.*

WOODS OF RAASAY

*The sunlit wood*
*joyful and sportive,*
*the many-winded wood,*
*the glittering-jewel found by chance;*
*the shady wood,*
*peaceful and unflurried,*
*the humming wood*
*of songs and ditties.*

*Above the wood of birch and hazel,*
*rowan and alder,*
*and above the green braes*
*where the young bracken*
*and the young grass are a carpet.*

BY SORLEY MACLEAN

around 600 BC, the Celts arrived in Britain, bringing skills in working iron and ploughing heavy soil. The timing of these events, especially in the Highlands, is vague, but they left enduring evidence of their activities in the west Highlands in the form of small stone forts or duns, many of which are marked on Ordnance Survey maps. People now began restructuring the woods. As the numbers of people and their domestic animals rose, the forest and the wild mammals went into retreat.

We know tantalisingly little of the lives of the early inhabitants of these woods, the significance of trees in their imagination and beliefs, or the practical uses they made of them. Much of our knowledge of the past history of the oakwoods is a matter of conjecture. We can only infer that the inhabitants of the west coast who were descended from Irish Celts and Scandinavian Vikings would have had an attitude towards the woods similar to that of their ancestors. The Celts had an affinity for trees, which was, and still is, expressed in their poetry. A hint of the importance of trees is given by Martin Martin, who wrote one of the first accounts of western Scotland in the late 17th century. He described a small wood in the north of Skye which 'none of the natives dare venture to cut the least branch of it, for fear of some signal judgement to follow upon it'. This suggests a reverence for trees that echoes the importance of sacred groves in early Celtic society.

There is no better place to get a feel of the conti-

John Davis *Arichonan village*
acrylics · 46 x 66 cm

*A bright day in a beautiful place. Perhaps a feeling of guilt at enjoying painting 'pretty pictures' in a spot that has seen its tenants evicted, but while they lived here it must have been a special site to them.*

nuity of human occupation of the oakwoods than Leitir Fura, an abandoned settlement in the Kinloch Hills of Skye. (It is also easy to reach along a path from a car park.) Even the name is evocative of the past. It is believed to be derived from *Fura Mhór* – a great oak tree which had shade for forty to fifty cattle on a hot summer's day – whose fate is an indication of the importance of trees in local life. There is a tradition that the family of Iain mac Mhaol-Chaluim (Malcolm) was evicted after his children lit a fire near the tree and burned it down. The settlement was abandoned in about 1790, when the inhabitants were removed during the infamous Clearances, but its occupation predates history. In 1996, a cave was found at the foot of the low cliff just behind the shore below Leitir Fura. Remains of domestic utensils on the floor showed that it had been occupied as a dwelling in the first half of the 19th century, but excavation revealed a history of near-continuous occupation from the 2nd century BC to the 6th century AD. Throughout this long span of time, the trees of Leitir Fura would have been a resource that was essential for the survival of the inhabitants. Then, through the 18th and 19th centuries, the Macdonalds of Sleat attempted to exploit the woods commercially to prop up shaky finances.

There is very little information about the relationship between trees and people in the Highlands before the 18th century. Indeed, even then the Highlands were Terra Incognita to the Lowland Scots. As Dr Johnson wrote of his travels through the Highlands in 1773, 'To the southern inhabitants of Scotland, the state of the mountains (Highlands) and the islands is equally unknown with that of Borneo or Sumatra. Of both they have only heard a little, and guess the rest.' Guesswork is now being supported by firmer evidence from archaeology and by what we know of life in similar situations elsewhere, but conjecture still colours ideas of how this tree-orientated culture operated.

A picture emerges of small, tight-knit communities living close to nature at little more than subsistence level. People were part of the ecosystem and their survival depended on the integrity of the ecosystem, just as is the case with any animal. Marion Campbell of Kilberry wrote, 'In the Gaeltacht (Gaelic-speaking region) the land owns the people, not the other way round.'

The importance of woods in the economy of these people is difficult to imagine as we walk around empty woods where the sound of a single chainsaw is an intrusion. The Highlands had a far higher population than now. (In the Sleat Peninsula of Skye, the population in 1841 was 2,706; in 1971 it was only 452, although the downward trend has since been reversed.) At times the woods would have been as busy as a high street, with scores of local people, old and young, at work. To get an idea of life in a tree-based culture, read Thomas Hardy's book *The Woodlanders*, set in Wessex at the other end of Britain. In these days of metal and plastic, when even expensive possessions are quickly discarded, it is not easy to appreciate how people lived when almost their only source of raw materials was what grew around them. If they wanted a length of rope, they made it out of birch twigs or heather. Anything that could not be simply made from whatever materials could be found nearby was virtually an heirloom, but of practical rather than sentimental value.

There are so few written records about the use of woodland in the western Highlands before the 17th and 18th centuries that the subject is full of conjecture and controversy. No doubt there was no universal legal or customary regulation, but the few records that do exist show that woods belonged to landowners and that there was no 'right of common' to give the local population access to woods, as there was in England. There were laws to protect woods from exploitation and destruction, or to restrict and manage their use. However, in practice, the niceties of law would not always have penetrated the Highlands, and supervision in these remote places would have been weak. There would have been unwritten arrangements with landowners for tenants to have privileges of wood use, and we can imagine there would have been local customs governing the privileges, much as the custom of souming governed the allocation of communal grazing. Parts of the woods were set aside for local use; landowners would reserve valuable oaks for themselves, while their tenants could use 'black wood' or 'barren timber', such as birch, alder and hazel, for their own purposes.

Yet, even without the final breaking of the clans at Culloden and its aftermath, daily life had been changing. The growing human population and a change towards a market economy were putting pressure on the woods. Although predominantly a subsistence economy, the Highlands had an income from traditional 'black' cattle. Herds were despatched annually to southern markets along a network of drove roads. In the mid-18th century William Pennant recorded that 3,000 head of cattle were sent annually from Lochaber alone. It is still possible to walk along the drove road from Kinloch to Kylerhea, where cattle had to swim the 500 metres of sea across the Kyle of Lochalsh to the mainland opposite. They were driven to markets as far away as southern England, where John Clare, the Northamptonshire poet, was struck by the outlandish appearance of:

*Men so oddly clad*
*In petticoats of banded plaid*

The accounts of the Macdonald estates in Sleat on Skye date from 1720. At this point, and presumably for many years earlier, the management of the woods was controlled by the laird and managed by his tacksmen and paid woodkeepers. No doubt practices varied from estate to estate, depending on the relationship between laird and tenants. Permission was needed to fell timber and take wood, and there are records of prosecutions for taking timber and removing bark for tanning. One man was evicted for taking timber to repair his house without permission and two women were prosecuted for collecting sticks.

Yet there are also records that show that parts of the wood were set aside for 'common country uses', as Dr Johnson put it. There still needed to be arrangements for grazing in the woods, because their shelter was vital for horses, cattle and sheep in winter, but goats, which could climb trees and eat the bark, were often banned. Around 1770, James Riddell of Ardnamurchan fined tenants the huge sum of £5 for each goat found on their land. This must have caused real hardship because goats were the mainstay of the common people's economy. Doctor Johnson found a family living by Loch Ness who were entirely dependent on their sixty goats. They were allowed to keep them in return for acting as woodkeepers. Presumably duties included controlling their own flock!

It seems that during this period a conflict was developing between the landlords, who wanted to reserve the woods to make a profit for supporting a lavish lifestyle, and the local people, who regarded taking timber for their own use as an age-old right, at least in practice. A Highland proverb stated that three things in life were free: 'A fish in the stream, a deer on the hill and a tree in the wood.' The Highland people were increasingly finding that this was not the case.

In 1763, Sir James Macdonald wanted to enclose the oakwoods in Sleat because they were 'entirely consumed by the cattle'. His object was the commercial development of the woods. However, rather than harvesting and selling wood products in an open market, landlords could make an easier profit by selling the timber or leasing the woods to entrepreneurs, who would then have the chore of extracting the raw material.

David Bennett *Ouzel and goat*
ink and watercolour · 43 x 57 cm

*Hidden in the dense heather and bracken on the edge of birch and oak scrub, I noticed a small group of feral goats. My attention was initially drawn to the area by an ouzel calling, a familiar sound from my home in Yorkshire. Ouzels can be very difficult to locate once breeding has started, and judging by the beak full of succulent morsels, this male had started in earnest.*

Feral Goat and Ring Ouzel. Summit June.

Pascale Rentsch *Ruined village of Inniemor, Morvern*
oilbar, conté and pencil · 38 x 55 cms

1

1. John Davis *Taynish Mill*
acrylics · 35.5 x 52 cm

*A wet day, spent painting under a fishing umbrella (like several other artists!). At one point the wind blew the umbrella into the stream – causing much cursing and a bruised shin.*

2

3

2. Duncan Currie *Autumn leaves, small stream, Kinloch woods I*
   watercolour (and bodycolour) · 27 x 18 cm
3. Duncan Currie *Autumn leaves, small stream, Kinloch woods II*
   watercolour (and bodycolour) · 27 x 18 cm

*In a way, water is the lifeblood of the wood, so it seemed appropriate to paint the fallen leaves caught in the pools of the burn running through the wood. The leaves represent several species of trees found in the wood, thus capturing a miniature snapshot of the environment here at Kinloch.*

1. Brin Edwards *Leitir Fura*
watercolour and gouache · 47 x 27 cm
2. Greg Poole *Leitir Fura settlement*
acrylic on paper · 55 x 39 cm

*The bare outlines of ancient lime-walled buildings, bare stone rectangles more like graves than habitations. Around the tops of the ruined walls, sprouting crowns of what I think was scaly male fern. Glowing copper-orange new growth, nodding shepherd's crook heads and clasping, unfurling filigree shoots.*

*Rocks softened by mossy hummocks, the empty compartments filled with tussocks of bleached straw molinia grass.*

1

2

Old Oak, Ardery, Sunart
©Keith Brockie
May 2004

# 4 Using woods

## WOOD PASTURE

At Ardery and Resipole, on the north banks of Loch Sunart, I have walked through woods that bear signs of a landscape that has almost disappeared from the rest of Britain. This is wood pasture, which provided grazing for livestock. The important part of the woodland was not the trees but the ground under them. Wood pasture is about as remote as woodland can be from the natural condition. It is more like the parks surrounding country houses in southern counties, where scattered trees are set in open grassland.

The trees in wood pasture were pollarded to protect them from browsing by animals. Pollard comes from the Norman word for 'head' (as in poll tax). The tops of the trees are cut off at head height to give a single stout trunk, 2.5–3.5 m high, from which new shoots spring. The shoots are either harvested on a rotation to provide poles for timber or lopped annually and thrown down for stock to eat. The advantage of pollarding is that the tender new growths are out of the reach of domestic animals and wild deer, so wood pasture had a dual function. The trees produced both timber and fodder, and the ground underneath provided pasture. Two further advantages are that there is no need to fence the woods to keep animals out and the trees provided cover for animals through the winter. This was important in the west Highlands, where winter storms sweep in from the Atlantic.

We can surmise that the system of wood pasture was viable only when a few cattle were reared for domestic use. Nevertheless, the woods were still important to the local economy, as is shown by the business records that still survive.

## VETERAN TREES

Walking through an old wood pasture, there is a sense of history. The oldest pollards – some dead, some barely alive – are centuries old and, not without reason, are known as veterans. Because their hearts have rotted away, ageing by tree rings is impossible, but Peter Quelch, the Forestry Commission Scotland Biodiversity Advisor, has estimated that they are at least 300 years old and perhaps double that, and so date from medieval times. The veterans are awe-inspiring structures to behold. With the broad girth of the trunk, the contorted branches and a covering of mosses and lichens, the veterans are the wildwood monsters of children's stories. Francis Kilvert described veterans in his diary for 1876 as 'misshapen oak men that stand waiting and watching century after century. They look as if they had been at the beginning and making of the world, and they will probably see its end.'

Hollow trees may look as if they are near the end of their lives and about to fall over. They are often felled as hazards to human life but this is in ignorance of the trees' biology. The living part of any tree is just under the bark. The bulk of wood in the trunk and branches is dead. In young trees, wood provides structural support, but as the tree grows, it becomes an increasing burden. Losing the surplus through the activities of fungi and woodboring insects is a positive advantage. A hollow tube is much stronger than a solid bar of the same weight: think of scaffolding or the structure of the Forth rail bridge. When a hurricane hit south-east England in 1987, 100-year-old trees with solid trunks were felled but hollow veterans survived.

For naturalists and conservationists the value of veterans lies in the wealth of wildlife they support. Woodpeckers, owls, treecreepers, tits, redstarts and bats breed and roost in holes. Hordes of insects and other invertebrates live in the rotting timber, which also supports flowers and small trees. Even the veteran feeds on its own dead tissues. It sends out

Keith Brockie *Old oak, Ardery*
watercolour · 53 x 39.5 cm

TAGHADH FIODH

*Tagh seileach nan allt,*
*tagh calltain nan creag*
*Tagh fearna nan lòn,*
*tagh beithe nan eas*
*Tagh uinnseann na dubhair,*
*tagh iubhar na leuma*
*Tagh leamhan na brùthaich,*
*tagh duire na grèine.*

CHOICE OF TIMBER

*Choose the willow of the streams,*
*choose the hazel of the rocks*
*Choose the alder of the marshes,*
*choose the birch of the waterfalls*
*Choose the ash of the shade,*
*choose the yew of resilience*
*Choose the elm of the brae*
*choose the oak of the sun.*

A. CARMICHAEL, CARMINA GADELICA

roots from the base of its branches to feed on the compost forming in the rotting trunk.

Eventually the veteran tumbles and comes to rest on the woodland floor. With the passage of many more years, it crumbles into dust and returns to the soil. Throughout this process it is home to a succession of species. The amount of dead wood in a wood is an indicator of its naturalness. Traditionally it was cleared for timber and firewood or because it was a reservoir for pests and diseases that could infect the living trees. Leaving dead wood is a simple way of increasing the wildlife value of a wood, and the Forestry Commission now manages its woods to increase the amount of dead wood.

### COPPICED WOODS

*'Travellers are delighted in passing through any district in which regular attention is paid to the forests, even when reared for the purpose of charcoal... No one can traverse the lands without a feeling of this kind; when the former waste state of that large tract is also contemplated, and contrasted with the marks of industry which appear, and the beautiful appearance of the regularly preserved and rising trees.'*

W. SINGERS 1829

Between 100 and 200 years ago, the oakwoods of Argyll went through a period of intensive management by coppicing to produce charcoal for iron smelting. The effects of this industry are still to be seen in the form of solid archaeological remains of enclosure walls, charcoal-burning hearths and packhorse roads, but especially by the structure of the woods. The 'regularly preserved and rising trees' noted by W. Singers are still there, and these coppice woods do not have the tangle of understorey, brambles and fallen logs that can make it so difficult to walk through more natural woods. They are more like plantations, with regular stands, almost monocultures, of even-age trees, cathedral-like with their soaring trunks, arched tracery of foliage and a clear floor underfoot.

Coppicing is a very ancient form of woodland management that dates back thousands of years and which is based on the ability of a tree to grow new stems from its base. It is used to produce thick poles, which could be used for tools and houses, and slender rods, which were needed for domestic uses such as wattles for fences, fishing creels and so on. Hazel, oak, ash and birch were managed in this way. Hazel coppices so well naturally that it is rare to find one with only a single stem. As the stems get taller, they lean out and leave space for new ones to grow up between them.

In its simplest form, suitable rods would have been cut as required. Then, at some point in prehistory, the observation that the stumps of felled trees sprouted new growth was put to good effect for increasing the yield. Trees were felled and new stems

1

2

allowed to sprout from the stump or stool. With a root system already well established, growth is rapid. It is believed that only a few stems would have been taken from a coppiced tree in a year. This had several advantages. There was less stress on the tree; the new growths were protected from browsing animals by the existing stems; and, for hazel, the trees continued to produce a valuable harvest of nuts.

The lack of tools made handling large timbers difficult, and even houses were built of slender poles. These were wattle and daub creel, or basket, houses, which were no more than simple huts. A report to the Duke of Gordon in 1767 describes the construction of houses as they must have been built for centuries:

*'First they place upright standarts about nine inches distant one from the other & about eight feet tall all round of the straightest young wood. Then with smaller wood they work up like a basket the height they design the side Walls and Gavells for Couples they use some old wood But the roof is finisht with wood like the standarts of the side walls. Those houses are annually repaird & often renewed from the foundation.'*

The annual repair and renewal would have recycled as much wood as possible, if only for the convenience of the builders, but there was a continual whittling away of the nearby woods as houses were built and rebuilt, and broken tools and utensils replaced. A simple creel house, like that described above, required an estimated 2,000 poles.

### TANBARK AND CHARCOAL

As Highland woods moved from providing local needs to generating a cash income, the harvesting of trees became more intensive and a major source of employment. Tree products could be exported in bulk to distant industries thanks to the proximity of the sea, which by-passed the problem of transport across the difficult Highland terrain. Oak was the main raw material.

The use of oak bark for tanning leather is an extremely old process. Leather was used locally for making brogues and domestic utensils, while boatmen preserved their sails and cordage by boiling them in an infusion of bark. Early in the 17th century, tanbark began to be exported from the western Highlands to Ireland, where a large leather industry became very profitable when the wars with France generated an enormous demand.

Oak provided the best bark because it had the highest tannin content. It was harvested in spring, from early May to early July, when the sap is rising and the bark is loose and easy to remove. Whole communities were involved. Larger trees were stripped where they stood, but smaller poles, down to 3 cm in diameter, were cut down and carried to a suitable place, where they were

3

1. Chris Rose *Hazel coppice*
   acrylic on paper · 47 x 66 cm

   *As I sat painting amongst the trees of this hazel coppice at Barnluasgan, a red squirrel approached, running expertly along familiar pathways up in the trees, leaping sure-footedly from branch to branch. It descended to the ground and foraged amongst the grasses, mosses and leaf litter, picking up hazel nuts and burying them for its winter larder.*
2. Andrew Sinclair *Birch woodland*
   oil on board · 80 x 100 cm
3. Nik Pollard *Path through silver birch, Taynish*
   acrylic on paper · 42 x 59 cm

stripped by the women and children. The bark was first loosened by beating with a mallet and then removed with a wedge or a special 'barking iron'. It was then dried and packed for transport.

The second half of the 18th century saw heavy industry come to the western Highlands. English ironmasters came north to seek ways of increasing their output. They found it was worth shipping their ore from Furness in Cumbria for processing because of the abundant and regular supplies of charcoal available from the local woods. Charcoal made up 60–70 per cent of the cost of smelting. It was cheap in Argyll because it could be transported by sea. It was a happy coincidence for the ironmasters and the landowners with trees to sell that oakwoods thrived on the coast, and packhorses were needed only to carry bags of charcoal to loading points on the shore.

Only two blast furnaces operated for any length of time in Argyll. Furnace, as Inverleachann was renamed, on Loch Fyne worked from 1755 to 1812 and The Lorn Furnace Company's ironworks, whose well-preserved ruins may still be visited at Bonawe, was on Loch Etive. Bonawe started operation in 1763 and continued until 1876. It produced up to 700 tons of iron and consumed charcoal from 700 acres of woodland every year.

Both ironworks relied on charcoal from scattered tracts of woodland to take advantage of the local labour force. The ironmasters brought in a system of coppicing that was widely used in England. Parcels of oakwood, called haggs, from a Norse word for 'hew', were cut on a rotation of about 25 years. The trees were felled and a mass of new shoots was allowed to sprout from the stump. It was not simply a matter of hacking off the poles. An early regulation stated that the cuts were to be 'raised and smoothed as to prevent the diminishing thereof by water'. In other words, the stool was shaped so that rainwater was shed and rotting prevented. At intervals of four, seven and 12 years, the new stems were thinned to allow room for the remaining half-dozen to grow. Not all the trees were coppiced; a scattering was left to mature into 'maidens' or ' standards' to provide large timbers.

Over the course of coppicing, other trees were 'weeded' out of the woods, and gaps were planted with more oak. Larch and other conifers were sometimes planted as 'nurses' to give shelter to the young oaks and were felled to yield an extra crop to help the cash flow as the oaks grew. Acorns often had to be imported from farther afield, because good crops of acorns are fickle in the Highlands and, at best, occur only at five- to seven-year intervals. Chris Marsh, the forester at Kinloch, told me how, with six companions, he spent a day collecting acorns at Aslaig. They returned with thirty-six! This was bad luck; in other years acorns carpet the floor and woodpigeons grow

1. Duncan Currie *Changing light, changing colour, shifting season*
mixed media · 23.5 x 51.5 cm

*I wanted to catch the leaves as they began to change into their autumn colours – just on the cusp between summer and autumn. It turned out to be fortunate, because when I returned later, gales had taken all the leaves. On this particular day I was very lucky, as there was a strong, low sun, which gave a lovely glowing light through the trees and accentuated the lovely yellows, oranges and greens of the changing leaves.*

2. Peter Partington *Redstart display – the oakwoods*
watercolour · 27 x 36.5 cm

1

2

fat. Nurseries, such as the one at Strontian, provided saplings for planting out when two or three years old. The resulting woods became monocultures of even-age oaks, whose remnants can still be seen. Some of the woods at Kinloch were planted by 18th-century Macdonalds, and recent DNA analysis of the trees suggests that the acorns came from Germany – an interesting provenance given the clan's antipathy to the House of Hanover!

### ENCLOSURES

After a round of cutting, the new shoots had to be protected from grazing by enclosure within stone or turf dykes or fences for six or so years, after which livestock was allowed back in. Many dykes are still to be seen in the woods, and they can be picked out on Ordnance Survey maps. In their present state they do not look as if they could have kept out goats, sheep or even agile cattle, but there is a record of tenants being required to build 'a dyke and ditch seven feet high and seven feet wide'. Low stone dykes were raised with layers of turf, into which branches could be stuck. Alternatively, less permanent enclosures were made from woven wattles. A third system involved reinforcing natural barriers by making a 'pareing brae', in which a steep slope was cut away to make a vertical wall, which might be reinforced with stones. Later in the 19th century the effective height of dykes was raised by the addition of strands of steel wire, whose rusting supports can still be seen. The effectiveness of the barriers was reinforced by the herders, usually the younger members of the family, who kept a watchful eye on their charges.

### CHARCOAL BURNING

The oakwoods of Argyll are studded with hundreds of charcoal burners' hearths. They are not conspicuous until you learn to look for flat circles, 6–12 metres across, set in the hillside. Here, again, I needed guidance from Jamie McIntyre, the Sunart Community Forester, who did much to impress on me the link between woods and people, both then and now. He showed me not only the hearths at Ardery but also the tracks, complete with bridges over burns, that were used by the packhorses. The

1

hearths were made by cutting into the slope and throwing the spoil out to build up a level platform behind a retaining wall of stones. Recent excavations have revealed that they may be of great antiquity and were originally bases for dwellings. It is likely, however, that they were reused by charcoal burners, but they are now called 'recessed platforms', a term that describes the structure without commenting on its function.

Making charcoal was a skilled business and was directed by a professional coaler. The cut and dried timber was stacked carefully around a central stake and covered with turf. The stake was then removed and a fire started in the 'flue' that it left. The coaler and his team had to maintain a continuous watch and stop any leaks that would let too much air into the stack. Otherwise the wood would burn into ash. The slow combustion converted the wood into charcoal over a period of several days, after which it had to cool before it was put into sacks ready for transport.

As well as providing the best bark for tanning, oak produced hard charcoal, which is best for smelting. It was stripped of its valuable bark in spring, but converted into charcoal later in summer. Other trees, such as ash and birch, were known as 'winter wood' because they were cut at the end of winter to prolong the coaling season and provide the furnaces with a steadier supply of charcoal.

At one time it was believed that commercial charcoaling had been a major cause of the deforestation of the Atlantic oakwoods. On the contrary, it is

1. Andrew Stock *Charcoal-burning hearth, Taynish*
watercolour · 18 x 25.5 cm

2. Chris Rose *Boggy tree (detail)*
acrylic on board · 75 x 94 cm

*This is a wet place – wet overhead, wet underfoot and wet in the middle – but I was captivated by it just the same. The trees literally drip with mosses and lichens, the moisture saturating the colours into vivid greens and oranges. I liked the way that the trees reflected darkly in the peaty water of this mire in the Taynish woods; and even when it wasn't raining, water dripped from the rain-soaked trees, spreading circular ripples on the water.*

2

1

clear now that the ironmasters are more likely to have preserved the woods and even extended them. It was in their interest to conserve trees as a renewable resource for their charcoal. What is true is that their demand for charcoal altered the nature of the woods, both in structure, by coppicing, and in nature, by the selective planting of oak and its attendant nurse trees.

Eventually coke replaced charcoal as the source of carbon in iron smelting but charcoal continued to be needed for other purposes. Coppice timber was used for barrels and wheel spokes. The ironworks at Furnace was converted into a gunpowder mill, in which soft charcoal from alder, aspen and willow was a main ingredient. The lead mine at Strontian also required charcoal, and there was a 'pyroligneous acid' works at Crinan. Acid making was the same process as charcoal burning but the vapours driven off the charring wood were condensed to yield acetic acid for the printing and dyeing industries.

When the market for charcoal collapsed, coppicing went into decline. Some trees were then singled – one stem only left to grow – to produce larger timber for shipbuilding. There were a few other outlets. The bobbin mill at Salen needed 1,400 tons of wood each year from the Sunart region for making bobbins or pirns for the weaving industry. But, in general, the woods became neglected and the enclosures fell into disrepair. Even the local use of woodland products gradually dwindled and by the end of the 19th century had almost ceased to exist. One of the last exports from the woods was sprigs of holly sent to Glasgow markets at Christmas.

1. Nik Pollard *Untitled*
   acrylic on paper · 42 x 59 cm
2. Matt Underwood *Rite of spring*
   gouache · 84 x 29 cm

   *I like the force of everything at this time, the upward feeling and battle for light and place. Looking into the wood it was so dark.*
3. Matt Underwood *Unfurling*
   mixed media · 84 x 33 cm

   *From a tight coil, through to violin forms, to an unfurling fern. This attracted me, as did the colours against the colours of the rocks – the orange. Warmer colours against the green are a sense of danger – the adder.*

2

3

1

1. John Busby *Venerable oak and young birches, Ardery*
   charcoal drawing · 32 x 24 cm
2. David Guy Measures *The pollarded oak*
   watercolour · 28.5 x 25 cm

   *Up the track on the hillside behind the caravans on the shore of Loch Sunart was the only pollarded oak that we found during the week. This was painted rapidly, in a haze of biting mosquitoes, on our last day.*

A white birch pole in front of
The only pollarded oak we saw
19 May 09 – in a haze of midges.

2

# 5 Woodland refuges

David Bennett *Otter family (detail)*
pencil and watercolour · 36 x 57 cm

*This family party appeared out of a golden, undulating carpet of weed. The cubs seemed a little giddy, and chased around before making their way back to mum, who was doing her scenting duties on a nearby rock. The cubs were very vocal, chittering loudly, a sound which could be heard from a considerable distance.*

The Atlantic oakwoods are important for conservation because of their great variety of wildlife. They form a marvellous refuge in the western Highlands for a rich, often unusual and sometimes unique, assemblage of animals and plants. They have survived partly through their remoteness and the poverty of the environment, which have discouraged the widespread industrialisation, urbanisation and intensive agriculture that swamped most of the country. Consequently, there is still enough space for preserving viable populations and communities of wildlife. This does not mean that nature can be left to her own devices. Space is not unlimited; many of the woods are small and human activity always poses a danger. Intervention is frequently necessary, even if it is no more intrusive than monitoring to check that all is well with key species of animals and plants.

It was only when Scotland's Atlantic oakwoods caught the attention of modern naturalists that their great diversity came to be appreciated. In the 1970s, when Brian Coppins began to study lichens on hazel trees, he found species that were new to Britain and even new to science. The white script lichen *Graphis alboscripta* is a species that has never been found outside the west coast of Scotland. Far from being 'scrub' of no particular interest, hazel woods have proved to have a unique collection of lichens, which are of great conservation value. This has been recognised possibly just in time. They were threatened by the revival of coppicing hazel, partly to provide wood products but also as a conservation tool. Many of these lichens only grow on old wood, so widespread coppicing would wipe them out.

It has been said that conserving diversity requires a 'diversity of conservationists'. Each one draws attention to their own speciality and prevents the management plan for somebody else's favourite species harming their own. So thinning a wood to allow more light for the benefit of flowers and the butterflies that feed on them could be detrimental to mosses and other shade-loving plants.

Preservation and restoration of the oakwoods is increasing the amount of habitat for rare species. Some may spread naturally to take advantage of these new opportunities but others may need help by reintroduction. This has been suggested for bringing back black grouse to the Kinloch Hills, but, more controversially, plans have been put forward for establishing the beaver on a trial basis in Knapdale, after an absence from Scotland of four centuries. Although this would be the return of a native, the ecosystem has changed in the intervening years, not least through Man's dominant role. The beaver's engineering would encourage wetland habitats and diversify woodlands, and so encourage a variety of species. However, there are those who regard a large tree-felling rodent as a serious threat to agricultural crops, trees and the fish that breed in the streams. The beaver's supporters point out the benefits to tourism and, if the new population became a problem, that it would be easy to contain such a conspicuous, slow-breeding animal.

### BLACK GROUSE

The black grouse is one of the most fascinating birds to be found in the west coast woods, although unfortunately one of the rarest. It is one of only three British birds with the extravagant mating displays

ORAN AN T-SAMHRAIDH

*Bi gach doire dluth, uaiguidh*
*'S trusgan uain' uim' a' fibs;*
*Bi an snodhach a' dìreadh*
*As gach freumaich is isle,*
*Troimh na cuisleanan sniòmhain*
*Gu meudachadh blath*
*Cuach is smeòrach 's an fheasgar*
*Seinn an leadain 'nam bàrr.*

THE SONG OF SUMMER

*O'er groves close and secret*
*A green mantle grows;*
*The juices ascending*
*From roots lowest bending,*
*Through arteries winding*
*To distribute the bloom;*
*On their tops thrush and cuckoo*
*Their sweet litanies hum.*

BY ALEXANDER MACDONALD

known as lekking. For most of the year, males – blackcock – gather every morning at traditional lekking grounds, perhaps in a grassy glade, on a forest track or in a rough pasture. There they defend small territories and, during April and May, compete for the attention of the females – greyhens. The males circle with tails spread to show off the white undertail-coverts, wings half-spread and red combs inflated. All the while, they utter a bubbling sound that can be heard a mile away in still conditions. It is worth getting up before dawn to get to a lek. The birds are very wary and easily driven off. A parked car makes a good hide but I once crawled behind a stone dyke to get a view.

At one time 30–40 blackcock made a good lek, but leks have been getting smaller and the last I saw had a lone male displaying by himself. Black grouse have been in decline throughout Europe over the last century, and during the 1990s the British population dropped by about 10 per cent per year. Black grouse now only occur in pockets through the country, and the species is a UK Biodiversity Action Plan Priority Species.

The natural habitat of black grouse is woodland clearings and edges, where there is a mix of trees, heather and blaeberry, and wet patches with plenty of insects for the young chicks. As the woodlands fragmented and disappeared, the grouse adapted to moorland fringes, and they thrived in young conifer forests. As grazing and forestry have intensified, the preferred mosaics of habitat have been replaced by monocultures. The grouse disappeared from the conifer woods when the canopy started to close. The hope is that by restructuring the woods through planned clearfelling, black grouse will be able to use the edges. Although not strictly birds of the oakwood, black grouse use them for feeding. They survive in birch woods and the edges of conifer forests, and they benefit from the fencing out of deer and sheep that is allowing the oakwoods to regenerate. There is, however, a real danger of collision with deer fences, but the Forestry Commission and other landowners have been removing redundant fences and making the remainder conspicuous to flying birds.

1

1. Chris Rose *Duel at dawn*
oil on board · 43 x 84 cm

*Early morning is the best time to witness blackcock lekking. The newly risen sun cast a dramtic light over this scene and made the dewdrops on the grass sparkle like jewels.*

*Although painted in Scotland, this picture was produced outside the project but serves to illustrate the species.*

2,3 John Busby *Sleeping pine marten*
pencil and watercolour sketches

2

3

PINE MARTENS AND RED SQUIRRELS

These are two tree-dwelling mammals which were once found throughout the country but subsequently struggled for survival. The pine marten is staging a recovery but the red squirrel seems to be going into free-fall.

Despite its name, the pine marten is found in both coniferous and broadleaved woods and even on open hills and moors. Persecution as a robber of game and poultry was so severe that by the 1920s it was confined to a small area of upland forest and rocky moor in north-west Scotland. However, by the 1960s, there were signs of a revival, and martens spread south and west into Argyll. They have continued to spread and increase, and they colonised Skye after they had been seen running across the Skye Road Bridge.

Pine martens hunt mainly on the ground, although they are excellent climbers. Their main prey is voles, with squirrels forming only a small part of their diet in Scotland. Birds, beetles, carrion and fungi are also eaten and berries are important in autumn. A good sign of their presence is droppings and small piles of half-digested rowan berries deposited on woodland paths. However, martens are now becoming known as visitors to bird tables, and people put out food to attract them into their gardens.

In the 18th and 19th centuries the red squirrel fared worse than the pine marten. It almost became extinct in Scotland but hung on in the Highlands, where the population was boosted by introductions from England and the Continent. Numbers recovered but there was another decline in the 20th century. The reasons are unclear, but habitat fragmentation and disease are believed to have played a part. Subsequently, the spread of the grey squirrel has driven out its smaller relative and once again the western Highlands have become one of the red squirrel's last refuges in Britain.

The red squirrel's home on the west coast is mature conifer woods with a mixture of pine, larch and Norway spruce, which gives a broad harvest of cones, but the squirrels also spread into adjoining hazel and oak. Places like the Sunart oakwoods and

Knapdale are refuges, which the grey squirrel has not yet reached. It is ironic that linking the fragments of woods improves the red squirrels' habitat but will also make it easier for the greys to spread.

### OTTERS

Thirty years ago there was alarm about the status of the otter in Britain. From inhabiting every stretch of water, it had vanished from most of lowland Britain. Its last stronghold was the Highlands and Islands of Scotland. The reappearance of the otter in some of the worst-hit regions over the last decade has been a conservation success story, but western Scotland is still the place where you have the best chance to see an otter.

If you are going to Skye, visit the Forestry Commission's Otter Haven at Kylerhea. The hide looks down on a stretch of shore favoured by otters and is equipped with CCTV for improving the chance of a sighting. Another good spot is the hide at Ard Airigh on the northern shore of Loch Sunart. However, there is just as good a chance of spotting an otter anywhere along the coast. According to a recent survey, there are more signs of activity on stretches with less human activity, which on the west coast leaves plenty of places where a quiet watch may be rewarding. The pleasure of watching an otter eating its prey at the surface is surpassed only by watching a mother with her cubs.

At one time, otters seen along the Scottish coast were confusingly called 'sea otters' as if they were different from 'river otters'. The same animals work both fresh and salt water. The focus of activity is the shore and shallow water, and the otters' main prey is fish, crabs and sea urchins. Most of the holts and couches are within 50 metres of the coast. However, signs such as spraints (droppings deposited in conspicuous places and surprisingly sweet-smelling) are commonly found on burns flowing down through the woods. Otters travel upstream to hill lochans 500 metres or so above sea level, especially when frogs and toads are gathering to spawn, and they enter the woods to make homes under boulders and uprooted trees. Access to fresh water is also vital for washing salt from their fur.

Despite being expert swimmers, otters are not so well adapted for an aquatic life in some respects. Time spent in the water is limited mostly to bouts of feeding, and otters suffer, as we do, from getting cold by spending too long in the water. A study at Taynish by Alan McCluskie of Glasgow University has shown how otters' feeding habits are influenced by sea temperature. In summer, when the water is warm, they dive in deeper water for edible crabs. When it is cold, long dives use up too much energy and more time has to be spent on land recovering after feeding. So it is more economical to hunt in shallow water, even though this means subsisting on poor food like sticklebacks and doing without their favourite edible crabs.

Another finding from otter studies shows why the best time to look for them is in the early morning. Apart from the lack of disturbance by people, they tend to feed at this time of day because their main prey, such as fish, are inactive and easier to catch.

1

1. William Neill *Otter*
felt pen · 9 x 16 cm

2,3 Keith Brockie *Otter, Sunart*
pencil · 19 x 23 cm

2

3

1

2

1. Esther Tyson *Otter and cub feeding, on the edge of Kinloch woods*
   acrylic on paper · 27 x 78 cm

   *Early evening. I have been painting for a couple of hours. The breeze has kept the midges away till now. I scan the point. Movement. Otter! Two. Three. A head above water. Gone. Closer. Head back, chewing something small. Gone. Head above water. Larger catch. Crunching. Crab claws either side of her mouth. Playing cubs clambering on her, trying to get food. Gone. Closer again. Female now has what looks like a white sack with long tentacles. She stretches them from the body, one by one. Cubs continually at her side.*

2. Esther Tyson *Otter and cub*
   charcoal and pencil on paper · 24 x 59.7 cm

*Two days ago we came across an otter's holt, some way into the woodland. I picked up a trail about 200 yards away, not wanting to get too close. The ground is very boggy; I should have worn my wellies! There is a definite trail leading toward the shore. Heading downward, I follow a small stream in a shallow ravine. The trail crosses to the far bank. Soft ground but no tracks other than roe deer. I have found roe droppings regularly along the way, and I am beginning to wonder if that is all I will find. Steep climb around boulders and rocks. Up to higher ground. The trail is running parallel to the shoreline. I sit for a while under an old oak. Bones. A skull. The lower jaw is missing but already I am interested. I find a stick and poke around in the leaves. First right, then left, lower jaw. One tooth. Another. The midges are in my face as I disturb the leaf litter. An almost complete otter skull. The midges are too much! I move on. The trail is close to the edge. Narrow in places. Boulders and rocky outcrops. Jump down. Another boulder. Crab remains! An otter has been here! I follow at a faster pace. The ground is well trodden. Signs of activity every place I look. Trails leading through gaps between boulders. Many secret places for an otter to hole up. Spraint! Fresh on a predominant rock. Exciting. I move on. Another small stream winding its way to the open water. Soft ground. Otter track! One single, clear paw print...*

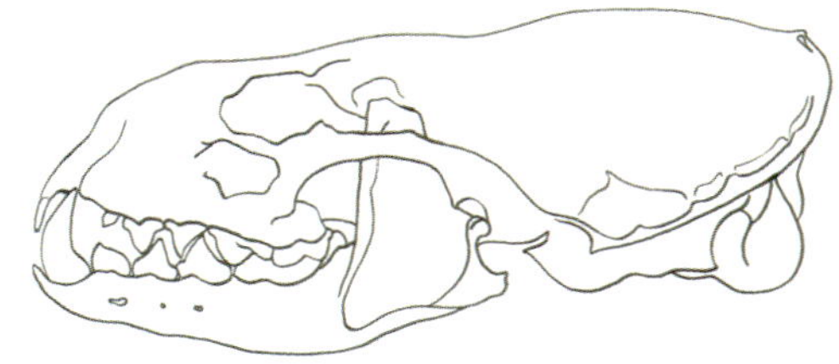

## LICHENS

You cannot look closely at the oakwood trees without noticing that they are smothered with a variety of lesser plant life – ferns, mosses, liverworts and lichens – growing on the bark. These are epiphytes, which means that they are simply growing on the tree and are not behaving as parasites by deriving sustenance from it, like mistletoe.

Epiphytes are an important part of the diversity of species that makes the Atlantic oakwoods a priority for conservation. Their profusion is a result of the high rainfall, which regularly soaks the bark and maintains a damp atmosphere, together with the long, uninterrupted existence of the woods, which allows their slow-developing communities to become established. Mosses and liverworts, collectively called bryophytes, are simple plants that grow in moist, sheltered conditions. In woods, lush growths are found in sheltered north-facing sites, at the bases of trees and in ravines. Lichens like more light and grow on sunny slopes in open woods, and along the edges of glades.

Early writers described lichens as 'scurf' or 'mould', and it is easy to dismiss them as no more than discoloration or perhaps a deformity of the bark. But lichens are one of the glories of the Atlantic oakwoods. The 10 hectares of Barnluasgan Wood in Knapdale, for instance, are known to support 300 kinds of lichens, most of which live on trees, and some of which are rare or scarce.

Whether rare or not, lichens are worth our attention because they are a unique life form. Not plants, they consist of a fungus and a green alga (in some cases a blue-green alga or cyanobacterium) living in a close relationship for mutual benefit, known as symbiosis. The alga manufactures carbohydrates by photosynthesis and shares them with the fungus. The fungus, in turn, gives the alga support and shelter. In particular, it protects the alga from the damaging rays of ultra-violet light and from desiccation in dry weather. So close is the relationship that neither alga nor fungus can live on its own.

A closer look at these lichens, preferably through a magnifying glass, reveals an exquisite variety of form and colour. The problem is that most lichens are difficult to identify. I was lucky to be shown around a small hazel wood in Knapdale, called Barrandaimh, and introduced to its lichens by Peter Quelch. As he put it, 'Some lichens are definitely not for amateurs', but he held my attention by pointing out interesting facts about the species we encountered. The scientific names were lost on me unless he pointed out some clear and interesting feature of the lichen by which I could remember them. *Usnea*,

1

2

3

or old man's beard, hangs in hairy festoons; *Platismatia glauca* looks like lettuce; and *Sphaerophorus globosus* has a remarkable resemblance to coral.

Lichens live in characteristic communities, with different collections of species on different trees. The types of lichen growing on a tree are partly a measure of the acidity of its bark. Birch, alder and oak are more acidic than hazel, willow and ash. The roughness of the bark also plays a part. Smooth bark is colonised by crusting lichens, which form a closely fitting mosaic on hazels and young oaks. One of these is grey, warty cudbear *Ochrolechia tartaria*, from which the Highlanders used to make a crimson dye by steeping it in rancid urine.

Our walk took us from birch and into hazel, and Peter pointed out how the characteristic lichens changed. When we moved among the hazel trees, there was *Parmelellia triptophylla,* which smells strongly of iodine. Much more striking were the four species of *Lobaria* lungworts. They are so named because the underside of the flat 'leaves' looks like lung tissue. On the strength of this resemblance they were once used for treating lung ailments. Peter also showed me how some common lichens were good colonisers and took up residence on twigs and saplings that were only two or three years old. As the tree grows, they are replaced by

6

1. Sîan Armstrong *Layered lichens*
   gouache, watercolour and ink · 17.5 x 17.5 cm
2. Sîan Armstrong *Recurring form, bracken and lichen*
   gouache and ink · 17.5 x 17.5 cm
3. Sîan Armstrong *Like a wave breaking*
   gouache, watercolour and ink · 17 x 17 cm
4. John Paige *Birch woodland, Taynish Mill*
   watercolour · 28 x 38 cm
5. Jane Leycester Paige *Colony of lichens on oak branch*
   watercolour and ink · 31 x 24 cm
6. Brin Edwards *Slow-worm with map-like lichens*
   watercolour and gouache · 20 x 36.5 cm

4

5

Brin Edwards *Slow-worm with map-like lichens*

*I was fascinated by the map-like lichens covering the rocks along the woodland paths. The slow-worm completed the picture, like a sinuous river.*

Sîan Armstrong *Layered lichens*

*At first I was overwhelmed by the variety of potential subjects and approaches, and I wandered around for ages – so much to see and take in. Eventually I decided to focus on 'pattern' – itself a huge, varied subject! I really liked the way these lichens 'arranged themselves' in rhythmic layers against the dark background of a tree trunk.*

species that need many years to become established. The rare ones need a century of tree growth to become established.

A walk through a wood of oaks would have revealed yet another community, although many species would have been the same, including tree lungwort growing to the size of dinner plates and sometimes falling off the tree under its own weight. There are several reasons why the Atlantic oakwoods are so well endowed with lichens. They thrive in the damp, mild air and they also like its purity. Lichens disappeared from industrial areas because they are so susceptible to acid rain. The remote west coast of Scotland is a sanctuary for rare species, and there are rich communities because the air has never been polluted. Linked with the absence of industrialisation there is the continuity of the woodlands, which enables slow-growing and slow-colonising species to maintain a presence. Despite the history of management by coppicing and pollarding, there has been continuous tree cover as a habitat for lichens.

There is more to the lichen community than lichens. The carpet of growth covering the trees is the foundation for a unique ecosystem of animals that feed on lichens, which hugely increases the diversity, and hence conservation value, of the lichens. It is not obvious because many of the animals are nocturnal and are, in any case, small and obscure. Earwigs and woodlice scavenge on dead tissues, while slugs and snails scrape the lichen with their rough tongues. If they are not visible, their presence is given away by the zig-zags trails where they have exposed the pale deeper tissues of the lichen. Moths that eat and rest on lichens, as either caterpillars or adults, are hard to spot because they are exquisitely camouflaged. These herbivorous animals are the prey of the ecosystem's carnivores, which include spiders, beetles, lacewing larvae, harvestmen and predatory flies.

1. John Paige *Lichen on rocks by the shore, Taynish*
   watercolour · 24 x 34 cm
2. Jane Leycester Paige *Dog lichen study*
   watercolour · 18 x 26 cm
3. Anna Kirk-Smith *Sea edge*
   mixed media · 68 x 50 cm

1

2

3

1

2

1. Chris Rose *Fungi*
acrylic on paper · 39 x 30 cm
2. Chris Rose *The living cloak*
acrylic on paper · 30 x 22 cm

*Everywhere you look in the oakwoods, there is evidence of the profusion of plant life. Every tree, log, stone and branch is covered in a bewildering array of lichens, mosses, ferns and fungi. This stem of a coppiced oak in the Taynish woods at Knapdale was typical.*

3. Barry W. Van Dusen *Oak forest epiphytes, Ardery Reserve*
watercolour · 27 x 34.5 cm
4. Richard Tratt *The silver ground carpet*
oil on canvas · 30.5 x 40 cm

*Painted outdoors amidst a cloud of midges, this is an ancient lichen-covered oak at Ceol na Mara woods. I couldn't resist painting in a moth – the silver ground carpet.*

3

4

1

1. Richard Tratt *Day moths – Loch Sunart area*
oil on paper · 23 x 30.5 cm

2

2. David Guy Measures *Speckled yellow moth*
pen and watercolour · 16 x 15 cm

23rd May 2004
Kinloch woods
large red Damsel
Four Spotted Chaser
newly emerged

1

26th May 2004
Kinloch Woods
four Spotted chaser

2

3

4

1,2 Paul Henery *Four-spotted chaser studies*
conté and pencil · 27 x 38 cm

3. David Bennett *Golden-ringed dragonflies emerging studies*
pastel and watercolour · 36 x 57cm

*A mere trickle of a stream was the setting for this mass emergence. Nine dragonflies were in various stages of unfolding. Their little bodies vibrating as fluid pumped around them. Truly a wild wonder.*

4. Richard Tratt *Beautiful demoiselles – sketchbook*
oil and pencil on paper · 15 x 20 cm

John Busby *Oaks, deer and bluebells, Ariundle*
oil on canvas · 27.5 x 35 cm

*The oak woods in early May. Trees in bud with few leaves out. Bluebells on the ground. All the many boulders covered with lichen, forming soft, golden-yellow, rounded shapes.*

1

1. John Paige *Yellow flag water meadow, Tayvallich*
acrylic · 56 x 76 cm

*We could see this water meadow from our cottage window. Full of yellow flag, ragged robin and hemlock water dropwort. A sedge warbler had his territory on our side and made frequent display flights, with slow, butterfly wing action. One morning a female roe deer jumped through the meadow.*

2. Keith Brockie *Stags in velvet*
watercolour on coloured paper · 35 x 32 cm

*There were stags in the woodland at Ardery but it was much easier to get to grips with them out on the open moorland. These were sitting in the sun amidst the nodding white heads of cotton grass. Their winter coats were worn and faded prior to moulting into a rich red summer pelage. The antlers were almost half grown and covered in 'velvet', which they would scrape off in the coming months, when the antlers had fully developed. The strong sunlight helped to highlight the strong sculptural facial form, and the play of shadows added more interest to the composition.*

2

1

1. John Davis *Towards Knapdale and Móine Mhôr*
   watercolour · 42 x 61 cm

   *A blustery, rainy day with occasional glimpses of the sun. The ochre expanse of Mòine Mhór, the steep hills of Knapdale and the Crinan Canal can all be seen. Ravens occasionally croaked as they enjoyed the buffeting winds.*

2. Keith Brockie *Raven brood*
   watercolour on paper · 35 x 49 cm

   *A brood of raven chicks sitting in a cliff nest overlooking a riverine gully in an oakwood above Glen More. I sat on the opposite bank and sketched and painted them via a telescope. One chick was panting in the strong sunlight, exposing a startling red gape.*

3. Keith Brockie *Raven sketch*
   pencil on paper · 24 x 33.5 cm

Raven brood, oakwood gorge,
Glen More, Ardnamurchan

2

Glen More Oakwood
Ardnamurchan
22nd May 2014

3

Katrina Cook

*Fore Druim to the island of Danna: as the raven flies.*
*Part I Looking south-west past Barnluasgan*
*Part II The Faery Isles, facing north-east*
*Part III Taynish and south-west out to sea*

A triptych in graphite · each panel 121 x 152 cm

*I wanted to produce a single piece of work accentuating the elongated ridges and lochs running* NE–SW, *which characterise the Knapdale region. I explored a number of options and travelled extensively during the residency, clocking up an astounding 600 miles during my stay. I drew each landmark from several directions, often being seen working from my car 'safari style', standing through the sunroof. I did become rather obsessed with getting the geography 'right' and was constantly buried in my map. From the beginning I knew an aerial view was necessary; Margaret and Mags were enormously helpful in providing me with aerial photographs taken previously, but I needed to get up there myself in order to really understand. I made a desperate plea to Mags to help me here, and on a memorable day this indeed came about. Many thanks to Mags for organising this, to Margaret for coming to find me and, of course, to Duncan McNair for the microlight flight and many subsequent photographs. I'll never forget that day. This work is dedicated to Duncan and Mags.*

*The next problem was physically producing the work, as I no longer have a studio of any sort. I tried renting a shared space for Part I, but this did not work out; so I had to move all the furniture in my bedroom out of the way and use the wall in there. I'll really miss being involved in these pictures, but it will be good to have my bedroom back!*

landing
Raven
Kinloch woods

2

1. Paul Henery *Raven studies*
   pencil and watercolour · 29 x 21 cm
2. Alastair Proud *Golden eagle mobbed by ravens*
   watercolour · 30 x 39 cm

   *It was a wonderful, sunny morning. I had gone up the forestry track towards Ben Aslak with the hope of seeing eagles. I was not disappointed as I was treated to a pair of eagles, one of them sunning itself for half an hour. Some ravens were also about, mobbing the eagles from time to time.*

Keith Brockie *Golden eagle pair on a ridge*
watercolour on paper · 24 x 42 cm

*A pair of golden eagles sitting on a ridge on cliffs high above the shores of Loch Sunart, sketched via a very powerful telescope from the road below.*

Darren Woodhead *White-tailed eagle sketchbook pages*
watercolour and pencil · 42 x 60 cm

*Both adults spent much time around the nest, watching the world below and manicuring feathers from their lofty precipice. Whenever they left the area, they were greeted by raucous attention from neighbouring buzzards, ravens and hooded crows. This would often be a physical clash, the eagle rising steadily with neck outstretched before flipping to one side and presenting talons. On one occasion whilst the male was engaged in combat, the female joined the crowd. This culminated in the male and female eagle talon grappling, where the adults clash in mid air, momentarily grasping each other's talons, to confirm their pairing and territory. The manoeuvre left me speechless and full of silent rapturous applause.*

Darren Woodhead *White-tailed eagle studies*
watercolour and pencil

David Bennett *White-tailed eagle*
watercolour · 41 x 57 cm

*I had seen the adult eagles visiting the nest, where a solitary juvenile sat looking quite pathetic in the persisting rain. On my return journey, I spotted an adult eagle landing nearby on a larch. It chose the very top of a spindly larch, like the star on a Christmas tree, the twigs bowing under its weight. Stretching out its wings to gain balance, it bounced, bungey style, for a short while, until a hooded crow flew in and mobbed it.*

Lochaline
25/7/04
David Bennett 04

6

# Saved in time

Nik Pollard *Harvesting (detail)*
conté on paper · 41 x 57 cm

The oakwoods survived into the 20th century as hundreds of scattered fragments, ignored, left to sheep and deer, and at the very edge of survival. Many continued to exist because they were on land that was too poor or too steep for any profitable use or else they were too remote to exploit. Only a few continued to be managed for timber. The woods in Sleat were reprieved twice. In the 1880s and again in World War I, clearfelling was contemplated but found not to be commercially worthwhile. Survival of these remnant, neglected woods finally depended on the longevity of trees. When I drove past stands of oakwoods around my home in Argyll back in the 1970s, I noticed that the trees were uniform in size. They were all around 120 years old and were survivors from the age of coppicing. I was concerned that when they eventually died, there would be nothing left but open grassland.

At this time, the Forestry Commission was determinedly planting every available patch of their land in Argyll with Sitka spruce. This included planting under the trees in native woodland. The oaks and other trees would act as nurses, protecting the young conifers from frost, but they would die, or be killed by ringbarking, when the spruces grew up through them. Apart from 'amenity' strips planted beside roads, broadleaved trees were being treated as worthless 'scrub'. I was sorry to see this because I could see older forests that had reached the 'thicket stage', in which the evergreen foliage was so dense that nothing grew in the mat of dead, brown needles that accumulated under the trees. Interestingly, as I have recently learned, the older conifer forests contain some of the rarer species of shade-requiring plants, especially if they are growing on or adjoining sites that were once ancient woodland.

I did not know it then but attitudes were beginning to change. The older generation of foresters had been brought up to produce the maximum volume of timber on their land, but a new generation was being allowed to have a regard for ecology and natural processes. This led to an appreciation that land could be used for purposes other than timber production, and now there are foresters who see woodland restoration as one of their most important duties.

At Dalavich, on the north bank of Loch Awe, there is an old coppice which once supplied charcoal to the Bonawe ironworks. When planted by the Forestry Commission in 1958, almost all the oaks had been ringbarked. The remaining 22 hectares were left as amenity for the village. In 1983 they were notified as a Site of Special Scientific Interest (SSSI) and a management plan was prepared. Forestry Commission staff also started to clear conifers from the rest of the site. Although there was little money for this type of pioneering work, it helped demonstrate what could be achieved. Much of the initiative for this woodland restoration work came from forest manager Alan Stevenson, who had seen how the old coppices were being restored at Grizedale in Cumbria. Appropriately, by a nice twist of fate, these woods had been exploited by the same ironmasters who had established the coppices in Argyll to feed their furnace at Bonawe.

Then, in 1984, came the European Year of the Environment. The Forestry Commission decided to back some conservation projects and expanded the restoration work at Dalavich. This was followed a year later by the Government's Broadleaf Policy Review, and the idea of preserving and restoring semi-natural woods took hold as a worthy aim for foresters. In 1992 the Earth Summit at Rio de Janeiro committed the British Government to sustainable forestry, which included better woodland management and the wider conservation of natural resources in the form of species, air, soil and water. Another consequence of the Earth Summit was a European Union Directive that led to the creation of the Natura Sites and Special Areas of Conservation. These include our three Aig an Oir sites. In 1994 David Bellamy helped the Forestry Commission launch an ambitious initiative to restore and expand the Atlantic oakwoods, and that year the Commission was awarded the Ford Conservation Project for its contribution to the conservation of the Atlantic oakwoods.

The Government's policy is being put into effect with a series of species and habitat action plans. The oakwoods in the Aig an Oir project fall into the *Habitat Action Plan for Upland Oakwoods*. Its target for the 15 years following 1998 is to maintain the existing areas of oakwood and extend them by planting new areas and restoring areas that had been converted to non-native forests. The woods are the home of species which need conserving, and these species have been given their own Action Plans. The species range from obscure lichens and fungi to the familiar red squirrel, song thrush and pearl-bordered fritillary butterfly. Each of these species plans states an objective – to restore the population to a certain level – and a method, which is usually a suitable form of habitat management. All these plans have a bearing on how the oakwood habitat will be managed.

Restoration of the oakwood habitat is being carried out in several ways, each of which can have a profound effect on the ecology of woodlands. The usual first step is to erect fences to exclude deer and sheep, or at least control their numbers. Deer are

1

2

4. John Davis *Rhododendron removal*
watercolour · 15 x 22 cm

not completely eliminated but in some areas populations have been reduced from 10–15 animals per square kilometre, or even more, to less than half that number. Lowering the pressure of grazing and browsing enables trees to start regenerating, but the presence of a small number of deer is acceptable because they prefer grass to seedling trees. An experiment on the island of Rum has shown that without a certain amount of grazing by deer, coarse grasses take over and the tree seedlings are crowded out. The woodland floor soon develops a characteristic flora with a scattering of tiny oak, birch and other seedlings, which now have the chance to grow into trees and shrubs.

4

Another major challenge has been to remove the rhododendrons that smother large areas of woodland on the west coast and prevent anything from growing under their thick, dark green canopy. Over 300 hectares have been removed in what has proved to be an expensive and often difficult process. Workers have had to dangle from ropes as they wield chainsaws to attack bushes growing out of rock faces. The cutting is backed up with chemical sprays to prevent regeneration from the stumps and the growth of seedlings. As with the fencing, the effects on tree regeneration have been dramatic.

1,2,3 Nik Pollard *Harvesting*
conté on paper · 41 x 57 cm

The greatest visual impact has been the removal of large areas of conifer forests planted from the 1920s onwards. Sitka spruces that I had seen being planted in the early 1970s and that had grown into 'Christmas trees' have been felled to let the native trees take back the ground. Sometimes the conifer timber has been removed and sold to help finance the operation. Elsewhere it has been left to rot. It looks unsightly but the process is called 'fell to recycle', and the dead trees will eventually provide nutrients for further growth. In the meantime the piles of dead brush provide shelter for young trees and other plants. Chris Marsh showed me a site in the Kinloch Hills where over 100 hectares of conifers had been felled in a project supported by lottery funding via the Millenium Forest for Scotland Trust. When I visited in 2004, regeneration was proceeding apace. The stark cut ends of the trunks and the stumps were covered by bright green mosses, while birch and rowan saplings were growing up through the shelter provided by brash –

3

1

1. Pascale Rentsch *Morvern Forest*
   mixed media · 67 x 51 cm
2. Katrina Cook *Stacked logs*
   pen · 15 x 42 cm

the piles of dead conifer branches. There were also good growths of brambles.

Natural ecological processes will slowly become re-established and the semi-natural habitat will be restored to something like it was before the 19th-century grazing and 20th-century planting all but destroyed it. Signs of felling, drainage channels and even-age stands of trees will slowly recede as a testament to the 20th-century planting, but the bottom line of the restoration process is the improvement in the diversity of native species and thus the conservation of threatened species in this habitat. This will be achieved either by natural colonisation of the restored habitat or by planned introductions.

TAOBH LOCH SEILE

*A' sealltainn gach àit' suas air dà thaobh Loch Seile*
*Còisir cheòlmhor nan craobh 's iad cho aobhach 's na meangain*
*'S a' ghrian thar na sgurr, 'togail smùid às an talamh.*
*Tha na bruthaichean cian, torach fiarach gu mullach*
*Tha gach lagan 's cùil dosrach, flùranach, lurach*
*Tha na craobhan 'sa choill 's iad a' boillsgeadh gu cladach*
*Agus cuid dhiu le loinn ag ath-shoillse sa chamas.*

BESIDE LOCH SHIEL

*On a warm, balmy day, I'm in the forest shade*
*Looking up and all around both sides of Loch Shiel*
*The musical choir of the trees so cheerful in the branches*
*And the sun above the crag creating a ground mist*
*The vast fertile banks inclining to the summit*
*Each little hollow and lovely, leafy, blossoming nook*
*The trees in the forest glitter to the shore*
*And some are elegantly reflected in the bay.*

DONALD MACCOLL

The Kinloch Hills, for instance, were once the home of the only black grouse in Skye but they died out a few years ago. Black grouse were once an important part of the ecosystem as food for golden eagles, as well as being interesting and spectacular birds in their own right. As the restoration of the woods progresses, the hope is that either the grouse will return on their own or a re-introduction programme will establish a viable population.

The programme of restoring old woods is being bolstered by planting native trees using local seed. This will not produce instant woodland habitat, but if the newly planted forests connect with old woods, species will have the chance to move in. Birds, mammals and some insects may move in quite quickly as trees mature and food and shelter become available, but specialists such as snails, beetles, lichens and fungi may take many years to become established. Not only do they spread very slowly but they also need a mature habitat to move into. Some will have to wait until the first trees have died.

Foresters have realised recently that there are more fragments of native woodland scattered around the Highlands than had been thought. There are several plants whose presence is an indication that a wood is ancient and has never been cleared. These include bluebell, dog's mercury, wood anemone, wood sorrel and wild strawberry, and small colonies of the decorative beech fern and false brome-grass are found on chalk or lime. Conversely, if these plants are found on open ground, they are an indication that the site was originally woodland.

It is a well-established fact in conservation that small fragments of habitat hold fewer species than large tracts and that small, isolated populations face a greater risk of extinction. Linking up these frag-

2

ments with the larger blocks of semi-natural woodland will raise the conservation status of the whole beyond the sum of the many parts. Part of the programme for preserving the oakwood habitat is to form cooperative links with private owners in order to join fragments and to prevent loss of woods that would isolate species into small, non-viable populations. This can be seen in Ardnamurchan, where the members of the North Sunart Woodland Group, which include the Forestry Commission, large landowners and crofters, work together to conserve a continuous swathe of 1,300 hectares of land, most of which is woodland.

## RESTORE TO WHAT?

Any habitat-restoration programme needs a decision about what to restore to. What precisely does restoring an oakwood mean? Should the aim be to try to turn a wood into primeval Mesolithic Wildwood or to revive a 19th-century coppice with its artificial preponderance of oak trees? The Sunart oakwoods are good examples of artificial woods. They are ancient woods, in that they have survived unbroken since the Wildwood, but they have been greatly modified by coppicing, pollarding and planting. Rather ironically, it is precisely their artificial nature that makes them so important from a conservation point of view. The coppices and pollards provide the right conditions for the rare assemblages of lichens and lower plants which are such a conservation feature of the Atlantic oakwoods.

Current restoration programmes are aiming to produce a more natural type of woodland, as opposed to commercial conifer planting. They will be maintained mostly by natural ecological processes. However, some of the new-look woodlands will be less suitable for the lichens and lower plants but they will have other valuable ecological features. It can be a delicate balancing act to reconcile the objectives of conserving a variety of wildlife forms with their different needs, as well as producing some timber for economic purposes. The preferred management option for any wood depends on both conservation and economic values, but the former is the prime consideration in the Atlantic oakwoods. George Peterken and Rick Worrell have advocated five options for sustainable management of the Sunart Oakwoods. *Natural reserves* are left to nature, although rhododendrons and other exotic plants would be removed and there would be no timber extraction. The other options involve some timber extraction, although this will not be commercially viable in such a remote and difficult terrain. *Ancient oak forest* is rather like natural reserves, with mature, old and rotting trees and a well-developed understorey. In *Native timber stands*, there is a long rotation of thinning trees and some felling of small areas at maturity. *Coppice* and *Wood pasture* recreate old economic management. *Coppices* are expensive to manage, while *Wood pasture* involves more or less constant grazing.

The option most likely to produce usable timber is the *Native timber stand* rotation. Stands can be produced by thinning of the old coppices, which are now made up of uniformly aged trees of about 130 years old. Thinning allows the crowns of the

Carry Akroyd *Tree harvesting, Knapdale*
acrylic on board · 55 x 98 cm

*As the efficient tree-harvesting machine steadily eats its way into the dark forest, small birds and red squirrels are disturbed. On a steep ridgeside, native deciduous trees hang on tenaciously. In the distance, the computer-graded logs are stacked by the forwarder, and slope cleared in previous years has flourishing birch and oak saplings.*

1

remaining trees to spread and bear more acorns, and the increased light penetrating to the ground favours sprouting seedlings. However, it is important that trees are individually selected for felling if the conservation interest of the wood is to be maintained. Trees with plenty of lichens, mosses and other epiphytes are candidates to be allowed to grow into the gnarled, hollow veterans of the future. Neighbouring trees can then be removed to reduce competition, but aspiring veterans must not be given too much space or they will lose the damp microclimate needed for their epiphytes. The moss *Plagiochila atlantica* is associated with ancient woodland and requires a balance of high humidity with warmth and light. This is achieved by neighbouring trees shading it from the afternoon sun when it is hot and the morning dew has evaporated. Removing the wrong tree could kill off a colony.

## THE WOODLAND COMMUNITY

The Atlantic oakwoods survived because they were valued by their inhabitants. They are now being conserved for their own sake, but the vision of the Forestry Commission and its partners is not that restored woodland becomes a nature reserve in which Man is no more than a warden or sightseer. The hope is that the woods will make a contribution to revitalising rural societies and economies.

Public money has been pumped into the

2

oakwoods to prevent their disappearance. The major threats – overgrazing and competition with exotic conifers and rhododendrons – have been removed. The woods are now much healthier and some are regenerating nicely. The question is now what the community – at the local and the national level – wants from these woods. They can be left to nature, which could lead to some rarities dying out, or they can be managed as described above to improve their conservation status, amenity value for local people and visitors, and maybe provide some timber.

Forestry used to provide a significant amount of employment from the 1950s to 1970s, when gangs of men were needed to plant the new conifer forests. New villages were built to house their families, but the workforce has since shrunk and people have often departed to find work elsewhere. Now employment is being created along different lines. There are some jobs in forestry, but with the provision of footpaths, signs and observation hides, the woods are being added to local tourist attractions (with tourists being housed in the former forestry villages!).

I find a more genuine link between woods and communities in the possibility of selling timber from the restored woods. The difficulties of extraction make commercial use unattractive, but there is a small niche market for veneer, which requires no more than a few high-quality, very valuable trees.

1. James Williamson-Bell *Timber loading I, Ardrishaig*
   pen and ink charcoal · 29 x 47 cm
2. James Williamson-Bell *Timber loading II, Ardrishaig*
   pen and ink charcoal · 28 x 47 cm

*I had decided not to produce 'wildlife subjects', as I felt that these would be well covered by the majority of artists. Instead I chose industrial aspects. The docks and the Crinan Canal were ideal. These drawings carried me back to the days when I was a shipbuilding draughtsman on the River Tyne.*

1

Dugie Cameron of Arivegaig, Lochaber, turns timber from 130-year-old oaks into high-quality bagpipes. At the other end of the market, local craftsmen use knotty timber for ornamental flooring and tables.

Although the numbers of jobs created by the woodlands would be so small as to be negligible in an urban setting, they can be significant in remote areas, where each job allows a family to stay in the community. They will help to keep shops, schools and transport services viable, so maintaining a community that is more than a dormitory for commuters and the retired and a landscape that is more than a theme park for visitors.

In almost every corner of the world, tourism is seen as a way of generating jobs and sustaining failing communities. It is also a cliché that tourism runs the danger of destroying what visitors come to see. The farming community forms the foundation of the Highland identity in terms of both the social fabric and the maintenance of the natural heritage of scenery and wildlife habitats. As the economics of small farming become more difficult, diversification is seen as the answer. Tourism can be the means of preserving what the visitors come to see. In the remote but scenic Highlands, tourism has become vital to the economy, and three-quarters of visitors say that they come for the wildlife and landscape. Restoring the oakwoods can only improve the quality of their visits and attract more visitors.

It has been said that Man preserves what he values but neglects or destroys what he does not. In the history of the Highlands, the Atlantic oakwoods were cared for when they were valued for sheltered pasture, timber, firewood, tanbark or charcoal. Thereafter there was a period of neglect, followed by woods being replaced by conifer forests. We have now entered a new era, in which native woods are valued for reasons divorced from human survival and profit. These are their aesthetic and recreational possibilities, which benefit people, and the richness of their animal and plant life, which is seen as a worthy end in itself. The future of the Atlantic oakwoods and their inhabitants is now assured.

1. Pascale Rentsch *Forest machinery, Barr, Morvern* pencil · 38 x 58 cm
2. Darren Woodhead *Forest machinery, Barr* watercolour · 47.5 x 71 cm
3. Pascale Rentsch *Processing timber, Lochaline* watercolour · 38 x 58 cm

2

3

1

1 Esther Tyson *Fencing*
acrylic on paper · 44 x 80 cm

2. Chris Rose *Tree harvesting*
acrylic on paper · 30 x 39 cm

*In an area of Knapdale being set aside for regeneration of the oakwoods, the final crop of Sitka spruce is being clear-felled. Three of us, intrepid artists, climbed, slipped and scrambled our way over steep terrain and treacherous fallen logs to this remote site to witness the operation. This modern, state-of-the-art tree-felling machine was an impressive and terrifying piece of hardware. We stood in awe as it gripped an 80-foot tree, cut it at the base, lifted it clear, ran its entire length through the cutting head, stripping all the branches off, and then cut it in to predetermined lengths, all in the space of a single minute. One man operated it, and alone he could fell and log 600 tons of timber in a week.*

*When we arrived, scrambling up the hill, this was the first view we saw. I was immediately struck by the symbolism of the darkly brooding and sterile spruce plantation contrasting with the bright optimism of the sunlit regenerated oakwoods, glimpsed at the left of the scene. In the midst of this, the machine, with its smooth, clean lines, marched unstoppably through the dark woods, cutting them down with clinical efficiency. While this operation was for the good, I was reminded of man's terrifying ability to destroy.*

*Painted on the spot, this picture was 'tidied up' later, in the studio.*

2

1

1. Darren Woodhead *Ruined village of Inniemore, Morvern*
   watercolour · 76 x 38 cm
2. Darren Woodhead *Fossil track, Morvern*
   watercolour · 76 x 38 cm

*Our first evening in Morvern , a memorable visit to a special area of woodland, with glorious ochre larches illuminating lichen-covered boughs. A flock of redwing cascade in to roost as a pair of raven croak overhead, sharply adjusting their course upon noticing the visitors below.*

2

Pascale Rentsch *Jake's workshop and chickens*
watercolour · 42 x 60 cm

15th May 20
John

# Appendices

John Busby *Oak woods, Ariundle, Loch Sunart*
conte crayon · 30 x 30 cm

# Study areas

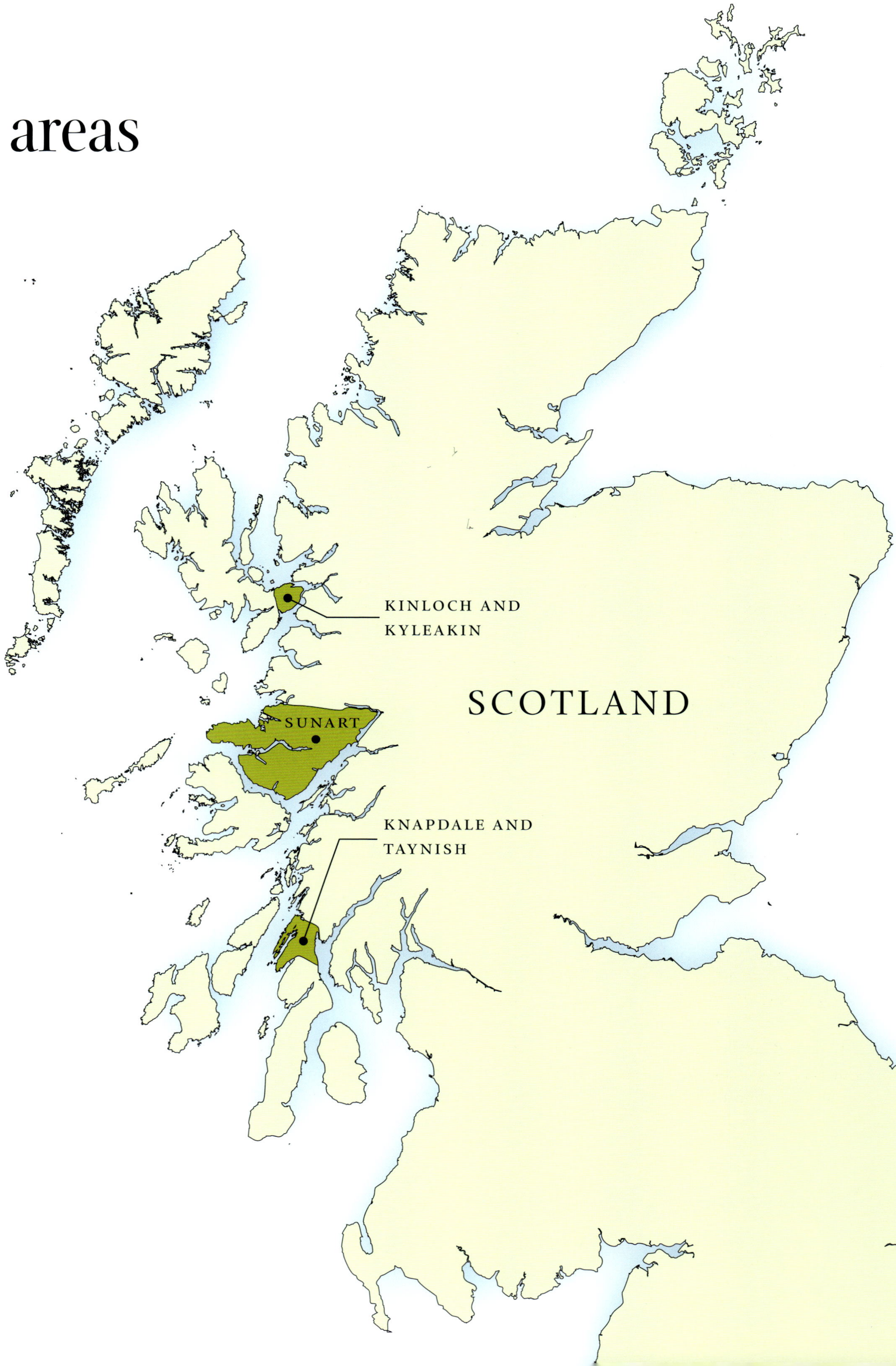
KINLOCH AND
KYLEAKIN
SCOTLAND
SUNART
KNAPDALE AND
TAYNISH

## KINLOCH AND KYLEAKIN

The attraction of the Isle of Skye for many visitors is the bare grandeur of the Cuillin Hills and the heritage of clan history. The scenic and historical associations of the island's native woods are all too easily overlooked. Many woods are remote from public roads and can be reached only by a determined walk along a forestry road or footpath. Woodland types are varied, most being birch with hazel, sometimes replaced by oak, ash, rowan or sallow. They are concentrated in the south end of the island, in Kyleakin and Sleat, where they are protected from the worst of the westerly Atlantic storms. Most are also on steep hillsides, where drainage has prevented the formation of bog and where past attempts at clearance have been difficult.

Forestry Commission Scotland owns the 7,400-hectare Kinloch and Kyleakin Estate in the south-east corner of Skye. Nearly one-third was planted with lodgepole pine and Sitka spruce over the last quarter-century, but significant areas of semi-natural woodland remain along the coastal fringes, mainly on steep, rocky slopes and along ravines. The largest of these are at Mudalach and Aslaig, both accessible only by rough walking or by boat, and the Kinloch Woods, which have access by a Forestry Commission road to a car park, from where the woods can be explored on footpaths. The woods at Kinloch are dominated by birch and oak, with abundant old hazel coppice, whereas those at Aslaig are almost pure oak of an even age, where grazing has prevented regeneration. It is likely that other kinds of trees have been 'weeded' to allow more space for oak. Mudalach has a totally different character; its woods are almost pure birch.

In partnership with the Scottish Forest Alliance (SFA) and with funding from BP, Forestry Commission Scotland has started to restore 700 hectares of woodland to oakwood habitat by allowing natural regeneration through reducing deer numbers and by planting with locally collected seed. This will effectively double the area of native woodland. An interesting feature of the new woodland is that it will range from the coastal fringe of existing semi-natural woodland to the treeline halfway up the hills.

The restoration project started with stands of conifer plantation being felled to recycle as a Millenium Forest for Scotland Trust project and natural regeneration being allowed to take place in the cleared ground. Then, in the summer of 2004, planting of oak and hazel seedlings started with three-dozen children from local primary schools planting three seedlings each in a plot outside Kyleakin. From this small start, around half a million tree seedlings will be planted over a five-year period. The schools are growing their own seedlings under the guidance of trained adults but the bulk will be grown in five nurseries, three of which have been set up on crofts which are diversifying from sheep farming with the aid of SFA funding.

As well as restoring the oakwood habitat, the Kinloch Hills Project plans the reintroduction of some vanished species. Black grouse no longer live on Skye, the last ones being seen in the Kinloch Hills. Regeneration of birch in the cleared areas will provide suitable grouse habitat where reintroduction may be possible. An artificial sea eagle nest has been placed in the canopy of an oak tree, which will hopefully attract eagles from the growing population that was introduced on Forestry Commission land on north Skye.

Access to the Forestry Commission's Kinloch and Kyleakin estate is very difficult at the moment, except for the paths leading to the abandoned settlement at Leiter Fura and an old drove road that continues on to the ferry at Kylerhea. Plans are under way for more footpaths and mountain-biking trails, and an otter hide has already been established at Kylerhea.

The area around Loch Sunart – Ardnamurchan to the north and Morvern to the south – contains some of the largest, and richest in terms of species, tracts of Atlantic oakwood in Scotland. It is also one of Britain's largest areas of ancient semi-natural woodland. Unusually there is often an unbroken transition from the seashore, through oakwood to birch wood and open hillside.

Unlike the other two areas visited by the Society of Wildlife Artists, Forestry Commission Scotland is only one of several landowners in the Sunart area; the others include national agencies, large private estates and small farmers and crofters. The area includes Ariundle National Nature Reserve north of Strontian and Scottish Natural Heritage's Glencripesdale National Nature Reserve on the south side of Loch Sunart. Several blocks of Forestry Commission land were planted with exotic conifers in the 1950s and 1960s and the oakwoods were often underplanted or felled.

There was a change in direction in 1994 when plans began to be formulated for restoring some plantations to native woodland, especially where they would link with remaining oakwood. At the same time many of the existing oakwoods required attention in order to control grazing by deer and livestock and to remove rhododendrons. The ecological and conservation values of the oakwoods are also being enhanced with new plantings to extend them into areas recently cleared of conifers or to link with neighbouring stands.

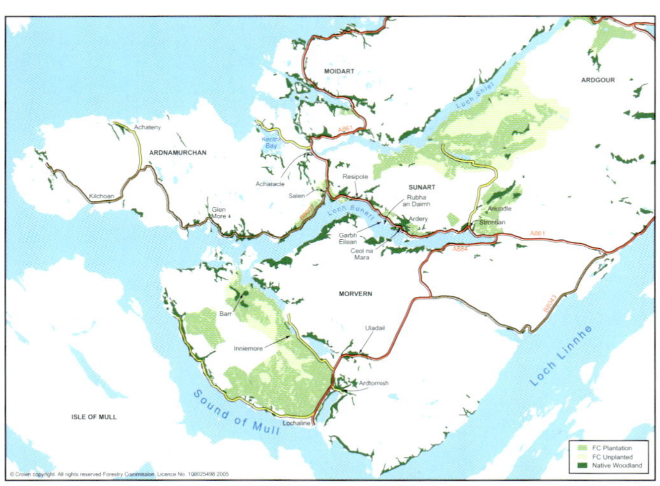


Part of the Forestry Commission's vision is that the restored woodland will make a significant contribution to the revitalisation of the rural economy. This hope is being tested in the Sunart area by a programme in which the local communities become involved with the sustainable management of the woods. This is the Sunart Oakwoods Initiative, which includes the agencies Forestry Commission Scotland, Scottish Natural Heritage, Lochaber Enterprise and the Highland Council as well as the communities. In 2003 the Initiative was extended into Morvern through the Morvern Woodland Project. As well as funding woodland restoration, the Initiative improves public access to the woods and develops community involvement through training, employment and events.

In 2001, private woodland owners on the north side of Loch Sunart joined forces with Forestry Commission Scotland in setting up the North Sunart Woodland Group, which controls a contiguous belt of 1,300 hectares of land, most of which is woodland. The Group had been set up informally in 1998 to share deer control and fence maintenance. Building a single deer fence around the entire belt was more economical and less intrusive than separate fences around each property. Subsequently the Group's objectives have been enlarged 'to optimise the combined conservation, recreation and economic value of the woodlands through sustainable management techniques'.

Sunart Oakwoods Initiative projects are aimed at linking local communities with the woods and providing employment. They include local utilisation of the conifer plantations with outlets in housing and boat building, and education in the value of the woods to conservation, local economy and culture. Schoolchildren, for instance, tend nurseries of native trees, and a Forest School (*Sgoil na Coille*) has been built at Salen, where both children and adults can gather in an oakwood to learn about the woodland habitat, its management and the use of its products. In the long term, there is the possibility of sustainable use of the restored oakwoods. This could include firewood as well as timber. Although no more than 20–70 tonnes of good timber might be produced from a 100-hectare oakwood per year, this would be sufficient for specialist uses and so would be significant at a local level. Producing high-class timber will require long-term management to produce straight-stemmed trees. Such an aim can sometimes lead to a clash between economics and conservation; for instance when felling one tree affects the lichens and mosses on its neighbour. Nevertheless, some careful felling is needed to maintain and improve the conservation interest of the woods. Some farmers are already attempting controlled grazing within the woods, and deer stalking is another option for generating income from woodland.

## KNAPDALE AND TAYNISH

Knapdale and Taynish are at the north end of the Kintyre peninsula, just south of the Crinan Canal. They have a unique landscape of parallel, rocky, wooded ridges and grassy bottoms, which give Knapdale its name, from the Gaelic *cnap* (hill) and *dall* (field). The 'fields' have been drained and planted with conifers.

From a viewpoint on one of the footpaths climbing over a knap, all stages of tree growth can be seen: from native woods to small stands of the original and now-maturing conifer planting and back to regenerating native woods. The woods are varied, with oak, ash, hazel and elm growing on the more fertile, drier and sunnier west-facing slopes of knaps, and birch and alder in damp hollows. Open spaces in the wet parts of the woods on the north-facing rocky slopes of knaps and around the lochs increase the local habitats for more species. The woods had once been coppiced for charcoal and there are also the remains of wood pasture. They include the important hazel wood at Barrandaimph. Knapdale was extensively planted with Sitka and Norway spruce, starting in 1933, but Taynish was planted with non-native hardwoods – beech, sycamore, lime and chestnut – in the early 19th century.

The richness of the area is shown by the tally of 336 species of lichens and 232 mosses and liverworts in Taynish. Knapdale is well known for the variety of bats, which include pipistrelle, Natterer's, Daubenton's and grey long-eared. Management of the woods has to take into account the use of the trees as bat roosts. There are also 10 species of dragonflies to be seen on the lochs, including the scarce hairy dragonfly, and rides have been cut through the woods so that dragonflies can easily find a way from one to another.

The Forestry Commission owns 6,000 hectares of Knapdale. Just to the north is Crinan Wood, which is owned by the Woodland Trust, while to the south lies Taynish Woods, a 350-hectare National Nature Reserve belonging to Scottish Natural Heritage.

Knapdale has 600 hectares of oakwood habitat, and 700 hectares of plantation on what was oakwood habitat are now being restored by felling to recycle of the conifers. Other plantations are being restructured to make corridors for wildlife to spread. With minimal intervention, a mix of thickets of young growth, mature trees and open spaces will develop, with old decaying veterans and fallen logs slowly returning to the soil. This sort of situation can already be seen on the knaps where there was very little disturbance in the past because the steep rocky ground was too difficult to manage profitably. I was told that these places are as good a natural Atlantic oakwood habitat as we are likely to get. So we do not have to wait for the restoration projects to mature before we can see how this part of Scotland looked before Man took charge.

The conifer plantations have their own conservation value. Small stands are being left for wood ants and black grouse, and around heronries. Pine martens have recently spread back into the area and prefer conifer woods, while black grouse have declined seriously and need habitat management to aid their survival.

Taynish Woods became a National Nature Reserve in 1977 and is now one of eight UNESCO Man and Biosphere reserves in Britain. The woods were grazed after coppicing stopped and they are now managed by 'limited intervention'. A core area is left untouched except for removing birch from small areas of bog. The surrounding management zone is used to demonstrate restoration techniques, which include coppicing, planting native trees in felled areas, excluding deer, and managed grazing by cattle.

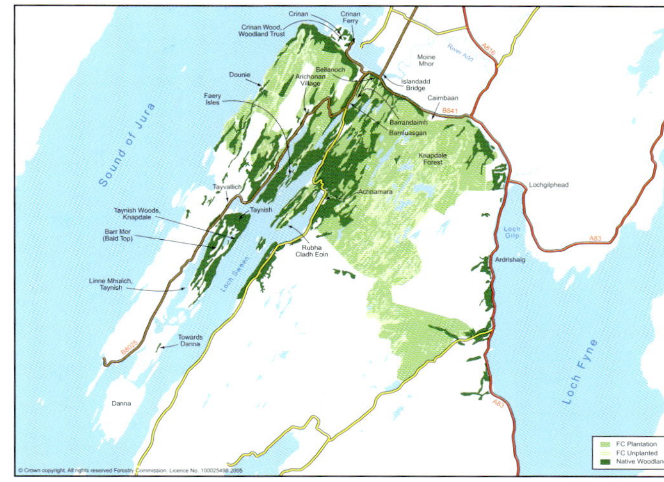


Both Knapdale and Taynish have a significant amenity value, with a network of footpaths and interpretive material for the public and schools. The Argyll Green Woodworkers Association has leased buildings at Barrandaimph, where they give demonstrations of the uses of hardwoods for furniture and building materials.

# The Artists

Ger Clancy *Cycle*
patinated copper and wood
height 46 cm · diameter 17 cm

## CARRY AKROYD

Carry has lived almost all her life in rural Northamptonshire, an unspectacular and unlabelled countryside, where wildlife struggles to survive alongside agribusiness. This arable landscape, and that of the nearby fens, has been the main source of her imagery, punctuated by forays to wilder regions. She spends a lot of time walking around with a notebook, trying to understand the landscape, to see what is going on in it – the history and geology, the botany and birds.

Carry likes to work in different media. Each process, she finds, provides stimulation for the others. Her paintings and prints are slowly distilled in the studio to try to find the right flavour. There is a lot of mapping and planning between the first sketches and the finished state.

Carry regularly shows work in a few small galleries around the country, and was elected as a member of the Society of Wildlife Artists in 2002.

## SÎAN ARMSTRONG

I have lived on Skye for the last 12 years but only resumed painting seriously approximately seven years ago, after a break of about 20 years. During that time I was involved in other things, e.g. hill farming, forestry, academic work and work with people who suffer from dementia.

Now, as an emerging artist, I have found that my approach to painting is developing, with both my increasing perception of the landscape and my – hopefully improving – technical abilities. The varying activities in which I have been involved in the landscape over the years tend to shape the subjects, compositions and the treatment of the paintings. I especially like the complexity and intricacy of details such as foliage, found objects and fur, placed in the wider context of hills, sea and light. More recently I have been exploring the movement and refraction of light on water.

## DAVID BENNETT

David specialises in producing, in his unique style, distinctive studies of wildlife in its natural habitat. David's paintings are an exciting blend of observation and painting, with an impressive use of colour and light. With strong drawing and painting, mainly produced in the field, David's work is a delight to see.

He travels widely and has been involved in major expeditions to Extremadura in Spain, County Wexford in Ireland and the Copper River Delta in Alaska.

Born in 1969 in Doncaster, he studied art at Doncaster College and Leeds Polytechnic, before obtaining a Masters degree in Natural History Illustration at the Royal College of Art in London.

A member of the Society of Wildlife Artists, he has had a number of successful one-man exhibitions and is the winner of several prestigious awards, including first prize for the RSPB *Birds* magazine painting competition in 2001, first prize for the *BBC Wildlife* Magazine Art Awards in 1998, and Winner of the Colour Section of the *Birdwatch* Harper Collins Artist of the Year in 1997.

## KEITH BROCKIE

Keith Brockie graduated from Duncan of Jordanstone College of Art, Dundee, in 1978, and after a short period working as an illustrator with Dundee Museums and Art Galleries he became a freelance artist specialising in wildlife.

Since then he has had six books published featuring his own work. In addition he has part or wholly illustrated many more books; the latest *Rural Portraits*, 2003, features the native farm animals of Scotland and the characters involved with them. A film, *One Man's Island*, featuring his work on the Isle of May was shown on the BBC 2 *World About Us* series in 1984.

In the course of his work he has travelled widely in countries as disparate as Scandinavia, North Yemen, Tanzania and North America. Also he has participated in expeditions to Greenland in 1982, 1988 and 1991, and Svalbard in 1993 as assistant leader with the British Schools Exploring Society, teaching about the wildlife and field sketching. Working with groups of artists, he has participated in environmental awareness projects in Schiermonikoog, Netherlands, 1990; Biezbra Valley, Poland, 1992; Copper River Delta, Alaska, 1995 and the Briere Marshes, Loire, France, 2001.

He now lives in the village of Fearnan on the shores of Loch Tay, Perthshire, where he has a studio/gallery.

## PHILIP BURTON

I studied Zoology at University College, London, and then taught for several years, carrying out my PhD study while doing so, finally gaining it in 1969. Two years before this, I joined the ornithological staff of the British Museum (Natural History).

I have participated in several expeditions as part of my museum work. I am a

Founder Member of the Society of Wildlife Artists, and have illustrated several books and other works.

### JOHN BUSBY

Born in Yorkshire. Drew animals and birds from an early age. Studied at Leeds and Edinburgh Colleges of Art, then taught drawing and painting at ECA from 1956 to 1988. Has illustrated over 30 natural history books. Mainly interested in expressing the behaviour of birds, and the forms and inner meaning of landscape. Lives near the Firth of Forth and the Bass Rock and has studied seabirds in Shetland, New Zealand, The Falklands and Galapagos Islands, and shared an expedition to Aldabra Island with Bryan Nelson in 1974. His own books include *Drawing Birds* (RSPB 1987), *John Busby: Nature Drawings* (Arlequin 1996); and a new *Drawing Birds* (RSPB 2004). He has exhibited widely, with one-man shows at The Scottish Gallery, Edinburgh in 1997, a retrospective exhibition at Cartwright Hall, Bradford in 2000, and solo shows at The Wildlife Art Gallery, Lavenham in 2001 and at The Shire Pottery Gallery, Alnwick in 2003 & 2004.

He has been involved with the Artists For Nature Foundation since its inception in 1991 and taken part in projects in Poland, Spain, Portugal, India, and Ireland. He is an Associate of the Royal Scottish Academy and Founder Member of the Society of Wildlife Artists.

### GER CLANCY

I was born in Ireland in 1980. I attended the National College of Art and Design in Dublin. Here, I specialised in fine art and sculpture. Since completing my studies, I have been working as a professional sculptor. My studio is in the Docklands area in Dublin port. I work with various materials. I am currently working on a commissioned piece and am building enough work for a solo show in Slovenia and Dublin for the end of the summer 2005. I have also worked in theatre and film-based work. At the moment I am lecturing in the IADT Dun Laoghaire teaching model making.

### KATRINA COOK

With the dual occupations of bird artist and Bird Group Curator at the Natural History Museum's ornithological collection at Tring, I am often asked whether I'm an artist who became interested in birds, or an ornithologist who started drawing. There's no straightforward answer. A serious involvement in natural history has gone hand in glove with my art in a diversity of ways. My pictures are inspired by nature and strengthened by my knowledge of it. As a ringer, the opportunity to handle a variety of bird species has certainly given me a greater three-dimensional understanding – vital for any observational drawing – and a feeling for the weight and form of my subjects.

My 'finished' pictures were, for many years, predominantly drypoints, a copperplate engraving technique. I also etch and I am now concentrating on graphite drawings. I no longer have a studio to work in, but I take full advantage of residency and travel opportunities, producing my large work *in situ*.

My best-kept secret is the many volumes of sketchbooks and illustrated travel diaries I have amassed over many years of field drawing. I have seldom shown them and keep them strictly as personal raw material, which may be referred to later. I also try to keep my drawing skills sharp by attending regular life-drawing sessions – the ultimate workout for eye–hand co-ordination.

### JOHN COX

As with most other bird artists, fieldwork is very important to John, and his sketchbooks have accompanied him to many parts of the world, from North America to Borneo. Although it is in no way possible to paint from life every bird that he is commissioned to illustrate, he believes that a good knowledge of as many species as possible in their natural habitat is essential to be able to create a lifelike image on the page.

John became a full-time wildlife illustrator in 1989, after winning *British Birds* magazine's prestigious Bird Illustrator of the Year award. He works mainly on illustrations for books, with his work appearing in, among others, *Handbook of Birds of the World* (Lynx Edicions), *Pigeons and Doves of the World* (Gibbs, Barnes and Cox), *Pheasants, Partridges and Grouse of the World* (Madge and McGowan), and *Petrels and their Allies* (Brook).

In 1993, John was elected a member of the Society of Wildlife Artists and wishes he could devote more time to producing 'gallery' paintings of subjects of his own choosing, especially from his many foreign trips. Born 9 April 1967 in Romford, Essex, England, John now lives with his family in Preston, Lancashire.

### DUNCAN CURRIE

Duncan completed his secondary education on the Isle of Skye when his parents settled on the island. He grew to love the spectacular mountain and maritime scenery of Skye and north-west Scotland. As a keen painter, he expressed his enthusiasm for the natural environment of the islands: 'landscape' forming the dominant theme of his degree show at Edinburgh College of Art in 1985.

At about the same time, he became interested in the fishing boats of Cockenzie, a village just along the coast from Edinburgh. Fishing boats are a recurrent theme in his work today, their vibrant colours and lively compositions contrasting with the more subtle hues and fleeting light effects of his landscape paintings.

Nowadays his inspiration comes from hill walking and long fly-fishing trips. This enables him to find unfamiliar views of the well-known Skye hills and lochs. There is a unique light about the landscape of the island. This, together with the spectacular rock formations found in the Cuillins and the mountains and hills in the north of the island, forms the basis of his work.

Duncan specialises in mixed media painting, using a combination of oil and wax-resist materials overlaid with acrylics, inks and water-based media. He also produces traditional watercolour paintings and pen and ink illustrations of wildlife.

### JOHN DAVIS

Born in 1956, John studied Wildlife Illustration at Dyfed College of Art in South Wales in the mid 1970s.

In 1987, he became a member of the Society of Wildlife Artists and also won the RSPB's Fine Art Award with a picture of a hunting Barn Owl. In 1991, he won the *British Birds*' Bird Illustrator of the Year award and the RSPB award again. More recently, he has won the black and white section of the *Birdwatch* Artist of the Year award.

Over the years his work has appeared in many books and journals, including RSPB's *Birds* magazine and *British Wildlife*, and he illustrated the 'new moon' page for *BBC Wildlife* magazine for several years. Books illustrated include *Downland Wildlife* with John Burton, *Badgers* with Ernest Neal, *Heathlands* with James Parry, and several field guides.

He is happiest in the field, painting either landscapes or wildfowl and waders at Pagham or Chichester harbours, or further afield such as Canada, Iceland, West Africa and lots of visits to Scotland. Paintings are often in watercolour, but increasingly in oils and acrylics. He has exhibited throughout England, and regularly at the Society of Wildlife Artists' annual exhibition at the Mall Galleries in London.

### BRIN EDWARDS

I studied biology at Exeter University, followed by ecology at Durham University, with a vague idea that I would spend the rest of my life in scientific research. I soon realised that I was infinitely more interested in the way the natural world looks than in any theories about how it works. I had sketched and painted wildlife all my life, so it seemed a logical, if risky, step to continue doing that as a career.

My illustrations cover all aspects of natural history and wildlife and combine a passion for the natural world with my background knowledge of the subject. I now have more than 15 years experience working for a variety of UK and European book and magazine publishers.

When left to my own devices, I produce paintings of birds in their habitats, which are altogether looser and more expressive, and this is rapidly becoming an important part of my work. The resultant images have an emphasis on strong design and pattern.

In 2002 I moved from Bristol to a small village on the Suffolk/Essex border. This has provided me with a seemingly endless supply of inspiration for paintings; indeed much of my recent work is derived from the sights of the surrounding countryside.

### CARL ELLIS

Since graduating from the Royal College of Art in 1994, I have been working as an artist, consultant and freelance illustrator, specialising in painting fish. I have worked with leading writers and artists on a variety of projects, such as John Bailey's *Freshwater Fishing*, Chris Yates' *The Secret Carp* and *The Wildlife of Britain* magazine.

In recent years my work has been selected for the Association of Illustrator's Images book and tour. My work has also been selected for the American Society of Illustrators Exhibition in New York and appeared in both their *Illustrators 40* and *Illustrators 41* annuals. Over the past few years I have been exhibiting my life drawings, studies and paintings of our British fish at galleries across the UK My work is also selected regularly for exhibitions organised by the Federation of British Artists, including the Pastel Society, the Royal Institute of Painters in Watercolours, the Royal Society of Marine Artists, and the Society of Wildlife Artists at the Mall Galleries in London.

My contribution to fish in art can be seen in a recent edition of *Wildscape* magazine. I am also excited about being included in the Febuary/March 2005 issue of *International Artist* magazine, for my fish work.

### ROBERT GREENHALF

Born 1950. Trained at Eastbourne and Maidstone Colleges of Art.

A painter in watercolours and oils, and a printmaker producing limited editions of woodcuts and drypoints, mainly wildlife and landscape subjects. He has been a Member of the RBA (Royal Society of British Artists) and the SWLA (Society of Wildlife Artists) since the 1980s.

He was involved in Artists for Nature Foundation projects in Poland, Extremadura, Wexford, The Fens, and the Netherlands. He participated in the SWLA New Forest Project, and was Artist in Residence at the Parc des Ecrins in the French Alps for four years. His work is reproduced in the books connected to these projects, as well as in *Twentieth Century Wildlife Artists* (1986, Croom Helm) and *Modern Wildlife Painting* (1998, Pica Press), both by Nicholas Hammond. *Towards the Sea* (1999, Pica Press) is the first book devoted solely to his work.

### PAUL HENERY

Born 1963 in Northumberland, Paul has studied Advertising, Graphics and Photography Illustration and Fine Art at the Newcastle College of Art and Northumbria University.

He was elected a member of the Society of Wildlife Artists in 2004 and has exhibited widely in galleries throughout Britain.

Paul has received a number of awards, including 1995 *Natural World* magazine readers' Award, 1997 Kittiwake Gallery Award, 1997 *British Birds*' PJC Award, 1998 *British Birds*' Bird Illustrator of the Year Award, 2002 *BBC Wildlife* magazine Art Award and, in 2004, the RSPB Fine Art Award.

Working in all mediums and outdoors in all weathers, Paul seeks to capture the essence of the elemental forces of nature and landscape.

### ANNA KIRK-SMITH

Born in 1972. After initially studying veterinary science, Anna attended the Wildlife Illustration course at Carmarthen College and then gained a master's degree in Natural History Illustration at the Royal College of Art. She has exhibited with the SWLA in recent years and was awarded bursaries in 2002 and 2004, the latter for participation in the 'Aig an Oir' project. Anna also received the PJC prize for drawing in the 2004 exhibition. She now works as a freelance artist.

### PETER MCDERMOTT

Peter entered the West Surrey College of Art and Design at the age of 15, becoming the college's youngest student. After 5 years of formal training, and following a period of 18 years spent in London, where he rose to the position of Creative Director within a highly respected agency, Peter felt the need to change direction, return to the country of his father, and pursue his first love, watercolours.

Now based on the Isle of Skye with his family, Peter has been painting professionally for just over 8 years, and in that time he has enjoyed several successful exhibitions. Peter's work is represented in private collections around the world.

As a child, landscape represented a connection to one's roots. Landscape evoked emotions of belonging and family. Later, the landscape became a demonstration of God's magnificent presence in creation, especially with the ever-changing light and dramatic weather patterns found particularly in the Western Isles. Because of this, my work is unashamedly representational, enabling everyone to recognise and react emotionally to the location and elements portrayed.

I draw my inspiration from James Fletcher-Watson, one of Britain's finest landscape watercolourists, Edward Wesson for his economy of brush strokes, and John Singer Sargent for his incredible ability to take the very ordinary and turn it into something beautiful.

### DAVID GUY MEASURES

Brought up amid a wealth of wildlife on the banks of the Avon in Warwick, his enthusiasm for the natural world developed at an early age. He went on to study painting and printmaking at the Slade, before lecturing at Nottingham Trent University. His life has been divided between his enthusiasm for art and his deep love of natural history. He is an acknowledged expert on butterflies, having published two books on the subject and contributed to others. He has exhibited throughout Britain, won the *BBC Wildlife* magazine's major award and has had a television programme made about him. Fundamental to all his work are the diaries he has kept since his teens. He observes, writes and paints in the field. In the natural history work, he attempts that elusive quality – the life of the creature. In his landscapes, he is free to begin a dialogue with place, its changes and his medium when chance and inclination can prevail.

### WILLIAM NEILL

William Neill was born in Middlewich, Cheshire, in 1943. He taught art in Britain and Australia, before moving to the Western Isles in 1980.

Since then he has worked as a wildlife and landscape artist and in nature conservation and biodiversity research. He is currently involved in a project to map the distribution of bumblebees in the Western Isles. He exhibits regularly at the Society of Wildlife Artists' exhibition at the Mall Galleries, London, where he was elected a member in 1990. He regularly facilitates courses in watercolour painting, wildlife art and natural history, both in the Western Isles and at the Nature in Art museum and art gallery, Gloucester.

### LOUISE OPPENHEIMER

Louise studied Fine Art at Maidstone College of Art (1970–4). Here her close relationship with weaving and wool was founded, a medium which has continued to inspire her throughout her artistic development.

In 1985, a move to Argyll saw her childhood dream of living in a landscape of exposed rock fulfilled, and the rich and varied landscape of the area revealed subject matters that have never ceased to inspire her. The vibrancy of her colours and textures stems from both a broad understanding of her surroundings and a close observation of the influence of season, weather and light.

Drawing forms the backbone of Louise's creative process. However, whilst drawing is a relatively controllable process, Louise's style of weaving is much more organic and unpredictable, with finished weavings often evolving into something quite different from their original sketch.

Louise's methods in both weaving and drawing determine a slow process, which allows her to enjoy in her artwork a wealth of detail, and development of ideas as she creates. One weaving may take weeks to complete, and this scope of work and the solidity of the final piece are aspects which she particularly enjoys.

### JANE LEYCESTER PAIGE

After studying botany, zoology and geography at A-level, Jane went on to do a Froebel teacher's training at Westhill Training College, Birmingham, taking art as her main subject.

From childhood, she was encouraged by her mother to identify and paint wildflowers and by her father to study and develop an interest in early English watercolours. These two interests continue to influence much of her work.

She was elected a Founder Member of the Society of Botanical Artists in 1982 and is a Fellow of the Chelsea Physic Garden Florilegium Society. She regularly illustrated gardening magazines as well as books for BBC Publications and the RSPB. Her work is featured in a new book, *The Watercolour Artist's Flower Sketchbook*, published by Quarto Publishing plc.

Her work has been exhibited with the RI and RWS and regularly with the SBA.

Jane and her husband, John Paige SWLA, run the Old Brewery Studios, King's Cliffe, Northamptonshire, where she teaches art generally and Botanical Illustration in particular. They are both involved with Artists for Nature Foundation projects, and for many years they led painting/birdwatching/botanising holidays for Wildlife Travel.

### JOHN PAIGE

Trained in graphic design at Birmingham College of Art.

Member of the Society of Wildlife Artists. Work in the permanent collections of the Leigh Yawkey Woodson Art Museum, USA, and Nature in Art, UK. Participant in Artists for Nature Foundation in Alaska and SWLA Drawn to the Forest projects. Draws from life in the field, but most finished work now produced in the studio. A keen printmaker, as well as a painter in oil and watercolour.

### PETER PARTINGTON

Peter grew up near Poole Harbour, which had a deep influence on his art. It was easy to escape from school and watch along the shoreline. He went on to art college, where he studied all aspects. He taught art students for many years, until demand for his work encouraged him to pursue painting and printmaking professionally. His preferred medium is watercolour, and more recently he has explored sculpture. He has had numerous one-man shows. He has written and illustrated many books on drawing and painting and writes regularly for art periodicals. He is currently illustrating for *BBC Wildlife* magazine; recent books include illustrations for the very successful *The Secret Life of Garden Birds*, published by the RSPB.

### BRUCE PEARSON

As often as the opportunity arises I work out in the wild, where wildlife and landscape, and sometimes people, interact. A painting might be completed directly in the field, while other paintings and printmaking work results from re-working field notes and re-evaluating ideas in the studio.

Elected a member of the Society of Wildlife Artists in 1976, and its President from 1994 to 2004, I have painted professionally for almost 30 years. In that time I have been lucky enough to travel widely in search of subjects. However, much of my time is spent in East Anglia – either working out in the field or in my Cambridgeshire studio.

For the past 10 years, my work has largely involved private commissions from individuals, museums and institutions; and, by invitation from the Artists for Nature Foundation (ANF), I have participated in various international art events and exhibitions.

Some of my work has been used to illustrate various books, journals and magazines, including writing and illustrating *An Artist on Migration*. A BBC film was made about one part of the journey that I made. Other film projects include the six-part Channel 4 *Birdscape* TV series.

I have shown work in a range of group and solo exhibitions in a number of overseas countries and widely in galleries throughout the UK.

### NIK POLLARD

Born 1970, England. Nik Pollard studied at the Royal College of Art, specialising in Natural History Illustration. He is a member of the SWLA and past winner of the Bursary for young artists. In 2001, he received the *BBC Wildlife* Art Award. He is a published author and illustrator of children's picture books.

Nik's work aims to convey a sensitive understanding of place, focusing on the inherent subtleties of landscape and natural history. Based in Kent, he spends most of the year painting on the Swale estuary, an area he has known since childhood.

### GREG POOLE

Greg Poole became an elected member of the Society of Wildlife Artists (SWLA) in 1991 and a Council member in 1997. In 1993, Greg gained the *Natural World* art award and the Artists for Nature Foundation (ANF) Award and was subsequently involved in four of their projects.

Greg has had a varied career path, which began with a Zoology degree at Cardiff University, conservation work in Avon, and wardening at Bardsey Island Bird Observatory, Wales and Long Point Observatory, Ontario. He now divides his time between illustration (largely computer graphics) and more personal fine art work.

'Producing finished work is a juggling act between fieldwork (mainly in charcoal and acrylic) and the studio, generally using printmaking based on ideas derived from collage.

'I'm making pictures about nature, above all trying to celebrate appreciation of nature – to hear, smell, touch and see it, marvel at how it all fits together. I am upset about how a lot of it is getting ripped apart, but I don't feel inclined to express unhappiness in my art. It seems better to point out how great things are and to try to show the way I see things. I use artwork as a means of investigation, and this can go from micro to macro in microseconds.'

### ALASTAIR PROUD

Alastair Proud was born and brought up in Co. Dublin. He went to Art College in Wales, leaving in 1978 to pursue a career as an artist. In 1985, he was elected to full membership of the Society of Wildlife Artists but had taken part in their annual exhibitions in the Mall Galleries, London, since 1976. The books he has illustrated include *Birds of Prey of the British Isles* and *Wildfowl of the British Isles*. His paintings are held in many private collections all over the world, including more than 50 works commissioned by the Sultan of Oman. He loves travelling and has been to both the Arctic and the Tropics in search of subjects to paint. His main venues for exhibitions are Dublin and London. Alastair lives in West Wales with his wife and two children.

### DARREN REES

Darren Rees was born in Hampshire in 1961 and studied Mathematics at Southampton University, teaching the subject for a short time before pursuing painting full time. As an artist he is self-taught.

He uses a variety of media, most commonly watercolour in the field, and acrylic and oil paint for larger landscapes and studio works. He lists his influences as John Busby, Lars Jonsson and John Singer Sargent.

His work has attracted many awards, including *BirdWatch* Artist of the Year, *Natural World* Fine Art Award, RSPB Fine Art Award, and the Countryman Art Award at the Mall Galleries, London. His first solo book, *Bird Impressions*, as greeted by much critical acclaim and was a runner-up in the Natural History Book of the Year Award. He is a member of the Society of Wildlife Artists in London and is a regular writer with *Birds Illustrated* magazine.

He has been a contributing artist to the Artists for Nature Foundation/WWF projects in Holland, Poland, Peru and Ecuador.

He lives in the Forth Valley west of Stirling, Scotland, with his wife and two children.

### PASCALE RENTSCH

Pascale was born and educated in Switzerland. She studied art at Brighton and Edinburgh. She has been a practising artist since 1999.

In July 2001, as part of winning the Artist for Nature Foundation prize in 2001, she was invited on to the ANF 'Spanish Pyrenees' project. In February 2000 she was invited on to the Society of Wildlife Artists' 'New Forest' project.

In October 1998 and July 1999 she was invited to work with seven other artists at the Minsmere RSPB Reserve, Suffolk, on two Society of Wildlife Artists' projects that involved screen-printing and hand designing two limited-edition handmade books, within the space of a week for each book.

She received the Isaac Howitt Award for the most promising Art and Design teacher, August 2003 – July 2004 and the Society of Wildlife Artists' bursary for travel and education in 1997 and 1998. She was elected as an associate member of the Society of Wildlife Artists in 2000.

Pascale was Artist in Residence at Edinburgh Zoo in 2000. She has taken part in several solo and mixed exhibitions and has exhibited annually at the SWLA exhibition at the Mall Galleries from 1997.

### ANDREA RICH

Andrea Rich has an international reputation as a printmaker, working in multiple-colour woodcut prints. She produces her prints from personal observations of wildlife in their natural habitats. Madagascar, New Zealand, Costa Rica, Africa and Europe are some of the places outside North America that she has visited in search of interesting subjects. To create an image, she carves and prints a separate block for each colour, and then hand pulls each print. A typical print requires ten to twenty blocks. Because the process is very time consuming, editions of her work generally number 30 or fewer. Her woodcuts are represented in numerous museums and universities, as well private collections. As well as her fine original prints, she has published a limited-edition letterpress book of collected works. If you have a question or comment, she'd love to hear from you.

### MARTIN RIDLEY

Upon completing the wildlife illustration course at Carmarthen in 1988, Martin was awarded course, faculty and college student of the year. May 2005 was his seventh Artist in Residency at The Society of Wildlife Art of the Nations at Nature in Art, Gloucestershire.

August 2003 saw his third successful exhibition at The Wildfowl and Wetlands Trust, Slimbridge. In 1999, a painting was selected for the prestigious Leigh Yawkey Woodson Art Museum *Birds in Art* exhibition in the USA.

A plethora of Martin's images have gone into printed circulation, including illustrations for books, prints, cards and calendar designs.

A painter of both mammals and birds, Martin has spent much time developing knowledge of the field, which is clearly reflected in his work. Combined with conceptual composition, his attention to animal behaviour, habitat detail and lighting creates an amazingly accurate and artistic record of his nature encounters.

### CHRIS ROSE

Chris Rose was born in 1959 in Uganda, where he lived until the age of six. He was educated in Surrey and gained a degree in Biology at Nottingham University. On graduating in 1981, and initially unable to find work as a biologist, he was offered a post as illustrator for the Dorset Heritage Coast Project for one year. Drawing and painting birds and other wildlife had been a paid hobby since his early teens and the year with the Dorset Heritage Coast Project convinced him that this was the career for him.

Chris is an active member of the Society of Wildlife Artists and currently serves on the SWLA council and on the Board of Governors of the Federation of British Artists. He has exhibited widely in the UK and abroad and has won several awards for his work, including Bird Illustrator of the Year and European Bird Artist of the Year.

Chris has travelled widely and recently joined an Artists for Nature Foundation project visiting the endangered dry forests of north-west Peru and south-west Ecuador in order to highlight the conservation value of this area by painting its wildlife. However, most of the inspiration for his paintings comes from the countryside around his home in the Scottish Borders.

### DAFILA SCOTT

After training as a zoologist, Dafila Scott turned to drawing and painting. Most of her work is inspired by wildlife and landscape, and features animals or places with which she has become familiar. As a member of the Society of Wildlife Artists, she has exhibited regularly at their annual exhibition at the Mall Galleries, as well as at regional shows. She has also illustrated books and articles.

Working mostly in oils, sometimes watercolours and more recently pastels, she paints either from life or from a combination of field sketches and memory. She has taken courses with painters and art teachers and is especially grateful for the inspirational teaching of Robin Child.

Recent work includes both figurative wildlife paintings and abstract landscapes inspired by visits to Wales and to the South African Kalahari. However, she is equally happy to gain inspiration at home in the garden or on the surrounding fenland. In 2003 she won the RSPB Fine Art Award.

### ANDREW SINCLAIR

Andrew Sinclair was born in Garderen, Holland in 1975. He studied Fine Art, Drawing and Painting at Duncan of Jordanstone College of Art, Dundee.

In 1999–2000 he travelled in Western Europe, spending three months living in Barcelona developing range of arts practice, including animation. In 2000–1 he took part in Artist for Gaelic art workshops at Acharacle School, Ardnamurchan. From 2000–4 he designed and developed Resipole Studios, Ardnamuchan, which opened in July 2004. He is now a professional painter and owner–manager of Resipole Studios.

His work is held in private collections in New Zealand, Holland, Kenya and the UK.

### JANE SMITH

After receiving a university degree in Zoology at Manchester, Jane became a researcher, producer and then photographer for the RSPB film unit. Jane was also Producer for the wildlife series *Operation Survival* for BBC Scotland. After a spell as a freelance camerawoman making films for the BBC and National Geographic (winning an Emmy for cinematography), Jane began to experiment with painting and printmaking.

With a young family, time is limited but she started painting for one day per week and says she is 'still feeling her way'. Jane has now stopped the constant travelling and is looking at her surroundings on a more intimate level. Regular walks in the Taynish oakwoods have given her much to look at and think about, which she is now expressing on paper.

### ANDREW STOCK

Andrew is a self-taught painter and etcher and has been painting full time since 1978. Personally encouraged by the late Sir Peter Scott, he held his first one-man exhibition at the age of 21, at the Malcolm Innes Gallery in London. As well as participating in many joint shows, Andrew has held eleven solo London shows. He has won several awards, including *British Birds* magazine's Bird Illustrator of the Year in 1995.

Etching has formed an important part of Andrew Stock's creative repertoire since 1991, and printmaking now represents a significant portion of his portfolio. He was elected an Associate of the Royal Society of Painter-Printmakers (RE) in 2001.

Andrew was elected a member of the Society of Wildlife Artists in 1983 and has exhibited with them every year since 1981. Last year he was elected President of the Society, having served nine years as Honorary Secretary.

Andrew usually works in water-based media but he also paints in oils. Subject matter has primarily been wildlife, especially birds. However, in recent years he has been painting still life, landscape and figures with great success.

Andrew has lived in West Dorset for the last twenty years and now works from his studio in the hamlet of Ryme Intrinseca, near Sherborne

### RICHARD TRATT

Richard Tratt was born in Enfield, North London, in 1953. As a young boy he developed a consuming interest in natural history, with a particular fascination for butterflies and moths. He began painting in his teens, and attended Northwich College of Art, Cheshire, and Dartington College of Arts, Devon (1970–4).

Richard spends a great deal of time observing and sketching his subjects in their environment. Most of his wildlife paintings are finished in the studio, but much of his landscape work is painted outdoors. He works mainly in oils or acrylics on canvas. Richard has been painting full time since 1979, and was elected a member of The Society of Wildlife Artists (SWLA) in 1981, and The Society of Botanical Artists (SBA) in 1986.

He exhibits at many galleries and venues throughout the country and shows regularly at the annual SWLA and SBA exhibitions. Richard has an international following. Recently his paintings have become popular in Japan, resulting in one-man exhibitions in Tokyo, in 1998 and 2000.

Work published by CK Art, Rosenstiel's, Medici, Reynard Fine Art, RSPB, and Sally Mitchell Fine Art. Paintings on permanent display at the International Centre for Wildlife Art, Gloucester. In 1996, first- prize winner of national competition 'Art in Nature', organised by *The Artist* magazine.

### ESTHER TYSON

Born in 1973, Esther Tyson was brought up in a small town at the edge of the Lake District, Cumbria. She currently lives and works in South Wales. Esther studied at Carlisle College of Art and Design, Carmarthenshire College of Technology and Art and then London's Royal College of Art. Esther has exhibited widely in the UK, and her work has also earned acclaim in London, where she was shortlisted for the prestigious Hunting Art Prizes in early 2004.

Esther is a painter whose work reflects her deep feeling for the natural world, without being sentimental. Painting from life, she seeks to capture the essence of her subject. Her painting is a response to the smell, sights and sounds. It emerges from her reactions, feelings and thoughts toward both her subject and the marks she makes.

### MATT UNDERWOOD

Matt was always curious about natural history as a child, and began drawing and keeping sketchbooks from an early age.

From school Matt went on to study art and art history at Salisbury College of Art, where his tutor provided him with many animal and bird skeletons to work from at weekends. Matt went on to study wildlife illustration at Carmarthenshire College of Art. After leaving college Matt began a career as a painter, his main subjects being landscapes and still life.

In recent years Matt has returned to his interest in natural history, producing eye-catching works in collage, mixed media and oil. Matt finds it is often a tiny piece of information, together with constant observation and drawing, which can trigger an idea for a painting; the real challenge for him is to convey his enthusiasm for the subject and to capture the feeling and wonder of seeing something for the first time.

Matt has exhibited his work at many galleries, including the Mall Galleries, where, in 2002, he won the RSPB Art Award at the Society of Wildlife Artists for his collage *Swallows over the dairy yard*. In April 2003 Matt had a very successful exhibition of his work in Amsterdam.

### BARRY W. VAN DUSEN

Barry was born in 1954 in Portland, Maine, USA. He studied Visual Design at Southeastern Massachusetts University, graduating in 1977. Beginning his career as a graphic artist and designer, he soon narrowed his focus to natural history subjects. Barry's work has appeared in a variety of nature books and pocket guides, many as the result of a long and productive association with the Massachusetts Audubon Society. His articles and paintings have been featured in *Birder's World* and *Bird Watcher's Digest* magazines, and his bird illustrations have been published by the American Birding Association, HarperCollins and Princeton University Press.

In 1994, Barry was elected a full member of the Society of Wildlife Artists, and he is an annual contributor to their exhibitions. His work has been selected numerous times for the prestigious Birds in Art show (Leigh Yawkey Woodson museum, Wausau, Wisconsin) and has appeared in galleries throughout the United States and Europe. At the invitation of the Artists for Nature Foundation (the Netherlands), Barry has travelled to Spain, Ireland, England, India and Peru, working alongside other wildlife artists to raise money for conservation of threatened habitats.

Barry resides in central Massachusetts, USA.

### MICHAEL WARREN

Michael Warren is a professional artist specialising in paintings of birds in their natural habitats. He has lived in Winthorpe, Nottinghamshire since 1975. His work has enabled him to travel widely, drawing and studying birds. These journeys have taken him to many European countries, all 50 American States, Micronesia, Peru, Ecuador, Africa and Australia.

His early training was at the College of Art, Wolverhampton. In 1972, on the offer of a one-man exhibition in Cork Street, London, he began to paint full time. Since then he has had numerous one-man exhibitions in England, New York, France, Spain and Mallorca. He is President of Nottinghamshire Birdwatchers and Treasurer of the Society of Wildlife Artists. He exhibits at their annual show at the Mall Galleries, London.

Michael has contributed to many publications and has had four books published. He has also designed postage stamps for the British Post Office and the Republic of the Marshall Islands and many conservation stamps.

All Michael's paintings are based on observations of birds in the field; immediate sketches provide the basis for paintings. Sometimes these are completed outdoors but more often in the studio. The paintings are done in watercolour and graphite on Arches or Fabriano paper.

### JAMES WILLIAMSON-BELL

Born Wallsend-on-Tyne, 1938, James left school in 1954, and then worked as a shipbuilding draughtsman at Swan Hunter's Wallsend Yard. After twenty years in shipbuilding, James decided to paint full time.

In 1976, he was awarded a Silver Medal for watercolour at the Paris Salon, followed the following year with a Gold Medal, again for watercolour, and a Silver Medal for sculpture. He has exhibited widely in the UK and abroad, receiving several awards in the USA and Kenya for his wildlife work. James is a member of various societies, including the SWLA and Societe des Artistes Francais, the Bilan d'l'art Contemporain and the Royal Society of Miniaturists.

Apart from wildlife painting, James also paints industrial landscapes, originating from his time in the shipyards. Recently he has concentrated more and more on oriental work, woodblock printmaking and Chinese Ink painting. In 1989 he received a travel grant to study for 3 months in Taiynan, Shannstic Province. His work has also taken him to Cuba, Italy and Vietnam. In 1999 he participated in the SWLA and Forestry Commission project in the New Forest.

### DARREN WOODHEAD

Darren was born in Leeds in 1971. After studying at Wakefield District College and Carmarthenshire College, he spent three years working on and around a small island off the Pembrokeshire coast, South Wales. He graduated with a Master's degree in Natural History Illustration at The Royal College of Art in 1997.

He has been a keen naturalist since a very early age, spending hours in his native Yorkshire Dales. Combining this interest with drawing was a natural step. All his work is produced in the field, trying to keep a sense of life and freshness in the images.

He has participated in several projects based on wildlife and conservation, including several Artists for Nature Foundation projects. He also participated in two handmade book projects at Minsmere RSPB Reserve, Suffolk, in October 1998 and July 1999.

Awards include: the Society of Wildlife Artists' bursary for travel and education, in 1994 and 1996; and the Artists for Nature Foundation Award 2000 at the SWLA Exhibition, Mall Galleries, London; *Birdwatch* Artist of the Year 1999. Elected a member of the Society of Wildlife Artists in July 2001, and currently serves on their council.

His first solo book of paintings and drawings is due to be published by Langford Press in October 2005.

Barry W. Van Dusen *Hooded crow, Ariundle Reserve*
watercolour · 30 x 35.5 cm